6/12/13
#217.00

Drug Injury
Liability, Analysis and Prevention

Third Edition

James T. O'Donnell,
Pharm.D., M.S., FCP, ABCP, FACN, R.Ph.

Contributors

Gopi Doctor Ahuja, MPH

Antonia Alafris, B.S., Pharm.D., CGP

Loyd V. Allen, Jr., B.S., M.S., Ph.D.

Peter D. Anderson, Pharm.D.

Robert S. Baratz, M.D., DDS, Ph.D.

Ramune E. Barkus, Esq.

Stephen Barrett, M.D.

David M. Benjamin, Ph.D., FCLM, FCP

David C. Clark, Ph.D.

Henry Cohen, B.S., M.S., Pharm.D., FCCM, BCPP, CGP

Victor Cohen, B.S., Pharm.D.

Kathleen M. Dahle, RN, B.S.N.

Paul N. Danese, Ph.D.

Armand Derian, Esq.

S. Albert Edwards, Pharm.D., RAC, FRAPS

Constantine John Falliers, M.D.

Todd W.B. Gehr, M.D.

Vincent Idemyor, Pharm.D.

Anne D. ImObersteg, M.S., J.D., MBA, B.A.

Patricia Iyer, MSN, RN, LNCC, CLNI

Christopher A. Keeys, B.S., Pharm.D., BCPS, RPh

William N. Kelly, Pharm.D., FISPE

Roger S. Klotz, R.Ph., BCNSP, FASCP, FACA, CDM

Charles R. Kozak, J.D.

Mary E. Kremzner, Pharm.D.

Rita Marcoux, R.Ph., MBA

Donald H. Marks, M.D., Ph.D.

Ned Milenkovich, Pharm.D., J.D.

Justina A. Molzon, M.S. Pharm., J.D.

Roger Morris, R.Ph., J.D.

Francis J. Muno, Jr., B.S., Pharm., R.Ph., MBA

Megan Musselman, B.S., Pharm.D.

Jadwiga Najib, Pharm.D.

Lori A. Nesbitt, Pharm.D., MBA

James J. O'Donnell III, M.S., Ph.D.

Kimberly O'Donnell, MBA

Damani Parran, Ph.D., DABT

Gourang Patel, B.S. Chem, Pharm.D., MSc, BCPS

Karen L. Pellegrin, Ph.D., MBA

Kip A. Petroff, Esq.

Domenic A. Sica, M.D.

John C. Somberg, M.D.

William J. Stilling, R.Ph., M.S., J.D.

Ed Sweeney, Esq.

F. Randy Vogenberg, R.Ph., Ph.D.

Saifi Vohra, Pharm.D., RPh, MBA, FASHP, FASCP

Vanessa M. Vullmahn, M.S.

Sondra Wacker, CIM

James P. Walters, J.D., M.S.

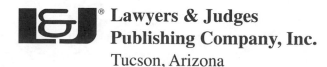 **Lawyers & Judges
Publishing Company, Inc.**
Tucson, Arizona

This publication is designed to provide accurate and authoritative information in regard to the subject matter covered. It is sold with the understanding that the publisher is not engaged in rendering legal, accounting, or other professional service. If legal advice or other expert assistance is required, the services of a competent professional person should be sought.

—From a Declaration of Principles jointly adopted by
a Committee of the American Bar Association
and a Committee of Publishers and Associations.

The publisher, editors and authors must disclaim any liability, in whole or in part, arising from the information in this volume. The reader is urged to verify the reference material prior to any detrimental reliance thereupon. Since this material deals with legal, medical and engineering information, the reader is urged to consult with an appropriate licensed professional prior to taking any action that might involve any interpretation or application of information within the realm of a licensed professional practice.

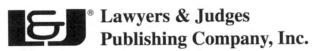 **Lawyers & Judges Publishing Company, Inc.**

P.O. Box 30040 • Tucson, AZ 85751-0040
(800) 209-7109 • FAX (800) 330-8795
e-mail: sales@lawyersandjudges.com
www.lawyersandjudges.com

Library of Congress Cataloging-in-Publication Data

O'Donnell, James, Pharm. D.
  Drug injury : liability, analysis and prevention / James T. O'Donnell ; contributing authors, Gopi Doctor Ahuja ... [et al.].
-- 3rd ed.
     p. cm.
  Includes index.
  ISBN-13: 978-1-936360-08-6 (hardcover : alk. paper)
  ISBN-10: 1-936360-08-X (hardcover : alk. paper)
  1. Products liability--Drugs--United States. 2. Drugs--Law and legislation--United States. 3. Trial practice--United States.
I. Ahuja, Gopi Doctor. II. Title.
  KF1297.D7O36 2012
  346.7303'8--dc23
                          2012023835

Printed in the United States of America
10 9 8 7 6 5 4 3 2 1

Dedication

To my son Jim
(James John O'Donnell III)
whose recent achievement in Pharmacology (Ph.D.)
launches his career in medical and pharmacology research
temporaneously with the launch of this third edition of *Drug Injury*.

—James Thomas O'Donnell
June 2012

Contents

Preface to Third Edition

Drug Injury, Liability, Analysis, and Prevention, Third Edition (2012) is designed to serve as a reference for attorneys, pharmacists, physicians, risk managers, nurses, drug manufacturers, and regulators—as well as anyone with any interest in drug use and drug injury. It summarizes the FDA's responsibility in monitoring drug development and safety. It reviews current drug-product-related liability issues that focus on the manufacturer's role in providing for drug safety. The book identifies important roles that pharmacists play in enhancing medication safety and effectiveness, and demonstrates what can happen when pharmacists and other practitioners and healthcare institutions do not perform adequately. By focusing on the most dangerous drugs, the reader can learn from the tragedies and mistakes of others, look at their own practice settings, and avoid making similar mistakes.

This third edition contains 48 chapters, 11 of which were contributed by lawyers, including those who practice at the FDA, healthcare, regulatory law, malpractice defense, and the prosecution of product liability and medical malpractice. The remaining chapters were contributed by accomplished physicians, pharmacologists, pharmacists, nurses, and other scientists, as well as one business executive. The book is divided into four sections:

I.   The Pharmaceutical Process: How are drugs developed?
II. High Risk Drug Therapies Resulting in Injury and Litigation: Which drugs cause the most injury?
III. Pharmacists, Pharmacy, and Pharmacy Practice: What can pharmacists and health systems do to minimize risk and improve drug safety?
IV   Forensic and Toxicology Issues: Recreational Drugs, Drug Testing, and Pain Equipotency

Most of the chapters are either new (14) or extensively revised since the publication of the second edition of this book. Five chapters that have not been updated contain information that remains timely: Chapter 4, *The Failed System of Drug Warnings in the United States*, Chapter 8, *Identification of Regulated Solid-Dosage Forms*, Chapter 19, *The*

Story of E-Ferol: Adding Insult to Injury, Chapter 29, *Hemophilia Holocaust Litigation Related to Blood Factor VIII and IX Products and AIDS Transmission*, and Chapter 40, *The NABP Model Act and Rules Initiative toward Pharmacy Technicians*.

Several chapters have been deleted, usually representing major drug litigation (Fen-Phen, Oxycontin, Rezulin, Baycol, Ephedra-Metabolide, PPA, anabolic steroids) that has now been resolved through global settlements, market withdrawal, product reformulation, or more restrictive regulation. Chapters new to the third edition include:

- Chapter 3, *The Pharmaceutical Revolution: Drug Discovery and Development*
- Chapter 9, *Counterfeit Drugs*
- Chapter 10, *General Principles of Pharmacology*
- Chapter 12, *Search and Analysis of the Food and Drug Administration's Adverse Event Reporting System*
- Chapter 13, *Liability, Litigation, and Lessons in New Drug Development*
- Chapter 25, *Anticoagulants: Therapeutics, Risks, and Toxicity—Special Focus on Heparin-Induced Thrombocytopenia*
- Chapter 27, *Dangers of Opioids*
- Chapter 28, *Acute Adverse Drug Events in Critical Care: Emergency Department and Intensive Care Units*
- Chapter 30, *HIV Pharmacotherapy and Its Complications*
- Chapter 31, *Fetal Drug Exposure*
- Chapter 32, *Nonscientific Uses and Illegal Marketing of Drugs and Dietary Supplements*
- Chapter 33, *Regulation of Pharmacy Practice*
- Chapter 35, *Pharmacist Malpractice and Liability*
- Chapter 38, *After-Hours Pharmacy Services, Medication Use and Safety in U.S. Hospitals*
- Chapter 46, *Postmortem Redistribution and Interpretation of Drug Levels*

The pharmacist's most important responsibility is to ensure that drugs are used safely and effectively. We have included updated chapters on many of the specialized pharmacist chapters from the second edition. We are fortunate to have an updated compilation of pharmacy case law (Chapter 34, Pharmacy Case Law Update: October 2009 through October 2010 by Morris and Stilling, two pharmacist/attorneys), adapted from a very popular presentation at the 2010 Annual Meeting of the American Society of Pharmacy Law.

Chapter 18, *Physician and Hospital Liability in Drug and Medical-Device Litigation,* is a revised chapter by medical malpractice defense attorneys Barkus and Derian, discussing the defense of physicians and hospitals in drug and medical device litigation.

The medication error chapters have been consolidated into one chapter, with extensive revisions (Chapter 17, *Medication Errors*). The 1999 Institute of Medicine (IOM) report, To Error Is Human, was updated by the IOM in 2006. Similar problems continue to be reported, and therefore the following is worth repeating. According to the Institute of Medicine's (IOM) report "To Err is Human," originally published in 1999, between 44,000 and 98,000 people die every year from medical errors that occur in hospitals. About 7,000 of these were attributable to medication errors in 1993—comprising one out of every 131 outpatient deaths and one out of every 854 inpatient deaths. This problem is not limited to hospital patients either. In fact, hospitalized patients represent only a small number of the total population at risk of experiencing a medication-related error. "Numerous studies document errors in prescribing medications, dispensing by pharmacists, and unintentional non-adherence on the part of the patient," reads the IOM report. "Medication errors have the potential to increase as a major contributor to avoidable morbidity and mortality as new medications are introduced for a wider range of indications." A *JAMA* article described the enormity of drug-related deaths as the equivalent of two 747s crashing every week. Of course, where there is injury, there may be litigation. When education and safe practice by healthcare practitioners fail, affected patients have a right to investigate and seek damages for their injuries. Many times, that is all that they can do, because their injuries are permanent or fatal.

Because drugs are ubiquitous, and because drugs affect people's lives and practice outside the walls of the hospital and the drugstore, we again include chapters on recreational drugs and the forensic pharmacist (see Part IV). As stated earlier, attorneys are a focused audience of this book, and they usually have no training in FDA, pharmacy, or regulatory law, and certainly have no training in pharmacology or the pathology of drugs. Yet, in a wide spectrum of practices, attorneys must master these complex topics to represent their clients. To assist in the apparently daunting learning curve facing the non-clinician in assessing drug injury matters, we have included an extensive review of the basic principles of pharmacology (Chapter 10, *General Principles of Pharmacology*), which contains principles applicable to all drugs. The first and second editions of *Drug Injury* were well-received by legal, medical, pharmacy, and nursing practitioners and scholars. The first and second editions of *Drug Injury* have been used as text and reference books in several universities, and can be found in numerous medical, pharmacy, manufacturer, and law libraries, the FDA library, and in private law offices throughout the United States.

Summary

In closing, *Drug Injury, Third Edition,* is intended to serve as a broad and deep reference for anyone with a professional or personal interest in drug use, development, testing, and the dangers of drug injury. This book shows how pharmacists play pivotal roles in the proper administration and use of prescription medications, and clearly highlights the perils of untrained or careless practitioners. I and all of the contributors to *Drug Injury* sincerely hope that readers will learn from the lessons contained within this text, collaborating together to create a safer future for all of us. Without these contributors, there would be no book!

On a personal note, it gives me great pride to include contributions by my children, Kimberly, who, while completing requirements for her MBA at the Kellogg Business School, investigated and reported on the (continuing) problem of counterfeit drugs (Chapter 9, *Counterfeit Drugs*), and my son Jim, who just completed his Ph.D. in Pharmacology and contributed to Chapter 10, *General Principles of Pharmacology*.

James O'Donnell, Pharm.D., M.S., FCP, ABCP, FACN, R.Ph.
Associate Professor of Pharmacology,
Rush University Medical Center, Chicago, IL
President, Pharmaconsultant Inc., Barrington, IL

Preface to Second Edition

Drug Injury, Second Edition was designed to serve as a reference for attorneys, pharmacists, physicians, risk managers, nurses, drug manufacturers, and regulators—as well as anyone with any interest in drug use and drug injury. It summarizes the FDA's responsibility in monitoring drug safety. It reviews drug-product-related liability issues that focus on the manufacturer's role in providing for drug safety. The book identifies important roles that pharmacists play in enhancing medication safety and effectiveness, and demonstrates what can happen when pharmacists do not function adequately. By focusing on the most dangerous drugs, the reader can learn from the tragedies and mistakes of others, look at their own practice settings, and avoid making similar mistakes.

The second edition contains 48 chapters, ten of which were contributed by lawyers, including those who practice at the FDA, in healthcare, regulatory law, malpractice defense, and the prosecution of product liability. The remaining 38 chapters were contributed by accomplished physicians, pharmacologists, pharmacists, nurses, and other scientists, in three areas of focus:

1. How are drugs developed?
2. What drugs cause the most injury?
3. What can clinicians and health systems do to minimize risk and improve drug safety?

With rare exception, all of the chapters are either new or extensively revised since the release of the first edition of this book. The two chapters that have not been updated contain information that remains timely. The Omniflox and Vaccine Litigation chapters have been deleted, since these topics have become dated. Chapters new to the Second Edition include Drugs for Asthma, Allergies, and Anaphylaxis: Harm from Use, Misuse and Non-Use, by Constantine John Falliers, MD, an eminent allergist; and Drug-Induced Nephrotoxicity, by nephrologists Sica and Gehr. Attorney Kip Petroff has also contributed two new chapters, including Dangers at the Drug Store: Practical Comments about the Pondimin and Redux Litigation, which completes the story of the diet pill Redux, as described in the First Edition by Restaino and O'Donnell. Petroff is recognized as a pioneer and legal authority in diet-drug litigation. Petroff's second new contribution, The Failed System of Drug Warnings in America, was written about a year ago, and is prophetic! Both the lay and trade presses are full of commentary and concerns about the Vioxx withdrawal. A Senate Committee hearing has since been held, with testimony from an FDA drug-safety officer that Vioxx and several other best-selling drugs were somehow not adequately tested, monitored, and warned. (More about Vioxx later!)

Chapters on the Pharmaceutical Industry, the FDA, and The Dietary Supplement Act have been updated for this edition. Additional chapters in this subject area include FDA Regulation of Clinical Investigations by Walters, a former FDA inspector; and Protection of Subjects in Clinical Research, by Clark and Ahuja. Dr. Clark has described himself as the "research police," and his review of requirements for clinical research will provide a thorough and up-to-date reference on the subject.

Chapters on ephedra, Rezulin, Baycol, E-Ferol, and blood-factor products reflect the latest news on these drug products, which have played large roles in drug-product liability and represent some very interesting theories of liability. Since the analysis of drug injury can help prevent recurrence by educating the entire healthcare profession, this book presents numerous case reports. Of interest, despite FDA's recognition of ephedra/caffeine dietary supplements in 1995 and a proposed rule to limit use and dosage, it still took the agency until 2004 to finally and officially ban the useless (and obviously dangerous) product. Up until this point, ephedra had been regulated as a "dietary supplement." In reality, this substance acted like a toxic drug. Finally, there is a peek at OxyContin litigation in the form of a report by this expert, as part of an updated chapter on Pain Medications.

Many chapters—such as Performance Enhancing Drugs—address toxic drug products, such as anabolic steroids, modified steroids, corticosteroids, hepatotoxins, diabetic drugs, and others. Some of these chapters include discussions and case reports on drug-product liability issues related to the individual drugs.

I believe that the pharmacist's most important job is to ensure that drugs are used safely and effectively. We included updated chapters on many of the specialized pharmacist chapters from the First Edition, and have recruited contributions in the areas of emergency-department care, the identification of drug dosage forms, the appropriate use of intravenous medications, the role of the pharmacoepidemiologist, and a new chapter on pharmacist errors. A special chapter by attorney Sweeney discusses the roles of pharmacy technicians. Del Konnor, a former Executive Director of the Managed Care Pharmacy Association, has contributed a chapter on pharmacy-benefits managers (PBMs), who currently affect millions of American lives, and who also have been involved in some high-profile litigation. We are fortunate to have a compiled Pharmacy Case-Law Update by Morris and Carpenter—both pharmacist/attorneys—adapted from a very popular presentation at the Annual Meeting of the American Society of Pharmacy Law.

Pharmacy got a big black eye, dropping a notch in the public trust, following the news of the Courtney case—the Kansas City pharmacist who was diluting chemotherapy drugs and cheating patients out of life-sustaining (or at least palliative) chemotherapy. This was not malpractice—more like greed-driven criminal acts. A special review of the Courtney story is included in a new chapter on Pharmacist Malpractice.

A chapter by medical-malpractice defense attorneys Barkus and Derian covers physician and hospital liability in drug and medical-device litigation. The medication error chapter has been extensively expanded. A collaboration amongst pharmacist O'Donnell, nurse Iyer, and physician Cohen brings three different analyses and points of view to this topic exploration. According to the Institute of Medicine's (IOM) report "To Err is Human," originally published in 1999, between 44,000 and 98,000 people die every year from medical errors that occur in hospitals. About 7,000 of these were attributable to medication errors in 1993—comprising one out of every 131 outpatient deaths and one out of every 854 in-patient deaths. One study referenced in the report found that almost 2 percent of all hospital admissions experienced a preventable adverse drug event, resulting in average increased hospital costs of $4,700 per admission, or about $2.8 million annually for a 700-bed teaching hospital. This problem is not limited to hospital patients either. In fact, hospitalized patients represent only a small number out of the total population at risk of experiencing a medication-related error. "Numerous studies document errors in prescribing medications, dispensing by pharmacists, and

unintentional non-adherence on the part of the patient," reads the IOM report. "Medication errors have the potential to increase as a major contributor to avoidable morbidity and mortality as new medications are introduced for a wider range of indications." A *JAMA* article described the enormity of drug-related deaths as the equivalent of two 747s crashing every week. Of course, where there is injury, there may be litigation. When education and safe-pharmacy practice fail, affected patients have a right to investigate and seek damages for their injuries. Many times, that is all that they can do, because their injuries are permanent or fatal.

Because drugs are ubiquitous, and because they affect people's lives and practice outside the walls of the hospital and drugstore, we again include chapters on Recreational Drugs and the Forensic Pharmacist. We have also added a new chapter on Drug Testing in the Workplace, by Anne D. ImObersteg, a toxicologist/attorney. As stated earlier, a focused audience is attorneys, who usually have no training in FDA, pharmacy, or regulatory law, and who certainly have no training in pharmacology or the pathology of drugs. Yet, in a wide spectrum of practices, attorneys must master these complex topics to represent their clients. The First Edition of *Drug Injury* was well received by legal, medical, pharmacy, and nursing practitioners and scholars. The First Edition is used as a textbook in several universities, and can be found in numerous medical, pharmacy, and law libraries, the FDA library, and in private law offices throughout the United States.

And, finally…Vioxx.

The only good thing about a delayed publication of this book is that the Vioxx withdrawal and some of its immediate fallout occurred before the final press date. As mentioned above, there has already been a Senate hearing on the topic, looking for answers on how this drug got to and stayed on the market with such serious toxicity. A short summary of the events to date gives a little bit of the story: Merck announced a market withdrawal of their $3 billion blockbuster drug, Vioxx, on September 29, 2004. The cardiovascular risk (heart attacks, blood clots, strokes) that had dominated the medical news for the prior three years was proven again in a second study. Merck stock price dropped 25 percent in one day, a $25 billion drop in the capitalization of the company. Patients, physicians, pharmacists, the news media, the FDA—everyone had comments and concerns. Questions were raised about a "class effect"—did this toxicity extend to other "COX-2 inhibitors," such as Celebrex (Pharmacia) or Bextra (Pfizer)? Lots of questions. Overnight, amidst Internet and television solicitations by attorneys recruiting Vioxx cases, Merck announced that there were several hundred lawsuits filed. Recently, Merrill Lynch estimated an $18 billion litigation price tag related to Vioxx.

Vioxx is another shocking and disturbing chapter in the pharmaceutical industry. Shocking because it scares patients who take prescription medications, and it disheartens physicians and pharmacists who prescribe and dispense the drugs. Since the publication of the First Edition, several other drugs have been removed from the market for safety reasons, and severe prescribing limitations have been applied to many more.

A review of the pharmacology of Vioxx may answer some questions as to what happened. Aspirin (acetylsalicylic acid) has been in use for over 100 years and it has had great success in relieving the pain and inflammation caused by arthritis. For several centuries prior to the chemical synthesis of acetylsalicylic acid, ground willow bark was used to relieve fever, pain, and inflammation. The willow bark worked because it contained salicylic acid. Even after it was chemically described, the mechanism of action of aspirin remained a mystery until about 30 years ago, when Sir John Vane described the chemical pathways of prostaglandin synthesis. The process identified prostaglandins. Prostaglandins are found throughout the body and serve as mediators of cell-membrane function and other physiological functions. Of course, we know that more than a dozen NSAIDs (non-steroidal anti-inflammatory drugs) were developed in the intervening 30 years. These NSAIDs worked on this prostaglandin cascade.

Two sites of possible drug action were discovered, both of which featured an enzyme called cyclooxegenase (COX). These two sites of biological synthesis of prostaglandins are called COX-1 and COX-2. COX-1 is thought to be a site used to protect cells and cell membranes, while COX-2 is thought to activate components of the body's inflammatory cell response to injury or infection. Prostaglandins can promote vasodilation, change capillary permeability, and modulate the degree and extent of inflammation. In conditions such as rheumatoid arthritis (RA), inflammation is accompanied by pain, swelling, and fever.

Aspirin is a member of the family of NSAIDs, which include Motrin, Advil, Butazolidin, Naprosyn (Aleve), Voltaren, Clinoril, and Indocin. All of these NSAIDs are effective and similar in effectiveness at therapeutic doses. All of them also have the potential for GI side effects, especially gastric ulcers and GI bleeding. All of the listed NSAIDs inhibit both COX-1 and COX-2, and because both COX-1 and COX-2 are found throughout the body, they have other influences that are still being discovered. One such function is that inhibition of COX-1 receptors interferes with the amount and thickness of the mucosal lining of the stomach, which results in gastric acid coming into contact with the underlying tissue with bleeding and ulcer formation. Another effect of COX-1 inhibition is an effect on platelets that renders them less "sticky," and therefore reduces their ability to form the platelet plugs that initiate thrombosis inside a blood vessel. It is now understood that in patients at risk for cardiovascular heart disease, it is a good thing for platelets to be less likely to aggregate (this diminishes the risk of coronary-artery thrombosis in arteries with damaged intimal linings due to atherosclerosis).

Vioxx was developed in response to the NSAIDs predictable risk of GI bleeding in the event of simultaneous COX-1 and COX-2 inhibition. If a chemical could be found that selectively inhibited only COX-2 and had little or no effect on COX-1, patients who had not been able to tolerate NSAIDs would be able to obtain relief from pain and inflammation, without the GI side-effect risks. Vioxx is considered to be a specific COX-2 inhibitor.

Vioxx is no more effective than non-specific NSAIDs in inhibiting inflammation. The manufacturer's claims and promotion of this product are based on the lack of adverse effect of Vioxx on the gastric mucosa. Researchers have hypothesized that there is more than one iso-enzyme form for COX-2. One iso-form of COX-2 might be associated with disease states, such as RA, and another iso-form of COX-2 might be involved with normal physiology.

COX-1 inhibition affects the following parts of the body: synovial joint tissue, platelet aggregation, gastric mucosa, and the kidneys. COX-2 inhibition affects the following body tissues and/or functions: synovial joint tissue, vascular endothelium, tissue repair, bone formation, and the kidneys.

Platelets are affected by non-selective COX-1 and COX-2 inhibitors, by reducing platelet production of thromboxane, A2 (TXA2). This product is part of the cascade of chemical reactions that the body uses to begin and limit coagulation in normal physiology. Non-selective NSAIDs, such as aspirin, slightly diminish the "stickiness" of platelets, which are literally physiological plugs. The effect is a slight degree of anti-coagulation, which is desirable in patients at risk for a coronary-artery thrombosis. With selective COX-2 inhibition, platelet agglutination increases (or, at least, does not provide the anti-coagulation benefit of non-selective NSAIDs). Selective COX-2 inhibition, as seen with celecoxib, elevates blood pressure and promotes leukocyte adherence.

In conducting clinical studies of safety and efficacy, the manufacturer limited its safety data to patients who had received Vioxx for up to nine months. After receiving market approval, this drug was highly promoted, and millions of doses have been taken. Postmarketing data shows that at around 18 months of Vioxx use, an increased incidence of cardiovascular adverse events was being reported. It was unclear whether this unexpected event is the result of an un-explained risk of Vioxx causing coronary and cerebral artery thrombosis, or whether it could be, instead, due to the lack of platelet inhibition and anti-coagulation provided by non-specific NSAIDs. Merck argued the latter. What is clear is that the adverse events were occurring after the time period employed in the clinical trials. In other words, the clinical trials had not evaluated the risk of these serious adverse effects prior to market release.

It is obvious that nine months was not a long-enough study period to successfully uncover the long-term risks of Vioxx in a population likely to continue to take this or another drug for several years. Secondly, if the increased CV risk is due to a failure to interact with COX-1 while inhibiting COX-2, then this should be considered a class effect, as the increased risk could be shared by other COX-2 inhibitors on the market, such as Celebrex and Bextra.

The FDA's AERS database contains voluntary reports from the population of adverse events reported in association with prescription medications. All of the AERS reports in the database through first quarter, 2002, were examined for the drug names Vioxx, Celebrex, and naproxen. All reports that listed one or more of these drug names were then searched for reports of thrombotic events involving the heart and brain. These data do not establish cause and effect, but they do show that the risk of acute myocardial infarction (almost always due to blockage caused by atherosclerosis and thrombosis) is twice as high with Vioxx than it is with non-selective NSAIDs, such as naproxen.

The populations studied in clinical trials are not a subset of the general population, and, therefore, may not be representative of the risk the population experiences after the release of a newly approved drug to the general prescription-drug market. The continuing influence of COX-2 inhibitors on cardiovascular and cerebrovascular adverse effects will require further study to evaluate the risk exposure faced by the general population. Prospective studies evaluating cardiac outcomes after long-term administration of rofecoxib (or other COX-2 inhibitors) in combination with aspirin have not been conducted. Prospectively designed studies to collect additional CV outcomes data from the selective COX-2 inhibitors are currently underway. Data from these prospectively designed studies, when added to the extensive data already available, will provide an even more comprehensive picture of the CV safety profile of the selective COX-2 inhibitors.

Summary

In closing, *Drug Injury, Second Edition* is intended to serve as a broad and deep reference for anyone with a professional or personal interest in drug use and the dangers of drug injury. The book shows how pharmacists play pivotal roles in the proper administration and use of prescription medications, and clearly highlights the perils of untrained or careless practitioners. I and all of the authors and editors of *Drug Injury* sincerely hope that readers will learn from the lessons contained within this text, collaborating together to create a safer future for all of us.

James O'Donnell,
Pharm.D., M.S., FCP, ABCP, FACN, R.Ph.
Associate Professor of Pharmacology,
Rush University Medical Center, Chicago, IL
President, Pharmaconsultant Inc., Chicago, IL

About the Editor

James O'Donnell, Pharm.D., M.S., FCP, ABCP, FACN, R.Ph., is a pharmacologist, pharmacist and nutritionist from Barrington Hills, Illinois. His career has included pharmacy practice in a variety of settings, as well as teaching, research, publications, and consultations in pharmacology, pharmacy, and nutrition to industry, government, health care, publishing and legal fields. He is Associate Professor of Pharmacology at the Rush University Medical Center in Chicago, where he serves as the Course Director for the Medical Pharmacology program. He also holds Faculty appointments at the University of Illinois Colleges of Medicine and Pharmacy. Dr. O'Donnell is a Diplomate of the American Board of Clinical Pharmacology, a fellow of the American College of Clinical Pharmacology, a fellow of the American College of Nutrition, Founding Editor-in-Chief of the Journal of Pharmacy Practice, and Editor of *Drug Injury: Liability, Analysis, and Prevention, First Edition* (2001) and *Second Edition* (2005), aand a Co of-Editor *Pharmacy Law: Litigating Pharmaceutical Cases* (1995), and*The Process of New Drug Discovery and Development, Second Edition* (CRC Press 2005). He consults and testifies in matters involving pharmaceuticals, medication errors, nutritionals, dietary supplements, alcohol and recreational drug toxicity, and drug injuries throughout the United States, for defense and plaintiffs' counsel. Dr. O'Donnell received a Bachelor of Science in Pharmacy from the University of Illinois, a Doctor of Pharmacy from the University of Michigan, and a Master of Science in Clinical Nutrition from Rush University.

About the Contributors

Gopi Doctor Ahuja, MPH, Burr Ridge, Illinois

Antonia Alafris, B.S., Pharm.D., CGP, Clinical Associate Professor, Arnold & Marie Schwartz College of Pharmacy of Long Island University; Assistant Director of Pharmacotherapy Services and Pharmacy Residency Programs, Kingsbrook Jewish Medical Center, Department of Pharmacy, Brooklyn, New York

Loyd V. Allen, Jr., B.S., M.S., Ph.D., Editor-in-Chief, *International Journal of Pharmaceutical Compounding*, Edmond, Oklahoma

Peter D. Anderson, Pharm.D., Consultant Pharmacist, Randolph, Massachusetts

Robert S. Baratz, M.D., DDS, Ph.D., Newton, Massachusetts

Ramune E. Barkus, Esq., Principal, Barkus & Associates, Burbank, California

Stephen Barrett, M.D., Pittsboro, North Carolina

David M. Benjamin, Ph.D., FCLM, FCP, Boston, Massachusetts

David C. Clark, Ph.D., Professor of Psychiatry, Assistant Dean for Clinical Research and Professor of Psychiatry, Department of Psychiatry and Behavioral Medicine, Medical College of Wisconsin, Milwaukee, Wisconsin

Henry Cohen, B.S., M.S., Pharm.D., FCCM, BCPP, CGP, Arnold & Marie Schwartz College of Pharmacy and Health Sciences of Long Island University; Chief Pharmacotherapy Officer, Director of Pharmacy Residency Programs, Kingsbrook Jewish Medical Center, Brooklyn, New York

Victor Cohen, B.S., Pharm.D., Assistant Professor of Pharmacy Practice, Arnold & Marie Schwartz College of Pharmacy and Health Sciences; Clinical Pharmacy Manager; Department of Emergency Medicine Residency Program Director, Divisions of Pharmacotherapy, Department of Pharmaceutical Services, Maimonides Medical Center, Brooklyn, New York

Kathleen M. Dahle, RN, B.S.N., Legal Nurse Consultant, The Dent Law Firm, Fort Worth, Texas

Paul N. Danese, Ph.D., Vice President, FDAble, LLC, Glastonbury, Connecticut

Armand Derian, Esq., Glendale, California

S. Albert Edwards, Pharm.D., RAC, FRAPS, Consultant and Drug Information Expert, Lincolnshire, Illinois

Constantine John Falliers, M.D., Clinical Professor, University of Colorado School of Medicine, Allergy and Asthma Clinic, P.C., Denver, Colorado

Todd W.B. Gehr, M.D., Professor of Medicine, Chairman Division of Nephrology, Virginia Commonwealth University, Richmond, Virginia

Vincent Idemyor, Pharm.D., Consultant, Chicago, Illinois

Anne D. ImObersteg, M.S., J.D., MBA, B.A. (Deceased)

Patricia Iyer, MSN, RN, LNCC, CLNI, President, Med League Support Services, Flemington, New Jersey

Christopher A. Keys, B.S., Pharm.D., BCPS, RPh, President, Clinical Pharmacy Associates, Laurel, Maryland

William N. Kelly, Pharm.D., FISPE, President, William N. Kelly Consulting, Inc., Oldsmar, Florida

Roger S. Klotz, R.Ph., BCNSP, FASCP, FACA, CDM, Regional Coordinator/Assistant Professor of Pharmacy Practice, Pamona, California

Charles R. Kozak, J.D., Law Offices of Charles Kozak, San Francisco, California

Mary E. Kremzner, Pharm.D., Center for Drug Evaluation and Research, U.S. Food and Drug Administration, Silver Spring, Maryland

Rita Marcoux, R.Ph., MBA, Assistant Research Professor, University of Rhode Island, Kingston, Rhode Island

Donald H. Marks, M.D., Ph.D., Clinical Assistant Professor, Voluntary, Division of General Internal Medicine, Department of Medicine, University of Alabama, Birmingham, Alabama

Ned Milenkovich, Pharm.D., J.D., McDonald Hopkins, Chicago, Illinois

Justina A. Molzon, M.S., Pharm., J.D., Associate Center Director for International Programs, Center for Drug Evaluation and Research, U.S. Food and Drug Administration, Silver Spring, Maryland

Roger Morris, R.Ph., J.D., Partner-Chairman Health Care Practice Group, Quarles & Brady Streich Lang, LLP, Phoenix, Arizona

Francis J. Muno, Jr., B.S., Pharm., R.Ph., MBA, Wayne, Illinois

Megan Musselman, B.S., Pharm.D., Clinical Pharmacist, Emergency Medicine, Saint Luke's Health System, Kansas City, Missouri

Jadwiga Najib, Pharm.D., Professor of Pharmacy Practice, Long Island University, Arnold and Mary Schwartz College of Pharmacy and Health Sciences, Long Island, New York

Lori A. Nesbitt, Pharm.D., MBA, Chief Executive Officer, Compass Point Research, Nashville, Tennessee

James J. O'Donnell III, M.S., Ph.D., Department of Medicine, Section of Pulmonary and Critical Care, University of Chicago, Chicago, Illinois

Kimberly O'Donnell, MBA, Senior Pricing Analyst and Program Manager, Rolling Meadows, Illinois

Damani Parran, Ph.D., DABT, Manager of Toxicology, Owner, Parran Consulting Group, Westfield, New Jersey; Manager, Global Personal Care Product Assurance and Regulatory, AkzoNobel Surface Chemistry, LLC, Bridgewater, New Jersey

Gourang Patel, B.S. Chem, Pharm.D., MSc, BCPS, Assistant Professor of Pulmonary Medicine and Pharmacology, Rush University Medical Center, Chicago, Illinois

Karen L. Pellegrin, Ph.D., MBA, University of Hawaii, College of Pharmacy, Hilo, Hawaii

Kip A. Petroff, Esq., Partner, Petroff & Associates, Dallas, Texas

Domenic A. Sica, M.D., Professor of Medicine and Pharmacology, Chairman, Section of Clinical Pharmacology and Hypertension, Division of Nephrology, Virginia Commonwealth University, Richmond, Virginia

John C. Somberg, M.D., Professor of Pharmacology and Medicine, Rush University, Chicago, Illinois

William J. Stilling, R.Ph., M.S., J.D., Attorney at Law, Parsons Behle & Latimer, Salt Lake City, Utah

Ed Sweeney, Esq., Wusinich, Brogan, and Stanzione, Downington, Pennsylvania

F. Randy Vogenberg, R.Ph., Ph.D., Senior Vice President and National Practice Council Leader, Aon Consulting, Providence, Rhode Island

Saifi Vohra, Pharm.D., RPh, MBA, FASHP, FASCP, Provider Solutions Inc., Westmont, Illinois

Vanessa M. Vullmahn, M.S., Graduate Student, Biopharmaceutics Department, University of Illinois at Chicago, Chicago, Illinois

Sondra Wacker, CIM, Vice President of Ethics and Compliance, Compass Point Research, Nashville, Tennessee

James P. Walters, J.D., M.S., Attorney at Law; Adjunct Professor of Law, The John Marshall Law School, Chicago, Illinois

Part I
The Pharmaceutical Process

Chapter 1

The FDA and Drug-Approval Process

Justina A. Molzon, M.S. Pharm., J.D., and Mary E. Kremzner, Pharm.D.

1.1 Introduction

In the United States, medical products are developed and used within a complex system involving players with various goals and responsibilities:

- manufacturers who develop and test products and submit applications for their approval to the FDA;
- the FDA, which has an extensive premarketing review and approval process and which uses a series of postmarketing surveillance programs to gather data on and assess risks;
- healthcare practitioners involved in the healthcare delivery system; and
- patients, who rely on this complex system to provide them with the necessary interventions to protect them from injury.

Although medical products are required to be safe, safety does not mean zero risk. A safe product is one that has reasonable risks when balancing the benefit expected and the available alternatives. All players in the complex medical product development and delivery system (see Figure 1.1) have a role to play in maintaining balance in the risk-benefit ratio by ensuring that medical products are developed, tested, manufactured, labeled, prescribed, dispensed, and used such that risk is minimized and benefit is maximized.

Disclaimer: The views expressed in this chapter are those of the author's and do not necessarily represent the views of the U.S. Food and Drug Administration.

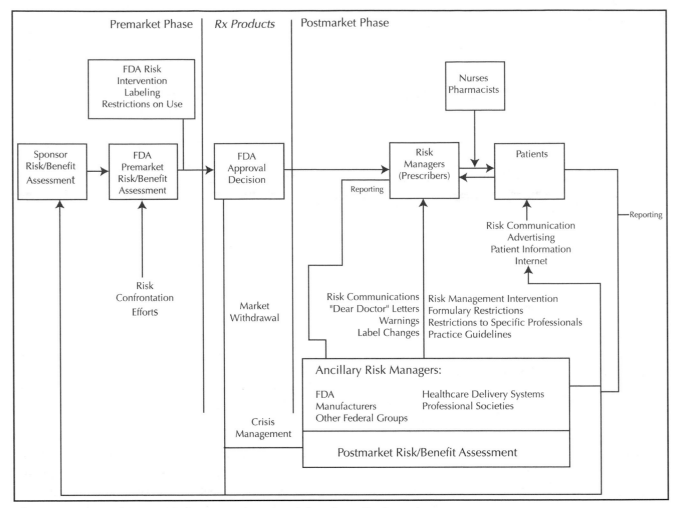

Figure 1.1 *Complex system for managing the risks of medical products.*

The FDA's responsibilities in this system—as laid out in the Federal Food, Drug, and Cosmetic Act—are largely devoted to pre- and postmarketing risk assessment. The FDA approval or non-approvable decision is the agency's central risk-management action. The FDA must ensure that beneficial medical products are available and labeled with adequate information on their risks and benefits while protecting the public from unsafe products or false claims.

The FDA approves a product when it judges that the benefits of using a product outweigh the risks for the intended population and use. A major goal of the premarketing review is to ensure that products are truthfully and adequately labeled for the population and use. Labeling is given considerable emphasis because it is the chief tool the agency uses to communicate risk and benefit to the healthcare community and patients.

However, once medical products are on the market, ensuring safety is principally the responsibility of healthcare providers and patients, who make risk decisions on an individual, rather than on a population, basis. They are expected to use the labeling information to select and use products wisely, thereby minimizing adverse events.

To assist with postmarketing risk management, the agency maintains a system of complex postmarketing surveillance and risk-assessment programs to identify adverse events that are not identified during medical product development and premarketing review. The FDA investigates suspected adverse events associated with the use of an approved medical product. The agency uses this information to initiate labeling updates and, on rare occasions, to reevaluate the marketing decision.

1.2 Clinical Studies (Overview)

The new drug application (NDA) is the vehicle through which drug sponsors formally propose that the FDA approve a new pharmaceutical for use in the United States (Figure 1.2). To obtain this authorization, a drug manufacturer submits an NDA nonclinical (animal) and clinical (human) test data and analyses, drug information, and descriptions of manufacturing procedures.

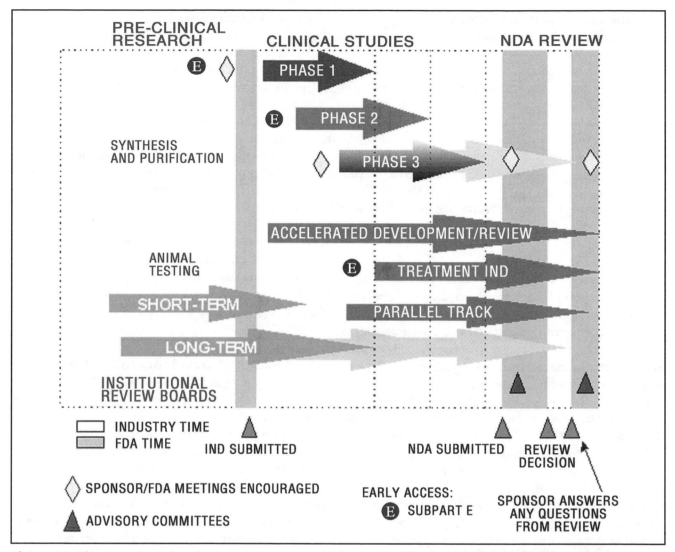

Figure 1.2 *The new drug development process: steps from test tube to new drug application review.*

An NDA must provide sufficient information, data, and analyses to permit FDA reviewers to reach several key decisions, including whether the

- drug is safe and effective for its proposed uses, and whether the benefits of the drug outweigh its risks;
- drug's proposed labeling is appropriate and, if not, what the drug's labeling should contain; and
- methods used in manufacturing the drug and the conditions used to maintain the drug's quality are adequate to preserve the drug's identity, strength, quality, and purity.

The purpose of pre-clinical work—animal pharmacology/toxicology testing—is to develop adequate data to support a decision that it is reasonably safe to proceed with human trials of the drug. Clinical trials represent the ultimate premarket testing for unapproved drugs. During these trials, an investigational compound is administered to humans and is evaluated for its safety and effectiveness in treating, preventing, or diagnosing a specific disease or condition. The results of this testing will comprise the single most important factor in the approval or disapproval of a new drug.

Although the goal of clinical trials is to obtain safety and efficacy data, the overriding consideration in these studies is the safety of those in the trials. The FDA's Center for Drug Evaluation and Research (CDER) monitors the study design and conduct of clinical trials to ensure that people in the trials are not exposed to unnecessary risks.

1.3 Phases of Clinical Studies

The four phases of clinical studies are:

- the initial introduction of an investigational new drug into healthy volunteers to evaluate safety,
- small clinical studies conducted with patients to obtain preliminary data on the effectiveness of the drug and further safety data,
- large clinical trials to evaluate safety and efficacy in groups of patients with the disease to be treated, and
- postmarketing commitments and postmarket requirements.

A. Phase 1 Clinical Studies

Phase 1 includes the initial introduction of an investigational new drug to human research subjects. These studies are closely monitored and may be conducted in patients, but are usually conducted in healthy volunteer subjects. These studies are designed to determine the metabolic and pharmacologic actions of the drug in humans, to determine the side effects associated with increasing doses, and, if possible, to gain early evidence on effectiveness. During Phase 1, sufficient information about the drug's pharmacokinetics and pharmacological effects should be obtained to permit the design of well-controlled, scientifically valid, Phase 2 studies.

Phase 1 studies also evaluate drug metabolism, structure-activity relationships, and the mechanism of action in humans. These studies also determine which investigational drugs are used as research tools to explore biological phenomena or disease processes. The total number of subjects included in Phase I studies varies with the drug, but is generally in the range of 20 to 80.

In Phase 1 studies, the CDER can impose a clinical hold (i.e., prohibit the study from proceeding or stop a trial that has started) for reasons of safety, or because of a sponsor's failure to accurately disclose the risk of study to investigators. Although the CDER routinely provides advice in such cases, investigators may choose to ignore any advice regarding the design of Phase 1 studies in areas other than patient safety.

B. Phase 2 Clinical Studies

Phase 2 includes the early controlled clinical studies conducted to obtain preliminary data on the effectiveness of the drug for a particular indication or indications in patients with the disease or condition. This phase of testing also helps uncover the common short-term side effects and risks associated with the drug. Phase 2 studies are typically well-controlled, closely monitored, and conducted in a relatively small number of subjects (usually several hundred people).

C. Phase 3 Clinical Studies

Phase 3 studies are expanded controlled and uncontrolled trials. They are performed after preliminary evidence suggesting effectiveness of the drug has been obtained in Phase 2, and are intended to gather the additional information about efficacy and safety that is needed to evaluate the overall benefit-risk relationship of the drug. Phase 3 studies also provide an adequate basis for extrapolating the results to the general population and transmitting that information in the prescribing information. Phase 3 studies usually include several hundred to several thousand people.

In both Phase 2 and 3, the CDER can impose a clinical hold if a study is unsafe (as in Phase 1), or if the protocol is clearly deficient in design in meeting its stated objectives. Great care is taken to ensure that this determination is not made in isolation, but that it reflects current scientific knowledge, agency experience with the design of clinical trials, and experience with the class of drugs under investigation.

1.4 Accelerated Development or Review

Accelerated development or review (*Federal Register*, April 15, 1992) is a highly specialized mechanism for speeding the development of drugs that promise significant benefit over existing therapy for serious or life-threatening illnesses for which no therapy exists. This process incorporates several novel elements aimed at making sure that rapid development and review is balanced by safeguards to protect both the patients and the integrity of the regulatory process.

Accelerated development or review can be used under two special circumstances: when approval is based on evidence of the product's effect on a "surrogate endpoint," or when the FDA determines that safe use of a product depends on restricting its distribution or use. A surrogate endpoint is a laboratory finding or physical sign that may not be a direct measurement of how a patient feels, functions, or survives, but is still considered likely to predict therapeutic benefit for the patient.

The fundamental element of this process is that the manufacturers must continue testing after approval to demonstrate that the drug indeed provides therapeutic benefit to the patient. If not, the FDA can withdraw the product from the market more easily than usual.

1.5 Treatment IND (T-IND)

Treatment investigational new drugs (*Federal Register*, May 22, 1987) make promising new drugs available to desperately ill patients as early in the drug-development process as possible. The FDA will permit an investigational drug to be used under a treatment IND if there is preliminary evidence of drug efficacy and the drug is intended to treat a serious or life-threatening disease, or if there is no comparable alternative drug or therapy available to treat that stage of the disease in the intended patient population. In addition, these patients are not eligible to be in the definitive clinical trials, which must be well underway, if not almost finished.

An immediately life-threatening disease means a stage of a disease in which there is a reasonable likelihood that death will occur within a matter of months, or in which premature death is likely without early treatment. For example, advanced cases of AIDS, herpes simplex encephalitis, and subarachnoid hemorrhage are all considered to be immediately life-threatening diseases. Treatment INDs are made available to patients before general marketing begins, typically during Phase 3 studies. Treatment INDs also allow the FDA to obtain additional data on the drug's safety and effectiveness.

More recently, in August 2009, the FDA issued two final rules to improve access to investigational drugs which amends regulations on expanded access. The first final rule clarifies existing regulations and adds new types of expanded access for treatment use. Under the final rule, expanded access to investigational drugs for treatment use will be available to individual patients, including in emergencies, intermediate-size patient populations, and larger populations under a treatment protocol or T-IND.

The second final rule amends the IND regulation on charging patients for investigational drugs. The rule elucidates the appropriate conditions for charging for an investigational drug in a clinical trial, provides criteria for charging for an investigational drug for the different types of expanded access for treatment use and clarifies what costs can be recovered.

1.6 Parallel Track

An older mechanism that permitted wider availability of experimental agents is the "parallel track" policy (*Federal Register*, May 21, 1990) developed by the U.S. Public Health Service in response to AIDS. Under this policy, patients with AIDS whose condition prevents them from participating in controlled clinical trials can receive investigational drugs shown in preliminary studies to be promising.

1.7 Subpart E

Subpart E in Section 312 of the Code of Federal Regulations establishes procedures to expedite the development, evaluation, and marketing of new therapies intended to treat people with life-threatening and severely debilitating illnesses, especially where no satisfactory alternatives exist (*Federal Register*, October 21, 1988).

1.8 Investigational New Drug (IND) Application

In many ways, the investigational new drug (IND) application is the result of a successful pre-clinical development program. The IND is also the vehicle through which a sponsor advances to the next stage of drug development known as clinical trials (human trials).

During a new drug's early pre-clinical development, the sponsor's primary goal is to determine whether the product is reasonably safe for initial use in humans, as well as whether the compound exhibits pharmacological activity that justifies commercial development. When a product is identified as a viable candidate for further development, the sponsor then focuses on collecting the data and information necessary to establish that the product will not expose humans to unreasonable risks when used in limited, early-stage clinical studies.

Generally, this includes data and information in three broad areas:

- Animal pharmacology and toxicology studies. Pre-clinical data to permit an assessment as to whether the product is reasonably safe for initial testing in humans.
- Manufacturing information. Information pertaining to the composition, manufacture, stability, and controls used for manufacturing the drug substance and the drug product. This information is assessed as to whether the company can adequately produce and supply consistent batches of the drug.
- Clinical protocols and investigator information. Detailed protocols for proposed clinical studies to assess whether the initial-phase trials will expose subjects to unnecessary risks. Also, information on the qualifications of clinical investigators—professionals (generally physicians) who oversee the administration of the experimental compound—to assess whether they are qualified to fulfill their clinical trial duties.

The IND is not an application for marketing approval. Rather, it is a request for an exemption from the federal statute that prohibits an unapproved drug from being shipped in interstate commerce. Current federal law requires that a drug be the subject of an approved marketing application before it is transported or distributed across state lines. Because a sponsor will probably want to ship the investigational drug to clinical investigators in many states, it must seek an exemption from that legal requirement. The IND is the means through which the sponsor technically obtains this exemption from the FDA; however, its main purpose is to detail the data that provide documentation that it is, indeed, reasonable to proceed with certain human trials with the drug.

Due to growing public interest in investigational new drugs, the Food and Drug Administration Modernization Act (FDAMA) of 1997 required the FDA to establish a clinical trial registry. This database, www.clinicaltrials.gov, contains information on more than 69,000 clinical trials conducted in more than 160 countries. The Food and Drug Administration Amendments Act of 2007 (FDAAA) increases the usefulness of this database by requiring the availability of more clinical trials and trial-related information. The Clinical Trials website (www.clinicaltrials.gov) has grown to include "basic results" information describing the results of certain trials.

1.9 New Drug Application (NDA)

For decades, the regulation and control of new drugs in the United States has been based on the New Drug Application (NDA). Since 1938, every new drug has been the subject of an approved NDA before U.S. commercialization. The data gathered during the animal studies and human clinical trials of an investigational new drug (IND) become part of the NDA.

The NDA has evolved considerably during its history. When the Food, Drug, and Cosmetic Act (FD&C) was passed in 1938, NDAs were required to contain only information pertaining to the investigational drug's safety. In 1962, the Kefauver-Harris Amendments to the FD&C Act required NDAs to contain evidence both that a new drug was effective for its intended use as well as that the established benefits of the drug outweighed its known risks.

The NDA was again the subject of change in 1985, when the FDA completed a comprehensive revision of the regulations pertaining to NDAs. While this revision, commonly called the NDA Rewrite, modified content requirements, it was mainly intended to restructure the ways in which information and data are organized and presented in the NDA to expedite FDA reviews.

Further modification of formatting of the NDA is currently underway as part of an initiative of the International Conference on Harmonisation of Technical Requirements for Registration of Pharmaceuticals for Human Use (ICH) (www.ich.org). Through the ICH process, considerable harmonization has been achieved among the three regions (Japan, Europe, and the United States) in the organization of a submission for the registration of pharmaceuticals for human use. The culmination of these efforts is the Common Technical Document (CTD) (www.ich.org/products/ctd.html), a modular presentation of technical documentation acceptable by ICH regulators.

A common format for regulatory submissions will significantly reduce the time and resources needed to compile applications for registration of human pharmaceuticals and will ease the preparation of electronic submissions. Regulatory reviews and communication with the applicant will be facilitated by a standard document of common elements. In addition, exchange of regulatory information between regulatory authorities will be simplified.

1.10 Fundamentals of NDA Submissions

Although the quantity of information and data submitted in NDAs can vary significantly, the components of NDAs are more uniform. The components of any NDA are, in part, a function of the nature of the subject drug and the information available to the applicant at the time of submission. As outlined in Form FDA-356h, "Application to Market a New Drug, Biologic or an Antibiotic Drug for Human Use," NDAs can consist of as many as 15 different sections:

- index
- summary
- chemistry, manufacturing, and control
- samples, methods validation package, and labeling
- nonclinical pharmacology and toxicology
- human pharmacokinetics and bioavailability
- microbiology (for anti-microbial drugs only)
- clinical data
- safety update report (typically submitted 120 days after the NDA's submission)
- statistics
- case-report tabulations
- case-report forms
- patent information
- patent certification
- marketing and advertising
- other information

1.11 NDA Classifications

CDER classifies NDAs with a code that reflects both the type of drug being submitted and its intended uses. The numbers one through seven are used to describe the type of drug:

1. new molecular entity
2. new salt of previously approved drug (not a new molecular entity)
3. new formulation of previously approved drug (not a new salt *or* a new molecular entity)
4. new combination of two or more drugs

5. already marketed drug product—duplication (i.e., new manufacturer)
6. new indication (claim) for already marketed drug (includes switch in marketing status from prescription to OTC)
7. already marketed drug product—no previously approved NDA

The following letter codes describe the review priority of the drug:

A. Standard review for drugs similar to currently available drugs
P. Priority review for drugs that represent significant advances over existing treatments

1.12 Labeling Review

Each statement proposed for drug labeling must be justified by data and results submitted in the NDA. The Code of Federal Regulations (C.F.R.) describes labeling requirements in 21 C.F.R. Part 201—Labeling. In January 2006, the FDA issued a final prescription drug labeling rule. The rule is based on research and focus groups addressing the usefulness of the current label and prescribing information. These revisions make it easier for healthcare providers to access, read, and use prescribing information, and enhance the safe and effective use of prescription drug products.

The new regulations phase in the requirement for drug manufacturers to submit prescription drug labeling, or prescribing information, in a new format. The new labeling format contains three main sections, highlights, contents, and full prescribing information. Format changes include consolidating and adding new sections, emphasizing *"Patient Counseling Information,"* which establishes a minimum font size, and encourages adverse event reporting.

These revisions make it easier for healthcare providers to access, read, and use prescribing information, and they enhance the safe and effective use of prescription drug products.

As a result of the new regulations the prescribing information is organized in the following sections:

*   Highlights—a concise summary of information most important to prescribers and refers prescribers to the appropriate section or sections in the Full Prescribing Information
*   Contents—an index of the Full Prescribing Information
*   Full Prescribing Information
*   Boxed Warning:

A. Indications & Usage
B. Dosage & Administration
C. Dosage Forms & Strengths
D. Contraindications
E. Warnings & Precautions
F. Adverse Reactions
G. Drug Interactions
H. Use in Specific Populations
I. Drug Abuse & Dependence
J. Overdosage
K. Description
L. Clinical Pharmacology
M. Nonclinical Toxicology
N. Clinical Studies
O. References
P. How Supplied/Storage & Handling
Q. Patient Counseling Information

When an NDA nears approval, agency reviewers evaluate draft-package labeling for accuracy and consistency with the regulatory requirements for applicable prescription or over-the-counter drugs. Each element of the proposed labeling—including indications, use instructions, and warnings—is evaluated in terms of conclusions drawn from animal and human testing. All claims, instructions, and precautions must accurately reflect submitted clinical results.

If the CDER has concerns about the draft labeling, the center will contact the sponsor detailing suggested revisions. CDER comments can relate to almost any aspect of the proposed labeling. For example, the CDER can comment on drug indications and warnings or suggest general changes in wording and format.

The labeling "negotiation process," through which a drug's final approved labeling is agreed on, can take from a few weeks to many months. The length of the process depends on the number of agency comments and an applicant's willingness to reach agreement. Sometimes a sponsor will submit several revisions of labeling before agreement with the FDA on the labeling can be reached. New regulations enhance FDA's ability to make suggested labeling changes when new safety information is identified. Manufacturers are limited to 30 days to respond to these suggestions although the timeline can be shortened if the change is necessary due to a public health threat.

New product labeling is now being cataloged on "DailyMed," a new interagency online health information clearinghouse that provides the most up-to-date drug product information to consumers, healthcare providers, others. Labeling can be accessed through the National Library of Medicine at http://dailymed.nlm.nih.gov.

1.13 Additional FDA-Approved Patient Labeling

- Patient package inserts: For some prescription medicines, the FDA approves special patient materials to instruct patients about the safe use of the product. These materials may be given to patients by their healthcare provider or pharmacist, and are considered part of FDA-regulated product labeling.
- Medication guides: The FDA may require distribution of Medication Guides. Medication Guides are FDA-approved patient information, for selected prescription drugs that pose a serious and significant public-health concern.

Medication guides are required if the FDA determines that one or more of the following circumstances exist:

- Patient labeling could help prevent serious adverse effects.
- The drug product has serious risks (relative to benefits) of which patients should be made aware because information concerning the risks could affect patients' decision to use, or to continue to use, the product.
- The drug product is important to health, and patient adherence to directions for use is crucial to the drug's effectiveness.

A list of medication guides is available at www.fda.gov/drugs/drugsafety/ucm085729.htm.

1.14 The Generic-Drug-Approval Process
A. Abbreviated New Drug Applications (ANDAs)

A generic-drug product is one that is comparable to an innovator drug product (also known as the reference listed drug [RLD] product as identified in the FDA's list of Approved Drug Products with Therapeutic Equivalence Evaluations) in dosage form, strength, route of administration, quality, performance characteristics, and intended use.

Abbreviated New Drug Applications (ANDAs) are submitted to the FDA's Center for Drug Evaluation and Research, Office of Generic Drugs, for review and approval. Once approved, an applicant may manufacture and market the generic-drug product, provided all patent protection and exclusivity associated with the RLD have expired.

Generic-drug applications are termed "abbreviated," because they are not required to provide clinical data to establish safety and efficacy, since these parameters have already been established by the approval of the innovator drug product (first approved version of the drug product marketed under a brand name).

B. Bioequivalence Review

The FDA requires an applicant to provide information to establish bioequivalence. Such information may include:

- a formulation comparison for products whose bioavailability is self-evident, for example, oral solutions, injectables, or ophthalmic solutions where the formulations are identical
- comparative dissolution testing where there is a known correlation between in vitro and in vivo effects
- in-vivo bioequivalence testing comparing the rate and extent of absorption of the generic to the reference product
- for non-classically absorbed products, a head-to-head evaluation of comparative effectiveness based on clinical endpoints

C. Chemistry or Microbiology Review

The chemistry or microbiology review provides assurance that the generic drug will be manufactured in a controlled, consistent manner. Areas such as manufacturing procedures, raw material specifications and controls, sterilization processes and validation, container and closure systems, and stability are reviewed to assure that the drug will perform in an acceptable manner.

D. Labeling Review

The labeling review ensures that the proposed generic-drug labeling is identical to that of the reference listed drug, except for differences due to a change in manufacturer, patent or exclusivity issues, or if approval is based on a suitability petition. Furthermore, the Division of Medication Error Prevention and Analysis in the Office of Surveillance and Epidemiology reviews the product labels. Labeling review serves to identify and resolve issues of confused or mistaken identity that may arise in drug labeling in an effort to avoid drug mix-ups and prevent medication errors.

E. ANDA Approval

After all components of the application are found to be acceptable, an approval letter is issued to the applicant, detailing the conditions of the approval, and providing the company with the ability to market the generic-drug product. If the approval occurs prior to the expiration of any patents or exclusivities accorded to the reference listed drug product, a tentative approval letter is issued to the applicant detailing the tentative approval of the generic-drug product until the patent or exclusivity condition has expired. A tentative approval does not allow the applicant to market the generic-drug product.

1.15 Over-the-Counter Drug Products

Over-the-counter (OTC) drug products are drugs available to consumers without a prescription. There are more than 80 classes (therapeutic categories) of OTC drugs, ranging from acne drug products to weight-control drug products. As with prescription drugs, the CDER oversees OTC drugs to ensure that they are properly labeled and that their benefits outweigh their risks.

OTC drugs play an increasingly vital role in America's healthcare system by providing easy access to certain drugs that can be used safely without the help of a healthcare practitioner. This enables consumers to take control of their own health care in many situations. There are more than 100,000 OTC drug products marketed, encompassing about 800 significant active ingredients. Most OTC drug products have been marketed for many years. For this reason, the FDA has been evaluating the ingredients and labeling of these products as part of "The OTC Drug Review Program." The goal of this program is to establish OTC drug monographs for each class of products. OTC drug monographs are a kind of "recipe book" covering acceptable ingredients, doses, formulations, and labeling. Monographs will continually be updated, adding additional ingredients and labeling, as needed. Products conforming to a monograph may be marketed without further FDA clearance, while those that do not must undergo separate review and approval through the "New Drug Approval System." The NDA system—not the monograph system—is also used for new ingredients entering the OTC marketplace for the first time. For example, the newer OTC products (previously available only by prescription) are first approved through the NDA system, and their "switch" to OTC status is approved via the NDA system.

1.16 Postmarketing Surveillance

The goal of the CDER's postmarketing surveillance system is to monitor the ongoing safety of marketed drugs. This is accomplished by reassessing drug risks based on new data obtained after the drug is marketed, and recommending ways to appropriately manage that risk. This is accomplished through a variety of activities and tools that are outlined below.

A. Adverse Event Reporting

Even the large, well-designed Phase 3 clinical studies that are conducted by drug manufacturers cannot uncover every problem that can come to light once a product is widely used. For this reason, receipt of adverse event reports after a product is FDA approved is critical in order to continuously evaluate product safety over its lifecycle. To capture this critical data—especially serious adverse-event data—the CDER receives adverse events from drug manufacturers, who are required by regulation to submit adverse event reports to FDA. In addition, the FDA has a medical products reporting program called "MedWatch" to promote and facilitate voluntary reporting of serious adverse events, medication errors, and product problems with drugs by healthcare practitioners and patients (www.fda.gov/safety/medwatch/howtoreport/default.htm).

The FDA is especially interested in learning of "serious" events that follow drug use. Serious events are generally defined as those that involve death, a life-threatening condition, hospitalization, disability, a congenital anomaly, or intervention to one of these serious outcomes. Additionally, the FDA is interested in learning of all medication errors regardless of patient outcome. In return, the FDA keeps healthcare professionals informed about new safety concerns and may issue a communication to the public describing the concern. The FDA shares information in the interest of informing doctors, other healthcare providers and patients. It generally includes information about the safety issue, factors to consider when making treatment decisions, and other information that patients need to know in order to safely use the drug. The FDA's information sharing is mainly accomplished through MedWatch Safety Alerts (www.fda.gov/safety/medwatch/safetyinformation/default.htm) and other FDA safety web postings.

B. Adverse Event Reporting System (AERS)

A powerful drug-safety tool is the Adverse Event Reporting System. This computerized system combines the voluntary adverse drug event and medication error reports from MedWatch and the required reports from manufacturers. These reports often form the basis of "signals" that there may be a potential for serious, unrecognized, drug-associated events and medication errors. When a signal is detected, further testing of the hypothesis is undertaken using various epidemiological and analytic databases, studies, and other instruments and resources. The reports in AERS are evaluated by clinical reviewers in the Center for Drug Evaluation and Research (CDER) to detect safety signals and to monitor drug safety. They form the basis for further epidemiological studies when appropriate. As a result, the FDA may take regulatory actions to improve product safety and protect the public health.

C. The Food and Drug Administration Amendments Act (FDAAA)

The Food and Drug Administration Amendments Act (FDAAA) was passed in 2007 and gave the FDA new authorities to require manufacturers to conduct necessary post-approval studies and post-approval clinical trials to assess a known serious risk related to the use of a drug, to assess signals of serious risk related to the use of a drug, or to identify an unexpected serious risk when available data indicates the potential for a serious risk. A postmarketing requirement (PMR) is a study or trial that a sponsor is required to conduct post-approval. PMRs are sometimes necessary as a condition of approval and are useful to collect more safety information. In contrast, a postmarketing commitment (PMC) is a study or trial to conduct post-approval that a sponsor agrees to in writing, but not required by law. The FDA tracks and monitors the progress of PMRs and PMCs to ensure that they are completed in a timely manner. Please refer to more information on FDAAA in Section 1.19.

1.17 Drug Safety

Drug safety is the focus of CDER's Office of Surveillance and Epidemiology (www.fda.gov/aboutfda/transparency/track/ucm206800.htm). The Office of Surveillance and Epidemiology (OSE) works with the Office of New Drugs and other programs in CDER to evaluate the safety profiles of drugs available to U.S. consumers using a variety of tools and disciplines throughout the lifespan of drugs. OSE maintains a system of postmarketing surveillance and risk-assessment programs to identify medication errors and adverse events that did not appear during the drug-development process. Adverse event data is collected through required reporting by companies and through voluntary reports submitted to the FDA's MedWatch program, which, together, total over 500,000 reports per year. Staffs in OSE use this information to identify drug-safety concerns and recommend actions to improve product safety and protect the public health. Potential actions include updating drug labeling, providing more information to the community, implementing or revising a risk-management program, and, on rare occasions, removing products from the market. OSE, OND and other CDER offices also evaluate data and initiate appropriate regulatory actions regarding medication errors related to confusing container labels, carton labeling, drug packaging, and drug names that look or sound similar.

The Office of Surveillance and Epidemiology (OSE) is organized in five program divisions whose staff works across division lines on multi-disciplinary drug safety teams within OSE and CDER.

1. Division of Epidemiology (DEPI)
2. Division of Medication Error Prevention Analysis (DMEPA)
3. Division of Pharmacovigilance I (DPV1) and Division of Pharmacovigilance II (DPV2)
4. Division of Risk Management (DRISK)

The Drug Safety and Risk Management Advisory Committee continues to advise the FDA on both general and product-specific safety issues. The Committee is comprised of nationally recognized experts in the areas of risk perception, risk management, pharmacoepidemiology, clinical pharmacology, clinical research, and medication errors.

A. Division of Epidemiology (DEPI)

DEPI consists of epidemiology teams and a drug use analysis team. Staff in DEPI are tasked with conducting epidemiology reviews of postmarketing safety issues (review of the literature, sponsor submitted postmarketing observational safety protocols and final study reports), and performing observational pharmacoepidemiology safety studies to confirm, quantify and characterize drug safety signals. DEPI is also tasked with performing drug utilization studies to characterize the extent and patterns of use of approved drugs by analyzing commercially available proprietary databases. Additionally, the division procures and maintains all drug use databases and participates in the procurement of epidemiology data resources for conducting pharmacoepidemiology drug safety research and collaborates with external research organizations and federal partners in drug safety research.

B. Division of Medication Error Prevention and Analysis (DMEPA)

The Division of Medication Error Prevention and Analysis (DMEPA) staff includes pharmacists and nurses trained in evaluating root causes of medication error. DMEPA staff performs premarketing reviews of proposed proprietary names and determines the overall acceptability of the name. The staff also evaluates container labels, carton labeling, and packaging design in CDER. This evaluation focuses on the medication error potential of a proposed product. DMEPA also detects, reviews, and assesses all medication error safety signals reported to CDER and determines appropriate action, such as public communication about new or emerging risks, or regulatory action such as requiring safety labeling changes. They also provide recommendations on Risk Evaluation and Mitigation Strategies (REMS).

C. Division of Pharmacovigilance I and II (DPVI and DPVII)

Division of Pharmacovigilance staff includes safety evaluators and medical officers whose primary role is to detect and assess safety signals for all marketed drug products. They work closely with medical reviewers in the Office of New Drugs, so that potential safety signals are considered in the context of existing pharmacologic, pre-clinical, clinical, and postmarketing knowledge of the drugs in question.

D. Division of Risk Management (DRISK)

The Division of Risk Management (DRISK) leads OSE's review of all patient-directed labeling, including Medication Guides, Patient Package Inserts, and Patient Instructions for Use. The Division provides input on appropriate risk mitigation measures for drugs with significant safety concerns and reviews all Risk Evaluation and Mitigation Strategies (REMS) proposals and other risk management plans submitted by the manufacturers. Finally, the Division reviews all REMS Assessments and oversees internal research designed to assess risk communication and mitigation strategies.

1.18 Drug Safety and Risk Management Advisory Committee

The Drug Safety and Risk Management Advisory Committee paired with OSE advise the FDA on both general and product-specific safety issues. The Committee is comprised of nationally recognized experts in the areas of risk perception, risk management, pharmacoepidemiology, clinical pharmacology, clinical research, and medication errors.

1.19 Recent FDA Initiatives Related to Drug Safety

CDER has taken steps to equalize its efforts and resources devoted to drug development and postmarket drug safety. The science of safety offers new opportunities for addressing a fundamental dilemma: the trade-off between safety and access. The "Safety First" initiative includes strengthening the Center's scientific and review capability and capacity, and increasing the overall presence of safety reviewers in drug regulatory decision-making.

The complementary component of the *Safety First* initiative is the *Safe Use Initiative*. "Safe use" is the term the FDA uses to describe a long-term effort to expand the Center's mission to ensure that medicines are used safely and appropriately throughout the lifecycle of the drug. This initiative is accomplished by working in partnership with other components of the health care system.

FDAAA also authorizes the FDA to require sponsorholders of certain applications for prescription drug and biological products to submit proposed risk evaluation and mitigation strategies (REMS) and to implement an approved REMS if the agency determines that a REMS is necessary to ensure that the benefits of a drug outweigh the risk of the drug and certain criteria are met. The FDA began to implement REMS in March 2008.

The FDA may require an REMS to include one or more of the following elements:

- a medication guide, which is a paper handout/pamphlet that is required to be distributed to patients with certain medications by the pharmacist. Medication Guides convey risk information that is specific to particular drugs and drug classes, and they contain FDA-approved information that can help patients avoid serious adverse events.
- a patient package insert, which is another form of FDA-approved patient-directed labeling that the FDA can require in a REMS if it may help mitigate the serious risks of the drug.
- a communication plan to healthcare providers to support implementation of the REMS.
- elements to assure safe use, which usually restrict the distribution of the drug in some manner.

For a list of approved REMS, visit www.fda.gov/drugs/drugsafety/postmarketdrugsafetyinformationforpatientsandproviders/default.htm. For Medication Guides, visit www.fda.gov/drugs/drugsafety/ucm085729.htm.

FDAAA also mandates that FDA develop a website with postmarket drug safety information for patients and providers, which is available at www.fda.gov/drugs/drugsafety/postmarketdrugsafetyinformationforpatientsandproviders/default.htm. This website contains links to postmarket drug safety information to improve transparency and communication to patients and healthcare providers. The FDA is required to post information from each summary analysis of adverse drug reaction reports received for newly approved drugs. These summary reports are prepared after a drug has been approved for 18 months or after 10,000 individuals have used the drug, whichever is later. This report must include the identification of any new risks not previously identified, potential new risks, or known risks reported in unusual number.

FDAAA includes an additional requirement for the FDA to conduct regular, bi-weekly screenings of the Adverse Event Reporting System and post a quarterly report on the reporting system website (www.fda.gov/drugs/guidancecomplianceregulatoryinformation/surveillance/adversedrugeffects/ucm082196.htm). The Center now posts on the Internet a quarterly report of new safety information or potential signals of a serious risk identified from the AERS. The appearance of a drug on this list does not mean that the FDA has concluded that the drug has this listed risk. It means that the FDA has identified only a potential safety issue. If after further evaluation the FDA determines that the drug is associated with the risk, it may take a variety of actions including some previously mentioned. Please refer to more information on FDAAA in Section 1.16.C.

In 2005, the FDA established a Drug Safety Oversight Board comprised of members from government, which include the FDA and medical experts from other health and human services agencies and government departments. The board's primary objectives are to provide independent oversight and advice to CDER leadership on the management of important drug safety issues, and manage the flow of emerging safety information to healthcare professionals and patients. An important drug safety issue is one that has the potential to alter the benefit/risk analysis for a drug in such a way as to affect decisions about prescribing or taking the drug.

1.20 *Sentinel System*

In September 2007, Congress passed, and the President signed, the Food and Drug Administration Amendments Act (FDAAA). Section 905 of FDAAA called for active postmarket drug safety surveillance and analysis. Specifically, it called for the HHS Secretary to develop methods to obtain access to disparate data sources and to establish a postmarket risk identification and analysis system to link and analyze healthcare data from multiple sources. The law set goals of accessing healthcare data from 25 million people by July 1, 2010, and 100 million people by July 1, 2012. The law also required the FDA to work closely with partners from public, academic, and private entities.

In May 2008, the Secretary of the Department of Health and Human Services (HHS) and the Commissioner of the Food and Drug Administration announced the *Sentinel Initiative*, a long-term effort to create a national electronic system for monitoring FDA-regulated medical product safety. The *Sentinel System*, which will be developed and implemented in stages as the science and technology matures, will expand FDA's existing postmarket safety surveillance systems by enabling the FDA to *actively* gather information about the safety and performance of its regulated products once they reach the market.

The active electronic safety surveillance system that will be established through the *Sentinel Initiative* will complement available methods for safety signal identification in several ways:

- improve capability to identify and evaluate safety issues in near real time
- expand capacity for evaluating safety issues
- improved access to defined populations (e.g., the elderly, patients with diabetes)
- improved access to longer term data
- improve capability to identify increased risks of common adverse events (e.g., myocardial infarction, fracture) that healthcare practitioners may not suspect are related to medical products

FDA has long been interested in expanding its safety monitoring capabilities in just such a manner. The combination of new authorities, progress in health information technology, and increased national interest in using the information that is collected in administrative and medical record databases to inform the understanding of medical product safety, has enabled the FDA to launch this ambitious program.

The *Sentinel System*, as currently envisioned, would utilize *active surveillance methodologies* to monitor postmarket medical product safety. The *Sentinel System* would employ a distributed model, in which all personally identifiable information would remain with its data holders in its local environment, protected by existing firewalls and managed by those most familiar with the data. The FDA would develop questions targeted to medical product–adverse event pairs of concern and submit them for evaluation to participating data holders, including academic centers, healthcare systems, and medical insurance companies. Participating data holders would evaluate the medical product–adverse event pair in their databases and return only summaries of results. Using active surveillance methodologies, the FDA would be able to enhance its understanding of postmarket safety issues to help inform regulatory decisions and, ultimately, inform healthcare decision-making.

1.21 Applicable Statutes and Implementing Regulations

A. Food and Drug Acts of 1906

This first drug law required only that drugs meet official standards of strength and purity. The burden of proof was on the FDA to show that a drug's labeling was false and fraudulent before it could be taken off the market.

B. Food, Drug and Cosmetic Act (1938)

A bill was introduced into the Senate in 1933 to completely revise the 1906 drug law—widely recognized then as being obsolete. But Congressional action was stalled. It took a tragedy in which 107 people died from a poisonous ingredient in "Elixir Sulfanilamide" to prompt passage of revised legislation that—for the first time—required a manufacturer to prove the safety of a drug before it could be marketed. Among other provisions, the law also eliminated the Sherley Amendment requirement to prove intent to defraud in drug-misbranding cases, provided for tolerances, authorized factory inspections, and added the remedy of court injunction to previous remedies of seizure and prosecution.

C. Durham-Humphrey Amendment (1951)

Until this law, there was no requirement that any drug be labeled for sale by prescription only. The amendment defined prescription drugs as those unsafe for self-medication and that should, therefore, be used only under a physician's supervision. Until this time, pharmacists could sell any drugs to patients without any physician's prescription.

D. Drug Amendments (1962)

News reports about the role of FDA medical officer Frances O. Kelsey, M.D., in keeping the drug thalidomide off the U.S. market, aroused public interest in drug regulation. Thalidomide had been associated with the birth of thousands of malformed babies in western Europe. In October 1962, Congress passed these amendments to tighten control over drugs. Before marketing a drug, firms now had to prove not only safety, but also effectiveness, for the product's intended use. The requirement was applied retroactively to 1938, when the FDC Act was passed. (Pre-1938 drugs were "grandfathered"—allowed to be sold because they were generally recognized as safe and effective—provided no evidence to the contrary developed.) To help implement the amendments, the FDA contracted with the National Academy of Sciences/National Research Council to review the efficacy of drugs approved solely on the basis of safety since 1938. This review was referred to as the Drug Efficacy Study Implementation (DESI). Firms were also required to send adverse-reaction reports to the FDA, and drug advertising in medical journals was required to provide complete information to doctors—the risks as well as the benefits, described as a brief summary. In fact, most ads now publish the entire package insert.

E. Orphan Drug Act (1983)

"Orphans" are drugs and other products for treating rare diseases. They may offer little or no profit to the manufacturer, because of the limited market, but may benefit people with the rare disease. To foster orphan product development, this law allows drug companies to take tax deductions for about three-quarters of the costs of their clinical studies. Firms also are given exclusive marketing rights for seven years for any orphan products that are approved.

F. Drug Price and Competition and Patent Term Restoration Act (1984)

This law expands the number of drugs suitable for an Abbreviated New Drug Application, or ANDA. ANDAs make it less costly and time-consuming for generic drugs, which are often sold at lower prices than brand-name drugs, to reach the market. "Patent term restoration" refers to the 17 years of legal protection given a firm for each drug patent. Some of that time allowance is used while the drug goes through the approval process, so this law allows restoration of up to five years of lost patent time.

Though not involving changes in law, the following changes in three of FDA's drug regulations are noteworthy.

1. Revision of New Drug Application Regulations (1985)

These changes provide for safety reports after an application for a new drug is submitted, more focused and better organized data, use of summaries and tables for easier review, earlier problem solving, and allowance of approval on the basis of foreign studies alone. It also strengthens the monitoring of adverse reactions from marketed drugs.

2. Revision of Investigational New Drug Application Regulations (1987)

Encourages problem-solving meetings with the FDA, requires deadlines in safety reports, and increases sponsor control over initial human test design, as long as subjects face no unreasonable, significant risks.

3. Treatment Use of Investigational New Drugs (1987)

Patients with serious or immediately life-threatening diseases, such as AIDS, may now get treatment with experimental drugs that show reasonable evidence of potential benefit—provided no satisfactory approved therapy exists. This applies only to drugs already being studied in controlled clinical studies. Also, the drugs cannot expose patients to unreasonable risks.

G. Prescription Drug User Fee Act (1992)

The Prescription Drug User Fee Act (PDUFA) provides the FDA with resources for a period of five years to accelerate the review of applications, without compromising safety and efficacy standards. The goal of PDUFA is to focus on reviewing timeliness. By improving FDA review efficiency, while concurrently improving the quality of submissions by the industry, overall approval times will improve and result in earlier patient access to safe and effective new therapies. (General Accounting Office report, *FDA Drug Approval:*

Review Time Has Decreased in Recent Years, www.fda.gov/aboutfda/reportsmanualsforms/reports/userfeereports/performancereports/pdufa/ucm117257.htm.)

H. FDA Modernization Act of 1997

The Modernization Act (FDAMA) implemented important provisions regarding patient access to experimental drugs and medical devices, information on clinical trials, pharmacy compounding, food safety and labeling, and other matters.

One provision of the act abolishes a prohibition on manufacturers' dissemination of information about unapproved uses of drugs and devices, permitting them to disseminate peer-reviewed journal articles, provided that they commit to file, within a specified timeframe, an application to establish the safety and effectiveness of the unapproved use for a period of five years. The statute also added a new provision requiring tracking of the status of postmarketing approval studies. One of the most important pieces of the legislation is one that reauthorizes, for another five years, user fees paid by manufacturers for prescription drugs. Since 1992, funding from the fees provided the Agency with resources to reduce (from 30 months to 15 months) the average time for new drug review. The act is available at www.fda.gov/regulatoryinformation/default.htm.

I. FDA Amendments Act of 2007

The FDA Amendments Act (FDAAA) of 2007 is a combination of six different pieces of prescription drug and medical device legislation reflecting new authorities given to the FDA.

Four sections of the Act are reauthorizations—the Prescription Drug User Fee Act, the Medical Device User Fee and Modernization Act, the Best Pharmaceuticals for Children Act, and the Pediatric Research Equity Act. The fifth legislative amendment expands the authority of the FDA to assess and manage drug risks. The sixth is new legislation to encourage specialized pediatric medical device development and to create a foundation (Reagan-Udall) to modernize product development, accelerate innovation, and enhance product safety.

1.22 Controlling Statute

The controlling statute concerning the approval of drugs in the U.S. is governed by 21 U.S.C. § 301 *et seq*. The Federal Food Drug and Cosmetic Act (FD&C) contains the basic definitions of a "drug" and a "new drug," for purposes of FDA approval. In particular, subsections 201 (g); 21 U.S.C. 321 (g); 21 C.F.R. parts 310 and 314 provide insight into this process.

As defined in FD&C Act 201 (g), a drug is an article recognized by the United States Pharmacopeia, or other officially recognized national formulary. The definition also includes articles intended for use in the diagnosis, cure, mitigation, treatment, or prevention of disease. The statute covers articles other than food that are designed to affect the structure or any function of the body.

The definition of a "drug" previously excluded "devices." In 1990, Congress removed this exclusion due to the wide acceptance of some products, drugs, and devices.

1.23 Classification as Food or Drug?

The classification of a product as a drug is based on the claims or representations made by the manufacturer in the labeling or advertising literature of the product. The definition of "labeling" is contained in FD&C Act, 201 (m), 201(n), 502; 21 U.S.C. §§ 321 (m), 321 (n), 352; 21 C.F.R. part 201 (see Chapter 11, *Important Code of Federal Regulations Applicable to Drug Product Liability Suits*).

It is important to note that because of the labeling requirement of a drug, a product can be regulated both as a food and a drug. This dual classification of a product can give rise to causes of action under different federal and state provisions. For example, see Chapter 32, *Nonscientific Uses and Illegal Marketing of Drugs and Dietary Supplements*. As with l-tryptophan, some products can be regulated both as foods and drugs. This often happens when the manufacturer makes both nutritional claims and medical claims. See *U.S. v. Vitasafe Formula M*, 226 F. Supp. 266 (DNJ 1964).

Chapter 2

Dietary Supplement and Health Education Act of 1994 (DSHEA) and Related FDA Activities

Justina A. Molzon, M.S. Pharm., J.D.

2.1 Definition of a Dietary Supplement

The FDA traditionally considered dietary supplements to be composed only of essential nutrients, such as vitamins, minerals, and proteins. The Nutrition Labeling and Education Act of 1990 added "herbs, or similar nutritional substances" to the definition of "dietary supplement."

DSHEA broadens the definition to include, with some exceptions, any product intended for ingestion as a supplement to the diet. This includes vitamins, minerals, herbs, botanicals, other plant-derived substances, amino acids and concentrates, metabolites, and constituents and extracts of these substances.

As a result, DSHEA covers substances such as ginseng, garlic, fish oils, psyllium, enzymes, glandulars, and mixtures of these.

It's easy to spot a supplement, because DSHEA requires manufacturers to include the words "dietary supplement" on product labels. Also, as of March 1999, a "Supplement Facts" panel is required on the labels of most dietary supplements.

Dietary supplements come in many forms, including tablets, capsules, powders, softgels, gelcaps, and liquids. Though commonly associated with health-food stores, dietary supplements also are sold in grocery, drug, and national discount-chain stores, as well as through mail-order catalogs, television programs, the Internet, and direct sales.

Dietary supplements are not drugs. A drug—which sometimes can be derived from plants used as traditional medicines—is an article that, among other things, is intended to diagnose, cure, mitigate, treat, or prevent diseases. Before marketing, drugs must undergo clinical studies to determine their effectiveness, safety, possible interactions with other substances, and appropriate dosages; and the FDA must review these data and authorize the drugs' use before they are marketed. The FDA does not authorize or test dietary supplements.

A product sold as a dietary supplement and touted in its labeling as a new treatment or cure for a specific disease or condition would be considered an unauthorized—and thus illegal—drug.

DSHEA established a formal definition of "dietary supplement" using several criteria. A dietary supplement:

Disclaimer: The views expressed in this chapter are those of the author's and do not necessarily represent the views of the U.S. Food and Drug Administration.

- Is a product (other than tobacco) that is intended to supplement the diet, bearing or containing one or more of the following dietary ingredients: a vitamin, a mineral, an herb or other botanical, an amino acid, a dietary substance for use by man to supplement the diet by increasing the total daily intake, or a concentrate, metabolite, constituent, extract, or combination of these ingredients
- Is intended for ingestion in pill, capsule, tablet, or liquid form
- Is not represented for use as a conventional food or as the sole item of a meal or diet
- Is labeled as a "dietary supplement"
- Includes products, such as an approved new drug, certified antibiotic, or licensed biologic that was marketed as a dietary supplement or food before approval, certification, or license (unless the Secretary of Health and Human Services waives this provision)

2.2 Overview of DSHEA

Signed by President Clinton on October 25, 1994, DSHEA acknowledges that millions of consumers believe dietary supplements may help to augment daily diets and provide health benefits. Congress' intent in enacting DSHEA was to meet the concerns of consumers and manufacturers and ensure that safe and appropriately labeled products remain available to those who want to use them.

In the findings associated with DSHEA, Congress stated that there may be a positive relationship between sound dietary practice and good health, and that while further scientific research was needed, there may be a connection between dietary supplement use, reduced healthcare expenses, and disease prevention.

The provisions of DSHEA define dietary supplements and dietary ingredients, establish a new framework for assuring safety, outline guidelines for literature displayed where supplements are sold, provide for use of claims and nutritional-support statements, require ingredient and nutrition labeling, and grant the FDA the authority to establish good-manufacturing-practice (GMP) regulations.

DSHEA also created an Office of Dietary Supplements in the National Institutes of Health to coordinate research on dietary supplements, and required the formation of an executive-level commission on dietary supplement labels to report on the use of claims in dietary supplement labeling.

DSHEA essentially gives consumers broad access to dietary supplements and gives supplement manufacturers the freedom to market more products as dietary supplements and to provide information about their products' benefits—

for example, in product labeling.

However, in choosing whether to use dietary supplements, consumers should be aware that under DSHEA, the FDA's requirement for premarket review of dietary supplements is less than that conducted for the other products it regulates, such as drugs and many additives used in conventional foods. This means that consumers and manufacturers have the responsibility of checking the safety of dietary supplements and determining the truthfulness of label claims.

Because of this, DSHEA also recognizes that there is a need for a rational regulatory framework that provides the FDA with the authority to remove products from the market that pose a "significant or unreasonable" risk to consumers (or that are otherwise adulterated), and to require accurate labeling for dietary supplements.

Since Congress considered dietary ingredients marketed prior to the passage of DSHEA to be generally safe, dietary supplements containing these ingredients are permitted to be freely marketed, just like regular foods (such as fresh fruits and vegetables).

If a supplement contains a new dietary ingredient that has not been in the food supply, however, Congress required the manufacturer to notify the FDA at least 75 days before marketing, and to include in the notification the manufacturer's basis for its conclusion that a dietary supplement containing the ingredient will reasonably be expected to be safe. There is no requirement that the firm wait for a safety determination from the FDA before marketing the product.

Should safety problems arise after marketing, DSHEA considers any dietary supplement that creates a "significant or unreasonable" risk to consumers to be "adulterated," thereby subjecting it to the FDA's enforcement action. Further, in particularly compelling cases, DSHEA allows the secretary to ban a dietary supplement if she finds it to be an "imminent hazard."

DSHEA grants the FDA explicit authority to establish good-manufacturing-practice (GMP) regulations for dietary supplements. Such regulations are intended to establish a mechanism to help assure purity and consistency in dietary supplement products.

In terms of labeling, DSHEA seeks to provide consumers with information to help guide their personal choices. This includes specially tailored requirements for ingredient labeling and nutrition labeling.

DSHEA also provides for the use of claims that a product affects the structure or function of the body, claims of general well-being from consumption of a nutrient or dietary ingredient, and claims of benefits related to classical nutrient-deficiency diseases.

These claims must include notification to the FDA

within 30 days after marketing, must be substantiated, and must be accompanied by the following disclaimer: "This statement has not been evaluated by the FDA. This product is not intended to diagnose, treat, cure, or prevent any disease."

Finally, DSHEA contains ground rules for publications used in connection with the sale of dietary supplements.

2.3 The FDA's Role in Implementation of DSHEA
A. Elements of the Dietary Supplement Program

The Center for Food Safety and Applied Nutrition (CFSAN) oversees the agency's activities related to dietary supplement products. The CFSAN has developed an overall dietary supplement strategy to address all elements of the dietary supplement program. This includes:

- Definitional boundaries between dietary supplements and conventional foods, between dietary supplements and drugs, and between dietary supplements and cosmetics
- Claims
- Good-manufacturing-practice regulations
- Adverse-event reporting, review, and follow-up
- Laboratory capability and research needs
- Enforcement needs
- Resource needs
- Stakeholder outreach

In its initial efforts under DSHEA, the agency concentrated on promulgating the many regulations mandated by DSHEA and began a number of other regulatory actions to establish the framework for implementation of the new statute.

Since passage of DSHEA, the FDA has published over 25 *Federal Register* notices regarding dietary supplements. A few specific DSHEA regulatory actions have included:

1. Good manufacturing practices

On February 6, 1997, the FDA published in the *Federal Register* an Advance Notice of Proposed Rulemaking, requesting comment on whether the FDA should institute rulemaking to develop current GMP regulations for dietary supplements and dietary ingredients. In February 1998, the FDA asked its Food Advisory Committee to establish a working group to assist it in defining GMP for dietary supplements.

The commissioner of the FDA at the time, Dr. Jane Henney, made the development and implementation of GMP regulations one of her priorities. Such regulations are an effective mechanism for consumer protection and would help assure the purity and consistency of dietary supplement products.

2. Labeling

On September 23, 1997, the FDA published a final rule in the *Federal Register* implementing the nutrition-labeling provisions of DSHEA. As of March 23, 1999 (the effective date of the regulation), all dietary supplements must bear nutrition information entitled "Supplement Facts." This labeling is similar to nutrition-content labeling for conventional foods, but is tailored to the special characteristics of dietary supplements.

3. Structure/function statements

On April 29, 1998, the FDA published in the *Federal Register* (and sought public comment on) a proposed rule defining the types of statements that could be made concerning the effect of a dietary supplement on the structure or function of the body. This action is intended to implement the provisions of DSHEA that permit structure/function claims but prohibit claims to treat or prevent disease. The comment period closed on September 28, 1998, and the agency received over 100,000 comments—many of which addressed the proposed definition of disease. As of publication of this book (2012), the agency was reviewing each of the comments and planned to re-evaluate each of the elements of the proposed rule in light of these comments.

4. Authoritative statement health claims

On January 21, 1999, the FDA published a proposed rule in the *Federal Register* to permit the use of health claims based on authoritative statements for dietary supplements under the notification procedures established in the Food and Drug Administration Modernization Act (FDAMA). This proposal tracks the language of Section 303 of the FDAMA and would place dietary supplements on an equal footing with conventional foods, with respect to health claims based on authoritative statements.

These proposals were open rulemakings that were still in progress as of publication of this book (2012).

B. Boundaries of Regulatory Classification

Before Congress passed DSHEA, dietary supplements (including vitamins and minerals) were regulated either as foods or as drugs, depending on their intended uses. If a product was used primarily for its taste, aroma, or nutritive value, it was regulated as a food. This meant that the ingredients used in such dietary supplements were subject to the food-additive provisions of the FD&C Act, which require the safety of an ingredient to be demonstrated before it may be marketed.

The supplement was also subject to regulation as a drug if therapeutic claims were made, such as claims to treat or prevent disease, if claims were made to affect the structure or function of the body through a non-nutritive mechanism, or if there was other evidence that the intended use of the product was as a drug. The supplement, with such claims, would have to meet the rigorous drug-safety and efficacy requirements of the FD&C Act, including—in the great majority of cases—premarket approval.

When Congress passed DSHEA, it created a previously non-existent regulatory framework for dietary supplements. The purpose of creating this new framework was to strike the right balance between providing consumers with access both to products and to truthful information about these products, while retaining the authority for the FDA to take action against products that presented safety problems or that were improperly labeled.

The FDA is now engaged in the difficult task of delineating boundaries between drugs, dietary supplements, and conventional foods. This is a task that requires great care, if the agency is to fulfill Congressional intent (with regard to the availability of dietary supplements), while still preserving the established food-additive and drug-regulatory frameworks for products that fall outside the dietary supplement boundaries.

For example, Congress has allowed dietary supplements that are designed to affect the structure or function of the body, but it has not permitted dietary supplements that are designed to treat, prevent, mitigate, cure, or diagnose disease (with the exception of dietary supplements bearing authorized health claims).

DSHEA required the FDA to draw a line between two types of intended uses that the agency never needed to distinguish previously. Congress also drew a line between conventional foods and dietary supplements, by saying that a dietary supplement may not be represented for use as a conventional food. This boundary also raises many complex issues that the agency is responsible for clarifying.

Aspects of DSHEA's dietary supplement definition that have proven especially problematic to implement include the statute's limitation of dietary supplements to products that are intended to supplement the diet, as well as its inclusion of dietary substances to supplement the diet as dietary ingredients that may be used in dietary supplements.

It is clear that the dietary ingredients specifically listed in DSHEA (vitamins, minerals, herbs or other botanicals, and amino acids) were intended by Congress to be broadly available under DSHEA, and many of these have a long history of safe use. Products are now being positioned as dietary supplements, however, by purporting to fall within the "dietary substance" language. The terms "dietary substance" and "intended to supplement the diet" are broad, but they must not allow the inclusion of ingredients never intended to fit within the universe of dietary supplements.

Currently, products that contain substances similar to those found in prescription drugs are marketed for children as dietary supplements. Likewise, products with ingredients that simulate illicit street drugs are marketed as dietary supplements to adolescents via the Internet and shops specializing in drug paraphernalia. The FDA is working toward a solution that will be consistent with the intent of DSHEA.

C. Labeling of a Dietary Supplement

The label of a dietary supplement must contain enough information about the composition of the product that consumers can make informed choices. The information must be presented in FDA-specified format. The manufacturer must make sure the label information is truthful and not misleading. The manufacturer is also responsible for making sure that all the dietary ingredients in the supplements are safe. Manufacturers and distributors do not need to register with the FDA or get FDA approval before producing or selling dietary supplements.

1. The new requirements for dietary supplement labels

Information required on the labels of dietary supplements includes:

- Statement of identity (e.g., "ginseng").
- Net quantity of contents (e.g., "60 capsules").
- Structure/function claim and the statement, "This statement has not been evaluated by the Food and Drug Administration. This product is not intended to diagnose, treat, cure, or prevent any disease."
- Directions for use (e.g., "Take one capsule daily").
- Supplement Facts panel (lists serving size, amount, and active ingredients).
- Other ingredients in descending order of predominance and by common name or proprietary blend.
- Name and place of business of manufacturer, packer, or distributor. This is the address to write for more product information.

2. "Supplement Facts" panel

As of March 23, 1999, the FDA began to request that more complete information appear on the labels of dietary supplement products. This information included an information panel titled "Supplement Facts," a clear identity statement, and a complete list of ingredients.

The "Supplement Facts" panel provides information, such as the quantity of specific nutrients in vitamin and mineral products, and the part of the plant used in herbal products. It is similar in format to the "Nutrition Facts" panel that appears on most processed foods.

Specifically, the "Supplement Facts" panel shows the following:

- The manufacturer's suggested serving size.
- Information about nutrients, when they are present in significant levels—such as vitamins A and C, calcium, iron and sodium—and the percentage of Daily Value, where a reference has been established (similar to nutrients listed in the "Nutrition Facts" panel on food labels).
- All other dietary ingredients present in the product, including botanicals and amino acids—those for which no daily value has been established.
- Herbal products are identified by the common or usual name and the part of the plant used to make the supplement (such as root, stem or leaf). If the common or usual name is not listed in Herbs of Commerce, published by the American Herbal Products Association, the Latin binomial name must be used.
- All ingredients in the product will be declared in the ingredient statement or within the "Supplement Facts" panel.
- A statement of identity will appear on the front panel of the product label.
- The statement must use the terms "dietary supplement" or a term identifying the contents of the product, such as "vitamin C supplement" or "herbal supplement."

The new labeling rule implements some of the major provisions of the Dietary Supplement Health and Education Act of 1994. The rule was published September 23, 1997, with an effective date of March 23, 1999—giving the industry 18 months to comply. Products labeled prior to that date can continue to be sold, until stocks are depleted.

The FDA surveys dietary supplement products on the market to check for compliance with the new labeling rules.

2.4 Claims Permitted under DSHEA

Claims that tout a supplement's healthful benefits have always been a controversial feature of dietary supplements.

Manufacturers often rely on them to sell their products. But consumers often wonder whether they can trust them.

Under DSHEA and previous food-labeling laws, supplement manufacturers are allowed to use three types of claims, when appropriate:

- Nutrient-content claims
- Disease claims
- Nutrition-support claims, which include "structure/function claims"

Nutrient-content claims describe the level of a nutrient in a food or dietary supplement. For example, a supplement containing at least 200 milligrams of calcium per serving may carry the claim "high in calcium." A supplement with at least 12 mg per serving of vitamin C may state on its label, "Excellent source of vitamin C."

Disease claims show a link between a food or substance and a disease or health-related condition. The FDA authorizes these claims based on a review of the scientific evidence.

Recently, the FDAMA authorized a second method for streamlined review of health claims. This involves the use of authoritative statements made by certain federal scientific bodies and the National Academy of Sciences in their publications. With this latter method, an interested party notifies the FDA of its intent to make a health claim based on an authoritative statement and provides information as to the source of the statement.

Certain dietary supplements may be eligible to carry disease claims, such as claims that show a link between:

- The vitamin folic acid and a decreased risk of neural tube defect-affected pregnancy, if the supplement contains sufficient amounts of folic acid
- Calcium and a lower risk of osteoporosis, if the supplement contains sufficient amounts of calcium

Nutrition-support claims can describe a link between a nutrient and the deficiency disease that can result if the nutrient is lacking in the diet. For example, the label of a vitamin C supplement could state that vitamin C prevents scurvy. When these types of claims are used, the label must mention the prevalence of the nutrient-deficiency disease in the United States.

A. Structure/Function Claims

Claims can also refer to the supplement's effect on the body's structure or function, including its overall effect on a person's well-being. As mentioned previously, these are known as structure/function claims. Examples of structure/function claims are:

- Calcium builds strong bones.
- Antioxidants maintain cell integrity.
- Fiber maintains bowel regularity.

Manufacturers can use structure/function claims without FDA authorization. They base their claims on review and interpretation of the scientific literature. Like all label claims, structure/function claims must be true and not misleading.

Structure/function claims are easy to spot because they must be labeled with the disclaimer: "This statement has not been evaluated by the Food and Drug Administration. This product is not intended to diagnose, treat, cure, or prevent any disease."

Manufacturers who plan to use a structure/function claim on a particular product must inform the FDA of the use of the claim no later than 30 days after the product is first marketed. While the manufacturer must be able to substantiate its claim, it does not have to share the substantiation with the FDA or make it publicly available.

B. The FDA's Dietary Supplement Proposal

Because dietary supplements are permitted to make disease-treatment and prevention claims without premarket review, the burden is on consumers to evaluate the validity of a myriad of claims about products marketed for serious and life-threatening conditions. For this reason the agency issued a proposed rule intended to provide direction to the industry as to the types of statements that can be made concerning the effect of a dietary supplement on the structure or function of the body and to clarify the line between disease and structure/function claims. This is important, because disease claims for drugs (as well as for conventional foods and dietary supplements) continue to require premarket authorization by the FDA.

The FDA's proposal, "Regulations on Statements Made for Dietary Supplements Concerning the Effect of the Product on the Structure or Function of the Body," published in the *Federal Register* on April 29, 1998, clarified for manufacturers what types of claims they may and may not use on the labels of dietary supplements.

The proposal, which is generally consistent with guidance provided by the Commission on Dietary Supplement Labels, describes allowable claims as truthful and non-misleading statements about the effect a substance has on a body system, organ, or function—provided that the context

in which the claim appears does not suggest that the product treats, prevents, or mitigates a disease.

The proposal describes and provides numerous examples of the various types of prohibited disease claims, and, when appropriate, contrasts them with examples of allowable structure/function statements.

Under the proposal, prohibited disease claims are statements that imply or state that:

- The product has an effect upon a specific disease or class of diseases. Examples of prohibited statements: "protects against the development of cancer," or "reduces the pain and stiffness associated with arthritis." Examples of allowable structure/function claims (no reference to a disease): "helps promote urinary-tract health," "helps maintain cardiovascular function," or "promotes relaxation."
- The product is in a drug class that is intended to be used to diagnose, mitigate, treat, cure, or prevent a disease. Examples of prohibited claims include description of the product as an "antibiotic," "antiseptic," "antidepressant," "laxative," "vaccine," or "diuretic." Examples of allowable product descriptions (no reference to disease treatment or prevention): an "energizer," a "rejuvenative."
- The product has an effect on one or more signs or symptoms that are recognizable to health professionals or consumers as being characteristic of a specific disease or diseases. Examples of prohibited claims: "lowers cholesterol," or "reduces joint pain." Examples of allowable claims (symptoms do not identify a disease): "reduces stress and frustration," "improves absentmindedness."
- The product is a substitute for, or augmentation of, a drug or other medical therapy. Examples of prohibited claims: product names such as "Herbal Prozac," or a suggestion that the product should be used "as part of your diet when taking insulin to help maintain a healthy blood-sugar level."
- The product has a role in the body's response to a disease or carrier of disease. Examples of prohibited claims: "supports the body's antiviral capabilities," "supports the body's ability to resist infection." Example of an allowable claim (effect on a normal body function): "supports the immune system."
- The product has an effect on a consequence of a natural state that presents characteristic signs or symptoms recognizable as constituting an abnormality of the body. Examples of prohibited claims:

"treats toxemia of pregnancy," or affects such abnormalities associated with aging as "decreased sexual function," "hot flashes," and "Alzheimer's disease."

- The product treats, prevents, or mitigates adverse events associated with a medical therapy or procedure. Examples of prohibited claims: "helps avoid diarrhea associated with antibiotic use," "reduces nausea associated with chemotherapy." Example of an allowable claim (no mention of a therapy or procedure): "helps maintain healthy intestinal flora."

- The product has an effect on a disease, made in one or more of the following ways:
  - The name of the product. Examples of prohibited product name: "Carpaltun" (implies effect on carpal-tunnel syndrome), "Raynaudin" (Raynaud's phenomenon) or "Hepatacure" (liver problems). Examples of allowable product names: "Cardiohealth," "Heart Tabs."
  - Statements about the formulation of the product—including the claim that the product contains an ingredient that is a well-known regulated drug, such as aspirin, laetrile, or digoxin.
  - Citation of a publication in which the title refers to a disease use. Example of a prohibited claim for vitamin E might be a reference to an article entitled "Serial Coronary Angiographic Evidence That Antioxidant Vitamin Intake Reduces Progression of Coronary Artery Atherosclerosis."
  - Use of the term "disease" or "diseased."
  - Suggestions of an effect on disease through pictures, vignettes, symbols, or other means. Since the passage of DSHEA, the FDA has received approximately 2,300 notifications from manufacturers about structure/function claims for their products. The agency has informed the manufacturers that about 150 of these claims are problematic, and it estimates that another 60 claims would not be permitted under the proposed criteria.

The FDA received over 150,000 comments on the proposed rule. Most of the comments objected to the proposed definition of disease or to some or all of the criteria for identifying disease claims.

Although the comments raised many issues, three issues received particular attention: (1) whether the FDA should retain the definition of "disease or health-related condition" issued for NLEA health claims, rather than issue a new definition of "disease"; (2) whether certain common conditions associated with natural states, such as hot flashes associated with menopause, or premenstrual syndrome associated with the menstrual cycle, should be considered "diseases"; and (3) whether dietary supplements may carry implied disease claims.

Because of the degree of controversy surrounding these issues, the FDA felt that further public discussion focused on the three issues would be useful. The FDA held a public meeting on August 4, 1999, to obtain further input on how to develop appropriate rules or policies that are consistent with the intent of DSHEA and with protection of the public health.

If the proposed rule becomes final, unacceptable structure/function claims will have to be removed from labeling, or the product will have to be approved as a drug under the Federal Food, Drug and Cosmetic Act.

C. Advertising

The FDA does not regulate advertisements for dietary supplements. The FDA oversees safety, manufacturing, and product information—such as claims in a product's labeling, package inserts, or accompanying literature. The Federal Trade Commission (FTC) regulates the advertising of dietary supplements and most other products sold to consumers. The FDA works closely with the FTC in this area, but different laws direct their work.

2.5 Monitoring the Safety of Dietary Supplements

For decades, the Food and Drug Administration regulated dietary supplements as foods, to ensure that they were safe and wholesome, and that their labeling was truthful and not misleading.

An important facet of ensuring safety was the FDA's evaluation of the safety of all new ingredients—including those used in dietary supplements—under the 1958 Food Additive Amendments to the Federal Food, Drug, and Cosmetic Act (FD&C Act).

With the passage of DSHEA, dietary supplements were deemed to be foods—except for purposes of the drug definition.

Congress specifically excluded "dietary ingredients" in dietary supplements from the definition of "food additive." As a result, dietary ingredients used in dietary supplements no longer require premarket documentation of safety for submission to the FDA, unless they are new dietary ingredients subject to the notification requirement in Section 413(a)(2) of the FD&C Act.

Food additives not generally recognized as safe must undergo the FDA's premarket approval process for new food ingredients. This requires manufacturers to conduct safety studies and to submit the results to the FDA for review before the ingredient can be used in marketed products. Based on its review, the FDA either authorizes or rejects the food additive.

In contrast, dietary supplement manufacturers who wish to market a new ingredient (i.e., an ingredient not marketed in the United States before 1994) have two options. The first involves submitting to the FDA, at least 75 days before the product is expected to go on the market, information that supports the conclusion that a new ingredient can reasonably be expected to be safe.

"Safe" means that the new ingredient does not present a significant or unreasonable risk of illness or injury under the conditions of use recommended in the product's labeling.

The information the manufacturer submits becomes publicly available 90 days after the FDA receives it.

Another option for manufacturers is to petition the FDA—asking the agency to establish the conditions under which the new dietary ingredient would reasonably be expected to be safe. To date, the FDA's Center for Food Safety and Applied Nutrition has received no such petitions.

Under DSHEA, once a dietary supplement is marketed, the FDA has the responsibility for showing that a dietary supplement is unsafe before it can take action to restrict the product's use. To monitor product safety, the agency must rely on adverse-event reports, product sampling, information in the scientific literature, and other sources of evidence.

This was the case when, in June 1997, the FDA proposed, among other things, to limit the amount of ephedrine alkaloids in dietary supplements (marketed as ephedra, Ma huang, Chinese ephedra, and epitonin, for example) and to provide warnings to consumers about the hazards associated with use of dietary supplements containing the ingredients. The hazards ranged from nervousness, dizziness, and changes in blood pressure and heart rate to chest pain, heart attack, hepatitis, stroke, seizures, psychosis, and death. The proposal stemmed from the FDA's review of the adverse-event reports it had received, in addition to the scientific literature and public comments.

The same year, the FDA uncovered a contamination of the herbal ingredient plantain with the harmful herb Digitalis lanata. The agency came to its conclusion after receiving and investigating a report of a complete heart block in a young woman. The FDA traced all use of the contaminated ingredient and asked manufacturers and retailers to withdraw these products from the market.

Beyond the FDA, individual states can take steps to restrict or stop the sale of potentially harmful dietary supplements within their jurisdictions.

Under DSHEA, a dietary supplement is considered adulterated if it or one of its ingredients presents "a significant or unreasonable risk of illness or injury" when used as directed on the label, or under normal conditions of use (if there are no directions).

A dietary supplement that contains a new dietary ingredient (i.e., an ingredient not marketed for dietary supplement use in the U.S. prior to October 15, 1994) may be considered adulterated when there is inadequate information to provide reasonable assurance that the ingredient will not present a significant or unreasonable risk of illness or injury.

The secretary of HHS may also declare that a dietary supplement or dietary ingredient poses an imminent hazard to public health or safety. However, like any other foods, it is a manufacturer's responsibility to ensure that its products are safe and properly labeled prior to marketing.

A. MedWatch

Supplement users who suffer a serious harmful effect or illness that they think may be related to supplement use should call a doctor or other healthcare provider. He, in turn, can report the suspected reaction to the FDA MedWatch, by calling 800-FDA-1088, or going to www.fda.gov/medwatch/report/hcp.htm on the MedWatch website. Patients' names are kept confidential.

Consumers can also report the suspected reaction through the same outlets. To file a report, consumers will be asked to provide the following:

- Name, address, and telephone number of the person who became ill
- Name and address of the doctor or hospital providing medical treatment
- Description of the problem
- Name of the product and store where it was purchased

Consumers also should report the problem to the manufacturer or distributor listed on the product's label and to the store where the product was purchased.

B. Good Manufacturing Practices (GMPs) to Assure Quality

DSHEA grants the FDA the authority to establish GMP regulations governing the preparation, packing, and holding of dietary supplements under conditions that ensure their safety.

These regulations are to be modeled after current GMP regulations in effect for the rest of the food industry. The

FDA intends to work with the supplement industry and other interested persons to develop GMPs and, in doing so, will seek public comment as to their scope.

Some supplement makers may already voluntarily follow GMPs devised, for example, by trade groups, as the industry strives to regulate itself.

The FDA is reviewing these GMPs as it considers whether to pursue mandatory industry-wide GMPs.

In a February 1997 advance notice of proposed rulemaking, the agency said it would establish dietary supplement GMPs if, after public comment, it determined that GMPs for conventional food are not adequate to cover dietary supplements.

GMPs would ensure that dietary supplements are made under conditions that would result in safe and properly labeled products. GMPs would help assure purity and consistency in dietary supplement products.

CFSAN has held two public meetings—on September 28, and October 21, 1999—to solicit comments to assist it in understanding the economic impact that any proposal to establish current good manufacturing practices (CGMP) regulations for dietary supplements may have on small businesses in the dietary supplement industry.

The meetings discussed manufacturing practices and standard operating procedures for: (1) personnel; (2) buildings and facilities; (3) equipment; (4) laboratory operations; (5) production and process controls; and (6) warehousing, distribution and post-distribution of raw, intermediate, and final products. The meeting also included a discussion about the verification of the identity, purity, and composition of dietary supplements and dietary supplement ingredients.

C. Literature Guidelines under DSHEA

DSHEA provides that retail outlets may make available "third-party" materials to help inform consumers about any health-related benefits of dietary supplements.

These materials include articles, book chapters, scientific abstracts, or other third-party publications. These provisions stipulate that the information must not be false or misleading, cannot promote a specific supplement brand, must be displayed with other similar materials to present a balanced view, must be displayed separate from supplements, and may not have other information attached (e.g., product promotional literature).

D. Commission on Dietary Supplements

DSHEA requires the formation of a commission to conduct a study and make recommendations on the regulation of label claims and statements for dietary supplements and procedures for the evaluation of the claims.

The members of the commission will evaluate how best to provide truthful, scientifically valid, and non-misleading information to consumers, so they can make informed and appropriate healthcare choices.

The commission is composed of seven members—appointed by the President—with experience in dietary supplements and in the manufacture, regulation, distribution, and use of supplements. Three members must be qualified by scientific training and experience to evaluate supplements' health benefits, and one of these must be trained in pharmacognosy, medical botany, traditional herbal medicine, or other related sciences. All commission members and staff should be unbiased about supplement use.

The commission was tasked with preparing a report to include recommendations and legislation related to label claims for dietary supplements to the President and to Congress within two years of convening.

The report of the President's Commission on Dietary Supplement Labels was released in November 1997, and provides a look at the future of dietary supplements.

It encourages researchers to find out whether consumers want and can use the information allowed in dietary supplement labeling under DSHEA. It encourages studies to identify more clearly the relationships between dietary supplements and health maintenance and disease prevention.

It urges the FDA to take enforcement action when questions about a product's safety arise. And it suggests that the FDA and the industry work together to develop guidelines on the use of warning statements on dietary supplement labels. Indeed, enforcement actions, seizures, and consumer warnings are promulgated weekly by the FDA, which is evidence of a multitude of problems in the industry. (For an archive of recent recalls and warnings related to dietary supplements, see www.consumerlab.com/recalls.asp#past. The FDA's archive of enforcement actions may be viewed at www.fda.gov/iceci/enforcementactions/warningletters/ucm282367.htm. The actions include foods, drugs, devices, and dietary supplements.)

The FDA generally concurred with the commission's recommendations in the agency's 1998 proposed rule on dietary supplement claims.

E. Office of Dietary Supplements

DSHEA also required the secretary of the HHS to establish an office within the National Institutes of Health (NIH) to explore the potential role of supplements to improve healthcare in the United States.

The office will also promote scientific study of supplements and their value in preventing chronic diseases; collect and compile scientific research, including data from foreign sources and the NIH Office of Alternative Medicine; serve as a scientific adviser to the HHS and the FDA; and compile a database of scientific research on supplements and individual nutrients.

2.6 Growth of Dietary Supplement Industry

Since DSHEA was passed in 1994, there has been a great increase in products claiming to be dietary supplements promoted on the Internet and elsewhere. The dietary supplement market has grown tremendously in just a few years. In 2010, consumers spent more than $28 billion on dietary supplements—more than double the amount spent in 2004—and sales continue to grow at a rate of just under 5 percent a year, according to a 2011 article in the *Wall Street Journal* (October 25, 2011).

The popularity of dietary supplements continues to rise. According to a national survey, 68 percent of respondents reported using vitamins, minerals, herbals, or other supplements in the third quarter of 1998, according to the Hartman Group, who estimates that 69 percent of the population are using vitamin and mineral supplements and 24 percent are using herbal supplements.

A small, but disturbing, number of these products have a potential for harm or bear unsupported claims. In this context, a rapidly expanding industry and a changing demographic of consumers eager to manage their own healthcare needs, provide a significant regulatory challenge for the FDA.

Just as the agency is committed to fully implementing DSHEA and ensuring that consumers have access to dietary supplements, the FDA is also committed to quickly removing unsafe products from the market or taking other timely actions to protect consumers.

The FDA has taken enforcement actions against dietary supplements found to have safety, labeling, or other violations of the FD&C Act, as amended by DSHEA.

The agency has used a variety of regulatory tools—from enforcement actions to rulemaking—when it has found dietary supplements that cause safety concerns. Table 2.1 lists significant recalls of supplements by the FDA for safety reasons.

2.7 Future FDA Activities Related to DSHEA

The FDA intends to issue a draft guidance for the botanical drug products industry. The draft guidance will explain the circumstances under which FDA approval of a new drug application (NDA) is required for marketing a botanical drug product and when such a product may be marketed under an over-the-counter drug monograph. The draft guidance also provides guidance to researchers and manufacturers on conducting initial and expanded clinical investigations of botanical drugs.

A. Guidelines for Evaluating Herbal Medicines

As previously discussed, the Federal Food, Drug, and Cosmetic Act characterizes a product based on its intended use. For a botanical product, the intended use may be as a food (including a dietary supplement), a drug (including a biological drug), or a cosmetic shown by—among other things—the product's accompanying labeling claims, advertising materials, and oral or written statements.

Botanical products are now used widely in the United States as foods—generally as dietary supplements. However, a botanical product that is marketed with a claim of diagnosing, mitigating, treating, curing, or preventing disease is considered a drug and must be marketed under either an OTC monograph or an approved NDA.

The Center for Drug Evaluation & Research is currently developing a guide for the industry, explaining the circumstances under which a botanical drug may be marketed under an over-the-counter (OTC) drug monograph and when FDA approval of an NDA is required for marketing. In addition, the document provides regulatory and scientific guidance to sponsors on conducting initial and expanded clinical investigations of botanical drug products, including those botanical products currently lawfully marketed as food and dietary supplements in the United States.

The guidance also discusses several areas in which—because of the unique nature of botanicals—the FDA finds it appropriate to apply regulatory policies that differ from those applied to synthetic, semi-synthetic, or otherwise highly purified or chemically modified drugs. In particular, the guidance states that the FDA will require minimal documentation on safety and on chemistry, manufacturing, and controls (CMC) to support an investigational new drug application (IND) for initial clinical studies on botanicals that have been marketed in the United States as dietary supplements or cosmetics.

A botanical product that has had a substantial marketing history in the United States for a specific OTC therapeutic indication may be eligible for inclusion in an OTC drug monograph. Currently, there are several botanical drugs—including cascara, psyllium, and senna—that are included in OTC monographs. For a botanical drug substance to be included in an OTC monograph, there must be data establishing general recognition of safety and effectiveness, including results of well-controlled clinical studies.

Table 2.1
Recalls and Enforcement Actions for Dietary Supplements

- FDA Warns Seller of Almased Weight Loss Product of Marketing Violations (Posted: 2/1/2012), www.consumerlab.com/recall_detail.asp?recallid=10290
- FTC Stops Fake News Sites About Acai Berry Products (Posted: 1/31/2012), www.consumerlab.com/recall_detail.asp?recallid=10289
- Recall of Calcium-Vitamin D Product That's Actually Glucosamine—Allergy Alert (Posted: 1/17/2012), www.consumerlab.com/recall_detail.asp?recallid=10287
- Hoodia Supplements Containing No Hoodia Are Banned from California Counties (Posted: 1/16/2012), www.consumerlab.com/recall_detail.asp?recallid=10288
- Herbal Extract Company Warned by FDA of Making Drug Claims (Posted: 1/11/2012), www.consumerlab.com/recall_detail.asp?recallid=10286
- Acai Berry Pill Marketers to Pay $1.5 Million to Settle FTC Charges (Posted: 1/10/2012), www.consumerlab.com/recall_detail.asp?recallid=10285
- Seller of "HCG Drops" for Weight Loss Warned by FDA and FTC of Violations (Posted: 1/4/2012), www.consumerlab.com/recall_detail.asp?recallid=10284
- Recall by Eclectic Institute of Supplements Containing Gotu Kola and Bladderwrack (Posted: 1/3/2012), www.consumerlab.com/recall_detail.asp?recallid=10282
- Manufacturing Violations for Multivitamin, Vitamin K and Other Supplements (Posted: 1/2/2012), www.consumerlab.com/recall_detail.asp?recallid=10279
- FDA Warns ION Labs of Manufacturing Violations Affecting Multiple Dietary Supplements (Posted: 1/2/2012), www.consumerlab.com/recall_detail.asp?recallid=10277
- FDA Warns XYMOGEN of Manufacturing and Labeling Violations Regarding Multiple Products (Posted: 1/2/2012), www.consumerlab.com/recall_detail.asp?recallid=10278
- Organic Celery Seed Products Recalled Due to Potential Salmonella Contamination (Posted: 12/20/2011), www.consumerlab.com/recall_detail.asp?recallid=10275
- DMAA Supplements Pulled from Military Stores After 2 Deaths (Posted: 12/19/2011), www.consumerlab.com/recall_detail.asp?recallid=10276
- HCG Diet Products Don't Work and Are Illegal Says FDA (Posted: 12/8/2011), www.consumerlab.com/recall_detail.asp?recallid=10274
- Maker of PowerGum and Colon Cleanser Warned of Violations by FDA (Posted: 12/7/2011), www.consumerlab.com/recall_detail.asp?recallid=10273
- FTC Stops Operator of Fake News Sites Offering Acai and Colon Cleanse Products (Posted: 12/6/2011), www.consumerlab.com/recall_detail.asp?recallid=10272
- Maker of Acai Product Warned by FDA of Manufacturing Violations (Posted: 11/30/2011), www.consumerlab.com/recall_detail.asp?recallid=10271
- FDA Seeks Permanent Injunction Against Dietary Supplement Maker—400+ Products Affected (Posted: 11/27/2011), www.consumerlab.com/recall_detail.asp?recallid=10270
- FDA Warns Maker of Milk Thistle and L-Carnitine Supplements of Serious Violations (Posted: 11/18/2011), www.consumerlab.com/recall_detail.asp?recallid=10269
- Hoodia Marketers Fined and Banned from Business (Posted: 11/3/2011), www.consumerlab.com/recall_detail.asp?recallid=10268
- FDA Warns Supplement Maker of Manufacturing Violations Affecting Many Products (Posted: 10/26/2011), www.consumerlab.com/recall_detail.asp?recallid=10267
- FDA Warns Consumers Against Eighteen Weight Loss Products Containing Drugs (Posted: 10/18/2011), www.consumerlab.com/recall_detail.asp?recallid=10266
- Recall of Whey Protein Powders Due to Allergens (Posted: 10/7/2011), www.consumerlab.com/recall_detail.asp?recallid=10265
- Testosterone Booster Supplement Recalled for Containing Synthetic Steroid (Posted: 10/6/2011), www.consumerlab.com/recall_detail.asp?recallid=10261
- FDA Warns Herbal Nitro of Manufacturing Violations (Posted: 10/5/2011), www.consumerlab.com/recall_detail.asp?recallid=10262
- FDA Warns Nature's Rite of Promoting 8 Supplements as Drugs (Posted: 10/5/2011), www.consumerlab.com/recall_detail.asp?recallid=10263

Table 2.1 (continued)

- FDA Warns Nutrition Center Inc (Nutri-West) of Manufacturing Violations (Posted: 10/5/2011), www.consumerlab.com/recall_detail.asp?recallid=10264
- Possible Concern with Fenugreek Based on Contamination in Europe (Posted: 9/9/2011), www.consumerlab.com/recall_detail.asp?recallid=10260
- FDA Warns Several Supplement Manufacturers Not Following Good Manufacturing Practices (Posted: 9/8/2011), www.consumerlab.com/recall_detail.asp?recallid=10259
- Recall of Prenatal Supplement Due to Egg Allergen (Posted: 9/1/2011), www.consumerlab.com/recall_detail.asp?recallid=10258
- Performance Enhancing Ingredient, DMAA, Not Really from Geraniums, Putting Its Use in Supplements in Doubt (Posted: 8/7/2011), www.consumerlab.com/recall_detail.asp?recallid=10257
- FDA Calls "Melatonin Brownie" Unsafe and Sends Warning to Manufacturer (Posted: 8/3/2011), www.consumerlab.com/recall_detail.asp?recallid=10256
- FDA Warns of Unsafe Drug in Slimming Supplements (Posted: 7/19/2011), www.consumerlab.com/recall_detail.asp?recallid=10255
- Recall of Enhancement Supplement for Men - Contains Drug Compounds (Posted: 7/19/2011), www.consumerlab.com/recall_detail.asp?recallid=10254
- FDA Inspection Finds Manufacturing Problems with Several Supplements Including Women's Multivitamin (Posted: 7/15/2011), www.consumerlab.com/recall_detail.asp?recallid=10253
- Use of "Sports Drinks" and "Energy Drinks" Discouraged by Pediatric Group (Posted: 7/11/2011), www.consumerlab.com/recall_detail.asp?recallid=10252
- Recall of Calcium & Magnesium Softgels Containing Excessive and Potentially Toxic Amounts of Vitamin D (Posted: 6/22/2011), www.consumerlab.com/recall_detail.asp?recallid=10247
- FDA Seizes Probiotics Over Marketing Claims (Posted: 6/21/2011), www.consumerlab.com/recall_detail.asp?recallid=10251
- FDA Warns Laboratory of Manufacturing Violations (Posted: 6/21/2011), www.consumerlab.com/recall_detail.asp?recallid=10250
- Vitamin Pitchman Indicted (Posted: 6/19/2011), www.consumerlab.com/recall_detail.asp?recallid=10248
- FTC Attacks Massive Online Fraud Regarding "Free Trials" of Supplements and Health Products (Posted: 6/18/2011), www.consumerlab.com/recall_detail.asp?recallid=10249
- FDA Seizes Elderberry Juice Concentrate Due to Unproven Claims (Posted: 6/7/2011), www.consumerlab.com/recall_detail.asp?recallid=10246
- FDA Finds Pesticides in Ginseng Supplement (Posted: 6/1/2011), www.consumerlab.com/recall_detail.asp?recallid=10245
- FDA Warns: Beware of Bogus STD Products (Posted: 5/3/2011), www.consumerlab.com/recall_detail.asp?recallid=10244
- FTC Targets Fake News Sites Making Deceptive Acai Claims (Posted: 4/21/2011), www.consumerlab.com/recall_detail.asp?recallid=10243
- FDA Warns Manufacturer of Soy Products of Violations (Posted: 4/7/2011), www.consumerlab.com/recall_detail.asp?recallid=10241
- Prostate Drug Found in Prostate Supplement— Recall Underway (Posted: 4/7/2011), www.consumerlab.com/recall_detail.asp?recallid=10242
- More Protein Supplements Recalled for Salmonella Risk (Posted: 3/30/2011), www.consumerlab.com/recall_detail.asp?recallid=10239
- Dangerously High Levels of Vitamins A and D in Product Prompt FDA Warning (Posted: 3/28/2011), www.consumerlab.com/recall_detail.asp?recallid=10240
- FDA Cracks Down on Violators of Supplement Manufacturing Rules (Posted: 3/28/2011), www.consumerlab.com/recall_detail.asp?recallid=10238
- 22 Brands of Whey Protein Recalled Due to Salmonella Concern (Posted: 3/14/2011), www.consumerlab.com/recall_detail.asp?recallid=10237
- Recall of "Raw" Vitamin C Supplement Containing Soy (Posted: 3/4/2011), www.consumerlab.com/recall_detail.asp?recallid=10236
- Weight Supplement Found by FDA to Contain Prescription Drug (Posted: 2/25/2011), www.consumerlab.com/recall_detail.asp?recallid=10234
- Recall of Counterfeit Extenze Tablets Containing Drugs (Posted: 2/24/2011), www.consumerlab.com/recall_detail.asp?recallid=10235
- Allergy Alert Issued for "Essentials" and "RightFoods" Brand Products (Posted: 2/9/2011), www.consumerlab.com/recall_detail.asp?recallid=10233

Table 2.1 (continued)

- Maker of Hoodia and Green Tea Products to Pay $2.65 Million Settlement for Unfair Business Practices (Posted: 2/7/2011), www.consumerlab.com/recall_detail.asp?recallid=10232
- Weight Loss Supplement Containing a Drug Can Cause Serious Adverse Events, Warns FDA (Posted: 1/4/2011), www.consumerlab.com/recall_detail.asp?recallid=10231
- Recall of Two Supplements Spiked with Erectile Dysfunction Drug (Posted: 1/1/2011), www.consumerlab.com/recall_detail.asp?recallid=10230
- Four Probiotic Products in Canada May Pose Serious Health Risks to Those with Milk or Soy Allergies (Posted: 12/26/2010), www.consumerlab.com/recall_detail.asp?recallid=10229
- FDA Steps Up Efforts to Battle Tainted Supplements (Posted: 12/17/2010), www.consumerlab.com/recall_detail.asp?recallid=10228
- FDA Warns Consumers to Avoid Man Up Now Capsules (Posted: 12/14/2010), www.consumerlab.com/recall_detail.asp?recallid=10226
- FDA Warns Consumers Not to Use Vigor-25 (Posted: 11/21/2010), www.consumerlab.com/recall_detail.asp?recallid=10225
- Misleading Claims by "One a Day Men's" Products Result in $3.3 Million Settlement (Posted: 11/9/2010), www.consumerlab.com/recall_detail.asp?recallid=10224
- Enzyte "Male" Supplement Found to Affect Heart (Posted: 10/22/2010), www.consumerlab.com/recall_detail.asp?recallid=10223
- "Red Flags" for Spotting Tainted Supplements (Posted: 10/8/2010), www.consumerlab.com/recall_detail.asp?recallid=10221
- FDA Warns of Stimulant in Slimming Capsules (Posted: 10/8/2010), www.consumerlab.com/recall_detail.asp?recallid=10222
- FDA Charges Deceptive Advertising by POM Wonderful (Posted: 9/27/2010), www.consumerlab.com/recall_detail.asp?recallid=10220
- Many Supplements Recalled for Hormone-Affecting Compounds (Posted: 9/20/2010), www.consumerlab.com/recall_detail.asp?recallid=10219
- Recall of Testosterone-Boosting Supplement (Posted: 9/15/2010), www.consumerlab.com/recall_detail.asp?recallid=10218
- ExtenZe Enhancement Supplements Seized in Canada (Posted: 9/13/2010), www.consumerlab.com/recall_detail.asp?recallid=10214
- Recall of Herbal Slimming Supplement Spiked with Drug (Posted: 9/13/2010), www.consumerlab.com/recall_detail.asp?recallid=10215
- Supplement for "Increasing Desire" Recalled for Containing Drug (Posted: 9/13/2010), www.consumerlab.com/recall_detail.asp?recallid=10217
- Mr. Magic Male Enhancer Recalled (Posted: 9/12/2010), www.consumerlab.com/recall_detail.asp?recallid=10216
- Government Finds Fraud in Personalized Supplements Sold with Genetic Tests (Posted: 8/13/2010), www.consumerlab.com/recall_detail.asp?recallid=10213
- Recall of Male Enhancement Supplement Sold in National Stores (Posted: 8/13/2010), www.consumerlab.com/recall_detail.asp?recallid=10212
- FDA Warns Against "Miracle" Mineral Supplement (Posted: 8/9/2010), www.consumerlab.com/recall_detail.asp?recallid=10211
- Choking Concern Prompts Eye Supplement Recall (Posted: 7/28/2010), www.consumerlab.com/recall_detail.asp?recallid=10210
- Recall of ED Supplement Containing Drug (Posted: 7/20/2010), www.consumerlab.com/recall_detail.asp?recallid=10209
- FDA Warns of Drug in Herbal Slimming Supplement (Posted: 7/19/2010), www.consumerlab.com/recall_detail.asp?recallid=10207
- Expansion of Pet Supplement Recall for Salmonella Risk; Many Brands Affected (Posted: 7/18/2010), www.consumerlab.com/recall_detail.asp?recallid=10208
- Supplement Company Pays $5.5 Million to Settle False Advertising Claims (Posted: 7/15/2010), www.consumerlab.com/recall_detail.asp?recallid=10206
- FDA Issues Warning on Herbal Weight Loss Supplement (Posted: 7/9/2010), www.consumerlab.com/recall_detail.asp?recallid=10205
- FDA Warns Seller of Pills Used to Treat Autism (Posted: 6/24/2010), www.consumerlab.com/recall_detail.asp?recallid=10204
- Pet Vitamin Recalled for Salmonella Risk (Posted: 6/22/2010), www.consumerlab.com/recall_detail.asp?recallid=10202
- FDA Warns Parents to Be Careful Giving Vitamin D Drops to Infants (Posted: 6/21/2010), www.consumerlab.com/recall_detail.asp?recallid=10203

Table 2.1 (continued)

- FDA Warns Consumers to Avoid Breath Supplement Contaminated with Lead (Posted: 5/3/2010), www.consumerlab.com/recall_detail.asp?recallid=10201
- Vitamin D Overload in Supplement Sickens Users (Posted: 4/29/2010), www.consumerlab.com/recall_detail.asp?recallid=10200
- Capsule for Men Spiked with Erectile Drug (Posted: 4/8/2010), www.consumerlab.com/recall_detail.asp?recallid=10198
- Nationwide Recall of Masxtreme Capsules Containing Drugs with Cardiovascular Side Effects (Posted: 4/7/2010), www.consumerlab.com/recall_detail.asp?recallid=10199
- FTC Warns of Deceptive Claims with Children's Omega-3 Supplements (Posted: 2/17/2010), www.consumerlab.com/recall_detail.asp?recallid=10197
- Glucomannan May Cause Choking if Not Taken with Fluid (Posted: 1/31/2010), www.consumerlab.com/recall_detail.asp?recallid=10196
- Recall of Body Building Supplements Containing Steroids (Posted: 1/16/2010), www.consumerlab.com/recall_detail.asp?recallid=10195
- Nationwide Recall of Sexual Enhancement Supplements Containing Drug-like Compound (Posted: 12/14/2009), www.consumerlab.com/recall_detail.asp?recallid=10194
- Warning on Acai Berry Supplements Spiked with Drug (Posted: 12/8/2009), www.consumerlab.com/recall_detail.asp?recallid=10193
- Steroids Found in More Body Building Supplements (Posted: 11/17/2009), www.consumerlab.com/recall_detail.asp?recallid=10192
- Nationwide Recall of a Weight Loss Supplement Found to Contain Undeclared Drug Ingredients (Posted: 11/15/2009), www.consumerlab.com/recall_detail.asp?recallid=10191
- FDA Warns that "Stiff Nights" Enhancement Supplement Contains Undeclared Drug (Posted: 11/6/2009), www.consumerlab.com/recall_detail.asp?recallid=10190
- Recall of 65 Dietary Supplements That May Contain Steroids (Posted: 11/3/2009), www.consumerlab.com/recall_detail.asp?recallid=10189
- FTC Charges Marketers with Baseless Weight-Loss Claims (Posted: 11/2/2009), www.consumerlab.com/recall_detail.asp?recallid=10188
- FDA Raids Online Retailer for Supplements with Steroids (Posted: 10/2/2009), www.consumerlab.com/recall_detail.asp?recallid=10187

- Court Orders Marketers of Supreme Greens and Coral Calcium to Pay Nearly $70 Million for Consumer Refunds (Posted: 8/31/2009), www.consumerlab.com/recall_detail.asp?recallid=10186
- Hepatitis Associated with Herbal Supplement Containing Artemisinin (Posted: 8/25/2009), www.consumerlab.com/recall_detail.asp?recallid=10185
- FDA Warns Against Body Building Supplements with Steroid-like Compounds (Posted: 7/29/2009), www.consumerlab.com/recall_detail.asp?recallid=10184
- Weight Loss Supplements Found to Contain Prescription Drug (Posted: 7/23/2009), www.consumerlab.com/recall_detail.asp?recallid=10182
- Six Male Enhancement Supplements Found Adulterated (Posted: 7/23/2009), www.consumerlab.com/recall_detail.asp?recallid=10183
- Recall of Whey Protein Products Due to Possible Salmonella Contamination (Posted: 7/9/2009), www.consumerlab.com/recall_detail.asp?recallid=10181
- FDA Warns of Loss of Sense of Smell with Zicam Nasal Gel/Nasal Swab (Posted: 6/16/2009), www.consumerlab.com/recall_detail.asp?recallid=10179
- Sexual Enhancement Supplement Recalled—Second Time Found with Drug-like Compound (Posted: 6/15/2009), www.consumerlab.com/recall_detail.asp?recallid=10180
- Body-Building Supplements Confiscated by FDA for Adulteration (Posted: 5/13/2009), www.consumerlab.com/recall_detail.asp?recallid=10178
- FDA Warns Consumers to Stop Using Hydroxycut—Product Being Tested by ConsumerLab.com (Posted: 5/1/2009), www.consumerlab.com/recall_detail.asp?recallid=10177
- Recall of "Slimming" Supplements Spiked with Drug (Posted: 4/23/2009), www.consumerlab.com/recall_detail.asp?recallid=10176
- QVC Settles Charges of False Claims for Supplements (Posted: 3/19/2009), www.consumerlab.com/recall_detail.asp?recallid=10175
- "The Truth About Nutrition" Marketers Agree to Pay $3 Million to Settle Charges of Deceptive Advertising of Dietary Supplements and Devices (Posted: 3/6/2009), www.consumerlab.com/recall_detail.asp?recallid=10174
- $4 Million Settlement by Supplement Maker for False Claims (Posted: 2/27/2009), www.consumerlab.com/recall_detail.asp?recallid=10173

Table 2.1 (continued)

- Generic Toprol XL (Metoprolol Succinate ER) Recalled Along with 60 Other Drugs (Posted: 1/30/2009), www.consumerlab.com/recall_detail.asp?recallid=10172
- Many Brands of Nutrition Bars Recalled Due to Potential Salmonella Contamination (Posted: 1/24/2009), www.consumerlab.com/recall_detail.asp?recallid=10171
- FDA Expands Warning to Consumers About Tainted Weight Loss Pills (Posted: 1/9/2009), www.consumerlab.com/recall_detail.asp?recallid=10170
- Generic Manufacturer Suspends Production of All Tablets—Including Generic Metoprolol Succinate ER (Posted: 12/26/2008), www.consumerlab.com/recall_detail.asp?recallid=10169
- FDA Warns Consumers About Tainted Weight Loss Pills (Posted: 12/22/2008), www.consumerlab.com/recall_detail.asp?recallid=10168
- Airborne Settles Over False Advertising—$7 Million to States (Posted: 12/17/2008), www.consumerlab.com/recall_detail.asp?recallid=10167
- Fat Loss Supplement Recalled for Containing Prescription Drug (Posted: 11/28/2008), www.consumerlab.com/recall_detail.asp?recallid=10166
- Sales of Weight-Loss Supplement Suspended—May Contain Diuretic Drug (Posted: 11/2/2008), www.consumerlab.com/recall_detail.asp?recallid=10165
- Possible Risk Rather than Benefit Found in Trial of Vitamin E and Selenium for Prostate Cancer (Posted: 10/30/2008), www.consumerlab.com/recall_detail.asp?recallid=10163
- Two Vitamin C Supplements Recalled in Canada for Vitamin A Risk (Posted: 10/29/2008), www.consumerlab.com/recall_detail.asp?recallid=10164
- FDA Permits Incorrect Labeling on Generic Wellbutrin XL, But May Require Drug to be Tested (Posted: 10/2/2008), www.consumerlab.com/recall_detail.asp?recallid=10162
- FDA Finds Fault with Generic Toprol XL—Problems Reported Earlier by ConsumerLab.com (Posted: 8/28/2008), www.consumerlab.com/recall_detail.asp?recallid=10161
- Airborne to Pay $30 Million for Deceptive Advertising of Cold Remedy—Refunds Available (Posted: 8/14/2008), www.consumerlab.com/recall_detail.asp?recallid=10160
- Stroke Attributed to Xenadrine Ephedra-Free Supplement (Posted: 8/11/2008), www.consumerlab.com/recall_detail.asp?recallid=10159
- Recall of Viapro Capsules Due to Potentially Harmful Ingredient (Posted: 7/30/2008), www.consumerlab.com/recall_detail.asp?recallid=10158
- Recall of Sexual Enhancement Supplements Containing Drug (Posted: 7/29/2008), www.consumerlab.com/recall_detail.asp?recallid=10157
- Seizure of Xiadafil VIP Tablets After Company Refuses Recall (Posted: 7/28/2008), www.consumerlab.com/recall_detail.asp?recallid=10156
- FDA Warns Groups to Stop Selling Fake Cancer 'Cures' (Posted: 6/19/2008), www.consumerlab.com/recall_detail.asp?recallid=10155
- Selenium Toxicity from a Supplement (Posted: 6/3/2008), www.consumerlab.com/recall_detail.asp?recallid=10154
- Recall of Virility Supplement (Posted: 5/29/2008), www.consumerlab.com/recall_detail.asp?recallid=10153
- FDA Requests Recall of Xiadafil VIP Supplements (Posted: 5/28/2008), www.consumerlab.com/recall_detail.asp?recallid=10152
- Feds Seek Millions from Seller of Enzyte Sexual Enhancement Supplement (Posted: 5/15/2008), www.consumerlab.com/recall_detail.asp?recallid=10151
- Court Upholds Order for Seasilver Marketers to Pay $120 Million (Posted: 4/22/2008), www.consumerlab.com/recall_detail.asp?recallid=10150
- Twelve Dietary Herbal Supplements Recalled—Possible Health Risk Associated with Ephedra, Aristolochic Acid and Human Placenta (Posted: 4/11/2008), www.consumerlab.com/recall_detail.asp?recallid=10148
- Update: Hazardous Levels of Selenium Confirmed by FDA in Two Supplements (Posted: 4/11/2008), www.consumerlab.com/recall_detail.asp?recallid=10149
- Federal Agents Seize Nearly $1.3 Million of Illegal Dietary Supplements (Posted: 4/7/2008), www.consumerlab.com/recall_detail.asp?recallid=10147
- FDA Warns of Adverse Reactions with Two Liquid Supplements—Selenium Toxicity Possible (Posted: 3/28/2008), www.consumerlab.com/recall_detail.asp?recallid=10146
- FDA Warns of Sexual Supplements with Drug-like Ingredients (Posted: 3/25/2008), www.consumerlab.com/recall_detail.asp?recallid=10145

Table 2.1 (continued)

- Airborne Settles Lawsuit Over False Advertising of its "Miracle Cold Buster" (Posted: 3/4/2008), www.consumerlab.com/recall_detail.asp?recallid=10143
- Two Supplements Recalled for Containing Viagra-like Compounds (Posted: 3/4/2008), www.consumerlab.com/recall_detail.asp?recallid=10144
- FTC Sues Sellers of Weight-Loss Pills for False Advertising (Posted: 2/29/2008), www.consumerlab.com/recall_detail.asp?recallid=10142

Source: ConsumerLab.com, accessed 02/09/2012.

An OTC drug monograph does not ordinarily contain CMC information for a drug product beyond the name of the active ingredients (i.e., the drug substances). However, tests and specifications for a botanical drug product, including its corresponding botanical raw materials and botanical drug substances, should be made part of the OTC monograph either directly or by cross-reference. In addition, FDA regulations on CGMPs apply to all OTC drug monograph products—including botanical drug products.

When a botanical drug product does not have previous marketing history or is a new drug, the manufacturer must obtain marketing approval from the FDA by submitting an NDA containing information on the quality, safety, and efficacy of the botanical drug.

The evidence required to demonstrate the safety and efficacy of a botanical drug product marketed under an OTC monograph is the same as that marketed through an NDA process. Also, the evidence required to demonstrate the safety and efficacy of a botanical drug product is not different from those for a synthetic drug product labeled for the same indication. Such evidence is derived by requiring adequate and well-controlled clinical studies, and, if the sponsor wishes to conduct a clinical trial in the United States it must submit an IND application. An IND should contain sufficient information to demonstrate that the drug product is safe for testing in humans and that the clinical protocol is properly designed for its intended objectives.

Botanical drug products have certain unique characteristics that should be taken into account in the application of FDA regulations and guidance. Botanical drugs are derived from vegetable matter and are usually prepared as complex mixtures. Their chemical constituents are not always well-defined. In many cases, even the active constituent(s) in a botanical drug is not identified, nor is its biological activity well characterized. Therefore, the CMC documentation that should be provided for botanical drugs will be different from that for synthetic or highly purified drugs, whose active constituents can be chemically identified and quantified.

B. Combination Drug Rule

The botanicals draft guidance likely will note that the FDA is considering revising its regulations on fixed-combination drugs to exempt certain botanical and other natural source drugs from those regulations (21 C.F.R. § 300.50). For such exempted drugs, the sponsor would not be required to demonstrate the contribution to the claimed effects of each constituent of the drug.

C. FDA Research Efforts

One of Dr. Henney's initiatives is science-based regulations. As a result, the FDA is engaged in several research initiatives related to botanicals.

The FDA is cultivating St. John's wort at the USDA in Beltsville, Maryland, and in Oxford, Mississippi, and is using it as the model botanical to establish product-quality approaches.

These approaches include the authentication and characterization of raw materials, safety profile (i.e., heavy metals analysis), and *in-vitro* and *in-vivo* assessment of bioavailability and bioequivalence.

2.8 Conclusion (Editor's Opinion)

Despite almost no evidence of efficacy, occasional withdrawal, and banning of supplements for serious health risks, the supplement industry continues to grow. Indeed, the product warnings and complaints regarding adulterations, false claims, marketing schemes, and credit care fraud continue to be reported. Responsible health professionals should warn their patients of the "dark side" of supplements, and encourage their patients to save the billions spent on these mostly useless and sometimes dangerous products.

Chapter 3

The Pharmaceutical Revolution: Drug Discovery and Development

John C. Somberg, M.D.

3.1 Introduction

The pharmaceutical industry as we know it is undergoing considerable change. The industry will be markedly changing as the impact of new technologies, biotechnology, genomics, proteomics takes effect. Additionally, the healthcare "reform" bill of 2010 has had a dramatic impact. The forces of technology and government are like fast-running rivers forever changing the topography of the landscape.

Change is part of the human condition. Over the last 100 years, the drug development process has undergone considerable, perhaps even revolutionary, change. But perhaps all that has passed will pale in comparison in the dramatic new information era, which will markedly alter the environment we work in and the drug development process.

Even the most powerful and financially stable companies engaged in drug discovery and development need to recognize the forces of change. The evolution of the computing age gave IBM the opportunity to expand and alter its business from analog systems and adding machines to punch cards and then to complex computer systems. As the computer age developed, IBM led the way with the innovative personal computer. The lead was then lost by IBM when "software" became the core of the information age, along with the chips that permit the exponential growth in machine computing performance. Thus, Microsoft, just a concept 30 years ago, is more dominant in today's information age than IBM. IBM remains a leader in technology advances and in new fundamental patents, and remains a formidable presence in the IT departments of large corporations. It kept up in technology, but its management failed to perceive the salient change in the information age from large computers to small, and then the importance of the software that controls information processing, analysis, and communication. But change has not stopped here and Microsoft is now challenged by the web and the likes of Google and the "open software" approach of other companies in the information age.

Drug development is in an analogous situation. We have seen an evolution from the age of botanicals to the age of chemical synthesis, discovery and now to the age of biotechnology and gene manipulation. Each area can still grow, but the shift in direction is fundamental to scientific development. Taking these major changes into account, drug discovery and development will be fundamentally altered by the information age. The concept of the information age had been discussed by Alvin Toffler and was correctly perceived to be revolutionary in its effects on society. The agricultural and the industrial revolutions brought about fundamental changes in society, as will the information age. In his book entitled *Future Shock*, Toffler describes an era when the pace of change in modern life is so great as to disenfranchise individuals from the process that society is undergoing (Toffler, 1970). While this is a real problem for society and a problem with political dimensions, failure of our institutions and of our corporate structures to adjust will bring considerable societal and economic disruption. For these reasons, an understanding of the evolution of drug discovery and development and how this evolution will be affected by the information age is essential for those working in these fields.

3.2 Drugs from Plants

From the earliest times dating at least to the hunter and gatherer societies, humans made use of herbals. Whether as foods, items of religious significance, or medication cannot be clearly discerned. As civilization progressed, remedies from plants further developed. Earliest folklore relates stories of plant medicinals. The bible contains passages eluding to medicinal herbs and plants. In fact, all the major religions discuss plant remedies as part of their sacred heritage. There are many stories in pharmacology relating to the use of medicinal plants and the work of herbalists in the early discovery of drugs. One example is the story of William Withering, the physician from Birmingham, England, who on his charity rounds in Shropshire saw that an herbal potion was used to treat a woman with dropsy (CHF) who then showed improvement. Withering's botanical training in Edinburgh permitted him to identify the probable active ingredient, the leaf of the foxglove plant. After 10 years of clinical experimentation, he developed a series of case studies explaining the dose range from minimal effective dose to toxicity. He categorized the adverse side-effect profile of the digitalis leaf and its potentially life-threatening toxicities. He noted the adverse outcomes and carefully chronicled the conditions that the drug was most useful in treating. While he thought the agent increased urine volume and, thus, had diuretic properties, he commented in his thesis that the drug had a powerful action on the motion of the heart and, thus, recognized its cardiotonic action years before this was actually proven. Withering was a masterful botanist (he chronicled the plants of Great Britain later in his life). He was an exemplary clinical pharmacologist and demonstrated the best in botanical drug discovery and testing given the skills of his day. But Withering's observations may not be unique. The effect of the foxglove plant on disease was known to be part of European plant folklore. The use of these glycoside-yielding plants and the use of the skin of the toad for medicinal purposes goes back to ancient Egypt, and is also mentioned in Chinese herbal writings. Confucius talks of glycoside plants for edematous states and cardiac glycosides are a significant component of Chinese herbal medications. While Withering's observations were a defining moment for modern medicine, botanicals of similar action were used for over 2,000 years. Clearly, botanicals have been an important component to therapeutic advances. Whether we are discussing digitalis or atropine or any number of other drugs, plants have contributed much to drug discovery. The use of quinidine in atrial fibrillation or quinine to treat malaria are other examples of the importance botanicals have had in therapeutics. In fact, in the 1700s and 1800s, botanicals were the only source of drugs. The anti-infective agents have depended on extracts from molds and fungus for a very long time. Recent therapies are derived from nature with some chemical modifications to improve activity. We often think of the age of botanicals as one that has gone by. Indeed, it was the first step in the field of drug discovery and development, but one that continues to play a major role to this day. While reserpine was used for a thousand years in India and parts of China, it was only in the 1950s that it was purified and used as an effective antihypertensive agent. The recent use of taxol in oncology is an example of a botanical turned into a drug and synthetic chemistry relieving a very scarce supply. Until a synthetic pathway for commercial production was developed, the bark of the hew tree became a very valuable commodity and caused the hew tree to be endangered. The cardiac anti-rejection drug Serlrelumos is an even more recent example of a soil sample taken years earlier from an atoll in the pacific that has lead to a major new therapy. The therapy is used as both an anti-rejection drug in transplantation surgery and a coating for coronary artery stents to prevent re-stenosis.

There was a trend for large companies to form alliances with botanical gardens, and with distant countries to explore to find new therapies. In fact a company called Schanan Pharmaceuticals was founded with a corporate purpose to discover and develop pharmaceuticals from botanical sources based on the folklore of "medicine men." However, these ventures and alliances were not quick to deliver new therapies and the impetus to continue this phase of development is fading. This is most unfortunate since this type of discovery has proven so fruitful in the past and there is nothing we know that would discourage this type of further exploration. In fact the one discouraging factor is the rapid "drop off" in the planet biodiversity that has been caused by the relentless expansion of human development with the emphasis on corporate agriculture, the clearing of the Amazon jungle, international travel contaminating the biomass and the rapid worldwide rampant growth of "non native species." To successfully deal with the challenge requires the application of the most modern techniques, the most important of which may well be those related to handling the vast amount of information that can be collected. Clearly, computer applications to the exploration of the plant world, its categorization, automated process for analysis, and chemical categorization with innovative storage, organization, and retrieval will be required to make the drug discovery process effective. The systematic computerization of knowledge in ethnobotany and pharmacognosy, with emphasis on plant categorization across primitive societies, will be helpful to sustain the discovery process. Using sophisticated computer techniques to look for similarities in medicinal plant use among primitive peoples to ascertain potentially useful observations can greatly aid the ethnobotanist. Hopefully, these computerized techniques will replace the hundreds, if not thousands, of years that are needed for serendipitous observations such as that made by William Withering 200 years ago, which led to the introduction of the digitalis glycosides in clinical medicine.

3.3 Synthetic Drug Discovery

For the last 75 years, the majority of new molecules have come from synthetic chemistry. In cardiology, the beta-blockers and calcium channel blockers have revolutionized cardiovascular therapeutics. Beta agonists in respiratory therapy and H_2 antagonists in gastrointestinal ulcer disease therapy are a few examples of the work of the synthetic chemist that has greatly changed our treatment of patients. The proven model of finding a useful transmitter in a physiologic system, finding a receptor to which the transmitter acts, and then modifying the agonist structure to find a specific antagonist has worked well with major advances in a number of fields. As new receptors and new physiological systems are revealed, the synthetic chemist will surely be making considerable contributions to the field of drug discovery. This process is indeed ongoing. For instance, as the role of the endothelium becomes better understood, its impact on pharmaceutical research greatly expands. What was once called endothelial derived relaxing factory (EDRF) has been characterized as a locally released gas, nitric oxide. Studies on endothelium function have found endogenous substances involved in the modulation of vasodilation and vasoconstriction at the local endothelial level. There are endogenous substances opposing the vasodilating properties of nitric oxide. Endothelin is one of these transmitters and the development of specific endothelin antagonists is an exciting field. Whether these endothelin antagonists will be effective therapies in angina, hypertension, or congestive heart failure remains to be determined, but the process shows that the synthetic discovery of drugs, combined with physiological transmitter research, is still spawning drugs of great potential. Even here, with well-established approaches, we see the influence of the information age. Employing computers to determine receptor structure and, thus, possible receptive blockers has become a useful tool in the drug discovery process. Computer-assisted drug synthesis has great potential. In fact, there is at least one company that has this technology central to its commercial activities. The revolution in this aspect of synthetic chemistry is analogous to the revolution where computers have very greatly changed the animation industry. Where once dozens of artists were necessary, computers have now replaced them, creating "lifelike" anima-

tions that were not previously feasible. The same type of revolution will occur in the chemical drug synthetic industry. Besides design, there are the categorization and synthetic pathways that are so readily applied to computerization. The application of computer sciences to chemistry will lead to considerable advances in this field. The application of computers to the steps beyond modeling systems, identifying chemical structures and automatically developing synthetic approaches, will be of considerable impact. Synthetic antagonists with optimum potency can be developed from a host of chemical possibilities. With a heightened receptor selectivity and potency, the increased yield of these procedures will be noticeable. The industry must target improved, as well as new and novel, therapies. A more potent, less toxic agent can be as useful and financially rewarding as a blockbuster. Still, there are significant pitfalls to this approach. We must not deviate too greatly from nature. Synthesizing millions of compounds that are unrelated to the norms of biochemistry leads to tens of thousands of compounds to evaluate that turn out to be of no biologic use. We need to integrate computerized chemistry with biology so as not to go off from accepted chemical templates.

The information age applications to synthetic modeling will be inherently limited unless we can improve screening techniques. For many years, there has been considerable thought given to the link between drug synthesis, discovery, and development. Almost 25 years ago, I had the good fortune to visit Janssen Pharmaceuticals and discuss the drug discovery process with the late Paul Janssen, a genius in the field of synthetic chemistry. His grasp of chemistry, his diverse interests, and his unparalleled success in the discovery of novel pharmaceuticals were most impressive. Janssen was a chemist looking for novel compounds that could then be assessed to find biological activity. A new promising compound would be processed through hundreds of models, looking for possible pharmacologic activity. The question arose about the ability to screen for biological activity. This is a critical linkage point in the discovery and development process, one to which the great potential of the information age can be effectively applied.

Janssen's approach is fascinating, but to this day has created deep abiding concerns. I was particularly interested in Janssen's approach as applied to anti-arrhythmic pharmacology since I have studied the field of anti- arrhythmic drug development for many years and have participated in all stages of anti-arrhythmic drug development from chemical synthesis to the design and execution of clinical studies. I had been working on Lorcainide, a drug Janssen developed at Bersa, and wondered how this compound came out of discovery and how it compared to other agents screened.

Janssen employed a costly dog model of PVC suppression, postcoronary artery ligation. Lorcainide, being a Ic Vaughan Williams agent, was a sodium channel blocker. With this profile, Lorcainide was predicted to be effective in the PVC suppression model. But PVC suppression and the Ic agents have not shown prolongation of life in post-MI studies. The type III agents appear to be most effective clinically, and a meta-analysis with amiodarone shows the drug to prolong life. This meta-analysis has reported that amiodarone is far more effective with much less proarrhythmia than the sodium channel blockers. This leads one to consider what would be the effect of the clinically valuable agent amiodarone in the screening model that Janssen was using to pick out his antiarrhythmic to go into clinical development. In fact, the records at Bersa were so accurate that the scientists in that department could look up the results in a few minutes and describe the actions of other known antiarrhythmic agents in the drug model. The answer they gave was that amiodarone was much less effective and, in fact, hardly effective at all in the model in which Lorcainide was extremely effective. It is no wonder that the pharmaceutical industry in the 1980s found a host of Ic agents (flecainide, encainaide, Lorcainide, propafenone, indecainide, ethmozine, etc.), since that is what their assays were best at picking up as active agents. Thus, the model is the important factor in the drug discovery process, and it will often determine if a compound is to undergo development. We could synthesize thousands of compounds and select for development a few that may not be optimum for therapy. These agents, though, would fit the characteristics being sought by the model employed in the screening process. This is a major problem and one not given enough consideration. We can only think of the possibility that there may be hundreds, if not thousands, of compounds buried in analytical hoppers such as Janssen's Bersa research establishment that could have been extremely useful, but were discarded because they were not identified as biologically active in an inherently flawed screening model.

In addition to the models used in drug screening is the fundamental difference in discovery between mass screening and receptor-targeted research. The latter has proved more successful in the last decade, but some major advances have come out of pure chemistry and follow-up screening to determine biological activity. Can the revolution of the information age and computer sciences be applied to synthesis and screening? These are questions that will challenge us in the coming years. I believe a revolution will occur in this area. Synthesis on a grand scale will be tied to automated focused biological activity screening that will permit the evaluation of tens of thousands of molecules on a daily basis. To date the large screening programs in the pharmaceutical industry have been very unsuccessful in identifying promising compounds and the few identified have caused serious toxicities in clinical trials. Screening for adverse toxicities is also a critical component. Clearly, the screens that are selected will determine the validity of this approach.

While we are in transition from the age of synthetic chemistry to biotechnology and gene manipulation, synthetic discovery will still play a major role in advancing the therapeutic armamentarium.

3.4 Biotechnology, Geneomics and Proteomics

The area of biotechnology and gene manipulation is in its early stages, but has already made considerable impact. The largest companies are busy positioning themselves by acquiring or "joint venturing" with the biotechnology companies, usually small startup enterprises. They are undertaking these acquisitions to be prepared to benefit from the coming revolution in biotechnology and gene manipulation. Biotechnology has not advanced as rapidly as some have predicted. The science has made tremendous strides, but a number of factors have limited the advances and commercialization. The scale-up and commercialization of biotechnology processes is limited by expense and the difficulties that are technologically imposed. The first generation of compounds have been effective, growth hormone and recombinant tissue plasminogen activator (rTPA). However, there have been major failures such as the antibodies to counteract the effects of septic shock. While science permits the creation of drugs to evaluate, the compounds themselves may not be effective. This dichotomy stems from our imperfect knowledge of the pathophysiology of disease states, such as is the case with gram-negative sepsis and shock which blocks the body's response and causes even more adversity, hypotension and decreased survival. Another problem revolves around a constantly changing target, such as the AIDS virus. Genetech and Amgen have been successful in bringing drugs to the marketplace, but even these companies have struggled to remain viable and continue adequate cash flow to undertake the research and development for the next generation of products leading to mergers and acquisitions to continue. The hundreds, if not thousands, of smaller companies may not fare as well, and it is safe to predict that only a small fraction will indeed find a successful product. Besides the discrepancy between the ability to make a compound and its clinical efficacy lies the problems of corporate capitalization and effective drug development. The mergers of biotech concerns and the established pharmaceutical industry will go beyond improved capitalization and will bring more expertise in drug development and the regulatory approval process to this fledgling industry. But there are further impediments to success. Many of the products of biotechnology synthesis are proteins that are not orally active. A major area of research is going to be to convert the intravenously active compounds to ones with a facilitated means of delivery, or a small chemical entity active analog. Novel drug delivery systems to overcome the problems of lack of oral activity will be crucial. Carrier molecules, topical transport enhancers, nasal absorption enhancers and methodologies are but a few of the possible solutions to the drug delivery problem that considerably hampers the biotechnology field. Another approach has been the development of chemical molecules that have similar key structural elements that may permit the chemical compound to act like the protein molecule. If this is possible, we may find ourselves using the tools of biotechnology to enhance the drug discovery process through chemical synthesis. Despite the problems and inherent limitations, the field of biotechnology will greatly increase the possible compounds available for drug development and, in fact, promote development in many novel areas that have been very much lacking effective therapies. The initial cost and the pressures for successful development are so great that the critical elements of the development process will need to be more effectively used if we are not to repeat the mistakes of yesterday. For example, demonstrating the blood clot lysing capabilities of rTPA and reversal of an acute MI in development was not enough for commercial viability of the product. Genetech persisted and undertook to perform a comparative study of rTPA with streptokinase demonstrating superiority of the rTPA product. The superiority of the rTPA combined with an aggressive marketing strategy permitted Genetech to dominate the thrombolytic market for a period of time. In the development process of biotechnology products, their value and place in the therapeutic armamentarium may be as important as the demonstration of efficacy of a pivotal trial. When we talk so often of pharmacoeconomic impact of new therapies and take into consideration the very great expense of the biotechnology-derived drugs, the benefits of the drug, its place in therapy, and especially its cost-benefit ratio will become critical factors in the product's success. This will be especially important in the age of socialized medicine where costs will mostly be borne by the government.

The area of oncology has been most promising of late regarding translating biotechnology into successful products. A number of specific products targeted to cancer have proven successful in clinical trials though possibly limited in overall impact on the treatment of cancer. Specifically antibodies used to target specific receptors turning off cell growth appears a fruitful approach in the oncology area. Still

the potential for proteins to affect genes and modify disease is tremendous and we are just touching the surface of the myriad of potential opportunities these fields have to offer. Especially interesting but disappointing to date is the field of angiogenesis, that involves factors inhibiting angiogenesis and the tumor growth, or increasing angiogenesis and thus decreasing organ ischemia, such as seen in coronary artery disease. While Avastin has proven effective in some GI tumors, its use in advanced breast cancer has been questioned. To date angiogenesis in the treatment of coronary artery disease has not proven effective. Perhaps these areas will become fruitful in the coming years.

3.5 Gene Therapy

Gene modification, substitution and inhibition strategies are a promising array of new strategies for the effective treatment of disease. That there would be a single gene responsible for a metabolic disease like gout or homocystinuria, for example, seems reasonable. That a single gene mutation could cause a condition like Eulers Danos syndrome also seems reasonable. But breast cancer, lupus erythematosus, or coronary artery disease caused by a single abnormal gene is surprising to say the least. An accumulating body of evidence supports many of these claims. These developments are exciting and may represent a new age of possible effective therapies for some of the most difficult to treat conditions affecting humans. But the identification of the gene itself, though an important first step, is only the initial part of a long process to cure the disease. The techniques for gene modification are rudimentary and certainly need further study. An area of cardiology where gene therapy should be most promising is restenosis following acute angioplasty. Angioplasty entails placing the catheter in the coronary vessel, inflating a balloon at the tip of the catheter, pushing aside the atherosclerotic lesion. This is rather a successful technique; however, a major problem limiting the success of angioplasty is restenosis. At the time of the initial angioplasty, there are stimuli that initiate cell proliferation of the media leading to restenosis.

The medial cells that proliferate are homogeneous and this process seems to occur quite rapidly in about 20 to 60 percent of individuals having a single-vessel angioplasty. But even this simple model for gene therapy has proven a difficult target. There has been some fascinating work done with antisense therapy, but it has been difficult to reproduce the results and commercialize a process. So much of the methodology is so new as to impede clinical development. The use of a viral vector to insert the material in the medial cells to turn off protein synthesis is limited by concern for the use of viral vectors. Major questions arise. Can the virus replicate? Will the gene be correctly inserted or will additional genetic material of the virus be inserted? Thus, validation and safety aspects are formidable and can markedly slow the development process. As experience increases with product development, manufacturing and skill in conducting clinical trials, the overall time for developing gene manipulation strategies will decrease. While anti-sense therapy has not proved clinically useful to date, the use of drug-coated stents has been introduced and become dominant. The changing therapeutic landscape influences commercial development. So while anti-sense therapies and other agents have failed thus far, the advances with drug-coated stents may render new therapies for restenosis moot. We are only at the initial frontiers of gene manipulation. The possibilities are phenomenal. Whether the promise will be realized cannot be answered at this time, but the concept of preventing or even treating serious diseases like cancer in advanced stages or incurable conditions is so exciting as to make the concept scientifically irresistible.

A worrisome problem that has developed is the penchant to patent a gene even when our knowledge of what it does is only partial. Supporters of gene patenting believe that the proprietary nature of a patent will spur commercial development. However, a gene is not a drug but part of the disease process. We don't patent diseases. One therapy directed at a given gene may be different from another. An antibody could block gene expression; a chemical could block a protein from being made by a gene; or a gene's action could be promoted instead of inhibited. But if the gene is patented then many facets of research can be blocked by the patent owners. Blocked not just by the cost of working with the gene due to royalty payments, but deliberately by the gene's owner who wants to ensure that its therapy directed at the gene is the only one available. Patenting genes will be a major inhibitor of research in this area and a grave error on the part of the Patent and Trademark Offices. The courts are now severely limiting this concept of patenting genes, following a recent Supreme Court decision.

3.6 Cell Therapy and Regenerative Therapies

The use of adult or stem cell therapy to cure disease is a slowly developing field gaining momentum. The possibility of using human skin to treat burn patients more effectively to the accelerated healing of bone fractures are areas in rapid development. The use of modified cells to treat patients following a myocardial infarction is another area undergoing study. The use of adult stem cells, as well as embryonic stem cells, to treat an MI has had mixed results. Are the cells properly developed, do they remain viable, do they cause

arrhythmias? These are just some of the concerns that arise. The ethical issue of where the cells are obtained has been problematic, and the potential to cause tumors has limited the more rapid development of this field. Rejection is still a problem, but new approaches to regenerative therapy, gene modification, blocking antibodies and other techniques make this area more promising than ever.

3.7 The Developers

Along with the evolution in the process of discovery and the tremendous influence of the revolution in information handling upon drug development, changes in the participants in the development process will also have considerable impact. There is also an evolution occurring in the parties to the development process. Observing the trends makes one think of the theories of the origins of the universe with oscillations in mass accumulating, exploding, and reaccumulating, forming large aggregates and small breakoff components. Perhaps the process started with the entrepreneurs who led the field successfully and developed the large corporate giants of today. Merck, Hoffman-LaRoche and Pfizer are examples of one-person entrepreneur-driven companies expanding into major international concerns. In fact, the major companies dominate the pharmaceutical industry to an unparalleled extent. The largest 10 companies represent over 90 percent of pharmaceutical sales. Over the last 20 years, mergers have continued, and indeed the last few years have seen even further consolidation of the pharmaceutical industry. One analyst reported in the *Wall Street Journal* that for a company to survive it must be able to compete with the major players in the pharmaceutical field. This is not just because of funding requirements for drug development programs, but because of the development impediments established by these very large competitors. Impediments can be something simple like the number of patients exposed to a new entity, or more complex such as a survival study or the use of experimental ancillary technologies that are prohibitively expensive and would not be automatically required for the development of a compound. These impediments can create an impression, both to the FDA and within other companies, that they are requisite making development of a second or third agent in the field much more difficult, time-consuming, and expensive. The time factor is especially important since the longer it takes to develop a compound, the more dominance in the market the first drug has gained. Time is the same as money and the loss of product lead can all but destroy the market potential for an agent.

Another result of industry consolidation is the tremendous pressure to develop blockbuster products. To sustain the pharmaceutical behemoths, $1 billion compounds are mandatory. Compounds that gross only $50 to $100 million are no longer of interest to the large companies, and the "niche" diseases they treat are no longer attractive targets for therapy. A company that loses one or two compounds in its pipeline can rapidly fall from favor and itself be a possible takeover target. The failure of Merck's pipeline led to a crisis at that company questioning its very survival. However, consideration and the focus on blockbuster products has created an opportunity for small companies to develop within the vacuum created by large multinational companies. This is an opportunity to develop not just "niche" compounds but also blockbuster therapies. An insightful discovery is not limited to large robotic labs. "Big science" is not the substitute for new ideas, new approaches and "thinking out of the box" which often are the requisites for new discoveries and blockbuster products.

Even a company with a very successful acquisition record for blockbuster products like Pfizer, can be undone by a failure of a lead compound (Torcetrapib) and the looming patent expirations of lead blockbusters such as atorvastatin (Lipitor).

3.8 Small Development Companies

Considering all these obstacles to development and the considerable regulatory maze, the trend to conglomeratization with bigger and bigger companies is not surprising. What is indeed surprising is the simultaneous opposing trend of the development of the very small niche startup companies proliferating along with the ever-increasing size of the major players in pharmaceutical development. In fact, it is not just how small these companies are, it is that they only encompass an aspect of the drug discovery and development process. Some companies are focusing on discovery; others specialize in clinical development. Some companies plan to license the product to a larger firm for marketing once the NDA is granted. Then there are other companies that neither discover nor develop drugs but place their energy in the marketing of developed pharmaceuticals. One may argue that the niche enterprises are doomed to failure. But a number of factors combine to make this approach viable. The total overhead of the very large companies limits development to compounds expected to have sales of at least $100 million. At times, a drug will have a smaller market and a large company will develop the product for public relations because of interest in the field to bolster sales of existing products in its product line or out of sheer miscalculation of market potential. However, the small companies look to a potential market of $5 to $50 million a year as a bonanza. Their costs are far lower, permitting adequate profit margins to be recouped after development, marketing, and discov-

ery costs are accounted for and expenses for sales covered. Small companies cannot carry out clinical trials at the same level expected of a Pfizer or a Merck. Thus, the studies are fewer, smaller, and aimed at proving the efficacy and safety as directly as possible. Clearly, though, the niche company will play a major role in drug development. They will service areas not considered appropriate in terms of market size by the larger companies. They will represent the dynamic growth of entrepreneurs from business and academia who look to the commercialization of ideas, especially in biotechnology and gene manipulation.

Additionally, an up and coming area is the reformularization of products, improving their clinical pharmacology. Drug delivery systems can administer a chemical topically to prolong action in the body or even target a drug's action to a specific site through liposome delivery and associated antibodies. This is an area in which many small companies are currently involved, and it has attracted the interest of Big Pharma.

3.9 Academicians and Entrepreneurs

Many of these companies are investor driven, and thus have intense dedication to development and success. But can a company with one or two products compete? It appears it can, although often the process takes the course of mergers or acquisitions by larger firms. Some start out as "spin offs" of an academic research, some license a product being developed by Big Pharma while others start as marketing or generic firms that grow from success. King Pharmaceuticals started small, made some brilliant acquisitions and through mergers has moved into research and development. Biovail is an example of a generic company now developing its own products but running into regulatory conflicts. In the biotechnology field most companies are small. The biotechnology industry seems most appropriate for the small company approach. Whether companies besides Genetech and Amgen can climb into the Big Pharma group remains to be seen. Centicor, Genzine, and US Bioscience have all made attempts to move into the large category of Big Pharma, some more successful than others; but it is difficult to develop a viable product and then sustain research and development to continue to grow.

Yet the trend is clearly established. Academicians with a novel idea no longer publish their results and go on to the next project. Rather, patents are obtained and a company is started. There are recent reports of a new technique in cardiothoracic surgery being performed using the laparoscopic approach. Instead of reading about the advances in JAMA, the discussion occurs in the *Wall Street Journal* and centers on the possible IPO that will be forthcoming for a company making the instruments essential for the procedure. Entrepreneurs and academicians are forming alliances that may speed a procedure or chemical entity into a viable product for development. While the free exchange of ideas may be limited and scientific discourse suffers a bit, the possibility of widespread clinical use facilitated by commercial development is enhanced. The pros and cons of this approach are not for us to debate, but rather to accept as a trend that is ongoing and growing considerably. The fast-moving nimbleness of these small dynamic companies, coupled with their lower overhead cost, offers considerable benefit to pharmaceutical discovery and development. Drugs are being developed that the larger concerns would not have considered. The advancement in niche areas like orphan drugs are for the most part being pursued by smaller companies. This is a healthy trend and one that will force all of the industry to streamline. Along with the trend of small niche companies in drug development has come the parallel corporate trend of downsizing and the hesitancy to expand divisions to take on temporary projects. More and more of the large companies are contracting out of critical aspects of drug discovery and development. Compounds can be manufactured under contract. Consultants can put together manufacturing specifications and preclinical testing and stability work can be done under contract. Clinical studies are performed by clinical research organizations (CROs) with the data handled by contract statistical analysis. A consulting team can put together an NDA all under the supervision of a small core group at corporate headquarters. This can be done for the small company or the very largest of the pharmaceutical giants. Parts of a project can be subcontracted. Indeed it is not uncommon for intermediate to small projects at the largest companies to be entirely subcontracted. For these reasons, the CROs and other contract service companies (CSAs) have been most successful. A bonanza of new business has created exponential growth for these types of companies. The companies are competitive and the work is relentless, but results are what make the industry thrive, and drug development has been accelerated considerably in some instances using this "piece work" approach. To some extent, the "virtual" pharmaceutical company has materialized.

There are dangers with the fragmented approach. Outside companies can be less dependable, projects can fall apart when the capitalization of the company is inadequate and they go under, and less than favorable schedules can sometimes develop since the project is not necessarily the highest priority of the contracting company. The fragmented approach can create situations where the contracting company may be less alert to important clinical findings that should alter the development program or less alert to serious toxicities that need to be taken into account. If studies are performed outside the U.S., as they often are, the quality of the data and the important aspects of clinical study acumen by the site investigators are often lacking. Important information about the drug may not be passed along and this can seriously impede the development process. In addition, corporate rapport with the site investigators may be lost and the important "seeding" of the market with experienced investigators who have experience with the product may not occur when contract organizations are involved and only non-U.S. studies are undertaken. However, there may be significant cost savings and increased patient accession with the CRO and foreign study data approaches, that may make their utilization advisable. Clearly, a balanced program giving careful considerations to the limitations of CROs running the studies, providing statistical analysis and monitoring services, as well as CROs coordinating non-U.S. studies, need to be carefully evaluated and balanced against the more traditional approaches to drug development.

3.10 Government, Regulation and Drug Development

The influences of the federal government are pervasive in our society, from our tax structure to the actions of regulatory agencies. All aspects of industry, and especially the pharmaceutical industry, are greatly influenced. In the 1990s, some manipulative politicians targeted the pharmaceutical industry in their rhetoric to pander to voters. This pseudopopulist approach has continued. The balanced tension between the Democrats representing more government and the Republicans representing less government and deregulation has vanished with one marked lurch to the left with the Health Care Reform Act of 2010. This is, of course, a simplification, but one with historic justification. Clearly, there is a trend against government as the provider of solutions. But recent events have gone against this trend. How the trend will develop in the future is difficult to predict. Even with the progression of government and regulation, the impact this trend has on the pharmaceutical industry will remain substantial. The specter of an unprotected public is a difficult "political cry" to oppose and one not readily challenged except by the most ardent of conservative Republicans. The industry itself, especially the larger pharmaceutical companies, appear to support the FDA rather vigorously. They operate successfully within its framework and, in a way, the FDA has become part of the process to limit competition and diminish the effectiveness of the smaller companies not able to compete against the more formidable pharmaceutical giants. Additionally, the FDA, especially at the scientific level, well serves industry, ensuring efficacy and safety and instilling a very high degree of confidence on the part of the public in pharmaceutical products. In addition, the FDA stands at the "gate" as the guardian of Big Pharma's market, with both having a vested interest against the re-importation of pharmaceuticals.

However, the reworking of the health care system under President Obama portends an age of hyper-regulation. This, combined with the dismal performance of the economy and projections of entitlement programs for cash infusion for their solvency, supports an environment of high taxes, slow growth and price pressure on the pharmaceutical industry. The age of ever-increasing drug prices is coming to an end. Costs by industry will need to be cut, and efficiency improved to maintain profitability. The Obama Administration will need to obtain further price concessions, foster the use of generic pharmaceuticals and generic biologics to begin to pay for the massive explosion of health care and to reduce Medicare and Medicaid costs. These pressures on pricing will extend to medical devices and new technologies for diagnosis and treatment, as well as the cost of pharmaceuticals.

3.11 Government Research

The importance of the defense and space-related technology on drug development has been minimal and will probably continue to be most disappointing. A more effective utilization of research funding coming from space research and the military defense research consortium could be obtained by a granting system based upon the National Institutes of Health (NIH) and National Science Foundation (NSF) with more decentralization. While the NSF and NIH are imperfect systems, they are far better at supporting the advancement of knowledge than the military or a space administration. The trend toward big scientific projects has slowed, with more emphasis on biologic research supported through NIH being preferred. This is especially encouraging since by supporting new programs, small programs, and diverse projects, we are more likely to see important advances as opposed to the results seen when only the established industrial scientific complex and its bureaucracy are the grantors of support.

Still, there is a paucity of support for pharmaceutical-related research, clinical pharmacology research, and research related to drug development in terms of governmental support. This is truly unfortunate since there is tremendous public health benefit to be obtained in this area. This is not to suggest that government should compete with industry; but in areas where industry is not working or in more fundamental areas that lead to the discovery and development process or are ancillary to drug discovery and development, gov-

ernment could and should play an important role. However, a major component of the nation's public health remains solely funded by for-profit pharmaceutical enterprises. The federal government's genome project appears much more promising for the biotechnology gene manipulation sector of drug discovery and development. This information is fundamental and will form the information base of so many discoveries in this area for the future. It is counterproductive that the government would patent its findings and not facilitate the dissemination and utilization of this information in research and practical product development. It is good that this approach has stopped, and the government is once again returning to its role as a facilitator, not a competitor, and one not aimed at accumulating wealth. That the direction of the genome project is recoiling from the concept of patenting in competition with the private sector is a sign that the federal bureaucracy can be modified and responsive to the needs of society.

One promising area coming from the recent Health Reform Act is the support for Comparative Effectiveness Research supported by the Federal government. This is an area that the NIH should control and one that can greatly improve physician use of pharmaceutical therapies. However, it can be misused by some parts of government to control health care supporting programs just to cut costs and not to address medical therapeutics. Identifying the best and most effective ways to treat disease is needed and the drug development process aims at drug approval and not comparative effectiveness. Hopefully, the U.S. will avoid the European system where market entry requires comparative research. Only prolonged clinical use can give information on effectiveness and side effects, permitting a drug to find its place in therapy.

3.12 The FDA Regulators

The drug development process occurs within the structure defined by the FDA. From initial clinical testing in Phase I to later Phase II and III clinical trials, the FDA has considerable influence and control while at the same time exercising a minimal degree of interference that is often surprising. Unlike European agencies, for example, the scientific levels of the FDA are most accessible at all stages of development—from pre-IND, pre-Phase II, or pre-NDA meetings, the FDA can provide meaningful guidance in a drug development program. Yes, it will be the judge of the data presented and the "keeper of the regulations," but its assistance comes more from experience in the drug development process. The scientific division chiefs and other senior individuals at the FDA see a tremendous number of clinical trials, have often encountered clinical development problems, and can, without the disclosure of confidential information, provide considerable assistance to those involved in drug development. While an individual in a company may be involved with only a couple of compounds over a career in terms of major development programs, the FDA senior people may see that many in one week, and from many different perspectives. Clearly, the FDA is the nexus of pharmaceutical development information and training that unfortunately has not been tapped into as effectively as it should be.

Those involved in drug development must work in concert with the FDA. The FDA and industry working together on a product will often bring about a development program that is more effective and more efficient in time and resources. Too many may take FDA's advice as dictum. There is what could be termed "the shadow FDA." Those regulatory advisors in industry telling us what the FDA requires and wants are all too often distortions and impediments to effective drug development. The FDA should be looked upon as an important resource, with whom those pivotally involved in drug development in industry should communicate directly. Regulatory advisors, consultants, past regulators, facilitators, and legal advisors all have their place, but should not be interposed between those at the companies who are the critical links in drug development. No advice should be binding; everything needs to be discussed; and reasonable approaches need to be taken. The individuals at the FDA are not omniscient. A development plan may not work out and may need substantial modification. Failure to realize this and blindly going forth after an FDA conference can lead to failure. Coming back to the FDA and saying, "But this is what we were instructed to do" is foolish and in a sense undercuts the free and open exchange of ideas between the regulators and the developers. Advice is given, but subsequent reproach because of changing circumstances, developments in the field, or just lack of efficacy of a compound is counterproductive. In fact, it may deter the critical assistance from the FDA that can be so helpful to a drug development team.

These impressions, of course, need to be modified in the context of the divisions and the individuals involved. There are differences among and between divisions and individuals and those at the FDA giving advice, and this needs to be factored into the equation. But, clearly, the most successful in development have created a working relationship with the FDA and made use of the extensive scientific experience these individuals have with drug development. Having been the organizer of a course on cardiovascular drug development, protocol design and methodology for 15 years, I can attest to the unselfish assistance of so many senior individuals at the FDA. Their knowledge of the drug development field and their interest in successful drug development and in finding scientific truth is clear cut. While the course involves many leading academics and industry physicians who have considerable knowledge, each year the symposium demonstrates that the FDA participants who are senior at the agency consistently demonstrate a broad knowledge of the field of drug development.

The FDA can facilitate drug development further than what is currently being done. There are times that the delays are needless, that the debate is not helpful, but the era of the "drug lag" behind Europe that so severely crippled therapeutics in the 1950s, 1960s, and the 1970s no longer exists. However, excessive drug regulation is not the goal. Rather, more expeditious, less costly development in the information age should be the goal of the FDA. A case-by-case review is no longer necessary. Each data point to be separately chronicled and meticulously reviewed for efficacy and toxicity by a junior reviewer is an immense waste of time. Having the primary reviewer recreate the NDA piece-by-piece and then producing their own summary is a laborious process that obviously can take a year or more. Quality assurance techniques are in place to ensure accuracy and integrity of an NDA database. The FDA could make use of these techniques and clearly it will need to strengthen procedures, applying sophisticated computer techniques to make analyses as expeditious as possible. To keep up with the information age, the FDA will be one of the links in the drug development process that is most stressed by forthcoming change. User fees and more FDA revenues are not the answer; placing the cost of submission beyond the capacity of small startup companies is ill advised. Using these funds for more and more reviewers, thus expanding the laborious approach to data review, is fallacious. Many of these programs are not objected to by the giants of industry and in fact are encouraged, since once again it appeases those who want to speed up the process and, at the same time, places impediments on the more formative, dynamic small companies, thus forming anticompetitive practices into which the FDA is lured as an unwitting ally.

The statement that the FDA needs to "take its time" to "plow through each data point" to protect the public is often heard. By never approving a drug, FDA would be the most protective, since no adversity would ensue from approved drugs. However, the adverse effects of no therapeutic advances would be intolerable. Thus, a compromise in the tension between the regulators charged to protect the public and the public's need for new effective therapies needs to be reached. The use of the information revolution to facilitate drug development needs to be explored. We are at the beginning of this exciting period and the government will evolve more slowly perhaps than other centers in the development process, but it will indeed evolve.

A number of approaches are possible. The use of quality assurance techniques for partial to comprehensive data verification on a random basis certainly needs to be validated and then applied. Perhaps data analysis performed by certified groups that are paid for by the company, but at the same time are licensed by the FDA, would eliminate the need for data reentry and reapplication of analytical techniques. Focusing on quick review techniques for the critical pivotal studies and ascertaining their veracity needs to be placed at the top of the review list. With the acceptance of efficacy, rapid computerized analysis of the product's toxicity and comparison of the results to those obtained with other agents could permit an estimation of the agent's potential benefits and toxicity. This could facilitate early presentation of the NDA material to an advisory committee that would be able to understand its place in the therapeutic armamentarium and decide whether a more prolonged and thorough evaluation is needed or an early release could be considered. Of course, an early release might be combined with a more prolonged preliminary period, where information is collected on adverse experiences and efficacy, and these items are then used for continued drug evaluation.

The process of approving a drug, getting very little additional information after the approval, and allowing the drug to remain on the market forever is as wrong as a very slow and time-consuming initial development process. In fact, the difficulty in getting a drug off the market and the scarcity of postmarketing information, reinforces the regulators' need to make the initial approval so stringent. It would be far better to look to a system such as that in Great Britain, where there may be a more provisional stage of approval, with a detailed program of postmarketing surveillance that is quite simple for practitioners to participate in. We must understand that drugs can be marketed; and then knowledge and information that has been developed can change our initial impression. A drug could be severely limited in its labeling, have warnings issued to physicians who will be using it, or possibly even taken off the market when our knowledge base on the product changes. A drug withdrawal should not be considered as a criticism of the FDA, but a realization that our knowledge continues to grow. Unfortunately, transcripts exist of congressional committees led by inquisitors who severely criticize regulators when adversity is later discovered from an agent that was approved on quite a meritorious application. We need to straighten out the ground rules and come to an understanding that our knowledge base expands constantly and that different regulatory decisions may be necessary with new knowledge. With this understanding

we can accept the early approval and later drug withdrawal, without faulting our regulatory colleagues. This approach is necessary if we are to fundamentally change for the better the drug development process. This is a difficult change, since so much of the process is developed by lawyers who view drug development as a litigious opportunity rather than a scientific pursuit, where knowledge is continuously increasing as more information is collected and there is no guilt or innocence, no liability to determine.

Unfortunately considerable tension has developed at the FDA between those groups supervising the drug development and approval process and those involved in adverse side effects surveillance post-approval. These groups differ from outlook to personality. Most toxicities will only be noted when large groups are exposed to a drug post-approval. Some at the FDA are far too ready to associate a side effect with toxicity, far too eager to remove a drug from the market when some patients find benefit from it. It is essential for physicians to have multiple therapies to chose from, weighing the risk to benefit ratio of a drug. All drugs have associated risks, but one would never know that when some zealots are screaming about a particular agent. Crusaders have advocated positions that are openly hostile to the pharmaceutical industry and they clearly have a temperament that would make medical practice impossible. They relentlessly oppose certain drugs despite those in clinical practice believing that these agents have a place in therapy and should remain on the market. Some at the FDA and in academia have severely criticized decisions about drugs, even recommendations from the FDA advisory panels after long and thoughtful deliberations. The Avandia controversy is just one example of the inability of some to accept opinions that differ from their conclusions. When an FDA advisory panel opposed the blanket removal of Avandia, those individuals retorted with statements that the pharmaceutical industry just "games" the system to continue to sell "dangerous drugs." What arrogance to believe that the careful review by academic physicians is pharmaceutical industry "gaming" of the system. These anti-industry zealots gain attention and medical community notoriety that fulfills some of their goals and we must expect their numbers and irresponsible attacks to increase.

Besides the tension at the FDA and the trend toward greater regulation, reviews are taking longer and more studies are requested for approval. There are a number of areas of genuine debate within the FDA regarding drug development. One example is with anti-infective agents. The FDA has now adopted the position that non-inferiority trials are not the appropriate way to develop these agents. They favor superiority or placebo-controlled trials. This is considered a significant impediment to drug development, since many in academia, as well as the pharmaceutical industry, believe it is not feasible to undertake placebo-controlled trials, and that asking for an agent to be superior is not possible or even wanted. Anti-infective agents are not developed to be superior, but often to be alternatives if bacterial resistance develops. Also, side effects in a given individual make the selection of an agent optimum when that has nothing to do with efficacy superiority. Even when the FDA will consider a non-inferiority study design, the margin of non-inferiority is requested to be so tight as to drastically increase sample size and thus cost of the study. While we might like these trends to reverse to encourage drug development and more approvals, we must expect the opposite with more difficult studies: less approvals and fewer changes facilitating drug development introduced.

What we need to strive for is not just intellectual rigor and statistical validity, but a feasible way to develop new agents given the clinical demand for new drugs, especially anti-infective agents. The public good must come first and thus these debates must be tempered.

3.13 Protecting the Domestic Drug Supply

The geopolitical situation remains perilous, and threats to the United States have continued to increase in the twenty-first century. While the United States is the only true "superpower," Russia has maintained a hostility and nuclear arsenal that is formidable. China has continued to increase in economic power that they are translating into military power they can project. North Korea and Iran have developed nuclear weapons and remain unstable rogue regions that are unpredictable and dangerous to friends and perceived foe alike. With these instabilities the ever present asymmetric threat of terrorists from al-Qaeda and other Muslim extremist groups is also present. These problems combined to pose a real problem for a reliable trade with many countries, especially in a time of war or terrorist action. With this context in mind the defense of the U.S. drug supply from parts of the world that are unstable is a real, but ignored problem. The clinical supplies for pharmaceuticals are produced in countries that could be unstable or outright hostile to the United States. India is becoming a major supplier of raw material. Would it be reliable if war with Pakistan or China develops? The U.S. has become dependent on China, a country with which hostility could develop. Heparin is just one example. The supply is unreliable due to potential contaminants; but even if it were reliable, can the U.S. depend solely on China for raw material supply of crucial pharmaceuticals?

Additionally, some critical drugs are made by only one company in the U.S., for example sub-lingual nitroglyc-

erin. A shortage developed when manufacturing problems developed at a factory in Puerto Rico. These are unacceptable vulnerabilities in the domestic drug supply. Given the vast buying power of the U.S. government through Medicare Prescription Benefits Program and the VA Administration, both Democrats and Republicans should be able to agree upon a strategy to diversify the pharmaceutical supply chain, to make it less dependent on foreign suppliers that could be unreliable at times of a terrorist attack or war. Our citizens with medical conditions should not be placed in danger due to international terrorism or hostility between nations. Securing the U.S. drug supply needs to be a national priority and can be readily accomplished through government procurement policies. This is an area where a role for government is appropriate.

3.14 Conclusion

Drug development and discovery is a most exciting field. It is creative, intellectually taxing, and organizationally demanding. Those involved are to be congratulated for undertaking efforts that are usually anonymous, but that impact clinical therapeutics to a considerable degree. The drug discovery process has gone through the botanical phase, the synthetic chemistry phase, and is now into an exciting era of biotechnology and gene manipulation. There is a tremendous evolution in our understanding of medicine, disease processes, and statistical evaluation of clinical trials. These are developing areas that are important, and they interact with the drug discovery process. The drug development process, is being markedly affected by the third wave, the information age. We can only think back to when a chapter like this would be handwritten, typed on a typewriter with carbon paper, corrections made and then a copy sent off to the publisher. Word processing has revolutionized this approach and will continue to revolutionize it in the next couple of years. This is the same revolution that is markedly changing the drug development process, facilitating it, and changing the FDA review of the data. All phases will undergo radical change and we will be better for it. This is a most exciting era and one that will be both exciting and worthwhile in which to participate.

Hopefully, government intrusion in the health care marketplace will be limited over time with the government bureaucracy and regulations not so intrusive as to degrade the quality of health care as it has done in Europe and Canada. While a lurch to the left has occurred in a time of financial panic that influenced the election process, the pendulum will move to the right, moderating the government's intrusions and costly policies over time.

References

Feldman, A.M., M.R. Bristow, W.W. Parmley, P.E. Carson, C.J. Pepine, E.M. Gilbert, J.E. Strobeck, G.H. Hendrix, E.R. Powers, R.P. Bain, and B.G. White BG for the Vesnarinone Study Group. "Effects of vesnarinone on morbidity and mortality in patients with heart failure." *N. Engl. J. Med.* 1993; 329(3):149-15.

Myerburg, R.J., K.M. Kessler, I. Kiem, K.C. Petkaros, C.A. Conde, D. Cooper D, and A. Castellanos. "Relationship between plasma levels of procainamide, suppression of premature ventricular complexes and prevention of recur- rent ventricular tachycardia." *Circulation* 1981; 64(2):280-289.

Packer, M., M. Gheorghiade, J.B. Young, P.J. Constantini, K.F. Adams, R.J. Cody RJ, L.K. Smith, L. van Voorhees, L.A. Gourley, M.K. "Jolly for the RADI- ANcE Study. Withdrawal of digoxin from patients with chronic heart failure treated with angiotensin-converting-enzyme inhibitors." *N. Engl. J. Med.* 1933; 329(1):1-7.

Scandinavian Simvastatin Survival Study Group. "Randomized trial of cholesterol lowering in 4444 patients with coronary heart disease: the Scandinavian simvastatin survival study (4S)." *Lancet* 1994; 344:1383-1389.

SOL VD Investigators. "Effect of enalapril on survival in patients with reduced left ventricular ejection fractions and congestive heart failure." *N. Engl. J. Med.* 1991; 325(5):293-302.

Toffler, A. *Future Shock*. New York: Random House, 1970.

Chapter 4

The Failed System of Drug Warnings in the United States

Kip A. Petroff, Esq.

4.1 Introduction

The current system for warning American consumers about side effects associated with prescription medications is seriously flawed and needs to be changed. The current system involves drug companies issuing initial warnings based primarily on side effects identified in small-scale, short-term clinical trials.[1] These warnings are disseminated to doctors and pharmacies through the *Physicians' Desk Reference* (or through similar written compendia) or through personal visits to doctors' offices, where the company's sales representatives discuss the features, benefits, and side effects of the drugs.[2] Drug companies are supposed to update these warnings, as they acquire new information (after the drugs

have received FDA approval and have been on the market awhile).

Such warnings are also required to be given directly to prospective patients, but only if the company chooses to market the drug directly to the consumers.[3] Generally, there is no duty for the drug company to directly warn consumers of anything—unless the drug company chooses to target advertising directly to potential consumers.[4,5]

The FDA relies on healthcare providers to report problems they see in the field as patients experience problems with the drugs. The drug companies disclose potential problems to doctors, and rely upon them to warn patients. The problem is that physicians drastically underreport drug-related side effects, and important new product warnings often go unheeded by the doctors. This chapter will discuss this system, address its flaws and shortcomings, and will suggest that the system needs drastic changes. It is hoped that this chapter will spark debate and discussion, and provoke possible improvements.

A. Overview of "The System"

The traditional method for providing information about the safety profile of a prescription drug entailed the drug manufacturer disclosing such information in the "product labeling."[6] The FDA defines "labeling" to include such things as "brochures, booklets, mailing pieces, calendars, letters, films, sound recordings, exhibits, literature, prints and similar types of printed, audio or visual matter descriptive of a drug and that contain drug information supplied by the manufacturer, and which are disseminated by or on behalf of its manufacturer, packer, or distributor."[6] Detailed federal regulations describe what information should be disclosed, including what section of the label should disclose certain information.[7] Such information was generally provided in the "Warnings, Contraindications, Precautions, and Adverse Reactions" sections of the product label.[8] The primary sources for such disclosures include the *Physicians' Desk Reference*, a several-thousand-page book published annually by Thomson Healthcare, as well as similar books, such as *Facts and Comparisons* (also another large tome that is published annually). Another traditional source was the actual written "product label" sent to the pharmacy or dispensing clinic when the drugs were shipped by the manufacturer.

The product label (also sometimes called a "package insert") includes information that fully discloses any warnings and supplies adequate directions for proper usage.[6] The package insert on a new drug is intended to disclose pertinent information from the clinical trials that were conducted before the FDA approved the drug for marketing. The FDA regulates what information goes in the package insert before the drug is approved for marketing and, thereafter, as new information about adverse reactions is acquired from actual use in the marketplace.

Other, less comprehensive, means of disclosing information about the safety profile of drugs include various forms of meetings with physicians and their staff members, either at the doctors' offices or at educational meetings that the drug companies sponsor and pay for. Drug companies also typically commission post-approval studies on their drugs, whereby physicians—typically at medical schools or in large clinical practices—would conduct studies and publish their results in medical journals. Not surprisingly, company-funded studies tend to favor that company's products. According to a 1996 study published in the *Annals of Internal Medicine*, 98 percent of company-sponsored drug studies published in peer-reviewed journals and symposium proceedings between 1980 and 1989 favored the funding company's drug.[9]

Drug companies typically did not provide information directly to the consumers, until the recent advent of direct marketing to consumers. The traditional explanation for not providing information directly to consumers was that such disclosure would interfere with the physician-patient relationship and would usurp the physician's responsibility and duty to the patient.[10] That rationale still applies today, but with one important exception: the manufacturer is required to disclose certain safety information directly to the consumer only when the manufacturer chooses to market its products directly to the consumers.[3]

B. Overview of the Problem

A major problem with the current "system" of dispensing safety information about prescription drugs is that such information is not adequately conveyed to the doctors or is not fully absorbed and acted upon by the doctors. Recent studies and other developments have dramatically demonstrated the

depth of this problem. One study revealed that physicians continued to prescribe Propulsid (Cisapride/Janssen) to patients who had a medical condition or who were on other medicines, despite a contraindication in the package insert that expressly recommended against prescribing the drug to such people.[11] The drug Baycol (Cerivastatin/Bayer) was removed from the market in August 2001,[12] in part because physicians continued to prescribe the drug in combination with Lopid (gemfibrozil/Warner-Lambert), despite a contraindication in the label and a "Dear Doctor" letter that was sent to physicians in December 1999.[13]

Numerous other recent examples can be cited where drugs were removed from the market reportedly, in part, because of physicians' prescribing practices. The drug Duract (sodium bromfenac/Wyeth), which caused rare but serious liver events associated with long-term use, was removed from the market on June 22, 1998—partly because physicians continued to prescribe the drug for longer than the ten days suggested by the manufacturer as the maximum course of therapy.[14] Perhaps one of the most well-known examples of drugs being removed due to adverse events associated with prescribing practices inconsistent with the prescribing information is the withdrawal of the drug Pondimin (fenfluramine/Wyeth) in September 1997.[15] The prescribing information for Pondimin always stated that it was a weight-loss medication indicated for "short-term (a few weeks)" duration.[16] The drug was removed when an association was observed between the use of the drug and the development of valvular heart disease. Importantly, numerous studies have revealed that the incidence of that disease occurs in patients at a statistically significant increased risk only when used in excess of 90 days.[17,18]

Other studies published in the medical literature have also demonstrated this problem. For some examples, see Lasser et al.'s article, entitled "Timing of New Black Box Warnings and Withdrawals for Prescription Medication," published in *JAMA*, in May 2002.[19] See also Figueiras et al.'s 1999 article published in *Med Care*, entitled, "Influence of Physicians' Attitudes on Reporting Adverse Drug Events: A Case Control Study,"[20] and Rogers et al.'s 1988 article in the *Archives of Internal Medicine*, entitled "Physician Knowledge, Attitudes, and Behavior Related to Reporting Adverse Drug Events."[21]

The ramifications to society, as a result of this problem have been enormous. People have died or suffered serious injuries. Lawsuits have been filed. Billions of dollars have been paid to injured patients and to lawyers who defend (and prosecute) such lawsuits, and to expert witnesses on both sides of these lawsuits. Equally important is the fact that drugs—important drugs that could help patients if used properly—have been completely removed from the market. The anticipated benefits of years of drug-company research and development (along with vast financial and human resources) were short-lived.

This chapter explores the system of drug warnings in America and discusses how and why this system is not accomplishing what it intends to achieve. Analysis of these areas will reveal that something needs to be changed in order to allow patients and physicians to have available to them a wider array of drugs and to lessen the number of adverse events experienced with the use of such drugs.

4.2 Underreporting of ADEs
A. Adverse Drug Events

1. Introduction

An adverse drug event (ADE), also referred to as an adverse drug reaction (ADR), may be defined as any undesirable or unexpected event believed to be caused by the taking of a prescription or over-the-counter drug that facilitates some change in the patient's case, including discontinuing the medication, modifying the dose, prolonging hospitalization, or initiating supportive care.[22] In particular, the Food and Drug Administration (FDA) is concerned about drugs that cause "serious" adverse events. An adverse event is serious if the patient outcome is death, a life-threatening event, hospitalization, disability, or if the product causes a congenital anomaly or a birth defect.[23] The FDA encourages, but does not require, all healthcare professionals to report any serious adverse drug events they detect. Through this voluntary reporting system, the FDA monitors the safety of all prescription drugs in the United States. This current method of tracking adverse events, however, has one glaring problem—roughly 90 to 99 percent of all adverse drug reactions never get reported.[24,25]

Increased reporting of adverse drug events is necessary because, at the time a drug is marketed, data relating to its safety is quite limited. Before any drug receives FDA approval, it is tested on only a limited number of people for only a short period of time.[5] "[M]ost Americans believe that the drug approval process is rigorous and complex, involving studies of thousands of people over a period of many years."[1] But in fact, "the scientific studies required for FDA approval generally last only about five to six weeks and involve a few hundred people at most."[1] Overall, 51 percent of approved drugs have serious adverse effects not detected prior to approval.[26] Therefore, uncommon or delayed effects may not be detected before a drug is released. Such effects only emerge when a drug is used in large numbers of people, in special (sometimes in "at-risk") populations, or over long periods of time.[21] Thus, underreporting of ADEs prolongs the time between initial marketing of the drug and a complete understanding of its actual safety profile.

2. ADE reporting

Administered by the Division of Pharmacovigilance and Epidemiology (DPE) of the FDA, the Adverse-Event Reporting System (AERS), formerly the Spontaneous Reporting System (SRS), is a computerized information database designed to support the FDA's postmarketing safety surveillance program for all approved drug and therapeutic biological products. The FDA relies on the AERS to flag safety issues and identify pharmaceuticals or therapeutic biological products that need further epidemiological study. The ultimate goal of the AERS is to improve the public's health by providing the best available tools for storing and analyzing safety reports.[27] This goal will be thwarted if the underreporting problem is not corrected.

AERS is a database of ADRs provided by healthcare providers, pharmacists, drug manufacturers, patients, and parents.[28] Drug manufacturers and distributors are required by regulation to submit adverse drug-reaction reports to the FDA. They must submit expedited reports for serious and unexpected (i.e., unlabeled) adverse events. Quarterly or annual periodic reports, depending on the date the FDA approved marketing of the drug, must be submitted for all other serious and non-serious events. Healthcare professionals and consumers, on the other hand, are not required to report anything; they may send reports voluntarily through the MedWatch program.

MedWatch is the FDA avenue through which health professionals can voluntarily report serious events and problems with such medical products as drugs, biologics, medical devices, radiation-emitting devices, and special nutritional products.[23] MedWatch, however, is not designed as the repository for reports of all adverse events, but rather for focused reporting of those events considered "serious and unexpected."[23] The term "serious" is defined above, and "unexpected" simply means the ADR being reported is not listed in the *Physicians' Desk Reference* for that particular drug. Thus, the FDA does not desire a report on every ADR—only on those where the patient outcome is death, a life-threatening event, hospitalization, disability, or a congenital anomaly. This is intended to maximize the efficiency of generating signals or trends of potential problems on the basis of report evaluation within a high-volume system.

While only serious adverse events should be reported to the FDA, proof of causality is not required. The FDA does not require that a doctor become thoroughly convinced of a drug's connection to an adverse event before making a report. That would be nearly impossible to determine, and would also be unworkable, because busy clinicians cannot be expected to thoroughly investigate the causation issues. Thus, mere suspicion that a drug may be related to a serious event is sufficient reason for a physician to submit a report.[25] Especially important for healthcare professionals to report are adverse effects from medications that have been on the market for a short time (i.e., three years or less), because that is when the most critical problems are discovered.[25] That is, undoubtedly, why the drug manufacturer is required to submit quarterly reports on its ADE experiences during the first three years that the drug is on the market.

The FDA hoped MedWatch would encourage an increased sense of responsibility among physicians and other healthcare providers about reporting adverse events that may be related to FDA-regulated products. To that end, the MedWatch reporting system encourages healthcare professionals to regard reporting of ADEs as a fundamental professional and public-healthcare responsibility. In an attempt to underscore the responsibility of healthcare providers in identifying and reporting adverse events, the FDA sought to: (1) make it easier for providers to report serious events, (2) make it clear to physicians what types of reports the FDA wants to receive, (3) more widely disseminate information on the FDA's actions that have resulted from adverse-event reporting, and (4) increase physician understanding and awareness of drug-induced disease.[25] The first part of this chapter will point out the shortcomings of the MedWatch program in achieving its goal of heightening the awareness and reporting of adverse drug events by healthcare professionals.

B. The Underreporting Problem

1. MedWatch: A seriously deficient approach

The problem of underreporting ADEs has been discussed for years in the scientific literature. A brief historical review of the problem is appropriate here.

In 1988 (five years prior to the introduction of Med-Watch), seven doctors performed a study on the underreporting of adverse drug events.[21] They discovered that only 57 percent of the doctors surveyed were even aware of the FDA reporting system. Furthermore, 18 percent of the doctors reported an adverse event during this study, but only 28 percent of those were reported directly to the FDA. Thus, only 5 percent of all detected ADEs were reported directly to the FDA. A second study estimates that as few as 1 percent of suspected serious adverse reactions were reported to the FDA during the 1980s.[29] When asked why they reported so few adverse events, doctors claimed the event was either not serious, the event was already known and documented, or the FDA form was unavailable when it was needed.

Even after the introduction of the MedWatch reporting system in 1993, a severe problem of underreporting still persists today in the United States. Because doctors, hospitals, and others report adverse events on a voluntary basis, the MedWatch reporting system captures only a small percentage of total adverse drug events.[30] Thomas J. Moore noted that "[o]ur surveillance system of drugs once they are approved is extremely weak....It relies entirely on voluntary reports [from physicians] and we know that a large majority of even serious and fatal adverse events are never reported."[31] More than 250,000 side effects linked to prescription drugs are reported each year. Many experts believe these reports represent only 1 to 10 percent of all such events,[32] which is no better than the rate at which ADEs were reported before MedWatch was ever implemented. Some believe that number should be reduced even further, because many reports are excluded on technicalities, such as insufficient information on the form, or because the patient had another problem complicating the picture.[33] It is for this reason that many believe the number of adverse events reported by physicians comprises less than 1 percent of all adverse events actually experienced.[24,34]

The introduction of the MedWatch program seems to have done nothing to alleviate the underreporting problem in the United States. Clinicians still give the reporting of ADEs a very low priority, so if this limited monitoring system reveals that a certain drug is causing hundreds of adverse events, thousands (or tens of thousands) of consumers are likely being affected. This high rate of underreporting indicates that the FDA reporting system is a seriously deficient approach.

2. Making the decision to report ADEs

Simply stated, adverse drug events are highly underreported because doctors often do not detect them. In addition, doctors frequently fail to report them—even when an adverse reaction is known or suspected. The voluntary monitoring system fails to entice physicians to report ADEs, because "[t]here's no incentive at all for a physician to report an adverse drug reaction."[32] When an adverse event occurs, a doctor must first recognize the potential association of the drug to the ADE, and then she must decide whether to report it. This decision is often influenced by the seriousness of the event, the perceived likelihood that it is due to the drug (including knowledge of previous reports), and the time and resources available to the doctor.[35] Many physicians cite the "hassle factor" as a reason for not reporting an adverse event, because such work is perceived as a burden without benefit.[36] One physician, Louis M. Soletsky, M.D., wrote the following commentary about the excessive burdens involved in reporting an ADE:

> Years ago I reported a Stevens-Johnson reaction to an antihistamine and a product defect in a particular brand of syringe. In each case the FDA responded to my short form by sending me a long, somewhat intimidating letter and an enormous multi-page form. In addition, they shared this information with the manufacturer, who proceeded to add to the paperwork....I would personally advise any busy practitioner to avoid having any involvement with [the FDA's reporting system] unless he or she has plenty of free time and secretarial services.[37]

Dr. Richard W. Parkinson remarked that the opinion of Dr. Soletsky is common among most doctors. He adds, "neither the FDA nor the manufacturer wants to hear about [any adverse reactions], but if [doctors] persist, then they're going to make it as difficult as possible."[37]

There are many reasons why doctors are reluctant or unmotivated to report or even identify a potential adverse reaction to a drug. Some of the factors associated with the low motivation to report ADEs are: (1) doctors believe that really serious ADEs are well-documented by the time a drug is marketed; (2) they fail to perceive the importance of their individual contribution to the overall knowledge of drug-treatment safety; (3) they believe it is nearly impossible to determine whether or not a drug is directly responsible for a particular adverse event (in other words, it is often difficult to discern whether or not a reported adverse reaction was from the medication or was a consequence of the underlying conditions that necessitated the medication); (4) they lack certainty about the diagnosis; (5) after a drug has been on the market for a few weeks, doctors and other healthcare professionals become aware of the possible adverse reactions and stop reporting them; (6) they do not have time for or interest in reporting ADEs; (7) they fear involvement in future litigation, including possibly having the report used against them if the patient sues for wrongfully prescribing the drug; (8) those healthcare professionals who consistently report adverse events appear less safe than non-reporting colleagues or competitors; and (9) they fear that reporting of several ADEs may damage their reputation.[20,36]

3. Need for improvement

There is, and undoubtedly has been, an inadequate system for reporting adverse drug reactions in the United States. Compared with the reporting rates of other devel-

oped countries, the United States ranks among the lowest in the world.[38] Although similarly low reporting rates are experienced in the Netherlands, France, Germany, and Belgium, United States reporting rates are, on the average, approximately 20 percent of those reported in Denmark, 40 percent of those reported in Canada, and 50 percent of those reported in the U.K.[36] The FDA MedWatch program focuses on rare reactions to medications not yet reported in the literature for a particular prescription drug. While this is a valuable service, it is not designed to identify signals or trends that point to serious safety problems. Without accurate and more complete reporting of adverse events and "near misses," it is difficult to identify and impossible to establish a baseline against which to gauge the success or failure of the various adverse-event-reporting initiatives that have been undertaken over the past decade.

The entire system for monitoring drug safety relies on doctors' thorough reporting of serious adverse events. Since doctors report such a low percentage of actual adverse events, dangers associated with many drugs are not discovered and, subsequently, important new product warnings are never disclosed. Even if warnings are issued, some doctors disregard them, as seen by the Propulsid and Baycol examples mentioned in the introduction to this chapter. This is a serious problem that must be remedied.

C. Solutions to the Problem

1. A mandatory system

A report released by the Inspector General of the Department of Health and Human Services in February 2000 recommended that the voluntary reporting system established by the FDA be replaced by a mandatory one.[36] While confidentiality protections and privileges that keep reports out of litigation are often proposed as solutions to the problem of underreporting, such measures may undermine public trust and create concerns about accountability. Therefore, the report concluded that, in cases of serious injury or death, a mandatory reporting system, with some degree of public access and potential for sanctions, is necessary for purposes of policing deficient reporting practices and ensuring accountability. This type of mandatory reporting system has, for years, been an obligation of doctors who suspected events (such as child abuse) in patients,[39] and it is difficult to understand why doctors who see potential adverse drug reactions should have a lesser duty to report to the FDA.

Separate, sanction-free voluntary-reporting systems were deemed necessary for purposes of prevention. This would cover the remainder of cases, picking up the "near misses" that would be exceedingly difficult to capture through a mandatory system. In both systems, reporting could be increased through standardization of forms, to lessen the paperwork burden and investment of resources in data analysis-and-feedback channels to healthcare providers who report them. A system that would encourage adverse-event reporting seems clearly indicated—especially since new drugs are being approved, but later withdrawn, at alarming rates.

2. Alternative: Avoiding new drugs altogether

Many serious ADRs are discovered only after a drug has been on the market for a few years. This sometimes requires only a year or two before serious trends and signals are detected, but half of newly discovered, serious ADRs are not detected or documented within seven years after drug approval, according to a recent study by Dr. Karen Lasser.[19] Over a 25 year period, the estimated probability of a new drug acquiring black-box warnings or being withdrawn from the market was 20 percent.[19] During that same period, new drugs had a 4 percent probability of being withdrawn from the market. Half of all drug withdrawals occurred within the first two years. Therefore, because of their limited exposure to the general public, new drugs should be avoided, said Dr. Lasser, when safe and effective alternatives already exist.

4.3 Problems at the FDA
A. The FDA in the 1990s

1. Introduction

In the early 1990s, the FDA received a considerable amount of criticism from those who said it was moving too slowly, was holding up the approval of new breakthrough drugs, and was lagging behind other countries. In response to these critics, the agency agreed in 1992 to put drug approvals on a "fast track." But by the end of the decade, new critics were saying this approach had backfired and bad drugs were slipping through. As will be seen below, Duract, Posicor, Redux, and Seldane were some of the many drugs approved during this time that were later removed from the market within a few years of their approvals.[40]

2. PDUFA (1992) and FDAMA (1997)

Since the early 1990s, there has been a debate about whether fast drug approval was more important than safe drug approval. Congress wanted to ensure that the American people had access to effective new medicines as quickly as possible. So, beginning in 1992, Congress authorized the FDA, via the Prescription Drug User Fee Act (PDUFA),[41] to take drug-company subsidies, called "user fees," to hire approximately 600 additional persons to review marketing

applications. Under this Act, any company wanting FDA approval of a new drug prior to marketing must submit an application, along with a fee, to support the review process. In addition, the company must pay an annual fee for each manufacturing establishment and for each prescription-drug product marketed. Previously, taxpayers alone paid for product reviews through budgets provided by Congress. Some entities thought this led to a needless delay in the drug evaluation-and-approval process.

In the new program, industry provides the funding, in exchange for the FDA agreeing to meet drug-review performance goals, which emphasize timeliness. President Clinton, for example, called for the FDA, by January 2000, to reduce "by an average of one year the time required to bring important new drugs to the American public."[42] Recent reports demonstrate a better compliance with PDUFA time requirements (www.fda.gov). Before the enactment of PDUFA, the FDA took an average of 30 months to approve a new drug. In consultation with industry and Congress, the FDA agreed to meet these goals, which became more stringent each year, so long as the FDA also received sufficient fee resources to enable goal achievement.[43] The primary goal of PDUFA, therefore, was to provide the FDA with additional revenue so it could hire more reviewers and support staff and upgrade its information technology to speed up the application-review process for human drug and biological products, without compromising review quality.[43]

The PDUFA, however, had a very limited purpose. Caving to the demands of the pharmaceutical industry, Congress prohibited the FDA from spending user fees for monitoring drug safety or any purpose other than reviewing marketing applications. By 1997, Congress had capped this industry-inspired effort by enacting "modernization" legislation lowering the barriers to approval of new drugs, partly with "fast-track" procedures. This resulted in an over-emphasis on getting drugs approved and an under-emphasis on making sure the newly approved drugs were adequately monitored in their first years of use.

Similarly, Congress passed the FDA Modernization Act of 1997 (FDAMA),[44,45] which instituted major reforms to the Federal Food, Drug, and Cosmetic Act of 1938. Through FDAMA, Congress emphasized that the FDA's mission is not only to prevent the distribution of unsafe products, but also to review and approve new drugs in a timely manner.[46] The Advisory Committee for the FDA noted, "the agency should be guided by the principle that expeditious approval of useful and safe new products enhances the health of the American people. Approving such products can be as important as preventing the marketing of harmful or ineffective products. This is especially true for people with life-threatening illnesses and for diseases for which alternative therapies have not been approved."[7] Accordingly, Congress set forth numerous provisions in FDAMA that would expedite the drug-approval process considerably.

By the late 1990s, the focus of the FDA seemed to shift. Instead of concentrating on drug safety, the FDA began looking more at speedy approval of new drugs. In 1999, then-FDA Commissioner Jane E. Henney appeared before Congress, not to report on what the agency had done to protect the public, in compliance with the drug-safety laws, but to boast how the agency "enhances U.S. competitiveness in global markets, provides a level playing field for industry, and strengthens the domestic economy as a whole by inviting increased foreign investment...."[47] These types of statements clearly reflect a "business attitude" of the FDA that is not necessarily consistent with trying to reduce the number of ADEs that are experienced with a given drug.

3. Pressure to approve

This legislation had a significant impact on FDA employees. "The pressure to meet deadlines [at the FDA was] enormous," said Dr. Solomon Sobel, director of the FDA's Metabolic and Endocrine Drugs Division during the 1990s. And the pressure was not merely to complete the reviews. "The basic message [was] to approve."[42] That message was clear to other employees as well. "[O]ne should be approving things, not questioning problems that arise, and...give the drug company the benefit of the doubt," said Elizabeth Barbehenn, who left the agency in frustration over the pressure to skim over safety concerns, after spending 13 years at the FDA monitoring the safety of certain experimental drugs.[40]

Another FDA employee, Michael Elashoff, worked at the FDA from 1995 to 2000, reviewing new drug applications. His job (so he thought) was to scrutinize the safety and effectiveness of emerging drugs. In 1999, he was assigned to review Relenza, a flu drug developed by Glaxo Wellcome. He recommended against approval, citing a lack of proven effectiveness and potential risks. An agency advisory committee agreed with Elashoff and, on February 24, 2000, voted 13-4 against approving Relenza. After the vote, senior FDA officials reprimanded Elashoff. They stripped him of his review of another flu drug, told him he would no longer make presentations to the advisory committee, and approved Relenza as a safe and effective flu drug.[30]

Through the efforts of Congress and the pharmaceutical industry, new drugs became available in the United States as fast or faster than anywhere else in the world by the late 1990s. However, this achievement came at a hefty cost. That cost was an under-funded drug-review staff working on too

many drugs in too little time. Between 1999 and 2011, 176 new drugs and biologics were approved (www.fda.gov).

4. Understaffed and overworked: A "sweatshop environment"

While pressuring the FDA to approve new drugs in record numbers, Congress simultaneously denied FDA safety monitors the resources required to meet the increased burdens these new drugs imposed. Federal money did not keep pace with the FDA's workload, as more than 1,300 drugs being tested on humans swamped the agency by the end of the decade.[48] This speed-up of approvals increased the burdens on the FDA's already indefensibly understaffed office responsible for monitoring the safety of marketed drugs. This resulted in the approval of numerous drugs that were withdrawn within three years of their approvals.

While the FDA had more than 1,400 employees with principal duties related to approving new drugs in 1998, a full-time staff of only 52 monitored the safety of approximately 5,000 brand-name, generic, and over-the-counter drugs already on the market.[26] Of those 52, only ten were professionally trained as physicians or epidemiologists.[47] Although all FDA employees play a role in promoting drug safety, the FDA continued to focus primarily on evaluating new drugs expeditiously, with only modest resources and staff to monitor the safety of drugs once they entered the marketplace. Janet Woodcock, M.D., director of the FDA's drug-review center at that time, acknowledged that a heavy workload and tight performance goals had created "a sweatshop environment that's causing high staffing turnover."[30] FDA employees worked long hours, with poor salaries and training opportunities, which caused high turnover. Clearly, this environment was breeding neglect of safety concerns. This was a difficult time for these FDA employees who were involved in analyzing these new drugs.

5. Compromising safety

The FDA was faced with the difficult task of protecting the public from drugs that could be dangerous, without delaying the availability of useful treatments. Before FDAMA was enacted, a reviewer who approved an unsafe drug would suffer tremendous consequences, while a reviewer who delayed or denied drug approval would be overlooked.[49] Congress was confident that FDAMA's provisions would not cause public health concerns. However, after FDAMA's enactment, the FDA appeared to focus on approving drugs for marketing as quickly as possible, which may have been detrimental to the FDA's duty to protect public health. There are numerous other authors who have addressed this topic. (See Timmerman, L. Feb. 19, 2002. "FDA Headache: Balancing Safety and Drug Approval." *Seattle Times*.[48] See also Mishbin[50] and Parver.[51])

Ultimately, the drug reviewer must reconcile the tension between speedy drug review and safety, and it appeared that, as a consequence of FDAMA's ambitious performance goals, a reviewer's productivity was linked to the number of drugs approved. Reviewers were under tremendous pressure to approve drugs from drug manufacturers, physicians, and Wall Street. The decision to approve or not approve was a $231 million question, and any decision other than "yes" would have been second-guessed.[51] In fact, the FDA appeared to be working too closely with drug manufacturers during the review process. "Consumer advocates, and even some of the agency's own drug reviewers, argue that the agency has become too cozy with the pharmaceutical industry and too lax, putting lives at risk."[52] Such a relationship resulted in a conflict of interest, leading to fatal approval errors.[52]

During the mid-1990s, the FDA and the pharmaceutical industry certainly developed a more partner-like relationship. This relationship grew even less adversarial as the 1990s progressed. In return for speeding along the approval of new drugs, the FDA got big money from the pharmaceutical industry in the form of user fees. The FDA feared that unless new drugs were approved in record time, companies would object and Congress would refuse to renew the user fees. As a result, safety took a backseat. With drug makers writing bigger checks to the drug-safety police, some physicians wondered whether the FDA could put public health first.

This neglect of consumer safety was evident in the unprecedented number of drugs withdrawn from the market because of adverse—and sometimes even deadly—effects. Since the late 1990s, the FDA has pulled 11 unsafe drugs off the market.[48] From 1993 to 2000, reports of serious side effects shot up 89 percent.[48] Between September 1997 and July 1998—a span of just ten months—five drugs were withdrawn from the market: the painkiller Duract (for causing liver failure, including four deaths and eight liver transplants); the blood-pressure drug Posicor (after 400 injuries and 24 deaths when it interacted dangerously with other medications); the diet drugs fenfluramine and Redux (for damaging hearts); and the antihistamine Seldane (which interacted lethally with a long list of other drugs).[40] In the previous ten years, the FDA had banned just six other drugs. This makes the early years of PDUFA look very bad in comparison to the previous ten years.

Thus, almost as many prescription drugs were yanked off the U.S. market in just ten months as were withdrawn in the entire previous decade. Never before has the FDA overseen the withdrawals of so many drugs in such a short time. One physician stated that the "FDA used to serve a purpose....A doctor could feel sure that a drug he was prescribing was as safe as possible. Now you wonder what kind of evaluation has been done, and what's been swept under the rug."[30]

Some experts said these recalls were evidence the FDA had begun allowing slack in its approval process, but the FDA repeatedly claimed that safety standards had not been lowered during this time period. While the total number of drugs withdrawn from the market increased dramatically in the late 1990s, the percentage of drugs approved each year that were later withdrawn due to adverse effects remained steady from year to year. In fact, that percentage has "stayed very consistent for the past thirty years at around 2.5%."[53] Thus, the FDA could argue it was doing its job well. Nevertheless, the number of hazardous drugs entering the marketplace escalated in the 1990s, and many people have been injured or even killed as a result. Therefore, it can be argued that the FDA essentially sacrificed safety for speed.

B. The Current and Future FDA

1. The modern FDA

The seven-year streak of faster approval times for new drugs, which began in 1992, ended at the turn of the millennium. In 1999, the average time it took FDA regulators to approve a new drug fell to as low as 12.6 months. By the next year, the FDA took almost 40 percent more time as the average approval time for a new drug shot up to 17.6 months in 2000.[54] That year, the FDA began the practice of issuing "approvable letters," which merely indicate that the agency is leaning toward approval. "Approvable letters are a tool in the FDA's satchel which basically allow the agency to take longer to look at things."[54] To win final approval, which can take months or even years longer, the FDA started requiring drug makers to submit new information or even entirely new studies on products under review. Alan Goldhammer, an executive with the Pharmaceutical Research and Manufacturers of America, remarked that, "[t]he FDA's review times have been coming down every year, until 2000, when all of a sudden there was a spike upwards....The slowdown has caught everyone pretty much by surprise and we're trying to find out the reasons for the delay."[54]

Although the reasons for the slowdown were numerous, the FDA is very concerned with drug safety, especially after several prescription medicines were pulled from the market in recent years, when patients died taking them or developed serious side effects. After being stung by criticism from the media and consumer-advocate groups because of the recalled drugs, the FDA slowed the entire review process down in order to take a harder look at things.[54] The FDA now also handles more drug-approval cases than ever before, which is taxing its staff and contributing to the slowdown.[55]

Other reasons for the unexplained delays include the fact that the FDA was leaderless from January of 2001 until November of 2002, when current Commissioner of Food and Drugs, Mark B. McClellan, M.D., Ph.D., was appointed. (Jane Heaney, former commissioner under the Clinton administration, resigned the day after President Bush's inauguration.) Without somebody sitting atop the FDA to make policy or to take the heat for controversial decisions, tough calls on new drug approvals were delayed or sent back to the companies for further study. "FDA employees are sitting on their hands, waiting for a new commissioner….As a result, there's been a slowdown in policy decisions, especially controversial policies, because no one wants to make a decision that will be second-guessed by the new boss."[56] The slowdown had many people in the pharmaceutical industry concerned. Without a commissioner, no one at the FDA was willing to go out on a limb and put forth written guidelines to address industry concerns.[53]

2. Proposed changes

At present, the DPE is limited to reporting its information and conclusions back to the FDA review divisions, even if these findings call into question the original decision to approve the drug. This creates an obvious bias, because people who recommended approval might be reluctant to recommend removal (since that might be seen as recognition that the original approval had been in error). The need for more independent safety monitoring has been long recognized. In the U.K., for instance, safety monitoring of marketed drugs is separated from the system for initial approvals more thoroughly than any U.S. report has ever recommended. In the British system, one major office reviews and recommends approval of new drugs, and an entirely separate unit monitors the safety of approved drugs. The monitoring unit may order changes in product labeling, and may even order outright drug withdrawal. France also has a different organizational plan, with a well-developed network of 30 regional pharmacovigilance centers, a national database that practitioners can query, and an important drug-safety journal.

In a 1998 article entitled "Time To Act On Drug Safety," the author pointed out four specific tasks that are (or should be) involved in the FDA's broader mission of "protecting the American public from health risks of marketed drugs."[26] They are: (1) estimating the number and cause of serious injuries and deaths, (2) identifying new, serious adverse reactions, (3) monitoring the effect of previous safety alerts, and (4) operating an early-warning system.

The first task would require a program to monitor all adverse effects from prescription drugs and annually report the number of injuries and deaths and their likely causes. As of 1998, neither the DPE nor any other office at the FDA collected, analyzed, or published any such information on a regular basis.

The second task in safety monitoring would involve a program to monitor side effects from new drugs. In 1998, the FDA's DPE had a staff of 52 people, but only eight of those had medical degrees, and only one had a Ph.D. in epidemiology. This small group collected anecdotal information about side effects of new drugs, but did not have the resources to be systematic or thorough. When the DPE identifies a drug problem, it can only pass the information along to the division of the FDA that approved the drug. That division can require the manufacturer to develop additional information. However, "[t]he most common corrective action is a change in the product disclosure label or package insert."[26] The next logical step would be to determine whether the new, stronger warnings were effective.

The third part of a competent drug-safety program would make sure that safety information is being disseminated and heeded by physicians. FDA officials have supported the use of package labels as a way to (in their own words) "manage" risks. Yet, the FDA typically has no way of knowing whether the labeling precautions, usually lengthy and in tiny print, are read and followed by doctors and their patients. While the FDA has access to up-to-date prescription-volume data, it has no organized program to check whether the most important warning messages are being heeded. The limited information available, however, suggests that some important safety information—such as boxed warnings on drug disclosure labels—either was not received or had little effect. (For example, in 2000, an article published in *JAMA* indicated that strengthened warnings for Cisapride, in the form of a strict contraindication in the product label, had virtually no effect on doctors' prescribing practices.[11])

The fourth task would aggressively seek out information about unsuspected adverse reactions to drugs. Instead of waiting passively for anecdotal information to filter in, the government needs to aggressively look for drug involvement in reported birth defects, heart problems, and other common disorders that are frequently caused by prescription drugs. In the same way that the world's public-health specialists aggressively seek out new strains of influenza, the FDA needs to be aggressively seeking out new side effects of drugs. "With limited resources and continuing pressures to act rapidly on new drug applications, the FDA focuses on improving its performance on the narrowly defined mission of identifying unlabeled serious adverse effects of newly marketed drugs. Without additional funds and a new mandate, the other three vital safety monitoring tasks will continue to be largely neglected."[26] The problem is that these words of warning from 1998 seem to be just as relevant today.

4.4 Conclusion

"No government body touches us where we live more than the Food and Drug Administration does. Whenever we eat, drink, take medicine, apply deodorant, fire up the microwave, feed the cat, take a pregnancy test, or don a condom, the FDA acts as our guardian and gatekeeper. It regulates products accounting for twenty-five cents of every dollar we spend."[53] Thus, any deficiencies with the FDA could have widespread consequences for the American people. As this chapter has shown, the number of hazardous drugs entering the marketplace escalated in the 1990s, and many people were injured and killed as a result. While this would be dreadful enough by itself, we must also keep in mind the severe underreporting problem in the United States. If the FDA's limited monitoring system reveals that a certain drug is causing hundreds of adverse events, then tens of thousands of consumers are likely being affected. The actual number of people adversely affected by the inadequacies of the FDA and the failed "system" of drug warnings could be astronomical. These problems need to be more carefully studied and solutions need to be considered and debated. Anything less would be a failure of our government in the regulation of prescription drugs in this country.

Endnotes

1. T.G. Whittle and J. Thorpe. "Buying Off the drug traffic cop," *Freedom Magazine* (1991). Available online at http://www.psychdrugs.freedommag.org/page05.htm.

2. C. Shepherd. "Doctors, pharmaceutical companies differ in priorities," *The Daily Universe*, December 11, 2001. Available online at www.newsnet.byu.edu/story.cfm/35623.

3. *See* 21 C.F.R. § 202.1(e)(1). 2002. "All advertisements for any prescription drug…shall present a true statement of information in brief summary relating to side effects, contraindications…and effectiveness."

4. See *Hall v. Merck, Sharpe & Dohme, a Div. of Merck & Co.*, F.Supp.774:604 (D.Kan. 1991) (stating that a drug manufacturer has no legal duty to warn the ultimate consumer of the risks associated with its prescription drugs if it adequately warns the consumer's physician of those risks); see also T.J. Moore, "In short drug tests, fatal flaws," *Boston Globe*, July 14, 2002. Available online at www.globe.com. "Companies have no legal obligation to make public such findings [of adverse effects caused by their drugs]."

5. P. Moore and M. Newton. "Prescription drug advertising on the Internet: A proposal for regulation," *W. Va. J. L. & Tech.*, February 14, 1998. Available online at www.wvu.edu/~law.

6. *Id.* (citing 21 C.F.R. § 202.1. (1997).

7. *See* 21 C.F.R. § 1.21. (2002).

8. Author unknown. "Pancrease MT." www.drugs.com/mtm/pancrease-mt-4.html. Accessed May 9, 2012.

9. *See* Moore, *supra* note 5.

10. T. Bodenheimer and R. Collins. "Telling the truth: What drug companies don't want you to know: Integrity in science: A CSPI project." www.cspinet.org/integrity/tell_truth.html [Referring to M.K. Cho and L.A. Bero, "The quality of drug studies published in symposium proceedings," *Ann. Intern. Med.* 124:485–9 (1996)].

11. FDA. "*Direct to You: TV Drug Ads That Make Sense.*" www.fda.gov/cder/about/whatwedo/testtube-11.pdf (August 21, 2002).

12. *See* 21 C.F.R., *supra* note 3.

13. W. Smalley et al. "Contraindicated use of cisapride: Impact of food and drug administration regulatory action," *JAMA* 2847:3036–9 (2002).

14. S. Sternberg. "Bayer pulls cholesterol drug linked to deaths," *USA Today*, August 8, 2001. Available online at www.usatoday.com/news/healthscience/health/2001-08-08-statin-drug.htm.

15. Richard K. Goodstein. "Dear Doctor" letter from Richard K. Goodstein, M.D., V.P., Scientific Relations, Bayer Corp., to healthcare professionals (1999).

16. FDA Talk Papers. "Yvyeth-Ayerst Laboratories Announces the Withdrawal of Duract from the Market," http://www.fda.gov/ohrms/dockets/ac/98/briefingbook/1998-3454B1_03_WL06.pdf (June 22, 1998).

17. Marc W. Deitch. "Dear Doctor" letter from Marc W. Deitch, M.D., S.V.P., Medical Affairs, Wyeth-Ayerst

Laboratories, to healthcare professionals. http://www.fda.gov/downloads/Safety/MedWatch/SafetyInformation/UCM189811.zip (September 15, 1997).

18. *Physicians' Desk Reference*, 50th ed. (Montvale, NJ: Medical Economics Company, 1996), p. 2066. "Pondimin is indicated in the management of exogenous obesity as a short-term (a few weeks) adjunct in a regimen of weight reduction based on caloric restriction."

19. "Long-term use of fen-phen causes aortic regurgitation," *J. Watch Cardiology* 6:6 (2000); *see also* J.G. Jollis et al., "Fenfluramine and phentermine and cardiovascular findings: Effect of treatment duration on prevalence of valve abnormalities," *Circulation* 101:2071–7 (2000).

20. "Adverse drug reaction reporting," HRTALERT. (2002).

21. S.A. Goldman and D.L. Kennedy. "MEDWatch: FDA's medical products reporting program," *Postgrad. Med.* 103:13–16 (1998).

22. J.A. Staffa . "Cerivastatin and reports of fatal rhabdomyolysis," *New Engl. J. Med.* 346:539–40 (2002); *see also* D.A. Kessler, "Introducing MEDWatch: A new approach to reporting medication and device adverse effects and product problems," *JAMA* 269:2765–68 (1993).

23. *See* Moore, *supra* note 4.

24. *See* Whittle, *supra* note 1.

25. *Id.*

26. T.J. Moore et al. "Time to act on drug safety," *JAMA* 279:1571–3 (1998).

27. A. Smith-Rogers et al. "Physician knowledge, attitudes, and behavior related to reporting adverse drug events," *Arch. Intern. Med.* 148:1596–600 (1988).

28. FDA. "Adverse event reporting system," www.fda.gov/cder/aers (31 July 31, 2001).

29. DIMACS. "Working Group on Adverse Event/Disease Reporting, Surveillance, and Analysis." http://dimacs.rutgers.edu/Workshops/AdverseEvent (December 10, 2001).

30. *See* Goldman, *supra* note 21.

31. *Id.*

32. *See* Kessler, *supra* note 22.

33. *Id.*

34. *Id.*

35. *See* Rogers, *supra* note 27.

36. L. La Grenade et al. "Underreporting of hemorrhagic stroke associated with phenylpropanolamine," *JAMA* 286:1226 (2001) (citing Scott et al., "Rhode Island physicians' recognition and reporting of adverse drug reactions," *R.I. Med. J.* 70:311–316 (1987)).

37. D. Willman. "FDA's expedited drug approvals cost lives," *Los Angeles Times,* December 29, 2000. Available online at http://members.fortunecity.com/siriusw/tracy.htm.

38. M.T. Willis. "Risk of the new: Research suggests greater risks accompany newly approved drugs," abcnews.com, May 1, 2002 (quoting Thomas J. Moore).

39. D. Willman. "How a new policy led to seven deadly drugs," *Los Angeles Times*, December 20, 2000. Available online at www.msbp.com/fda.htm.

40. T.J. Moore. "FDA in crisis," *Boston Globe* (April 2, 2000).

41. *See* Staffa, *supra* note 22; *see also* T.J. Moore, *Prescription for Disaster 5* (NY: Dell, 1998).

42. *See* Willman, *supra* note 39.

43. A. Herxheimer. "Possible harm from drugs: When and how to inform doctors and users," *Médecine Légale Hospitalière.* (2000).

44. Anderlik, M.R. "Mandatory reporting for medical mishaps: Is there middle ground?" *Texas Med. Center News,* www.tmc.edu/tmcnews/02_01_00/page_18.html (February 1, 2000).

45. L.M. Soletsky and R.W. Parkinson. "Reporting of adverse drug reactions," *Postgrad. Med.* 102:35–36 (1997).

46. *Id.*

47. A. Figueiras et al. "Influence of physicians' attitudes on reporting adverse drug events: A case control study," *Med. Care* 37:809–14.

48. *See* Anderlik, *supra* note 44.

49. S.A. Edlavitch. "Adverse drug event reporting: Improving the low U.S. reporting rates," *Arch. Intern. Med.*
148:1499–503 (1988).

50. *Id.* at 1499.

51. *See* Anderlik, *supra* note 44.

52. K.A. Petroff."The challenge of child abuse cases," *J.
Legis.* 9:127–39 (1982).

53. K.E. Lasser et al. "Timing of new black box warnings
and withdrawals for prescription medication," *JAMA*
287:2215–20 (2002).

54. *Id.*

55. "Critics question FDA safety net after drugs get
yanked." *Associated Press*, July 12, 1998. Available
online at www.antidepressantsfacts.com/th6.htm.

56. *See generally* Pub. L. No. 102-571, 106 Stat. 4491
(1992).

Chapter 5

Clinical Research:
Testing Treatments in Humans

Lori A. Nesbitt, Pharm.D., MBA and Karen L. Pellegrin, Ph.D., MBA

5.1 Introduction

Humans participate in research projects every day. Some of this research comes in the form of surveys. Other research is designed to test the effectiveness of an intervention. We get calls from marketing analysts to determine our attitudes, preferences, and brand loyalties. We fill out customer-satisfaction surveys after purchasing a car or staying in a hotel to quantify our experiences with the product or service. And we complete employee-satisfaction surveys at work to allow management to determine levels of worker morale and loyalty. In response to these baseline data, those conducting the research may implement interventions designed to change purchasing behaviors, increase our brand loyalty, or reduce employee turnover.

In its most general sense, research can be defined as a systematic search for facts. This would include criminal investigations, as well as survey research and studies of the effectiveness of treatments. According to the Department of Health and Human Services (45 C.F.R. Part 46), research is defined as "a systematic investigation, including research, development, testing and evaluation, designed to develop or contribute to generalizable knowledge." It is this "generalizable knowledge" component that narrows the definition and differentiates between a physician who systematically searches for facts (e.g., obtains a medical history, blood pressure, and physical exam) in order to diagnose and treat a patient and a physician who systematically searches for facts among a sample of patients with the intention of drawing conclusions about the effectiveness of a treatment across a larger population.

While much of this chapter focuses on industry-sponsored research of experimental medications, the basic principles of research for testing treatments or interventions in humans are the same—regardless of the source of funding or the type of intervention. The first section of this chapter focuses on the process pharmaceutical companies must follow to bring a new drug to market. Next, this chapter describes the basic scientific principles behind the evaluation of any experimental intervention or treatment. The final section of the chapter discusses clinical-trial service providers.

5.2 Testing Drugs in Humans

Drugs intended to treat people must be studied in people. However, long before potentially new drugs are tested in people, researchers analyze the physiologic and chemical properties in vitro (laboratory testing and/or bench research) and pharmacologic and toxic effects in laboratory animals (animal testing and/or animal modeling). According to the Pharmaceutical Research and Manufacturers of America and the Tufts Center for the Study of Drug Development, only one in 5,000 compounds makes it from the petri dish in the laboratory to the pharmacy shelves.

When laboratory and animal studies show a promising efficacy-versus-risk profile for a compound, the sponsor can apply to the FDA to begin human clinical trials (via an Investigational New Drug Application). Only five out of 5,000 compounds make it from this pre-clinical stage of testing to human testing. If permission is granted, the FDA will assign an Investigational New Drug (IND) number. The sponsor must then submit the investigational plan (clinical-trial protocol) to the FDA and an institutional review board (IRB) for review and approval. Once approval from both entities is granted, the sponsor may begin human clinical trials. Of those five compounds that make it to human trials, only one of these will be approved for sale.

Because of this intensive, long-term, high-risk investment, coupled by the overwhelming odds of failure, it should not be a surprise that the retail cost of drugs is so high. According to a November 2001 report by the Tufts Center for the Study of Drug Development, the average cost to develop a new prescription drug is $802 million. In addition, DiMasi et al. (*J. Health Econ.* 2003; 22: 151–185; *Drug Inf. J.* 2004; 38: 211–223) estimate expenditure on new drug development using publicly available data. The paper estimates that average expenditure on drugs in human clinical trials is around $27 million per year, with $17 million per year on drugs in Phase 1, $34 million on drugs in Phase 2 and $27 million per year on drugs in Phase 3 of the human clinical trials. Most recently Adams et al. repeated the DiMasi study by combining a 12-year panel of research and development expenditure for 183 publicly traded firms in the pharmaceutical industry with panel of drugs in human clinical trials for each firm over the same period. The paper estimates drug expenditure by estimating the relationship between research and development expenditure and the number of drugs in development for 1,682 company/years (183 firms multiplied by the number of years for which we have financial and drug development information). In summary, the study estimates the cost of drug development is actually $1 billion.

Also noteworthy was the finding that, although the costs have increased for all phases of development, the inflation-adjusted cost increase of the clinical phase of new drug development was more than five times greater than the cost increase for pre-clinical phases.

Human clinical trials are divided into four distinct phases. Key points regarding each phase are outlined below.

A. Phase 1

Phase 1 studies are designed to assess the acute safety profile of a drug. Phase 1 studies are also usually "dose ranging." (In other words, the studies are examining the maximum tolerated dose of the investigational agent.) Initial clinical studies also begin to clarify the drug's pharmacokinetic (absorption, distribution, metabolism, and excretion) profile. Unless significant adverse events are expected, as in many cancer treatments, Phase 1 studies are often conducted in normal, healthy volunteers.

B. Phase 2

In the event that Phase 1 studies do not reveal any major concerns, such as unacceptable toxicities, the next step is to assess efficacy, while further defining the safety profile. Phase 2 studies are most often conducted in patient volunteers, rather than normal, healthy volunteers. Specifically, the investigational agent is administered to patients who have been diagnosed with the disease or condition the drug is intended to treat. Phase 2 studies are the first real opportunities researchers and patients get to determine effectiveness of the drug. Furthermore, since greater numbers of patients receive the investigational agent in Phase 2 studies than in Phase 1 studies, the opportunity to observe untoward side effects is enhanced. Each new phase of a clinical trial utilizes information from the earlier phases. In this case, if the investigational agent shows positive activity against the intended disease or condition and the side effects are tolerable, a Phase 3 trial will usually ensue.

C. Phase 3

Phase 3 studies require large numbers of patients and are most often designed to compare currently available or standard-of-care treatments against an investigational agent. Patients are usually randomized to receive either the investigational treatment or the currently available comparator.

Phase 3 trials are the studies that really determine the effectiveness of the drug. In addition, the results of the Phase 3 trials are the best indicators of the benefit-versus-risk ratio for the drug once it is introduced into the general population. If the drug still looks favorable after Phase 3 trials, the sponsor submits a New Drug Application, which includes all of the data. The NDA is typically 100,000 pages or more in length. Once the FDA has sufficient evidence to support a drug's safety and efficacy, it may grant marketing approval.

D. Phase 4

Phase 4 studies occur once a drug has been marketed. Unlike Phase 1 through III studies, the FDA does not typically require Phase 4 studies. Phase 4 studies are most often conducted to collect postmarketing surveillance data. These data are extremely important, as study-entry criteria are often less stringent and more accurately reflect general use. For example, Phases 1 through 3 studies often exclude patients with co-morbid illnesses or conditions, such as hypertension and diabetes. However, once marketed, the new drug is often used in patients with co-morbid disease states, with no data on drug-disease or drug-drug interactions. If designed properly, Phase 4 studies can add valuable information to the profile of the new agent (see Table 5.1).

According to the FDA, new drug development takes, on average, 8.5 years for marketing approval. Pre-clinical testing, from initial synthesis to animal testing, ranges from one to three years, with an average of 18 months. Clinical trial Phases 1 through 3, require two to ten years, with an average of five years. The FDA then requires two months to seven years to review a New Drug Application, with an average of 24 months. Postmarketing surveillance begins following marketing approval.

Table 5.1
Key Elements of Clinical-Trial Phases

Phase	Trial Characteristics	Information Gathered	Study Design	Data Focus	Examples
1	*Duration*: Short-term (up to thirty days) *Population*: twenty to eighty healthy volunteers *Aim*: Safety and tolerance in humans	• Physiologic effects • Pharmacokinetics • Bioavailability • Bioequivalence • Dose-proportionality • Metabolism	• Single, ascending dose • Maximum tolerated dose	• Safety • Vital signs • Cognitive tests • Plasma/serum levels	Pharmacokinetic study of a single dose of test drug A in normal volunteers
2	*Duration*: Short-medium (up to a few months) *Population*: 200-300 study subjects *Aim*: Define dose; establish effectiveness for a specific population and disease	• Safety • Efficacy • Pharmacokinetics • Bioavailability • Drug-drug interactions • Drug-disease interactions • Efficacy at varying doses	• Controlled comparisons with placebo or active controls • Well-defined patient-eligibility criteria	• Dose-response • Tolerance • Adverse events • Efficacy versus placebo • Efficacy versus approved drug • Efficacy versus approved therapeutic regimen	Double-blind study evaluating the safety and efficacy of 1mg versus 2mg of study drug A in alleviating chronic pain
3	*Duration*: Parallels anticipated treatment *Population*: Hundreds to thousands *Aim*: Safety and efficacy with a selected dose	• Efficacy and safety • Dosing interval • Drug-drug interactions • Drug-disease interactions • Risk/benefit profiles	• Broader subject-eligibility criteria • Studies may have two or three treatment groups	• Efficacy • Safety profiles • Laboratory data • Adverse events	Study of relative safety and efficacy of test drug A versus placebo in hypertensive patients
4	*Duration*: Ongoing *Population*: May involve additional age or ethnic groups *Aim*: Monitors continued safety in large groups	• Additional Safety • Drug-drug interactions • Drug-disease interactions • Patient satisfaction	• Broad subject-eligibility criteria • Post-marketing surveillance	• Adverse events • Pharmaco-economic data • Additional efficacy data	Pharmaco-economic study of approved drug A versus approved drug B in patients with arthritis

Table 5.2
New Drug Development Timeline[1]

Pre-Clinical Research and Development:	FDA Safety Review	Clinical Research and Development			FDA Review of NDA	Post-Marketing Surveillance
Range: 1-3yrs Average: 18 mos. Initial Synthesis Animal Testing	30 Days	Range: 2-10 years Average: 5 years			Range: 2mo--7yrs. Average: 24 mos.	Adverse-reaction reporting Surveys/Sampling/Testing Inspections
		Phase 2	Phase 2	Phase 3		

Interestingly, another source reports that the process takes longer than the FDA admits. According to the Pharmaceutical Research and Manufacturers of America and the Tufts Center for the Study of Drug Development, the average time from laboratory testing to drug approval is 10 to 15 years. This source reports an average of 6.5 years in pre-clinical testing, seven years in Phase 1–3 clinical testing, and 1.5 years for FDA review and approval (see Table 5.2[1]).

E. Translational Research

According to the National Institutes of Health, translational research is defined as a way of thinking about and conducting scientific research to make the results of research applicable to the population under study and is practised in the natural and biological, behavioral, and social sciences. In the field of medicine, for example, it is used to translate the findings in basic research more quickly and efficiently into medical practice and, thus, meaningful health outcomes, whether those are physical, mental, or social outcomes. In medicine in particular, governmental funders of research and pharmaceutical companies have spent vast amounts internationally on basic research and have seen that the return on investment is significantly less than anticipated. Translational research has come to be seen as the key, missing component.

With its focus on removing barriers to multi-disciplinary collaboration, translational research has the potential to drive the advancement of applied science. An attempt to bridge these barriers has been undertaken particularly in the medical domain where the term translational medicine has been applied to a research approach that seeks to move "from bench to bedside" or from laboratory experiments through clinical trials to actual point-of-care patient applications.[10]

F. Health Outcomes Research

Health Outcomes Research (HOR), also called outcomes research, refers to research (usually medically related) which investigates the outcomes of health care practices. It can use epidemiology to link health care outcomes (quality of care, quality of life) with independent variables such as geography, income, or lifestyle. In addition, outcomes research seeks to understand the end results of particular health care practices and interventions. End results include effects that people experience and care about, such as change in the ability to function. In particular, for individuals with chronic conditions—where cure is not always possible—end results include quality of life as well as mortality. By linking the care people get to the outcomes they experience, outcomes research has become the key to developing better ways to monitor and improve the quality of care.

The urgent need for outcomes research was highlighted in the early 1980s, when researchers discovered that "geography is destiny." Time and again, studies documented that medical practices as commonplace as hysterectomy and hernia repair were performed much more frequently in some areas than in others, even when there were no differences in the underlying rates of disease. Furthermore, there was often no information about the end results for the patients who received a particular procedure, and few comparative studies to show which interventions were most effective. These findings challenged researchers, clinicians, and health systems leaders to develop new tools to assess the impact of health care services.

For clinicians and patients, outcomes research provides evidence about benefits, risks, and results of treatments so they can make more informed decisions. One group of researchers, for example, studied the outcomes of patients with pneumonia, a common cause of hospitalization in elderly people. They developed a way for clinicians to determine which patients with pneumonia can be treated safely at home, an option that not only reduces costs but is preferred by many patients. In areas such as cancer, where outright cure is often not the only goal, outcomes research has provided the information to help patients make choices that will improve their quality of life.

For health care managers and purchasers, outcomes research can identify potentially effective strategies they can implement to improve the quality and value of care. AHRQ-sponsored outcomes studies, for example, have shown that even when treatments are known to be effective, many people who could benefit from them are not getting them. Beta blocker medication, given after heart attacks, can reduce mortality; blood-thinning medication can prevent strokes; and thrombolytic ("clot-buster") therapy given immediately after a heart attack can reduce the damage from the attack. Yet in each case, many eligible patients are not getting these treatments. By identifying and addressing the barriers to better care—for example, through development of a tool to help doctors know which patients with suspected heart attacks will benefit from thrombolytic treatment—AHRQ researchers have helped translate these findings into practical strategies to improve care.

G. Comparative/Clinical Effectiveness Research

Comparative Effectiveness Research (CER) is the direct comparison of existing health care interventions to determine which work best for which patients and which pose the greatest benefits and harms. The core question of comparative effectiveness research is which treatment works best, for whom, and under what circumstances. Comparative clinical effectiveness research has been discussed as a source of information for health care decision makers that may aid them in reaching evidence-based decisions. The premise that "what is newest is not always the best" is the core of the rationale behind comparative effectiveness research. Diverse governmental and non-governmental organizations have publicly expressed their support and reservations about comparative effectiveness research. Although publicly supported by many governmental and non-governmental entities in the abstract, controversy about comparative clinical effectiveness research lies in its practice and implementation.

Impressive gains made in Americans' health over the past decades provide only a preview of what might be possible when data on treatment effects and patient outcomes are systematically captured and used to evaluate their effectiveness. Needed for progress are advances as dramatic as those experienced in biomedicine in our approach to assessing clinical effectiveness. In the emerging era of tailored treatments and rapidly evolving practice, ensuring the translation of scientific discovery into improved health outcomes requires a new approach to clinical evaluation. A paradigm that supports a continual learning process about what works best for individual patients will not only take advantage of the rigor of trials, but also incorporate other methods that might bring insights relevant to clinical care and endeavor to match the right method to the question at hand.

5.3 Clinical Research: Not an Exact Science

On the surface, and often to the general population, the clinical-trial process appears straightforward—simply recruit groups of patients to participate in a study, administer the drug to those who consent to participate, and see if it works. Sounds easy enough (and sometimes it is). In what may be medicine's most celebrated clinical trial, Louis Pasteur treated patients exposed to rabies with an experimental anti-rabies vaccine. Every one of the treated patients survived. Since scientists knew that untreated rabies was 100 percent fatal, it was not hard to conclude that Pasteur's treatment was effective.[1]

The rabies example was a highly unusual case. Drugs do not usually miraculously reverse fatal illness. More often, drugs reduce the risk of death from a particular disease, but do not entirely eliminate it. Drugs usually accomplish this by relieving the symptoms of the illness, such as pain, nausea, anxiety, fatigue, shortness of breath, or edema (swelling). In addition, drugs may alter a clinical measurement or a physiologic process (such as lowering blood pressure or cholesterol levels) in a way that is advantageous for patients. Although important, these effects are generally subtler and harder to qualify and quantify than curing rabies.

Subtle improvements in symptoms and clinical measurements are more difficult to evaluate, because diseases are highly variable. For example, the common cold affects people very differently. One person may experience a severe sore throat while another complains mainly of rhinitis. In addition, each episode for a given individual may vary. During one episode of the flu, a person may experience fever and malaise. The following year, another episode of the flu for the same individual may cause only nausea and vomiting. Furthermore, many illnesses resolve spontaneously. Thus, it is most difficult to discern the "cure causality" or clinical relevance of a new agent. If a drug could decrease the length of a cold by one day, is it worth the millions spent on discovery?

Clinical-trial results for chronic conditions—such as arthritis, depression, multiple sclerosis, Parkinson's disease and asthma—are also difficult to evaluate, due to periods of remission, "on/off phenomenon" or varying courses. Often, symptoms of these diseases can improve or worsen for no apparent reason. Heart attacks and strokes have widely variable mortality rates, depending on treatment, length of time for intervention, age, co-morbid illness, and other factors, so that the "expected" mortality can be hard to predict. Without baseline predictors of mortality or disease progression, clinical relevance of an investigational agent is, again, difficult to establish.

A further obstacle in gauging the effectiveness of an investigational drug is that, in some cases, measurements of disease are subjective, relying in part on interpretation by the investigator and/or patient. In those circumstances, it is difficult to tell whether a treatment is having a favorable effect, no effect, or even an adverse effect. The best way to answer the real-life scenarios posed is to subject the investigational agent to a controlled clinical trial.[1]

5.4 Study Design

The primary difference between anecdotes and science is methodology. Drawing a conclusion about whether a medication or other treatment works based on anecdotes is logically flawed. The reason is that there are numerous alternatives, other than the treatment, that could explain anecdotal findings (these are called "confounding variables"). Anecdotes include what may be seen in clinical practice, testimonials, and case studies published in professional journals or at conferences. These all reflect a non-experimental, pre-test or post-test design, as reflected in Figure 5.1.

In Figure 5.1, containing hypothetical data, one or more subjects are given a drug to reduce their total cholesterol levels. Baseline (i.e., pre-treatment) cholesterol is measured, the treatment (in this case a drug) is given, and then cholesterol is measured again after treatment. Many looking at this figure would conclude that the drug worked—that the drug caused the reduction in blood cholesterol. Yet, such a conclusion is unwarranted. This study design cannot be used for making reliable decisions about treatment efficacy.

Some additional graphs demonstrate why we cannot use the non-experimental pre-test/post-test design to draw

reliable conclusions about the treatment's effects. In Figure 5.2, the data above are put into context by showing some additional hypothetical data points. This chart would indicate that the drug was not the cause of the cholesterol reduction, but that the decrease in lipid levels was due to some pre-existing trend (i.e., some other factor, like a gradual improvement in diet, that influenced the patient's health prior to or during the drug administration).

Finally, Figure 5.3 shows—also through hypothetical data—that the decrease in cholesterol seen in Figure 5.1 could have been simply a function of random variation in the measurement of cholesterol. Any one data point that is high or low is likely to be followed by a measurement that is closer to the mean. This "regression to the mean" can lead to an erroneous assumption that there was a special cause of the decrease (see Figure 5.3).

Although non-experimental designs cannot be used to draw conclusions about a given treatment, anecdotal evidence is often used to formulate hypotheses that can then be tested using experimental designs.

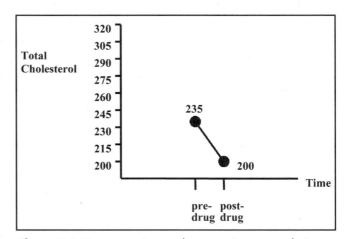

Figure 5.1 *Non-experimental pre-test/post-test design (hypothetical data).*

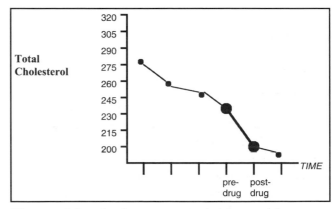

Figure 5.2 *Results due to a pre-existing trend (hypothetical data).*

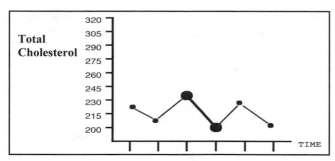

Figure 5.3 *Results due to chance and regression toward the mean (hypothetical data).*

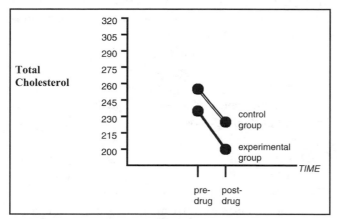

Figure 5.4 *Change in cholesterol for both experimental and control groups (hypothetical data).*

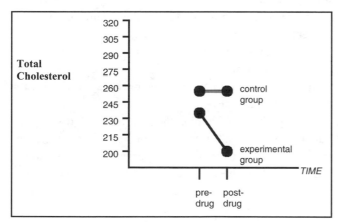

Figure 5.5 *Change in cholesterol for experimental group only (hypothetical data).*

The scientific method is the application of experimental or quasi-experimental designs to control for confounding variables. The appropriate study design varies depending on the research question or hypothesis under consideration. While there are many different types of experimental designs, the gold standard for determining safety and efficacy is the randomized, double-blind, placebo-controlled study. This research design is so valuable because it controls for

virtually all potentially confounding variables. Therefore, the results of the study can be used to reliably determine whether the treatment is effective and whether side effects are significant. (See Section 5.5.E, "Statistical Design," for an explanation of why this design does not result in 100 percent certainty in its conclusions.) The following section explains the key components of this experimental design.

A. Control Groups

Control groups are essential in research attempting to determine safety and efficacy. Without a control group, there is no way to know whether any improvements are due to the treatment or to something else, such as a naturally occurring improvement or a placebo effect (psychological benefits that often result from simply believing in a treatment—see Section 5.4.C, "Double-Blind," below). In addition, given that all people experience adverse events periodically (e.g., headaches, dizziness, illness, and even death), the control group also permits analyses regarding whether adverse events are more common in the treatment group. Figure 5.4 demonstrates the results of the hypothetical cholesterol medication study, in which both the treatment and the control group showed similar results, suggesting that the treatment does not work.

Whether the treatment works to improve a health indicator, or simply to reduce its rate of decline, control groups are essential to determining treatment efficacy. Figure 5.5 shows the results of the cholesterol-medication study in which the treatment group shows improvement, while the control group does not—suggesting that the treatment does work.

There are two basic types of control groups: placebo and active. The purpose of placebo controls is to determine whether the treatment works. The placebo group receives an inert pill or receives an inert treatment that is administered in the exact same method as the treatment itself. Research participants in an active control group are given an active treatment that has already been shown to work. The purpose of this type of control group is to determine whether the experimental treatment works better or worse than the existing treatment. Some study designs include three treatment arms (i.e., experimental, placebo control, and active control). The purpose of this design is to answer the questions "Does the treatment work?" and "How well does it work, relative to existing treatments?" in one fell swoop.

Ethical considerations are important in determining what types of control groups should be used in a study. The use of placebo control groups means that there will be some research participants who receive no treatment at all. The ethics of such a control group depend on the impact of the disease being studied and the types of existing treatments available. If the disease being studied is not severe and there are no effective treatments available (e.g., the common cold), a placebo control group is not likely to be seen as unethical. If the disease is serious and there are existing treatments (e.g., high cholesterol, hypertension), a placebo group would be considered unethical by many.

More ambiguous is the case in which the disease is not severe, but existing treatments are available (e.g., chicken pox and acne). There is growing sentiment that even in this low-risk situation, the use of a placebo control is unethical. This is based on the principle that risks must be balanced against the benefits both to the individual and to society. This includes the societal benefits of new knowledge. It could be argued that use of placebo control does not contribute important "new" knowledge. That is, even if the new treatment were shown to work, this does not help clinicians determine which is the better treatment (i.e., existing treatment or new treatment). The only way to answer the practical question about best practice is to use an active control group. Thus, it could be argued that use of a placebo control group is unethical any time there is an existing treatment.

According to the FDA, healthy, fully informed patients can consent to take part in a controlled, randomized, blinded clinical trial, even when effective therapy exists, as long as they are not denied therapy that could alter survival or prevent irreversible injury. They can voluntarily agree to accept temporary discomfort and other potential risks in order to help evaluate a new treatment.[1]

In disease states where using a placebo would be unethical, investigational drugs are often studied by being added to the patient's current treatment regimen. Examples of these include chemotherapy for the treatment of cancer, antipsychotics for the treatment of schizophrenia, and anti-seizure drugs for the treatment of epilepsy. In this type of trial, study participants receive the approved therapy, but those in the treatment group also receive the investigational drug. The control group receives either no added treatment or a placebo. Differences between the two groups are then analyzed for statistically significant treatment effects. While the "add-on" trial design may not be as methodologically sound as a double-blinded, randomized, placebo-controlled study, ethical considerations must outweigh scientific rationale.

After a treatment has been shown to be efficacious (i.e., works in a controlled study), "open-label" studies are often performed. These studies have no control group. That is, all research participants are given the active treatment. The design of these studies is more epidemiological in nature. Research participants are tracked over time to collect additional data on safety and side effects and to determine whether the positive results found in the controlled studies prove applicable to the "real world" practice of medicine.

B. Random Assignment

Another fundamental component of the gold standard of experimental design is the use of random assignment to groups. The purpose of randomly assigning research participants to groups is to ensure that the only difference between groups is the type of treatment received (i.e., experimental, placebo, or active control). Given inter- and intra-subject variability, random assignment is key in eliminating bias in either group. While study-entry inclusion and exclusion criteria screen for major differences in the disease process that can affect treatment outcomes, random assignment serves to even out differences in age, gender, weight, and overall general health status between groups. Random assignment is accomplished by assigning participants to groups using random number tables, which is similar to drawing numbers from a hat or flipping a coin.

C. Double-Blind

The final key element of the gold-standard design is double-blinding. A double-blind study is one in which neither the investigator nor the research participant knows which group they are in. A study in which the research participants are blinded but the investigator is not is called a single-blind study. This is clearly a less rigorous design than a double-blind study. The purpose of blinding the research participant, as mentioned earlier, is to control for the placebo effect. If the participant knows which group he is in, the psychological impact can lead to measurable changes that are not due to the experimental treatment. The only way to control for this is to blind the participants.

The purpose of blinding the investigator and the study staff is to ensure that they do not bias the results either intentionally or unintentionally. For example, if a researcher had her own hypothesis about which treatment worked better (perhaps based on anecdotal evidence), she might interpret lab results, X-ray tests, or other outcome data in a manner biased to confirm the original hypothesis. In addition, knowledge of the treatment groups might lead the researcher to interact with the research participants in such a way that they could figure out which groups they were in. The study assignment code is broken only after the study data have been collected, or if a serious adverse event causes the researchers to alter treatment decisions based on the study assignment.

The placebo effect is a well-documented phenomenon in the history of the scientific evaluation of treatments. For example, participants receiving an inactive medication for pain have reported complete remission of symptoms. On the other hand, if the active treatment has a well-known side effect of constipation, patients receiving the placebo may report feeling constipated. A fascinating recent report of the power of belief in a treatment (i.e., the placebo effect) further demonstrates the placebo effect in treatment outcome studies. This research was conducted at the Veteran's Affairs Medical Center in Houston to assess the effectiveness of arthroscopy of the knee for osteoarthritis, a common surgical procedure performed on approximately 650,000 patients each year at a cost of $5,000 each.

The Houston study design was a randomized, placebo-controlled trial in which 180 patients with osteoarthritis of the knee were randomly assigned to receive arthroscopic debridement, arthroscopic lavage, or placebo surgery. In the placebo group, patients were sedated, received skin incisions, and underwent a simulated debridement without insertion of the arthroscope. The patients and the assessors of the outcome were blinded to the treatment-group assignment. Patient reports of pain and function, as well as an objective test of walking and stair climbing were measured over a 24-month period. The results indicated that the patients in the placebo group reported the same amount of pain reduction and improved function as those who received the active surgery. However, on the one objective test of function, none of the patients improved, whether they were in one of the active surgery groups or the placebo group.[2]

The power of the placebo effect reinforces the need to blind the studies in order to tease out the true effect (or lack thereof) of an experimental treatment. It also demonstrates the need to conduct randomized, controlled, and blinded studies of treatments that are commonly used but whose reported efficacy is based only on anecdotal reports of success. Patients and physicians alike are prone to believe in treatments that have no real effect because humans naturally draw inappropriate conclusions based on personal experiences and the testimonials of others. Since the placebo effect is almost impossible to quantify, study blinding is essential for the scientific evaluation of human clinical-trial data.

D. Crossover Design

Another common design is the crossover design. In this type of design, each research participant serves as his own control, because each receives both the experimental and the control treatment during the course of the study. For example, a participant might start the study receiving treatment A and end the study with treatment B. In this type of design, the order of treatments is varied from one subject to another to control for order effects (i.e., effects that are due to the order in which treatments are received, rather than to the treatment itself). In this design, random assignment to treat-

ment order and blinding procedures are just as important as in the control-group designs. This type of design is only appropriate with treatments that are short acting, such as pain medication.

E. Historical Control

In some cases, a study utilizes a "historical control," as opposed to an active comparator. Historical controls compare patients given the investigational drug with similar patients treated with the control drug at a different time and place. Sometimes the historical control is a form of long-term follow-up. Here, the patient is followed for a period of time after receiving the investigational drug and health status is compared before and after treatment. Historical control studies are usually conducted as Phase 4 trials. In order for historical control design to be plausible, the disease state under study must have a high rate of predictable death or illness.[1]

5.5 Elements of the Clinical-Trial Protocol

In order to evaluate the merits, risks, and benefits of a given research study, it is important for the investigator, research coordinators, and IRB members to understand the elements of a sound clinical-trial protocol. The most common elements found in a scientifically based clinical-trial protocol include: background and significance, specific aims or endpoints, inclusion and exclusion criteria, study procedures, and statistical design.

A. Background and Significance

Each clinical protocol includes a section that describes the background and significance of the current study. The purpose of this section is to provide a sound rationale for conducting the current proposed study. The following elements are typically included:

- importance of the line of research/treatment for addressing health problems (e.g., number of people affected by the disease or condition, costs in lost productivity, existing treatment options)
- the development or discovery of the experimental treatment
- the theory of the mechanism of action of the new treatment
- the progression of research that has been completed to date and a summary of the research findings from these previous studies
- a description of the gap in the extant literature that is being addressed by the current study (i.e., study rationale)

B. Specific Aims or Endpoints

The specific aims basically serve as the hypotheses of the study. A theory is rarely proven in a single study. Instead, a series of studies testing one or more aspects of the treatment in question are conducted before drawing conclusions about a theory. The endpoints are the clinical outcomes that are measured to determine whether the treatment works for the indication in question.

For example, in the study of a cancer treatment, the clinical endpoints will depend upon the question that is being addressed in the study. If the purpose of the study is to determine whether a treatment affects the progression of a tumor, the response of the tumor, including tumor measurement, is the clinical endpoint. If the purpose of the study is to determine whether the treatment affects mortality, survival rate, and/or amount of time that patients' lives are extended, then these become the important factors to evaluate.

Clinical endpoints can include a variety of outcomes, and may include laboratory, pathology, imaging data, autopsy reports, physical descriptions, and any other data deemed relevant. The key is to operationally define "success," and then design the study around this measurement system. In order to accomplish this, it is important to be able to reliably and validly measure these clinical endpoints.

C. Inclusion and Exclusion Criteria

The inclusion and exclusion criteria define the population that will be included in the study. This includes both demographic and clinical parameters. Development of these criteria is critical for the implementation of the study. If the criteria are too narrow, subject recruitment may be difficult. In addition, narrow criteria limit the ability to generalize the findings to a broader population. On the other hand, criteria that are too broad reduce the level of control in the design by increasing the possibility that, by chance, the groups will differ on some relevant variable. If the groups differ in any way other than the treatment, it is considered a confounding variable that could lead to incorrect conclusions about the treatment's safety or efficacy. In addition, broader criteria can obscure significant findings that would only be detected in specific subgroups within the population.

In evaluating the inclusion and exclusion criteria, it is important to ensure that no group of people is included or excluded for any unscientific reason. This would violate the ethical principle of justice. This principle asserts that both the benefits and risks of research should be evenly distributed. On the heels of the Tuskegee experiment, where research participants were all economically disadvantaged African-Americans suffering from syphilis, the United States

has become acutely sensitive to this issue. In the Tuskegee experiment, not only were the research participants not informed that they were participating in a study, they were denied treatment for this disease. Clearly, this study, which offered no benefits and only risks, was concentrated in a disadvantaged population. The reverse case is also important to examine. That is, for study designs that offer potential benefits, no groups should be excluded unless there is a legitimate need to do so.

Because of the difficult balance in creating appropriate inclusion and exclusion criteria, many sponsors will grant "waivers" or "exceptions" to these criteria on a case-by-case basis. Despite the fact that this is a common practice, the investigator should neither pursue nor accept these exceptions, unless these exceptions are approved by the IRB prior to implementation.

D. Study Procedures

The study procedures section includes a day-by-day description of the study activities. Most protocols contain a chart called a "schedule of events" or "study flow chart" that succinctly summarizes the key study procedures. This section also specifies the time frames in which each study activity must be completed. Virtually all studies have the following study procedures:

- requirement of informed consent
- completion of a screening visit to determine eligibility (based upon inclusion and exclusion criteria)
- baseline data collection that will be used to compare with post-treatment assessments
- treatment phase in which subjects receive the active treatment or the control treatment
- assessment of endpoints

E. Statistical Design

The statistical design section specifies how the outcome measures will be analyzed statistically. This section should include a statistical analysis for each specific aim identified in the protocol. The basic concept behind the use of statistical analyses is to make inferences about a population, based on a sample of representative subjects. Two common analyses are described briefly below.

Analysis of variance (ANOVA). The purpose of this analysis is to determine whether differences between group means are statistically significant, by examining the amount of variation around each mean.

Survival analysis. The purpose of a survival analysis is to compare the time between entry to a study and some subsequent event, such as death, myocardial infarction, or time for a wound to heal.

Statistics sections will indicate the "p-value" or confidence level that will be used in the analyses. A common p-value is 0.05. This means that, if the analysis shows a statistically significant result, we can be 95 percent sure that the effect is real, rather than being due to chance variation between groups. What this also means, however, is that there is a 5 percent chance that this conclusion is wrong—that the difference between groups is due to random chance and not the treatment. This is called a type-I error. We can reduce the likelihood of this kind of error by decreasing the p-value (e.g., to 0.01). A significant statistical result would mean we could be 99 percent sure that the treatment worked. However, reducing the p-value means we increase the risk of missing a true treatment effect when one in fact exists. This is called a type-II error. Thus, the researcher must attempt to strike a balance between type-I and II errors when selecting a p-value. Either way, we can never be 100 percent certain about our conclusions from research, especially from one study.

Interim analysis of clinical-trial data allows decisions to be made regarding treatment effectiveness or toxicity. This is especially important when a possible effect on survival is being assessed. An example of this occurred in the first clinical trials of an acquired immune deficiency syndrome (AIDS) drug. It became readily apparent during the clinical trial that patients receiving active treatment had a clear survival advantage over the placebo group. The trial was then concluded early and the FDA authorized a protocol allowing patients to receive the drug before it was approved for marketing.

5.6 Clinical-Trial Service Providers

Although it is estimated that $24 billion was spent in human drug development (phases 1–3) last year, the industry is quite small and very specialized. In fact, most Americans have a limited knowledge of how new medications actually end up in their pharmacies.[3] The service providers challenged with bringing new treatments and cures to the masses include: the Food and Drug Administration, clinical-trial sponsors, contract research organizations, study monitors, clinical-trial sites, site-management organizations, institutional review boards, and study participants.

A. The Food and Drug Administration

The FDA's very noble mission is "to promote and protect public health by helping safe and effective products reach the market in a timely way, and monitoring products for continued safety after they are in use." The scope of this mission has grown substantially over the past century. In addition to its consumer-protection in regulating all prescription and over-the-counter drugs, the FDA establishes and enforces standards for all food (except meat and poultry); all blood products, vaccines, and tissues for transplantation; all medical equipment; all devices that emit radiation; all animal drugs and food; and all cosmetics.

Given the complex and diverse tasks performed by the FDA, it is not surprising that there are critics on both sides of the drug-approval fence. Many argue that the FDA has taken away the human right to make an informed choice regarding whether to take an investigational drug. Others argue that the FDA acts too hastily in approving drugs that later are shown to be unsafe. Thus, there is a constant tension between those who want greater consumer protection and those who want greater freedom of choice.

In 1992, Congress passed the Prescription Drug User Fee Act (PDUFA). The purpose was to establish a mechanism for financing the resources that would be needed to speed up the process of reviewing New Drug Applications (NDAs). PDUFA allows the FDA to collect user fees from pharmaceutical companies to support the review of applications. A recent report by the U.S. General Accounting Office (September 2002; "Food and Drug Administration: Effect of User Fees on Drug Approval Times, Withdrawals, and Other Agency Activities") concludes that "PDUFA has been successful in providing FDA with the funding necessary to hire additional drug reviewers, thereby making new drugs available in the United States more quickly."

Supporting this conclusion is the fact that approval times have decreased from 27 months to 14 months. However, the General Accounting Office (GAO) also reported a small increase in the drug-withdrawal rate since the implementation of PDUFA. That is, a higher percent of approved drugs have been withdrawn from the market due to safety issues. FDA officials argue that the increase is insignificant, from 3.10 percent in the eight-year period before PDUFA to 3.47 percent in the eight-year period after PDUFA. See Chapter 13, *Liability, Litigation, and Lessons in New Drug Development,* for more statistical figures.

This protection versus freedom dynamic is even more intensive when it comes to drugs being tested for use in patients with terminal illnesses that have no other viable treatment options. In these situations, the FDA receives tremendous pressure to approve these drugs rapidly. The rationale is that the most serious risk of death from an experimental drug is no risk at all compared to the certainty of death in patients with a lethal disease.

B. Clinical-Trial Sponsor

The clinical-trial sponsor ("sponsor") is defined as an individual, company, institution, or organization that assumes responsibility for the initiation, management, or financing of the clinical trial. The sponsor is required by the FDA to conduct clinical trials to determine safety and efficacy of the investigational agent. Safety data are usually derived through documented occurrence of adverse pharmacokinetic or pharmacodynamic effects. Alternately, efficacy data may be evaluated by the prevention of a medical condition or through improvement of specific symptoms of a disease process.

In the proper procedures for clinical trial, according to the Code of Federal Regulations (C.F.R.), the study sponsor is responsible for all aspects of the study including, but not limited to: maintaining quality assurance and quality control, medical expertise, trial design, trial management, data handling, record keeping, investigator selection, allocation of duties and functions, determining compensation to subjects and investigators, financing, notification/submission to regulatory authorities, product information, preparing and supplying study medications, and monitoring and assuring that all clinical-trial sites comply with federal regulatory requirements.[4]

The sponsor bears ultimate responsibility for the success, failure, and safety of the treatment under study, even after FDA approval. In addition, the sponsor is the true innovator in the clinical-trial process. Innovation is expensive, causing newly available treatments to be costly to the end user. Thus, due to the escalating price of medications, it is the innovators that are under increased scrutiny by consumers and policymakers. Paradoxically, as the population ages, it is the consumers that are driving the demand for new cures and better treatments.

Given the high rate of "failure" in the drug industry, it is reasonable to hypothesize that drug development would take place in economies characterized by relatively free markets and prices. The ideal environment would provide adequate incentives for investing in high-risk ventures. Such an environment exists in the United States. Although the United States is home to only about 5 percent of the world's population, roughly 36 percent of the worldwide pharmaceutical research and development is conducted in the U.S. on a yearly basis.[3]

That said, being the world's quantitative and qualitative leader in drug development comes with a price.[3] Many U.S. taxpayers and consumers are outraged at the high cost of prescription drugs compared to those nations with price controls, such as Canada, Mexico, and the United Kingdom. USA Today recently featured a front-page story that compared the price of ten innovator drugs that were still under patent. According to the article, the sample of drugs was 100 to 400 percent higher in the United States compared to

Canada, Mexico, and a few European nations, where direct price controls exist.[5] Having established this disparity, the writer concluded that what was a good deal for these other countries would be a good deal for the United States. What escaped the writer's attention, however, was the fact that if such controls were in effect here, many of the sampled drugs would never have been developed and made available to price-controlled countries in the first place.

Citizens and policymakers misunderstand that while drug development is expensive, production costs of the drugs themselves are comparatively low. It is the formula, not the ingredients, that racks up the large costs. In addition, drug expenditure is just part of the overall expense of healthcare and must not be looked at in a vacuum. For example, it is estimated that U.S. citizens spend about 12 percent more per capita on pharmaceutical goods—about $44 more per person, per year—than price-controlled nations.[3] However, a study completed by the Battelle Institute estimated that pharmaceutical research will save more than $750 billion in treatment costs for just five illnesses—Alzheimer's, AIDS, heart disease, arthritis, and cancer—over the next 25 years.[3] Being the world's leader in drug discovery is probably well worth the extra $44.

C. Contract Research Organizations

The daily attendance of the clinical-trial process can require time, manpower, and training that many sponsors feel do not match their current capabilities. Therefore, sponsors may elect to outsource any or all of their trial-related duties to a contract research organization (CRO). Full-service CROs offer data monitoring, data management, protocol development, medical writing, statistical analysis, contract management, site selection, and investigational supplies, shipping and handling. Niche CROs may elect to provide only a few of these services, such as data monitoring or medical writing. The CRO should maintain its own system of quality assurance and quality control. However, regardless of the duties assumed by the CRO, the final responsibility for the quality and integrity of the data always resides with the sponsor, and any duties not specifically transferred to a CRO remain the responsibility of the sponsor.

Contract research organizations are growing and mutating, making it difficult to spot CRO-specific trends. However, one thing is certain: pharmaceutical, biotechnology, and medical-devices sponsors expect to increase outsourcing to the several hundred CROs. In fact, pharmaceutical companies have increased CRO usage from 28 percent of clinical studies in 1993 to 61 percent in 1999. This reflects increased spending on CRO traditional services of Phase 3 study monitoring, data management, pharmaco-economic analysis, and medical writing. While these services remain the most highly utilized, CROs are also offering new services to satisfy sponsors' demands for faster trials and globalization.[6]

Several years ago, to meet this challenge, CROs seemed to be strategically planning to become either mega-CROs or niche providers, and industry observers believed that the mid-sized CRO would disappear. According to a study conducted in 2011 by Industry Standard Research, as a group, mid-sized CROs performed quite well or even better than their larger counterparts and they received higher marks for service, quality and loyalty overall. The strong performance of mid-sized CROs was evident in the category for speed of site and investigator recruitment. The top five attributes that pharmaceutical companies are looking for in a CRO are therapeutic expertise, low cost, a global footprint, quality clinical research associates and upfront contingency planning.[7] Today, mid-size CROs play an important role in the pharmaceutical ecosystem with their focus on quality of service and their ability to specialize in therapeutic areas. They also leverage their low administrative overhead as a competitive advantage.[11] The overall outlook for the CRO industry is strong because more and more sponsors plan to complete their clinical studies through outsourcing, but the costs of these studies is growing as a factor in how pharmaceutical companies select CROs. Years ago, pharmaceutical companies might not have ranked cost as a high selection factor for some drug studies. Pharmaceutical companies are increasingly indicating a stronger preference for recruiting efficiency over cost efficiency. But even that preference has a basis in cost. If it takes longer to recruit for clinical trials, that lost time costs money.[7]

As the CRO industry consolidates, some large publicly traded CROs are making acquisitions that diversify the breadth of service beyond study-conduct activities. This move enables sponsors to do one-stop shopping, instead of contracting with multiple companies throughout the discovery-development process. In addition, CROs are positioning themselves to gain access to populations in emerging markets, such as Israel, Russia, Latin America, China, and India.

D. Study Monitors

Study monitors or clinical research associates (CRAs) can be directly employed by the study sponsor or CRO, or independently contracted for a specific study. According to the *Guideline for Good Clinical Practice*, the CRA's purpose is the following:[9]

- to verify that the rights and well-being of human subjects are protected
- to verify that the reported trial data are accurate, complete, and verifiable from source documentation

- to verify that the conduct of the trial is in compliance with the currently approved protocol or amendments, with good clinical practices, and with applicable regulatory requirements

CRAs achieve the above through frequent visits to the clinical-trial site. During these visits, the monitor will source-verify data, audit the regulatory documents for accuracy and completion, perform drug accountability, and communicate about any concerns, problems, or new information with the study staff.

E. Clinical-Trial Site

The front line of clinical trials is the site. It is at the site level that participants are given informed consent, study-related procedures are being conducted according to the clinical-trial protocol, and data is being collected and reported. It is these data, in aggregate from all of the sites, that will ultimately determine the fate of the investigational drug or device. Given the rigor with which clinical trials must be conducted today, site-research personnel usually include the principal investigator, sub-investigators, study coordinators, and regulatory managers. However, depending on the amount of research being conducted at a given location, the study coordinators are often also responsible for the regulatory compliance.

The principal investigator (PI) is the individual who is ultimately responsible for the clinical trial at the trial site and who verifies that the data reported to the study sponsor is accurate. Although not required by the FDA, the PI is usually a physician. In the event that the PI is not a physician, adequate physician oversight of the trial must be readily evident. As addressed by ICH and GCP, the PI should be qualified through education, training, and experience to assume responsibility for the proper conduct of the trial and should meet all of the qualifications specified by the applicable regulatory requirements.[8]

Not all physicians are well-suited for clinical research. A successful investigator has distinct characteristics:

- has an intrinsic interest in science
- is knowledgeable of the protocol
- always places patient care above all other priorities
- is willing to carve out time for the study
- is very involved in medical oversight
- knows her limitations and when to ask for help
- is tolerant of the increased need for regulatory scrutiny
- understands that being a respected clinician does not mean being a good researcher, and is open to learning about the conduct of clinical research

- is able to deliver documentation with a quick turn-around
- meets participant recruitment and enrollment goals established with the sponsor

As defined by ICH and GCP, a sub-investigator is any individual member of the clinical-trial team designated and directly supervised by the PI to perform trial-related procedures or make trial-related decisions.[8] Examples of sub-investigators include other physicians, pharmacists, nurses, and study coordinators.

Clinical research coordinators (CRCs) are the research personnel that assist with patient visits and perform study-related procedures not required of a physician (phlebotomy, vital signs, adverse-event and concomitant-medication discussions, and so on). CRCs provide the PI and physician with data required for interpretation, medical decisions (inclusion or exclusion, dosage adjustment, patient withdrawal, adverse events, causality, and so on), and trial oversight. In addition, CRCs are usually responsible for transcribing source documentation (medical records, clinic notes, laboratory reports, and so on) into case report forms (CRF) supplied by the study sponsor.

Another important function of the CRC is to interact with the sponsor or CRO-appointed CRA. As an agent for the sponsor, the CRC/CRA relationship is one that can make or break a study. If a CRC is doing an excellent job and the documents are available and accurate, the CRA's interactions with the site should be positive and productive. Unfortunately, this does not always happen. There are dynamics on both sides of the case-report form. Some common complaints are:

- The CRA assigned to a given study changes frequently. Each CRA communicates different directives to the site, causing the site to re-do work.
- The CRA has a condescending attitude towards the site, including the investigator.
- The CRA is not well trained.
- The CRC is inexperienced.
- The CRA cannot obtain rapid answers to questions, often creating patient-care issues.
- The CRC cannot obtain rapid answers to queries, often extending timelines for study closure.
- The CRC makes numerous errors in the case-report forms.
- The CRC does not seem dedicated to the study.

In an industry where there is virtually full employment, it is difficult to find trained CRCs and CRAs. So, conflict may arise from interaction between untrained or inexperienced personnel. Sometimes, however, personality conflicts are the main culprit. There is no question that technology may eliminate some of the need for CRA/CRC interaction, but until that time, all parties should seek to understand the others' roles and pressures.[9] For example, many CRAs travel four days a week and see various levels of work quality at different sites. On the other hand, CRCs are often responsible for more than one study and have requests from multiple CRAs on any given day. In addition, the CRA must respond to the needs of the research participant first, which can cause time delays in completing data queries.

Regulatory managers are usually charged with submission of regulatory documents to the institutional review board (IRB) and study sponsor, and charged with maintaining a regulatory binder. A regulatory binder should contain a protocol; protocol amendments; IRB approvals and correspondence; all versions of the IRB-approved, patient-informed consent; investigators brochure; sponsor correspondence; curriculum vitas and licensures of the PI and sub-investigators; and any safety reports.

F. Site-Management Organizations

As the number of clinical-research sites has grown, a new entity called site-management organizations (SMOs) has emerged. SMOs, in the traditional sense, were established to offer the sponsor consolidated services at the site level. SMOs took the business model of the CROs and brought it to the front lines. For example, CROs offer a variety of services for the sponsor, such as site monitoring, contract administration, shipping and receiving of study supplies, and data management. SMOs offer PI recruitment, patient recruitment, and regulatory and contract management for multiple sites. As sponsors often must recruit between 50 and 200 clinical-trial sites, SMOs offer a one-stop shop. SMOs can provide the sponsors with multiple PIs and centralized contract and regulatory services, expediting study initiation.

SMO models vary widely in the industry. Some SMOs hire physician investigators as employees of the company. Others simply sub-contract for investigator services. However, few offer true turnkey solutions for investigators who wish to be involved in clinical research, but who lack the specialized training or necessary personnel to conduct a study. Full-service SMOs act as liaisons between the pharmaceutical, device, or biotechnology company (and the CRO) and the research patient. Services often include patient and investigator recruitment, regulatory-document preparation and compliance, and study coordination.

SMOs provide an interesting entry for investigators into the clinical-trial business. Specifically, some SMOs can present new investigators with clinical-trial opportunities, essential training and qualified research personnel. In turn, the investigator assumes ultimate responsibility for the ethical conduct of the study. By relieving the physician, hospital, and respective staff members from time-consuming, non-clinical tasks, SMOs can make research not only feasible—but actually lucrative—for investigators and hospitals. This risk-sharing model can be beneficial to all parties.

For SMOs that sub-contract investigators, perceived drawbacks include shared reimbursement, variable performance among the sites within the SMO, and lack of on-site medical expertise. First, some investigators may feel that they could realize more revenue from clinical research by maintaining the infrastructure. This way, the revenue earned from the grant is not shared with the SMO. While this may be true, the investigator must consider the cost of personnel and overhead. In addition, the time required to gain a reputation as an investigator and achieve an adequate pipeline of clinical-trial opportunities may prohibitively impact return on investment.

Second, from the SMO and sponsor perspective, there is little recourse for poor performance. As the investigators are not employees of the SMO, enforcement of company standard operating procedures of the organization may be difficult. However, if expectations are communicated early and proper training transpires, these problems can be averted. Furthermore, it is the responsibility of the SMO to develop a strong rapport and teamwork with investigators affiliated with the organization and to recommend only those investigators with a proven track record to the sponsor customer.

Third, the quality of medical oversight is often questionable, since the investigators (almost always physicians) are not physically on-site. Also, sponsors may feel the SMO does not have strong clinical expertise. Again, communicating expectations and logistics early is critical. The SMO research personnel must have immediate access to the investigator for medical backup. In addition, SMOs that retain coordinators that are also strong clinically (nurses, pharmacists, and so on) are the most equipped to be successful with this model. Furthermore, SMOs that sub-contract investigators have the luxury of selecting the most appropriate investigators on a study-by-study basis. For example, if the study is for brittle diabetics, the SMO is free to approach a diabetologist about the study. SMOs that have investigators as company employees may not have a physician with this specialized expertise or patient population. It is unlikely that the SMO would hire a physician as an employee for a particular study. It is likely that the physician already on staff would act as the principal investigator, without the specialized expertise.

SMOs that hire physician investigators as employees of the company have a perceived lack of access to patients. This type of SMO often uses advertising as a principal method of patient recruitment. As research participants are not patients of the physician investigator, sponsors may have concerns that this causes logistical problems when attempting to audit study documents. Medical records may be housed at the participant's regular physician's office and at the research clinic. Sponsors are also concerned with the overuse or "recycling" of research participants. Furthermore, the potential research participant's regular physician may or may not advise their patients to participate in a clinical trial. Also, referring physicians are often concerned that they might lose patients to the investigator. Local physicians must understand that the investigator will not assume the care of the patient once the study has concluded. Community awareness and strong support with local physicians is important for this model to be effective.

G. Institutional Review Board

The sole mission of the institutional review board (IRB) is to protect the rights and welfare of human subjects. In general, the IRB is charged with overseeing patient informed-consent forms, evaluating the benefit versus the risk of clinical-trial protocols, reviewing safety reports, and ensuring that the qualifications of the investigators are adequate to perform the duties required by the protocol and the FDA. Guidelines for institutional review boards are vast, and are discussed in detail in Chapter 6, *FDA Compliance and Inspection Programs Governing Clinical Investigations.*

H. Research Participants

Research participants drive the whole clinical-trial process. Without a sufficient number of volunteers, it would be impossible to derive valid conclusions about new drugs or medical devices. It is important to protect these stalwarts by building in mechanisms to ensure that each subject is able to make an educated decision regarding his study participation. This is where the subject informed-consent form comes in. In lay terms—and in great detail—the form describes the potential risks and benefits of the study regimen (see Chapter 7, *The Protection of Subjects in Clinical Research*). In addition, the informed-consent form explains who will have access to the trial documents.

Regulations also exist to protect the confidentiality of the research participants. All information collected throughout the clinical trial remains with the study staff. For the purpose of data capture, each subject is identified only by his initials and study number.

Research participants are the true pioneers of medicine. Their participation has made the development of novel therapeutic cures and treatments possible. Furthermore, their contribution has protected the public from the approval of drugs that have a poor risk-to-benefit ratio. (See Figure 5.6.)

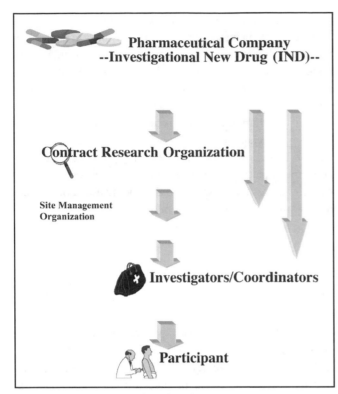

Figure 5.6 The clinical trial industry.

5.7 Industry Trade Organizations and Support Services

As stated earlier, the pharmaceutical industry must concede to a high failure rate. In order to minimize failures due to poor performance on the part of any niche service providers, there is a clear need for structured education, training, and communication. The largest trade organizations devoted to the clinical-trial industry include Associates of Clinical Research Professionals (ACRP), Drug Information Associates (DIA), and Pharmaceutical Research and Manufacturers Association (PhRMA). In addition, the FDA offers multiple training sessions and hosts a website for consumers and researchers. CenterWatch (www.centerwatch.com) is the leading publication and website for clinical-trial information and industry news. Publications, such as the *Good Clinical Practice Handbook* (available online at www.fda.gov/aboutfda/centersoffices/officeofmedicalproductsandtobacco/officeofscienceandhealthcoordination/ucm2018191.htm), the Code of Federal Regulations (available online at www.fda.gov/medicaldevices/deviceregulationandguidance/overview/ucm134499.htm), and "ICH Guidelines" (available online at www.ich.org/products/guidelines.html) outline industry-specific standards and regulations. Online versions of these documents are free.

Endnotes

1. K. Flieger. "FDA consumer special report: Testing drugs in people," www.fda.gov (January, 1995).

2. Adams, C. P. and Brantner, V. V. (2010), Spending on new drug development. Health Economics, 19: 130–141. doi: 10.1002/hec.1454

3. CRS Report for Congress. Comparative Clinical Effectiveness and Cost-Effectiveness Research: Background, History, and Overview. Jacobson, Gretchen A. (October, 2007)

4. LeighAnne Olsen and J. Michael McGinnis; Roundtable on Value & Science-Driven Health Care; Institute of Medicine. Redesigning the Clinical Effectiveness Research Paradigm: Innovation and Practice-Based Approaches: Workshop Summary. National Academies Press (2010).

5. Agency for Healthcare Research and Quality (AHRQ, formerly the Agency for Health Care Policy and Research). Outcomes Research Fact Sheet.

6. R. Winslow. *Wall Street Journal*, July 11, 2002.

7. Frank Vinluan, "Midsized CROs perform as good or better than larger ones, survey says," *MedCity News*, June 14, 2011. www.medcitynews.com/2011/06/midsized-cros-perform-as-good-or-better-than-larger-ones-survey-says. Accessed June 2012.

8. J.B. Moseley et al. *New England Journal of Medicine*. 347(2):81–3 (2002).

9. Title 21. Foods and Drugs. ICH Guideline for Good Clinical Practice: Subpart D (Part 312:50). 1999. *Code of Federal Regulations and ICH Guidelines.* 34–42.

10. National Institutes of Health. www.commonfund.nih.gov/clinicalresearch/overview-translational.aspx. Accessed April 30, 2012.

11. Prasad Sristi and Ron Kolanitch, "Workflow management systems for mid-sized CROs," Applied Clinical Trials, April 18, 2012. www.appliedclinicaltrialsonline.com/appliedclinicaltrials/Online+Extras/Workflow-Management-Systems-for-Mid-size-CROs/ArticleStandard/Article/detail/769709?contextCategoryId=47497. Accessed June 2012.

Recommended Reading

Code of Federal Regulations and ICH Guidelines. Title 21. Foods and Drugs. ICH Guideline for Good Clinical Practice. 1.56. 1997:9.

Chapter 6

FDA Compliance and Inspection Programs Governing Clinical Investigations

James P. Walters, J.D., M.S.

6.1 Introduction

The 1962 Kefauver–Harris Drug Amendments[1] to the Food, Drug, and Cosmetic Act (FDCA) of 1938[2] defined a *new drug* as one that is not generally recognized as safe and effective by qualified experts under the intended conditions of use.[3] The amendments changed the provisions of the Act so that drugs would no longer be approved by default. Before those changes, drugs that the Food and Drug Administration (FDA) *failed to disapprove* could be marketed. After the amendments, a drug's manufacturer had to prove the drug's safety and efficacy before it could be marketed.[4]

The amended FDCA prohibited anyone from marketing a drug without FDA approval.[5] For manufacturers to bring a new drug to market, they must now submit an investigational new drug (IND) application to the FDA, and the FDA must approve the application as proof of the drug's safety and efficacy.[6] Clinical studies must be done to prove safety and efficacy. Unapproved new drugs may need to be shipped interstate to facilitate clinical investigations, so the amendments authorize a shipping exemption for investigational purposes only.[7] That exemption is known as the *investigational new drug exemption.*

By 1963, the FDA had begun promulgating a series of IND regulations.[8] The core of the regulations are in Title 21, Part 312 of the Code of Federal Regulations (C.F.R.),[9] which defines clinical investigations and some of the parties involved in the IND process. A *clinical investigation* is any use of a drug by human subjects that is not a marketed drug prescribed by a doctor. An *investigator* is someone who conducts a clinical investigation, and the *sponsor* is the person, corporation, or government entity that initiates and is responsible for a clinical investigation (usually the pharmaceutical company that wants to market the drug). The *subject* is anyone who participates in an investigation as either a recipient of an investigational new drug or a control.[10]

Section 312 of Title 21 also sets forth the duties and responsibilities of investigators and sponsors. Those duties create other regulated parties, and regulations for those other parties are found in separate sections of the C.F.R. Chief among these other parties is the institutional review board (IRB).[11] Because an investigator must submit a proposed clinical investigation for initial approval and for continuing review and approval to an IRB, regulations were written to govern IRBs.[12] The investigator is also responsible for obtaining informed consent from each subject,[13] and required regulations must be written for obtaining informed consent.[14] The sponsor has the duty to select a monitor[15] to ensure that investigators comply with all applicable laws, regulations, and sponsor requirements.[16] A *contract research organization* (CRO) is an entity that assumes all or part of the duties of the sponsor or the monitor. By regulation, a CRO is subject to FDA action as if it were a sponsor.[17]

All parties regulated under the IND rules are subject to FDA inspection. The investigation records and reports of investigators,[18] sponsors,[19] and IRBs[20] are subject to inspection. The financial records of an investigator are also subject to inspection so that the FDA can determine whether the investigator has a financial interest in the drug under investigation.[16] The *monitor* is considered part of the sponsor and is also subject to FDA inspection.[16,19]

This chapter summarizes and comments on the FDA's compliance programs governing clinical investigations and the relevant regulations. The formal compliance programs and the inspection process are outlined, and the chapter ends with a discussion of FDA warning letters.

6.2 FDA Regulations for Clinical Investigators

This chapter covers only the regulations of drug products, but under the FDCA, therapeutic biological products are considered drugs,[21] so this section applies to them as well. Separate regulations cover the clinical investigations of medical devices.[22]

A. 21 C.F.R. Part 312: Investigator Regulations

The importance, as well as the scope and depth, of the relationship between an investigator and the sponsor may be why the C.F.R. commingles its regulations.[9] To avoid confusion, this chapter discusses the investigator and sponsor regulations separately.

1. § 312.60: General Responsibilities

The general responsibilities of investigators include conducting investigations according to the signed investigator statement (FDA Form 1572)[64] and the investigational plan (or protocol).[13] The investigator is also required to adhere to all regulations protecting the rights, safety, and welfare of research subjects and the informed consent regulations.[14]

2. § 312.61: Control of the Investigational Drug

The investigator must control the use of the drug being studied. That control means limiting who can use the drug to the subjects under the investigator's personal supervision or under the supervision of a sub-investigator responsible to the investigator. The investigator cannot give the drug to anyone, including a physician, who is not authorized to receive it or identified as a sub-investigator on the investigator statement.

3. § 312.62: Recordkeeping and Retention

Investigational records must be prepared and retained by the investigator, including records of the disposal of the study article.[24] The records must document the dates and quantity of the drug given to each subject as well as any drug disposed of or returned to the sponsor.

Clinical investigators must prepare and maintain adequate case histories on each subject. The case histories document all observations and data pertinent to the investigation, regardless of whether the subject receives the drug being studied or a control.[65] Case histories include case report forms (CRFs), which are typically supplied by the sponsor for documentation and data compilation. Case histories also include supporting data, such as signed and dated consent forms, progress notes, hospital charts, and nurses' notes. Relevant laboratory reports, operative notes, and any other document relevant to a subject's participation in the clinical investigation are also part of the subject's case history.

All required records must be retained by the clinical investigator for two years following the approval date of the marketing application—the new drug application (NDA). If after investigation, no NDA is submitted to the FDA, the records must be retained for two years following the date that the FDA is notified that the investigation has been discontinued.

4. § 312.64: Reports

Progress reports must be submitted to the sponsor responsible for collecting and evaluating the results of the investigation. Safety reports and any adverse effects that might reasonably be associated with the drug must be reported to the sponsor. If the adverse effect is alarming, the investigator must report it to the sponsor immediately. An adequate final report must be submitted to the sponsor shortly after completion of the investigator's participation in the study. The investigator must also provide sufficient, accurate information so the sponsor can submit to the FDA adequate certification or disclosure statements about that investigator's financial interests.[23] Any changes in that information must also be reported to the sponsor.

5. § 312.66: Assurance of Institutional Review Board Review

The investigator is responsible for ensuring that a qualified IRB[12] reviews and approves the clinical investigation. The investigator must submit to continuing review and approval as required, and must promptly report to the IRB any changes in the research activity as well as any unanticipated problems that put the subjects or others at risk. No changes in the research activity can be made without IRB approval, except where necessary to eliminate an immediate hazard to the subjects.

6. § 312.68: FDA Inspections

If properly requested,[66] an investigator must provide all study-related records and reports for FDA inspection, copying, and verification. The investigator is not required to divulge subject names, unless the records of particular subjects require more detailed inspections or unless there is reason for the FDA to believe that the records do not represent actual case studies or do not represent actual results obtained.[67]

7. § 312.69: Controlled Substances

If the study article is subject to the Controlled Substances Act,[25] the investigator must make adequate safeguards to prevent the drug from being stolen or diverted. Such safeguards include storing the article in a locked and substantially constructed cabinet and limiting access to the drug.

B. 21 C.F.R. Part 312: Sponsor Regulations

The responsibilities of sponsors are elaborated in Title 21 C.F.R. Part 312.50–312.59 and Title 21 C.F.R. Part 54. The sections of Part 312 address the primary responsibilities.

1. § 312.50: General Responsibilities

Sponsors must select qualified investigators and provide them with the information needed to conduct the investigation properly. The sponsor must also monitor the investigators conducting the study. That responsibility includes ensuring that the investigation is conducted in accordance with the protocol, and the IND is kept in effect throughout the study. The sponsor must promptly inform the FDA and all investigators of any significant new adverse effects or risks associated with the study article.

2. § 312.52: Contract Research Organizations

A sponsor may transfer any or all of its responsibilities to a CRO. Such transfers must be in writing, and if only parts of the study are being transferred, the written transfer must describe each of the transferred obligations. Any obligation not described in the writing is deemed by the FDA as remaining the responsibility of the sponsor.

A CRO that assumes an obligation assigned a sponsor must comply with the applicable regulations as if it were a sponsor. The CRO is subject to the same regulatory sanctions that the sponsor would be for any violations.

3. § 312.53: Selecting Investigators and Monitors

The sponsor must select only qualified investigators who have the training and experience to make them appropriate experts for investigating the study article. The sponsor must also control the distribution of the study drug and supply the article only to investigators participating in the investigation. Before permitting an investigator to participate in a sponsored investigation, the sponsor must obtain the following information:

- a signed investigator agreement (Form FDA-1572)[1]
- a curriculum vitae
- a clinical protocol[68]
- financial disclosure information sufficient for the sponsor to comply with the investigator financial disclosure requirements[23]

4. § 312.54: Emergency Research

The sponsor must monitor all investigations involving emergency treatment for informed consent (see Section 6.2.C, "21 C.F.R. Part 50: Informed Consent," below). When an IRB sends a sponsor information on required public disclosures,[27] the sponsor must promptly submit copies of that information to the FDA. The sponsor must monitor emergency use investigations, looking specifically for instances where an IRB refused to approve an informed consent exception. When such information is found, the sponsor must inform the FDA, other potential investigators, and other involved IRBs.

5. § 312.55: Informing Investigators

Before an investigation begins, a sponsor must provide investigators with an investigator's brochure.[28,69] Throughout the study, the sponsor must keep the investigator informed of new observations discovered by or reported to the sponsor, particularly those related to the safe use of the study article. That information can be sent to the investigator in a revised investigator brochure, in reprints or published studies, by reports or letters, or any other appropriate means. Those reports must, however, comply with the IND safety-report regulations.[29]

6. § 312.56: Review of Ongoing Investigations

The sponsor must monitor the conduct of clinical investigations testing its IND. When a sponsor discovers that an investigator is not complying with the signed investigator's statement, the protocol, or any applicable FDA regulations, the sponsor must promptly secure compliance or discontinue shipping the study article to the investigator and end the investigator's participation.

If an investigator's participation is ended, the sponsor must ensure that the investigator properly disposes of or returns all of the investigational drug.[30] The sponsor must review and evaluate that investigator's evidence relating to the safety and efficacy of the study drug and report the findings to the FDA.[29] The sponsor must also make annual reports on the progress of any IND-related investigation.[31]

When a sponsor determines that the investigational drug presents an unreasonable and significant risk to the subjects, the sponsor must discontinue the investigation and notify the FDA, all involved IRBs, and all investigators who participated in the study at any point. The sponsor must ensure the proper disposition of all study article stocks and furnish the FDA with a full report of the sponsor's actions in discontinuing the investigation. The investigation must be discontinued as soon as possible—but no later than five working days—after making the determination that the study should be discontinued. The FDA then confers with the sponsor on the reasons for discontinuing the study.

7. § 312.57: Recordkeeping and Retention

The sponsor must maintain adequate records documenting all receipts, shipments, and other dispositions of the investigational drug. Those records include the name of the investigator to whom the drug is supplied and the date, quantity, and batch or code mark of each shipment. The sponsor must keep complete and accurate records of the financial interests of the investigator, including payments by the sponsor, and all other financial interests of the investigators as required.[23]

Similar to the rules for recordkeeping by investigators, sponsors must retain all required records for two years after a marketing application (an NDA) has been approved for the drug. If no application is submitted, the sponsor must retain the records for two years after the shipment and delivery of the investigational drug is discontinued.

The sponsor must maintain reserve samples of any test article and reference standard used in any of the bioequivalence or bioavailability studies.[32,33] If requested, the reserve samples must be released to the FDA.

8. § 312.58: FDA Inspections

Sponsors, like investigators, must allow FDA inspection and copying of any required records and reports, and if requested, the sponsor must submit all required records and reports (or copies of them) to the FDA.[70] The sponsor must discontinue shipments of the investigational drug to any investigator who fails to provide all required records and reports to the sponsor. The regulations also specifically provide for inspection by the Drug Enforcement Administration of the distribution records of any controlled substances involved in IND-related clinical investigations.

9. § 312.59: Disposition of Unused Supplies

The sponsor must secure the return of all unused supplies of the investigational drug from any discontinued or terminated investigator. Alternative disposition can be authorized, as long as such disposal does not expose people to risks. Written records must be maintained of all dispositions of investigational drugs.

10. 21 C.F.R. Part 54: Financial Disclosure

When all required clinical investigations are completed, the sponsor can submit an NDA to the FDA. The FDA, an advisory panel, and the FDA commissioner must approve the application before marketing can commence. When the application is submitted, the sponsor must either certify that no investigators involved in the clinical investigations had a financial interest in the drug or disclose whatever financial interest any investigator had.[23]

Because the FDA believes that an investigator's financial interest might bias her in favor of the safety and efficacy of the drug, the FDA will use disclosed financial interest to evaluate the reliability of the data submitted in the NDA.[34] Financial interests that must be disclosed include:

- compensation affected by the outcome of the clinical studies conducted by the investigator
- significant equity interest (of $50,000 or more) in the sponsor of the clinical studies during the time of the investigator's participation in the drug's clinical trials
- any proprietary interest in the study drug, such as a patent, trademark, copyright, or licensing agreement
- significant payments (of more than $25,000, excluding the cost of doing the studies) made to the investigator by the sponsor

It is the sponsor's responsibility to supply the financial certification or disclosure, but the investigator must cooperate in supplying the sponsor with the information.

C. 21 C.F.R. Part 50: Informed Consent

The regulations in Part 50 of Title 21 are meant to ensure the protection of human subjects involved in investigational studies and clinical trials.

1. § 50.20: General Requirements

Except as specifically provided in the regulations,[28] no investigator can include a subject in a study before obtaining legally effective informed consent from the subject or the subject's legally authorized representative. Securing an informed consent must allow the subject the opportunity to consider whether or not to participate in the study. The subject must not be subjected to undue influence or coercion. Information provided to the subject or the legal representative must be presented in language that the consenting party can understand. Exculpatory language, which waives or appears to waive the subject's legal rights, cannot be included in the consent process. The exculpatory exclusion applies to the investigator, the sponsor, the institution, and any agents of the institution.[71]

The first time an investigational drug or control is administered does not necessarily determine the point when a subject is considered part of a study. For randomized clinical trials, the FDA considers a subject to have entered the study at the time of the randomization. If laboratory or other tests are necessary to determine a subject's eligibility, the subject is considered part of the trial as soon as the tests begin.

2. § 50.23: Exceptions

Informed consent is deemed feasible unless both the investigator and a physician who is not otherwise participating in the clinical study certify in writing that:

- the potential subject is confronted by a life-threatening situation that necessitates the use of the investigational article
- informed consent cannot be obtained from the subject because of the inability to communicate with or obtain an informed consent from the subject
- there is not sufficient time to obtain consent from the subject's representative
- there is no available, approved alternative or generally recognized therapy that provides for an equal or greater likelihood of saving the subject's life

If a clinical investigator makes use of this exception and uses the drug without consent, that decision must be evaluated within five working days of that use. The clinical investigator's use of the drug without consent and the use itself must be reviewed in writing by a physician who is not participating in the investigation. That required documentation[27] must be submitted to the IRB within five days after using the drug under these regulations. The regulations specifically provide for special exceptions to informed consent for military use of an unapproved drug.

3. § 50.24: Exception for Emergency Research

The regulations allow use of an unapproved drug during an emergency, when it might be possible to secure informed consent before treatment. It is the IRB's responsibility to determine—after consulting a licensed physician who is either a member of the IRB or a consultant to the IRB—whether use under these provisions is appropriate.

To determine whether or not an investigational drug can be given without consent during an emergency, the IRB must make and document certain findings of fact. The IRB must find that the human subjects are in life-threatening situations, that alternative available treatments are unproven or unsatisfactory, and that scientific investigation is needed to prove the safety and efficacy of the intervention to be studied.

The IRB must also find that informed consent is not feasible because:

- the subjects are not able to give consent because of their medical conditions
- it is not feasible to obtain informed consent from the subject's legally authorized representative

- prospective identification of subjects who may need the intervention is not reasonable

The IRB must then find that the participation in the study will provide the subject with direct benefits because:

- the subjects are facing a life-threatening situation requiring intervention
- appropriate animal and other preclinical studies have been conducted, and the studies support the potential that the intervention will provide a direct benefit to the subjects
- the risks associated with the intervention are reasonable in relation to what is known about the medical condition of the potential class of subjects, the risks and benefits of standard therapy, if any, and what is known about the risks and benefits of the proposed intervention

The IRB must find that the investigation would not be feasible without this general waiver. The proposed protocol defines the length of the therapeutic window under this exemption. Investigators must commit to attempt to find an authorized representative during the therapeutic window and to document those attempts.

The IRB reviews and approves the consent procedures to be used where informed consent is feasible from the subject or his representative. The IRB also reviews and approves of protocol procedures that provide a family member with the opportunity to object to the subject's participation.

The IRB then makes a determination about additional safeguards required for subjects who are treated without obtaining their consent. Minimum safeguards include:

- consultation with members of the community where the investigation is to be carried out
- public disclosure of the investigation in the community
- public disclosure after completion of the study with sufficient information to inform the community of the characteristics of the treated subjects and the results of treatment
- establishment of an independent data-monitoring committee to exercise oversight of the investigation

The IRB is responsible for ensuring that procedures are in place to inform each subject, her representative, or a family member at the earliest feasible opportunity that the subject has been included in the clinical investigation and other pertinent information. Such information includes explaining the contents of the approved consent form and explaining that the subject, her representative, or a family member can discontinue the subject's participation at any time without penalty or loss of benefits. If the representative or family member is initially informed and the patient subsequently improves and is able to understand the information, the subject must then be informed. If the subject dies before the representative or family member can be informed, the disclosure must still be made, if feasible.

All records of all required findings and any other documentation must be retained by the IRB for three years after the investigation is completed. These records must be made available to the FDA for inspection and copying.

A protocol that involves the emergency exception requires a separate IND, which clearly identifies the research as involving subjects who may not be able to give informed consent. That separate IND is required even if an IND already exists for the drug. An application to amend an existing IND to include emergency research will not be accepted by the FDA.

When an IRB decides that it cannot approve an emergency research protocol—because the protocol does not meet the criteria in the regulations or for some other ethical reasons—the IRB must document its reasons and promptly inform the clinical investigator and sponsor of those findings in writing. The sponsor is responsible for promptly informing the FDA, other investigators, and other IRBs if there are any negative findings by an IRB against allowing an exception to informed consent under the emergency research regulations.

4. § 50.25: Elements of Informed Consent

The regulations specify both basic and additional elements of informed consent.[35] The basic elements that must be included in all informed consent procedures are a statement that the subject's involvement includes research, an explanation of the purposes of the research, and the expected duration of the subject's participation. There must be a description of the procedures included in the research, identifying any experimental procedures. A description of any reasonably foreseeable risks or discomforts to the subject must be included. A description of any reasonably expected benefits to the subject or others must also be provided. Appropriate alternative treatments, if any, must be disclosed. The informed consent must include a statement describing the protections employed to keep the subject's records confidential.[72]

For research that involves more than minimal risk, the consent must include a statement of any compensation to be provided to the subject. The consent must also state whether or not medical treatment will be provided for any research-related injuries and provide the subject with a contact that he can use to report any research-related injuries, to answer questions about the research, and to answer questions about his rights.[73]

Basic elements of an informed consent also include a statement that participation is voluntary and that refusing to participate will not result in a penalty or loss of benefits to which the subject might otherwise be entitled. The subject must be informed that he can discontinue participation at any time without penalty or loss.

When appropriate, an informed consent should include the following additional elements:

- a warning about risks to a pregnant woman or fetus
- anticipated circumstances under which the subject may be terminated from the study
- any additional costs to the subject that may result from participation
- consequences of a subject's decision to withdraw from the study and an orderly procedure for withdrawing
- a statement that significant new findings that develop during the course of research and that might affect the subject's willingness to continue will be provided to the subject as they occur
- the approximate number of subjects involved in the study

The regulation specifically states that the informed consent does not preempt any other federal, state, or local laws. The regulation states that the informed consent does not limit a physician's authority to provide any emergency medical care that is permitted under federal, state, or local law.

5. § 50.27: Documentation of Informed Consent

Except as provided for in the IRB regulations,[36] informed consent must be documented in a written form approved by the IRB and signed by the subject or the subject's legally authorized representative.[37] A copy must be given to the person signing the form. The consent form can be either of the following:

- a written consent document that contains all of the required elements of informed consent[35,74]
- a short form stating that all of the required elements

have been verbally presented to the subject or the subject's representative

When the second alternative is used, a witness must observe the oral presentation, and the IRB must approve a written summary of the information to be orally presented. Only the short form must be signed by the subject or the subject's representative, but the witness must sign both the short form and a copy of the summary. The person obtaining the subject's consent must sign a copy of the summary. Copies of both the short form and the summary must then be provided to the subject or the subject's representative.

D. 21 C.F.R. Part 56: Institutional Review Board

Title 21 Part 56[12] describes the people who can become part of an IRB and the operating standards and responsibilities of those boards.

1. § 56.107: IRB Membership

Each IRB must have a minimum of five members of various backgrounds to adequately review the research before it.[38] The IRB must be composed of members sufficiently qualified by experience and expertise and must be diverse to promote respect for its advice and counsel in protecting subjects' rights. The IRB members must be competent to evaluate the proposed research. Membership competence should include determining institutional commitments and applicable regulations, laws, and standards of professional conduct. If an IRB regularly reviews research involving vulnerable subjects (such as children, prisoners, pregnant women, or handicapped or mentally disabled people), the IRB should consider appointing a member knowledgeable and experienced in working with such subjects.

No appointment to the board can be made based on gender, but every nondiscriminatory effort should be made to ensure that the IRB does not consist solely of men or of women. No IRB can consist solely of members of one profession. Every IRB must have at least one member whose primary concerns are in a scientific area and at least one other member whose primary concerns are in a nonscientific area. The IRB must have at least one member who is not otherwise affiliated with the institution and is not a member of the immediate family of someone affiliated with the institution.

No IRB member who has a conflicting interest can participate in initial or continuing reviews of the research, except to provide information requested by the IRB. The IRB can consult outside experts, but the consultants are not allowed to vote on any proposed investigation.

2. § 56.108: IRB Functions and Operations

The IRB must have a written procedure for fulfilling the requirements of the regulations.[39] That procedure must cover:

- the initial and continuing review of proposed investigations and how findings will be reported to the investigator and to the institution
- the steps for determining which investigations require reviews more than once a year and which require verification from sources other than the investigator to ensure that no material changes have occurred since the previous IRB review and approval[75]
- how promptly reporting about any changes made to the study protocol will be secured from an investigator
- how to ensure that changes in the research activity are not initiated until after IRB review and approval (except where necessary to eliminate immediate hazards to subjects)

IRB written procedures must ensure that investigators promptly report to the IRB, to appropriate institutional officials, and to the FDA any

- unanticipated problems involving risks to human subjects or others
- serious or continuing noncompliance with regulations or with the requirements of the IRB[76]
- suspension or termination of an IRB research approval

Except when an expedited review procedure[40] is used, the IRB must review proposals at meetings convened with a majority of the members present. Regulations also require that at least one member be present whose primary concerns are nonscientific. No proposal can be approved unless the majority of the members present vote in favor of the proposal.

3. § 56.109: Review of Research

The IRB must have the authority to review and approve all regulated research conducted at its institution.[36] The IRB can require modifications to a research proposal as a condition for approval or disapproval of the proposal. The IRB must state what information it requires to be given to subjects in any proposed investigation, meeting at least the minimum requirements.[35] If the IRB determines that further information would add meaningful protection to the subjects,

it can require the additional information also be included in the consent process.

Generally the IRB must require the investigator to document informed consent.[37] There are, however, exceptions. If the IRB finds that a proposed investigation presents no more than minimal risks and involves no procedures for which informed consent would be required outside of the investigation, it can waive the requirement for a written consent form. The IRB can also determine if requirements have been met for a waiver under the emergency research regulations,[27] and can then waive the requirement.

The IRB must notify the investigator and the institution in writing of its decision to approve or disapprove a research proposal. Such notification is also required for proposals the IRB approves conditioned on modifications. When the IRB decides to disapprove a proposal, the written notification to the investigator must include a statement of the reasons for disapproval and provide the investigator an opportunity to respond to those reasons. As previously discussed, if a request under the emergency research regulations[27] is rejected, the IRB must inform the investigator and the sponsor in writing. That notice must also include the reasons for rejection.

The IRB must conduct continuing review of approved research at intervals appropriate to the risk presented by the investigation. However, the IRB must review all research activities at least once a year.[77] The IRB also has the authority to observe both the consent process and the research or to have a third party observe.

When an IRB approves of an exception to the informed consent requirements,[27] it must promptly provide the sponsor a copy of all of the information required under the public disclosure provisions of that section. In turn, the sponsor must provide copies of that information to the FDA.

4. § 56.110: Expedited Review Procedures for Certain Kinds of Research

The FDA has published a list of research categories that qualify for expedited review.[41,78] The IRB can use an expedited procedure to review any category of research found on the published list that presents no more than minimal risk. Expedited review can also be used for minor changes in previously approved research (although the annual review requirement still applies). Expedited reviews can be performed by the IRB chair or by any experienced reviewer selected by the chair. However, a proposed investigation can be disapproved only after full review.[39]

Any IRB that uses an expedited review must adopt a method of informing its members of proposals approved under the procedure. The FDA specifically reserves the right to restrict, suspend, or terminate an IRB's use of an expedited review procedure if the agency finds that full reviews are necessary to protect the rights or welfare of subjects.

5. § 56.111: Criteria for IRB Approval of Research

The IRB must make certain findings about a research proposal before it can be approved.[42] Sound research designs must be used to minimize the risks subjects are exposed to.[79] Whenever appropriate, the procedures used in the research should be those typically used on subjects outside of the research activity. The IRB must find that the risks to subjects by the research are reasonable in relation to subjects' anticipated benefits. The IRB can also consider the importance of the probable results of the research in balancing the findings. The IRB can consider only the therapies directly required by the research, not those that the subjects could receive outside the investigation. The IRB should not consider long-range effects of applying knowledge gained in the research. For example, the IRB should not consider the possible effects of the research on public policy.

The IRB must find that the selection of subjects is equitable. In making this determination, the IRB should take into account the research purpose and the setting in which it is to be carried out. The IRB should be aware of special problems that might be caused by the research, such as the involvement of vulnerable subject populations.

The IRB ensures that informed consent will be obtained from each subject and documented.[14] It ensures that the research protocol includes appropriate monitoring of the data collected to protect the safety of the subjects. Where appropriate, the protocol must make provisions for protecting the privacy of subjects and the confidentiality of the data. When the subject class might be vulnerable to coercion or undue influence, the IRB must find that the protocol provides safeguards to protect the rights and welfare of those subjects. The classes specifically contemplated by the regulation include (among others) the economically or educationally disadvantaged.

6. § 56.112: IRB Review by Institution

The IRB is subject to oversight by other authorities in the institution.[43] An IRB's favorable decision on a proposal can be disapproved by other institutional authorities. However, if an IRB issues a negative decision on a proposal, the regulations prohibit its decision from being overridden by other institutional authority.

7. § 56.113: Suspension or Termination of Research

An IRB has the authority to suspend or terminate approval of ongoing research that is not conducted in accord with the IRB's requirements or which has been associated with unexpected serious harm to subjects.[44] All suspensions and terminations should be promptly reported to the investigator, institutional officials, and the FDA, with a statement of the reasons for the decision.

8. § 56.114: Cooperative Research

To avoid duplication of effort, multi-institutional studies can be jointly reviewed, be reviewed by qualified IRBs, or by similar arrangements.[45] Although not specifically required by the regulation, the FDA has required that such arrangements be documented in writing.

9. § 56.115: Records and Reports

The IRB must prepare and maintain certain documents.[46] Copies of all research proposals presented for approval must be kept. Scientific evaluations, if any, which accompany the proposal must also be kept. Copies of the approved consent form and all progress reports presented by the investigator must be maintained.

Minutes of IRB meetings must be kept. Those minutes must show attendance, actions taken, votes on each action (including the number of members voting for, against, or abstaining), the basis for requiring changes or disapproving a proposal, and a written summary of the discussion and resolution of contested issues. Records of continuing review activities must be maintained, as must copies of all correspondence between the IRB and an investigator.

A list of IRB members—identified by name, degrees earned, the capacity represented, indications of experience (board certifications, licenses, and the like), and any employment or other relationship with the institution—must be kept. The IRB must maintain a copy of its required written procedures.[39] Statements of significant new findings provided to subjects as required[35] must be kept as well.

All required records must be retained for at least three years after completion of the research. The records must be accessible to the FDA for inspection and copying when requested. If an IRB refuses to allow FDA inspection, the FDA can refuse to consider any clinical investigation done at the institution when reviewing a premarket NDA.

6.3 Guidance for FDA Compliance Programs

The FDA publishes a *Compliance Program Guidance Manual* for all major enforcement programs. Those manuals define the relationship between headquarter divisions and the district offices that are generally responsible for conducting regulatory inspections. The manuals provide guidelines for how inspection assignments are made, the depth and scope of inspections to be performed, documentation and reporting requirements, inspection classification procedures, and enforcement actions. This section outlines the compliance program manuals and chapters that relate to clinical investigations. The chapters are available from the FDA's website.[80]

The FDA is split into centers, primarily by the type of commodities regulated. For example, the Center for Drug Evaluation and Research (CDER) is responsible for regulating drug products. The Center for Biologics Evaluation and Research (CBER) is responsible for biologics, including therapeutic biologics.[81]

The Office of Regulatory Affairs (ORA) is responsible for field operations, including inspection activities. ORA management is located at FDA headquarters. The head of the ORA has the same rank and authority as a center head. The FDA district offices that are located in major cities throughout the United States are part of the ORA.

Inspections of clinical investigators, sponsors (including monitors), CROs, and IRBs are typically conducted by district office personnel commonly known as *investigators*. Investigators are a special subsection of the FDA's Consumer Safety Officers (CSOs). (To avoid confusion with clinical investigators, district office investigators will be referred to as CSOs.) Headquarters personnel sometimes accompany CSOs on inspections to provide such staff with field experience and familiarity with inspection procedures and industry conditions and practices. Headquarters occasionally sends a representative who has a particular interest in an inspection or who has some special qualification needed for the inspection.[82] A CSO is the lead FDA employee responsible for an inspection.[8]

A. Compliance Program 7348.811: Clinical Investigators

FDA form 2438 contains the *Compliance Program Guidance Manual* information for clinical investigators.[48] The purpose of the compliance program is to ensure the quality and integrity of safety and efficacy data submitted to the FDA in support of a premarketing application (an NDA). The objective of the program is to obtain the compliance of clinical investigators with the FDA regulations and to evaluate through onsite inspections whether the clinical investigator records substantiate the data submitted to the FDA.

Before approving an NDA, FDA headquarters routinely issues an assignment to inspect the clinical investigators who provide the safety and efficacy data in support of the application. Terms commonly used to describe these inspections include *routine*, *directed*, and *for cause*. These

terms, particularly *directed* and *for cause*, are used loosely. However, *routine* generally means an inspection that is issued without any special reason (other than an FDA compliance program). Routine inspections are general in scope and depth and follow the program guidance manual. *Directed* inspections generally refer to inspections that focus on one particular aspect of the clinical investigation or its records. *For cause* inspections mean there is an *a priori* reason to believe that a violation has occurred, and the FDA inspects to determine whether the violation has occurred and, if so, to document it.

All inspection assignments are issued from headquarters, but any FDA field office can recommend to the appropriate center that a particular investigator be inspected. Inspections requested by field units are often issued as *for cause* inspections because the field unit has information that leads it to believe a violation has occurred. Any regulated individual has the right to ask what type of inspection the CSO is planning to conduct. CSOs are generally forthright in answering that question, but they are not obligated to divulge all of the information about why a given inspection may be *for cause*. In practice, a CSO may decline to characterize an inspection as *for cause*,[83] particularly when the CSO has reason to believe that the individual has repeatedly or deliberately violated FDA laws or regulations.[84]

Inspections of clinical investigators are typically made by appointment, but should be done within ten working days of initial contact. Refusing to allow an inspection or restricting the CSO's access to required records can constitute a *refusal to inspect* under the Food, Drug, and Cosmetic Act.[2] Such a refusal is a violation of law and can result in appropriate enforcement actions. Whether the investigator's actions constitute a refusal is determined by FDA headquarters in consultation with appropriate field personnel.

If a CSO discovers violations that in her judgment can affect data validity or endanger subjects, the CSO immediately notifies headquarters. Headquarters determines, based on information provided by the CSO, if such conditions exist and decides on appropriate actions. While that determination is being made, the CSO will continue the inspection.

Inspection procedures—including an inspection's scope and depth, materials to be inspected, and inspection documents—are covered in great detail in the guidance manual. Compliance with every regulation that applies to investigators and to investigator's relationships with subjects, sponsors (including monitors), and IRBs, must be documented. In an assignment request, headquarters attaches records and reports submitted to the sponsor by the investigator. The CSO compares those documents to on-site copies and other data or information located on site to verify that there are no inconsistencies. When an investigator discovers a possible violation, he documents it. A written summary of all violations is presented to the investigator at the close of the inspection. That document is commonly known as the *483*; officially, it is FDA Form 483–Inspectional Observations.

After the inspection, the CSO writes an official report—the establishment inspection report (EIR). All documentation of observed violations and all documents routinely collected (and specified in the manual) are attached to the EIR. The district office evaluates the EIR and determines its classification (see below). The headquarters, however, has the final authority to evaluate the EIR, so the EIR and all its attachments are forwarded to the appropriate (as identified in the compliance manual) headquarters office.

EIR classification refers to the FDA's evaluation of whether the inspectional observations warrant agency action and whether such actions are supported by the documented evidence. The EIR classifications are:

- **NAI**. No significant objectionable conditions or practices were found.
- **VAI**. Objectionable conditions or practices were found, but the FDA is not prepared to take or recommend any official action.
- **OAI**. Regulatory or administrative actions will be recommended.

After headquarters makes a classification, the center informs the district office and the investigator in writing of its determination. If the classification is NAI or VAI, the investigator is sent a letter stating that no violations were found or requesting voluntary corrections. An OAI classification generally requires a warning letter be issued to the investigators (see the later section on warning letters).

B. Compliance Program 7348.810: Sponsors

The *Compliance Program Manual* for sponsors, CROs, and monitors is found in FDA Form FDA 2438j.[51] The objective of the program is show whether an investigational product is safe and effective for its intended use. The purpose is to determine whether the drug sponsor ensures the validity of the data submitted by its clinical investigators and whether the sponsor, CROs, and monitors have complied with all applicable regulations.

This compliance program for sponsors is essentially the same as the one for clinical investigators in terms of intra-agency relationships and responsibilities, inspections, documentation, reporting, EIR evaluations, and follow-up. There are four differences. Under this compliance program, inspections:

- do not require prior notice,
- emphasize organizational structure and responsibility,
- determine if adverse events are reported properly, and
- determine if independent quality assurance audits follow internal protocols.

Inspections conducted under this program are initiated without prior notification. No reason is given for this difference, but under the Act, the FDA has no obligation to provide prior notice of inspection.[52] The FDA provides prior notice to investigators as a courtesy because the agency realizes that physicians may not always be available at a moment's notice and because it may take time to locate and gather the records a CSO needs to inspect (especially patient records). On the other hand, the sponsor is in the business of developing new drugs, and typically has full-time employees dedicated to that process, including employees dedicated to cataloging and storing records pertaining to clinical investigations. In recent years, however, the FDA has begun to adopt a policy of initiating inspections by appointment, including inspections under this compliance program.[85] Undue delay, however, in allowing the inspection or in providing access to appropriate documents and reports will, at a minimum, put the agency on alert and can constitute a *refusal to inspect*, which is a prohibited act.[2]

The sponsor's compliance program emphasizes determining and documenting the sponsor's or CRO's organizational structure and responsibilities. In particular, the CSO documents:

- the sponsor officials responsible for developing protocols, selecting investigators, analyzing statistical and investigational data, providing investigational supplies, monitoring investigator performance, and ensuring quality assurance;
- the party with the authority to review and approve study reports and data; and
- the individuals responsible for final adverse experience evaluations.

The third major difference between the sponsor and clinical investigator programs is that this program emphasizes determining whether the sponsor has complied with adverse experience reporting as required by the regulations.[29] For each *life-threatening* or *fatal adverse event*, the CSO verifies that the FDA was notified by telephone within seven calendar days of the event. For each *serious* or *unexpected adverse event*, the CSO determines if the FDA was notified in writing within 15 calendar days. The CSO must also determine if adverse events reported to the sponsor by the investigators were subsequently relayed to the FDA. The sponsor's method of reporting adverse events to investigators is documented, and copies of those notifications are attached to the EIR.

The fourth major difference in this compliance program concerns quality assurance units (QAUs). A QAU is a group within a sponsor's organization that is responsible for performing independent audits of the sponsor's or monitor's compliance with internal policies and procedures and with FDA regulations. The *Compliance Program Guidance Manual* recognizes that QAUs are not required by the regulations, but it states that many sponsors have such units. The manual requires the CSO to determine if the sponsor has such a unit. If it does, the CSO must determine if the QAU is independent in its routine monitoring or quality control functions. QAU results are not inspected by the CSO unless authorized to do so by FDA headquarters.

C. Compliance Program 7348.809: Institutional Review Boards

The *Compliance Program Guidance Manual for Institutional Review Boards* is found in FDA Form 2438.[54] The objective of the program is to provide information and guidance to improve IRB performance and to apply administrative sanctions when an IRB is found to be seriously out of compliance with the regulations.

The IRB compliance program is also substantially the same as that for clinical investigators, including provisions for appointments before inspection. One noteworthy difference is that this program specifies various types of inspections. *Surveillance inspections* are undefined, but include an *initial inspection* and a *subsequent inspection*. An initial inspection request comes from headquarters when it becomes aware of an IRB because the IRB has approved a clinical investigation regulated by the FDA.[86] *Follow-up inspections*, which result when an initial inspection was classified NAI or VAI, are also referred to as *surveillance inspections*. Such inspections are made five years after the initial inspection.

The program defines *directed inspections* as those assigned when headquarters receives information on questionable IRB practices. Directed inspections may be limited to one area of FDA concern or assigned to cover the entire compliance program.

6.4 FDA Inspection Procedures

Inspection procedures are based on statutory requirements.[52]

As previously discussed, inspections of investigators and IRBs are typically made by appointment. Inspections of sponsors are unannounced. On arriving at a site, a CSO provides the investigator or the chair of the IRB with her name and title (FDA Investigator) and presents duly-authorized inspection credentials.[87] Inspections of sponsors or monitors are initiated when a CSO arrives at the site and requests to speak to the most responsible person present (typically a CEO or corporate president). Thereafter, the sponsor procedures are the same as investigator or IRB inspection procedures. Before starting an inspection, the CSO must fill out and issue a notice of inspection (Form FDA-482: Notice of Inspection). The notice includes the name and title of the responsible parties and the CSO's signature.[53]

Because inspections of clinical investigators are made by appointment, all necessary documents and reports are usually compiled and waiting for CSO review. For IRB surveillance inspections, the CSO typically asks for a list of all study proposals received by the IRB during the past two to five years. The CSO then selects certain proposals and requests all relevant documentation, including:

- the protocols
- the approved consent forms
- all correspondence between the IRB and investigators
- meeting minutes
- a list of IRB members (present and historical, as appropriate)
- the IRB written procedures

For directed IRB inspections, the CSO may request all records pertinent to the FDA's *a priori* concerns or questions. For sponsor or monitor inspections, the CSO will specifically request the records he wants to review. The CSO then reviews and evaluates the records for compliance.

During the inspection, the CSO can request an informal conference with the responsible party to provide further records or answer questions. Also during the inspection, the CSO can offer the appropriate parties an opportunity to clear up misunderstandings or explain apparent violations. If there are conditions or practices, which in the opinion of the CSO are violations, the CSO will arrange for a closing discussion. At that closing meeting, the CSO will provide the responsible party with a Form FDA-483: Inspectional Observations, which summarizes the violations.[52] The CSO will allow the responsible party to respond to the points on the FDA-483. The CSO can, at his discretion, remove a point from the 483 if he finds the response acceptable.

6.5 Warning Letters to Clinical Investigators

As discussed, FDA headquarters can issue a warning letter to a clinical investigator after reviewing the EIR submitted by a CSO. The following section presents the analysis of FDA warning letters issued to clinical investigators from November 1996 through August 2002. This section describes those warning letters, presents the results of this analysis, and includes some comments.

A. FDA Warning Letters

Warning letters are issued by the appropriate headquarters unit when the FDA believes that significant violations of the Food, Drug, and Cosmetic Act[2] or its own regulations have been violated. Warning letters describe the violations (referencing the law or regulation) and usually give examples of objectionable conditions or practices. All warning letters should state that a written response is required within 15 business days of receipt.[88] Warning letters also state that failure to respond could result in official action against the investigator. Examples of possible official actions are typically given, and they include disqualification of the investigator. The warning letter usually provides specific items to be addressed in the response or specific questions to be answered.

B. Analysis of FDA Warning Letters from 1996 to 2002

Ninety-four warning letters received by clinical investigators between 1996 and 2002 were downloaded from the FDA's online "Freedom of Information Reading Room."[89] Four of those letters were rejected from the analysis because they contained no reference to specific laws or regulations.[90] During the period of the study, CDER issued 16 warning letters, CBER issued 35, and the Center for Devices and Radiologic Health (CDRH) issued 39. For each warning letter, the legal and regulatory citations were recorded. That data was compiled by the center (CDER, CBER, and CDRH) and by the statutory or regulatory section cited. The CDRH data is not presented here (except in Section 6.5.E, below, which comments on warning letters in general).

C. FDA's Apparent Trend Toward an Increased Use of Warning Letters

Beginning in 1998, the FDA seems to have become more active in enforcing the clinical-investigation regulations. On June 9, 1998, the Director of Scientific Investigations (CDER), David A. Lepay, M.D., Ph.D., publicly announced that his division would step up compliance surveillance.[55]

Figure 6.1 shows the number of warning letters issued by CDER and CBER from November 1996 through August 2002 (by year). The data show that, beginning in 2000, the FDA began issuing more warning letters. Keeping in mind that there can be a significant amount of time between inspection and issuance of a warning letter,[91] the data seem to support the increased commitment to clinical investigation surveillance announced by Dr. Lepay.

It is also interesting to note that CBER issued almost twice as many warning letters as CDER. During the period of the study, CBER issued 35 warning letters, and CDER issued 16. This is interesting because the surveillance of clinical investigations was, in September 2002, transferred from CBER to CDER.

D. Regulations Most Often Cited in Warning Letters

Figure 6.2 shows the regulation sections most often cited in the CDER and CBER warning letters. The x-axis showing regulatory sections, uses "62" to refer to Title 21 C.F.R. § 312.62: Investigator Recordkeeping and Retention; 60 to refer to Title 21 C.F.R. § 312.60: General Responsibilities of Investigators; and 66 to refer to Title 21 C.F.R. § 312.66: Assurance of IRB Review.

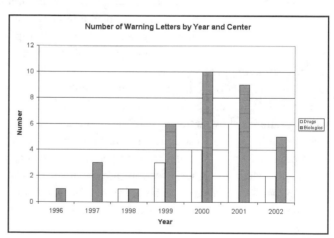

Figure 6.1 *The number of warning letters issued by Center for Drug Evaluation and Research (CDER) and Center for Biologics Evaluation and Research (CBER) from November 1996 through August 2002 (by year). The data show that, beginning in 2000, the FDA began issuing more warning letters. CBER issued almost twice as many warning letters as CDER: during the period of the study, CBER issued 35 warning letters, and CDER issued 16. About September 2002, the surveillance of clinical investigations was transferred from CBER to CDER.*

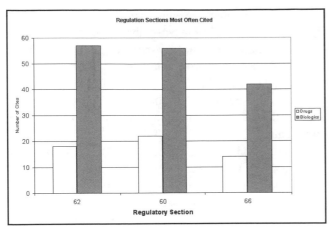

Figure 6.2 *The regulation sections most often cited in the Center for Drug Evaluation and Research (CDER) and Center for Biologics Evaluation and Research (CBER) warning letters between November 1996 and August 2002. The x-axis showing regulatory sections, uses "62" to refer to Title 21 C.F.R. § 312.62: Investigator Recordkeeping and Retention; "60" to refer to Title 21 C.F.R. § 312.60: General Responsibilities of Investigators; and "66" to refer to Title 21 C.F.R. § 312.66: Assurance of IRB Review.*

Because of the way the warning letters were written, it was not possible to obtain accurate or meaningful data on references to subsections of a regulation. The letters typically cite a major regulatory section such as 21 C.F.R. § 312.62. Sometimes subsections are cited, but often they are not. After the citation, the warning letter usually gives specific examples of objectionable practices. Careful reading of the examples showed that they often fit into a subsection that was not cited. A few times, the facts asserted by the FDA did not seem to fit in the regulatory section cited at all. Therefore, when the general sections are discussed below, the comments are based on general impressions gained by reading the examples of objectionable practices, and not on hard data.

Section 312.62[24] requires the investigator to keep complete and accurate records of the use of a study article and the disposition of unused supplies, as well as case histories for all subjects. It also requires that the records be retained and made available for FDA inspection for two years after the article is approved for marketing or the clinical investigation is discontinued. CDER cited this section 18 times, whereas CBER cited it 57 times.

Based on the examples given, there were numerous violations regarding drug inventories and case histories. Most of the violations were for incomplete recordkeeping or inconsistencies found by the CSO. There were numer-

ous times when C.F.R.'s referenced in the records conflicted with source documents, such as the patient progress notes or laboratory reports. There were some instances in which the investigator failed to retain the required records. Occasionally, an investigator failed to provide records to the FDA when requested to do so.

Section 312.60[13] requires an investigator to comply with all regulations covering clinical investigations, to protect the rights and welfare of subjects (particularly to obtain adequate informed consent under 21 C.F.R. Part 50), and to control the use of the investigational drug. CDER cited violations to this section 22 times, and CBER cited it 56 times. There were numerous alleged violations of the regulations in general, some instances of failing to protect subjects (most often having to do with technical violations of the informed consent regulations), and some instances of failure to control the use of the drugs.

Section 312.66[11] requires an investigator to submit to initial and continuing review of an IRB. Violations to this section were cited 14 times by CDER and 42 times by CBER. There were numerous alleged violations for failing to submit to continuing review that consisted of either incomplete or inaccurate reports to the IRB. Only a few investigators failed to obtain initial IRB review and approval.

E. Comments on Warning Letters

Any warning letter can be a precursor to an FDA administrative, regulatory, or legal action. However, a proper response can often dispose of the matter. Therefore, every effort should be made to respond to a warning letter within 15 business days of receipt. If an investigator believes she cannot meet that time frame, the investigator should telephone the agency contact person provided in the letter and request an extension. Where the warning letter provides specific topics to be addressed, the response should be limited to those items. If the warning letter presents specific questions to be answered, the response must address those questions.

Some warning letters contain phrases or assertions of fact that indicate the FDA is particularly concerned about the investigator's conduct and often indicate that the FDA is predisposed towards taking further official action. Of all of the warning letters included in this analysis, only 10 percent contained one or more of these statements (three warning letters each for CDER, CBER, and CDRH). Those phrases almost always are associated with findings of seriously objectionable practices. The remainder of this chapter will describe those phrases or assertions of fact and provide examples. Any warning letter that contains any one or combination of the following phrases should be taken very seriously.

1. Repeated or deliberate violations

As previously discussed,[84] repeated or deliberate violations are not only specific grounds for disqualification,[49] they are also criteria traditionally used by the FDA in considering criminal prosecution.[50]

A CDER warning letter stated, "Based on evaluation of the information obtained during the inspection, we have determined that you have repeatedly or deliberately violated regulations governing the proper conduct of clinical studies involving investigational new drugs." Among other violations, the investigator allegedly altered pulmonary function test results, resulting in the inclusion of three subjects who would otherwise have been excluded from the study.[56]

A CBER warning letter reads in part, "On the basis of the above, we believe that you have repeatedly and deliberately failed to comply with the cited regulations and we propose that you be disqualified as a clinical investigator." Among other things, the investigator allegedly did not follow IRB- and sponsor-approved eligibility criteria when enrolling subjects, and thereby put the subjects at undue risk.[57]

2. Investigator disqualification statements and Part 16 hearing offers

As discussed above, every warning letter should require a response within 15 days and may state that the investigator may be disqualified should he fail to do so. However, very few warning letters directly state that the investigator may be disqualified for specific violations or offer a Part 16 hearing.[92]

A CDER warning letter stated, "If, in the future, you do not strictly abide by the 1991 Agreement signed by you, we may consider steps that will lead to your disqualification." The instant inspection (1999) found that the investigator continued to make the violations found in a previous inspection, even though the investigator signed a consent agreement not to repeat those violations.[58]

A CBER warning letter proposed that the clinical investigator be disqualified and offered a consent agreement to dispose of the matter, but then stated, "If we cannot come to terms on an agreement, or if your written or oral responses to our allegations are unsatisfactory, you will be offered a regulatory hearing before the Food and Drug Administration, pursuant to Part 16 and section 312.70 of the regulations." The warning letter alleged that the investigator failed to protect the safety and welfare of the subjects by violating the eligibility criteria for enrolling subjects. The warning letter stated that the IRB and the sponsor provided the eligibility criteria to protect the subjects.[59]

3. Consent agreement offers

As used in warning letters, a consent agreement appears to be a written agreement that the investigator will not repeat violations in the future and agrees to certain restrictions imposed by the FDA or will not participate in future clinical investigations. Any consent agreement offered by the FDA should be carefully considered, as the offer is usually accompanied by a specific threat of a disqualification proceeding.

A CDER warning letter alleged that the investigator repeatedly or deliberately violated regulations by submitting false information to the FDA or to the sponsor. The last paragraph of the letter states, "If you do not wish to submit a corrective action plan, you may wish to consider entering into a consent agreement with the agency regarding your future use of investigational new drugs."[60]

A CBER warning letter alleged repeated and deliberate violations and proposed that the investigator be disqualified but offered a consent agreement to dispose of the matter. The letter states, "If you agree with our findings or do not wish to avail yourself of the opportunity for an informal conference and do not wish to make a reply to our findings, you may consider entering into a consent agreement with the FDA regarding your future eligibility to receive investigational drugs. Such an agreement would terminate further administrative proceedings."[61]

4. Cease and desist orders and requests

There does not appear to be any specific statutory or regulatory authority for the FDA to issue or enforce a cease and desist order to a clinical investigator.[93] Even so, a few warning letters include such an order. (Some warning letters clearly make it an order; others present it in terms of a request.) If such an order is ignored, it seems probable that the FDA will consider such an action as a repeated and deliberate violation of the regulations or statutory law.

A CBER warning letter stated, "You should immediately cease administering the investigational [redacted] to human subjects outside of sponsor-approved protocols, and immediately discontinue use of [redacted] until the clinical hold issues are satisfactorily resolved."[94] The investigator allegedly violated a clinical hold by continuing to treat subjects after being notified by the sponsor to stop. The warning letter also alleged that the investigator diverted an investigational article for use outside of a sponsor-approved study.[62]

A CDRH warning letter stated, "You may not use your laser beyond the conditions of approval of your IDE. Therefore, you must immediately stop clinical use of your excimer laser upon receipt of this letter." The letter alleged that the investigator failed to abide by his conditionally approved investigational device exemption (IDE) in that he failed to provide the FDA with requested information (not specified), initiated the investigation including treatment of subjects without IRB approval, and refused FDA inspectors access to investigational records.[63]

Endnotes

1. "Kefauver–Harris drug amendments of 1962." (1962). *Congressional Record.* 87th Cong., 2d sess. Washington DC: U.S. Government Printing Office.

2. "Food, Drug, and Cosmetic Act of 1938 (FDCA)." (June 25, 1938). *Congressional Record.* 75th Cong. 3rd sess. Public Law 75-717. Washington DC: U.S. Government Printing Office. Also 21 U.S.C. 301–397.

3. "Definitions." (2002). 21 U.S.C. § 321(g).

4. Hutt, P.B. and Merrill, R.A. (July 1991) *Food and Drug Law: Cases and Materials,* 2nd ed. St. Paul, MN: Foundation Press. p. 477.

5. "New drugs: necessity of effective approval of application." (2003). 21 U.S.C. § 355(a).

6. "New drugs: filing application; contents." (2003). 21 U.S.C. § 355(b).

7. "New drugs: exemptions of drugs for research; discretionary and mandatory conditions." (2002). 21 U.S.C. §355(i), pp. 51–52.

8. "Clinical Investigators: Implementation." (October 1997), *Compliance Program Guidance Manual.* 7348.811. Part II. p. 1–3.

9. "Investigational new drug application." (2003). 21 C.F.R. Part 312.

10. "Investigational new drug application: definition and interpretations." (2003). 21 C.F.R.'312.3(b) pp. 51–52.

11. "Investigational new drug application: assurance of IRB review." (2003). 21 C.F.R. '312.66. p. 78.

12. "Institutional review boards." (2003). 21 C.F.R. Part 56.

13. "Investigational new drug application: general responsibilities of investigators." (2003). 21 C.F.R. '312.60. p. 77.

14. "Protection of human subjects." (2003). 21 C.F.R. Part 50.

15. "Investigational new drug application: Selecting investigators and monitors." (2003). 21 C.F.R. § 312.53 (Subpart D). p. 74.

16. "Investigational new drug application: review of ongoing investigations." (2003). 21 C.F.R. §§ 312.56(a) and (d) and § 312.56.6(b)(2). pp. 75–76.

17. "Investigational new drug application: transfer of obligations to a contract research organization." (2003). 21 C.F.R. § 312.52(b). pp. 73–74.

18. "Investigational new drug application: inspection of investigator's records and reports." (2003). 21 C.F.R. § 312.68. p. 78.

19. "Investigational new drug application: inspection of investigator's records and reports." (2003). 21 C.F.R. § 312.58. pp. 76–77.

20. "Institutional review boards: IRB records." (2003). 21 C.F.R. § 56.115(b). pp. 305–306.

21. *Fed. Reg.* Vol. 38, (February 13, 1973). p. 4319.

22. "Investigational device exemptions." (2003). 21 C.F.R. Part 812.

23. "Financial disclosure by clinical investigators." (2003). 21 C.F.R. Part 54.

24. "Investigational new drug applications: investigator recordkeeping and record retention." (2003). 21 C.F.R. § 312.62 p. 77).

25. "Comprehensive drug abuse prevention and control act of 1970: controlled substances act." (1970). *Congressional Record.* 91st Cong., 2d sess. Washington, DC: U.S. Government Printing Office. Also at 21 U.S.C. 801. (2003).

26. "Investigational new drug application: phases of an investigation." (2003). 21 C.F.R. § 312.21. pp. 53–54.

27. "Protection of human subjects: exception from informed consent requirements for emergency research." (2003). 21 C.F.R. § 50.24(a). pp. 290–291.

28. "IND content and format: investigator's brochure." (2003). 21 C.F.R. § 312.23(a)(5). p. 56.

29. "Investigational new drug applications: IND safety reports." (2003). 21 C.F.R. § 312.32. pp. 61–63.

30. "Investigational new drug applications: disposition of unused supply of investigational drug." (2003). 21 C.F.R. § 312.59. p. 77.

31. "Investigational new drug applications: annual reports." (2003). 21 C.F.R. § 312.33. p. 63.

32. "Bioavailability and bioequivalence requirements: retention of bioavailability samples." (2003). 21 C.F.R. § 320.38. pp. 192–193.

33. "Bioavailability and bioequivalence requirements: retention of bioequivalence samples." (2003). 21 C.F.R. § 320.63. p. 193.

34. "Financial disclosure by clinical investigators: purpose." (2003). 21 C.F.R. § 54.1. p. 295.

35. "Protection of human subjects: elements of informed consent." (2003). 21 C.F.R. § 54.25. pp. 291–292.

36. "Institutional review boards: IRB review of research." (2003). 21 C.F.R. § 56.109(c). p. 303.

37. "Protection of human subjects: documentation of informed consent." (2003). 21 C.F.R. § 50.27. pp. 292–293.

38. "Institutional review boards: IRB membership." (2003). 21 C.F.R. § 56.107. p. 302.

39. "Institutional review boards: IRB functions and operations." (2003). 21 C.F.R. § 56.108. pp. 302–303.

40. "Institutional review boards: expedited review procedures for certain kinds of research involving no more than minimal risk and for minor changes in approved research." (2003). 21 C.F.R. § 56.110. p. 304.

41. "Institutional review board; research categories list; expedited review procedure." (1998). Fed. Reg. 63(216). Doc. 98-29748. pp. 60353–60356.

42. "Institutional review boards: criteria for IRB approval of research." (2003). 21 C.F.R. § 56.111. pp. 304–305.

43. "Institutional review boards: review by institution." (2003). 21 C.F.R. § 56.112. p. 305.

44. "Institutional review boards: suspension or termination of IRB approval of research." (2003). 21 C.F.R. § 56.113. p. 305.

45. "Institutional review boards: cooperative research." (2003). 21 C.F.R. § 56.114. p. 305.

46. "Institutional review boards: IRB records." (2003). 21 C.F.R. § 56.115. pp. 305–306).

47. Personal experience as a former Bioresearch Monitoring Specialist. (1993–1997). FDA Chicago District Office.

48. "Bioresearch monitoring: clinical investigators." (September 2, 1998). Compliance Program Guidance Manual for FDA Staff. Ch. 48. Prog. 7348.811. Form 2438.

49. "Investigational new drug application: disqualification of a clinical investigator." (2003). 21 C.F.R. § 312.70(a). pp. 78–79.

50. Fine, S.D. (1976) "The Philosophy of Enforcement, Food Drug Cosmet. Law J. 31(324).

51. "Bioresearch monitoring: sponsors, contract research organizations, and monitors." (February 23, 2001). Compliance Program Guidance Manual for FDA Staff. Ch. 48. Prog. 7348.810. Form 2438j.

52. "Inspection: right of agents to enter; scope of inspection; notice; promptness; exclusions." (2002). 21 U.S.C. § 374(a) and (b).

53. "Inspection procedures: pre-inspection procedures." and "Notice of inspection." (2002). Investigations Operations Manual. § 510 and '511.

54. "Bioresearch monitoring: institutional review boards." (August 18, 1994). Compliance Program Guidance Manual for FDA Staff. Ch. 48. Prog. 7348.809. Form 2438.

55. D.A. Lepay. (June 22, 1998). GCP Compliance: FDA Expectations and Recent Findings, Rockville, MD: CDER. Available at www.fda.gov/cder.

56. J.L. Rhoads. (June 11, 2002). Warning letter to Leonard J. Caputo, M.D. Rockville, MD: CDER.

57. J.C. Simmons. (November 19, 1996). Warning letter to Huibert Vriesendorp, M.D. Rockville, MD: CBER.

58. D.A. Lepay. (March 29, 2000). Warning letter to Cal K. Cohn, M.D. Rockville, MD: CDER.

59. J.C. Simmons. (November 19, 1996). Warning letter to Huibert Vriesendorp, M.D. Rockville, MD: CBER.

60. J.L Rhoads. (June 11, 2002). Warning letter to Leonard J. Caputo, M.D. Rockville, MD: CDER.

61. J.C. Simmons. (November 19, 1996). Warning letter to Huibert Vriesendorp, M.D. Rockville, MD: CBER.

62. S.A. Masiello. (April 19, 2000). Warning letter to N. Franklin Adkinson, Jr., M.D. Rockville, MD: CBER.

63. L.J. Gill. (June 11, 1997). Warning letter to Mark Kislinger, M.D., Ph.D. Rockville, MD: CDRH.

64. Form FDA 1572 (1/03) Statement of Investigator. This form must be submitted by the investigator before beginning any clinical investigation. (Previous versions of the form are obsolete.) The form includes a description of the party or parties who will conduct the study and where the study will be done. The form commits the investigator to performing the investigation in accordance with FDA regulations including informed consent and IRB review and approval.

65. Many clinical investigations are double-blind, which means the investigator does not know which patients receive the drug being studied and which receive controls until after the study is complete or until after a subject is dropped from the study and it becomes necessary for that subject's safety or welfare to determine which treatment was administered.

66. There are four parts to a proper FDA request: the request must be made by an FDA employee; who presents the investigator with an FDA Form 482, Notice of Inspection; who provides FDA credentials as identification; and who makes such a request at a reasonable time and in a reasonable manner.

67. As a practical matter, investigators routinely provide the names of study subjects to FDA inspectors because patient medical records, which are required by 21 C.F.R. § 312.62,24, are found in hospital files identified by the patient name. Moreover, unless some tedious, burdensome, and perhaps unworkable system of blinding ensures that each patient's medical record relates to the given subject, there is no way for the FDA representative to know which patient records relate to which subject.

68. How extensive a protocol must be depends on whether the clinical trial is a Phase 1, 2, or 3 study. Clinical investigation phases are described in 21 C.F.R. § 312.21.26 The sponsor usually supplies the protocol to the investigator, primarily because almost all clinical trials (especially Phase 2 and 3) are multicenter trials, and for statistical and other reasons, the protocol must be uniform among the centers. The investigator, nevertheless, must obtain IRB approval of the protocol before commencing the investigation.

69. The investigator's brochure contains a brief description of the drug (including the structural formula, if known), a summary of the pharmacological and toxicological effects of the drug in animals and humans, a summary of the pharmacokinetics and biological disposition of the drug in animals and humans, a summary of the information on safety and efficacy in humans obtained from prior clinical studies, a description of the possible risks and side effects to be anticipated on the basis of earlier experience with the drug or related drugs, and the precautions or special patient monitoring to be done as part of the investigational use of the drug.

70. The regulations seem to provide specifically for the option of sending records to the FDA in lieu of an FDA site visit. That option, however, appears to be only at FDA discretion. Perhaps the most frequent use of the inspection provision has to do with inspecting clinical investigators. Before approving an NDA, the FDA will inspect clinical investigators involved in the study. The FDA will request certain records from the sponsor that were submitted it by investigators (especially the case report forms). Those records requested are supplied to the relevant FDA field office so that they can be compared to the onsite records as part of the inspection.

71. Most clinical investigations are conducted at large medical centers, which are usually part of a university.

72. The regulations specifically state that the subject must be informed that the FDA may inspect patient records. The FDA has interpreted this section to mean that consents include a statement disclosing that the sponsor may inspect subject records.

73. The FDA generally considers it appropriate for the investigator to serve as the contact for an injury report or for questions about the research, but discourages the investigator from being the contact about a subject's rights. The FDA has faulted clinical investigators for using consent forms that identify the investigator as the contact regarding the subject's rights. Appropriate contacts about a subject's rights include the chair of the IRB, a hospital minister, a social worker employed by the hospital, or the patient's rights representative at the hospital. FDA would probably deem it inappropriate to identify the hospital risk manager or other corporate officials—who have a duty to protect the corporation—as the contact regarding a subject's rights.

74. The form may be read to the subject or to the subject's representative, but the investigator must provide an opportunity for the subject or the representative to read the form before signing.

75. For example, the investigator may include in an application for continuing approval that no material changes have been made, but the IRB may determine that it needs verification from the sponsor that such is the case. Sometimes the study may be partially or wholly conducted at a location remote from the institution. In those cases, the IRB may determine it is necessary to interview sub-investigators, the study coordinator, or subjects to ensure that no material changes have been made.

76. The IRB can impose its own requirements on an investigator before approving a research plan, or it might make approval conditional on additional requirements that are not necessarily required by the FDA.

77. The FDA interprets this section to mean that all IRBs must convene meetings at least annually. Moreover, if an inspection of an IRB reveals that it has not continued ongoing reviews of any investigation for more than a year, the FDA considers the IRB to be in violation of this section and will take appropriate action.

78. A complete and current list of research categories is located in the *Federal Register*. Vol. 63, No. 216 (November 9, 1998). See also note 41.

79. The FDA has interpreted § 56.11040 to require IRBs to make specific findings or consider whether the proposed protocols are scientifically sound; that is, whether they will provide legitimate results, if properly performed, and offer the possibility of therapeutic gain.

80. Compliance Manual chapters can be found on the FDA's web site at www.fda.gov/ora/cpgm/default.htm#bimo.

81. The responsibility for oversight of clinical investigations has passed back and forth between the Center for Drug Evaluation and Research (CDER) to the Center for Biologics Evaluation and Research (CBER). Throughout the 1990s, CBER had that responsibility; before that, CDER was responsible. During the last months of 2002, the obligation for oversight of clinical trials returned to CDER.

82. District-office investigators sometimes train health officials of foreign governments. Representatives of South Korea, Spain, India, and Greece have all received such training. See also note 47.

83. Perhaps reflecting the FDA's reluctance to characterize inspections as *for cause*, the IRB compliance program manual defines a *directed* inspection of an IRB as one which may issue, "...when the assigning Center receives information that calls into question the IRB's practices."[48]

84. Clinical investigators who deliberately or repeatedly violate FDA regulations can be disqualified. See note 49. Criteria that the FDA traditionally uses in determining if a criminal prosecution is warranted include violations ordinarily shown to be continuing in nature and those violations that are deliberate attempts to circumvent FDA laws and regulations. Examples of deliberate attempts to circumvent the law include submission of false data and falsification of records. See note 50.

85. The FDA's *Investigations Operations Manual* (at § 510) provides guidance to CSOs on when appointments can be used to initiate inspection. See also note 53.

86. Current FDA laws and regulations do not require IRBs to register with the FDA. The FDA becomes aware of an IRB when a sponsor reports to the agency that an IRB has approved or disapproved a sponsored study or when an investigator declares he will conduct a study under the authority of a specified IRB.

87. Credentials are signed by the FDA commissioner. CSOs are prohibited from allowing their credentials to be copied or reproduced in any way. Another problem that sometimes comes up during inspections is the presence or absence of a badge. Some district offices have traditionally provided badges (like those worn by police officers) to CSOs. Badges are not official and are not required. They are useful to CSOs as quick identification in emergency situations because they can be penned on an outside garment. CSOs can be called to serve in emergency situations (sometimes during martial law), such as natural disaster relief including hurricanes. CSOs commonly inspect drug warehouses after hurricanes to make sure the drugs have not been damaged. Where such damage has occurred, the CSO is responsible for initiating proper procedures to ensure the product does not get into distribution.

88. The FDA usually uses the U.S. Postal Service certified, return receipt requested service to document when a warning letter was received. However, other delivery services that verify receipt have been used.

89. The FDA's Freedom of Information (FOI) Reading Room is located at www.fda.gov/foi/warning.htm. There may be some warning letters that were issued

during the timeframe of this study that were not available through the FOI Reading Room, obtained through personal communication with another attorney involved in private litigation.

90. Three letters issued by Center for Devices and Radiologic Health (CDRH) redacted all citations to law and regulation. One letter issued by the Center for Veterinary Medicine did not cite law or regulation.

91. My review found at least one warning letter that was sent out two years after the inspection was completed. Typically, warning letters were sent out about four months to one year after the inspection.

92. Title 21 C.F.R. Part 16: "Regulatory Hearing Before the Food and Drug Administration," as it applies to investigators, is a hearing to determine if the investigator should be disqualified from participating in clinical investigations. The investigator has the right to representation, but formal rules of evidence do not apply. See also note 49.

93. Title 21 C.F.R. § 312.42: "Clinical Holds and Request for Modification" states that the FDA can order a sponsor to delay initiation of a clinical investigation or suspend one that is ongoing.

94. Apparently, the FDA issued a clinical hold in this case, directing the sponsor to suspend the investigator.

Chapter 7

The Protection of Subjects in Clinical Research

Sondra Wacker CIM, Gopi Doctor Ahuja, MPH and David C. Clark, Ph.D.

7.1 The Safety Net: The Web of Responsibilities That Minimizes Human Subjects' Risks

All clinical trials have one common factor—human subjects. Protecting their rights should be the first priority of all those involved, including investigators, sponsors, institutional review boards, compliance offices, and anyone that may be directly or indirectly responsible for the study. Before the establishment of rules, laws, and regulations that govern medical research, human subjects' rights were not a moving consideration. Gaining knowledge for the greater good took precedence over individuals and small groups. Vulnerable populations (i.e., the poor, the uneducated, the mentally ill, prisoners, children, and pregnant women) were often exploit-

ed by researchers. Vulnerable subjects are sometimes easy to deceive and exploit for the ostensibly altruistic motive of maximizing study sizes and statistical power. The majority of these people were good, honest people who credulously put their trust and lives in the hands of medical professionals.

It is not ethically defensible to preferentially risk subjects' health and welfare for the "good of science" without their full understanding and voluntary consent—and excessive risk is never defensible. Since some subjects do not have the education and political power to speak for themselves, it is the responsibility of the medical and research professionals—clinicians and administrators alike—to minimize risk, and advocate for and educate the subjects.

7.2 The Beginning of Evolution of Ethical Principles of Clinical Research

Although not the first example of harmful research on unwilling subjects, the history of the development of formal ethical principles of research with humans can be traced back to World War II. Physicians in Nazi Germany performed "medical experiments" on thousands of concentration camp prisoners. These included experiments to determine how long humans would survive in freezing water and high altitudes, injecting people with viruses, and forcing them to ingest poison. While German physicians argued that the experiments were medically justified, the Nuremberg Military Tribunal declared them to be "crimes against humanity." In December 1946, the War Crimes Tribunal at Nuremberg indicted 20 physicians and three administrators for their participation in these so called "medical experiments." The Tribunal found that the defendants had corrupted the ethics of the medical and scientific professions and repeatedly and deliberately violated the rights of the subjects. Sixteen of the 23 were found guilty and imprisoned and seven were put to death.

Professional ethics are supposed to guide a physician's professionalism and conduct. The principles of medical ethics are inherent in the Oath of Hippocrates and the Oath of Maimonides, among numerous other writings through the

95

ages.[1] The concept of "human research ethics," however, did not emerge until the last 60 to 70 years. Clinical research is "hybrid"—part real medical care and part research activity. Historically, the custodians of medical research have failed, time and again, to uphold the ethical standards laid down by Hippocrates to "keep them from harm and injustice."[1] From 1932, the beginning of the Tuskegee syphilis study, to the modern-day studies such as the Johns Hopkins hexamethonium study incident, human subjects' rights have been repeatedly violated. There has been a multitude of outcries against unethical human research, but there was never any general agreement about what fundamental principles regulated human research until after World War II and the "medical experiments" carried out by the Nazis in the concentration camps. In 1947, the Nuremberg Code of Ethics (see Table 7.1) was the first set of principles developed in response to the inhumane medical experiments conducted by 23 German physicians and administrators during World War II.[1] The Nuremberg Code outlines the ten directives for human experimentation, and is the foundation for all current ethical standards in research. It is also the basis for what has evolved into today's medical research laws and regulations, and the governing bodies (see Table 7.2). The first item in the Nuremberg Code emphasizes obtaining informed consent as a primary responsibility of the researcher:

> The voluntary consent of the human subject is absolutely essential. This means that the person involved should have legal capacity to give consent; should be so situated as to be able to exercise free power of choice, without the intervention of any element of force, fraud, deceit, duress, over-reaching, or other ulterior form of constraint or coercion; and should have sufficient knowledge and comprehension of the elements of the subject matter involved as to enable him to make an understanding and enlightened decision. This latter element requires that before the acceptance of an affirmative decision by the experimental subject there should be made known to him the nature, duration, and purpose of the experiment; the method and means by which it is to be conducted; all inconveniences and hazards reasonable to be expected; and the effects upon his health or person which may possibly come from his participation in the experiment.
>
> The duty and responsibility for ascertaining the quality of the consent rests upon each individual who initiates, directs or engages in the experiment. It is a personal duty and responsibility which may not be delegated to another with impunity.

Table 7.1
The Ten Directives of the Nuremberg Code

1. The voluntary consent of the human subject is absolutely essential.
2. The experiment should be such as to yield fruitful results for the good of society, unprocurable by other methods or means of study, and not random and unnecessary in nature.
3. The experiment should be so designed and based on the results of animal experimentation and a knowledge of the natural history of the disease or other problem under study that the anticipated results will justify the performance of the experiment.
4. The experiment should be so conducted as to avoid all unnecessary physical and mental suffering and injury.
5. No experiment should be conducted where there is an *a priori* reason to believe that death or disabling injury will occur.
6. The degree of risk to be taken should never exceed that determined by the humanitarian importance of the problem to be solved by the experiment.
7. Proper preparations should be made and adequate facilities provided to protect the experimental subject against even remote possibilities of injury, disability, or death.
8. The experiment should be conducted only by scientifically qualified persons. The highest degree of skill and care should be required.
9. The human subject should be at liberty to withdraw at any time.
10. During the course of the experiment the scientist in charge must be prepared to terminate the experiment at any stage, if he has probable cause to believe, in the exercise of the good faith, superior skill and careful judgment required of him that a continuation of the experiment is likely to result in injury, disability, or death to the experimental subject.

Table 7.2
Timeline: Ethics, Laws, and Regulations

~ 400 B.C.	Hippocrates
1798	U.S. Public Health Service (PHS)
1862	Division of Chemistry (preceding department of FDA)
1901-1927	Bureau of Chemistry (preceding department of FDA)
1927-1930	Food, Drug and Insecticide Administration
1906	Food and Drug Administration (FDA)
1887	Laboratory of Hygiene (preceding agency for NIH)
1930	National Institutes of Health (NIH)
1906	Center for Drug Evaluation and Research (CDER)
1947	Nuremberg Code
1948	Declaration of Human Rights
1953	Department of Health and Human Services (DHHS)
1964	Declaration of Helsinki
1972	Office for Protection from Research Risks (OPRR) → 2000 Office of Human Research Protections (OHRP)
1979	Belmont Report
1987	IND Regulations (21 C.F.R. 312)
1991	Common Rule (45 C.F.R. 46)
1991	Office of Human Subjects Research (OHSR)

Some of these are subdivisions of a larger body of regulations:
FDA → CDER → IND Regulations
DHHS → PHS → NIH → OHSR

7.3 Other Violations of the Rights of Human Subjects and the Ethical Principles Brought Forth

A. Tuskegee Syphilis Study: 1932–1972

In 1964, the World Medical Association adopted the Declaration of Helsinki to guide researchers in the ethical conduct of medical research. This document has been revised several times since it was adopted. These guidelines reinforced the importance of informed consent, outlined by the Nuremberg Code and added a provision to allow for the consent process to be performed with a legal guardian for people unable to provide consent for themselves.

At the same time this history of medical research ethics was unfolding internationally, a heinous medical experiment, the Tuskegee syphilis study, was being conducted in the United States by the U.S. Public Health Service. The purpose of the research which began in the 1930s, was to study the natural history of untreated syphilis. More than 400 poor, uneducated, African-American men were recruited to participate in this study without informed consent. Although arsenic and bismuth were available treatments at the time the study began,[2] the subjects were deceived during the study, being told that some study tests were "special free treatment." During the course of the study, the researchers learned that the mortality rate was twice as high in subjects with syphilis compared to controls without the disease. Additionally, in 1947, penicillin became a standard effective treatment for syphilis, but still the study continued with subjects never being told of or given the available treatment.

Reports of the Tuskegee syphilis study began appearing in the media in 1972. Overwhelming and justified public outrage resulted in federal action to compensate for these egregious ethical breaches and to prevent them from recurring. The National Commission for Protection of Human Subjects of Biomedical and Behavioral Research was established in 1974 to identify basic ethical principles to guide all research with humans. The Commission's work was documented in *The Belmont Report: Ethical Principles and Guidelines for the Protection of Human Subjects*. This report presented the three principles that guide the work of modern researchers and became the foundation for federal regulations governing research with humans: respect for persons, beneficence, and justice.

The first of these three principles reflects the Nuremberg Code's emphasis on informed consent—that is, respect for the research participant means treating her as an autonomous agent. The Belmont Report defines "autonomous agent" as "an individual capable of deliberation." This means that the informed consent process is needed so that potential participants are given all the information they need to determine whether participating in the study is in their best interest. The principle of respect also means that researchers conducting research with a "vulnerable" population (e.g., children, people who are cognitively impaired) should ensure that extra provisions are made to protect those potential participants with diminished autonomy. Additionally, the principle of respect includes the concept that the consent process must be completed with no pressure or coercion from the researcher for the potential subject to participate.

The principle of beneficence refers to the need to ensure that all aspects of the study must be designed to obtain the desired knowledge in a way that maximizes benefits and minimizes risks to participants. This also means that a risk/benefit analysis must be performed on every proposed study. In determining if this ratio is ethical, consideration must be given to the impact on the participants and on society.

The principle of justice refers to the fairness or equity involved throughout the selection of the research participants. The point is to ensure that the risks or benefits incurred by research participants are not unfairly concentrated in one portion of the population.

B. Radiation Experiments: 1940s–1950s

Testing radiation and radioactive treatments has been commonplace since the 1940s. One such study took place at the State Residential School in Fernald, Massachusetts, in the 1950s. The investigators were gathering information about metabolism and absorption of iron and calcium.[3] Seventeen mentally retarded boys were fed a breakfast cereal that contained a radioactive iron tracer, and 45 were fed milk with radioactive calcium.[3] The children were told that they were joining a "science club" that entitled them to extra portions of milk, occasional dinners out, and trips to baseball games and the beach.[4] A letter of consent to the parents misleadingly stated that "blood samples are taken after one test meal which consists of a special breakfast meal containing a certain amount of calcium."[4] Proper consents were not obtained prior to enrollment, and parents were not aware of the potential risks to their children. In 1994, a review study concluded that the radiation caused no medical harm to the subjects in the Fernald study, but clearly, their civil rights and their right to give informed consent had been violated.[4]

7.4 Violations of the Rights of Human Subjects: Drug Studies
A. Thalidomide Use: 1956–1961

Among the incidents that led to the emergence of U.S. laws that address drug safety, drug efficacy, informed consent, and systematic reporting of adverse events was a major study involving the use of thalidomide. In many European countries, pregnant women used thalidomide to treat nausea from 1956 to 1961.[5] In 1960, an application to market thalidomide was rejected by the U.S. Food and Drug Administration (FDA), due to insufficient toxicity studies, and, thus, a dearth of data related to absorption, distribution, metabolism, and excretion.[1,6] The following year, data linking thalidomide to birth defects emerged.[1] The teratogenic effects of thalidomide were devastating. Children were born with missing or stunted arms or legs, neurological disorders, internal defects, and sensory defects.[5] It was also found that long-term use of thalidomide caused tingling, numbness,

and burning pain in the fingers and toes.[6] It was speculated that thalidomide damaged nerves in those parts of the body.[6] With these new findings, thalidomide was never approved in the United States, and the number of subjects harmed by research with thalidomide in the U.S. was minimized (there were 16 or 17 cases, maximum) compared to the experience with thalidomide in Europe (thousands of cases).

B. Willowbrook State School Study: 1960s

Another propelling factor to the development of research ethics, among many, was the hepatitis study at the Willowbrook State School—an institution for "mentally defective persons." Similar to the Tuskegee study, investigators were studying the natural course of a disease (hepatitis A) and the effects of gamma globulin in preventing or treating the disease.[7] The pediatric subjects were deliberately infected with the hepatitis A virus.[1,7] The children were fed diluted amounts of stool extracts from other infected children.[7] During the course of the study, students were only admitted to the school if their parents agreed to enroll in the hepatitis program.[1] Outside of the study, the school was not accepting new enrollees due to "overcrowded conditions."[7] Parents that could no longer care for their children and had no other recourse were effectively coerced into consenting for the study. The consent form falsely stated that the children would receive a vaccine against hepatitis. This was another example of deception and exploitation of vulnerable populations—in this case, retarded, institutionalized children.

C. Hexamethonium: 2001

Many laws, rules, and regulations have been established and revised over the years to protect the rights of human subjects. This has not foolproofed the system, by any means. However, there has been a definite advance in creating a better system of checks and balances in the research community, and penalties for violations are harsher than they were in the past.

Several more recent events have jeopardized subject safety. This does not imply that it was intentional, but subject safety was put at risk, nonetheless. An incident that took place at the Johns Hopkins Asthma Center is a particularly interesting one that received much attention from the media, government, and the research community. In 2001, a healthy 24-year-old lab technician at the Johns Hopkins Asthma Center named Ellen Roche volunteered to take part in an asthma study.[8,9] The goal of the study was to understand the natural defenses of healthy people against asthma.[9] The volunteers were required to inhale hexamethonium to induce a mild asthma attack.[8] The young volunteer lost one-third of her lung capacity within 24 hours of inhaling the drug, and died within one month.[8]

There were many flaws with this study, from the beginning to the end. First, hexamethonium was found to cause fatal lung inflammation back in the 1950s, but these safety studies were not incorporated into safety planning by the investigator or safety evaluation by the institutional review board (IRB). This was a crucial oversight on the part of both. In 1972, the FDA withdrew the approval for hexamethonium, leaving it classified as an experimental therapy, and thereby requiring an Investigational New Drug (IND) approval by the FDA. The investigator had not obtained an IND approval before administering it to volunteers.

There were mistakes made by others, as well. The IRB's analysis of the protocol was inadequate—it overlooked the fact that the investigator did not have an IND. Further along the process, the investigator amended the protocol without the knowledge and approval of the IRB. Thus, negligence put a healthy volunteer in harm's way. An investigator who is inducing pathophysiological occurrences—especially in an otherwise healthy volunteer—cannot afford to be careless. The investigator created and conducted a haphazard study at the cost of a human life.

D. Dangers of Off-Label Therapy

Children may be seen as "little people," but, physiologically speaking, they are very different than adults. Many drugs are not labeled for pediatric use, yet they are prescribed for children on a regular basis. The toxic and lethal doses for children vary significantly when absorption, volume of distribution, metabolism, and excretion are taken into account. Children's organs, depending on their age, can be developing in ways that affect how much of the drug will get absorbed, how well and at what rate it will metabolize, and the rate of excretion. Depending on the height and weight of the child, the volume of distribution will be different too. It is not always a safe assumption that a drug approved for adults is safe for children. Pediatricians normally determine total dosage of drugs by calculating the milligrams required per kilogram of body weight. This method is more accurate than adult dosing. However, until the minimum effective and toxic doses are determined for children, it may not be wise to prescribe off-label drugs.

The pediatric studies rule from the Federal Register requires pediatric labeling for all new drugs, and may require further studies for drugs already on the market in certain compelling circumstances when pediatric labeling could avoid significant risks to kids. Serious pediatric adverse drug reactions that can occur in the absence of pediatric labeling include:

- jaundice in newborns from sulfa drugs

- seizures and cardiac arrests from the local anesthetic bupivacaine
- withdrawal symptoms from prolonged use of the painkiller fentanyl
- staining of teeth from the antibiotic tetracycline

Legally, physicians are allowed to provide pediatric prescriptions for drugs that are approved for adults only. Ethically, physicians face the dilemma of either prescribing a drug that may have harmful effects, or withholding a drug that may be able to cure an illness or alleviate its symptoms.

Despite the need for pediatric drug studies, many argue that clinical studies put children at risk, for a multitude of reasons. Others believe that the benefit outweighs the risk. After all, clinical trials place a small number of children at risk (in a controlled environment). Furthermore, the children enrolled in clinical studies will have illnesses and, therefore, stand to (hopefully) benefit from the experimental treatment. The ultimate benefit will be appropriate pediatric labeling for the drug and safe use on children in the future.[10]

Another example of the dangers of off-label therapy is fen-phen. Three drugs commonly found in weight-loss pills were dexfenfluramine, fenfluramine, and phentermine. A drug combination therapy known as fen-phen, consisting of the latter two drugs, had been approved and used in many diet pills to manage obesity.[11] Many physicians were prescribing an off-label cocktail of these and other similar drugs.[12] Off-label use of drugs comes with its own set of risks. Drugs labeled for similar therapeutic effects may produce undesirable or unexpected side effects when taken simultaneously. Some hold the misconception that similar drugs will have a synergistic effect when used in a drug combination therapy. Unless the drugs have been tested for such enhanced effects, this is not a safe assumption to make.

On July 8, 1997, the Mayo Clinic reported that 24 subjects had developed heart-valve disease after taking fen-phen.[13] This unusual surge in cases of valvular diseases, specifically in fen-phen users, triggered a suspicion that it may be a drug-related adverse event. The Food and Drug Administration immediately issued a Public Health Advisory describing the findings at Mayo Clinic.[14] As a result, over 100 cases were reported, including the original 24 from Mayo Clinic.[14] There was plenty of anecdotal evidence to cause the FDA to re-assess the safety of the drugs and to withdraw them from the market, if necessary. Based on further research, the products were, in fact, found to be unsafe, and were withdrawn from the market. It was recommended that research subjects stop taking the drugs.[14] Subsequent studies published in 1998 indicated that the use of any of these three drugs—whether alone or in combination—increased the risk of valvular diseases.[13,14] These studies did not produce identical results, but they corroborated previous findings and supported the FDA's decision.

The potential for adverse events is present in all clinical trials. In this case, cardiac-valve disease was not detected, because it was not screened for. After all, a weight-loss trial would not be likely to screen for heart-valve disease, especially asymptomatic heart-valve disease (why would it?).[14] It is not feasible to screen every subject in every clinical trial from head-to-toe for the remote possibility that something could go wrong.

7.5 Preventive Measures: Protecting Human Subjects
A. Why Do We Need Research Oversight?

Today, protecting human subjects is a requirement for federally regulated studies; it is not an option. Being able to conduct research is a privilege, and protecting the subjects, who ultimately grant researchers this privilege, must not be taken lightly.

As seen in previous sections, investigators have landed in varying unethical situations, from blatantly unethical studies exploiting vulnerable populations, to a careless oversight leading to human subjects' violations. Can an investigator guarantee subject protection? This is a difficult question to assess, since even well-intentioned investigators, in their zeal for new discoveries, may get blindsided by the goal of the study, which should be to uncover any immediate dangers posed to the subjects. Without regulations to guide them, investigators left to their own devices may not be good judges of what is ethical or not. They have a tendency to tailor their ethical analysis to the goals of their study.

It is the collaborative effort between investigators, institutional officials, IRB, federal agencies, and the compliance officials that will help establish the balance between providing optimal human-subject protection and allowing investigators to conduct research with as few impediments as possible. Gaining the trust of subjects is vital to conducting a study. Subjects should be able to take comfort in knowing that someone is protecting their rights. They should feel comfortable enough to make themselves and their time available for science and for the benefit of future generations. Without subjects, there can be no research. Without research, medical science cannot advance.

B. Federal Agencies

Federal agencies take the lead in protecting human subjects by creating the regulations that investigators, institutions,

IRBs, and sponsors must abide by. The Code of Federal Regulations, Title 45, Part 46—referred to as the Common Rule—is invoked by almost all the federal agencies that conduct or fund research involving human subjects. Among others, the three key aspects of the Common Rule are: (1) requiring voluntary informed consent from the subjects, (2) that the risks be reasonable in relation to anticipated benefits and knowledge gained, (3) and IRBs are required to conduct regular, independent reviews.

As more and more institutions are penalized for violating human subjects' rights, more IRBs are created, and more research comes under close scrutiny by these IRBs. The burden of reviewing and re-reviewing studies is a time-consuming and painstaking process. At many institutions, the IRB members are not reimbursed for their time and effort. Members of the IRB are generally faculty and staff who are volunteering their time as a service to the institution, which, in most cases, takes them away from their daily departmental work obligations or personal time. Over the last two years, the Food and Drug Administration and the National Institutes of Health have required more and more from the IRB members, in terms of responsibility, education, expertise, and professional accountability.[15] It is mandatory for a research facility to provide an adequately staffed IRB if they want to continue receiving federal funds and doing research. If the IRB process is to improve, the IRBs and their members need to be provided with the proper sources and funding required to perform an outstanding job in protecting the human subjects.[15]

The Department of Health and Human Services (HHS) regulations apply to research involving human subjects conducted by the HHS, or to studies funded (solely or partly) by the HHS. The FDA regulations apply to research involving products regulated by the FDA, regardless of the funding source. When research involves products regulated by the FDA and is funded, supported, or conducted by the FDA and/or HHS, both the HHS and FDA regulations apply.[16]

Institutions conducting federally funded studies bind themselves to the Common Rule by means of a federal assurance.[17] Federal assurance is an agreement between the Office of Human Research Protections (OHRP) and the institution, stating that the institution will comply with federal regulations.[17] There is overlap between the jurisdiction of the FDA (which regulates the testing of new drugs and devices) and the Common Rule. The Office for Good Clinical Practice, established by the FDA, oversees the application of the FDA human-subject protection regulations.[18] However, unlike the Office of Human Research Protection, the Office for Good Clinical Practice goes beyond overseeing institutions.[18] It oversees many clinical investigators, commercial sponsors, IRBs, groups that monitor clinical trials, and contract research organizations.[18] Failure to comply with these regulations may result in the shutdown of all human research at a facility being audited by the OHRP or the FDA (or both). A research shutdown can be detrimental to the credibility of the institution and its investigators, and can lead to a sizeable loss of research revenue, as well as considerable expense for the reconstruction of an improved human-subjects protection program.

C. Institutional Review Board

The Institutional Review Board (IRB) is a committee that is required, under the Common Rule and FDA regulations, to review and monitor human studies and review all research documents and activities that pertain directly to the rights and welfare of the participants of proposed research. The IRB has the authority to approve, require modification in, or disapprove all research activities as specified in the federal regulations. Institutions wishing to conduct research must form internal IRBs to review studies, or must contract out to independent national IRBs (e.g., Western Institutional Review Board, Schulman Associates IRB, Patient Advocacy Council IRB, etc.). The IRB is responsible for ensuring the safety of study participants, and to make certain that the protocol follows all federal and institutional guidelines. It is the federally mandated charge of the IRB to ensure the safety of the research participant. This is achieved by assembling an IRB that has medical experience and knowledge, and is culturally and educationally diverse. The diversity in membership is required in order to provide expertise in and sensitivity to a broad range of scientific and ethical considerations.[19]

The IRB is required to include at least five members with varying backgrounds to promote the complete and adequate review of all protocols.[19] One person's expertise and experience may prompt him to bring up issues that others may not think of as a necessary point of discussion. The IRB must have at least one scientific, one non-scientific, and one non-affiliated member.[19] A non-affiliated member is someone that represents the community in general. This person brings the perspective of subjects or their family members, whether they have concerns about the safety of the drug and their side effects, or the simplicity of the explanation in the informed consent. (It is important to write the informed consent in layperson's terms, so that all subjects can understand what will be done to them and what will be expected of them.) The ultimate key to all studies is that the subjects understand the study, so that the investigator may truly obtain an informed consent. The experience, expertise, and diversity of the members—as well as their race, gender, cultural background, and sensitivity to community attitudes—enhances the IRB, and promotes respect for its advice and counsel in protecting human subjects.[19]

An IRB may not allow any individual who has conflicting interests to participate in an initial or continuing review of that project, except to provide additional information requested by the IRB.[19] Conflict of interest can manifest in many ways. The members need to be aware of these possible situations, and recuse themselves when appropriate. An IRB should have policies that define potential conflicts of interest and procedures for managing them. Any relationship to the study, sponsor, or investigator may qualify as conflict of interest. On the other hand, an IRB may invite expert individuals to assist in the review of issues that are beyond the scope of the available IRB (however, these persons may not vote).[19] Even a diverse IRB may not have enough members to handle all protocols. And sometimes, an outside expert consultant can contribute a considerable amount of knowledge required to make the right decision.

The primary purpose of the IRB is to ensure, in advance and by periodic review, that appropriate measures are taken to safeguard the rights, safety and well-being of human participants involved in a clinical trial. Board members must determine that the following requirements are satisfied:

- Human participants are protected from ill-advised research or research protocols in light of both ethical and scientific concerns.
- Risks to participants are minimized.
- Risks to participants are reasonable in relation to anticipated benefits and the importance of the knowledge expected to result.
- Selection of participants is equitable.
- Informed consent will be obtained from each prospective participant or the participant's legally authorized representative and will be documented in accordance with IRB, FDA, and International Committee on Harmonization (ICH) informed consent regulations and guidelines.
- Adequate provisions are made for monitoring the data collected to ensure the safety of participants.
- Adequate provisions are made to protect the privacy of participants and maintain confidentiality of data.
- Appropriate additional safeguards have been included to protect the rights and welfare of participants who are members of a particularly vulnerable group.
- Participant selection and exclusion criteria includes justification of the use of special participant popu-

lations, such as children, pregnant women, human fetuses and neonates, or people who are mentally handicapped.

• Study design includes discussions of the appropriateness of research methods.[20]

When subjects are likely to be exposed to coercion or undue influence ("vulnerable subject populations"), additional safeguards need to be in place. Vulnerable populations may include the poor, the uneducated, children, fetuses, pregnant women, the elderly, those with decreased decisional capacity, prisoners, and, sometimes, employees or students. The IRB needs to make sure that there is no undue influence on these subjects to participate. Influence could take the form of monetary pressure (including bribery or threats of salary cuts for non-participation), intimidation, or a lack of comprehension. Some people may be convinced to participate in studies out of fear of: being terminated from their jobs, receiving bad grades, or being denied adequate healthcare services. Some might participate because they do not understand that it is an experimental protocol with risks involved. The IRB ensures that the information in the consent form is clear, that the risks are clearly defined, and that extra precautions are imposed for vulnerable subjects. This must all be stated in simple language, without medical jargon or complicated explanations.

When enrolling children, for example, parental consent on behalf of a child is required. In some cases, consent of both parents may be required depending on the risk/benefit ratio. Researchers must also obtain the child's assent in order to proceed. The procedures of the study, direct benefits (or lack thereof), and risks of suffering discomfort or pain due to procedures must be explained to the child in language that is appropriate to the child's age and maturity level. Lastly, failure to oppose does not imply assent.[21]

It is very easy to deceive and exploit children. The burden of protecting children does not fall to one person (even if that person is the parent). Everyone has self-interests—for example, the investigator may need to enroll more subjects or the parents may need the money. These possibilities must be considered. The IRB system—a system of checks and balances—is designed to ensure that participation in a study would be in the child's best interest. This system includes a panel of pediatric experts on the IRB (for studies involving children), the investigator, the parents, and the child. The IRB, having the most significant role, must render the study safe and plausible in order for it to commence. If done correctly and according to the federal regulations, the IRB's unbiased decision is probably the most reliable of all.

As another example, college students may be coerced into participation in order to get better grades or not receive bad grades.[22] If extra credit or rewards are offered for participation, students must be provided with and informed of non-research alternatives involving comparable time and effort to obtain the extra credit in order for the possibility of undue influence to be minimized. However, if participation in research is a course requirement, students must be informed of non-research alternatives involving comparable time and effort to fulfill those requirements in order for the possibility of undue influence to be minimized. Moreover, students must not be penalized for refusing to participate in research (45 CFR 46.116(a)(8)).[22] Some proper methods for recruiting vulnerable populations are outlined in the Informed Consent Frequently Asked Questions of the Policy and Guidance Section of the OHRP website and in the Code of Federal Regulations, Title 45, Part 46. In a study that calls for a student population as participants, the school or investigator is instructed to advertise on the school campus, and not to recruit individual students directly.[22]

D. Informed Consent

As previously discussed, one of the most important aspects of a research trial is the informed consent of the research participant. However, the signature on an informed consent document does not constitute the end of the informed consent. It is very important for the research community (the sponsor, investigator, and the IRB) to remember that informed consent is not just a document, but a continuing process that carries through to the end of the individual's participation in the trial. The informed consent process begins with the recruitment of participants, whether through advertisements or initial contact with the principal investigator or the research staff. The process includes initial consent where all aspects of the trial are explained including the risks, benefits, procedures, alternatives, purpose, and so on, to the potential participant. The subject is allowed to ask questions and he is provided satisfactory answers to those questions. New information is shared throughout the trial and the participant determines whether he is willing to continue in the study. For long-term studies the consent should be periodically reviewed in light of possible capacity changes. The consent should be presented in language that is easily understandable to the potential participant. The informed consent should be reviewed to determine that complete, accurate, and pertinent study-related information is being provided to the potential participants and that medical terms are clearly defined in simple language that the study population can understand.

Human participant protection is a shared responsibility among the sponsor, the investigator and the IRB. It is their responsibility as a team to ensure that the participants remain well-informed and that their rights and welfare are protected. It is important that all members of the research team understand the informed consent form regulations [21 CFR Part 56.108] as well as their part of the informed consent process. This knowledge should be applied to each informed consent form that is reviewed, presented and distributed to a potential participant.

As listed in 45 C.F.R. 46 and FDA regulations, the elements of proper informed consent are:

1. a statement disclosing that the study involves research, an explanation of the purposes of the research, the expected duration of the subject's participation, a description of the procedures to be followed, and the identification of any experimental procedures
2. a description of any reasonably foreseeable risks or discomforts to the subject
3. a description of any possible benefits to the subject or to others as a result of the research
4. a disclosure of appropriate alternative procedures or courses of treatment—if any exist—that might be advantageous to the subject
5. a statement describing how the confidentiality of the subjects' medical records will be maintained (or a description of how information will be used or disclosed)
6. for research involving more than minimal risk, a description of any possible injury that could occur, accompanied by an explanation of (and instructions on how to obtain) any available compensation or medical treatment for an adverse effect
7. contact information for resources who can answer pertinent questions about the research and research subjects' rights, as well as a contact list to be used in the event of a research-related injury to the subject
8. a statement that (1) participation is voluntary, that (2) refusal to participate will not involve any penalty or loss of benefits to which the subject would otherwise be entitled, and that (3) the subject may discontinue participation at any time—without penalty or loss of benefits to which the subject would otherwise be entitled

When appropriate, one or more of the following elements of information must also be provided to each subject:

1. a statement that the particular treatment or procedure may involve currently unforeseeable risks to the subject (or to the embryo or fetus, if the subject is, or may become, pregnant)
2. anticipated circumstances under which the subject's participation may be terminated by the investigator—without regard to the subject's consent
3. any additional costs to the subject that may result from participation in the research
4. the consequences of a subject's decision to withdraw from the research, as well as the proper procedures for orderly termination of participation
5. a statement that researchers will communicate any significant new findings developed during the course of the research to the subjects, if the findings might reasonably impact their willingness to continue participating in the study
6. the approximate number of subjects involved in the study

In addition to these required elements, an IRB can and may require additional standard Information and/or required signatures to be added to all informed consent forms being reviewed by the IRB.

E. Investigators' Responsibilities

As discussed earlier, the protection of research subjects is shared among regulatory agencies, sponsors, investigators and the IRB; however, the investigator conducting the study has the *primary* responsibility to ensure that participants in research are fully informed of their rights, and properly protected. The investigator, not the IRB, FDA, or sponsor, has direct contact with each human subject.

The investigator should be qualified by education, training, and experience to assume responsibility for the proper conduct of the trial, and should meet all qualifications specified by applicable regulatory requirements. Evidence of such qualifications should be provided to the sponsor, the IRB/IEC, and/or regulatory authorities. The investigator should also be thoroughly familiar with the appropriate use of the investigational product as described in the protocol, in the current investigator's brochure, and any other product information provided by the sponsor.

The investigator is responsible from the time the study is conceptualized until the research has been completely terminated. Ideally, the investigator will devise a study that protects human subjects, that does not duplicate previous studies, and that obtains information that will directly benefit the subject or (indirectly) the greater good. Prior to burdening the IRB with additional work, the investigator should make sure that the study is feasible, have necessary resources at her disposal, and have the proper administrative approval. The investigator must obtain an IND approval for any drug or device used in research, though an exemption may apply for most FDA-approved drugs and devices.

The investigator should have the time to properly conduct the study, and have an adequate number of qualified staff available and adequate facilities for the foreseen duration of the study. The investigator should ensure that all persons assisting with the trial are adequately informed about the protocol, the investigational product and their trial-related duties and functions. Additionally, the investigator should be aware of and comply with GCP guidelines, all applicable federal regulations, local/state law (as applicable), IRB SOPs, site SOPs, and institutional policies and procedures (as applicable).

For the initial IRB review, the investigator must provide complete information—protocol, consent form, investigator's brochure, results from any previous study that may be useful in approving the study, and any other relevant materials. Once approved by the IRB, the investigator needs to keep track of periodic submissions at intervals determined by the IRB (never greater than 365 days) for continuing review and amendments.

The research staff—the investigator or another designated person—is also responsible for educating the subjects about the study and their rights. The education process includes, but goes well beyond, the consent process. The subjects are made aware of the key points (also mentioned in section 7.5.D, above) via the consent form. In addition, they are informed of prior studies and their results (this is an ongoing process, as well). When new information arises regarding the safety of the drug or its previously unknown side effects, the subjects are immediately notified. This information may come from the study itself or from another study utilizing the same drug. At this point, the subjects may be asked to cut down on the dose or to cease taking the medication altogether.

Another necessary consideration is that potential subjects may want to discuss their possible participation with family members. The staff needs to be prepared to answer questions that these relations may have. Especially when recruiting vulnerable populations, it is crucial to allow a minimum of 24 hours for subjects to discuss with their families and consider their options before signing a consent form. It is the investigators' duty to advise the subjects that they should take the given time period to make their final decision. On rare occasions, a subject may be asked to give consent in advance for future research activities. For example, if, for some reason, a study population is expected to

become incapable of making decisions (e.g., patients with incipient Alzheimer's disease), they would need to sign a consent form ahead of time, outlining the conditions under which they would want to continue enrollment, and specifying the point at which they would want to withdraw from the study. The subject may choose to leave that decision in the hands of the person who has Durable Power of Attorney for Healthcare (DPOAH). In an unforeseeable situation, when neither a consent nor a DPOAH is available, the Healthcare Surrogate Act may be invoked. Either case must be precisely documented. (See Table 7.3.)

F. Serious and Unexpected Adverse Events

The reporting of serious and/or unexpected adverse events (SAEs) is a mechanism to ensure future safety and continued monitoring of drug use. There are two reporting mechanisms: mandatory and voluntary. The FDA MEDWATCH forms for reporting are 3500A and 3500, respectively.

Mandatory reporting applies to all drugs that have not been FDA-approved. While taking the medication, if a subject experiences a reaction that was not foreseen by the investigator, it needs to be reported. "Foreseen reactions," in this case, are only those that are listed in the "side effects" section of the protocol or consent, as long as the severity and frequency of those side effects are consistent with what was anticipated in the protocol or consent. If a reaction is foreseen by the investigator, but not listed as a potential side effect, it must be reported as an SAE. Not all reactions will occur as a result of the medication or device, but the report must be submitted, along with the principal investigator's assessment of whether or not it is believed to be drug-related. Compilation of SAEs helps the FDA and the sponsor assess the safety of the drug and, consequently, affects the FDA's decision for approval. This FDA reporting occurs outside of, and in addition to, the reporting requirements of the sponsor, the local IRB, and so on.

Voluntary reporting also applies to drugs that have already been FDA-approved. This allows continued monitoring of approved drugs. If there is a trend in SAEs, it will direct the FDA to consider a possible withdrawal of the drug approval (and, subsequently, the withdrawal of the drug from the market). Institutional policy is the guiding force for the requirements of voluntary reporting. A key point to remember is that voluntary reporting is not exclusive to research—it pertains to drugs used for non-research (clinical care) as well.

In complying with SAE policies and regulations, an institution needs to develop policies for how the progress of a study and the accumulation of adverse events will be monitored. The IRB can either assume the responsibility

Table 7.3
Investigators' Responsibilities as Described in the FDA Regulations (21 C.F.R. § 312)

General Responsibilities § 312.60:
- Ensuring adherence to the protocol, the signed investigator statement, and applicable regulations
- Protecting rights, safety, and welfare of subjects
- Control of drugs
- Obtain informed consent form in accordance with 21 C.F.R. 50, except as provided by § 50.23 and § 50.24

Control of Investigational Drug § 312.61:
- Drug must be administered in the presence of the investigator or a co-investigator
- Drugs shall not be supplied to any person not authorized under this part to receive it

Investigator Record-keeping and Record Retention § 312.62:
- Disposition of drug
- Case histories
- Records are required to be maintained for a period of two years following the date a marketing application is approved for the drug for the indication for which it is being investigated
- If no application is filed, the records are required to be retained for two years after the investigation is discontinued and FDA is notified

Investigator Reports § 312.64:
- Progress reports to the sponsor
- Safety reports to the sponsor
- Financial disclosure reports to the sponsor

Assurance of IRB Review § 312.66:
- An IRB that complies with part 56 of this chapter will be responsible for initial and continuing review and approval of the proposed clinical study
- Investigator shall report all changes to the IRB, including all unanticipated problems involving risk to human subjects or others
- No changes will be made without IRB approval, except to remove apparent immediate hazards to human subjects

Inspection of Investigators Records and Reports § 312.68:
- Shall, upon request from any properly authorized officer or employee of FDA, at reasonable times, permit such officer or employee to have access to, and copy and verify any records or reports made by the investigator pursuant to § 312.62
- Investigator is not required to divulge subject names unless the records of particular individuals require a more detailed study of the cases, or unless there is reason to believe that the records do not represent actual results obtained

Handling of Controlled Substances § 312.69:
- If the investigational drug is subject to the Controlled Substances Act, the investigator shall take adequate precautions

continued on next page...

Table 7.3 (continued)

21 C.F.R. 50.24 and 45 C.F.R. 46.101(I):

- Identify how criteria are met
- Life-threatening situation
- This research is needed now (basic science and animal work are supportive)
- Consent is not feasible
- Benefit/risk assessment
- Study with consent not practicable
- Document in protocol
- Therapeutic window
- How to attempt consent
- Write documents
- Informed consent form
- Information form
- Define (in conjunction with IRB)
- Community
- Methods of community consultation
- Methods of public disclosure
- Submit/obtain IND/IDE (FDA regulations only)
- Submit information for continuing review
- Provide data to Data Monitoring Committee
- Inform subject, representative, family

for performing this task or form a subcommittee of the IRB (in some cases, this may be a completely independent entity). Sometimes, the investigator creates an independent data-monitoring board for a single study. The purpose of this board is to review SAEs and make a ruling on whether the complication is drug-related or not, and whether there should be any action taken by the investigator.

G. Subjects' Responsibilities

Subjects are the key component of all clinical trials and, therefore, have the most control over their participation. Subjects need to take advantage of this power. They should ask questions and obtain as much information as possible before agreeing to participate in a study. The questions can be as simple as, "What is a clinical trial?" or as detailed as, "What class of drugs will I be taking and at what dosage?" All research staff is obligated to provide any information that the subjects request. Most of the information is provided in the informed consent, but anything that is not clear will be clarified, and anything that is missing will be provided. The subject will forget some details over time and will have to be reminded. During different stages of a study, new questions may arise. It is the responsibility of the investigator

and staff to answer questions throughout the duration of a study. The subject should also take some responsibility for his own safety. He can either research the topic on his own or get input from family, friends, or other sources.

There are many good reasons to participate in a study. A study may facilitate advancement of knowledge that will be helpful to future generations, or may generate a little extra money. Regardless of why one wants to participate in a study, one must carefully weigh all available options. For example, some subjects may be okay with taking oral medications, but may not be okay with being injected. Prior to enrolling, the subject should have a complete understanding of the study. If, for some reason, the subject does not fully understand the study, he should ask as many questions as necessary, until he feels comfortable with the decision to enroll (or not enroll, as the case may be). Some standard questions are usually answered in the consent form. The designated research staff member must review all aspects of the study mentioned in the consent form. They are also obligated to answer other questions that the subject may have. These details are covered in Sections 7.5.D, and 7.5.E, above. A list of sample questions is available in Appendix 7.2.

H. Sponsors' Responsibilities

The study sponsor is the individual, company, institution or organization that assumes responsibility for the initiation, management, or financing of the study. The sponsor is required by the FDA to conduct study trials to determine the safety and efficacy of the investigational agent. Safety data are usually derived through documented occurrence of adverse pharmacokinetic or pharmacodynamic effects. Alternatively, efficacy data may be evaluated by the prevention of a medical condition or through improvement of specific symptoms of a disease process.[23]

In the conduct of the study, according to the *Code of Federal Regulations*, the study sponsor is responsible for all aspects of the study including, but not limited to, the following:

- Maintaining quality assurance and quality control;
- Medical expertise;
- Study design;
- Study management;
- Data handling;
- Record keeping;
- Investigator selection;
- Allocation of duties and functions;
- Determining compensation to subjects and investigators;
- Financing;
- Notification/submission to regulatory authorities;
- Product information;
- Preparing and supplying study medications;
- Monitoring and ensuring that all clinical study sites comply with federal regulatory requirements.[23]

Sponsors are also responsible for gathering and distributing information regarding unexpected serious and adverse events associated with the drug, including any side effects not previously listed. This information should be passed on to the subjects via the investigator.

The sponsor bears ultimate responsibility for the success, failure, and safety of the treatment under study, even after FDA approval. In addition, the sponsor is the true innovator in the study process.[23]

I. Institutional Responsibilities

The institution provides the compliance assurance on behalf of all of its investigators. Therefore, it is the institution's responsibility to monitor all investigators and assure compliance with all federal standards. Establishing a Research Compliance Office whose duty is to "police" all studies is the first step. The compliance office is responsible for devising an audit plan to monitor activities across the institution on a regular basis. Auditing can range from a mock FDA audit to reviewing IRB minutes. These internal auditing systems are developed to find out how studies are actually being conducted, in addition to educating everyone on how studies should be conducted. The purpose of the compliance office is to prevent unnecessary deviations or violations from occurring, and to discover problems before they become serious or harm someone. IRB minutes may be reviewed to make certain that the review is thorough and that it covers at least the minimum requirements of the review process, if not more. Audit systems can be set up for all aspects of studies, from the initial paperwork, to reporting of serious adverse events. Lab visits, personal interviews, and file review are all examples of an audit system. In light of recent FDA audits in the last two to three years, many institutions have established a compliance office and/or an internal audit group in hopes of avoiding violation of human subjects' rights (and consequent penalties).

The Public Health Service Policy on Instruction in the Responsible Conduct of Research, issued on December 1, 2000, was mainly developed in response to the death of a human research subject, Jesse Gelsinger, in September 1999.[24] When institutions neglect subject safety, the government issues stricter new policies. These policies come with harsher penalties. The main focus of this policy is human-subject protections. There are nine core instructional areas that the institutions are required to cover.[24] Except for animal studies, the remaining eight areas directly or indirectly influence clinical trials. The nine areas are:[24]

1. data acquisition, management, sharing, and ownership
2. mentor/trainee responsibilities
3. publication practices and responsible authorship
4. peer review
5. collaborative science
6. human subjects
7. research involving animals
8. research misconduct
9. conflict of interest and commitment

The institutions have flexibility in deciding how much education is necessary for individual research staff members, and in determining the mode of training employed.[24]

J. Ethical Dilemmas in Clinical Research and Subjects' Safety

In today's world, as the clinical research industry grows rapidly, so do knowledge, medical innovations, new technology and scientific breakthroughs. However, even with all its good, many ethical issues and dilemmas have been raised with regard to clinical research.

Ethical violations, conflicts of interests, coercion, and misrepresentation date back to the 1930s. As described earlier, examples of ethical breaches include the Tuskegee syphilis study, the "medical experiments" performed on concentration camp prisoners, the Willowbrook Hepatitis Study and others. Clearly, these human subjects were deceived, coerced and treated unjustly. All of the above are examples of unethical acts, coercion, conflicts of interest, and misrepresentation.

The ethical standards and regulations that emerged after the Nuremberg Trials exposed the studies that had taken place in Germany. While this may have been the turning point, Germany was not the only place that unethical studies were taking place. Ethics and benevolence are international concerns. With time, regulations have molded and shaped research into a respectable career. There are thousands of investigators and their staff participating in clinical trials who are dedicated to advancing science and the development of new therapeutic treatments and who are using the highest ethical standards when protecting the rights, safety and welfare of the subjects who participate in their research trials. Federal and institutional oversight can bring some assurance that someone is looking out for subjects' welfare. The research community is charged with effectively protecting human subjects and ensuring that research is conducted ethically. Often, ethical violations in research are caused by lack of awareness rather than malice. However, without clinical research, medical innovations would not be possible. So, practicing ethical conduct, seeking continued training, and complying with the governing regulations will promote good, sound and ethical research, which will in turn benefit society.

And, if the IRB, the sponsor, the investigator, and the institution work smoothly together in the spirit (not just the letter) of existing human-subjects protection regulations, today's subjects will be empowered in a way that allows them to make educated decisions and to refuse experimental treatment without fear of any repercussions. An educated subject who gives informed consent for research is the first indication of the ethical conduct of an investigator. The second indication is the investigator's respect for these subjects and the understanding that the subjects have put their trust in the investigator, and that it is the investigator's job to protect their rights.

Endnotes

1. K. McCarty. "Protecting people who take part in medical research: Laws and ethics govern research at Gillette and elsewhere: Gillette children's specialty," *Healthcare Research Review* 1(2) (2002).

2. A.O. Jech. "Everyday ethics for nurses." (NurseWeek online course; see http://69.3.158.146/nurse/courses/nurseweek/nw1700/course.htm) (2001).

3. J. Hylton. "MIT investigates involvement in past radiation experiments," *The Tech* 65(113) (1994), http://tech.mit.edu/V113/N65/radiation.65n.html.

4. Harkins, Don. "Federal government publishes confession; 1995 report to Clinton documents 30 years of radiation experiments." *May 1999 Idaho Observer*. http://proliberty.com/observer/19990504.htm.

5. Prater, Alecia M. "Facts about the thalidomide tragedy." *Helium*. www.helium.com/items/1215795-thalidomide-birth-defects. Accessed May 9, 2012.

6. R. Spiegel. "Thalidomide gets a second chance," *Research in the News* (1997), http://science-education.nih.gov/snapshots.nsf/story?openform&rtn~Thalidomide.

7. University of California, Santa Barbara, Office of Research. "Willowbrook hepatitis study," http://hstraining.orda.ucsb.edu/training/willowbrook.htm.

8. P. Suber. "The Ellen Roche story," *Free Online Scholarship Newsletter* (2001). http://dash.harvard.edu/bitstream/handle/1/4725003/suber_roche.htm?sequence=1. Accessed May 9, 2012.

9. *Report of Internal Investigation into the Death of a Volunteer Research Subject* (2001), www.hopkinsmedicine.org/press/2001/july/report_of_internal_investigation.htm.

10. T. Nordenberg. "Pediatric drug studies: Protecting pint-sized patients," *FDA Consumer Magazine*, May–June, 1999, www.highbeam.com/doc/1G1-54612390.html. Accessed May 9, 2012.

11. U.S. Food and Drug Administration, Center for Drug Evaluation and Research. "Questions and answers about withdrawal of fenfluramine (Pondimin) and dexfenfluramine (Redux)," (1997), www.fda.gov/Drugs/DrugSafety/PostmarketDrugSafetyInformationforPatientsandProviders/ucm180078.htm. Accessed May 9, 2012.

12. F.F. Seghatol and V.H. Rigolin. "Appetite suppressants and valvular heart disease," *Current Opinions in Cardiology* 17(5):486–492.

13. M.A. Khan et al. "The prevalence of cardiac valvular insufficiency assessed by transthoracic echo-cardiography in obese patients treated with appetite-suppressant drugs," *N. Engl. J. Med.* 339(11):713–718 (1998).

14. H. Jick et al. "A population-based study of appetite-suppressant drugs and the risk of cardiac-valvular regurgitation," *N. Engl. J. Med.* 339(11):719–724 (1998).

15. J. Kaufman. "Protecting research subjects," *N. Engl. J. Med.* 346(26):2093–2094 (2002).

16. U.S. Food and Drug Administration. "IRB information sheets: Guidance for institutional review boards and clinical investigators: 1998 update," www.fda.gov/oc/ohrt/irbs/appendixe.html.

17. Code of Federal Regulations, Title 45 C.F.R. 46 Subpart 103.

18. R. Steinbrook. "Health policy report: Improving protection for research subjects," *N. Engl. J. Med.* 346(18): 1425–1430 (2002).

19. Code of Federal Regulations, Title 45 C.F.R. 46 Subpart 107.

20. Code of Federal Regulations, Title 45 C.F.R. 46 Subpart 111.

21. Code of Federal Regulations, Title 45 C.F.R. 46 Subpart 408.

22. Informed Consent FAQs. U.S. Department of Health & Human Services, Office of Human Research Protections. http://answers.hhs.gov/ohrp/categories/1566.

23. Lori A. Nesbitt. *Clinical Research: What It Is and How It Works* (2004), Boca Raton: CRC Press.

24. D. Maloney. "Instruction in responsible conduct of research," *Human Research Report* 16(1):2–3 (2001).

Appendix 7.1
Resources for Further Reading

- Belmont Report: http://ohrp.osophs.dhhs.gov/humansubjects/guidance/belmont.htm
- Center for Biologics Evaluation and Research: www.fda.gov/cber
- Center for Drug Evaluation and Research: www.fda.gov/cder
- Code of Federal Regulations: www.gpo.gov/fdsys/browse/collectionCfr.action?collectionCode=CFR
  - 45 C.F.R. 46
  - 21 C.F.R. 50
  - 21 C.F.R. 56
  - 21 C.F.R. 312
  - 21 C.F.R. 812
- Declaration of Helsinki: www.wma.net/en/30publications/10policies/b3
- Declaration of Human Rights: www.un.org/en/documents/udhr/
- Department of Health and Human Services: www.hhs.gov
- Food and Drug Administration: www.fda.gov
- Food and Drug Law Institute: www.fdli.org
- National Institutes of Health: www.nih.gov
- Nuremberg Code: http://ohsr.od.nih.gov/guidelines/nuremberg.html
- Office of Human Research Protections: www.hhs.gov/ohrp
- Office of Human Subjects Research: http://ohsr.od.nih.gov
- Office of Research Integrity: http://ori.dhhs.gov
- U.S. Department of Energy: http://science.energy.gov

Appendix 7.2
Examples of the Types of Questions That
a Subject Should Ask the Investigator or
Research Coordinator

1. What are the phases of a clinical trial?
2. Which phase is this particular study?
3. What is the study about?
4. What is the purpose of the study?
5. What will be done with the results?
6. Is this study being done at other places, as well as at this particular facility?
7. What do you hope to learn from this study?
8. Who put this study together?
9. Who are the researchers, scientists, or doctors?
10. Have they done studies like this before?
11. Is the government part of this study?
12. Who is paying for the study?
13. Who will make money from this study?
14. Can I share ideas during the study?
15. To whom can I go with ideas, concerns, or complaints?
16. How can I find out how the study is going and what is learned from the study?
17. Who will be in the study?
18. Why are you looking for people like me?
19. Are people younger than 18 included in the study?
20. Will I have to pay to be in this study?
21. Who will pay for my medications, labs, and so forth?
22. Can I quit the study after signing the consent?
23. Will my name be used in the study?
24. How will my confidentiality be maintained?
25. Will my care be affected if I do not qualify for the study?
26. What will I get out of the study?
27. What are the benefits?
28. Is payment involved? How will I get paid?
29. If I am removed from the study, will I get payment for the time invested?
30. Can I still get the medications if I leave the study?
31. What are my risks? Could I be harmed?
32. If I am harmed, who will take care of me, and who will pay for treatments?
33. Do I have any legal avenues if I am harmed by the study?

Chapter 8

Identification of Regulated Solid-Dosage Forms

Francis J. Muno, Jr., B.S., Pharm., R.Ph., MBA

8.1 Introduction

Solid dosage forms (SDFs), as identified by the United States Pharmacopeia (USP), include tablets, capsules, softgels, gelcaps, geltabs, vaginal tablets, chewable tablets, and wafers. These types of solid dosage forms have not changed for more than half of a century. No new dosage form has been developed since the capsule (gelcaps and geltabs are a hybrid of tablet and capsule dosage forms). New technology has been applied to some solid dosage forms in terms of formulation—sustained release, delayed release, and release in a specific segment of the gastro-intestinal tract—and in coatings, to aid in the preservation of the drug or alter drug absorption. None of the new technology has increased or decreased the number of solid dosage forms requiring identification.

The goal of this chapter is to survey the several methods by which a solid dosage form may be identified by product name, drug content, strength, and marketer—and thereby identify its national drug code, pharmacological activity, and legal status in the United States (see Table 8.1). Emphasis will be placed upon recent improvements in the art of using the imprint—as the marking on solid dosage form is known—as the direct means of making the identification. A secondary means of identification will be drug-product appearance. Development of imprints now allows patients and professionals to use a novel search engine and an innovative website to directly identify drug products. For the first time since Robertson declared in 1964 the need for marking solid dosage forms with imprints and for a ready means to identify them,[1] the technology is finally adequate to fulfill the task.

8.2 Physical Chemical Analysis

Natural and synthesized drug products are chemical agents that affect bodily functions or ameliorate disease processes. Physio-chemical analysis applies the body of knowledge of chemistry and physics in the service of identifying the chemical components in drug products.

Table 8.1
Characteristics of Methods of Solid Dosage Forms Identification

Method	Response/ Delay	Time Consuming	Not Always Possible (Examples)	Competence	Expense
physical/ chemical	typically 8 weeks	yes	multi-ingredient	scientist	high
accompanying documents	immediate	no	tampered with	professional	none
imprint and appearance	immediate	little	virtually never	anyone	low

The identification by physical chemical analysis is pursued for two reasons: No other practicable method of identification is available, nor is any other legally required (in a judicial process or court proceedings). Chemical analysis has historically been accepted forensically, and has the cachet of being incontrovertible.

Physio-chemical techniques, however, may be hindered by contaminants or by the presence of multiple ingredients in a sample. No single type of analysis is applicable to every unknown sample. The two principal techniques of high-pressure chromatography and spectrophotometry are exemplary of modern analytic methods. In the presence of multiple ingredients in the unknown sample, chemical elements or groups may overlay or be unrecognizable, leading to an inability to certify a "proof-positive" identification by these methods. To remedy this situation further, chemical separation becomes an additional expense of both time and money. Multiple ingredients may be represented both by the principal drugs in the solid dosage form, as well as by inactive ingredients (e.g., dyes, fillers, and binders that constitute the solid dosage form itself). While these techniques are legally recognized, physio-chemical analysis may not be definitive for every sample of drug product.

Physio-chemical analysis requires access to specialized personnel and equipment. The analysis is also labor-intensive, time-consuming, and expensive, and is often accompanied by a delay in getting the unknown solid dosage form to the analyzer. For these reasons, physio-chemical analysis is available only to well-funded organizations, such as pharmaceutical companies and law-enforcement agencies. Relatively little identification of solid dosage forms is made by this method, principally for law-enforcement and judicial agencies. Physio-chemical analysis is not routinely available to the public, to healthcare professionals, or to teaching professionals and organizations.

For all of the above reasons, the choice to identify solid dosage forms by physio-chemical analysis is not taken casually. If another means of making the ID is available, a prudent person would take the alternative.

8.3 Accompanying Documents

Solid dosage forms are usually accompanied by documents referring to their packaging. The package may be a blister pack that isolates a solid dosage form individually, or it may be a container of several tablets, capsules, softgels, or the like. Both types of packaging are the product of the packager of solid dosage forms. Another layer of packaging may also be in evidence, such as a consumer sleeve (box) or shelf-packer. The solid dosage form within the package may or may not be produced by the packager.

The package of the solid dosage form includes not only the physical container itself, but also labeling, as required by the United States Food and Drug Administration (FDA). By regulation, a label must appear directly on the packaging containing the solid dosage form (the single-dose blister or the multiple-dose container). "Labeling" refers to more than the label itself—it includes further descriptive and instructional information on the sleeve and inserts providing extensive professional and consumer-product information. The solid dosage form and packaging together is commonly referred to in the pharmaceutical industry as the "drug product," a commercial—not a scientific or professional—term.

Drug products must be identified by a number appearing on their packaging. For prescription drug products (for human, veterinary, and homeopathic use) and controlled substances (narcotics, certain stimulants, certain depressants, and steroids controlled by both federal law and state statutes), this number is the national drug code (NDC). Over-the-counter drugs have a Consumer Product Code. Requirements originate from several federal regulations. The NDC is unique to the packager, as well as to the name of the active drug(s), dosage form, and quantity of the dosage form in the package. NDC is principally a drug-product-identification and marketing code, devised in the 1960s and subsequently revised several times since then. The NDC may be in any one of three formats, all of which are represented in an 11-digit number.

It is important to note here that the NDC does not necessarily identify the maker of the solid dosage form, per se. The solid dosage form may be made by the packager (typical in the case of brand- and generic-drug manufacturers). Alternatively, the packager may purchase solid dosage forms in bulk from its maker, package them under its own labeling, and subsequently market the drug product as a distributor. Another iteration is the drug product in which each of the three functions—production of solid dosage forms, packaging, and marketing—are performed by separate parties. In the latter case, the NDC or Consumer Product Code may identify the marketer only. The NDC identifies the maker only if the maker also is the packager, distributor, or marketer. It is important to note that the NDC specifically identifies the drug name, dosage form, and quantity in the package unequivocally—so long as, and only when, the drug package is sealed and in tamper-proof packaging. Once the drug package is opened, the principle of the "chain of custody" must be invoked, and is the only means of safely determining the package content. Should doubt arise over the contents of an opened package, then physio-chemical analysis or the imprint on the solid dosage form must be used for identification.

Importantly, with a drug product intact (i.e., if the blister or container is sealed in a tamper-proof manner), the package labeling is reliable documentation from which an identification of the drug product can immediately be made. Most identification is made in this way (e.g., the pharmacist choosing the right drug to fill a prescription or the patient choosing the right medicine to take). This method of identification is certainly not labor-intensive, time-consuming, or expensive, and it does not incur a delay, as in the case of getting an unknown solid dosage form to an analyzer. All of these advantages contribute to the orderly distribution, handling, and storage of the drug product.

That said, the neatly assembled, easily identifiable, tamper-proof drug product depends upon the human element—the maker, packager, distributor, and dispenser—as well as upon the consumer. The weakest links in the chain are the dispenser and consumer. The principle of "chain of custody" comes into play, since both the dispenser and consumer require that the package must be opened—tampered with—for them to perform their functions. So long as the pharmacist and patient maintain a responsibility towards the drug product(s) in their possession, the minimal criteria of safety for the drug product—its identity—is maintained. The pharmacist demonstrates that responsibility with her professional and business-liability coverage.

The concept of the consumer's responsibility has radically changed throughout the past several decades. In the past, when consumers were admonished to properly discard a solid dosage form found separately from its labeling, drug identifications were needed less frequently. During these times, a respect for prescribed and OTC medicines was prevalent. The "drug culture" was yet to be born. All of this is now history!

These days, it is the expense of medicines and the quantity that we use that keeps us from discarding them. The necessity to take medications at different times and places leads to medicines being separated from their original containers and labeling. (Have you ever placed tablets or capsules in a small plastic bag, a daytime medicine box, a purse, a wallet, or your luggage?) Each of these situations creates risks concerning the loss of potency or identity, as well as the risk of contamination.

A means for an inexpensive method of making a proof-positive ID when no labeled container is in evidence is now widely sought. The remainder of our attention in this chapter will be focused on the goal of providing the reader with the expertise to make drug identifications from websites, search routines, and databases.

8.4 Imprints and Appearance

The search for the "grail" of making identifications from the appearance of the solid dosage form alone has been long-standing. In 1962, the article *Identification Guide for Solid Dosage Forms* by Hefferren et al.[2] (hereafter referred to as "the Guide") described an attempt to identify approximately 5,000 different tablets, capsules, and softgels by their size, shape, color, and markings. The method used physical measurement of size, assignment of the unknown drug product to predetermined shapes, matching color to a standard color reference (similar to paint chips), and markings on solid dosage forms known within the industry (imprints). Only a few drug products bore an imprint at that time. The Guide was of particular benefit in emergency rooms and coroners' laboratories because of their need to know, as well as their ability to physically manipulate the unknown drug product. However, in many cases, the process of identification destroyed the drug product. At each step of the Guide's decision tree, the user's choices were "narrowed to one or, at most, a relatively few drugs." A tentative identification was thus established.

Compared to today's "information age" standards, 1962's state-of-the-art in tablet and capsule identification was primitive. Experts, such as forensic scientists, pharmacists, and specialists in poison centers, could be relied upon to use the Guide, but it had little utility in non-expert hands. The Guide has not been formally maintained, and no new products have been cataloged since June 1962.

A system to make any physical identification must rely on objective (as opposed to subjective) information or data points. Size is objective, but its measurement is fraught with difficulties. Standard tools and methods and their immediate availability are needed in expert hands. Shape is subjective. It is difficult at times to describe the overall appearance of a drug product verbally. The descriptors of a solid dosage form—such as oblong, oval, or caplet—do not provide a definitive description. Similarly, color is subjective. It is difficult to describe the color of a solid dosage form verbally without the use of a color chip (pink, coral, peach, flesh, and rose are all common descriptors of colors used by drug makers).

In the 1960s, before the widespread marketing of generic drug products, brand manufacturers were all too ready to identify their products, as they faced an influx of counterfeit products.[3] Trade dress was yet another means of protecting branded products in the marketplace. From a marketplace where one manufacturer systematically imprinted its solid dosage forms in the late 1960s came elegant-looking products marked with a growing number of logos specifically identifying the drug maker. Using maker-specific markings on the dosage form—logos, alphabetic letters, and numeric characters—drug makers identified drug products by content, strength, dosage form, and route of administration, all independent of size, shape, or color. Imprints were the solution to identifying solid dosage forms. What remained was the intractable problem of identifying solid dosage forms from imprints, which is the thrust of this chapter.

The 1970s saw a burgeoning market for generically produced drug products. Generic manufacturers introduced repetitive lines of drug products, each bearing an imprint to legitimize their appearance among branded products, before a federal regulation to do so was required. The number of imprints in use in the marketplace changed as generic manufacturers found success or failure for their product lines.

The principal organizations that moved for better identification of drug products were poison centers across the U.S. In 1975, the FDA passed regulations requiring prescription and narcotic drugs (a subset of prescription drugs), to bear identifying marks on solid dosage forms. While the implementation of these regulations had a long run-in period, it was a major break-through in the art of making an identification. The regulation did not, however, include over-the-counter (OTC), vitamin, veterinary, homeopathic, and herbal products, which spoke to the extent that any one of these classes was important at the time. Furthermore, no public provision was made to catalog the myriad of resulting imprints—existing or extant.

During the 1970s and early 1980s, the number of poison centers in the U.S. grew to well over 100. The resources and practices of the poison centers expanded, and the response from the public grew accordingly. Because poison center services were authoritative, as well as free to the public, calls for tablet and capsule identifications soon overshadowed the very reason that poison centers came into existence. Poison centers continued to provide immediate help in poisonings and drug information to callers for more than a decade.

By the early to mid-1990s, however, the ever-increasing number of callers overwhelmed the budgets of many poison centers. Calls for drug identification were often the fastest-growing kind of call. These calls competed for the resources devoted to the primary mission of poison centers (to prevent poisoning and advise on treatment). A number of poison centers began to have severe budgetary constraints. Closures occurred. (In the 1980s, there were about twice as many poison centers operating as there are today.) A growing number of poison centers now turn away or refer calls for tablet/capsule identifications.

For quite some time, it has been evident that there is a strong need for a comprehensive, easy-to-use, definitive, current tablet- and capsule-identification database for pub-

lic use. Survey of the available resources is instructive: No print resource or existing electronic catalog is or has been adequate to fully meet the demands of drug-identification professionals and the public at large. The commonly available print and electronic resources fail to include non-numeric, non-alphabetic information, leave the user with the final choice of making an identification, and—in the former case—are dated from the day they were reproduced and further decline in value thereafter. Inclusion of imprints in these references is often several revision-quarters away, as noted by the introduction date of the drug product and the catalog revision in which it first appears.

In 1974, a privately held medical-information company acquired the first copyright for an electronic catalog. Its methodology presented imprints only in textual format, even though many logo-bearing drug products were already in common use. (For example, it expressed Teva Labs' acetaminophen 325 mg and codeine 30 mg tablet as the number *93 150 3*. The number *93* signifies Teva Labs, and the number *150 3* means that the drug is an acetaminophen 325 mg and codeine 30 mg tablet.) This catalog increased the possibility of finding the imprint by listing all possible combinations of imprint features, although redundancy reduced its ease of use.

The burden of these combinations within the catalog soon becomes obvious to the user. Lacking any discriminating routine for attacking imprints, the user has 398 choices from which to make an identification if the feature 93 is used for the initial search, 140 choices if the feature 150 is chosen, and 210 choices if the feature 3 is chosen. Each of these choices may require the user to assess them individually to make an identification. Users may also be impeded by the multiplicity of screens that must be reviewed—in the exemplary imprint *93 150 3* above, the electronic catalog presents nine or ten screens in order to make an identification. In yet another example, the imprint *BRA 200* may be identified by first approaching the *BRA*, and then the *200*, but not vice-versa. After examining a list of 359 possibilities containing the feature 200, the user finds that the feature BRA is absent. In yet another example from the electronic catalog, the imprint *230*, the user must evaluate 16 records to make a rather simple identification. The electronic catalog presents a multiplicity of choices, but makes no definitive declaration of identification for users. It is users alone who make the final choice.

Furthermore, because of the text-only format of the electronic catalog, direct representation of logo features is precluded. The catalog contrives, as an example, the Abbott logo (see Figure 8.1) with either the capital letter *A* or *E*, while a lower-case printed letter *a* might be a better expression (while still not a direct expression) of the logo itself. Other logos may not lend themselves to such contrivances, nor even to be represented by a cipher in the catalog—consequently overlooking a valuable feature within the imprint. The user may be left with no direct representation of logo-imprint features, or, at times, an outright absence of information—all serious deficiencies for the leading reference in the field. For these reasons, the electronic catalog cannot be definitive in making an identification.

Yet logos do lend themselves to direct representation. While a logo may be described textually, lengthy, often arcane, descriptive texts for sometimes similar-looking logos (Figure 8.2) can be avoided by presenting logos graphically. An innovative database has recently included graphics for over 200 logos found on solid dosage forms in the United States and made them searchable. This innovation has lead to the realization of a definitive and declarative identification.

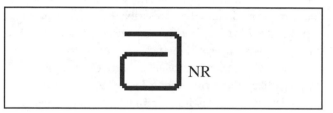

Figure 8.1 *Exemplary logo. Abbott logo as it appears in the imprint for Depakote® tablet 250 mg. More than 200 logos are used to identify solid dosage forms in the United States.*

From the above examples and absent any logos therein, a reasonable strategy for the publisher of the electronic catalog might be to limit its use to experts. In fact, each resultant informational screen bears the legend "All POISON-DEX®[4] product information is CONFIDENTIAL, intended for use by healthcare professionals, and may not be released to nonmedical personnel." In addition, this imprint catalog, initially and for more than a decade afterward, overlooked the National Drug Code (NDC); consequently, no search to confirm a drug product by its NDC—a particular need of healthcare professionals—is currently available.

Regardless of its dated features and reflecting the burgeoning drug market, the current electronic catalog has had a market for its more than 30,000 imprint records and their combination for nearly three decades.

Several websites offer direct searches of their databases for tablet and capsule identifications, specifically www.rxlist.com and www.identadrug.com. The former two sites are not easy to use, nor are they comprehensive with regard to the number of drug products and imprints. More tellingly, these sites use no more technology in the search for a specific imprint than a simple "grep"—an input of a string of characters, as seen in the imprint. They return a search result of multiple records containing the same string somewhere therein, and may or may not be related to the imprint itself. The user is left with making a choice. Again, no definitive declaration of an identification is provided. The technology is reminiscent of the 1974 electronic catalog discussed above.

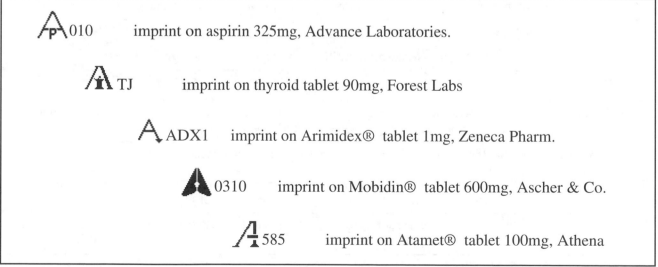

Figure 8.2 *Logos within imprints are better seen than described. Viewers immediately perceive differences among logos and can make the comparison between logo and its graphical representation. The alternative of matching a descriptive text to graphics may be a more difficult task. Example: Capital letter P inserted on the crossbar of the letter A may not be perceived as different from a mortar and pestle forming the crossbar of the capital letter A, using the first two examples above.*

Yet another database leased on a CD-ROM resorts to input of color, shape, and scoring, along with any alphabetic or numeric characters in the imprint. Again, the user is left with choices from a multiplicity of records in order to make the identification. This type of database reverts to concepts reminiscent of the 1962 Hefferren Guide. If the user misrepresents color, shape, or scoring, it is likely that no records will be found. Worse yet, an incorrect choice may be made.

The need for solid-dosage-form identification (see Table 8.2) goes beyond those of personnel in poison centers, forensic labs, and health professions, and extends to the public as a whole—specifically parents, elders, caregivers, travelers, and drug-abusers, when their usual sources of information are mislaid, separated from the SDF, or unavailable. Anyone who has found a stray tablet or capsule in his home, automobile, business location, or even among personal items, has wondered what it might be.

Even as fewer poison centers are able to extend their services to tablet and capsule identification, demand continues to increase for the pharmaceutical industry to introduce new products in all drug product categories. The number of generically dispensed prescriptions has grown from a small percentage of all prescriptions dispensed in the 1960s to nearly 40 percent of all prescriptions in the late 1990s. Patients are seeing different colors, shapes, and markings on tablets and capsules from one prescription refill to another.

Patients know so little about their medicines that they lose confidence when the slightest change occurs, even if there is only a change in the appearance of the medication. Because pharmacists choose among several generic manufacturers in order to meet prescription insurers' reimburse-

ment rates, patients will continue to experience the discomfort of seeing variously shaped and colored tablets and capsules, even as they return to the same drugstore.

To further complicate the situation, pharmacies are increasingly unable to make an identification of a tablet or capsule for patients that they directly serve, let alone for the requests made by the public at large. The limited inventories of pharmacies and pharmacists' limited success in making an identification are no match for the thousands of drug products never stocked nor seen by pharmacists or no longer in stock since the patient's last refill. They have no better resources than the general public in trying to make an identification. In fact, pharmacists must resort to using the very resources available to the public (see Table 8.3) and function as intermediaries in making the identification.

Patients, parents, elders, and caregivers with no answers to drug-identification questions may turn to their physicians. Physicians have little opportunity to see the physical dosage forms of the medicines they prescribe. In turn, the physician consults the *Physician's Desk Reference* (PDR),[5] which is chiefly an advertiser's reference and guide for frequently used or newly marketed products, discovers its limited utility and—like other print references—finds that it has been out of date from the day it was printed. Physicians and pharmacists alike routinely send patients and the public with identification questions back and forth among themselves and to poison centers and other resources.

More recently, the unprecedented number of prescription and controlled substances available on the street has increased the number of calls for tablet and capsule identifications. Some of these illicit drug products originate in

Table 8.2
The Need to Make an Identification of Solid Dosage Forms

Party	Situations
General public	Found medicines, medicines separated from label, confirming accuracy of a prescription recently dispensed, or by caregiver about to give medicine
Law enforcement	Found in a traffic stop, purchased undercover, or for evidence in a judicial process.
School districts	Confirming identity of found medicines on premise, on floor, in locker, on person of student or employee or prior to administering a prescribed dose of medicine.
Pharmacies	Identifying medicines at request of public or customer, confirming the identification by descriptors on the prescription label.
Hospitals	Confirming identity of patients own medicines or of medicines for patients in emergency room.
Doctor s office	Confirming identity of patients own medicines.
Nursing home	Confirming identity prior to scheduled administration of a prescribed medication

Table 8.3
Drug Identification Resources Typically Used by Venue and Their Availability

Resource	PDR	F&C	Identa	MDX Drug	Identadrug	Clinical Pharmacology	http://www. drugid.info	http://www. rxlist.com	http://www. identadrug.com	http://www. pdr.net
Media	print	print	print	CD-ROM	CD-ROM	CD-ROM	World Wide Web	World Wide Web	World Wide Web	World Wide Web
Typically used by										
Drug store		sub.	sub.			sub.				
Physician	sub.									
Poison center	sub.	sub.		sub.						
Anyone	library		sub.		sub.	sub.	fee	fee	sub.	fee

- PDR is Physicians Desk Reference®, a registered trademark of Thomson Healthcare which operates www.pdr.net.
- F&C is Facts and Comparisons®, a registered trademark of Lippincott Williams & Wilkins, Inc.
- Identadrug® is a registered trademark of Therapeutic Research Center which operates www.identadrug.com.
- MDX is Micromedex®, a registered trademark of Thomson Healthcare.
- Clinical Pharmacology® is a registered trademark of Gold Standard Multimedia which operates www.goldstandard.com.
- www.drugid.info is operated by Drug Identity Information, Inc.
- www.rxlist.com is operated by RxList LLC.

the failure of a few drug-manufacturing companies to secure controlled substance products within their own facilities.

Another factor driving the demand for solid dosage form identification is the growing number of prescriptions filled by mail-order pharmacies. Mail-order prescriptions are now approaching 8 percent of all prescriptions dispensed. With no direct professional relationship to a pharmacist, nor any independent means of checking the accuracy of the dispensed prescription, the patient in receipt of prescriptions by mail often turns to poison centers, other pharmacies, or any knowledgeable pharmacist. These informational intermediaries are hard-pressed to provide the time to make an identification, having neither the budget, the resources, nor the mission to do so. Consequently, these intermediaries are routinely turning away the public and do not provide the comfort of a positive identification for drug products.

Yet another factor is patient discomfort in the growing revelation that errors occur in the filling of prescriptions in pharmacies every day. Errors range from the wrong drug going to the wrong patient, to the wrong administration time, route of administration, quantity, and to any combination of the above. The opportunities for error are extensive.

The public wants and needs assurances that they are receiving the right drug. The imprint provides that reassurance, yet few resources readily make the identification via the imprint. A recent approach to providing reassurance to the public has been introduced by the Board of Pharmacy in the State of Oregon, which requires that the imprint of the solid dosage form in the container and its physical descrip-

tion appear on the prescription label.

The need for a readily available identification of imprints on solid dosage forms has become a public health problem of growing proportions. Over the years, the literature has been replete with references to patient errors and patients mistakenly taking one drug for another. The admission rate to hospitals because of patient misadventures with their prescribed medicines is now estimated to be more than 20 percent, due in part to the lack of a basic safety measure: the proper identity of the drug product. The introduction of additional regulations in 1995 related to imprinting solid dosage forms may be interpreted as an attempt by the FDA to meet this need.

The 1995 FDA regulations extended the requirement for imprints to three additional classes of drug products—OTC, veterinary, and homeopathic. Vitamins, dietary supplements, and herbal products still remain beyond the requirement for imprints. As in 1974, the need for a public, state-of-the-art facility directed at making imprint identifications still goes unmet, even as the number of new imprints in circulation has increased by the thousands. Such a facility—public or private—would go a long way towards capitalizing on the FDA imprint regulations.

Finally, the demand for tablet and capsule identifications is larger than the need for the public alone. For the same reason that the public needs to have drugs identified, professionals in law enforcement, healthcare, and education need an accurate, reliable means of making an identification from the imprint on drug products. The public and the professionals each have their own motivations for seeking accurate tablet/capsule identifications.

Drug task forces are special entities within the law-enforcement community. Their mission is to investigate illegal and illicit drug traffic, and then arrest those involved in the trade. A source of immediate, accurate, reliable tablet and capsule identification is invaluable. A need exists, often in the hours after midnight, for the identification of controlled substances—by phone, and from the marks on the potentially offensive drug product as reported by a police officer in the field. Such an identification, including a fax back of information, provides the officer with a statement of probable cause from an expert. The expert statement permits the offender to be held and arraigned the next court day. Reliable and immediate tablet and capsule identifications save time in "wrapping up" the case, and avoid the expenditure of time and equipment formerly required to "round up" the offender based on physio-chemical analyses prepared weeks later (in turn giving the potential offender time to leave the jurisdiction). Such identifications require a method and routines for a definitive identification, as well as professionals, applicable databases, and search programs.

If law enforcement has the charge of characterizing the nature of the "drug problem" in the community, teachers at all levels of practice are the observers of the problem and bear the brunt of this problem, along with parents. It falls to practitioners of this profession to deal with the consequences of the "drug problem" on a day-to-day basis. Teachers have a daily need to identify a scurrilous drug found in lockers, on school floors, or in the possession of a student. Teachers, like all of us, have a need to know what drugs are being abused by students, and yet have no ready resource—not in law enforcement, not in pharmacists, and not in poison centers.

Lately, a new, more intensive activity related to drugs in our schools has become prevalent—the proper supervision and administration of scheduled medicines during school hours. These drugs are prescribed for students to ameliorate or alter behavior or disease. The drugs must be properly identified, yet are often delivered by the parent or student in unlabeled containers or in a mix of several different tablets or capsules in a single container. Proper identification is required to limit the school district's liability. Failing to make a proper identification means the medicine may not be administered. If no medicine is administered, no potential exists for the amelioration of behavior or illness in the affected student.

Drugs are ubiquitous in our culture. Everywhere we turn, we come across prescriptions, controlled substances, over-the-counter drugs, veterinary drugs, "recreational" drugs, homeopathics, vitamins, and dietary supplements. They may be legal, illegal, or illicit. Consequently, the demand for the service is large, but diffuse. It is for these reasons that there exists a need for special means to be used to make drug identification readily accessible.

What are the consumer and professional to do? Immediately, the Internet comes to mind. In Table 8.3, resources for solid-dosage-form identification are summarized by user venues, media type, and availability.

8.5 Conceptually, Imprints are Unique

After nearly 30 years with little development in the field, current technology applied to SDF identification now accommodates all types of imprint features types—non-numeric, non-alphabetic graphics, as well as textual numeric and alphabetic features. Innovative technology organizes the three types of imprint features with an eye toward the fewest number of decisions required to arrive at a declaration of unique identification and confirms the identification with associated descriptors. The technology revolves around (1) A method of arranging all, including heretofore unrecognized, imprint features; (2) routines that present a hierarchical decision-tree for each feature within the imprint; (3) novel methods and routines that ignore the fallibility of making identifications by physical characteristics of solid dosage forms, partial catalogs, or data sets; and (4) the absence of a concept that imprints are unique.

Imprints then become the sole independent variable, and physical characteristics become descriptors and dependent variables. By using all features of imprints, and not overlooking or discarding the logo feature, imprints are, indeed, virtually unique.[6] These methods and routines definitively identify an imprint of a solid dosage form, thereby identifying the drug and its strength and dosage form and confirming its physical appearance. The method depends upon the single requirement, established by FDA regulations in 1975 and 1995, that solid dosage forms bear an imprint with no other limits placed upon it.

Even an exemplary database with a plurality of classified imprint features—without a means of accommodating the graphic features therein—cannot, alone, definitively identify the imprint of a solid dosage form. Something more than "grepping" a string of characters is needed. Search routines, when presented in a hierarchical scheme—including the choice of a logo—direct the user to a unique outcome, thereby definitively identifying the solid dosage form.

Routines of the innovative website www.drugid.info permit users to compare a plurality of imprint features, including logo, numeric, and alphabetic. Data is presented serially by feature classes, until all features of the imprint are exhausted, thereby deducing an identification of the imprint on the solid dosage form. Feature classes are correlated one to the other for the several features of an imprint: solid dosage forms may be selected from choices including tablets, capsules, softgels, gelcaps, geltabs, vaginal tablets, chewable tablets, and wafers. Feature classes are selected from logos, numbers, letters, and the remainder of the imprint classes.

The search routines include confirmation of unique descriptors of the identified imprint. The unique descriptors include color, opacity, scoring, shape, drug name, strength, dosage form, and route of administration.

Two websites providing the public with the best chance of making an identification are www.drugid.info and www.identadrug.com. The two websites are accessed for a small user fee and by subscription, respectively. Both sites' main goal is drug identification, whereas the other resources in Table 8.3 make drug identification a secondary feature. The above two websites provide the highest probability of success with the least time committed.

The website www.drugid.info uses all of the information contained in an imprint—logos, as well as the alphanumeric letters and characters—to make the identification. Because of this innovation, the website leads to a declaration of identification. The www.identadrug.com site lists choices based upon alphanumeric characters alone, leaving the user the final decision in making the identification.

The reader is encouraged to select an imprint of an existing drug product or from those in Figure 8.2 as examples, and attempt to identify the drug product using the various resources within reach, or using those seen in Table 8.3. Because of its ubiquity of access, the Internet is an easy and frequent choice and is the special means needed for the public and professionals to identify medicines separated from their labeling. The examples illustrate the accessibility of each website and its capacity to provide an identification. The Internet thrives on content, and solid-dosage-form identification has an obvious place there. Prior to the advent of new technology in the art and access to the Internet, the above invitation would have been an exercise in futility.

Historically, two intermediaries—pharmacists at the local drugstore and specialists in poison-control centers across the country—were available to identify solid dosage forms. Both of these parties use the same resources as found in Table 8.3. More and more pharmacists are referring requests for identifications to the poison centers because the principal activity of pharmacies is dispensing medications quickly to waiting patients. Poison centers, on the other hand, have instituted a national toll-free number (800-222-1222) to take all calls related to exposures, including bites by, contacts with, or ingestions or inhalations of, a toxic animal or substance.

Poison centers provide limited drug-product identification services after callers provide the poison specialist with their personal identity and satisfy the specialist of their urgency of need. Poison centers nationally do not encourage drug-product identification, except as related to their principal mission. Their mission and list of services may be seen at the website, www.1-800-222-1222.info, along with links to participating centers across the country.

8.6 Conclusion

For the public, as well as for the professional, definitive identification of drug products is imperative as a starting point in understanding if a specific set of circumstances represents a drug problem, a misadventure with prescribed medication, or evidence in judicial proceedings.

In any case, the Internet is clearly the place to go for solid dosage form (SDF) identification. Imprints on SDFs are required by the FDA for regulated classes of drug products, and these can be used for identification.

Imprints are unique in at least one database and search engine. This uniqueness is a product of using all of the information of the imprint—logos as well as alphanumeric letters and characters—and presenting that information hierarchically to arrive at a definitive identification. The website www.drugid.info has the capacity to achieve a definitive identification, and supports that identification with its liability.

Endnotes

1. W.O. Robertson. "Letter: Drug-imprint code," *JAMA* 229: 766 (1974).

2. J.J. Hefferren. "Identification guide for solid dosage forms," *JAMA* 182:1145–1302 (1962).

3. Counterfeits are illicit and look like a legal, branded drug product, typically with a high commercial value.

4. POISONDEX® is a registered trademark of Thomson Health Care.

5. PDR is a registered trademark of Thomson Health Care.

6. Imprint M2 is the only case where imprint, color, shape and scoring is inadequate; the database must further provide, in this one case, the imprint location—face, obverse or both—to make an identification.

Chapter 9

Counterfeit Drugs

Kimberly O'Donnell, MBA

9.1 Introduction and Definition

Drug counterfeiting is a global issue across the entire pharmaceutical supply chain. The World Health Organization (WHO) has defined counterfeit drugs as drugs that are deliberately and fraudulently mislabeled with respect to identity and/or source. Counterfeiting may apply to both branded and generic products and may include products with the correct ingredients but fake packaging, with the wrong ingredients, without active ingredients, or with insufficient active ingredients. Pharmaceutical companies are concerned about counterfeiting drug issues and are more willing to take additional security measures to protect their products and brand image, as well as reduce liability costs despite a lack of standards of security measures in the pharmaceutical industry. Firms that import drugs from third-party manufacturers or those that have significant repackaging are most at risk.

A. Scope of the Problem

According to the Center for Medicine in the Public Interest, worldwide counterfeit sales are increasing at about 13 percent annually—approximately double the rate of legitimate pharmaceuticals—estimated to become a $75 billion industry by 2010.[1] Reports continue to be made with intentional criminal involvement. The WHO estimates that the pervasiveness of counterfeit medicines ranges from 1 percent of sales in developed countries to up to 30 percent in developing countries. Figures 9.1 and 9.2 (courtesy of the Pharmaceutical Security Institute) provide the number of reported counterfeit drug incidents over time and by region of the world.

B. Greatest Problems in the Poorest Parts of the World

Counterfeiting is of greater prominence in the poorest parts of the world (India, China, and Africa) and in those regions where regulatory and legal oversight is weaker. Many countries in Africa and parts of Asia and Latin America have areas where more that 30 percent of the medicines on sale can be counterfeit, while other developing markets have less than 10 percent; overall, the range is between 10 and 30 percent for these countries. Many of the former Soviet republics have a proportion of counterfeit medicines which is above 20 to 30 percent of market sales.

In developing countries and areas of the world where the problem is most severe, the issue is not tracked as quantitatively; however, there are several documented incidents of deaths in such countries due to counterfeit medicines. In Niger in 1995, during a meningitis epidemic, 2,500 people died from counterfeit vaccines. Eighty-nine deaths in Haiti, 30 deaths in India, and 80 deaths in Nigeria were caused by cough syrup made with diethylene glycol (used in antifreeze).[1,2]

Year	Number of Incidents	Percent Increase
2002	196	N/A
2003	484	146.94%
2004	964	99.17%
2005	1123	16.49%
2006	1412	25.73%
2007	1759	24.58%
2008	1834	4.26%

Figure 9.1 Total number of incidents by year: 2002–2008. Courtesy of the Pharmaceutical Security Institute. Pharmaceutical Security Institute. Incident trends, last accessed March 15, 2010, from www.psi-inc.org/incidenttrends.cfm.

Region	Number of Incidents	Percent of Total
Asia	835	38.30%
Latin America	402	18.44%
Europe	347	15.92%
Eurasia	202	9.27%
North America	175	8.03%
Near East	170	7.80%
Africa	49	2.25%

Figure 9.2 Incidents by geographic region. Courtesy of the Pharmaceutical Security Institute. Pharmaceutical Security Institute. Geographic distribution, last accessed March 15, 2010, from www.psi-inc.org/incidenttrends.cfm.

9.2 Problem Increases in Industrialized Countries

Most industrialized countries with effective regulatory systems and market control (e.g., U.S., most of EU, Australia, Canada, Japan, and New Zealand) have a low proportion of counterfeit drugs, that is, less than 1 percent of market value.[1] However, incidents of counterfeit drugs in the United States and Europe are on the rise. Medicines purchased over the Internet from sites that conceal their physical address are counterfeit in over 50 percent of cases.[1] A 2009 Pfizer study found that 21 percent of Western Europeans surveyed admitted to buying prescription medications from illicit sources, and that there was a 630 percent increase the two years from 2005 to 2007 in counterfeit medications being found at EU borders.[1]

9.3 Global and U.S. Pharmaceutical Market Sizes

As of 2012, the global pharmaceutical retail market value (branded and generic) was estimated at approximately $500 billion. The U.S. market is the largest market in the world and the main source of global pharmaceutical manufacturers. The retail portion of the U.S. market has been estimated at approximately $250 billion as of 2012,[1] over half of the global pharmaceutical market. The U.S. is also one of the most regulated pharmaceutical markets in the world, establishing benchmarks and compliance that are readily adopted by foreign countries. U.S. pharmaceutical companies spend significantly on R&D in the hopes of discovering the next patentable blockbuster drug. Drug counterfeiting is of concern to major drug brand owners because it can lead to threats to consumer safety, liability issues, loss of brand loyalty, loss of revenue and profits, and brand devaluation.

9.4 Where Counterfeiting is Most Likely to Occur

Counterfeiting problems typically occur with high-cost prescription drugs more so than OTC medicines or kits (e.g., oxygen-sensitive drug kit, hydration kit for babies, etc.). This makes sense, since prescription drugs represent a majority of drug sales globally, and present higher profit possibilities. Kits are less likely to be counterfeited since they are much more complex than pills and therefore more difficult to counterfeit. OTC drugs are typically not counterfeited, as the profit potential is much less as compared to prescription drugs. Accutane is one such prescription drug that is counterfeited and sold on the Internet, which is especially dangerous, due to its myriad of side effects, including serious mental health problems, and birth defects if taken while pregnant. The FDA issued a news release in March 2007, to highlight these risks, and is also working with Google and other search providers to position their consumer warning website as a search result when a consumer searches for Accutane by any of its four names.[1] Also, high demand for a drug in insufficient supply can cause counterfeiting to occur. In the fall of 2009, due to the H1N1 influenza virus severity and shortage of Tamiflu, enough counterfeit Tamiflu has been sold over the Internet for the FDA to issue a warning and provide information to consumers about how to safely purchase drugs online.[1]

Lifestyle-related prescription drugs (Viagra, Cialis, OxyContin, Alli, etc.) are typically among the most counterfeited. In January 2010, the FDA issued a warning about counterfeit Alli, a weight-loss drug, being sold over the Internet. The Internet version is being sold with a different active ingredient, causing different side effects and especially dangerous to people with certain medical problems. The FDA warning website includes side-by-side photos of the authentic and counterfeit product to assist the consumer in determining if they have a counterfeit product.

9.5 Preventing Drug Counterfeiting

Preventing drug counterfeiting involves pharmaceutical companies, drug wholesalers, drug distributors, pharmacies, and governments. The products affected by counterfeiting include prescription drugs, over-the-counter (OTC) drugs, medical devices, and other pharmaceutical and medical products. The FDA and World Health Organization (WHO) keep track of these problems in the United States and across the globe, respectively. They provide basic information on anti-counterfeit regulations and recommend anti-counterfeiting techniques and technologies. Additional organizations, consulting firms, and universities provide more specific and up-to-date information on the latest anti-counterfeit technology.

Given the size and scope of the counterfeiting problem, research and discussion of anti-counterfeiting measures for pharmaceuticals is on-going, and the market potential is quite huge. Serialization of products with technologies such as 2-D bar-coding or radio-frequency identification (RFID) security technologies were anticipated to have been required by 2011. Many pharmacies and wholesalers have already self-regulated to more tightly define distribution channels, and several state laws have been passed to define distributor/wholesaler licensure regulation.[1] In March 2008, the FDA issued a Request for Information on technologies for prescription drug identification and/or authentication (see Appendix 9.1).[2]

9.6 Legislative Measures in the U.S.

Since 1987, the FDA has encouraged the pharmaceutical industry to tighten its supply chain's vulnerability to counterfeits. The FDA recommends, and several states now mandate, a drug pedigree, which is a certificate of authenticity that details a drug's movement through the supply chain. Without the pedigree, it is nearly impossible to determine where a drug has been and if it is safe. The federal government also regulates the wholesale distributors; they banned the sale of drug samples and drug coupons, banned re-importation (limited exceptions), and also set requirements for sample distribution and storage and required state licensing of wholesale distributors.[3] The FDA recommends that drug makers and wholesalers take a dynamic and multi-layered approach to protecting their products from counterfeiters.

9.7 Understanding the Pharmaceutical Market Distribution Process[4,5]

The U.S. pharmaceutical distribution process can be broken down into five steps, as follows:

A. Step 1: API Creation

Most U.S. pharmaceutical companies manufacture the active pharmaceutical ingredient (API) outside of the U.S., in countries with lower labor costs. The API is manufactured into final formulation: capsule, liquid suspension, patch, tablet, vial, etc. The most common formulation is the tablet, so that formulation will be considered in the following steps. Once the tablets are stamped, they are packaged into bulk configurations, which are generally shipped in palletized steel drums.

B. Step 2: Customs

Federal customs agents check the FDA paperwork as the product enters the U.S. Assuming the paperwork is satisfactory, the product will clear customs in a few days. The agents do have authority to dissemble the bulk packaging and audit the product. The customs-clearing step in the process is a point of potential, although unlikely, product theft.

C. Step 3: Repackaging

The bulk configurations of product are then shipped from customs to packaging facilities, where they are disassembled and repackaged into FDA-approved commercial trade configurations that are then labeled and given a tamper-evident induction seal. This typically includes various sized bottles that hold frequently utilized tablet counts. For the most popular prescriptions, tablet counts might include only 30, 60, or 90 tablets per bottle. However, most drugs are assembled into stock bottles and these counts often are 500, 1,000, or 5,000 tablets per bottle. Commercially packaged bottles may then be reconfigured into larger pallet configurations in preparation for shipments to wholesale distributors.

Larger pharmaceutical companies may do the packaging in-house, whereas smaller pharmaceutical companies are more likely to utilize contract packagers. Contract packagers include Catalent Pharma Solutions—the world's largest contract manufacturer and packager. Efficient packaging facilities are highly sought after to realize true economies of scale in the product packaging process.

D. Step 4: Sale to Distributors

Approximately 90 to 95 percent of the pharmaceutical industry's retail product supply is sold to the top three wholesale distributors: McKesson, Cardinal Health, and AmerisourceBergen.[6] These distributors have relationships with all major retail pharmacies and provide efficient distribution of product to these pharmacies in line with pharmacy product demand. Once the wholesalers determine pharmacy product demand, they aggregate the commercial trade packaging (bottles) and assemble into quantities in line with demand requirements at the retail pharmacies. During periods of inventory fluctuations, the three main wholesale distributors engage in inventory sales with smaller distributors that make up the remaining 5 to 10 percent of the wholesale distributors. Counterfeit drugs have a higher likelihood of entering the distribution chain during these transactions. Manufacturers do conduct audits of their products at the wholesale distributor's facilities to ensure counterfeit drugs are not entering the supply chain during these transactions. During these audits, the drug manufacturers *look for compliance with their sourcing agreements, which require wholesalers to purchase their products directly from the drug manufacturer and to sell only to authorized end users.* Many past counterfeit drug problems stemmed from these smaller "secondary" wholesalers selling directly to pharmacies or healthcare providers. There has been a crackdown on these secondary wholesalers in the U.S., and as of 2003, many states now require these secondary wholesalers to be licensed.

E. Step 5: Retail Pharmacy Dispense

At the retail pharmacy, pharmacists dispense drugs to patients to fill written prescriptions. Medications are provided to patients either in original manufacturer packaging if available in smaller count bottles (30, 60, or 90) or in retail pharmacy bottles. The retail pharmacist may never open the smaller count bottles before filling a patient prescription. Large count stock bottled products do require pharmacists to remove the drug from the stock bottle, count out the prescribed number of units, and place the medication in a retail branded container. Experts do not believe that pharmacists or pharmacies would be supportive of conducting authentication of drugs as an additional step in their drug-dispensing procedure, given their existing responsibilities and their hectic workload.[7,8]

9.8 Anti-Counterfeit Packaging

Pharmaceutical corporations are increasingly concerned with counterfeiting problems, and interested in advances in anti-counterfeiting technology. Since repackaging is one of the highest areas of opportunity for counterfeit product to enter the supply chain, drug manufacturers and wholesalers primarily take measures to mitigate the risks here. A range of anti-counterfeiting packaging exists today. The FDA suggests that the industry use a combination of track-and-trace

technologies and product authentication technologies in order to employ multi-layer protection. Industry standards and FDA requirements for anti-counterfeit measures are still evolving (e.g., e-Pedigree/RFID still yet to be implemented). These technologies can be segmented into four categories: overt, covert, forensic, and serialization/track-and-trace devices.

A. Overt Anti-Counterfeit Packaging

Overt anti-counterfeit packaging is visible to the naked eye. The positive attributes of overt anti-counterfeit packaging is that it is user verifiable, is more secure than in the past, can be incorporated into brand-identity images, and may deter counterfeiters. Negative attributes are that end consumers do not know exactly what real packaging is supposed to look like, and some packaging can be easily replicated by counterfeiters. Overt devices include:

- Optical variable devices (OVD): Holograms make pharmaceutical packaging significantly more difficult to counterfeit.
- Optical variable inks (OVI): Provide an easy means of identification on films, labels, bar codes.
- Security papers: Invisible fibers embedded into paper stock. Stocks can also employ chemical reactivity as an added counterfeiting measure.
- Microtext: Effective, economical safety measure.
- Tamper-proof/tamper evident techniques: Immediately alert users to products that may have been altered or contaminated.

B. Covert Anti-Counterfeit Packaging

Covert devices are invisible to the naked eye and are often more difficult for counterfeiters to duplicate successfully. They also have little or no effect on the design of the packaging. Positives of covert devices include the fact that inks, images, PCIDs, etc., can easily be added or modified, can be applied in-house to reduce security threats, and can be expensive to replicate. Minuses are that the invisible inks, images, etc., can be replicated if not implemented under secrecy. Covert features include invisible printing, embedded images, elements visible with only specialized equipment utilizing ultraviolet/infrared light, watermarks, anti-scan designs, microscopic nanotext and hidden images and odors.

C. Forensic Anti-Counterfeit Packaging

These solutions require lab testing or field test kits to test for authenticity. These are considered a subset of covert technologies; these are covert technologies that require scientific testing to prove authenticity. Positive attributes include that they provide positive authentication and are high-tech to secure against copying. Negative attributes include significant costs, and the fact that they are not available to authorities or the public.

Physical-chemical identifiers (PCIDs): the use of inks, pigments, or flavors. In some cases, the PCID may be detected easily by wholesalers or pharmacists to determine if they have authentic products. In other cases, special analytical instruments may be necessary to identify whether the PCID is present (depending on the PCID this could be either overt or covert):

- Chemical taggants: cannot be detected with conventional analysis, but require specific test systems.
- Biological taggants: require specific kits to authenticate.
- DNA taggants: only detectable with a dedicated device, where marker and reagent pair are in a matrix of random DNA strings.

D. Serialization/Track-and-Trace Anti-Counterfeit Packaging

Serialization/track-and-trace technology means a unique identifier is assigned to each package, which allows for package tracking through the entire supply chain. Pluses include that it is secure against copying, facilitates recalls, and can also assist with increasing supply efficiencies. Minuses include that cost is a significant barrier at the single item-level (such as per tablet), it could be vulnerable to computer hacking, and remote reading may be considered in conflict with consumer privacy and patient confidentiality issues.

Serialization/track-and-trace devices include:

- Radio frequency identification technology (RFID): An electronic track-and-trace technology that provides close control of product authenticity, inventory and location. Also allows fast, rapid recalls.
- Laser images: Covert markings on bottles, containers, lids, packaging, etc. Images can be as small as 20 microns and placed directly on pills and tablets.
- Taggants: Codes supplied in a variety of clear films, directly in the film including laminate, holographic, shrink sleeve, tamper evident, and all other polymer resin films. Codes and information is validated through machine reading and verification with specialized handheld readers.

- Linear or two-dimensional barcodes: Linear bar coding is used as a complementary technology to identify counterfeit drugs before they are administered. Two-dimensional barcodes are similar to one-dimensional barcodes but with more advanced special pattern technology.

E. 2010 Anti-Counterfeiting Measure Utilizing Cell Phones

In January 2010, a new type of consumer-oriented counterfeit-drug test was being trialed in Nigeria. Sproxil Inc., started by Dartmouth-trained entrepreneur Ashifi Gogo, utilizing a technology that allows consumers to scratch-off areas of labeling to reveal an ID number, and then send a text message via their cell-phone to see if the drugs are authentic. The trial took place with the diabetes drug Glucophage. This drug is manufactured in France by Merck Serono, and is so frequently copied that legitimate sales of Glucophage dropped 75 percent in 2009.[9]

9.9 Shutting Down Illegal Websites

Drugmakers could do more to fight illicit Internet sites selling counterfeit drugs. Their perception may be that there is nothing they can do about illicit Internet sites, but the reality is that they can get illicit Internet sites shut down. Domain-name registrars, such as Verisign, have the authority to shut down websites that conduct illegal activity, do not need court orders to do so (a common misconception), and, in fact, may lose their accreditation for not doing so. NanoGuardian, a provider of nanotechnology-based anti-counterfeiting measures, says that manufacturers could police the Internet for illegal websites, and get them shut down by working with authorities and domain name registrars.[10]

9.10 When FDA Approval is Required

Any anti-counterfeiting technology applied underneath the lid or inside the container, not in place during initial FDA approval, does require additional FDA approval. This is because any alterations to shape, size, moisture control, or tamper proofing underneath a bottle's lid requires a two-year FDA approved stability study. To avoid this process, the anti-counterfeiting technology would need to be placed outside the bottle to ensure it would not interfere with the drug's stability or storage environment.

An additional issue that requires consideration is the disposal of the authentication packaging. Counterfeiting organizations could more easily and cheaply recreate the technology by benchmarking and analyzing the discards of pharmacies. Thus, it would be highly recommended to create a disposal process at the pharmacy.

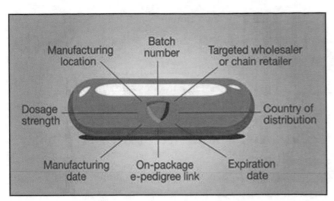

Figure 9.3 *E-Pedigree. Reproduced by permission from NanoGuardian, a division of NanoInk, Inc., Skokie, IL. © 2008.*

9.11 Nanotechnology

The most effective anti-counterfeiting technology would be placed at the lowest unit level (i.e., tablet). Nanotechnology research is already taking place by companies such as NanoGuardian to determine how to efficiently achieve this. Information including product strength, expiration date, manufacturing location, batch, and lot number can be written on individual doses. This data could then be linked to on-package e-pedigree technologies. At the overt level, a simple field inspection can reveal if a dose is authentic. The forensic-level codes would only be detected with highly specialized, proprietary tools within NanoGuardian.[11]

9.12 E-Pedigree and RFID

Currently there are state and federal laws that require chain-of-custody documentation, or pedigree, for pharmaceuticals passing state lines. These records are typically paper-based, and as such are difficult to review and search, and are easily falsified. The new federal law proposes that the pedigree be electronic, or electric pedigree, e-pedigree for short. Radio-frequency identification (RFID) is the most discussed solution to an e-pedigree requirement.

A. Florida and California

Florida and California are leading the country with their own Prescription Drug Safety Acts. In 2006, the State of Florida required a pedigree starting with the wholesaler. The State of California is requiring manufacturers to create a unique serial number for each saleable unit[12] and tracked electronically from the manufacturer through the wholesaler to the pharmacy.[13] Originally, this requirement was to be met by January 1, 2009; this date was moved to January 1, 2011, for various reasons. These reasons include more time needed to ensure RFID does not affect blood products, technology compatibility problems, or standards development, and the California budget crisis (California Dept. of Corrections, state mental hospitals, State University campus clinics, and University of California hospitals will need to purchase expensive equipment to be in compliance).[14]

B. Supply Chain Benefits

Although the costs to meet e-pedigree requirements are high, there are supply chain benefits. For example, in the case of recalls, since record keeping is currently paper-based, distributors usually just return their entire inventory of a drug, instead of trying to wade through all of the paper records to see which product matches lot numbers or date ranges. This can cost millions of dollars to drug manufacturers. If the product returned in a recall was limited to the product actually being recalled, the potential cost savings would be huge.

C. RFID

RFID is believed to be the most promising approach in meeting the e-pedigree requirement. In 2004, Sun Microsystems, Inc., and SupplyScape introduced a Pharmaceutical Anti-Counterfeit RFID Package. According to the FDA report, "Reliable RFID technology will make the copying of medications either extremely difficult or unprofitable."[15] Although highly recommended by the FDA, RFID is not widely used in the pharmaceutical industry yet. Based on a survey in 2007 on 143 industry leaders, 95 percent of which were manufacturers, only one in five pharmaceutical companies were evaluating the benefits of RFID technology, and only 15 percent of companies were adopting RFID in some capacity. The three major reasons for the lack of adoption were: 1) cost and a lack of demonstrated return-on-investment, 2) lack of radio frequency standards, and 3) security/consumer privacy concerns. The survey also indicates that the average company spends only $25,000 on RFID technology, indicating that most must still be in the evaluation stage since that level of investment is not high enough to support RFID implementation. RFID is still considered an inventory control device rather than an anti-counterfeiting device. RFID is still being developed and is being closely watched by pharmaceutical manufactures and wholesalers. RFID is not yet cost effective or functionally reliable enough to use.

Recommended Reading

Eban, Katherine. (2005) *Dangerous Doses, How Counterfeiters are Contaminating America's Drug Supply.* Harcourt Books.

Appendix 9.1
Food and Drug Administration Documents and Publications

March 20, 2008

Technologies for Prescription Drug Identification, Validation, Track and Trace, or Authentication; Request for Information

SECTION: FOOD AND DRUG ADMINISTRATION
REGULATORY DOCUMENTS

SUMMARY: The Food and Drug Administration (FDA) is requesting comments and information regarding technologies used for the identification, validation, tracking and tracing, and authentication of prescription drugs. This request is related to FDA's implementation of the Food and Drug Administration Amendments Act of 2007 (FDAAA).

DATES: Submit written or electronic comments and information by May 19, 2008.

ADDRESSES: Submit written comments and information to the Division of Dockets Management (HFA-305), Food and Drug Administration, 5630 Fishers Lane, rm. 1061, Rockville, MD 20852. Submit electronic comments and information to www.regulations.gov.

FOR FURTHER INFORMATION CONTACT: Ilisa Bernstein, Office of Policy (HF-11), Food and Drug Administration, 5600 Fishers Lane, rm. 14C-03, Rockville, MD 20857, phone: 301-827-3360, FAX 301-594-6777, e-mail: ilisa.bernstein@fda.hhs.gov

SUPPLEMENTARY INFORMATION: On September 27, 2007, FDAAA (Public Law 3580) was signed into law. Section 913 of this legislation requires the Secretary of Health and Human Services (the Secretary) to develop standards and identify and validate effective technologies for the purpose of securing the drug supply chain against counterfeit, diverted, subpotent, substandard, adulterated, misbranded, or expired drugs. Specifically, section 913 created section 505D(b) of the Federal Food, Drug, and Cosmetic Act (the act), which directs the development of standards for the identification, validation, authentication, and tracking and tracing of prescription drugs. Section 505D(b)(3) states that the standards developed under 505D "shall address promising technologies, which may include—(A) radio-frequency identification; (B) nanotechnology; (C) encryption technologies; and (D) other track and trace or authentication technologies."

FDA has previously identified counterfeit drugs as a threat to the safety of the public and the pharmaceutical supply chain.

1. In 2004, FDA's Counterfeit Drug Task Force issued a report (Task Force Report) on the threat of counterfeit medications and measures that can be taken by private and public stakeholders to make the U.S. drug supply chain more safe and secure. The 2004 Task Force Report stated, among other things, that:

- Widespread use of electronic track and trace technology would help secure the integrity of the drug supply chain by providing an accurate drug "pedigree," which is a record of the chain of custody of the product as it moves through the supply chain from manufacturer to pharmacy;
- Radio Frequency Identification (RFID) is a promising technology as a means to achieve e-pedigree; and
- Widespread adoption and use of electronic track and trace technology would be feasible by 2007.

2. In 2006, the Task Force issued an update report which stated that the goal of widespread use of e-pedigree and track and trace technologies by 2007 would probably not be met. The voluntary approach taken did not provide enough incentives for the adoption and implementation of the technologies and e-pedigree.

As part of the efforts listed above, we received information about various technologies for the identification, track and trace, and authentication of prescription drugs, and we met with companies to learn more about these technologies. We are aware that significant progress has been made and new technologies are emerging for the identification, track and trace, and authentication of prescription drugs. In order to address the "promising technologies" related to standards development, as described in section 505D(b)(3) of the act, we are seeking information from technology vendors and others. Rather than meet individually with companies, for efficiency and to further our understanding and knowledge, we are requesting that information be submitted to the docket number listed above.

Elsewhere in this issue of the Federal Register, FDA is publishing a related document entitled "Standards for Standardized Numerical Identifier, Validation, Track and Trace, and Authentication for Prescription Drugs; Request for Comments." Under section 505D(b)(1) and (b)(2) of the act, this related document seeks information from drug manufacturers, distributors, pharmacies, other supply chain stakeholders, foreign regulators, standards organizations, and other Federal agencies and interested parties on issues related to standards for identification, validation, tracking and tracing, and authentication for prescription drug products.

We are particularly interested in the following information regarding available and emerging technologies for identification, validation, track and trace, and authentication of prescription drugs:

1. What are the RFID technologies, encrypting technologies, and nanotechnologies that are relevant? What are other relevant technologies?
2. Please provide information related to:
   - Strengths for identification, validation, track and trace, or authentication;
   - Limitations for identification, validation, track and trace, or authentication;
   - Costs of implementation and use;
   - Benefits to the public health;
   - Feasibility for widespread use;
   - Utility for e-pedigree.
3. Is the technology interoperable with other technologies? If so, describe.
4. What standards are necessary for supply chain use of the specific technology? What is the status of development of such standards?

II. Comments

Interested persons may submit to the Division of Dockets Management (see ADDRESSES) written or electronic comments and information. Submit a single copy of electronic comments and information or two paper copies of any mailed comments and information, except that individuals may submit one paper copy. Comments and information are to be identified with the name of the technology and the docket number found in brackets in the heading of this document. A copy of this notice and received comments may be seen in the Division of Dockets Management between 9 A.M. and 4 P.M., Monday through Friday.

Please note that on January 15, 2008, the FDA Division of Dockets Management Web site transitioned to the Federal Dockets Management System (FDMS). FDMS is a Government-wide, electronic docket management system. Electronic comments or submissions will be accepted by FDA through FDMS only.

Dated: March 13, 2008.
Jeffrey Shuren,
Assistant Commissioner for Policy.
[FR Doc. E8-5599 Filed 3-19-08; 8:45 A.M.]
BILLING CODE 4160-01-S
Notice; request for information.
Citation: "73 FR 14991"
Document Number: "Docket No. FDA-2008-N-0121"

Federal Register Page Number: "14991"
"Notices"

LOAD-DATE: March 20, 2008

LANGUAGE: ENGLISH

JOURNAL-CODE: HF

Copyright 2008 Federal Information and News Dispatch, Inc.

Appendix 9.2
Top Ten Drugs by Sales, Worldwide[16]

1. Lipitor (Pfizer)
2. Plavix (Sanofi/Aventis)
3. Nexium (AstraZeneca)
4. Advair (GlaxoSmithKline)
5. Enbrel (Amgen)
6. Zyprexa (Eli Lilly)
7. Risperdal (Janssen)
8. Seroquel (AstraZeneca)
9. Singulair (Merck)
10. Aranes p (Amgen)

Endnotes

1. *Current status of safety of the U.S. prescription drug distribution system.* Accenture. (June, 2008)

2. *Technologies for prescription drug identification, validation, track and trace, or authentication; request for information.* Department of Health and Human Services. Docket No. FDA-2008-N-0211.

3. FDA. Docket No 2006N-0081. Federal Register: June 2, 2006. (71)106. Retrieved from www.fda.gov/OHRMS/DOCKETS/98fr/E6-8569.htm.

4. Primary Research Interview with Director—Trade & Distribution, Top 15 global pharmaceutical company.

5. *Counterfeit pharmaceuticals—a serious threat to patient safety.*(2007)

6. F. Kermani. *Pharmaceutical Distribution in the US, Current and Future Perspectives.* Urch Publishing. (2009)

7. J. O'Donnell, *Drug Injury, Second Edition.* Boca Raton: CRC Press. (2005) chap. 15.13 and 15.14.

8. *Current Status of Safety of the U.S. Prescription Drug Distribution System.* Accenture. (June, 2008).

9. W. Connors. *awash in fake drugs, Nigerians fight back; text messaging will enable consumers to check authenticity; spate of fatalities included antifreeze-laced cough syrup. The* Wall Street Journal (Online and Print). (March 12, 2010)

10. Washington Business Information, Inc. *Manufacturers make mistakes in counterfeit fight, experts say.* Drug GMP Report. (March 1, 2010). (212) .

11. *NanoGuardian.* Retrieved on March 15, 2010 from www.nanoguardian.net/what.htm.

12. P. Faber. *RFID strategy—pharmaceutical e-pedigree—biggest supply chain topic of 2008.* Industryweek.com. Retrieved March 15, 2010 from www.industryweek.com/articles/rfid_strategy_--_pharmaceutical_e-pedi-gree_--_biggest_supply_chain_topic_of_2008_15664.aspx.

13. E. Koutnik-Fotopoulus. *E-pedigree: A Key Solution to Combat Counterfeiting.* Pharmacy Times. (May 1, 2008) Retrieved March 15, 2010 from www.pharma-cytimes.com/issue/pharmacy/2008/2008-05/2008-05-8541.

14. *PhRMA statement on California's e-pedigree law.* Retrieved March 15, 2010 from www.phrma.org.

15. U.S.D.A. *The U.S. Food and Drug Administration report.* (February 18, 2004).

16. IMS Health, Inc. *Retail drug monitor report 2007.* Retrieved June 15, 2008, at www.imshealth.com.

Chapter 10

General Principles of Pharmacology

James J. O'Donnell III, M.S., Ph.D., James T. O'Donnell, Pharm.D., MS, FCP, and Vanessa M. Vullmahn M.S.

10.1 Introduction

Pharmacology can be defined as the study of drug action on a living organism through chemical processes. It involves the analysis of normal and abnormal interactions between the substance and the living organism. These substances may be administered to achieve either therapeutic or toxic effects to the patient's metabolic processes or hosted parasites, respec-

Note: The contents of this chapter represent the first seven lectures of a pharmacology course taught by James J. O'Donnell, Ph.D and James T O'Donnell, Pharm.D. at Rush University Medical College in Chicago, Illinois. As such, the source of most of the information is the course textbook: Katzung, Bertram G., Susan B. Masters, and Anthony J. Trevor. *Basic and Clinical Pharmacology*. Eleventh Edition. New York: McGraw-Hill Medical, 2009.

tively. To achieve an effect, the substance binds, or attaches, to specific targets within the body, which then causes a specific activation or inhibition of chemical processes.

The concept of rational therapeutics (e.g., the administration of the correct dose to achieve the desired effect) was introduced into medicine only about 65 years ago. Only then did it become possible to accurately evaluate therapeutic claims. Therapeutic agents referenced within this chapter are based on experimental evidence, and supported by the scientific method.

During the last half-century, many fundamentally new drug groups and new members of old groups were introduced. Drugs are derived from a number of sources: chemicals, animals, minerals, proteins, carbohydrates and fats. All drugs can be toxic; chemicals in botanicals (plants) and natural/organic products can be just as toxic as synthetic chemicals. As stated by Paracelsus, the father of toxicology, "All things are poison, and nothing is without poison; only the dose permits something not to be poisonous." This is more commonly summarized as "The dose makes the poison."

The last three decades have seen an ever more rapid growth of information and understanding of the molecular basis for drug action. Studies of the local molecular environment of receptors have shown that receptors, effectors (molecules that interact with receptors) and other proteins do not function in isolation; they are strongly influenced by surrounding regulatory proteins.

10.2 Basic Principles

In the broadest sense, human pharmacology can be considered as the interaction between a drug and the body. At the next level of complexity, the interaction can be broken down into pharmacodynamics and pharmacokinetics (see Figure 10.1).

Pharmacodynamics is defined as the drug's effect on the body. In other words, it is the mechanism of action of that specific drug/substance. Pharmacokinetics is defined as the effect that the body has on the drug, which includes the processes of absorption, distribution, metabolism and elimination/excretion (ADME). Both pharmacodynamics and pharmacokinetics are interconnected.

When a drug is administered, it undergoes absorption within the body. Drugs administered orally usually undergo a first pass effect in the liver which alters the drug's bioavailability, or the amount of unchanged drug that reaches the circulation blood (systemic circulation). The drug is then distributed to a number of physical sites, where it binds to a specific receptor on a particular bodily tissue, or organ, which functions through the combined cooperation of individual cells. Processes induced by this interaction include a number of second messenger cascades which lead to a particular cellular response. A second messenger is a particular biomolecule which relays information from the receptor on the cell surface to a targeted organelle within the cytoplasm. After binding with a receptor, a drug is metabolized, or biotransformed, by key enzymes. This metabolic biotransformation causes the drug to inactivate and to be more easily excreted from the body.

A. Absorption

Absorption can be defined as the process by which a drug enters systemic circulation from the site of administration. Generally, a drug is absorbed either orally (mouth), dermally (skin) or by inhalation (Figure 10.2). Following absorption is migration to the site of action in another bodily compartment (e.g., the brain, in the case of an anti-seizure medication). This inter-compartmental navigation requires permeation through various barriers including: the stomach/intestine, the blood and veins, and the blood brain barrier.

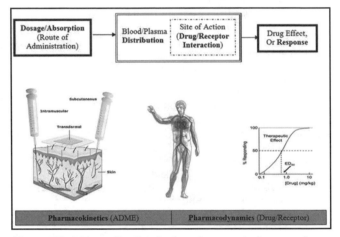

Figure 10.1 *Pharmacological pathways. A drug undergoes both pharmacokinetics (absorption, distribution, metabolism and elimination) and pharmacodynamics (mechanism of action, drug-receptor binding) within the body. Sources of digital images (left to right): (1) Skin + syringes: ABCs of Pharmacology: A Drug's Life. Digital Image. National Institute of General Medical Sciences, 2006. Web. 12 Oct. 2011. <http://publications. nigms.nih.gov/medbydesign/chapter1.html>. (2) Human body: Wikipedia Commons: Blutkreislauf. Digital Image. Wikipedia, 2006. Web. 12 Oct. 2011. <http:// commons.wikimedia.org/wiki/File:Blutkreislauf.png> (3) Graph – Therapeutic Effect: Clarkson, Craig W. Basic Principles of Pharmacology: Drug Safety and the Therapeutic Index. Digital Image. Tulane Pharmwiki, 2009. Web. 9 Oct. 2011. http://tmedweb.tulane.edu/pharmwiki/doku.php/drug_receptor_theory. Reproduced by permission from Craig W. Clarkson, PhD. ©2011 Craig W. Clarkson, Tulane University, New Orleans, LA.*

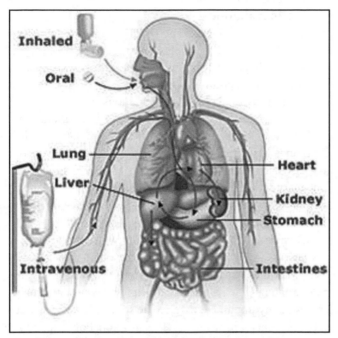

Figure 10.2 Drug's absorption in the body. Medicines taken orally pass through the liver before they are absorbed into the blood. Other forms of drug administration enter the blood directly. Source: ABCs of Pharmacology: A Drug's Life. Digital Image. National Institute of General Medical Sciences, 2006. Web. 12 Oct. 2011. http://publications.nigms.nih.gov/medbydesign/chapter1.html.

B. Lipid Diffusion

Lipid bilayer diffusion, or passage, is the most important limiting factor for drug permeation. The compartments or organs of the body are separated by cellular membranes, or walls, made up of lipids. These cellular membranes are made up of two layers of lipids called the lipid bilayer. Lipids are a group of naturally occurring molecules which include: fats, waxes, and fat-soluble vitamins (A, D, E and K).

Passive transport, which includes both simple and facilitated diffusion, is the usual process by which drugs pass lipid bilayers. Facilitated diffusion involves transport via carrier proteins embedded within the lipid bilayer, while simple diffusion, the most common mechanism, allows easy passage of a drug either directly through the bilayer, or through a protein channel.

C. Determinants of Absorption

There are several physical characteristics of a drug that determine its ability to absorb across cellular membranes. These determinants can be divided into two categories: mechanical and physiochemical.

1. Mechanical:
   - Disintegration—the time for the preparation (e.g., pill) to be reduced to fragments.
   - Dissolution—the time for the drug to disperse into a solution, i.e., to dissolve.

Mechanically, both disintegration and dissolution are significant determinants of drug absorption. Disintegration, the reduction of the drug into small fragments, results in increased mobility. The efficacy of a drug mixture depends on the time it takes for the tablet or capsule to disintegrate in the patient's gastrointestinal tract. Dissolution is the dispersion of the drug within a solvent or digestive fluid. The rate of the dissolution is the primary variable used to control the duration that the drug will be in effect. For example, extended release tablets have a longer dissolution time and therefore take longer to achieve maximal effect.

2. Physiochemical:
   - Molecular size—the larger the molecule, the less likely it is to cross membranes.
   - Degree of ionization—the stronger the charge, the less likely it is to cross membranes.

Physiochemically, molecular size and degree of ionization are significant determinants of drug absorption. Molecular size or molecular weight (MW), critical for cellular receptor fit and activation, is inversely proportional to a drug's ability to diffuse across cellular membranes.

The (MW) of drugs varies from very small (lithium ion MW = 7 kDal) to very large (alteplase protein MW = 59,050 kDal). However, most therapeutic drugs have molecular weights between 100 kDal and 1,000 kDal. Drugs beyond this range (usually proteins) do not diffuse readily between compartments of the body, and therefore must often be administered directly into the compartment where they have their effect. For example, alteplase, a clot-dissolving enzyme, is administered directly into the affected blood vessel by intravenous (IV) administration.

A drug's ability to become ionized or charged is another key physiochemical determinant of absorption. Molecules can hold either a positive charge, a negative charge, or no charge at all (neutral). If the molecules within the drug mixture gain a positive or negative charge, they are less capable of crossing cellular membranes, and less likely to reach a specific compartment within the body. Neutral molecules, on the other hand, readily diffuse through membranes and can easily reach a number of compartments. Most drugs are organic (carbon-containing) compounds and can be categorized as/by:

1.   Non-electrolytes, e.g., glucose. These drugs do not
     ionize, and pH changes do not affect the absorption
     and distribution of this kind of drug.
2.   Weak acids or bases. Those drugs that donate pro-
     tons (positively-charged particles) are weak acids
     (aspirin, barbiturates). Those drugs that accept
     protons are weak bases (epinephrine (adrenaline)).
     Strong acids or bases are not used systemically as
     medicines. Found in the stomach, hydrochloric
     acid (HCl) is the body's only strong acid. The most
     important point to remember is that ionized drugs
     do not readily pass through membranes.

1. Lipid/aqueous partition coefficient and pH

Because lipid barriers separate aqueous compartments,
the lipid/aqueous partition coefficient of a drug determines
how readily the molecule moves between aqueous and lipid
media. In the case of weak acids and weak bases (which
gain or lose electrical charge-bearing protons, depending on
the pH), the ability to move from aqueous to lipid, or vice
versa, varies with the pH of the medium, because charged
molecules attract water molecules. The pH is quantified on
a scale between 1 and 14. A water-friendly, or aqueous, environment has a more neutral pH (~7). Acidity is inversely
proportional to pH (less than 7), while basicity is directly
proportional to pH (greater than 7).

The ratio of the lipid-soluble form to water-soluble form
for a weak acid or weak base is expressed by the Henderson-
Hasselbach equation. The equation exists in two forms, one
for an acidic drug and another for a basic drug.

Acidic drug:

$$pH = pK_a + \log\left(\frac{[A^-]}{[HA]}\right)$$

Where:
A^- = the conjugate base of the corresponding acid HA
pK_a = –log(K_a), where K_a = acid dissociation constant
$[A^-]$ = molar concentration of A^-.
$[HA]$ = molar concentration of HA.

Basic drug:

$$pOH = pK_b + \log\left(\frac{[BH^+]}{[B]}\right)$$

Where:
BH^+ = the conjugate acid of the corresponding base B
pK_b = –log(K_b), where K_b = base dissociation constant
$[BH^+]$ = molar concentration of BH^+.
$[B]$ = molar concentration of B.

2. Bioavailability

The amount and means by which we absorb a drug determines bioavailability, or the unchanged drug concentration in the blood. Our first and simplest task is to relate a
dose to the concentration of the drug in the body. For the
purposes of pharmacokinetic calculations, we will assume
the one-compartment model. That is, we will assume that
once the drug is absorbed into systemic circulation, that it
distributes instantaneously and homogenously throughout
the vascular space. The first thing we need to find is the
amount of the dose that reaches systemic circulation. This is
simply the fraction of drug that reaches systemic circulation
(bioavailability, F) multiplied by the dose.

Bioavailability is determined by how easily the drug is
absorbed as well as the amount lost due to first pass metabolism. Maximum absorption occurs when a drug is hydrophobic enough to pass through the lipid bilayer of cell membranes but hydrophilic enough to be soluble. Bioavailability
is 100 percent for intravenous (IV) injection. For simplicity's
sake, pharmacokinetic (PK) equations are sometimes represented in the form assuming IV injection as this obviates the
need to explicitly include the bioavailability. However, a PK
equation that contains dose and assumes IV administration
can be modified for oral or other routes of administration by
simply replacing (dose) by the expression $F \times dose$.

Some reasons for bioavailability:

1.   Tableting—dosage form must disintegrate and dis-
     solve to be absorbed
2.   Stability in the stomach
3.   Degradation by bacterial enzymes
4.   First pass effect

3. First pass effect

Due to its anatomical arrangement, the blood supply
from the GI tract goes first to the liver. Drugs taken orally
can therefore be metabolized in the GI tract, the liver, or both
before absorption to systemic circulation. This phenomenon
is variously known as first pass effect or presystemic drug
elimination. In some cases, the majority of a drug dose can
be lost this way, necessitating increased dosage or different
routes of administration (e.g., IV).

Following absorption across the gut wall, the portal blood
delivers the drug to the liver prior to entry into systemic circulation. A drug can be metabolized in the gut or even in the portal blood, but most commonly it is the liver that is responsible.
In addition, the liver can excrete the drug into the bile. Any
of these metabolic precursors can contribute to a reduction in
bioavailability. The effect of first-pass hepatic elimination (on
bioavailability) is expressed as the extraction ratio (ER).

A drug such as morphine is almost completely absorbed, so that loss in the gut is negligible. However, the hepatic extraction ratio for morphine is 0.67, so ER is 0.33. The bioavailability of morphine is therefore expected to be about 33 percent, which is close to the observed value. The clinical value of this phenomenon is that a 10 mg IV dose of morphine is equivalent to a 30 mg oral dose.

10.3 Routes of Administration

Drug administration can be divided into two broad categories—intravascular (within the vein) and extravascular (outside the vein).

Intravascular (e.g., intravenous injection) is the type of administration in which the drug is placed directly into systemic circulation. Because there is no drug lost upon administration, bioavailability is 100 percent.

Extravascular (e.g., oral dosing, intramuscular injections) may be associated with drug loss due to the first pass effect. When a drug is administered extravascularly, the time of onset and intensity of action are determined by the characteristics of absorption from the site of administration.

Bioavailability (F) is determined by dividing the amount of a drug which reached systemic circulation after extravascular administration by the amount of a drug which reached systemic circulation after IV administration (same drug, same dose). This is done by taking blood samples at timed intervals, measuring the concentration of the drug, and plotting concentration vs. time on a graph (see Figure 10.3). The resulting area under the curve (AUC) is proportional to the total mass which reached systemic circulation between the first and last sampling intervals. If the oral and IV doses are unequal, one can normalize by dividing the AUC for each administration by the respective dose:

For equal doses:

$$F = \frac{AUC_{oral}}{AUC_{IV}}$$

For different doses:

$$F = \left(\frac{AUC_{oral}\,Dose}{AUC_{IV}\,Dose} \right)$$

For direct comparison of two drugs:

$$\text{relative bioavailability} = \left(\frac{AUC_T / Dose_T}{AUC_Q / Dose_Q} \right)$$

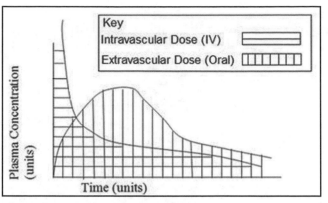

Figure 10.3 *Difference in blood plasma concentration of an intravascular vs. extravascular drug dose.*

10.4 Extravascular Administration
A. Oral Administration

Approximately 80 percent of drugs prescribed in the U.S. are for oral administration. This route is used largely for convenience, ease of administration, minimal toxicity, and lower expense (see Figure 10.4). The first oral absorptive surface is the buccal mucosa (between the inside cheek and gums). Due to the rapid transit time, usually very little absorption takes place here. Special drug formulations are sublingual (SL), or under the tongue. Nitroglycerin is an example of a drug which is formulated to dissolve quickly in the mouth and is rapidly absorbed in approximately one to two minutes. This route will also eliminate the first pass effect.

The next absorptive surface is the stomach/gastric pouch. The minimum absorption time for drugs in the absence of food is about 20 minutes. With food, absorption time becomes quite variable depending upon fat content, viscosity (resistance of a fluid) and volume. The pH of gastric contents is 1-2 (highly acidic). However, the absorbing surface (gastric mucosa) appears to absorb drugs best at pH 3-3.5. Weak acids (aspirin), water, and lipid-soluble non-electrolytes (ethyl alcohol) are readily absorbed by passive diffusion.

Because some drugs would be adversely affected by acid and digestive enzymes, many are formulated with an enteric coating which resists dissolution in low pH environments. The enteric coating provides a protective effect which, depending on the extent and type, may provide for a delayed or sustained absorption. It at least prevents destruction by gastric acid, thus allowing the dosage form to pass into the small intestine. Enteric coatings, such as those used on aspirin, also provide protection of the gastric pouch from irritation leading to possible ulcerations.

Absorption from the small intestine takes 30 to 90 minutes. The rate at which drugs reach the small intestine will

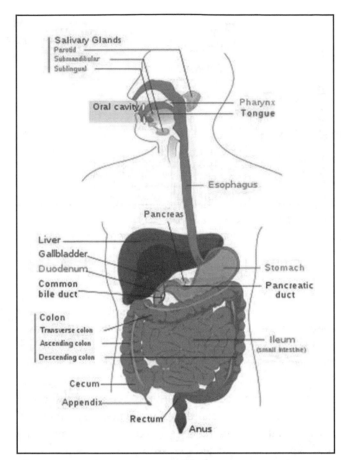

Figure 10.4 The gastrointestinal tract (GIT). The success of oral administration depends upon the drug absorption through the GIT. Adapted from Wikipedia Commons: Ruiz, Mariana. Diagram of the Human Digestive System. Digital Image. Wikipedia, 2006. Web. 12 Oct. 2011. http://commons.wikimedia. org/wiki/File:Digestive_system_diagram_edit.svg.

depend upon gastric emptying time. Emptying time is decreased by taking a drug with 6-8 oz. of water and increased by the presence of food. These pharmaceutical characteristics will prompt instructions such as "take on empty stomach" or "take with food."

The small intestine, with its large blood circulation, is the primary absorptive surface for most orally administered drugs, largely because its surface, covered with thousands of cellular membrane protrusions, or microvilli, has an area of approximately 120 m² (≈1000 times that of the stomach).

Malabsorptive function, due to reduced residence time in the small intestine, may be caused from disease, genetics, or a side effect of other (or the same) medication. The pH of the small intestine is more alkaline (pH 6.3-6.5) than the stomach. Therefore, drugs which have a pKa in this range will be better absorbed.

Usually very little drug is absorbed in the large intestine, either because most of the drug has already been absorbed, or because of the smaller surface area and blood supply relative to the small intestine. All drugs absorbed in the stomach or small intestine will undergo the first pass (hepatic) effect mentioned above.

B. Rectal Administration

Rectal administration is useful for drugs which may be inactivated via the oral route and for drugs which are irritating (cause nausea and vomiting). Rectal administration can be used for giving antiemetics to control nausea and vomiting. This route is not used frequently for other types of drugs because absorption is less predictable. It does have the advantage of avoiding the first pass effect intrinsic to the oral route.

C. Other Routes of Administration

Other routes of administration include:

Intrathecal	Injection into cerebral spinal fluid (CSF) to obtain effective concentration in the central nervous system (CNS).
Intradermal	Injection into the skin (e.g., local anesthesia with lidocaine).
Intramuscular (IM)	Injection into muscles of the arm or buttocks; used for irritating drugs, drugs not absorbed by the oral route or when a depot of drug is required. The rate of absorption can be altered by formulation (type of suspension, size of crystal) and application of heat, cold, or exercise. This route of administration was quite popular before the onset of the AIDS/HIV epidemic, and as a caution against occupational needle sticks, a switch to intravenous administration occurred. Risks of IM include local infections, accidental intravascular administration, and pain experienced by the patient.
Subcutaneous (SQ)	Injection under the skin; absorption is slower than for IV or IM and less predictable. Insulin and heparin are administered SQ.
Topical	Application on the skin; usually for local effect such as rash.

Transdermal	Patches used with drugs like fentanyl, nicotine, nitroglycerin, scopolamine, and hormones are applied topically for sustained absorption into systemic circulation. This is an area of rapid product development.
Inhalation	Gaseous anesthetics are often given for systemic effect. This route is rapid due to the large surface area of the lung. Used with gaseous anesthetics, bronchodilators for asthma, and emergency administration of resuscitative medications.
Eye and ear drops	Applied topically for local effects. May lead to systemic toxicity.

10.5 Intravascular Administration

Intravenous (IV) and intra-arterial (IA) administration involves introducing a drug directly into the blood vessel and therefore into the systemic circulation. The bolus IV push (hypodermic needle) is the fastest means of getting a drug into the systemic circulation. Circulation throughout the body takes about 2 minutes. One must take precautions with any bolus injection as the dose cannot be recovered. Other disadvantages include:

a)   Transient high blood level concentrations.
b)   Only small volumes can be injected.

   IV infusion (Figure 10.5) is a useful means to control both the rate of administration and obtain a desired response (even over an extended period of time). This method is used when drugs would be inactivated by gastric enzymes or acid. It is also used for drugs which are poorly absorbed, or can cause irritation in tissues if injected intramuscularly. IV infusion is fast and can be used to maintain a desired blood level over a long period of time. IV drip is a special case where the drug is administered dropwise (i.e. so many drops per unit time). By increasing the time over which the dose is given, one can obtain a lower concentration for a longer period of time.

   Due to inherent difficulty and risk, the intra-arterial route is used only for special circumstances (e.g., vasodilator drugs in the treatment of vasospasm and thrombolytic drugs for treatment of embolism).

10.6 Distribution

This section will discuss how drugs distribute throughout the body and what factors can affect this distribution. The

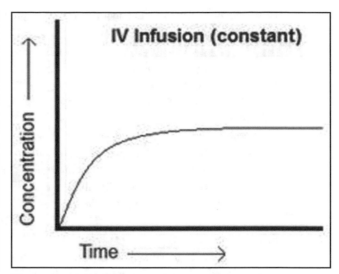

Figure 10.5 *IV diffusion is fast and is used to maintain a target drug level in the blood over time.*

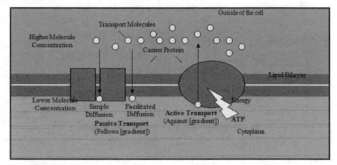

Figure 10.6 *Drug transport and means of distribution: simple diffusion, facilitated diffusion and active transport.*

extent of distribution of a drug away from the blood is indicated by the volume of distribution (V_D). Once the drug has been absorbed, it can be distributed to the rest of the body. This distribution is done in two main ways:

1.   *Bulk flow* via the blood. In this phase the physiochemical (i.e. drug size) properties are not important. However, this phase can result in patterns of distribution. The tissues that are well-perused will receive more of the drug than the less well-perused tissues. This is highly relevant in intravascular administration.

2.   *Diffusional transfer* determines where and how quickly the drug distributes. This depends upon the drug's ability to cross the cell membranes that separate the various aqueous compartments of the body. In general there are four ways by which most drug molecules cross cell membranes (see Figure 10.6):

a. Passive Diffusion: Diffusion through lipid membranes.

b. Facilitated Diffusion: Diffusion through pores in, or between, membranes.

c. Active Transport: Transport across the membrane by carriers into or out of cells.

d. Pinocytosis or phagocytosis: Pinocytosis is the process of engulfing fluid and nutrients by a cell. Phagocytosis is the engulfing of particulates by a cell. Both require cellular energy. Drugs with large MW (>900 kDal) may cross tissue barriers by these processes.

A. Diffusion

Drugs move across biological barriers by diffusion. The driving force is the concentration gradient. Drugs move down the concentration gradient (from high to low concentration). It is only the concentration of the unbound, unionized drug which contributes to the diffusion gradient.

B. Volume of Distribution

Now we have determined how much of the dose reaches the systemic circulation. How can we determine the drug concentration? Since concentration = mass/volume, concentration is related to mass (drug dose) through the volume in which it is dissolved (volume of distribution). Since we are assuming the one-compartment model where the drug is homogenously distributed throughout all the space it occupies in the body, the volume of distribution is a theoretical abstraction.

In reality, the drug will only be homogenously distributed within the blood stream; it will be heterogeneously distributed to the tissues and other spaces of the body depending on the physical composition of the patient and the properties of the drug. Drug concentration, which counts both free molecules and those bound to proteins, can only be measured in the blood compartment. The concentration in other compartments cannot be measured. By necessity, we assume that the drug is just as concentrated (or just as diluted) in the other compartments of the body as it is in the blood compartment; our estimate of volume of distribution is derived from this assumption. As such, the volume of distribution (V_D) is given by the following equation:

$$V_D = \text{total amount of drug in the body / drug blood plasma concentration}$$

An organizing principle for how the volume of distribution changes in various conditions is as follows: anything that causes the distribution of the drug to shift from the blood compartment to the tissues and other compartments will increase the volume of distribution. This is not due to the patient receiving a blood transfusion—it is merely a mathematical adjustment used to account for the drug's behavior. The concept is similar to wind chill factor. The actual temperature does not change when the wind is blowing, but is adjusted lower to more accurately portray how it feels. In the same manner, the actual volume of water in a patient's body does not change when factors cause a shift in drug distribution from tissues and other compartments to the blood stream, but is adjusted lower to more accurately calculate the dosage. See Table 10.1.

Table 10.1
Physical Volumes (in L/kg Body Weight) of Some Body Compartments into Which Drugs or Toxins May Be Distributed

Compartment and Volume Water	Examples of Drugs or Toxins
Total body water (0.6 L/kg)	Small water-soluble molecules: e.g., ethanol
Extracellular water (0.2 L/kg)	Larger water-soluble molecules: e.g., gentamicin
Blood (0.08 L/kg); plasma (0.04 L/kg)	Strongly plasma protein-bound molecules and very large molecules: e.g., heparin
Fat (0.2–0.35 L/kg)	Highly lipid-soluble molecules: e.g., DDT
Bone (0.07 L/kg)	Certain ions: e.g., lead, fluoride

For example, the more lipophilic a drug, the more affinity it will have for fatty tissues and the more it will be pulled out of the blood, increasing V_D. Similarly, the more obese a patient is, the more drug molecules will be pulled out of the blood and distributed in the fatty tissues, increasing V_D. A drug which has a high degree of protein binding will be pulled into the blood compartment more, decreasing V_D. Affinity or binding of the drug in the blood compartment versus the other compartments of the body causes a shift in distribution in accordance with the basic chemical law of Le Chatelier's principle—if a chemical system at equilibrium experiences a change in concentration, temperature, volume, or partial pressure, then the equilibrium shifts to counteract the imposed change and a new equilibrium is established. Once the pharmacokinetic parameter of volume of distribution has been established, concentration can be calculated by dividing the mass of drug (dose in systemic circulation) by the volume of distribution.

Values over 40 L represent a drug which is mostly found somewhere in the body other than the plasma. So the larger the V_D, the more of the drug dose is outside of systemic circulation. In the equation

V_D = total amount of drug in the body /
drug blood plasma concentration

there are three parameters. Knowing any two of them allows the calculation of the third.

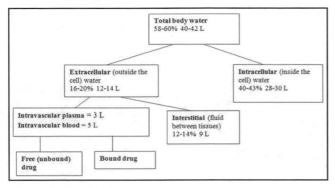

Figure 10.7 *Bodily compartments.*

In medicine, for descriptive purposes, one can use a standard patient weighing 70 kg. The major compartments of this body are shown in Figure 10.7.

Example: If 40 mg of drug is given by IV push to a 70 kg man and the drug distributes into total body water, what was the starting drug concentration in the plasma?

$$V_D = \frac{D}{C_O}$$

Where:
V_D = Volume of distribution
D = Dose
C_O = Initial concentration

$$V_D \times C_O = D$$

$$C_O = \frac{D}{V_D}$$

From Figure 10.7, we can determine that the volume of distribution for a 70 kg patient, total body water, is 40 L.

C. Binding to Plasma Proteins and Cellular Constituents

Plasma, a yellow fluid component of the blood that surrounds the blood cells, contains mostly water, but also proteins, glucose, minerals and hormones. Plasma albumin constitutes about 50 percent of the plasma proteins and is usually responsible for drug binding. Binding to plasma albumin is generally reversible and involves ionic, hydrogen, and Van der Waals forces. There are multiple binding sites with differing polarities so different drugs may bind. Albumin usually binds acidic drugs while α-glycoprotein binds basic drugs. Equilibrium is established between the free and the bound drug.

D. Re-Distribution

Highly lipid soluble drugs will move into muscles and fat where they have no physiological activity, and this represents a type of sink. This movement will tend to show an increased V_D for the drug, but it will also have an effect upon the duration of the drug's action. For drugs that act in the CNS, sequestration into fat deposits represents a loss of activity. For example, the drugs diazepam and lorazepam (benzodiazepines) are used for epilepsy. They have a long half-life in the blood. But they have only a limited duration of action in epilepsy because they come out of the CNS and are sequestered into the fat where they are physiologically inert. Therefore, the duration of action is not associated with the half-life of the drug, but rather with the rate of sequestration into the fat deposits.

E. Blood-Brain Barrier (BBB)

The blood brain barrier separates the circulating blood from the brain extracellular fluid (see Figure 10.8). Not all substances present in the bloodstream can gain access to the brain. Endothelial cells (layer of cells that line the inside of a

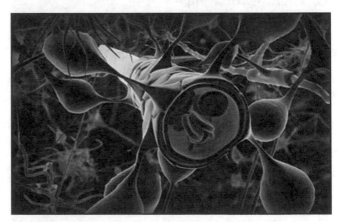

Figure 10.8 *Blood brain barrier, which separates blood and the brain's extracellular fluid. Reproduced from Wikipedia Commons: Mohammed, Ben Brahim. The Blood Brain Barrier and Astrocytes. Digital Image. Wikipedia, 2010. Web. 12 Oct. 2011. http://commons. wikimedia.org/wiki/File:Blood_Brain_Barriere.jpg.*

blood vessel) appear to be a barrier for some drugs and substances against entry into the brain. Inflammation may increase the permeability of the blood-brain barrier and under these conditions even ionized compounds may penetrate.

Some of the properties which determine drug entry into the brain are:

a)   Molecular weight—compounds with MW >60, 000 Dal will not penetrate

b)   Lipid solubility—the greater the lipid solubility the better the penetration

c)   Fraction of drug un-ionized at physiological pH— the larger the un-ionized fraction, the greater the penetration since the concentration gradient is larger

d)   Protein binding—only the free fraction contributes to the concentration gradient

F. Placental Barrier

The blood supply of the mother is separated from the blood supply of the fetus by several tissue layers known as the "placental barrier." Drugs must diffuse across this barrier to enter fetal circulation.

Passage across the placental barrier is regulated by the same requirements as passage across the blood-brain barrier. However, only very large molecules (e.g., Heparin, proteins, etc.) do not cross the placenta. Small molecules, which represent the overwhelming majority of therapeutic agents, will cross the placenta, and represent potential risk to the fetus. In this case, with rare exception, the "barrier" is a myth!

G. Therapeutic Range

The therapeutic range is the broadness of plasma concentrations within which the plasma drug levels produce the maximum benefit and the least toxicity. Important factors indicated in a drug's therapeutic range are:

•   Time to onset of activity: Time from first taking the drug until it starts to work.

•   Duration of action: Time during which the dose is effective in the body.

H. Bioequivalence vs. Bioinequivalence

Bioequivalence compares two different manufacturers' products of the same drug (e.g., brand name Drug A vs. generic preparation Drug B) or two different drugs. Bioinequivalence may occur even if Drugs A and B have equal bioavailability. Bioequivalence has two requirements:

a)   Same maximum bioavailability

b)   Same maximum rate of absorption

Drug A and Drug B have similar bioavailability according to their AUC's and similar rates of absorption. Drug B, however, is slightly slower. The slower rate of absorption has a lower maximum concentration (*Cmax B*) attained over a longer period of time (*Cmax* and *Tmax*). To quantify the bioequivalence ratio, Drug A's AUC and Drug B's AUC are calculated. The FDA allows for a leeway in the *Cmax* and *Tmax* in approving generic equivalents; equality is not required. To be accepted as bioequivalent, the area ratio would need to fall between 0.8 and 1.25. See Figure 10.9.

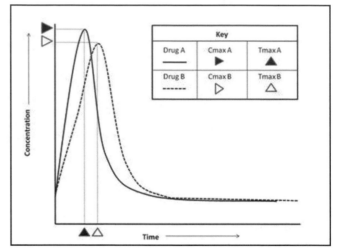

Figure 10.9 Bioequivalence of Drugs A and B. Drug A is the name brand and Drug B is the generic. (Cmax: maximum plasma drug concentration, Tmax: time required to achieve a maximal concentration, AUC: total area under the plasma drug concentration-time curve)

Drug A: Calculated AUC =   100.0 mg.h/L
Drug B: Calculated AUC =   90.0 mg.h/L
                               90.0/100.0 = 0.9

The ratio of the areas, and therefore the relative bioavailability, is 0.9.

10.7 Drug Metabolism (Biotransformation)

Drug metabolism, or biotransformation, is the process by which a drug is converted to another form which is more amenable to excretion, which negates the drug's action, or both. Foreign chemicals or drugs are also called xenobiotics. Membrane associated proteins called cytochrome P450s play an important role in xenobiotic metabolism, especially for lipophilic drugs. The metabolism of these compounds takes place in two phases.

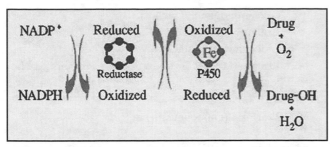

Figure 10.10 Phase I drug oxidation. Source: "Preventable Adverse Drug Reactions: A Focus on Drug Interactions." US Food and Drug Administration. N.p., n.d. Web. 29 Oct. 2011. www.fda.gov/drugs/developmentapprovalprocess/developmentresources/druginteractionslabeling/ucm110632.htm.

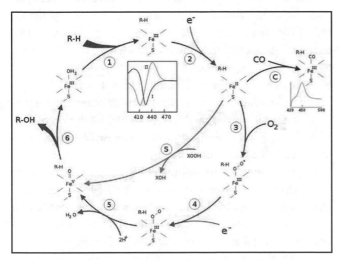

Figure 10.11 Phase I reaction catalytic cycle induced by cytochrome P450. Public domain, via Wikimedia Commons: Richfield, David. Accessed 03-23-2012. http://commons.wikimedia.org/wiki/file:p450cycle.svg.

Phase I reactions (Figures 10.10 and 10.11), which usually convert the parent drug to a more polar metabolite by introducing or unmasking a functional group (–OH, –NH2, –SH), are mediated by the cytochrome P450 enzymes in the liver. Phase I is chemical modification in order to add a functional group that can be used to attach a conjugate. The conjugate makes the modified compound more water soluble so it can be excreted in the urine. Many P450s add a hydroxyl group (-OH) in a Phase I step of drug metabolism. The hydroxyl then serves as the site for further modifications in Phase 2 drug metabolism—the conjugation.

Endogenous substrates such as glucuronic acid, sulfuric acid, acetic acid, or an amino acid combine with the newly incorporated functional group to form a highly polar conjugate. Such conjugation or synthetic reactions are the hallmarks of Phase II metabolism.

The liver is the primary site of drug metabolism, although there is some metabolism in the intestinal wall with p-glycoprotein. Furthermore, there may be some metabolism in the lungs, skin, kidneys, and the brain. Some orally administered drugs (clonazepam, chlorpromazine, and cyclosporine) are more extensively metabolized in the intestines than the liver.

Both intestinal and hepatic metabolism contribute to the first pass effect. First-pass effects may circumscribe the bioavailability of orally administered drugs to such a degree that alternative routes of administration must be used to achieve therapeutically effective blood levels.

Mutations in cytochrome P450 genes or deficiencies of the enzymes are responsible for several human diseases. This is termed a polymorphism. Induction of some endogenous P450s is a risk factor in several cancers since these enzymes can convert procarcinogens to carcinogens.

A. Phase I Reactions

Many drug-metabolizing enzymes are located in the lipophilic endoplasmic reticulum membranes of the liver and other tissues. Biotransformation acts upon endogenous (already found within the body) as well as exogenous substrates (also termed xenobiotics).

Biotransformation (drug metabolism) is the process by which a drug is chemically converted in the body to its metabolite. Cytochrome P450s (CYP450s) are the main Phase I endogenous proteins that act as drug metabolizing enzymes and also have endogenous enzymatic processes that are used to make cholesterol, steroids and other important lipids such as prostacyclins and thromboxane A2.

P450 enzymes are primarily located in the liver, but are also found in the kidneys, lungs, intestines, skin and eyes. The name cytochrome P450 derives from the fact that these proteins have a heme group, and an unusual spectrum. Mammalian cytochrome P450s are membrane bound. They were originally discovered in rat liver microsomes, hence the name microsomal enzymes.

P450s catalyze three main types of chemical reactions: oxidation, reduction and hydrolysis. The reaction that is most important, however, is hydroxylation.

A quick biotransformation rate may be due to the affinity of the drug molecule for the enzyme receptor. Other drugs biotransform slowly and thus a high molecular burden cannot be tolerated. The CYP enzyme(s) which degrade it will become saturated and the drug may accumulate in the body. If enzymes cannot metabolize a drug quickly, toxicity can result. Sometimes a drug may be biotransformed at a decent rate but has low potency, which means the effective dose must be high. Thus, the molecular burden will be high, which may push the kinetics into zero order.

Different biotransformation rates may be due to the structure of the drug molecule, as different drugs metabolized by the same CYP isoform (such as, for example, CYP3A4) may have different affinities for the enzyme and therefore different metabolization rates. Alternatively, in some cases the enzyme itself may have a different structure in different people (polymorphisms of the enzyme). In the latter case, some people may be fast metabolizers and others may be slow metabolizers. The most prominent CYP enzyme which has different drug metabolism polymorphisms is CYP2D6, which metabolizes most of the neurological drugs and is second only to CYP3A4 in the number of drugs it metabolizes.

1. The families of human P450s

The P450 proteins are categorized into families and subfamilies by their sequence similarities. Sequences that are greater than 40 percent identical at the amino acid level belong to the same family. Sequences that are greater than 55 percent identical are in the same subfamily. There are more than 2500 cytochrome P450 sequences known.

Biotransformation utilizing P450 pathways are integral to the biosynthesis of many mammalian compounds such as bile acids and hormones. These enzymes tend to be in families with one or two members and they have only one substrate. Most of these enzymes use steroids or steroid precursors as their substrates.

2. Induction of P450 enzymes

Inducers of P450 enzymes accelerate metabolism, lower the effect of the substrate drug, and may rob the patient of the beneficial effect. P450 enzymes have a variety of gene regulatory mechanisms. Many of these genes can be turned on or induced by a chemical signal. An example is the induction of steroid biosynthetic P450s by ACTH adrenocorticotropic hormone.

Some of the chemically dissimilar P450 substrate drugs, on repeated administration, induce P450 expression by enhancing the rate of its synthesis or reducing the rate of P450 degradation. Induction accelerates substrate metabolism, which usually hinders the pharmacologic action of the inducer and co-administered drugs. However, in the case of drugs metabolically transformed to reactive metabolites, enzyme induction may exacerbate metabolite-mediated toxicity. For example, ethanol induces the CYP2E enzymes.

The CYP3A subfamily is one of the most important drug metabolizing families and is "the most abundantly expressed P450 in human liver." CYP3A4 is known to metabolize more than 120 different drugs.

Examples of CYP3A4 substrates:

- Acetaminophen (Tylenol),
- Codeine (narcotic),
- Lidocaine (anaesthetic),
- Lovastatin (HMGCoA reductase inhibitor, a cholesterol lowering drug),
- Taxol (cancer drug),
- Warfarin (anticoagulant).

3. P450 Inhibition

P450 inhibitors slow down metabolism, increase the effect of the substrate drug and may cause toxicity of the substrate.

There are common drugs given for special purposes that inhibit P450 enzymes. These include erythromycin (an antibiotic), ketoconazole, and itraconazole (both antifungals that inhibit the fungal CYP51 and unintentionally inhibit CYP3A4). If these drugs are given with other drugs that are normally metabolized by P450 enzymes, the lifetime of these other drugs will be prolonged, and plasma levels will be increased, since they will not be cleared as fast.

If these drugs affect heart rhythms or other critical systems, the result can be fatal. For example, inhibition of CYP3A4 in a patient taking warfarin can cause bleeding (common cause of adverse drug interactions).

An important factor in drug dosage is interference from food. Grapefruit juice contains a CYP3A4 inhibitor that causes about a twelvefold increase in some drug concentrations. The effect may last several days. It is advisable to discourage your patients from drinking grapefruit juice while on medication metabolized by CYP3A4. Pharmacists will automatically place caution labels on prescriptions for such medications (e.g., cholesterol-lowering "statins").

B. Phase II Reactions

Parent drugs or their Phase I metabolites that contain suitable chemical groups often undergo coupling or conjugation reactions with an endogenous substance to yield drug conjugates. In general, conjugates are polar molecules that are readily excreted and often inactive. Generally, biotransformation of a drug results in a metabolite that is not only inactive, but more polar than the parent compound. This facilitates excretion of the metabolite.

There are five main Phase II reactions: glucuronidation, acetylation, glutathione conjugation, sulfation and methylation.

1. Metabolism of drugs to toxic products

Metabolism of drugs and other foreign chemicals may not always be an innocuous biochemical event leading to detoxification and elimination of the compound. Several compounds have been shown to be metabolically transformed to reactive intermediates that are toxic to various organs. Such toxic reactions may not be apparent at low levels of exposure to parent compounds when alternative detoxification mechanisms are not yet overwhelmed or compromised and when the availability of endogenous detoxifying co-substrates (GSH, glucuronic acid, sulfate) is not limited. However, when these resources are exhausted, the toxic pathway may dominate, resulting in organ toxicity or carcinogenesis.

10.8 Factors Affecting Drug Metabolism
A. Disease
Diseases such as hepatitis, alcoholic liver disease, fatty liver, and biliary cirrhosis can decrease biotransformation pathways and affect drug metabolism. Decrease in hepatic blood flow as a result of cardiac insufficiency or use of beta blockers may also affect metabolism. Therefore, caution must be exercised when treating hepatic-disease-afflicted patients with drugs which are extensively metabolized in the liver, such as lidocaine, verampamil, or morphine.

B. Age
Newborns typically have slower rates of Phase 1 biotransformation vs. adults. Impairment of bilirubin conjugation (Phase 2), a primary cause of jaundice, is not uncommon in newborns. Older adults demonstrating decreased liver mass and hepatic blood flow have an overall slower rate of biotransformation. Once again, this slow rate of biotransformation may potentiate the effect of drugs extensively metabolized by the liver.

C. Gender
Androgenic and estrogenic hormones may influence drug metabolism. Clinical reports suggest that sex-dependent differences in drug metabolism exist in humans for ethanol, propanolol, some benzodiazepines, estrogens, and salicylates.

D. Genetic Factors
Genetic factors that influence enzyme levels account for some of these differences. Succinylcholine, for example, is metabolized only half as rapidly in people with genetically determined defects in pseudocholinesterase. See Table 10.2.

10.9 Drug Excretion
Through the concepts of bioavailability and volume of distribution, we have established the relationship between drug dosage and plasma concentration. How can we determine how this drug concentration will change with time? The increase in drug concentration due to drug absorption is countered by the simultaneous elimination of the drug. For our purposes, we assume that the drug absorption is instantaneous (though this is only true for IV administration). Elimination of the drug is primarily governed by metabolism in the liver and excretion from the kidney.

The termination of drug activity in the body occurs when:

a. The drug is metabolized.
b. The redistribution of the drug into other tissues removes it from its site of action, e.g., redistribution of thiopental into fat.
c. The drug is excreted.

As a very general rule, polar compounds are excreted unchanged and nonpolar compounds are metabolized to more polar compounds. There is a difference between elimination and excretion. In a minority of drug classes, for example, elimination via metabolism without excretion may occur.

In drug excretion, the main routes are via urine and feces, with the kidney (urine producer) being the principal excretion organ. Volatile drugs, such as inhalation anesthetics, are mostly excreted via the lungs, but lungs play only a very small part in elimination for the remainder of drugs.

Excretion via sweat and breast milk have very small contributions to the overall elimination of drugs, but can have very important clinical consequences (breast milk excretion with toxicity to the neonate/infant).

With fecal excretion, the passage of drugs and metabolites may be by passive diffusion or active transport. In passive diffusion the same physiochemical factors that affect absorption and distribution of the drugs are important (e.g., pH, pKa, and protein binding).

With biliary excretion, the mechanisms by which the body directs some compounds to the bile and others to urine are not clear. Two of the important requirements for biliary excretion are a fairly large MW (>300 kDal), and some polar characteristics.

Some conjugates such as glucuronides (formed by Phase II metabolism) and amino acid conjugates are principally excreted into bile. From the bile these compounds pass into the GI tract where they are exposed to bacteria. The bacteria can act on these drugs, sometimes resulting in recovery of the parent drug which can be reabsorbed to again exert its effect. This is known as enterohepatic recycling and is thought to be responsible for the prolongation of action of drugs such as ethinyl, estradiol and digoxin.

Table 10.2
Examples of Genetic Polymorphisms in Drug Metabolism

Defect	Enzyme Involved	Drug and Therapeutic Use	Clinical Consequences (Observed or predictable)
Oxidation	CYP2D6	Bufuralol (-adrenoceptor blocker)	Exacerbation of blockade, nausea
Oxidation	CYP2D6	Codeine (analgesic)	Reduced analgesia
Oxidation	CYP2D6	Debrisoquin (antihypertensive)	Orthostatic hypotension
Oxidation	Aldehyde dehydrogenase	Ethanol (recreational drug)	Facial flushing, hypotension, tachycardia, nausea, vomiting
N-Acetylation	N-acetyl transferase	Hydralazine (antihypertensive)	Lupus erythematosus-like syndrome
N-Acetylation	N-acetyl transferase	Isoniazid (antitubercular)	Peripheral neuropathy
Oxidation	CYP2C19	Mephenytoin (antiepileptic)	Overdose toxicity
S-Methylation	Thiopurine methyltransferase	Mercaptopurines (cancer chemotherapeutic)	Myelotoxicity
Oxidation	CYP2A6	Nicotine (stimulant)	Lesser toxicity
Oxidation	CYP2D6	Nortriptyline (antidepressant)	Toxicity
O-Demethylation	CYP2C19	Omeprazole (proton pump inhibitor)	Increased therapeutic efficacy
Oxidation	CYP2D6	Sparteine	Oxytocic symptoms
Ester hydrolysis	Plasma cholinesterase	Succinylcholine (neuromuscular blocker)	Prolonged apnea
Oxidation	CYP2C9	S-warfarin (anticoagulant)	Bleeding
Oxidation	CYP2C9	Tolbutamide (hypoglycemic)	Cardiotoxicity

A. Urinary Excretion

The three processes involved in urinary excretion are glomerular filtration, tubular secretion, and tubular reabsorption.

1. Glomerular filtration

The overall rate of filtration depends on the plasma concentration and the glomerular filtration rate (GFR) within the kidney. Only the free drug fraction is filtered; therefore binding of drug to plasma proteins retards excretion, while displacement from proteins enhances filtration. Disease may affect filtration; however drugs usually do not.

2. Tubular secretion (active secretion)

Proximal tubules in the kidney (nephrons) actively transport a lot of drugs, for example, glucose and amino acids. There are also two non-specific systems: one for anions (negative-charged, e.g., organic acids) and one for cations (positively-charged, e.g., organic bases). Consequently, drugs being eliminated via the same system may compete for the same transport sites. This may be good or bad. There have been no clinically significant drug interactions reported for the basic system, but there are some problems with the acid secretion system, for example, some diuretics compete with the active secretion of uric acid leading to hyperuricemia.

On the other hand, probenecid, a uricosuric (increases uric acid excretion) agent that prevents the nephrotic reabsorption of uric acid, can also inhibit the anion secretory pathway. This delay in excretion has been used to clinical advantage for dozens of years with a variety of therapeutic agents. It can be used to prevent the secretion of acidic drugs such as penicillin, thereby decreasing their excretion and prolonging their action.

In active secretion, as the free drug is secreted, the plasma level of the drug decreases. This leads to the dissociation of the drug-protein complexes in the plasma, thus increasing the free drug's supply. See Figure 10.12.

3. Tubular reabsorption

There are specific active transport mechanisms for some drugs (e.g., glucose), but most pass back into the body by passive diffusion in the kidney's distal tubules. By then, urine has been concentrated so that a concentration gradient exists. Only the unionized drug contributes to the gradient. The ionized drug acts as a pool from which more unionized drug may be obtained. Consequently, the pH of urine is very important because of the degree of ionization that will

occur (see Figure 10.13). Ionized drugs are not passively reabsorbed. The amount of the drug going out via the urine will then be the sum of the three processes:

Urinary excretion =
GFR + active secretion reabsorption (active + passive)

4. Effects of pH on urinary excretion of ionizable drugs

Ionization increases renal clearance of drugs:

1. Both ionized and unionized drugs are filtered.
2. Passive reabsorption is only associated with unionized drugs.
3. Ionized portions of a drug are water soluble and can be filtered, but cannot be reabsorbed. They are therefore trapped in the filtrate. This trapping increases removal of the drug from the body. For example, in acute toxicity from overdoses of aspirin, alkalinization of the urine will increase the ionization of salicylic acid in the filtrate and thus eliminate it faster by decreasing reabsorption.

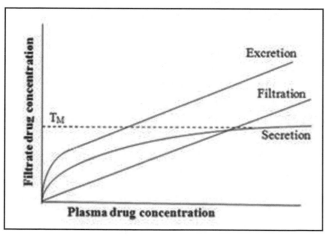

Figure 10.12 Elimination of drug through glomerular filtration.

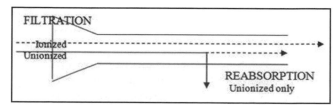

Figure 10.13 Drug reabsorption from the kidney (ionized vs. unionized drugs). Unionized drug molecules readily passed the renal membrane and are therefore likely to be reabsorbed back into the blood.

10.10 Pharmacokinetics
A. Introduction

Pharmacokinetics (PK) is the study of the how the concentration of a drug changes in the various compartments of the body over time. Pharmacokinetics describes how the body acts upon a drug. In contrast, pharmacodynamics is the relationship between drug concentration at the site of action and the pharmacologic responses (i.e. the intensity and time course of therapeutic and adverse effects). Pharmacodynamics describes what the drug does to the body.

The study of pharmacokinetics is not purely academic. One of the responsibilities of a physician is to prescribe how much (dose) and how often (dosing interval) a drug should be taken by the patient. In order to determine the proper dose and dosing interval of a drug, one must (1) know what drug concentration this dose would correspond to after absorption and distribution, and (2) be able to predict how quickly this concentration will decrease due to elimination. Too much drug or too short a dosing interval could be toxic or fatal. In fact, too much therapy is the most common cause of toxicity. For example, if the dose and thus effects of the anticoagulant warfarin gets too high, the patient could have an intracranial bleed. Conversely, if the dose is too small or the dosing interval is too long, the drug will not be effective, and clotting may occur. Other possible consequences of insufficient dosage include an antibiotic not controlling an infection, a blood pressure medication not being able to prevent blood pressure from rising to dangerous levels, or a birth control pill not preventing pregnancy.

The basic assumption in utilizing pharmacokinetics is that drug responses are proportional to blood levels that one can measure. Therefore, PK can be used for predictive purposes to answer the following questions:

- What is the appropriate dose or dosing interval to maintain adequate blood levels, thereby optimizing the therapeutic response?
- How would a disease (such as renal failure) affect the drug concentration in the body?
- Is therapeutic failure due to use of the wrong drug or inadequate dosing?

Using PK principles, one may predict plasma concentration at any future time, thereby achieving optimal dosing with minimal oversight. For drugs in which the dosage required for therapeutic effect is close to the dosage eliciting toxicity and thus have a small safety margin (i.e., narrow therapeutic index), PK-predicted concentrations may be verified by measuring the drug concentration clinically (therapeutic drug monitoring—TDM).

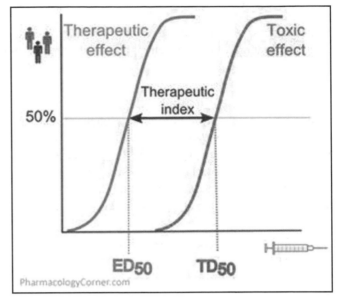

Figure 10.14 *Therapeutic index compares the amount of drug that causes a therapeutic effect versus a toxic effect in humans. Source: Guzman, Flavio. Therapeutic Index. Digital Image. Pharmacology Corner, 2011. Web. 12 Oct. 2011. http://pharmacologycorner.com/therapeutic-index. Reproduced by permission from PharmacologyCorner.com. Copyright © 2011 Pharmacology Corner.*

B. Therapeutic Window and Therapeutic Index

Indeed, it is vital to operate in a therapeutic window of drug concentration—high enough to be effective but not so high that it is toxic. This is determined by the average responses of the larger population to a drug. The median effective dose, ED50, is the dose at which the drug is effective in 50 percent of individuals. Naturally, toxic and lethal doses are not established by experimenting on human patients! Rather, they are modeled using animal studies. The median lethal dose, LD50, is the dose at which death would result in 50 percent of the population. The median toxic dose, TD50, is the concentration at which 50 percent would experience a specific side effect. Since a drug can have many different side effects, it can have different TD50s—one corresponding to each side effect.

The safety of a drug is expressed as the therapeutic index (TI), or the ratio of TD50 / ED50. A high TI indicates the drug may be safe even if the drug concentration unexpectedly rises somewhat (as could happen due to a drug interaction). If a drug has a low TI, such as is the case for anesthetics, then even a relatively small increase in concentration could lead to toxicity or death. In other words, TI is an indication of the size of the safety margin a drug possesses in terms of its dosage. See Figure 10.14.

$$\text{Therapeutic index} = \frac{TD50}{ED50}$$

Where:
TD = Toxic dose
ED = Effective dose

Narrow therapeutic index drugs:

- Warfarin
- Phenytoin
- Valproic Acid
- Carbamepazine Theophylline
- Cylclosporin
- Digoxin

With narrow therapeutic index (NTI) drugs, slight alterations in systemic concentration can lead to significant changes in a patient's pharmacodynamic response. This may result in toxic effects, especially in patients who are receiving a number of medications, are ill, or are of old age. Bioavailability between generic and brand drug products does not equal bioequivalence, especially when referring to NTI drugs. Warfarin is an anticoagulant NTI drug for which substitution is now available and may indeed be substituted without the knowledge of the patient or the practitioner. When the brand name drug is preferred by the practitioner, "no substitution" must be clearly indicated on the prescription to avoid the generic replacement of warfarin and other NTI drugs.

C. Blood Levels for Narrow Therapeutic Index (NDI) Drugs

When a dose of a drug is given either orally, rectally or intravenously, it ultimately accumulates in the blood (plasma or serum). One may measure drug concentrations by obtaining blood specimens at various times. Of course, the concentration of the drug in blood is constantly changing, so it is important to know when the last dose was given when evaluating serum or plasma drug concentration.

The minimum effective concentration is the concentration below which a drug is known to lack effectiveness. Likewise, the maximum effective concentration indicates the level above which increasing the drug concentration has no additional therapeutic benefit. This latter dose phenomenon is called a maximum effect. The maximum effective concentration is less than or equal to the toxic concentration. The area between the minimum and maximum effective concentrations is termed the therapeutic window.

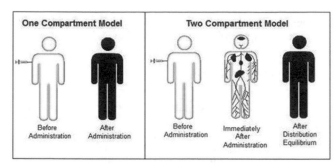

Figure 10.15 Compartment models. The one compartment model assumes even distribution (equilibrium) throughout the body immediately after drug administration. The two compartment model indicates specific sites of action, or targets, immediately after drug administration and equilibrium after full distribution. Adapted from: Tharp, Rick. Pharmacokinetic Modeling. Digital Image. Rx Kinetics. Web. 12 Oct. 2011. www.rxkinetics.com/pktutorial/1_5.html.

D. Kinetic Modeling

Kinetic models attempt to quantify how the body acts upon a drug over time, utilizing mathematical "compartment" models. In compartment modeling, one assumes the body is equivalent to one or more compartments in which the drug moves. A change in drug concentration in any one body compartment will affect the concentration in any other model compartment. In these models, a change in concentration within a single compartment results in an immediate re-equilibration of the drug within the compartment. See Figure 10.15.

The number of compartments a drug exhibits may be estimated by examination of the plasma drug concentration vs. time curve. Each break in the absorption or elimination curves represents a body compartment.

The concentration decay (kinetics) over time usually proceeds by first order kinetics (explained below). First order elimination occurs when the amount of drug eliminated from the body in a specific time is dependent on the amount of drug in the body at that time. For first order elimination, the fraction of drug eliminated in the body per unit of time remains constant.

E. Drug Absorption and Elimination

Absorption rate depends on many factors such as dosage form, drug dissolution and gastric emptying time. The absorption rate constant (ka) is the fraction of the administered dose that leaves the site of administration per unit time. The larger the ka the faster the drug is absorbed. The time required for a drug to reach maximal blood concentration is termed *Tmax*. The concentration of drug in the blood at this time is termed *Cmax*.

1. Absorption rate
a. Zero order

Absorption rate is constant, independent of amount of drug administered:

$$ko = mg/min \text{ or } mg/ml/min$$

Intravenous (IV) infusion demonstrates zero order absorption kinetics.

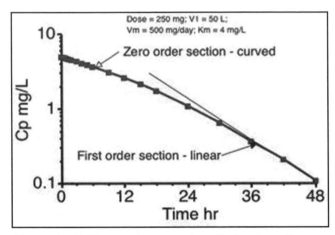

Figure 10.16 *First and zero order elimination. Source: Bourne, David. Non-linear Pharmacokinetic Models. Digital Image. Boomer, 2010. Web. 12 Oct. 2011. www.boomer.org/c/p4/c21/c2103.html. Reproduced by permission from David W.A. Bourne. Copyright © 2001-3 David W.A. Bourne.*

b. First order

Absorption rate is proportional to the amount of drug present (ka), which is the fraction of the drug absorbed per unit of time. The larger the *ka* the faster the drug is absorbed. See Figure 10.16.

2. Elimination rate

Like absorption rate, the rate of elimination for drugs follows either first order or zero order kinetics. First order means the rate of elimination is proportional to the amount of drug. The concentration vs. time graph will exhibit exponential decay. Zero order means that rate of elimination is constant. The concentration vs. time graph for zero order will be a straight line. Almost all drug elimination is governed by first order kinetics, although some notable exceptions are alcohol, phenytoin, and some cardiac drugs (at high concentrations); these follow zero order kinetics. Also, drugs can

follow first order kinetics at one dosage but then transition to zero order kinetics at higher doses. To understand why a drug would follow first order or zero order kinetics, one must examine drug elimination at a molecular level.

As mentioned, most drug metabolism takes place in the liver. A drug molecule is metabolized by binding with a CYP enzyme, where it is cleaved or otherwise modified (elimination). At first, the more drug molecules that are presented to the liver, the more bind to CYP enzymes and are degraded. Hence, the rate of the elimination or processing of the drug molecules is proportional to the number of drug molecules. However, the number of CYP enzymes is finite. As the number of drug molecules increases, the CYP enzymes are increasingly occupied until saturation occurs and no more receptor sites are open. Before any more drug molecules can bind to enzymes and be eliminated, the bound drug molecules must be degraded.

At this point, the elimination follows zero order kinetics. It does not matter how many drug molecules are presented to the liver, the elimination is constant as the drug molecules are in essence waiting in line to get processed by the CYP enzymes. In this sense, the elimination of drug molecules by the numerous liver CYP enzymes is analogous to getting into a football stadium through the numerous turnstiles at the gate. Instead of molecules being processed through degradation or chemical modification, people are "processed" from one side of the gate to the inside of the stadium.

Assume there are ten turnstiles at a gate, and it takes a person one second to get through them. If one person shows up to the gate, than that person will be processed in one second and the rate of processing (elimination) is one person per second. If two people show up to the gate, then the two people go through two separate turnstiles and the rate of processing is two people per second. Hence, the rate of elimination is proportional to the number of people, so by definition it follows first order kinetics.

If this is a game between the Bears and the (abysmal) Detroit Lions, perhaps the number of people showing up to the gate will not exceed ten people per second and therefore no one has to wait for a turnstile. However, for a Bears-Packers game, a ton of people will show up at the gate to see the game—more than ten people per second. However, the turnstiles will be saturated, and the rate of processing of people from one side of the gate to the other will be constant as the people are slowly funneled through the ten turnstiles. Whether there are 10,000 or 20,000 people that show up, the rate of processing people in the stadium will be constant at 10 people per second. This describes zero order kinetics. Further, if a few people show up early to beat the lines and the bulk of the people show up later, then the rate of processing would transition from first order to zero order kinetics.

a. First order

The rate of drug elimination is proportional to the amount of drug remaining. The rate constant k relates the rate of drug elimination to the amount in the body at any time t:

$$k = \frac{\text{rate of elimination}}{\text{amount of drug in body}}$$

By definition, first order kinetics means the rate of change in concentration (elimination) is proportional to the concentration. Mathematically, this is represented as follows:

$$\text{Rate of elimination}\,(mg/\min) = \frac{d[C]}{dt} = ke[C]$$

Where:
ke = the rate constant ($min - 1$)
$[C]$ = concentration
t = time

From the equation, it is clear that the rate constant is the fraction of drug eliminated per unit time. This concept is very useful in developing PK equations, as the rate constant is part of many of them.

A more useful equation for first order kinetics is represented by the following equation for exponential decay, which will allow one to calculate the concentration of drug remaining after a certain period of time:

$$[C] = C_o e^{-kt}$$

Where:
$[C]$ = concentration
C_o = initial concentration
k = the rate constant (also called ke or rate of elimination)
t = time

A similar equation applies if you are dealing with the amount of drug rather than concentration, though it should be noted that the mass of the drug refers to that which has reached systemic circulation ($F \times dose$):

$$m_{drug} = m_o e^{-kt}$$

Other versions of the first order equation can be converted from concentration to mass of drug in the same fashion by merely substituting $[C]$ for m_{drug} and the initial concentration for the initial mass. If you are solving for time, the following integrated equation is more useful:

$$-kt = ln\,([C]\,/\,C_o)$$

b. Zero order

Zero order elimination means the mass of drug decreases at a constant rate (e.g., a decline in serum concentration of 5 mg/ml per hour). The units of rate of elimination are mg/hr or mg/ml/hr.

Zero order kinetics means that the rate of elimination is constant. Therefore, the amount eliminated is just this constant multiplied by the time:

$$\begin{array}{c}\text{Amount of drug eliminated} = \\ \text{(elimination rate)} \times \text{(time)}\end{array}$$

Elimination rate in this case is in units of mg/min. The arrows represent a given interval of time, the following progression is an example of how the mass of a zero order elimination drug would change with time:

$$50\text{ mg} \rightarrow 40\text{ mg} \rightarrow 30\text{ mg} \rightarrow 20\text{ mg} \rightarrow 10\text{ mg} \rightarrow 0\text{ mg}$$

Dividing by volume yields a similar equation for concentration:

$$\begin{array}{c}\text{(Change in drug concentration)} = \\ \text{(elimination rate)} \times \text{(time)}\end{array}$$

Elimination rate is in units of mg/ml/min.

One way to check that your equation is probably correct is to make sure the units cancel to yield the same thing on each side of the equation.

The most useful case of zero order kinetics is alcohol elimination.

3. Clearance (CL)

Clearance is a volume of blood from which the drug is completely removed per unit time. Instead of the drug remaining homogenous throughout the volume of distribution as it becomes more dilute, clearance is modeled as if a certain volume of the blood containing the drug is removed repeatedly from the body. Since the rate constant k_e is the fraction of drug removed per unit time, and the total volume the drug is dissolved in is estimated as the volume of distribution (V_D), the volume being cleared per unit time is $ke \times V_D$.

$$CL = ke \times V_D$$

Units for clearance are volume per unit time (ml/min).

Rate of elimination (mg/min) =
CL (ml/min) × concentration (mg/ml)

Since the total amount eliminated is the dose, the total body clearance can also be calculated from the AUC.

$$CL = \frac{Dose}{AUC} = \left(\frac{mg}{mg \, / \, (ml \, / \, min)} \right) = \frac{ml}{min}$$

4. Area Under the Curve (AUC)

As mentioned previously, the AUC is the area under the plot of plasma concentration of drug vs. time after drug administration (see Figure 10.17). The AUC is of particular use in estimating bioavailability of drugs and in estimating total clearance of drugs (CL). Following single intravenous doses, $AUC = dose \, / \, CL$, for single compartment systems obeying first-order elimination kinetics. For routes other than the intravenous:

$$AUC = F \times \frac{Dose}{CL}$$

Where:
F = the bioavailability of the drug

$$AUC = \frac{Dose}{CL} = mg \, / \, ml \text{ per min}$$

For equal doses:

$$F = \frac{AUC_{Oral}}{AUC_{IV}}$$

For different doses:

$$F = \left(\frac{AUC_{Oral} \, / \, Dose}{AUC_{IV} \, / \, Dose} \right)$$

5. Elimination (k)

You have already learned about concepts and processes of hepatic and renal elimination. In this context, elimination is simply defined as follows:

k = rate of drug elimination/amount of drug in the body (i.e., the fractional rate of drug removal per unit time).

Elimination may be broken into two components: metabolism and excretion.

Metabolism: chemical biotransformation of the parent drug within the body to one or more products or compounds.

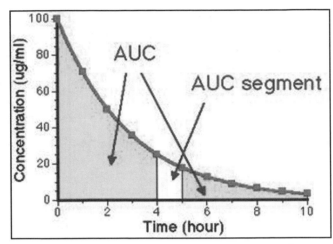

Figure 10.17 *Area under the curve (AUC) graph. Source: Bourne, David. Area Under the Plasma Concentration Time Curve. Digital Image. Boomer, 2010. Web. 12 Oct. 2011. www.boomer.org/c/p3/c02/c0210.html. Reproduced by permission from David W.A. Bourne. Copyright © 2001-3 David W.A. Bourne.*

Excretion: Physical removal of parent drug or metabolite from the body.

6. Elimination half-life

Elimination half-life ($t_{1/2}$) is the time it takes for 50 percent of the concentration of the drug to be eliminated from the body. It is only constant for first order kinetics, so it is only used in that context. Elimination half-life is dependent upon volume of distribution (V_D) and clearance (CL) in the same way k is.

The half-life is inversely proportional to the rate constant:

$$t_{1/2} = ln \, (2) \, / \, k_e = 0.7 \times V_D \, / \, CL$$

There are two methods to determine half-life: calculation and graphical. Graphically, half-life is determined by measuring drug concentrations periodically, plotting them as in Figure 10.18, and determining the time it takes for the concentration to be halved. Calculation of half-life is shown below.

The percent of drug lost in a certain number of half-lives is as follows:

$$\text{Percent of drug eliminated} = 1 - \left(\frac{1}{2} \right)^n$$

$$\text{Percent of steady state achieved} = 100 \times \left[1 - \left(\frac{1}{2} \right)^n \right]$$

Where:
n = number of half-lives elapsed

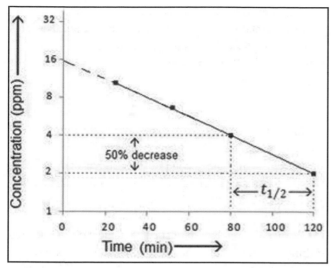

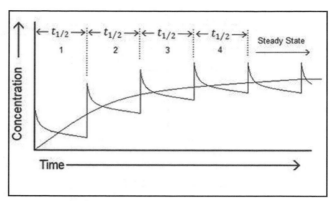

Figure 10.18 *Drug elimination half-life. When represented using a logarithmic scale on the Y axis, the concentration vs. time curve of a first order elimination drug yields a straight line. Adapted From: Tharp, Rick. Pharmacokinetic Modeling. Digital Image. Rx Kinetics. Web. 12 Oct. 2011. www.rxkinetics.com/pktutorial/1_5.html.*

Figure 10.20 *Steady state curve. Steady state is reached after 4 half lives. Adapted From: Tharp, Rick. Pharmacokinetic Modeling. Digital Image. Rx Kinetics. Web. 12 Oct. 2011. www.rxkinetics.com/pktutorial/1_5.html.*

As successive doses of drug are administered, drug begins to accumulate in the body. The amount of drug added to the system with each administration is the same (in Figure 10.19, the concentration increases 10 mg/mL with every dose). However, the drop in concentration during the elimination phase is greater with each subsequent dose. This is because the concentration at the beginning of the elimination phase (right after the dose) is higher with each subsequent dose, and first order elimination dictates that the amount of drug eliminated per unit time is proportional to the amount of drug in the body. Therefore, drug in the body will accumulate until the rate of elimination equals the rate of drug entering the body—steady state.

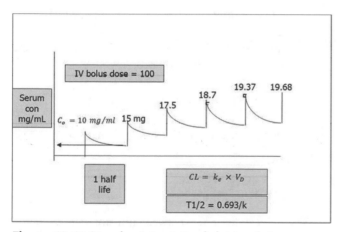

Figure 10.19 *Steady state. Actual data points are interpolated and extrapolated by an appropriate software application.*

7. Steady state

Steady state is a condition of equilibrium in which the rate of drug administration equals the rate of elimination. We may assume that steady state is reached after five half-lives of the drug have elapsed, regardless of the dosing regimen. The figures that follow will serve to discuss these concepts of half-life, steady state, the size of the dose and the frequency at which it is given to determine the height of the plateau.

As the rate of drug elimination approaches that of drug administration (i.e., approach steady state), the maximum (peak) and minimum (trough) drug concentrations in the blood increase until equilibrium is reached. At this point, no more drug will accumulate in the body, and the peak and trough drug concentrations will be constant. When peak and trough drug concentrations are roughly the same in two or more successive doses, steady-state (Css) has been reached (Figure 10.20).

The table below represents graphical data in which the time required to reach steady state is predicted based on a drug's half-life.

Drugs with a higher comparative k_e (shorter half-life) will reach steady state sooner than drugs with a lower k_e (longer half-life). Drugs eliminated quicker reach steady state quicker because the time it takes for the rate of drug elimination to equal the rate of drug absorption is faster compared to drugs eliminated slowly.

Number of half-lives	Percent steady-state
1	50
2	75
3	87.5
4	93.75
5	96.88
6	98.44
7	99.22

F. Dosing

Now that the important concepts of pharmacokinetics have been established, we can discuss the calculation of dosage. Loading dose is the dose to immediately establish therapeutic levels. Maintenance dose is the amount of drug and dosing interval needed to keep the drug concentration in the therapeutic range.

When a continuous intravenous infusion (IV drip) of a drug is started, it takes approximately five half-lives to reach steady state. In some cases, an immediate drug response is required that cannot wait five half-lives. If a very large dose is given immediately, followed by smaller doses, the result is that therapeutic concentrations can be immediately achieved. This initial dose is termed a "loading dose." The subsequent smaller doses are termed "maintenance doses" (*MD*).

1. Loading dose

Loading dose, the amount of drug that needs to be in the systemic circulation to establish a certain desired concentration, can be found using the formula for concentration:

$$\text{(Dose in systemic circulation)} = C \times V_D$$

For IV administration the dose in systemic circulation equals the dose prescribed:

$$\text{Dose} = C \times V_D$$

For other routes of administration, the equation must include the bioavailability *F*.

$$F \times \text{Dose} = C \times V_D$$

2. Maintenance doses (*MD*)

For some drugs, maintenance of a specific blood concentration is imperative to therapeutic success. Therefore, we can administer drugs at specific times on an ongoing basis to maintain adequate blood concentration. The goal of the maintenance dose is to replace the drug lost through elimination. If 10 mg of drug is lost in an hour, then the maintenance dose must be 10 mg every hour (10 mg / hr). Hence, maintenance dose is calculated by finding the amount of drug eliminated per unit time.

In multiple dosing, the second dose is given before the first dose is completely eliminated; therefore, the maximum concentration after the second dose is higher than the first. Patient compliance is greatest with once a day dosing. Ideally, the dose interval should be selected as a factor of 24 so doses can be given at the same time each day.

We have already established that the volume cleared of drug per unit time is the clearance. So the total volume cleared is the clearance multiplied by the time. Let the time equal the dosing interval (*tau*) so the volume cleared is equal to *CL* × *tau*. The amount of drug in this cleared volume is the maintenance dose. The amount of drug in any specific volume is given by (mass of drug) = (volume cleared) × concentration. Substituting for the volume cleared (volume cleared = *CL* × *tau*), the expression becomes:

$$\text{Mass of drug} = \text{concentration} \times CL \times tau$$

Taking bioavailability into account, the equation for the maintenance dose (*MD*) is as follows:

$$F \times MD = \text{concentration} \times CL \times tau$$

For IV administration, *F* = 1, so the maintenance dose is:

$$MD = \text{concentration} \times CL \times tau$$

The clinical difference between infusion rate and maintenance dose is that maintenance dose yields a sawtoothing (see Figure 10.19) of concentration while infusion is more tightly controlled. Maintenance doses have more potential for toxicity (right after the dose) or loss of effectiveness (right before the next dose) in comparison to infusion.

Units of the continuous infusion rate have the same units as the zero order rate constant (e.g., mg/min).

3. Example—dosage adjustment in renal impairment

Diseases such as renal impairment can reduce clearance, and so the maintenance dose must be adjusted in these cases to compensate for this. The loading dose remains the same as that for healthy patients.

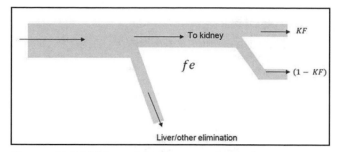

Figure 10.21 *Kidney function mathematics.*

In order to estimate glomerular filtration and, therefore, identify renal impairment, one must look at certain markers within the urine, such as insulin or creatinine. Creatinine is an endogenous compound secreted by the muscle and is usually produced at a constant rate by the body depending on body mass.

Creatinine is filtered out of the blood by the kidneys by glomerular filtration and proximal tubular secretion, and there is minimal reabsorption (entrance back into the blood) from the kidney. If kidney filtration is deficient, then creatinine blood levels increase. Therefore, creatinine levels in the blood or in the urine are a reliable marker to reflect glomerular filtration rates (GFR). See Figure 10.21.

For patients with renal impairment, alteration in dosing regimen is determined from creatinine clearance calculations.

Calculation of kidney function (*KF*):

- Individualized kidney function assessment
- Based on a comparison of an impaired individual to one with "normal" kidney function
- *KF* = Creatinine *CL* (impaired) / Creatinine *CL* (normal)

Normalize *CrCL* to a 70 kg individual:

$$CrCL = \frac{\left[(140 - \text{age}) \times LBW\right]}{72 \times SrCr}$$

Normalize to 70 kg:

$$CrCL\left(\frac{ml/\min}{70}kg\right) = \frac{140 - \text{age}}{SrCr}$$

Assume:
CrCL = 120 ml/min / 70 kg in normal renal function

Dosage adjustment for renal impairment determined to compensate for the associated reduction in clearance.

For renal impairment, the magnitude of impact on drug clearance depends on:

- Degree of kidney dysfunction
- Fraction of drug excreted unchanged in kidney (*fe*)

Changes in drug clearance can be estimated by determining kidney function and the fraction of drug excreted renally:

$$(CL \text{ renally impaired}) = [1 - fe \times (l - KF)] \times (CL \text{ normal})$$

Where:
fe = fraction of drug excreted unchanged in urine

By knowing the percent loss in *CL* due to renal impairment, one can estimate an approximate drug dose using the equation for maintenance dose.

G. Therapeutic Drug Monitoring (TDM)

The goal of therapeutic drug monitoring (TDM) is to use serum or plasma drug concentrations as an aid to optimize drug therapy and maximize the probability of an appropriate therapeutic effect while minimizing the chance for toxicity.

The therapeutic range (window) is defined as the range of drug concentration in the serum or plasma necessary to achieve a therapeutic response. Although the therapeutic range defines a desirable concentration in the majority of patients, the specific concentration may vary greatly from patient to patient (idiosyncrasy). Moreover, some patients may require dosage in an otherwise toxic or sub-therapeutic range.

Some common misconceptions regarding therapeutic range:

1. Drug concentrations in the therapeutic range automatically result in the desired therapeutic response.
2. Toxicity is not encountered in the therapeutic range.

In general, the therapeutic range should be considered as a probability, that is, high probability of therapeutic success without toxicity. However, therapeutic ranges are derived from population-based studies and are only general guidelines for the general population. Conditions such as age, disease or drug interaction may alter therapeutic range for a particular patient. The patient's response is always more important than absolute serum or plasma drug concentrations and should be used as a basis for altering dosing patterns.

H. Pharmacokinetics Summary

Pharmacokinetics is a valuable tool to accurately determine the dosage of a drug to target the therapeutic concentration. It utilizes physiological parameters of the patient and chemical properties of the drug in kinetic models to achieve this end, and accounts for the effects of renal impairment on drug elimination kinetics. While pharmacokinetics has great predictive power, ultimately the patient's response should determine how the dose should be adjusted.

10.11 Drug Receptor and Pharmacodynamics

Therapeutic and toxic effects of drugs result from their interactions with molecules in the patient. Most drugs act by associating with specific macromolecules in ways that alter the macromolecules' biochemical or biophysical activities. This idea, more than a century old, is embodied in the term receptor: the component of a cell or organism that interacts with a drug and initiates the chain of events leading to the drug's observed effects.

A. Agonists and Antagonists

Most drugs exert their effects in the body by interacting with discrete parts of a cell called receptors. Receptors are the central focus of investigation of drug effects and their mechanisms of action (pharmacodynamics). See Figure 10.22.

Receptors determine the quantitative relationships between dose, or concentration, of the drug and the pharmacological response. They do so by having selectivity for a drug. That is, they recognize distinct drugs or ligands. Affinity for binding a drug determines the concentration of drug required to form a significant drug-receptor complex. See Figure 10.23.

Mediating the actions of a drug, or ligand, by transducing information from the binding of the drug to a response within the cell produces the physiological effect. Drugs modify only naturally occurring effects, and do not generate new effects.

B. Drug-Receptor Interactions

There are three variables involved in drug-receptor interactions: dose, effect, and time. Time is eliminated as a variable by considering the effect at maximal response. When quantifying the dose response, the following assumptions are made:

1. The intensity of the response is directly proportional to the number of receptors occupied.
2. One drug molecule binds to one receptor.

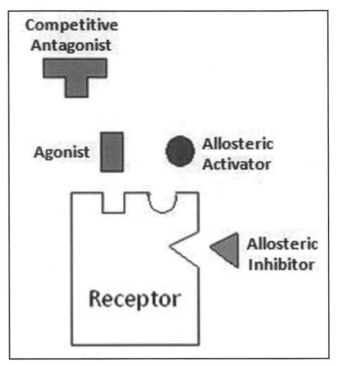

Figure 10.22 *Receptor and ligands (pharmaceutical modifiers).*

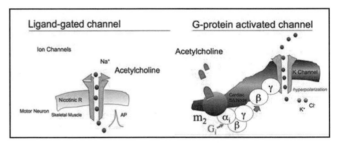

Figure 10.23 *Drug-receptor interactions. Ligand-gated channels are bound by a specific ligand/drug (i.e. acetylcholine), which causes activation of the channel. In this case, acetylcholine is opening the channel and inducing the influx of Na+ ions. G-protein activated channels are attached to G proteins within the cell and cause signal transduction, or an alteration of intracellular molecules to create a certain response. Source: Clarkson, Craig W. Basic Principles of Pharmacology: Direct Activation and G-Protein Activation of an Ion Channel. Digital Images. Tulane Pharmwiki, 2009. Web. 9 Oct. 2011. http://tmedweb.tulane.edu/pharmwiki/doku.php/ drug_receptor_theory. Reproduced by permission from Craig W. Clarkson, PhD. ©2011 Craig W. Clarkson, Tulane University, New Orleans, LA.*

3.   The amount of drug binding to the receptors is so small compared to the total drug available, that practically the amount of uncombined drug equals the total drug present.
4.   The binding is reversible and of short duration.
5.   The binding of one receptor does not affect another.

Mathematically the drug receptor interaction can be represented by:

$$D + R \underset{k_2}{\overset{k_1}{\rightleftarrows}} DR \xrightarrow{k_3} \text{response}$$

Where:
D = Drug
R = Receptor

The preceding equations demonstrate two principles:

1.   Affinity is k_1 / k_2 and is a measure of the preference that a drug exhibits for a receptor.
2.   Efficacy (intrinsic activity) is k_3 and describes the biological effectiveness of the drug-receptor complex in generating a response.

10.12 Dose Responses

Dose responses (DR) are an integral aspect of the drug and effect relationship. DRs are used ubiquitously to determine the therapeutic, toxic and lethal effects of a particular drug on the body. These tests are done in animals and are an essential step before a drug is tested in humans.

Several statistical concepts are used as a guideline to categorize the safety of a drug. As mentioned before, the therapeutic index plays a significant role in determining drug safety.

There are responses to a drug which can be quantified by a yes/no response, for example, sleep, protection from a seizure, etc. Continuous responses may be changed to quantal responses by setting a goal, for example, a drug (will/will not) decrease blood pressure by 20 mm Hg. The construction of a quantal dose-response curve is associated with measurement of population responses. Because of individual variations, a single dose of a drug will then exhibit a variance of responses in the population.

The response (given enough individuals) will be the familiar bell-shaped curve found in statistics and can be defined by knowing the median and standard deviation. Note that in a large enough population a single dose can elicit a response gradient from no effect to toxicity. Log dose response curves (LDRs—see Figure 10.24) can be useful in identifying similarly acting drugs.

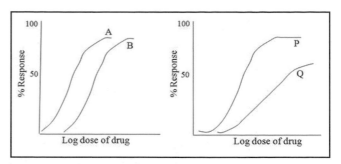

Figure 10.24 *Log dose-response curves. A and B have different potencies, and P and Q have different efficacies.*

Regarding Figure 10.24:

1.   If the two drugs have the same pharmacological mechanism in the body they will produce parallel curves. Therefore A and B are likely to have the same mechanism, while P and Q do not.
2.   Potency can be measured only for drugs binding to the same receptor and producing the same physiological activity. Therefore the potencies of A and B can be compared. On a graph, affinity is indicated by the position of the LDR on the X axis. The closer to the Y axis, the greater is the potency (i.e. a lower dose is needed for a given response). Therefore A has a greater potency than does B. Because P and Q have different slopes, they have different mechanisms of action and therefore their affinities cannot be compared.
3.   Efficacy is measured by the maximum response of the LDR. One looks at the size of response not how it is produced. Therefore in the graphs above, A and B have the same efficacy and P has greater efficacy than Q.

A. Potency

Potency is the measure of the amount of drug necessary for a given response. The less drug needed to elicit a response, the more potent the drug. It is important not to equate greater potency with therapeutic superiority since other factors like side effects have to be considered.

Potency of a drug depends in part on the affinity (Kd) of receptors for binding the drug and in part on the efficiency with which drug-receptor interaction is coupled to respond. Potency refers to the concentration or dose of a drug required to produce 50 percent of that drug's maximal effect (ED50).

B. Agonism and Antagonism

An agonist is a drug that when combined with a receptor leads to a physiologic response, essentially causing a specific

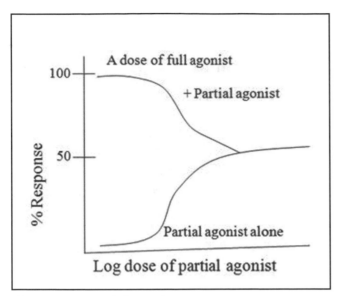

Figure 10.25 *Partial agonism.*

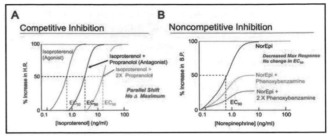

Figure 10.26 *Antagonist inhibition. (A) Competitive inhibition does not change maximum drug response. (B) Noncompetitive inhibition decreases the maximum drug response. Source: Clarkson, Craig W. Basic Principles of Pharmacology, Antagonists: Competitive vs. Noncompetitive. Digital Images. Tulane Pharmwiki, 2009. Web. 9 Oct. 2011. http://tmedweb.tulane.edu/pharmwiki/doku.php/ drug_receptor_theory. Reproduced by permission from Craig W. Clarkson, PhD. ©2011 Craig W. Clarkson, Tulane University, New Orleans, LA.*

action. An antagonist is a drug that when combined with a receptor blocks the agonist's (drug or natural agonist) action and leads to no physiologic response.

Pharmacologic antagonists bind to receptors but do not activate the generation of a signal; they interfere with the ability of an agonist to activate the receptor. The effect of a so-called "pure" antagonist on a cell or in a patient depends entirely on its preventing the binding of agonist molecules and blocking their biologic actions. Some of the most useful drugs in clinical medicine are pharmacological antagonists.

1. Partial agonists

Most drugs fall in the range between a full agonist and an antagonist. Those drugs are known as partial agonists and they exhibit affinity and only moderate efficacy.

Partial agonists exhibit slopes that are parallel to those of full agonists but their maximal response is less.

Many drugs used clinically as antagonists are actually weak partial agonists. For example, buprenorphine, a partial agonist of the mu-opioid receptors, is a generally safer analgesic drug than morphine because it produces less respiratory depression in overdose.

a. Duality of partial agonists
Regarding Figure 10.25:

1. The bottom curve is generated by a partial agonist being added to a tissue. The response maxes out at the maximum response for the partial agonist. The net is a gain in activity, or agonism.
2. The upper curve is generated by pretreating the tissue with a full agonist and obtaining the maximum

possible response. The full agonist is discontinued and replaced with a partial agonist. As the full agonist is displaced from the receptors by the partial agonist the response declines. Eventually, all of the full agonist will be displaced and the response will be completely due to the partial agonist. The net is a loss of activity or antagonism.
3. The partial agonist is the only class of drug that can be used either as an antagonist or as an agonist.

10.13 Competitive Antagonism

An antagonist alone produces no response. An agonist alone produces its normal LDR curve. The addition of antagonist to tissue before the addition of agonist will result in some receptors being occupied by antagonist. Therefore, more agonist is necessary to displace the antagonist from those receptors. Eventually, given high enough doses of agonist, all of the antagonist will be displaced and the maximum response will be elicited (curves parallel and of same height).

Changes in agonist concentration-effect (dose-response) curves are produced by a competitive antagonist or by an irreversible antagonist. In the presence of a competitive antagonist, higher concentrations of agonist are required to produce a given effect. Thus, the agonist concentration required for a given effect is shifted to the right, as shown in Figure 10.26. High agonist concentrations can overcome inhibition by a competitive antagonist. This is not the case with an irreversible (or noncompetitive) antagonist, which reduces the maximal effect the agonist can achieve, although it may not change its EC50.

10.14 Non-Competitive Antagonism

Non-competitive antagonism occurs when the antagonist cannot be displaced from the receptor and consequently the number of possible receptors available to the agonist decreases. This means that the agonist can never obtain full effect. The resulting curve has a lower slope and height (nonparallel and unequal heights). See Figure 10.27. There are three different types of antagonism:

1. Pharmacological antagonism (1 receptor)—both the agonist and antagonist compete for the same receptor.
2. Physiological antagonism (2 receptors)—two agonists bind to two different receptors. Each agonist elicits a physiological response. Those responses tend to oppose each other. Although glucocorticoids and insulin act on quite distinct receptor-effector systems, the clinician must sometimes administer insulin to oppose the hyperglycemic effects of a glucocorticoid hormone.
3. Chemical antagonism (0 receptors)—the antagonist directly interacts with the agonist, for example, antacids neutralizing HCl, or chelating agents. (e.g., protamine, a positively charged protein that neutralizes negatively charged heparin, thus making the heparin unavailable for interactions with proteins involved in blood clotting).

Classical theories have to be modified to explain things like:

a. Partial agonists
b. Tachyphylaxis—a sudden unresponsiveness to a drug; a phenomenon in which the repeated administration of some drugs results in a rapid and marked decrease in effectiveness.
c. Signaling mechanisms (see Figure 10.28) and drug action:
   1. A lipid-soluble drug crosses the plasma membrane and acts on an intracellular (inside the cell) receptor, R (which may be an enzyme or a regulator of gene transcription) such as for steroids, Vitamin D, thyroid hormone.
   2. The drug ligand binds to the extracellular (outside of the cell) domain of a transmembrane receptor, thereby activating an enzymatic activity ($A \rightarrow B$) of its cytoplasmic domain.
   3. The ligand binds to the extracellular domain of a transmembrane receptor bound to a protein kinase enzyme (Y), which it activates.

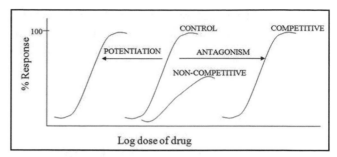

Figure 10.27 Effects of antagonism and potentiation.

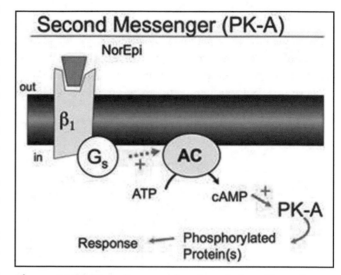

Figure 10.28 Signaling mechanism A drug/ligand (norepinephrine) binds to a beta 1 adrenergic receptor which is linked to a G protein. The G protein relays a signal to adenylyl cylase (AC) which induces the second messenger (PKA) to cause a response. Source: Clarkson, Craig W. Basic Principles of Pharmacology: G protein Activation of a Second Messenger Cascade. Digital Images. Tulane Pharmwiki, 2009. Web. 9 Oct. 2011. http://tmedweb.tulane.edu/pharmwiki/doku.php/drug_receptor_theory. Reproduced by permission from Craig W. Clarkson, PhD. ©2011 Craig W. Clarkson, Tulane University, New Orleans, LA.

4. The ligand binds to and directly regulates the opening of an ion channel such as sodium, calcium and potassium channels. Many of the most useful drugs in clinical medicine act by mimicking or blocking the actions of endogenous ligands that regulate the flow of ions through plasma membrane channels. Natural ligands include acetylcholine, serotonin, GABA, and glutamate—all synaptic transmitters.

5. The ligand binds to a cell-surface receptor linked to an effector enzyme (E) by a G protein, a signal relay protein that is attached to the receptor and acts during receptor activation.

10.15 Conclusion

These general principles (absorption, distribution, metabolism, excretion [ADME], kinetics, and drug receptor site activity) serve as a foundation for all learning and understanding in pharmacology. Separate and apart from the specific action of a particular drug, if there are interferences in ADMS, then the drug may have no effect, or be toxic. Several examples of alterations or interferences in the ADME are presented throughout the book. A good understanding of these principles will assist the reader in appreciating the examples.

Chapter 11

Important Code of Federal Regulations Applicable to Drug Product Liability Suits

Compiled by S. Albert Edwards, Pharm.D., RAC, FRAPS

NOTE: All Code citations are current as of May 2012 and are presented in chronological, ascending, numerical order. The table below provides an index for topics and the pertinent Code of Federal Regulation citation. All Code citations are from Title 21.

Term / Topic	Code of Federal Regulation(s), 21 CFR
Adverse event reporting	310.305, 312.32, & 314.80
Approved drug, adverse event reports	314.80
Investigational drug, adverse event reports	312.32
Informed consent, elements required	50.25
Institutional Review Boards, IRBs	56.109
Labeling, approved drug	201.56 & 201.57
Labeling, changes prior to FDA approval	314.70(c)(6)(iii)
Labeling, changes to promotional labeling	314.70(c)(4)
Mailing important information on drugs	200.5
Marketed drug, adverse events reports	310.305
OTC drug, identity statement	201.61
OTC drug, labeling format/content req.	201.66
OTC drug, meeting monograph standards	330.1

Term / Topic	Code of Federal Regulation(s), 21 CFR
OTC drug, net contents declaration	201.62
OTC drug, calcium labeling	201.70
OTC drug, magnesium labeling	201.71
OTC drug, potassium labeling	201.72
OTC drug, sodium labeling	201.64
Pregnancy categories, labeling	201.57(i) 8.1 Pregnancy
Review of research, IRB duties	56.109
Side effect reporting, approved drugs	314.80
Side effect reporting, investigational drugs	312.32
Side effect reporting, marketed drugs	310.305

Sec. 50.25 Elements of informed consent.

(a) *Basic elements of informed consent.* In seeking informed consent, the following information shall be provided to each subject:

(1) A statement that the study involves research, an explanation of the purposes of the research and the expected duration of the subject's participation, a description of the procedures to be followed, and identification of any procedures which are experimental.

(2) A description of any reasonably foreseeable risks or discomforts to the subject.

(3) A description of any benefits to the subject or to others which may reasonably be expected from the research.

(4) A disclosure of appropriate alternative procedures or courses of treatment, if any, that might be advantageous to the subject.

(5) A statement describing the extent, if any, to which confidentiality of records identifying the subject will be

maintained and that notes the possibility that the Food and Drug Administration may inspect the records.

(6) For research involving more than minimal risk, an explanation as to whether any compensation and an explanation as to whether any medical treatments are available if injury occurs and, if so, what they consist of, or where further information may be obtained.

(7) An explanation of whom to contact for answers to pertinent questions about the research and research subjects' rights, and whom to contact in the event of a research-related injury to the subject.

(8) A statement that participation is voluntary, that refusal to participate will involve no penalty or loss of benefits to which the subject is otherwise entitled, and that the subject may discontinue participation at any time without penalty or loss of benefits to which the subject is otherwise entitled.

(b) *Additional elements of informed consent.* When appropriate, one or more of the following elements of information shall also be provided to each subject:

(1) A statement that the particular treatment or procedure may involve risks to the subject (or to the embryo or fetus, if the subject is or may become pregnant) which are currently unforeseeable.

(2) Anticipated circumstances under which the subject's participation may be terminated by the investigator without regard to the subject's consent.

(3) Any additional costs to the subject that may result from participation in the research.

(4) The consequences of a subject's decision to withdraw from the research and procedures for orderly termination of participation by the subject.

(5) A statement that significant new findings developed during the course of the research which may relate to the subject's willingness to continue participation will be provided to the subject.

(6) The approximate number of subjects involved in the study.

(c) The informed consent requirements in these regulations are not intended to preempt any applicable Federal, State, or local laws which require additional information to be disclosed for informed consent to be legally effective.

(d) Nothing in these regulations is intended to limit the authority of a physician to provide emergency medical care to the extent the physician is permitted to do so under applicable Federal, State, or local law.

Sec. 56.109 IRB review of research.
(a) An IRB shall review and have authority to approve, require modifications in (to secure approval), or disapprove all research activities covered by these regulations.

(b) An IRB shall require that information given to subjects as part of informed consent is in accordance with 50.25. The IRB may require that information, in addition to that specifically mentioned in 50.25, be given to the subjects when in the IRB's judgment the information would meaningfully add to the protection of the rights and welfare of subjects.

(c) An IRB shall require documentation of informed consent in accordance with 50.27 of this chapter, except as follows:

(1) The IRB may, for some or all subjects, waive the requirement that the subject, or the subject's legally authorized representative, sign a written consent form if it finds that the research presents no more than minimal risk of harm to subjects and involves no procedures for which written consent is normally required outside the research context; or

(2) The IRB may, for some or all subjects, find that the requirements in 50.24 of this chapter for an exception from informed consent for emergency research are met.

(d) In cases where the documentation requirement is waived under paragraph (c)(1) of this section, the IRB may require the investigator to provide subjects with a written statement regarding the research.

(e) An IRB shall notify investigators and the institution in writing of its decision to approve or disapprove the proposed research activity, or of modifications required to secure IRB approval of the research activity. If the IRB decides to disapprove a research activity, it shall include in its written notification a statement of the reasons for its decision and give the investigator an opportunity to respond in person or in writing. For investigations involving an exception to informed consent under 50.24 of this chapter, an IRB shall promptly notify in writing the investigator and the sponsor of the research when an IRB determines that it cannot approve the research because it does not meet the criteria in the exception provided under 50.24(a) of this chapter or because of other relevant ethical concerns. The written notification shall include a statement of the reasons for the IRB's determination.

(f) An IRB shall conduct continuing review of research covered by these regulations at intervals appropriate to the degree of risk, but not less than once per year, and shall have authority to observe or have a third party observe the consent process and the research.

(g) An IRB shall provide in writing to the sponsor of research involving an exception to informed consent under 50.24 of this chapter a copy of information that has been publicly disclosed under 50.24(a)(7)(ii) and (a)(7)(iii) of this chapter. The IRB shall provide this information to the sponsor promptly so that the sponsor is aware that such disclosure has occurred. Upon receipt, the sponsor shall provide copies of the information disclosed to FDA.

(h) When some or all of the subjects in a study are children, an IRB must determine that the research study is in compliance with part 50, subpart D of this chapter, at the time of its initial review of the research. When some or all of the subjects in a study that is ongoing on April 30, 2001 are children, an IRB must conduct a review of the research to determine compliance with part 50, subpart D of this chapter, either at the time of continuing review or, at the discretion of the IRB, at an earlier date.

Sec. 200.5 Mailing of important information about drugs.

Manufacturers and distributors of drugs and the Food and Drug Administration occasionally are required to mail important information about drugs to physicians and others responsible for patient care. In the public interest, such mail should be distinctive in appearance so that it will be promptly recognized and read. The Food and Drug Administration will make such mailings in accordance with the specifications set forth in this section. Manufacturers and distributors of drugs are asked to make such mailings as prescribed by this section and not to use the distinctive envelopes for ordinary mail.

(a) Use first class mail and No. 10 white envelopes.

(b) The name and address of the agency or the drug manufacturer or distributor is to appear in the upper left corner of the envelope.

(c) The following statements are to appear in the far left third of the envelope front, in the type and size indicated, centered in a rectangular space approximately 3 inches wide and $2^{1}/_{4}$ inches high with an approximately $^{3}/_{8}$ inch-wide border in the color indicated:

(1) When the information concerns a significant hazard to health, the statement:

IMPORTANT
DRUG
WARNING

The statement shall be in three lines, all capitals, and centered. "Important" shall be in 36 point Gothic Bold type. "Drug" and "Warning" shall be in 36 point Gothic Condensed type. The rectangle's border and the statement therein shall be red.

(2) When the information concerns important changes in drug package labeling, the statement:

IMPORTANT
PRESCRIBING
INFORMATION

The statement shall be in three lines, all capitals, and centered. "Important" shall be in 36 point Gothic Bold type. "Prescribing" and "Information" shall be in 36 point Gothic Condensed type. The rectangle's border and the statement therein shall be blue.

(3) When the information concerns a correction of prescription drug advertising or labeling, the statement:

IMPORTANT
CORRECTION
OF DRUG
INFORMATION

The statement shall be in four lines, all capitals, and centered. "Important" shall be in 36 point Gothic Bold type. "Correction," "Of Drug," and "Information" shall be in 36 point Gothic Condensed type. The rectangle's border and the statement therein shall be brown.

Sec. 201.56 Requirements on content and format of labeling for human prescription drug and biological products.

(a) *General requirements.* Prescription drug labeling described in 201.100(d) must meet the following general requirements:

(1) The labeling must contain a summary of the essential scientific information needed for the safe and effective use of the drug.

(2) The labeling must be informative and accurate and neither promotional in tone nor false or misleading in any particular. In accordance with 314.70 and 601.12 of this chapter, the labeling must be updated when new information becomes available that causes the labeling to become inaccurate, false, or misleading.

(3) The labeling must be based whenever possible on data derived from human experience. No implied claims or suggestions of drug use may be made if there is inadequate evidence of safety or a lack of substantial evidence of effectiveness. Conclusions based on animal data but necessary for safe and effective use of the drug in humans must be identified as such and included with human data in the appropriate section of the labeling.

(b) *Categories of prescription drugs subject to the labeling content and format requirements in 201.56(d) and 201.57.* (1) The following categories of prescription drug products are subject to the labeling requirements in paragraph (d) of this section and 201.57 in accordance with the implementation schedule in paragraph (c) of this section:

(i) Prescription drug products for which a new drug application (NDA), biologics license application (BLA), or efficacy supplement was approved by the Food and Drug Administration (FDA) between June 30, 2001 and June 30, 2006;

(ii) Prescription drug products for which an NDA, BLA, or efficacy supplement is pending on June 30, 2006; or

(iii) Prescription drug products for which an NDA, BLA, or efficacy supplement is submitted anytime on or after June 30, 2006.

(2) Prescription drug products not described in paragraph (b)(1) of this section are subject to the labeling requirements in paragraph (e) of this section and 201.80.

(c) *Schedule for implementing the labeling content and format requirements in 201.56(d) and 201.57.* For products described in paragraph (b)(1) of this section, labeling conforming to the requirements in paragraph (d) of this section and 201.57 must be submitted according to the following schedule:

(1) For products for which an NDA, BLA, or efficacy supplement is submitted for approval on or after June 30, 2006, proposed conforming labeling must be submitted as part of the application.

(2) For products for which an NDA, BLA, or efficacy supplement is pending on June 30, 2006, or that has been approved any time from June 30, 2005, up to and including June 30, 2006, a supplement with proposed conforming labeling must be submitted no later than June 30, 2009.

(3) For products for which an NDA, BLA, or efficacy supplement has been approved anytime from June 30, 2004, up to and including June 29, 2005, a supplement with proposed conforming labeling must be submitted no later than June 30, 2010.

(4) For products for which an NDA, BLA, or efficacy supplement has been approved anytime from June 30, 2003, up to and including June 29, 2004, a supplement with proposed conforming labeling must be submitted no later than June 30, 2011.

(5) For products for which an NDA, BLA, or efficacy supplement has been approved anytime from June 30, 2002, up to and including June 29, 2003, a supplement with proposed conforming labeling must be submitted no later than June 30, 2012.

(6) For products for which an NDA, BLA, or efficacy supplement has been approved anytime from June 30, 2001, up to and including June 29, 2002, a supplement with proposed conforming labeling must be submitted no later than June 30, 2013.

(d) *Labeling requirements for new and more recently approved prescription drug products.* This paragraph applies only to prescription drug products described in paragraph (b)(1) of this section and must be implemented according to the schedule specified in paragraph (c) of this section.

(1) Prescription drug labeling described in 201.100(d) must contain the specific information required under 201.57(a), (b), and (c) under the following headings and subheadings and in the following order:

Highlights of Prescribing Information
Product Names, Other Required Information
Boxed Warning
Recent Major Changes
Indications and Usage
Dosage and Administration
Dosage Forms and Strengths
Contraindications
Warnings and Precautions
Adverse Reactions
Drug Interactions
Use in Specific Populations
Full Prescribing Information: Contents
Full Prescribing Information
Boxed Warning
1 Indications and Usage
2 Dosage and Administration
3 Dosage Forms and Strengths
4 Contraindications
5 Warnings and Precautions
6 Adverse Reactions
7 Drug Interactions
8 Use in Specific Populations
8.1 Pregnancy
8.2 Labor and delivery
8.3 Nursing mothers
8.4 Pediatric use
8.5 Geriatric use
9 Drug Abuse and Dependence
9.1 Controlled substance
9.2 Abuse
9.3 Dependence
10 Overdosage
11 Description
12 Clinical Pharmacology
12.1 Mechanism of action
12.2 Pharmacodynamics
12.3 Pharmacokinetics
13 Nonclinical Toxicology
13.1 Carcinogenesis, mutagenesis, impairment of fertility

13.2 Animal toxicology and/or pharmacology
14 Clinical Studies
15 References
16 How Supplied/Storage and Handling
17 Patient Counseling Information

(2) Additional nonstandard subheadings that are used to enhance labeling organization, presentation, or ease of use (e.g., for individual warnings or precautions, or for each drug interaction) must be assigned a decimal number that corresponds to their placement in labeling. The decimal numbers must be consistent with the standardized identifying numbers listed in paragraph (d)(1) of this section (e.g., subheadings added to the "Warnings and Precautions" section must be numbered 5.1, 5.2, and so on).

(3) Any reference in Highlights to information appearing in the full prescribing information must be accompanied by the identifying number (in parentheses) corresponding to the location of the information in the full prescribing information.

(4) Omit clearly inapplicable sections, subsections, or specific information. If sections or subsections required under paragraph (d)(1) of this section are omitted from the full prescribing information, the heading "Full Prescribing Information: Contents" must be followed by an asterisk and the following statement must appear at the end of Contents: "* Sections or subsections omitted from the full prescribing information are not listed."

(5) Any risk information that is required under 201.57(c)(9)(iv) is considered "appropriate pediatric contraindications, warnings, or precautions" within the meaning of section 505A(l)(2) of the Federal Food, Drug, and Cosmetic Act (the act) (21 U.S.C. 355A(l)(2)), whether such information appears in the "Contraindications," "Warnings and Precautions," or "Use in Specific Populations" section of labeling.

(e) *Labeling requirements for older prescription drug products.* This paragraph applies only to approved prescription drug products not described in paragraph (b)(1) of this section.

(1) Prescription drug labeling described in 201.100(d) must contain the specific information required under 201.80 under the following section headings and in the following order:

Description
Clinical Pharmacology
Indications and Usage
Contraindications
Warnings
Precautions
Adverse Reactions

Drug Abuse and Dependence
Overdosage
Dosage and Administration
How Supplied

(2) The labeling may contain the following additional section headings if appropriate and if in compliance with 201.80(l) and (m):
Animal Pharmacology and/or Animal Toxicology
Clinical Studies
References

(3) Omit clearly inapplicable sections, subsections, or specific information.

(4) The labeling may contain a "Product Title" section preceding the "Description" section and containing only the information required by 201.80(a)(1)(i), (a)(1)(ii), (a)(1)(iii), and (a)(1)(iv) and 201.100(e). The information required by 201.80(a)(1)(i) through (a)(1)(iv) must appear in the "Description" section of the labeling, whether or not it also appears in a "Product Title."

(5) The labeling must contain the date of the most recent revision of the labeling, identified as such, placed prominently immediately after the last section of the labeling.

(6) The requirement in 201.80(f)(2) to reprint any FDA-approved patient labeling at the end of prescription drug labeling or accompany the prescription drug labeling must be implemented no later than June 30, 2007.

Sec. 201.57 Specific requirements on content and format of labeling for human prescription drug and biological products described in 201.56(b)(1).
The requirements in this section apply only to prescription drug products described in 201.56(b)(1) and must be implemented according to the schedule specified in 201.56(c), except for the requirement in paragraph (c)(18) of this section to reprint any FDA-approved patient labeling at the end of prescription drug labeling or accompany the prescription drug labeling, which must be implemented no later than June 30, 2007.

(a) *Highlights of prescribing information.* The following information must appear in all prescription drug labeling:

(1) *Highlights limitation statement.* The verbatim statement "These highlights do not include all the information needed to use (*insert name of drug product*) safely and effectively. See full prescribing information for (insert name of drug product)."

(2) *Drug names, dosage form, route of administration, and controlled substance symbol.* The proprietary name and the established name of the drug, if any, as defined in section 502(e)(3) of the Federal Food, Drug, and Cosmetic Act

(the act) or, for biological products, the proper name (as defined in 600.3 of this chapter) including any appropriate descriptors. This information must be followed by the drug's dosage form and route of administration. For controlled substances, the controlled substance symbol designating the schedule in which the controlled substance is listed must be included as required by 1302.04 of this chapter.

(3) *Initial U.S. approval.* The verbatim statement "Initial U.S. Approval" followed by the four-digit year in which FDA initially approved a new molecular entity, new biological product, or new combination of active ingredients. The statement must be placed on the line immediately beneath the established name or, for biological products, proper name of the product.

(4) *Boxed warning.* A concise summary of any boxed warning required by paragraph (c)(1) of this section, not to exceed a length of 20 lines. The summary must be preceded by a heading, in upper-case letters, containing the word "WARNING" and other words that are appropriate to identify the subject of the warning. The heading and the summary must be contained within a box and bolded. The following verbatim statement must be placed immediately following the heading of the boxed warning: "See full prescribing information for complete boxed warning."

(5) *Recent major changes.* A list of the section(s) of the full prescribing information, limited to the labeling sections described in paragraphs (c)(1), (c)(2), (c)(3), (c)(5), and (c)(6) of this section, that contain(s) substantive labeling changes that have been approved by FDA or authorized under 314.70(c)(6) or (d)(2), or 601.12(f)(1) through (f)(3) of this chapter. The heading(s) and, if appropriate, the subheading(s) of the labeling section(s) affected by the change must be listed together with each section's identifying number and the date (month/year) on which the change was incorporated in labeling. These labeling sections must be listed in the order in which they appear in the full prescribing information. A changed section must be listed under this heading in Highlights for at least 1 year after the date of the labeling change and must be removed at the first printing subsequent to the 1 year period.

(6) *Indications and usage.* A concise statement of each of the product's indications, as required under paragraph (c)(2) of this section, with any appropriate subheadings. Major limitations of use (e.g., lack of effect in particular subsets of the population, or second line therapy status) must be briefly noted. If the product is a member of an established pharmacologic class, the concise statement under this heading in Highlights must identify the class in the following manner: "(Drug) is a (name of class) indicated for (indication(s))."

(7) *Dosage and administration.* A concise summary of the information required under paragraph (c)(3) of this section, with any appropriate subheadings, including the recommended dosage regimen, starting dose, dose range, critical differences among population subsets, monitoring recommendations, and other clinically significant clinical pharmacologic information.

(8) *Dosage forms and strengths.* A concise summary of the information required under paragraph (c)(4) of this section, with any appropriate subheadings (e.g., tablets, capsules, injectable, suspension), including the strength or potency of the dosage form in metric system (e.g., 10-milligram tablets) and whether the product is scored.

(9) *Contraindications.* A concise statement of each of the product's contraindications, as required under paragraph (c)(5) of this section, with any appropriate subheadings.

(10) *Warnings and precautions.* A concise summary of the most clinically significant information required under paragraph (c)(6) of this section, with any appropriate subheadings, including information that would affect decisions about whether to prescribe a drug, recommendations for patient monitoring that are critical to safe use of the drug, and measures that can be taken to prevent or mitigate harm.

(11) *Adverse reactions.* (i) A list of the most frequently occurring adverse reactions, as described in paragraph (c)(7) of this section, along with the criteria used to determine inclusion (e.g., incidence rate). Adverse reactions important for other reasons (e.g., because they are serious or frequently lead to discontinuation or dosage adjustment) must not be repeated under this heading in Highlights if they are included elsewhere in Highlights (e.g., Warnings and Precautions, Contraindications).

(ii) For drug products other than vaccines, the verbatim statement "To report SUSPECTED ADVERSE REACTIONS, contact (*insert name of manufacturer*) at (*insert manufacturer's phone number*) or FDA at (*insert current FDA phone number and Web address for voluntary reporting of adverse reactions*)."

(iii) For vaccines, the verbatim statement "To report SUSPECTED ADVERSE REACTIONS, contact (*insert name of manufacturer*) at (*insert manufacturer's phone number*) or VAERS at (*insert the current VAERS phone number and Web address for voluntary reporting of adverse reactions*)."

(iv) For manufacturers with a Web site for voluntary reporting of adverse reactions, the Web address of the direct link to the site.

(12) *Drug interactions.* A concise summary of the information required under paragraph (c)(8) of this section, with any appropriate subheadings.

(13) *Use in specific populations.* A concise summary of the information required under paragraph (c)(9) of this section, with any appropriate subheadings.

(14) *Patient counseling information statement.* The verbatim statement "See 17 for Patient Counseling Information" or, if the product has FDA-approved patient labeling, the verbatim statement "See 17 for Patient Counseling Information and (insert either FDA-approved patient labeling or Medication Guide)."

(15) *Revision date.* The date of the most recent revision of the labeling, identified as such, placed at the end of Highlights.

(b) *Full prescribing information: Contents.* Contents must contain a list of each heading and subheading required in the full prescribing information under 201.56(d)(1), if not omitted under 201.56(d)(4), preceded by the identifying number required under 201.56(d)(1). Contents must also contain any additional subheading(s) included in the full prescribing information preceded by the identifying number assigned in accordance with 201.56(d)(2).

(c) *Full prescribing information.* The full prescribing information must contain the information in the order required under paragraphs (c)(1) through (c)(18) of this section, together with the headings, subheadings, and identifying numbers required under 201.56(d)(1), unless omitted under 201.56(d)(4). If additional subheadings are used within a labeling section, they must be preceded by the identifying number assigned in accordance with 201.56(d)(2).

(1) *Boxed warning.* Certain contraindications or serious warnings, particularly those that may lead to death or serious injury, may be required by the FDA to be presented in a box. The boxed warning ordinarily must be based on clinical data, but serious animal toxicity may also be the basis of a boxed warning in the absence of clinical data. The box must contain, in uppercase letters, a heading inside the box that includes the word "WARNING" and conveys the general focus of the information in the box. The box must briefly explain the risk and refer to more detailed information in the "Contraindications" or "Warnings and Precautions" section, accompanied by the identifying number for the section or subsection containing the detailed information.

(2) *Indications and usage.* This section must state that the drug is indicated for the treatment, prevention, mitigation, cure, or diagnosis of a recognized disease or condition, or of a manifestation of a recognized disease or condition, or for the relief of symptoms associated with a recognized disease or condition.

(i) This section must include the following information when the conditions listed are applicable:

(A) If the drug is used for an indication only in conjunction with a primary mode of therapy (e.g., diet, surgery, behavior changes, or some other drug), a statement that the drug is indicated as an adjunct to that mode of therapy.

(B) If evidence is available to support the safety and effectiveness of the drug or biological product only in selected subgroups of the larger population (e.g., patients with mild disease or patients in a special age group), or if the indication is approved based on a surrogate endpoint under 314.510 or 601.41 of this chapter, a succinct description of the limitations of usefulness of the drug and any uncertainty about anticipated clinical benefits, with reference to the "Clinical Studies" section for a discussion of the available evidence.

(C) If specific tests are necessary for selection or monitoring of the patients who need the drug (e.g., microbe susceptibility tests), the identity of such tests.

(D) If information on limitations of use or uncertainty about anticipated clinical benefits is relevant to the recommended intervals between doses, to the appropriate duration of treatment when such treatment should be limited, or to any modification of dosage, a concise description of the information with reference to the more detailed information in the "Dosage and Administration" section.

(E) If safety considerations are such that the drug should be reserved for specific situations (e.g., cases refractory to other drugs), a statement of the information.

(F) If there are specific conditions that should be met before the drug is used on a long term basis (e.g., demonstration of responsiveness to the drug in a short term trial in a given patient), a statement of the conditions; or, if the indications for long term use are different from those for short term use, a statement of the specific indications for each use.

(ii) If there is a common belief that the drug may be effective for a certain use or if there is a common use of the drug for a condition, but the preponderance of evidence related to the use or condition shows that the drug is ineffective or that the therapeutic benefits of the product do not generally outweigh its risks, FDA may require that this section state that there is a lack of evidence that the drug is effective or safe for that use or condition.

(iii) Any statements comparing the safety or effectiveness of the drug with other agents for the same indication must, except for biological products, be supported by substantial evidence derived from adequate and well-controlled studies as defined in 314.126(b) of this chapter unless this requirement is waived under 201.58 or 314.126(c) of this chapter. For biological products, such statements must be supported by substantial evidence.

(iv) For drug products other than biological products, all indications listed in this section must be supported by substantial evidence of effectiveness based on adequate and well-controlled studies as defined in 314.126(b) of this chapter unless the requirement is waived under 201.58 or 314.126(c) of this chapter. Indications or uses must not be implied or suggested in other sections of the labeling if not included in this section.

(v) For biological products, all indications listed in this section must be supported by substantial evidence of effectiveness. Indications or uses must not be implied or suggested in other sections of the labeling if not included in this section.

(3) *Dosage and administration.* (i) This section must state the recommended dose and, as appropriate:

(A) The dosage range,

(B) An upper limit beyond which safety and effectiveness have not been established, or beyond which increasing the dose does not result in increasing effectiveness,

(C) Dosages for each indication and subpopulation,

(D) The intervals recommended between doses,

(E) The optimal method of titrating dosage,

(F) The usual duration of treatment when treatment duration should be limited,

(G) Dosing recommendations based on clinical pharmacologic data (e.g., clinically significant food effects),

(H) Modification of dosage needed because of drug interactions or in special patient populations (e.g., in children, in geriatric age groups, in groups defined by genetic characteristics, or in patients with renal or hepatic disease),

(I) Important considerations concerning compliance with the dosage regimen,

(J) Efficacious or toxic concentration ranges and therapeutic concentration windows of the drug or its metabolites, if established and clinically significant. Information on therapeutic drug concentration monitoring (TDM) must also be included in this section when TDM is necessary.

(ii) Dosing regimens must not be implied or suggested in other sections of the labeling if not included in this section.

(iii) Radiation dosimetry information must be stated for both the patient receiving a radioactive drug and the person administering it.

(iv) This section must also contain specific direction on dilution, preparation (including the strength of the final dosage solution, when prepared according to instructions, in terms of milligrams of active ingredient per milliliter of reconstituted solution, unless another measure of the strength is more appropriate), and administration of the dosage form, if needed (e.g., the rate of administration of parenteral drug in milligrams per minute; storage conditions for stability of the reconstituted drug, when important; essential informa-

tion on drug incompatibilities if the drug is mixed in vitro with other drugs or diluents; and the following verbatim statement for parenterals: "Parenteral drug products should be inspected visually for particulate matter and discoloration prior to administration, whenever solution and container permit.")

(4) *Dosage forms and strengths.* This section must contain information on the available dosage forms to which the labeling applies and for which the manufacturer or distributor is responsible, including:

(i) The strength or potency of the dosage form in metric system (e.g., 10 milligram tablets), and, if the apothecary system is used, a statement of the strength in parentheses after the metric designation; and

(ii) A description of the identifying characteristics of the dosage forms, including shape, color, coating, scoring, and imprinting, when applicable. The National Drug Code number(s) for the drug product must not be included in this section.

(5) *Contraindications.* This section must describe any situations in which the drug should not be used because the risk of use (e.g., certain potentially fatal adverse reactions) clearly outweighs any possible therapeutic benefit. Those situations include use of the drug in patients who, because of their particular age, sex, concomitant therapy, disease state, or other condition, have a substantial risk of being harmed by the drug and for whom no potential benefit makes the risk acceptable. Known hazards and not theoretical possibilities must be listed (e.g., if severe hypersensitivity to the drug has not been demonstrated, it should not be listed as a contraindication). If no contraindications are known, this section must state "None."

(6) *Warnings and precautions.* (i) *General.* This section must describe clinically significant adverse reactions (including any that are potentially fatal, are serious even if infrequent, or can be prevented or mitigated through appropriate use of the drug), other potential safety hazards (including those that are expected for the pharmacological class or those resulting from drug/drug interactions), limitations in use imposed by them (e.g., avoiding certain concomitant therapy), and steps that should be taken if they occur (e.g., dosage modification). The frequency of all clinically significant adverse reactions and the approximate mortality and morbidity rates for patients experiencing the reaction, if known and necessary for the safe and effective use of the drug, must be expressed as provided under paragraph (c)(7) of this section. In accordance with 314.70 and 601.12 of this chapter, the labeling must be revised to include a warning about a clinically significant hazard as soon as there is reasonable evidence of a causal association with a drug; a causal relationship need

not have been definitely established. A specific warning relating to a use not provided for under the "Indications and Usage" section may be required by FDA in accordance with sections 201(n) and 502(a) of the act if the drug is commonly prescribed for a disease or condition and such usage is associated with a clinically significant risk or hazard.

(ii) *Other special care precautions.* This section must contain information regarding any special care to be exercised by the practitioner for safe and effective use of the drug (e.g., precautions not required under any other specific section or subsection).

(iii) *Monitoring: Laboratory tests.* This section must identify any laboratory tests helpful in following the patient's response or in identifying possible adverse reactions. If appropriate, information must be provided on such factors as the range of normal and abnormal values expected in the particular situation and the recommended frequency with which tests should be performed before, during, and after therapy.

(iv) *Interference with laboratory tests.* This section must briefly note information on any known interference by the product with laboratory tests and reference the section where the detailed information is presented (e.g., "Drug Interactions" section).

(7) *Adverse reactions.* This section must describe the overall adverse reaction profile of the drug based on the entire safety database. For purposes of prescription drug labeling, an adverse reaction is an undesirable effect, reasonably associated with use of a drug, that may occur as part of the pharmacological action of the drug or may be unpredictable in its occurrence. This definition does not include all adverse events observed during use of a drug, only those adverse events for which there is some basis to believe there is a causal relationship between the drug and the occurrence of the adverse event.

(i) *Listing of adverse reactions.* This section must list the adverse reactions that occur with the drug and with drugs in the same pharmacologically active and chemically related class, if applicable. The list or lists must be preceded by the information necessary to interpret the adverse reactions (e.g., for clinical trials, total number exposed, extent and nature of exposure).

(ii) *Categorization of adverse reactions.* Within a listing, adverse reactions must be categorized by body system, by severity of the reaction, or in order of decreasing frequency, or by a combination of these, as appropriate. Within a category, adverse reactions must be listed in decreasing order of frequency. If frequency information cannot be reliably determined, adverse reactions must be listed in decreasing order of severity.

(A) *Clinical trials experience.* This section must list the adverse reactions identified in clinical trials that occurred at or above a specified rate appropriate to the safety database. The rate of occurrence of an adverse reaction for the drug and comparators (e.g., placebo) must be presented, unless such data cannot be determined or presentation of comparator rates would be misleading. If adverse reactions that occurred below the specified rate are included, they must be included in a separate listing. If comparative rates of occurrence cannot be reliably determined (e.g., adverse reactions were observed only in the uncontrolled trial portion of the overall safety database), adverse reactions must be grouped within specified frequency ranges as appropriate to the safety database for the drug (e.g., adverse reactions occurring at a rate of less than 1/100, adverse reactions occurring at a rate of less than 1/500) or descriptively identified, if frequency ranges cannot be determined. For adverse reactions with significant clinical implications, the listings must be supplemented with additional detail about the nature, frequency, and severity of the adverse reaction and the relationship of the adverse reaction to drug dose and demographic characteristics, if data are available and important.

(B) *Postmarketing experience.* This section of the labeling must list the adverse reactions, as defined in paragraph (c)(7) of this section, that are identified from domestic and foreign spontaneous reports. This listing must be separate from the listing of adverse reactions identified in clinical trials.

(iii) *Comparisons of adverse reactions between drugs.* For drug products other than biological products, any claim comparing the drug to which the labeling applies with other drugs in terms of frequency, severity, or character of adverse reactions must be based on adequate and well-controlled studies as defined in 314.126(b) of this chapter unless this requirement is waived under 201.58 or 314.126(c) of this chapter. For biological products, any such claim must be based on substantial evidence.

(8) *Drug interactions.* (i) This section must contain a description of clinically significant interactions, either observed or predicted, with other prescription or over-the-counter drugs, classes of drugs, or foods (e.g., dietary supplements, grapefruit juice), and specific practical instructions for preventing or managing them. The mechanism(s) of the interaction, if known, must be briefly described. Interactions that are described in the "Contraindications" or "Warnings and Precautions" sections must be discussed in more detail under this section. Details of drug interaction pharmacokinetic studies that are included in the "Clinical Pharmacology" section that are pertinent to clinical use of the drug must not be repeated in this section.

(ii) This section must also contain practical guidance on known interference of the drug with laboratory tests.

(9) *Use in specific populations.* This section must contain the following subsections:

(i) *8.1 Pregnancy.* This subsection may be omitted only if the drug is not absorbed systemically and the drug is not known to have a potential for indirect harm to the fetus. For all other drugs, this subsection must contain the following information:

(A) *Teratogenic effects.* Under this subheading, the labeling must identify one of the following categories that applies to the drug, and the labeling must bear the statement required under the category:

(1) Pregnancy category A. If adequate and well-controlled studies in pregnant women have failed to demonstrate a risk to the fetus in the first trimester of pregnancy (and there is no evidence of a risk in later trimesters), the labeling must state: "Pregnancy Category A. Studies in pregnant women have not shown that (*name of drug*) increases the risk of fetal abnormalities if administered during the first (*second, third, or all*) trimester(s) of pregnancy. If this drug is used during pregnancy, the possibility of fetal harm appears remote. Because studies cannot rule out the possibility of harm, however, (*name of drug*) should be used during pregnancy only if clearly needed." The labeling must also contain a description of the human studies. If animal reproduction studies are also available and they fail to demonstrate a risk to the fetus, the labeling must also state: "Reproduction studies have been performed in (kinds of animal(s)) at doses up to (x) times the human dose and have revealed no evidence of impaired fertility or harm to the fetus due to (name of drug)." The labeling must also contain a description of available data on the effect of the drug on the later growth, development, and functional maturation of the child.

(2) Pregnancy category B. If animal reproduction studies have failed to demonstrate a risk to the fetus and there are no adequate and well-controlled studies in pregnant women, the labeling must state: "Pregnancy Category B. Reproduction studies have been performed in (*kind(s) of animal(s)*) at doses up to (x) times the human dose and have revealed no evidence of impaired fertility or harm to the fetus due to (*name of drug*). There are, however, no adequate and well-controlled studies in pregnant women. Because animal reproduction studies are not always predictive of human response, this drug should be used during pregnancy only if clearly needed." If animal reproduction studies have shown an adverse effect (other than decrease in fertility), but adequate and well-controlled studies in pregnant women have failed to demonstrate a risk to the fetus during the

first trimester of pregnancy (and there is no evidence of a risk in later trimesters), the labeling must state: "Pregnancy Category B. Reproduction studies in (*kind(s) of animal(s)*) have shown (*describe findings*) at (x) times the human dose. Studies in pregnant women, however, have not shown that (name of drug) increases the risk of abnormalities when administered during the first (*second, third, or all*) trimester(s) of pregnancy. Despite the animal findings, it would appear that the possibility of fetal harm is remote, if the drug is used during pregnancy. Nevertheless, because the studies in humans cannot rule out the possibility of harm, (*name of drug*) should be used during pregnancy only if clearly needed." The labeling must also contain a description of the human studies and a description of available data on the effect of the drug on the later growth, development, and functional maturation of the child.

(3) Pregnancy category C. If animal reproduction studies have shown an adverse effect on the fetus, if there are no adequate and well-controlled studies in humans, and if the benefits from the use of the drug in pregnant women may be acceptable despite its potential risks, the labeling must state: "Pregnancy Category C. (*Name of drug*) has been shown to be teratogenic (or to have an embryocidal effect or other adverse effect) in (*name(s) of species*) when given in doses (x) times the human dose. There are no adequate and well-controlled studies in pregnant women. (*Name of drug*) should be used during pregnancy only if the potential benefit justifies the potential risk to the fetus." The labeling must contain a description of the animal studies. If there are no animal reproduction studies and no adequate and well-controlled studies in humans, the labeling must state: "Pregnancy Category C. Animal reproduction studies have not been conducted with (*name of drug*). It is also not known whether (*name of drug*) can cause fetal harm when administered to a pregnant woman or can affect reproduction capacity. (*Name of drug*) should be given to a pregnant woman only if clearly needed." The labeling must contain a description of any available data on the effect of the drug on the later growth, development, and functional maturation of the child.

(4) Pregnancy category D. If there is positive evidence of human fetal risk based on adverse reaction data from investigational or marketing experience or studies in humans, but the potential benefits from the use of the drug in pregnant women may be acceptable despite its potential risks (for example, if the drug is needed in a life-threatening situation or serious disease for which safer drugs cannot be used or are ineffective), the labeling must state: "Pregnancy Category D. See `Warnings and Precautions' section." Under the "Warnings and Precautions" section, the labeling must

state: "(*Name of drug*) can cause fetal harm when administered to a pregnant woman. (*Describe the human data and any pertinent animal data.*) If this drug is used during pregnancy, or if the patient becomes pregnant while taking this drug, the patient should be apprised of the potential hazard to a fetus."

(5) Pregnancy category X. If studies in animals or humans have demonstrated fetal abnormalities or if there is positive evidence of fetal risk based on adverse reaction reports from investigational or marketing experience, or both, and the risk of the use of the drug in a pregnant woman clearly outweighs any possible benefit (for example, safer drugs or other forms of therapy are available), the labeling must state: "Pregnancy Category X. See `Contraindications' section." Under "Contraindications," the labeling must state: "(*Name of drug*) may (*can*) cause fetal harm when administered to a pregnant woman. (*Describe the human data and any pertinent animal data.*) (*Name of drug*) is contraindicated in women who are or may become pregnant. If this drug is used during pregnancy, or if the patient becomes pregnant while taking this drug, the patient should be apprised of the potential hazard to a fetus."

(B) *Nonteratogenic effects.* Under this subheading the labeling must contain other information on the drug's effects on reproduction and the drug's use during pregnancy that is not required specifically by one of the pregnancy categories, if the information is relevant to the safe and effective use of the drug. Information required under this heading must include nonteratogenic effects in the fetus or newborn infant (for example, withdrawal symptoms or hypoglycemia) that may occur because of a pregnant woman's chronic use of the drug for a preexisting condition or disease.

(ii) *8.2 Labor and delivery.* If the drug has a recognized use during labor or delivery (vaginal or abdominal delivery), whether or not the use is stated in the Indications and Usage section, this subsection must describe the available information about the effect of the drug on the mother and the fetus, on the duration of labor or delivery, on the possibility that forceps delivery or other intervention or resuscitation of the newborn will be necessary, and the effect of the drug on the later growth, development, and functional maturation of the child. If any information required under this subsection is unknown, it must state that the information is unknown.

(iii) *8.3 Nursing mothers.* (A) If a drug is absorbed systemically, this subsection must contain, if known, information about excretion of the drug in human milk and effects on the nursing infant. Pertinent adverse effects observed in animal offspring must be described.

(B) If a drug is absorbed systemically and is known to be excreted in human milk, this subsection must contain one of the following statements, as appropriate. If the drug is associated with serious adverse reactions or if the drug has a known tumorigenic potential, the labeling must state: "Because of the potential for serious adverse reactions in nursing infants from (*name of drug*) (or, "Because of the potential for tumorigenicity shown for (*name of drug*) in (*animal or human*) studies), a decision should be made whether to discontinue nursing or to discontinue the drug, taking into account the importance of the drug to the mother." If the drug is not associated with serious adverse reactions and does not have a known tumorigenic potential, the labeling must state: "Caution should be exercised when (*name of drug*) is administered to a nursing woman."

(C) If a drug is absorbed systemically and information on excretion in human milk is unknown, this subsection must contain one of the following statements, as appropriate. If the drug is associated with serious adverse reactions or has a known tumorigenic potential, the labeling must state: "It is not known whether this drug is excreted in human milk. Because many drugs are excreted in human milk and because of the potential for serious adverse reactions in nursing infants from (*name of drug*) (or, "Because of the potential for tumorigenicity shown for (*name of drug*) in (*animal or human*) studies), a decision should be made whether to discontinue nursing or to discontinue the drug, taking into account the importance of the drug to the mother." If the drug is not associated with serious adverse reactions and does not have a known tumorigenic potential, the labeling must state: "It is not known whether this drug is excreted in human milk. Because many drugs are excreted in human milk, caution should be exercised when (*name of drug*) is administered to a nursing woman."

(iv) *8.4 Pediatric use.* (A) Pediatric population(s)/pediatric patient(s): For the purposes of paragraphs (c)(9)(iv)(B) through (c)(9)(iv)(H) of this section, the terms *pediatric population(s)* and *pediatric patient(s)* are defined as the pediatric age group, from birth to 16 years, including age groups often called neonates, infants, children, and adolescents.

(B) If there is a specific pediatric indication different from those approved for adults that is supported by adequate and well-controlled studies in the pediatric population, it must be described under the "Indications and Usage" section, and appropriate pediatric dosage information must be given under the "Dosage and Administration" section. The "Pediatric use" subsection must cite any limitations on the pediatric indication, need for specific monitoring, specific hazards associated with use of the drug in any subsets of the pediatric population (e.g., neonates), differences between pediatric and adult responses to the drug, and other information related to the safe and effective pediatric use of the drug. Data summarized in this subsection should be discussed in more detail, if appropriate, under the "Clinical Pharmacology" or "Clinical Studies" section. As appropriate, this information must also be contained in the "Contraindications" and/or "Warnings and Precautions" section(s).

(C) If there are specific statements on pediatric use of the drug for an indication also approved for adults that are based on adequate and well-controlled studies in the pediatric population, they must be summarized in the "Pediatric use" subsection and discussed in more detail, if appropriate, under the "Clinical Pharmacology" and "Clinical Studies" sections. Appropriate pediatric dosage must be given under the "Dosage and Administration" section. The "Pediatric use" subsection of the labeling must also cite any limitations on the pediatric use statement, need for specific monitoring, specific hazards associated with use of the drug in any subsets of the pediatric population (e.g., neonates), differences between pediatric and adult responses to the drug, and other information related to the safe and effective pediatric use of the drug. As appropriate, this information must also be contained in the "Contraindications" and/or "Warnings and Precautions" section(s).

(D)(*1*) When a drug is approved for pediatric use based on adequate and well-controlled studies in adults with other information supporting pediatric use, the "Pediatric use" subsection of the labeling must contain either the following statement or a reasonable alternative:

The safety and effectiveness of (*drug name*) have been established in the age groups ___ to ___ (note any limitations, e.g., no data for pediatric patients under 2, or only applicable to certain indications approved in adults). Use of (*drug name*) in these age groups is supported by evidence from adequate and well-controlled studies of (*drug name*) in adults with additional data (*insert wording that accurately describes the data submitted to support a finding of substantial evidence of effectiveness in the pediatric population*).

(*2*) Data summarized in the preceding prescribed statement in this subsection must be discussed in more detail, if appropriate, under the "Clinical Pharmacology" or the "Clinical Studies" section. For example, pediatric pharmacokinetic or pharmacodynamic studies and dose response information should be described in the "Clinical Pharmacology" section. Pediatric dosing instructions must be included in the "Dosage and Administration" section. Any differences between pediatric and adult responses, need for specific monitoring, dosing adjustments, and any other information related to safe and effective use of the drug in pediatric patients must be cited briefly in the "Pediatric use" subsection and, as appropriate, in the "Contraindications," "Warnings

and Precautions," and "Dosage and Administration" sections.

(E) If the requirements for a finding of substantial evidence to support a pediatric indication or a pediatric use statement have not been met for a particular pediatric population, the "Pediatric use" subsection must contain an appropriate statement such as "Safety and effectiveness in pediatric patients below the age of (__) have not been established." If use of the drug in this pediatric population is associated with a specific hazard, the hazard must be described in this subsection, or, if appropriate, the hazard must be stated in the "Contraindications" or "Warnings and Precautions" section and this subsection must refer to it.

(F) If the requirements for a finding of substantial evidence to support a pediatric indication or a pediatric use statement have not been met for any pediatric population, this subsection must contain the following statement: "Safety and effectiveness in pediatric patients have not been established." If use of the drug in premature or neonatal infants, or other pediatric subgroups, is associated with a specific hazard, the hazard must be described in this subsection, or, if appropriate, the hazard must be stated in the "Contraindications" or "Warnings and Precautions" section and this subsection must refer to it.

(G) If the sponsor believes that none of the statements described in paragraphs (c)(9)(iv)(B) through (c)(9)(iv)(F) of this section are appropriate or relevant to the labeling of a particular drug, the sponsor must provide reasons for omission of the statements and may propose alternative statement(s). FDA may permit use of an alternative statement if FDA determines that no statement described in those paragraphs is appropriate or relevant to the drug's labeling and that the alternative statement is accurate and appropriate.

(H) If the drug product contains one or more inactive ingredients that present an increased risk of toxic effects to neonates or other pediatric subgroups, a special note of this risk must be made, generally in the "Contraindications" or "Warnings and Precautions" section.

(v) *8.5 Geriatric use.* (A) A specific geriatric indication, if any, that is supported by adequate and well-controlled studies in the geriatric population must be described under the "Indications and Usage" section, and appropriate geriatric dosage must be stated under the "Dosage and Administration" section. The "Geriatric use" subsection must cite any limitations on the geriatric indication, need for specific monitoring, specific hazards associated with the geriatric indication, and other information related to the safe and effective use of the drug in the geriatric population. Unless otherwise noted, information contained in the "Geriatric use" subsection must pertain to use of the drug in persons 65 years of age and older. Data summarized in this subsection must be discussed in more detail, if appropriate, under "Clinical Pharmacology" or the "Clinical Studies" section. As appropriate, this information must also be contained in the "Warnings and Precautions" and/or "Contraindications" section(s).

(B) Specific statements on geriatric use of the drug for an indication approved for adults generally, as distinguished from a specific geriatric indication, must be contained in the "Geriatric use" subsection and must reflect all information available to the sponsor that is relevant to the appropriate use of the drug in elderly patients. This information includes detailed results from controlled studies that are available to the sponsor and pertinent information from well-documented studies obtained from a literature search. Controlled studies include those that are part of the marketing application and other relevant studies available to the sponsor that have not been previously submitted in the investigational new drug application, new drug application, biologics license application, or a supplement or amendment to one of these applications (e.g., postmarketing studies or adverse drug reaction reports). The "Geriatric use" subsection must contain the following statement(s) or reasonable alternative, as applicable, taking into account available information:

(1) If clinical studies did not include sufficient numbers of subjects aged 65 and over to determine whether elderly subjects respond differently from younger subjects, and other reported clinical experience has not identified such differences, the "Geriatric use" subsection must include the following statement:

Clinical studies of (name of drug) did not include sufficient numbers of subjects aged 65 and over to determine whether they respond differently from younger subjects. Other reported clinical experience has not identified differences in responses between the elderly and younger patients. In general, dose selection for an elderly patient should be cautious, usually starting at the low end of the dosing range, reflecting the greater frequency of decreased hepatic, renal, or cardiac function, and of concomitant disease or other drug therapy.

(2) If clinical studies (including studies that are part of marketing applications and other relevant studies available to the sponsor that have not been submitted in the sponsor's applications) included enough elderly subjects to make it likely that differences in safety or effectiveness between elderly and younger subjects would have been detected, but no such differences (in safety or effectiveness) were observed, and other reported clinical experience has not identified such differences, the "Geriatric use" subsection must contain the following statement:

Of the total number of subjects in clinical studies of (name of drug), __ percent were 65 and over, while __ percent were 75 and over. (Alternatively, the labeling may state the total number of subjects included in the studies who were 65 and over and 75 and over.) No overall differences in safety or effectiveness were observed between these subjects and younger subjects, and other reported clinical experience has not identified differences in responses between the elderly and younger patients, but greater sensitivity of some older individuals cannot be ruled out.

(3) If evidence from clinical studies and other reported clinical experience available to the sponsor indicates that use of the drug in elderly patients is associated with differences in safety or effectiveness, or requires specific monitoring or dosage adjustment, the "Geriatric use" subsection must contain a brief description of observed differences or specific monitoring or dosage requirements and, as appropriate, must refer to more detailed discussions in the "Contraindications," "Warnings and Precautions," "Dosage and Administration," or other sections.

(C)(1) If specific pharmacokinetic or pharmacodynamic studies have been carried out in the elderly, they must be described briefly in the "Geriatric use" subsection and in detail under the "Clinical Pharmacology" section. The "Clinical Pharmacology" and "Drug Interactions" sections ordinarily contain information on drug/disease and drug/drug interactions that is particularly relevant to the elderly, who are more likely to have concomitant illness and to use concomitant drugs.

(2) If a drug is known to be substantially excreted by the kidney, the "Geriatric use" subsection must include the statement:

This drug is known to be substantially excreted by the kidney, and the risk of adverse reactions to this drug may be greater in patients with impaired renal function. Because elderly patients are more likely to have decreased renal function, care should be taken in dose selection, and it may be useful to monitor renal function.

(D) If use of the drug in the elderly appears to cause a specific hazard, the hazard must be described in the "Geriatric use" subsection, or, if appropriate, the hazard must be stated in the "Contraindications" or "Warnings and Precautions" section, and the "Geriatric use" subsection must refer to those sections.

(E) Labeling under paragraphs (c)(9)(v)(A) through (c)(9)(v)(C) of this section may include statements, if they are necessary for safe and effective use of the drug, and reflect good clinical practice or past experience in a particular situation, e.g., for a sedating drug, it could be stated that:

Sedating drugs may cause confusion and over-sedation

in the elderly; elderly patients generally should be started on low doses of (*name of drug*) and observed closely.

(F) If the sponsor believes that none of the requirements described in paragraphs (c)(9)(v)(A) through (c)(9)(v)(E) of this section are appropriate or relevant to the labeling of a particular drug, the sponsor must provide reasons for omission of the statements and may propose an alternative statement. FDA may permit omission of the statements if FDA determines that no statement described in those paragraphs is appropriate or relevant to the drug's labeling. FDA may permit use of an alternative statement if the agency determines that such statement is accurate and appropriate.

(vi) *Additional subsections.* Additional subsections may be included, as appropriate, if sufficient data are available concerning the use of the drug in other specified subpopulations (e.g., renal or hepatic impairment).

(10) *9 Drug abuse and dependence.* This section must contain the following information, as appropriate:

(i) *9.1 Controlled substance.* If the drug is controlled by the Drug Enforcement Administration, the schedule in which it is controlled must be stated.

(ii) *9.2 Abuse.* This subsection must state the types of abuse that can occur with the drug and the adverse reactions pertinent to them, and must identify particularly susceptible patient populations. This subsection must be based primarily on human data and human experience, but pertinent animal data may also be used.

(iii) *9.3 Dependence.* This subsection must describe characteristic effects resulting from both psychological and physical dependence that occur with the drug and must identify the quantity of the drug over a period of time that may lead to tolerance or dependence, or both. Details must be provided on the adverse effects of chronic abuse and the effects of abrupt withdrawal. Procedures necessary to diagnose the dependent state and the principles of treating the effects of abrupt withdrawal must be described.

(11) *10 Overdosage.* This section must be based on human data. If human data are unavailable, appropriate animal and in vitro data may be used. The following specific information must be provided:

(i) Signs, symptoms, and laboratory findings associated with an overdosage of the drug;

(ii) Complications that can occur with the drug (for example, organ toxicity or delayed acidosis);

(iii) Concentrations of the drug in biologic fluids associated with toxicity or death; physiologic variables influencing excretion of the drug, such as urine pH; and factors that influence the dose response relationship of the drug, such as tolerance. The pharmacokinetic data given in the "Clinical

Pharmacology" section also may be referenced here, if applicable to overdoses;

(iv) The amount of the drug in a single dose that is ordinarily associated with symptoms of overdosage and the amount of the drug in a single dose that is likely to be life threatening;

(v) Whether the drug is dialyzable; and

(vi) Recommended general treatment procedures and specific measures for support of vital functions (e.g., proven antidotes, gastric lavage, forced diuresis, or as per Poison Control Center). Such recommendations must be based on data available for the specific drug or experience with pharmacologically related drugs. Unqualified recommendations for which data are lacking for the specific drug or class of drugs must not be stated.

(12) *11 Description.* (i) This section must contain:

(A) The proprietary name and the established name, if any, as defined in section 502(e)(2) of the act, of the drug or, for biological products, the proper name (as defined in 600.3 of this chapter) and any appropriate descriptors;

(B) The type of dosage form(s) and the route(s) of administration to which the labeling applies;

(C) The same qualitative and/or quantitative ingredient information as required under 201.100(b) for drug labels or 610.60 and 610.61 of this chapter for biological product labels;

(D) If the product is sterile, a statement of that fact;

(E) The pharmacological or therapeutic class of the drug;

(F) For drug products other than biological products, the chemical name and structural formula of the drug; and

(G) If the product is radioactive, a statement of the important nuclear physical characteristics, such as the principal radiation emission data, external radiation, and physical decay characteristics.

(ii) If appropriate, other important chemical or physical information, such as physical constants or pH, must be stated.

(13) *12 Clinical pharmacology.* (i) This section must contain information relating to the human clinical pharmacology and actions of the drug in humans. Pharmacologic information based on in vitro data using human biomaterials or pharmacologic animal models, or relevant details about in vivo study designs or results (e.g., drug interaction studies), may be included in this section if essential to understand dosing or drug interaction information presented in other sections of the labeling. This section must include the following subsections:

(A) *12.1 Mechanism of action.* This subsection must summarize what is known about the established mechanism(s) of the drug's action in humans at various levels (e.g., receptor, membrane, tissue, organ, whole body). If the mechanism of action is not known, this subsection must contain a statement about the lack of information.

(B) *12.2 Pharmacodynamics*. This subsection must include a description of any biochemical or physiologic pharmacologic effects of the drug or active metabolites related to the drug's clinical effect in preventing, diagnosing, mitigating, curing, or treating disease, or those related to adverse effects or toxicity. Exposure-response relationships (e.g., concentration-response, dose-response) and time course of pharmacodynamic response (including short-term clinical response) must be included if known. If this information is unknown, this subsection must contain a statement about the lack of information. Detailed dosing or monitoring recommendations based on pharmacodynamic information that appear in other sections (e.g., "Warnings and Precautions" or "Dosage and Administration") must not be repeated in this subsection, but the location of such recommendations must be referenced.

(C) *12.3 Pharmacokinetics*. This subsection must describe the clinically significant pharmacokinetics of a drug or active metabolites, (i.e., pertinent absorption, distribution, metabolism, and excretion parameters). Information regarding bioavailability, the effect of food, minimum concentration (Cmin), maximum concentration (Cmax), time to maximum concentration (Tmax), area under the curve (AUC), pertinent half-lives ($t^1/_2$), time to reach steady state, extent of accumulation, route(s) of elimination, clearance (renal, hepatic, total), mechanisms of clearance (e.g., specific enzyme systems), drug/drug and drug/food (e.g., dietary supplements, grapefruit juice) pharmacokinetic interactions (including inhibition, induction, and genetic characteristics), and volume of distribution (Vd) must be presented if clinically significant. Information regarding nonlinearity in pharmacokinetic parameters, changes in pharmacokinetics over time, and binding (plasma protein, erythrocyte) parameters must also be presented if clinically significant. This section must also include the results of pharmacokinetic studies (e.g., of metabolism or interaction) that establish the absence of an effect, including pertinent human studies and in vitro data. Dosing recommendations based on clinically significant factors that change the product's pharmacokinetics (e.g., age, gender, race, hepatic or renal dysfunction, concomitant therapy) that appear in other sections (e.g., "Warnings and Precautions," "Dosage and Administration" or "Use in Specific Populations") must not be repeated in this subsection, but the location of such recommendations must be referenced.

(ii) Data that demonstrate activity or effectiveness in in vitro or animal tests and that have not been shown by

adequate and well-controlled clinical studies to be pertinent to clinical use may be included under this section only under the following circumstances:

(A) In vitro data for anti-infective drugs may be included if the data are immediately preceded by the statement "The following in vitro data are available but their clinical significance is unknown."

(B) For other classes of drugs, in vitro and animal data that have not been shown by adequate and well-controlled studies, as defined in 314.126(b) of this chapter, to be necessary for the safe and effective use may be included in this section only if a waiver is granted under 201.58 or 314.126(c) of this chapter.

(14) *13 Nonclinical toxicology*. This section must contain the following subsections as appropriate:

(i) *13.1 Carcinogenesis, mutagenesis, impairment of fertility*. This subsection must state whether long term studies in animals have been performed to evaluate carcinogenic potential and, if so, the species and results. If results from reproduction studies or other data in animals raise concern about mutagenesis or impairment of fertility in either males or females, this must be described. Any precautionary statement on these topics must include practical, relevant advice to the prescriber on the significance of these animal findings. Human data suggesting that the drug may be carcinogenic or mutagenic, or suggesting that it impairs fertility, as described in the "Warnings and Precautions" section, must not be included in this subsection of the labeling.

(ii) *13.2 Animal toxicology and/or pharmacology*. Significant animal data necessary for safe and effective use of the drug in humans that is not incorporated in other sections of labeling must be included in this section (e.g., specifics about studies used to support approval under 314.600 or 601.90 of this chapter, the absence of chronic animal toxicity data for a drug that is administered over prolonged periods or is implanted in the body).

(15) *14 Clinical studies*. This section must discuss those clinical studies that facilitate an understanding of how to use the drug safely and effectively. Ordinarily, this section will describe the studies that support effectiveness for the labeled indication(s), including discussion of study design, population, endpoints, and results, but must not include an encyclopedic listing of all, or even most, studies performed as part of the product's clinical development program. If a specific important clinical study is mentioned in any section of the labeling required under 201.56 and 201.57 because the study is essential to an understandable presentation of the information in that section of the labeling, any detailed discussion of the study must appear in this section.

(i) For drug products other than biological products, any

clinical study that is discussed in prescription drug labeling that relates to an indication for or use of the drug must be adequate and well-controlled as described in 314.126(b) of this chapter and must not imply or suggest indications or uses or dosing regimens not stated in the "Indications and Usage" or "Dosage and Administration" section. For biological products, any clinical study that is discussed that relates to an indication for or use of the biological product must constitute or contribute to substantial evidence and must not imply or suggest indications or uses or dosing regimens not stated in the "Indications and Usage" or "Dosage and Administration" section.

(ii) Any discussion of a clinical study that relates to a risk from the use of the drug must also refer to the other sections of the labeling where the risk is identified or discussed.

(16) *15 References.* When prescription drug labeling must summarize or otherwise rely on a recommendation by an authoritative scientific body, or on a standardized methodology, scale, or technique, because the information is important to prescribing decisions, the labeling may include a reference to the source of the information.

(17) *16 How supplied/storage and handling.* This section must contain information on the available dosage forms to which the labeling applies and for which the manufacturer or distributor is responsible. The information must include, as appropriate:

(i) The strength or potency of the dosage form in metric system (e.g., 10 milligram tablets) and, if the apothecary system is used, a statement of the strength in parentheses after the metric designation;

(ii) The units in which the dosage form is ordinarily available for prescribing by practitioners (e.g., bottles of 100);

(iii) Appropriate information to facilitate identification of the dosage forms, such as shape, color, coating, scoring, imprinting, and National Drug Code number; and

(iv) Special handling and storage conditions.

(18) *17 Patient counseling information.* This section must contain information necessary for patients to use the drug safely and effectively (e.g., precautions concerning driving or the concomitant use of other substances that may have harmful additive effects). Any FDA-approved patient labeling must be referenced in this section and the full text of such patient labeling must be reprinted immediately following this section or, alternatively, accompany the prescription drug labeling. Any FDA-approved patient labeling printed immediately following this section or accompanying the labeling is subject to the type size requirements in paragraph (d)(6) of this section, except for a Medication Guide

to be detached and distributed to patients in compliance with 208.24 of this chapter. Medication Guides for distribution to patients are subject to the type size requirements set forth in 208.20 of this chapter.

(d) *Format requirements.* All labeling information required under paragraphs (a), (b), and (c) of this section must be printed in accordance with the following specifications:

(1) All headings and subheadings required by paragraphs (a) and (c) of this section must be highlighted by bold type that prominently distinguishes the headings and subheadings from other labeling information. Reverse type is not permitted as a form of highlighting.

(2) A horizontal line must separate the information required by paragraphs (a), (b), and (c) of this section.

(3) The headings listed in paragraphs (a)(5) through (a)(13) of this section must be presented in the center of a horizontal line.

(4) If there are multiple subheadings listed under paragraphs (a)(4) through (a)(13) of this section, each subheading must be preceded by a bullet point.

(5) The labeling information required by paragraphs (a)(1) through (a)(4), (a)(11)(ii) through (a)(11)(iv), and (a)(14) of this section must be in bold print.

(6) The letter height or type size for all labeling information, headings, and subheadings set forth in paragraphs (a), (b), and (c) of this section must be a minimum of 8 points, except for labeling information that is on or within the package from which the drug is to be dispensed, which must be a minimum of 6 points.

(7) The identifying numbers required by 201.56(d) and paragraphs (c)(1) through (c)(18) of this section must be presented in bold print and must precede the heading or subheading by at least two square em's (i.e., two squares of the size of the letter "m" in 8 point type).

(8) The information required by paragraph (a) of this section, not including the information required under paragraph (a)(4) of this section, must be limited in length to an amount that, if printed in 2 columns on a standard sized piece of typing paper (8½ by 11 inches), single spaced, in 8 point type with ½-inch margins on all sides and between columns, would fit on one-half of the page.

(9) Sections or subsections of labeling that are identified as containing recent major changes under paragraph (a)(5) of this section must be highlighted in the full prescribing information by the inclusion of a vertical line on the left edge of the new or modified text.

(10) For the information required by paragraph (b) of this section, each section heading must be in bold print. Each subheading within a section must be indented and not bolded.

Sec. 201.61 Statement of identity.

(a) The principal display panel of an over-the-counter drug in package form shall bear as one of its principal features a statement of the identity of the commodity.

(b) Such statement of identity shall be in terms of the established name of the drug, if any there be, followed by an accurate statement of the general pharmacological category(ies) of the drug or the principal intended action(s) of the drug. In the case of an over-the-counter drug that is a mixture and that has no established name, this requirement shall be deemed to be satisfied by a prominent and conspicuous statement of the general pharmacological action(s) of the mixture or of its principal intended action(s) in terms that are meaningful to the layman. Such statements shall be placed in direct conjunction with the most prominent display of the proprietary name or designation and shall employ terms descriptive of general pharmacological category(ies) or principal intended action(s); for example, "antacid," "analgesic," "decongestant," "antihistaminic," etc. The indications for use shall be included in the directions for use of the drug, as required by section 502(f)(1) of the act and by the regulations in this part.

(c) The statement of identity shall be presented in bold face type on the principal display panel, shall be in a size reasonably related to the most prominent printed matter on such panel, and shall be in lines generally parallel to the base on which the package rests as it is designed to be displayed.

Sec. 201.62 Declaration of net quantity of contents.

(a) The label of an over-the-counter drug in package form shall bear a declaration of the net quantity of contents. This shall be expressed in the terms of weight, measure, numerical count, or a combination or numerical count and weight, measure, or size. The statement of quantity of drugs in tablet, capsule, ampule, or other unit form and the quantity of devices shall be expressed in terms of numerical count; the statement of quantity for drugs in other dosage forms shall be in terms of weight if the drug is solid, semisolid, or viscous, or in terms of fluid measure if the drug is liquid. The drug quantity statement shall be augmented when necessary to give accurate information as to the strength of such drug in the package; for example, to differentiate between several strengths of the same drug "100 tablets, 5 grains each" or "100 capsules, 125 milligrams each" or "100 capsules, 250 milligrams each": *Provided,* That:

(1) In the case of a firmly established, general consumer usage and trade custom of declaring the quantity of a drug in terms of linear measure or measure of area, such respective term may be used. Such term shall be augmented when

necessary for accuracy of information by a statement of the weight, measure, or size of the individual units or of the entire drug; for example, the net quantity of adhesive tape in package form shall be expressed in terms of linear measure augmented by a statement of its width.

(2) Whenever the Commissioner determines for a specific packaged drug that an existing practice of declaring net quantity of contents by weight, measure, numerical count, or a combination of these does not facilitate value comparisons by consumers, he shall by regulation designate the appropriate term or terms to be used for such article.

(b) Statements of weight of the contents shall be expressed in terms of avoirdupois pound and ounce. A statement of liquid measure of the contents shall be expressed in terms of the U.S. gallon of 231 cubic inches and quart, pint, and fluid-ounce subdivisions thereof, and shall express the volume at 68 deg. F (20 deg. C). See also paragraph (p) of this section.

(c) The declaration may contain common or decimal fractions. A common fraction shall be in terms of halves, quarters, eights, sixteenths, or thirty-seconds; except that if there exists a firmly established, general consumer usage and trade custom of employing different common fractions in the net quantity declaration of a particular commodity, they may be employed. A common fraction shall be reduced to its lowest terms; a decimal fraction shall not be carried out to more than two places. A statement that includes small fractions of an ounce shall be deemed to permit smaller variations than one which does not include such fractions.

(d) The declaration shall be located on the principal display panel of the label, and with respect to packages bearing alternate principal panels it shall be duplicated on each principal display panel.

(e) The declaration shall appear as a distinct item on the principal display panel, shall be separated, by at least a space equal to the height of the lettering used in the declaration, from other printed label information appearing above or below the declaration and, by at least a space equal to twice the width of the letter "N" of the style of type used in the quantity of contents statement, from other printed label information appearing to the left or right of the declaration. It shall not include any term qualifying a unit of weight, measure, or count, such as "giant pint" and "full quart," that tends to exaggerate the amount of the drug in the container. It shall be placed on the principal display panel within the bottom 30 percent of the area of the label panel in lines generally parallel to the base on which the package rests as it is designed to be displayed: *Provided,* That:

(1) On packages having a principal display panel of 5 square inches or less the requirement for placement within

the bottom 30 percent of the area of the label panel shall not apply when the declaration of net quantity of contents meets the other requirements of this part; and

(2) In the case of a drug that is marketed with both outer and inner retail containers bearing the mandatory label information required by this part and the inner container is not intended to be sold separately, the net quantity of contents placement requirement of this section applicable to such inner container is waived.

(3) The principal display panel of a drug marketed on a display card to which the immediate container is affixed may be considered to be the display panel of the card, and the type size of the net quantity of contents statement is governed by the dimensions of the display card.

(f) The declaration shall accurately reveal the quantity of drug or device in the package exclusive of wrappers and other material packed therewith:*Provided,* That in the case of drugs packed in containers designed to deliver the drug under pressure, the declaration shall state the net quantity of the contents that will be expelled when the instructions for use as shown on the container are followed. The propellant is included in the net quantity declaration.

(g) The declaration shall appear in conspicuous and easily legible boldface print or type in distinct contrast (by typography, layout, color, embossing, or molding) to other matter on the package; except that a declaration of net quantity blown, embossed, or molded on a glass or plastic surface is permissible when all label information is so formed on the surface. Requirements of conspicuousness and legibility shall include the specifications that:

(1) The ratio of height to width of the letter shall not exceed a differential of 3 units to 1 unit, i.e., no more than 3 times as high as it is wide.

(2) Letter heights pertain to upper case or capital letters. When upper and lower case or all lower case letters are used, it is the lower case letter "o" or its equivalent that shall meet the minimum standards.

(3) When fractions are used, each component numeral shall meet one-half the minimum height standards.

(h) The declaration shall be in letters and numerals in a type size established in relationship to the area of the principal display panel of the package and shall be uniform for all packages of substantially the same size by complying with the following type specifications:

(1) Not less than one-sixteenth inch in height on packages the principal display panel of which has an area of 5 square inches or less.

(2) Not less than one-eighth inch in height on packages the principal display panel of which has an area of more than five but not more than 25 square inches.

(3) Not less than three-sixteenths inch in height on packages the principal display panel of which has an area of more than 25 but not more than 100 square inches.

(4) Not less than one-fourth inch in height on packages the principal display panel of which has an area of more than 100 square inches, except not less than one-half inch in height if the area is more than 400 square inches.

Where the declaration is blown, embossed, or molded on a glass or plastic surface rather than by printing, typing, or coloring, the lettering sizes specified in paragraphs (h) (1) through (4) of this section shall be increased by one-sixteenth of an inch.

(i) On packages containing less than 4 pounds or 1 gallon and labeled in terms of weight or fluid measure:

(1) The declaration shall be expressed both in ounces, with identification by weight or by liquid measure and, if applicable (1 pound or 1 pint or more) followed in parentheses by a declaration in pounds for weight units, with any remainder in terms of ounces or common or decimal fractions of the pound (see examples set forth in paragraphs (k) (1) and (2) of this section), or in the case of liquid measure, in the largest whole units (quarts, quarts and pints, or pints, as appropriate) with any remainder in terms of fluid ounces or common or decimal fractions of the pint or quart (see examples set forth in paragraphs (k) (3) and (4) of this section). If the net weight of the package is less than 1 ounce avoirdupois or the net fluid measure is less than 1 fluid ounce, the declaration shall be in terms of common or decimal fractions of the respective ounce and not in terms of drams.

(2) The declaration may appear in more than one line. The term *net weight* shall be used when stating the net quantity of contents in terms of weight. Use of the terms *net* or *net contents* in terms of fluid measure or numerical count is optional. It is sufficient to distinguish avoirdupois ounce from fluid ounce through association of terms; for example, "Net wt. 6 oz" or "6 oz net wt.," and "6 fl oz" or "net contents 6 fl oz."

(j) On packages containing 4 pounds or 1 gallon or more and labeled in terms of weight or fluid measure, the declaration shall be expressed in pounds for weight units with any remainder in terms of ounces or common or decimal fractions of the pound; in the case of fluid measure, it shall be expressed in the largest whole unit (gallons, followed by common or decimal fractions of a gallon or by the next smaller whole unit or units (quarts or quarts and pints)) with any remainder in terms of fluid ounces or common or decimal fractions of the pint or quart; see paragraph (k)(5) of this section.

(k) Examples:

(1) A declaration of $1\frac{1}{2}$ pounds weight shall be ex-

pressed as "Net wt. 24 oz (1 lb 8 oz)," or "Net wt. 24 oz (1½ lb)" or "Net wt. 24 oz (1.5 lb)."

(2) A declaration of three-fourths pound avoirdupois weight shall be expressed as "Net wt. 12 oz."

(3) A declaration of 1 quart liquid measure shall be expressed as "Net contents 32 fl oz (1 qt)" or "32 fl oz (1 qt)."

(4) A declaration of 1¾ quarts liquid measure shall be expressed as "Net contents 56 fl oz (1 qt 1 pt 8 oz)" or "Net contents 56 fl oz (1 qt 1.5 pt)," but not in terms of quart and ounce such as "Net 56 fl oz (1 qt 24 oz)."

(5) A declaration of 2½ gallons liquid measure shall be expressed as "Net contents 2 gal 2 qt," "Net contents 2.5 gallons," or "Net contents 2½ gal" but not as "2 gal 4 pt."

(l) For quantities, the following abbreviations and none other may be employed. Periods and plural forms are optional:

(m) On packages labeled in terms of linear measure, the declaration shall be expressed both in terms of inches and, if applicable (1 foot or more), the largest whole units (yards, yards and feet, feet). The declaration in terms of the largest whole units shall be in parentheses following the declaration in terms of inches and any remainder shall be in terms of inches or common or decimal fractions of the foot or yard; if applicable, as in the case of adhesive tape, the initial declaration in linear inches shall be preceded by a statement of the width. Examples of linear measure are "86 inches (2 yd 1 ft 2 in)," "90 inches (2½ yd)," "30 inches (2.5 ft)," "¾ inch by 36 in (1 yd)," etc.

(n) On packages labeled in terms of area measure, the declaration shall be expressed both in terms of square inches and, if applicable (1 square foot or more), the largest whole square unit (square yards, square yards and square feet, square feet). The declaration in terms of the largest whole units shall be in parentheses following the declaration in terms of square inches and any remainder shall be in terms of square inches or common or decimal fractions of the square foot or square yard; for example, "158 sq inches (1 sq ft 14 sq in)."

(o) Nothing in this section shall prohibit supplemental statements at locations other than the principal display panel(s) describing in nondeceptive terms the net quantity of contents, provided that such supplemental statements of net quantity of contents shall not include any term qualifying a unit of weight, measure, or count that tends to exaggerate the amount of the drug contained in the package; for example, "giant pint" and "full quart." Dual or combination declarations of net quantity of contents as provided for in paragraphs (a) and (i) of this section are not regarded as supplemental net quantity statements and shall be located on the principal display panel.

(p) A separate statement of net quantity of contents in terms of the metric system of weight or measure is not regarded as a supplemental statement and an accurate statement of the net quantity of contents in terms of the metric system of weight or measure may also appear on the principal display panel or on other panels.

(q) The declaration of net quantity of contents shall express an accurate statement of the quantity of contents of the package. Reasonable variations caused by loss or gain of moisture during the course of good distribution practice or by unavoidable deviations in good manufacturing practice will be recognized. Variations from stated quantity of contents shall not be unreasonably large.

(r) A drug shall be exempt from compliance with the net quantity declaration required by this section if it is an ointment labeled "sample," "physician's sample," or a substantially similar statement and the contents of the package do not exceed 8 grams.

Gallon gal
quart qt
pint pt
ounce oz
pound lb
grain gr
kilogram kg
gram g
milligram mg
microgram mcg
liter l
milliliter ml
cubic centimeter cc
yard yd
feet or foot ft
meter m
centimeter cm
millimeter mm
fluid fl
square sq
weight wt

Sec. 201.64 Sodium labeling.

(a) The labeling of over-the-counter (OTC) drug products intended for oral ingestion shall contain the sodium content per dosage unit (e.g., tablet, teaspoonful) if the sodium content of a single maximum recommended dose of the product (which may be one or more dosage units) is 5 milligrams or more. OTC drug products intended for oral ingestion include gum and lozenge dosage forms, but do not include dentifrices, mouthwashes, or mouth rinses.

(b) The sodium content shall be expressed in milligrams

per dosage unit and shall include the total amount of sodium regardless of the source, i.e., from both active and inactive ingredients. The sodium content shall be rounded-off to the nearest whole number. The sodium content per dosage unit shall follow the heading "Other information" as stated in 201.66(c)(7).

(c) The labeling of OTC drug products intended for oral ingestion shall contain the following statement under the heading "Warning" (or "Warnings" if it appears with additional warning statements) if the amount of sodium present in the labeled maximum daily dose of the product is more than 140 milligrams: "Ask a doctor before use if you have [in bold type] [bullet][1] a sodium-restricted diet." The warnings in 201.64(c), 201.70(c), 201.71(c), and 201.72(c) may be combined, if applicable, provided the ingredients are listed in alphabetical order, e g., a calcium or sodium restricted diet.

(d) The term *sodium free* may be used in the labeling of OTC drug products intended for oral ingestion if the amount of sodium in the labeled maximum daily dose is 5 milligrams or less and the amount of sodium per dosage unit is 0 milligram (when rounded-off in accord with paragraph (b) of this section).

(e) The term *very low sodium* may be used in the labeling of OTC drug products intended for oral ingestion if the amount of sodium in the labeled maximum daily dose is 35 milligrams or less.

(f) The term *low sodium* may be used in the labeling of OTC drug products intended for oral ingestion if the amount of sodium in the labeled maximum daily dose is 140 milligrams or less.

(g) The term *salt* is not synonymous with the term sodium and shall not be used interchangeably or substituted for the term *sodium*.

(h) The terms *sodium free, very low sodium,* and *low sodium* shall be in print size and style no larger than the product's statement of identity and shall not be unduly prominent in print size or style compared to the statement of identity.

(i) Any product subject to this paragraph that contains sodium bicarbonate, sodium phosphate, or sodium biphosphate as an active ingredient for oral ingestion and that is not labeled as required by this paragraph and that is initially introduced or initially delivered for introduction into interstate commerce after April 22, 1997, is misbranded under sections 201(n) and 502 (a) and (f) of the Federal Food, Drug, and Cosmetic Act (the act).

(j) Any product subject to paragraphs (a) through (h) of this section that is not labeled as required and that is initially introduced or initially delivered for introduction into inter-

state commerce after the following dates is misbranded under sections 201(n) and 502(a) and (f) of the Federal Food, Drug, and Cosmetic Act.

(1) As of the date of approval of the application for any single entity and combination products subject to drug marketing applications approved on or after April 23, 2004.

(2) September 24, 2005, for all OTC drug products subject to any OTC drug monograph, not yet the subject of any OTC drug monograph, or subject to drug marketing applications approved before April 23, 2004.

(k) The labeling of OTC drug products intended for rectal administration containing dibasic sodium phosphate and/or monobasic sodium phosphate shall contain the sodium content per delivered dose if the sodium content is 5 milligrams or more. The sodium content shall be expressed in milligrams or grams. If less than 1 gram, milligrams should be used. The sodium content shall be rounded-off to the nearest whole number if expressed in milligrams (or nearest tenth of a gram if expressed in grams). The sodium content per delivered dose shall follow the heading "Other information" as stated in 201.66(c)(7). Any product subject to this paragraph that contains dibasic sodium phosphate and/or monobasic sodium phosphate as an active ingredient intended for rectal administration and that is not labeled as required by this paragraph and that is initially introduced or initially delivered for introduction into interstate commerce after November 29, 2005, is misbranded under sections 201(n) and 502(a) and (f) of the act.

Sec. 201.66 Format and content requirements for over-the-counter (OTC) drug product labeling.

(a) *Scope*. This section sets forth the content and format requirements for the labeling of all OTC drug products. Where an OTC drug product is the subject of an applicable monograph or regulation that contains content and format requirements that conflict with this section, the content and format requirements in this section must be followed unless otherwise specifically provided in the applicable monograph or regulation.

(b) *Definitions*. The following definitions apply to this section:

(1) *Act* means the Federal Food, Drug, and Cosmetic Act (secs. 201 *et seq.* (21 U.S.C. 321 *et seq.*)).

(2) *Active ingredient* means any component that is intended to furnish pharmacological activity or other direct effect in the diagnosis, cure, mitigation, treatment, or prevention of disease, or to affect the structure or any function of the body of humans. The term includes those components that may undergo chemical change in the manufacture of the drug product and be present in the drug product in a

modified form intended to furnish the specified activity or effect.

(3) *Approved drug application* means a new drug (NDA) or abbreviated new drug (ANDA) application approved under section 505 of the act (21 U.S.C. 355).

(4) *Bullet* means a geometric symbol that precedes each statement in a list of statements. For purposes of this section, the bullet style is limited to solid squares or solid circles, in the format set forth in paragraph (d)(4) of this section.

(5) *Established name* of a drug or ingredient thereof means the applicable official name designated under section 508 of the act (21 U.S.C. 358), or, if there is no designated official name and the drug or ingredient is recognized in an official compendium, the official title of the drug or ingredient in such compendium, or, if there is no designated official name and the drug or ingredient is not recognized in an official compendium, the common or usual name of the drug or ingredient.

(6) *FDA* means the Food and Drug Administration.

(7) *Heading* means the required statements in quotation marks listed in paragraphs (c)(2) through (c)(9) of this section, excluding subheadings (as defined in paragraph (a)(9) of this section).

(8) *Inactive ingredient* means any component other than an active ingredient.

(9) *Subheading* means the required statements in quotation marks listed in paragraphs (c)(5)(ii) through (c)(5)(vii) of this section.

(10) *Drug facts labeling* means the title, headings, subheadings, and information required under or otherwise described in paragraph (c) of this section.

(11) *Title* means the heading listed at the top of the required OTC drug product labeling, as set forth in paragraph (c)(1) of this section.

(12) *Total surface area available to bear labeling* means all surfaces of the outside container of the retail package or, if there is no such outside container, all surfaces of the immediate container or container wrapper except for the flanges at the tops and bottoms of cans and the shoulders and necks of bottles and jars.

(c) *Content requirements.* The outside container or wrapper of the retail package, or the immediate container label if there is no outside container or wrapper, shall contain the title, headings, subheadings, and information set forth in paragraphs (c)(1) through (c)(8) of this section, and may contain the information under the heading in paragraph (c)(9) of this section, in the order listed.

(1) (Title) "Drug Facts." If the drug facts labeling appears on more than one panel, the title "Drug Facts (continued)" shall appear at the top of each subsequent panel

containing such information.

(2) "Active ingredient" or "Active ingredients" "(in each [insert the dosage unit stated in the directions for use (e.g., tablet, 5 mL teaspoonful) or in each gram as stated in 333.110 and 333.120 of this chapter])," followed by the established name of each active ingredient and the quantity of each active ingredient per dosage unit. Unless otherwise provided in an applicable OTC drug monograph or approved drug application, products marketed without discrete dosage units (e.g., topicals) shall state the proportion (rather than the quantity) of each active ingredient.

(3) "Purpose" or "Purposes," followed by the general pharmacological category(ies) or the principal intended action(s) of the drug or, where the drug consists of more than one ingredient, the general pharmacological categories or the principal intended actions of each active ingredient. When an OTC drug monograph contains a statement of identity, the pharmacological action described in the statement of identity shall also be stated as the purpose of the active ingredient.

(4) "Use" or "Uses," followed by the indication(s) for the specific drug product.

(5) "Warning" or "Warnings," followed by one or more of the following, if applicable:

(i) "For external use only" [in bold type] for topical drug products not intended for ingestion, or "For" (select one of the following, as appropriate: "rectal" or "vaginal") "use only" [in bold type].

(ii) All applicable warnings listed in paragraphs (c)(5)(ii)(A) through (c)(5)(ii)(G) of this section with the appropriate subheadings highlighted in bold type:

(A) Reye's syndrome warning for drug products containing salicylates set forth in 201.314(h)(1). This warning shall follow the subheading "Reye's syndrome:"

(B) Allergic reaction warnings set forth in any applicable OTC drug monograph or approved drug application for any product that requires a separate allergy warning. This warning shall follow the subheading "Allergy alert:"

(C) Flammability warning, with appropriate flammability signal word(s) (e.g., 341.74(c)(5)(iii), 344.52(c), 358.150(c), and 358.550(c) of this chapter). This warning shall follow a subheading containing the appropriate flammability signal word(s) described in an applicable OTC drug monograph or approved drug application.

(D) Water soluble gums warning set forth in 201.319. This warning shall follow the subheading "Choking:"

(E) Alcohol warning set forth in 201.322. This warning shall follow the subheading "Alcohol warning:"

(F) Sore throat warning set forth in 201.315. This warning shall follow the subheading "Sore throat warning:"

(G) Warning for drug products containing sodium phosphates set forth in 201.307(b)(2)(i) or (b)(2)(ii). This warning shall follow the subheading "Dosage warning:"

(H) Sexually transmitted diseases (STDs) warning for vaginal contraceptive and spermicide drug products containing nonoxynol 9 set forth in 201.325(b)(2). This warning shall follow the subheading "Sexually transmitted diseases (STDs) alert:"

(iii) "Do not use" [in bold type], followed by all contraindications for use with the product. These contraindications are absolute and are intended for situations in which consumers should not use the product unless a prior diagnosis has been established by a doctor or for situations in which certain consumers should not use the product under any circumstances regardless of whether a doctor or health professional is consulted.

(iv) "Ask a doctor before use if you have" [in bold type] or, for products labeled only for use in children under 12 years of age, "Ask a doctor before use if the child has" [in bold type], followed by all warnings for persons with certain preexisting conditions (excluding pregnancy) and all warnings for persons experiencing certain symptoms. The warnings under this heading are those intended only for situations in which consumers should not use the product until a doctor is consulted.

(v) "Ask a doctor or pharmacist before use if you are" [in bold type] or, for products labeled only for use in children under 12 years of age, "Ask a doctor or pharmacist before use if the child is" [in bold type], followed by all drug-drug and drug-food interaction warnings.

(vi) "When using this product" [in bold type], followed by the side effects that the consumer may experience, and the substances (e.g., alcohol) or activities (e.g., operating machinery, driving a car, warnings set forth in 369.21 of this chapter for drugs in dispensers pressurized by gaseous propellants) to avoid while using the product.

(vii) "Stop use and ask a doctor if" [in bold type], followed by any signs of toxicity or other reactions that would necessitate immediately discontinuing use of the product. For all OTC drug products under an approved drug application whose packaging does not include a toll-free number through which consumers can report complaints to the manufacturer or distributor of the drug product, the following text shall immediately follow the subheading: "[Bullet] side effects occur. You may report side effects to FDA at 1-800-FDA-1088." The telephone number must appear in a minimum 6-point bold letter height or type size.

(viii) Any required warnings in an applicable OTC drug monograph, other OTC drug regulations, or approved drug application that do not fit within one of the categories listed in paragraphs (c)(5)(i) through (c)(5)(vii), (c)(5)(ix), and (c)(5)(x) of this section.

(ix) The pregnancy/breast-feeding warning set forth in 201.63(a); the third trimester warning set forth in 201.63(e) for products containing aspirin or carbaspirin calcium; the third trimester warning set forth in approved drug applications for products containing ketoprofen, naproxen sodium, and ibuprofen (not intended exclusively for use in children).

(x) The "Keep out of reach of children" warning and the accidental overdose/ingestion warning set forth in 330.1(g) of this chapter.

(6) "Directions," followed by the directions for use described in an applicable OTC drug monograph or approved drug application.

(7) "Other information," followed by additional information that is not included under paragraphs (c)(2) through (c)(6), (c)(8), and (c)(9) of this section, but which is required by or is made optional under an applicable OTC drug monograph, other OTC drug regulation, or is included in the labeling of an approved drug application.

(i) Required information about certain ingredients in OTC drug products (e.g., sodium in 201.64(b), calcium in 201.70(b), magnesium in 201.71(b), and potassium in 201.72(b)) shall appear as follows: "each (insert appropriate dosage unit) contains:" [in bold type (insert name(s) of ingredient(s) (in alphabetical order) and the quantity of each ingredient). This information shall be the first statement under this heading.

(ii) The phenylalanine/aspartame content required by 201.21(b), if applicable, shall appear as the next item of information.

(iii) Additional information that is authorized to appear under this heading shall appear as the next item(s) of information. There is no required order for this subsequent information.

(8) "Inactive ingredients," followed by a listing of the established name of each inactive ingredient. If the product is an OTC drug product that is not also a cosmetic product, then the inactive ingredients shall be listed in alphabetical order. If the product is an OTC drug product that is also a cosmetic product, then the inactive ingredients shall be listed as set forth in 701.3(a) or (f) of this chapter, the names of cosmetic ingredients shall be determined in accordance with 701.3(c) of this chapter, and the provisions in 701.3(e), (g), (h), (l), (m), (n), and (o) of this chapter and 720.8 of this chapter may also apply, as appropriate. If there is a difference in the labeling provisions in this 201.66 and 701.3 and 720.8 of this chapter, the labeling provisions in this 201.66 shall be used.

(9) "Questions?" or "Questions or comments?," followed by the telephone number of a source to answer questions about the product. It is recommended that the days of the week and times of the day when a person is available to respond to questions also be included. A graphic of a telephone or telephone receiver may appear before the heading. The telephone number must appear in a minimum 6-point bold type.

(d) *Format requirements.* The title, headings, subheadings, and information set forth in paragraphs (c)(1) through (c)(9) of this section shall be presented on OTC drug products in accordance with the following specifications. In the interest of uniformity of presentation, FDA strongly recommends that the Drug Facts labeling be presented using the graphic specifications set forth in appendix A to part 201.

(1) The title "Drug Facts" or "Drug Facts (continued)" shall use uppercase letters for the first letter of the words "Drug" and "Facts." All headings and subheadings in paragraphs (c)(2) through (c)(9) of this section shall use an uppercase letter for the first letter in the first word and lowercase letters for all other words. The title, headings, and subheadings in paragraphs (c)(1), (c)(2), and (c)(4) through (c)(9) of this section shall be left justified.

(2) The letter height or type size for the title "Drug Facts" shall appear in a type size larger than the largest type size used in the Drug Facts labeling. The letter height or type size for the title "Drug Facts (continued)" shall be no smaller than 8-point type. The letter height or type size for the headings in paragraphs (c)(2) through (c)(9) of this section shall be the larger of either 8-point or greater type, or 2-point sizes greater than the point size of the text. The letter height or type size for the subheadings and all other information described in paragraphs (c)(2) through (c)(9) of this section shall be no smaller than 6-point type.

(3) The title, heading, subheadings, and information in paragraphs (c)(1) through (c)(9) of this section shall be legible and clearly presented, shall have at least 0.5-point leading (i.e., space between two lines of text), and shall not have letters that touch. The type style for the title, headings, subheadings, and all other required information described in paragraphs (c)(2) through (c)(9) of this section shall be any single, clear, easy-to-read type style, with no more than 39 characters per inch. The title and headings shall be in bold italic, and the subheadings shall be in bold type, except that the word "(continued)" in the title "Drug Facts (continued)" shall be regular type. The type shall be all black or one color printed on a white or other contrasting background, except that the title and the headings may be presented in a single, alternative, contrasting color unless otherwise provided in an approved drug application, OTC drug monograph (e.g.,

current requirements for bold print in 341.76 and 341.80 of this chapter), or other OTC drug regulation (e.g., the requirement for a box and red letters in 201.308(c)(1)).

(4) When there is more than one statement, each individual statement listed under the headings and subheadings in paragraphs (c)(4) through (c)(7) of this section shall be preceded by a solid square or solid circle bullet of 5-point type size. Bullets shall be presented in the same shape and color throughout the labeling. The first bulleted statement on each horizontal line of text shall be either left justified or separated from an appropriate heading or subheading by at least two square "ems" (i.e., two squares of the size of the letter "M"). If more than one bulleted statement is placed on the same horizontal line, the end of one bulleted statement shall be separated from the beginning of the next bulleted statement by at least two square "ems" and the complete additional bulleted statement(s) shall not continue to the next line of text. Additional bulleted statements appearing on each subsequent horizontal line of text under a heading or subheading shall be vertically aligned with the bulleted statements appearing on the previous line.

(5) The title, headings, subheadings, and information set forth in paragraphs (c)(1) through (c)(9) of this section may appear on more than one panel on the outside container of the retail package, or the immediate container label if there is no outside container or wrapper. The continuation of the required content and format onto multiple panels must retain the required order and flow of headings, subheadings, and information. A visual graphic (e.g., an arrow) shall be used to signal the continuation of the Drug Facts labeling to the next adjacent panel.

(6) The heading and information required under paragraph (c)(2) of this section shall appear immediately adjacent and to the left of the heading and information required under paragraph (c)(3) of this section. The active ingredients and purposes shall be aligned under the appropriate headings such that the heading and information required under paragraph (c)(2) of this section shall be left justified and the heading and information required under paragraph (c)(3) of this section shall be right justified. If the OTC drug product contains more than one active ingredient, the active ingredients shall be listed in alphabetical order. If more than one active ingredient has the same purpose, the purpose need not be repeated for each active ingredient, provided the information is presented in a manner that readily associates each active ingredient with its purpose (i.e., through the use of brackets, dot leaders, or other graphical features). The information described in paragraphs (c)(4) and (c)(6) through (c)(9) of this section may start on the same line as the required headings. None of the information described in

paragraph (c)(5) of this section shall appear on the same line as the "Warning" or "Warnings" heading.

(7) Graphical images (e.g., the UPC symbol) and information not described in paragraphs (c)(1) through (c)(9) of this section shall not appear in or in any way interrupt the required title, headings, subheadings, and information in paragraphs (c)(1) through (c)(9) of this section. Hyphens shall not be used except to punctuate compound words.

(8) The information described in paragraphs (c)(1) through (c)(9) of this section shall be set off in a box or similar enclosure by the use of a barline. A distinctive horizontal barline extending to each end of the "Drug Facts" box or similar enclosure shall provide separation between each of the headings listed in paragraphs (c)(2) through (c)(9) of this section. When a heading listed in paragraphs (c)(2) through (c)(9) of this section appears on a subsequent panel immediately after the "Drug Facts (continued)" title, a horizontal hairline shall follow the title and immediately precede the heading. A horizontal hairline extending within two spaces on either side of the "Drug Facts" box or similar enclosure shall immediately follow the title and shall immediately precede each of the subheadings set forth in paragraph (c)(5) of this section, except the subheadings in paragraphs (c)(5)(ii)(A) through (c)(5)(ii)(G) of this section.

(9) The information set forth in paragraph (c)(6) of this section under the heading "Directions" shall appear in a table format when dosage directions are provided for three or more age groups or populations. The last line of the table may be the horizontal barline immediately preceding the heading of the next section of the labeling.

(10) If the title, headings, subheadings, and information in paragraphs (c)(1) through (c)(9) of this section, printed in accordance with the specifications in paragraphs (d)(1) through (d)(9) of this section, and any other FDA required information for drug products, and, as appropriate, cosmetic products, other than information required to appear on a principle display panel, requires more than 60 percent of the total surface area available to bear labeling, then the Drug Facts labeling shall be printed in accordance with the specifications set forth in paragraphs (d)(10)(i) through (d)(10)(v) of this section. In determining whether more than 60 percent of the total surface area available to bear labeling is required, the indications for use listed under the "Use(s)" heading, as set forth in paragraph (c)(4) of this section, shall be limited to the minimum required uses reflected in the applicable monograph, as provided in 330.1(c)(2) of this chapter.

(i) Paragraphs (d)(1), (d)(5), (d)(6), and (d)(7) of this section shall apply.

(ii) Paragraph (d)(2) of this section shall apply except that the letter height or type size for the title "Drug Facts

(continued)" shall be no smaller than 7-point type and the headings in paragraphs (c)(2) through (c)(9) of this section shall be the larger of either 7-point or greater type, or 1-point size greater than the point size of the text.

(iii) Paragraph (d)(3) of this section shall apply except that less than 0.5-point leading may be used, provided the ascenders and descenders do not touch.

(iv) Paragraph (d)(4) of this section shall apply except that if more than one bulleted statement is placed on the same horizontal line, the additional bulleted statements may continue to the next line of text, and except that the bullets under each heading or subheading need not be vertically aligned.

(v) Paragraph (d)(8) of this section shall apply except that the box or similar enclosure required in paragraph (d)(8) of this section may be omitted if the Drug Facts labeling is set off from the rest of the labeling by use of color contrast.

(11)(i) The following labeling outlines the various provisions in paragraphs (c) and (d) of this section:

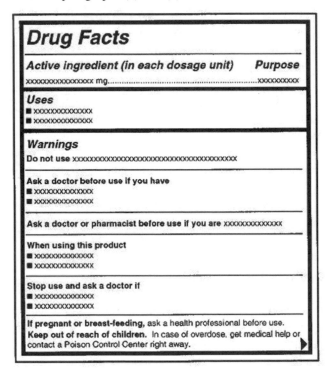

(ii) The following sample label illustrates the provisions in paragraphs (c) and (d) of this section:

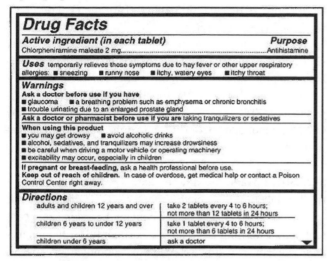

(iii) The following sample label illustrates the provisions in paragraphs (c) and (d) of this section, including paragraph (d)(10) of this section, which permits modifications for small packages:

Drug Facts

Active Ingredients (in each tablet)   Purpose
Aluminum hydroxide gel 200 mg.....................................Antacid
Magnesium hydroxide 200 mg.......................................Antacid
Simethicone 25 mg...Antigas

Uses
■ relieves symptoms referred to as gas
■ relieves: ■ heartburn   ■ acid indigestion   ■ sour stomach
    ■ upset stomach due to these symptoms

Warnings
Ask a doctor before use if you have kidney disease

Ask a doctor or pharmacist before use if you are taking a prescription drug. Antacids may interact with certain prescription drugs.

Stop use and ask a doctor if symptoms last for more than 2 weeks

Keep out of reach of children.

Directions ■ chew 1 to 4 tablets 4 times daily
■ do not take more than 16 tablets in 24 hours or use the maximum dosage for more than 2 weeks

Inactive Ingredients D&C red no. 30, D&C yellow no. 10, dextrose, FD&C blue no. 1, glycerin, magnesium stearate, mannitol, saccharin sodium, sorbitol, starch, sugar, talc

(iv) The following sample label illustrates the provisions in paragraphs (c) and (d) of this section for a drug product marketed with cosmetic claims:

(e) *Exemptions and deferrals.* FDA on its own initiative or in response to a written request from any manufacturer, packer, or distributor, may exempt or defer, based on the circumstances presented, one or more specific requirements set forth in this section on the basis that the requirement is inapplicable, impracticable, or contrary to public health or safety. Requests for exemptions shall be submitted in three copies in the form of an "Application for Exemption" to the Food and Drug Administration, 5630 Fishers Lane, rm. 1061, Rockville, MD 20852. The request shall be clearly identified on the envelope as a "Request for Exemption from 21 CFR 201.66 (OTC Labeling Format)" and shall be directed to Docket No. 98N-0337. A separate request shall be submitted for each OTC drug product. Sponsors of a product marketed under an approved drug application shall also submit a single copy of the exemption request to their application. Decisions on exemptions and deferrals will be maintained in a permanent file in this docket for public review. Exemption and deferral requests shall:

(1) Document why a particular requirement is inapplicable, impracticable, or is contrary to public health or safety; and

(2) Include a representation of the proposed labeling, including any outserts, panel extensions, or other graphical or packaging techniques intended to be used with the product.

(f) *Interchangeable terms and connecting terms.* The terms listed in 330.1(i) of this chapter may be used interchangeably in the labeling of OTC drug products, provided such use does not alter the meaning of the labeling that has been established and identified in an applicable OTC drug monograph or by regulation. The terms listed in 330.1(j) of this chapter may be deleted from the labeling of OTC drug products when the labeling is revised to comply with this section, provided such deletion does not alter the meaning of the labeling that has been established and identified in an applicable OTC drug monograph or by regulation. The terms listed in 330.1(i) and (j) of this chapter shall not be used to change in any way the specific title, headings, and subheadings required under paragraphs (c)(1) through (c)(9) of this section.

(g) *Regulatory action.* An OTC drug product that is not in compliance with the format and content requirements in this section is subject to regulatory action.

Sec. 201.70 Calcium labeling.

(a) The labeling of over-the-counter (OTC) drug products intended for oral ingestion shall contain the calcium content per dosage unit (e.g., tablet, teaspoonful) if the calcium content of a single maximum recommended dose of the product (which may be one or more dosage units) is 20 milligrams or more. OTC drug products intended for oral ingestion include gum and lozenge dosage forms, but do not include dentifrices, mouthwashes, or mouth rinses.

(b) The calcium content shall be expressed in milligrams or grams per dosage unit and shall include the total amount of calcium regardless of the source, i.e., from both active and inactive ingredients. If the dosage unit contains less than 1 gram of calcium, milligrams should be used. The calcium content per dosage unit shall be rounded-off to the nearest 5 milligrams (or nearest tenth of a gram if over 1 gram). The calcium content per dosage unit shall follow the heading "Other information" as stated in 201.66(c)(7).

(c) The labeling of OTC drug products intended for oral ingestion shall contain the following statement under the heading "Warning" (or "Warnings" if it appears with additional warning statements) if the amount of calcium present in the labeled maximum daily dose of the product is more than 3.2 grams: "Ask a doctor before use if you have [in bold type] [bullet][1] kidney stones [bullet] a calcium-restricted diet." The warnings in 201.64(c), 201.70(c), 201.71(c), and 201.72(c) may be combined, if applicable, provided the ingredients are listed in alphabetical order, e.g., a calcium or sodium restricted diet.

(d) Any product subject to this paragraph that is not labeled as required by this paragraph and that is initially introduced or initially delivered for introduction into interstate commerce after the following dates is misbranded under sections 201(n) and 502(a) and (f) of the Federal Food, Drug, and Cosmetic Act.

(1) As of the date of approval of the application for any single entity and combination products subject to drug marketing applications approved on or after April 23, 2004.

(2) September 24, 2005, for all OTC drug products subject to any OTC drug monograph, not yet the subject of any OTC drug monograph, or subject to drug marketing applications approved before April 23, 2004.

Sec. 201.71 Magnesium labeling.

(a) The labeling of over-the-counter (OTC) drug products intended for oral ingestion shall contain the magnesium content per dosage unit (e.g., tablet, teaspoonful) if the magnesium content of a single maximum recommended dose of the product (which may be one or more dosage units) is 8 milligrams or more. OTC drug products intended for oral ingestion include gum and lozenge dosage forms, but do not include dentifrices, mouthwashes, or mouth rinses.

(b) The magnesium content shall be expressed in milligrams or grams per dosage unit and shall include the total amount of magnesium regardless of the source, i.e., from both active and inactive ingredients. If the dosage unit contains less than 1 gram of magnesium, milligrams should be used. The magnesium content shall be rounded-off to the nearest 5 milligrams (or nearest tenth of a gram if over 1 gram). The magnesium content per dosage unit shall follow the heading "Other information" as stated in 201.66(c)(7).

(c) The labeling of OTC drug products intended for oral ingestion shall contain the following statement under the heading "Warning" (or "Warnings" if it appears with additional warning statements) if the amount of magnesium present in the labeled maximum daily dose of the product is more than 600 milligrams: "Ask a doctor before use if you have [in bold type] [bullet][1] kidney disease [bullet] a magnesium-restricted diet." The warnings in 201.64(c), 201.70(c), 201.71(c), and 201.72(c) may be combined, if applicable, provided the ingredients are listed in alphabetical order, e.g., a magnesium or potassium-restricted diet.

(d) Any product subject to this paragraph that is not labeled as required by this paragraph and that is initially introduced or initially delivered for introduction into interstate commerce after the following dates is misbranded under sections 201(n) and 502(a) and (f) of the Federal Food, Drug, and Cosmetic Act.

(1) As of the date of approval of the application for any single entity and combination products subject to drug marketing applications approved on or after April 23, 2004.

(2) September 24. 2005, for all OTC drug products subject to any OTC drug monograph, not yet the subject of any OTC drug monograph, or subject to drug marketing applications approved before April 23, 2004.

Sec. 201.72 Potassium labeling.

(a) The labeling of over-the-counter (OTC) drug products intended for oral ingestion shall contain the potassium content per dosage unit (e.g., tablet, teaspoonful) if the potassium content of a single maximum recommended dose of the product (which may be one or more dosage units) is 5 milligrams or more. OTC drug products intended for oral ingestion include gum and lozenge dosage forms, but do not include dentifrices, mouthwashes, or mouth rinses.

(b) The potassium content shall be expressed in milligrams or grams per dosage unit and shall include the total amount of potassium regardless of the source, i.e., from both active and inactive ingredients. If the dosage unit contains less than 1 gram of potassium, milligrams should be used. The potassium content shall be rounded-off to the nearest 5 milligrams (or nearest tenth of a gram if over 1 gram). The potassium content per dosage unit shall follow the heading "Other information" as stated in 201.66(c)(7).

(c) The labeling of OTC drug products intended for oral ingestion shall contain the following statement under the heading "Warning" (or "Warnings" if it appears with additional warning statements) if the amount of potassium present in the labeled maximum daily dose of the product is more than 975 milligrams: "Ask a doctor before use if you have [in bold type] [bullet][1] kidney disease [bullet] a potassium-restricted diet." The warnings in 201.64(c), 201.70(c), 201.71(c), and 201.72(c) may be combined, if applicable, provided the ingredients are listed in alphabetical order, e.g., a magnesium or potassium-restricted diet.

(d) Any product subject to this paragraph that is not labeled as required by this paragraph and that is initially introduced or initially delivered for introduction into interstate commerce after the following dates is misbranded under sections 201(n) and 502(a) and (f) of the Federal Food, Drug, and Cosmetic Act.

(1) As of the date of approval of the application for any single entity and combination products subject to drug marketing applications approved on or after April 23, 2004.

(2) September 24, 2005, for all OTC drug products subject to any OTC drug monograph, not yet the subject of any OTC drug monograph, or subject to drug marketing applications approved before April 23, 2004.

Sec. 310.305 Records and reports concerning adverse drug experiences on marketed prescription drugs for human use without approved new drug applications.

(a) *Scope.* FDA is requiring manufacturers, packers, and distributors of marketed prescription drug products that are not the subject of an approved new drug or abbreviated new drug application to establish and maintain records and make reports to FDA of all serious, unexpected adverse drug experiences associated with the use of their drug products. Any person subject to the reporting requirements of paragraph (c) of this section shall also develop written procedures for the surveillance, receipt, evaluation, and reporting of post-marketing adverse drug experiences to FDA.

(b) *Definitions.* The following definitions of terms apply to this section:-

Adverse drug experience. Any adverse event associated with the use of a drug in humans, whether or not considered drug related, including the following: An adverse event occurring in the course of the use of a drug product in professional practice; an adverse event occurring from drug overdose whether accidental or intentional; an adverse event occurring from drug abuse; an adverse event occurring from drug withdrawal; and any failure of expected pharmacological action.

Disability. A substantial disruption of a person's ability to conduct normal life functions.

Life-threatening adverse drug experience. Any adverse drug experience that places the patient, in the view of the initial reporter, at *immediate* risk of death from the adverse drug experience as it occurred, *i.e.*, it does not include an adverse drug experience that, had it occurred in a more severe form, might have caused death.

Serious adverse drug experience. Any adverse drug experience occurring at any dose that results in any of the following outcomes: Death, a life-threatening adverse drug experience, inpatient hospitalization or prolongation of existing hospitalization, a persistent or significant disability/incapacity, or a congenital anomaly/birth defect. Important medical events that may not result in death, be life-threatening, or require hospitalization may be considered a serious adverse drug experience when, based upon appropriate medical judgment, they may jeopardize the patient or subject and may require medical or surgical intervention to prevent one of the outcomes listed in this definition. Examples of such medical events include allergic bronchospasm requiring intensive treatment in an emergency room or at home, blood dyscrasias or convulsions that do not result in inpatient hospitalization, or the development of drug dependency or drug abuse.

Unexpected adverse drug experience. Any adverse drug experience that is not listed in the current labeling for the drug product. This includes events that may be symptomatically and pathophysiologically related to an event listed in the labeling, but differ from the event because of greater severity or specificity. For example, under this definition, hepatic necrosis would be unexpected (by virtue of greater severity) if the labeling only referred to elevated hepatic enzymes or hepatitis. Similarly, cerebral thromboembolism and cerebral vasculitis would be unexpected (by virtue of greater specificity) if the labeling only listed cerebral vascular accidents. "Unexpected," as used in this definition, refers to an adverse drug experience that has not been previously observed (*i.e.*, included in the labeling) rather than from the perspective of such experience not being anticipated from the pharmacological properties of the pharmaceutical product.

(c) *Reporting requirements.* Each person identified in paragraph (c)(1)(i) of this section shall report to FDA adverse drug experience information as described in this section and shall submit one copy of each report to the Central Document Room, Center for Drug Evaluation and Research, Food and Drug Administration, 5901-B Ammendale Rd., Beltsville, MD 20705-1266.

(1) *Postmarketing 15-day "Alert reports."* (i) Any person whose name appears on the label of a marketed prescription drug product as its manufacturer, packer, or distributor shall report to FDA each adverse drug experience received or otherwise obtained that is both serious and unexpected as soon as possible, but in no case later than 15 calendar days of initial receipt of the information by the person whose name appears on the label. Each report shall be accompanied by a copy of the current labeling for the drug product.

(ii) A person identified in paragraph (c)(1)(i) of this section is not required to submit a 15-day "Alert report" for an adverse drug experience obtained from a postmarketing study (whether or not conducted under an investigational new drug application) unless the applicant concludes that there is a reasonable possibility that the drug caused the adverse experience.

(2) *Postmarketing 15-day "Alert reports"—followup.* Each person identified in paragraph (c)(1)(i) of this section shall promptly investigate all serious, unexpected adverse drug experiences that are the subject of these postmarketing 15-day Alert reports and shall submit followup reports within 15 calendar days of receipt of new information or as requested by FDA. If additional information is not obtainable, records should be maintained of the unsuccessful steps taken to seek additional information. Postmarketing 15-day Alert reports and followups to them shall be submitted under separate cover.

(3) *Submission of reports.* To avoid unnecessary duplication in the submission of, and followup to, reports required in this section, a packer's or distributor's obligations may be met by submission of all reports of serious adverse drug experiences to the manufacturer of the drug product. If a packer or distributor elects to submit these adverse drug experience reports to the manufacturer rather than to FDA, it shall submit each report to the manufacturer within 5 calendar days of its receipt by the packer or distributor, and the manufacturer shall then comply with the requirements of this section even if its name does not appear on the label of the drug product. Under this circumstance, the packer or distributor shall maintain a record of this action which shall include:

(i) A copy of each adverse drug experience report;

(ii) The date the report was received by the packer or distributor;

(iii) The date the report was submitted to the manufacturer; and

(iv) The name and address of the manufacturer.

(4) Each report submitted to FDA under this section shall bear prominent identification as to its contents, *i.e.*, "15-day Alert report," or "15-day Alert report-followup."

(5) A person identified in paragraph (c)(1)(i) of this section is not required to resubmit to FDA adverse drug experience reports forwarded to that person by FDA; however, the person must submit all *followup* information on such reports to FDA.

(d) *Reporting form.* (1) Except as provided in paragraph (d)(3) of this section, each person identified in paragraph (c)(1)(i) of this section shall submit each report of a serious and unexpected adverse drug experience on an FDA Form 3500A (foreign events may be submitted either on an FDA Form 3500A or, if preferred, on a CIOMS I form).

(2) Each completed FDA Form 3500A should pertain only to an individual patient.

(3) Instead of using Form FDA Form 3500A, a manufacturer, packer, or distributor may use a computer-generated FDA Form 3500A or other alternative format (e.g., a computer-generated tape or tabular listing) provided that:

(i) The content of the alternative format is equivalent in all elements of information to those specified in FDA Form 3500A, and

(ii) The format is agreed to in advance by MedWatch: The FDA Medical Products Reporting Program.

(4) FDA Form 3500A and instructions for completing the form are available on the Internet at *http://www.fda.gov/medwatch/index.html.*

(e) *Patient privacy.* Manufacturers, packers, and distributors should not include in reports under this section the names and addresses of individual patients; instead, the manufacturer, packer, and distributor should assign a unique code number to each report, preferably not more than eight characters in length. The manufacturer, packer, and distributor should include the name of the reporter from whom the information was received. Names of patients, individual reporters, health care professionals, hospitals, and geographical identifiers in adverse drug experience reports are not releasable to the public under FDA's public information regulations in part 20 of this chapter.

(f) *Recordkeeping*. (1) Each manufacturer, packer, and distributor shall maintain for a period of 10 years records of all adverse drug experiences required under this section to be reported, including raw data and any correspondence relating to the adverse drug experiences, and the records required to be maintained under paragraph (c)(4) of this section.

(2) Manufacturers and packers may retain the records required in paragraph (f)(1) of this section as part of its complaint files maintained under 211.198 of this chapter.

(3) Manufacturers, packers, and distributors shall permit any authorized FDA employee, at all reasonable times, to have access to and copy and verify the records established and maintained under this section.

(g) *Disclaimer*. A report or information submitted by a manufacturer, packer, or distributor under this section (and any release by FDA of that report or information) does not necessarily reflect a conclusion by the manufacturer, packer, or distributor, or by FDA, that the report or information constitutes an admission that the drug caused or contributed to an adverse effect. The manufacturer, packer, or distributor need not admit, and may deny, that the report or information submitted under this section constitutes an admission that the drug caused or contributed to an adverse effect.

Sec. 312.32 IND safety reports.

(a) *Definitions*. The following definitions of terms apply to this section:-

Associated with the use of the drug. There is a reasonable possibility that the experience may have been caused by the drug.

Disability. A substantial disruption of a person's ability to conduct normal life functions.

Life-threatening adverse drug experience. Any adverse drug experience that places the patient or subject, in the view of the investigator, at immediate risk of death from the reaction as it occurred, *i.e.*, it does not include a reaction that, had it occurred in a more severe form, might have caused death.

Serious adverse drug experience : Any adverse drug experience occurring at any dose that results in any of the following outcomes: Death, a life-threatening adverse drug experience, inpatient hospitalization or prolongation of existing hospitalization, a persistent or significant disability/incapacity, or a congenital anomaly/birth defect. Important medical events that may not result in death, be life-threatening, or require hospitalization may be considered a serious adverse drug experience when, based upon appropriate medical judgment, they may jeopardize the patient or subject and may require medical or surgical intervention to prevent one of the outcomes listed in this definition. Examples of such medical events include allergic bronchospasm requiring intensive treatment in an emergency room or at home, blood dyscrasias or convulsions that do not result in inpatient hospitalization, or the development of drug dependency or drug abuse.

Unexpected adverse drug experience : Any adverse drug experience, the specificity or severity of which is not consistent with the current investigator brochure; or, if an investigator brochure is not required or available, the specificity or severity of which is not consistent with the risk information described in the general investigational plan or elsewhere in the current application, as amended. For example, under this definition, hepatic necrosis would be unexpected (by virtue of greater severity) if the investigator brochure only referred to elevated hepatic enzymes or hepatitis. Similarly, cerebral thromboembolism and cerebral vasculitis would be unexpected (by virtue of greater specificity) if the investigator brochure only listed cerebral vascular accidents. "Unexpected," as used in this definition, refers to an adverse drug experience that has not been previously observed (e.g., included in the investigator brochure) rather than from the perspective of such experience not being anticipated from the pharmacological properties of the pharmaceutical product.

(b) *Review of safety information*. The sponsor shall promptly review all information relevant to the safety of the drug obtained or otherwise received by the sponsor from any source, foreign or domestic, including information derived from any clinical or epidemiological investigations, animal investigations, commercial marketing experience, reports in the scientific literature, and unpublished scientific papers, as well as reports from foreign regulatory authorities that have not already been previously reported to the agency by the sponsor.

(c) *IND safety reports* —(1) *Written reports* —(i) The sponsor shall notify FDA and all participating investigators in a written IND safety report of:

(A) Any adverse experience associated with the use of the drug that is both serious and unexpected; or

(B) Any finding from tests in laboratory animals that suggests a significant risk for human subjects including reports of mutagenicity, teratogenicity, or carcinogenicity. Each notification shall be made as soon as possible and in no event later than 15 calendar days after the sponsor's initial receipt of the information. Each written notification may be submitted on FDA Form 3500A or in a narrative format (foreign events may be submitted either on an FDA Form 3500A or, if preferred, on a CIOMS I form; reports from animal or epidemiological studies shall be submitted in a narrative format) and shall bear prominent identification of its contents, *i.e.*, "IND Safety Report." Each written notification to FDA shall be transmitted to the FDA new drug review division in the Center for Drug Evaluation and Research or the product review division in the Center for Biologics Evaluation and Research that has responsibility for review of the IND. If FDA determines that additional data are needed, the agency may require further data to be submitted.

(ii) In each written IND safety report, the sponsor shall identify all safety reports previously filed with the IND concerning a similar adverse experience, and shall analyze the significance of the adverse experience in light of the previous, similar reports.

(2) *Telephone and facsimile transmission safety reports.* The sponsor shall also notify FDA by telephone or by facsimile transmission of any unexpected fatal or life-threatening experience associated with the use of the drug as soon as possible but in no event later than 7 calendar days after the sponsor's initial receipt of the information. Each telephone call or facsimile transmission to FDA shall be transmitted to the FDA new drug review division in the Center for Drug Evaluation and Research or the product review division in the Center for Biologics Evaluation and Research that has responsibility for review of the IND.

(3) *Reporting format or frequency.* FDA may request a sponsor to submit IND safety reports in a format or at a frequency different than that required under this paragraph. The sponsor may also propose and adopt a different reporting format or frequency if the change is agreed to in advance by the director of the new drug review division in the Center for Drug Evaluation and Research or the director of the products review division in the Center for Biologics Evaluation and Research which is responsible for review of the IND.

(4) A sponsor of a clinical study of a marketed drug is not required to make a safety report for any adverse experience associated with use of the drug that is not from the clinical study itself.

(d) *Followup.* (1) The sponsor shall promptly investigate all safety information received by it.

(2) Followup information to a safety report shall be submitted as soon as the relevant information is available.

(3) If the results of a sponsor's investigation show that an adverse drug experience not initially determined to be reportable under paragraph (c) of this section is so reportable, the sponsor shall report such experience in a written safety report as soon as possible, but in no event later than 15 calendar days after the determination is made.

(4) Results of a sponsor's investigation of other safety information shall be submitted, as appropriate, in an information amendment or annual report.

(e) *Disclaimer.* A safety report or other information submitted by a sponsor under this part (and any release by FDA of that report or information) does not necessarily reflect a conclusion by the sponsor or FDA that the report or information constitutes an admission that the drug caused or contributed to an adverse experience. A sponsor need not admit, and may deny, that the report or information submitted by the sponsor constitutes an admission that the drug caused or contributed to an adverse experience.

Sec. 314.70(c) Supplements and other changes to an approved application.

(c) *Changes requiring supplement submission at least 30 days prior to distribution of the drug product made using the change (moderate changes).* (1) A supplement must be submitted for any change in the drug substance, drug product, production process, quality controls, equipment, or facilities that has a moderate potential to have an adverse effect on the identity, strength, quality, purity, or potency of the drug product as these factors may relate to the safety or effectiveness of the drug product. *If the supplement provides for a labeling change under paragraph (c)(6)(iii) of this section, 12 copies of the final printed labeling must be included.*

(4) The applicant must promptly revise all promotional labeling and advertising to make it consistent with any labeling change implemented in accordance with paragraphs (b) and (c) of this section.

(5) *Except for a supplement providing for a change in the labeling*, the applicant must include in each supplement and amendment to a supplement providing for a change under paragraph (b) or (c) of this section a statement certifying that a field copy has been provided in accordance with 314.440(a)(4).

(6) The agency may designate a category of changes for the purpose of providing that, in the case of a change in such category, the holder of an approved application may commence distribution of the drug product involved upon receipt by the agency of a supplement for the change. These changes include, but are not limited to:

(iii) *Changes in the labeling to reflect newly acquired information*, except for changes to the information required in 201.57(a) of this chapter (which must be made under paragraph (b)(2)(v)(C) of this section), to accomplish any of the following:

(A) *To add or strengthen a contraindication, warning, precaution, or adverse reaction* for which the evidence of a causal association satisfies the standard for inclusion in the labeling under 201.57(c) of this chapter;

(B) *To add or strengthen a statement about drug abuse, dependence, psychological effect, or overdosage*;

(C) *To add or strengthen an instruction about dosage and administration that is intended to increase the safe use of the drug product;*

(D) *To delete false, misleading, or unsupported indications for use or claims for effectiveness*; or

(E) *Any labeling change normally requiring a supplement submission and approval prior to distribution of the drug product that FDA specifically requests be submitted under this provision.*

(7) If the agency disapproves the supplemental application, it may order the manufacturer to cease distribution of the drug product(s) made with the manufacturing change.

Sec. 314.80 Postmarketing reporting of adverse drug experiences.

(a) *Definitions.* The following definitions of terms apply to this section:-

Adverse drug experience. Any adverse event associated with the use of a drug in humans, whether or not considered drug related, including the following: An adverse event occurring in the course of the use of a drug product in professional practice; an adverse event occurring from drug overdose whether accidental or intentional; an adverse event occurring from drug abuse; an adverse event occurring from drug withdrawal; and any failure of expected pharmacological action.

Disability. A substantial disruption of a person's ability to conduct normal life functions.

Life-threatening adverse drug experience. Any adverse drug experience that places the patient, in the view of the initial reporter, at *immediate* risk of death from the adverse drug experience as it occurred, *i.e.*, it does not include an adverse drug experience that, had it occurred in a more severe form, might have caused death.

Serious adverse drug experience. Any adverse drug experience occurring at any dose that results in any of the following outcomes: Death, a life-threatening adverse drug experience, inpatient hospitalization or prolongation of existing hospitalization, a persistent or significant disability/

incapacity, or a congenital anomaly/birth defect. Important medical events that may not result in death, be life-threatening, or require hospitalization may be considered a serious adverse drug experience when, based upon appropriate medical judgment, they may jeopardize the patient or subject and may require medical or surgical intervention to prevent one of the outcomes listed in this definition. Examples of such medical events include allergic bronchospasm requiring intensive treatment in an emergency room or at home, blood dyscrasias or convulsions that do not result in inpatient hospitalization, or the development of drug dependency or drug abuse.

Unexpected adverse drug experience. Any adverse drug experience that is not listed in the current labeling for the drug product. This includes events that may be symptomatically and pathophysiologically related to an event listed in the labeling, but differ from the event because of greater severity or specificity. For example, under this definition, hepatic necrosis would be unexpected (by virtue of greater severity) if the labeling only referred to elevated hepatic enzymes or hepatitis. Similarly, cerebral thromboembolism and cerebral vasculitis would be unexpected (by virtue of greater specificity) if the labeling only listed cerebral vascular accidents. "Unexpected," as used in this definition, refers to an adverse drug experience that has not been previously observed (*i.e.*, included in the labeling) rather than from the perspective of such experience not being anticipated from the pharmacological properties of the pharmaceutical product.

(b) *Review of adverse drug experiences.* Each applicant having an approved application under 314.50 or, in the case of a 505(b)(2) application, an effective approved application, shall promptly review all adverse drug experience information obtained or otherwise received by the applicant from any source, foreign or domestic, including information derived from commercial marketing experience, postmarketing clinical investigations, postmarketing epidemiological/surveillance studies, reports in the scientific literature, and unpublished scientific papers. Applicants are not required to resubmit to FDA adverse drug experience reports forwarded to the applicant by FDA; however, applicants must submit all followup information on such reports to FDA. Any person subject to the reporting requirements under paragraph (c) of this section shall also develop written procedures for the surveillance, receipt, evaluation, and reporting of postmarketing adverse drug experiences to FDA.

(c) *Reporting requirements.* The applicant shall report to FDA adverse drug experience information, as described in this section. The applicant shall submit two copies of each report described in this section to the Central Document

Room, 5901-B Ammendale Rd., Beltsville, MD 20705-1266. FDA may waive the requirement for the second copy in appropriate instances.

(1)(i) *Postmarketing 15-day "Alert reports."* The applicant shall report each adverse drug experience that is both serious and unexpected, whether foreign or domestic, as soon as possible but in no case later than 15 calendar days of initial receipt of the information by the applicant.

(ii) *Postmarketing 15-day "Alert reports"—followup.* The applicant shall promptly investigate all adverse drug experiences that are the subject of these postmarketing 15-day Alert reports and shall submit followup reports within 15 calendar days of receipt of new information or as requested by FDA. If additional information is not obtainable, records should be maintained of the unsuccessful steps taken to seek additional information. Postmarketing 15-day Alert reports and followups to them shall be submitted under separate cover.

(iii) *Submission of reports.* The requirements of paragraphs (c)(1)(i) and (c)(1)(ii) of this section, concerning the submission of postmarketing 15-day Alert reports, shall also apply to any person other than the applicant (nonapplicant) whose name appears on the label of an approved drug product as a manufacturer, packer, or distributor. To avoid unnecessary duplication in the submission to FDA of reports required by paragraphs (c)(1)(i) and (c)(1)(ii) of this section, obligations of a nonapplicant may be met by submission of all reports of serious adverse drug experiences to the applicant. If a nonapplicant elects to submit adverse drug experience reports to the applicant rather than to FDA, the nonapplicant shall submit each report to the applicant within 5 calendar days of receipt of the report by the nonapplicant, and the applicant shall then comply with the requirements of this section. Under this circumstance, the nonapplicant shall maintain a record of this action which shall include:

(A) A copy of each adverse drug experience report;

(B) The date the report was received by the nonapplicant;

(C) The date the report was submitted to the applicant; and

(D) The name and address of the applicant.

(iv) *Report identification.* Each report submitted under this paragraph shall bear prominent identification as to its contents, *i.e.*, "15-day Alert report," or "15-day Alert report-followup."

(2) *Periodic adverse drug experience reports.* (i) The applicant shall report each adverse drug experience not reported under paragraph (c)(1)(i) of this section at quarterly intervals, for 3 years from the date of approval of the application, and then at annual intervals. The applicant shall sub-mit each quarterly report within 30 days of the close of the quarter (the first quarter beginning on the date of approval of the application) and each annual report within 60 days of the anniversary date of approval of the application. Upon written notice, FDA may extend or reestablish the requirement that an applicant submit quarterly reports, or require that the applicant submit reports under this section at different times than those stated. For example, the agency may reestablish a quarterly reporting requirement following the approval of a major supplement. Followup information to adverse drug experiences submitted in a periodic report may be submitted in the next periodic report.

(ii) Each periodic report is required to contain: (*a*) a narrative summary and analysis of the information in the report and an analysis of the 15-day Alert reports submitted during the reporting interval (all 15-day Alert reports being appropriately referenced by the applicant's patient identification number, adverse reaction term(s), and date of submission to FDA); (*b*) a FDA Form 3500A (Adverse Reaction Report) for each adverse drug experience not reported under paragraph (c)(1)(i) of this section (with an index consisting of a line listing of the applicant's patient identification number and adverse reaction term(s)); and (*c*) a history of actions taken since the last report because of adverse drug experiences (for example, labeling changes or studies initiated).

(iii) Periodic reporting, except for information regarding 15-day Alert reports, does not apply to adverse drug experience information obtained from postmarketing studies (whether or not conducted under an investigational new drug application), from reports in the scientific literature, and from foreign marketing experience.

(d) *Scientific literature.* (1) A 15-day Alert report based on information from the scientific literature is required to be accompanied by a copy of the published article. The 15-day reporting requirements in paragraph (c)(1)(i) of this section (*i.e.*, serious, unexpected adverse drug experiences) apply only to reports found in scientific and medical journals either as case reports or as the result of a formal clinical trial.

(2) As with all reports submitted under paragraph (c)(1)(i) of this section, reports based on the scientific literature shall be submitted on FDA Form 3500A or comparable format as prescribed by paragraph (f) of this section. In cases where the applicant believes that preparing the FDA Form 3500A constitutes an undue hardship, the applicant may arrange with the Office of Surveillance and Epidemiology for an acceptable alternative reporting format.

(e) *Postmarketing studies.* (1) An applicant is not required to submit a 15-day Alert report under paragraph (c) of this section for an adverse drug experience obtained from a postmarketing study (whether or not conducted under an investigational new drug application) unless the applicant concludes that there is a reasonable possibility that the drug caused the adverse experience.

(2) The applicant shall separate and clearly mark reports of adverse drug experiences that occur during a postmarketing study as being distinct from those experiences that are being reported spontaneously to the applicant.

(f) *Reporting FDA Form 3500A.* (1) Except as provided in paragraph (f)(3) of this section, the applicant shall complete FDA Form 3500A for each report of an adverse drug experience (foreign events may be submitted either on an FDA Form 3500A or, if preferred, on a CIOMS I form).

(2) Each completed FDA Form 3500A should refer only to an individual patient or a single attached publication.

(3) Instead of using FDA Form 3500A, an applicant may use a computer-generated FDA Form 3500A or other alternative format (e.g., a computer-generated tape or tabular listing) provided that:

(i) The content of the alternative format is equivalent in all elements of information to those specified in FDA Form 3500A; and

(ii) The format is agreed to in advance by the Office of Surveillance and Epidemiology.

(4) FDA Form 3500A and instructions for completing the form are available on the Internet at *http://www.fda.gov/medwatch/index.html.*

(g) *Multiple reports.* An applicant should not include in reports under this section any adverse drug experiences that occurred in clinical trials if they were previously submitted as part of the approved application. If a report applies to a drug for which an applicant holds more than one approved application, the applicant should submit the report to the application that was first approved. If a report refers to more than one drug marketed by an applicant, the applicant should submit the report to the application for the drug listed first in the report.

(h) *Patient privacy.* An applicant should not include in reports under this section the names and addresses of individual patients; instead, the applicant should assign a unique code number to each report, preferably not more than eight characters in length. The applicant should include the name of the reporter from whom the information was received. Names of patients, health care professionals, hospitals, and geographical identifiers in adverse drug experience reports are not releasable to the public under FDA's public information regulations in part 20.

(i) *Recordkeeping.* The applicant shall maintain for a period of 10 years records of all adverse drug experiences known to the applicant, including raw data and any correspondence relating to adverse drug experiences.

(j) *Withdrawal of approval.* If an applicant fails to establish and maintain records and make reports required under this section, FDA may withdraw approval of the application and, thus, prohibit continued marketing of the drug product that is the subject of the application.

(k) *Disclaimer.* A report or information submitted by an applicant under this section (and any release by FDA of that report or information) does not necessarily reflect a conclusion by the applicant or FDA that the report or information constitutes an admission that the drug caused or contributed to an adverse effect. An applicant need not admit, and may deny, that the report or information submitted under this section constitutes an admission that the drug caused or contributed to an adverse effect. For purposes of this provision, the term "applicant" also includes any person reporting under paragraph (c)(1)(iii) of this section.

Sec. 330.1 General conditions for general recognition as safe, effective and not misbranded.

An over-the-counter (OTC) drug listed in this subchapter is generally recognized as safe and effective and is not misbranded if it meets each of the conditions contained in this part and each of the conditions contained in any applicable monograph. Any product which fails to conform to each of the conditions contained in this part and in an applicable monograph is liable to regulatory action.

(a) The product is manufactured in compliance with current good manufacturing practices, as established by parts 210 and 211 of this chapter.

(b) The establishment(s) in which the drug product is manufactured is registered, and the drug product is listed, in compliance with part 207 of this chapter. It is requested but not required that the number assigned to the product pursuant to part 207 of this chapter appear on all drug labels and in all drug labeling. If this number is used, it shall be placed in the manner set forth in part 207 of this chapter.

(c)(1) The product is labeled in compliance with chapter V of the Federal Food, Drug, and Cosmetic Act (the act) and subchapter C *et seq.* of this chapter, including the format and content requirements in 201.66 of this chapter. An **otc drug** product that is not in compliance with chapter V and subchapter C, including 201.66 of this chapter, is subject to regulatory action. For purposes of 201.61(b) of this chapter, the statement of identity of the product shall be the term or phrase used in the applicable **otc drug** monograph established in this part.

(2) The "Uses" section of the label and labeling of the product shall contain the labeling describing the "Indications" that have been established in an applicable **otc drug** monograph or alternative truthful and nonmisleading state-

ments describing only those indications for use that have been established in an applicable monograph, subject to the provisions of section 502 of the act relating to misbranding and the prohibition in section 301(d) of the act against the introduction or delivery for introduction into interstate commerce of unapproved new drugs in violation of section 505(a) of the act. Any other labeling under this subchapter and subchapter C*et seq.* of this chapter shall be stated in the exact language where exact language has been established and identified by quotation marks in an applicable **otc drug** monograph or by regulation (e.g., 201.63 of this chapter), except as provided in paragraphs (i) and (j) of this section.

(d) The advertising for the product prescribes, recommends, or suggests its use only under the conditions stated in the labeling.

(e) The product contains only suitable inactive ingredients which are safe in the amounts administered and do not interfere with the effectiveness of the preparation or with suitable tests or assays to determine if the product meets its professed standards of identity, strength, quality, and purity. Color additives may be used only in accordance with section 721 of the act and subchapter A of this chapter.

(f) The product container and container components meet the requirements of 211.94 of this chapter.

(g) The labeling for all drugs contains the general warning: "Keep out of reach of children." [highlighted in bold type]. The labeling of drugs shall also state as follows: For drugs used by oral administration, "In case of overdose, get medical help or contact a Poison Control Center right away"; for drugs used topically, rectally, or vaginally and not intended for oral ingestion, "If swallowed, get medical help or contact a Poison Control Center right away"; and for drugs used topically and intended for oral use, "If more than used for" (insert intended use, e.g., pain) "is accidentally swallowed, get medical help or contact a Poison Control Center right away." The Food and Drug Administration will grant an exemption from these general warnings where appropriate upon petition, which shall be maintained in a permanent file for public review by the Division of Dockets Management, Food and Drug Administration, 5630 Fishers Lane, rm. 1061, Rockville, MD 20852.

(h) Where no maximum daily dosage limit for an active ingredient is established in this part, it is used in a product at a level that does not exceed the amount reasonably required to achieve its intended effect.

(i) The following terms may be used interchangeably in the labeling of **otc drug** products, provided such use does not alter the meaning of the labeling that has been established and identified in an applicable monograph or by regulation. The following terms shall not be used to change in any way the title, headings, and subheadings required under 201.66(c)(1) through (c)(9) of this chapter:

(1) "Abdominal" or "stomach" (in context only).

(2) "Administer" or "give."

(3) "Aggravate(s)" or "make(s) worse."

(4) "Application of this product" or "applying."

(5) "Are uncertain" or "do not know."

(6) "Ask" or "consult" or "contact."

(7) "Asking" or "consulting."

(8) "Assistance" or "help" or "aid."

(9) "Associated with" or "due to" or "caused by."

(10) "Avoid contact with eyes" or "do not get into eyes."

(11) "Avoid inhaling" or "do not inhale."

(12) "Before a doctor is consulted" or "without first consulting your doctor" or "consult your doctor before."

(13) "Beverages" or "drinks."

(14) "Clean" or "cleanse."

(15) "Consulting" or "advising."

(16) "Continue(s)" or "persist(s)" or "is persistent" or "do(es) not go away" or "last(s)."

(17) "Daily" or "every day."

(18) "Develop(s)" or "begin(s)" or "occur(s)."

(19) "Difficulty" or "trouble."

(20) "Difficulty in urination" or "trouble urinating."

(21) "Discard" or "throw away."

(22) "Discontinue" or "stop" or "quit."

(23) "Doctor" or "physician."

(24) "Drowsiness" or "the drowsiness effect."

(25) "Drowsiness may occur" or "you may get drowsy."

(26) "Enlargement of the" or "an enlarged."

(27) "Especially in children" or especially children."

(28) "Exceed" or "use more than" or "go beyond."

(29) "Exceed recommended dosage" or "use more than directed."

(30) "Excessive" or "too much."

(31) "Excitability may occur" or "you may get excited."

(32) "Experience" or "feel."

(33) "For relief of" or "relieves."

(34) "For temporary reduction of" or "temporarily reduces."

(35) "For the temporary relief of" or "temporarily relieves."

(36) "For the treatment of" or "treats."

(37) "Frequently" or "often."

(38) "Give to" or "use in."

(39) "Immediately" or "right away" or "directly."

(40) "Immediately" or "as soon as."

(41) "Immediately following" or "right after."

(42) "Improve(s)" or "get(s) better" or "make(s) better."

(43) "Increased" or "more."

(44) "Increase your risk of" or "cause."

(45) "Indication(s)" or "Use(s)."

(46) "Inhalation" or "puff."

(47) "In persons who" or "if you" or "if the child."

(48) "Instill" or "put."

(49) "Is (are) accompanied by" or "you also have" (in context only) or "(optional: that) occur(s) with."

(50) "Longer" or "more."

(51) "Lung" or "pulmonary."

(52) "Medication(s)" or "medicine(s)" or "drug(s)."

(53) "Nervousness, dizziness, or sleeplessness occurs" or "you get nervous, dizzy, or sleepless."

(54) "Not to exceed" or "do not exceed" or "not more than."

(55) "Obtain(s)" or "get(s)."

(56) "Passages" or "passageways" or "tubes."

(57) "Perforation of" or "hole in."

(58) "Persistent" or "that does not go away" or "that continues" or "that lasts."

(59) "Per day" or "daily."

(60) "Presently" or "now."

(61) "Produce(s)" or "cause(s)."

(62) "Prompt(ly)" or "quick(ly)" or "right away."

(63) "Reduce" or "minimize."

(64) "Referred to as" or "of."

(65) "Sensation" or "feeling."

(66) "Solution" or "liquid."

(67) "Specifically" or "definitely."

(68) "Take" or "use" or "give."

(69) "Tend(s) to recur" or "reoccur(s)" or "return(s)" or "come(s) back."

(70) "To avoid contamination" or "avoid contamination" or "do not contaminate."

(71) "To help" or "helps."

(72) "Unless directed by a doctor" or "except under the advice of a doctor" or "unless told to do so by a doctor."

(73) "Use caution" or "be careful."

(74) "Usually" or "generally" (in context only).

(75) "You" ("Your") or "the child" ("the child's").

(76) "You also have" or "occurs with."

(77) "When practical" or "if possible."

(78) "Whether" or "if."

(79) "Worsen(s)" or "get(s) worse" or "make(s) worse."

(j) The following connecting terms may be deleted from the labeling of **otc drug** products, provided such deletion does not alter the meaning of the labeling that has been established and identified in an applicable monograph or by regulation. The following terms shall not be used to change in any way the specific title, headings, and subheadings required under 201.66(c)(1) through (c)(9) of this chapter:

(1) "And."

(2) "As may occur with."

(3) "Associated" or "to be associated."

(4) "Consult a doctor."

(5) "Discontinue use."

(6) "Drug Interaction Precaution."

(7) "Due to."

(8) "Except under the advice and supervision of a physician."

(9) "If this occurs."

(10) "In case of."

(11) "Notice."

(12) "Or."

(13) "Occurring with."

(14) "Or as directed by a doctor."

(15) "Such as."

(16) "Such as occurs with."

(17) "Tends to."

(18) "This product."

(19) "Unless directed by a doctor."

(20) "While taking this product" or "before taking this product."

(21) "Within."

Chapter 12

Search and Analysis of the Food and Drug Administration's Adverse Event Reporting System

Paul N. Danese, Ph.D.

12.1 Introduction

In the United States, the Food and Drug Administration (FDA) monitors the safety of marketed prescription and non-prescription medications using an electronic database known as the Adverse Event Reporting System (AERS). Although the FDA routinely mines the AERS to search for unexpected drug safety issues, this database is effectively inaccessible to the lay-public and to many other interested parties. This chapter discusses the AERS database in depth, discussing how the FDA and others can use the AERS to increase drug safety and promote public health.

12.2 Background

The FDA approves and regulates the sale of prescription and non-prescription medications in the United States. In particular, FDA approval of prescription drugs is usually based on the results of randomized, controlled, Phase III clinical trials, which are often designed to assess both drug safety and efficacy.[1-3]

Although clinical trials do much to assess drug safety, they are limited in their ability to identify all possible drug safety issues. These limitations are due to the following characteristics of clinical trials.

A. Small Clinical Trial Population

Although clinical trials can recruit thousands of patients for safety and efficacy testing,[1,3] such trial populations are almost always relatively small in comparison to the number of patients who will be exposed to a medication after its approval. As such, the clinical trials that are used to assess drug safety are often underpowered with respect to their ability to identify rare drug-related adverse events.[4,5]

B. Narrow Patient Demographics

Second, patients recruited into clinical trials usually belong to narrowly defined demographic groups. For example, children rarely participate in drug clinical trials.[6] However, once approval is granted, the spectrum of patients exposed to a drug often expands beyond the demographic boundaries established in the clinical trial. As a consequence, drug exposure of previously untested groups can also reveal drug safety issues that were not apparent from the clinical trials that were used as the basis for drug approval.[7,8]

C. Tightly Regulated Co-Administration of Concomitant Medications

Third, clinical trials will often impose restrictions on the types of medications that may be co-administered with the drug being tested.[1,9] In contrast, once a medication is approved for marketing, there is less control, aside from explicit contraindications that may be incorporated into a drug's prescribing information, over the types and quantities of medications that are co-administered with a newly approved medication. As a result, administration of a medication to members of the general public can reveal drug-drug interactions that might not have been observed in the more controlled settings of a clinical trial.

Because of the limitations in the ability of conventional clinical trials to identify rare and/or unanticipated drug safety issues, the FDA has established a number of surveillance systems to identify drug safety issues that arise after a drug has been approved for sale.

This chapter focuses on the FDA's primary pharmacovigilance tool, the Adverse Event Reporting System (AERS), which monitors safety issues of approved drug and biologic agents,[10] and also briefly discusses other surveillance systems that are used to monitor the safety of approved vaccines and medical devices.

12.3 History of the FDA's Drug Safety Surveillance Systems

From 1968 to 1997, the FDA collected over 1.6 million reports of suspected drug safety issues from manufacturers, healthcare professionals, and the lay-public using the Spontaneous Reporting System (SRS).[11,12] SRS reports captured patient demographic information (e.g., age and gender), adverse reaction information and patient outcomes. In late 1997, the FDA replaced the SRS with the AERS,[12] which differs from the SRS in that it:

1)   captures a wider array of information, and

2)   allows for the electronic submission of adverse event reports, in anticipation of the increasing importance of the Internet as a means of information exchange.

Today, the AERS is used to collect and analyze suspected safety issues for all FDA-approved prescription and non-prescription medications. Since its inception, the AERS has received over 4 million adverse event reports with almost every successive year seeing an increase in the number of submissions (Figure 12.1). Remarkably, even though there were more than 782,969 reports submitted to the FDA in 2011, only a small minority of suspected drug adverse reactions is reported to the FDA (see Section 12.8.C for a detailed discussion).[13,14]

12.4 Submission of Adverse Event Reports to the FDA

There are two classes of reports submitted to the AERS: mandatory reports submitted by drug and biologic manufacturers, and voluntary reports submitted by the lay-public and their representatives.

A. Mandatory Reports

The overwhelming majority of adverse event reports (more than 92 percent) are submitted to the FDA by drug and biologic manufacturers. Manufacturers are obligated to submit to the FDA reports of both serious and non-serious adverse events in a timely manner. Specifically, manufacturers must report serious and unexpected adverse events to the FDA within 15 calendar days of their notification of an adverse event. These reports are sometimes referred to as Expedited Reports. In addition, manufacturers must also submit quarterly reports summarizing all adverse events (serious and non-serious) associated with their marketed medications for the first three years after approval of a New Drug Application or Biologics License Application. After three years, manufacturers must submit annual summaries of adverse events associated with their marketed medications.[15]

B. Voluntary Reports

The FDA also receives a small fraction (less than 8 percent) of its adverse event reports directly from healthcare professionals (physicians, pharmacists, nurses and other healthcare providers) as well as consumers and consumer representatives (patients, family members, lawyers and others). These reports are voluntarily submitted to the FDA and are not subject to the reporting deadlines mandated for manufacturers.

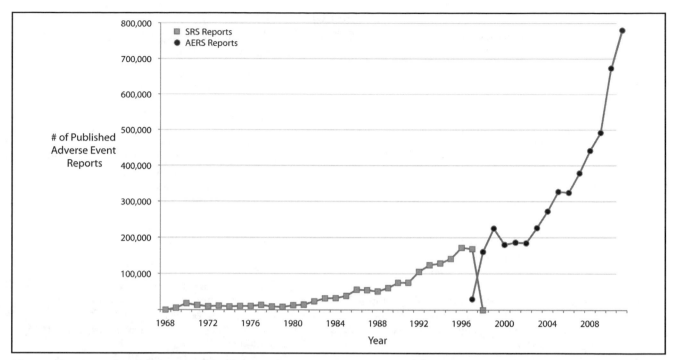

Figure 12.1 Number of drug and biologic adverse event reports published by the FDA from 1968 to 2011. Squares represent reports from the Spontaneous Reporting System (SRS). Circles represent reports from the Adverse Event Reporting System (AERS).

12.5 Adverse Drug Reaction Information Captured by the AERS

Each adverse event report submitted to the FDA contains an array of information that attempts to provide a clear picture of the patient who suffered the adverse event, the medications taken during the time surrounding the event, the specific adverse events suffered by the patient and the overall patient outcome after the adverse event. Table 12.1 summarizes the information that can be captured within each report. Note that although each report can contain the information outlined in Table 12.1, the actual information included in a report will vary depending on the extent of information known at the time the report is submitted. As an example, the AERS allows persons submitting a report to list the lot number for each administered medication. However, this information is not always known to the submitter, and, therefore, this information may or may not be included in any particular report.

12.6 Searching AERS Data to Identify Possible Safety Problems

With over 4 million existing reports and more than 150,000 newly submitted reports arriving in recent quarters, one may ask how the FDA, and other organizations, analyze the adverse event database.

A. Statistical Methods to Identify Drug Safety Signals

Researchers at the FDA, as well as those in academia and the pharmaceutical industry, chiefly use AERS data to search for drug *safety signals*—unexpected adverse reactions that may be causally linked to the administration of a drug or biologic agent.[16]

The methods employed to search for safety signals are statistical in nature, and in general, they attempt to identify adverse reactions that are more frequently, or disproportionately, co-reported with one drug (or class of drugs) than with a comparator drug (or class of drugs).[17] Adverse reactions that are disproportionately associated with a particular drug represent safety signals that warrant further investigation to assess the possibility of a causal link between the drug and the adverse reaction.

Figure 12.2 shows a safety signal analysis of the intra-nasal spray, Zicam®, using AERS data from early 2005 and using a statistical method known as the Proportional Reporting Ratio (PRR) that measures reporting disproportionality.[17–19] Interestingly, the strongest safety signals shown in Figure 12.2 are primarily related to dysfunctions in smell and taste (anosmia, dysgeusia). Note, these signals were present using AERS data available four years before a 2009 FDA public advisory that warned the public of the relationship between intra-nasal Zicam® and anosmia.[20]

Table 12.1
An Abridged List of Information Captured in Individual Safety Reports
Submitted to the FDA's Adverse Events Reporting System

- Patient Information
- Date Information
- Adverse Event Date
- Date of Death (when applicable)
- Demographic Information
- Age
- Weight
- Gender
- Reporter Information
- Date Information
- Date Report Was Submitted
- Manufacturer Notification Date
- FDA Notification Date
- Name of Manufacturer Sending Report (when applicable)
- Manufacturer's Internal Report Identification Code
- Occupation of the Person Submitting the Report
- Whether a Reporter Requested that His Identity Not Be Disclosed to the Manufacturer
- Reporter's Country
- Drug Information
- Drug Name

- Administration Route
- Drug Dose
- Drug's Reported Role (Primary Suspect, Secondary Suspect, Interacting or Concomitant)
- Dechallenge Information (Was the severity of the adverse reaction ameliorated when administration of the drug was stopped?)
- Rechallenge Information (Did the severity of the adverse reaction increase after a medication was re-administered?)
- Drug's Lot Number
- Drug's Expiration Date
- Drug's Start Date
- Drug's End Date
- Duration of Drug Therapy
- Adverse Reaction and Outcome Information
- Preferred Term for Adverse Reaction (medical term describing the adverse event using MedDRA, the Medical Dictionary for Regulatory Activities)
- Patient Outcome(s) (Congenital Anomaly, Death, Disability, Life-Threatening, Other, Required Intervention to Prevent Permanent Impairment / Damage)

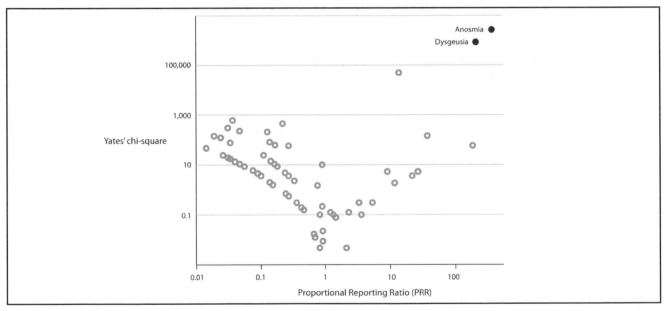

Figure 12.2 *Safety signal analysis of Zicam® using AERS data from 1997 to Q1 of 2005. Each data-point represents a single adverse reaction, and the position of each data point represents the degree to which an adverse reaction is more (or less) co-reported with Zicam® when compared to all cases that do not report Zicam®. Adverse reactions in the upper-right (filled circles) are those that are most disproportionately co-reported with Zicam®, and therefore represent the strongest safety signals for this medication. Yates' chi-square serves as a measure of the statistical significance of an observed reporting disproportionality (as indicated by a PRR ≠ 1). A higher Yates' chi-square value corresponds to a lower probability that the observed reporting disproportionality occurred solely by chance.*

Researchers at the FDA have published a number of peer-reviewed manuscripts devoted to their analysis of AERS data. It is clear from these manuscripts that the FDA uses statistical methods that measure reporting disproportionality, including the PRR and the Multi-item Gamma Poisson Shrinker methods to identify safety signals.[17–19] However, it is unclear as to whether these approaches are used to systematically mine all adverse event data or whether other quantitative and qualitative methods are also employed to search for safety signals.

B. Dechallenge and Rechallenge Data

Although it is not always possible to definitively demonstrate a causal relationship between a drug and a particular adverse reaction using AERS data alone, AERS reports sometimes contain data that help support a causal relationship. Specifically, individual safety reports often include information on whether the severity of an adverse reaction was ameliorated when administration of a drug was discontinued (known as a positive dechallenge), or whether the severity of an adverse reaction increased with the re-administration of a medication (known as a positive rechallenge), or both. When analyzing AERS data, dechallenge and rechallenge information can provide evidence of a link between a drug and a particular adverse reaction.[21,22]

C. Identifying Drug-Drug Interactions

Recent research has also shown that the FDA's AERS data can be used to search for previously unexpected drug-drug interactions. Specifically, Tatonetti et al. mined the AERS database in an attempt to identify medications that, only when co-administered, were disproportionately associated with adverse reactions relating to increased blood glucose levels.[23] This approach identified two medications, paroxetine and pravastatin, which do not appear to increase blood glucose levels unless they are co-administered. Tatonetti et al. subsequently tested the hypothesis that co-administration of paroxetine and pravastatin interfered with blood glucose homeostasis by mining an independent registry of medical records, whose data also support the link between increased blood glucose and co-administration of these medications.[23]

D. Timelines and Deadlines of Adverse Event Reporting

AERS reports also contain a wealth of date-related information, including the date when a manufacturer receives an adverse event report. It is therefore possible to use the AERS to determine when a manufacturer was first notified of a possible link between a medication and a specific adverse reaction. It is also possible to use the AERS to determine whether manufacturers have complied with FDA-mandated reporting deadlines for serious adverse reactions.

Specifically, because AERS reports contain information on when a manufacturer was notified of an adverse event and when the manufacturer subsequently notified the FDA, it is possible to use the AERS to determine whether a manufacturer has forwarded reports of serious and unexpected adverse reactions to the FDA within the mandated 15 calendar day period. This issue has recently been thrust into the spotlight when the FDA released a statement indicating that Pfizer and other unnamed organizations had submitted adverse event reports related to the medication varenicline through "improper channels" and had initially submitted adverse event reports to the FDA "in a way that did not allow for [the FDA to conduct] comprehensive evaluation." These improper submissions included reports of varenicline-associated suicides and serious psychiatric episodes that were submitted to the FDA as periodic summaries rather than as expedited, 15-calendar-day, reports.[24]

12.7 The Food and Drug Administration's Use of the AERS in Regulatory Decisions

As noted above, the FDA uses the AERS to search for unexpected safety issues associated with marketed medications. The FDA subsequently uses the information that it gathers as part of its strategy to communicate drug safety issues with the public and to guide changes in the regulation of marketed medications. In 2008, the FDA began releasing lists of newly identified "Potential Signals of Serious Risks/New Safety Information Identified from the Adverse Event Reporting System."[25] These lists, which are released quarterly, include three items:

- the name of the drug or class of drugs being investigated
- the potential adverse reaction (safety signal) associated with the drug in question
- additional information on what steps the FDA has taken or is taking to further its investigation

From 2008 to the first quarter of 2011, the FDA has published 171 potential signals of serious risks based on its examination of the AERS. The safety signals identified by the FDA are a remarkable testament to the diverse types of adverse reactions that can be revealed by analyzing AERS data. They include:

- overdoses related to confusion over packaging (e.g., arginine hydrochloride)

- organ and tissue failure (e.g., liver failure and dronedarone)
- drug-drug interactions (e.g., ranolazine and simvastatin)
- age-related adverse reactions (e.g., serious adverse events in neonates associated with lopinavir/ritonavir)

The range of actions taken by the FDA in response to its investigation of these safety signals also covers a wide range.

A. Boxed Warnings

The most serious changes include addition of boxed warnings to the prescribing information of several medications (e.g., extraneal, lapatinib, trastuzumab[25]) and recommendations that prescribers limit the use of high doses of certain medications like simvastatin.[26,27]

B. Other Changes to a Medication's Prescribing Information

The FDA has also used its investigation of AERS data to orchestrate more moderate changes to the prescribing information of numerous medications (e.g., minocycline, tapentadol, saquinavir).[25] In these cases, prescribing information of an investigated drug is changed to include the newly identified safety signals as part of a list of adverse reactions that have been observed in postmarketing reports. These changes often do not include the more serious addition of a boxed warning.

C. Determination That No Action is Needed and Continuing Investigations

The bulk of the remaining medications under investigation for potential safety issues are either still under investigation, or the FDA has determined that no regulatory action is needed at the time, either because there is insufficient evidence to support the initial safety signal or because the FDA believes that the medication's existing prescribing information adequately addresses the potential safety issue (e.g., mefloquine[28]).

12.8 Limitations of the AERS

Although analysis of AERS data can identify rare and unexpected drug safety issues, the FDA notes that the AERS does have certain limitations, including the following.

A. Lack of Demonstration of Causality for Individual Reports

For any individual report, the information contained therein does not necessarily demonstrate that a particular medication caused the reported adverse reactions. However, as noted above, dechallenge and rechallenge data, when available in the reports, may help support causality.

B. Reporting Biases

The voluntary nature of AERS reporting can make the number of reports filed for a particular medication susceptible to publicity surrounding a particular medication.[10,13]

C. Extensive Underreporting

The AERS is a voluntary drug safety surveillance system. That is, drug safety reports are either voluntarily submitted directly to the FDA by members of the public or they are voluntarily submitted to manufacturers who are then obligated to submit the reports to the FDA. As a result of its voluntary underpinnings, most suspected drug adverse reactions are not reported to the AERS. A number of studies have attempted to estimate the degree of underreporting:

1) within the AERS, and
2) within all voluntary pharmacovigilance adverse event reporting systems.

A 2006 analysis estimates that only 6 percent of known, suspected or expected adverse drug reactions are reported in voluntary pharmacovigilance systems like AERS (with an interquartile range of 2 to 18 percent).[14] Similar conclusions were drawn by a 2008 FDA study, which estimated the degree of underreporting for the serious adverse reaction, rhabdomyolysis for the class of drugs colloquially known as statins (3-hydroxy-3-methyl-glutaryl coenzyme A [HMG-CoA] reductase inhibitors). The FDA study estimated that only 5–15 percent of rhabdomyolysis adverse events were reported for the statins in general. Moreover, even after the FDA publicized the safety issue by disseminating a "Dear Health Care Provider" letter urging healthcare practitioners to be aware of this potential issue and to submit suspected cases to the FDA, the FDA estimates that the reporting frequency was still only 5–30 percent for the entire class of statin medications.[13]

D. Lack of Comparator Populations (Lack of a Denominator)

Under ideal conditions, one would be able to determine the frequency at which a particular adverse reaction is associated with a particular drug (Equation 12.1):

$$\text{Frequency of association} = \frac{\text{Number of cases where Adverse Event X occurs when patients are exposed to Drug Y}}{\text{Total number of patients exposed to Drug Y}}$$

(12.1)

One could then compare this frequency to the frequency of occurrence of Adverse Event X in the population as a whole (or in another suitable control population). Comparisons of this type would then allow investigators to calculate the strength of association of a particular adverse event for a particular drug. However, it is often difficult to estimate the total number of patients exposed to a particular medication. Therefore, many analyses of AERS cannot compute an incidence frequency owing to a lack of a denominator in the equation shown above.[29] As noted in Section 12.6.A, however, other statistical methods have been employed to address this issue, primarily by identifying adverse reactions that are disproportionately co-reported with specific medications.[17–19]

12.9 Forthcoming Changes to the Adverse Event Reporting System
A. FAERS
In 2009, the FDA announced that it is developing a successor to the AERS, termed the FDA Adverse Event Reporting System (FAERS). Although the FAERS is not currently implemented, the FDA's description of the system suggests that it will merge several existing surveillance systems and allow users to report new types of adverse events that are not currently captured with the AERS. This includes reports of adverse events from clinical trials (premarket reports), medical-device adverse events, food-related adverse events and adverse events related to veterinary medications. The FDA has stated that implementation of the FAERS will be completed in stages, with full integration having been expected in 2011.[30]

B. FDA's Transparency Initiative
The Administration of President Obama has made an effort to increase public access to all branches of the federal government. In an effort to align itself with this goal of greater openness, the FDA and the Department of Health and Human Services launched the Transparency Initiative, whose goals are four-fold:

- to better explain FDA decisions
- to provide more data to doctors and patients
- to illuminate FDA enforcement efforts
- to support innovation for rare diseases

As part of the effort to achieve these goals, the members of the Transparency Initiative[31] have sought public comment on specific proposals that would help the FDA achieve its four stated goals. Notably, the first draft proposal issued by the members of the Transparency Initiative is to expand public access to its adverse event data, including the data found in the AERS. As of this writing, the FDA continues to solicit public comment on its Transparency Initiative proposals and has yet to render a formal decision on which proposals it will ultimately enact.[31]

12.10 Search and Retrieval of Adverse Event Reports from the FDA's AERS
For researchers outside the FDA, there are two significant hindrances in analyzing the FDA's AERS data. First, only a portion of the AERS data set is publicly available. Second, the subset of data that is publicly available is effectively unsearchable by the general public.

Specifically, even though the AERS was initiated in 1997, the FDA has made available on its website only AERS data from 2004 to the present, thus preventing public access to more than 1.1 million adverse event reports.[32] In addition, although the FDA makes some of its AERS data available to the public, it does not provide a mechanism to search or analyze these data. Instead, it provides the public with raw text files of adverse event data that can only be searched efficiently using advanced computational methods.

As a consequence, there are only two general mechanisms by which one may search the complete AERS database, as follows.

A. FOIA Requests
First, interested parties can file a Freedom of Information Act (FOIA) request with the FDA and specify the search parameters (e.g., all cases reporting both ibuprofen and cardiac arrest) that should be used to query the FDA's AERS database. Upon receipt of a FOIA request, the FDA will perform a search using its internal database and return electronic copies of the case reports that match the submitted search criteria. The FDA charges a fee for FOIA requests that is dependent on the complexity of the search and on the amount of time and expertise required to conduct the search. The time required for the FDA to complete these requests varies from a few weeks to longer periods.[33]

B. Commercial Vendors
Second, commercial organizations have built search engines that allow users to mine and analyze the complete AERS data set more rapidly than is possible by means of a conventional FOIA request.[34,35] Depending on the commercial vendor, search results can provide end-users with both raw data and statistical analysis of their search results, allowing users to search for safety signals (Figure 12.2) and to see such statistics as patient outcome distributions, and the frequency of co-reported adverse reactions (Figure 12.3).

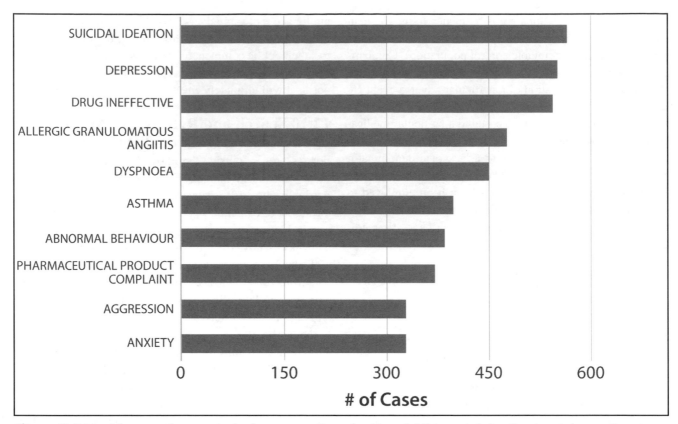

Figure 12.3 *Most frequently reported adverse reactions for Singulair® (montelukast) using Adverse Event Reporting System data from 1997 to 2010.*

12.11 Other FDA Adverse Event Reporting Systems

As noted above, the AERS is not the only postmarketing surveillance system employed by the FDA. Rather, the FDA uses a number of surveillance systems, each of which is designed to monitor adverse events for a specific type of medical treatment.

A. VAERS

For example, the FDA (in conjunction with the Centers for Disease Control and Prevention) monitors reports of vaccine adverse events using a separate electronic database known as VAERS. VAERS has been in existence since 1990 and contains over 250,000 adverse event reports. The FDA and CDC use VAERS to search for vaccine safety signals in a manner similar to that employed for safety signal analysis of the AERS.[36,37]

B. MAUDE

The FDA also maintains a separate database that collects adverse event reports for medical devices and medical facilities. This database is known as MAUDE (Medical Device and User Facility Device Experience). MAUDE reports are

available from approximately 1991 to the present and the database currently contains more than 1.4 million reports.[38]

Although the AERS, VAERS and MAUDE databases each capture different sets of information, the FDA may merge these data sets into the FAERS system described above. It remains to be seen whether this unification will change the types of information captured in drug, device and vaccine adverse event reports.

C. *Sentinel Initiative*

In May 2008, the FDA announced a new program, termed the *Sentinel Initiative*, whereby it would track all FDA-approved products by mining electronic health record systems and insurance claims databases from a number of external organizations. The *Sentinel Initiative* is still in a pilot stage known as the Mini-Sentinel Pilot.[39,40]

12.12 Summary

This chapter has discussed the Food and Drug Administration's Adverse Event Reporting System (AERS), the primary tool used to monitor the safety of marketed medications in the United States. The FDA uses the AERS to identify unexpected drug safety issues and guide regulatory changes in response to these safety issues. The FDA has used the AERS to identify a diverse array of drug safety issues, including unexpected drug-drug interactions, organ failure, overdoses related to confusion over drug packaging and age-related adverse reactions. Although it is difficult for others to search and analyze the AERS through the FDA's website, commercial vendors do provide access to the electronic database, allowing interested parties the ability to search for drug safety signals and compile statistical data on medications of interest. Ultimately, expanded access to these data should enhance drug safety efforts and promote greater public health.

Endnotes

1. Gad, S.C., ed. *Clinical Trials Handbook*. (NJ: Wiley, 2009).

2. U.S. Food and Drug Administration. (October 19, 2010). *Drug Study Designs—Information Sheet*. Available at www.fda.gov/RegulatoryInformation/Guidances/ucm126501.htm

3. National Institutes of Health. (March 18, 2008). *Glossary of Clinical Trial Terms*. Available at http://clinicaltrials.gov/ct2/info/glossary#phaselll

4. Alsheikh-Ali, A.A. et al. "The safety of rosuvastatin as used in common clinical practice: a postmarketing analysis," *Circulation*, 111(23):3051–3057 (2005).

5. Strangfeld, A. and J. Listing. "Infection and musculoskeletal conditions: Bacterial and opportunistic infections during anti-TNF therapy," *Best Pract. Res. Clin. Rheumatol.* 20(6):1181–1195 (2006).

6. U.S. Food and Drug Administration. (July 18, 2011). *Should Your Child Be in a Clinical Trial?* Available at www.fda.gov/ForConsumers/ConsumerUpdates/ucm048699.htm

7. Johann-Liang, R. et al. "Pediatric drug surveillance and the food and drug administration's adverse event reporting system: an overview of reports, 2003–2007," *Pharmacoepidemiol. Drug Saf.* 18(1):24–27 (2008).

8. Rivkees, S., and A. Szarfman. "Dissimilar hepatotoxicity profiles of propylthiouracil and methimazole in children," *J. Clin. Endocrinol. Metab.* 95(7):3260–3267 (2010).

9. National Institutes of Health. (July 18, 2011). *ClinicalTrials.gov*. Available at www.clinicaltrials.gov.

10. U.S. Food and Drug Administration. (August 20, 2009) *Adverse Event Reporting System (AERS)*. Available at www.fda.gov/Drugs/GuidanceComplianceRegulatoryInformation/Surveillance/AdverseDrugEffects/default.htm

11. Rossi, A.C., and D.E. Knapp. "Discovery of new adverse drug reactions: a review of the food and drug administration's spontaneous reporting system," *JAMA*. 252(8):1030–1033 (1984).

12. Trontell, A.E. "How the U.S. Food and Drug Administration defines and detects adverse drug events." 2001. *Current Therapeutic Research*. 62(9):641–649 (2001).

13. McAdams, M. et al. "Estimating the extent of reporting to FDA: a case study of statin-associated rhabdomyolysis," *Pharmacoepidemiol. Drug Saf.* 17(3):229–39 (2008).

14. Hazell, L. and S.A.W. Shakir. "Under-reporting of adverse drug reactions: a systematic review," *Drug Saf.* 29(5):385–396 (2006).

15. "Postmarketing reporting of adverse drug experiences." (2010). 21 C.F.R. '314.80'

16. Edwards, I.R. and C. Biriell. "Harmonisation in pharmacovigilance," *Drug Saf.* 10(2):93–102 (1994).

17. Almenoff, J.S. et al. "Comparative performance of two quantitative safety signalling methods: implications for use in a pharmacovigilance department," *Drug Saf.* 29(10):875–887 (2006).

18. W. DuMouchel. "Bayesian data mining in large frequency tables, with an application to the FDA Spontaneous Reporting System," *Am. Stat.* 53(3):177–202 (1999).

19. Evans, S.J. et al. "Use of proportional reporting ratios (PRRs) for signal generation from spontaneous adverse drug reaction reports," *Pharmacoepidemiol. Drug Saf.* 10(6):483–486 (2001).

20. U.S. Food and Drug Administration. (June 16, 2009) *FDA Advises Consumers Not To Use Certain Zicam Cold Remedies: Intranasal Zinc Product Linked to Loss of Sense of Smell*. Available at www.fda.gov/Newsevents/Newsroom/PressAnnouncements/ucm167065.htm

21. Wysowski, D.K., et al. "Postmarketing reports of QT prolongation and ventricular arrhythmia in association with cisapride and food and drug administration regulatory actions," *Am. J. Gastroenterol.* 96(6):1698–1703 (2001).

22. Bremner, J.D. and P. McCaffery. "The neurobiology of retinoic acid in affective disorders," *Prog. Neuropsychopharmacol. Biol. Psychiatry.* 32(2):315–331 (2008).

23. Tatonetti, N.P., et al. "Detecting drug interactions from adverse-event reports: interaction between paroxetine and pravastatin increases blood glucose levels," *Clin. Pharmacol. Ther.* 90(1):133–142 (2011).

24. U.S. Food and Drug Administration. (May 19, 2011). *Chantix: Quarterwatch Article.* Available at www.fda.gov/Drugs/DrugSafety/ucm255918.htm

25. U.S. Food and Drug Administration. (July 14, 2011). *Potential Signals of Serious Risks/New Safety Information Identified from the Adverse Event Reporting System (AERS).* Available at www.fda.gov/Drugs/GuidanceComplianceRegulatoryInformation/Surveillance/AdverseDrugEffects/ucm082196.htm

26. U.S. Food and Drug Administration. (July 14, 2011) *Potential Signals of Serious Risks/New Safety Information Identified from the Adverse Event Reporting System (AERS) between April–June 2010.* Available at www.fda.gov/Drugs/GuidanceComplianceRegulatoryInformation/Surveillance/AdverseDrugEffects/ucm223734.htm

27. U.S. Food and Drug Administration. (June 8, 2011). *FDA Drug Safety Communication: New restrictions, contraindications, and dose limitations for Zocor (simvastatin) to reduce the risk of muscle injury.* Available at www.fda.gov/Drugs/DrugSafety/ucm256581.htm

28. U.S. Food and Drug Administration. (July 14, 2011). *Potential Signals of Serious Risks/New Safety Information Identified from the Adverse Event Reporting System (AERS) between July–September 2008.* Available at www.fda.gov/Drugs/GuidanceComplianceRegulatoryInformation/Surveillance/AdverseDrugEffects/ucm085925.htm

29. Baciu, A. et al., ed. *The Future of Drug Safety: Promoting and Protecting the Health of the Public.* (Institute of Medicine of the National Academies, 2007).

30. U.S. Food and Drug Administration. (May 22, 2009) *MedWatchPlus / FAERS.* Available at www.fda.gov/ScienceResearch/SpecialTopics/CriticalPathInitiative/SpotlightonCPIProjects/ucm083295.htm

31. U.S. Food and Drug Administration. (May 26, 2011) *FDA Transparency Initiative,* Available at www.fda.gov/AboutFDA/Transparency/TransparencyInitiative/default.htm

32. U.S. Food and Drug Administration. (April 18, 2011). *The Adverse Event Reporting System (AERS): Older Quarterly Data Files.* Available at www.fda.gov/Drugs/GuidanceComplianceRegulatoryInformation/Surveillance/AdverseDrugEffects/ucm083765.htm

33. U.S. Food and Drug Administration. (March 22, 2011). *How to Make a FOIA Request.* Available at www.fda.gov/RegulatoryInformation/FOI/HowtoMakeaFOIARequest/default.htm

34. FDAble, LLC. Available at www.fdable.com.

35. United BioSource Corporation. Available at www.unitedbiosource.com.

36. Department of Health and Human Services. (July 13, 2011). *Vaccine Adverse Event Reporting System.* Available at http://vaers.hhs.gov/index

37. Iskander, J. et al. "Data mining in the U.S. using the Vaccine Adverse Event Reporting System," *Drug Saf.* 29(5):375–384 (2006).

38. U.S. Food and Drug Administration. (June 9, 2011). *Manufacturer and User Facility Device Experience Database—(MAUDE).* Available at www.fda.gov/MedicalDevices/DeviceRegulationandGuidance/PostmarketRequirements/ReportingAdverseEvents/ucm127891.htm

39. U.S. Food and Drug Administration. (June 23, 2011). *FDA's Sentinel Initiative.* Available at www.fda.gov/Safety/FDAsSentinelInitiative/ucm2007250.htm

40. Mini-Sentinel. (July 14, 2011). Available at http://mini-sentinel.org.

Chapter 13

Liability, Litigation, and Lessons in New Drug Development

James T. O'Donnell, Pharm.D., M.S., FCP, ABCP, FACN, R.Ph.

13.1 Liability: The Downside of Drug Development

Therapeutic agents, such as vaccines and antibiotics, have changed the course of modern medicine and prolonged the average life span of the population by abating diseases that used to be associated with mortality. New classes of medications contribute to further treatment and disease eradication. All drugs can, however, be harmful. Table 13.1 defines how the Food and Drug Administration (FDA) differentiates "adverse drug reactions" (ADRs) from "adverse drug events" (ADEs) and other terms.

Richard Merli, managing editor of *Pharmaceuticals Insiders*, believes that increased public concern presents drug companies with the difficult choice of either "implementing expensive risk management strategies that might involve taking a blockbuster drug off the market or risking huge court awards and irreparable public relations damage."[1] For instance, the blockbuster drug Vioxx, with sales of several billion dollars each year, was withdrawn from the market in late 2004. Several years later, a multi-billion dollar global settlement was finalized. The Vioxx withdrawal and widespread effect on the NSAID market will be addressed later in this chapter.

Merli states that a proactive risk management plan reduces product liability lawsuits but can also reduce drug sales "for reasons that turn out to be ephemeral."[1] He warns pharmaceutical companies, however, that being defensive—such as described by Fitzgerald[2]—is extremely risky. "Ongoing product liability litigation can damage a company's bottom line for years." He recommends companies adopt a risk management plan that closely monitors ADRs and includes a communication channel for quick decisions if serious side effects begin to show up. "It's much more to a company's advantage to make a decision to voluntarily withdraw a drug from market," says John Morris, global chair of KPMG in London, "rather than be forced to withdraw the drug."[1] Poor public relations and stiff liability verdicts for not acting quickly on ADRs or for withholding drug safety information can bankrupt a company, as was seen with asbestos and several ephedra manufacturers, for example, Metabolife. The FDA issued strong concerns and warnings in 1996; the ephedra manufacturers refused to withdraw the products. It took 8 years to force the market withdrawal of these dangerous, and now banned substances.

Another example involves Bayer Pharmaceuticals, which in September 2004 settled 2,861 product liability cases for $1.09 billion for its cholesterol medicine cerivastatin (Baycol), which was linked to 100 deaths and withdrawn from the market in 2001. After that settlement, Bayer still had several thousand cases in litigation that were eventually resolved or dismissed.[3] (See 13.4.D.4, "Noteworthy class actions: Rezulin, Baycol" for additional information). In another case, a $1 billion jury verdict was upheld against Wyeth for its fenfluramine or dexfenfluramine and phentermine (Fen-Phen) drug combination, which was linked to primary pulmonary

Table 13.1
Glossary of Drug Misadventure Terms

Term	Definition
Accelerated approval	A process for speeding approval of drugs that "promise significant benefit over existing therapy for serious or life-threatening illnesses." FDA usually approves the drug on condition that the drug company will conduct phase IV studies on the actual clinical benefit of the drug.
Adverse drug event / experience (ADE)	Any untoward medical occurrence in a patient or clinical-investigation subject administered a pharmaceutical product. It is not necessary for the event to have a causal relationship with this treatment.
Adverse drug reaction (ADR)	A negative, undesirable, or harmful reaction to a particular drug. In marketed drugs, an ADR is an unintended reaction that happens at a normal dose. In clinical trials, where the drug is not yet approved for marketing, any and all unintended and noxious reactions to a drug are considered ADRs and reported accordingly.
Advisory committee	A panel of outside experts convened periodically to advise the FDA on safety and efficacy issues about drugs and other FDA-regulated products. The FDA is not bound to take committee recommendations, but usually does.
Beers list or Beers criteria	Criteria for safe medication use in older adults, people over 65 years of age, the Beers list was first issued in 1991, and the criteria have been repeatedly revised and updated. Named for Dr. M.H. Beers, principal author of the original 1991 criteria.
Brand name drug	A brand name drug is a drug marketed under a proprietary, trademark-protected name.
Clinical trial	Any investigation in humans to identify any ADRs and to assess a drug's safety and efficacy.
Deception	In clinical trials, intentionally misleading or withholding information about results or reactions in the trial.
Discontinued drug	A discontinued drug is one that has been removed from the market in the United States for reasons other than safety or effectiveness.
Drug interaction	An altered reaction of the body to one drug when another is taken as well. An interaction between a drug and another substance that prevents the drug from performing as expected. This definition applies to interactions of drugs with other drugs (drug–drug interactions) as well as drugs with food (drug–food interactions) and other substances.
Efficacy	The ability of a drug to produce beneficial effects in the duration or course of a disease.
Institutional review board (IRB)	An independent group that reviews and approves material about a clinical trial to ensure that the study is safe and effective and adheres to FDA regulations.
Kaplan-Meier survival analysis	A statistical technique used to test the significance of differences between the survival curves associated with two different treatments. It is often used to analyze survival (life/death) data when there are censored observations (observations that are unknown because a subject has not been in the study long enough for the outcome to be observed) or to analyze the effects of different treatment procedures (Dukes, M.N.G., Risk and Safety in Medicine, 1996 Meyler's Side Effects of Drugs, Elsevier, Amsterdam).
Label	The FDA-approved label is the official description of a drug product and includes what the drug is used for; who should take it; adverse events (side effects); instructions for use in pregnancy, children, and other populations; and safety information for the patient. Labels are often found inside drug product packaging.

Table 13.1 (continued)

Term	Definition
Medication Guide	A medication guide is required by the FDA when a drug poses serious health concerns. It contains information for patients' understanding of how to safely use a drug product.
MedWatch program	An FDA program to monitor ADRs by analyzing voluntary health professional reports and required drug manufacturer reports.
Morbidity	An adverse effect caused by a treatment. A state produced by any departure, subjective or objective, from a state of physiological or psychological well-being.
Off-label	The unauthorized use of a drug for a purpose not approved by the FDA.
Orphan drug	An FDA designation for a therapy developed to treat a rare disease (one which afflicts less than 200,000 people in the United States). Because there are fewer financial incentives for drug companies to develop these therapies, the U.S. government offers additional incentives (tax advantages and extended marketing exclusivity) to the companies that develop these drugs.
Over-the-counter drugs (OTC)	FDA defines OTC drugs as safe and effective for use by the general public without a doctor's prescription.
Patient package insert (PPI)	A PPI contains information for patients' understanding of how to safely use a drug product.
Phase IV study	After a drug has been approved by the FDA, Phase IV studies are conducted to compare the drug to a competitor, explore additional patient populations, or further study any ADRs.
Postmarketing surveillance	The FDA's ongoing safety monitoring of marketed drugs.
Review	A comprehensive analysis of clinical trial data and other information that forms the basis of the FDA's decision to approve an application.
Safety	No drug is completely safe or without potential side effects. Before a drug is approved for marketing, tests show a drug is "safe" under the conditions on the proposed label. "Safety" is therefore determined on a case-by-case basis and reflects the risk–benefit ratio.
Serious adverse drug event	A serious adverse event is any untoward medical occurrence that results in death, is life-threatening, requires in-patient hospitalization, prolongs a hospital stay, results in persistent or significant disability or incapacity, or causes a congenital anomaly or birth defect.
Serious adverse event (SAE)	Any ADE that is fatal, life-threatening, permanently disabling, or that results in hospitalization or prolonged hospital stays.
Side effects	Secondary or unwanted effects. Problems that occur when treatment affects healthy cells. For instance, the common side effects of chemotherapy include fatigue, nausea, vomiting, decreased blood cell counts, and hair loss. Most treatment-related side effects can be managed.
Supplement	An application to allow a company to make changes in a product that has already been approved. The FDA must approve all important changes (in packaging or ingredients, for instance).
Unexpected Adverse Drug Reaction	A reaction that is not consistent in nature or severity with study application.

Sources

"Clinical Trials Glossary | CenterWatch." The Global Source for Clinical Trials Information | CenterWatch. Web. 15 Dec. 2011. www.centerwatch.com/health-resources/glossary.

"FDA Glossary." FDAReview.org, a Project of The Independent Institute. Web. 15 Dec. 2011. www.fdareview. org/glossary.shtml.

hypertension (PPH). Wyeth has set aside $16.6 billion to cover future liability on the drug . It was eventually described as a $22 billion scandal by Kip Petroff.[4] (See Section 13.4.D.2, *Fen-Phen and other diet drugs*, for more on this case).[5]

13.2 History of Drug Liability and Milestones in Drug Regulation

Physician liability is nothing new; from the beginning of civilization, people have been concerned about the quality and safety of their food and medicines. In approximately 1700 B.C., the Babylonian "Codex of Hammurabi" decreed that a physician who caused the death of a noble patient should lose his hands.[6] In 1202, King John of England proclaimed the first English food law, the Assize of Bread, which prohibited adulteration of bread with such ingredients as ground peas or beans.[7] Food regulation in the United States started in colonial times. Federal control of the drug supply began with the inspection of imported drugs in 1848.[7] Regulations continued to evolve throughout the nineteenth century. In today's environment, medical mistakes often become career-ending errors that cost healthcare providers millions or billions in settlements.

Table 13.2 traces the chronology of laws, regulations, and litigation intended to ensure drug safety and efficacy in the United States.

13.3 Classification of Adverse Drug Reactions (ADRs)

An ADR is any unintended or undesirable response obtained from the appropriate dose of a drug or diagnostic agent. ADRs have been conventionally classified into six different categories: overdose, intolerance, unexpected side effects, secondary effects, and idiosyncratic and hypersensitivity reactions. Although drug interactions are included with other ADRs, they are also classified into seven categories:

1. Those that occur outside the body.
2. Those that occur at the site of entry.
3. Those that occur at storage sites within the body.
4. Those that occur at the site of action.
5. Those that inhibit enzymes from metabolizing.
6. Those that stimulate enzymes.
7. Those that affect drug excretion.

Although these classifications have been used in both reviews and textbooks, it is unnecessary and confusing to separate ADRs from drug interactions.

Drug manufacturers are required to promptly report all serious or unexpected ADRs from spontaneous sources and from any clinical or epidemiological investigation—inde-

pendent of design or purpose. It also applies to cases not reported directly to a sponsor or manufacturer (for instance, those found in regulatory ADR registries or in publications). There are situations in addition to single case reports of serious ADRs that may necessitate rapid communication to regulatory authorities, such as information that might materially influence the risk-benefit assessment of a medicinal product or that would be sufficient to consider changes in administering the product or in the overall conduct of a clinical investigation. Examples include clinically important increases in the rate of occurrence for an "expected," serious ADR; significant hazards to the patient population—such as lack of efficacy with a drug used to treat a life-threatening disease; or major safety findings from a newly completed animal study (such as a study on carcinogenicity).

13.4 Adverse Drug Reactions (ADRs): A Major Cause of Litigation

The reported incidence and frequency of ADR vary depending on the source of the report and the methods used to describe the event. One reason for the discrepancy is that the cause of an ADR can be difficult to ascertain. ADRs listed in hospital admission reports have ranged from less than 1 percent to 28 percent. Most studies report an incidence rate of 10 to 20 percent, reflecting the different methods used to detect and report ADRs.

A. Extent of the Problem: Incidence of ADRs

In reviewing ADRs, Jick determined that the incidence of ADRs ranged between 1 in 10,000 (0.01 percent) to 1 in 200 (0.5 percent).[8] ADRs with an incidence of 1 in 10,000 would be difficult to identify at the clinical trial stage, where data are usually available on only about 1,000 patients. ADRs with an intermediate frequency (greater than 1 in 10,000 but less than 1 in 200) might be identified in postmarketing surveillance studies, whereas ADRs of low frequency (less than 1 in 10,000) might be verified only in cohort or case-control studies. Many important ADRs are pharmacologically unpredictable with an incidence of 1 in 10,000 or less, entailing a follow-up of a cohort of drug users. This has important implications for the sample size needed in postmarketing surveillance studies. Sample-size limitations mean that serious but infrequent reactions will not be picked up unless cohort samples are of 100,000 or more.

The mortality from ADRs has been estimated within the hospitalized patient population to be 0.01 to 0.3 percent. Estimates of deaths annually from ADRs have ranged from 2,000 to 140,000, and annual hospitalizations due to ADRs range from 160,000 to 1.5 million.[9] It is estimated that up to 30 percent of hospitalized patients experience an ADR.[10]

Table 13.2
History and Milestones in U.S. Drug Regulation

1820	Physicians establish the *U.S. Pharmacopoeia*, the first U.S. drug standards.
1848	The *Drug Importation Act* passed to stop the entry of adulterated drugs.
1862	The Bureau of Chemistry, predecessor of the FDA, is created.
1880	Chief chemist Peter Collier recommends a national food and drug law; during the next 25 years, more than 100 such bills are introduced.
1883	Chief chemist Harvey W. Wiley (called the "Crusading Chemist" and "Father of the Pure Food and Drugs Act") campaigns for a federal drug safety law.
1902	*The Biologics Control Act* passes to ensure purity and safety in vaccines.
1906	The *Food and Drugs Act* prohibits interstate commerce of adulterated drugs.
1911	In *U.S. v Johnson*, the Supreme Court rules that the *Food and Drugs Act* does not prohibit false therapeutic claims.
1912	The *Sherley Amendment* passes to prohibit false therapeutic claims in medicines.
1914	The *Harrison Narcotic Act* requires prescriptions for products exceeding the allowable limit of narcotics and mandates increased record-keeping for physicians and pharmacists.
1924	The *U.S. v 95 Barrels Alleged Apple Cider Vinegar* ruling says that any statement, design, or device on a label that may mislead or deceive is prohibited.
1927	Regulatory functions of the Bureau of Chemistry become the Food, Drug, and Insecticide Administration, which is shortened to Food and Drug Administration (FDA) in an agricultural appropriations act three years later.
1933	FDA recommends revision of the *Food and Drugs Act*, launching a five-year legislative battle.
1937	Elixir of Sulfanilamide, containing a poisonous solvent, kills 107 people including children, dramatizing the need to enact the pending food and drug law.
1938	The *Federal Food, Drug, and Cosmetic (FD&C) Act* passes requiring new drugs be shown safe before marketing, eliminating the requirement in the *Sherley Amendment* that "intent to defraud" must be proven in misbranded drugs, requiring that safe tolerances be set for unavoidable poisonous substances, authorizing factory inspections, and adding injunctions to seizures and prosecution as remedies for violations.
1940	FDA is transferred from the Department of Agriculture to the Federal Security Agency, with Walter G. Campbell appointed the first Commissioner of Food and Drugs.
1941	The *Insulin Amendment* requires the FDA to test and certify the purity and potency of insulin.
1943	*U.S. v Dotterweich* makes corporations and officials of corporations liable for violations without the need to prove intent or knowledge.
1944	The *Public Health Service Act* passes to regulate biological products, the control of communicable diseases, and other health issues.
1945	The *Penicillin Amendment* requires the FDA to test and certify the safety and effectiveness of all penicillin products (later extended to all antibiotics).
1948	The *Miller Amendment* ensures the FD&C Act applies to all goods regulated by FDA and transported from one state to another.
1949	FDA publishes the first *Guidance to Industry*.
1950	*Alberty Food Products Co. v U.S.* finds that drug labels must include the drug's purpose.
1951	The *Durham-Humphrey Amendment* defines drugs that cannot be used without a prescription from a licensed practitioner.
1952	*U.S. v Cardiff* finds that factory inspection in the 1938 FD&C Act is too vague to be enforced as criminal law. FDA consumer consultants are appointed in each field district.
1953	The *Factory Inspection Amendment* clarifies FD&C and requires FDA to provide written inspection reports.

continued on next page...

Table 13.2 (continued)

1955 The Division of Biologics Control becomes an independent entity within the National Institutes of Health (NIH) after a polio vaccine is linked to about 260 cases of polio.

1958 The FDA publishes the first list of "Substances Generally Recognized as Safe" (GRAS), containing nearly 200 substances.

1962 The sleeping pill thalidomide causes birth defects in thousands of babies in western Europe. News reports about FDA medical officer Dr. Frances Kelsey keeping the drug from U.S. markets arouse public support for stronger drug regulation. The *Kefauver-Harris Drug Amendments* pass to ensure drug efficacy and safety; manufacturers are required to prove the effectiveness of their drugs before marketing them.

1966 The FDA has the *effectiveness* of 4,000 drugs (approved on safety only) evaluated. The *Fair Packaging and Labeling Act* requires all labels to be honest and informative.

1968 The FDA becomes part of the Public Health Service (PHS). The *Drug Efficacy Study Implementation (DESI)* is the FDA's response to the investigation on the effectiveness of drugs.

1970 *Upjohn v. Finch* upholds enforcement of the 1962 drug effectiveness amendments by ruling that commercial success alone does not constitute substantial evidence of drug safety and efficacy. The FDA requires the first patient package insert.

1972 Over-the-counter (OTC) drug review begins to ensure the safety, effectiveness, and appropriate labeling of drugs sold without prescription. Regulation of biologics (serums, vaccines, and blood products) is transferred from NIH to the FDA.

1973 The Supreme Court upholds the 1962 drug effectiveness law and endorses FDA action to control classes of products by regulation rather than litigation.

1976 The *Medical Device Amendments* pass to ensure safety and effectiveness of medical devices including diagnostic products, requiring some quality control, premarket approval, and performance standards on some products.

1982 Tamper-resistant packaging required after the deaths from cyanide placed in Tylenol, and the *Federal Anti-Tampering Act* makes it a crime to tamper with packaged consumer products.

1983 The *Orphan Drug Act* passes, enabling the FDA to promote research and marketing of drugs needed to treat rare diseases.

1984 *Fines Enhancement Laws* of 1984 and 1987 increase penalties for all federal crimes, with double fines for corporations. The *Drug Price Competition and Patent Term Restoration Act* expedites the availability of less-costly generic drugs by permitting the FDA to approve generics without repeating the safety and effectiveness research.

1985 The FDA approves the AIDS test on blood to protect patients from infected donors.

1986 The *Childhood Vaccine Act* requires vaccine makers to provide patient information, gives the FDA authority to recall biologics, and authorizes civil penalties.

1987 Regulations on experimental drugs for patients with serious diseases and no alternative therapies.

1988 The *Food and Drug Administration Act* puts the FDA within the Department of Health and Human Services (HHS) and spells out research, enforcement, and education requirements. The *Prescription Drug Marketing Act* prevents the resale of diverted drugs, requires drug wholesalers be licensed, restricts reimportation, and bans the sale, trade, or purchase of drug samples or counterfeit drug coupons.

1989 The FDA recalls all OTC dietary supplements containing L-tryptophan because of a clear link to an outbreak of eosinophilia-myalgia syndrome (EMS). By 1990, more than 1,500 cases of EMS 38 deaths are confirmed, with an estimated 3,000–10,000 unreported cases.

continued on next page...

Table 13.2 (continued)

1990	The *Safe Medical Devices Act* requires reporting of medical devices that probably caused the death, serious illness, or injury of a patient. Postmarket surveillance on permanently implanted devices required with methods for tracing and locating patients depending on such devices. The FDA is authorized to recall device product.
1991	Regulations are published to accelerate the review of drugs for life-threatening diseases.
1992	The *Generic Drug Enforcement Act* imposes debarment and other penalties for illegal acts involving abbreviated drug applications. The *Prescription Drug User Fee Act* (PDUFA) requires manufacturers of drug and biologics to pay fees for product applications and supplements. The *Mammography Quality Standards Act* requires facilities to be accredited and federally certified by 1994, with annual inspections.
1997	The *Food and Drug Administration Modernization Act* reauthorizes PDUFA and mandates accelerated reviews and regulates drug advertising of unapproved uses.
1998	The first phase begins of consolidating FDA labs from 19 facilities to nine (by 2014).

Source: Milestones in U.S. Food and Drug Law History, www.fda.gov/opacom/backgrounders/miles.html

B. Who Is Most at Risk?

PIAA conducted a medication-error study in 1993[11] and another in 1999[12] to analyze high-frequency and severe malpractice claims. The data collected included loss description and causation information, expense and indemnity payments, and the demographics of policyholders, claimants, and institutions. PIAA companies insured almost 87,000 physicians in the United States, ranging from the smallest to the largest physician-owned malpractice insurers.

PIAA found in both studies that prescriptions were the second-most frequent and second-most expensive item in the claims reported. The authors of the study concluded that medication injury claims are a significant source of loss for malpractice carriers and the physicians they insure.

We can extrapolate from the PIAA data to determine who is most at risk of experiencing ADRs. More female than male patients were involved in the claims studied by PIAA (ratio: 1.5 female to one male).[12] Two-thirds of all claims involved patients between 18 and 59 years. Although the number of claims in the 6 to 12 and 13 to 17 age brackets were predictably low, these brackets had the highest average indemnities, reflecting the serious consequences of medication errors in young patients.

The elderly represent the group taking the largest amount of drugs (one-third of all medications prescribed each year)[13] and suffering the greatest number of ADRs. In a recent study, Curtis et al. found that 21 percent (162,370 of 765,423 subjects) of elderly Americans were being prescribed drugs that could possibly harm them (defined as drugs on the Beers list, see Table 13.1), 15 percent received

two or more of these medicines, and 4 percent received three or more of the risky drugs.[13]

Routine monitoring for drug safety should include patients in various subsets (the elderly, children, and patients with specific disease states, such as kidney or liver disease) where there may be a particular liability to ADRs.

The PIAA studies also emphasize that medication errors can cause significant injuries.[11,12] A substantial percentage (42.4 percent) of the claims involved significant permanent injuries, with 24 percent of all claims resulting in death. Close analysis of the death claims shows that medication errors were either the direct cause or a major contributing factor in the deaths in 84.3 percent of the claims. In a 1998 study of 33 million hospital admissions, the number of serious injuries from ADRs was 2.2 million; 2.1 percent of all in-patients experienced a serious ADR.[14] Lazarou et al. found that 4.7 percent of all admissions were due to serious ADRs, and fatal ADRs occurred in 0.19 percent of in-patients and 0.13 percent of admissions. The authors concluded that 106,000 deaths occur annually from ADRs. The Institute of Medicine (IOM) Landmark reports in 1999 and 2006 estimate 7,000 deaths from ADRs per year.[15,16]

C. Beyond Malpractice: Reasons for the High Incidence of ADRs

When investigating an ADR, the many syndromes and conditions can have multiple causes that occur in only a small percentage of the population and which often have vague or obscure onsets.[17] These data complicate the causal relationship. Often a drug has been on the market for years before its ADRs become known. In a study of the Physicians' Desk Reference (PDR) black box warnings, only half of the serious ADRs were detected and documented within seven years of the drug's approval.[18] Half of all drug withdrawals occur within two years of approval.[18,19] As mentioned, pre-marketing drug trials frequently miss ADRs because of their limited sample size (see Table 13.3 for a list of prescription drugs withdrawn since 1997).[18,20,21]

1. Inadequate testing

The FDA has been criticized from at least two different sides. Industry and certain patient groups argue that the agency takes far too long to approve new drugs, whereas public interest groups argue that the agency is not thorough enough in its reviews of new drugs. Before drugs can be sold in the United States, the manufacturers must apply to the FDA for the right to test them in humans, submit their test results to the agency, and then apply for the right to sell the drugs. Compounding the issue of serious ADRs which elude premarketing trial investigation are those which are detected but fail to prevent a drug's release.[22] According to Lasser et al., there were reports that alosetron hydrochloride (Lotronex, GlaxoWellcome) was associated with ischemic colitis before its approval and subsequent withdrawal.[18] In another example, David Willman of the *Los Angeles Times* blamed new policies at the FDA for the failure to prevent the marketing approval of grepafloxacin hydrochloride (Raxar, GlaxoWellcome, now GlaxoSmithKline), which was implicated in prolonging QT intervals (an electrocardiogram measurement), possibly leading to two deaths.[23] Willman blamed the release and withdrawal since 1993 of seven drugs suspected in 1,002 deaths on an FDA decision to "partner" with the pharmaceutical industry. After a two-year investigation, the newspaper found "that the FDA approved each of those drugs while disregarding danger signs or blunt warnings from its own specialists."[23]

The *Los Angeles Times* alleged that the FDA often asks companies to conduct additional studies after a product is approved if unresolved safety questions remain, but that the "suggestion" is often ignored.[23] According to research by *Public Citizen*, in only 13 percent (11 of 88) of the drugs approved, contingent on postmarketing studies, did the companies actually complete the tests.[24] Although the FDA has the authority to withdraw drugs from companies that have not performed required postmarketing research, by April 2000, they had not done so. According to Willman, FDA officials conceded that they do not know how often the studies are performed.[23]

Of the seven drugs cited in the Willman research that were approved and then withdrawn from market, none

were needed as a life-saving therapy, and all had alternatives that could have been substituted: alosetron hydrochloride (Lotronex, GlaxoSmithKline) was for irritable bowel syndrome, dexfenfluramine (Redux, Wyeth-Ayerst) was a diet pill, grepafloxacin (Raxar, Glaxo Wellcome, now GlaxoSmithKline) was an antibiotic, mibefradil (Posicor, Roche Laboratories) treated high blood pressure, bromfenac (Duract, Wyeth-Ayerst) was a pain killer, Troglitazone (Rezulin, Warner-Lambert, now Pfizer) was for diabetes, and cisapride (Propulsid, Janseen Cilag) treated heartburn.[23] The 2004 withdrawals of Vioxx and Bextra are also examples of medications that were used to treat non-life threatening conditions. These COX-2 specific NSAIDs were most likely overprescribed (beyond any gastro-protective effect), and now that they are no longer on the market, other medications have readily replaced them. As Lasser et al. suggest, "Some drugs represent a significant advance over existing drugs in the reduction of morbidity and mortality and warrant use despite limited experience. However, the drugs that do not represent a significant advance should be considered second-line drugs until their safety profile is better known."[18] Unfortunately, patent life, blockbuster swings, investor and stockholder demands, direct-to-consumer advertising, and prescribing habits mean that new medicines are often rushed to market.[18,25-31]

2. Inadequate warnings

Medical errors, which include ADRs, are believed to be one of the leading causes of death in the United States.[12,32] Patient exposure from new drugs with unknown toxic effects may be extensive. For instance, nearly 20 million patients in the United States took at least one of the five drugs withdrawn from the market between September 1997 and September 1998.[33] Three of the five drugs were new, having been on the market for less than two years.

"Boxed warnings" on medicine labels are described in the Code of Federal Regulations as follows:

> Special problems, particularly those that may lead to death or serious injury, may be required by the Food and Drug Administration to be placed in a prominently displayed box. The boxed warning ordinarily shall be based on clinical data, but serious animal toxicity may also be the basis of a boxed warning in the absence of clinical data.[34]

Because this description lacks adequate criteria on when boxed warnings should be required, missing and inconsistent warnings are one of the causes of the high incidence of ADRs. For instance, the antipsychotic drug ziprasidone

Table 13.3

Prescription drugs withdrawn from market for safety reasons in the United States from 1997–2011

Drug	Brand Name	Manufacturer	Type of Drug	Date Approved	Date Withdrawn	Time on Market	Primary Health Risk	Estimated U.S. Sales
Acetaminophen; Propoxyphene napsylate	Darvocet	Eli Lilly and Co.	Opioid Analgesic	9/10/2003	11/19/2010	7 years	Addictiveness, Heart problems	Not available
Drotrecogin alfa	Xigris	Eli Lilly and Co.	Human Activated Protein C	11/21/2001	10/25/2011	10 years	Increased bleeding	$200 million
Sibutramine	Meridia	Abbott Laboratories	Oral anorexiant	11/1997	10/08/2010	3 years	Heart attack/stroke	Not available
Gemtuzumab ozogamicin	Mylotarg	Wyeth/Pfizer, Inc.	Monoclonal antibody	5/2000	06/21/2010	10 years	Veno-occlusive disease	Not available
Efalizumab	Raptiva	Genentech, Inc.	Monoclonal antibody	10/27/2003	6/8/2009	5.67 years	Progressive Multifocal Leukoencephalopathy (PML)	$500 million
Aprotinin	Trasylol	Bayer	Basic pancreatic trypsin inhibitor	12/29/2003	5/14/2008	4.42 years	Liver and cardiovascular toxicity	Not available
Tegaserod Maleate	Zelnorm	Novartis	5-HT4 agonist	7/24/2002	3/30/2007	4.67 years	Adverse cardiovascular effects	Not available
Pergolide Mesylate	Permax	Valeant Pharm International	Dopamine Receptor Agonist	12/30/1988	3/29/2007	18.25 years	Valvular dysfunction	Not available
Hydromorphone Hydrochloride	Palladone	Purdue Pharma	Opioid analgesic	9/24/2004	7/2005	10 months	Fatal interaction with alcohol	Not available
Premoline	Cylert	Abbott Laboratories	Dopamine reuptake inhibitor	1975	3/2005	30 years	Hepatotoxicity	Not available
Natalizumab	Tysabri*	Biogen	Monoclonal antibody	11/23/2004	2/28/2005	3 months	Progressive Multifocal Leukoencephalopathy	Not available
valdecoxib	Bextra	Pfizer, Inc.	Cox-2 Inhibitor	11/1/2002	4/7/2005	2.5 years	Serious and potentially life-threatening skin reactions	Not available
rofecoxib	Vioxx	Merck & Co.	Cox-2 Inhibitor	5/21/1999	9/30/2004	5.33 years	Heart attack and stroke	$2.5 billion

continued on next page....

Table 13.3 (continued)

Drug	Brand Name	Manufacturer	Type of Drug	Date Approved	Date Withdrawn	Time on Market	Primary Health Risk	Estimated U.S. Sales
cerivastatin sodium	Baycol	Bayer	cholesterol lowering	6/26/1997	8/8/2001	4.17 years	Rhabdomyolsis	$554 million in 2000.
rapacuronium bromide	Raplon	Organon	anesthetic, muscle relaxant	9/19/1999	3/30/2001	7 months	Bronchospasm	$23 million
alosetron hydrochloride	Lotronex	Glaxo Wellcome	gastrointestinal	2/9/2000	11/28/2000	9 months	Ischemic colitis	$50.4 million
cisapride monohydrate	Propulsid	Janssen Pharmaceuticals	heartburn	7/29/1993	7/14/2000	7 years	Heart rhythm abnormalities	$2.5 billion
troglitazone	Rezulin	Warner-Lambert	type 2 diabetes	1/29/1997	3/21/2000	2.16 years	Liver failure	$2.1 billion worldwide
asternizole	Hismanal	Janssen Pharmaceuticals	antihistamine	12/19/1988	5/18/1999	6 months	Heart rhythm abnormalities	$23 million
grepafloxacin	Raxar	Glaxo Wellcome	antibiotic	11/6/1997	11/1/1999	2 years	Heart rhythm abnormalities	$23.5 million
mibefradil	Posicor	Roche Laboratories	blood pressure, cardiovascular	6/20/1997	6/8/1998	1 year	Drug interaction, lowered heart rate in women	not available
bromfenac	Duract	Wyeth-Ayerst	pain reliever	7/15/1997	6/22/1998	1 year	Liver failure	$89.7 million
terfenadine	Seldane, Seldane-D	Hoechst Marion Roussel	antihistamine	5/8/1985	2/27/1998	2.75 years	Heart rhythm abnormalities	not available
fenfluramine hydrochloride	Pondimin	Wyeth-Ayerst	appetite suppressant	6/14/1973	9/15/1997	23.25 years	Valvular heart disease	not available
dexfenfluramine hydrochloride	Redux	Wyeth-Ayerst	appetite suppressant	4/29/1996	9/15/1997	1.42 years	Valvular heart disease	$255.3 million

*Returned to U.S. market.

Sources:

Drug Recalls. *U S Food and Drug Administration Home Page.* Web. 16 Dec. 2011. www.fda.gov/Drugs/DrugSafety/DrugRecalls/default.htm.

Drugs@FDA. *U S Food and Drug Administration Home Page.* Web. 16 Dec. 2011. www.accessdata.fda.gov/scripts/cder/drugsatfda.

List of Withdrawn Drugs. *Wikipedia, the Free Encyclopedia.* Web. 16 Dec. 2011. http://en.wikipedia.org/wiki/List_of_withdrawn_drugs.

(Geodon, Pfizer), linked to heart toxicity, was not required to have a black box warning even though such a warning was required on six other drugs with prolonged QT intervals. Sidney Wolfe writes, "Although this is a dangerous inconsistency, it is somewhat predictable given the lack of clear FDA criteria for deciding on when a black box warning is necessary."[35]

In the PDR study, Lasser et al. found that between 1975 and 1999, 548 NCEs were approved, and 56 (10.2 percent) acquired a new black box warning or were withdrawn from the market.[18] The authors found, using a Kaplan-Meier survival analysis (see Table 13.1), that there was a 20 percent probability of a new drug acquiring black box warnings or being withdrawn from the market within 25 years and a 4 percent probability of a new drug being withdrawn from the market, half of which occurred during the first two years the drug was marketed. The authors also noted inconsistencies in the PDR safety warnings. For instance, four beta-blockers contained black box warnings about the dangers of abruptly discontinuing the drugs (which can exacerbate coronary artery disease), but three other beta-blockers had no such warning. They also found asynchronous dates on the warnings for drugs from the same class.

A relationship between inadequate warnings and liability should be clear. Since physicians rely on manufacturers' warnings, if a physician is sued for an ADR in her patient, and it is discovered that information related to precautions and warnings are deficient, the plaintiff/injured party and/or the physician may in turn file litigation against a manufacturer. Indeed, in 20 years of consulting work in litigation, this author has observed that an overwhelming number product liability claims against a pharmaceutical manufacturer are based on inadequate warnings, which are claimed to render the product defective. Since FDA regulations provide for manufacturers to strengthen their warning based on a reasonable association of risk, the manufacturer cannot (but frequently tries to) claim that the warnings were approved by the FDA and could not be changed without approval. The specific regulation is as follows:

21 USC 201.57 (e)

Warnings. Under this section of the section heading, the labeling shall describe serious adverse reactions and potential safety hazards, limitations in use imposed by them, and steps that should be taken if they occur. The labeling shall be revised to include a warning as soon as there is reasonable evidence of an association of a serious hazard with a drug; a causal relationship need not have been proved.

21 USC 314.70 (c) Supplements for changes (in labeling) that may be made before FDA approval "Special Supplement-Changes Being Effected."
....(2) changes labeling to accomplish any of the following:
(i) to add or strengthen a contraindication, warning, precaution, or adverse reaction:
(ii) to add or strengthen a statement about drug abuse, dependence, or overdosage; or
(iii) to add or strengthen an instruction about dosage and administration that is intended to increase the safe use of the product
(iv) to delete false, misleading, or unsupported indications for use or claims for effectiveness.

3. Quality control, safety, manufacturing

Robert Rhoades' book, *Risky Business: Managing The Quality of America's Medicines*, is a revealing look at the pharmaceutical industry.[36] Rhoades, a veteran of 25 years in the quality control industry, writes the book to those in the FDA-regulated quality control industry, offering an insider's view on the complexity and intricacy of the industry. The book describes how established quality systems in manufacturing and distribution are necessary to help protect the integrity of the product, the safety of the patient, the reputation of the company, and stockholders' investments. While most drug liability litigation flows out of inadequate warnings, sometimes ineffective manufacturing controls and procedures are to blame. This book is recommended to anyone working in the pharmaceutical industry, not just those involved in quality control.

D. Types of Drugs Most Frequently Involved in Litigation

Although almost any drug can cause an adverse reaction in a handful of individuals, a number of drugs can be singled out as causing approximately 90 percent of reported drug reactions: adrenal steroids, aminoglycosides, anticoagulants, antimicrobials, antineoplastics, aspirin, bronchodilators, digitalis, diuretics, insulin, and nonsteroidal anti-inflammatories (NSAIDs). These agents have commonly been cited for the past 20 years. With the exception of digitalis, the use of which is declining, the "usual suspects" continue to be drawn from the same drug classes. It should be noted that old drugs, which have undergone many upgrades and enhancements to their warnings, are usually not subject to product liability litigation. Litigation involving the older drugs is usually limited to medical and pharmacy malpractice.

Generally, the more learned about the drug, the more information is in the package insert, and the less the drug company/manufacturer faces liability for inadequate warnings. The new drugs are usually the subject of product liability suits.

The PIAA studies[11,12] found that the most frequent drug classes involved in errors and claims were antibiotics (failure to note documented allergy, most appropriate drug not used, drug inappropriate for medical condition); glucocorticoids (incorrect dosage, communication failure between physician and patient, failure to monitor for drug side effects); and narcotic and nonnarcotic analgesics or narcotic antagonists (drug inappropriate for medical condition, incorrect dosage, failure to monitor for drug side effects, drug dependence).[37] The following sections describe drugs of note—those that have been or are currently the subject of large or highly publicized lawsuits (See Table 13.4).

1. Vaccines

Because the government has an interest in preventing the spread of diseases, vaccines have followed a somewhat different historical path than that of other drugs. Most vaccines have been hailed as major advances in modern medicine. During the 1920s, several vaccines were introduced: diphtheria and tetanus toxoids, whole-cell pertussis, and bacille Calmette-Guérin (BCG) (to protect against tuberculosis). The chorioallantoic membrane used to culture viruses allowed a yellow fever vaccine to be developed by 1935. After World War II, many of today's modern vaccines emerged, including those for polio (inactive and oral), measles, mumps, and rubella. Despite the undeniable benefits of reduced pathogeneticity, vaccine regulation and litigation has a tumultuous history.

In the early 1960s, drug companies began to lobby for government indemnity for the vaccines they developed, tested, and produced.[17] Because so many people are vaccinated at one time, particularly school-age children, ADRs from a vaccine can carry considerable liability. As more diseases have become vaccine-preventable, more ADRs have been reported.[38] In 1974, impetus for indemnity increased when the courts upheld a jury verdict of $200,000 for a child who developed polio from the Sabin live-polio vaccine.[5]

After a suspected case of the 1918 Spanish flu virus (which, in a global pandemic during World War I, affected half the world's population and killed almost 25 million people in 18 months) was identified in 1976, Congress passed the National Swine Flu Immunization Program, releasing manufacturers from liability so a flu vaccine could be produced.[39] Forty million people in the United States were vaccinated against this flu in less than three months.[40] ADRs were reported shortly after the massive vaccination program began, and it was found that those who had received the vaccine had a tenfold increase of Guillain Barre Syndrome (GBS). The swine flu program is a milestone in vaccine litigation history because it was a precursor to federal involvement and to no-fault vaccine compensation programs.[17]

In response to continued concerns about vaccine safety, the National Childhood Vaccine Injury (NCVI) Act of 1986 established a no-fault compensation process for people injured by them.[41] The NCVI also mandated that the Institute of Medicine (IOM) review scientific evidence of vaccine-related ADRs in children. In 1996, the Department of Health and Human Services (HHS) made changes to the NCVI, which lessened its usefulness.[17] In response to the problems this generated, the Vaccine Injured Children's Compensation Act of 2001 was introduced in Congress.[42] This bill, however, also has its problems, and in April 2001, the bill was referred to the House subcommittee on health, where it remains.[43]

Vaccine liability issues were also covered in Section 304 of the Homeland Security Act (HSA) of 2002.[44] As amended in April 2003, Congress enacted liability protection for manufacturers of smallpox vaccines.[45] Vaccine liability can be handled in four different ways: the government can substitute itself as the defendant, it can decide nobody need be liable and provide no-fault compensation, it can indemnify manufacturers after they have been sued and lost, or it can alter the normal rules of litigation.[46] In the HSA, the government substitutes itself as the defendant if the HHS Secretary declares "an actual or potential bioterrorist incident or other actual or potential public health emergency makes advisable the administration of a covered countermeasure,"[46] such as a vaccine. Secretary Tommy Thompson issued the first such declaration on January 24, 2003.

The HSA states, however, that "covered countermeasures" apply only to smallpox vaccines at this time, and although HSA protects manufacturers and others against liability, it does not directly set forth compensation procedures for vaccine recipients. Under Part C of HSA, compensation for death benefits is capped at $262,100. If a case goes to court, the plaintiff must "prove culpability equal to or rising above the level of negligence."[46] Given its history, vaccine regulations and litigation will continue to evolve.

Although vaccines are relatively safe, they have caused problems in the past, and any vaccine can cause an ADR in a "predisposed individual."[17] As mentioned, the government has an interest in controlling disease outbreaks, so vaccines are routinely given to millions of people. With that many people receiving a vaccine, even a low incidence of ADRs can result in high rates of litigation; and because children receive a large number of vaccines (often several vaccines at once), jury awards can be high.

Table 13.4
Drugs and Claimed Injuries

Drug Name	Claimed Injury—Drug Defect	Drug Name	Claimed Injury—Drug Defect
Accutane	Depression/Suicide/IBD	Darvon/Darvocet	Fatal Heart Rhythm Abnormalities/Withdrwan)
Acetaminophen	Acute Liver Damage/Failure	Definity	Cardiopulmonary Reactions
Actos	Congestive Heart Failure (CHF)	Depakote	Congenital Malformations in Infants; Suicide
Advair	Severe Bronchospasms (bronchial sensitivity and inflammation)	Desmopressin	Hyponatremia-related Seizures and Death
Proton Pump Inhibitors (PPI)	Bone Fracture	Diethylstilbesterol	Clear Cell Adenocarcinoma 2nd & 3rd gen daughters
Aranesp	Blood Clots; Cardiac Arrest	Dexedrine	Heart Risk; Sudden Death
Arava	Liver Damage	Digitek Recall	Digitalas Toxicity / Manufacturing Defect
Aredia	Osteonecrosis of the Jaw (ONJ)	Dilantin	Purple Glove Syndrome; Fetal Dilantin Syndrome
Aricept	Deleterious Effects on Thinking Skills and Physical Activity	Ditropan	Hallucinations and Other Central Nervous System Risks
Avandia	Hepatitis or other Liver Injury; Cardiovascular Problems and CHF	Dostinex/Permax	Severe Heart Valve Problems
Avonex	Flu-like Symptoms and Injection-site Reactions	Duragesic Patches (Fentanyl)	Overdose Due to Manufacturing Defect / Rx Ignorance
Betaseron	Hepatotoxicity	Effexor	Suicide/Depression
Campath	Severe Idiopathic Thrombocytopenic Purpura (ITP)	Elidel	Cancer (Skin or Lymphoma)
		Epogen/Procrit	Intracranial Hemorrhage
Cardizem	Male Infertility	Evista	Increased Risk of Death Due to Stroke
CellCept	Fetal Defects; Miscarriage		
Chantix	Psychosis	Fen-Phen	Heart Valve Abnormalities/ PPH
Cipro	Tendon Ruptures and Irreversible Neurological Conditions	Fosamax	Dead Jaw or Osteonecrosis
		Gardasil and Cervarix	Guillain-Barre Syndrome; Blood Clots; Miscarriage
Cleocin	Clostridium Difficile Diarrhea; Pseudomembranous Colitis	Geodon	Hyperglycemia and Diabetes
		Gleevec	Congestive Heart Failure (CHF)
Heparin (chondroitin contamination)	Severe Hypotension and Serious Allergic-type Hypersensitivity	Hormone Replacement Therapy	Breast Cancer; Heart Conditions
		Ketek	Acute Liver Damage/Failure
Crestor	Kidney Damage; Rhabdomyolysis; Cardiomyopathy	Lamictal	Fetal Cleft Lip; Suicidal Thoughts
Cytotec	Torn Uterus	Levaquin	Tendinitis and Tendon Rupture

continued on next page…

Table 13.4 (continued)

Drug Name	Claimed Injury—Drug Defect	Drug Name	Claimed Injury—Drug Defect
Levodopa	Dyskinesia	Renu	Serious Eye Injuries
Lyrica	Intent to Mislead for Use in Fibromyalgia	Requip	Compulsive Behavior
Macugen	Anaphylaxis/Anaphylactoid Reactions	Risperdal	Leukopenia/Neutropenia and Agranulocytosis
Methadone	Overdose Dangers	Rituxan	Progressive Multifocal Leukoencephalopathy (PML)
Metoclopramide	Tardive Dyskinesia	Seroquel	Neuroleptic Malignant Syndrome (NMS); Tardive Dyskinesia
Monoamine Oxidase Inhibitors	Hypertensive Crisis; Hyperserotonemia; Intracerebral Hemorrhage	Simponi	Fungal Infections; Lymphoma
Myfortic	Miscarriage; Congenital Anomalies	Singulair	Neuropsychiatric Events
Ortho Evra	Blood Clots, Stroke, Heart Attack	SSRIs	SSRI Discontinuation Syndrome
Paxil	Cardiovascular Malformations; Suicidal Thoughts	Thiazolidinedione	Bone Fracture
		Terbutaline	Birth Defects
Permax	Heart Valve Disease; Falling Asleep with Little Warning	Thimerosal	Brain Development Disorders
Phenylpropanolamine	Hemorrhagic Stroke/ Withdrawn	Trasylol	Cardiovascular and Kidney Toxicity
Pristiq	Discontinuation Syndrome	Tussionex	Impair Thinking or Reactions/ abuse
Procrit	Heart Attack; High Blood Pressure	Viagra, Cialis, Levitra	Blindness/Hypotension
Propylthiouracil	Fetal Abnormalities; Hepatotoxicity	Vioxx	Serious Heart Problems/ Thrombolytic / Withdrawn
Fluoroquinolone	Tendon Injuries	Yaz	Hyperkalemia
Razadyne/Reminyl	Bradycardia; Syncope	Zelnorm	Heart Complications
Reglan	Tardive dyskinesia	Zetia	Drug Does Not Work
Regranex	Cancer	Zicam	Loss of Sense of Smell
Remicade	Lymphoma and Other Cancers	Zocor	Drug interaction— rhabdomylolysis
		Zyprexa	Diabetes

Source: Pharmaceutical Injury Attorneys. Personal Injury, 2011. Web. Access date 14 Oct., 2011. www.personalinjury.com/pharmaceutical_injury_lawyers.html.

The production of vaccines has marched hand-in-hand with production mistakes, medication errors, and ADRs. For example, in October 1954, the National Foundation for Infantile Paralysis, which had paid for the development of the Salk vaccine to prevent polio, announced it was ordering enough of the drug to vaccinate 9 million children—without waiting for the results of a field trial.[47] This became the famous "Cutter Incident," when the doctor who conducted the field trials stated the vaccine was 60 to 90 percent effective, assuming that it was ineffective for the children in the trial who developed polio. Newspapers, parades, air raid sirens, and erroneous statements all helped create the euphoria over the treatment. After vaccine shortages, conspiracy charges, and somewhat unregulated manufacturing to increase production, postinnoculation polio was being seen in children inoculated by the vaccine from the Cutter Laboratories in Berkeley, California, which turned out to have live polio virus in some of its batches.

In 1976, another vaccine case illustrated how dangerous a mistake involving vaccines can be. Between October 1, 1976, and December 14, 1976, more than 40 million people were vaccinated against swine flu (a virus similar to the 1918 Spanish flu virus that killed so many during World War I). The feared epidemic never manifested, but there was a tenfold increase in GBS (in which the body's immune system attacks its peripheral nerves), which thousands of people contracted.

Numerous other vaccines have been linked to a variety of autoimmune disorders, such as encephalitis, lupus-like reactions, arthritis syndromes, arthropathies, and transverse myelitis.[17] Other vaccines have been linked to ADRs:

- Rotavirus—the most common cause of severe diarrhea in infants, with approximately 125 million cases worldwide per year and 600,000 deaths—vaccines have been linked with intussusception (a problem with the intestine in which one portion of the bowel slides into the next) at a rate of between 1 in 5,000 and 1 in 11,000 infants.[48] The only rotavirus vaccine approved in the United States, RotaShield (Wyeth-Ayerst), was withdrawn from market on October 22, 1999, about one year after licensure.
- The diphtheria, pertussis, and tetanus (DPT) vaccine, which has prevented more than 95 percent morbidity from these diseases, has been linked with convulsions, encephalitis, and sudden infant death syndrome.[49]
- The hepatitis B vaccine has been linked to anaphylaxis.
- The measles vaccine has been linked to thrombocytopenia and anaphylaxis.
- Tetanus toxoid-containing vaccines to GBS, brachial neuritis, and anaphylaxis.

What is, perhaps, most disturbing is the assertion by Coulter and Fisher in 1985 that the ADRs from DPT should not have happened.[50] They document that Japan switched to an acellular form of the DPT virus in 1981, which was just as effective in preventing the diseases but had fewer ADRs. Shoemaker reports that "In Japan, the Ministry of Health, instead of trying to cover up problems with the vaccines, chose to find a solution."[17] According to Shoemaker, it took almost 20 years for the United States to stop using the whole-cell version of the vaccine, and manufacturers are still distributing the whole-cell version in third world countries "undoubtedly because it is cheaper to make."[17]

Vaccines are currently in development for Cholera, ETEC, Rotavirus, Shigellosis, Typhoid Fever, Influenza virus, Parainfluenza virus type 3 (PIV-3), Respiratory Syncytial Virus (RSV), Severe acute respiratory syndrome (SARS), Streptococcus pneumonia (pneumococcal disease), Tuberculosis, Anthrax, *Neisseria meningitides (Groups A, C, Y, W135), Neisseria meningitides (Group B),* Plague, Group A *Streptococcus,* Group B *Streptococcus, Chlamydia trachomatis,* Herpes simplex type 2 (HSV-2), HIV / AIDS, Dengue Fever, Japanese Encephalitis, West Nile virus, Hookworm Disease, Leishmaniasis, Malaria, Schistosomiasis, *Helicobacter pylori,* hepatitis B, hepatitis C, hepatitis E, Human papillomavirus, Epstein-Barr Virus, and Poliovirus.[51]

2. Fen-Phen and other diet drugs

The use of drugs to treat obesity has had limited success because of the danger of unintended side effects. Some of these side effects are a nuisance, but some can be life threatening. Compounding the risk of diet drugs is taking them in doses exceeding the recommended amount or in an "off-label" manner. Using larger doses, extending the duration of treatment, or combining two or more drugs to enhance the same effect are examples of this practice. The Fen-Phen diet was an example of combining two drugs for assistance in achieving weight loss. Each had been tested and approved as safe and effective for short-term use in morbidly obese subjects. The combined therapy proved to be so well received that millions of prescriptions were written for two drugs that were not approved or tested for safety in combined use. In addition, the duration of therapy was arbitrarily extended from the approved six to eight weeks (short term), to more than one year. The result was that a population experiment in which a potentially deadly adverse effect, primary pulmonary hypertension (PPH), was discovered after millions of doses had been prescribed and administered.

PPH was a problem in Europe in the 1960s for an appetite suppressant, Aminorex. There is no method for screening potential dexfenfluramine patients for susceptibility to PPH: it is a silent killer, with no early symptoms, affects predominately women in their early thirties and forties, and there is no cure. The risk of PPH among anorexic agents is significantly elevated, but the absolute incidence is still small: 28 cases per 1 million person-years of exposure, comparable to the fatality risk from penicillin-caused anaphylaxis. The risk of death from untreated obesity is perhaps 20 times higher than the estimated mortality from PPH among patients given appetite-suppressant drugs.[52]

The Chairman of the FDA's Advisory Committee commented on the risk of death from developing PPH. "We have had what I think appears to be a reasonable estimate of the risk of deaths from pulmonary hypertension. We need to understand clearly that if 1 million patients take this drug, at least a couple dozen of them will die annually as a result of this complication. That seems the best estimate. This is something that has to be weighed seriously." The appearance of heart valvulopathies in otherwise asymptomatic people in their thirties or forties was unexpected and caught patients and practitioners by surprise. Both fenfluramine and phentermine cause an increase in the amount of serotonin available in the body, which can cause the cardiac valvulopathies.[52]

On September 15, 1997, the FDA asked the manufacturers of dexfenfluramine (Redux, manufactured for Interneuron Pharmaceuticals by Wyeth Ayerst) and fenfluramine (Pondimin, Wyeth Ayerst) to voluntarily withdraw both treatments from the market because of findings that indicate approximately 30 percent of patients taking the combined drugs had abnormal echocardiograms, even if they had no symptoms.[52] Both companies agreed. The FDA is not requesting the withdrawal of phentermine, the third widely used medication for obesity.

Additional ADRs linked to diet pills include psychosis[53]; myocardial ischemia[54]; drug interactions, such as the interaction of fenfluramine with imipramine, fenfluramine with amitriptyline or desipramine, or the toxic reaction between fluoxetine and phentermine; and the release of serotonin while inhibiting its reuptake,[55] contributing to hyperserotonin reactions. When the next craze takes hold of patients, hopefully physicians and pharmacists will take a more vocal position and recommend restraint, until some proof of efficacy and lack of toxicity is shown for new faddish off-label combinations. Fen-Phen was described as one of the worst and most extensive cases of drug product liability in modern day drug history. Full discussions of the Fen-Phen story may be found in the first and second editions of this book.

3. Nonsteroidal Anti-inflammatories (NSAIDs)

The efficacy of NSAIDs in the treatment of a wide variety of disorders is well-established. An estimated 1.2 percent of the U.S. population takes NSAIDs regularly, and more people take them intermittently. NSAIDs have also been involved in the prescription-to-OTC shift (Motrin to Advil; Naprosyn to Aleve) so more—and more potent—NSAIDs are being used. The NSAIDs, according to the FDA, account for the largest number of ADR reports.

NSAIDs have been increasingly incriminated in chronic peptic ulcerations. Patients on short- and long-term therapy should be instructed in the signs of GI bleeding and ulcer perforation, and periodic monitoring of renal function is advisable. Four NSAIDs that have caused concern recently include rofecoxib, valdecoxib, benoxaprofen and ketorolac. Two are discussed here: rofecoxib and vadecoxib.

Rofecoxib, a COX-2 Specific inhibitor NSAID, is one of the drugs most recently withdrawn from market (Table 13.3). Rofecoxib (Vioxx, Merck & Co.) was voluntarily withdrawn from the U.S. and worldwide markets on September 30, 2004, because of an increased risk of heart attacks and strokes confirmed during investigations to determine if Rofecoxib was effective in preventing the recurrence of colon polyps. Thousands of lawsuits against the manufacturer were filed; a multidistrict litigation was established to manage the massive litigation. Four years later, a global settlement was entered in the In RE Vioxx litigation involving 50,000 plaintiffs. The settlement was $4.85 billion:

(574 F.Supp.2d 606 (2008)
In re: VIOXX PRODUCTS LIABILITY LITIGATION.
This Document Relates to: All Cases.
MDL No. 1657.
United States District Court, E.D. Louisiana.
August 27, 2008.)

In late 2011, Merck has agreed to pay $950 million to settle federal criminal charges and civil claims for off-label promotion of pain drug Vioxx, which was removed from the U.S. market in 2004. The settlement ends a seven-year Justice Department investigation. The company will enter into a corporate integrity agreement with the HHS Office of Inspector General. Among other mandates, the agreement requires company executives to complete annual compliance certifications and forces Merck to post information about physician payments on its website. (FDA News Drug Daily Bulletin, Vol. 8, No. 231, Nov. 28, 2011.)

A post-withdrawal Advisory Committee questioned the need to withdraw the drug, and the Company has released statements suggesting that Vioxx may be re-introduced to the market. This COX-2 selective NSAID has been on the market for more than five years for treating osteoarthritis, rheumatoid arthritis, acute pain, and menstrual symptoms. On approval, it had gone through an expedited (six months) "priority review" because the drug "potentially provided a significant therapeutic advantage over existing approved drugs due to fewer gastrointestinal side effects, including bleeding," according to the FDA.

The original safety database on Vioxx included approximately 5,000 patients on rofecoxib and did not show an increased risk of heart attack or stroke. A June 2000 study, VIGOR (Vioxx GI Outcomes Research), was primarily designed to look at the effects of rofecoxib on ADRs such as stomach ulcers and bleeding. The study showed that patients taking rofecoxib displayed fewer of the side effects than patients taking naproxen. The study also showed a greater number of heart attacks in patients taking rofecoxib. The FDA response to the VIGOR study was to include new safety information on the Vioxx label in April 2002. Merck then began to conduct longer-term trials to obtain more data on the risk for heart attack and stroke with chronic use of Vioxx. Additional information on Vioxx is available at www.fda.gov/cder/drug/infopage/vioxx.

Vadecoxib (Bextra, Pfizer), a second COX-2 specific inhibitor NSAID, was taken off the market a few months after Vioxx. In addition to a higher risk of serious skin toxicity, patients given Vioxx after coronary bypass surgery had a higher rate of myocardial infarctions.

In the aftermath of the Vioxx and Bextra withdrawals, the FDA has studied the cardiovascular and gastrointestinal risks in great detail. A recent request for strengthening the warnings and precautions on all NSAID products was released, and reads as follows:

MedWatch—The FDA Safety Information and Adverse Event Reporting Program

FDA has requested that sponsors of all non-steroidal anti-inflammatory drugs (NSAID) make labeling changes to their products. FDA recommended proposed labeling for both the prescription and over-the-counter (OTC) NSAIDs and a medication guide for the entire class of prescription products. All sponsors of marketed prescription NSAIDs, including Celebrex (celecoxib), a COX-2 selective NSAID, have been asked to revise the labeling (package insert) for their products to include a boxed warning, highlighting the potential for increased risk of cardiovascular (CV) events and the well described, serious, potential life-threatening gastrointestinal (GI) bleeding associated with their use. FDA regulation 21CFR 208 requires a Medication Guide to be provided with each prescription that is dispensed for products that FDA determines pose a serious and significant public health concern.

Read the complete MedWatch 2005 safety summary, including a link to the updated Drug Information Page and Medication Guide, at: www.fda.gov/medwatch/SAFETY/2005/safety05.htm#NSAID.

4. Noteworthy class actions: Rezulin, Baycol

Rezulin (troglitazone, Warner Lambert, now Pfizer) was approved in January 1997 to treat adult-onset diabetes and was hailed as a drug to treat patients who have failed other therapies (untreated diabetes can cause heart and kidney failure, blindness, and other problems). It was a "fast track" drug with an approval process that took only six months, despite objections from several FDA scientists and the death from liver failure of one of the study participants. The FDA received reports of liver failure and in December 1997 it was banned in Great Britain. The FDA, at that time, however, only ordered stronger liver toxicity warnings on the drug label—the warning was strengthened four times between 1997 and June 1999—even though several patients who had monthly liver tests still experienced sudden liver failure and died.[56] In March 1999, an FDA epidemiologist warned that "Rezulin was among the most dangerous drugs on the American market," and that "patient monitoring would not protect them from liver failure."[56] An advisory committee recommended the drug be made available only to patients whose diabetes was not well-controlled by other drugs. In March 2000, an FDA official Robert Misbin wrote Congress, "I am writing to enlist your aid in convincing my superiors at FDA that Rezulin should be removed from the market because of its unacceptably high risk of causing liver failure."[57]

Even the efficacy of troglitazone was suspect. After the drug was removed from the market, one FDA official wrote that it had been approved and kept on the market so long because it was "shown to reduce or delay long-term serious effects of diabetes, including death." But when asked about the basis of that claim, an FDA spokesperson said that "those findings were not intended as definitive scientific observations."[56] With the help (and possible conflicts of interest) of FDA officials and the physicians carrying out an NIH study,[58] the drug manufacturer was able to keep the FDA from banning troglitazone for 27 months.[59] The drug was eventually withdrawn from the market in the United States on March 21, 2000, but keeping the drug on the market as long as possible was profitable. At its peak sales in January 1999, 488,000 prescriptions were filled, and during its three years on the U.S. market, troglitazone generated $2.1 billion for Warner Lambert.

The withdrawal of troglitazone came only after a whistleblower shared his findings and internal e-mail with a *Los Angeles Times* reporter. A series of articles by David Willman, raised questions about irregularities and conflicts of interest in the study and approval of the drug.[23,56,58] Litigation over troglitazone is still ongoing. In 2003, an appeals court overturned a lower court, which had denied class action status to Rezulin cases. In January 2004, Pfizer set aside $975 million to cover 35,000 settled or withdrawn injury claims. In March 2004, a federal grand jury requested testimony from former Warner-Lambert employees. In April 2004, a jury awarded $2 million in compensatory damages to a woman. In June 2004, a Los Angeles jury found that facts about the drug did not support responsibility for the death of two patients and the injury of another. In July 2004, an Illinois class action lawsuit was settled for $60 million, and an $11.55 million award was upheld for a man who died one month after starting the drug.[60]

5. Drug-induced hepatotoxicity

Of course, Rezulin is not the only drug implicated in liver toxicity. In fact, the FDA posted a notice on its website (www.fda.gov) describing a special interest and monitoring of drug-induced hepatotoxicity:

Drug-Induced Liver Toxicity

Momentum and interest continue to grow concerning the rising incidence of liver toxicity, uncommon but serious, caused by prescription drugs, over-the-counter medications, or dietary supplements that are often combined with special diets and alcohol consumption, in addition to environmental chemicals. The liver is a most marvelous organ that usually protects us against injury from foreign substances, and is very robust in its capacity to withstand damage and heal itself. In a few people, the ability to resist and heal is not adequate, or the injury is so great that serious liver damage results, with progression to acute failure, and to death or transplantation. *Drug-induced liver injury has become the most frequent cause of acute liver failure in the United States, exceeding all other causes combined. Drug-induced liver injury also remains the major single reason for regulatory actions concerning drugs, including failure to approve, withdrawal from the market, restrictions on use, and warnings to physicians.* (emphasis added).

Per the emphasized text in the quote above, drug-induced hepatotoxicity is the leading cause of acute liver failure and the number one reason for regulatory actions against drugs in the United States.

Baycol (cerivastatin, sold as Lipobay in Europe, Bayer) is a statin, a class of cholesterol-lowering drugs. Statins are the most prescribed drugs in the United States, with more than 12 million people taking them. More than 700,000 people in the United States took cerivastatin.[61] It received

marketing approval on June 26, 1997, and was voluntarily removed from the market on August 8, 2001, because of its link to 100 deaths and several injuries from potentially the muscle disease rhabdomyolysis. The other statins—lovastatin (Mevacor, Merck); pravastatin (Pravachol, Bristol-Myers Squibb); simvastatin (Zocor, Merck); fluvastatin (Lescol, Novartis); atorvastatin (Lipitor, Parke-Davis); rosuvastatin (Crestor, Astra-Zeneca); and lovastatin + niacin (Advicor, Kos Pharmaceutical)—that can also cause rhabdomyolysis remain on the market. Although scientists agree that the other statins "seem to have essentially identical safety profiles and benefit–risk ratios,"[62] the FDA said the ADRs associated with Baycol "have been reported significantly more frequently than for other approved statins."[61]

When initially recommending cerivastatin for approval, after testing in 3,343 patients from the United States, Japan, and China, an FDA official cited rhabdomyolysis as one of four potentially serious ADRs. After approval, a warning was added in 1999, and the labeling was changed again in June 2001. Just two months later, Baycol was withdrawn from the market. In 2003, the first Baycol lawsuit went on trial in Texas and involved a victim who did not die or require kidney transplant; the verdict favored Bayer.[63] The primary legal complaint in subsequent lawsuits is that the manufacturer failed to adequately warn of the known dangers and complications of the drug. "In clinical trials, there is a "filtering" of adverse events in drug-treated groups in that if the principal investigator expresses the opinion that the adverse event was not related to the drug, one researcher says, "the adverse event is excluded from analysis."[62] Kauffman, discussing Lipitor, suggests that the cost-benefit analysis of statins is another possible area of litigation, saying, "The absolute risk reduction is…one in 667 per year. The cost of a month's supply of Lipitor at 40 mg/day is $1,500/year, reflecting a cost of $1 million to prevent one death among 667 people taking the drug for one year."[64]

In March 2004, Bayer settled with its insurance carriers, eliminating the insurers' rights of litigation and settlement and setting the limits of liability at $1.2 billion. In July 2004, the company settled 2,771 cases for $1.06 billion. In September 2004, Bayer settled another 2,861 product liability cases for $1.09 billion. There are still 7,577 such suits pending.[3] For more discussion of drug-induced liver disease, see Chapter 24, *Drug-Induced Liver Disease.*

13.5 Market Entry and Subsequent Withdrawal

In 1997, 39 new drugs were approved by the FDA. By 2004, five of them have been taken off the market, and an additional two have new boxed warnings. Thus, seven drugs approved that year (18 percent) have already been withdrawn or had a black box warning four years after approval. According to one study, 20 percent of drugs will be withdrawn or have a black box warning within 25 years of coming on the market.[18]

In ten years (1988–1998) the number of drugs approved first-in-the-world by the FDA jumped from 4 to 66 percent. The FDA approved 80 percent of the new drug applications at the end of the 1990s but only 60 percent at the beginning of the decade. Furthermore, it has recently been slow in removing drugs that have already been withdrawn in Europe. There are increasing reports of drug approvals despite counter recommendations from FDA scientists and drug advisory committees. Conflict of interest accusations have recently been leveled against researchers and advisory committee members responsible for deciding on a drug's safety and approval. Several medical researchers have concluded that new drugs should only be given with extreme caution. It is not surprising that some drugs are withdrawn due to safety reasons. Due to limited sample size, clinical trials usually uncover only the more frequent ADR's. For example, a trial with a sample size of 10,000 patients (no adverse reactions) will only yield a 95 percent confidence interval that an ADR with a frequency of 1 in 10,000 will not occur. In order to increase the confidence interval for detecting an ADR of the same frequency (1 in 10,000) to 99 percent, a sample size of 46,000 is needed.[65] These numbers lie in stark contrast to a 2005 FDA standard which recommends that the clinical trial of a drug used to treat a non-life-threatening condition expose 1,500 subjects to the investigational product (with 300 to 600 exposed for 6 months, and 100 exposed for 1 year).[66]

The FDA argues that many good therapies are lost because physicians fail to read and heed the drug warnings it issues. There are many reasons that drugs might be approved and later withdrawn, and there are many people and groups pointing fingers at others. A new Drug Safety Board has been appointed, constituted by members primarily from the Agency; and Congress has substantially increased the funding for FDA Safety monitoring.

Many drugs are simply discontinued for reasons that may not have to do with safety. OTC drugs and drug products used as a compound in other drugs may also be withdrawn, leading to a discrepancy in the number of withdrawn drugs reported. Table 13.3 lists prescription drugs withdrawn from the market for safety reasons between 1997 and 2011.

13.6 Product Liability Case Report: Fluoroquinolone Tendonopathy

Fluoroquinolones represent a class of antibiotics that have widespread use in the community for a variety of common infections. Early on in their clinical use, a warning was added contraindicating their use in children due to animal toxicology findings. As use increased, many reports of tendon ruptures were received by various manufacturers and the FDA. The following discussion reports a case of serious tendonopathy and rupture in a woman who consumed fluoroquinolone over an extended period of time (pseudonyms used for persons and institutions). The case demonstrates the effect of black box warnings.

Facts of the case

Diann Queen was first prescribed Cipro (Ciprofloxacin) in 2004 (3 days) following her passing a kidney stone. She developed a chronic urinary tract disorder, and subsequently was prescribed Cipro in March 2005 (100 tablets). December 2005, according to the Complaint, July 17, 2006, new prescription #6787 (100 tablets—Dr. Poland), refills to #6787 on November 17, 2006 (100 tablets—Dr. Poland), February 2007 (100 tablets—Dr. Poland), May 31, 2007 (100 tablets—Dr. Poland), September 4, 2007 (100 tablets—Dr. Poland). A new prescription (# 7821) for 100 Cipro tablets was prescribed and filled on February 13, 2008, and refilled on June 9, 2008.

In March 2007, Diann Queen suffered from right foot and ankle pain. She saw Dr. R. Bone, an orthopedic surgeon. In December 2007, Dr. Bone operated on Diann's right Achilles tendon for chronic calcific insertion Achilles tendonitis. In June 2008, Diann suffered a fracture and a ligament tear of her right ankle on the inside of her foot and a second surgery had to be performed. She continues to have limited mobility due to her orthopedic injuries in both lower extremities. She was treated intermittently with analgesics (opiates and NSAIDS) and prednisone (Delta) and methylprednisolone (Medrol).

Relevant facts include the following:

Ms. Queen has been an LPN for about 27 years at Southern Medical Center . She has a long history of kidney stones associated with bladder spasm and infection. She has testified that she first received IV Cipro in the 1970s from Dr. Murphy. Ms. Queen recalls that she started to use PO Cipro in 1998 or 1999 for treatment of bladder infections. She has had recurrent kidney stones since around 1970.

She did not take PO Cipro for bladder infection until 1998 or 1999 and took her last dose in May 2008. The Cipro prescription she received was for 500 mg, BID for 7 to 14 days, PRN. Usually she would tell Dr. Poland she was having problems, but she felt she was free to start taking Cipro PRN, as needed, on her own. If after 14 days of Cipro the bladder infection persisted she would take off a few days and then resume Cipro. It was usually about a week between courses.

Ms. Queen would often speak to the physicians when she had bladder infection symptoms rather than schedule an office visit. Did she ever request Cipro for an infection? "Like my physician, Dr. Poland, it could be a desk conference right there in the nurse's station. And he would just say, 'Do you have any more Cipro?' Or, 'Get back on your antibiotics since it works.' And we would just renew the prescription." Ms. Queen denies ever receiving any literature about Cipro from her physicians or pharmacists. She was not aware of any association between her Achilles problems until her mother saw an ad on television or the Internet offering legal advice for patients who had received Cipro and developed a tendonopathy. Her mother told her not to take another Cipro tablet. This was after the first tendon surgery in March or April 2008.

Ms. Queen saw orthopedic surgeon Dr. Bone who performed some tests in his office in March 2008. She did not mention her use of Cipro to Dr. Bone and he did not inquire. When orthopedic surgeon Dr. Ankle saw Ms. Queen in December 2007, he told her the MRI indicated a need for surgery. The Achilles tendon was disintegrated. Dr. Poland did not discuss her use of Cipro and did not discuss possible causes. Dr. Ankle put her in a walking boot until surgery. Surgery was performed on December 14, 2007. Post Op she was in a cast until March 2008 and then was placed in a walking boot. She went back to work in May 2008 but then suffered an ankle fracture on June 11, 2008. Dr. Bone reduced a fibula fracture on June 13, 2008.

Ms. Queen first began to have pain and swelling in her left ankle in February 2009. After this new problem she asked Dr. Poland and Dr. Bone if Cipro could have been the cause. Dr. Poland said he could not say yes or no but both doctors told her to stop taking Cipro. Ms. Queen has been scanned for osteoporosis but she has never been given that diagnosis.

The hospital pharmacy did not provide her with product information because she was a hospital employee. If it was a non-employee patient they probably would have. Ms. Queen was given corticosteroid for her foot swelling and foot pain: Medrol dosepaks in 2001, 2002, 2004, two in 2008, and 2009. Ms. Queen also received Prednisone in April 2007 for her foot and ankle pain. Did she discuss the risks of steroid therapy with Dr. Poland? "I take it on faith that he is giving me what I need." "The Cipro gave me the relief. That's why I have never had any question about it doing anything else to me." Ms. Queen states that she does not discuss risk/benefit with her doctors for Cipro or other medications. "These are my friends. I take it on faith they are giving me what I need."

From 2003 onward all of her Cipro prescriptions were for #100 tablets. Ms. Queen thinks that it was probably the cheapest way for the hospital pharmacy to dispense the drug to her. If Ms. Queen was at work she might consult the doctor about starting on Cipro but if it was the weekend she would start it on her own. Ms. Queen has not consulted the PDR about Cipro since she started taking it. She knows that Cipro is in the class of fluoroquinolones and denies taking any other drug in this class. Ms. Queen states that she had not done any investigation of her own as to any association between Cipro and her tendon problems because she did not relate the two together. The only hospital she ever used for her Cipro Rx was the hospital pharmacy.

Ms. Queen recalls that her first tendon problem was pain and swelling in her right ankle in January 2007 which worsened over time. She was taking Cipro at the time these symptoms began. When she went to see Dr. Poland she did not mention her Cipro use neither to him nor to any of her other doctors. On April 17, Dr. Bone examined the patient and did tests. He recorded: Left (sic) Achilles tendonitis. Surgery on the R Achilles tendon occurred in December 2007. Ms. Queen had R Achilles tendon surgery on December 14, 2007 performed by Dr. Lillich. She was discharged and returned to work in May 2008 and worked for about two weeks before she broke her left leg (ankle) and had additional surgery in June 2008. Dr. Jointfix was the orthopedic surgeon who treated her broken fibula. Dr. Ankle did all of the Achilles tendon procedures. She currently takes Prilosec and Urocet for her kidney stone problem. She had L Achilles tendon surgery on June 2, 2010 by Dr. Ankle. She is currently using a walking boot to ambulate.

Dr. Poland is Ms. King's primary care physician. She usually sees him for urinary tract infections associated with stones and for the flu. Dr. Poland is familiar with Cipro and it worked in relieving Ms. Queen's bladder symptoms. "It worked well and it was cheap." Cipro was indicated for treatment of UTI. Dr. Poland denies being aware of case reports associating Cipro with tendonopathy prior to the Dear Doctor letter and label change (Black Box—October 22, 2008). Dr. Poland reads selected part of the package insert but does not read all of it. Dr. Poland does not remember if he read the entire warnings section in the PDR for Cipro. "I don't read all the drugs' warning. I mean, there's no way I can read them all." The first thing that came to his mind about Cipro warnings was pseudomembranous colitis, not tendon rupture. Dr. Poland concedes that since the label change and Dear Doctor letter, he is now aware that Cipro and fluoroquinolones are more frequently associated with tendon rupture. He still prescribes Cipro and takes its risk/benefit ratio into account.

Dr. Poland also prescribed steroids (Medrol) to Ms. Queen and also has given her IM steroid injections for UTI and bronchitis. He has recently learned that steroids also have a risk of tendon rupture. Dr. Poland does not treat Achilles tendon patients. He refers them to an orthopedic surgeon. Dr. Poland's last Cipro Rx was given on February 13, 2008, #100 with 2 refills. First Cipro Rx was on March 14, 2005 #100 with 3 refills. Reason he wrote the Rx? A: Because she asked for it. "You know, she works in the hospital. She was a nurse here. So, you know, sometimes she would approach me saying that she would have a urinary tract infection or she was burning or she had symptoms, and if she could have a prescription for antibiotics. And you know, I guess I could have said, you know, 'You need to come to the office and see me before I prescribe anything,' but, you know, I've been doing it for a lot of patients, and they just grab me in the hallway. You know, 'Can I have penicillin for my tooth?' You know, 'Can I have some Motrin for my back?' You know, 'Can I have a mammogram?' So I would write a prescription." Dr. Poland does not recall advising Ms. Queen of any risks in taking Cipro.

In Dr. Poland's clinic records there is no mention of Cipro. "If I knew that she had problems with the tendons, and with all those new warnings about Cipro quinolone, I wouldn't prescribe her Cipro no more. The label change and Dear Doctor letter of October 22, 2008 changed emphasis on the risk of tendon rupture while using Cipro. This was new and significant. When Dr. Poland wrote Ms. Queen's Cipro Rx he was unaware of the depth and scope of this risk."

Dr. Ankle specializes in surgery of the foot and ankle. He last saw his patient, Ms. Queen, on September 7, 2010. He first saw this patient on referral by Dr. Bone (Ortho). A tendon transplant was performed on December 14, 2007. Diagnosis? "It was chronic calcific insertional Achilles tendonitis." Both pre and post Op, Dr. Bone states that there are multiple possibilities for the cause of this condition.

Cipro and generic ciprofloxacin warnings

The FDA announced on July 28, 2008, that a new Black Box warning must be added to fluoroquinolones (the Class of Cipro) labels to emphasize the increased risk they pose for developing tendinitis and tendon ruptures.

> WARNING: Fluoroquinolones, including CIPRO, are associated with an increased risk of tendinitis and tendon rupture in all ages. This risk is further increased in older patients usually over 60 years of age, in patients taking corticosteroid drugs, and in patients with kidney, heart or lung transplants.

Despite a prior warning about tendon risk (appended to this report), in effect since 1996, the FDA felt that the prior warning was ineffective, based on the continuing large number of tendon damage reports received. A medication guide was developed to further help the patients recognize the symptoms and use the drug more safely.[I]

Black Box warnings will raise the level of consciousness over the risk. Doctors will need to caution patients to be aware of and report any arthritic or tendon pains, as these may be premonitory of tendonopathies.[II]

In addition to hundreds of case reports received by the FDA and reported in the scientific literature, pharmacoepidemiology studies have reported an increased (and growing) risk since the mid- to late 1990s. These reports and studies are presented in the "Bases for Opinions" section of this report.

Of further note, Public Citizen, in 2006, petitioned the FDA to require a Black Box warning related to tendon rupture, based on several hundred reports that the agency had received. Of note, the Attorney General of Illinois petitioned the FDA for a Black Box warning in 2005 (referenced below).

FDA Should Warn of Tendon Ruptures Linked to Cipro, Levaquin, Other Antibiotics in Same Class

Public Citizen and Illinois Attorney General Petition FDA to Place "Black Box" Warning on Fluoroquinolones

WASHINGTON—August 29—The U.S. Food and Drug Administration (FDA) should strongly warn the public about the risk of tendon rupture associated with Cipro and other fluoroquinolone antibiotics, Public Citizen said today in a petition to the agency. The FDA should do this by requiring a "black box" warning on the drugs' packaging and requiring pharmacists to give patients FDA-approved medication guides that also carry the warning, the group said.

Public Citizen joined with Illinois Attorney General Lisa Madigan's office, which also sent the FDA an addendum to its earlier petition urging the agency to act. Both Public Citizen's petition and the Illinois Attorney General's office letter to the FDA are available at www.WorstPills.org.

"The numbers are startling. Tendon ruptures associated with these drugs continue to occur at a disturbing rate but could be prevented if doctors and patients were more aware of early warning signals, such as the onset of tendon pain, and switched to other antibiotics," said Dr. Sidney Wolfe, director of Public Citizen's Health Research Group. "The FDA must act and require black box warnings and patient information guides."

Public Citizen's review of the FDA's adverse event database shows 262 reported cases of tendon ruptures, 258 cases of tendonitis and 274 cases of

other tendon disorders between November 1997 and December 31, 2005, associated with the fluoroquinolone antibiotics, with 175 of those occurring since the beginning of 2003. Sixty-one percent of the ruptures were associated with Levaquin, which has accounted for 45 percent of all fluoroquinolone prescriptions in the past four years, while 23 percent of the ruptures were associated with Cipro.

The tendon that most frequently ruptures is the Achilles tendon, which causes sudden and severe pain, swelling and bruising, and difficulty walking. Other tendon ruptures have occurred in the rotator cuff (the shoulder), the biceps, the hand and the thumb. One theory is that fluoroquinolones are toxic to tendon fibers and may decrease blood supply in tendons that already have a limited blood supply.

These antibiotics, which are widely prescribed for gastrointestinal, respiratory and genito-urinary tract infections, include Cipro (Ciprofloxacin, made by Bayer), Penetrex (Enoxacin, made by Aventis), Tequin (Gatifloxacin, made by Bristol-Myers Squibb), Levaquin (Levofloxacin, made by Ortho-McNeil), Maxaquin (Lomefloxacin, made by Unimed), Avelox (Moxifloxacin, made by Bayer), Noroxin (Norfloxacin, made by Merck) and Floxin (Ofloxacin, made by Daiichi-Sankyo).

The Public Citizen's petition follows a 1996 petition the nonprofit group filed seeking a warning on the label of fluoroquinolones. The FDA that year granted the petition, but the warning is buried in the list of possible adverse reactions and so has been inadequate. In April 2005, the Illinois Attorney General's office petitioned the FDA to place a black box warning on the drugs, but the FDA has never responded substantively to the petition. A black box warning is in bold type and surrounded by a black box to make it stand out.

"Consumers and physicians have a right to know the adverse effects associated with prescription medicines," Illinois Attorney General Lisa Madigan said. "We join with Public Citizen in urging the FDA to take prompt action on these petitions."

The prior warning, in effect since 1996, (referenced above) is as follows:

TENDON EFFECTS: Ruptures of the shoulder, hand, Achilles tendon or other tendons that required surgical repair or resulted in prolonged disability have been reported in patients receiving quinolones, including ciprofloxacin. Post-marketing surveillance reports indicate that this risk may be increased in patients receiving concomitant corticosteroids, especially the elderly. Ciprofloxacin should be discontinued if the patient experiences pain, inflammation, or rupture of a tendon. Patients should reset and refrain from exercise until the diagnosis of tendinitis or tendon rupture has been excluded. Tendon rupture can occur during or after therapy with quinolones, including ciprofloxacin.

An earlier (and 2006) warning discussed risks discovered in animals and a warning against use in children:

ANIMAL PHARMACOLOGY:

THE SAFETY AND EFFECTIVENESS OF CIPROFLOXACIN IN PEDIATRIC PATIENTS, ADOLESCENTS (LESS THAN 18 YEARS OF AGE), PREGNANT WOMEN, AND LACTATING WOMEN HAVE NOT BEEN ESTABLISHED. (See PRECAUTIONS, Pediatric Use, Pregnancy, Teratogenic Effects, Pregnancy Category C and Nursing Mothers) Ciprofloxacin causes lameness in immature dogs. Histopathological examination of the weight-bearing joints of these dogs revealed permanent lesions of the cartilage. Related quinolone-class drugs also produce erosions of cartilage of weight-bearing joints and other signs of arthropathy in immature animals of various species. (See ANIMAL PHARMACOLOGY.)

Ciprofloxacin and other quinolones have been shown to cause arthropathy in immature animals of most species tested (See WARNINGS.) Damage of weight bearing joints was observed in juvenile dogs and rats. In young beagles, 100 mg/kg ciprofloxacin, given daily for 4 weeks, caused degenerative articular changes of the knee joint. At 30 mg/kg, the effect on the joint was minimal. In a subsequent study in beagles, removal of weight bearing from the joint reduced the lesions but did not totally prevent them.

Opinions

All my opinions are expressed with reasonable pharmacological and pharmaceutical certainty.

The tendonopathies and tendon rupture injuries suffered by Diann Queen were probably caused by prolonged and cumulative exposure to ciprofloxacin. The biochemistry, animal toxicology, and accumulated pharmacovigilance evidence strongly supports this causation.

Westward and Apotex, as generic manufacturers of ciprofloxacin, had a duty to monitor the literature and use of their products, and to evaluate the effectiveness of their warnings regarding the safety of ciprofloxacin.

Westward and Apotex were negligent and departed from the standard of care of reasonable pharmaceutical companies by not enhancing and promulgating the warning regarding tendon risk. Regulatory protocol provides, where a safety change in text is intended to add or strengthen warnings, the company can actually implement a new product labeling (change) without obtaining prior approval by the FDA (Changes Being Effected) (21 CFR 314.70(c)(2)).

The negligence and departure of these companies is proximately related to Ms. Queen's injuries. Had a Black Box and/or Dear Doctor letters been petitioned and implemented earlier, Ms. Queen would have been advised of the risk and how to recognize the injury. Her treating physicians, those that prescribed the Cipro (Polonad) and diagnosed and treated her tendon injuries (Drs. Bone and Ankle) would have recognized association earlier and made further inquiry into Ms. Queen's fluoroquinolone exposure, and prevented further exposure after the first complaint of tendon pain and the first orthopedic intervention.

Westward and Apotex knew or should have known of the risk of tendon injury, and the ineffectiveness of the 1996 warnings. The only reasonable remedy to the continual unawareness of the prescribing and consuming public was to initiate a Black Box Warning and Dear Doctor letters.

Bases for opinions

Public Citizen and the Illinois Attorney General's actions and promulgation of the information, referencing the accumulated MedWatch reports of tendon rupture and risk of tendonitis, and the ineffectiveness of the pre-existing warning provided notice to these manufacturers.

The published literature, in the form of case reports, but more importantly in the form of pharmacoepidemiology studies that demonstrated relative risks and odds ratios of greater than 2 provide compelling information documenting the continuing risk, and the need for warning the prescribers and patients of that risk. A summary of the literature, especially published pharmacoepidemiology studies demonstrating an increased risk and continuing reports, is appended to this report.

Case summary

Apotex and Westward were negligent and departed from the standard of care of reasonable pharmaceutical manufacturers by not providing a stronger and more effective warning, which could have been implemented without prior approval of the FDA. The more prudent action by these manufacturers would have been, based on the evidence and experience of the drug (class) use, to petition the FDA to strengthen the warning by implementing a Black Box warning and Dear Doctor letters. Had they done so in 2005 or 2006, Ms. Queen's long-term cumulative exposure to Ciprofloxacin would have been avoided and her injuries would not likely have occurred.

Case references

I. FDA Warns of Levaquin Tendon Rupture & Injuries. Prod. schmidtandclark. 2009. YouTube. Web. 19 Dec 2011. www.youtube.com/watch?v=ByZXSwkyyX4&feature=related>

II. FDA Issues Black Box Warnings for Fluoroquinolones. Prod. medvidblog. 2008. YouTube. Web. 19 Dec 2011. <www.youtube.com/watch?v=yiwUE80v_oI>

13.7 Summary and Conclusions

Careful monitoring by pharmaceutical manufacturers during clinical trials, during early postmarketing, and throughout the life of the product, with labeling updates and adequate warnings to prescribers and patients, will improve the safety of medicines and limit the liability of the pharmaceutical manufacturers.

The best science in the world, as evidenced and described in this book, has to be balanced and tempered with thorough safety monitoring in order to safely provide new drug discoveries to patients.

Endnotes

1. Merli, R., Lawsuits against drug companies put a premium on risk management. *Pharm. Insider*, July 9 2004.

2. Fitzgerald, G., PhD, former FDA officer in the Center for Drug Evaluation and Research. (Personal communication, 1992).

3. American College of Clinical Pharmacology, Bayer settles 2,861 more Baycol cases for another $1 billion, *FDAnews Drug Daily Bulletin*, 1(184), September 28, 2004.

4. Petroff, Kip. *Battling Goliath: Inside a $22 Billion Legal Scandal* (Frame House Press, Dallas, 2011).

5. *Reyes v. Wyeth Laboratories*, 498 F.2d 1264 (5th Cir. 07/31/1974).

6. Sontheimer, Richard. "The Cost of Medical Care—Then (1700 B.C.) and Now." *Dermanities*. Captus Solutions. Web. 15 Dec. 2011. www.dermanities.com/detail.asp?article=149.

7. "Milestones in U.S. Food and Drug Law History." *U.S. Food and Drug Administration Home Page*. Web. 15 Dec. 2011. www.fda.gov/AboutFDA/WhatWeDo/History/Milestones/default.htm.

8. Jick, H., Adverse drug reactions: the magnitude of the problem, *J. Allergy Clin. Immunol.*, 74(4 Pt 2), 555–557, 1984.

9. Stetler, C.J., Drug-induced illness, (letter) *JAMA* 229, 1043–1044, 1974.

10. Miller, R.R., Interpretation of studies on adverse drug reactions. Am. J. Hosp. Pharm., 34, 753–754, 1977.

11. Physician Insurers Association of America, Medication Error Study, PIAA, Washington, DC, June 1993

12. Physician Insurers Association of America, Statistical data from the PIAA cumulative data sharing report, January 1, 1985–December 31, 1999, as reported in *Reporter*, Texas Medical Liability Trust, 1–8, September/October 1999.

13. Curtis, L.H. et at., Inappropriate prescribing for elderly Americans in a large outpatient population, *Arch. Intern. Med.*, 164, 1621–1625, 2004.

14. Lazarou, J., Pomeranz, B.H., and Corey, P.N., Incidence of adverse drug reactions in hospitalized patients: a meta-analysis of prospective studies. *JAMA*, 279(15), 1200–1205, 1998.

15. Kohn, Linda T. *To Err Is Human: Building a Safer Health System*. Washington: National Academy, 1999. Print.

16. Aspden, Philip. *Preventing Medication Errors*. Washington, DC: National Academies, 2006. Print.

17. Shoemaker, Cliff. "A Call To Arms: The History of Vaccines" *Shoemaker & Associates*. Web. 18 Dec. 2011. www.shoemakerassociates.com/index.php?option=com_content&view=article&id=51:vaccine-litigation-history&catid=15:vaccine-litigation&Itemid=35.

18. Lasser, K.E. et al. Timing of new black box warnings and withdrawals for prescription medications, *JAMA*, 287(17), 2215–2220, 2002.

19. Bakke, O.M. et al. Drug safety discontinuations in the United Kingdom, the United States, and Spain from 1974 through 1993: a regulatory perspective. *Clin. Pharmacol. Ther.*, 58, 108–117, 1995.

20. Brewer, T. and Colditz, G., Postmarketing surveillance and adverse drug reactions: current perspectives and future needs, *JAMA*, 281, 824–829, 1999.

21. Thase, M.E., How should efficacy be evaluated in randomized clinical trials of treatments for depression? *J. Clin, Psychiatry*, 60(suppl. 4), 23–31, 1999.

22. Lurie, P. and Sasich, L.D., Safety of FDA-approved drugs, *JAMA*, 282, 2297–2298, 1999.

23. Willman, D., How a new policy led to seven deadly drugs, *Los Angeles, Times*, Section A1, December 20, 2000.

24. Sasich, L., Lurie, P., and Wolfe, S.M., The drug industry's performance in finishing postmarketing research (Phase IV) studies, letter and report from *Public Citizen, Health Research Group Publication #1520*, Washington, DC, April 13, 2000.

25. Peay, M.Y. and Peay, E.R., The role of commercial sources in the adoption of a new drug, *Soc. Sci. Med.*, 26, 1183–1189, 1988.

26. Stross, J.K., Information sources and clinical decisions, *J. Gen. Intern. Med.*, 2, 155–159, 1987.

27. Jones, M.I., Greenfield, S.M., and Bradley, C.P., Prescribing new drugs: qualitative study of influences on consultants and general practitioners, *BMJ*, 323, 378–381, 2001.

28. Basara, L.R., The impact of a direct-to-consumer prescription medication advertising campaign on new prescription volume, *Drug Inf. J.*, 30, 715–729, 1996.

29. Petersen, M. Pushing pills with piles of money: Merck and Pharmacia in arthritis drug battle, *New York Times*, C1, October 5, 2000.

30. Hurwitz, M.A. and Caves, R.E., Persuasion or information? promotion and the shares of brand name and generic pharmaceuticals. *J. Law. Econ.*, 31, 299–320, 1988.

31. Murphy, M.N., Smith, M.C., and Juergens, J.P., The synergic impact of promotion intensity and therapeutic novelty on market performance of prescription drug products, *J. Drug Issues*, 22, 305–316, 1992.

32. Starfield, B., Is U.S. health really the best in the world? *JAMA*, 284, 483–485, 2000.

33. Wood, A.J., Thrombotic thrombocytopenic purpura and clopidogrel: a need for new approaches to drug safety, *N. Engl. J. Med.*, 342, 1824–1826, 2000.

34. Specific requirements on content and format of labeling for human prescription drugs: warnings Title 21 *Code of Federal Regulations*, Part 201.57(e), pp. 23, revised 2003.

35. Wolfe, S.M., Letter from Health Research Group to Margaret Heckler, Department of Health and Human Services, Washington, DC. December 28, 1983.

36. Rhoades, Robert. *Risky Business: Managing The Quality of America's Medicines, Second Edition*. FDAnews. (2008).

37. Connors, P.J., Medication error study: a summary. *Physician Insurers Association of America Medication Error Study*, PIAA, Washington, DC, June 1993.

38. CDC, Update: vaccine side effects, adverse reactions, contraindications, and precautions recommendations of the advisory committee on immunization practices (ACIP), *MMWR*, 45(RR12;001), September 6, 1996.

39. Carl Vinson Institute of Government, The University of Georgia chronology of the 1918 Spanish Influenza Epidemic in Georgia, 1999. Available at http://georgiainfo. galileo.usg.edu/1918flu.htm.

40. Neustadt, R.E. and Fineberg, H.V., *The Swine Flu Affair: Decision-Making on a Slippery Disease, Department of Health, Education, and Welfare*, Washington, DC, 1978.

41. *The National Childhood Vaccine Injury Act of 1986*, Section 2125, Public Health Service Act as codified at 42 U.S.C. 300aa-(suppl), 1987.

42. Vaccine Injured Children's Compensation Act of 2001, HR 1287, March 29, 2001.

43. Bill Summary and Legislative Action: Vaccine Injured Children's Compensation Act of 2001, HR 1287, March 29, 2001, last major action April 16, 2001. Available at www.govtrack.us/congress/bills/107/hr1287.

44. *Homeland Security Act of 2002*, Pub. L. 107-296, January 24, 2003 (codified at 42 *USCS* § 233).

45. Smallpox Emergency Personnel Protection Act of 2003, Pub. L. 108-20, April 30, 2003 (retroactive effective date January 24, 2003).

46. Mair, J.S. and Mair, M. Vaccine liability in the era of bioterrorism, *Biosecurity Bioterror. Biodefens Strat. Pract. Sci.*, 1(3), 169–, 2003.

47. Who is responsible, and shy, for the chaotic confusion over the polio inoculations? *Harper's Magazine*, August 1995.

48. Bellanti, J.A., ed. *Immunology III*. Philadelphia, PA: WB Saunders Co., 1985.

49. Jonville-Bera AP, et al. Sudden unexpected death in infants under three months of age and vaccination status: a case-control study, *Br. J. Clin. Pharmacol.*, 51(3), 271–276, 2001.

50. Coulter, H.L. and Fisher, B.L., *DPT: A Shot in the Dark: Why the P in DPT May Be Hazardous to Your Health*, Avery Publishing, Vonore, TN, 1985.

51. "New Vaccines against Infectious Diseases: Research and Development Status, IVR, WHO, April 2005, Updated February 2006." *WHO | Vaccine Research and Development*. World Health Organization. Web. 19 Dec. 2011. www.who.int/vaccine_research/documents/ en/Status_Table.pdf.

52. Voelkel, N.F., Clarke, W.R., Hegenbottam, T., Obesity dexfenfluramine, and pulmonary hypertension: a lesson learned? *Am. J. Resp, Crit. Med.*, 155, 786–788, 1997.

53. Cleare, A.J. Phentermine, psychosis, and family history, *J. Clin. Psychopharmacol.*, 16(6), 470–471, 1996.

54. Kokkinos, J. and Levine, S.R., Possible association of ischemic stroke with phentermine, *Stroke*, 24, 310–313, 1993.

55. Bostwick, J.M., Brown, T.M., A toxic reaction from combining fluoxetine and phentermine." *J. Clin. Psychopharmacol.* 16(2):189–190. 1996.

56. Willman, D., Drug tied to deaths is pulled; Safety: Baycol is a cholesterol-lowering medication that may lead to kidney failure, *Los Angeles, Times,* Section A1, August 9, 2001.

57. Jury Finds Rezulin diabetes drug not liable for deaths, Defeat Diabetes Foundation. Available at www.defeatdiabetes.org/articles/drugs040603.htm, posted June 3, 2004.

58. Lehmann, J., Statins and Baycol: questionable cholesterol control, in O'Donnell JT, Ed. *Drug Injury: Liability, Analysis, and Prevention*, 2005; 469–472.

59. *Haltom v. Bayer Corp.*, No. 02-60165-00-0-4 (Nueces Co., TX, Dist. Ct.).

60. Kauffman, J.M., 2001.

61. *Horn v. Thoratec Corp.*, No. 02-4597 (3d Cir. May 11, 2004).

62. Klein, A., Taylor, M.A., and Nelson, C.E., Another circuit bars tort suits under the MDA, Duane Morris, LLP, New York, NY, August 13, 2004.

63. *Buckman Co. v. Plaintiffs' Legal Comm.* (98-1768) 531 US 341 (2001) 159 F.3d 817, reversed, Argued December 4, 2000–Decided February 21, 2001.

64. *McCain-Kennedy-Edwards Patients' Bill of Rights* of 2001, S-283.

65. Jacobsen, Thomas M., and Albert I. Wertheimer. *Modern Pharmaceutical Industry: a Primer*. Sudbury, MA: Jones and Bartlett, 2010. Print.

66. *Guidance for Industry Premarketing Risk Assessment*. Rockville, MD: U.S. Dept. of Health and Human Services, Food and Drug Administration, Center for Drug Evaluation and Rresearch, 2005. Print.

Part II
High Risk Drug Therapies
Resulting in Injury and Litigation

Chapter 14

Adverse Drug Reactions: Focus on Drug Allergy

James T. O'Donnell, Pharm.D., M.S., FCP, ABCP, FACN, R.Ph.

14.1 Adverse Drug Reactions (ADRs): How Large is the Problem? What Drugs are Involved? What are the Injuries?

Although there is no doubt that therapeutic agents such as vaccines and antibiotics have changed the course of modern medicine and prolonged the average life span of the population, we must still assume that all drugs can potentially be harmful. Pharmacovigilance is a relatively new term that describes efforts to monitor human drug experience. In the United States, the Food and Drug Administration's Med-Watch system maintains a database of voluntary reports of postmarketing (i.e., after the manufacturer's data has been reported and published in the drug's package insert) adverse drug reactions. Pharmacoepidemiology is "the application of epidemiologic knowledge, methods and reasoning to the study of the effects (beneficial and adverse) and uses of drugs in human populations."[1] This task involves the identification, analysis, research, and interventions intended to decrease the incidence and severity of drug-induced injuries.

A. Historical Perspective

The reported incidence and frequency of adverse drug events varies, depending on the source of the report and on the methods used to describe the event. One reason for these discrepancies is that it is sometimes difficult to determine the causality of the adverse event with absolute certainty. Hospital-admission reports have ranged from between less than 1 percent and up to 28 percent. However, most studies report an incidence of between 10 and 20 percent. This disparity reflects differences in the methods used to detect and report adverse drug reactions (ADRs).

The first ADRs probably occurred when humans began to experiment with plants as medications and learned how to brew alcohol and to smoke tobacco. However, the history of ADRs remained relatively sparse until this century. ADRs slowly grew in frequency until the end of the Second World War. Since that time, there has been an explosion of new drugs and a corresponding increase in ADRs.

B. ADR Incidence

The human life span has increased tremendously over the last several hundred years. Most attribute this life extension to the development of life-saving medications and medical devices, in addition to industrialization.

There are currently 4,750 drugs available on the U.S. market, in a total of 17,992 drug products.[2] With so many drugs, it is no surprise that the medication-error rate is high in this country, estimated at nearly one in five doses at the typical hospital and skilled nursing facility (different studies report different rates). The percentage of errors rated potentially harmful is 7 percent—more than 40 per day per 300 in-patients, on the average, according to one study. Drug allergies and introductions are an important subset of these errors, representing 5 to 10 percent of all drug injuries that occur, estimates show.

In a review article, the incidence rate of drug-related hospital admissions was reported to vary from 0.2 to 21.7 percent, with the median rate of drug-related hospitalizations at 4.9 percent.[3] The author defined drug-related hospitalizations as adverse events that could cause a side effect,[4] excessive effect, idiosyncratic effect, or hypersensitivity. In another review, the rate of drug-related hospital admissions ranged from 0.3 to 16.8 percent of all hospital admissions, with a median value of 5.6 percent.[5]

A recent *New England Journal of Medicine* article reviews the topic of emergency hospitalizations for adverse drug events in older americans.[6] The authors analyzed adverse event data from the National Electronic Injury Surveillance System—Cooperative Adverse Drug Event Surveillance project (2007 through 2009) to estimate the frequency and rates of hospitalization after emergency department visits for adverse drug events in older adults. The review included nearly 100,000 emergency hospitalizations, half of which were in-patients over 80 years of age. Two-thirds were due to unintentional overdoses. Four medications or medication classes were implicated alone or in combination: warfarin (33.3 percent), insulins (13.9 percent), oral antiplatelet agents (13.3 percent), and oral hypoglycemic agents (10.7 percent). Frequently, warfarin and anti-platelet medications were combined. Other medications classes reported include opiates (4.8 percent), antibiotics (4.2 percent), Digoxin (3.5 percent), rennin an-

giotensin inhibitors (2.9 percent) and sedative hypnotics (2.5 percent). The authors recommend that improved management of antithrombotic and antidiabetic drugs has the potential to reduce hospitalizations for adverse drug events in older adults. The reader will find extensive discussion of anticoagulant toxicity in Chapter 25, *Anticoagulants*, and of diabetic drug toxicity in Chapter 22, *Adverse Effects of Diabetic Drugs,* and of opiate toxicity in Chapter 27, *Dangers of Opioids.*

Following a 1999 report by the Institute on Medication Safety entitled "To Err is Human," drug-injury prevention has become a major focus of healthcare organizations nationally.[7] This has resulted in many innovative ideas, including the use of bar coding—both at the bedside, as well as on the medication labeling (and sometimes on the administrator of the drug itself), as well as drug-counting/weighing machines, and complicated software products. Drug-injury prevention has become a multi-million dollar industry.

A drug-induced disease is an unintended effect of a drug that may result in mortality or morbidity with symptoms sufficient to prompt a patient to seek medical attention and/or require hospitalization. Fortunately, many drug-induced diseases are preventable.

Every health care student learns the "Five Basic Rights of Medication Administration" (Table 14.1). These "rights" represent the "right" way to administer medication without errors.

Table 14.1
The Five Basic Rights of Medication Administration

- Right Patient
- Right Medication
- Right Dosage
- Right Time (Frequency)
- Right Route of Administration

Furthermore, healthcare practitioners should also know the "Four Additional Rights of Medication Administration": 1) Right Documentation, 2) Right Reason, 3) Right to Know (Patient Education), and 4) Right to Refuse.

Unfortunately, this simple system cannot catch every error. In fact, although covered under "right medication," the system offers no way to determine whether that "right medication" might produce a drug allergy in any particular patient at any particular time. Likewise, without being able to predict allergic reactions, it is almost impossible to predict cross-reactions (reactions with similar drugs in the same class).

Hopefully, with today's pharmacy software and checks and balances, the number of interactions will continue to decrease. Pharmacy software flags such interactions, helping medical personnel prevent them before they occur. According to the American Heart Association, total estimated morbidity and mortality costs for drug-related diseases was $76.6 billion in 1995.[8] A follow-up study in 2001, using the same cost-of-illness model, reported annual drug-related morbidity and mortality costs (in 2000 dollars) of $177.4 billion.[9] In comparison, the cost of cardiovascular diseases and stroke were estimated to be $393.5 billion in 2005, and the cost for all cancers in 2004 was about $190 billion.[9]

Due to limited sample size, clinical trials usually uncover only the more frequent ADRs. For example, a trial with a sample size of 10,000 patients (no adverse reactions) will only yield a 95 percent confidence interval that an ADR with a frequency of 1 in 10,000 will not occur. In order to increase the confidence interval for detecting an ADR of the same frequency (1 in 10,000) to 99 percent, a sample size of 46,000 is needed.[10] These numbers lie in stark contrast to a 2005 FDA standard which recommends that the clinical trial of a drug used to treat a non-life-threatening condition expose 1,500 subjects to the investigational product (with 300 to 600 exposed for 6 months, and 100 exposed for 1 year).[11]

Delays in sounding an alert are a function of the need for verification and the initiation of any regulatory action. Alerting others usually occurs through published anecdotal reports. Voluntary reporting and other early-warning systems have made a negligible contribution to alerting. The MedWatch system is valuable for generating and forming hypotheses for epidemiological studies. Routine monitoring for drug safety should include patients in various subsets (the elderly, children, and patients with specific disease states, such as kidney or liver disease), where there may be a particular liability to ADRs. The elderly represent the group taking the largest amount of drugs and suffering the greatest number of ADRs. Life expectancy—the probability of living a longer life—has increased from around 50 years at the dawn of the twentieth century to an anticipated 75 years at the turn of the twenty-first century. With the greater life expectancy, both the total number of elderly, as well as the number of elderly as a percentage of the population, increases. In actual numbers, this means that the number of people 75 years of age and over will rise from about 10 million (or 4.4 percent of the population) in 1980 to close to 30 million (9.1 percent of the population) in 2050. For the population over 85 years of age, these values will change from about 3 million in 1980 (1 percent) to about 18 million (5.2 percent) in 2050. This latter group, then, represents the most rapidly growing segment of the population. Remarkably, even though there were more than 650,000 reports submitted to the FDA in 2010, only a small minority of suspected drug adverse reactions is reported to the FDA (see the extensive discussion in Section 12.8.C for more information).

C. FDA Reporting Requirements

Currently, the United States has a voluntary, spontaneous reporting system called MedWatch. Healthcare professionals and drug companies report ADRs to the FDA with the MedWatch Drug Experience Report Form (See Chapter 11, *Important Code of Federal Regulations Applicable to Drug Product Liability Suits*). Since 1962, drug manufacturers have been required to report all ADRs brought to their attention. The drug companies file the majority of the 200,000-plus ADRs reported annually.

The FDA is interested in receiving reports of serious new reactions associated with the use of drugs and biologic products used in the course of medical practice. In addition, there is interest in reactions to new drugs during their first three years of marketing in the United States. The FDA does not collect reports of inappropriate use, prescriber errors, or administration errors. "Serious" reports are generally considered to be those that are life threatening, or those that result in death, hospitalization or prolonged hospitalization, or permanent or severe disability. The determination of seriousness is up to the discretion of the reporter. If there is any doubt, the report should be considered serious and should be submitted to the FDA—a causality assessment is not required.

The ICH (International Conference on Harmonization) Technical Requirements for Registration of Pharmaceuticals for Human Use brings together as equal partners the regulatory authorities of Europe, Japan, and the USA with experts from the pharmaceutical industry in these regions to discuss scientific and technical aspects of product registration. The United States' spontaneous reporting system has many good features. The input is global—covering the entire population of patients treated with drugs. Thus, it includes all drugs and all physicians in "real-life" situations of drug use, unlike the controlled settings of clinical drug trials. It is inexpensive, requires a minimum amount of time, and does not interfere with the practice of the physician. Unfortunately, the overall effectiveness of the Drug Experience Report system has been found to be wanting.[12,13] Leading a list of its limitations is underreporting—few physicians ever fill out reports. It has been conservatively estimated that 95 percent of ADRs go unreported.[14] Some of the reasons that doctors may neglect to report ADRs are listed in the next section.

The FDA has been under fire from at least two different sides. First, the industry (as well as certain patient groups) argues that the agency takes far too long to approve new drugs. Second, public-interest groups argue that the agency is not thorough enough in its reviews of new drugs. Before drugs can be sold in the United States, the manufacturers must apply to the FDA for the right to test them in humans, submit their test results to the agency, and then apply for the right to sell the drugs. Experts agree that the clinical trials completed before approval cannot detect all side effects that may be caused by the drugs. Because the testing is done in groups of people ranging from a few hundred to a few thousand, it is unlikely that clinical testing will uncover side effects that occur in, say, one person in 10,000.

D. The "Seven Deadly Sins": Why Doctors Fail to Report ADRs[15]

The following are the main failures of MedWatch, the FDA's voluntary reporting system:

1. **Complacency**—the result of a mistaken belief that only safe drugs are allowed on the market.
2. **Fear** of involvement in litigation or of an investigation of prescribing habits.
3. **Guilty feelings** about the damage physicians may have caused their patients.
4. **Ambition** to collect and publish a personal series of cases.
5. **Ignorance** about what should be reported, the reporting process, and the value of the reporting.
6. **Difference** in reporting mere suspicions.
7. **Indifference** to the responsibility that an individual doctor has to contribute to the general body of knowledge about the effects of drug treatment.

Most drugs are sold to hundreds of thousands (sometimes millions) of people, so rare side effects are often seen only after the drug reaches the market. These side effects are then reported to the FDA by the drug's manufacturers and—to a lesser extent—by healthcare professionals. A General Accounting Office (GAO) study counted as "serious" all those "adverse reactions that could lead to hospitalization, increases in the length of hospitalization, severe or permanent disability, or death."[16] These reactions, whether they are seen in a small or large number of patients, have caused the FDA to withdraw drugs from the market or to add warnings to their labels, so that doctors might avoid their use or be more careful in deciding who should use them.

A GAO report suggests that some lives could be saved if the Food and Drug Administration monitored after-market hazards more closely and communicated them more quickly to doctors and the public. Critics of the agency say it can take up to five years from the time a serious side effect is observed to the time that doctors and the public are told. Among the reactions noted by the GAO were a great variety of ailments, including heart failure, shock, respiratory arrest, convulsions, kidney and liver failure, birth defects, and blindness. Some cases have become quite well known, like the birth defects that can be caused by the anti-acne drug Accutane.

The GAO study found that certain classes of drugs, including heart, anti-inflammatory, psychopharmacologic, fertility, dermatologic, and antibiotic drugs, had a much higher percentage of post-approval risks and adverse reactions than other categories of medications.

E. Attitudes Toward ADRs

Fitzgerald, while researching crisis management and ADRs, said:

> The initial response of those working within an organization, particularly product champions, both technical and commercial, is that of denial. Until this moment, the whole culture within the pharmaceutical company has been positively and energetically to promote the advantage of the drug. Thus, before accepting that the drug is associated with a potentially serious disadvantage, drug champions tend to demand, firstly, proof of causality; secondly, to seek out alternative explanations for the clinical syndrome; and thirdly, to try to implicate other agents in the same drug class, in order to diminish the impact on the specific product.[17]

Replies published by companies concerning published ADRs are not too dissimilar to this pattern, giving a very one-sided viewpoint, and certainly not giving the reader a balanced opinion of the problem. These letters usually contain some of the following:

- No admission of a causal relationship.
- No acknowledgment of the validity of any of the comments in the original publication.
- A list of all possible alternatives, however tenuous.
- No mention of the number of cases that the company has received.
- References, some of which seem to have little to do with the original problem.
- Implications that it is a class effect.
- Remarks from a clinician who has been involved with the company as a trialist or adviser, without any acknowledgment of an association with the pharmaceutical company.

In an editorial in *Risk and Safety in Medicine*, Dr. M.N.G. Dukes said there are still "serious instances where risk data have been concealed in the interests of commerce."[18]

F. Investigator Fraud

Another problem in detecting and reporting adverse drug effects (ADEs) has been the discovery of numerous instances of proven investigator fraud. In the field of ADEs, the investigator's attitude can vary from bewildered ignorance to deliberate dishonesty:

- Some fail to document and report what they should clearly recognize as an ADE.
- Some are so "invested" in the study drug, believing so strongly in its safety, that their enthusiasm overshadows sound scientific and regulatory standards.
- Some choose not to report ADEs—either because it requires too much effort, or because they are deliberately attempting to defraud.
- Some are confused over what constitutes an ADE.
- Many ADE reports lack essential information.
- Most are weak in causality assessment. (Did the drug actually cause the ADE?)

14.2 Classification of ADRs

In essence, an ADR is any unintended and undesirable response obtained from the appropriate dose of a drug or diagnostic agent. Adverse drug reactions have been conventionally classified as: (1) overdosage, (2) intolerance, (3) unexpected side effects, (4) secondary effects, (5) idiosyncrasy, and (6) hypersensitivity reactions.

Drug interactions have been categorized into those occurring (1) outside the body, (2) at the site of entry, (3) at storage sites within the body, (4) at the site of action, (5) by inhibition of metabolizing enzymes, (6) by stimulation of enzymes, and (7) by affecting drug excretion. Drug interactions are also included with other ADRs. Although these classifications have been used both in reviews and textbooks, it is unnecessary and confusing to separate ADRs from drug interactions.

The term "drug-drug interactions" refer to interactions between prescription or nonprescription drugs. The broader term "drug interaction" is often substituted. Many drug interactions cause undesirable effects and account for a significant number of adverse events. They can also limit bioavailability or block desired effects. (See Table 14.2.)

All serious or unexpected ADRs must be promptly reported. This applies to reports from spontaneous sources and from any type of clinical or epidemiological investigation—independent of design or purpose. It also applies to cases not reported directly to a sponsor or manufacturer (e.g., those found in regulatory authority-generated ADR registries or in publications). The source of a report (investigation, spontaneous, other) should always be identified.

Expedited reporting of reactions that are serious, but expected, will ordinarily be inappropriate. Expedited reporting is also inappropriate for serious events from clinical investigations that are considered unrelated to the study product, regardless of whether the event is expected or not.

Table 14.2
Terminology Concerning Drug Misadventures

---

adverse event (or adverse experience). Any untoward medical occurrence in a patient or clinical-investigation subject administered a pharmaceutical product. It is not necessary for the event to have a causal relationship with this treatment.

adverse drug reaction (ADR). In the pre-approval clinical experience with a new medicinal product or its new usages, particularly as the therapeutic doses may not be established, "all noxious and unintended responses to a medicinal product related to any dose should be considered adverse drug reactions."

unexpected adverse drug reaction. An adverse reaction, the nature or severity of which is not consistent with the applicable product information (e.g., an investigator's brochure for an unapproved investigational medicinal product).

serious adverse event. A serious adverse event, experience, or reaction is any untoward medical occurrence that at any dose may: (1) result in death, (2) be life-threatening, (3) require in-patient hospitalization or prolongation of existing hospitalization, (4) result in persistent or significant disability or incapacity, (5) results in a congenital anomaly or birth defect. (Note: the term "life-threatening" refers to an event in which the patient was at risk of death at the time of the event; it does not refer to an event which hypothetically might have caused death if it were more severe.)

There are situations, in addition to single case reports of "serious" adverse events or reactions, that may necessitate rapid communication to regulatory authorities. Appropriate medical and scientific judgment should be applied for each situation. In general, this includes information that might materially influence the risk-benefit assessment of a medicinal product, or that would be sufficient to consider changes in medicinal product administration or overall conduct of a clinical investigation. The following are some examples:

- A clinically important increase in the rate of occurrence for an "expected" serious ADR.
- A significant hazard to the patient population—such as lack of efficacy with a medicinal product used in treating life-threatening disease.
- A major safety finding from a newly completed animal study (such as a study on carcinogenicity).

A. Categories of ADRs[19]

Traditionally, ADRs have been divided into two types. Type A reactions are dose-related and arise from the normal pharmacological action of a drug. Type B reactions represent an abnormal or novel response to a drug.

1. Type A reactions: Augmentation of the pharmacological response

These reactions are usually the result of an exaggerated, but otherwise normal, pharmacological action of a drug given in the usual therapeutic doses. An example of this type of reaction would be the postural and exercise hypotension (low blood pressure) in a patient taking an adrenergic neuronal blocking agent such as guanethidine (used to treat severe high blood pressure), or drowsiness in those taking phenobarbital (a barbiturate central-nervous system depressant used as a sedative hypnotic and also commonly as an anticonvulsant). Type A reactions are largely predictable on the basis of the known pharmacological properties of a drug. They are frequently dose-dependent. Although the incidence of morbidity (side effects) in the population is often high, the mortality rate is usually low.

2. Type B reactions: Bizarre (idiosyncratic)

These reactions are unusual effects that would not be expected from known pharmacological actions of a drug when it is given in the accepted therapeutic doses to such a patient whose body handles that drug in a normal manner. Example of this type of reaction includes malignant hyperthermia caused by anesthesia. Many of the immunological (allergic-hypersensitivity) reactions would fall into this category (although these would constitute medication errors if the allergy is known).

Anaphylaxis—a classic Type B hypersensitivity reaction—is one of the most serious, potentially life-threatening ADRs.[20] This IgE-mediated reaction generally occurs within 20 minutes of exposure to an antigen. It is most common after an injection, but it can occur with any route of administration. The symptoms of anaphylaxis are produced by a variety of chemical mediators, most notably histamine.[21] While the incidence of anaphylaxis is low, the mortality rate from these reactions is high. These reactions are usually unpredictable and are not observed during conventional toxicological screening programs.

14.3 Types of Drug Allergy and Hypersensitivity
A. The Nature of Drug Allergy

Drug allergies are the body's overreaction to a foreign substance, be it dust, pollen, or a medication. Histamine is released in response to what the body perceives as a threat, and the results can be deadly. Of course, the immune system is designed to protect the body from dangerous invaders, which are usually viruses and bacteria, but can also be medications on occasion.[22]

Unfortunately, there is no way to predict with 100 percent accuracy who will develop an allergic reaction to a medication. Allergies may develop at any time, even when an agent has been taken in the past. Indeed, multiple exposures actually raise the odds of developing an allergy to a particular substance. Additionally, some allergies do not develop for days or weeks after ingestion of or injection with a medication, which can make the reaction difficult to trace to the substance. Causation assessment can be challenging due to all these variables. Although some other adverse drug reactions (ADRs) are dependent upon the amount of the drug administered, this is not the case with a drug allergy. Even a tiny amount of the medication can trigger a life-threatening anaphylactic episode.

Some types of drugs induce allergic reactions more readily than others, and result in a spectrum of symptoms that may affect a range of tissues and organs. Medications with larger drug molecules seem to be more likely to cause reactions than those with smaller drug molecules.

Some examples of medications comprised of larger drug molecules include:

- insulin
- antiserum containing antibodies
- recombinant proteins produced by genetic engineering

Many other allergens have molecules too small to set off alarm bells for the immune system. For examples, drugs such as antibiotics cannot induce an immune response—unless they combine with a body cell or a carrier protein in the blood. Furthermore, drug allergies often are caused by the breakdown products or metabolites of the drug rather than by the drug itself. Sometimes the same drug, such as penicillin, can induce different types of allergic reactions. The most common drug sensitivity is to aspirin (ASA). Nearly 1 million Americans, primarily adults, are sensitive to ASA. However, many medications, including ASA and other nonsteroidal anti-inflammatory drugs (NSAIDs) such as ibuprofen (Advil, Motrin, and others), can trigger an asthma attack in children. It is estimated that up to 10 percent of all people develop allergies to penicillin or other antibiotics at some point in their lives. Those taking multiple medications or frequent courses of antibiotics appear to be more at risk for developing drug allergies.

Children represent a large segment of the population that is affected by drug allergy. Many times, these allergies manifest as asthma—a common chronic respiratory condition in children. Attacks occur when the air passages from the lungs to the nose and mouth are narrowed causing difficulty breathing. ASA and ASA-like medications are common triggers for asthma attacks in as many as 30 percent of asthmatic children.[22]

Children also frequently develop allergies to the following agents:[22]

- barbiturates
- ASA
- anticonvulsants
- sulfa-based drugs
- dyes that are injected into blood vessels before taking X-rays
- insulin preparations

Interestingly enough, insect stings and the intravenous injection of certain drugs are the most common causes of anaphylaxis, the most severe and frightening allergic response, often marked by respiratory distress (swelling of the throat, preventing breathing) and death.

Skin conditions, including a measles-like rash, hives, and photosensitivity, are the most common drug reactions.

Uncommon—but more serious—symptoms of a drug allergy include the following:[23]

- Fever
- Muscle and joint aches
- Lymph node swelling
- Inflammation of the kidney
- Difficulty breathing, wheezing

- Low blood pressure, fainting
- Rapid or irregular heartbeat
- Swelling of face, tongue, lips, throat, joints, hands, or feet

B. Dangerous Drug-Allergy Reactions

1. Angioedema usually occurs within a few minutes of exposure to a drug, often in conjunction with urticaria. Angioedema often is asymmetrical: for example, only one side of the lip may be affected. This allergic symptom may become life-threatening if the swelling affects the larynx and the air passages become blocked. Emergency symptoms of a drug allergy include obstruction of the throat from swelling, severe asthma attack, and/or anaphylaxis. Angioedema is the most well-known and serious of the drug-induced throat disorders. Ototoxicity is manifested by hearing loss, tinnitus (continued ringing in the ear), and vertigo. Hyposmia is a diminished ability to detect or recognize a smell, while anosmia is the absolute absence of the sense of smell. All of these may be symptoms of angioedema.

2. Anaphylaxis involves the entire body. Although it is rare, several hundred Americans die of anaphylaxis every year. These deaths are most common in children who are allergic to penicillin and similar antibiotics—drugs that cause 97 percent of all deaths from drug allergies. Anaphylaxis, by definition, requires a prior exposure to the drug acting as the allergen.

3. Allergic reactions to drugs are the most common cause of tubulointerstitial nephritis, which can occur between five days and five weeks after exposure to penicillin, sulfonamides, diuretics, ASA and other NSAIDs.

C. Drug Sensitivities Mimic Allergy Symptoms

Sometimes, an allergy is not an allergy—it is actually just a hypersensitivity reaction. However, these types of reactions, especially pulmonary hypersensitivity, can still be dangerous and often mimic the symptoms of an actually drug allergy (such as rashes, urticaria, and angioedema). For example, children may have drug sensitivities to ASA; other NSAIDs; opiates such as morphine and codeine; and some antibiotics, including erythromycin and ampicillin. Anaphylactoid drug reactions are similar to anaphylactic reactions. However, they are caused by drug sensitivity (rather than a drug allergy) and can occur upon the first exposure to a drug. Anaphylactoid reactions can occur in response to the following:

- opiates
- *radiopaque* dyes (radiocontrast media) used in X-ray procedures; 2 to 3 percent of patients have immediate generalized reactions to these dyes
- ASA and other NSAIDs in some people, usually adults
- pentamidine

Drug-induced diseases have a considerable impact on American society. They cost billions of dollars annually, cause considerable morbidity, and are often fatal. Some adverse drug effects are not clinically significant; however, many people would contend that any condition that results in hospitalization is significant.

With so many types and manifestations of drug allergies, they can be difficult to detect, and if missed, the reaction can worsen. The most important factor is awareness. With vigilance (being aware of patient's allergies, and cross-allergies), most drug reactions can be caught early, or prevented altogether.

D. Definitions of Allergic/Hypersensitivity Reactions[19]

The definition of an adverse drug reaction is any response to a medication that was not desired or intended by its prescriber. These reactions occur at doses that would normally—according to package instructions—bestow a positive benefit on the patient, be it therapeutic, diagnostic, or prophylactic. These reactions also usually occur within a proximate time of administration of the medication. Studies show that allergic drug reactions account for only 6 to 10 percent of all observed ADRs. Yet, as many as 15 percent of adults believe themselves to be allergic to one or more drugs. The danger? A lifesaving medication may be withheld because of a faulty belief. Although many patients with a history of reacting to a drug could safely receive that drug again, the outcome could be serious if that patient is truly allergic. Hence, a suspicion of drug hypersensitivity must be evaluated carefully. For example, some ADRs that are perceived to be allergy related (but are not) may influence future use of a particular medication, when, in fact, a drug-induced side effect may be corrected simply be reducing its dose. However, it is important to keep in mind that if the reaction was indeed an allergy, the drug cannot be used or may require other special considerations.

There are two major categories of ADRs used to define and distinguish between the different types. The first is predictable adverse reactions, which are often dose-dependent, appear in otherwise normal patients, and are common enough to fall into this category. The other type is unpredictable reactions, which are usually dose independent, unrelated to the drug's pharmacological properties, or related to a patient's immunological responsiveness or susceptibility due to genetics. Something else to watch out for are reactions that are unrelated to the drug administered but can be caused by the administration (either events that occur, or through the route of administration). For example, sometimes parenteral administration of a drug can cause psycho-physiologic reactions (hysteria, vasovagal, hyperventilation, etc.). Some of these reactions may be attributable to the placebo effect (even anaphlyactoid symptoms have been observed in placebo-treated patients). And, of course, ADRs may be mistaken for other, coincidental health conditions.

E. Idiosyncratic Reactions[19]

Idiosyncratic reactions are qualitatively abnormal, unexpected responses to a drug that are uncharacteristic of its pharmacologic actions and that resemble hypersensitivity. These ADRs do not involve allergy. In contrast, allergic drug reactions are unpredictable and quantitatively abnormal, and are unrelated to the pharmacologic action of the drug. They involve immune responses to a drug following previous exposure to the same drug or to an immunochemically related substance that had resulted in the formation of specific antibodies, of sensitized T lymphocytes, or of both.

F. Intolerance[19]

Another type of ADR is intolerance, a characteristic pharmacologic effect of a drug that is quantitatively increased and/or produced by an unusually small dose of a medication. Although similar to intolerance, idiosyncratic and allergic reactions are qualitatively aberrant and often inexplicable, in terms of the normal pharmacology of the drug given in usual therapeutic doses.

G. Toxicity[19]

One type of predictable ADR is related directly to dosage. These ADRs can be expected in almost any patient administered too much or too little of a drug. Additionally, side effects from this type of ADR are usually known to be characteristic of the drug itself. Every drug's overdosage symptoms are different.

Sometimes, a drug overdose is not an acute event. It can be chronic, due in some cases to accumulation resulting from a patient's inability to process and excrete the medication properly. For example, a patient with a liver disorder may render a particular medication (such as morphine) even more toxic than a particular dose would be for another person.

As discussed earlier,[19] drugs with high molecular weight are most likely to cause reactions. Fortunately, most drugs are simple organic chemicals of low molecular weight, usually less than 1.000 daltons. For such low molecular weight drugs to become immunogenic, the drug or a drug metabolite must be bound to a macromolecular carrier, often by covalent bonds, for effective antigen processing. Macromolecular drugs, such as heterologolls, antisera, and insulin, are complex antigens and can potentially sensitize any patient.

H. Hypersensitivity Vasculitis[19]

Characterized by inflammation and necrosis of blood vessels, vasculitis is a condition that often involves organs or systems with a rich supply of blood vessels. Thus, the skin is often involved in vasculitic syndromes. According to Ditto: "In the systemic necrotizing vasculitis group (polyarteritis nodosa. allergic granulomatosis of Churg-Strauss) and granulomatous vasculitides (Wegener granulomatosis, lymphomatoid granulomatosis, giant cell arteritides), cutaneous involvement is not as common a presenting feature as seen in the hypersensitivity vasculitides (HSV)."[19] Drugs do appear to be causative or associated with HSV—especially in patients over 50, who are more frequently prescribed medications that have been associated with this syndrome (for example, diuretics or cardiac drugs). Other frequently implicated agents include penicillin, sulfonamides, thiouracils, hydantoins, iodides, and allopurinol, the author contends. Signs and symptoms to watch out for include fever, malaise, rash, hepatocellular injury, renal failure, leukocytosis, and eosinophilia. That said, the most common clinical feature of HSV is palpable purpura, making the skin the most likely place that vasculitis is recognized. The lesions are usually distributed in a symmetric pattern on the lower extremities and sacral area.

I. Predominantly Organ-Specific Reactions[19]
1. Dermatologic Manifestations

Studies show that skin lesions are among the most common ADRs, occurring in between 2 and 3 percent of hospitalized in-patients. The most common culprits include:

- anticonvulsants and central-nervous system depressants
- sulfonamides (especially TMP·SMX)
- NSAIDs
- β·lactam antibiotics (especially ampicillin and amoxiclllin)

With cutaneous reactions, eruptions are usually exanthematous or morbiliform in nature. Outside of Stevens-Johnson syndrome and toxic epidermal necrolysis (TEN), most are of mild or moderate severity, abate within a few days, and pose no threat to life or subsequent health.

J. Urticaria[19]

Urticaria is the second most frequent drug-induced eruption. It may occur alone or may be part of an acute reaction, such as anaphylaxis or serum sickness. An allergic IgE-mediated mechanism is often suspected (but it may be the result of other mechanisms).

K. Fixed Drug Eruptions[19]

Fixed drug eruptions—lesions that continue to appear in the same places each time a medication is administered are indications of drug hypersensitivity. Men and children appear to be more frequently affected than women. The lesions are usually well-defined and rounded, varying in size, and usually presenting as a purple, raised spot.

"Lesions are most common on the lips and genitals but may occur anywhere on the skin or mucous membranes," Ditto writes. "Usually, a solitary lesion is present, but the lesions may be more numerous, and additional ones may develop with subsequent administration of the drug. The length of time from exposure to the drug to the onset of symptoms is 30 minutes to 8 hours (mean, 2.1 hours). The lesions usually resolve within 2 to 3 weeks after drug withdrawal, leaving transient desquamation and residual hyper pigmentation."[19]

Because it is so difficult to absolutely prove the presence or the absence of a drug allergy, it remains the physician's responsibility to collect whatever evidence he can and evaluate it thoroughly. Only the skillful and practiced physician will notice the subtle signs of any cutaneous hypersensitivity reaction. To make sure you know how to recognize cutaneous drug hypersensitivity reactions, review the clinical criteria and manifestations. Most of these cases are very treatable, especially when recognized early.

With Stevens-Johnson syndrome, some studies show effective early management with high-dose corticosteroids (160 to 240 mg methylprednisolone a day, initially). This is a bit controversial, however. Proponents say that corticosteroids hasten recovery, produce few major side effects, and can result in almost a 100 percent survival and full recovery. This strategy should never be used to the management of (TEN) drug challenges to establish whether a patient can tolerate a drug following a reaction.

L. Photosensitivity Reactions[19]

Almost regardless of the route of administration (topical, oral, parenteral), photosensitivity reactions are always a possibility. These reactions occur when a drug present in the skin interacts with the light energy from direct sunlight or filtered or artificial light with sufficient UV light. Individuals with lighter skin seem most susceptible to these reactions, which are most likely to occur on the face, the neck, the forearms, and the backs of the hands. Usually, photosensitivity is a phototoxic, non-immunologic reaction caused by oxidative energy being transferred to tissues, resulting in damage to tissues. Every drug has its own specific light-absorption spectrum. These types of reactions look a lot like bad sunburns—occasionally with vesiculation. A photosensitivity reaction should be expected if the patient has been taking tetracycline or amiodarone.

When a photosensitive reaction is the result of a photoallergic immunologic reaction, the picture is slightly altered. In this scenario, the radiant light energy alters the drug in the skin to form reactive metabolites that combine with cutaneous proteins to form a complete antigen, provoking an immunologic response. These reactions may be difficult to trace, because they can occur or recur days to months after light exposure (even without continuing the drug). Unlike non-immunologic reactions, window glass cannot protect against a reaction. A patch test can confirm the presence of such a reaction. Most likely culprits are sulfonamides (antibactericals, hypoglycemics, diuretics), phenothiazines, NSAIDs, and griseofulvin.

M. Generalized Exfoliative Dermatitis[19]

A potentially life-threatening skin disease, exfoliative dermatitis presents as excessive scaling of the skin, resulting in peeling over virtually the entire body, including hair and nails. Symptoms can include fever, chills, and malaise, as well as large extra-renal fluid loss. Fatalities occur most frequently from this type of reaction in elderly or debilitated patients. Pre-existing skin disorders (psoriasis, seborrheic dermatitis, etc.) may be at the root of this reaction, but it is often difficult to track down. The reaction does not immediately cease upon stopping the drug. It may continue on for months after withdrawal of the culprit. Most frequent causes are sulfonamides, penicillins, barbiturates, carbamezepine, phenytoin, phenylbutazone, allpurinol, and gold salts.

N. Thrombocytopenia[19]

A well-recognized complication of drug therapy, thrombocytopenia is not usually fatal. Clinical manifestations include petechiae and ecchymoses and, upon occasion, gastrointestinal bleeding, hematuria, and/or vaginal bleeding. This complication can be identified through examination of bone marrow, which will show normal or increased numbers of normal appearing megakaryocytes. Prompt recovery (within two weeks) is expected upon withdrawal of the drug.

O. Hemolytic Anemia[19]

There are three mechanisms for the provocation of drug-induced immune hemolytic anemia. The first is an immune complex type, the second, a hapten or drug adsorption type, and the final is an autoimmune reaction. In general, however, the immune complex mechanism is the most frequent mechanism for the development of this reaction.

P. Agranulocytosis[19]

Usually occurring six to 10 days after initial drug therapy, patients suffering agranulocytosis may experience high fever, chills, arthalgias, and severe prostration. The granulocytes disappear within a matter of hours or persist five to ten days after withdrawal. This drug-induced neutropenia is mediated by immunologic mechanisms.

Q. Treatment: Withdrawal of the Suspected Drug[19]

If an allergic drug reaction is suspected, a detailed history of all drugs taken within the past month or two should be examined. Upon reasonable suspicion, treatment should be discontinued. If the reaction resolves, the answer is clear.

R. Symptomatic Treatment[19]

Some drug-induced allergy or hypersensitivity reactions do not require any treatment at all. Other types may be uncomfortable or dangerous enough that they require treatment aimed at alleviating the symptoms until the reaction subsides. The best examples are probably urticaria, which can be treated with corticosteroids, and drug-induced serum sickness, which can be treated with antihistamines and NSAIDs. More severe manifestations require treatment with prednisone 40 to 60 mg daily to start, with tapering over seven to 10 days. The most prominent types of reactions—those that may lead to anaphylaxis or anaphylactoid reactions—require the most aggressive treatment, or (in many cases) withdrawal from the suspect drug(s).

S. Prevention of Allergic Drug Reactions[19]

The best way to prevent drug allergy is to limit exposure to medications, prescribing only those that are clinically essential. Also, prescribing as few medications as possible simplifies identification of a potential allergen. The number of adverse reactions is proportional to the number of drugs prescribed, studies show. It is also possible to administer antihistamines and/or corticosteroids (alone, or in combination with α-adrenergic agonists) in advance; this has been found to reduce the number and severity of anaphylactoid reactions.

Alternatively, desensitization is employed to help the patient better tolerate the drug. This is only for patients with a history of an IgE-mediated immediate generalized reaction to a drug, confirmed by skin testing. The desensitization produces a temporary, nonresponsive state lasting as long as therapy continues. Analphylatic sensitivity may return within 48 hours of withdrawing the drug. Caution, and continuation of an agent, such as insulin, is therefore advised. Drugs that are not clearly indicated should also be stopped. If a drug is necessary but possibly cross-reactive, it may be prudent to search for a non cross-reactive drug in the same class.

With allergies, this means the mechanism should be based on the identification of specific antibodies and/or sensitized lymphocytes. Although many drugs will evoke an immune response, only a small number of patients will actually experience a clinical hypersensitivity reaction. Penicillin alone has been associated with many of these reactions. See Table 14.3.

Table 14.3
Immunopathology of Allergic Reactions to Drugs

Classification	Clinical Presentation
Type I	Anaphylaxis, urticaria, angioedema, asthma, rhinitis.
Type II	Immune cytopenias. Some organ inflammation.
Type III	Serum sickness, vasculitis.
Type IV	Contact dermatitis. Some exanthems.

Adapted from Kay, A. Concepts of allergy and hypersensitivity. In: Kay, A. Allergy and allergic diseases. Oxford, UK: Blackwell Science, 1997:23.

Anaphylaxis and urticaria following penicillin administration are examples of type I reactions, and associated with high-dose penicillin therapy is a type II reaction. A serum sickness-like reaction, now most commonly associated with penicillin treatment, is a type III reaction. Finally, the contact dermatitis that occurred when penicillin was used topically in the past is an example of a type IV reaction.

Anaphylaxis occurs most commonly after parenteral administration, but it has also followed oral, percutaneous, and respiratory exposure. Although symptoms, which usually appear within 30 minutes of exposure, can be ameliorated with treatment, they may last 24 hours or longer, or recur several hours after apparent resolution. Without treatment, death can occur within minutes of initial presentation.

T. Pseudoallergy[20]

Some reactions mimic an allergy, but are not associated with antibody production or sensitized T-lymphocytes. This is difficult, if not impossible, to observe clinically or distinguish from hypersensitivity. Pseudoallergy is an inflammatory reaction originating from mast cells, basophils, or other body tissues. A few examples:

- skin flushing
- local red skin rashes
- bronchospasm
- angioedema
- hypotension

Pseudoallergy is also called drug intolerance or anaphylactoid reactions (e.g., bronchospasm, angioedema, urticaria, hypotension), although the anaphylactoid reactions are non-IgE mediated.

U. Angioedema

Angioedema is a reaction causing swelling in the tissue just below the surface of the skin, most often around the lips and eyes. It generally results from an allergic reaction to either a food or medication, wherein histamine causes blood vessels to swell. Sometimes the condition is unilateral, affecting only one side of the body and not the other. The condition is mild in most cases, but severe angioedema can cause bronchoconstriction or swelling of the tongue, both of which can block the airway and cause death.[25]

According to the University of Maryland Medical Center, "The characteristic lesion is well delineated and round or oval; it varies in size from a few millimeters to 25 to 30 cm. Edema appears initially, followed by erythema, which then darkens to become a deeply colored, reddish purple, dense raised lesion....Lesions are most common on the lips and genitals but may occur anywhere on the skin or mucous membranes...."[24]

Angioedema usually presents as a solitary lesion. Sometimes, however, the lesions may be more numerous, and additional ones may develop with re-exposure to the drug. Angioedema usually develops between 30 minutes and eight hours after administration of the offending substance. The average is about two hours.

Common symptoms of angioedema include:[25]

- Sudden appearance of red welts, especially near the eyes and lips, but also on the hands, feet, and the inside of the throat.
- Burning, painful, swollen areas; sometimes itchy.

- Hoarseness, tight or swollen throat, breathing trouble.
- Discolored patches or rash on the hands, feet, face, or genitals.
- Vomiting, abdominal pain, diarrhea, and reduced appetite.
- In a form called angioedema-eosinophilia syndrome, hives, itching, fever, muscle pain, decreased urine, weight gain, and high white blood cell count occur (UNM).

Studies show that more than 50 percent of patients presenting to the ED with angioedema were taking ACE inhibitors. In patients with idiopathic anaphylaxis, ACE inhibitors are contraindicated at least on a relative basis until it has been ruled out as a cause of the reaction.[26]

V. Hypersensitivity Reactions[20]

Allergies and drug reactions that elicit immune responses are not completely understood, perhaps because of the lack of a validated animal model for hypersensitivity. It is also difficult to isolate the antigenic components and metabolites of potential drug allergens. Although much is unknown about the mechanisms of hypersensitivity reactions, it is known that a drug can cause a number of different hypersensitivity reactions (via different mechanisms, even). On the basis of current evidence and existing models of hapten-mediated allergy, a number of complex stages appear to be involved in the generation of an immune response to a drug. These stages are:

1. Formation of a complete antigen.
2. Processing of the complete antigen by antigen-presenting cells.
3. Recognition of the antigenic determinant by the T lymphocytes.
4. Generation of a drug-specific antibody or sensitized T-cells.
5. Elicitation of a clinical immune response.

Sylvia writes:

To be recognized by the immune system, a drug must bind, usually covalently, to a high molecular weight carrier protein, thereby forming a complete antigen. The hapten hypothesis, first described in 1966, offers an understanding of this stage of immune processing. The parent drug rarely has the ability to bind to tissue or cellular proteins and serve as a hapten. For most low molecular weight

drug allergens, the hapten is a reactive metabolite of the parent drug, formed via metabolism in the liver, skin keratinocytes, or white blood cells. 1M-55 As an example, sulfamethoxazole is well recognized as a highly allergenic compound; however, a reactive metabolite, the mitroso-sulfamethoxazole derivative, not the parent compound, serves as the primary hapten.[20]

14.4 Risk Factors, Drugs and Patients
A. Hypersensitivity Risk Factors[20]

Drug hypersensitivity usually involves contributory or predisposing factors—usually drug or patient (host) related. Although numerous studies and ample controversy continues to be the influence of these factors on the risk of hypersensitivity, causes still remain largely unknown.

Besides molecular weight over 4,000 Da, other factors may include chemical composition consisting of protein or peptides, and the ability of the drug to form a covalent bond with a carrier protein. The presence of proteins of non-human origin or the inclusion of antigenic excipients (peanuts, for example) also increases the risk of drug reactivity. As mentioned earlier in this course, another possible hypersensitive provocateur may include the route of drug administration, as well as the dose, and/or frequency of administration.

For example, parenteral routes of administration—perhaps because they provide a higher rate of drug delivery than oral or other routes of administration—seem to provoke more severe reactions (after an initial sensitization).

Dosage also plays a role in provoking hypersensitivity. In general, the amount given is usually proportional to the immune response mounted by the patient's body.

Certain allergic reactions are reported more frequently among specific age groups. For example, anaphylaxis with penicillin has been reported more commonly in patients between the ages of 20 and 49 years compared with children. It is thought, however, that this fact is related more to the possibility of more exposures to the drug throughout an adult individual's lifetime, creating a higher risk of sensitivity.

Over-prescription of antibiotics can also cause hypersensitivity, particularly in those who receive frequent courses of antibiotics (children with chronic otitis media or bronchitis, for example). So, the frequency and number of exposures are more likely to increase risk compared with age.

Gender may be a risk factor for drug allergy. Bigby et al. reported a 35 percent higher incidence of drug-induced allergic cutaneous reactions in women than in men.[27] More recently, in a study of penicillin allergy, Macy et al. also found that women were more likely to present with hypersensitivity reactions.[28]

B. Identification of a Drug Allergy

Drug allergies can sometimes be difficult to identify because so many factors may be involved and contributing to the patient's reaction. Additionally, some symptoms of drug allergy mimic other conditions, such as hypersensitivity reactions.

The key distinguishing factor with allergies, however, is an exaggerated immune response. The physiopathology of these diseases is not well understood. For this reason, physicians must immediately identify risk factors—before an allergic response ever happens. Although clinical and biologic tests are helpful diagnostic tools, they cannot predict who will develop an allergic reaction. For this reason, we must turn to the epidemiological characteristics of the demographic that develops a reported drug allergy reaction.

The factors most associated with drug allergies are:[29]

- Female gender.
- Concomitant infections (HIV, herpes).
- Concurrent illnesses (systemic lupus erythematosis).
- Genetic predisposition (certain ethnic groups have been found to have similar allergies and sensitivities amongst individuals. For example, some ethnic groups seem to be prone to certain types of ADRs. A study by Easterbrook[30] found that being a member of the Caucasian race raised the incidence of hypersensitivity to abacavir. African Americans were found to be more susceptible to developing ACE-related angioedema than other ethnic groups).[26]
- Use of anticonvulsants.
- Insulin-dependent diabetics.
- Use of local injectable anesthetics.
- Use of topical anesthetics.
- Host-related factors can predispose to drug allergy especially by acting on the way the drug is processed.
- Frequent exposure to a drug (such as an anti-retroviral drug used to treat a patient with HIV).

Certain drugs also seem to be more prone to causing reactions than others. The drugs that seem to cause the most problems include:[31]

- Penicillin
- Sulfa drugs

- Anticonvulsants
- Insulin preparations (particularly animal sources of insulin)
- Iodinated (containing iodine) X-ray contrast dyes (these can cause allergy-like anaphylactoid reactions)

C. Penicillins and Cephalosporins

It is estimated that 10 percent of the population is allergic to penicillin. Healthcare students are always taught to specifically ask about an allergy when penicillin is considered. This risk is exacerbated by the fact that more than a dozen other "penicillins" are marketed, but their names do not specifically include "penicillin." A patient allergic to one type of penicillin is at risk for an allergic reaction to another. To further complicate the issue, there is a group of drugs that share the beta lactam ring—the cephalosporins. As a result of this common chemical structure, there is a risk of "cross-allergenicity" when cephalosporins are given to penicillin allergic patients, and vice versa.[32]

In addition to being the most common cause of drug allergy in general, β-lactam antibiotics are also considered to be the most common non-serum causes of serum sickness-like reactions. Other drugs occasionally incriminated include ciprofloxacin, metronidazole, streptomycin, sulfonamides, allopurinol, carbamazepine, hydantoins, methimazole, phenylbutazone, propanolol, and thiouracil.[19]

D. Case Report: Cross-Allergencity

A case in Montana demonstrates the serious nature of allergic reactions and cross-allergenicity of drugs (*Re: Estate of Frank Hamilton v. F. John Allaire, M.D.*, Montana Eighth Judicial District Court, Cascade County CDV-91-303). In this case, a 51-year-old patient suffered anaphylaxis and death in the Montana Deaconess Medical Center following one intramuscular (IM) dose of Ancef (cefazolin). He had a history of penicillin allergy, which he had noted on consent forms to receive drugs and treatments. His physician was aware of the allergy, and the pharmacist also called the physician's attention to the allergic caution. According to Mr. Randy Dix, the attorney representing the family, the hospital pharmacist stated that it was not his job to "second guess" the doctor, and filled the Ancef as ordered. The order read "penicillin sensitive, give one gram Ancef IM." The pharmacist filled the order, and the nurse administered the injection. Shortly thereafter, the patient suffered a cardiopulmonary arrest and died.

In his defense, the physician stated that the patient said that he had suffered a mild rash reaction to previous penicillin. Mild reactions (delayed hypersensitivities) are not a contraindication to cephalosporin. However, when the attending nurse was deposed, she specifically remembered the patient always anxious and asking to be sure that he was not receiving penicillin, because he had a serious reaction to penicillin in the past. The nurse testified that she was not aware of the penicillin-cephalosporin cross-reactivity and obvious contraindication in her patient.

Before initiation of cephalosporin therapy, careful inquiry should be made concerning previous hypersensitivity reactions to cephalosporins, penicillins, and other drugs. Cephalosporins should be avoided in patients who have had an immediate-type (anaphylactic) hypersensitivity reaction to penicillins and should be administered with caution to patients who have had a delayed-type (e.g., rash, fever, eosinophilia) reaction to penicillin.

Experts in the case, including a physician (infectious-disease specialist) and a former hospital pharmacist, stated that other non-cross-reactive drugs were available to treat the patient's suspected pneumonia.

The case was presented to the Montana Medical Legal Panel, who found substantial evidence that such acts or omissions constituted a departure from the accepted standards of healthcare and that there was a reasonable probability that the claimant was injured by such a departure. The hospital settled the lawsuit early in the case. The physician settled the case after experts for the plaintiff gave their reports and depositions.

Unfortunately, it seems that there exists an almost cavalier attitude about this well-described risk of cross-reactivity. Pharmacists should realize that it is their responsibility to monitor for allergic cross-reactivity. Perhaps if the pharmacist in this case had advised the physician of the danger, had called the nurse, or had interviewed the patient, he would have discovered the history of this serious reaction, and this death could have been avoided.

14.5 Erythema Multiforme, Stevens-Johnson Syndrome and Toxic Epidermal Necrolysis[19,20,33-43]

A. Fixed Drug Eruptions

In contrast to most other drug-induced dermatoses, fixed drug eruptions (lesions that continue to recur in the same locations on the body every time a specific allergen is encountered) are considered to be a certain indicator of drug hypersensitivity. Men and children seem to be affected by this reaction more frequently than women. Drugs that have frequently been found to be associated include:

- phenolphthalein
- sulfonarnides

- tetracycline
- barbiturates
- NSAIDs

B. Erythema Multiforme-Like Eruptions

Erythema multiforme (EM minor) is often a benign cutaneous illness with or without minimal mucous membrane involvement. A more severe cutaneous reaction that does affect mucous membranes (at least two mucosal surfaces) and constitutional symptoms is called *erythema multiforme major* (EM major).

EM major is synonymous with Stevens-Johnson syndrome (SJS). In addition, some have considered toxic epidermal necrolysis to represent the most severe form of this disease process, while others think it should be classified separately.

Most instances of drug-induced erythema multiforme can be classified as EM major, or Stevens-Johnson syndrome. This form of EM produces bulbous-erosive lesions and is usually accompanied by high fever, headache, and malaise. It also affects mucosal surfaces. There is often more pronounced truncal involvement. Painful oral and pharyngeal mucous membrane lesions may stop patients from eating. The border of the lips all but disappears and develops serosanguinous crusts. Eighty-five percent of patients develop hyperemia and/or extensive pseudomembrane formation.

Both SJS and TEN are most commonly caused from drugs, especially the following:[20]

- sulfonamides
- cephalosporins
- penicillins
- fluoroquinolones
- anticonvulsants (phenytoin, phenobarbital, and carbamazepine)
- allopurinol
- NSAIDs

TEN (Lyell syndrome) is a sudden, potentially lethal condition presented by widespread blistering of the skin, extensive epidermal necrosis and exfoliation. Some research suggests that TEN may represent the extreme manifestation of EM major. Other studies challenge this position. Further, some write that TEN is a worsening of SJS. All agree that extensive skin involvement with SJS and TEN is best treated in a burn unit.

C. Fluoroquinolones

Effective against both negative and gram-positive organisms, fluoroquinolones are antimicrobial agents with a broad range of activity. Adverse reactions may include skin rash and pruritis, phototoxicity and/or Achilles tendon inflammation and rupture.

D. ASA and NSAIDs

Second to the β-lactam antibiotics, ASA and NSAIDs are the most likely drugs to cause allergic drug reactions. Reactions may include exacerbated urticaria (in 21 to 30 percent of patients who suffer from idiopathic urticaria or angioedema), bronchoconstriction in patients with nasal polyps, persistent erythema, and anaphylaxis. Sometimes, in perfectly healthy patients, there have been reports of urticaria and analphylactoid reactions within minutes after taking ASA or a nonselective NSAID. Respiratory reactions occur in about 10 to 20 percent of asthmatic patients older than 10 years. That said, those with known sensitivities present with reactions in 66 to 97 percent of cases.[19] There is less risk of reaction in asthmatic children under the age of 10, but the risks appear to increase in the teenage years, equaling the number of asthmatic adults who suffer an ADR. Usually, the patients who suffer from respiratory reactions already had established respiratory problems for months or years before a clear, causative reaction from ASA or NSAIDs. Reactions usually occur within two hours of drug ingestion. These reactions may be quite severe, even fatal. They consist of severe nasal congestion, rhinorrhea, and eye problems.

E. NSAIDs Cross Reactivity Case Report

The following is a preliminary report prepared in a case in which an aspirin-allergic patient suffered a serious allergic reaction when prescribed Naproxen, an NSAID. Pharmacists' duties and responsibilities are discussed in the report. The case is in litigation as of the time of publication (2012). The identity of the parties have been anonymized.

I reviewed the following materials in this matter:

1. General Hospital Emergency Room visit for back pain and admission to the hospital the following day following an anaphylactic reaction and angioedema caused by an allergic reaction to Naproxen. Mr. Gonzalez reported that he was allergic to aspirin, and this fact was noted multiple times in the ER record.
2. Subsequent admissions starting with 9/29/09 through 11/19/08 wherein he was treated for airway complications of his initial treatment for his anaphylactic reaction.
3. Pharmacy records for Mr. Gonzalez.

4. Standards of Practice for the Profession of Pharmacy.
5. The Illinois Pharmacy Practice Act.
6. Neighborhood Healthcare records, September, 2006.
7. Authoritative references in pharmacology, pharmacotherapeutics, and allergy related to the cross-sensitivity of Naprosyn (naproxen), an NSAID, and Aspirin (ASA).
8. The PDR (Physician's Desk Reference)—package insert for Naprosyn, 2006 edition.

Facts of the case

Mr. Gonzalez, a 64-year-old, complained of back and leg pain which prompted him to seek care at the Suburban General (SGH) ER on the evening of 9/21/06. He was evaluated and prescribed Lortab (hydrocodone and acetaminophen), and Naprosyn (naproxen), 500 mg twice a day. He filled the prescriptions at a local pharmacy (Naprosyn 500 mg #30). At home, he took one capsule/tablet of naproxen, and reported that within 5 minutes he had difficulty breathing, and returned to the SGH ER. At SGH, he required mechanical ventilation for several days, and was discharged home again. A few days later, he again had severe respiratory complaints, which prompted his return to SGH, where he entered a long and complicated treatment for airway complications following his intubation.

Examination of the Neighborhood Healthcare records indicates an aspirin/ASA allergy (1999 and 2000), as well as treatment for an allergic reaction to Advil (ibuprofen—an NSAID) in 1999. NSAIDs were also listed in his allergy history following an allergic reaction to Advil.

After litigation began, the ER resident physician who prescribed the Naproxen was deposed. He testified that he was unaware of the cross-allergenicity between aspirin and naproxen, and if the pharmacist had called, he would have discontinued the naproxen and avoided NSAIDs in this aspirin-allergic patient.

Opinions

1. Naprosyn/naproxen, an NSAID, is contraindicated in a patient with a history of aspirin allergies. Contraindication means—DO NOT USE! The cross-reactivity of aspirin and NSAIDs is well known and promulgated.

2. The initial allergic/anaphylactic reaction with angioedema was caused by the allergic reaction to Naprosyn.

3. Mr. Gonzalez's history of aspirin allergy (anaphylaxis) was known to Walgreens. Salicylate is listed in the allergy window. Aspirin is listed in another pharmacy profile location. Entry of Naprosyn (naproxen) in the pharmacy system therefore should have precipitated a serious warning to the technician and/or pharmacist. Such a warning should have prompted the pharmacist to inquire further with Mr. Gonzalez regarding his allergy history, which would have verified the aspirin allergy, thus contraindicating the dispensation (SHOULD NOT FILL). The pharmacist(s) who over-rode the computer alert and verified and checked/verified/dispensed the Naprosyn prescription for Mr. Gonzalez violated the standard of care of pharmacists. This violation is a proximate cause of his allergic reaction. This violation put Mr. Gonzalez in danger of a fatal anaphylactic reaction to Naprosyn, which we know occurred.

Had the pharmacist(s) exercised his duty and complied with the standard of care for screening allergies with all prescriptions and responding to the allergy warning, Mr. Gonzalez would not have suffered his acute life-threatening allergic reaction and the subsequent morbidity.

F. Radiographic Contrast Media (RCM)

Non-fatal, immediate generalized reactions to non-iodinated, gadolinium-based contrast agents for magnetic resonance imaging (MRI) occur in about 1 to 2 percent of cases. Severe anaphylactoid reactions are rare (1:350,000 infections).

This is another instance in which risk factors are the best predictors of a possible reaction. The following groups are most like to suffer an ADR after receiving an injected RCM:

- history of a previous reaction to these agents
- severe coronary artery disease
- unstable angina
- advanced age
- female gender
- exposure to large volumes of contrast media
- atopic individuals
- asthmatics

The following patients are just slightly more likely to suffer an ADR after RCM administration:

- patients who react to iodides
- patients with allergies to shellfish

The most common side effects are nausea and vomiting. More generalized reactions include:

- pruritus,
- urticaria,
- angioedema,
- bronchospasm,
- hypotension, and
- syncope.

G. Local Anesthetics

Patients who experience any ADRs following administration of a local anesthetic are often told that they are allergic to the entire range of agents in this classification. This is untrue and dangerous, considering that such patients may not be able to receive routine dental care or outpatient surgical procedures.

The most common reactions to local anesthetics include:

- vasovagal reactions
- toxic reactions
- hysterical reactions
- epinephrine side effects
- contact dermatitis

To manage these patients, use a different local anesthetic agent. For example, substitute an amide for an ester. Amides are not known to cross react with other amides.

As a side note, latex-containing products—such as gloves and rubber dams—are often used in dental and surgical practices. If a patient is allergic to latex, this factor should be considered while testing for adverse reactions that might otherwise be attributed to the local anesthetic.

Among other analgesics, morphine and codeine are most likely to activate mast cells and cause flushing or acute urticaria. Meperidine, tramadol, and fentanyl are much less likely to cause mast-cell activity.

Sometimes, the side effect of opioid painkillers may mimic hypersensitivity. However, if a patient has a history of codeine- or morphine-induced urticaria, alternative agents are recommended when narcotics are required.

H. Anticonvulsants

Phenytoin hypersensitivity syndrome is rare. It usually begins a couple of months after initiation of the drug. Reactions may include fever, marked erythematous papules that may blister, necrosis from vasculitis, liver enlargement and mouth ulcers. These symptoms may actually be an indicator of Stevens-Johnson syndrome (SJS), discussed later in this course. Lab tests may reveal atypical lymphocytes, elevation of serum creatinine, eosinophilia (sometimes pulmonary), leucopenia, and hepatic abnormalities.

Carbamazepine can cause similar reactions and is contraindicated in patients who are hypersensitive to phenytoin, because of their shared structures and metabolism. According to Ditto:

> The mechanism may relate to inadequate detoxification by epoxide hydrolase of hepatic microsome-generated metabolites of phenytoin and carbamazepine. The relatives of affected patients who are themselves non-epileptic and not exposed to phenytoin may have findings of delayed metabolism. The metabolites are thought to cause neoantigen formation with the clinical hypersensitivity syndrome.[19]

14.6 Conclusion

Allergic reactions to drugs may be deadly. Initial dose reactions cannot be avoided. For drugs with high risk for severe allergic reactions, close monitoring, and even pretreatment with an antihistamine and corticosteroid is common (contrast media), or observation of the patient (injections of penicillin). Once an allergic reaction is experienced, the patient should be advised to write down the reaction, tell it to all physicians, pharmacists, and other health providers, and wear a medic alert bracelet. Providers should inquire of allergies, without relying on the patient to volunteer. Allergies should be prominently posted on the patient chart, over the patient's bed, on all drug order and medication administration sheets.

Serious allergic reactions to drugs for which the patient had a known or knowable history is an avoidable adverse reaction—it should not happen. Finally, patients allergic to one drug in a class (penicillin, aspirin) are at risk for an allergic reaction to another drug in the same class (ampicillin, ibuprofen). This is known as a cross-allergenicity. History of hypersensitivity to a member of the class should be considered as a contraindication—do not do it!

Endnotes

1. Trontel, A. CDER/CBER PDUFA3 Risk Management Working Group, April 9, 2003

2. Litaker, John R., and James P. Wilson. "Epidemiology and Public Health Impact of Drug-Induced Diseases." In James E. Tisdale, Douglas A. Miller, *Drug-induced diseases: prevention, detection, and management.* Bethesda, Md.: American Society of Health-System Pharmacists, 2005. 3. Print.

3. Hallas J. "Drug related hospital admissions in sub-specialities of internal medicine." *Dan Med Bull.* 1996;43:141–155.

4. Einarson TR. "Drug-related hospital admissions." *Ann Pharmacother* 1993;27:832–40.

5. Johnson, Jefferey A., and Lyle Bootman. "Drug-Related Morbidity and Mortality: A Cost-of-Illness Model." *Journal of Managed Care Pharmacy* 2.1 (1996): 39-47. Print.

6. Budnitz, Daniel S., Maribeth C. Lovegrove, Nadine Shehab, and Chesley L. Richards. "Emergency Hospitalizations for Adverse Drug Events in Older Americans." *New England Journal of Medicine* 365.21 (2011): 2002-012. Print.

7. Kohn, Linda T. *To Err Is Human: Building a Safer Health System.* Washington: National Academy, 1999. Print.

8. Drug-Related Morbidity and Mortality: A Cost-of-Illness Model, 9 OCTOBER 1995, Johnson and Bootman 155 (18): 1949

9. American Heart Association. Heart Disease and Stroke Slatistics-2005 Update. Dallas, TX:American Heart Association; 2005

10. Jacobsen, Thomas M., and Albert I. Wertheimer. *Modern Pharmaceutical Industry: a Primer.* Sudbury, MA: Jones and Bartlett, 2010. Print.

11. *Guidance for Industry Premarketing Risk Assessment.* Rockville, MD: U.S. Dept. of Health and Human Services, Food and Drug Administration, Center for Drug Evaluation and Rresearch, 2005. Print.

12. Paul, H. "Risks vs. benefits: How a drug firm deals with disputes over its medicines," *NEJM* 300:1046 (1979).

13. Wardell, P. et al. "Postmarketing surveillance of new drugs II: Case study," *J. Cl. Pharm.*, June 1, 1984, p. 1.

14. Wardell, P. "Can post marketing surveillance permit earlier approval?" *Drug Therapy*, Febraury, 1992, p. 143.

15. Schiff, G. "Monitoring and reporting adverse drug reaction," *Infusion* 9(6) (1985).

16. Seligman, P: *Risk Management; The FDA Role*. Office of Pharmacoepidemiology and Statistical Science, Center for Drug Evaluation and Research. GAO, January 17, 2002.

17. Fitzgerald, G. (former FDA officer in the Center for Drug Evaluation and Research). Personal communication, 1992.

18. Dukes, M.N.G., ed. *Side Effects of Drugs Annual 8: A Worldwide Yearly Survey of New Data and Trends* (NY: Elsevier, 1984).

19. Ditto, Marie Anne. "Drug Allergy." In Patterson, Roy, Leslie Carroll. Grammer, and Paul A. Greenberger, *Patterson's Allergic Diseases*. Seventh ed. Baltimore, MD: Wolters Kluwer Health/Lippincott Williams & Wilkins, 2009. 238-70. Print.

20. Sylvia, Lynne M."Drug Allergy and Pseudoallergy" In James E. Tisdale, Douglas A. Miller, *Drug-induced diseases: prevention, detection, and management*. Bethesda, Md.: American Society of Health-System Pharmacists, 2005. 27-50. Print.

21. Savitsky, M.E. "Recognizing hospital adverse drug reactions," *J. Pharm. Pract.* 2(4):203–208 (1989).

22. Alic, Margaret. "Drug Allergies/Sensitivities: Information from Answers.com." *Answers.com: Wiki Q&A Combined with Free Online Dictionary, Thesaurus, and Encyclopedias*. Answers Corporation. Web. 13 Jan. 2009. www.answers.com/topic/drug-allergies-sensitivities.

23. Keim, Samuel M., MD "Drug Allergy Causes, Symptoms, Treatment—Drug Allergy Symptoms on EMedicineHealth." *EMedicineHealth*. Ed. Melissa C. Stoppler, MD. WebMD, Inc. Web. 08 Dec. 2011. www.emedicinehealth.com/drug_allergy/page3_em.htm.

24. Ehrlich, Steven D. "Angioedema." *University of Maryland Medical Center*. University of Maryland Medical System. Web. 23 Jan. 2009. www.umm.edu/altmed/articles/angioedema-000011.htm.

25. Blankenship, Crystal S. "Auditory Nose and Throat Disorders." *Drug-induced Diseases: Prevention, Detection, and Management*. By James E. Tisdale and Douglas A. Miller. Bethesda, MD: American Society of Health-System Pharmacists, 2005. 752. Print.

26. Gibbs, Lip and Beevers (1999), Angioedema due to ACE inhibitors: increased risk in patients of African origin. British Journal of Clinical Pharmacology, 48: 861–865. doi: 10.1046/j.1365-2125.1999.00093.x

27. Bigby M, Jick S, Jick H, Arndt K. Drug-induced cutaneous reactions; a report from the Boston Collaborative Drug Surveillance Program on 152,438 consecutive inpatients, 1975 to 1982. JAMA 1986; 256: 3358–63

28. Macy, Eric, Ripdeep Mangat, and Raoul J. Burchette. "Penicillin Skin Testing in Advance of Need: Multiyear Follow-up in 568 Test Result-negative Subjects Exposed to Oral Penicillins1." *Journal of Allergy and Clinical Immunology* 111.5 (2003): 1111-115. Print.

29. Joint Task Force on Practice Parameters. Disease management of drug hypersensitivity: a practice parameter. Ann Allergy Asthma Immunol. 1999;83:665-700

30. Easterbrook PJ, Waters A, Murad S, et al. Epidemiological risk factors for hypersensitivity reactions to abacavir.HIV Med 2003; 4: 321–324.

31. "Drug Allergies." *University of Pennsylvania Health System | Penn Medicine*. Web. 09 Dec. 2011. www.pennmedicine.org/encyclopedia/em_PrintArticle.aspx?gcid=000819.

32. "Penicillin Allergy—Amoxicillin Allergy—Cephalosporin Allergy." *Allergies — Allergy*. 01 Nov. 2010. Web. 09 Dec. 2011. http://allergies.about.com/od/medicationallergy/a/penicillin.htm.

33. Tripathi A, Peters NT and Patterson R: Chapter 16, Erythema Multiforme, Stevens-Johnson Syndrom, and Toxic Epidermal Necrolysis in Grammer LC and Greenberger PA, Editors: Patterson's Allergic Diseases. Lippincott Williams & Wilkins, Philadelphia, 2002

34. Margolis RJ, Tonnesen MG, Harrist TJ, et. al., Lymphocyte Subsets and Langerhans Cells/Indeterminate Cells in Erythema Multiforme. The Journal of Investigative Dermatology; 81, 1983:403-406

35. Patterson R, Dykewicz MS, Gonzalez A, et al. Erythema Multiforme and Stevens-Johnson Syndrome, Descriptive and Therapeutic Controversy. Chest 1990; 98: 331-336

36. Shiohara T, Chiba M, Tanaka Y, et al. Drug-induced, photosensitive, erythema multiforme-like eruption: Possible role for cell adhesions molecules in a flare induced by Rhus dermatitis. Journal of the American Adademy of Dermatology. 1990;22:647-50

37. Levenson DE, Arndt KA, and Stern RS: Cutaneous Manifestations of Adverse Drug Reactions. Journal of Allergy Clinics of North America, Vol. II, No. 3, August 1991:493-507

38. Patterson R, Grammar LC, Greenberger PA, et al. Stevens-Johnson Syndrome (SJS): Effectiveness of Corticosteroids in Management and Recurrent SJS. Allergy Proceedings, Vol. 13, No. 2, March-April 1992: 89-95

39. Patterson R, Miller M, Kaplan M: Effectiveness of early therapy with corticosteroids in Stevens-Johnson syndrome: experience with 41 cases and a hypothesis regarding pathogenesis. Annals of Allergy; Volume 73, July, 1994: 27-34

40. Cheriyan S, Patterson R, Greenberger PA, et al. The Outcome of Stevens-Johnson Syndrome Treated with Corticosteroids. Allergy Proceedings; 16,4:151-155, 1995

41. Schlienger RG, Knowles SR, and Shear NH: Lamotrigin-associated anticonvulsant hypersensitivity syndrome. Neurology 1998;51:1172-1175

42. Tripathi A, Ditto AM, Grammer LC: Corticosteroid Therapy in an Additional 13 Cases of Stevens-Johnson Syndrome: A Total Series of 67 Cases. Allergy and Asthma Proceedings 21:101-105, 2000

43. Pichler WJ: Delayed Drug Hypersensitivity Reactions. Annals of Internal Medicine, 2003;139:683-693

Recommended Reading

Cheriyan S, Patterson R, Greenberger PA, et al. The Outcome of Stevens-Johnson Syndrome Treated with Corticosteroids. Allergy Proceedings; 16,4:151-155, 1995

Committee on Safety of Medicines. "Suspension of products licenses for benoxaprofen," Lancet 2:396 (1982).

Jick, H. et al. "A population-based study of appetite suppressant drugs and the risk of cardiac-valve regurgitation," New England Journal of Medicine 332(11):719–724 (1998).

O'Donnell, J.T. "Injuries from drugs," Am. Jur. Proof of Facts, 3rd. series (San Francisco: Bancroft Whitney, 1990).

O'Donnell, J.T. "Introduction to adverse drug reactions," Infusion 9(4):112–115 (1985).

Patterson R, Dykewicz MS, Gonzalez A, et al. Erythema Multiforme and Stevens-Johnson Syndrome, Descriptive and Therapeutic Controversy. Chest 1990; 98: 331-336

Patterson R, Grammar LC, Greenberger PA, et al. Stevens-Johnson Syndrome (SJS): Effectiveness of Corticosteroids in Management and Recurrent SJS. Allergy Proceedings, Vol. 13, No. 2, March-April 1992: 89-95

Pichler WJ: Delayed Drug Hypersensitivity Reactions. Annals of Internal Medicine, 2003;139:683-693

Shiohara T, Chiba M, Tanaka Y, et al. Drug-induced, photosensitive, erythema multiforme-like eruption: Possible role for cell adhesions molecules in a flare induced by Rhus dermatitis. Journal of the American Adademy of Dermatology. 1990;22:647-50

Stephens, M.D.B., J.C.C. Talbot and P.A. Routledge. Detection of New Adverse Drug Reactions, 4th ed. (Hampshire, England: MacMillan, 1998).

Tisdale JE and Miller DA. Chapter 4: Drug-Induced Diseases, Prevention, Detection, and Management. American Society of Health-System Pharmacists, Bethesda, Maryland, 2005

Tripathi A, Ditto AM, Grammer LC: Corticosteroid Therapy in an Additional 13 Cases of Stevens-Johnson Syndrome: A Total Series of 67 Cases. Allergy and Asthma Proceedings 21:101-105, 2000

Tripathi A, Peters NT and Patterson R: Chapter 16, Erythema Multiforme, Stevens-Johnson Syndrom, and Toxic Epidermal Necrolysis in Grammer LC and Greenberger PA, Editors: Patterson's Allergic Diseases. Lippincott Williams & Wilkins, Philadelphia, 2002.

Chapter 15

Evaluation of Medical Causation

Donald H. Marks, M.D., Ph.D.

15.1 What is Causation

Medical causation is the determination of whether an adverse effect was caused by the use of a medication, biological, vaccine, device or procedure, generally referred to as "treatments." An adverse effect refers to an untoward physical sign, symptom, abnormal assessment (lab value, vital sign, ECG, etc.), or cluster of signs, symptoms, abnormal assessments within the definition of FDA reg 21 CFR.[1] Physical signs can include fever, hypertension, weight loss or other physical findings. A symptom can include any complaint from a patient, including nausea, headache, abdominal pain or others. A medication can refer to any FDA-approved prescription drug or to an over-the-counter preparation. Biologicals refer to prepared synthetic materials of living origin. Vaccines are preparations designed to induce a protective or therapeutic immune response. Medical devices include both large units (MRI) and miniature units (intravascular stents).

15.2 Importance of Establishing Causation

Patients who receive a treatment for an illness generally can be expected to have, as a result of their illness, physical signs and symptoms as manifestations of their illness. As a general statement, all treatments also can cause their own array of physical signs and symptoms separate from the underlying illness being treated, and these new signs and symptoms are referred to as adverse effects. This illustrates the crux of medical causation's difficulty—distinguishing adverse effects of treatments from signs or symptoms of the underlying illness they are being given to treat.

This problem is illustrated by the medication Lotronex (Alosetron, Glaxo Wellcome), an antagonist of the 5-HT3 (serotonin) receptor. Lotronex was indicated for the treatment of severe, chronic, diarrhea-predominant irritable bowel syndrome (IBS) in women who had failed conventional therapy. IBS patients can typically present with a wide range of GI symptoms and signs. Unfortunately, Lotronex can act both as serotonergic drug and as a Serotonin Reuptake Inhibitor (SRI). Serotonin is a potent neurotransmitter (NM) which activates a muscle at the neuromuscular (NM) endplate. The intensity and duration of the muscle activation is directly related to the concentration of serotonin at the NM end plate. Lotronex mimics serotonin at the active receptor and blocks serotonin resorption, thereby causing an inordinately high level of serotonin activity in the GI NM endplate. This high serotonin level can be associated with severe vasoconstriction and ischemia.[2]

These elevated serotonin levels are known and accepted causes of many of the serious side effects of Lotronex, including obstruction, perforation, impaction, toxic megacolon, and secondary ischemia. This led to the quandary that the signs and symptoms of an adverse effect[3] from the medication Lotronex, which could have warned of an adverse event (AE) and led to the drug's discontinuation, were similar to the not unexpected signs and symptoms of the underlying disease (IBS) being treated. Ultimately this difficulty of use led to the removal of Lotronex from the market.

Another example is the development of depression leading to suicidal thought from use of metoclopramide.[4] This drug has both central (nausea) and peripheral (gastric motility) actions, can be an antagonist of dopamine, and sensitize gastric smooth muscle to the effects of acetylcholine stimulation. Metoclopramide (Reglan) has a varied CNS effect, including drowsiness, extra pyramidal syndrome (dystonias, akathesia), depression, dizziness and insomnia. It should not be surprising that a drug with antipsychotic efficacy, and which can cause akathesia, may cause an increased risk of suicide, as is pointed out in the prescribing information for Reglan.

15.3 Definitions

In general, both the pharmaceutical industry and the regulatory bodies use the same definitions for adverse events (AE), effects, and for the FDA these are contained in 21CFR.[1] Providers who observe potential AE, and patients who experience AE, can use different definitions or meanings of commonly used terms such as causation, probable, possible, severe, serious. This potentially imprecise use of terms can lead to some confusion when AE are reported to regulatory agencies. This potential for discrepancy is one of the reasons why primary MedWatch reports need to be thoroughly evaluated, rather than simply tabulated. MedWatch reports can supply critical information on unsuspected, previously unreported adverse events (e.g., heart valve thickening and pulmonary hypertension after Fen-Phen), or an incidence rate which is greater than previously known (rhabdomyolysis with statins). The following are definitions of some commonly used terms, which are found in 21CFR 312.32 (revised as of April 1, 2011):

1. **Adverse events**: any unfavorable and unintended diagnosis, symptom, sign (including an abnormal laboratory finding), syndrome or disease which either occurs during the drug's use, having been absent at baseline, or, if present at baseline, appears to worsen. Any untoward medical occurrence associated with the use of a drug in humans should be considered in a broader sense to be an adverse event, whether or not considered drug related.

2. **Life-threatening adverse events** or suspected life-threatening adverse reactions are those which, in the view of either the investigator or sponsor, place the patient or subject at immediate risk of death. They do not include adverse events or suspected adverse reactions which, had they occurred in a more severe form, might have caused death.

3. **Serious adverse events**: any untoward medical occurrences that (1) result in death, (2) are life threat-

ening, (3) require (or prolong) hospitalization, (4) cause persistent or significant disability/incapacity, (5) result in congenital anomalies or birth defects, or (6) are other conditions which in the judgment of the physician represent significant hazards. Important medical events that may not result in death, be life-threatening, or require hospitalization may still be considered to be serious when, based upon appropriate medical judgment, they may jeopardize the patient or subject and may require medical or surgical intervention to prevent one of the outcomes listed in this definition. Examples of such medical events include allergic bronchospasm requiring intensive treatment in an emergency room or at home, blood dyscrasias or convulsions that do not result in inpatient hospitalization, or the development of drug dependency or drug abuse.

15.4 Degree Adverse Effects Relate to Intervention

Causation can be described as definitely, probably, possibly or unrelated to the treatment. Each of the degrees of relatedness has definite meanings, and their structured and consistent application is important for patients receiving the medication and for prescribing physicians. These terms are defined in 21CFR,[1] and their use is consistent throughout the pharmaceutical industry, the FDA, CDC and WHO. Under the revised (April 1, 2011) reporting FDA requirements (21CFR 312.32) for adverse events (AEs) which occur in an investigational new drug application (IND), the definition of "suspected adverse reaction" imposes a greater burden on sponsors to determine whether the drug caused the event. A wider application to these revised rules and definitions should be anticipated.

The determination of a degree of causation must occur within structured guidelines,[5] such as those of Koch,[24] Hill[6,7] or Riddell.[8] A practical definition scheme for assessing the degree of causality is as follows:

Unrelated:
The adverse event is clearly due to extraneous causes (e.g., underlying disease, environment).

Unlikely (must have 2):
The adverse event:
1) does not have temporal relationship to intervention,
2) could readily have been produced by the subject's clinical state,

3) could have been due to environmental or other interventions,

4) does not follow a known pattern of response to intervention,

5) does not reappear or worsen with reintroduction of intervention.

Possible (must have 2):

The adverse event:

1) has a reasonable temporal relationship to intervention,[9]

2) could not readily have been produced by the subject's clinical state,

3) could not readily have been due to environmental or other interventions,

4) follows a known pattern of response to intervention.

Probable (must have 3):

The adverse event:

1) has a reasonable temporal relationship to intervention,

2) could not readily have been produced by the subject's clinical state or have been due to environmental or other interventions,

3) follows a known pattern of response to intervention,

4) disappears or decreases with reduction in dose or cessation of intervention.

Definite (must have all 4):

The adverse event:

1) has a reasonable temporal relationship to intervention,

2) could not readily have been produced by the subject's clinical state or have been due to environmental or other interventions,

3) follows a known pattern of response to intervention,

4) disappears or decreases with reduction in dose or cessation of intervention and recurs with re-exposure.

Under the revised (April 1, 2011) reporting FDA requirements (21CFR 312.32) for AEs which occur in an IND, the relationship of "unknown" is not an option for causality of serious adverse events. In the revised regulations, there is greater burden to establish a cause. If there is *no* cause clearly determined in the evaluation of an SAE then the SAE would be stated to be *definitely associated* or caused

by the product. The burden then shifts from the investigator to the sponsor to determine with aggregate data that the SAE is not associated with the product being tested.

15.5 Methodology to Investigate Causation

Signs or symptoms associated with both regulated treatments and non-regulated supplements can be observed in any phase of development ranging from clinical trial (before a drug is on the market), through initial marketing, up to many years. Clinical studies beyond the initial and characteristically small Phase I study are designed primarily to demonstrate efficacy—safety data is collected as a secondary parameter. Clinical studies, which can be conducted in a randomized, blinded or non-randomized, non-blinded setting, are varied in their design, and strongly influenced by the disease studied, the drug, and the types of information sought (safety, dosing, efficacy, disease-specific). It is for these reasons that referring to the randomized clinical trial (RCT) as the gold standard for demonstrating causation is overly simplistic and deceptive. Important safety data which has allowed the discovery of new counter indications for already-licensed drugs, and caused the removal from market of others, has even come from a few cases presented in collected case series.[10–12]

Some of the structured settings in which adverse effects can be evaluated include:

RCT—however, efficacy is almost always the primary parameter, and safety is collected as a secondary parameter. An example would be adverse effects which are collected during the efficacy trial of an antihypertensive medication. Data can be collected actively (for example, actively questioned for, and data collected in case report forms, or passively collected, as when patients volunteer information on adverse effects that are not actively questioned for).

Epidemiologic studies—non-randomized, non-blinded studies which can collect incidence and prevalence data on adverse events in a specific population.

Case-controlled studies—patients who exhibit an adverse event are matched with multiple demographically similar but non-exposed patients.[13–15]

Individual case reports[16] or series—physicians (used here as a general term to include other health-care providers) publish their observations of novel, unreported adverse effects in individual patients (cases) or groups of patients (series).

15.6 Structured Algorithms for Determination of Causation

Koch was perhaps the first to set down rules of causation, albeit not for adverse events.[24] The famous Koch postulates were designed to demonstrate whether a disease was caused by an infectious organism. Some have attempted to adapt Koch's postulates from infectious disease to drug AE causation, but this has generally been unsatisfactory.

Koch's Postulates:
1) The suspected agent must be isolated from a patient with the disease in question.
2) The agent must be grown in the laboratory in pure culture.
3) The isolated agent, grown in pure culture, when infected into a healthy host produces exactly the same clinical disease.
4) One is able to isolate the same infective organism from the newly diseased person.[24]

Not only are Koch's postulates not useful for determining AE causation for medications, they are also not practical for many diseases, including HIV (intentional application of the third postulate). In contrast, other criteria, such as those defined by Hill and Riddell, are well-suited for drug adverse causation.

With a set of eight or nine rules, Hill and also Riddell established systematic methods for evaluating potential drug adverse effect causation. Not all of their rules need to be met for causation to be established, and some are more important than others. One of the first rules to meet is temporality, for it is obvious that symptoms of a putative adverse event which occur before the introduction of a treatment could not have been caused by the treatment. However, the symptom or symptom complex, even if pre-existing, can be exacerbated by the introduction of the medication.

Hill Criteria[17]	Riddell Criteria
• Strength of association	• Temporal eligibility
• Consistency of results	• Latent period
• Specificity	• Exclusion
• Temporal relationship	• De-challenge
• Dose response	• Re-challenge[18,19]
• Biologic plausibility	• Singularity of the drug
• Biologic coherence	
• Experimentation	• Pattern
• Analogy	• Drug identification

A. Hill Criteria—Expanded Discussion

1. Strength of Association
A strong association gives support to a causal hypothesis. A weak association requires other information but can be equally as important.

2. Consistency of Results
Repeated findings in different populations and different settings.

3. Specificity
Strengthens confidence in association. Lack of specificity does not rule out causation.

4. Temporal Relationship
Required: exposure must come before disease.

5. Dose Response
Increased dose = increased risk. This holds true for both drugs and for vaccines.

6. Biological Plausibility
Known mechanism not required. For example:

- Cigarettes and lung cancer
- Asbestos and lung cancer
- Fen-Phen and valvular heart disease and PPH

7. Biological Coherence
Does not conflict with what is known.

8. Experimentation
RCT is close to experimentation. Removal or reduction of exposure reduces disease. Challenge—de-challenge—re-challenge.

9. Analogy
Similarities with other like exposure. For example:

- Aminorex and PPH
- Ergot drugs and VHD

All of these systems for determination can be simplified in an algorithm-based analysis:

1. Temporal relatedness
2. Known or reported AE of medication
3. Presence of concurrent illnesses or medications which could present similarly

4.   Challenge—de-challenge—re-challenge

15.7 Comments on the Individual Riddell Criteria for Causation

Temporal Eligibility: As previously discussed, an effect must occur after a treatment in order to establish causation. The effect should not occur *too* long after the treatment. Inevitably, the question becomes: how long is too long? Regardless of the context, this question, asked without accompanying details, can only have one answer: it depends. Some drugs, such as PCP and Lariam, are known to have neuropsychiatric adverse effects that can last for years after the drug was last taken.

Latent Period: Although the closer the interval between the introduction of the treatment and the adverse effect the better, a long latent period can still be consistent with a causal relatedness. Some adverse effects can have immediate action, or a latent period in seconds, such as immediate hypersensitivity reactions. Other adverse effects are more subtle, although equally lethal, such as acetaminophen liver toxicity.

Exclusion: It is important to rule out the effect of concurrent medications or underlying medical conditions such as alternative hypothesis. Liver enzyme elevations in a diabetic patient with underlying fatty liver, and simultaneously taking a statin for hyperlipidemia, can be a challenge for determination of causation. Regardless, with careful attention to the timeline and details, even in such cases, a determination can be made.

Challenge: The disappearance or improvement of an adverse event after the withdrawal of the treatment is a positive indication of relatedness. Adverse events can however persist after the treatment is withdrawn, which indicates either that there was no relatedness, or that the adverse effect causes persistent injury.

Re-challenge: Reintroduction of a treatment which is associated with the same or similar adverse event is a good indication of causation. If the adverse event does not reappear, this can be a sign of lack of causation, but may also indicate the development of tolerance. Of course, since the potential association in the first place may prevent the reintroduction of the suspect treatment, this is not always possible to see.

Singularity of the Drug: It is important to determine whether there is something unique about the adverse reaction experience that is not consistent with any other drug taken or any existing disease condition. Even when a supposed unique adverse reaction is noted (heart valve thickening and pulmonary hypertension with FenPhen), careful investigation can show that a pharmacologically similar medication is known to cause similar adverse effects.

Pattern: It is important to determine whether similar adverse effects have been described in the literature with the treatment in question or by another medication in the same therapeutic class. A characteristic morphologic pattern in a target organ may suggest an association with a particular drug or group of drugs. For example, "Pseudo tumor cerebri with hypervitaminosis" provides a literature precedent, and a biological plausibility for neurologic injury with Accutane.

Drug Identification: Identification of the causative agent is of major utility in toxicity and overdose cases. In some cases, such as over-the-counter ephedra associated with intracranial hemorrhage, there may be neither a package insert, nor an established laboratory procedure for measuring blood level concentration. It is important to take into account drug metabolism, as it may affect the drug level detected. In some cases, for example with vaccines and biologicals, quantitative determination is not possible, and demonstration of an immune response will suffice.

15.8 *Daubert* and the Evolution of Causation[20,21]

The accurate determination of causation is a crucial part of every investigation of an adverse effect. Causation can determine whether a treatment receives a marketing authorization, whether a treatment is withdrawn from market, and if the AE frequency will be reported in the accompanying labeling (which has a great influence on the competitive market position). The *Daubert* ruling (*Daubert v. Merrell Dow Pharmaceuticals, Inc.,* 509 U.S. 579, 113 S.Ct. 2786, 125 L.Ed.2d 469, 1993) set the stage for the Federal Rules of Evidence,[22] which is the standard for admitting testimony about scientific evidence. Many, if not most, expert reports concerning causation can expect to have a *Daubert* challenge over scientific validity. The United States Supreme Court upheld the trial court's exclusion of evidence in the *Daubert* case, giving as part of its opinion, four criteria that the trial judge should consider in determining if evidence should be admitted:

1.   The theory's testability,
2.   whether it "has been a subject of peer review or publication,"
3.   the "known or potential rate of error," and
4.   the "degree of acceptance" within the relevant scientific community.

The court stressed that this analysis was intended to be flexible, with the trial judge determining how and whether the factors applied in a given case. Although not comparable to the Hill or Riddell criteria, they are just as important, and determinations of causation, while not needing to address all criteria, need to be consistent with them. Any inconsistencies should have a logical and factual basis.

Daubert v. Merrell Dow Pharmaceuticals, Inc., 43 F.3d 1311, 1317 [9th Cir., 1995] expanded on these rules, listing the following as important considerations:

1. The cases versus controls must have a relative risk or odds ratio of ≥ 2.0 .
2. The data must be from double or triple-blind clinical trials.
3. The evidence cited should be from relevant peer-reviewed scientific journals.
4. Challenge/de-challenge/re-challenge studies are useful in suggesting causation.
5. Perform or cite epidemiological studies with adequate samples, controls, and appropriate statistical analyses.
6. Theories or methods utilized should be generally accepted in the relevant scientific community or discipline.
7. The investigator must make every effort to account for or rule out alternative explanations of the outcome.
8. Testimony by scientific experts should be non-litigation driven.
9. Purported outcome effects should be from similar purported causes.

Each of these criteria is briefly explained below:

1. Cases versus controls with a relative risk or odds ratio of ≥ 2.0 is a relative and arbitrary standard and not applicable to all conditions, such as idiosyncratic reactions.
2. Blind, randomized, clinical trials are in general supported by drug companies, to demonstrate efficacy as a means to achieving licensure. Safety data is collected as a secondary parameter.
3. Even evidence cited from relevant peer-reviewed scientific journals can be questionable. Ghost writing is a common practice in research supported by the pharmaceutical industry. There also have been a number of recent examples of scientific falsification of data, questionable methods and conflict of interest in several prominent peer-reviewed medical journals.
4. Challenge/de-challenge/re-challenge studies are useful in suggesting causation.

5. Cite epidemiological studies with adequate samples, controls, and appropriate statistical analyses. There are many instances where the RCT is not appropriate to evaluate a causal relatedness, including:
   a. the difficulties in definition of the population to be studied,
   b. the large sample size needed to detect an event of low incidence (such as suicide, suicide ideation or homicide), and
   c. the bias introduced by employing multiple investigators in order to generate a large sample size.[23]

   In these cases, an alternative study design, such as challenge-rechallenge, has the potential to better determine whether or not a drug effect is present. These alternative study designs do employ components of the RCT, but can remove bias inherent in epidemiologic studies, view patients at higher risk from a wide variety of sources, and employ objective experimental measures to clarify patient selection, diagnostic, and response parameters.
6. Theories or methods utilized should be generally accepted in the relevant scientific community or discipline. This is always important, but not all physicians in all cultures and localities agree on the existence, importance or cause of some diseases.
7. The investigator must make every effort to account for or rule out alternative explanations of the outcome. However, a drug may be a proximate cause without being *the* proximal cause, and still be causal. A drug may be a necessary (that without which not) condition without being a sufficient (the only) condition. "Ruling out" is not always possible. Further, alternative explanations can still exist.
8. Testimony by scientific experts should be non-litigation driven. This is important as a demonstration of honesty and objectivity; however many if not most experts have ties to one side of the issue or another, and are compensated for their expert opinions. Applying these criteria to FDA Advisory Committee membership, very few experts would be able to serve.
9. Purported outcome effects should be from similar purported causes. No comment is necessary.

15.9 Does Causation Need to be Established Before a Warning is Given?

This is an area of concern for the pharmaceutical industry, for the prescribing clinician and for the patient. The FDA gives guidance on this issue in 21CFR 201.57. This section provides specific requirements on the content and format (warnings) for human prescription drugs. Section (e) states:

> e. Warnings: Under this section heading, the labeling shall describe SAE and potential safety hazards, limitations in use imposed by them, and steps that should be taken if they occur. The labeling should be revised to include a warning as soon as there is reasonable evidence of an association of a serious hazard with a drug, a causal connection need not have been shown.

Key points that can be taken from 21CFR 201.57 are:

1. The FDA regulations provide a broad duty to warn: "all serious and potential." The FDA threshold is not proven causation, but as soon as an "association" is detected. This explains why it states, "a causal connection need not have been shown."
2. The duty to warn is also a continuing duty to amend and revise: "...as soon as there is..." The duty to warn is placed on the manufacturer, not on the FDA: Warnings for prescription drugs are typically directed to prescribing physicians, but there are also occasions where warnings must be made directly to the consumer.

15.10 Summary

The determination of causation of an adverse effect by a medical treatment is complex. Only by applying a structured, scientific approach consistent with established criteria can an accurate causal assessment be reached.

Endnotes

1. "Title 21: Food and Drugs; Part 310.305(b): New Drugs; Records and Reports; Definitions." *Code of Federal Regulations*. Washington DC: U.S. Government Printing Office.

2. Camilleri, M. Jan. 14, 2003. "Safety concerns about alosetron." *Arch. Intern. Med.* 162(1):100–101.

3. Karch FE, Lasagna L. Towards the operational identification of adverse drug reactions. Clin Pharmac & Ther. 1977; 21: 247-253;

4. Marks DH. *Depression Leading to Suicide As An Adverse Effect of Metoclopramide*. www.ispub.com/ostia/index.php?xmlFilePath=journals/ijge/vol5n2/depression.xml. Internet Journal of Gastroenterology [peer-reviewed serial on the Internet]. 2007. Volume 5(2).

5. Hutchinson TA, Lane DA. Assessing methods for causality assessment. J Clin Epidemiol 1989, 42: 5-16.

6. Doll R. Sir Austin Bradford Hill and the progress of medical science.

7. Morabia A. On the origin of Hill's causal criteria. Epidemiology (1991 Sep) 2(5):367-9

8. Riddell RH., ed. Pathology of Drug-Induced and Toxic Diseases. Churchill Livingstone, New York, 1982 (3-9).

9. Horwitz RI, Feinstein AR, Harvey MR. Temporal Precedence and other problems of the exposure-disease relationship. Archives of Internal Medicine. 1984;144:1257-1259.

10. Connolly, H.M., Crary, J.L., McGoon, M.D., et al. Aug. 28, 1997. "Valvular heart disease associated with fenfluramine–phentermine." *N. Engl. J. Med.* 337(9):581–588.

11. Jick H, Vessey MP. Case-control studies in the evaluation of drug-induced illness. American Journal of Epidemiology. 1978;107:1-7.

12. Jones JK. Determining Causation from Case Reports, in Strom BL, Pharmacoepidemiology, Second Edition, Wiley, New York, 1994

13. Austin H, Hill HA, Flanders D, Greenberg RS. Limitations in the applications of case-control methodology. Epidemiologic Reviews. 1994;16:65-76.

14. Breslow NE, Day NE. Statistical Methods in Cancer Research. Volume I -The Analysis of Case-Control Studies Lyon: International Agency for Research on Cancer; 1980.

15. Schlesselman JJ. Case-Control Studies. Design, Conduct, Analysis New York: Oxford University Press; 1982.

16. Kazdin A. Single-Case Research Designs. New York: Oxford University Press; 1982.

17. Hill AB. The environment and disease: association or causation. Proc Roy Soc Med. 1966; 58: 295-300.

18. Girard M. Conclusiveness of rechallenge in the interpretation of adverse drug reactions. Brit J Clin Pharmacology. 1987; 23: 73-79.

19. Stevens M. Deliberate drug rechallenge. Human Toxicology. 1983; 2: 573-577.

20. *Daubert v. Merrell Dow Pharmaceuticals, Inc.*, 509 U.S. 579, 113 S.Ct. 2786, 125 L.Ed.2d 469 (1993).

21. *Daubert v Merrill Dow Pharmaceuticals, Inc.*, 43 F.3d 1311, 1317 (9th Cir. 1995).

22. Reference Manual On Scientific Evidence, 2nd ed., Federal Judicial Center, 2000

23. Sackett DL. Bias in analytic research. Journal of Chronic Diseases. 1979;32:51-63.

24. Koch Robert (1893). "Über den augenblicklichen Stand der bakteriologischen Choleradiagnose" (in German). Zeitschrift für Hygiene und Infectionskrankheiten 14: 319–333; Koch Robert (1884). "2 Die Aetiologie der Tuberkulose". Mitt Kaiser Gesundh. pp. 1–88.

Chapter 16

The Role of Pharmacoepidemiology and Expert Testimony

William N. Kelly, Pharm.D., FISPE

16.1 Introduction

It is natural to look for blame when someone is harmed by a medication, something that is supposed to confer a benefit. All drugs have side effects and are potentially dangerous. Additionally, people vary in how they react to medication.

It is often difficult to discover whether a medication caused the drug misadventure, and if the drug misadventure was avoidable. If the drug caused the misadventure and was avoidable, then the questions are: (1) was the drug misadventure because of negligence of a healthcare provider? or (2) was the product (drug) defective? And, if defective, was the defect known before the drug mishap?

Some answers to these questions are possible through the discipline of *pharmacoepidemiology*—a long and fancy word for the study of drug risk—and the testimony of an expert in drug safety.

This chapter will:

* define common terms used in pharmacoepidemiology,
* discuss the nature of drug misadventures,
* discuss the four mechanisms by which drug misadventures occur,
* discuss methods used to discover the likelihood of a drug causing a drug misadventure,
* define the term "evidence-based medicine" as it relates to drug misadventures,
* discuss the four types of studies used to discover the safety of medication,
* discuss how the quality of the evidence is determined,
* discuss the duties and responsibilities doctors, pharmacists, and patients have for preventing drug misadventures, and
* discuss the role of pharmacoepidemiologists in drug injury testimony.

16.2 Drug "Misadventures"

The term "drug misadventures" was coined by Henry Manasse in 1989.[1] The definition is complex: An iatrogenic hazard or incident (1) that is an inherent risk when drug therapy is indicated; (2) that is created through either omission or commission by administering a drug or drugs during which a patient is harmed, with effects ranging from mild discomfort to fatality; (3) whose outcome may be independent of the preexisting pathology or disease process; (4) that may be attributable to error (human or systemic, or both), immunological response, or idiosyncratic response; or (5) that is always unexpected and thus unacceptable to patient and prescriber.

Later, Manasse simplified drug misadventures to mean "when something goes wrong with drug therapy and is unexpected."[2] What can go wrong with drugs that *is* expected? The answer is: side effects. Side effects are known, expected, minor, annoying effects of the drug that are experienced by many people taking it. An example is the drowsiness that occurs with older antihistamine drugs used for allergies and the common cold. What follows are the four different types of drug misadventures that can occur.

A. Adverse Drug Reactions

Some drugs can cause more dangerous conditions called "adverse drug reactions" (ADRs). These are unwanted, and usually more serious, adverse effects of the drug than side effects, and occur in a much smaller proportion of patients. ADRs can be divided into two major categories—type A and type B. ADRs classified as type-A reactions have a basis in the pharmacology of the drug, are dose-related, and are thus predictable. The toxicity experienced as the result of a type-A ADR is an expected effect that has gone too far. An example is morphine: a known adverse effect of morphine is that it affects the part of the brain that controls breathing. Giving too much morphine heightens analgesia, but can also potentially reduce breathing—even to the point of death.

ADRs classified as type-B reactions are much different. These are unpredictable events that are often called "bizarre" or "idiosyncratic." These reactions are not based on the drug's pharmacology, nor is the adverse effect dose-related. An example would be if someone took a drug and their hair turned green.

B. Allergic Drug Reactions

Another drug misadventure is the allergic drug reaction. Some feel these are a subcategory of ADRs. Patients allergic to a drug or an ingredient in the medication—even a color dye—can experience drug reactions that vary from a minor annoyance to a life-threatening event. These reactions are antigen/antibody-based, and are termed immunologic.

In allergic drug reactions, the drug is the antigen. A person experiencing a true allergic reaction must have been exposed to the drug at least once previously without experiencing any major adverse effects. Once exposed to the drug, for reasons unknown, some people produce antibodies to the drug. The next time the person is exposed to that drug, the antigen (the drug or something in the drug) reacts with the previously produced antibodies.

Antigen-antibody reactions set a cascade of adverse effects in motion, some of which are based on the release of histamine. An example of an allergic drug reaction would be someone experiencing flushing, low blood pressure, and breathing difficulty (anaphylaxis) after taking penicillin, or experiencing a warm, itchy, red rash (urticaria).

C. Drug Interactions

Another category of drug misadventures is drug interactions. Some drugs interact with other drugs or with food or drink the patient is taking. One drug can make another drug less or more active. An example is the interaction between the asthma drug theophylline and the antibiotic ciprofloxacin. In this case, ciprofloxacin increases the serum levels of theophylline, which may induce theophylline toxicity. Some people feel drug interactions are a subcategory of ADR.

D. Medication Errors

The last category of drug misadventures is medication errors. Medication errors are sometimes the result of human error, but are commonly the result of a faulty "safety net" in the medication-use system. The medication-use system is complex, and healthcare professionals, especially pharmacists, have built safeguards that protect patients from experiencing a medication mishap. However, the medication system is getting even more complex, and more and more medication is being prescribed. This increases the likelihood of a medication error.

No health professional wants to make a medication error. Medication errors are often the result of poor systems or systems that break down. There are two types of human error—slips and mistakes.[3] "Slips" are defined as "attention-deficit" errors. In other words, the person knew better, but because of inattention or distraction, she did something wrong. Almost everyone has made these errors. An example is going to the supermarket and inadvertently bringing home a sugared cola drink, rather than a diet drink. The cans look similar.

The other type of error is a "mistake." A mistake is an error made because of lack of knowledge, education, or understanding. An example would be a doctor—out of ignorance—writing a prescription for a drug, such as propranalol (a drug contraindicated in patients with respiratory distress), for an asthma patient.

1. Prevalence of medication errors

a. In hospitalized patients

The prevalence of adverse drug reactions in hospitalized patients has been well-studied. A meta-analysis of high quality studies was completed in 1998.[4] Results suggest that 1 in 15 hospital patients in the United States can expect to suffer from a serious reaction to a prescription or over-the-counter drug, and about 5 percent of these may die. These figures are for reactions to drugs when the medication was administered correctly.

There have been many studies on the prevalence of medication errors in hospitals. Results differ, depending on how errors are counted. The prevalence of medication errors cannot accurately be determined by reporting medication errors through an incident-reporting system like those present in hospitals. The result is a gross underreporting and lack of a proper denominator (doses administered, patient days, and so on) to determine the actual error rate. The observation method (observing how medication is processed) of discovering medication errors is the most valid and reliable way to study medication errors.[5]

Medication error rates also vary because of the disparate definitions of what makes up an "error." For example, in a recent study of medication errors observed in 36 hospitals and skilled nursing facilities in the United States, 19 percent of doses were administered in error.[6] The frequency of errors by category were:

- Wrong time: 19 percent
- Omission: 30 percent
- Wrong dose: 17 percent
- Unauthorized drug: 4 percent

Seven percent of the errors were judged to be "potentially harmful." This translates into more than 40 medication errors each day in a typical 300-bed facility, not all of which cause harm. Some studies of medication errors do not count medication given at the wrong time as an error, and thus report lower medication-error rates. Some studies also include misspelled patient names as errors.

b. Long-term care facilities

There have been some studies of medication errors in long-term care facilities. One study discovered an observed error rate of 12.2 percent.[7]

c. Ambulatory care

The extent of ADEs in the ambulatory environment has not been well-studied. Thus, it is like an iceberg, submerged 95 percent below the waterline. The frequency with which ambulatory patients experience drug misadventures and the number of patients who seek the attention of their doctors when they experience an adverse effect is still a guess. No one knows for sure. Also unknown is the extent and kind of medication errors in community pharmacy. This information is a closely guarded secret. However, there is some evidence to indicate the medication error rate in retail pharmacies is less than medication error rates in hospitals.[8] There is some evidence that medication error rates in mail order pharmacies are much lower than in other pharmacy settings, largely because of automation.[9]

d. Emergency room and clinic visits

Studies suggest that 1.7–3.9 percent of patients visiting an emergency room are there because of a drug misadventure, and that 66 of these were preventable errors.[10,11] One study suggests that 0.19 percent (4.77 visits for every 100,000 people) of visits to ambulatory clinics are because of adverse effects of medication.[12]

2. Hospitalization

Many studies have been conducted in an effort to discover how often patients are admitted to the hospital because of adverse medication effects. One large study suggested that 3.7 percent of hospitalizations are a result of ADEs.[13]

The National Coordinating Committee for Medication Error Reporting and Prevention (NCCMERP) has made a strong statement about the dangers of trying to compare medication-error rates between healthcare organizations.[14] They cite four reasons for not comparing error rates: (1) differences in organizational culture, (2) differences in defining error, (3) differences in patient populations, and 4) differences in the systems used to detect and document errors.

Healthcare workers have known about drug misadventures for a long time. The significance of this problem did not become widely known to the public until the Institute of Medicine (IOM) released a report in 1999. This report was the "tipping point" for a heightened awareness of America's "other" drug problem.[15]

3. Severity and patient outcomes

Not all medication errors (prescribing, dispensing, or administration) reach the patient. Many nurses and pharmacists catch medication errors by a system of checks and balances. The United States Pharmacopeia (USP) developed an anonymous medication-error reporting system (MedMARx) for over 519 hospitals. In 2006, only 47.5 percent of medication errors reported to USP reached the patient. Of these, 1.3 percent caused patient harm.[16]

Table 16.1
The Naranjo Adverse Drug Reaction Probability Scale[25]

To assess the adverse drug reaction, please answer the following questionnaire and give the pertinent score.

	Yes	No	Do not know	Score
1. Are there previous *conclusive* reports on this reaction?	+1	0	0	
2. Did the adverse event appear after the suspected drug was administered?	+2	-1	0	
3. Did the adverse reaction improve when the drug was discontinued or a *specific* antagonist was administered?	+1	0	0	
4. Did the adverse reaction reappear when the drug was readministered?	+2	-1	0	
5. Are there alternative causes (other than the drug) that could have caused the reaction?	-1	+2	0	
6. Did the reaction reappear when a placebo was given?	-1	+1	0	
7. Was the drug detected in the blood (or other fluids) in concentrations known to be toxic?	+1	0	0	
8. Was the reaction more severe when the dose was increased, or less severe when the dose was decreased?	+1	0	0	
9. Did the patient have a similar reaction to the same or similar drug in *any* previous exposure?	+1	0	0	
10. Was the adverse event confirmed by any objective evidence?	+1	0	0	

Definite = >9; Probable = 5-8; Possible = 1-4; Doubtful = ≤ 0.

The severity of the ADEs that cause harm range from a minor discomfort (like GI upset from erythromycin), to a moderate ADR (like a skin reaction from sulfa drugs), to a severe ADR (like deafness from an aminoglycoside antibiotic), to death (like an anaphylactic reaction to penicillin).

The prevalence of permanently disabling, life-threatening, and fatal ADEs is unknown (we know how often they are reported, but do not know how often they occur).[17-20] The number of deaths associated with the legitimate use of medication in the United States has been highly debated. Estimates range as high as 140,000 people each year. This figure is difficult to discover and may never be known due to multiple variables.[21]

4. Treatment
Treatment of a patient undergoing an adverse reaction to a medication varies, but is based on the signs and symptoms the patient is presenting. Minor allergic or skin reactions are usually treated with anti-itching and anti-inflammatory drugs or ointments and creams. Moderate allergic reactions are usually treated with diphenhydramine and tapering doses of oral corticosteroids. More serious reactions may need a specific antidote (for example, naloxone for an opioid overdose), or an injectable corticosteroid. There are guidelines for treating anaphylactic reactions, and for cardiac and respiratory arrests.

16.3 Did the Drug Cause the Adverse Event?
Just because it rains and you see frogs on the lawn and sidewalk does not mean that it rained frogs. Likewise, when a person suffers an adverse event after taking a medication, it does not mean that the drug caused the adverse event. It is easy to blame the drug when it could easily be something else. *Association* is not equivalent to *causation*.

It is often difficult to determine causality. The adverse effect could be caused by another drug the patient is taking or by another substance to which the person is exposed. Or, the patient may be experiencing a new symptom of their disease, or showing symptoms of a new health problem. For example, someone starts taking a medication in the evening. The next day, the person has a rash on his shoulders, back, and chest. Did the medicine cause this? In this case it was not the medicine, but a dye in a shampoo the patient used in the morning.

Sir Austin Hill was one of the first to identify what to consider when determining causation.[22] Today, the Naranjo method (see Table 16.1) is the easiest and most reliable method for estimating the probability that a drug caused an adverse reaction.[23] Hansten and Horn have developed a modified Naranjo probability scale (Table 16.2) for assessing the likelihood of a drug-drug interaction.[24] Usually, the reaction among attorneys who view this method of drug causation is

Table 16.2
A Drug Interaction Probability Scale[26]

	Yes	No	Unsure or N.A.	Score
1. Are there previous credible reports of this interaction in humans (i.e., rating "possible" or higher on this algorithm)?	+1	0	0	
2. Is the observed interaction consistent with the known interactive properties of the precipitant drug (the one causing the interaction)?	+1	-1	0	
3. Is the observed interaction consistent with the known interactive properties of the object drug (the drug affected by the interaction)?	+1	-1	0	
4. Is the event consistent with the known or reasonable time course of the interaction (onset and/or offset)?	+1	-1	0	
5. Did the interaction remit upon dechallenge of the precipitant drug with no change in the object drug? If no dechallenge, use NA.	+1	-2	0	
6. Did the interaction reappear when the precipitant drug was readministered in the presence of continued use of object drug?	+2	-1	0	
7. Are there alternative reasonable causes for the event?*	-1	+1	0	
8. Was the object drug detected in the blood or other fluids in concentrations consistent with the proposed interaction?	+1	0	0	
9. Was the drug interaction confirmed by any objective evidence consistent with the effects on the object drug (other than drug concentrations from question 8)?	+1	0	0	
10. Was the reaction greater when the precipitant drug dose was increased or less when the precipitant drug dose was decreased?	+1	-1	0	

Highly Probable >8; Probable = 5-8; Possible = 2-4; Doubtful = <2
*Consider the patient's diseases and clinical condition, other drugs, lack of compliance, risk factors for the object drug toxicity (e.g., age, inappropriate doses of object drug). A "no" answer presumes that enough information was presented so that one would expect any alternative causes to be mentioned. When in doubt, use unsure.

that the method is too subjective. However, other methods are too complex. The Naranjo algorithm has been validated and has wide acceptance in the medical community.

16.4 Patient Risk Factors for ADEs

To be sure, not all patients have the same degree of risk for experiencing an ADE. For example, females incur more ADEs then males. Other risk factors might include being young or old, the number of other drugs used, the number of active diseases, ethnicity, abnormal kidney or liver function, the abuse of alcohol or other drugs, the severity of illness, history of allergy, history of ADEs, the drug in question, and genetic predisposition to the drug.

It would seem that patients have the same degree of risk for experiencing a medication error, but this is not so. Some risk factors for medication errors include the name and medication prescribed, how the drug is packaged, the knowledge, attention, and thoroughness of those who care for the patient, and the quality of the systems in which these healthcare professionals work.

16.5 Preventability

If the risk of an adverse event occurring is well-known, or if the adverse event appears in the warnings in the drug's official labeling, then the event is foreseeable and potentially preventable. In general, the following four types of adverse events are preventable: (1) known drug allergies, (2) known drug interactions, (3) type-A ADRs, and (4) medication errors. In cases where the patient has told her healthcare provider that she is allergic to a drug, but still receives the drug, the ADE is a clear error.

16.6 Cost

Preventable ADEs in hospitalized patients, on average, cause an additional 4.6 days in the hospital with an average additional cost of $5,857.[25] This represents about $2.8 million yearly for the average 700-bed teaching hospital.

In the ambulatory-care settings, Johnson and Bootman estimated that drug-related morbidity and mortality costs $76.6 billion yearly (ranging from $30.1 to $136.8 billion).[26]

To put this in perspective, the annual cost of all diabetes care for one year in the United States is $50 billion.

A series of studies by Kelly described awards for judgments and settlements in drug-misadventure cases litigated and published between the mid-1970s and the mid-1990s. For drug-induced death, the mean payout was $1,061,318 (range $35,000 to $9 million).[17] For drug-induced permanent disability, the mean payout was $4.3 million (range $20,000 to $127 million).[18] For drug-induced threats to life, the mean payout was $1,152,182 (range $32,000 to $8 million).[19] The payout for all outcomes (death, permanent disability, and threats to life) sharply increased from 1988 to 1995.[20]

16.7 Supporting Evidence

From a legal perspective, knowing whether a specific adverse effect has previously been reported is of prime importance. There are three questions to answer. First, was the adverse effect noted in clinical trials before the drug was approved for use? Second, after the Food and Drug Administration (FDA) approved the drug for marketing, was the drug labeled for the adverse effect? Third, after FDA approval, have there been any studies showing the adverse effect indeed happens? If yes, how well known is the adverse effect? What is its incidence or prevalence?

A. Pre-FDA Approval Studies

Before a potential new drug can be considered for approval, it must pass animal tests and three phases of human testing. Phase 1 investigation is completed in 20 to 30 healthy volunteers and is mainly to test dose-response. Phase 2 investigation takes place in several hundred patients with the disease for which the drug is intended, and is mainly to demonstrate short-term safety and effectiveness. In Phase 3 investigation, the drug is studied in several hundred to several thousand patients—some who will receive the drug (study patients) and some who will not (control patients). Phase 3 investigations usually take place in multi-hospital settings. The groups are compared for drug efficacy and safety.

During these trials, side effects and ADRs are closely observed and documented. If the manufacturer seeks new drug approval (NDA) for the drug, the drug-safety information and recommended labeling is submitted to the FDA with the rest of the information on the drug.

B. Drug Labeling

The FDA decides how the drug will be labeled and what information will be required in the package insert. This is called "official labeling," as opposed to the "label" which is the physical paper attached to a drug's container. Official labeling is available in the product's package insert, some of which may be (but not always) reproduced in the *Physicians' Desk Reference*® (published annually by Thomson Healthcare—see www.pdr.net). The FDA can require additional labeling as more information becomes known about the drug. All official labeling is dated. Thus, what was required in the product's labeling when the drug first came onto the market may change with time.

This latter point is important in legal work. The precautions required when the drug was prescribed are important—not the requirements at the time of litigation, or the requirements that existed on the date of the drug's original approval.

C. Postmarketing Surveillance

It is impossible to identify all possible ADRs associated with a new drug by the study of a mere few thousand patients during the period before FDA approval. Suddenly, after the drug is approved for marketing, many more patients will be exposed to the drug. New ADRs will be identified. There are several ways these new ADRs become known.

1. Spontaneous reporting

Spontaneous reporting is the first step in the postmarketing surveillance of ADRs. Doctors use their subjective clinical judgment and experience to help determine whether a new drug may be causing an ADR. Once a doctor sees a few cases of the same ADR, she may conclude that a new drug is associated with the adverse effect. In these cases, she should report her findings to the FDA's *MedWatch* system (www.fda.gov/medwatch/index.html).

The FDA is interested in new and serious ADRs. The Centers for Disease Control and Prevention (CDC) and the FDA jointly sponsor a similar reporting system for vaccines called the Vaccine Adverse Event Reporting System (VAERS), where healthcare professionals and patients can document an ADR to a vaccine (http://vaers.hhs.org). Access to information in these databases is through the freedom of information office (www.usdoj.gov/oip/oip.html).

The FDA and CDC constantly review incoming ADR reports to scout for "signals"—trends that may indicate problems associated with specific drugs or vaccines. All signals are assessed scientifically and statistically to determine whether a signal is true or false.

2. Case reports

Another way of reporting a possible ADR is by publishing case reports in the medical and pharmaceutical literature. Sometimes a doctor will submit information to a medical journal about several patients who have taken the same drug and experienced the same ADR. This is called a case series.

Doctors write these case reports to alert other prescribers that a drug may cause a certain adverse effect. They describe the patient, the patient's disease states, the drug therapy involved, and the adverse effect. These can be helpful; however, the quality of these reports has recently been questioned, chiefly because few reports contain any formal causality assessment.[27] Guidelines to help reporters write complete and valid ADE reports for publication are now available.[28]

3. Evidence-based medicine studies

Signals from MedWatch or VAERs, or information from case reports or case series, are considered hypothesis-generating information, rather than cause-and-effect information. Thus, the information from these sources needs to be investigated using more rigorous study methods. A study using simple rules of logic and science that can be applied to improve the clinical care of patients is called "evidence-based medicine" (EBM).[29] There are several types of EBM studies.

a. Observational (epidemiologic) studies

The first EBM drug safety study is observational or pharmacoepidemiological studies. These studies compare the records of many patients who received the drug with records of many patients who did not receive the drug, which is why they are sometimes called *population-based studies*. There are three basic types of observational studies—cross-sectional, case-control, and cohort.

- *Cross-sectional studies.* The first type of observational study is called the cross-sectional study. A cross-sectional study is the simplest observational study and is done in present time (concurrently) to capture a snapshot of the prevalence of an adverse effect at a certain point in time (see Figure 16.1). For example, let's say we select 100 patients on one day and divide them into those that received and those that did not receive aspirin within the last 30 days. All patients are checked (endoscopically) to see if they have GI bleeding. Bleeding rates are calculated and compared for those taking or not taking aspirin. Cross-sectional studies can be done quickly and are inexpensive. However, since the results of these studies are limited (cannot calculate incidence), they are usually used to generate hypotheses.
- *Case-control studies.* The second type of pharmacoepidemiological study is the case-control study. In these studies, patients are selected by outcome (they are displaying the adverse effect being studied). As such, these are usually retrospective studies (looking back in time) to see

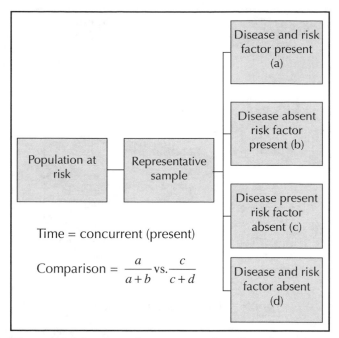

Figure 16.1 *Design of a cross-sectional study and computation of results.*

whether a person received the drug of interest (see Figure 16.2).

Case-control studies are designed to determine the odds or odds ratio (OR) of a person receiving a drug when he has the ADR of interest versus someone who does not experience the ADR of interest. For example, let's say we select 100 patients and divide them into those two groups—those with and without GI bleeding. We look back in time to see which patients received aspirin during the last 30 days and calculate an OR. Case-control studies are relatively inexpensive and can be done quickly. However, they cannot be used to calculate an incidence rate (the number of new cases with time) for the adverse effect.

- *Cohort studies.* The third type of observational study is the cohort study, sometimes called a "longitudinal" or "follow-up" study. Patients are selected based on their exposure to the drug (whether they received or did not receive the drug), then followed prospectively (forward in time) to see if they develop the adverse effect of interest (see Figure 16.3). Cohort studies can discover the true incidence of an adverse effect (the rate per so many people per so many years). They also determine the relative risk (RR) of a person experiencing a particular adverse effect when they have taken a drug, as opposed to someone who has not taken the drug.

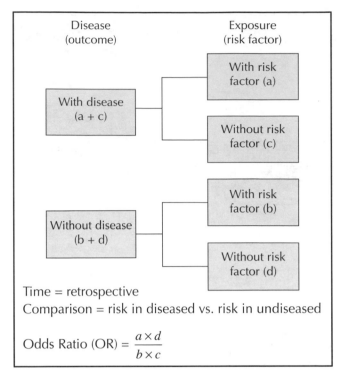

Figure 16.2 *Design of a case control study and computation of an Odds Ratio (OR).*

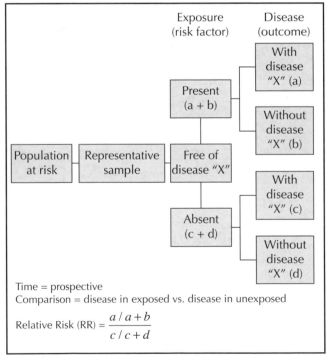

Figure 16.3 *Design of a cohort study and computation of Relative Risk (RR).*

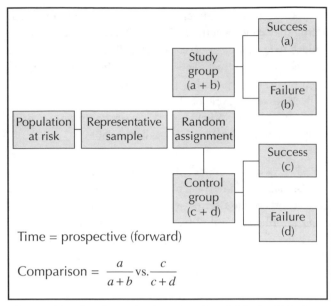

Figure 16.4 *Design of a Randomized Clinical Trial (RCT) and computation of results.*

For example, let's say we start with 100 patients and divide them into those who are taking aspirin and those who are not taking aspirin. We follow all patients for three months, look to see who has GI bleeding, then calculate an RR.

b. Randomized clinical trials (RCTs)

Observational or epidemiologic studies are done when one cannot randomly assign patients to the study or control groups. In observational studies, the investigator has little to no control over the study and control groups. The investigator gets what she gets when patients are selected. The groups may not be comparable.

In a randomized clinical trial (RCT), the study is a true experiment and conditions are controlled by an investigator. The investigator draws potential patients from a population of similar individuals and randomizes them into a study sample and a control sample (see Figure 16.4). This increases the chance that the groups are comparable except for the exposure (drug versus no drug, drug versus placebo, or drug A versus drug B).

The investigator in an RCT is also able to size the groups to make sure there is enough statistical power to show a significant difference between groups (if one exists). The patients and investigator can also be blinded (made unaware of whether the drug or a placebo was given) and the studies are prospective (moving forward in time). These added conditions increase control over the study, which is why the RCT is the gold standard for investigation. But they are expensive and take time.

- Calculations: All studies use a 2×2 (two columns by two rows) contingency table (see Figure 16.5) to calculate RRs, ORs, or to compare proportions. The table is always laid out in the same fashion. Quadrant A contains the number of people who were exposed to the drug and who experienced the adverse effect of interest. Quadrant B contains the number of people exposed to the drug who did not experience the adverse effect of interest. Quadrant C contains the number of people who were not exposed to the drug, but who experienced the adverse effect of interest. Quadrant D is for the number of people not exposed to the drug and who did not experience the adverse effect of interest.

The formula for calculating an OR is shown in Figure 16.2. Figure 16.3 contains the formula for calculating a RR. ORs and RRs are expressed as point estimates of risk and are computed with confidence intervals. For example, OR = 2.4 (1.8, 3.1), CI = 95 means that we are 95 percent confident that the actual risk estimate lies between 1.8 and 3.1.

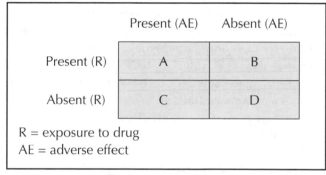

Figure 16.5 *The 2 x 2 contingency table used to calculate the results of research studies on drugs.*

For cross-sectional studies (Figure 16.1) and RCTs (Figure 16.4), proportions are compared. The comparison is between the proportion (percentage) of patients who receive the drug and experience the adverse effect, versus the proportion of patients who did not receive the drug but still experienced the adverse effect (during the same time period).

- Interpretation. What does an OR or RR of 1.5 mean? Let's say we are trying to discover the risk of GI bleeding when taking nonsteroidal anti-inflammatory drugs (NSAIDs), such as ibuprofen. When interpreting point estimates, the statement starts with how the study started. For example, in a case control study, an OR of 1.5 would be interpreted as: people with GI bleeding are 50 percent

more likely to be taking NSAIDs than those people without GI bleeding. In a cohort study, an RR of 1.5 would be interpreted as: people taking NSAIDs are 50 percent more likely to have GI bleeding than people who are not taking NSAIDs.

An OR or RR of 1.0 means there is no difference between groups. ORs and RRs less than one (<1) mean that there is a protective effect of the exposure (drug). However, because of limits inherent in observational studies, most pharmacoepidemiologists do not feel that point estimates are significant unless both confidence limits are greater than 1. The following point estimate would be significant: OR = 1.6 (1.1, 2.0), while this one would not be considered significant: OR = 1.6 (0.8, 2.0). When the adverse effect is rare, the OR and RR are about the same.

The proportion of people experiencing the adverse effect from the drug in an RCT (let's say 8 percent) can be divided by the proportion of people experiencing the adverse effect that are not taking the drug or that are taking the placebo (let's say 2 percent). This provides a ratio (8:2 or 4:1) that can be interpreted (for example, those taking the drug may be four times more likely to experience the adverse effect than those not taking the drug). However, there is danger in doing this. Typically, RCTs use relatively small numbers of patients that decreases the precision of this estimate.

c. Systematic reviews

A systematic review is a process of using statistical methods to combine the results of different studies. A frequent application has been to pool results from a set of RCTs that, by themselves, may not be powerful enough to show statistically significant differences (but may do so in the aggregate). Systematic reviews are also used to see a net effect when the results of trials conflict with one another.

The most common systematic review today is the meta-analysis. Meta-analyses can be powerful tools if done correctly. Meta-analyses can be used to assess combinations of RCTs and observational studies. Assessing the quality of each study in the meta-analysis is of primary importance and must be performed according to strict criteria.[30]

16.8 Grading the Strength of the Evidence

All studies have limitations—flaws in methodology, bias, or deviations from the truth. Major flaws should be detected by peer review before the manuscript is accepted for publication. Minor flaws and bias should be identified by the author and discussed as a limitation in the discussion section of the manuscript. An example of bias is in selecting patients for a study. If not done carefully, one group (the control group or the study group) may not be comparable (except for the drug exposure) to the other group. This is called selection bias. There are many kinds of bias.

In July 2002, the Women's Health Initiative (WHI) stopped a large randomized trial assessing the risk and benefits of estrogen plus progestin in healthy postmenopausal women.[31] The study was stopped after 5.2 years of follow-up because the overall health risks exceeded the benefits of taking the medication. Specifically, there was an increased risk for cardiovascular disease and invasive breast cancer.

The result of the WHI study has caused concern among some in the healthcare community. The results are the opposite of what was believed before this, most of which was based on observational studies. These differing results may be the result of an inherent limitation in observational studies—*confounding by indication*—which is "a distortion of the effect of a treatment on the outcome that is caused by the presence of a sign or symptom that is associated both with the treatment and with the outcome."[32]

In general, well-designed RCTs > (are better than) well-designed cohort studies > well-designed case-control studies > well-designed cross-sectional studies. Well-designed systematic studies may be better than well-designed RCTs. However, sometimes, a well-designed case-control study may be better than a poorly designed cohort study. It is critical that guidelines on how to conduct studies—like the ones by the International Society for Pharmacoepidemiology—are followed to produce the most accurate results.[33]

16.9 Risk Communication and Possible Actions by the FDA

The FDA is charged with assuring that drugs are safe and effective. The FDA continually oversees each drug for safety once the drug is approved. The FDA watches the safety of drugs primarily through its MedWatch program. Drug manufacturers are required to report (through MedWatch) all ADR case reports they receive. This is not so with health professionals, for whom reporting ADRs to MedWatch is voluntary. The agency watches ADR case reports, case series, and drug-safety studies published in the literature. It also monitors what actions pharmacovigilance centers in other countries are doing on the safety of drugs.

The FDA aggressively monitors the risks of the drugs it approves. When more evidence starts to show more risk, the agency has several actions available. First, it can tighten the drug's labeling by requiring more precautions and recommendations about the drug's use. It can also write "Dear Doctor," "Dear Pharmacist," or "Dear Health Professional" letters that heighten awareness of a drug's increased risk. If

this has minimal effect, the FDA may require a "black-box warning" in the drug's product labeling.

The last action the FDA can take is to ask a manufacturer to remove its drug from the market. If the manufacturer does not remove the drug, the FDA has the power to make them remove it.

16.10 Communicating Drug Risks to Patients

There is a set of laws governing the use of investigational drugs in patients and on acquiring patient consent for the drug's use that is beyond the scope of this chapter. The following are some of the duties of doctors and pharmacists in handling the risks of approved drugs.

A. Doctors' Duties

Doctors have duties about the safe prescribing and monitoring of FDA-approved medication in patients. This is not an easy task. Just see the long and detailed information in a typical drug's labeling. What risks should be shared with patients? Certainly not every side effect and ADR listed in the package insert. Is the minimum requirement what a reasonable and prudent doctor would share with the patient?

Reaching consensus on what risks should be shared with patients for each drug is impossible. Most doctors would agree that they have a duty to counsel patients about any known, major problems associated with the drug, and let the patient know what he (the patient) should do if he experiences any of these negative effects. Documenting that the patient has been counseled about the drug is always good.

B. Pharmacists' Duties

As per the results of several court decisions, pharmacists are bound to three different types of responsibilities, as follows.

1. Ethical responsibilities

Under the profession of pharmacy's code of ethics, the pharmacist places the concern for the welfare of the patient at the center of professional practice.[34] Furthermore, the pharmacist promises to help individuals achieve the best benefit from their medications and to be committed to their benefit.

2. Duty to warn

Some courts have ruled that the pharmacist has a duty to warn of unusual drug risks. In *Dooley v. Everett*, 805 S.W. 2d 380 (Tenn. App. 1990), the appellate ruling established that pharmacists have a legal duty to detect and warn the prescribers about harmful drug interactions.[35]

In *Lasley v. Shrake's Country Club Pharmacy, Inc.*, 1994, Westlaw 109647, the Court of Appeals of Arizona ruled that the pharmacist may have a duty to warn (either the patient or the doctor) that prolonged use of a drug in combination with other drugs may lead to addiction or adverse effects.[36]

In *Gassen v. East Jefferson General Hospital*, 1993 Westlaw 514862 (La. App. Dec. 15, 1993), the court ruled that the pharmacist has a duty to detect and correct clear errors and mistakes in a doctor's prescription.[37]

It is becoming clear that "if a pharmacist knows (or should know) of a risk, and there is a reasonably foreseeable possibility of the adverse effect occurring, then he must warn the patient. If there is a risk, but the pharmacist has no knowledge of it (or could not reasonably be expected to have such knowledge of it), or if the pharmacist knows (or should know) of a risk, yet harm to the patient is not reasonably foreseeable, then there is no requirement for a warning."[35]

What duty does that pharmacist have when a doctor insists on dispensing a medication that could harm the patient? According to *Gassen v. Jefferson General Hospital*, the pharmacist has a duty to notify the doctor of potential problems, and should document her conversation and recommendation. Once the pharmacist does this, she has fulfilled her duty and can defer to the doctor's expertise. "However, that general rule may not apply when the medication prescribed has potential to kill the patient. The threat of imminent death imposes an extra duty on the pharmacist to impress on the doctor the gravity of the situation."[38]

3. Duty to counsel patients

In January 1993, pharmacists became legally required to offer counseling to patients about their medication (OBRA 90). The legislature specifically required that pharmacists offer to counsel Medicaid patients about their medication. However, most state boards of pharmacy subsequently required that the pharmacist must make an offer to counsel all patients about their medication. Clearly, the intent of the law is to reduce the risk of using medication and to improve patient compliance with taking the medication as the doctor had intended.

Unfortunately, most pharmacists are not personally offering to counsel the patient about the patient's medication. There are several reasons for this. First, some pharmacists do not have a clear understanding of the law—they do not know that they, rather than someone else (like a clerk or technician) must make the offer to counsel. Second, some pharmacists feel that as more and more prescriptions are written, less time is available to counsel patients—thus making dispensing (which is a technical function that can

be automated) more important than having contact with patients. Third, those who employ pharmacists (mostly chain store pharmacies) are having clerks ask the patient to "sign here." Most patients do not realize that what they are signing is waiving their rights to be counseled by the pharmacist. Many patients think they are signing for insurance reasons or that they have picked up their medication.[39]

C. Patients' Duties

Patients also have duties associated with the safe use of medication. First, they have a duty to reveal to all healthcare professionals caring for them what medications they take regularly. They also have a duty to reveal their medication allergies. Patients should also commit themselves to learning as much as possible about the medications they take, and should be as compliant as possible in taking the medication as prescribed. Additionally, patients should report any problems they have with their medications to their doctors and pharmacists.

16.11 Human Error and Disciplinary Decision Making

Human error is a risk for harm from medication. Health professionals are trained "to do no harm." If they do harm, it is almost always unintentional, and they usually—of course—feel terrible. There are four behavioral concepts important to an understanding of the inter-relationship between discipline and safety: human error, negligence, intentional rule violations, and reckless conduct.[40] The reference provided defines the differences in these behavioral concepts and how they should be disciplined.

16.12 Drug-Injury Testimony

Expert witnesses are often necessary in cases of alleged drug-induced injury. Common questions to be answered are: Can it occur? Did it occur? How did it occur? Why did it occur? The expert witnesses to retain in alleged drug-induced injury cases depends on the definition of "it" (in the above questions), and if an error is involved.

A. Can It Occur?

The people best trained to determine whether cases of the alleged drug-induced drug injury have occurred include pharmacoepidemiologists and drug-information specialists. Drug-information specialists—pharmacists working in 89 drug information centers in the United States (many with the Pharm.D. degree)—are best at locating previous cases of the ADE in question.[41] Pharmacoepidemiologists (many with M.D., Ph.D., and M.P.H. degrees) may be better at interpreting the results of these literature searches, and are experts in assessing risk. They are experts at reviewing, assessing, and interpreting the risk evidence gathered on a drug.

B. Did It Occur?

The best person to retain as expert witnesses for answering the question "did it occur?" or "what happened?" depends on what exactly has occurred. If the question is "Did the drug cause the ADR in this patient?" the best person to ask may be a pharmacoepidemiologist or a practicing physician. If the question is "Did the drug kill the patient?" then the expert of choice may be a medical practitioner, a toxicologist (forensic or otherwise), or an expert in drug safety (usually, but not always, a pharmacoepidemiologist).

C. How Did It Occur?

Pharmacologists can answer questions on a drug's action, its mechanisms of action, dosage, and dose-response. There are two types of pharmacologists—basic science and clinical. Basic-science pharmacologists are scientists who have an M.S. or Ph.D. degree, while clinical pharmacologists confine their practice to humans and are usually physicians.

If there are questions about the absorption, distribution, metabolism, or excretion of the drugs, and calculations are needed to interpret levels (serum, urine, etc.) of the drug, the best person to do this is an expert in pharmacokinetics. This could be a Ph.D., Pharm.D., or M.D. who specializes in that area. In cases of allergic reactions, the best experts are board-certified allergists.

D. Why Did It Occur?

Once an expert witness establishes causality in the case of significant morbidity or mortality from a drug and other experts prove how the drug caused its adverse effect, it is natural to ask why the event occurred and whether or not it was preventable. Was it an allergic reaction? A drug interaction? An ADR? A medication error? In cases of medication error, it is helpful to seek an expert in medication safety or the opinion of a health professional with the same background as the person accused of committing the error. Keep in mind that most experts believe preventable drug misadventures include known allergic reactions, known drug interactions, Type-A ADRs, and all medication errors.

16.13 Summary

Drugs can cure and relieve the symptoms of disease. Drugs have improved the quality of life for many patients and have helped increase life expectancy. Unfortunately, they can also cause misadventures—unexpected and unwanted harm from allergic drug reactions, adverse drug reactions, drug interaction, or errors.

It is often difficult to determine whether or not a drug was the cause of the adverse effect, whether or not the adverse effect has appeared before in others, and/or how a drug misadventure came to pass. Pharmacoepidemiologists—experts in assessing drug risk—can use the sciences of epidemiology and pharmacology to determine if the adverse effect can occur and if it did occur.

Endnotes

1. H.R. Manasse. "Medication use in an imperfect world: Drug misadventuring as an issue of public policy: Part 1," *Am. J. Hosp. Pharm.* 46(5):929–44 (1989).

2. H.R. Manasse. "Toward defining and applying a higher standard of quality for medication use in the United States." *Am. J. Health-Syst. Pharm.* 52:374–379 (1995).

3. L.L. Leape. "Error in medicine," *JAMA* 272(23):1851–1857 (1994).

4. J. Lazarou, B.H. Pomeranz and P.N. Corey. "Incidence of adverse drug reactions in hospitalized patients: A meta-analysis of prospective studies," *JAMA* 279(15):1200–1205 (1998).

5. B. Dean and N. Barber. "Validity and reliability of observational methods for studying medication administration errors," *Am. J. Health-Sys. Pharm.* 58:54–59 (2001).

6. K.N. Barker. "Medication errors observed in 36 health-care facilities," *Arch. Intern. Med.* 162(16):897–1903 (2002).

7. K.N. Barker. "Medication errors in nursing homes and small hospitals," *Am. J. Hosp. Pharm.* 39:987–991 (1982).

8. Flynn EA, Barker KN, Carnahan BJ. National observational study of prescription dispensing accuracy and safety In 50 pharmacies. *J Am Pharm. Assoc.* 2003;43(2):191-200.

9. Teagarden JR, Nagle B, Aubert RE, et al. Dispensing error rate in highly automated mail-service pharmacy practice. *Pharmacotherapy.* 25(11):1629-1635.

10. O. Scheitman. "Medication misadventures resulting in emergency room visits at an HMO medical center," *Am. J. Health-Sys. Pharm.* 53:1416–1422 (1996).

11. C.E. Dehhenh, D.T. Kishi and C. Louie. "Drug-related illness in emergency department patients," *Am. Health-Sys. Pharm.* 53:1422–26 (1996).

12. R.R. Aparasu and D.L. Helgeland. "Visits to hospital outpatient departments in the United States due to the adverse effects of medication," *Hosp. Pharm.* 35: 825–831 (2000).

13. T.A. Brennan et al. "Incidence of adverse events and negligence in hospitalized patients," *N. Engl. J. Med.* 324:370–376 (1991).

14. National Coordinating Committee for Medication Error Reporting and Prevention. "Use of medication error rates to compare healthcare organizations is of no value," June 11, 2002. Available online at www.ncc-merp.org/council/council2002-06-11.html.

15. M. Gladwell. *The Tipping Point: How Little Things Can Make a Big Difference* (Boston: Little, Brown, 2000).

16. United States Pharmacopeia. *A report on the relationship of drug names and medication errors in response to the Institute of Medicine's call for action.* (Rockville, MD: United States Pharmacopeia, 2008).

17. W.N. Kelly. "Potential risks and prevention: Part 1: Fatal adverse drug events," *Am. J. Health-Sys. Pharm.*, July 15, 2001.

18. W.N. Kelly. "Potential risks and prevention: Part 2: Drug-induced permanent disabilities," *Am. J. Health-Sys. Pharm.*, July 15, 2001.

19. K. Marcellino and W.N. Kelly . "Potential risk factors and prevention: Part 3: Drug-induced threats to life," *Am. J. Health-Sys. Pharm.*, August 1, 2001.

20. W.N. Kelly. "Potential risks and prevention, part 4: Reports of significant adverse drug events," *Am. J. Health-Sys. Pharm.*, August 1, 2001.

21. W.N. Kelly. "Can the frequency and risks of fatal adverse drug events be determined?" *Pharmacotherapy* 21(5): 521–527 (2001).

22. A.B. Hill. "The environment and disease: Association or causation?" *Proc. R. Soc. Med.* 58:295–300 (1965).

23. C.A. Narnajo et al. "A method for estimating the probability of adverse drug reactions," *Clin. Pharm. Ther.* 30(2):239–245 (1981).

24. P.D. Hansten and J.R. Horn, eds. *Hansten and Horn's Drug Interactions Analysis and Management* (Vancouver, WA: Applied Therapeutics Inc., 1998).

25. D.W. Bates et al. "The costs of adverse drug events in hospitalized patients," *JAMA* 277:307–311 (1997).

26. J.A. Johnson and J.L. Bootman. "Drug-related morbidity and mortality: A cost-of-illness model," *Arch. Intern. Med.* 155:1949–1956 (1995).

27. W.N. Kelly. "The quality of published adverse event reports." *Annals of Pharmacotherapy.* 2003;37:1774-1778,

28. Kelly WN, Arellano FM, Barnes J, Bergman U, Edwards IR, Fernandez SB, Goldsmith DI, Huang KA, Jones JK, McLeay R, Moore N, Stather RH, Trenque T, Troutman WG, van Puijenbroek E, Williams F, and Wise RP. Guidelines for submitting adverse event reports for publication. *Pharmacoepidemiology and Drug Safety.* 2007;16:581-587.

29. Evidence-Based Medicine Working Group. "Evidence-based medicine: A new approach to teaching the practice of medicine," *JAMA* 268:2420–2425 (1992).

30. A.P. Verhagen et al. "The Delphi list: A list for quality assessment of randomized clinical trials for conducting systematic reviews developed by Delphi consensus," *J. Clin. Epidemiology* 51(12):1235–1241 (1998).

31. Women's Health Initiative. "Risks and benefits of estrogen plus progestin in healthy post-menopausal women," *JAMA* 288:321–333 (2002).

32. Last JM. A Dictionary of Epidemiology. Oxford University Press. Oxford. 2001.

33. International Society for Pharmacoepidemiology. "Guidelines for Good Pharmacoepidemiology Practices (GPP)," Revised April 2007. Available online at www.pharmacoepi.org/resources/guidelines_08027.cfm.

34. L.D. Vottero. "Code of ethics for pharmacists," *Am. J. Health-Sys. Pharm.* 52:2096–2131 (1995).

35. K.G. Williams. "Pharmacists' duty to warn of drug interactions," *Am. J. Hosp. Pharm.* 49:2787–2789 (1992).

36. G.G. Cacciatore. "Pharmacist's duty to warn," *Am. J. Hosp. Pharm.* 51:2824–2826 (1994).

37. D.B. Brushwood. "Hospital pharmacists' duty to ques-
    tion clear errors in prescriptions," *Am. J. Hosp. Pharm.*
    51:2031–203 (1994).

38. Anonymous. "Physician-pharmacist standoff: Legal les-
    sons for the hospital pharmacist," *Am. Soc. for Pharm.
    Law* 2(1):3 (1993).

39. K. Marcellino. "What do Georgia patients expect from
    their pharmacist?" *Ga. Pharm. J.*, October, 2001, 22–
    23.

40. D. Marx. Patient Safety and the "Just Culture": A
    Primer for Healthcare Executives (Medical Event Re-
    porting System—Transfusion Medicine, Trustees of
    Columbia University in the City of New York, 2001).

41. Rosenberg JM, Schlit S, Nathan JP, et al. Update on
    the status of 89 drug information centers in the United
    States. *Am J Health-Syst.* 2009;66(19):1718-1722.

Chapter 17

Medication Errors

James T. O'Donnell Pharm.D., M.S., FCP, ABCP, FACN, R.Ph.,
Patricia Iyer MSN, RN, LNCC, CLNI, and David Benjamin PhD, FCP, FCLM

17.1 Introduction

Medication errors affect patients in all aspects of healthcare. The true number of medication errors is unknown, either because of lack of awareness that an error has occurred, dismissal of the error as unimportant to report because the patient was not harmed, or fear of reporting an error because of possible reprisals. Perhaps the most difficult aspect of discussing this topic is that no one seems to know the true scope of the problem. Reported medication error rates range from a fraction of a percent up to nearly 20 percent of all doses given in hospitals. Vast differences are seen depending on the methodologies used to measure rates. One group of researchers compared three methods: process observation, chart review, and incident reporting and found 11.7 percent dosing errors by the observer method compared with 0.7 percent error rate from chart review and less than 0.2 percent rate (only one case) using incident reports. Further, they observed a fairly high rate of false negatives and false positives as compared to an expert research pharmacist. This same group estimates one in five doses results in an error.[1]

Drug mishaps are nothing new. In fact, studies dating back several years show that about 2 percent of hospital patients experience preventable adverse drug events, although the majority are not fatal.[2] Medication error has been cited as the cause of death for one out of every 131 outpatient deaths and one in 854 in-patient deaths. After being read a common definition of a medical error, about one in three people (34 percent) say they, or a family member, have experienced one at some point in their life. This includes 21 percent of all Americans who say that a medical error caused "serious health consequences," such as death (8 percent), long-term disability (11 percent), or severe pain (16 percent).[3]

Approximately 50 percent of people with chronic conditions experience a medical error in either their own care or that of a family member. This is far more than those without a chronic illness (30 percent).[4] Studies from Canada, New Zealand, Denmark, Australia, and the United Kingdom show that approximately 10 percent of all patients in acute care settings experience significant injury from medical care.[5] A Danish study performed through direct observation, unannounced control visits, and chart reviews detected 1,065 errors in 2,467 opportunities for errors, or 43 percent. The frequency of medication errors was:

1. Ordering: 39 percent
2. Transcribing: 56 percent
3. Dispensing: 4 percent
4. Administering: 41 percent
5. Discharge summaries: 76 percent[6]

MEDMARX, a voluntary, Internet-accessible system for reporting medication errors, was being used by more than 775 hospitals and healthcare systems as of 2003. In the five–year period of 1999-2003, a total of 580,759 errors were reported, although 98 percent did not result in patient harm.[7]

Healthcare facilities supplement data about voluntarily reported errors by computer detection of errors, chart re-

views, observational studies, and other ways to generate a more accurate picture of the kinds of errors that take place. Computer alerts note when a medication error may have occurred by identifying orders for antidotes used to treat medication errors. Certain significant laboratory results may reveal subtherapeutic or toxic levels of medications.[8]

The Harvard Medical Practice Study, which was based on review of New York patients' medical records, is perhaps the most well-known example of the use of chart review to detect medical errors. Of 30,000 records examined, the investigators found that 1 percent of the patients had experienced errors that caused injury. This study was based on 1980s records and published in the 1990s.[9] It revealed that most (56.8 percent) adverse events that occur to hospitalized patients result in no or minor impairment, with complete recovery in one month. Twenty-two percent of these adverse events were caused by negligence. Another 13.7 percent of the adverse events led to disabilities that lasted more than one month but less than six months. However, 2.6 percent of adverse events resulted in permanent, total disability, with one-third of these caused by negligence. While 13.6 percent of the adverse events resulted in the death of the patient, half of these deaths were caused by negligence.

Although healthcare providers were somewhat aware of the results of the Harvard Medical Practice study, the press remained uninformed. When the study was described in an Institute of Medicine report published in 1999, the public first learned that 44,000–98,000 people die each year as a result of medical errors. The actual numbers are unknown, as the Harvard Practice Study relied on examination of hospital charts. The investigators did not review physician office records, nursing home records, or clinic records, or detect unrecorded errors. HealthGrades announced in July 2004 that as many as 195,000 people could be dying in U.S. hospitals because of easily preventable errors. Their data was based on three years of Medicare data in all 50 states and Washington, D.C. In July 2006, the Institute of medicine reported that 1.5 million Americans suffer from a medication error annually.

17.2 Detection of Errors
A. Concealment of Errors
Methods of detecting medication errors reveal widely varying results. Some medication errors are not reported because they are not noticed by the person who made them. Accurate information regarding errors relies on voluntary reporting of errors by those who make or observe them. A study reported in June 2005 revealed that many nurses, physicians, and pharmacists fear punitive action would be taken by their licensing boards in the wake of a medication error,

whether it was a near miss or a fatal error with many system-based causes. Fear of punishment from licensing boards may greatly contribute to underreporting of medication errors. Thirty percent of all respondent nurses felt they would receive a verbal or written reprimand, or be required to undergo education, even if the error never reached the patient. Refer to *ISMP Survey on State Licensing Boards Response to Medical Error* for details of the results are found at www. ismp.org.[10]

B. Observation

While chart review may detect errors in medication orders, observational studies are considered to be more valid in detecting errors in dispensing or administering medications. Observation was proven to be most effective in detecting errors made when 2,556 doses of medications were administered. Using a combination of incident report review, chart review, and direct observation at 36 hospitals and skilled nursing facilities in Colorado and Georgia, observers detected 300 of 457 pharmacist-confirmed errors. This represented an error rate of 11.7 percent. Only 17 errors were detected by chart review (0.7 percent error rate) and one error was detected by incident report review (0.04 percent error rate). All errors detected involved the same 2,556 doses.[11]

C. Subtherapeutic Levels or Exaggerated Levels of Medications

Drug levels are infrequently tested in hospital and other organized healthcare settings (nursing homes, home health care), with the exception of drugs classified as "narrow therapeutic windows," such as Digoxin, phenytoin, Gentamicin and other aminoglycosides, and Vancomycin. With these drugs, the drug levels are routinely ordered as part of a therapeutic drug monitoring effort (TDM), usually coordinated by the pharmacist in the institution. If a medication error is suspected with one of these medications, the attorney or expert should closely examine the physicians' or pharmacists' notes to determine if blood levels were ordered, if appropriate clinical laboratory testing was ordered, if the frequency and timing of the testing was appropriate, and then examine and interpret what levels were reported. Were the levels subtherapeutic, therapeutic, or toxic?

PRACTICE TIP: If a drug overdose is suspected clinically, the physician might order a toxicology level on the blood or other fluids of the patient (or decedent), as well as the contents of any drug administration delivery systems (syringes, syringe pumps, IV bags, and so on) to determine the identity and concentration of any suspected substances. This is particularly important in

death investigations. If a suspect drug or medication is unknown to the medical examiner, it is unlikely an analysis for its identity and concentration will be performed, and therefore, it will be missed. If it is early enough in the case investigation, the sample may still be stored at the medical examiner's office or at some off-site toxicology laboratory. Consult with a pharmacologist or toxicologist to determine the potential for identification of toxic substances stored in biological fluids taken during an acute event or postmortem. Many attorneys petition the court to order preservation of any existing biological fluid specimens for future forensic evaluations; contrary to most hospital clinical labs, forensic labs maintain samples for at least six months, or longer if requested.

D. Antidotes

Computerized surveillance may also play a role in uncovering certain errors. Medication errors involving narcotics may be detected by searching for Narcan (naloxone) orders for patients (Narcan reverses narcotics overdoses). Several hospital computerized medication order-entry systems have the potential for identifying adverse drug events.[12] Another sentinel antidote is Benadryl (diphenhydramine) "stat," the drug of choice for allergic reactions. The order may not say, "patient has a rash," but the order of an antihistamine is the classic first-line response for a drug allergic reaction. The next line of severity includes corticosteroids (Solu Medrol or Hydrocortisone), which mitigate the inflammatory response, and sympathomimetics like Adrenalin (epinephrine) used to stimulate cardiovascular function and overcome pulmonary toxicity. Orders for any of these critical intervention drugs are strong evidence that a drug reaction has occurred, and dictates a very thorough review of the medical records, or later in discovery, interrogatories, or questions to treaters involved in the care of the patient.[13]

E. Statements in the Progress Notes/Discharge Summary

Discussions or notations of drug reactions are not always recorded in progress notes by attending physicians, and are rarely documented in the discharge summary. Even when the discharge summary or operative notes are made after an adverse event or death, notes about the drug event are frequently absent.

17.3 Investigating the Claim

The first thing to establish is what happened to the patient as a result of the medication error. Table 17.1 identifies different categories of errors, according to the National Coordinating Council for Medication Error Reporting and

Prevention. It is unlikely a plaintiff's attorney is willing to assume responsibility for reporting a medication error that could be categorized as A-D. Category E errors may be questionable depending on the amount of time the patient was temporarily affected as a result of the error. A Category F error may not be deemed serious enough to institute a suit. The administration of a medication to which the patient had a known allergy may have resulted in a trip to the emergency department and an overnight admission, but no lasting damages. Category G, H, and I medication errors may result in the patient seeking the services of an attorney.

Table 17.1

Error Category	Result of Error
A	Circumstances or events with the capacity to cause error
B	An error occurred but the error did not reach the patient
C	An error occurred that reached the patient but did not cause patient harm
D	An error occurred that reached the patient and required monitoring to confirm that it resulted in no harm to the patient and/or required intervention to preclude harm
E	An error occurred that may have contributed to or resulted in temporary harm to the patient and required intervention
F	An error occurred that may have contributed to or resulted in temporary harm to the patient and required initial or prolonged hospitalization
G	An error occurred that may have contributed to or resulted in permanent patient harm
H	An error occurred that required intervention necessary to sustain life
I	An error occurred that may have contributed to or resulted in the patient's death

Reprinted with permission of USP. Hicks, R., Santell, J, Cousins, D. and Williams, R., MEDMARX 5th Anniversary Data Report: A Chartbook of 2003 Findings and Trends 1999-2003, Rockville, MD: USP Center for the Advancement of Patient Safety, 2004.

A. Establishing the Details Regarding the Error

The attorney or legal nurse consultant involved in the screening of the case must analyze the client's understanding of what occurred. The following questions should be asked:

1. What medication was involved?
2. What type of error was made?
3. What caused the error?

1. What medication was involved?

High-risk medications include chemotherapeutic drugs, opioids (narcotics), anticoagulants (blood thinners), hormones, and cardiovascular agents. The medications most frequently involved in Category E-I errors are shown in Table 17.2. Medication information may be obtained by reading the *Physician's Desk Reference*, a nursing drug book produced by one of the major nursing publishers, or by performing an Internet search for the drug literature provided by the manufacturer.

2. What type of error was made?

The error may have occurred at any of the steps from prescribing to administration. The error could have been made by a prescriber (physician, physician's assistant, nurse practitioner), a dispenser (pharmacist or pharmacy technician), or someone who administered the medication (physician, nurse, medical assistant, or medication aide). According to the data analyzed and reported by MEDMARX, the four most common types of errors were omission, improper dose/quantity, prescribing error and unauthorized drug given to the patient.[14]

3. What caused the error?

It may be unclear at the screening stage what caused the error. Sometimes the patient or family was given an explanation of the cause. The five most common causes of medication errors are performance deficits, not following procedures or protocols, inaccurate or omitted transcription of information, incorrect computer entry, and documentation errors. Healthcare providers cited the top five contributing factors to errors as distractions, workload increases, inexperienced staff, insufficient staffing, and shift change.[15] Causes of the errors are explored as discovery proceeds. Refer to Section 17.4 for more information on causes of errors.

Table 17.2
Most Commonly Reported Products Involved in Medication Errors in 2003

Name of medication and action	Number of errors in MEDMARX data from 10 percent of U.S. hospitals	Percentage
Insulin* (controls blood sugar)	362	8.7
Morphine* (pain reliever)	218	5.3
Heparin* (thins blood)	160	3.9
Potassium chloride* (electrolyte necessary for cardiac functioning)	122	2.9
Warfarin/Coumadin* (thins blood)	109	2.6
Fentanyl* (fast acting pain reliever)	108	2.6
Hydromorphone/Dilaudid* (pain reliever)	94	2.3
Vancomycin* (antibiotic)	75	1.8
Furosemide/Lasix (reduces blood pressure by increasing urination)	64	1.5
Meperidine/Demerol* (pain reliever)	55	1.3
Enoxaparin/Lovenox* (thins blood)	53	1.3
Lorazepam/Ativan (sedative)	52	1.3
Ceftriaxone/Rocephin (broad spectrum antibiotic)	44	1.1
Dopamine* (increases blood pressure)	44	1.1
Diltiazem/Cardizem (anti-anginal)	40	1.0

* Denotes high-risk medication.
Reprinted with permission of USP. Hicks, R., Santell, J, Cousins, D. and Williams, R., MEDMARX 5th Anniversary Data Report: A Chartbook of 2003 Findings and Trends 1999-2003, Rockville, MD: USP Center for the Advancement of Patient Safety, 2004.

B. Screening the Client

Make note of the initial impression of the potential client. Is the client able to answer questions clearly? Does the client seem to be exaggerating? Is he believable? Does the information provided sound reliable, or does the story seem too fantastic to be true? Carefully observe the nonverbal body language of the client. Read the narrative of the patient. Does it have a ring of truth? The wilder the narrative, the less likely there is a case. Is the person simply angry over the way he was treated? Attorneys generally avoid a client with an extensive criminal record or a prisoner who complains of the quality of medical care. These folks are notoriously poor witnesses. If a patient is admitted to a facility who is heavily intoxicated or in a drug-induced condition and then suffers from a medication error, he typically makes an unsympathetic plaintiff.

C. Use an Intake Sheet

The law firm intake or client interview sheet is an important form. Not only does it give the attorney vital, personal information on the client in the case, but a properly prepared intake sheet will allow the attorney to secure information for discovery requests. Also, intake questions and questionnaires may be the single best source to jog the client's memory so that facts which may otherwise be forgotten are revealed.

D. Obtaining Medical Records

In an effort to avoid alerting the medical records department or risk manager to a potential suit, many plaintiff attorneys request that the client obtain a copy of the medical record to screen a potential nursing malpractice case. Some attorneys ask a physician to obtain the record on behalf of the client, for the same reason. Medical records departments often notify their risk manager when a record request comes from a plaintiff attorney's office. The healthcare professionals involved in the care of the patient may be informed of this request and, therefore, may take this opportunity to review the medical record.

Some attorneys prefer to obtain the records rather than ask the client to do so to ensure the records needed to properly evaluate the case are obtained. It is essential to have the client sign medical authorizations to send out HIPAA-compliant requests for copies of any medical reports and information needed to fully evaluate the case. Many attorneys request a second copy of the medical record before the case goes to trial. This enables the attorney to detect changes made in the medical record after the initiation of a lawsuit. Although this type of tampering with the record is rare, it can have a profound impact on a malpractice case.

The basic information needed to obtain medical records includes:

1. Name of patient upon entry to the facility
2. Date of birth
3. Social security number
4. Dates of treatment or admission
5. In-patient treatment versus outpatient treatment in the ER, clinic, and so on
6. Physician's name and address[16]

A full certified copy of the medical record is needed to review a medication error case. Although a record is sent to the attorney or insurance carrier with the letter from the medical records department stating that it is a certified copy, this does not mean that both sides of every page have been properly copied. It is not unusual for a medical records clerk or an employee of a copying service to fail to turn over a page, or omit some of the pages of a multi-page flow sheet.

The attorney and paralegal should expect that an expert witness or a legal nurse consultant reviewing the medical records will draw these omissions to the attention of the attorney. A nurse is in a better position to spot the omissions than an attorney or a paralegal because the nurse understands how the typical record is maintained and organized. Once the medical records are obtained, further investigation of the claim proceeds. The factors below are important to both the plaintiff and defense attorney.

E. Mitigation of Damages

1. How was the plaintiff's health prior to the medication error?
2. Did the plaintiff have any chronic conditions?
3. Was the plaintiff employed before the medication error?
4. Is there any evidence the plaintiff made disability claims, or received work excuses or releases prior to or at the time of the medication error?
5. Has the plaintiff had any diagnostic testing prior to the medication error that documents preexisting injuries?
6. What medications was the plaintiff taking before the medication error?

7. Did the plaintiff report involvement in other medication errors or injuries either before or after the current medication error?
8. Did the plaintiff fail to seek follow-up medical care?
9. Are there any potentially damaging statements in the medical records about the plaintiff?
10. Are there inconsistencies in the medical records?
11. What comments about how the medication error occurred were recorded in the medical records?
12. Are there discrepancies about how the medication error happened?
13. Is there evidence the patient withheld information from the treating doctor?
14. Has the patient refused to have certain diagnostic tests performed? What is the explanation for the refusal?
15. Was the plaintiff compliant with medical treatment?
16. Did the plaintiff take the medications as prescribed?
17. Did the patient keep the appointments?

F. Physician Factors That Affect Medication Error Cases

1. Does the patient's treating doctor support the medical diagnosis with a description of the patient's symptoms?
2. Are the facts in the history correct?
3. How often did the doctor see the patient after the injury?

G. Attorney Factors That Affect Medication Error Cases

1. Who did the plaintiff contact first after the medication error? Was it the plaintiff attorney or a physician?
2. Did the plaintiff contact the plaintiff attorney before contacting a doctor after the medication error?
3. Do the doctor's records state the patient was referred by the plaintiff attorney?
4. Do the doctor's medical records contain any references to phone calls with the plaintiff attorney?
5. Do the doctor's records contain any implications that the plaintiff attorney is directing the patient's care?
6. Do the doctor's records contain any implications that the plaintiff attorney has requested a revision of a report to favor the plaintiff?

7. Does the plaintiff attorney's name appear on the medical billing?

H. Identifying the Defenses

The most obvious way to defend a medication error case is to dispute damages. A Category A-F error that does not result in permanent injury has limited or no damages, permitting the defense attorney to use the "so what?" defense. Another commonly used defense is to point to the known risks associated with taking a medication. A side effect may be the necessary price the patient has to pay for taking the medication, but side effects signal a need to discontinue the medication. Decreased hearing as a side effect of certain antibiotics signifies a need to stop the medication. Questions then arise concerning how quickly the complication or adverse reaction was recognized. Was it immediate or did the doctor miss the diagnosis?

Medication errors may occur when a critically ill patient is under the care of healthcare providers. Two of the high-risk medications, Dopamine and Ativan, are typically used in the critical care unit. A complicated case involving a patient with a long list of underlying problems permits the defense to point out that the causation of death is in question. Invariably, the alleged malpractice becomes inexplicably tied to the underlying disease processes from which the patient suffers. The seriousness of the underlying medical problem often makes proving causation more difficult.

Novel or sophisticated medical issues intertwined with a medication error may make a case defensible. If the alleged malpractice involves an emerging area of medicine, plaintiff attorneys may be less inclined to pursue the case. It will make obtaining competent experts much more difficult since there probably are only a select few individuals competent to testify on the case. The jury may be sympathetic towards medical pioneers trying new techniques.

17.4 Factors that Contribute to Errors

From a nursing systems perspective, there are both system and individual factors that contribute to errors.

A. Systems Factors

1. Research and education

Research studies that advance nursing's knowledge of evidence-based best practices are not easily or quickly transferred to the clinical setting. It can take years for recommendations based on solid research to be integrated into nursing educational programs and memorialized in current clinical policies and procedures. Nursing educational settings may not understand or have enough time to teach students about new and evolving technologies and their impact on medication administration. Busy medical surgical units in hospitals, where students typically spend a significant amount of their clinical time, are complex environments in which to teach medication administration.

2. Nursing administration

Although the Joint Commission on Accreditation of Healthcare Organizations stresses the need for the same quality of care to be delivered throughout an organization, there is often lack of standardization of policies. For example, IV conscious sedation may be delivered in the operating room, emergency department, or endoscopy area, among other sites. The degree of monitoring and assessment for complications should be identical wherever this procedure is performed. If policies for this procedure were developed by anesthesiologists without nursing input or without regard to best practices, potential for error may occur.

Nursing administration may also be implicated in setting up an environment for errors by:

1. not providing sufficient nursing staff,
2. not acknowledging the importance of adequate safeguards to provide patient safety,
3. not remaining current in best practices,
4. not involving bedside nurses in decision making about implementing new technologies,
5. not changing practices that drain nursing time away from the bedside,
6. not planning how to address patient safety when technology fails to work,
7. not helping other healthcare departments communicate with nursing about patient safety issues, and
8. not detecting methods nurses are using to work around or sabotage safeguards.

Although individuals perform work and provide services, it is best to think of them as part of a system, and a system is more than the sum of its parts. There are a multitude of interactions and interrelationships in the system involved in providing medications to patients. Lucien Leape, M.D., one of the authors of the IOM study, has estimated that up to 20 steps are involved with the prescribing, transcribing, dispensing, and administration process in a paper-based (non-computerized) hospital setting. With so many interim steps to traverse, it is no wonder errors occur. Contrast that scenario to one in which a physician writes a prescription for a patient in an outpatient setting. The patient takes the prescription to the pharmacy and the pharmacist fills it. Simplicity supports safety. The fewer steps involved in the process, the lower the likelihood for error.[17] The challenge is to examine which steps are necessary, eliminate unnecessary and error-prone steps if possible, and build quality assurance and safety nets to detect mistakes before they become medication errors.

3. Staffing issues

Staffing issues never seem to be solved. It is clear that if resources, professional staff (pharmacists and nurses), and support staff (technicians, nursing assistants or nursing aids) are unavailable, the existing staff will be stretched beyond limits, which creates a dangerous situation. Stopgap measures of voluntary or mandatory overtime, with staff routinely working double shifts, solve the immediate staffing issue, but create an increased error-prone environment by introducing fatigue and sleep-deprivation issues.

Another staffing issue that can increase the risk of errors is the use of temporary, or "agency," employees. Nurses without orientation into or experience in the system are less invested and cannot be expected to get up to speed in a setting that normally provides weeks to months for new-employee orientation. This staffing issue is confounded by institutions that rely heavily on temporary employees—who are at an increased risk of errors—rather than invest in regular employees. The agency employee will probably cost more in wages and agency fees than a regular employee, but there are no long-term employee costs or benefit costs, as with a regular employee. This is not unique to healthcare. It is prevalent throughout many industries for the same reasons.

4. Shift change

"It fell through the cracks" is a common explanation for an omission. For example, the order for Heparin for the newly admitted stroke patient was received at 2:30 P.M. The order did not have the patient's weight, which is required for calculating the dose of Heparin based on an agreed-upon protocol. The day pharmacist called the day nurse, who agreed to get the weight and call back the pharmacist. The day nurse did not get the weight and went home at 3:30 P.M. The day pharmacist did not hear from the nurse, left the order in the pending orders box, and went home at 4 P.M. Neither the nurses nor the pharmacist on subsequent shifts raised questions about the lack of clarification and the absence of a Heparin dose for the patient. The order was discovered "overlooked" 16 hours after it was written; a weight was obtained; the doses prepared, and the first dose was administered to the patient 28 hours after the order was written. His condition severely deteriorated, and he suffered

an acute massive stroke. In this case, the order "fell through the cracks," which is not uncommon at shift changes. The patient did not recover from the stroke—he died. The family sued, claiming the nurses and pharmacists departed from the standard of care by not providing timely medication subsequent to the physician's orders. While there were experts who provided opinions that the delay in administration of the Heparin did not contribute to the stroke, the delayed order subjected the hospital and its employees to litigation (unpublished case). The facility should have a clear communication method for resolution of orders, and make sure any unresolved matters at shift change are endorsed to the next shift, which can resolve it and provide timely services.

5. Medication errors across a continuum

Failure to monitor in the outpatient setting has a different appearance. A typical scenario may look like this: A patient is transferred to a nursing home. The nurse filling out the list of medications the patient was receiving in the hospital makes transcription errors, omitting two medications and recording an incorrect dose of a third medication. The nurse in the nursing home accepted this list as accurate and transcribed it onto the physician order sheet. The physician in the nursing home signed off on the orders, assuming they were accurate. This is an all-too-common situation. To avoid medication errors of this type, The Joint Commission has listed among its 2006 National Patient Safety Goals the need to "Reconcile Medication Across a Continuum of Care." This means that a Joint-Commission-accredited facility must ensure that upon admission and upon discharge the changes in a patient's medication regimen are "reconciled" (listed) and that changes in medications and dosages are correctly recorded and implemented.

Some hospitals utilize nurses or pharmacists to call patients after discharge to verify that new prescriptions have been filled and that the patient is taking her medications according to the most recent orders of the prescribing physician. The Visiting Nurse Association (VNA) and other home health nursing agencies can also play a valuable role in helping to ensure that newly prescribed medications are taken as directed.[17]

6. Computer and technology related errors

Table 17.3 shows the results of studies conducted by the Agency for Healthcare Research and Quality (AHRQ) to determine at what stage in the Medication Use Process (MUP) errors occurred. Up to 68 percent of errors occurred during the prescribing/ordering phase. Twenty-five to 38 percent of errors occurred during administration, followed by transcription errors and pharmacy dispensing errors.[18,19]

**Table 17.3
Occurrence of Medication Errors
in Studies of Hospitalized Patients**

Physician ordering	39-49 percent
Nursing administration	26-38 percent
Transcription	11-12 percent
Pharmacy dispensing	11-14 percent

Modified from: Bates, D. W., D. L. Boyle, and N. Laird, et al., "Incidence of Adverse Drug Events and Potential Adverse Drug Events," *JAMA* 274, no. 1 (1995): 29–34.
Leape, L. L., D. W. Bates, and D. J. Cullen, et al., "Systems Analysis of Adverse Drug Events," *JAMA* 274, no. 1 (1995): 35–43.

Avoiding medication errors requires communication of the right drug, right dose, right route, and right frequency of administration from one healthcare professional to another.

Illegible medication orders, look-alike drug names, and confusion of brand and generic names lead to medication errors.[20] When an error is made in the prescribing/ordering phase of the process, it can permeate the MUP and result in an adverse experience for the patient. Much attention has been given to instituting new practices for prescribing, such as Computerized Physician Order-Entry (CPOE), because of the prevalence of errors during the prescribing/ordering phase of the MUP. One study showed that in the hospital setting, CPOE decreased serious medication errors by 55 percent and potential Adverse Drug Events (ADEs) by 84 percent.[21]

Computerized systems are defined as computer programs that maintain patient drug profiles and generate prescription-fill or dispensing lists. They may also interface with laboratory and other hospital departments. Computerization assists in the initial monitoring of a patient's drug therapy and decreases the chance of drug interactions. Most systems used today have built-in programs to detect potential drug interactions. Computerization also decreases the likelihood of drug sensitivities (allergies) and therapeutic duplications of medications going unnoticed, and warns of high or low dose alerts. Some systems include drug/disease contraindications. These enhancements improve medication safety and documentation. Technological advances are heralded as safety benefits for patients and potential cost and resource savers for institutions. However, the healthcare professional should be aware that with any system, errors can creep in. Factors associated with medication errors, such as inexperience, distractions, and lack of knowledge, apply to computer and other technology- related errors.

CPOE eliminates transcription and interpretation of the handwriting of the prescriber, but other types of error can be

introduced. One such incident occurred in the early 1990s. A rehabilitation institute patient was being treated for HIV. The resident physician intended to select azidothymidine (an antiviral used early in the AIDS epidemic), but somehow selected azathioprine (the drug listed just above azidothymidine on the computer screen). Azathioprine is an immunosuppressant. When the order was entered into the computer, it was noted by the pharmacist who provided daily doses. The computer created a MAR (medication administration record) used to chart the administration of the incorrect azathioprine (an immunosuppressant in an immunosuppressed patient). The MAR was also available to the patient's physicians. The patient received the wrong drug for seven days; he did not receive his azidothymidine for that period as well. On discovery of the error, HIV specialists assessed the effect of the wrong drug and not receiving the correct drug. A lawsuit was filed against the hospital. There was no question of liability; it was admitted. The only question was of causation. Did the consequences of the error harm the patient? The hospital settled the case early in the litigation. This is called the parallax error. All pharmacists, and perhaps nurses, are taught that when pouring a liquid in a measuring container, the measurement read will differ according to the angle of view. This is called parallax. In this case, the resident physician saw the aziothymidine, but selected the line above it.

Further systems failures followed. The pharmacist should have realized that an HIV patient, already immunosuppressed, should not receive an immunosuppressant. The pharmacist should be assessing the reason for prescribing. The nurses should be making similar assessments. The physician resident should have noticed the error when he viewed the MAR on daily rounds.

Many facilities use computerized medication carts (Pyxis and others) to reduce medication errors and improve efficiency. In these systems, the patient's medication record is stored on a computer built into the medication cart. The nurse presses a button to select the medication required for the patient. The computer identifies the exact bin number and drawer for each medication. The drawer containing the medication opens so the nurse can remove the dose, similar to a vending machine. The system is designed to reduce the chance the nurse will administer the wrong medication. Experts in safe medication practices[22] point out potential sources of error with this system:

1. A nurse can retrieve a drug from an automated medication cart before a pharmacist screens the order for allergies or double-checks the dose.
2. Some computerized medication carts are poorly designed, allowing a drug to easily drop into the wrong

slot. Some medication carts are stocked haphazardly. For example, a baby received an adult concentration of Digoxin (which slows the heart rate) because the adult and pediatric strengths of the medication were side-by-side in the cart. Filling several medication orders at once from a computerized cart further adds to the potential for medication mix-ups.

3.   If the bins are filled with the wrong drug by the pharmacy employee, usually a technician, the wrong drug can be dispensed, leading to an error.

4.   Not all drugs can be accommodated in the automatic-dispensing system, especially refrigerated drugs. Lack of inclusion in the system causes the system to revert to the antiquated "Floor Stock System," a system cluttered with flaws and prone to error that led to a strong movement in hospitals 30 years ago to initiate unit dose dispensing.

The following case provides an example of how the Pyxis system failed, and how classic errors led to brain damage in one patient.

A 46-year-old patient went to the emergency department of a suburban Chicago hospital complaining of severe gastric distress following dinner at a Mexican restaurant. The ED physician prescribed Pepcid (famotidine). Pepcid requires refrigeration. Since the Pyxis machine does not accommodate refrigerated storage, any medications requiring refrigeration are stored in a medication refrigerator. Pepcid vials are small, 2ml, with a small, blue label. They were stored in an organizer tray on one of the ED medication refrigerator shelves. The nurse mistakenly selected Pavulon (pancuronium, Organon), which paralyzes the diaphragm, instead of Pepcid, and administered the Pavulon intravenously. Ten minutes later, the patient's husband called out for help, "my wife stopped breathing," after she let out a loud gasp. The ED resident quickly recognized the potential problem, asked to see the vial of Pepcid, and discovered that Pavulon was mistakenly given. The patient was emergently intubated with difficulty, and it was estimated that she was "down" for 10 to 15 minutes (inadequate or no breathing). She was resuscitated; however, she was seriously brain damaged, requiring specialized care. This is a classic case of "confirmation bias." The nurse saw Pepcid in her mind's eye when she took the vial out of the refrigerator. She saw it when she drew the medication out of the vial with the syringe, and she thought she was administering it when she administered the drug intravenously. The case went to trial. Liability was admitted; the only fight was how much the hospital had to pay. The jury returned a verdict of $6 million (unpublished case).

B. Individual Factors

1. Psychological aspects of human error: mistakes and slips

Cognitive psychologists and human-factors specialists have been concerned with the biology, psychology, and sociology of errors for decades. They have learned a great deal about why people make errors and how to prevent them by developing models of human cognition and studying complex environments such as airplane cockpits and nuclear power plant control rooms. Most mental functioning is automatic, effortless, and rapid. We do not have to "think" to eat or to drive a car to work. This automatic mode is unconscious, rapid, and effortless; like the new microprocessors, it occurs in parallel-processing mode. While our minds are under "intentional control," we have to pay attention only when there is a change.[23] Psychologists consider an error a disorder of intentional acts, and they distinguish between errors in planning an act and errors in its execution. If a prior intention to reach a specified goal leads to action, and the action leads to the goal, then all is well. A mistake occurs if the plan of action contains some flaw (for example, planning to give a medicine to a child, but failing to realize the child requires a different dose than an adult). A "slip" or "lapse" occurs in carrying out the action. A slip is a form of human error defined to be "the performance of an action that was not what was intended." A slip of the pen, when a nurse intends to write chlorpromazine but distractedly writes chlorpropamide, is an example. Lapses are covert slips, particularly errors of memory. Slips and lapses are errors due to failures of skill: picking the wrong medicine or administering the medicine to the wrong patient when two patients have the same surname.

Slips are errors that occur when an individual is functioning in the automatic mode. They usually result from distractions or failure to pay attention at critical moments. A common error mechanism is loss of activation, in which attention is distracted and a thought process is lost.[24] Slips can occur at the point in which an intention to act is formed if the situation that demands action is misclassified, and thus the wrong schema is chosen. A prescriber who habitually orders meperidine 100 mg as a postoperative analgesic might specify the dosage of morphine as 100 mg as the result of such an error. Errors in carrying out the sequence of events specified in the schema, such as omitting or duplicating some steps, are a further important class of slips. An example would be when a nurse, having already added 20 mEq of potassium chloride to a bag of infusion fluid, forgets having done so and adds an additional 20 mEq of potassium chloride. There can also be faults in activation of the schema that lead to slips. For example, when several things are happening at the same time, two schemata can become confused. A verbal slip that illustrates this is when a person may be thinking of both "closed" and "shut," but says "clut."

Slips and lapses are distinguished from mistakes. Mistakes can be subdivided into those due to lack of expertise (knowledge-based errors), when there is ignorance of the rule required and thus a need to plan an action from first principles; and those due to failure of expertise (rule-based errors), when rules are applied inappropriately.

Psychological factors include other activity ("busyness") as well as emotional states such as boredom, frustration, fear, anxiety, and anger. All lead to preoccupations that divert attention. Psychological factors, though considered internal or endogenous, may be triggered by external factors, such as overwork, interpersonal relations, and other forms of stress. Environmental factors, such as noise, heat, visual stimuli, and motion, can divert attention and lead to slips.[25]

2. Inexperience, ignorance (knowledge deficit), inattention

Lesar, Lomaestro and Pohl[26] reported on an analysis of data from a nine-year study of medication prescribing errors in a teaching hospital. Antibiotics were most often involved in a prescribing error. One-third of the errors were overdoses of antibiotics, with the rest of the errors defined as underdoses (26.3 percent) or allergy to the antibiotic (22.3 percent). The authors concluded that 30-50 percent of all adverse drug events were preventable. The following factors were cited as contributing to prescribing errors:

1. Increased workload
2. Intensity of care
3. Inadequate prescriber knowledge of medications and drug therapies
4. Inadequate performance in managing drug therapy

Ensuring appropriate medication use is a complex process that requires knowledge of drugs, timely access to accurate and complete patient information, and a series of interrelated decisions over a period of time. In a study conducted by Lesar,[27] the most common factors associated with errors were decline in renal or hepatic function requiring alteration of drug therapy (13.9 percent); patient history of allergy to the same medication class (12.1 percent); using the wrong drug name, dosage form, or abbreviation (11.4 percent for both brand and generic name orders); incorrect dosage calculations (11.1 percent); and atypical or unusual and critical dosage frequency considerations (10.18 percent). The most

common groups of factors associated with errors were those related to knowledge and application of knowledge regarding drug therapy (30 percent); knowledge and use of knowledge regarding patient factors that affect drug therapy (29.2 percent); and nomenclature: incorrect drug name, dosage form, or abbreviations (13.4 percent).[28]

3. Violations of policies, procedures, or protocols

A policy is a statement of the goal of the process, the intention of what is done; a protocol or procedure is a menu checklist of how the act is accomplished, how the service is provided, and who provides the service. Procedures and protocols are carefully written by accomplished practitioners across multidisciplinary lines to provide checks and balances so that medication errors of all types—slips, mistakes, inexperience, inattention, ignorance, commission, and omission with respect to prescribing, dispensing, and administration—can be avoided. Established policies and procedures provide a road map for patient safety; all healthcare workers should be knowledgeable of the relevant policies and procedures in the institution, and quality-assurance efforts should include monitoring compliance with policy and procedures.

A reproduction (with permission) of a recent case provides a poignant example of the serious consequences of failure to follow procedure. This case also demonstrates a systems failure.

The following case involves a patient who received intrathecal Vincristine. He did not die, but was permanently paralyzed as a result of this medical error. This case provides a good study of systems design, the value of systems, and what happens when the system breaks down (i.e., when the system is not followed).

This patient, a 69-year-old farmer, was scheduled to complete a successful methotrexate/Vincristine treatment for lymphoma at a major university medical center. His prognosis was good. He was planning on retiring soon, and knew that he would be the primary caregiver for his wife, who was beginning to show signs of Alzheimer's disease. His children had grown and moved away.

One fateful day in May 2000, he arrived at the oncology clinic for his scheduled methotrexate intrathecal and Vincristine intravenous treatment. Because the intrathecal injection must be performed under guided fluoroscopy, the oncologist reserved a radiology suite. No nurse was available to accompany or assist the oncologist who was to administer the injection. The oncologist, not wanting to miss the appointment, stopped at the clinic pharmacy and asked the pharmacist for the "methotrexate and flush (preservative-free NaCl)." The syringes for both the Vincristine IV and the methotrexate intrathecal had already been prepared. The staff pharmacist on duty in the clinic pharmacy asked the oncologist: "Would you like the complete order?" The oncologist confirmed, and the pharmacist proceeded to place both the Vincristine and the methotrexate syringes in the container, which the oncologist then took to the radiology suite. There the oncologist injected what he knew was methotrexate, followed by the Vincristine syringe (which he assumed was preservative-free NaCl).

The patient was taken back to the clinic where, he believed, he would receive the intravenous Vincristine, but the Vincristine could not be found. A call to the pharmacy led to the discovery that the Vincristine had been given to the oncologist who immediately went to Radiology and retrieved the discarded syringes from the sharps container. To his horror, he realized the Vincristine had mistakenly been administered intrathecally in place of the saline flush.

Physicians immediately conducted an emergency spinal-fluid dialysis/replacement, saving the patient's life. Sadly, the patient was completely paralyzed below the nipple line of his body. The oncologist, devastated over the event, quickly settled with the patient for $500,000.

Had the system been followed, this accident probably never would have occurred. First, a nurse should have accompanied the oncologist, who while engaged in a delicate intrathecal injection, did not read the label of the syringe he was administering. Next, although the pharmacy department had a policy in place for utilizing the Vincristine manufacturer's syringe label, which read "FATAL IF GIVEN INTRATHECALLY. FOR INTRAVENOUS USE ONLY," and the red-bordered syringe overwrap that warned: "FATAL IF GIVEN INTRATHECALLY. FOR IV USE ONLY. DO NOT REMOVE COVERING UNTIL MOMENT OF INJECTION," the oncology clinic pharmacy manager decided these were unnecessary for adult patients, because the oncology-clinic staff was competent and well-informed. The staff pharmacist, who knew about the policy in the main hospital's sterile-products-compounding room, followed this unofficial exemption. That same staff pharmacist, given a verbal order for the "methotrexate and the flush" gave both the methotrexate and the Vincristine to the physician, thereby violating another system rule: never to place the methotrexate and Vincristine in the same container. Since many staff pharmacists rotated through the oncology-clinic pharmacy, it was common knowledge that the precautionary syringe label and overwrap were not being used.

A lawsuit was brought against the university hospital, staff pharmacist, oncology clinic pharmacy manager, and director of pharmacy. The lawsuit alleged the "Hospital and its employees failed to properly promulgate and enforce appropriate policies, procedures, and protocols relating to

the ordering, packaging, delivery, dispensing, and administration of Vincristine; that the Hospital and its employees failed to properly train and supervise employees, and that those failures were substantial factors in causing the plaintiffs' injuries and damages." The lawyers for the hospital and the pharmacists argued it was the oncologist who was to blame, and the pharmacists and the university were not negligent. While the oncologist was admittedly negligent, an overriding theme of the litigation was that this was a systems failure—that if adequate systems controls had been in place and enforced, the accident would not have happened. One of the authors (JOD) consulted on and testified in this case. In his testimony, he described the patient and the oncologist both as victims of this systems failure.

Although a good system was in place, the system had been violated in several instances. There was no nurse to accompany the oncologist. The pharmacist provided Vincristine in place of the saline flush, did not question the systems violation (not using the syringe label and overwrap), and provided both drugs in the same container. The pharmacy clinic manager violated the system policy and the manufacturer's precautionary labeling. The director of pharmacy allowed an environment in which a manager could change and/or elect not to follow policies. Another important systems violation was that the safety policies were exempted with the *assumption* of a competent and informed staff.

This was an unnecessary error. After protracted mediation and settlement negotiations, an additional $1.6 million was added to the settlement package—thus providing a $2.1 million settlement, which would almost cover all future medical expenses and economic losses. Some other provision would have to be made for care of the patient's frail wife, whose Alzheimer's disease had advanced.[29]

4. Inaccurate or omitted transcription of information

The following is a case that illustrates the harm that can come when a pharmacist or another healthcare professional fails to maintain a "holistic" point of view when evaluating a patient's medications.

This case involves a lawsuit waged by the family of a 90-year-old woman who had a thyroidectomy and had been taking levothyroxine sodium (Levoxyl) for several years. She was a patient at a nursing home in the area and, subsequent to a transient ischemic attack (TIA), was admitted to a local tertiary-care hospital for treatment. Hospital staff noted the patient's thyroidectomy history and continued her Levoxyl therapy. When the patient was transferred to her new nursing home, staff prepared a discharge summary along with a copy of the electronic medication administration record (MAR). For some reason, the patient's medication list was transcribed by hand and sent with the patient (instead of the hospital printing and sending the electronic MAR). Somehow, the Levoxyl was omitted from the patient transfer form. The nursing home's attending physician did not notice the thyroidectomy history or Levoxyl therapy, despite the fact that both were mentioned several times in the medical records that accompanied the patient.

The attending physician wrote admitting orders using the handwritten medication list. Consequently, the Levoxyl was never ordered or administered to the patient. About two weeks after the patient's admittance to the nursing home, a consultant pharmacist visited the nursing home to perform the monthly medication reviews. This pharmacist signed the medication order sheet, certifying the patient's chart had been reviewed at the facility by the pharmacy consultant. Like the doctor, the pharmacist failed to detect the patient's history of thyroidectomy, hypothyroidism, or Levoxyl therapy.

After approximately nine weeks without thyroid medication, the patient's condition deteriorated. She was urgently transferred back to the hospital in a myxedema coma (severe acute hypothyroidism). The Levoxyl omission was discovered during a resident physician's review of her chart. Despite the subsequent reinstitution of the thyroid medication, the patient died a week later.

The hospital and the attending physician at the nursing home were sued. All parties contributed to a settlement.

5. Failure to educate patient on importance of home monitoring

A significant problem can occur if patients are inadequately informed of required follow-up care for outpatients after discharge from the hospital. One such example related to Coumadin (warfarin sodium, a blood thinner). Even under the best of circumstances, one out of 10 patients has problems with Coumadin. An absolute essential for monitoring the efficacy and safety of Coumadin is outpatient INR (International Normalized Ratio for prothrombin time, a measure of the degree of blood thinning). The INR must be maintained in a certain range. If it is too low, the patient risks clotting. If it is too high, the patient risks bleeding. Arrangements must be made for outpatient laboratory testing for INRs. An assessment must be made of the patient's understanding of the need for:

1. testing,
2. the scheduling for the testing,
3. an understanding of the signs and symptoms of Coumadin toxicity, and
4. immediate contact with the physician.

Failure to provide such necessary educational information can result in serious morbidity or mortality. This educational need is critical with more complex therapies provided to patients at home, coupled with early discharge from the hospital. In addition to teaching, nurses follow up with the patient in the form of reminders of treatment schedules, and confirm testing has occurred as an additional method of providing the safest ambulatory treatment to patients on critical drug therapies.

17.5 Ordering Stage Errors

The potential for medication errors by nurses begins when the healthcare provider orders a medication. Medications may be ordered by physicians, nurse practitioners, physician assistants, and pharmacists in many states. For simplicity, the term "healthcare provider" is used to refer to the individual prescribing the medication. Each medication order must consist of these components: name of the medication, dose, route, and frequency.

A. The Order-Entry Process

The order for the medication can be brought to the nurse's attention in a number of ways. It may be handwritten onto the order sheet that is part of the patient's medical record or entered into a computer system. Handwritten orders are transcribed, or copied, onto the medication administration record (MAR) by either a unit secretary or nurse. Many agencies require the registered nurse to review the unit secretary's transcription for accuracy. The unit secretary usually does not need a medical background to be qualified for the job. Computer order-entry by physicians may result in the order being communicated electronically to the pharmacy for filling and dispensing to the nursing unit, with addition of the medication to the computerized medication-administration record.

B. Hazards Associated with the Ordering Stage

1. Handwriting, stray marks and letters

A recent report by the Committee on the Quality of Health Care in America has drawn attention to the prevalence of errors in day-to-day medical care delivery, with a major source attributable to illegible, poorly written, or difficult to interpret prescriptions.[30]

Stray marks, such as initials, check marks, or letters indicating transcription of the order has occurred may lead to a misinterpretation of an order. For example, some facilities use letters such as "M" to indicate the order was placed on the medication administration record, "K" to state it was

Table 17.4
Examples of Look Alike Drug Names

Acetohexamide	Acetazolamide
Advair	Advicor
Amaryl	Reminyl
Avinza	Evista
Celebrex	Celexa
Chlorpromazine	Chlorpropamide
Cisplatin	Carboplatin
Clonidine	Klonopin
Diabeta	Zebeta
Diflucan	Diprivan
Epinephrine	Ephedrine
Fentanyl	Sufentanil
Hespan	Heparin
Humulin	Humalog
Hydromorphone	Morphine
Lamisil	Lamictal
Lente	Lantus
Leukaran	Leucovorin Calcium
Novolin	Novolog
Prilosec	Prozac
Primacor	Primaxin
Protonix	Protomine
Retrovir	Ritonavir
Serzone	Seroquel
Taxol	Taxotere
Vincristine	Vinblastine
Xanax	Zantac
Zyprexa	Zyrtec
Zyrtec	Zantac

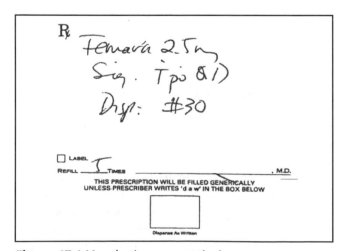

Figure 17.1 Handwritten prescription.

up on a kardex or "O" to indicate it was ordered. Accupril was interpreted as Monopril in one setting because a unit secretary placed an "M" in front of the order to note it was transcribed onto the MAR.[31]

Many drugs have similar appearing names. Refer to Table 17.4 for examples. Nurses are expected to match the patient's diagnosis with the drug before transcription of the order and administration of the medication. Drugs with look-alike names may be used for very different purposes.[32] Refer to Figure 17.1 for an example of a handwritten prescription. The physician intended to prescribe Tenormin. The prescription was filled as Femara, and administered to the patient. This female hormone was contraindicated given her history of uterine cancer.

While computerized prescribing systems might cut the quantity and severity of medication ordering errors, they cannot eliminate them completely. It is still possible for a prescriber to enter an order into the wrong electronic record. Not all the performance problems defined in the study below are alleviated by an electronic prescribing system.

A study performed to assess medical students' and housestaffs' knowledge, attitudes, and behaviors regarding safe prescribing used anonymous, self-administered questionnaires about safe prescribing. Of 175 respondents, results indicated they did the following:

1. Checked prescribing information before prescribing new drugs: 89 percent
2. Checked for drug allergies: 59 percent
3. Checked for renal impairment: 56 percent
4. Checked for potential drug to drug interactions: 30 percent

The authors of the study concluded that routine use of safe medication-prescribing behaviors were poor. Contributing factors may have been inadequate training and a culture that did not support safe prescribing.[33]

2. Unapproved abbreviations

Potential for error occurs when the healthcare provider uses a confusing abbreviation. This issue has been highlighted in recent years with the Joint Commission's requirement to avoid dangerous abbreviations. Healthcare providers are expected not to use U for units; IU for international units; QD, Q.D., qd, or q.d. for every day; QOD, Q.O.D., qod, q.o.d. for every other day; trailing zeros for X.0 mg; MS or MS04 for morphine; or MgS04 for magnesium sulfate.[34] See The Joint Commission website for strategies used by facilities to eliminate dangerous abbreviations.[35] Implementation of this goal requires healthcare organizations to revise existing medical record forms. Specialized order sheets might include these abbreviations. Any transcription or interpretation error involving a zero or a decimal point means the patient could potentially receive at least 10 times more medication than indicated, or only one-tenth of the ordered dose. Ask the hospital to provide the approved list of abbreviations, and ask if it has a list of unauthorized abbreviations.

Abbreviations contribute to or cause many errors. Reports of such errors have been published routinely. The abbreviation "TAB," meant to signify "triple antibiotic" (a name for a hospital sterile topical antibiotic mixture), caused patients to have their wounds irrigated with a diet soda. A prescription could be written with directions as follows: "OD OD OD" to mean one drop in the right eye once daily! Abbreviations should not be used for drug names because they are particularly dangerous. The writer may, through mental error, confuse two abbreviations and use the wrong one. Similarly, the reader may attribute the wrong meaning to an abbreviation. To further compound the problem, some drug name abbreviations have multiple meanings (ASA can stand for aspirin or for aluminum subacetate).

3. Telephone and verbal orders

Misunderstandings or documentation of wrong orders are prevalent when orders are received orally or by phone. Telephone orders may be taken in noisy, distracting environments. Accents and healthcare workers for whom English is a second language may add to confusion in interpreting verbal orders. Most agencies discourage verbal orders in circumstances other than emergencies. Every facility should have well-known and enforced policies that specify the criteria for dictating and accepting oral and phone orders. The Joint Commission brought this issue to the forefront when it was included as one of the 2006 Patient Safety Goals. The second patient safety goal states the commitment to improve the effectiveness of communication among caregivers. The accredited facilities must implement a process for taking oral or telephone orders that require a verification "read-back" of the complete order by the person receiving the order. Simply repeating back the order is not sufficient. Whenever possible, the receiver of the order should write down the complete order or enter it into a computer, then read it back, and receive confirmation from the individual who gave the order. This goal applies to all oral and telephone orders.[36]

There are many assonant medications. For example Celexa (citalopram) and Cerebyx (fosphenytoin) sound alike. Xanax, used to treat anxiety, may be confused with Zantac, the histamine blocker that treats ulcers. Patients frequently mistake these two names. A nurse who cannot clearly interpret a spoken order should ask the speaker to repeat the

name of the drug and the dosage. The nurse should also ask the prescriber to spell the name of the drug.

When taking a spoken order, the nurse should ask for the drug's indication. The Institute for Safe Medications Practices recommends including indications in written orders, as well. Nurses should ask the prescriber to countersign the spoken order within 24 hours.

4. Not using critical thinking

Nurses are expected to recognize and question inappropriate medication orders. Examples include inappropriate drugs, dosages, routes, frequencies, and interactions. A nurse who questions an order would ordinarily discuss the concerns with the prescriber. If a satisfactory resolution to the concern is not achieved, the nurse is expected to consult with the nurse's direct supervisor, and allow the supervisor to continue up the chain of command until the concern is resolved.

17.6 Dispensing Stage Errors

The following discussion focuses on pharmacists and provides specific examples. The reader will recognize that the general factors leading to errors are also specific factors in the pharmacist's arena. Nurses play a role in dispensing errors when they do not recognize the wrong medication or strength of medication has been dispensed, or become involved in the dispensing function.

Pharmacists have an independent duty to protect their patients from harm, and must consult with prescribing physicians in a positive way so mistakes and misunderstandings are avoided or corrected. Pharmacists are increasingly becoming the target of malpractice litigation. This phenomenon has resulted in the development of strategies to reduce the risks of medication errors, as well as to manage pharmacist liability.[37]

Pharmacists Mutual (see Figure 17.2) has identified the most common categories of errors and omissions responsible for claims against pharmacists for malpractice. They are, in order of frequency:

1. Wrong drug
2. Wrong strength of drug
3. Wrong directions
4. Lack of drug review (which can result in allergies or contraindicated combinations of drugs being administered)
5. Failure to properly counsel patients on medication usage
6. Non-bodily injury
7. Other (miscellaneous)

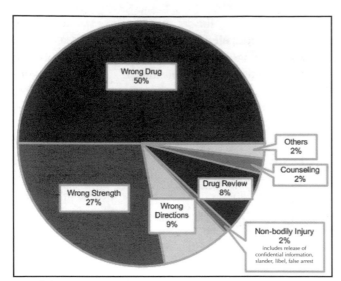

Figure 17.2 *Categories of errors and omissions most responsible for claims against pharmacists for malpractice. Reproduced by permission from Pharmacists Mutual Insurance Company, Algona, IA. © Pharmacists Mutual Insurance Company, 2011.*

A. Wrong Drug

Since 1990, the number of "wrong drugs" administered has remained relatively consistent, although the reasons for these errors appear varied. In one case, the pharmacist took a prescription for Digoxin over the phone from a doctor's office. The pharmacist prepared the label, counted the correct drug into the tray, and poured it into the bottle. As he placed the bottle next to the completed label, the phone rang again, with a request for warfarin. The pharmacist filled the prescription for warfarin in the same manner, but somehow, the two labels were mixed up. The warfarin bottle received the Digoxin label and was given to the wrong patient.

In another case, a technician simply took the wrong bottle from the shelf. If a busy pharmacist does not catch the error when performing his check, or does not check the technician's work, the results can be serious.

Distractions in the pharmacy are another common and unavoidable part of every workday. Label switches can result due to "multi-tasking" or filling multiple prescriptions for a single patient. A patient may have a prescription for Coumadin (Warfarin) once a day and Lasix twice a day. If the labels are switched, and the patient ends up taking Coumadin twice a day, she may suffer a serious hemorrhage from the Coumadin and congestive heart failure from under-treatment of the Lasix (Furosemide).

Sometimes drug names look alike. Prescriptions for Navane can be mistaken for Norvasc, Prilosec for Prozac, Lasix for Losec. Interestingly, the Lasix/Losec error precipitated a name change by the Losec manufacturer (it was

renamed Prilosec). After that, Prilosec and Prozac were mistakenly dispensed in place of one another. This problem occurs so frequently that a special committee of the United States Pharmacopeia (USP) has been formed to look at the selection of new drug names. There is an evolving science in understanding and preventing this error of fine distinction.

The physicians' handwriting is another cause of pharmacist error. Often the subject of jokes, the typical physician's scrawl presents the most dangerous type of pharmacist error. An increased interest in electronic prescribing would help obviate such interpretative errors between physician and pharmacist.

B. Wrong Drug Strength

The second largest category of claims (24.4 percent) shown in the Pharmacists Mutual Study is wrong strength. A common example would be receiving a prescription for Digoxin 0.125 mg, and filling it in error with Digoxin 0.25 mg. Misplacement of a decimal point is a very common way these errors occur. Another error is picking up the wrong bottle when filling the prescription. Perhaps the drug is correct, but the dosage is wrong. Depending upon the drug prescribed, the results of selecting the wrong strength can be dangerous, even fatal. Another common outcome is a lack of efficacy. An underdosage of an anticoagulant (such as coumadin) could fail to prevent a fatal clot. Even old, familiar drugs are subject to this error. Drugs filled most frequently are involved in more errors, simply as a matter of incidence. For example, Haldol is used for senile dementia. It would be unusual for Haldol 5 mg to be prescribed for an ambulatory elderly patient. A more common dosage is 0.5 mg. The drugs with the greatest number of available dosage forms offer the greatest probability for a dosage error. The drugs that can cause the most toxicity will result in claims. These drugs have the lowest "therapeutic index"; the relationship between a therapeutic level and toxic level is small. If the patient suffers from damage or adverse effect—even if the patient only has to present to an emergency room—this can result in a cause of action against the pharmacist and pharmacy.

C. Wrong Directions

At 7.8 percent of all claims, "wrong directions" represents a significant number reported in the Pharmacists Mutual Study. These cases involve incorrect directions in the computer. In one case, a pharmacist entered a new prescription for birth-control tablets into the computer and inadvertently typed, "Take two tablets daily." For nine months, this patient refilled her birth control prescription every 15 days while following the erroneous label directions, without anyone at the pharmacy noticing the discrepancy. The most dangerous "wrong directions" claims are for children's prescriptions, especially children under the age of 6.

To avoid labeling the prescription with the wrong directions, pharmacists should always check the label directions against the hard copy prescription. Another good practice is for the pharmacist to follow a standard procedure of removing the prescription from the bag as he counsels each patient. The pharmacist should read the written directions to the patient and ask, "How did your doctor explain you were to take this medication?" The pharmacist can use similar words to determine whether the patient understands what the directions mean. The pharmacist should ask the patient to repeat the directions on the prescription. This serves two purposes: it allows the pharmacist to double-check the label directions, and, by removing the prescription from the bag, it creates the appearance of a professional service rather than the mere sale of a "commodity" in a sack.

D. Lack of Drug Review

OBRA-90 (Omnibus Budget Reconciliation Act) requires pharmacists to review all prescriptions prior to filling them and check for interactions, allergies, and a list of other potential problems. Especially because pharmacy technicians are increasingly used to reduce the pharmacist's workload, this area of claims—previously almost unheard of—now represents over 9 percent of all claims.

Drug review was first described in The Standard of Practice of the Profession of Pharmacy.[38] The American Pharmaceutical Association (APHA), in concert with the American Association of Colleges of Pharmacy (AACP), defined standards of practice for the profession of pharmacy. Many or all of the requirements eventually legislated and mandated by the OBRA were components of the standards of practice. OBRA requires medication profiles, as well as review for therapeutic duplication, allergy, cross sensitivity, drug disease, and contraindications. Failure to provide meaningful patient drug review has resulted in claims and lawsuits that plead error of omission.

17.7 Administration Stage Errors
A. The Five Rights

A number of serious reported medication errors have resulted in fatal overdoses. As with most such errors, more than one safeguard within the medication administration system either failed or simply was not in place. Medication errors are preventable. Nurses are taught the "five rights" of medication administration in nursing school.

1. Right drug

The nurse is expected to question any unclear order or one that seems inappropriate. As part of the medication-administration process, the nurse must read labels and obtain information from authoritative sources (references, pharmacy consultation) about correct drug usage when encountering unfamiliar drugs. Many nurses were taught to read the order for the medication three times: when first reviewing the medications to be administered to the patient, when removing the medication from the drawer, and just before administering it to the patient.

2. Right patient

The nurse must check the patient's identification band to make sure the name on the medication administration record (MAR) matches the identification band. When the identification band has been removed for any reason, such as swelling in the arm due to an intravenous infiltration, the nurse is responsible for ensuring another identification band is applied to the patient. When medications are labeled with the patient's name, the nurse should check the medication package to ensure a match. The Joint Commission National Patient Safety Goals stress the importance of using patient identifiers to correctly confirm the patient's identity. The use of bar codes on medication packages and patient identification bands helps to reduce the risk of administering the medication to the wrong patient.

3. Right dose

The third "right" requires the nurse to understand all abbreviations and measurements used at the facility. When confronted with a questionable dose, the nurse must consult authoritative sources to verify the dose is correct. Errors in dosage may occur if calculations are performed incorrectly. A wrong dose error typically occurs when the patient receives an amount of medicine greater or less than the amount ordered.

4. Right route

The nurse is expected to administer the medication according to the route specified in the order. Some medications can only be given intramuscularly, and not intravenously or orally. Nurses are taught how to administer injections using recommended sites and to document the site of the injection on the MAR. A good nursing library contains several well-illustrated basic textbooks that describe the techniques for proper administration of injections.

5. Right time

Pharmacology courses in nursing school teach nurses the expected frequency of certain categories of medications.

For example, most antibiotics are given more than one time a day to maintain a consistent blood level.

B. Examples of When the Five Rights Go Wrong

Many medication errors clearly fall within the scope of the five rights of medication administration. This section of the chapter presents information on cases involving deviations from the five rights. Review of published reports of settlements and verdicts is useful for locating expert witnesses and networking with attorneys who have been involved in similar cases.

1. Wrong drug

Misinterpretation of a prescriber's handwriting, a dispensing error, or selecting the wrong drug from the supply can result in administration of the incorrect drug. Responses to a 2004 survey of 1,600 hospitals showed that less than half (41 percent) always label containers (including syringes, basins, and other vessels used to store drugs) in the sterile field of an operating room, physician's office, cardiac catheterization suite, endoscopy or radiology suite, and other areas. An alarming 18 percent did not label medications and solutions on the sterile field at all, and another 42 percent reported inconsistent labeling of solutions. A 2006 Joint Commission National Patient Safety Goal now highlights the need to label all drugs and solutions in perioperative and procedural settings.[39]

2. Wrong patient

The MARs for two infants were mixed up, resulting in administration of Synagis (palivizumab), used to prevent respiratory syncytial virus, to the wrong child. The infants were side-by-side in isolettes, and both their MARs were on the counter between the two isolettes. Coincidentally, both infants had the same first name along with very similar hospital identification numbers. The nurse failed to notice she was referring to the wrong MAR and administered a dose of Synagis to the wrong infant.[40] Clearly, the nurse did not check the newborn's identification band before administering the medication intended for another.

3. Wrong dose

The miscalculation of a dosage is a common source of error in both the prescribing and administration of medications. Lesar reports that errors in the use of dosage equations account for more than 15 percent of all medication prescribing errors. These types of errors have significant potential for producing adverse events. Children are at particular risk for this error as the broad range of sizes and ages require individualized calculation of dosages.[41] Wrong doses of medication may be administered, leading to overdose or underdose.

A 47-year-old woman undergoing an outpatient endoscopic lithotripsy procedure for removal of a kidney stone was involved in a procedure that took over six hours. She died 12 hours later from fluid overload caused by absorption of the irrigating fluid used, and by the resulting low sodium, high potassium, pulmonary edema, general tissue edema, acidosis, renal failure, and other conditions. The plaintiffs claimed the defendants committed numerous acts of malpractice related to the irrigating fluid used, including the use of distilled water rather than saline, failure to keep track of the volume of irrigating fluid used, and failure to verify that adequate drainage of the bladder was taking place. The parties settled for a confidential amount following mediation.[42]

4. Wrong route

Wrong route errors occur when the correct form of drug is administered, but in the incorrect site on the patient's body, such as ear drops administered in the eye or intramuscular (IM) injections given intravenously (IV). In one case, a liquid diet that should have been given through a tube into the patient's stomach was by mistake administered intravenously. In another case, Maalox was administered into an intravenous line instead of through a tube inserted into the stomach. In some instances, medications meant to be applied on the skin (topically) have been injected into the body.

Listing topical medications on the MAR, even when they are technically part of a treatment plan, can help avoid error. Clear labeling of all medications and double-checking labels before use are also important. Keeping treatment solutions on the bedside table increases the likelihood of staff error and may be dangerous if they are within a patient's reach. Many institutions use large, brightly colored or luminescent stickers and labels that read, "For topical use only."

5. Wrong time

Administering the medication before it is due or delays in the administration of medications are considered wrong time errors. Some medications must be given at specific times to maintain an appropriate blood level. Timing of meals or other medications may also affect the therapeutic impact of a medication. The following case illustrates the potential consequences of this occurrence.

When one patient arrived at an emergency department with a fever of 103.2 degrees, low blood pressure, weakness, dizziness, and chills, she was diagnosed with a kidney infection. She was transferred to a second hospital without having received any antibiotics. The physician ordered antibiotics to be given at 2 P.M., but these were not administered. Around 5 P.M., the patient was admitted to a nursing unit, accompanied by a dose of antibiotics. Medical records did not document that this dose was administered. At 8 P.M., the first dose of antibiotics was given to the patient. By 1 A.M., the patient's condition deteriorated and she was transferred to the intensive care unit in septic shock. She suffered a cardiac arrest within seven hours and died. Plaintiff's experts were critical of the nurses and physicians for the delay in administration of antibiotics. The defense argued that the infecting organism was so virulent that no treatment would have saved her life. The case was settled for $2.1 million.[43]

C. Additional Types of Medication Errors

This section provides more information on the types of medication errors described in the previous section. Examples of cases involving these types of errors are included.

1. Omitted dose

An omission error takes place when a patient has not received her medication by the time the next dose is due. When a dose is not administered, the usual practice is for the nurse to put her initials in the box for the designated dose. The nurse draws a circle around the initials to indicate the dose was omitted. Following this, the nurse documents the reason for the omitted dose on the medication administration record or on the medical record. The nurse may fail to administer a medication for a variety of reasons. These may include any of the following:

1. The medication order was not transcribed onto the medication record.
2. The medication was not available in the nursing unit at the time it was to be given.
3. The patient was not in the nursing unit at the time the medication was to be given.
4. More than one medication administration record was in use. When the nurse was administering medications, the second sheet was overlooked.
5. When the nurse was preparing the medications for the patient, one or more of the medications was overlooked.
6. The medication was administered to another patient in error.
7. The medication record was recopied when all of the spaces were used up and in the recopying process the medication was not copied onto the new record.

Other than when the patient or the medication was not available at the specified time, the remaining reasons for omissions of a medication constitute errors. Omission errors may be difficult for the attorney to detect if the nurse covered up the omission and signed the medication administration record to indicate the dose was given. If the drug was one for which therapeutic blood levels can be checked, consistent omissions of the medication would result in subnormal blood levels.

2. Duplicate dose

A duplicate dose may be administered to a patient if a nurse does not follow the procedures for documenting a medication dose, and a second nurse comes along and administers the medication. For example, the following situation resulted in a duplicate dose.

A nursing home patient died of an overdose of Fentanyl. When the decedent was taken to a hospital, she had three patches of Fentanyl on her back for treatment of rheumatoid arthritis. Proof showed that each patch contained Fentanyl, which is considered to be 50 to 100 times stronger than Morphine. The jury returned a $1 million verdict.[44]

3. Unordered drug error

An unordered drug error occurs when a patient receives a medication for which the physician did not write an order. Some authors refer to this as an unauthorized drug error. This category includes outcomes that result when a nurse switches medications for two patients; each patient is the victim of an unordered drug error (as well as an omission).

A Texas woman who had a previous cesarean section was pregnant, and in the defendant hospital for labor and delivery. Pitocin was started. While in labor, the woman's uterus ruptured and the baby was found to have been without oxygen for an indeterminate amount of time. The plaintiffs claimed the hospital, doctors, and nurses were negligent in giving Pitocin to the patient. The doctor claimed he did not remember ordering the Pitocin, and he did not believe he would have ordered it under the circumstances. The jury found the doctor not negligent, but the hospital negligent. They awarded the plaintiff $1,587,000 in damages.[45]

17.8 High-Risk Medications

The Joint Commission on Accreditation of Health Care Organizations (Joint Commission) has identified high-risk sentinel medications. Even though the original list was compiled in 1999, the same drugs continue to be problematic. This fact in itself certainly demonstrates the failure of educators, regulators, and legislators to effectively rectify the problems associated with getting information about drugs to

Table 17.5
Identifying High-Risk Drugs

Characteristic	Prototypes
Narrow Therapeutic Index (NTI)	Digoxin, anticoagulants
Inherent Undesirable Effect(s)	Steroids, chemotherapy antibiotics/allergy
Class of Drugs Which Shares Toxicity	NSAIDs*, ACEIs**
Narcotics—Patient Controlled Analgesia	Morphine, all opiates
Newly-Approved Drugs	Temofloxacin (unknown safety profiles)
"Off-Label" Uses of Drugs	Fen-Phen
Pharmacokinetic Drug Interactions	SSRIs*** (Zoloft, Paxil, Prozac)
Direct-to-Consumer Promoted	Add-a-med

Modified from Benjamin DM and O'Donnell JT. "Medication Errors," In Sandbar S, Ed. Legal Medicine. American College of Legal Medicine. Schaumburg, IL 2006.
*NSAID   NonSteroidal Anti-inflammatory Drug
**ACEI   Angiotension Converting Enzyme Inhibitor
***SSRI   Selective Serotonin Reuptake Inhibitor

the prescriber. The Joint Commission's high alert medications include:

1. Insulin
2. Opiates/PCA
3. Concentrated solutions of KCl and Potassium Phosphate
4. IV anticoagulants (Heparin)
5. NaCl solutions above 0.9 percent
6. Intrathecal administration of chemotherapy by the wrong route[46]

Extensive discussions in earlier sections of the chapter have addressed the anticoagulants Warfarin (Coumadin) and Heparin (which would include low molecular weight heparins Lovenox, Organon, and Fragmin). Additional discussion follows, with several case examples. Drugs are high-risk if they have a low therapeutic index, or are intrinsically toxic. The therapeutic index is defined as the ratio of the toxic dose to the therapeutic dose. Such low therapeutic index drugs provide little margin for overdose. Drugs intrinsically toxic include narcotics, anticoagulants, digitalis, and

chemotherapy. Table 17.5 provides a list of common high-risk drugs, based on their pharmacologic properties.

A. Insulin

Insulin is the mainstay for treatment of virtually all type-I and many type-II diabetic patients. Frequently, hospitalized non-diabetic patients who have elevated glucose readings due to high glucose intravenous solutions are subject to insulin errors in the ordering of insulin, interpretation of the order, or preparation of the insulin injection, which can have disastrous consequences. Some agencies and institutions require a nurse preparing to give an insulin injection to have another nurse review the order and the prepared syringe to verify the correct dose has been drawn up. Insulin is ordered in units. The prescriber should spell out the word "units" and not abbreviate it. The dosage may be misunderstood if the order contains the symbol "U," which has been confused for a "0." Some of the most serious errors are due to misinterpretations of abbreviations used in medical writing in patient charts. A slash mark (/) has been mistaken for a "1," causing a patient to receive a 100-unit overdose of NPH insulin when the slash was used to separate an order for two insulin doses: 6 units regular insulin/20 units NPH insulin.[47]

The primary risk associated with insulin therapy is hypoglycemia. While insulin is used to lower blood sugar in hyperglycemia (overly high blood sugar), those who have normal levels and hyperglycemia who have their blood-sugar levels lowered accidentally face morbidity and mortality of hypoglycemia.[48] Since the brain depends on glucose as its primary fuel, hypoglycemia, or low blood-glucose level, has a marked impact on brain metabolism. Alterations of brain function are responsible for the characteristic symptoms of hypoglycemia. As glucose levels fall, prodromal signs and symptoms may appear. Such manifestations include hunger, salivation, an overall ill-at-ease feeling, or even nausea. Hypoglycemia may lead to convulsions resulting in brain damage, as well as serious musculoskeletal injuries. The essential biochemical event is a blood sugar level of less than 25–30 mg/100 ml, lasting one to two hours, and leading to exhaustion of the store of cerebral glucose and glycogen. Within this brief span of time, as cerebral oxidation proceeds without exogenous glucose, the structural component of neurons are metabolized and irreversible damage occurs. The cerebral cortex suffers major damage; cortical nerve cells degenerate and are replaced by micogliacytes and astrocytes.[49]

In a Minnesota case, the plaintiff was admitted to the hospital for treatment of shoulder pain. Her blood sugar was to be monitored and maintained through insulin administration by hospital staff. Within five hours of admission, the plaintiff was overdosed with insulin. She suffered severe hypoglycemia, which resulted in severe brain damage. She was placed on life support, but this was removed after one week. A $675,000 settlement was reached in this case involving a 64-year-old, wheelchair-bound woman.[50]

Nursing responsibilities include accurately transcribing insulin orders, questioning inappropriate doses, accurately drawing up insulin in the correct number of units, and observing patients for signs and symptoms of hypo- or hyperglycemia.

B. Opiates

The opiate drug class—morphine, Demerol, and Dilaudid—consists of high-risk drugs. Morphine is the opiate against which all others are measured. Opiates depress respiratory drive even at therapeutic doses; therein lies the risk. The patient may not know breathing is impaired. A sleeping patient is at greater risk. Opiates given with other central nervous system depressants (phenothiazines, benzodiazepines) further increase the risk.[51]

In a Minnesota case, the plaintiff's decedent went to the hospital because of a two-day history of abdominal pain. An epidural catheter was placed for pain control after surgery for his intra-abdominal abscess. The infusion was initially ordered at 2 mcg/ml to be infused at a rate of 10/ml per hour. This resulted in an hourly dose of 20 mcg per hour. Around noon the next day a nurse wrote a telephone order from the defendant doctor for a dose change in the Fentanyl infusion. The order was to increase the dose of Fentanyl in the epidural infusion to 10 mcg/ml to run at the same rate as before. This resulted in an hourly dose of 100 mcg/hour of Fentanyl. This new infusion began around 2 P.M. When the nurses checked the decedent around 4:30 A.M. the next day, he had no pulse and was not breathing. A code was called and resuscitation begun, which was unsuccessful. An autopsy revealed that the decedent had a blood level of Fentanyl that was 13 mg/ml. The plaintiff claimed the defendants were negligent in ordering and administering an excessive dose of Fentanyl and in failing to properly assess and monitor changes in the decedent's condition. A confidential settlement was reached.[52]

Nursing responsibilities include preparing and administering correct doses of narcotics, questioning inappropriate doses, withholding opiates from a patient when such medications are contraindicated, and observing for and intervening when respiratory depression is noted.

C. PCA (Patient Controlled Analgesia)

PCA became popular in the late 1980s, and today is the standard and most frequent method for administering opiates for acute pain, in the hospital and sometimes at home. The Institute for Safe Medication Practices has identified safety issues with PCA. PCA has considerable potential to improve pain management by allowing patients to self-administer more frequent, but smaller, doses of pain medications. The ISMP performed a review of actual errors involving PCA therapy consisting of cases reviewed, including those reported voluntarily by healthcare practitioners to the USP-ISMP Medication Errors Reporting Program and those solicited by ISMP for the project. Some of the most serious errors occurred because the basic premise of PCA was violated. PCA is to be controlled by the patient only. A patient already sedated by an opiate or opioid pain medication will not activate the PCA pump to deliver another dose. This built-in safeguard protects the patient from overdose. However, family members and nurses have innocently pushed the button for patients, hoping to keep them comfortable. The well-intentioned "PCA by proxy" has led to oversedation, respiratory depression, and even death.

Other factors leading to PCA errors include:

1. Improper patient selection
2. Product mix-up, wrong drug, or wrong concentration
3. Inadequate patient education
4. Ineffective monitoring of the patient's vital signs
5. Insufficient staff training
6. Practice-related problems (inaccurate programming, incorrect transcription of orders, compounding errors, similar to the routine medication error factors discussed earlier in the chapter)
7. Prescribing errors
8. Design flaws in the PCA pumps[53]

Nursing responsibilities for the use of PCA pumps include the need to:

1. Question the use of the PCA pump in patients with sleep apnea, obstructed airways, or the inability to self-medicate
2. Correctly program the pump
3. Accurately record the amount of opiate received by the patient per shift.
4. Observe the patient at ordered intervals and more frequently
5. Accurately count respiratory rate
6. Report changes in patient condition
7. Provide patient education about the use of the pump and the need to avoid medication by proxy

D. Coumadin and Heparin

Another class includes Coumadin and Heparin, both anti-coagulants. Patients who need anticoagulants are at risk for clotting, with complications of deep vein thromboses, pulmonary embolism, coronary thrombosis, and cerebral thrombosis. Other thrombotic conditions can affect any part of the vasculature. With too much anticoagulation, however, the patient may bleed internally and risk grave results, including death. The following is a case report related to Heparin.

A 53-year-old man entered the hospital for femoral by-pass surgery. Before his surgical procedure, an inadequate preoperative cardiac workup was performed. Twenty hours after the uneventful surgery, the patient's hemoglobin and hematocrit were low, indicative for possible bleeding. After the surgery, the doctor ordered 7,500 units of Heparin to be administered over a 24-hour period or 2,500 units every eight hours continuously. One hour after the order was written, the nursing staff misread the instructions. Instead of administering 2,500 units of Heparin, they administered 25,000 units of Heparin. This caused the patient to continuously bleed, his urine output to decline to zero, and his heart rate to increase to over 130. Consultation with a nephrologist and cardiologist was ordered, to see if they could determine the cause of the continuing abdominal pain and the renal failure. At no time did the doctor believe his orders were not followed with respect to Heparin administration. Finally, about eight hours after the first Heparin infusion, the patient was taken back to surgery for an exploratory laparotomy. However, a nurse again prepared him with an additional (negligently misinterpreted) 25,000 units of Heparin. Profound and serious bleeding was apparent, but the physician team had no idea what was causing the bleeding. The patient died from a coronary thrombus. The plaintiff claimed the cause of death was the failure to adequately perform a preoperative cardiac workup, as well as the negligent administration of toxic levels of Heparin. The defendant hospital admitted liability regarding the actions of the nurse, but denied the actions of the nurse had anything to do with the patient's death. The matter settled for $2.5 million after the jury was selected. *Marie Lenoure, Special Administrator for the Estate of Victor LePore v. Oak Park Hospital*, Cook County (IL).[54,55]

Trauma complicates the risks associated with giving Coumadin, Heparin, and other medications which prolong clotting time. Nursing responsibilities include questioning whether anticoagulants should be continued after trauma, increasing the risk of bleeding.

In an Alabama case, the plaintiff's decedent previously suffered a stroke and was on Coumadin therapy. She suf-fered a fall in her home and was admitted to the defendant hospital. The nurse assigned to watch for changes in the decedent's physical presentation did not inform the doctor the decedent was lethargic and manifested changes in her blood pressure, heart rate, and respiration. The physician released the decedent to return home. The next day, the patient fell into a coma, and was readmitted to the hospital. She died several days later from a subdural hematoma. The plaintiff claimed the hospital's staff failed to obtain copies of the decedent's coagulation studies, investigate the history of Coumadin therapy, order a CT scan, order a blood test, report the changes in physical condition, and obtain a neurological consultation. The defendants claimed there was no negligence and that the decedent would not have survived even if surgery was performed. A $2.5 million verdict was returned.[56]

E. Cancer Drugs

Antineoplastics always occupy the list, but not due to the inherent toxicity associated with these cancer chemotherapy drugs, for it is extremely rare for litigation to arise following routine chemotherapy, despite frequent devastating toxicity associated with it. Litigation arises when mistakes are made (the wrong dose, frequency, or route of administration), often with devastating results. The following case report is an example.

The plaintiff's decedent, a 54-year-old man, was diagnosed with cancer of the tongue. The treatment plan included surgery, radiation therapy and chemotherapy. The patient was admitted to the hospital for 5 FU after treatment with Cisplatin. The 5 FU was given by bolus instead of continuous infusion. When switching from continuous infusion to a bolus, the dose needs to be significantly reduced. In the decedent's case, the dosage was never decreased during the five-day course, so he received 1,500 mg per day. He suffered from a very low platelet count, low red blood cell count, sepsis, acidosis, and died. The plaintiffs claimed the defendant's negligent administration of the wrong dosage of 5 FU caused the death. The defense admitted liability for settlement discussion purposes only, but also claimed the decedent's life expectancy was less than five years. The case settled for $1,358,000.[57]

F. Methotrexate

Methotrexate is used for chemotherapy, to treat arthritis, or dissolve ectopic pregnancies and other conditions. It has complicated dosing schedules and potential for toxicity due to potentially confusing frequencies. It is commonly indicated for weekly dosing and has been involved in several severe and fatal reactions as a result of being dispensed erroneously as daily doses. Because of the number of fatalities from errors with oral methotrexate, clinicians should consider it a "high-alert" medication. The ISMP recommends the following measures to reduce the risk of an error when oral methotrexate is prescribed:

1. Build alerts in electronic prescribing systems and pharmacy computers to warn clinicians whenever doses of oral methotrexate have been entered (and to remind staff to check the indication with the patient in a retail setting). Configure the systems to avoid defaulting to a daily dosing schedule.

2. Have a pharmacist conduct a prospective drug-utilization review before dispensing oral methotrexate to determine its indication for use, verify proper dosing, confirm the correct dosing schedule on medication administration records and prescription labels, ensure staff and patient education, and promote appropriate monitoring of the patient.

3. Establish a system that ensures outpatients receive counseling when picking up new prescriptions and refills (e.g., mark the bag with a red flag to alert clerical staff that counseling is required).

4. Provide patients with clear written instructions that name a specific day of the week for taking the tablet(s). When possible, avoid choosing Monday since it could be misread as "morning." Prepare instructions in large print to assist elderly patients with poor eyesight.

5. Advise patients to contact their physician if they miss a dose. Tell them a flare-up of the disease is unlikely with one missed dose.

6. Ensure written drug information leaflets are given to patients and they contain clear advice about the weekly dosage schedule, not a daily dosage schedule.

7. Explain to patients that taking extra doses is dangerous. Encourage feedback to ensure the patient understands the weekly dosing schedule and the medication should not be used as needed for symptom control.

8. Solicit help from a responsible caregiver if the patient appears to have cognitive or severe sensory difficulties.

9. Prescribe the drug as a dose pack (e.g., RHEU-MATREX by Lederle), which helps reinforce the weekly dosing schedule.[54]

17.9 High-Risk Populations

The effects of medication errors can range from insignificant to deadly. Failure to monitor levels of certain medications can result in either toxic responses from levels too high or a lack of therapeutic effect from levels too low. A vulnerable patient may receive the wrong medication, dose, or route of administration, or not receive the medication at all. Interactions between medications can result in toxic effects or one medication making another ineffective.

A. Pediatrics

Children are at particular risk of medication errors for a number of reasons. Unlike adults, they cannot question an unfamiliar medication or provide details of medical conditions which stimulate a healthcare professional to question the appropriateness of a medication order. All of the child's systems function closer to their maximum capacity than an adult's in order to meet metabolic demands. In the face of illness, metabolic demands are increased even more, especially with fever, infection, injuries, or burns. Although children generally have healthy hearts and lungs that allow them to compensate for deficits, their immature systems have fewer reserves when stressed, leading to the possibility of rapid decompensation.[58] A medication error taxes a child's already limited ability to respond to physiological stresses. Additionally, children are at risk for medication errors due to the:

1. Different and changing drug dosages needed to treat children of different ages and sizes

2. Need for calculating individualized doses based on the patient's age, weight, body surface, and clinical condition

3. Lack of available dosage forms and concentrations appropriate for administration to neonates, infants, and children

4. Need for precise dose measurement and appropriate drug delivery systems

5. Lack of a published information or Food and Drug Administration-approved labeling regarding dosing, safety, efficacy, and clinical use of drugs in the pediatric population[59]

B. Elderly

Medication errors affect elderly individuals in all healthcare settings. Risk factors that put the elderly at especially high-risk for adverse medication outcomes include:

1. age-related decline in liver and kidney function,

2. greater sensitivity to the effects of medications,

3. reduced ability to tolerate usual adult doses,

4. multiple chronic diseases requiring multiple chronic medications, and

5. under-representation of the elderly in clinical trials.[60]

Medications control the symptoms of the elderly, prevent complications of disease, improve the quality of the frail senior's life, and maintain or improve physiological status.[61] Polypharmacy, or the prescribing of several medications at the same time, is common among the elderly. The more medications a resident is taking, the greater the chance of interactions, and the greater the risk of errors. Medicaid data for one state showed that during a 30-day period, 68 percent of long-term care residents had received nine or more prescription drugs, and 32 percent had received 20 or more prescription drugs.[62]

An Atlanta Legal Aid Society, Inc. study found that 21 percent of nursing home residents interviewed said they had been given the wrong medications, but 38 percent said the error was corrected when they pointed it out to the nurse. Fourteen percent said they actually ingested the wrong medication.[63]

A study of adverse drug events, some of which are due to medication errors, revealed the most common causes of prescribing errors in nursing homes. These were wrong dose (63 percent), failure to consider drug interaction (22 percent), and wrong choice of a drug (9 percent). Physicians also failed to order monitoring associated with the medication (83 percent) and did not respond to signs and symptoms of drug toxicity or to laboratory evidence of drug toxicity (41 percent).[64]

C. Allergic Versus Intolerant

Perhaps the most preventable, and certainly among the most lethal, of medication errors is the administration of a drug for which the patient has an allergic history. Every patient should be asked: "Are you allergic to aspirin, iodine, sulfa, or penicillin? Have you ever had an allergic reaction to any drug?" Some patients do not consider over-the-counter medications as drugs, so the nurse must ask the question. Data about allergies should be documented on the front of the chart, on the patient's history and physical, on the nursing admission sheet, and on the medication administration record. Some facilities even include information about allergies on the patient's identification band, on the wall above the hospital bed, and on every physician order sheet.

Many patients report having allergic reactions to medications. However, on closer questioning, it can be determined they had nausea, vomiting, or diarrhea, not an allergy

in a true immunologic sense. These symptoms are more accurately termed an intolerance, which would not preclude subsequent administration. The patient should be warned about the possibility of these symptoms and how to combat them, such as taking with food to avoid an upset stomach, and so on. The nurse is expected to question the patient who reports an allergy to a medication to find out what occurred. Nurses are expected to question an order that directs the nurse to administer a medication to which the patient is allergic, and to be able to identify drugs related to the one in question. If the patient says she is allergic to penicillin, the nurse would question an order for Ampicillin. A patient allergic to steroids should not be given Prednisone, Cortisone, or any of the many forms of steroids.

A New York woman's allergy to steroids was manifested by becoming psychotic. Before and after surgery on her shoulder for a displaced fracture of the surgical neck of the right humerus, she was given steroids to treat an asthmatic condition. The steroids were administered first in the form of Solu-Cortef, an intravenous form of hydrocortisone, followed by prednisone, an oral form. Following several doses of steroids, she became psychotic and was seen wandering around the hospital unit from room to room. In her confusion, she would not keep her sling on the operated arm. The inability to keep her arm immobilized resulted in damage to the surgical site. After the steroids stopped, she became alert and oriented. When she returned to the hospital a month later to redo the surgery on her shoulder, she reported an allergy to prednisone, but the nurse who obtained that information did not ask her what type of allergic reaction she had. She was again given Solu-Cortef, despite the notation on the order sheet that she was allergic to prednisone. The plaintiff's nurse expert witness was prepared to testify that the nurse should have recognized Solu-Cortef and prednisone as steroids and questioned this order. The order was filled by the night nursing supervisor, who also did not note the allergy. Again, following the Solu-Cortef administration, the plaintiff became confused, was seen banging on the hospital window with the arm that had been operated on, convinced her grandchildren were playing in the trees outside the hospital. She again damaged her shoulder. There were no more attempts to surgically repair her shoulder. The case settled for $250,000 in the midst of trial after the orthopedic surgeon admitted liability (unpublished case).

PRACTICE TIP: Carefully review the medical record for evidence of documentation of allergies. The attorney will encounter the following abbreviations indicating that an inquiry was made and the patient denied allergies: NKA (No Known Allergies) or NKDA (No Known

Drug Allergies). The nurse has fulfilled the standard of care by inquiring about allergies and should not be liable if the patient conceals a history of allergies.

D. Critically Ill Patient

The critically ill patient is particularly vulnerable to serious medication errors. This individual is already high-risk for dying or having a reduced quality of life. There are five categories of critically ill patients.

1. People who suffer life-threatening medical problems in the community. This includes a wide array of people and problems, including severe infections, heart attacks, stroke, drug and alcohol-related emergencies, liver, lung, kidney failure, and other less common disorders. Some may be in the intensive care unit (ICU) due to a delay or failure of diagnosis and delay in treatment.

2. People with life-threatening, potentially surgical conditions, such as multiple traumas, head injury, ruptured and/or dissecting aorta, and acute abdominal emergencies. Some of these individuals may be in the ICU as a result of trauma related to a personal injury suit.

3. Elective surgical patients undergoing high-risk procedures that normally require an ICU bed (e.g., coronary artery bypass surgery, lung resection, or removal of a brain tumor), or have enough existing medical problems to warrant admission to an ICU post op (e.g., a patient with heart failure undergoing gall bladder surgery).

4. Patients who deteriorate while in the hospital and need to be admitted or readmitted to an ICU for medical or surgical problems. The list of conditions that cause these problems is long but is usually one of seven: chest pain, cardiac rhythm disturbance, low blood pressure, infection, bleeding, respiratory failure, cardiac arrest, or some combination thereof. Patients with unexpected problems at the time of low-risk elective surgery are also included. Medical malpractice cases may result from alleged deviations associated with deterioration, such as failure to diagnose or appropriately intervene before the patient's condition becomes life threatening.

5. The chronically, critically ill. This is a varied group of patients who continue to have critical care issues such as requiring a respirator for prolonged periods of time, sometimes indefinitely. In this group are patients who return to ICUs on multiple occasions

for reasons such as recurring severe infections or bouts of respiratory failure. The hospital mortality rate of this group is extremely high.[65]

An overdose, an inadequate amount of medication, a medication infusion hung at the wrong rate, or any other type of serious medication error may be the only thing necessary to cause physiological stress to an individual already in a compromised state.[66]

Detection of a medication error may be difficult because critically ill patients may deteriorate independent of an error. Furthermore, the skills of an intensivist may be needed to separate the impact of the error from the factors resulting in the critically ill condition.

17.10 Litigation of the Medication Error Claim

The hospital risk manager investigating the incident—as well as the attorney for the family or injured patient—first must determine an injury has occurred. Without an injury, and solid scientific evidence supporting causation of the injury by the drug (or absence of the drug), there should be no litigation. Causation can be determined by a toxicologist, pharmacologist, or physician trained in a particular specialty (such as a cardiologist or nephrologist evaluating cardiac and kidney toxicities).

A. Useful Discovery Items

In addition to medical records, internal pharmacy records not part of the medical record should be subpoenaed. Prior to computers, these records were retained only for relatively short periods of time. With computers, these records are usually available indefinitely. An additional benefit to the computer record is a "fingerprint" of any authorized person making entries or changes to the record. No records can be replaced. If controlled substances are involved a separate record requirement of five years by the Drug Enforcement Administration usually exceeds local record retention requirements for departmental records outside the chart. If there are toxicology issues, the raw data of the toxicology analysis should be reviewed. Often called the "litigation package," commercial toxicology laboratories are frequently asked for chromatographs, standards, controls, and so on, beyond the basic toxicology report.

Policies and procedures of the nursing and pharmacy department for safe medication use outline the mission and objective of the various departments related to medication use. Additional policies and procedures related to PCA may be found in the anesthesia policies. Operating rooms and intensive care units may have specific policies and procedures.

B. Types of Experts Needed

Once causation is established as described above, many jurisdictions require a certificate of merit or affidavit of a healthcare professional to affirm a particular professional violated the standard of care, and the violation was a cause or contributing cause of the injury to the patient. The expert recruited must be from the same profession as the patient's caregiver (i.e., physician, nurse, or pharmacist).

C. When Early Settlement is Advised

Early settlement is advised when causation is determined and an error occurred. Even though the phrase "to err is human" is pertinent, patients do not expect to be harmed by error, and arguing an error was innocent and not a violation of the standard of care will probably be ineffective with the jury. One prominent attorney who represented an insurance company representing pharmacists was quoted: "If your pharmacist fills the prescription with the wrong drug or the wrong strength, admit liability. Focus on the causation only. Patients expect perfection when getting their prescriptions filled—don't you?"

17.11 Summary

The prevention of medication errors is a multifaceted and multidisciplinary problem. The serious repercussions from a medication error, both from a clinical sense and a legal perspective, drive healthcare professionals to adhere to the basics of medication ordering, transcription or transmission of orders, and dispensing and administering of medications. A medication error can result in a patient's death. Therefore, there cannot be any relaxing from adherence to the standard of care. Patients demand and deserve it!

References

1. Institute of Medicine. *To Err is Human: Building a Safer Health System.* Washington, D.C.: National Academy of Sciences, 1999.

2. Lazarou, J., B.H. Pomeranz, and P.N. Corey, "Incidence of adverse drug reactions in hospitalized patients: a meta-analysis of prospective studies," *JAMA* 279, no. 15 (April 15, 1998): 1200–1205.

3. Kaiser Family Foundation. "Five years after IOM Report on medical errors, nearly half of all consumers worry about the safety of their health care," 2004. Retrieved online at www.kff.org/kaiserpolls/pomr111704nr.cfm, last accessed 03/28/2012.

4. Reason, J., "Safety," American College of Endocrinology/American Association of Clinical Endocrinologists, Patient Safety and Medical System Errors in Diabetes and Endocrinology Consensus Conference, Washington, D.C., 2005.

5. Lisby, M., L. P. Nielsen, and J. Mainz, "Errors in the medication process: frequency, type, and potential clinical consequences," *International Journal of Quality Health Care* 1 (February 17, 2005): 15–22.

6. Hicks, R., et al., *MEDMARX 5th Anniversary Data Report.* Rockville, Maryland: US Pharmacopeia, 2004.

7. Anonymous, "Medication Safety Issue Brief: A Fully Stocked Toolkit," *Hospitals and Health Networks* 77, no. 6 (June 2003). Medication safety issue brief. A fully stocked toolkit. Series II, Part 1, 2.

8. Brennan, T. A., L. L. Leape, and N. M. Laird, "Incidence of Adverse events and negligence in hospitalized patients: results from the Harvard medical practice study," *New England Journal of Medicine* 324 (1991): 370–376. *Perspectives in Healthcare Risk Management*, 2-8, as quoted in Kohn, L., J. Corrigan, and M. Donaldson (eds.) *To Err is Human,* Washington, D.C.: National Academy Press, 2000.

9. Institute of Medicine. *To Err is Human: Building a Safer Health System.* Washington, D.C.: National Academy of Sciences, 2000.

10. "ISMP Survey on State Licensing Boards Response to Medical Error," www.ismp.org/Survey/surveyResults.asp, accessed 05/14/2012.

11. Flynn, E., et al., "Comparison of methods for detecting medication errors in 36 hospitals and skilled-nursing facilities," *American Journal of Health-System Pharmacy* 59, no. 5 (March 1, 2002): 436–446.

12. Wald, H. and K. G. Shojania, "Incident reporting," In *Making Health Care Safer: A Critical Analysis of Patient Safety Practices.* Rockville, Maryland: Agency for Healthcare Research and Quality, 2001.

13. Iyer, P., L. Cohen, and J. T. O'Donnell, "Medical Legal Aspects of Medication Error," In *Drug Injury: Liability, Analysis, and Prevention,* Second edition, ed. J. T. O'Donnell. Tucson, Arizona: Lawyers & Judges Publishing Co., 2005.

14. See note 6.

15. Id.

16. Iyer, P., "Obtaining and Organizing Medical Records," In *Medical Legal Aspects of Medical Records,* eds. P. Iyer, B. Levin, and M. A. Shea. Tucson, Arizona: Lawyers & Judges Publishing Co., 2006.

17. Benjamin, D. M. and J. T. O'Donnell, "Medication Errors," In *LegalMedicine,* Eighth edition, ed. S. Sandbar. Schaumburg, Illinois: American College of Legal Medicine, 2010.

18. Wilson D. G., R. G. McArtney, and R. G. Newcombe, "Medication Errors in Paediatric Practice: Insights from a Continuous Quality Improvement Approach," *European Journal of Pediatric Surgery* 157 (1998): 769–774.

19. Cohen, M. R., *Medication Errors*, 2–3, Washington, D.C.: American Public Health Association, 1999.

20. Burnum, J. G. "Preventability of Adverse Drug Reaction" *Annals of Internal Medicine* 85 (1976): 810.

21. Bates, D. W., L. L. Leape, and D. J. Cullen, et al., "Effect of Computerized Physician Order Entry and a Team Intervention on Prevention of Serious Medication Errors," *JAMA* 280, no. 15 (1998): 1311–1316.

22. Cohen, M. and H. Cohen, "Following a game plan for continued improvement, medication errors," *Nursing 95* (November 1995): 34–37.

23. See note 18.

24. Id.

25. See note 22.

26. Lesar, T., B. Lomaestro, and H. Pohl, "Medication prescribing errors in a teaching hospital," *Archives of Internal Medicine* 157 (1997): 1569–1574.

27. Lesar, T. S., L. Briceland, and D. S. Stein, "Factors Related to Errors in Medication Prescribing," *JAMA* 277, no. 4 (1997): 312–317.

28. See note 9.

29. O'Donnell, J. T., "From the Courtroom: Systems Failure-An Intrathecal Vincristine Tragedy," *Pharmacy Practice News* (January 2004).

30. See note 1.

31. "Bad 'marks' for order communication," *ISMP Medication Safety Alert,* www.ismp.org/newsletters/acutecare/articles/20020918.asp, accessed 03/28/2012.

32. "All is not as it seems," *ISMP Medication Safety Alert* 3, no. 9 (September 2005).

33. Garbutt, J. G., et al., "Safe medication prescribing: training and experience of medical students and housestaff at a large teaching hospital," *Academic Medicine* 6 (June 2005): 594–599.

34. www.jointcommission.org/assets/1/18/Official_Do_Not_Use_List_6_111.pdf.

35. www.jointcommission.org/assets/1/18/SEA_23.pdf.

36. Iyer, P., "Legal Aspects of Charting," In *Medical Legal Aspects of Medical Records*, eds. P. Iyer, B. Levin, and M. A. Shea. Tucson, Arizona: Lawyers & Judges Publishing Co., 2006.

37. O'Donnell, J. T. "Pharmacist Malpractice and the Infamous Courtney Case," In *Drug Injury: Liability, Analysis, and Prevention,* Second edition, ed. J. T. O'Donnell. Tucson, Arizona: Lawyers & Judges Publishing Co., 2005.

38. Kalman and Schlegel, "Standards of Practice for the Profession of Pharmacy," *American Pharmacy* 19, no. 3 (March 1979).

39. "Positive identification: not just for patients, but for drugs and solutions," *ISMP Medication Safety Alert* 3, no. 8 (August 1, 2005).

40. Green, M., "Nursing error and human nature," *Journal of Nursing Law* 9, no. 4 (2004): 7–44.

41. "Oops, sorry, wrong patient! Applying the JCAHO 'two-identifier' rule beyond the patient's room," June 3, 2004, http://www.ismp.org/newsletters/acutecare/articles/20040603.asp, accessed 03/28/2012.

42. Lesar, T., "Errors in the use of medication dosage equations," *Archives of Pediatric and Adolescent Medicine* 152 (April 1998): 340–344.

43. Laska, L. (ed.),"Woman dies after endoscopic lithotripsy procedure for removal of kidney stone," *Medical Malpractice Verdicts, Settlements, and Experts* (April 2003): 58.

44. Laska, L. (ed.), "Failure to promptly administer antibiotics for kidney infection, resulting in death," *Medical Malpractice Verdicts, Settlements, and Experts* (June 2004): 17.

45. Laska, L. (ed.), "Patient dies after Fentanyl patches induce overdose," *Medical Malpractice Verdicts, Settlements, and Experts* (July 2003): 35.

46. Laska, L. (ed.), "Pitocin administered to pregnant woman who had undergone previous cesarean section," *Medical Malpractice Verdicts, Settlements, and Experts* (April 2003): 36.

47. www.jointcommission.org/assets/1/18/SEA_11.pdf.

48. Davis, N. M., *Medical Abbreviations: 24,000 Conveniences at the Expense of Communications and Safety.* Eleventh edition. Huntington Valley, Pennsylvania: Neil M. Davis Associates, 2003.

49. O'Donnell, J. T., "Adverse Effects of Diabetic Drugs," In *Drug Injury: Liability, Analysis, and Prevention, Second edition,* ed. J. T. O'Donnell. Tucson, Arizona: Lawyers & Judges Publishing Co., 2005.

50. "Metabolic and nutritional diseases of the nervous system," In *Harrison's Principles of Internal Medicine,* Seventh edition, eds. Wintrobe, M. M., et al. New York: McGraw-Hill, 1974.

51. Laska, L. (ed.), "Diabetic overdosed with insulin soon after hospitalization," *Medical Malpractice Verdicts, Settlements, and Experts* (April 2005): 18.

52. O'Donnell, J. T., "Pain Medications and OxyContin," In *Drug Injury: Liability, Analysis, and Prevention.* Second edition, ed. J. T. O'Donnell, Chapter 30. Tucson, Arizona: Lawyers & Judges Publishing Co., 2005.

53. Laska, L. (ed.), "Overdose of Fentanyl following surgery for sigmoid diverticulitis," *Medical Malpractice Verdicts, Settlements, and Experts* (May 2005).

54. www.ismp.org.

55. *Marie Lenoure, Special Administrator for the Estate of Victor LePore v. Oak Pak Hospital,* Cook County (IL) _ Circuit Court, Case No. 98 L 7257.

56. Laska, L. (ed.), "Failure to perform preoperative cardiac work up and administration of excessive Heparin blamed for man's death following femoral bypass surgery," *Medical Malpractice Verdicts, Settlements, and Experts* (July 2002): 19.

57. Laska, L. (ed.), "Doctors fail to order proper tests and nurses fail to inform doctor of change in status in woman following fall while on Coumadin," *Medical Malpractice Verdicts, Settlements, and Experts* (April 2005): 21.

58. Laska, L. (ed.), "Failure to administer proper dose of 5-Fluoroouracil to tongue cancer patient," *Medical Malpractice Verdicts, Settlements, and Experts* (September 2005): 38.

59. Engleman, S., "Pediatric Records," In *Medical Legal Aspects of Medical Records,* eds. P. Iyer, B. Levin, and M. A. Shea. Tucson, Arizona: Lawyers & Judges Publishing Co., 2006.

60. Levine, S., et al., "Guidelines for preventing medication errors in pediatrics," *The Journal of Pediatric Pharmacology and Therapeutics* 6 (2001): 426–442.

61. Iyer, P., "Nursing home liability and its consequences," In *Nursing Home Litigation: Investigation and Case Preparation,* Second edition, ed. P. Iyer. Tucson, Arizona: Lawyers & Judges Publishing Co., 2006.

62. Clark, T., "Medications and the Nursing Home Survey: Introduction," In *Medication Guide for the long-term care nurse,* ed. T. Clark. American Society of Consultant Pharmacists, 2003.

63. Vance, J., "Reducing medication errors in nursing homes," www.amda.com/publications/caring/april2003/mederrors.cfm.

64. Atlanta Legal Aid Society, Inc., "The silenced voice speaks out," www.atlantalegalaid.org/abuse.htm.

65. Gurwitz, et al., "Incidence and preventability of adverse drug events in nursing homes," *American Journal of Medicine* 109 (2000): 87.

66. Cohen, I., "Pain and Suffering in the Intensive Care Unit," In *Medical Legal Aspects of Pain and Suffering,* ed. P. Iyer. Tucson, Arizona: Lawyers & Judges Publishing Co., 2003.

Chapter 18

Physician and Hospital Liability in Drug and Medical-Device Litigation

Ramune E. Barkus, Esq. and Armand Derian, Esq.

18.1 Introduction

Physician and hospital liability for drug-related injuries is usually based upon medical negligence, which may include lack of informed consent, negligent treatment, and/or failure to treat. Lack of informed consent is a failure to advise a patient of the risks and potential hazards of the proposed treatment, including all material information that would enable the patient to make an informed decision regarding treatment. Affirmative defenses available to a physician might include liability of a manufacturer because of a defectively manufactured product; concealment or failure to warn of known risks by the manufacturer; direct-to-consumer advertising by the manufacturer; and, possibly, direct-to-consumer advertising and negligent prescription by a web doctor/pharmacy ("cyber treatment"). In many jurisdictions, a physician cannot be sued for drug injuries based upon product liability, breach of warranty, or strict liability. These bases for liability are restricted to the manufacturer, distributor, wholesaler, or other person or entity in the chain of distribution. Defenses available to the manufacturer who is sued for negligence and product liability might include the learned-intermediary defense or the negligence of the treating physicians. Other theories of liability—such as elder abuse—are statutory. This might involve withholding medications or prescribing the wrong medication, for example.

This chapter will address situations where physicians and hospitals may be insulated or avoid liability in claims arising out of the use of prescription drugs or medical devices. It provides an overview of the law as it relates to issues in medical-malpractice litigation, centered on drug injury.

18.2 Informed Consent

The act of sufficiently warning a patient of the risks and side effects associated with certain prescription drugs and medical therapies is not only a solid defense for a physician in a medical-malpractice action, it is often the predominant issue in the litigation. The patient's claim is often that had he known of the risks, he never would have consented to take the drug. Once the manufacturer of a drug properly informs the physician of the risk associated with its use, the company—to a great extent—has discharged its duty to warn the end user (the patient). The duty to warn a patient rests mostly upon the doctor. Although this aspect of informed consent has been affected by "direct-to-consumer" advertising[1] (discussed in detail later), the concept of the physician obtaining informed consent is still an important one in the field of prescription-drug use and medical malpractice. It can be the determinative factor in the finding of either a defense or patient's (plaintiff's) verdict.

The legal doctrine of informed consent in this setting has its roots in the intentional tort of battery. As Justice Benjamin Cardoza so aptly stated in 1914, "Every human being of adult years and sound mind has a right to determine what shall be done with his own body; and a surgeon who performs an operation without his patient's consent commits an assault, for which he is liable in damages."[2] A doctor avoids liability for such an assault by securing his patient's consent prior to performing any surgery or invasive procedure.[3]

Over time, this idea of obtaining informed consent has become an established doctrine in the field of medical-negligence law, and complying with it has become as important for doctors as properly diagnosing symptoms and treating illnesses. Although some jurisdictions have codified the requirements for disclosure and obtaining informed consent, some physicians still fail to properly and adequately warn a patient about the risks and side effects associated with the drugs they prescribe. Although some jurisdictions, through their codes, have specifically identified the extent of disclosure required in certain procedures and treatments, physicians have not and cannot be given any clear mandate as to exactly what they must disclose to their patients. The medical community sets the standards within the practice of medicine, and as a result, physicians are given some latitude in deciding what information to give a patient.

At the very least, a physician is required to disclose any significant or material risks associated with the treatment, as well as any available alternatives. The physician determines what is significant or material, depending upon the needs, capabilities, and wishes of the patient. It is impossible and impractical for a doctor to disclose every single risk and benefit associated with a drug she prescribes to her patient. This is due to the sheer amount of information available and the limited amount of time a doctor has with her patient during a typical visit. It could arguably take hours to explain and have a patient comprehend every risk and every benefit associated with the drug. Furthermore, "overly" warning patients could frighten patients away from obtaining therapy with drugs they truly need.

As discussed later in this chapter, under the "Learned Intermediary Doctrine," an individual who suffers a drug injury due to lack of informed consent has a cause of action against the prescribing physician, and probably not against the drug manufacturer. These actions are usually based on the premise that the patient was not sufficiently warned about the risks, contraindications, and side effects associated with the drug and was, thereby, harmed by its use.

So who knows best—the doctor or the patient? The answer depends on whom you ask. Two schools of thought have developed as it relates to the standards for disclosure and obtaining informed consent: Some jurisdictions follow a "professional-opinion standard" and look to the medical community to establish the applicable standards for disclosure. In these jurisdictions, what is material will depend upon what a reasonable physician—under similar circumstances—would disclose.[4] Based on this view, a physician is only required to reveal the dangers and side effects that a reasonable practitioner—under the same circumstances—would have revealed. Such a view shows great deference to the medical community and provides a nearly impregnable defense. Typically, the states with codified disclosure requirements follow this "professional-opinion standard" view.

Other jurisdictions take a more patient-centered approach and operate under the premise that a patient has the ultimate right to determine what is to be done to his own body. In these jurisdictions, what is material is what a reasonable person or patient—under similar circumstances—would regard as important. Or, "the scope of the physician's communication to the patient must be measured by [the] patient's need, and whatever is material to the decision. Thus, the test for determining whether a potential peril must be divulged is its materiality to the patient's decision."[5] This does not mean, however, that a physician must, in a sense, "provide a 'mini-course' in medicine. A polysyllabic discourse is not required."[5] Some jurisdictions also look to the prior knowledge and past preferences of the individual patient while assessing the importance of the information to that patient.[6]

Independent investigation by the patient and direct-to-consumer advertising can both be mitigating factors in a claim of alleged lack of informed consent. If a patient independently obtains information about a drug through the Internet (including the manufacturer's website), in medical journals, or via advertising prior to taking the drug, actual knowledge of known risks is a defense available to the physician.

To illustrate the effects of the different disclosure standards in lack of informed consent claims, we analyze the claims surrounding Gentamycin ototoxicity. In these cases, the patients alleged permanent hearing loss as a result of being given the drug. They claim they were never advised of the possible side effect and/or the probability of its occurrence under the circumstances. Had they known this information, they claim they would never have taken the drug, even though it was necessary to potentially save their lives. There are objective tests that can help prove true ototoxicity.

Under the "reasonable-patient standard," a jury would hear expert testimony about the risks versus the benefits of taking the drug for the plaintiff/patient. It would then decide whether a reasonable patient, under the same circumstances, would have consented if she had known of the risk of hearing loss. If the answer is affirmative, the patient has failed to prove lack of informed consent.

Under the "professional-opinion standard," expert opinion by a physician for each side would establish whether, given the circumstances, the standard of care would have required the physician to advise the patient of the risk of hearing loss.

Even under the broader, patient-centered scope of determining the materiality of certain risks, side effects and dangers, there are some exceptions to the disclosure requirement. In the case of drug therapy, a physician may withhold material information regarding risks and side effects from a patient if the doctor thinks such disclosure would have a negative impact on the patient's care. This exception derives from the deference shown to the medical community in those jurisdictions that follow the professional standard of determining materiality. Other exceptions to informed consent—such as exigent/emergency circumstances, patient incompetence, and waiver—also apply in drug-related claims.

Physician ignorance is not an exception to the requirement of obtaining informed consent. For example, a physician who undertakes to prescribe an anti-malarial medication should know where the patient is traveling and the specific malaria prophylaxis known to be effective in the travel destination. If the wrong medication is prescribed and the patient contracts malaria, the physician may correctly argue that the patient was warned that no anti-malarial medications are 100 percent effective in the prevention of malaria. However, this informed consent will not relieve the physician from liability for failing to comply with the standard of care by prescribing the wrong malaria prophylaxis.

Both the professional standard and the reasonable-patient standard require expert opinion to establish what a physician should have known regarding the risks, side effects, and contraindications associated with the medication he prescribes. Expert testimony is also necessary to determine whether a patient is a proper candidate for the proposed drug therapy.

Regardless of the standard employed in judging materiality, plaintiffs must still demonstrate a causal link between the injury they suffered and the non-disclosure. In cases centered on the question of informed consent, courts will undoubtedly look to ascertain whether a reasonable patient would have refused the prescribed treatment had the information in question been given to him. Thus, a failure of a physician to adequately obtain informed consent may still yield a defense verdict if it can be found that despite the failure, the patient would not have reasonably refused treatment if he had known all the risks. Furthermore, a medical practitioner has a formidable defense to a lack-of-informed-consent-based claim if the plaintiff would have consented to treatment, even if another fully informed, reasonable person would not.[7]

18.3 Off-Label Use

"Off-label use" refers to the practice of prescribing a manufactured drug for purposes other than those indicated on the product's federally mandated labeling. Off-label use of pharmaceuticals and devices by physicians raises additional issues in the area of informed consent. In 1998, prescriptions for off-label use of drug products accounted for somewhere between 25 and 60 percent of the 1.6 billion prescriptions written each year.

The whistleblower lawsuits concerning the drugs Seroquel and Lexapro shed an enormous amount of light on the practice of prescribing off-label pharmaceuticals. The issues of unauthorized promotion and misbranding vis-a-vis the Food and Drug Administration (FDA) guidelines and disclosure requirements for off-label drugs were important issues in those cases. For example, in the case of the Seroquel actions, the FDA approved use of this drug for treatment of schizophrenia and bipolar disorder, while the off-label uses that were allegedly promoted included Alzheimer's disease, anger management, anxiety, and dementia. The Lexapro litigation involved allegations that the drug was used to treat depression in children and adolescents, whereas the FDA originally approved the drug as an antidepressant for adults. In 2010, the manufacturers for these medications reached multi-million dollar settlements amidst allegations that the manufacturers illegally promoted off-label uses for the drugs.[8]

Is a physician's prescription of a drug for a use other than those indicated on the product's labeling below the standard of care? If not, does off-label use, in and of itself, require anything more than the standard warnings?

The first question is easily answered. Off-label use can be, and often is, within the standard of care. "It is well-accepted that once the FDA determines that a drug or device can be marketed, a physician's discretionary use of that product is not restricted to the uses indicated on the FDA-regulated labels. Off-label use is widespread in the medical community and is often essential in giving patients optimal medical care."[9] For example, the use of orthopedic bone screws into the pedicles of the spine is not considered a deviation from the standard of care.[10]

Although common in its practice, some schools of thought believe that off-label use is inherently "experimental" and that patients should be informed of this fact. Under this rationale, physicians would have to follow a higher burden of disclosure to patients when prescribing drugs for uses beyond their stated purpose. Others believe that off-label use is not inherently experimental, but merely part of the overall practice of medicine. Thus, prescribing a drug for off-label use would carry with it the same standards for disclosure and informed consent as the product's indicated use.

This latter philosophy is more in line with the FDA's stance on off-label use by physicians. The FDA is not involved in, and has never sought to regulate the practice of, medicine. Once approved for market distribution by the FDA, the use of a drug is not restricted to those indicated on the

FDA-regulated labeling. It is well established that once a drug is FDA approved, physicians may use legally marketed drugs in any way that they believe will best serve their patients.[10] Prescriptions of drugs, as well as the sufficiency of the informed consent, are judged by expert opinion regarding the standard of care. In most cases, a plaintiff would have to submit expert testimony for a jury to determine whether the off-label use by the physician and the warnings given conformed to the applicable standard of care in the medical community. In many such cases, courts have held that the uses described by the product's labeling only provided some evidence as to the physician's compliance with the applicable standard of care.[11] In others, it was found that the labeling provided no legal significance and that a physician who did not follow the use prescribed by the label was not necessarily liable for a breach of professional standards.[12] Also, the *Physicians Desk Reference* (PDR), which recites a product's labeling, cannot be referred to or relied upon as "the last word" when it comes to the product's use or indications.

Medical journal articles regarding off-label use in controlled studies or anecdotal individual case studies regarding successful off-label use can be strong grounds for justifying a specific drug therapy.

In jurisdictions that face a high burden of disclosure for off-label use, a physician would be required to disclose to the patient that the off-label use was "experimental" in nature prior to obtaining informed consent. The courts are consistent with this philosophy when it comes to clinical trials for "experimental" non-FDA-approved drugs and/or devices. There are federal and state regulations that specify the extent and type of disclosure necessary in the use of non-FDA-approved, experimental drugs. Compliance with these regulations is mandatory, and failure to follow them can result in monetary or criminal penalties.[13] It remains questionable whether this heightened disclosure is required in off-label use of pharmaceuticals by physicians in the ordinary course of practice.

18.4 Product Liability

It is well-established that manufacturers of defective products who know their wares will be used without inspection will be held strictly liable in tort for placing those products in the marketplace.[14] Furthermore, Section 6 of the Restatement (Third) of Torts provides that a manufacturer of a prescription drug or medical device who sells or otherwise distributes a defective drug or medical device is subject to liability for harm to persons caused by the defect. A prescription drug or medical device is one that may be legally sold or otherwise distributed only pursuant to a health-care provider's signature.[15]

Relying on these classic theories of strict products liability, plaintiffs often attempt to assert strict liability claims against physicians and hospitals that perform and facilitate medical procedures utilizing a defective medical device or product. However, many jurisdictions are unwilling to impose strict liability on these healthcare providers—especially where medical services could not have been rendered without the use of the product or device, or where the predominant purpose of the transaction involving the product or device was to provide medical services.[16]

Exceptions to the application of strict liability have long existed in cases dealing with hospitals and blood transfusions. The supplying of blood by a hospital is entirely subordinate to its paramount function of furnishing trained personnel and specialized facilities in an endeavor to restore a patient's health.[17] Providing medicine or supplying blood is simply a chemical aid or instrument utilized to accomplish the objective of cure or treatment. The patient who enters a hospital goes there not to buy medicine, pills or blood, but to obtain a course of treatment.[17]

This same thinking is now applied to cases involving defective medical devices and drugs. In California, courts have repeatedly held that strict liability may not be imposed against healthcare providers for injuries suffered by their patients.[18] In *Carmichael v. Reitz*, the court concluded that a physician prescribing drugs could not be held strictly liable for a patient's injuries.[19] The court distinguished between those who are "mere conduits" for distributing a product to a consumer and the physician who furnishes her services as a healer of illnesses.[19] Essentially, the healthcare provider—whether a hospital or a physician—is not in the business of supplying medical devices or drugs, and is, therefore, not strictly liable for defects that cause injury to their patients.

Although attempts have been made to argue that hospitals and physicians are within the stream of commerce, it is commonly held that they are providing a service, not a product, and so cannot be held strictly liable for alleged product defects utilized in treatment. Even in instances where a hospital adds an additional surcharge for a device used in an operation, courts have been reluctant to classify the hospital as a seller of the device, rather than as a provider of services.[20] A hospital, by completing a purchase requisition and charge ticket, and by forwarding the charge ticket to the patient billing office, is not acting as a conduit, in the stream of commerce, to the distribution of the product to the consumer, but is actually furnishing medical services.[20]

If a hospital is engaged in activities not integrally related to its primary function of providing medical services, like selling items in a hospital gift shop, it is not immune from strict liability with regard to those items.[21] However, while a hospital, as an entity, does not use its own medical skills or knowledge in providing services in connection with the provision of certain medical devices, the hospital is still engaged in the process of providing everything necessary to furnish a patient with a course of treatment.[22]

California is not the only jurisdiction to follow this rationale. Courts in New York,[23] Pennsylvania,[24] New Hampshire,[25] Missouri,[26] Florida,[27] Washington,[28] New Jersey,[29] as well as others, have also been reluctant to hold hospitals and physicians strictly liable for defective drugs and medical devices.

18.5 "Direct-to-Consumer" (DTC) Advertising and its Effect on Physician Liability in Drug Product Claims

"Our medical-legal jurisprudence is based on images of health care that no longer exist."

These were the New Jersey State Supreme Court's opening remarks in a landmark opinion that has since changed the focus in pharmaceutical products liability litigation—*Perez v. Wyeth Laboratories, Inc.*, (1999) 734 A.2d 1245. In its decision, the court in *Perez* held that the "learned intermediary doctrine" does not apply to circumstances involving the direct marketing of prescription drugs to consumers. The result of that decision is a likely shift in litigation targets for lack of informed consent claims arising from adverse results in the use of prescription drugs. A manufacturer who engages in direct-to-consumer advertising will have a hard time claiming it was only the doctor who was negligent.

The "learned intermediary doctrine" (LID) has long stood for the premise that a manufacturer's duty to warn the ultimate user of the prescription drug is satisfied if the manufacturer adequately warns physicians by supplying them with information and warnings about the drug's risks, benefits, and side effects. By warning the physician, the manufacturer has constructively warned the patient, thereby meeting its duty. A manufacturer who provides adequate warnings to the prescribing physician could claim a physician's lack of communication with the patient as an affirmative defense to claims arising out of the patient's use of its drugs. The duty to warn the user, in many circumstances, would be the ultimate responsibility of the prescribing physician.

A number of rationales have supported the LID, including the traditional doctor-patient relationship. Doctors are in the best position to warn patients and to provide information to them. They have close—often personal—relationships with their patients and can communicate warnings more effectively than manufacturers who have little or no

contact with the general public. The physicians are, thus, the "learned intermediaries" who stand between the manufacturer and the consumer. Since 1966, manufacturers of pharmaceuticals have been able to limit or decrease product-liability claims based on the LID. Instead of seeking to hold the manufacturer solely responsible for unwanted side effects, plaintiffs would direct some allegations against the prescribing physician for medical malpractice.

Situations where the LID defense has not been applicable have been cases involving mass immunization, the use of certain contraceptives, and cases where the drug has a risk or side effect that was not disclosed by the manufacturer to the physicians. A fourth exception is related to compliance with Food and Drug Administration mandates. If the FDA mandates that a manufacturer warn a consumer directly, it may not avail itself of the LID defense.

The practices of medicine and pharmaceutical marketing have changed significantly over the last decade. With the advent of managed care, physicians now have very little time to get to know their patients during the course of a visit. Manufacturers, who once had little contact with the buying public, now bombard them with slick ads, designed to implant the minds of consumers with powerful images extolling the benefits of their products. An individual cannot open a magazine, turn on the television, or surf the Internet without being exposed to any one of the hundreds of prescription drugs now being marketed directly to consumers.

In a review of DTCA spending between 1997 and 2005, the U.S. Government Accountability Office noted that "drug companies concentrate their spending on DTC advertising in specific forms of media and on relatively few drugs. Television and magazine advertising represented about 94 percent of all spending on DTC advertising in 2005. DTC advertising also tends to be concentrated on relatively few brand name prescription drugs—in 2005, the top 20 DTC advertised drugs accounted for more than 50 percent of all spending on DTC advertising....Many of the drugs most heavily advertised to consumers in 2005 were for the treatment of chronic conditions, such as high cholesterol, asthma, and allergies."[30] The result of all this advertising is that 30 percent of all patients now know exactly what drug they want before they go to the doctor's office, and 40 percent of those patients actually end up receiving the drug they went to the physician to obtain.[31] Where once pharmaceutical manufacturers spent their resources on marketing primarily to physicians, they are now focused on the consumer.

The onslaught of marketing and advertising aimed directly at consumers by the pharmaceutical companies is what prompted the New Jersey Supreme Court to carve out the DTC exception to the LID. This new exception will likely expose pharmaceutical companies to an area of liability for informed consent they once could shift to the doctor.

According to the *Perez* court, the direct marketing of drugs to consumers generates a corresponding duty requiring manufacturers to warn of defects in the products. Given the amount of money spent on DTC advertising and marketing, it can no longer be said that pharmaceutical companies lack the means to effectively communicate with patients.[32] As a result, manufacturers who market directly to consumers may be subject to a user's claims if the advertising fails to provide adequate warnings of the drug's dangerous propensities.[33] Although the *Perez* court focused on an elective "life style" drug,[34] it is not unreasonable to carry this concept to other drugs likewise directly marketed to consumers.

It remains to be seen what effect *Perez* will have on medical-malpractice litigation. However, the implications of this ruling are quite significant in the field of healthcare litigation, and, more specifically, with regard to the liability of doctors who ultimately write prescriptions for these drugs. Arguably, a plaintiff who has suffered an unwanted, adverse reaction from a prescribed drug is no longer limited in his choice of defendants on the issue of informed consent. He can target the drug's manufacturer as well as the physician.

Prescription pharmaceuticals purchased over the Internet directly from a web pharmacy/doctor, or the patient obtaining certain medications without seeing any physician would be another form of direct-to-consumer advertising, and would likely shield a physician from liability. The action by a plaintiff would provide the physician with a complete defense against liability, since she was not involved in the patient obtaining the medication via the Internet. When consumers learn of a drug through direct-to-consumer advertising and then order the drug through an Internet doctor/pharmacy, the consumer fills out a questionnaire regarding medical history, drug history and complaints. This is reviewed by a physician and, if approved, prescribed directly to the patient without a physical exam or any personal physician/patient interaction. Arguably, the patient could sue the cyber physician, although this would be complex and difficult. The cyber physician could claim assumption of the risk by the patient.

In the end, it may be more advantageous for a plaintiff to seek indemnification from a huge corporate entity, rather than a lone physician. These companies have seemingly limitless financial resources, and carry the social stigma of being large, profit-driven corporations. In jurisdictions that have placed limitations on recovery of non-economic losses against healthcare providers,[35] the statutory limitations enacted to protect healthcare providers would not apply to drug manufacturers, since they are not considered healthcare providers. Where a plaintiff might be limited to $250,000 in non-economic damages[35] against a physician, he may be awarded significantly more against a pharmaceutical company.

18.6 Mass Tort Litigation

Over the past ten years, mass tort litigation involving drugs and devices has dramatically increased. Thousands of individual plaintiffs have sued for alleged injuries caused by a particular drug or device. Both the manufacturer and distributor have been the target defendants. In response to the thousands of claims nationwide, the federal district courts now consolidate all claims involving a specific drug or device to one federal court in one state. This is known as "multi-district litigation," or MDL.

In lawsuits against the manufacturers of silicone implants, Phen-Fen, Redux, Ephedra, and Rezulin, all of the cases have been consolidated and transferred to one federal district court. Unlike class-action lawsuits, each case remains separate for purposes of litigation and/or settlement. However, discovery (the fact finding and investigation phase of litigation) as to the manufacturer(s) is consolidated. A disadvantage of MDL for plaintiffs and defendant healthcare providers is that the litigation is long distance and the process can be prolonged because of the number of cases. In response to the long-distance problem associated with the MDL and statewide-coordinated cases, private companies regularly give seminars where claimants and individual defendants are updated on the recent developments in the litigation. Additionally, "liaison counsel" are appointed/elected for each class of defendants and the plaintiffs for travel and court appearances. Eventually, the manufacturer may negotiate a settlement with all parties, based upon a pre-determined formula for payment and upon the severity of the plaintiffs' injuries, age, prognoses, and other injury-specific criteria.

In order to avoid MDL litigation or to include another theory of liability, some plaintiffs name the physicians or other healthcare providers as defendants. Most of these cases are filed in state court and stay there because the physician/healthcare provider—a resident of the state—is a defendant. Some states consolidate all cases involving a specific drug or device and assign them to one court within the state. These cases are coordinated for discovery as to the manufacturer defendants. Discovery from defendants to plaintiffs is standardized for general background information and drug or device usage. Some cases are individually set for trials where the depositions of plaintiffs and physicians are allowed. Many of the state cases settle before anything is resolved in the MDL litigation. Therefore, keeping a mass tort drug or device case within the state court can be advantageous for the plaintiff.

A physician or healthcare provider named as a co-defendant with a manufacturer in mass tort litigation has several defenses, such as direct-to-consumer advertising, failure of the manufacturer to provide all information regarding risks and side effects of the drug or device, and fraud or concealment by the manufacturer. Affirmative defenses against the claim would include assumption of the risks because of direct-to-consumer advertising and independent research on the Internet. A physician/defendant would have the same defenses as if the coordinated case were an independent lawsuit.

A physician may consider tendering the defense and/or indemnity of her case to the manufacturer. This could be advantageous to the manufacturer. By accepting the tender of defense, the manufacturer may have an overview of specific instances of treatment, avoid finger pointing when not necessary, and, when possible, control mediation/settlement negotiations without the involvement of the physician. This situation is also advantageous to the physician, who would be provided a defense and indemnity via the manufacturer. Physicians who have been sued many times can especially benefit from this added protection. A settlement and/or verdict for the individual physician would be satisfied by the manufacturer, despite professional liability policy limits.

Tendering the defense and indemnity to the manufacturer is also considered when a physician is the only named defendant and the case involves a drug injury. However, the facts stated in the tender letter should be limited to facts alleged in the complaint, or to facts that are public record. The recent privacy requirements of the Health Insurance Portability and Accountability Act of 1996[36] (HIPAA) may preclude giving any other information to the manufacturer without the written consent of the plaintiff. Before tendering the defense, it may be advisable to get the written consent of the plaintiff, including the patient's records. This may be risky, in that it may prompt the plaintiff's attorney to sue the manufacturer, thereby possibly eliminating the possibility of obtaining defense and indemnity from the manufacturer.

18.7 Conclusion

In creating these various limits and shields to liability, the courts support public policy that seeks to limit the possible adverse effects that unchecked and massive amounts of medical-malpractice litigation inevitably produces. As state legislative bodies—and even the federal government—debate issues and seek to create boundaries in the field of medical-malpractice litigation, the courts have also had a hand in

shaping this area of the law. The limits and shields to liability discussed in this chapter will only expand and increase, as both the courts and the legislature attempt to control the current medical-malpractice crisis.

Endnotes

1. *Perez v. Wyeth Labs*, 734 A.2d 1245 (1999).

2. *Schloendorff v. The Society of New York Hospital*, 105 N.E 92 (1914).

3. *Pratt v. Davis*, 79 N.E. 562 (1905).

4. *Aikeb v. Clary*, 396 SW.2d 668 (1965).

5. *Cobbs v. Grant*, 8 Cal.3d 229 (1972).

6. *Hart v. McKelway*, 707 F.2d 1544 (1983); *Korman v. Mallin*, 858 P.2d 1145 (1993); *Macy v. Blatchford*, 8 P.3d 204 (2000).

7. *Warren v. Schecter*, 57 Cal.App.4th 1189, 67 Cal. Rptr.2d 573, 583 (2d Dist.1997), and *Truman v. Thomas*, 27 Cal.3d 285 (1980), 165 Cal.Rptr. 308, 611 P.2d 902.

8. Molly Cohen, Study: Whistleblower Cases Involving Off-Label Promotion Pervade Industry, DRUG INDUS. DAILY, Apr. 11, 2011.

9. Beck, J.M., and Azari, E.D. 1998. "FDA Off-Label Use and Informed Consent: Debunking the Myths and Misconceptions." Food & Drug L.J. (53)71.

10. *Buckman Company v. Plaintiffs Legal Committee*, 531 U.S. 341 (2001).

11. *Ellington v. Bilsel* 626 NE.2d 386 (1993).

12. *Grassis v. Retik* 521 N.E.2d 411 (1988).

13. Protection of Human Subjects in Medical Experimentation Act, CA HLTH & S Sections 24170–24179.5

14. *Greenman v. Yuba Power Products*, (1963) 59 Cal.2d 57.

15. Restatement (Third) of Torts, Section 6: Liability of Commercial Seller or Distributor for Harm Caused by Prescription Drugs and Medical Devices.

16. *Porter v. Rosenberg*, (1995) 650 So.2d 79.

17. *Perlmutter v. Beth David Hospital*, (1954) 308 N.Y. 100.

18. *San Diego Hospital Association v. Superior Court of San Diego County*, (1994) 30 Cal.App.4th 8.

19. *Carmichael v. Reitz*, (1971) 17 Cal.App.3d 958.

20. *Hector v. Cedars-Sinai Medical Center*, (1986) 180 Cal.App.3d 493.

21. *Siverhart v. Mount Zion Hospital*, (1971) 20 Cal.App.3d 1022.

22. *Hector v. Cedars-Sinai Medical Center*, (1986) 180 Cal. App. 3d 493, 506

23. *Perlmutter v. Beth David Hospital*, (1954) 308 N.Y. 100.

24. *Cafazzo v. Central Medical Health Servs., Inc.*, (1995) 668 A.2d 521.

25. *Royer v. Catholic Medical Center*, (1999) 741 A.2d 74.

26. *Budding v. SSM Healthcare System*, (2000) 19 S.W.3d 678.

27. *Russell v. Community Blood Bank*, (1966) 185 So.2d 749.

28. *McKenna v. Harrison Memorial Hospital*, (1998) 960 P.2d 486.

29. *Perez v. Wyeth Labs*, 734 A.2d 1245, 1251, 52.

30. United States Government Accountability Office. Prescription Drugs: Improvements Needed in FDA's Oversight of Direct-to-Consumer Advertising. November 2006. Available at www.gao.gov/htext/d0754.html. Accessed May 10, 2012.

31. *Perez*, note 29 at 1255.

32. *Perez*, note 29 at 1257.

33. Norplant Contraceptive System by Wyeth-Ayerst Laboratories, 1990.

34. California Civil Code Section 3333.2. Recovery of Noneconomic Losses.

35. PL 104-191, 1996 HR 3103.

36. United States. Cong. Promotional Spending for Prescription Drugs. By Sheila Campbell. Congressional Budget Office: Economic and Budget Issue Brief, December 2009.

Chapter 19

The Story of E-Ferol: Adding Insult to Injury

Kathleen M. Dahle, RN, B.S.N.

19.1 Introduction

The development of E-Ferol Aqueous Solution (E-Ferol), a high-potency vitamin E solution, was prompted by the need for an intravenous form of vitamin E to combat retrolental fibroplasia (RLF), a disease that causes impaired vision or permanent blindness in premature infants. During this time, clinical research had many neonatologists supporting the hypothesis that vitamin E was useful in reducing the incidence and severity of RLF in ventilated neonates. Before intravenous E-Ferol was placed on the market, the two principal forms of vitamin E available to neonatologists were an oral preparation and an intramuscular injection, both sold as nutritional supplements and not represented as safe and effective for use in premature infants. One exception to this was an intravenous multivitamin preparation containing a much smaller amount of vitamin E, and also marketed as a nutritional supplement.

Carter-Glogau Laboratories, Inc. (Carter-Glogau), the manufacturer of E-Ferol, was then located in Glendale, Arizona. Its president was Ronald M. Carter, Sr. (Carter). O'Neal, Jones & Feldman, Inc. (OJF), now known as O'Neal, Inc., the distributor of E-Ferol, was located in Maryland Heights,

Missouri. OJF's president was Larry K. Hiland (Hiland); under Hiland was James B. Madison (Madison), the Executive Vice-President of Operations for OJF. Madison was the purveyor of E-Ferol, who baited Carter into developing and manufacturing the drug for OJF's marketing, sale and distribution.

Carter and Madison had a long history together. Up until 1981, the two companies had been owned by the same parent, Chromalloy American Corporation (Chromalloy), at which time they were sold to their respective parent companies: Carter Glogau to Revco, D.S., and OJF to Northwestern Management Corporation of Delaware, a holding company for DKM Industries, Inc. (a company protected within the liabilities of the Dyson-Kissner-Moran Corporation).

OJF, within the pharmaceutical business, was a small-scaled manufacturer and distributor of pharmaceuticals. Carter-Glogau, had grown to be one of the country's largest manufacturer of me-too, copycat or generic-based injectables. Carter-Glogau was the principal manufacturer of OJF's injectable products, a complementary business relationship that remained steadfast subsequent to the split sale by Chromalloy in 1981.

For a number of years prior to the development of the intravenous product, OJF was distributing an intramuscular vitamin E solution, also called E-Ferol, and manufactured for OJF by Carter-Glogau. This product, as well as an oral vitamin E solution, was being used throughout the country by neonatologists for the unlabeled use to prevent RLF, though both routes of administration presented various drawbacks for the neonate patient. Nationwide, many neonatologists were concurrently aware that an intravenous vitamin E solution was under investigation and seeking approved new drug status from the FDA, and were therefore anxiously awaiting its approval to use in the treatment of their patients. Because of this foreseen approval, the salesmen for OJF, in conversing with physicians on marketing calls, were enlightened of this anticipated product and subsequently advised Madison in 1982.

19.2 E-Ferol Beginnings

On August 25, 1982, after being detailed by the OJF's sales force, Madison wrote to his colleague, Ronald Carter, Sr., and apprised him that the pharmaceutical lord, Hoffman-La-Roche, was currently investigating under an IND, a vitamin E injection for retrolental fibroplasia in premature infants and that this vitamin E injection was for intravenous use, "solubilized in some way."

Madison went on in his letter recapping the fact that "…Practically all the Vitamin E injection you sell to us is for the same use. It can only be used intramuscularly, and in infants this is not as easy to administer as the IV Roche product….My question, of course, is can you make the 50 mg. soluble in water…we could always label it for Vitamin E supplementation." And then, the motivation for the cheat: "*I'm afraid that when Roche gets their Vitamin E approved, we will lose the business, unless you can come up with something.*" (Emphasis added.)

Approximately four months earlier, Carter had received a similar letter from another regular customer, Malcolm H. Baker (Baker) of Hyrex Pharmaceuticals (Hyrex), channeling questions he receives "4 or 5 times a month." The questions: "Can Vitamin E be put up aqueous? Can Vitamin E be in a water miscible base? Can Vitamin E be put up for I.V. use? Please advise. There must be a Hell of a market out there."

Immediately Carter forwarded Baker's questions to two of his consultants and advised Baker of the same—he concluded with his "off-the-cuff" comments "…that you can make an aqueous solution of Vitamin E but it has to be solubilized." "…Small dosages of Vitamin E are used for IV use in the neighborhood of 5 or 10 units per ml. I am not aware of higher dosages. *The problem of solubilization of higher dosages is that the amount of polysorbates needed which may be detrimental.*" (Emphasis added.)

The consultants confirmed Carter's off-the-cuff comments, advising that vitamin E could not be put in an aqueous solution at such extreme concentrations, specifically warning that the levels of polysorbate 80 would be too high. In turn, Carter passed on this information to Baker, adding "Frankly, I don't recommend it in the injectable form."

Regardless of the system check that one delineates from the above, it failed to generate a categorical denial from Carter to Madison. Instead, Carter responded to Madison's letter on August 30, 1982, advising him that it was possible to manufacture a solubilized vitamin E, though he wasn't certain that a 50 mg/ml concentration could be administered. According to Carter, "The best way to approach this is to try to find out the formulation which Roche was using," enabling them to "exactly duplicate the 'benchmark' product." Carter added a direct, and unfortunately self-fulfilling prophesy: "*If we make some attempt to solubilize the Vitamin E and use the wrong proportions and kill a few infants, we'd have some serious problems.*" (Emphasis added.)

Madison's response to Carter's final comment: "You bet!" Nonetheless, he challenged Carter to "use your ingenuity" and question Hoffman-LaRoche about their product.

Following this exchange, Carter replied to Madison with a September 15, 1982 memorandum, indicating a willingness to move forward. He advised Madison that an inquiry to Hoffman-LaRoche would follow, seeking information on their IND vitamin E formula. Despite Carter's show of support, he again prudently outlined for Madison a precautionary foresight: "Solubilization of Vitamin E in a water-miscible base requires extraordinary amount of surfactants and other carriers."

Intravenous administration of such a product in neonates "without appropriate clinical work concerning toxicity will undoubtedly lead to an exposure in terms of product liability" which neither company would wish to assume. "After all, one neonatal death is one too many."

He recognized, as a pharmaceutical manufacturer, that an IND application involves intensive and systematic clinical research and testing. Therefore, once Hoffman-LaRoche marketed their vitamin E intravenous product, "they will undoubtedly have done major work including toxicity studies."

His final question to Madison was, "Is it not much better to wait and see what they come up with or, conversely, try to find out their formulation?"

Without heeding Carter's warnings, Madison was (concurrently) researching the medical literature, seeking information on the intended use of supplemental vitamin E in premature infants, its recommended dosage strengths, concentration and duration of use. It became apparent, that Madison selectively extracted the information that supported his intent and consciously ignored the explicit dangers that would eventually manifest at the cessation of his parsimonious crusade.

According to testimony in the criminal trial, discussions regarding the development of this intravenous vitamin E product ceased until the summer of 1983, when the topic resurfaced in a telephone conversation between Carter and Madison. In late June 1983, Madison packaged his plan in a memorandum to Hiland for approval. As president of OJF, only Hiland had the authority to add to the product line. Madison strategically advised Hiland of the anticipated fate of the current E-Ferol Injection (intramuscular), citing that it:

goes to hospitals for the treatment of Retrolental Fibroplasia in newborn infants....At the present time this injection is given intramuscularly because Vitamin E is in an oil solution. We have had numerous telephone calls from hospitals asking if we had a Vitamin E in water solution for IV infusion. I have suggested to Carter that he make up for us a Vitamin E Injection in water solution suitable to IV solution....Carter thinks he can do this....Of course, the labeling for such a product would be as the present labeling of our E-Ferol Injection, that is, a Vitamin E supplement. However the hospitals and other physicians can use it any way they please.

Madison wrapped up his presentation with numbers: "...With the new product we could conceivable sell 24,000 vials or $100,000.00....When our salesmen visit hospitals... they could drop off a single page brochure on this Vitamin E...."

After reading Madison's proposal, Hiland granted his request and the intravenous E-Ferol Aqueous Solution would be added to OJF's product line. Hiland's affirmative triggered manufacturing of their new product even though no testing, by OJF or by Carter, was ever done to determine whether E-Ferol would be a safe and effective drug for use in premature infants.

19.3 The Fruition of E-Ferol

By July 1983, Carter requested his product development officer formulate a water-soluble vitamin E product based on the dosage amount requested by Madison and the solubilizers of polysorbate 80 and polysorbate 20. As testified, the basis of the finalized formula was solely dependent on its ultimate esthetic appearance: dl-alpha tocopheryl acetate 25 USP units, 9 percent polysorbate 80 and 1 percent polysorbate 20 per ml in water for injection—the new E-Ferol aqueous injection for intravenous infusion. In criminal testimony, Carter admitted that he personally made the final decision as to the type of vitamin E and the proportions of polysorbates. Further, admission was made that at no time did he have any idea as to what level of polysorbate was safe for injection into premature infants.

In September 1983, Hiland approved Madison's marketing campaign for E-Ferol. OJF's initial marketing consisted of a mass mailing of "Dear Doctor" letters, accompanied by a brochure and a copy of the package insert. Promotional materials were mailed twice, in late October 1983 and in January 1984. Approximately 1,000 directors of neonatal intensive care units received the brochure that read: "New-Vi-

tamin E E-FEROL INJECTION—For Neonatal Care When Hyperalimentation is Ordered." The attached package insert read: "...Reports in literature indicate that substantial doses of Vitamin E will reduce the severity of retrolental fibroplasia in neonatals, which are administered oxygen because of their low weight, under 1500 grams." This was decreed even though no indications were asserted that E-Ferol had been tested or had been proven to be safe and effective for the treatment of RLF in premature infants.

Simultaneously, the FDA had yet to approve the IND Hoffman-LaRoche was intensively researching, a plight which ultimately added to Madison's urgency. This unspoken urgency was evident by the intensive and collaborative efforts of Carter and Madison, thus, by November 8, 1983, E-Ferol Aqueous Solution for intravenous infusion was in the channels of intrastate commerce.

Carter and Madison's haste to manufacture and distribute E-Ferol overruled all notices and warnings concerning the issues associated with the intravenous product. These critical issues were silently ignored until ultimately exposed by the subsequent federal investigation. The entire preparatory process of E-Ferol was the collaborative efforts of Carter and Madison. Carter himself testified that he relied on Madison for guidance and considered him the "expert" on E-Ferol. One must question Carter's definition of *expert*; later testimony would reveal that Madison had no formal pharmaceutical or chemistry education or training.

Salesmen were given the *E-Ferol Aqueous Injection Fact Sheet* to detail them on the new OJF product. They were instructed to recite specific information to hospital pharmacists and physicians. This fact sheet included a rhetorical question and answer monograph that gravely impacted their fraudulent deceit:

The question has been asked..."Is E-Ferol Aqueous approved by the FDA for I.V. infusion?" The answer is "yes." The M.V.I. solutions mentioned above have been approved; E-Ferol Aqueous is made exactly the same way except it has higher potency than M.V.I.

Throughout its brief product life, Madison continued to spend considerable time researching the literature on vitamin E; his intent was not for the acquisition of knowledge regarding its safety and effectiveness, but for issues of profit. He explored premature births and their frequency, as well as the average length of time premature babies required intravenous vitamin E, as a supplement, due to intervening mechanical ventilation. Madison shared his accumulated knowledge in his third edition of *Sales Potential of E-Ferol*

Aqueous: "...we could conservatively estimate 3 boxes or 18 vials per baby....Each year, there are 27,000 babies, who weigh 1500 grams or less. These require oxygen and Vitamin E nutrition....Thus we can see a potential market of: 27,000 × 3 boxes × $20.00 = $1,620,000." This self-memorandum to Madison's vitamin E file was written following the initial two months of sales. In his manifesto, Madison quotes the cliché: "We have just scratched the surface."

19.4 Final Exposure

During the five months that E-Ferol was on the market, OJF (specifically Madison), received numerous inquiries about the product—including three reports of severe adverse reactions associated with its use. The first one occurred within the first 40 days of distribution. The subsequent two reports, in January and March, reported infant deaths to Madison, and questioned their association to the E-Ferol product. The third inquiry received by Madison was from a pharmacist at the University of Tennessee Hospital. Concurrently (and unknown to OJF), this hospital also reported its cluster of illness and death to the Federal Centers for Disease Control (CDC) in Atlanta, Georgia. The CDC, already acting on an inquiry received on March 9, 1984, from Good Samaritan Hospital in Cincinnati, immediately acted on their call and began an on-site investigation. The CDC's investigation exposed a correlating link with E-Ferol as the suspected cause of the cluster of a specific complexity of symptoms, illnesses and deaths, subsequently known as the E-Ferol syndrome, that concurrently plagued the two hospitals. The CDC immediately notified the FDA.

19.5 FDA Alert

The CDC contacted the appropriate regulatory divisions of the FDA on April 2, 1984 and inquired about E-Ferol's approval status, complaints and reports of adverse events. FDA investigators convened immediately, including an on-site visit to OJF on April 6, 1984. By April 9, 1984, the FDA had declared E-Ferol IV an unapproved product. The FDA representatives, including the Director from the Office of Compliance, the Chief of the Prescription Drug Compliance Branch, a member of the Litigation and Recall Staff from the Office of Compliance, the Deputy Director from the Office of Biologics Research and Review and a medical officer from the Division of Metabolism and Endocrine Drug Products made an immediate regulatory conference call to Madison at OJF. Madison was informed that OJF's intravenous E-Ferol product was regarded to be an "unapproved new drug...in violation of Section 505 of the Federal Food, Drug and Cosmetic Act." The product was considered illegal, with the likelihood that the product was associated with a number of reported adverse reactions, including deaths, in premature infants. The medical officer in attendance outlined for Madison the adverse effects suspected to be related the E-Ferol, which included ascites, hepatomegaly, splenomegaly, cholestatic jaundice, thrombocytopenia and azotemia. Madison had heard the same, previously, in phone calls from users of his E-Ferol product.

This conference call was made in lieu of a regulatory letter to OJF, and the FDA requested that OJF respond to the FDA by April 10, 1984, with its intentions with regard to outstanding stocks of the drug. During this phone conference, Madison advised the FDA that distribution of E-Ferol stopped immediately on April 6, 1984, following the FDA's initial visit to OJF. On April 10, OJF agreed to recall all stocks of E-Ferol. The FDA declared this recall to be a Class I, that was to be completed on the user level.

19.6 The Recall of E-Ferol

On April 11, 1984, OJF's initial action was by phone, contacting all their direct hospital and wholesale accounts. OJF did not agree with the proposal made by the FDA to issue recall notices to all hospitals in the United States, limiting their notices of recall to all their direct hospital and wholesale accounts and their indirect hospital accounts made known through the drug wholesalers. Because of OJF's position, the FDA advised them on April 12, 1984 that, due to the seriousness of the situation, which included the potential toxicity of E-Ferol and possible need for follow-up patient care, the FDA would assume immediate responsibility for notification. Over the next several days, the FDA sent Class I recall notices to 6,600 hospitals (administrators and directors of pharmacy) and to 25,000 pediatricians—advising each professional entity of the problems reportedly associated with E-Ferol and the discerning indication for close monitoring of infants who had received the drug. Specifically, the FDA advised physicians, hospital administrators and directors of hospital pharmacies "...that physicians closely monitor infants who have received E-Ferol Aqueous Solution because of the possibility of delayed onset of symptoms." Doctors were notified that this advice went to all hospital administrators and pharmacy directors by letter. Further, those letters advised that "hospital staff be informed of the possible association of the drug product with the above described syndrome."

By April 23, 1984, the FDA had completed recall audits of all the wholesale distributors and the 159 hospitals that had received E-Ferol. All of the product was out of user channels, and all manufactured product was accounted for.

19.7 Congressional Hearing

On May 4, 1984, a Congressional hearing was held before the House Subcommittee on Intergovernmental Relations and Human Resources, chaired by Representative Ted Weiss. In his opening statement, Chairman Weiss communicated clearly the purpose of the noticed hearing: "We are here today to find out what bureaucratic blundering has enabled this tragedy to occur and to search to find ways to assure that this situation is never allowed to happen again."

Testifying at this hearing was Mark Novitch, M.D., acting Commissioner of the FDA, and various health professionals who had encountered or heard about E-Ferol. Several issues surfaced during the hearing. First, the FDA's policies and procedures were criticized for failing to detect the E-Ferol problem in advance and for having a compliance policy that did not require government clearance for newly marketed drug products that were similar to products that had been on the market since prior to 1962. Second, following the testimony of a neonatologist from Spokane, that he had reported adverse effects and death to Madison in January 1984, the FDA was criticized that neither the physician nor OJF submitted this inimical report (to the FDA)—asserting that such actions exposed incomprehensible communication defects in the regulated system. The FDA was publicly reprimanded and given a detail of system changes that demanded immediate intervention.

In closing comments, Dr. Novitch stated

…we will do what is needed to provide better scrutiny over the system for governing drugs that are on the market without benefit of a new drug application and do everything in our power to see that that kind of incident can never happen again. It is tragic and I think that we just do everything we can to prevent it again….I think that the system failed badly in this instance….But with all respect, I must reject the idea that the agency is a failing agency, it does not work well, it does not have conscientious people, and is not working in the best interest of the public health and American people.

Chairman Weiss responded, "If this is the example of a successful agency, I'd hate to see the others."

Representative Weiss concluded, warning OJF, Carter-Glogau, Carter, Madison and Hiland that their future would be left up to the criminal justice system.

19.8 Criminal Ramifications

Ultimately, the fraudulent practices of OJF, Carter-Glogau, Carter, Madison and Hiland resulted in a 25-count criminal indictment in 1987. By the time trial commenced on August 8, 1988 (Case No. 87-172CR(4) *United States of America v. Carter-Glogau Laboratories, Inc., now known as Retrac, Inc., Ronald M. Carter, Sr., Larry K. Hiland and James B. Madison*), the companies OJF and Carter-Glogau no longer existed and all three executives were no longer employed in their esteemed capacity. A two-month jury trial ensued, which led to guilty verdicts and the criminal convictions of Carter-Glogau, Carter and Hiland.

Notably, the other two defendants, OJF and Madison, entered guilty pleas pursuant to plea agreements. On the first day of trial, OJF plead guilty to one count of conspiracy, four counts of mail fraud, and 12 Federal Food, Drug, and Cosmetic Act (FDCA) felony counts. Approximately two weeks into trial, Madison entered a plea agreement, with admissions of guilt to two counts of wire fraud and one FDCA felony count. In his plea agreement, Madison testified for the government.

At the conclusion of the criminal trial, Carter-Glogau, Carter and Hiland were convicted on one count of conspiracy to commit mail and wire fraud, and to violate the FDCA, in violation of 18 U.S.C. § 371; six counts of introducing a new drug not approved by the FDA into interstate commerce with the intent to defraud or mislead, in violation of 21 U.S.C. §§ 331(d), 333(a)(2); and six counts of introducing a misbranded drug into interstate commerce with the intent to defraud or mislead, in violation of 21 U.S.C. §§ 331(a), 333(a)(2). Hiland was also convicted on five counts of committing mail fraud, in violation of 18 U.S.C. § 1341. Carter-Glogau and Carter were both acquitted on the counts of mail fraud. Carter-Glogau, Carter and Hiland were all acquitted on seven counts of committing wire fraud, in violation of 18 U.S.C. § 1343.

The ramifications of the guilty verdicts resulted with Carter and Hiland each sentenced to nine years imprisonment, of which all but six months was suspended, and fined $130,000. In lieu of the fine, each could pay $65,000 within one year of judgment to the neonatal intensive care units of certain hospitals victimized by the sale of E-Ferol—both opted for this choice. Carter-Glogau was required to pay $100,000 toward the government's cost of litigation, in addition to a $130,000 fine.

OJF, whose plea was placed under seal until the trial was concluded, was ultimately fined $115,000 and ordered to pay $100,000 toward the cost of prosecution. James Madison was sentenced to eight years in prison (all but six months was suspended) and fined $12,000. Like Carter and Hiland, in lieu of the fine, Madison could pay $10,000 to the neonatal intensive care units of court-specified hospitals who were victimized (to various degrees) by the sale of E-Ferol.

Carter-Glogau, Carter and Hiland appealed their convictions. United States Court of Appeals for the Eighth Circuit: No. 89-1222EM *United States of America, Appellee, v. Larry K. Hiland, Appellant*; No. 89-1223EM *United States of America, Appellee, v. Carter-Glogau Laboratories, Inc., now known as RETRAC, Inc., Appellant*; and No. 89-1224EM *United States of America, Appellee, v. Ronald M. Carter, Sr., Appellant*. Awaiting appeal, Carter and Hiland were denied deferment of their sentences and due process was served.

Following petition by briefs and oral argument, on July 19, 1990 the U.S. Court of Appeals, Eighth Circuit, affirmed the judgment of the district court.

One of the issues appealed by Carter, Carter-Glogau and Hiland was that the court erred in admitting prejudicial medical testimony specific to the effects E-Ferol had on premature infants. Both Carter and Hiland contended that the district court abused its discretion in admitting the testimony of physicians and pharmacists referencing the effects of E-Ferol on their premature infant patients. Carter and Hiland referenced specific testimony that cited the manifold of symptoms, including such descriptives as "oozing," "bleeding," and abdominal "bloating." Review of the trial transcripts revealed that such adjectives were used in limited context. For the most part, the witnesses limited themselves to strictly clinical terms when describing the symptoms observed. Further, testimony did not unduly emphasize E-Ferol's association with certain infant deaths. In fact, the very fact that E-Ferol was associated with infant deaths was disclosed to the jury by other channels of properly admitted evidence. The counsel for the defendants had pled to the district court that the testimony was prejudicial—firmly asserting that such testimony would only be proper if their clients (Carter and Hiland) were being tried for manslaughter, which they were not.

In the opinion of the appellate court, commendation was extended to the district court for their diligent efforts to limit the potential for unfair prejudice. The appellate court cited that the court had twice cautioned the jury that the defendants were not being tried for the causing of harm or death to infants. This was explicitly reiterated by the court in its final instructions to the jury. It was the opinion of the appellate court that, after careful review of the challenged medical testimony, the testimony presented did not substantially outweigh its probative value.

19.9 Hospital Policy and Procedure

Many hospitals nationwide bypassed this monumental tragedy by strictly adhering to hospital-implemented policies, whereby the medications within and added to their hospital

drug formulary were controlled by a Pharmaceutical and Therapeutics Committee. The procedures implemented by such a committee assured that all new drugs requested by physicians were evaluated and investigated before their administration to patients. Despite this safety net, many hospitals throughout the nation ignored this prudent practice and began to stock and dispense E-Ferol immediately.

Many of the neonatologists who had ordered E-Ferol had been previously apprised that an intravenous vitamin E solution (for premature infants) was being clinically investigated for FDA approval. Therefore, when E-Ferol became available, it seemed obvious to them that this had been the clinically investigated product now approved for use.

At the criminal trial, pharmacists and physicians testified that, based on E-Ferol's labeling, they believed the product was being promoted for the treatment of RLF in premature infants. In addition, they believed it to be tested and approved and proved to be safe for use in premature infants, especially because of the lack of warnings or suggestions to the contrary. Physicians and pharmacists further testified that they had assumed E-Ferol had been approved by the FDA because of its specified indications and targeted recipients: the treatment of RLF in premature infants.

19.10 Morbidity and Mortality Untold

The district judge in the criminal case of the Carter, Hiland and Madison and their respective pharmaceutical companies, instructed the jury: "I don't want the jury to make a decision based on the babies....I don't want the defendants to be blamed for something they are not charged with."

Who is accountable for this blame? What about the babies? A toxic drug was administered to helpless infants and children, with known cause of injury, disease and death. Families have been dismantled and betrayed. Two decades have passed since the E-Ferol tragedy. The survivors have reached majority age. Those, whose parents pursued legal action against the drug companies, are far too few compared with those whose death and injuries are silently unaccounted for.

In the criminal trial, the FDCA counts charged that E-Ferol was an unapproved "new drug" and "misbranded" under the FDCA, and that the defendants introduced it into interstate commerce with the intent to defraud and mislead—including recommending and suggesting conditions which ultimately caused danger to the health and well-being of premature infants. The government contended that the essence of the fraud against the neonatologists and other medical professionals was that the defendants intentionally represented E-Ferol as safe and effective for intravenous use in premature infants, despite knowing that no testing had been done to establish their very contentions. Further, the defendants continued to do so after receiving reports associated with severe adverse reactions and death.

In turn, the very core of these criminal violations have been perpetuated to this day. The ultimate victims of this tragedy are the babies, children and parents. Injury, illness and death permanently marked the lives of the over 1,000 patients who received this toxic drug from November 1983 to April 1984. Unfortunately, for the majority of these victims, due process has not been theirs. The very tactics manipulated by Madison, Hiland and Carter in the manufacturing, distributing and marketing of E-Ferol, were ultimately manifested by those caring for the infants and children themselves. Approximately 144 claims for injuries have been tolled, at least 866 have not. The same fears that hindered Madison when he was told of injuries and death, *silenced* physicians, pharmacists and hospital administrators throughout the nation. The 144 claims represents a selected cluster from eight states, representing fewer than 18 hospitals. (Re: CA 7-03-CV-102-R, *Klein and Swadley v. O'Neal, Inc. et al.*)

According to the intervening investigation by the FDA, over 25,800 vials of E-Ferol were distributed to 159 hospitals nationwide. Over 67 hospitals administered it. (Sixty-seven hospitals used two or more boxes, or 12 vials, of E-Ferol. Of the remaining 92 hospitals, those that used it, divided up the remaining 37 boxes that were distributed and accounted for as used.) A total of 12,036 vials were administered to over 1,008 premature infants, two children and three adults. Of the 67 hospitals, 1,008 infants (including two children) received it. The FDA, based on its limited review and qualified investigators, distinguished that 642 infants at 34 hospitals were cases of E-Ferol syndrome; the remaining 366 infants were reported from 33 hospitals as non-affected recipients of the drug (FOI Document, Faich, June 11, 1984).

The FDA is in no way criticized for its efforts. Investigators varied in education and experience, and, like the parents of the infants, relied on the physicians' honest evaluation of the vulnerable neonates. In addition, the cooperation of hospital administrators was crucial. Despite a distinct correlation of symptoms and illness directly associated with the administration of E-Ferol, more physicians than not dismissed E-Ferol as the cause of their patients' mysterious symptoms, deteriorating clinical conditions, prolonged hospitalizations and, all too often, death. After all, it was argued, premature infants are the most vulnerable patient group. It was an argument of fact that many neonatologists relied on.

The FDA was forthright in recognizing the limitations of its investigation. In a June 11, 1984, internal memorandum generated by Gerald A. Faich, M.D., MPH, Director of

Epidemiology and Biostatistics for the FDA, he summarized evaluation of the field investigation and recall of E-Ferol. Dr. Faich made notice to several factors that thwarted the field investigation:

(a) time pressure to ensure that the recall was complete and the drug was off all shelves; (b) lack of standard definitions and data collection instruments…; (c) varying methods used by field investigators to obtain information ranging from telephone contacts to medical record abstraction; (d) varying access to information, and (e) the inherent complexity of clinical information on severely ill neonates. (FOI document, Faich, June 11, 1984.)

Dr. Faich prudently warned (internally) that, because of these factors,

…all the data from the survey must be viewed cautiously. It is likely that data on boxes of E-Ferol used and perhaps number of infants exposed *are* fairly reliable. On the other hand the counts of cases of illness or death in exposed infants *may not be* accurate or complete. In some cases…when E-Ferol associated signs were present they may have not been appropriately attributed because they were incorrectly ascribed to the underlying conditions or were not recognized at all. (FOI document, Faich, June 11, 1984.)

Dr. Faich concluded his June 11, 1984 memo stating that several key questions remain:

1.   What is the full expression of the syndrome and its range of manifestations?
2.   How often were heavier babies affected?
3.   What was the precise dose-response relationship?
4.   Was the toxic agent vitamin E or polysorbate? Was the form of Vitamin E (acetate) a factor?
5.   Was there any residual damage in infants who apparently recovered?

Civil litigation alone *has* substantiated the doubts of Dr. Faich and proved the numbers to be invalid. Numerous claims of injury and death, medically conclusive to E-Ferol, have been litigated. In addition, medical professionals and researchers, primarily those closely related to the CDC investigation and those where a familiarity existed due to the administration of E-Ferol, made cause to answer the lingering questions above. E-Ferol and its components have been skillfully researched and meticulously investigated, with their conclusions and findings published in respectable peer-reviewed medical journals. The correlation to the injuries and death established the polysorbate as the primary toxin. The subsequent research which followed the E-Ferol incident continues to be referenced with credibility within the pharmaceutical and medical communities today.

19.11 Long-Term Aftermath

One of Dr. Faich's questions remains unanswered: "Was there any residual damage in infants who apparently recovered?" (As well as any in those who were ill but did not succumb to death from the toxic drug?) The medical literature alone affirms this question. The problem was that those affected were in all probability never made aware that they received this toxic drug.

The cause: failure to disclose to the patients, or their parents or guardians that the patient received this toxic drug. Carter-Glogau and OJF are considered shielded on this matter because of the "learned intermediary" doctrine. The learned intermediary doctrine allows the manufacturer of drugs to set up a defense that the physician was warned, thus the responsibility to warn the patient rests with the physician.

Is the E-Ferol situation exempt from the above? The perilous warnings were disclosed at the time of the recall, and the FDA clearly established by its actions that a *duty* existed, beyond the patient-physician relationship. The FDA took the authority to advise physicians, pharmacists and hospital administrators to closely monitor infants who have received E-Ferol Aqueous Solution because of the possibility of delayed onset of symptoms.

19.12 Implicit Duty

The concluding focus of this chapter is the issue of who had the duty to notify the parents of these infants and children.

The distributor, OJF, complied with the minimal requirements set forth by the FDA in the implementation and interventions covering the recall. Initial telephone contact was made with all hospital pharmacists and wholesalers, followed by a drug-recall letter to every account in their chain of distribution: direct and indirect hospital accounts and wholesalers. In conflict with the requests made by the FDA, OJF refused, due to cost, to put every pediatrician on notice with a recall letter.

The FDA thought differently. The fragility of the intended patient population and the potential virulent ramifications, beseeched an accountability for the Administration to make known the morbid and tenacious repercussions of this vitamin E compound. The impact and ramification of

the injuries speculated to be associated with this drug had the FDA on attentive alert in clearly every regulatory department thereof. E-Ferol was classified by the FDA as a Class I recall, with 100 percent product accountability to the user level.

On April 12, 1984, the FDA commenced a nationwide location site investigation at every hospital that had E-Ferol stocked on their shelves from early November 1983 through April 12, 1984. Additional measures taken immediately on April 12 by the FDA was the distribution of letters to all directors of hospital pharmacies and hospital administrators, approximately 6,600 hospitals nationwide with the following header: "Important Drug Warning Information and Urgent Class I Drug."

The CDC reported the association of illness and E-Ferol in the April 13, 1984 issue of its *Morbidity and Mortality Weekly Report*.

And, responsibly, on April 16, 1984, the FDA furthered its duty and mailed a letter to approximately 25,000 pediatricians in the United States, headed "Important Drug Warning Information and Urgent Class I Drug," notifying them of the problems reportedly associated with E-Ferol and the importance of monitoring the infants for delayed onset of symptoms.

Hospital administrators, pharmacists, physicians: how many of those accommodated the circumspection of the government and heeded the equivalent to their patients and their parents victimized by the E-Ferol tragedy? The question of *duty* begins here.

Pharmacist: the first hand in the admixture of the product.

Doctor: by and through the manufacturer, as *learned intermediary*.

Hospital administrator: who accommodates the medical profession with the dependent resources to take care of their patients: beds, operating facilities and staff, nurses, a multiform of therapists and therapies, medications and the pharmacists to dispense and compound them, and all of the multitudinous technical resources and innovations required to prudently administer to *their* patients.

Twenty years later, the E-Ferol story continues and the *duty* still remains.

Twenty years later and the litigation continues.

The medical profession is quick to routinely insist that the trial court system is inundated with frivolous lawsuits. It contends that the ethics of medicine, alone, should govern patient care and need not converge with the captious circus of lawyers, jurors, and judges. Yet, following the recall of E-Ferol, there may be cause to pause. The crimes of Madison, Hiland, and Carter appear to be replicated on the paradoxical continuum of (patient) care. The issues here raise questions concerning a prevailing movement of silence in the cover-up of injuries and deaths caused by E-Ferol. Innocent babies were injured and died because of E-Ferol, far more than the numbers produced by the prudent investigations of the CDC and FDA. Moreover, the babies that lived are feared to be with injury today.

The issue of *duty* has been litigated over the past decade. Through countless years of litigation and thousands of documents produced, the answer continues to be perplexed.

The 236th Tarrant County District Court, Fort Worth, Texas has litigated E-Ferol cases for years. The exposure of victim after victim disclosed two elements of commonality: (1) the baby received E-Ferol, and (2) not one parent was told that their child received the noted toxin. The injuries litigated have been devastating, including cerebral palsy, blindness and death.

19.13 The Exposure of Duty (and Ethics) through Litigation

Excerpts from deposition testimony on October 11, 2000.
Re: Cause No. 236-181122-99; *Gary Mills et al. v. O'Neal, Inc. et al.*

Deponent: Ed Eason, R.Ph., Director of Pharmacy at Fort Worth Children's Hospital (in April of 1984 and currently), d/b/a Cook Children's Medical Center, Fort Worth Texas.

Attorney for plaintiffs: Dwain Dent, the Dent Law Firm, Fort Worth, TX.

Attorney Dent: …For instance, I'm quite certain that you would have had a conversation with other pharmacists alerting them to E-Ferol, and "here's what it is and here's the effects of it, and we need to look and see, you know, if A: E-Ferol has been removed, and B: do we have any children that are having any serious side effects from this drug." That would have been something that you would have gathered; is that correct?

Pharmacist Eason: No. It would not have been the pharmacy's responsibility to evaluate the clinical conditions of the patients to see if they were having any of the effects that were described or in the recall.

Attorney Dent: All right.

Pharmacist Eason: That would have been the medical staff call.

Attorney Dent: If the—if the FDA asked you to gather that information, would it have been your responsibility to respond to the FDA inquiry?

Eason: …The FDA would expect from the pharmacy department to identify for them the patients that received it.

Dent: All right.

Eason: Then they were directed to the medical staff for the gathering of other information.

Dent: Okay. Did you sit down at any time with either Russell Tollman (Hospital Administrator) or somebody else from administration and any of the doctors that were acting out of or in charge of the neonatal intensive care unit and discuss E-Ferol anytime after you received the first two phone calls and the visit from the FDA?

Eason: The—first step that was taken when we received the calls or the notification to recall was to remove the E-Ferol from all possible distribution, to stop….Second—the second step in that then was to—for us to identify active patients. The third step was to communicate with the ordering physicians that—of those patients that had received or were receiving E-Ferol….So, from that standpoint, yes, sir, we had communications…we did indeed communicate with the ordering physicians as soon as we were notified of the recall.

Dent: All right. And I assume that that was a fairly urgent and emergent situation then….

Eason: It was immediate…It was immediately pulled and immediately not available…for use, and…the reasoning behind that and the information that we received relevant to the recall was provided to the ordering physicians.

Dent: …when you received the phone call, you were aware that babies were receiving E-Ferol in the NICU as you received the phone call, correct?

Eason: Yes.

Dent: And it was an emergent situation. It was an emergency to get this drug out of the neonatal intensive care unit, correct?

Eason: An emergency situation. It definitely was important that we stop distributing E-Ferol to our—to our patients, yes.

Dent: All right. So the communication with the doctors and administration that you testified a few minutes ago, that would have been in conjunction with stopping the flow of E-Ferol into the veins of children, correct?

Eason: I don't believe I said I discussed it with administration...I discussed with the physicians.

Dent: All right. Great. That's all I'm trying to establish is that it was an emergency situation, and you made phone calls down to the NICU to stop the use of the drug, correct?

Eason: Yes.

Dent: And that was the correct thing to do, wasn't it?

Eason: Yes.

Dent: Because as a pharmacist you have an obligation to look out for the welfare of patients, children and families receiving the drugs, correct?

Eason: Yes.

Dent: You have an obligation if a patient or a child, a neonate, a baby, who—who depends on others to take care of it and for life, you have an obligation if a—an incorrect drug is given the baby, you have an obligation to go down there and correct the situation and advise the patient, the baby and its family, correct?

Eason: No sir. I disagree with that statement....As an in-patient pharmacy, if we were in that scenario, our starting point would be with the physician to take care of the patient to begin with...if an error is made, you start with the physician so that you do whatever needs to be done for the care of the patient.

The part of your question that I—that I'm hesitant...is do I have a responsibility to tell the parent or the—or the baby or the child at that point.

Dent: Do you have an independent professional obligation to advise a citizen or a child if a medication error has been made or a lethal drug has been given to a parent or a child? Do you have a professional obligation to make sure that the family is advised?

Eason: A professional obligation to see that the family is advised? Yes.

Dent: ...If [in] practicing pharmacy...give a...prescription by mistake and them the wrong drug or...a lethal drug, do [you] have an obligation to tell the patient, or the patient's family if they're a baby, would...you as a pharmacist have an obligation?

Eason: ...if you have made an error, you have dispensed a medication error, there is absolutely no question that that is your responsibility to communicate. If you—if you have—if circumstances is that you have identified now that this drug is not really safe, after the fact, that this drug is not safe for this patient—

Dent: It is a lethal drug, that was my phrase. Lethal drug.

Eason: Okay. If this is a lethal drug, that was identified after the fact and is not what I term a medication error, but was dispensed according to order, and after the fact is defined as potentially lethal for this child, the starting point with that is the ordering physician.

Dent: Let's assume there is no physician around...by the time you get the call that it was a lethal drug, she has been placed in the ground and buried, and there is no treating physician. Do you as a pharmacist have an obligation to make sure that the family knows that their baby was given a lethal drug?

Eason: Under the condition, the scenario that you described, no, sir...they still have an ordering physician, the physician that was in care of that child, and that is where that communication should start.

Dent: Who in the—the chain of possession of that drug has an obligation, other than the doctor, to tell the family that this baby or family member received a lethal drug?

Eason: I...believe sir, that that is a physician responsibility, that that was the starting—the physician that ordered the drug for that family is the one that has the obligation to—to—to inform that family.

Dent: ...What did the policy and procedures say that you were required to do about notifying a patient... or the mom and dad back in April 1984.

Eason: It would have been very similar to what the policy exists today sir...it would have been similar. A decision would have been made in discussions with the physician who was going to communicate with the *patients*.

Excerpts from Deposition Testimony on October 27, 1999.

Re: Cause No. 236-181122-99; *Gary Mills et al. v. O'Neal, Inc. et al.*

Deponent: Peggy Troy, RN, M.S.N, President of Fort Worth Children's Hospital, d/b/a Cook Children's Medical Center, Formerly (November 1983–April 1984) Director of NICUs, Fort Worth Children's Hospital, d/b/a Cook Children's Medical Center and Harris Methodist Fort Worth Hospital, Fort Worth, Texas.

Attorney for plaintiffs: Dwain Dent, the Dent Law Firm, Fort Worth, TX.

Dent: Your position in 1984 with Fort Worth Children's Hospital...?

Troy: Director of neonatal nursing.

Dent: So the very unit where the drug was being dispensed, you are the nurse in charge or the director of that entire unit?

Troy: Yes.

Dent: When did you first learn—learn that the drug E-Ferol had been used at Fort Worth Children's.

Troy: I became aware of that really when...there was a filing in 1995...that there was a problem with E-Ferol. So that's when I became aware that was being used in the nursery....

Dent: So your first information or knowledge about the drug E-Ferol was sometime in 1995?

Troy: At the time this became an issue...yes.

Dent: Has somebody told you not to give notice to these children and their parents?

Troy: No.

Dent: That they received this drug?

Troy: No.

Dent: No one has told you not to do it?

Troy: No one has told me not to give notice.

Dent: And does the decision—does the ability to make that decision to either tell these families or not tell them stop on your desk as president of the medical center?

Troy: That is a physician's decision.

Dent: All right. Is—would it be in your power as president of the hospital to notify these families that they had received E-Ferol through your hospital?

Troy: That would be a physician's decision.

Dent: Okay. I understand what you're saying, but are you telling me that—you do not have the authority under law to advise a patient that an illegal drug or recalled drug had been given to their children?

Troy: I don't feel I have the sole authority to do that.

Dent: Do you have the responsibility?

Troy: I don't feel I have the sole responsibility to do that.

Dent: Okay. You're one of several people in the medical chain that might have the responsibility to do that?

Troy: Our position is that it is the physician's responsibility to notify or discuss things with the parents.

Dent: And when you say "our position" who do you mean, because I'm just asking you—right now. What do you mean by "our"?

Troy: It is—it is my position that the doctors are responsible to notify the parents...and discuss the children.

Dent: ...So are they the only ones that are obligated to tell a patient that they have been injured or harmed?

Troy: I feel it is the doctor's responsibility.

Dent: I understand. So you're saying that it's only the doctor that has the obligation to tell a patient if he's been injured or harmed?

Troy: Yes.

Dent: Or given an illegal drug like E-Ferol?

Troy: Yes.

Dent: Okay. What does the Nurse Practice Act say about advising a patient if they've been injured or harmed, or there is some dangerous condition that they're suffering from. What is the nurse's obligation to the patient?

Troy: I don't recall that.

Dent: You came to Fort Worth Children's in 1981... what was your entry level position with Fort Worth Children's?

Troy: Director of Nursing for the neonatal intensive care nursing.

Dent: So, did you start as director of nursing for Harris and Fort Worth Children's or just Fort Worth Children's?

Troy: For both.

Dent: For both. Okay. And as I understand, as director of nursing, that you were overseeing the day-to-day operations for the neonatology units for Fort Worth Children's and Harris.

Troy: Yes sir.

Dent: ...Has your job changed—

Troy: Yes, sir.

Dent: —since 1984? What's your position now?

Troy: President of Cook Children's Medical Center.

Dent: And—that means you're in charge of the whole organization?

Troy: Yes.

Dent: And when—when did you get that promotion?

Troy: February 1999.

Dent: And before February of 1999, what was your position?

Troy: Chief operating officer of Cook Children's Medical Center.

Dent: And how long had you held that position?

Troy: 1989.

Dent: And before 1989, what was your position with the hospital?

Troy: I was the vice president of patient services.

Dent: What is your job?

Troy: ...I was in charge of the clinical areas in the hospital for patient care.

Dent: ...How long were you vice president of patient services?

Troy: 1985 to 1989.

Dent: ...When is it that you told me earlier that you first heard of the drug E-Ferol.

Troy: I became aware of that drug as it relates to the neonatal nursery when we receive our notice in 1995.

Dent: In 1995. All right. And when is the first time you heard that there was a Class I FDA drug recall of E-Ferol?

Troy: ...subsequent to that time, after 1995.

Dent: After. So all your information—totally comes after you received a letter from my law firm saying we were pursuing an action on behalf of several families whose children has been at Fort Worth Children's during 1984; is that correct?

Troy: Yes.

Dent: And you have no knowledge of E-Ferol or any of its fatal consequences or serious side effects or—or anything about the drug until after 1995?

Troy: Yes.

Dent: ...I'm asking if you, as the executive officer of the hospital, have (you) visited with any committees about notifying the parents of these children that they received this Class I Recall Drug during 1984 in your hospital?

Troy: No.

Dent: And is it on any agenda for the future?

Troy: No.

Dent: And do you intend to ever give them notice?

Troy: No.

Excerpts from deposition testimony on July 10, 2002
Re: Cause No. 236-181122-99; *Gary Mills et al. v. O'Neal, Inc. et al.*

Deponent: Richard Sidebottom, M.D., neonatologist at Fort Worth Children's Hospital, d/b/a Cook Children's Medical Center and Harris Methodist Fort Worth Hospital, Fort Worth, Texas.

Attorney for plaintiffs: Fred L. Streck, III, the Dent Law Firm, Fort Worth, TX.

Fred Streck, III: Is it correct that if you believe that there wasn't any adverse effect at that time from E-Ferol, you didn't tell the parents?

Richard Sidebottom, M.D.: That's true.

Streck: Do you recall advising any of the pediatricians of any of these babies that this baby received E-

Ferol, here's the syndrome, you need to keep an eye on these babies for that particular reason?

Sidebottom: ...to specifically tell them about some—I mean, the kids that went home that got...I don't typically do that. I mean, this is—no.

Streck: Well, I guess back at that time you did—there was a syndrome, correct?

Sidebottom: There was an alleged syndrome.

Streck: Okay.

Sidebottom: It still has yet to be proven as far as I can tell.

Streck: And at that time there are no particular studies on long-term effects of this particular drug, correct?

Sidebottom: That's correct.

Streck: All right. So at that—at that time you don't have any basis to assume that there's not going to be any problems in the future associated with the drug E-Ferol, did you back then?

Sidebottom: I think we did. I think that polysorbate—I mean, Vitamin E had been given for a long period of time so—I mean, at least the current medical feeling amongst physicians and all was that the vitamin E wasn't causing the problem. So then you have to say it's probably the polysorbate in there because there was—we have known about other carriers or other things that drugs are mixed in that can cause toxicity if it's given in too big a doses or—and so you have to assume that probably it's the polysorbate that was—that was being given if it's causing a problem....And I think there was a little bit of history with the polysorbate and also the fact that once you metabolize polysorbate, it should be gone and the toxicity should be gone.

Streck: Okay. Have you conducted any kind of research on the long-term effects of polysorbate?

Sidebottom: No.

Streck: Doctor, if the hospital or the hospital pharmacist back at that time were to disclose or would have disclosed to the patients' parents that their babies received E-Ferol, do you believe in any way that would violate your doctor-patient privilege?

Sidebottom: No, I don't think so.

Streck: Okay. If the hospital pharmacist chose to tell the parents back at that time, you wouldn't have a problem with it?

Sidebottom: No.

Streck: And you never had any discussions with them regarding not telling the parents, correct?

Sidebottom: That's correct.

19.14 The Revelations from Litigation

The issue of *duty* came to fruition in the 236th District Court in Fort Worth, Tarrant County, Texas and relative conclusion in the Court of Appeals, Second District of Texas, Fort Worth. The underlying case of the original proceeding is a healthcare liability suit arising out of the care and treatment of four premature infants who were patients at Fort Worth Children's Hospital, d/b/a Cook Children's Medical Center, between January and April 1984 (Cause No. 236-181122-99, *Gary Mills et al. v. O'Neal, Inc. et al.*). These infants were recipients of the drug E-Ferol. Cook Children's was included in this liability claim because its pharmacy dispensed the E-Ferol to the infants based on physician written orders. The pharmacy, along with the hospital and its administration, participated in the recall of this product in 1984. None of the infants or their parents were told that they had received this drug.

Throughout the litigation, the plaintiffs in this case had made several discovery requests to Cook Children's to reveal the names and addresses of all patients who were administered E-Ferol while at Cook Children's. Cook objected to these requests on the basis that the information requested was protected by physician-patient privilege. A motion to compel was filed by the plaintiffs, followed by numerous hearings on the issue. In the end, the trial court had concern, based upon the evidence, that non-party patients and their parents had not been informed that the children had received E-Ferol while a patient at Cook Children's.

On October 18, 2002, the trial court signed an order requiring Cook Children's to produce the names and "face sheets" of all patients who received E-Ferol from January to April 1984. (The face sheet of the medical record contains information regarding admission and discharge date, patient's date of birth, parents' names and addresses, social security numbers and employment information.) The court did not order the information to be produced directly to the plaintiffs, but to a court appointed *guardian ad litem*. (An emergency motion was filed following this original preceding to appoint the *guardian ad litem*, who had been acting in this capacity for several years. The court stated in its order that the non-party patients were of minor age when the case commenced and may currently be incompetent. The district court appointed the *guardian ad litem* in a December 10, 2002 order.)

In its order, the court authorized the *guardian ad litem* to contact non-party patients and their parents, informing them that as infants they had received the drug E-Ferol while at Cook Children's. The order specifically stated that the *guardian ad litem* was not to reveal any information about non-party patients to any persons other than the pa-

tients, their parents, and any other court-appointed guardian without a further court order. The trial court's order states that it is "[o]f concern to this Court that some child may be suffering consequences of E-Ferol toxicity and may not know of it" and that the court "believes the patients and their parents have a right to be informed of the administration of this drug."

In response to this discovery ruling, defendant Fort Worth Children's Hospital, d/b/a Cook Children's Medical Center, filed a petition for writ of mandamus in the Second Court of Appeals, Fort Worth, Texas, Cause No. 02-02-00373-CV, *In Re: Fort Worth Children's Hospital d/b/a Cook Children's Medical Center, Relator,* from Cause No. 236-181122-99, 236th Judicial District Court of Tarrant County, Texas, Honorable Tom Lowe, presiding.

The summation of Cooks' plea was to impede the District Court's ruling requiring the hospital to release the "face sheet" with identifying information, to the *guardian ad litem*. In Cook's reply to response to petition for writ of mandamus, Cook declares it has "no duty to inform the patients whose records are the subject of this proceeding that they were administered E-Ferol." Further cited:

> First, such a duty would infringe on the relationship between those patients and their physicians who ordered the administration of the drug. If a duty to inform exists, it rests upon the patient's treating physician. Second, if Cook, through non-physician employees, informed former patients that they had been exposed to a particular recalled drug and attempted to explain the possible consequences of that exposure, such conversation would constitute the practice of medicine without a license....Even if this Court were to find that Texas law (of which none is cited) creates a duty for Cook to disclose E-Ferol treatment, which Cook denies, the Plaintiffs do not have standing to enforce that duty because it is irrelevant to any claim in the underlying lawsuit, and the trial court's order does not require Cook to disclose anything to anyone but a guardian ad litem who was improperly appointed.

On February 28, 2003, the Court of Appeals of Texas, Fort Worth, set forth their decision and opinion in Cause No. 2-02-373-CV *In re Fort Worth Children's Hospital d/b/a Cook Children's Medical Center, Relator*. For brevity, the court's analysis and conclusion is summarized.

Cook Children's contended that the trial court abused its discretion in ordering Cook Children's to produce the names and face sheets of the non-party patients, citing that the face sheets were subject to the patient-physician privilege and, for that reason, were protected from disclosure. Cook Children's also contested the trial court's appointment of a *guardian ad litem* for the non-party patients, that for the purpose contemplated within the order, no provision in Texas law existed for the appointment of a *guardian ad litem* in that situation. (The trial court appointed the *guardian ad litem* for the non-party patients on the basis that the non-party patients were, at the beginning of the discovery dispute, minors and that even though at the time of the order, the non-party patients would not be minors, they may be incompetent.) In addition, Cook Children's contended that the information in the face sheet of the medical record was not relevant to the underlying lawsuit, though, even if it were, the trial court failed to properly balance the need for the information against the patients' right to privacy.

The appellate court concluded, on analysis of Cook Children's brief and argument, that Cook had failed to provide evidence that the face sheet of the patient's record was completed and maintained by physicians rather than hospital employees and it failed to prove that such record was subject, by law, to the physician-patient privilege. Further, the court concluded that asserting the physician-patient privilege is a limited right of the patient, the patient's representative or the physician on behalf of the patient. Therefore, Cook Children's, as a hospital, cannot assert the privilege on behalf of non-party patients.

Using the above finding, the appellate court concluded that the information requested (face sheets) was discoverable by the plaintiffs if it proved to be relevant to any issue in the underlying lawsuit, not just a party's physical, mental or emotional condition. *In the underlying lawsuit, two of the claims of the real parties in interest are that Cook Children's fraudulently concealed the fact that its pharmacy administered E-Ferol to infants and that Cook, upon the recall of E-Ferol by the FDA, breached a duty to notify them. Therefore, according to the appellate court, it appeared to be a relevant issue to the underlying case—whether or not Cook Children's informed non-party patients about E-Ferol.*

Concerning the contention of the non-party patients' right to privacy, Cook asserted that a patient's medical records are within a constitutionally protected "zone of privacy," *without* contending that the court's order had restricted the discovery of the non-party patients' identities to third persons, that is, the trial court had ordered the release of the names and face sheets to the *guardian ad litem* and required the *guardian ad litem* to keep the information confidential. *Therefore, the appellate court ruled that Cook Children's did not show that the non-party patients' right to privacy would be violated under these conditions. The face sheets were ruled discoverable under these facts.*

Concerning the *guardian ad litem*, Cook contended that there was no provision in Texas law providing for such an appointment in this situation; therefore, the trial court had abused its discretion. On review of the argument and supporting law presented by Cook Children's, the appellate court held that the trial court had abused its discretion in appointing a *guardian ad litem* for non-party patients, for reasons including that the non-party patients were no longer minors, nor had evidence been presented that supported that any of them were incompetent.

In conclusion, the appellate court conditionally granted Cook Children's *writ of mandamus*, ordering the trial court to vacate its order of October 18, 2002 (ordering release of the names and face sheet to a court appointed guardian ad litem) and its order of December 10, 2002 (the appointment of the *guardian ad litem* for non-party patients whose names and face sheets were to be released).

On September 26, 2003, in a separate cause of action (Re: CA 7-03-CV-102-R, *Klein and Swadley v. O'Neal, Inc. et al.*), the plaintiffs filed a motion for class certification with the United States District Court for the Northern District of Texas. The plaintiffs defined the class as:

...all persons in the United States, including any estate representatives or heirs of deceased persons, who, during the period from November 1, 1983 until April 30, 1984, were administered E-Ferol. Included in the class are parents, spouses, children, guardians, and legal representatives of such persons with direct or derivative claims. (Re: CA 7-03-CV-102-R, *Klein and Swadley v. O'Neal, Inc. et al.*)

Administration of E-Ferol to premature infants caused death and serious immediate injuries in numbers of over 1000 infants that received this illegal substance. Even those infants whose conditions were worsened by E-Ferol, but without immediate and apparent serious consequences, are nevertheless subject to the long term risks and serious health consequences set out in the affidavit of Robert Brown, M.D., a board certified pathologist, now of Geisinger Medical Center, Dansville, Pennsylvania, and formerly of W.I. Cook Fort Worth Children's Medical Center, in Fort Worth, Texas, whose seminal article in *Pediatrics* and research attests to his status as the acknowledged expert on E-Ferol. Dr. Brown's affidavit is attached and sets out the criteria needed to medically monitor all recipients of E-Ferol, most of whom have never even been told they were administered this illegal substance. (Re: CA 7-03-CV-102-R, *Klein and Swadley v. O'Neal, Inc. et al.*).

The motion further addressed the rampant willful silence to the accountability of *duty* exacted by the FDA in April 1984 to hospital pharmacists, hospital administrators and physicians, staged in the scene of this historic tragedy. As pled:

...The fact that after so many years there have been so few individual actions brought by victims of E-Ferol attest to the defacto conspiracy of silence between the medical community and the Defendant manufacturers of this drug to lessen any potential liability that may come from informing the members of the class of what happened to them many years ago. (Re: CA 7-03-CV-102-R, *Klein and Swadley v. O'Neal, Inc. et al.*)

The plaintiffs' motion concluded with the issue of due notice from hospitals, exonerated by the appellate court in Cause No. 02-02-00373-CV, In Re: Fort Worth Children's Hospital d/b/a Cook Children's Medical Center, Relator. The motion for class certification cited:

The Plaintiffs propose that notice be made individually to each and every member of the class whose identity will be determined by a court order which orders each and every hospital to which E-Ferol was marketed to prepare and forward to the Plaintiffs the list of recipients of E-Ferol and their last known address, date of birth, Social Security number and any other information about the parents and guardians so as to facilitate location of these victim.... (Re: CA 7-03-CV-102-R, *Klein and Swadley v. O'Neal, Inc. et al.*)

On December 11, 2003, before the Honorable Jerry Buckmeyer, United States District Judge, a hearing was held in respect to the plaintiffs' motion for class certification. In 2010, a Texas judge issued a final settlement order, ending a long, sad saga.

References

FDA's Regulation of the Marketing of Unapproved New Drugs: The Case of E-Ferol Vitamin E Aqueous Solution; Hearing before a Subcommittee of the Committee On Government Operations, House of Representatives, Ninety-Eighth Congress, Second Session, May 4, 1984; United States Government Printing Office, Washington, 1984.

Trial transcript and exhibits from United States District Court for the Eastern District of Missouri: Cause No. 87-172CR(4) *United States of America v. Carter-Glogau Laboratories, Inc., now known as Retrac, Inc., Ronald M. Carter, Sr., Larry K. Hiland and James B. Madison.*

Judgment, opinion and exhibits from United States Court of Appeals for the Eighth Circuit: No. 89-1222EM *United States of America, Appellee, v. Larry K. Hiland, Appellant*; No. 89-1223EM *United States of America, Appellee, v. Carter-Glogau Laboratories, Inc., now known as RETRAC, Inc., Appellant*; and No. 89-1224EM *United States of America, Appellee, v. Ronald M. Carter, Sr., Appellant.* Appeals from the United States District Court for the Eastern District of Missouri.

Depositions and exhibits from Cause No. 236-181122-99, *Gary Mills et al. v. O'Neal, Inc. et al.*; 236th Judicial District Court of Tarrant County, Texas.

Cases

Cause No. 87-172CR(4) *United States of America v. Carter-Glogau Laboratories, Inc., now known as Retrac, Inc., Ronald M. Carter, Sr., Larry K. Hiland and James B. Madison*; United States District Court for the Eastern District of Missouri.

No. 89-1222EM *United States of America, Appellee, v. Larry K. Hiland, Appellant*; No. 89-1223EM *United States of America, Appellee, v. Carter-Glogau Laboratories, Inc., now known as RETRAC, Inc., Appellant*; and No. 89-1224EM *United States of America, Appellee, v. Ronald M. Carter, Sr., Appellant.* Appeals from the United States District Court for the Eastern District of Missouri; United States Court of Appeals for the Eighth Circuit.

Cause No. 236-157240-95, *Alice Hernandez et al. v. O'Neal, Jones & Feldman Pharmaceuticals, Inc. et al.*; 236th Judicial District Court of Tarrant County, Texas.

Cause No. 236-181122-99, *Gary Mills et al. v. O'Neal, Inc. et al.*; 236th Judicial District Court of Tarrant County, Texas.

Cause No. 2-02-00373-CV, *In Re: Fort Worth Children's Hospital d/b/a Cook Children's Medical Center, Relator;* Second Court of Appeals of Texas, Fort Worth.

CA 7-03-CV-102-R, *Klein and Swadley, Plaintiffs, v. O'Neal, Inc., d/b/a O'Neal, Jones & Feldman Pharmaceuticals, CVS Revco D.S., Inc. and Retrac, Inc., Defendants*; United States District Court for the Northern District of Texas, Wichita Falls Division.

Appendix 19.1
A Plaintiff's Expert Report on the *Duty* of the Pharmacist in the Recall of E-Ferol

July 8, 2003
RE: E-FEROL/Pharmacists' Duty
Baby B.B. a/k/a Baby Boy Doe

This report is prepared after reviewing the following materials:

1. Deposition testimony of David Turbeville, M.D., with exhibits, taken on July 8, 2002;
2. Deposition testimony of Richard Sidebottom M.D., with exhibits, taken on July 10, 2002;
3. Deposition testimony exhibits (no testimony reviewed), April 16, 1995;
4. Deposition testimony of Ed Eason, Pharmacist, Cook Children's Medical Center, taken on October 11, 2000;
5. Deposition testimony of Peggy Troy, RN, MSN, Nurse Manager for the NICUs of Harris Methodist Fort Worth and Cook Children's Medical Center, during the time of E-Ferol distribution and recall (subsequently became President of Cook Children's Medical Center);
6. Past discovery responses of Harris Methodist Forth Worth including—HMFW's Objections and Responses to Plaintiffs' First Request for Admissions, HMFW's Objections and Answers to Plaintiffs' First Set of Interrogatories, and HMFW's Objections and Responses to Plaintiff's' First Request for Production;
7. Harris Methodist Fort Worth medical records of Baby Boy Doe;
8. Expert report and attachments of Robert E. Brown M.D., dated April 7, 2003;
9. Plaintiffs' Seventh Amended Petition;
10. Standards of Pharmacists' Practice, FDA and Industry correspondence, FD&C laws and regulations regarding recalls of pharmaceuticals, literature, and consideration of the instant case issues in this matter, to wit, Pharmacists' responsibilities following a Class I Recall. (Referenced herein).

My declaration and summation of facts in this matter are as follows:

1. I based my opinions on my background, skill, education, training, and experience, as well as my specialized scientific and pharmaceutical knowledge in the field of pharmacy. Throughout my practice in the pharmaceutical field, I have consulted with physicians and nurses in the treatment of patients and advised hospital and pharmacy administrators as to the practice of pharmacy.

2. I am a pharmacist licensed to practice pharmacy since 1969. I have specialized in various fields throughout my career, including pharmacy administration, nutritional support, pediatric pharmacy, clinical pharmacology, research and education, and publishing. I currently hold the position of Assistant Professor of Pharmacology at the Rush Medical College and a Lecturer in Medicine at the University of Illinois College of Medicine. I am the Founding Editor of the *Journal of Pharmacy Practice*. I have edited two books which address issues relevant to this case: *Pharmacy Law: Litigating Pharmaceutical Cases*, and *Drug Injury: Liability Analysis and Prevention*.

3. I was employed as an Assistant Director of Pharmacy at the Cook County Hospital from 1971 to 1976 and at the Rush Presbyterian St. Luke's Hospital from 1976 to 1988. My responsibilities at both hospitals included management of pharmacies and consultation regarding patient care, including inventory control and recalls of pharmaceuticals, and the use of drugs for investigational purposes. In addition to my hospital employments, I have been employed by a number of outside organizations, including as a systems consultant for institutional pharmacy services. I consulted to the pharmaceutical industry in the areas of therapeutic nutrition and parenteral drugs. I have also served on the instructional faculty of the Colleges of Pharmacy at the University of Illinois and Purdue University.

4. My qualifications for offering those opinions are reflected in my curriculum vitae, a copy of which is attached to this report. Also included in my curriculum vitae is a list of 170+ publications authored or co-authored by me during the course of my professional career as a pharmacist, pharmacologist, and nutritionist, clinical researcher and scientific researcher. I am a Diplomate of the American Board of Clinical Pharmacology, a Fellow

of the American College of Clinical Pharmacology, a Fellow in the American College of Nutrition, and a Certified Nutrition Specialist. My curriculum vitae includes papers in pharmacy, pharmacology, nutrition, adverse reactions, practice standards, and litigation related to pharmaceuticals and pharmacists. I have presented 150 lectures throughout the United States and Canada regarding topics in my areas of expertise.

5. My training and experience during the period from pharmacy school graduation until joining the Cook County Hospital includes a Hospital Pharmacy Residency at the University of Illinois Hospitals and an Academic program leading to the Doctor of Pharmacy degree from the University of Michigan in 1971.

6. Over the last 34 years I have been an active member of many local, regional, and national professional associations and societies, including local and state-wide officer, committee memberships, editorial boards, and governmental appointments.

7. Baby Boy Doe was a premature infant born on 1/11/84 and died on 2/11/84. During the hospitalization, the child was administered E-Ferol in this TPN (total parenteral nutrition) solution. After his death, two autopsies were conducted. The initial autopsy was performed at the time of Baby Boy Doe's death on February 11, 1984, by Pathologist F.Q. Graybeal, Jr. M.D. A second autopsy was performed by R.E. Brown, M.D., in the summer months of 1984, immediately following the recall of E-Ferol, at the request of Michael Stanley, M.D., Director of Neonatology at Harris Methodist Fort Worth, who issued the following pathologic findings:

Final Diagnoses: Morphologic findings consistent with E-Ferol Syndrome (emphasis added) to include:

A. Hepatopathy:
   1. Vasculopathic characterized by:
       a. Sinusoidal dilatation with focal attenuation of liver cell trabeculae
       b. Exfoliation of sinusoidal lining (primarily Kupffer) cells
       c. Endophlebitis involving central veins (rare).
   2. Cholestatic, intralobular, marked.

B. Nephropathy associated with:
   1. Acute Tubular necrosis
   2. Intraluminal oxalate-type crystals involving distal convoluted and collecting tubules and minor calyces.
   3. Siderosis involving hepatocytes and Kupffer cells.
   4. Morphologic evidence of peroxidative-type insult to proximal convoluted tubular epithelium.

Dr. R.E. Brown, opined in his report:

...the clinical and histopathologic features of the E-Ferol Syndrome were reported in the literature and that coupled with some experimental observations in our laboratory and those reported in the literature, enabled me to conclude with confidence that BB (Baby Boy Doe) was a victim of the E-Ferol Syndrome. These findings and conclusions are contained in my consultative reports #AC84-12...

8. Two physicians (Turbeville and Sidebottom), a pharmacist (Ed Eason), and a nurse (Peggy Troy) were deposed in this case. I reviewed and considered the testimony. My summary of their deposition testimony follows (emphasis added): Harris' interrogatory responses, Answers to Interrogatories 25, 26 and 27 serve as a source for some of the following information.

Drs. Turbeville, Stanley, Sidebottom et al. were neonatologists who administered E-Ferol in the PICU of Fort Worth Children's Hospital (connected by tunnel with Harris Medical Center) in 1984. Nurse Peggy Troy was the Director of Nursing for the PICU but did not have contact with the pharmacy, medical staff or nursing staff about the recall. The Director of Pharmacy feels that he responded to the recall appropriately and that it was the physician's responsibility to inform the parents if it was appropriate about the recall.

If the preemies were well enough to go home they were considered to be unharmed by the E-Ferol and no future monitoring would be necessary because any possible toxicity had resolved. The autopsy performed by Pathology Department Head, Dr. Brown, was apparently done at the request of Dr. Sidebottom, and Dr. Brown reported that he found evidence of damage consistent with an E-Ferol syndrome. The neonatologists discount Dr. Brown's credibility because his findings could be explained by the immaturity of premature infants who often have such findings.

No one bothered to inform the pediatricians caring for the babies given E-Ferol to watch for any continuing toxicity. Pharmacist Eason (Director of Pharmacy for the Fort Worth Children's Hospital) created a file for the hospital handling of this recall but the file was destroyed during a 1989 facility move. (The testimony of Pharmacist Marlin Rose, Director of Pharmacy at the Harris Methodist Fort Worth is not available.)

Dr. Turbeville does not recall the conversation but he does recall a pharmacist coming to the nursery at Harris or Cook's saying that the FDA had withdrawn E-Ferol. It was not a total surprise because he had read or heard that there had been some problems with it. The problems Dr. Turbeville had heard of prior to recall were edema, kidney failure and liver failure and infant deaths from E-Ferol. Not all of the kids who got E-Ferol had complications. There was no treatment for patients who had received E-Ferol other than stopping the medication. After the recall, Dr. Turbeville did not order it anymore.

How did Dr. Turbeville advise the parents of babies who had received E-Ferol by his order? A. If any babies had symptoms, he discussed it with those parents. Babies who got E-Ferol but did not have problems, he did not discuss this with the parents. Dr. Turbeville did not expect the pharmacists, nurses or hospital administrators to communicate directly with the parents of the neonates who had received E-Ferol about its possible effect on their children. Dr. Turbeville is not aware that the E-Ferol withdrawal was a Class I recall. "I–I wasn't–didn't know that's the way it was tagged." Dr. Turbeville does recall one of the chief Hospital Pharmacists at Cook or Harris coming to the nursery to let him know that the drug had been recalled. Dr. Turbeville's two partners (Dr. Michael Stanley and Dr. Richard Sidebottom) had been notified by telephone that the drug had been recalled. Dr. Turbeville did not bother to inform the nurses or pharmacy techs about the recall because he assumed that since the pharmacists knew they wouldn't be using E-Ferol in the hyperalimentation preparations anymore, it wouldn't be dispensed.

What about babies who had already gone home? "Well, a baby that went home from the hospital, generally they–they go home well." "So those babies we felt like if there had been side effects, they had resolved." At the time of the recall, Dr. Turbeville did not know the long term effects of this particular drug. If something had come up later and they had to contact the families

of babies who had received E-Ferol, "we could have pulled those charts in a heartbeat and contacted the families and told the doctor what to have done, contact the parents if we'd had to." Dr. Turbeville did not order autopsies on patients who had been given E-Ferol. He recalls that one of these had received an autopsy and the pathologist indicated that E-Ferol may have played a significant role. Dr. Turbeville recalls some discussion with "our physicians whether or not we agreed with the conclusion about E-Ferol."

Did Dr. Turbeville have a duty to inform the parents of the babies given E-Ferol? "The ones who I felt like it didn't, I don't know that–I didn't feel like they needed to be informed at all–until we had more information about it." "In those cases I thought it might have affected them, I contacted them." Dr. Turbeville has no opinion as to whether Pharmacy Director Eason should have notified the parents that their babies had been given an illegal drug. "And I think to alarm a family unnecessarily would be to some degree unethical." Two E-Ferol babies at Cook Children's and Harris died in early 1984 and autopsies were performed by staff at Cook's (including Rachel Eskew) and the parents were not informed of the results of the postmortem exam.

Pharmacy Director Eason says that he notified the neonatologists about the recall but not the pediatricians who assumed care after the preemies were discharged from the NICU. Eason agrees that it is reasonable to "Maintain a written log of all recalls, the actions taken and their results." Eason did do this but the log was destroyed in 1989. Pharmacy should fill out the adverse events forms. "I would pass it on to the people I felt like were responsible and leave the ball in their court. If some form were to be filled out, I would leave that up to them to fill out." (No similar information or details of Pharmacist Marlin Rose's actions are available to this expert.)

In the 1980s, Lynette Hill was a staff pharmacist (and is now Mrs. Eason) and prepared a staff pharmacist report on the pharmacy formulary products that contained polysorbate 80 and turned the report into the Pathologist, Dr. Robert Brown. Pharmacist Eason has no criticism of Dr. Brown as a Pathologist. Pharmacist Eason says that Dr. Brown's research was important and needed to be done to clarify things about polysorbate and E-Ferol. "I believe that Dr. Brown's conclusions in his research were that additional research needed to be done." Pharmacist Eason does not know that doctors across America concluded that children died from E-Ferol.

Back in 1984, Pharmacist Eason just didn't check to verify claims of FDA approval. "I think it's reasonable for us to expect the pharmaceutical manufacturer to be honest." Pharmacist Eason is asked if it was his job to verify representations of FDA approval in 1984: "Yeah. I guess it was, yes." Pharmacist Eason says it was also his job and the P&T committee to evaluate the literature supplied in support of the new drug to see if it was appropriate for the patient population who would receive it.

Pharmacist Eason has no prior knowledge of (James) O'Donnell or criticism of him but he totally disagrees with (James) O'Donnell's report and Eason's conduct during the recall. In what areas does Eason disagree with O'Donnell? First, "the fact that communication with the physician is a starting point and if the pharmacist is requested to communicate with the families, that that be done. That is, I believe, the standard of care in our institution. Was then and is now the standard of care in our institution."

Pharmacist Eason is surprised to hear that none of the plaintiffs in this case have reported that they had been informed that their child had received E-Ferol. Eason: "I thought that it would have been communicated." "It seemed that in most circumstances, yes, he (a father) should have been told."

Dr. Sidebottom recalls that he was notified by the pharmacies of both Cook's and Harris on the same day that E-Ferol had been recalled. Both pharmacies told them that the product had been taken off the market and that "we needed to quit using it." Dr. Sidebottom has no recollection of what specific acts Pharmacist Eason or the pharmacy staff took in response to the recall. The day he was notified he informed the nurses on the unit that they were not going to use E-Ferol anymore and told the charge nurse. He also recalls talking about it at a nursing management meeting. Whose responsibility is it to inform the families what medications are being given to their babies? A. "So it's the physician's responsibility." And it was the physician's responsibility to inform the families whose babies had received the E-Ferol that the FDA had recalled the drug. Dr. Sidebottom did not expect the pharmacists, the nurses or the administrators to directly contact the parents and advise them that E-Ferol had been withdrawn from the market.

Peggy Troy was the director of the NICUs at both Cook's and Harris. On the day of the recall, Dr. Sidebottom did not speak with Peggy Troy but he did speak with the head nurse Maude Proctor. Were all of the nurses informed of the recall? Dr. Sidebottom recollects

that there was a monthly nursing management meeting in which this was discussed with the charge nurses.

What is Dr. Sidebottom's opinion of Pathologist Dr. Brown? A. "On more than one occasion he seemed to have crusades that he would go on that weren't necessarily accepted by the mainstream." "...There were times when he was right but there were a lot of times he was wrong, too." Dr. Sidebottom does not recall speaking to Dr. Brown about the second postmortem exam or receiving his bill for his services with respect to performing an autopsy on baby Eskew with regard to E-Ferol toxicity. The recall was based on 17 suspicious cases. Dr. Sidebottom feels that in a population of such sick patients it is difficult to sort out an alleged syndrome with only 17 cases.

Nurse Troy did not become aware that E-Ferol had actually been used at Fort Worth Children's Hospital until 1995 when this became an issue with the Medical staff. In April 1984, Peggy Troy was Director of Neonatal Nursing. The neonatologists would inform the floor nurses. Ms. Troy is not in the loop on this particular issue. The decision of whether to inform the parents of the Class I recall: "That's a physician decision." "I don't feel I have the sole responsibility to do that." "It is my position that the doctors are responsible to notify the parents."

In 1984 for a Class I Recall, "The practice would be that the pharmacist notify the physician in the unit, and the charge nurse of the unit." "In those days, it's my recollections that it was done verbal. The patient's chart would not be noted because it wasn't a practice. The nurses could tell the parents about nursing care for the preemies but it was not their responsibility to tell them the purpose of medications of the implications for the medications." Ms. Troy was not aware that E-Ferol was being given to patients in the NICU in 1984 at Fort Worth Children's Hospital.

9.   In 1983, the Carter Glogau company, through O'Neal Jones and Feldman manufactured and distributed an intravenous formulation of vitamin E (alphatocopherol, 25 U/ml, in a 10 percent emulsion of Polysorbate (91 percent) 80 and Polysorbate (1 percent) 20, emulsifiers, to facilitate the solubility of the oily formulation of the Vitamin E. This intravenous product was promoted for use in premature infants, without conducting requisite tests of safety and efficacy, nor seeking regulatory approval of the Food and Drug Administration (FDA). Shortly after the release, physicians started reporting problems, toxicity, and suspected deaths in the premature infants treated, leading

to a Class I recall by the company at the initiation of the FDA on or about April 11 or April 12, 1984. According to protocol, the company sent out notices to hospital pharmacists and wholesalers. The FDA also sent out urgent recall notices to hospital administrators, directors of hospital pharmacies, and pediatricians, and the topic of the recall and reasons therefor were reported in the FDA and pharmaceutical press and pediatric and toxicology literature. On April 16, 1984, the FDA HHS Important Drug Warning and Urgent Class I Drug Recall, repeated "The FDA advises that physicians closely monitor infants who have received E-Ferol Aqueous Solution because of the possibility of delayed onset of symptoms." FDA notices requested that reports of patient exposures be reported in order to determine the extent of the problem.

10. Epidemiologic investigation, including autopsy analysis of some of the dozens of children who died lead to the association of the Polysorbate component of the IV formulation as the toxic component, and possibly identified the Vitamin E as a possible toxicant.[1,2]

11. The Minimum Standard for Pharmacies in Institutions[3] states as follows:

> Pharmaceutical services in institutions have numerous components, the most prominent being. (1) The procurement, distribution and control of all pharmaceuticals used within the facility (2) the evaluation and dissemination of comprehensive information about drugs and their use to the institutions staff and patients, (3) the monitoring and assurance of the quality of drug use.

> Standard I: Administration
> An operations manual governing all pharmacy functions should be prepared. It should be continually revised to reflect changes in procedures, organization, etc. All pharmacy personnel should be familiar with, the contents of the manual. The relevant standards and guidelines of the American Society of Hospital Pharmacists and the Joint Commission on Accreditation of Hospitals should be adhered to regardless of the particular financial and organizational arrangements by which pharmaceutical services are provided to the facility and its patients.

> Standard III: Drug Distribution and Control
> The pharmacy shall be responsible for the pro-

curement, distribution and control of all drugs used within the institution....In doing so, it is essential that the pharmacist routinely visit all patient care areas to establish rapport with their personnel and to become familiar with medical and nursing procedures related to drugs.

> The pharmacist should maintain an up to date formulary of drug products approved for use in the institution. While the items to be included in the formulary are selected by the pharmacy and therapeutics committee (or its equivalent), it is the pharmacist's responsibility to establish specifications for these drug products and to select their source of supply. In doing so, it is advisable that written specifications for multi-source items be prepared and utilized in the acquisition process.

> The pharmacist must institute the control procedures needed to insure that patients receive the correct drugs at the proper times, In accomplishing this, it is necessary that all drugs used in the institution (including I.V. fluids) be distributed by the pharmacy.

> There shall be a system for removing from use any drugs subjected to a product recall.

> Standard IV: Drug Information
> The pharmacy is responsible for providing the institution's staff and patients with accurate, comprehensive information about drugs and their use, and shall serve as its center for drug information,...

> The pharmacist must keep the institution's staff well informed about the drugs used in the institution and their various dosage forms and packaging. This is accomplished through newsletters, seminars, displays, etc., developed by the pharmacy. No drug shall be administered unless the medical and nursing personnel have received adequate information about, and are familiar with its therapeutic use, adverse effects and dosage.

> The pharmacist must insure that all patients receive adequate information about the drugs they receive. This is particularly important for ambulant and discharge patients.

The ASHP Statement on the Pharmacy and Therapeutic Committee includes relevant passages as follows:

...it is necessary that hospitals have an organized, sound program for maximizing rational drug use. The Pharmacy and Therapeutics committee, or its equivalent is he organizational keystone of this program. The P&T committee is an advisory group of the medical staff and serves as the organizational line of communication between the medical staff and the pharmacy department. This committee is composed of physicians, pharmacists and other health professionals selected with the guidance of the medical staff. It is a policy-recommending body to the medical staff and the administration of the hospital on matters related to the therapeutic use of drugs, including the adoption of, or assists in the formulation of broad professional policies regarding evaluation, selection and therapeutic use of drugs in hospitals.[4]

The ASHP Guidelines on Hospital Drug Distribution and Control (with references) is excerpted for relevance to this case:

- Because the drug control system interfaces with numerous departments and professions, the P&T committee should be the focal point for communications relating to drug control in the institution.
- The pharmacist must be aware of and comply with the laws, regulations, and standards governing the process. Many of these standards and regulations deal with aspects off drug control....The FDA is responsible for implementing and enforcing the federal Food Drug and Cosmetic Act. The FDA is responsible for the control and prevention of misbranding and of adulteration of food, drugs, and cosmetics moving in interstate commerce. The FDA also sets label requirements for food, drugs; sets standards for investigational drug studies and for marketing of new drug products; and compiles data on adverse drug reactions...standards and guidelines for services have been established by The Joint Commission and the ASHP. The United States Pharmacopoeia Convention also promulgates certain pharmacy practice procedures as well as official standards for drugs and drug test. Professional practice guidelines and standards

generally do not have the force of law, but rather, are intended to assist pharmacists in achieving the highest level of practice.

- Among the records needed in the drug distribution and control system are records of medication orders and their processing...
- Once a (physician's) order has been approved, it is entered into the patients medication profile. A medication profile must be maintained in the pharmacy for all inpatients and those outpatients routinely receiving care at the institution. (The record also may be useful in retrospective review of drug use.)
- Appropriate records of each medication order and its processing in the pharmacy must be maintained. Such records must be retained in accordance with applicable state laws and regulations....A way should be provided to determine, for all doses dispensed, who prepared the dose, the date of dispensing, the source of the drug. and the person who checked it.

SPECIAL CONSIDERATIONS CONTRIBUTING TO DRUG CONTROL

In the case of product recalls of substantial clinical significance, a notice should go to the recipients that have a recalled product. The course of action they should take should be included. In the case of outpatients, caution should be exercised, not to cause undue alarm. The uninterrupted therapy of the patients must be assured, i.e., replacement of the recalled drugs generally will be required. The hospital's administration and nursing and medical staffs should be informed of any recalls having significant therapeutic implications. Some situations also may require notifying the physicians of patients receiving drugs that have been recalled. (Page 1102)

The Accreditation Manual for Hospitals, 1983, states the following:

There shall be a written drug recall procedure that can be implemented readily and the results documented. This requirement shall apply to both in-patient and ambulatory care patient medications.

12. E-Ferol recall was a Class I Recall, which is defined as: "A situation in which there is a reasonable probability that the use of or exposure to a violative product will cause serious adverse health consequences or death."[5]

In 1978, a Federal Register set forth six elements to be considered in making the required health hazard evaluation, although they also state that the pertinent Bureau's Health Hazard Evaluation Committee, which makes the evaluation for the FDA, need not be limited to these factors.[6]

    a.   Whether any disease or injuries have already occurred from the use of the violative product(s).

    b.   Whether any existing conditions could contribute to a clinical situation that could expose humans or animals to a health hazard. Any conclusion shall be supported as completely as possible by scientific documentation and/or statements that OR: conclusion is the opinion of the individual(s) making the health hazard determination.

    c.   Assessment of hazard to various segments of the population, such as children, surgical patients, pets, livestock, etc., who are expected to be expose to the product being considered, with particular attention paid to the hazard to those individuals who may be at greatest risk.

    d.   Assessment of the degree of seriousness of the health hazard to which the populations at risk would be exposed.

    e.   Assessment of the likelihood of occurrence of the hazard.

    f.   Assessment of the consequences (immediate or long-range) of occurrence of the hazards.

Responsibility of recipient. Consignees that receive a recall communication should immediately carry out the instructions set forth by the recalling firm.[7]

13. FDA Enforcement report and the Practice Standards of the ASHP (American Society of Hospital Pharmacists) describe the following actions to be taken in the Class I Recall:

    a.   Whenever feasible, notation of the drug manufacturer's name and drug lot number should appear on outpatient prescriptions, in-patient drug orders or profiles, packaging control records, and stock requisitions and their associated labels.

    b.   Review of these documents; (prescriptions, drug orders, and so forth) to determine the recipients (patients, nursing stations), of the recalled lots. Optimally, this would be done by automated means.

    c.   In the case of product recalls of substantial clinical significance, a notice should go to the recipients that they have a recalled product (received, need to be monitored.) The course of action they should take should be included. In the case of outpatients, caution should be exercised, not to cause undue alarm. The uninterrupted therapy of the patients must be assured, i.e., replacement of the recalled drugs generally will be required. The hospital's administration and nursing and medical staffs should be informed of any recalls having significant therapeutic implications. Some situations also may require notifying the physicians of patients receiving drugs that have been recalled.

    d.   Personal inspection of all patient care areas should be made to determine if any of the recalled products are present.

    e.   Quarantine of all recalled products obtained (marked "Quarantined-Do Not Use")- until they are picked up by or returned to the manufacturer.

    f.   Maintenance of a written log of all recalls, the actions taken, and their results.[8]

Standard IV of The Joint Commission: Written policies and procedures that pertain to the intra-hospital drug distribution system shall be developed by the director of the pharmaceutical department/service in concert with the medical staff and, as appropriate, with representatives of other disciplines:

There shall be a written drug recall procedure that can be implemented readily and the results documented. This requirement shall apply to both inpatient and ambulatory patient medications.[9]

14. Ed Eason, the Director of Pharmacy, at the Fort Worth Children's Hospital was aware of the recall. Pharmacist Marlin Rose at the Harris Methodist Ft. Worth was also aware of the recall. Both pharmacists were aware of the use of the volatile product, and the patients in whom it

was used clinically. Both communicated with the FDA and with the company related to reporting the use and returning the unused products for credit following the recall.

15. The parents of the exposed patients (plaintiffs' children and plaintiffs in this case), alive and deceased, had no knowledge nor were they informed of the potential toxicity or morbidity associated with the use of E-Ferol in their children.

16. The hospital staff (physicians and pharmacists) were aware of the association between the use of E-Ferol, the recalled product, and toxicity and morbidity in general, and in Baby Boy Doe.

17. Neither the pharmacist employed by HMFW, the physicians employed by or practicing in the HMFW, nor the administrators employed by HMFW notified or advised the parents of the E-Ferol-treated children of the exposure to this toxic drug and the potential association of that toxicity to any illness or death experienced in these premature babies.

18. In my opinion, with reasonable pharmaceutical certainty, Pharmacist Marlin Rose departed from the standard of care of reasonable and prudent hospital pharmacist and was negligent in failing to notify the families of these E-Ferol-exposed infants after the recall notice was received. The standards of practice and The Joint Commission, and the recall notice promulgated by the FDA, clearly direct that patients be notified, closely monitored, and cautioned, and that appropriate hospital and medical personnel be notified when significant clinical issues are involved. Further, in my opinion, Pharmacist Marlin Rose was negligent in failing to notify the hospital administrators of the significant clinical issues involved in the recall of the E-Ferol Aqueous Solution and failing to notify medical personnel and nursing staff of this Class I drug recall and its applicable directives for immediate, as well as long-term monitoring.

19. The aforementioned negligence has caused injury to the children and their parents who received E-Ferol at Harris Methodist Hospital Ft. Worth.

I reserve the right to supplement this report after reviewing additional information or being informed of additional facts.

Very truly yours,
James O'Donnell, Pharm.D., MS, FCP, ABCP, FACN, R.Ph.
Diplomate American Board of Clinical Pharmacology
Certified-Board of Nutritional Specialties

Endnotes for Appendix

1. Alade Brown and Paguet: Polysorbate 80 and E-Ferol Toxicity; *Pediatrics,* Vol. 77, No. 4.

2. Brown RE and Krouse M: Polysorbates and Renal Oxalate Crystals in E-Ferol. *JAMA* Letter to the Editor; vol 255, No. 18, May 9, 1986.

3. *American Journal of Hospital Pharmacy* 34:1356-1358 (Dec) 1988.

4. *American Journal of Hospital Pharmacy*, Vol 35, July 1978, 813, 814.

5. *Food Drug Cosmetic Law Journal.* July, 1978, Page 351.

6. *Federal Register,* Vol. 43, No. 117 Friday, June 16, 1978. Page 26219.

7. *Federal Register*, Vol. 43, No. 117 Friday, June 16, 1978. Page 26220.

8. ASHP Guidelines on Hospital Drug Distribution and Control (with References). *American Journal of Hospital Pharmacy*, Vol. 37, August 1980, 1097-1103 (special considerations Contributing to Drug control, Paragraph 3 at page 1102).

9. Joint Commission for the Accreditation of Hospitals (Joint Commission), Accreditation Manual for Hospitals, Pharmaceutical Services 1983, Standard IV, 142-143. Chicago, IL 60610.

Chapter 20

Antidepressants: Clinical Use and Litigation

Henry Cohen, B.S., M.S., Pharm.D., FCCM, BCPP, CGP and Antonia Alafris, B.S., Pharm.D., CGP

20.1 Major Depressive Disorders

Seventeen percent of the U.S. population will suffer from a major depressive disorder at least once in their lifetime, and more than 10 percent had an episode within the last ten months.[1] Depression is twice as common in women as it is in men: 21 percent of women have been diagnosed with major depression compared with 13 percent of men.[2,3] The average onset of a major depressive disorder is in patients in their late twenties. More than 50 percent of patients have their first episode by age 40. The duration of these episodes is between six months and two years when left untreated. Eighty percent of untreated patients have recurrent episodes.

Seventy-five percent of patients who have suffered from depression also suffer from another psychiatric disorder. The primary additional disorders include

- posttraumatic stress (19.5 percent),
- generalized anxiety (17.2 percent),
- social phobia (27.1 percent),
- panic (9.9 percent), and
- alcohol dependence (23.5 percent).

In this chapter, we discuss several scenarios involving antidepressants and the possible basis for litigation in those scenarios.

20.2 Antidepressant Pharmacology

The high incidence of depression in the United States is consistent with the 1998 sales of three antidepressants—Prozac (fluoxetine hydrochloride, Eli Lilly), Zoloft (sertraline hydrochloride, Pfizer), and Paxil (paroxetine hydrochloride, SmithKline Beechham)—that were among the ten top-selling prescription drugs in the world.[4] Nevertheless, only 31 percent of depressed adults actually seek treatment.[5] Antidepressants are the primary treatment in the management of depression.

The foremost antidepressant, Tofranil (imipramine hydrochloride, Novartis), was introduced in the late 1940s. Currently, antidepressants are classified as tricyclic antidepressant (TCA) agents or first-generation antidepressants, such as Tofranil or Elavil (amitriptyline, Merck); or second-generation agents, such as Serzone (nefazodone hydrochloride, Bristol-Myers Squibb). Second-generation antidepressants include the selective serotonin reuptake inhibitors (SSRIs), such as Prozac, Zoloft, Paxil, Lexapro, Celexa and the serotonin/norepinephrine reuptake inhibitors (SNRIs) such as Effexor, Pristiq, and Cymbalta. The term *cyclic antidepressant* can refer to either first- or second-generation antidepressants. Table 20.1 provides a list of the entire class of cyclic antidepressants.

Table 20.1
Generic and Brand Name Tricyclic and Second Generation Antidepressants

Generic Name	Brand Name
Tricyclic Antidepressants	
amitriptyline	Elavil
amoxapine	Asendin
clomipramine	Anafranil
desipramine	Norpramin
doxepin	Sinequan
imipramine	Tofranil
nortriptyline	Aventyl, Pamelor
protriptyline	Vivactil
trimipramine	Surmontil
Second Generation, Non-Tricyclic Antidepressants	
bupropion	Wellbutrin,[a] Zyban
desvenlafaxine	Pristiq
duloxetine	Cymbalta
maprotiline	Ludiomil
mirtazapine	Remeron[b]
nefazodone	Serzone
trazodone	Desyrel
venlafaxine	Effexor[c]
Second Generation, Selective Serotonin Reuptake Inhibitors Antidepressants	
citalopram	Celexa
escitalopram	Lexapro
fluoxetine	Prozac[d]
fluvoxamine	Luvox
paroxetine	Paxil[e]
sertraline	Zoloft

a. Also available in sustained-release formulations (Wellbutrin SR, Wellbutrin XL, Budeprion SR, Budeprion XL)
b. Also available in orally disintegrating tablets
c. Also available in extended-release formulation (Effexor XR)
d. Also available in weekly dosage form (Prozac weekly)
e. Also available in controlled-release formulation (Paxil CR)

TCAs can often cause a range of adverse effects:[2]

- peripheral antimuscarinic effects (dry mouth, blurred vision, constipation, urinary retention, rapid heart rate, increased blood pressure, increased body temperature, and mydriasis);
- central antimuscarinic effects (agitation, hallucinations, confusion, sedation, coma, and seizures);
- antihistaminic effects (sedation, drowsiness, dizziness, and weight gain);
- adrenergic effects (low blood pressure and subsequent fainting spells);
- heart rhythm and rate disturbances; and
- seizures.

SSRIs have supplanted TCAs as the first-line treatment for depressive disorders primarily because their adverse effect profiles are better. The SSRIs do not generally produce antimuscarinic, antihistaminic, or adrenergic adverse effects, and they are less cardiotoxic or seizuregenic.[2] Because SSRIs have fewer adverse effects, patients tolerate them better and comply better with their prescription regimen. SSRIs also appear to be safer in patients with suicidal ideation. The SNRI's neurohormonal effects are more similar to TCAs because they affect both norepinephrine and serotonin. The SNRIs generally produce less antimuscarinic, antihistaminic, or adrenergic adverse effects, and they are less cardiotoxic or seizuregenic than TCAs but slightly greater than the SSRIs.

20.3 Antidepressant Overdose

Despite the distinct pharmacological advantages of the SSRIs, TCAs are still widely prescribed, which may be because TCAs have less-expensive generic equivalents. The American Association of Poison Control Centers (AAPCC) recently reported[6] that antidepressants are second only to analgesics as the cause of overdose-related deaths. Sixty-nine percent of antidepressant fatalities involve TCAs.[6]

In the early 1990s, the annual incidence of TCA overdose in the United States was approximately 500,000.[7] Cyclic antidepressants (tricyclics, bicyclics, and monocyclics) are among the most common causes of self-poisoning. Morbidity has also been associated with the SSRIs, however, but with less frequency. More than 50,000 antidepressant exposures annually have been reported to poison control centers throughout the United States.[6]

20.4 Antidepressants and the Patient with Suicidal Ideation

Depressive disorders and suicides tend to cluster in families and in first-degree relatives of patients. Females are two to three times more likely to attempt suicide than males. Males, however, succeed three times more often.[8] All depressed patients should be assessed for suicidal ideation. Myths regarding suicide include:

- that suicide attempts are just a call for attention,
- that suicidal people are crazy or insane, and
- that if you ask someone who is considering commit-

ting suicide about their intentions, they will be more likely to follow through with the suicide attempt.

When suicidal ideation is suspected, patients should be asked about their desire to harm or kill themselves. Patients often attempt suicide by using prescription drugs. Adults tend to poison themselves with several different drugs at once. Combinations of antidepressants—benzodiazepines, barbiturates, alcohol, and over-the-counter pain relievers—are commonly used in suicidal attempts. Prescribing antidepressants to patients with suicidal ideation must be done carefully.

TCA overdose is often fatal when the adverse effects are pronounced and simultaneous. Symptoms of a TCA overdose include drowsiness, lethargy, cardiac arrhythmias, hypotension, and seizures. In hospital emergency rooms, life-threatening effects from TCA overdose usually begin within two to six hours of the patient's arrival at the hospital. Antidotes are unavailable for TCA overdose: gastric decontamination, activated charcoal, sodium bicarbonate, and supportive care are the usual treatment. To minimize the risk of overdose, doctors should prescribe no more than a one-week supply of a TCA and no more than 1 gram of the drug at any one time.[2] If refills are allowed, the pharmacist must not dispense them prematurely. Larger drug quantities through mail-order pharmacies should be prohibited.

In patients with suicidal ideation, prescribing a less-toxic antidepressant is critical: SSRIs or Desyrel (trazodone hydrochloride, Apothecon) are preferred. Although these second-generation agents are generally safer, overdose fatalities have also been reported using them. The FDA and the AAPCC have recorded 52 overdose deaths that involved only an SSRI: 34 overdoses using Prozac, ten using Zoloft, seven using Paxil, and one using Luvox (fluvoxamine maleate, Solvay Pharmaceuticals).[9] In most instances, the doses taken were many times greater than the usual therapeutic dose. Another factor that increases a depressed patient's risk of suicide is the slow therapeutic onset of cyclic antidepressants—generally about two to four weeks. The frustrated, depressed patient may double or triple their dose in an attempt to increase the efficacy.

SSRIs should be favored over TCAs for depressed patients with suicidal ideation. If a TCA must be used (such as for a patient with a history of SSRI failure), only small doses, not exceeding 1 gram, should be prescribed and dispensed. Furthermore, family members of patients with suicidal ideation should be notified, psychiatric care should be sought, and hospital admission should be considered.

A. Prozac and Suicidal Ideation

Eli Lilly & Co. first marketed Prozac in 1987. Since then, the drug has been accused of causing patients to commit

violent crimes and become suicidal. In the early 1990s, several lawsuits were filed against Eli Lilly, including a suit by Abbie Hoffman and another by the rock star Del Shannon.[10] Epidemiological studies have since demonstrated that Prozac was not associated with more incidents of violent crimes or suicidal behavior. The behavior was, instead, a consequence of an affective or mood disorder.

Comprehensive meta-analysis of clinical data was explored to assess a possible association of fluoxetine and suicidal acts or ideation.[11] The incidence of suicidal acts did not differ significantly between fluoxetine and placebo or between fluoxetine and tricyclic antidepressants. A marginally significant drop in suicidal ideation was found with fluoxetine when compared with a placebo, and a slightly larger gap was found between fluoxetine and TCAs. No worsening of suicidal ideation was found between fluoxetine and a placebo or between fluoxetine and TCAs. Nevertheless, Prozac's package insert,[12] and the inserts of all other SSRIs, has the following precautionary statement:

> The possibility of a suicide attempt is inherent in depressed patients and may persist until significant remission occurs. Close supervision of high-risk patients should accompany initial drug therapy. Prescriptions for Prozac should be written for the smallest quantity of capsules consistent with good patient management to reduce the risk of overdose.[12]

1. *Woulfe v. Eli Lilly & Co.*

In *Woulfe v. Eli Lilly & Co.* the plaintiff Daniel Clinton Woulfe was the father of Jack Wayne Woulfe, who committed suicide by hanging on February 1, 1991.[13] Woulfe brought action against Eli Lilly & Co. claiming that its failure to warn about the risk of suicide from Prozac caused or contributed to Woulfe's death and suffering. In particular, the plaintiff claimed that the warnings provided in the package insert for Prozac sold in the United States were deficient when compared with the language used in the package insert for the German market. The German insert advised prescribing physicians that

- Prozac did not have a general sedative effect on the central nervous system (CNS);
- patients, for their safety, had to be sufficiently observed until the antidepressive effect of Prozac set in; and
- the use of an additional sedative might be necessary in some cases.

The deceased was prescribed Prozac by his physician on January 4, 1991. The doctor believed that the warnings Eli

Lilly provided about Prozac were adequate and that any additional warnings about its use would not have changed his decision to prescribe the antidepressant to the deceased. Jack Wayne Woulfe did not exhibit or have a history of anger, anxiety, agitation, impulsivity, agitated ruminating, or volatile outbursts that might have suggested to the physician the need for additional treatment or referral to a psychiatrist.

Under Oklahoma law, Eli Lilly did not have the duty to personally warn Jack Wayne Woulfe of the possible risks associated with the use of Prozac. Under this "learned intermediary doctrine," the manufacturer of a prescription drug is shielded from liability if it adequately warns prescribing physicians of the dangers associated with the drug. Based on that argument, Eli Lilly's motion for summary judgment on the plaintiff's "failure to warn" claim was granted, and the case was dismissed.

2. *Espinoza v. Eli Lilly & Co.*

In *Espinoza v. Eli Lilly & Co.* the surviving family of Vera Espinoza claimed that she shot and killed her two children and immediately thereafter committed suicide as a result of her ingestion of Prozac.[14] She was diagnosed with major depression and dependent personality disorder. Espinoza was treated with Prozac for several years before her death, and during the last three months of her life, her dosage was increased from 20 mg to 40 mg. The deceased, however, was known to adjust her dosage as she saw fit, and it is uncertain how much Prozac she was taking when she died. Autopsy results revealed concentrations of Prozac and its metabolite norfluoxetine at ten times the approved therapeutic concentration.

In the days before her death, Espinoza was calm. She began giving away possessions, suggesting that she planned her suicide. She was not exhibiting symptoms of akathisia (restlessness), a mixed state (mania and depression), mania, or hypomania at that time. The family members offered a psychiatrist and suicidology expert as their sole expert in determining the cause of these homicides and suicide. The psychiatrist concluded that Prozac was a contributing cause of Espinoza's suicide because the medication disinhibited her, limiting her self-control, increasing her impulsivity, and making it difficult for her to control aggression.

The court noted a controversy within the psychiatric community in determining whether the observed association—between ingestion of certain types of antidepressants and suicidal or violent behavior—was causal. The expert's opinion on causation relied on an article that showed a causal connection between Prozac and akathisia and an association between akathisia and suicidal ideation. The court held, however, that the expert's opinion did not "fit" the facts of

this case, because Espinoza did not suffer from akathisia. Without expert testimony that the drug caused the deaths, it was not possible to show that any inadequacy in the drug's warnings was a substantial factor in bringing about the deaths. As a result, Eli Lilly's motion for summary judgment was granted on the grounds that the plaintiffs lacked admissible expert testimony and a proximate cause.

20.5 Broken Heart Syndrome: Tako Tsubo Cardiomyopathy Associated with Use of Antidepressants

Broken heart syndrome which was first described in the early 1990s is also known as Tako Tsubo (meaning octopus trap in Japanese) cardiomyopathy. It is a reversible condition that mimics an acute myocardial infarction or heart attack. It is primarily diagnosed in postmenopausal women following abrupt emotional or physical stress.[15,16] Patients present with chest pain and shortness of breath which appear within hours of the event. The left ventricle of the heart enlarges; an electrocardiogram (ECG) depicting the beating of the heart shows abnormal heart contractions and, overall, there is not enough oxygenated blood in the body, since the heart is failing. However, the heart arteries are not blocked and patients are not experiencing a heart attack.[17] Although the exact cause of this condition remains unclear, it is believed to be the result of increased catecholamines such as serotonin and norepinephrine. Since antidepressants exert their efficacy by enhancing the concentrations of serotonin and norepinephrine, dosages above those therapeutically recommended may be associated with Tako Tsubo cardiomyopathy. This condition is treated by discontinuation of the offending agent(s) and management of symptoms. The mortality rate is less than 8 percent and patients experience full recovery within 6–8 weeks.

Christoph et al. describe the case of a 43-year-old woman who developed Tako Tsubo cardiomyopathy after an accidental overdose of venlafaxine, which increases serotonin and norepinephrine concentrations.[2] A 24-hour urine collection showed increased concentrations of norepinephrine. The serum levels of venlafaxine and its active metabolite desmethylvenlafaxine were elevated above the therapeutic range. Upon discontinuation of the antidepressant and management of the heart symptoms, the patient fully recovered in 6 weeks.

Perry et al. describe the case of a 60-year-old female who presented to the emergency department with chest pain, lightheadedness, nausea and diaphoresis. At home, the patient was taking the antidepressant, duloxetine for the management of peripheral neuropathy (nerve pain).[18] While taking the antidepressant, she developed a urinary tract infection and was prescribed the antibiotic ciprofloxacin. This antibiotic has the ability to inhibit the metabolism of duloxetine, leading to supratherapeutic concentrations of the antidepressant. At the hospital, further workup ruled-out the diagnosis of a heart attack and the patient was eventually found to have Tako Tsubo cardiomyopathy that may have been the result of increased duloxetine concentrations. The antidepressant was discontinued and the patient's heart symptoms were managed. Full recovery was observed in about 6 weeks.

Since all antidepressants exert their efficacy by increasing the concentrations of norepinephrine and serotonin, doses above those therapeutically recommended can potentially lead to Tako Tsubo cardiomyopathy. Importantly, the co-administration of medications that can dangerously increase the concentrations of antidepressants can potentially cause this heart condition, which when left untreated can be fatal.

20.6 The Adverse Effects of Antidepressants and the Duty to Warn

TCAs are associated with many more adverse effects than SSRIs. SSRIs, however, cause a higher incidence of gastrointestinal side effects, such as nausea, vomiting, diarrhea, and erectile dysfunction. Pharmaceutical manufacturers have a duty to inform prescribers and pharmacists of all indications, contraindications, allergies, adverse effects, cautions, precautions, drug-drug and drug-food interactions, and dosing schedules. Both the prescriber and the pharmacist are responsible for monitoring a drug for its efficacy and toxicity and counseling the patient about the therapy. Is there, however, a duty to warn someone for whom a drug was not prescribed? If so, who would be responsible for performing that duty—the pharmaceutical manufacturer, the physician, or the pharmacist?

A. *Docken v. Ciba-Geigy*

In *Docken v. Ciba-Geigy*, the court was asked to determine whether the manufacturer, the physician, or the pharmacist owed a "duty of care" to warn someone who was not prescribed a drug.[19] In 1979, a physician prescribed the TCA Tofranil, manufactured by Ciba-Geigy and dispensed by a hospital pharmacy, for the plaintiff's son Tim. A hospital pharmacist dispensed it. In 1983, the plaintiff's other son Terry ingested several Tofranil tablets, hoping that it would remedy the same enuresis (bedwetting) problem that his brother had. Terry died as a result of ingesting the Tofranil. The plaintiff filed a lawsuit against the pharmaceutical manufacturer, physician, and pharmacist. The plaintiff's product liability theory alleged that the drug was dangerous and defective because of its inadequate labeling. Specifically, the plaintiffs said the defendants:

- failed to label Tofranil in a manner adequate to ensure its safe use;

- failed to warn that Tofranil must be taken and administered with extreme caution because of the potentially fatal effect of excessive dose;
- failed to warn that Tofranil must be disposed of properly after use because of the potential fatal effect of an overdose;
- failed to warn that Tofranil must be stored safely, away from children;
- failed to warn that Tofranil does not quickly leave a person's body, resulting in potentially fatal drug accumulation; and
- failed to warn that an excessive dose of Tofranil can result in death, especially in children.

The plaintiff alleged that the defendants were negligent by failing to warn of these dangers. The plaintiff failed to allege that the physician and the hospital pharmacy were in the business of selling drugs, so the plaintiff's complaint was missing an important element, failing to state a cause of action based on strict product liability. Therefore, Ciba-Geigy was the only defendant left to face liability claims regarding negligence and failure to warn. Had this case been presented differently and had the plaintiff proved that the physician and pharmacist did not warn the patient, it is plausible that one or both of them might have been held liable as well.

B. *Stebbins v. Concord Wrigley Drugs, Inc. et al.*

In *Stebbins v. Concord Wrigley Drugs, Inc. et al.* the plaintiff Bonnie Stebbins had been seriously injured when a car driven by Joseph Zagone struck her automobile.[20] A psychiatrist had prescribed Tofranil for Zagone's psychiatric illness. Concord Discount Drugs dispensed the drug to Zagone. After eating breakfast one day, Zagone got in his car and ran a red light, hitting Stebbins' automobile and seriously injuring her. Stebbins filed a lawsuit against Zagone, his physician, the pharmacy, and the pharmacist, claiming that they had failed to warn the motorist of the adverse effects and hazards of Tofranil. Stebbins alleged that Zagone should have been told not to drive while receiving Tofranil therapy. Zagone subsequently settled out of court with Stebbins.

The physician claimed that he had told Zagone to use Tofranil at bedtime. Zagone had been taking 75 mg of Tofranil at bedtime for some time without any adverse effects or daytime drowsiness. Zagone was confused, however, about whether he took Tofranil at bedtime or in the morning on the day of the accident. The court granted the physician's motion for summary judgment, concluding that he had given due warning. At the time in 1987, the court ruled that the pharmacist had no duty to warn the patient of possible side effects when the prescription was proper and when neither the physician nor the manufacturer had required the pharmacist to warn the patient. However, the Omnibus Budget Reconciliation Act (OBRA) enacted in 1990 required pharmacists to counsel all patients about adverse effects, drug interactions, and drug doses.[21] So, if the case was tried today, the pharmacist may have assumed some liability.

C. *Morgan et al. v. Wal-Mart Stores, Inc.*

In *Morgan et al. v. Wal-Mart Stores, Inc.*, Jacquelyn Morgan and Charles Pettus, the parents of Cameron Pettus, alleged that their son's death in August 1993 was caused by an adverse reaction to desipramine.[22] In 1989, Cameron Pettus was diagnosed with attention deficit hyperactivity disorder (ADHD). He also experienced mood swings, so desipramine was prescribed to control them. Cameron did not start taking the antidepressant until April 1991. Some months later and on various occasions, he complained of chest pains, and his mother took him to a hospital emergency room. No healthcare professional attributed Cameron's chest pains to desipramine. Until the time of her son's death, no pharmacist ever counseled Cameron's mother about the medication's adverse events when she picked up the prescription.

Cameron was later prescribed an antibiotic to heal a lymph node infection, thought to be the result of a mosquito bite. In the following weeks, Cameron's lymph node remained swollen, and he continued to experience chest pains. Finally he was diagnosed with hypereosinophilic syndrome, a disorder that consists of a high number of eosinophils in the blood and bone marrow, which can damage the heart, lungs, liver, and other internal organs. A few days later, Cameron slipped into a coma, was declared brain dead, and was eventually removed from life support. The medical staff concluded that Cameron's death was the result of hyper-eosinophilic syndrome caused by reaction to the desipramine. Wal-Mart was alleged to be negligent in the sale of desipramine "...by failing to properly warn intended users of the hazards and harms associated with the use of the product." The jury assigned 14 percent responsibility to Wal-Mart and the rest was assigned to Cameron's physicians and the other pharmacies from which Cameron's desipramine was purchased.

On appeal, the court ruled that "...pharmacists have no generalized duty to warn patients of potential adverse reactions to prescription drugs...pharmacists are not legally obligated to do so." The judgment of the trial court was reversed in favor of Wal-Mart. The interesting part of this case is that the Wal-Mart pharmacist testified that, although the standard of practice required patient counseling and warnings, the law did not require them, so she did not warn the patient.

D. *Penelope A. Carafelle et al. v. Brockton Oaks CVS, Inc.*

In *Penelope A. Carafelle et al. v. Brockton Oaks CVS, Inc.*, the parents of 13-year-old Jennifer Lynne Carafelle ("Jennifer"), alleged that their daughter's death on July 3, 1991, was the result of CVS Pharmacy's negligence in filling prescriptions by supplying medications to the deceased at a rate faster than that prescribed.[23] On July 2, 1991, Jennifer had an asthmatic attack—she had suffered from severe asthma since infancy—and used, and eventually emptied, her Proventil (albuterol) inhaler in an attempt to stabilize her breathing. Later that evening, she was transported to the emergency department suffering from respiratory distress. Jennifer died in the early morning of July 3, 1991, caused by asthma with acute exacerbation and severe acute respiratory distress.

A year before her death, Jennifer was prescribed the Proventil inhaler, to be used "as needed," together with TheoDur (theophylline) tablets, either an Intal (cromolyn sodium) or an Alupent (metaproterenol sulfate) nebulizer, Alupent tablets, and Azmacort (triamcinolone acetonide). The Proventil inhaler contained 200 metered doses, and at eight puffs per day, it should have lasted approximately one month. Jennifer's primary doctor stated that he had explained to the deceased and her mother the dangers of overusing the inhaler: accelerated heart rate or cardiac arrhythmia and the masking of worsening asthma symptoms.

Jennifer had filled all of her Proventil prescriptions at CVS Pharmacy, where the pharmacist was equipped with a computer with the ability to view a patient's entire medication history. The computer also issued a warning prompt for any prescription that was refilled too soon for insurance purposes. The pharmacist had to manually override the warning prompt to fill a prescription early. In Jennifer's case, her Proventil prescriptions were filled three times more frequently than standard practice or than is recommended for use of the inhaler.

The plaintiff argued that the CVS pharmacists should have refused to refill the prescription before its normal time and should have warned the deceased, her parents, and her physician of the possible overuse and the potential dangers of such overuse. CVS Pharmacy argued that it only had a duty to accurately refill the prescriptions and that it had no affirmative duty to warn. The court denied the motion for summary judgment, stating that a pharmacist owed his customers a duty of ordinary care to conduct his business as any other ordinary, skillful pharmacist would under similar circumstances. The defendant also had a duty to properly refill medications at the correct intervals; and when the pharmacy computer warned the pharmacist that a customer may have been refilling medications too soon, the pharmacist had a duty to alert the prescribing physician.

20.7 Antidepressants and Alcohol

The TCAs and several of the second-generation antidepressants possess potent CNS-depressant effects and should not be taken with alcohol, which is also a CNS depressant. The combination of alcohol and a cyclic antidepressant can lead to additive or synergistic CNS-depressant effects, including drowsiness, dizziness, confusion, and impaired motor activity. Operating heavy machinery, such as driving a vehicle or flying a plane, should be avoided. Patients with a known history of alcohol abuse should not be treated with CNS-depressing antidepressants. Some agents, such as Prozac, do not cause CNS depression but instead cause CNS excitation. CNS excitation manifests as tremor, nervousness, anxiety, and dizziness, so similar warnings regarding the operation of heavy machinery apply. Perhaps the agent least likely to cause CNS depression or excitation is the SSRI Zoloft. Paxil may also be a safer option; however, there have been several reports of Paxil-induced drowsiness.

It is the duty of the pharmaceutical manufacturer to provide warnings and information to healthcare providers about effects from antidepressant and alcohol combinations. Both the prescriber and the pharmacist must counsel the patient regarding this interaction. Patients should be told that alcohol is contraindicated while using antidepressants. Because of the long half-life of many antidepressant agents, residual blood concentrations and pharmacologic effects can remain after discontinuing the therapy. Therefore, alcohol should be avoided for at least 24 to 96 hours after the last dose of an antidepressant. To minimize CNS depression, antidepressants are usually taken at bedtime. To limit the CNS excitation and sleep disturbances of Prozac, it should not be taken after 2:00 P.M. Patients with suicidal ideation might also combine alcohol with their antidepressant, so a safer agent, such as Prozac, Zoloft, or Paxil, might be a more prudent prescription choice.

A. *Kirk v. Michael Reese Hospital*

In *Kirk v. Michael Reese Hospital* the issue was whether a hospital and its physicians have a duty to warn a patient before his discharge that the drugs given at the hospital might impair physical abilities.[24,25] A passenger injured in a car accident sued Michael Reese Hospital, two psychiatrists, and two drug companies for failing to warn the car driver about the danger of his drinking alcohol in combination with the psychotropic drugs—Prolixin (fluphenazine hydrochloride) and Thorazine (chlorpromazine)—he had been given. Both of the psychotropics possess a pharmacological adverse effect profile similar to TCAs. The driver received a Prolixin injection and oral Thorazine on the day of his discharge from the hospital. He also consumed alcohol that day as well. The patient later lost control of his car and smashed into a tree.

The plaintiff alleged that the two drugs diminished the patient's mental and physical abilities, impairing his driving skills, and causing him to get into the accident. The plaintiff further alleged that the pharmaceutical manufacturers had failed to provide adequate warnings, and the physicians and hospital had failed to warn the patient before discharge that the medications could impair his motor skills and should not be taken with alcohol. The court first addressed the foreseeability of the plaintiff's injury. The court held that the injury was sufficiently foreseeable to the pharmaceutical manufacturers, physicians, and hospital. The court further ruled that the failure to warn of the adverse effects and interactions of the drugs could result in injury to the plaintiff or to other members of the public. The court noted that the defendants had a duty to warn, rather than a duty to control or to prevent.

The hospital argued that it could not be liable for negligence because the administration of these drugs was within the purview of the physician. The physicians were neither employed nor controlled by the hospital. The court concluded that the hospital's negligence was for failure to warn and not because the treatment was inappropriate. Hospitals plainly do far more than merely furnish an edifice for treatment. They regularly employ on a salaried basis a staff of physicians, nurses, and pharmacists...the cost for these personnel are factored into the amount that patients are charged by the hospital. It follows that hospitals must assume certain responsibility for the care and treatment of their patients.

The court concluded that if the hospital knows, or should have known, that medications administered in the hospital can have adverse effects that might impair a patient's motor skills, or if mixing those agents with foods or beverages, such as alcohol, could intensify those adverse effects, they must warn the patient.[24]

Two years later, the Illinois Supreme Court reversed the appellate court decision because the plaintiff had failed to establish the existence of a legal duty.[25] The court recognized that there was a duty to warn and that such a duty may extend to those outside the purchasing chain. That duty, however, extends only to conduct that is reasonably foreseeable. The pharmaceutical manufacturers could not control physicians or hospitals that dispensed their drugs without warnings. The court reasoned that holding a hospital responsible for the harmful acts committed by its patients would place an unreasonable burden on hospitals. Additionally, the court took notice that the state was attempting to decrease the burden on healthcare providers from overzealous plaintiffs suing for medical malpractice. The physicians did have a duty to warn; that duty, however, is to warn the patient and does not extend to unknown nonpatients in the public. Evidently, a hospital and physicians might have been liable if the driver—who was administered the Prolixin and Thorazine but not warned about their side effects or their interaction with alcohol—had pursued this case.

B. *Hand v. Krakowski*

In *Hand v. Krakowski*, the issue of whether a pharmacist has a duty to warn an alcoholic of the possible dangers of concurrent administration of psychotropic drugs was evaluated.[26] The executor of the estate of a known alcoholic brought a lawsuit. For more than six years, the employees of the defendant pharmacy had dispensed various psychotropics prescribed by the patient's physicians. The pharmacist knew that the patient was an alcoholic. In the six months preceding the patient's death, the pharmacy dispensed 728 units of psychotropic drugs, even though it was known that these agents included opiates that were contraindicated with concurrent alcohol use. The autopsy report revealed that the cause of death was pancreatitis secondary to severe hepatic cirrhosis. The hepatic cirrhosis may have resulted from concurrent use of psychotropics, opiates, pain relievers (acetaminophen), and alcohol. Alcohol abuse may have predisposed the patient to hepatic disease induced by alcohol, psychotropics, opiates, and pain relievers.

The pharmacy moved for summary judgment, and the motion was granted. The executor of the estate appealed, and the summary judgment was reversed. The court found that the pharmacist had a duty to warn the decedent of the adverse sequelae incurred when combining psychotropic drugs, including opiates, with alcohol. The court stated that "the rule of ordinary care as applied to the business of a druggist means the highest practical degree of prudence, thoughtfulness, and vigilance commensurate with the dangers involved and the consequences which may attend inattention."

The court concluded that dispensing psychotropic drugs to a known alcoholic is a breach of a pharmacist's duty of ordinary care by knowingly ignoring the danger and consequences of an alcoholic's ingestion of medications for which alcohol is known to be contraindicated. However, the court was not willing to dismiss the notion that in certain settings and with appropriate monitoring and dosing adjustments, it is plausible to administer contraindicated psychotropics to a known alcoholic. The issue in this case was whether the pharmacist breached the standard of care required, rather than the pharmacist's duty to warn the patient. Nevertheless, the pharmacist was found liable.

20.8 Selective Serotonin Reuptake Inhibitors and the Serotonin Syndrome

When the SSRIs, Prozac, Zoloft, and Paxil are combined with serotonergic agents (see Table 20.2 for a list of selected serotonergic agents), serotonin levels in the CNS can become abnormally high, which can produce the *serotonin syndrome*.[2] The serotonin syndrome is a constellation of mental status changes and nervous system and neuromuscular effects that result from an excess of serotonin. A diagnosis of serotonin syndrome can be made when three of the following effects develop in the presence of high serotonin levels: agitation, diaphoresis, diarrhea, fever, hyperreflexia, incoordination, mental status changes, myoclonus, shivering, or tremor. Other manifestations include seizures and muscle rigidity. The onset of serotonin syndrome symptoms usually takes place within minutes or hours, and so does the resolution.

Table 20.2
A List of Selected Serotonergic Categories and Agents

Increase Synthesis	Serotonin Reuptake Inhibitors	Inhibit Serotonin Metabolism	Serotonin Agonists	Increase Serotonin Release
l-tryptophan	amphetamines citalopram cocaine dextromethorphan escitalopram fluoxetine fluvoxamine meperidine paroxetine pentazocine sertraline TCAs venlafaxine	phenelzine selegiline linezolid St. John's Wort	buspirone LSD lithium mescaline Sumatriptan Rizatriptan Naratriptan Zolmitriptan	amphetamines cocaine fenfluramine mirtazapine

Management consists of gastric decontamination, activated charcoal, and supportive care, which may require ventilator support or admission to an intensive care unit. There is no antidote for the serotonin syndrome. Anecdotally, however, serotonin antagonists such as methysergide, cyproheptadine, and propranolol have been of some success.

Combinations of meperidine and the popular cough suppressant dextromethorphan—both serotonin reuptake inhibitors that can significantly increase serotonin concentrations within the neuronal synapses—can potentially produce a severe serotonin syndrome that can be deadly. Any combination of serotonergic agents or a high dose of a single serotonergic agent can predispose a client to the dangerous serotonin syndrome. Healthcare providers must counsel patients on the dangers of using over-the-counter products such as l-tryptophan with an SSRI. l-tryptophan, used for the management of depression and as a sedative hypnotic, decarboxylates into serotonin, increasing serotonin synthesis. Furthermore, the popular alternative-medicine product, St. John's wort, possesses serotonin reuptake or releasing properties and should not be administered with SSRIs.

20.9 Hepatic Cytochrome P450 Drug Interactions and Cyclic Antidepressants

The SSRIs, Prozac, Paxil, and Zoloft, are potent inhibitors of the hepatic cytochrome (CY) P450-2D6 isoenzyme system. Therefore when meperidine, a popular analgesic, is administered, an SSRI can inhibit its hepatic metabolism and cause elevated meperidine levels. Elevated meperidine concentrations can result in severe CNS depression and seizures. Additionally, both meperidine and the SSRIs may increase serotonin concentrations, increasing the risk of the serotonin syndrome. The combination of SSRIs and CY P450-2D6 substrates should be avoided to diminish the possibility of an exaggerated substrate effect and subsequent toxicity.

The SSRIs can be ranked by the strength with which they inhibit CYP450-2D6 in this order from greatest inhibition to weakest:

- Prozac
- Paxil
- Zoloft
- Celexa

Despite Zoloft's weaker inhibitory properties, it is associated with significant increases in substrate blood concentrations. Celexa and Lexapro are considered weak inhibitors of CYP450-2D6 and would be good alternatives to avoid a significant drug interaction. Drug-drug interactions can also affect several other hepatic CYP450 enzymes such as 1A2, 2C9,

2C19, and 3A4. Pharmacists must screen for antidepressant drug interactions, notify prescribers, and recommend safer alternatives that do not interact. A list of antidepressant substrates, inhibitors, and inducers may be found in Table 20.3.

20.10 Antidepressants and Herbal Agents Drug Interactions

Herbal agents such as Ginkgo, Ginseng, Kava-Kava, Licorice, Ma Huang, Saw palmetto, St. John's wort, and Valerian are usually depicted as benign since they are not prescription medications and are readily available over-the-counter to be purchased at pharmacies, health food stores, supermarkets, and even grocery stores. In fact, the FDA does not strictly regulate herbals and supplements and hence, there is no guarantee of the purity of the product and most herbals have not been thoroughly tested for drug interactions.[27-28] However, published literature has shown that herbals can mimic, increase, decrease, or antagonize the effects of prescription drugs. Herbal-drug interactions are as common as drug-drug and drug-food interactions. In a study by Taylor et al., it was found that 71 percent of patients who used herbal agents never informed their healthcare provider of such use because they were either never asked about it; did not deem it important to let their physician know about it; herbals are not drugs; or expected their physician to disapprove the use of the herbal.[29] In the same study, 15 potential drug-herbal interactions were identified in 9 patients and an astounding number of 97 theoretical potential interactions in 51 patients.

St. John's wort (*Hypericum perforatum*) is a popular herbal agent that is being marketed for multiple indications including depression, anxiety, and seasonal affective disorder.[30] It is common for patients suffering from depression to start taking St. John's wort thinking that it will complement the efficacy of the prescription medication. However, St. John's wort shares the pharmacology of SSRIs, and its concomitant use with prescription antidepressants can lead to increased serotonin levels leading to serotonin syndrome (discussed previously in this chapter). Such cases have been reported with the concomitant use of St. John's wort and sertraline and nefazodone. Lethargy and grogginess have been reported in a patient taking the herbal with paroxetine. A few isolated case reports have documented serotonin syndrome with the use of St. John's wort alone. St. John's wort may also have the ability to increase the metabolism of amitriptyline and nortriptyline potentially leading to treatment failure.[27-31]

Ginkgo (*Ginkgo biloba*) is an herbal agent marketed for the treatment of dementia, peripheral vascular diseases and tinnitus (ringing in the ears).[28] There has been one case report of an 80-year-old woman who was prescribed Ginkgo

Table 20.3
Antidepressant Substrates, Inhibitors, and Inducers of Select CYP450 Isoenzyme Systems

1A2 CYP450 Isoenzyme System		
Substrates	**Inhibitors**	**Inducers**
Amitriptyline Clomipramine Duloxetine Fluvoxamine Imipramine Mirtazapine	Fluvoxamine	Barbiturates Carbamazepine Phenytoin Rifampicin Smoking tobacco

2C9 CYP450 Isoenzyme System		
Substrates	**Inhibitors**	**Inducers**
Amitriptyline Fluoxetine Sertraline	Fluoxetine Fluvoxamine Lovastatin	Phenytoin Phenobarbital Rifampicin Secobarbital

2C19 CYP450 Isoenzyme System		
Substrates	**Inhibitors**	**Inducers**
Amitriptyline Citalopram Clomipramine Escitalopram Imipramine Sertraline	Escitalopram Fluoxetine Fluvoxamine	Barbiturates Carbamazepine Phenytoin Prednisone Rifampicin

2D6 CYP 450 Isoenzyme System		
Substrates	**Inhibitors**	**Inducers**
Citalopram Duloxetine Escitalopram Fluoxetine Fluvoxamine Mirtazapine Paroxetine Tricyclic antidepressants Venlafaxine	Antipsychotics Bupropion Cimetidine Citalopram Duloxetine Escitalopram Fluoxetine Fluvoxamine Mirtazapine Methadone Paroxetine Quinidine Ritonavir Sertraline Venlafaxine	Dexamethasone Rifampicin

3A4 CYP 450 Isoenzyme System		
Substrates	**Inhibitors**	**Inducers**
Escitalopram Imipramine Mirtazapine Nefazodone Sertraline Venlafaxine	Erythromycin Fluoxetine Fluvoxamine Grapefruit juice HIV Protease inhibitors Itraconazole Nefazodone Ritonavir Verapamil	Barbiturates Phenytoin Rifampicin St. John's wort

Sources:
Ereshefsky L et al. 2009. "The use of pharmacotherapy for depression. The importance of drug-drug interactions." *Clinical Symposia.* 59:19-26.
Lexi-Comp Online. 2010. "Selective serotonin reuptake inhibitors (SSRIs) cytochrome P450 inhibition profile." Accessed online on June 25, 2010.

and a low dose trazodone after treatment failures for the management of dementia.[32] After 3 days of taking the herbal agent and the prescription medication together, she fell into a coma. Subsequently, she was taken to the hospital where she was quickly managed with intravenous medication and awoke immediately. Ginkgo and trazodone were never restarted and 2 months later, the patient remained stable. It is hypothesized that Ginkgo may have increased the metabolism of trazodone via CYP3A4 and hence, increased the production of the antidepressant's active metabolite, a potent hypnotic agent.

Herbal-drug interactions are common and far from benign. Patients and healthcare providers should be educated on their use, toxicities, and interactions, and discussion should be encouraged in order to avoid harmful combinations.

20.11 Serzone and Liver Disease

Serzone is a second-generation, non-TCA that has been associated with severe liver disease (hepatotoxicity).[33-35] The incidence of hepatic injury associated with Serzone is 29 cases per 100,000 patient-years.[36] In 2002, the FDA required a "black box warning" concerning the hepatotoxicity risk for patients taking Serzone.[37] The manufacturer (Bristol-Myers Squibb) also sent out "Dear Doctor" letters that described several instances of liver failure—some of which were fatal or required a liver transplant—with a reported rate in the United States of one case per 250,000 to 300,000 patient-years.[38] The Canadian Adverse Drug Reaction Monitoring Program database identified 32 cases of liver injury due to Serzone, of which 81 percent were classified as severe.[33] Out of those 32 cases, 11 patients were taking only Serzone and liver injury developed in 88 percent of the cases within the first six months of therapy. Interestingly, 70 percent of the 32 cases of liver injury were women, which is consistent with the greater incidence of depression among women.[39]

Current recommendations suggest caution in prescribing Serzone to any patient taking other drugs metabolized by the hepatic cytochrome P450-3A4 isoenzyme system. This precaution is to avoid drug interaction with Serzone, which is a substrate and an inhibitor of that metabolic pathway. A warning is also issued *not* to prescribe Serzone to any patient with preexisting liver disease. In addition, it is recommended that liver enzyme tests be monitored periodically (the time to liver injury generally ranges from two weeks to six months). Patients should also be advised about the signs and symptoms of liver injury (such as nausea, vomiting, abdominal pain, and yellow-discoloration of the skin), so that the drug can be stopped if they occur, and patients can be evaluated. Serzone should be stopped in patients who experience liver enzyme elevations of more than three times the upper limit of normal.

20.12 High Blood Pressure Associated with Venlafaxine Use

Venlafaxine, a second generation, non-tricyclic antidepressant, was approved in 1994 as the first agent to inhibit both norepinephrine and serotonin. It is FDA approved for the management of generalized anxiety disorder, panic disorder with or without agorophobia (the fear of being in public places), and social phobia.[40-41] It has been observed that 0.4 to 13 percent of patients taking venlafaxine experience persistent increases in blood pressure also known as hypertension. However, the incidence of hypertension varies depending on the dose and dosage form prescribed. Venlafaxine is available as immediate release tablets and extended release tablets and capsules. The immediate release tablets are dosed at least twice daily and the extended release formulations only once daily. The incidence of hypertension with the immediate release tablets is 3 to 7 percent (at doses between 100 mg and 300 mg daily) to 13 percent (at doses of 300 mg or greater daily). The incidence of high blood pressure with the extended release formulations is much less at 0.4 to 3 percent.[40,42]

Venlafaxine-induced hypertension is a dose-dependent effect that results from its pharmacologic mechanism of action. At doses above 150 mg per day, venlafaxine increases only the concentrations of norepinephrine, a catecholamine known to increase blood pressure. In addition, the risk of hypertension while taking venlafaxine is hypothesized to occur more likely in patients who are at risk for high blood pressure (pre-hypertensives) and in those already diagnosed with hypertension than in patients with normal blood pressure (normotensives).[43] Therefore, it is vital that patients monitor their blood pressure daily while taking venlafaxine, especially with dose escalations and if they are already at risk for high blood pressure.

Khurana et al. describe the case of a 37-year-old woman who developed hypertensive crisis, a condition where blood pressure is so high that is considered a medical emergency, while taking venlafaxine 75 mg once daily.[44] After 9 days of taking the antidepressant, the patient developed blurry vision which progressed to cotton wool spots in the eyes, right arm and leg numbness and headache. Upon hospital admission, hypertensive crisis was diagnosed and all of her medications were withheld. The patient was successfully treated with intravenous medications. In this case, the patient was taking a low dose of venlafaxine; however, when the antidepressant was prescribed, the patient was already taking disulfiram for anxiety. Disulfiram has the ability to inhibit the metabolism of venlafaxine and hence, increase venlafaxine's concentrations and its potential to increase blood pressure. Physicians should be cognizant that even at low doses, venlafaxine has the ability to increase blood pressure when it is co-administered with medications that can inhibit its metabolism.

20.13 The Pharmacist's Role

Pharmacists are the healthcare professionals most qualified to help consumers make the best use of their medications. Pharmaceutical education before 2000 required a minimum of five years of education and training leading to a B.S. degree in pharmacy. For the past three years, graduating pharmacists hold entry-level doctor of pharmacy (Pharm. D.) degrees. This degree requires a minimum of two to four years of pre-pharmacy training, followed by a four-year pharmacy program. The Pharm.D. program is rigorous and specialized, and concentrates on pharmacotherapy and the application of pharmaceutical care. A number of Pharm.D. graduates choose to continue their training for an additional one to two years, then pursue either a pharmacy practice or a specialty-pharmacy residency program. Pharmacy residents are intensely trained to develop, hone, and maximize pharmacotherapy skills. They receive comprehensive, intense, individualized training in all aspects of pharmacotherapy.

Pharmacists are experts on the thousands of medications available today, how each works in the body, and the ways to use each safely. The public should be aware that the pharmacist is obligated by law to provide pharmaceutical care. Pharmaceutical care requires that the pharmacist review the client's prescribed drug regimen, intervene and adjust medication regimens as necessary, and educate the patient, with the goal of maximizing patient care to ensure a positive outcome. The pharmacist's role is vital to patient care. It is paramount that the consumer seek out an effective pharmacist willing to provide pharmaceutical care services.

20.14 The Omnibus Budget Reconciliation Act

OBRA[21] requires pharmacists in all states to ensure appropriate answers to the following questions for every prescription filled:

- Is the medication prescribed indicated?
- Does the patient have any contraindications to the medication prescribed?
- Is the dosing schedule and route of administration appropriate?
- Are there existing or potential problems with drug side effects, drug-drug interactions, drug-nutrient interactions, or adverse drug reactions?
- What recommendations can be made to minimize adverse effects while maximizing therapeutic efficacy?

For a pharmacist to maximize the positive benefit and outcome of a medication therapy, she must be a good pharmaceutical historian and take a thorough history from the client. The client must inform the pharmacist of: all adverse events experienced with any medication; any allergies; dietary regimens followed; vaccination schedules; and all medications used, including over-the-counter drugs, homeopathic agents, and home remedies.

Under the OBRA of 1990, pharmacists are also required to perform prospective and retrospective drug utilization reviews (DURs). DURs contain explicit criteria for drug indications, drug contraindications, drug interactions, adverse reaction detection, monitoring parameters, tailored drug regimens, and expected outcomes. A prospective DUR ensures an appropriate use of a drug with every prescription. A retrospective DUR studies trends and adverse outcomes to detect inappropriate prescribing patterns.

20.15 How Safe is it to Buy Prescription Medications Over the Internet?

With the proliferation of the Internet, it has become very easy for patients to buy their medications at a minimum cost online. Multiple advertisements for less expensive prescription medications are e-mailed to millions of consumers daily. But, how safe is it to buy prescription medications online?

On February 16, 2007, the FDA alerted consumers of unsafe, misrepresented drugs purchased over the Internet.[45] A number of patients who purchased, among other medications, citalopram over the Internet, received instead a product that contained haloperidol, a potent antipsychotic medication used to treat schizophrenia. Many of the patients ended up in the hospital with difficulty breathing, muscle spasms and stiffness, all of which are symptoms of haloperidol toxicity. The consumers named multiple websites where the products were purchased; however, it is difficult to identify the vendors due to the deceptive practices of many commercial outlets over the Internet.

One of the FDA's website links is devoted to warning patients about the possible dangers of buying medications over the Internet.[46] Even though there are many legitimate websites that operate legally, there are many more that offer to sell medications that have not been reviewed for safety and efficacy. In fact, some of the products sold on the illegal websites may contain too much or too little of the active ingredient or may contain dangerous ingredients. Signs of a legitimate online pharmacy include the following: located in the USA; licensed by the state board of pharmacy; a licensed pharmacist available to answer questions; requires prescription; provides contact information and allows you to talk to a person. Another way is to look for the National Association Boards of Pharmacy's Verified Internet Pharmacy Practice Sites Seal, also known as VIPPS® Seal.

20.16 In a Perfect World

The ideal scenario for a patient starting and receiving drug therapy would be for a client and pharmacist to be able to spend 15 to 30 minutes in an office-based counseling session. Today most pharmacies have a private consultation area because pharmacies that do not have them cannot provide clients with the privacy conducive to effective counseling. No client wants his health profile and medication recommendations discussed within the confines of a noisy, cluttered area, with a crowd of customers and clerks and a busy cash register. Preferably, caregivers would attend the counseling sessions to maximize patient compliance.

Failure to use the services pharmacists are trained for can be life-threatening. Having a prescription filled by a nonpharmacist health professional prevents the crucial quality checks that detect and prevent harmful drug interactions, reactions, and mistakes. Most healthcare professionals are not familiar with all the pharmacological effects of a drug, the potential side effects, or the drug's interactions. All healthcare professionals must familiarize themselves with their client's prescribed regimen and thoroughly review each drug's pharmacology. Cross-checking by pharmacists, nurses, physicians, and other healthcare professionals helps to minimize drug toxicity and to maximize the therapeutic efficacy. In addition, clients must be encouraged to choose one pharmacy for all their medications. Most clients will see several physicians concurrently, increasing the risk of drug interactions and contraindications. Patients who choose one pharmacy enable a pharmacist to maintain an accurate medication profile and to detect any potentially harmful drug combinations.

20.17 Conclusion

It is obvious that appropriate prescriptions and counseling are critical in minimizing a patient's risks of an adverse outcome. The pharmacist plays a vital role in protecting the patient and the prescriber by using her pharmacotherapy knowledge and offering appropriate counseling and monitoring a patient's therapy. It is the duty of the pharmaceutical manufacturers to provide adequate and current information to the medical community. It is the responsibility of the hospital or medical institution to ensure that its healthcare providers are knowledgeable and skilled in their disciplines and to provide the resources for them to practice safely. Almost every state mandates continuing education for physicians and pharmacists, and quality assurance ensures the upkeep of that continuing education. Finally, it is evident that when prescribing antidepressants, the SSRIs are generally a safer alternative to the TCAs.

Endnotes

1. Depression Guideline Panel. Depression in Primary Care. Vol 1: Detection and Diagnosis. Clinical Practice Guideline No. 5. Rockville, MD: Agency for Health Care Policy and Research. 1993.

2. Cohen, H., Hoffman, R.S. and Howland, M.A. 1997. "Antidepressant poisoning and treatment: a review and case illustration. J. Pharm. Pract. 10(4):249–270.

3. Murphy, J.M. et al. 2000. "A 40-year perspective on the prevalence of depression: the Stirling County study." Arch. Gen. Psychiatry. 57:209–215.

4. Bloomberg, L.P. "World's Top Selling Prescription Drugs in 1998." www.bloomberg.com.

5. Regier, D.A., Burke, J.D. and Burke, K.C. 1990. "Comorbidity of affective and anxiety disorders in NIMH epidemiologic catchmen area program." Comorbidity of Mood and Anxiety Disorders. J.D. Maser and C.R. Cloninger, Eds. Washington DC: American Psychiatric Press. 113–122.

6. Litovitz, T.L. et al. 2001. "The 2000 annual report of the American Association of Poison Control Centers toxic exposure surveillance system (TESS). Am. J. Emerg. Med. 19:337–395.

7. Nicholson, D.P. 1991. "The immediate management of overdose." Med. Clin. North Am. 67:461–498.

8. Vaillant, G.E. and Blumenthal, S.J. 1990. "Risk factors and life span development." Suicide Over the Life Cycle. S.J. Blumenthal and D.J. Kupfer, Eds. Washington, DC: American Psychiatric Press. 1–16.

9. Barbey, J.T. and Roose, S.P. 1998. "SSRI safety in overdose." J. Clin. Psychiatry 59 (suppl 15):45–48.

10. Neuman, S.M. and Borja, A. 1995. "Prozac: A question of which came first, the chicken or the egg?" in J.W. Moch, A. Borja, and J. O'Donnell, eds. Pharmacy Law: Litigating Pharmaceutical Cases. Tucson, AZ: Lawyers and Judges Publishing Co. 121–131.

11. Beasley, Jr., C.M. et al. 1991. "Fluoxetine and suicide: a meta-analysis of controlled trials of treatment of depression. B.M.J. 21:685–692.

12. "Prozac Tablets: Package Insert." 1999. Physicians' Desk Reference. 53rd ed. Montvale, NJ: Medical Economics Company. 859–863.

13. *Woulfe v. Eli Lilly & Co.*, 965 F. Supp. 1478, (ED Okla. 1997).

14. *Espinoza v. Eli Lilly & Co.*, 207 F.Supp.2d 308 (2002); Lexis 16740 Case No. 2:00-cv-256 consolidated with case no. 2:00-cv-393.

15. T. Hanson. 2009. "Takotsubo cardiomyopathy: A case study of stress induced transient left ventricular apical ballooning syndrome." The Internet Journal of Advanced Nursing Practice. 10:2.

16. Christoph, M. et al. 2010. "Broken heart syndrome: Tako Tsubo cardiomyopathy associated with an overdose of the serotonin-norepinephrine reuptake inhibitor Venlafaxine." European Neuropsychopharmacology. Article in Press. Available online 7 May 2010.

17. Bybee, K.A. et al. 2004. "Systematic review: Transient left ventricular apical ballooning: A syndrome that mimics ST-segment elevation myocardial infarction." Ann. Intern. Med.141:858-865.

18. R. Perry. 2008. "Duloxetine-induced Takotsubo Cardiomyopathy: A Case Report." College of Psychiatric and Neurologic Pharmacists Award Finalists for the 2008 Poster Abstracts. Journal of Pharmacy Practice.21:60-61.

19. *Docken v. Ciba-Geigy*, 739 P.2d 591 (Ore. Ct. App. 1987).

20. *Stebbins v. Concord Wrigley Drugs, Inc. et al.*, 416 N.W.2d 381 (Mich. App. 1987).

21. Omnibus Budget Reconciliation Act of 1990. Public Law 101–508. Section 4401. 101st Cong., 2d sess. (Nov. 5, 1990).

22. *Morgan et al. v. Wal-Mart Stores, Inc.*, 30 S.W.3d 455 (Tex. App. 2000).

23. *Penelope A. Carafelle et al. v. Brockton Oaks CVS, Inc.*, 94-0414A. LEXIS 421 (Mass. Super. 1996).

24. *Kirk v. Michael Reese Hospital*, 483 N.E.2d 906 (Ill. App. 1 Dist. 1985).

25. *Kirk v. Michael Reese Hospital* 513 N.E. 2d 387 (Ill. S.Ct. 1987).

26. *Hand v. Krakowski*, 453 NYS.2d 121 (NY App. 1982).

27. Natural Standard Research Collaboration. 2009. "Drugs & supplements: St. John's wort (Hypericum perforatum L.)." www.nlm.nih.gov/medlineplus/druginfo/natural/patient-stjohnswort.html Accessed on March 29, 2012.

28. Wood AJJ. 2002. "Herbal Remedies." N Engl J Med. 347:2046-2056.

29. Taylor DMcD et al. 2006. "Potential interactions between prescription drugs and complementary and alternative medicines among patients in the emergency department." Pharmacotherapy. 26:634-640.

30. "St. John's Wort" Drug monograph. 2010. Micromedex(R) 2.0. Thompson Reuters.

31. University of Michigan Health System Drug Information Service. 2010. "Selected herb-drug interactions." www-personal.umich.edu/~mshlafer/Lectures/herb-drug.pdf Accessed on March 29, 2012.

32. Galluzzi S et al. 2000. "Coma in a patient with Alzheimer's disease taking low dose trazodone and gingko biloba." Letter to the Editor. J Neurol Neurosurg Psychiatry. 68:679-680.

33. Novak, D. and Lewis, J.H. 2003. "Drug-induced liver disease." Curr. Opin. Gastroenterol. 19:203–215.

34. Health Canada. July 1999. "Hepatotoxicity associated with Nefazodone (serzone)." Can. Med. Assoc. J. 161(1):74–75.

35. Aranda–Michel, J. et al. 1999. "Nefazodone-induced liver failure: report of three cases. Ann. Intern. Med. 130(4):285–288.

36. Carvajal, G.P. et al. 2002. "Hepatotoxicity associated with the new antidepressants." J. Clin. Psychiatry. 63:135–137.

37. Katz, R. Letter to Bristol Myers Squibb Company re: Black box warning required for Serzone. NDA 20-152/S-028. Rockville, MD: FDA. (Dec. 7, 2001).

38. Jody, D.M. Letter to Health Care Professional re: Important drug warning including black box information. Princeton, NJ: Bristol Myers-Squibb Company. (June 2001).

39. Stewart, D.E. 2002. "Hepatic adverse reactions associated with nefazodone." Can. J. Psychiatry. 47:375–377.

40. Cole, S. et al. 2008. "Depression." In Feldman and Christensen JF editors. Behavioral Medicine in Primary Care: A Practice Guide. 3rd ed. McGraw-Hill Medical Companies. 199-226.

41. "Effexor XR(R) (venlafaxine hydrochloride) extended release capsules: Package Insert." 2009. Wyeth Pharmaceuticals Inc. Philadelphia, PA.

42. Thase ME et al. 1998. "Effects of venlafaxine on blood pressure: a meta-analyis of original data from 3744 depressed patients." J Clin Psychiatry. 59:502-508.

43. Feighner JP et al. 1995. "Cardiovascular safety in depressed patients: focus on venlafaxine." J Clin Psychiatry. 56:574-579.

44. Khurana R et al. 2003. "Hypertensive crisis associated with venlafaxine." Letter to the Editor. Am J Med. 115:676.

45. U.S. Food and Drug Administration (FDA). 2007. www.fda.gov/NewsEvents/Newsroom/PressAnnouncements/2007/ucm108846.htm Accessed on March 29, 2012.

46. U.S. Food and Drug Administration. 2010. "The possible dangers of buying medicines over the Internet." FDA Consumer Information. March 1–3.

Chapter 21

Drugs for Asthma, Allergies, and Anaphylaxis: Harm from Use, Misuse, and Non-Use

Constantine John Falliers, M.D.

21.1 Introduction: Care and Harm

> Oh, what damage
> Can the brain (truly a carnage)
> Quickly cause…[1]

According to a thoughtful Southern Californian clinical allergist, "life is a drug-deficient state." However, while drugs for allergic and most other disorders cannot be considered "replacement therapy," some drugs, such as epinephrine and cortisol, are normal physiologic hormones. Medication is basically intended to control symptoms and to allow adequate life function. There are patients, however, who still prefer some persistent symptoms, such as stuffy nose or sneezing, to the risk of side effects from drugs. Therapeutic outcomes are ultimately determined by the brain (rather than by the properties of any specific pharmaceutical compounds), as they depend on the perception of need and a personal treatment choice.

The increasing prevalence of acute and chronic illnesses attributed to allergies[2,3] and asthma has precipitated[4,5] the widespread use of all kinds of drugs[6]—including drugs that are prescribed, over-the-counter (OTC) or (not infrequently) shared with others similarly afflicted. The cost may indeed represent a socioeconomic "injury." At this point, neither the pharmaceutical industry nor the healthcare practitioners can adequately monitor, control, or prevent possible adverse reactions[7] from the use, misuse, or, at times, the failure to use necessary medications for the respiratory, dermatological, or other systemic manifestations attributable to allergy.[8,9] Nevertheless, the recognition of possible or actual adverse reactions to medication—some common and predictable and others extraordinary and unexpected—continues to be the duty of the providers, as well as of the consumers of pharmaceutical healthcare.[10] Errors, regrettably, are not uncommon. In fact, a recent survey of 36 healthcare facilities

351

detected a 19 percent incidence of incorrect therapy (due to wrong dose in 3 percent of the cases and timing in 8 percent).[11]

Although self-preservation and care are natural behavior patterns, "the belief that it is a personal duty to take care of oneself is only one of several conceptions of individual existence."[12] No matter how attuned the prescribing doctor is to the full meaning and implications of "care,"[12] it is the patients who decide what information (or promotional messages) to follow and how to employ symptomatic and/or preventive medication, based on the demands of their individual lifestyles and their responses to their illness.[10] The often unexpected variability between objective airway function measurements and self-perceptions of ventilatory impairment[13] is reflected in the marked inconsistencies in self-care (see Section 21.2 below). Physically active persons may rush for medication (overuse of inhalers or even oral corticosteroids) to keep breathing function from dropping by even 15 percent (self-measurements of expiratory flow have now become rather common among asthmatics[14]), while others with peak expiratory flow rates (PEFR) not much better than 50 percent of predicted remain inactive and take no medication for fear of adverse effects. The unwelcome consequences of excessive dependence on medication[15] and of its opposite—the undue fear of drugs—can be defined, respectively, as either *pharmacophilia* or *pharmophobia*.[16] In this respect, the role of "pharmacist care" for patients with "reactive airways disease" (another term for asthma) is not limited to dispensing prescriptions, and must include guidance and individual monitoring. This role has been assessed again recently in controlled multi-center studies.[17]

The fact that the use of medication is often an individual choice does not diminish the importance of shared responsibility. Consumers must be told and convinced that medications, essential as they may be, can cause harm. Any users of the spectrum of the currently available drugs should also be made aware that harm might involve not only themselves, but others as well.

A. Young Boy Attacks Brother After Taking Theophylline

A preadolescent boy was given his first full doses of oral theophylline for asthma. In uncontrollable anger during a minor dispute with his brother, he grabbed a knife and attacked him. He was forcibly restrained and no more theophylline was given. This was reported to the author after the family moved from Texas to Colorado for further care.

B. Nurse Disrupts Home and Work with Steroid Psychosis

A practicing registered nurse received a relatively high dose of oral prednisone for persistent asthma. Her changed behavior puzzled her family and her co-workers. Doctors diagnosed her with steroid-induced psychosis. Her condition threatened to destabilize both home and work, until psychiatric in-patient care allowed a cautious medication withdrawal. A few years later, this nurse obtained her Master's degree and moved to Colorado, where the author met her professionally.

More broadly, harm from legitimate drugs can affect the entire environmental and human ecosystem. Metered-dose aerosol preparations for asthma are gradually switching from chlorofluorocarbon (CFC) propellants to hydrofluoroalkanes (HFA) to diminish the ozone-layer-depleting effect of the former.[18] Drugs—particularly antibiotics and hormones excreted in the urine—have been found to contaminate water systems[19] and injure animal and plant life, ultimately affecting humans too. It can be expected that other medicinal substances may follow the same route through sewage, so harm can go beyond the individual consumer and will only be reduced or avoided if care becomes the concern of everyone. Returning to the introductory quotation, we may refer again to the versatile collection of "icon versions and eye conversions"[1] for which this author had the privilege (as KI Fallieros, aka CJ Falliers) of contributing the Foreword and Forewarning: *"Though self-service is not rare....We must time and effort spare / to serve others, if we dare."*

21.2 Information, Interpretations, Attitudes

The proliferation of information on allergy and asthma—a verifiable data-flood—in the form of printed, recorded, electronic, and live educational services, has paralleled the increase in the incidence and, at times, the severity of respiratory and other illnesses attributed to hypersensitivity or "altered reactivity" (the original 1906 definition of allergy). A number of popular publications, such as the 1977 *People's Pharmacy* and the subsequent *Allergy Self Help Book*,[20] informed, but also, at times, frightened. What is needed is an enlightened guide, not only about drugs, but also about how to select important messages that one can trust and must retain,[21,22] including a reliable method for an objective assessment of the medical problem and its management.[23] Serious overtreatment and undertreatment can result from an incorrect medical estimate of respiratory distress, such as is associated with asthma.[24,25]

As much as the general public expects health maintenance not to be primarily dependent on medication, in recent years media exposure seemed to promote the use of pharmaceutical products as the solution for allergies and other major medical problems.[21] Ultimately, it is the professional healthcare provider who must explain the purpose and the differences among antihistamines, decongestants, "sinus" remedies, and even breathing aids (not to mention the multiplicity of topical—nasal, ophthalmic, and dermal—preparations) and why, for instance, skin rashes or nasal congestion can get worse, not despite treatment, but because of it.

Particularly critical is the recognition and interpretation of product labels. Medications that contain a sulfonamide, a penicillin congener, theophylline, or a sedating antihistamine cannot always be clearly identified. The cases summarized below were included in a recent presentation at a national medical meeting.[5]

A. Life-Threatening Sulfonamide Reaction After Pediamycin

A six-year-old girl was taken to the emergency department of a small Midwestern hospital for acute respiratory symptoms and fever. Her medical records (she had been in that hospital before) clearly noted what the parents also knew—that she was allergic to sulfa. The doctor on duty, who had never seen the child before, diagnosed a respiratory infection and gave samples from the medical cabinet of a suspension labeled Pediamycin. Neither he, nor the parents, nor the nurse recognized that the medication was a combination of erythromycin and sulfisoxazole (the product has not been listed in later editions of the *Physicians' Desk Reference*, but other similar combinations are still available). Because these were free medical samples, no pharmacist was involved.[26] Soon after the first dose at home, the child developed mucosal and skin lesions later diagnosed as manifestations of the Stevens-Johnson syndrome. Besides the oral and ophthalmic lesions, she suffered a marked esophageal stricture that required tube feeding for more than six months. It took several years for the youngster to resume partially normal age-appropriate activities. Both the physician and the hospital were considered negligent and were sued for damages. The author received detailed medical records and photographs of the acute phase of the little girl's face and body and supported the claim. (The author later learned that the claim was satisfactorily settled for the family, although their pain and suffering was hard to forget.)

Current reality makes it practically essential that an allergist (generalists are often too busy)—someone other than the dispensing pharmacists—ought to be involved in coordinating the multiple exposures of all ages of consumers[8,9,27] to prescription drugs, OTC drugs, and "natural" herbal remedies. Awareness of each patient's attitudes toward "drugs" will be needed to determine choices of management and to anticipate the degree of compliance. But when it comes to emergency situations, only the alertness of the physician—combined with the thoroughness of the medical (now commonly electronic) records—will determine a favorable outcome.

B. Sudden Death after Intravenous Primaxin

A 44-year-old woman who suffered persistent upper abdominal pain after horseback riding, had a difficult and not adequately justified gastroduodenoscopy. This procedure caused acute pancreatitis, which resulted in extremely high blood-glucose levels and markedly abnormal serum electrolytes. Though "allergy to penicillin" was clearly marked on her chart, she received an intravenous bolus dose of the beta-lactam antibiotic Primaxin (imipenem with cilastatin). Despite her serious infection and metabolic abnormalities, she was not in an intensive-care unit (ICU) and was only checked intermittently. A second dose of Primaxin was given and, about two hours later, this woman was found dead in her hospital bed. That was attributed to the antibiotic, though no rash was detected, and neither blood pressure nor cardiographic monitoring prior to her death were recorded. As a possibly avoidable and poorly managed anaphylactic death, the case went to trial in a small town near Saint Louis, and the author was asked to be an expert witness.

C. Fatal Anaphylactic Shock after Multiple Fire Ant Bites

The use of the Internet has been advocated as a way to improve patient care and understanding.[10] However, no electronic or remote source information (including the Internet or the telephone) can be a substitute for personal communications and judicious decision-making. The next case is an example of regrettable misinformation and misjudgment resulting in a fatality.

A 43-year-old Florida woman with a history of repeated reactions to fire ant (*Solenopsis geminate*) bites was bitten many times on her legs, around the ankles. A medical doctor from her new health plan, who did not know the patient, advised Benadryl over the telephone. The husband went to a drugstore to buy the drug. Returning home, he found his wife unconscious on the bathroom floor. Transferred by ambulance to the hospital, she remained in a coma and died there about a month later, from what was considered an irreversible anoxic encephalopathy. The author was called to testify and to discuss the risks of unrecognized severe allergic reactions and the medical standards of care for systemic anaphylaxis.

D. Blood Clots and Amputation after EACA for Angioedema

The human organism is certainly more complex than the most sophisticated machinery. The difference is that humans can rely on self-service and self-healing. That is where reliable guidance and appropriate warning become crucial.[26,28] But there are also cases of apparent self-destruction. In the following case, the author testified on behalf of the defending physician who had saved a life, though not without harm. He was acquitted.

A 62-year-old woman in Georgia, with a history of hereditary angioneurotic edema associated with C-1 esterase deficiency, was seen in the emergency department (ED) of a large hospital for severe swelling of her tongue that interfered with air exchange. No laryngeal edema or urticaria was noted. She was treated with subcutaneous epinephrine and intravenous (IV) diphenhydramine, followed by methylprednisolone sodium succinate (SoluMedrol) and famotidine (Pepcid). She improved only slightly and then received aminocaproic acid (EACA), a plasmin activator inhibitor. She had also been concomitantly on chemotherapy for lymphatic leukemia. Six years earlier, she had an aortofemoral graft, which had left her with a residual stenosis. Within hours after the ED treatment, she showed signs of disseminated intravascular coagulation and was transferred to the operating room where, despite anticoagulants and several thrombectomies, she had to have her right leg amputated. The thromboses were blamed on the EACA (which may have saved her life), but other considerations, such as the femoral grafts and her leukemia, helped to exonerate the defendant hospital and medical staff.

This case shows the importance and the limits of clinical data from each patient's history and how medical interventions may be interpreted differently, with sometimes unpredictable results.

21.3 Vehicles, Propellants, and Other "Inert" Ingredients

Allergists (and most primary-care physicians) must be well-acquainted with adverse patient reactions not attributed to drugs, but to so-called "inert" (i.e., therapeutically inactive) ingredients as well. Food colors and preservatives contaminate pharmaceutical products. Familiar are the cases of persons taking, for example, a cough syrup or an antibiotic, and getting worse, or developing abdominal symptoms or a generalized skin eruption caused by substances such as the dye

tartrazine or yellow #5. That particular food dye has gradually been removed from a number of anti-allergic preparations that were coated with it or had it included in liquid form. For instance, women taking hormonal-replacement therapy reported that their recurring hives subsided after the yellow tablet of one dosage form of Premarin was replaced by two half-strength tablets without the yellow dye.

The purpose of this section is not a detailed discussion of the diverse allergic reactions to ingested chemicals, but to focus on systemic and topical reactions to common asthma treatments.

Although specific reference to propellants such as the CFC and HFA is not to be found in standard allergy or clinical pharmacology texts, randomly selected patients with asthma, in a double-blind, controlled trial of inhalations of albuterol propelled either by freon or HFA showed comparable beneficial responses over a 12-week period.[29] While individual patients have been noted to prefer CFC (presumably because of a more distinct pressure effect), the possible adverse effects of fluorocarbon aerosols' proponents to the environment—that is, harm to others (see Section 21.1)—are well-recognized. More direct injury to the airways of patients receiving aerosol inhalation therapy on a regular basis have been considered,[30] but have still not been adequately documented.

Another possible (but relatively transient) undesirable effect of certain metered-dose inhalers, or MDIs, may be due to the oleic acid they contain to facilitate valve delivery of larger molecular weight compounds, such as corticosteroids. In one study, MDIs caused bronchial irritation and cough severe enough to induce some patients to discontinue their much-needed treatment.[31] The possible problems with propellants (and with some patients' ability to coordinate actuation and inhalation of the aerosol) may be avoided by the use of the newer dry powder single-dose disks. The lactose powder they contain may conceivably cause adverse reactions among sensitive patients, but no significant problems—other that some pharyngeal irritation and reflex cough—have been reported.

21.4 Adrenergic Agonists

Soon after adrenaline (also known by its trade name, Adrenalin, or—from the Greek—epinephrine) was first identified in 1901, physicians began to use it to treat asthma[32] and related conditions. While both epinephrine and cortisol (see Section 21.9) are endogenous physiologic hormones, their therapeutic applications are based on their pharmacologic properties and do not represent a treatment for deficiency (see Section 21.1), unless an alteration of individual stress-response mechanisms can account for their need. Adverse effects, likewise, are conditioned by individual susceptibility, except when they can be blamed on significant overdoses. It may be surprising that intelligent and talented persons may misjudge their medical needs (and also persuade sympathetic physicians that they are treating themselves appropriately) while they in fact alternate between under- and over-treatment with self-administration of adrenergic aerosols and adrenaline injections.[15]

Therapeutic compounds of adrenergic agonists are available for oral (ephedrine, in the form of the Chinese herb ma huang, has been used for over 2,000 years), inhalational, and parenteral administration.

For more than two generations, patients relied on oral combination compounds of ephedrine and theophylline with a sedative (phenobarbital or hydroxyzine) added to counteract some of the CNS-stimulating effects of these drugs. Interestingly, long after new compounds became available, some patients sought their customary relief from such (by that time) over-the-counter (OTC) compounds, seldom complaining of side effects, or perhaps even welcoming the associated "high" mental state.

Some early inhalational aerosolized preparations, such as the one containing racemic epinephrine, also went OTC, but have been known to cause considerable neuropsychiatric and cardiovascular problems.[33] At times, patients have arrived in the emergency department with serious tachycardia, but failed to inform the medical staff that they had been overusing a sympathomimetic OTC inhaler. Many of these cases were not managed quite appropriately.

A bevy of deaths in the 1960s and 1970s was attributed to patients' overuse of newer adrenergic compounds, such as isoproterenol[34] and fenoterol. The culprit was identified as reliance on patients' self-administration, which, apparently, led to overuse (the more an inhaler was used, the less it seemed to work). The phenomenon was so common that it was dubbed an "epidemic."[16,35,36] When better public information and medical controls were introduced, the fatalities seemed to become infrequent. Later on, the recognition of distinct types of adrenergic cellular receptors and of the variable responses in target organs led to the synthesis and clinical application of presumably safer selective beta-2 adrenergic agonists for asthma.

The characteristic pathway of beta-2 adrenoreceptor signaling involves the activation of G-protein-coupled receptors, with an increased production of cyclic adenosine monophosphate (cAMP). Receptor desensitization and down regulation can result in diminished cellular responses to endogenous or exogenous adrenergic agonists.[37] Interference with glucocorticoid receptor regulation[38] has a similar effect. The life-threatening development of epinephrine-re-sistant status asthmaticus[24] and of "near fatal asthma"[39] have been attributed to such receptor desensitization processes, which may be corrected or prevented with the appropriate use of corticosteroids.

The loss of adrenergic reactivity, defined as tachyphylaxis, can be a serious adverse consequence of the chronic or the frequently repeated use of adrenergic agonists, which may or may not spare the airways.[32,40] Hypoxemia increases the risk of adrenergic unresponsiveness, which can, in turn, aggravate the hypoxic state to the point of ventilatory failure (a vicious circle). Low oxygen saturation is also associated with a higher risk for serious cardiovascular adverse effects. Besides tachycardia (more common among infrequent users), acute arrhythmias, angina, and myocardial infarction have all been associated with the administration of adrenergic bronchodilators, in excessive and, at times, in ordinary doses.[32] The lowering of serum potassium (hypokalemia) caused by adrenergic agonists and also aggravated by hypoxia, may be contributing to their cardiac toxicity. An individual "low threshold" may be an additional predisposing factor and these cardiovascular reactions can be amplified by theophylline.[32] The hypoglycemic effect of adrenergic stimulants is primarily a potential problem in diabetes. Tremor and other neuromuscular adverse effects, more common with orally ingested compounds, can be disabling for certain occupational groups.

Chronic dependence on inhaled adrenergic bronchodilators has also been reported to have the opposite of a beneficial effect, by increasing airway reactivity and topical inflammatory changes associated with mast cell degranulation. Clinically this has been called "paradoxical," because it is the opposite of the expected bronchodilation. Continuous use of short-acting adrenergic bronchodilators for asthma may, in fact, worsen the disease and aggravate the characteristic bronchial hyperreactivity, an adverse effect not associated with the maintenance daily use of the long-acting compounds.[41] The possible advantages of the recently introduced enantiomers, such as levalbuterol for asthma, are still under investigation.[42]

Less-selective adrenergic drugs with both alpha- and beta-agonist activity may be indicated and can, in fact, be lifesaving for acute respiratory and systemic allergic and anaphylactic reactions, when vasoconstriction is a further therapeutic goal to alleviate mucosal edema and systemic hypotension. Epinephrine in a portable form is dispensed in "kits" (Ana-kits). The main concern about adverse reactions is lack of patient compliance, or a poorly preserved and deteriorated product in which metabolic alterations (such as adrenochrome, possibly) may cause serious cardiovascular and, at times, even psychotic reactions. The widely consumed OTC vasoconstrictor decongestants, which are commonly added to the popular new non-sedating antihistamines compounds (marked with the suffix "D"), may also produce broader sympathomimetic stimulation. Their effect is mediated by the activation of B-1 adrenergic receptors in venous erectile vessels. But B-2-mediated contraction of arterioles may cause mucosal damage by impairing circulation and nutrition. Continuous daily use of sympathomimetic nasal-decongestant sprays frequently causes rhinitis medicamentosa and persistent nasal symptoms that can only subside when such treatment is stopped. Additionally, while they produce a desirable vasoconstriction in the upper airways, the decongestants may also increase systemic and, possibly, pulmonary arterial tension. However, the side effects of the widely used pseudoephedrine (not a "true" ephedrine) are not as serious as those of the now-discontinued phenylpropanolamine. With the exception of a pediatric case pertaining to the incorrect use of the then-available Tussionex antitussive compound (around 1973), the author has not personally encountered any of the reported sometimes-fatal cardiovascular events caused by the misuse of this sympathomimetic amine as a dietary aid. The fairly common (but mostly reversible and relatively innocuous) undesirable effects of the "decongestant" adrenergic drugs, whether administered orally or in nasal and ophthalmic topical preparations, cannot be considered an "injury" and do not need further consideration in this section.

The composition of available adrenergic drugs is less the cause for confusion and misuse than is their timing.[43,44] Slow-acting compounds may lead to disastrous (even fatal) consequences when they are substituted for indicated, rapidly effective anti-asthmatic drugs. For example, there have been many reports of patients dying because of their reliance on the useful (but long-acting/maintenance) bronchodilator aerosol of salmeterol xinafoate when their progressive ventilatory impairment required quick relief with a fast-acting preparation. This has occurred despite headlines in the lay media, and has led to the development of an appropriate warning (in bold capital letters) in the *Physician's Desk Reference* (PDR) and on package inserts.

The following cases are from the author's files as an expert witness. They demonstrate the results of poor judgment concerning timing[11] and failure to recognize the need for immediately effective treatment.

A. Anaphylactic Death in a Medical Office

A 26-year-old lawyer collapsed during allergy skin testing in an allergist's office. The patient gasped for breath, but only faint wheezing was audible on auscultation of the lungs. The allergist could not obtain his blood pressure, and adminis-

tered injections of a slow-acting epinephrine suspension (Susphrine, the only preparation the doctor commonly used) and dexamethasone intramuscularly, but the patient showed no response, forcing the physician to call an ambulance. The patient was pronounced dead on the way to the hospital. The doctor was sued for causing the death with his intradermal tests (though only some two-plus reactions were noted), but that claim was disproved when postmortem gastric analysis turned out positive for peanut antigen. The patient was known to have had anaphylactic reactions to peanuts in the past. In this case, the patient had eaten at a restaurant, where a knife that had been used to prepare a peanut-butter sandwich was used again to butter his sandwich. The substandard (in this author's opinion) handling of the anaphylactic emergency was not included in the litigation, and so the author was able to defend the doctor. Regardless, he might have handled the emergency more effectively.

B. Death from Asthma in the Emergency Room

A 28-year-old South Florida woman with perennial asthma had been to her local hospital's emergency department ten times in six months. Her condition seemed to be under inadequate control. She came back again one evening after having used her albuterol inhaler more than every two to three hours all day, with diminishing results. She had consistently resisted taking steroids on the advice of her psychotherapist, who had warned her that these drugs might cause a psychotic reaction. In the ED, she persistently asked for an injection of epinephrine, which had always helped in the past, but the doctor on duty insisted (perhaps relying on some new medical reports) that additional respiratory therapy with albuterol should be similarly effective. When there was no change, and the patient still struggled for breath, she asked again for a "shot." Instead, the ED physician ordered more inhalation therapy with albuterol. Therapy was again initiated, and the doctor left to see a car accident victim in another room. About 10 or 15 minutes later, he returned to the patient's room, only to find her dead. He and the hospital were sued for underestimating the severity of the patient's asthma[39,45] and for refusing to administer a bronchodilator by injection to a patient who had obviously failed to get any relief from inhaled albuterol after frequent repeated use.

C. Death from Asthma after Leaving the Doctor's Office

Another instance of miscommunication and misjudgment concerning severe asthma involved a 49-year-old mechanic who, on a Saturday morning, was taken by his female companion to a medical clinic in their small mountain town in

Colorado. He had had an exacerbation of his chronic asthma, possibly after a "cold," and had used his bronchodilator nebulizer every two to three hours all night, without much benefit. At the clinic, the doctor ordered another bronchodilator treatment with inhalations of albuterol (despite the obvious lack of previous efficacy). When asthmatic dyspnea persisted and oxygen saturation remained low (84 percent), the patient was given (supposedly for faster action) an intramuscular injection of DepoMedrol, a delayed-action preparation (see Section 21.9). He was then advised to go to an oxygen-supply store for continuing treatment at home. But when the couple arrived at the oxygen-supply store that Saturday afternoon, they found it closed. The asthma was getting even worse, and the couple rushed to the nearest emergency facility. Before they reached the hospital, however, the patient collapsed on his car seat and lost consciousness. He remained comatose with what was diagnosed as anoxic brain damage, and died in an extended-care facility three weeks later.

21.5 Methylxanthines

The widespread popularity of the methylxanthine bronchodilator drug theophylline was summarized in an earlier edition of this book[46] with the statement that "theophylline is the most widely used medication for chronic asthma." In truth, the drug ruled the market for over 25 years. By the late 1990s, however, prescriptions for the products of "over 30 manufacturers"[46] began to decline. At the time of this writing, most preparations of theophylline have been withdrawn from the market. Curiously (the pattern of individual preferences is considered in Sections 21.1 and 21.2), the unavailability of some of these has distressed some chronic sufferers, who seemed to prefer specific drugs and insisted on avoiding substitutes. The rise and fall in the applications of methylxanthines for asthma ought to prompt clinicians to develop independent, objective judgment, uninfluenced by promotional messages. One wonders whether the apparent current enthusiasm for anti-inflammatory corticosteroids in this field will be followed by similar drop-off in usage (see Section 21.9).

Methylxanthines for asthma were introduced in 1921 with a study of a prominent xanthine called caffeine.[47] In various forms, methylxanthines became valuable therapeutic adjuncts for nearly 50 years. Eventually, their mode of action was attributed to their ability to inhibit the breakdown of adenosine monophosphate (cyclic AMP) or adenosine cellular receptors. When new, long-acting preparations became available, they were vigorously promoted with advertising and generous supplies of physicians' samples. A series of medical articles and lectures stressed the significance of theophylline kinetics and the need for blood-level monitoring. On the average, doses of 800–1,600 mg/day were considered necessary, with first-order pharmacokinetics, to attain the recommended therapeutic "window" of 10–20 m/ml. The reports also extolled or condemned particular commercial products for ensuring or failing to sustain optimal therapeutic blood levels. Practitioners reacted to such scientific and commercial messages not only by enthusiastically prescribing their favorite compound, but, in many cases, by also acquiring the equipment to measure blood levels, a practice that proved to be profitable both for healthcare practitioners and for clinical testing laboratories. Only gradually did the limited therapeutic applications, the considerable adverse effects, and the unpredictability of individual responses become more widely recognized. The current expanding promotion of corticosteroids (see Section 21.9) may have helped displace theophylline from its primary position for the management of asthma (a role it should never have attained in the first place).[48]

The author was one of the few specialists who relied only infrequently on blood-level theophylline assays. Clinical judgment has always seemed more dependable (and more economical). Several times, the author saw patients with serum levels no higher than 7 m/ml, who—after being strongly pressured by their physicians to increase their daily intake—simply changed doctors (because even at that level, theophylline was associated with significant neuromuscular, cardiovascular, and/or gastrointestinal disturbances). There were also some patients who had significant breathing difficulties when their theophylline levels were allowed to drop below 20 m/ml. These patients usually only felt comfortable with levels at 25 m/ml or above, and they seemed to tolerate these higher levels well. The relatively common adverse effects of theophylline—nervousness, headaches, insomnia, palpitations, gastric irritation, and cardiac arrhythmias—have often been aggravated when adrenergic agonists were administered concomitantly (see Section 21.4). Combinations with other drugs, fever, and varying individual susceptibility are factors that can influence the outcome by modifying theophylline kinetics. It may be appropriate to quote a statement the author made over 25 years ago: "Knowledge of theophylline kinetics cannot be consistently correlated with better patient care" as "patients developed an intense dislike both for the medication and for the physician who prescribed it."[48]

In contrast, the rationale for phosphodiesterase inhibitors in the treatment of asthma—reversible obstructive airways disease, or ROAD—has remained valid. New chemical compounds without the side effects of theophylline are currently undergoing controlled clinical trials. If these are successful, a welcome alternative to adrenergic and corticosteroid therapy (see Sections 21.4 and 21.9) may become available.

A. Convulsive Seizure from Intravenous Aminophylline

One instance of extraordinary aggressive anger related to theophylline was cited in Section 21.1.A as an example of harm to others. Here is another: A 48-year-old woman had been in intensive care in a suburban Denver hospital for severe asthma and had failed to improve, despite intensive therapy with adrenergic bronchodilators and corticosteroids in doses above the maximum recommended. Her family was visiting when physicians began an intravenous infusion of aminophylline. Less than 30 minutes later, someone had to call the nurse in charge, because the patient had developed an acute convulsive reaction. The aminophylline dosage was adjusted, and the next day the author was called for consultation. Relief was obtained with inhalations of the anticholinergic drug atropine sulfate (see Section 21.8), which, at that time, was available only in a solution administered through a pressure nebulizer. No permanent neurological sequelae were noted.

B. Permanent Brain Damage from Double Theophylline Doses

An eight-year-old boy was taken to the family pediatrician in a large city one Friday for severe, persistent asthma. The family was given a prescription for a theophylline suspension. The next day, the child was not any better and the family contacted the on-call pediatrician. He called in a prescription to the pharmacy for a different theophylline preparation, not realizing that the child was already taking a similar drug. The different brand names prevented the parents from realizing that there was duplication, so they continued giving their child both drugs in high doses. The boy suffered a comatose seizure-like episode the same night and was subsequently diagnosed with a resultant permanent neurological convulsive disorder.

More extensive legal documents pertaining to theophylline-related injuries were included in an earlier edition of this book.[49]

21.6 Mast-Cell Stabilizers and Anti-IgE

For the last two or three decades, the inability to avoid or suppress the development of allergic diseases has directed investigational interest and therapeutic efforts towards the possible blockade of specific steps known to be involved in the sequence of clinical manifestations. After a specific immunoglobulin (IgE—identified in 1966-67 by K. and

T. Ishizaka in Denver, and dubbed "E" for erythema) was found to be accountable for mast-cell activation and for experimental and clinical allergic reactions, pharmacologic substances were developed: to interfere with IgE binding to sensitized cells, and to disrupt the antigen-antibody reactions that lead to chemical mediator release.

It was difficult to apply a classic risk-benefit formula to clinical studies and broader therapeutic applications of IgE, because the effects of treatment were often considerably delayed. Although physicians did not observe any immediate adverse effects or harm, the interference with physiologic defense mechanisms continued to raise logical questions about undesirable long-term consequences. (For example, might inflammation play a useful role in sustaining the functional integrity of a living organism?)

Cromolyn sodium—also called disodium cromoglycate[50]—possessed no direct anti-mediator or anti-inflammatory properties. Its anti-allergic effects were thought to be due to the stabilization of sensitized mast cells and the inhibition of mediator release that follows their activation. Except for rare cases of systemic eosinophilia/eosinophilic pneumonia, no undesirable side effects have been observed—even after long-term bronchial inhalational or topical nasal or ophthalmic use. Despite the few adverse effects, the drug was at a clinical disadvantage because of its inconsistent therapeutic results. So despite the initial enthusiasm, cromolyn sodium has not remained a part of the standard anti-asthmatic and anti-allergic armamentarium: neither has its later-introduced derivative, nedocromil, which is now available only as a 2 percent ophthalmic solution. Strictly speaking, the main harm from the clinical use of these compounds might have been attributable to the neglect of other more effective (although perhaps less safe) treatments.

Current therapeutic approaches for asthma have included strategies for blocking IgE, which can be achieved with a recombinant, humanized monoclonal antibody against IgE. Similar strategies have been employed in the development of therapies designed to prevent anaphylaxis from food allergy (such as allergy to peanuts, for example). With a series of regular injections of the fraction of the IgE molecule that binds to the cellular receptor for sensitizing IgE antibodies, this treatment aims to prevent the pathogenic cascade of allergy.[51] The inconvenience and cost of the necessary series of (at least monthly) injections—as well as the still-uncertain role of IgE antibodies in the majority of patients with asthma—may not be the only negative aspects of this still-experimental modality. As pointed out earlier, interference with physiologic mechanisms may be found to lead to injury and harm not easily detectable at the early stages of therapy. It will be regrettable if some decade or two from now the potential risks of the newer experimental therapies become recognized.

21.7 Histamine and Leukotriene Antagonists

The identification of histamine and certain leukotrienes (to a lesser extent bradykinine too) as messengers responsible for allergic inflammatory processes has led to the development of a succession of antihistaminic (mainly anti-H-1) drugs and, more recently, antileukotrienes—the former mainly for upper respiratory, and the latter against the inflammatory edema and the bronchoconstriction of asthma. For dermatologic problems such as urticaria and angioedema, a combination of H-1 and H-2 antihistamines was often found more effective. Until the advent of the second generation of the relatively non-sedating antihistamines, the main concern about adverse effects of these drugs was suppression of CNS function. That danger was partly due to the relatively low cost of the standard compounds, as well as to their availability without medical prescription as single-entity drugs or in combinations (often not easily identified in "cold," "sinus," and cough remedies).

The author observed the following case as a bystander; there was no legal follow-up involving litigation.

A 21-year-old female student—new to the city of Denver—had an acute upper-respiratory infection (a "cold"), for which she was taking frequent doses of an OTC cough elixir containing diphenhydramine. She went through a red light in her compact car and was hit by another car from the right side. A passenger in her car suffered minor injuries. Upon an on-scene examination, she was found to have a fever, be congested, and feeling rather "drowsy" from her medication.

The new generation of prescribed antihistamines (one of them, loratadine, recently became available OTC) have not been known to cause significant harm.[52–54] Still some patients claim that they "cannot take" (possibly due to CNS effects) one particular formulation, and readily choose another—without any consistent preference patterns. The relatively minor side effects of ordinary doses of loratadine, desloratadine, fexofenadine, and cetirizine include somnolence, fatigue, dry mouth, and others. They are listed in the *PDR* and on package inserts, as required. The serious and potentially fatal cardiac arrhythmias and conduction disorders reported with the first nonsedating antihistamines (namely terfenadine and astemizol), though rare (roughly one in 10,000), alerted the prescribing physicians to the risk and led to their withdrawal from the market. These risks were compounded when other drugs that similarly affected hepatic cytochrome enzymes were taken concomitantly. Questions have been raised about whether similar adverse effects and drug interactions might be associated with the other non-sedating antihistamines,[55] but no subsequent, unequivocal confirmation of such risks has ever been reported.

The selective leukotriene-receptor antagonists—montelukast, zafirlukast and others—aim to block the cysteinyl leukotrienes C-4, D-4, and E-4. Their place in the management of chronic asthma has been reviewed in objective perspective.[56] The potential for adverse interactions with other drugs is cited in standard reference texts; the long-term safety of the suppression of defensive inflammatory reactions remains to be determined. As for immediate problems, allergic reactions (including urticaria and angioedema) have been infrequently reported. Because there is a rare possibility of systemic and, more specifically, hepatic eosinophilia (at least one earlier compound was also associated with accompanying serious liver abnormalities, as well), this treatment approach requires watchful monitoring.

21.8 Anticholinergics

Inhalations of steaming vapors or smoke from belladonna leaves were employed empirically for the relief of asthma before the beginning of the twentieth century. Later, such therapy lapsed to practical non-use, except among a few herbal enthusiasts, until newer synthetic compounds became available in metered-dose aerosol canisters. Prior to that, atropine aerosols for inhalation therapy via pressurized nebulizers were occasionally tried in refractory cases (see case described in Section 21.5). The only adverse effect that has come to the author's attention is briefly blurred vision, which panicked some patients. This was due to mydriasis when eyes were inadvertently sprayed by some drops of the aerosol. It is worth recalling that the word *belladonna*, meaning beautiful lady, came from women's intentional use of herbal mydriatic drops (it made their pupils larger, which was considered attractive in the eighteenth and nineteenth centuries).

The drug currently in use, ipratropium bromide, is applied to alleviate bronchial and nasal hyperreflexia and hypersecretion. It may be more applicable for COPD than for ROAD. Excessive mucosal dryness, including dry mouth (xerostomia), is the most frequently reported adverse effect. A newer, long-acting 24-hour topical preparation, tiotropin (currently under investigation[57]), may improve compliance among patients who find it difficult to remember the four-to-six hour schedule for ipratropium. Another possible concern about ipratropium is that it blocks M-2 receptors (in addition to M-1 and M-3 muscarinic receptors). Antagonism of M-2 may enhance acetylcholine release and thus interfere with the therapeutic benefits of M-3 anticholinergic blockade.

21.9 Corticosteroids

Sudden deaths began to occur during the several-year span following the 1949 introduction of the anti-inflammatory glucocorticoids in the treatment of rheumatoid arthritis. The same happened after the drugs became *de rigueur* for the treatment of other inflammatory disorders. These fatalities were due either to the drugs' masking symptoms of a more serious condition (such as pneumonia or meningitis), or because treatment was abruptly withdrawn, leaving patients vulnerable, with suppressed adrenal cortical function. Since then, correct use and gradual withdrawal of the sequentially available synthetic corticosteroids (CS)—which include prednisone, prednisolone, methylprednisolone, triamcinolone, dexamethasone,[58] and others—made it possible to prevent or minimize such risks. Nevertheless, many of the immediate and delayed CS adverse effects have continued to present significant medical and, at times, legal problems.[46]

In the early 1960s, a prominent New York City pediatric allergist (V. Fontana) insisted that the use of corticosteroids in pediatric allergy should be considered malpractice. Four decades later, one notes the opposite attitude. It is now stated that these corticosteroid drugs are "the most common group of medications…in the treatment of allergic and autoimmune disorders."[59] It seems very unlikely that the statement was influenced by the fact that the publication of that "educational activity" was supported by a manufacturer of widely used CS aerosol inhalers. So it may be concluded that resorting to CS basically reflects the failure of etiologic management. Few may remember the time when appropriate environmental changes, including relocation, were associated with a practical disappearance of symptoms and apparent clinical cures.[60] Alternatively, the dependence on prescribed anti-inflammatory hormonal drugs may be simply a time-saving measure, intended to limit the effort of handling rather complex clinical problems.

Doses above the average physiologic daily cortisol secretion (which varies markedly along the 24-hour circadian cycle[44] and more than tenfold in response to physical and mental stress) are considered pharmacological, which means that the corticosteroids are classified as drugs. The therapeutic benefits may not necessarily be dose-related. Low doses can be sufficient to control symptoms and to prevent acute exacerbations, and dosages near or above the recommended maximum may offer no further advantages.[61,62] Increasing potency of the CS does not appear to reduce the need for ER treatment, while the risk of undesirable side effects rises steadily higher as the dose and duration of the CS increases.[63] Similarly, while the beneficial effects of most inhaled CS aerosols attain a plateau at about 1,600 mcg/day, the risk of side effects continues to increase when higher doses are taken. The most common CS aerosol side effects are oral and (rarely) laryngeal candidiasis, with thrush, dysphonia, and dysphagia. The newly available dry powder or disc inhalational devices may permit a better intrabronchial deposition of the drug, but also incur greater risks of systemic absorption and secondary adverse effects.[64]

Both the therapeutic efficacy and the adverse effects of CS are attributed to their metabolic biochemical and molecular activity. The standard pharmacologic model aimed to interfere with the arachidonic acid inflammatory cascade at a level more central than that of the various NSAIDs.[65] More specifically, the anti-inflammatory effects of CS can now be linked to their capacity to activate cellular receptors that modulate inflammatory gene expression.[59] Such receptors are akin to those for mineral corticoids, androgens, estrogens, and other steroid molecules, but no problems due to receptor competition have been documented. The gene transcription requires several additional molecular steps. Refractoriness to the therapeutic effect of the corticosteroids has been defined as the inability to detect at least a 15 percent increase in the FEV-1 (baseline may be a determining factor) after a daily (recommended, although not necessarily safe) dose of 40 mg prednisone for 7 to 14 days.[59] Diverse molecular mechanisms involving cytokines have been thought to account for such unresponsiveness to CS, but chronic systemic administration has not been blamed for it. It is an intriguing clinical observation that relatively unresponsive patients, who require significantly higher-than-ordinary CS doses, also appear less likely to experience some of the common side effects, such as Cushingoid features ("moon face"), fluid retention, hypertension, and (possibly) hyperglycemia.

The catabolic effects of systemic CS have been associated with growth suppression in children, which is partially corrected when long-term treatment is terminated. High doses of topical, inhaled CS may have a similar, but lesser, catabolic effect. Oral administration on alternate days[66] and standard maintenance therapy of CS aerosols for bronchial[31] and nasal[18] application are recommended because they are less likely to produce any of the adverse effects of chronic CS administration. However, the possibility of mucosal atrophy—analogous to the dermatologic atrophic changes after long-term topical applications—ought to be kept in mind. The recent report of steroid-induced apoptosis in airway epithelium, epithelial cell shedding, and "programmed death"[67] raises the possibility of serious, irreversible injury that may be detected in humans only decades after continuous use. The argument that no other asthma drugs can rival corticosteroids[68] is like saying that nothing is as effective as a rocket when it comes to killing game birds!

Although an early survey detected no eye changes among children on long-term steroid treatment for asthma,[69] the incidence of subcapsular cataracts in CS-treated patients continues to cause concern. A less-common systemic effect that requires prompt recognition is "benign" (in the sense that it is not associated with a malignancy) intracranial hypertension, reported to occur after discontinuation,[70] but also when one preparation is suddenly exchanged for another. More common are behavioral changes (one such case is cited in Section 21.1). It is best to administer only the most minimally effective doses of these drugs to avoid these adverse effects.[62]

A. Diabetes after a Short Course of Oral Prednisone

The metabolic abnormalities associated with systemic steroids (even after a short treatment course of only a few days) are usually considered reversible upon termination of therapy or after a significant dose reduction. However, there are cases when the abnormalities induced by CS become permanent. In the following case, the author was consulted as an allergist, with an endocrinologist also involved.

A 26-year-old South Dakota man visited his doctor's office weekly for a regular allergen immunotherapy injection. On the occasion in question, the man received a dose that was 25 times stronger than intended, from a vial meant for another patient with the same last name. The injection caused a systemic anaphylactic reaction and generalized urticaria, for which he was given injections of epinephrine, plus antihistamines and a prescription for prednisone. After only five days on a daily dose of prednisone 40 mg, he developed hyperglycemia and permanent diabetes mellitus (a diagnosis confirmed by appropriate tests). There was no change—not even weeks after steroid administration was terminated. The author was asked for an opinion concerning the allergen injection and the management of anaphylaxis. An endocrinologist testified about the causation and prognosis of diabetes.

B. AVN after Dexamethasone for the Prevention of Postoperative Scars

The most devastating and chronically disabling adverse effect of corticosteroid administration is osteonecrosis, that is, bone death. (This should not to be confused with osteoporosis, a softening of the bones due to catabolic mineral loss. Osteoporosis is generally reversible.) Osteonecrosis, generally called avascular necrosis (AVN), is attributed to interference with proper vascularization of the heads of the large bones (most commonly hip and knee), caused by lipid microemboli. The term aseptic necrosis is also used, because

no infection, or sepsis, can be blamed for the destruction of skeletal tissue in these cases. Among the cases of AVN the author has been asked to review (or provide expert testimony for), the majority pertained to respiratory problems within the author's own medical specialty. In view of my clinical research and publications on the benefits and risks of corticosteroid therapy, a number of different, non-respiratory cases have also been brought to my attention. The following is a prime example.

A 35-year-old woman in the Chicago area had a fallopian tuboplasty in an attempt to treat her infertility. She received intramuscular injections of dexamethasone to reduce the risk of scar formation after surgery (10 mg QID, totaling 40 mg/day, for three days). Although the maximum recommended daily dose of dexamethasone is 10 mg, the higher prescribed dose was continued by mouth for a total dose of 380 mg in 17 days. The early side effects, mainly pronounced Cushingoid facial features ("moon face") subsided, but eight months later, she developed bilateral AVN of the femoral heads, first on the right side and, some weeks later, on the left side. She required bilateral surgical hip replacement.

C. High-Dose Prednisone for Contact Dermatitis

A 29-year-old professional golfer had a third seasonal episode of poison ivy contact dermatitis. This case was much worse than previous episodes. Previously, he had been treated effectively with topical and oral anti-inflammatory steroids. This time, a poor response to oral prednisone prompted his general physician to keep increasing the dose—up to 50 mg per day over a period of three weeks. Only later was the lack of improvement thought to have been attributable to a secondary skin infection. About six months later, the patient developed bilateral femoral head AVN and required surgery.

D. Wheezing Pneumonitis Treated as Severe Asthma

Both specialists (mainly pulmonologists) and generalists have resorted to systemic steroid administration for respiratory problems in asthmatic patients who experience an acute exacerbation of breathing difficulty. Three cases are summarized in the following sections, in order to illustrate the tendency to persist with hormonal anti-inflammatory therapy (even when unsatisfactory responses should indicate that the inflammation may not be that of uncomplicated asthma).

A 46-year-old woman in the southeastern United States had a history of recurrent paranasal sinusitis for eight years and intermittent asthma for four years (requiring only occasional bronchodilator inhalations and no daily medication), prior to an episode that was tentatively diagnosed as pneumonitis. Failing to improve after oral antibiotic therapy with Biaxin, inhalations of albuterol, and oral prednisone, she was hospitalized and treated with intravenous (IV) SoluCortef (hydrocortisone), then switched to SoluMedrol (methylprednisolone). She was discharged in a somewhat improved condition with a prescription for oral prednisone. Five days later, she was again seen in the emergency department (ED) with a cough, tight chest, and breathing difficulty, and required readmission. Variable wheezing was noted, but no cyanosis or dyspnea was observed upon exertion. An injection of epinephrine and inhalations of albuterol provided no relief. Her lung function, tested with a simple peak expiratory flow rate (PEFR) meter, remained unchanged at about 270 L/min (62 percent of predicted). Her oxygen saturation while breathing room air (i.e., without O_2 therapy) did not drop below a normal 95 to 97 percent. SoluMedrol IV was resumed at 125 mg every six hours. Parenteral (IV) and, later, oral steroid administration was continued for 134 days, with a total of 3,123 mg of prednisone equivalent (Medrol is converted to prednisone at a 4:5 ratio). Even when—three weeks after her discharge—her pulmonary function was as high as 76 to 84 percent of what was predicted, she was kept on the prednisone, with the instruction to cut it down from 30 mg to 20 mg daily. Four months after her steroid therapy was finally stopped, she complained of hip pain, and a diagnostic MRI confirmed a clinical diagnosis of bilateral femoral head AVN. Two months later, physicians discovered that both shoulders were also affected by AVN. Six months after the first AVN diagnosis, there was evidence of knee involvement. Unsuccessful attempts at orthopedic decompression were followed by successive bone-replacement operations that only partially relieved her disability and chronic pain.

E. Massive Steroids for Refractory Bronchitis Complicating Asthma

A 45-year-old woman—a schoolteacher and former police officer in Northern Florida—had a history of episodic asthma (not requiring regular treatment) for about eight years. She had been a cigarette smoker until three years before her treatment (she was treated first by a general practitioner and then by two pulmonologists). Although she began as an ambulatory patient, she spent 13 days in the hospital for an acute respiratory condition. This condition was first diagnosed as atypical pneumonia, then as bronchitis and asthma. She received a succession of six different antibiotics, including intravenous erythromycin (which may have affected her steroid pharmacokinetics), in addition to oral prednisone 40 mg to 60 mg

per day, with no significant improvement. Her management in the hospital consisted mainly of IV corticosteroids—first dexamethasone, followed by methylprednisolone (SoluMedrol) in dosages of 60 mg every four hours. Due to the lack of improvement, the dosage was increased to 125 mg every six hours for the next five days. No dyspnea was noted. Oximetry indicated normal arterial oxygen levels. Chest X-rays showed left upper-lobe infiltrates, possibly representing atelectatic areas created by mucous plugs. No arterial blood-gas determinations or lung spirometry records were obtained. There was no evidence of coagulopathy (blood-clotting disorder) or hyperlipidemia that might raise concern about vascular circulation. The patient was discharged from the hospital with a reduction in her oral prednisone prescription, from 60 to 40 mg per day. She discontinued the medication on her own, after having taken an estimated total of 3,110 mg of prednisone equivalent. Hip symptoms began about five months later. Two months after that, she was diagnosed with bilateral femoral-head AVN. Two orthopedic core decompressions did not prevent the need for bilateral hip replacement. Her serious activity limitation and discomfort persisted, and the case was tried in the regional district court.

F. Overtreatment with Steroids Prescribed by Telephone

A 38-year-old Kansan farmer with a history of asthma experienced acute-onset chest "congestion" that was unresponsive to his usual at-home breathing treatments with a metered-dose inhaler (MDI). He was then prescribed prednisone 60 mg per day by an allergist, without any tests to help diagnose reversible obstructive airways disease (ROAD). He was not better after two weeks of daily high-dose steroids, so he called his doctor, who recommended doubling the dose to 120 mg prednisone daily for another two weeks. The only significant improvement the patient noticed was when, some weeks later, he left the area and spent a month in Arizona. But toward the end of his stay there, he began to experience severe pain in both hips. AVN was diagnosed and hip replacement became his only therapeutic option.

Although the allergist had been trained in a well-recognized international center, the author felt obligated to support the plaintiff's claim, due to the obvious deviations from the established standards of medical diagnosis and care. The author's support was (apparently) effective. Prescribing physicians who claim that they have administered high doses of corticosteroids for more than one to two weeks each time without adverse consequences must be reminded that driving at very high speeds under the influence of alcohol or drugs does not invariably result in an accident—but the risk definitely increases with speed. So does the risk of permanent harm from increasing doses and duration of CS therapy. Prevention should be our primary concern. The extraordinary delay (seldom noted with other drugs) of more than 6 to 12 months in the detection of AVN makes it imperative that physicians, patients and—when the occasion demands it—attorneys, remain cognizant of the potential for steroid-induced bone destruction. As a practicing medical specialist with particular interest in therapeutic studies, the author has considered his own contributions as an expert witness an important educational function,[71] aiming not only at the recognition of—but hopefully also the prevention of—irreversible steroid-induced harm.

21.10 Antitussives and Expectorants

"Cough medicines" with many names and only slightly varying ingredients are sold OTC in large quantities. The possible untoward effects of the antihistamines contained in some of these admixtures are cited in Section 21.7. Antitussives (cough suppressants)—at times irrationally paired with expectorant secretory stimulants—commonly rely on the efficacy of codeine and its congeners. The case of an infant from California overdosed with a prescription drug, Tussionex, was described in Section 21.4, in reference to its phenylpropanolamine content. The case was brought to the author's attention over 30 years ago, when the baby died after the parents used a vitamin dropper to administer a dose much larger than the prescribed "half-dropperful" of a medicinal dispenser. The preparation in question is no longer available. The relatively common CNS and other suppressive effects of codeine-like compounds are listed in standard medical reference texts, but the author has not encountered a serious injury due to such treatment.

For several decades, iodine salt (or potassium iodide, or KI) was a widely used component of liquid- and tablet-form expectorants. Pediatric formulations attempted to use flavored elixirs or syrups to cover up the unpleasant taste. Besides hypersensitivity skin rashes and acneform eruptions, an adverse effect of chronic iodide intake is thyroid suppression and goiter. In the 1960s, the author saw a little girl from Arizona who had developed thyromegaly as a result of KI administration for her asthma. Oddly and inexcusably, instead of having her iodide therapy stopped, she had her thyroid gland surgically removed.

These days, the most common expectorant in both prescription and OTC cough medicines is guaifenesin. Small doses are no more effective than placebo or generous fluid intake.[72] Doses from 600 to 1,200 mg every 6 to 12 hours may be helpful for irritating dry cough (but may cause gastric irritation and discomfort). No major harm from such expectorant use has come to the author's attention.

21.11 Herbal and "Recreational" Drugs

Headings such as "integrative" or "alternative" medicine did not seem appropriate for this section, because there are no comparable alternatives to reliable, scientific healthcare. Standard pharmaceutical products, such as digitalis, quinine, atropine, the salicylates, and many others (not to mention nutritional supplements, including vitamins), are known to be purified chemical ingredients of natural botanical plants. A continuing search is likely to convert herbal remedies into recognizable, pure molecules for reliable and quantifiable therapeutic application. But, as has been generally recognized, "faith in the possibility of curing" does not always wait for the emergence of "complete scientific proof."[20] As a result, many who are disappointed by science's (hopefully diminishing) inadequacy find themselves encouraged to search for unproven "alternatives." Sadly, most of these alternatives only enrich their promoters.

A. Anaphylaxis from Herbal "Bee Pollen" Ingestion

For more than a decade, the centuries-old reliance on untested "natural" remedies has enjoyed unprecedented growth, despite repeated words of caution, especially in the most accessible communications media.[73] The lack of any evidence of objective or reproducible benefits—and the risk of direct or indirect harm (by interaction with other commonly prescribed drugs)—have been extensively documented. Recent attempts to introduce "complementary and alternative medicine" (CAM) to the programs of scientific and educational medical establishments have been compared to a "Trojan Horse" that may abolish resistance by entering the camp of the opposition.[74] Any possible injury caused by current "integrative" medical practices—besides the obvious financial waste—may relate to the concomitant neglect of established standard therapeutic approaches and the subsequent medical, surgical, and psychiatric harm that can ensue. An example of a more direct adverse effect is a case observed over 15 years ago.

The father of an adolescent asthmatic patient was bringing his son from Wyoming for a follow-up medical visit. On their arrival in town, they stopped at a health-food store. The father had seasonal "hay fever" symptoms, but had never seen an allergist and did not like OTC antihistamines (they made him feel drowsy). He bought a "bee-pollen" preparation that, he was told, helped seasonal allergies. Within minutes after his ingestion of the powder, he began to sneeze and itch all over. By the time he arrived at the medical office, he was in obvious anaphylactic shock, with generalized urticaria and facial angioedema. He had a history of large local reactions to bee or wasp stings, but no anaphylactic hypersensitivity to hymenoptera. Injections of epinephrine and diphenhydramine slowly relieved his symptoms. No legal action followed.

B. Worsening of Asthma Perceived as a Cure with Marijuana

The use of illegal, "recreational" drugs may appear as an attempt to escape an otherwise unpleasant reality. Such a case came to the author's attention in the form of a lengthy, rambling letter from a former patient who had just moved from Colorado to California.

A bright high-school student with rather severe asthma (repeatedly requiring emergency care and systemic steroids) had come to Colorado with his family. The new environment seemed to help his asthma improve. About 18 months later, he went to Southern California to begin college. A few weeks afterwards, the author received a five-page, handwritten letter from the young patient, describing an experience he had had on the beach while smoking marijuana. The young man thought that the marijuana seemed to make his asthma "go away." That impression was corrected when his father called me a few days later to report that his son had to be taken to a hospital for a severe asthma attack. Evidently, the street drug made the young patient unaware of his breathing problem. No further documentation was provided.

21.12 Communications and Monitoring

Inadequate patient databases and deficient information exchange inevitably result in diagnostic and therapeutic errors. Important communications between patients and physicians[75]—along with proper understanding of individual expectations and attitudes[21] that influence clinical decisions—have been reviewed in Sections 21.1 and 21.2. The fundamentals are adequately covered in standard medical-reference texts. The cases reported in this concluding section have been taken from the author's experience as an expert witness[5] for cases requiring initial medical opinions or, as required, for court depositions or testimony. Such referrals originated from law firms from various parts of the U.S., and often relied on available electronic databases. The first two cases—which are, perhaps, typical of a large number seen in medical practice—illustrate a deficiency in communications among physicians of the same or complementary specialties.

A. Three Steroids Taken Together for Orthopedic Inflammation

A 45-year-old airline pilot hurt his neck carrying his little daughter on his shoulders in a swimming pool in Florida. No bone pathology was detected, but because the pain persisted,

he consulted a group orthopedic practice, and was seen by a different doctor on duty on each of three successive visits. Each doctor gave him a different corticosteroid prescription—first prednisone, then Medrol (methylprednisolone) and, on the last visit, dexamethasone—all in oral tablet form. The doctors, apparently, did not check their partners' notes. The patient took all three drugs concomitantly for about ten days, not knowing that it was a duplication of anti-inflammatory medication. About six months later he began to experience hip pain. Shortly afterward, he was diagnosed with bilateral avascular necrosis (AVN) of the femoral heads, which required surgical replacement.

B. Liver Failure Due to Phenytoin Hypersensitivity

A 46-year-old Maryland schoolteacher had an uncomplicated brain surgery for a subarachnoid intracranial aneurism. Concern about seizures prompted the surgeons to administer oral capsules of phenytoin (Dilantin) postoperatively. Within two days, doctors noted an erythema multiforme eruption, which indicated a hypersensitivity reaction. The neurosurgeons prescribed antihistamines, alternating with small doses of Medrol. The order was changed almost every day as the rash worsened, but no allergist was ever consulted. Within three or four days, the patient developed multiple skin and mucosal signs of Stevens-Johnson syndrome, with evidence of progressive hepatic failure. She died about two weeks later, while waiting for a liver transplant.

C. Unanticipated Death of an Asthmatic Child

A six year-old girl in Texas with a history of intermittent asthma, who had been treated irregularly with oral theophylline "sprinkles" and albuterol inhalations, had a "choking spell" and was seen by a pediatric physician's associate, who did not detect any serious problem. The child returned home under the care of her grandmother, with no further treatment. She died just a few hours later, with what was called "cardiopulmonary arrest." Asphyxia and/or anaphylaxis to a food allergen were considered as causative factors. Autopsy findings were consistent with a diagnosis of severe asthma. The pediatric group was sued for failing to anticipate a possible fatal outcome and for not providing sufficient warning, instructions, or supervised management.

D. Missed Diagnosis of Pulmonary Carcinoma

A 48-year-old woman with a history of heavy cigarette smoking developed a persistent cough, which was treated by an allergist with weekly immunotherapy injections for presumed respiratory allergies for over a year without benefit. No diagnostic radiology or other tests were requested. After another consultation 14 months later, she was operated on, and a diagnosis of squamous-cell pulmonary carcinoma was made. Despite subsequent chemotherapy, she suffered multiple metastases and died ten months after the operation. The allergist was found liable for missing the diagnosis and for failing to implement appropriate therapy.

E. Inappropriate Attribution of Blame

A woman was 43 years old when she saw an internist in Denver for what was diagnosed as nephrotic syndrome. She was treated with oral steroids to suppress the inflammatory condition and to maintain adequate kidney function. She then left the area and returned four years later—at which time she sued the physician, alleging that his treatment was responsible for causing an avascular necrosis of her right hip. Study of her medical record in the interval revealed that she had been treated in another state with courses of corticosteroids for what was thought to be allergic asthma. The case against the physician and also the steroid (Medrol) manufacturer could not be supported, both because the prescription of an anti-inflammatory steroid was appropriate (and probably life-saving), and because similar medication had been prescribed by other physicians for quite a different medical problem.

F. Exacerbation of Asthma after a Riot-Control Spray

A 27-year-old woman with intermittent asthma had an acute attack of respiratory distress during lunch in a Las Vegas restaurant, when a security guard used an anti-riot "pepper spray" to break up a fight among some other customers. She was treated effectively in the emergency room. For nearly two months afterward, the patient continued to go to her personal physician almost daily for "breathing treatments" (charged at $200 per visit), which consisted mainly of oxygen inhalations, without any other standard anti-asthma medication, and without sufficient documentation (such as medical examinations or tests) of her therapeutic needs. The plaintiff was unable to prove causation or justify the need for her costly physician visits. The claim against the restaurant, the security guard, and their insurance company was eventually dismissed.

21.13 Conclusion

Prescription drugs and other medical treatments have caused adverse effects, permanent disability, and even death. These situations are not as unusual as they should be—especially in cases of severe allergic reactions, or where drugs are used for respiratory and other systemic hypersensitivity and inflammatory conditions. The care and caution of even the

most conscientious and well-informed health professionals must naturally be supplemented by the consumer's awareness of potential risk. That awareness, however, should not lead to inappropriate anxiety and/or unreasonable antagonism toward or lack of confidence in the medical establishment. Unjustified legal action can be as detrimental as the uncritical acceptance of therapeutic intervention—the ultimate safety of which may never be assured.

Endnotes

Additional extensive bibliographic references are contained in the author's publications, cited here selectively to avoid a lengthier list.

1. Fallieros, K.I. 2002. Foreword to *Self Serve Island* (D.A. Thalpor, I. d'Erge). Denver: Isos Publishers.

2. Matricardi, P.M.; Rosmini, F.; Panetta, V. 2002."Hay fever and asthma in relation to markers of infection in the United States." *J. Allergy Clin. Immnunol.* 110:381–7.

3. Falliers, C.J. 2002. "Atopy and asthma: Prevalence contrasts." *Ann. Allergy Asthma Immunol.* 89:326.

4. Falliers, C.J. 1966. "Asthma and cybernetics." *J. Allergy* 38:264–267.

5. Falliers C.J. July 24-6, 2002. "Medical liability in allergy practice." Poster, 20th Annual Aspen Allergy Conference.

6. Weiss, K.B.; Sullivan, S.D. 1993. "The economic costs of asthma: a review and conceptual model." *Pharmacoeconomics.* 4:14–30.

7. Falliers, C.J. 1988. "The asthma specialist and the law." *J. Asthma.* 25:255–7.

8. Barr, R.G.; Somers, S.C.; Spetzer, F.E.; Camargo, C.A. 2002. "Patient factors and medication guideline adherence among older women with asthma." *Arch. Int. Med.* 162:1761–8.

9. Kaushal, R.; Barker, K.N.; Bates, D. 2001. "How can information technology improve patient safety and reduce medication errors in children's health care?" *Arch. Pediatr. Adolesc. Med.* 155:1002–7.

10. Gurwitz, J.H.; Field, T.S.; Harrold, L.R. 2003. "Incidence and preventability of adverse drug events among older persons in the ambulatory setting." *JAMA.* 289:1107–1116.

11. Barker, K.N.; Flynn, E.A.; Pepper, G.A. 2002. "Medication errors observed in 36 health care facilities." *Arch. Int. Med.*162:1897–1903.

12. Falliers, C.J. 1998. "Care, Human and Humane." *Humane Care Internat.* 13:162.

13. Falliers, C.J. 1998. "Ventilatory impairment in asthma—Perceptions vs. measurements." *Chest.* 113:265.

14. Falliers, C.J. 1974. "Self-measurements for asthma." *JAMA.* 230:537.

15. Falliers, C.J. 1995. "Asthma, drugs and drinking in the life of an American poet, Elizabeth Bishop (1911-1979)." *J Asthma.* 32:235–8.

16. Falliers, C.J. 1988. "Iatroepidemics." *Am. Rev. Respir. Dis.* 137:491.

17. Weinberger, M.; Murray, M.D.; Marrero, D.G. 2002. "Effectiveness of pharmacist care for patients with reactive airways disease: a randomized controlled trial." *JAMA.* 288:1594–1602.

18. Tinkelman, D.G.; Falliers, C.J.; Gross, O. 1990. "Multicenter evaluation of triamcinolone acetonide nasal aerosol in the treatment of adult patients with seasonal allergic rhinitis." *Allergy Clin. Immunol. J.* 64:234–240.

19. Raloff, J. 2002. "Pharm pollution." *Science News.* 161:406–7

20. Raloff, J. 2002. "Contraceptive patch worry." *Science News.* 162:245–6.

21. Falliers, C.J. 1983. Foreword to the *Allergy Self-help Book.* S. Faelten, Ed. Emmaus: Rodale Press.

22. Robinson, A.R.; Hohman, K.B.; Rifkin, J.I. 2002. "Physician and public opinions on quality of health care and the problem of medical errors." *Arch. Int. Med.* 162:2186–2190.

23. Doerschug, K.C.; Peterson, M.W.; Dayton, C.S.; Kline, J.N. 1999. "Asthma guidelines: an assessment of physician understanding and practice." *Am. J. Respir. Crit. Care Med.* 159:1735–1741.

24. Falliers, C.J. 1978. "Prevention of status asthmaticus." *JAMA.* 239:1393.

25. Wolfenden, L.L.; Diette, G.B.; Krishman, J.A. 2003. "Lower physician estimate of underlying asthma severity leads to undertreatment." *Arch. Int. Med.* 163:231-6.

26. Diamond, S.; Salter, J.; Hummel, D. 2003. "The role of pharmacists in anaphylaxis education." *J. Allergy Clin. Immunol.* 111:S128.

27. Falliers, C.J. 1987. "Characteristic patterns and management of asthma in adolescence." In *Childhood Asthma: pathophysiology and treatment.* D.G. Tinkelman, C.J. Falliers, C.K. Naspitz, eds. New York: M. Dekker.

28. Falliers, C.J. 1983. "Beware of everything: The ever-present danger of anaphylaxis." *J. Asthma.* 20:175–6.

29. Tinkelman, D.G.; Bleecker, E.H.; Ramsdell, J. 1998. "Proventil HFA and Ventolin have similar safety profiles during regular use." *Chest.* 113:290–6.

30. Taylor, G.J.; Harris, W.S. 1970. "Cardiac toxicity of aerosol propellants." *JAMA.* 214:81–5.

31. Falliers, C.J. 1976. "Triamcinolone acetonide aerosols for asthma: I. Effective replacement of systemic corticosteroid therapy." *J. Allergy Clin. Immunol.* 57:1–11.

32. Sears, M.R. 2002. "Adverse effects of beta-agonists." *J Allergy Clin. Immunol.* 110:S322–8.

33. Suissa, S.; Hemmelgam, B.; Blais, L. "Bronchodilators and acute cardiac deaths." *Am. J. Respir. Med.* 154:1598–1602.

34. Molk, L.; Falliers, C.J. 1970. "Isoproterenol aerosols in perspective." *Excerpt Med. Internat. Congress. Series.* 211:126–7.

35. Spitzer, W.O.; Suissa, S.; Ernst, P. 1992. "The use of -agonists and the risk of death and near death from asthma." *N. Engl. J. Med.* 326:501–6.

36. Abramson, M.J.; Bailey, M.J.; Couper, F.J. 2001. "Are asthma medications and management related to deaths from asthma?" *Am. J. Resp. Crit. Care Med.* 163:12–18.

37. Benovic, J.L. 2002. "Novel -2-adrenergic receptor signaling pathways." *J. Allergy Clin. Immonol.*110:S229–235.

38. Tseng, Y-T., Wadhawan, R., Stabila, J.P. 2002. "Molecular interactions between glucocorticoid and catecholamine signaling pathways." *J. Allergy Clin. Immunol.* 110:S247–254.

39. Castro, M. 2002. "Near-fatal asthma: what have we learned?" *Chest.* 121:1394–5.

40. Lipworth, B.J.; Struthers, A.D.; McDevitt, D.G. 1989. "Tachyphylaxis to systemic but not to airway responses during prolonged therapy with high dose inhaled salbutamol in asthmatics." *Am. Rev. Respir. Dis.* 140:586–592.

41. Van Schayck, C.P.; Cloosterman, S.G.; Bijl-Hofland, I.D. 2002. "Is the increase in bronchial responsiveness or FEV-1 shortly after cessation of beta-2-agonsists reflecting a real deterioration of the disease in allergic asthmatic patients? A comparison between short-acting and long-acting beta2-agonists." *Respir. Med.* 96:155–162.

42. Milgrom, H. Skoner, D.P.; Bensch, G. 2001. "Low-dose leval buterol in children with asthma: Safety and efficacy in comparison with placebo and racemic albuterol." *J. Allergy. Clin Immonol.* 108:938–945.

43. Falliers, C.J. May 1971. "The importance of timing drug treatment for asthma." *Pharm. Times.* 56–62.

44. Falliers, C.J. 1983. "Chronobiology in relation to allergy." Chapter from *Allergy Principles & Practice*. E. Middleton, ed. Saint Louis: Mosby.

45. Falliers, C.J. 1986. "Deaths from asthma: Mistakes, myths and mysteries." *J Asthma.* 23:239–240.

46. O'Donnell, J.T. 2001. "Theophylline & Corticosteroids." Chapter from *Drug Injury: Liability, Analysis and Prevention*. Tucson: Lawyers & Judges Publishers.

47. Falliers, C.J. 1982. "Clinical and experimental contribution on the spasmolytic effect of purine derivatives, by S. Hirsch, 1922." *J. Asthma.* 19:219–221.

48. Falliers, C.J. 1988. "Is theophylline a 'primary drug'?" *Ann Allergy.* 60:461.

49. O'Donnell, J.T. 2001. In *Drug Injury: Liability, Analysis and Prevention*. Tucson: Lawyers & Judges Publishers. Chapters 19.6–19.8.

50. Falliers, C.J. 1971. "Cromolyn sodium (disodium cromoglycate)." *J. Allergy.* 47:298–305.

51. Kay, A.B. 2001. "Allergic diseases and their treatment." *N. Engl. J. Med.* 344:109–113.

52. Falliers, C.J. May 4–10, 1986. "The new non-sedating antihistamine loratadine." *Chairman's introductory remarks*. XIII Congress, Europ. Acad. Allerg. Clin. Immunol. Budapest.

53. Falliers, C.J.; Brandon, M.L.; Buchman, E. 1991. "Double-blind comparison of cetirizine and placebo in the treatment of seasonal rhinitis." *Ann. Allergy.* 66:257–262.

54. Bronsky, E.A.; Falliers, C.J.; Kaiser, H.B.1998. "Effectiveness and safety of fexofenadine, a new non-sedating H-1 receptor antagonist in the treatment of fall allergies." *Allergy Asthma Proc.* 19:135–141.

55. Lindquist, M.; Edwards, I.R. 1997. "Risks of non-sedating antihistamines." *Lancet.* 349:1322.

56. Drazen, J.M.; Israel, E.; O'Byrne, P.M. 1999. "Treatment of asthma with drugs modifying the leukotriene pathway." *N. Engl. J. Med.* 340:197–206.

57. Panning, C.A.; DeBisschop, M. 2003. "Tiotropium: An inhaled, long-acting anticholinergic drug for chronic obstructive pulmonary disease." *Pharmacotherapy.* 23:183–9.

58. Falliers, C.J.; Bukantz, S.C.1959. "Dexamethasone in childhood asthma." *Ann. Allergy.* 17:887–894.

59. Leung, D.Y.M.; Bloom, J.W. 2003. "Update on glucocorticoid action and resistance." *J. Allergy Clin. Immunol.* 111:3–22.

60. Falliers, C.J. 1970. "Treatment of asthma in a residential center: A fifteen-year study." *Ann. Allergy.* 28:513–521.

61. Suissa, S.; Ernst, P.; Benayoun, S. 2000. "Low-dose inhaled corticosteroids and the prevention of death from asthma." *N. Engl. J. Med.* 343:332–6.

62. Kayani, S.; Shannon, D.C. 2002. "Adverse behavioral effects of treatment of acute exacerbation of asthma in children: A comparison of two doses of oral steroids." *Chest.* 122:624–5.

63. Williams, C. 2003. "Potency of inhaled corticosteroid fails to predict reduced emergency department visits." *Arch. Int. Med.*163:247.

64. Allen, D.B. 2002. "Sense and sensitivity: Assessing inhaled corticosteroid effects on the hypothalamic-pituitary-adrenal axis." *Ann. Allergy Asthma Immunol.* 89:537–9.

65. Hardman, J.G.; Limbird, L.E. *Goodman & Gilman's The Pharmacological Basis of Therapeutics, Tenth edition.* New York: McGraw-Hill.

66. Falliers, C.J.; Chai, H. Molk, L.; Cardoso RR 1972. "Pulmonary and adrenal effects of alternate-day corticosteroid therapy." *J Allergy Clin Immunol.* 49:155–166.

67. White, S.R.; Dorscheid, D.R. 2002. "Corticosteroid-induced apoptosis of airway epithelium: A potential mechanism for chronic airway epithelial damage in asthma." *Chest.* 122:S278–284.

68. Hamelmann, E.; Schleimer, R.P. 2003. "Corticosteroid treatment in bronchial asthma: For better or for worse?" *J. Allergy Clin. Immunol.* 111:248–9.

69. Ley, A.P.; Bukantz, S.C.; Falliers, C.J. 1965. "Corticosteroid therapy and subcapsular cataracts." *JAMA.* 191:753.

70. Neville, B.G.R.; Wilson, J. 1970. "Benign intracranial hypertension following corticosteroid withdrawal in childhood." *Br. Med. J.* 3:554.

71. Falliers, C.J. 2003. "Malpractice claims, re: corticosteroids." *Arch. Int. Med.* 163:1112–3.

72. Falliers, C.J. 1983. "Antitussive effect of guaifenesin." *Chest.* 84:118.

73. Kolata, G. June 17,1996. "On fringes of health care, untested therapies thrive." *NY Times.* A1-C11.

74. Marcus, D.M. 2002. "Integrative medicine is a Trojan horse." *Arch. Int. Med.* 162:2381–3.

75. Forster, H.P.; Schwartz, J.; De Renzo, E. 2002. "Reducing legal risk by practicing patient-centered medicine." *Arch. Int. Med.162:1217–19.*

Chapter 22

Adverse Effects of Diabetic Drugs

Gourang Patel, B.S. Chem, Pharm.D., MSc, BCPS and
James T. O'Donnell, Pharm.D., M.S., FCP, ABCP, FACN, R.Ph.

22.1 Diabetes Demographics and Epidemiology

Millions of patients with diabetes are treated with insulin and sulfonylureas, oral drugs which lower blood sugar. Occasionally, patients receive either insulin or the oral sugar lowering drugs in error. In diabetic patients, and in those patients who receive these drugs in error, the toxic effects may be devastating or fatal. Further, the pharmacology of insulin and sulfonylureas are in themselves the topics of review articles and chapters. For the purposes of this chapter, these topics are briefly reviewed to assist in understanding the disease, and the use of agents that treat diabetes along with the factors leading to hypoglycemia are presented. Hypoglycemic injuries will be demonstrated by a thorough discussion of the pathophysiology and elucidated through case discussion from the literature and litigation files.

For a more comprehensive review, the reader is referred to endnotes one through six, which include several excellent reviews on these topics.

22.2 Insulin

The first patient to receive the active extracts of the pancreas prepared by Banting and Best lived in Toronto. The administration of Banting and Best's extracts induced a reduction in the concentration and excretion of blood glucose (sugar). Daily injections were then begun, and there was immediate improvement. Thus, replacement therapy with the newly discovered hormone, insulin, had interrupted what was clearly an otherwise fatal metabolic disorder.[1] Stable extracts were eventually obtained, and patients in many parts of North America were soon being treated with insulin.[2,3] The Nobel Prize in Medicine and Physiology was awarded to Banting and Macleod with remarkable rapidity in 1923.

22.3 Insulin Preparations

Insulins available in the United States differ in concentration, time of onset and duration of action, purity, and species of origin. Clinically significant differences among them have been reviewed. Each of these factors plays a role in determining the type and dose of insulin that is best suited to an individual patient. Insulin U-100 (100 units/ml) is the most commonly used concentration. (The numeral following the "U" indicates the number of units of insulin per milliliter.) Although the vast number of diabetics today use U-100 insulin, U-40 and U-500 insulins are available. U-40 syringes are color-coded "red"; U-100 products are color-coded "orange with black lettering." Recombinant-engineered insulin products, primarily used in the U-100 concentration, have replaced natural insulin (beef and pork origin) in most clinical settings. These "engineered" insulins are claimed to cause less insulin resistance and have less hypersensitivity risk. In addition, there are additional insulin preparations on the market available for clinicians to prescribe. While this may create an opportunity for better glucose control for patients, it also greatly introduces an opportunity for medication errors. The insulin preparations that have been added to the market for use include three ultra-short acting drugs (i.e., activity ranging from 5-15 minutes). Examples of ultra-short acting insulin medications include lispro, aspart, and glulisine. There are also extended-action preparations now available. Examples of extended-acting insulin include glargine and detemir.[4,5]

22.4 Clinical Use of Insulin

Insulin is the mainstay for treatment of virtually all type 1 and many type 2 diabetic patients, including type 2 diabetics who are not adequately controlled by diet and/or oral hypoglycemic agents, and for patients with post-pancreatectomy diabetes or gestational diabetes.[2,4,5] In addition, insulin is critical for the management of diabetic ketoacidosis (commonly abbreviated in medical documentation as DKA), and it has an important role in the treatment of hyperglycemic, nonketotic coma (commonly abbreviated in medical documentation as HHNK) and in the perioperative management of both type 1 and type 2 diabetic patients. When necessary, insulin may be administered intravenously or intramuscularly; however, long-term treatment relies on subcutaneous injection of the hormone. In all cases, the goal is the normalization not only of blood glucose, but also of all aspects of metabolism. Optimal treatment requires a coordinated approach to diet, exercise, and the administration of insulin.[6]

A. Dosing

There are a number of methods for dosing insulin. For the hospitalized patient, many clinicians prefer a "sliding scale" approach. Blood glucose concentrations are ordered several times a day (e.g., every four hours, every six hours, or at specified times—7 A.M., 11 A.M., 4 A.M., and midnight) such that fasting values and values before meals are obtained. The concept of sliding scale has been adjusted in clinical practice as scheduled dosing three times daily based on meal consumption. Subcutaneously-administered regular insulin is then ordered in an amount that increases corresponding to an increase in blood glucose. When the patient's insulin requirement has stabilized over two to three days, the number of units required during the previous 24 hours is totaled. The patient can then be given a single injection of an intermediate-acting insulin; the beginning dose is two-thirds to three-fourths of the 24-hour regular insulin dose, and is given 30 minutes before breakfast. The dose can then be "fine-tuned" and adjusted based on blood sugar values over the next several days.[5]

As the type 2 diabetic is usually not prone to ketoacidosis, there is less urgency to initiate aggressive therapy. This individual can be started on a single injection of 15–20 units/day of an intermediate-acting insulin. Blood glucose levels can then be followed and the insulin adjusted accordingly. Recent studies have shown that almost 90 percent of type 2 diabetics can be initially controlled on less than 20 units of insulin per day.[6] Patients should use the same preparation continuously to avoid a change in dosage requirement. In some patients, human insulin may have a more rapid onset and shorter duration of action than a comparable pork product.

22.5 Hypoglycemia (Low Blood Sugar)

Among the most frequent causes of hypoglycemia are the administration of insulin and ingestion of oral anti-diabetic agents, both of which are usually prescribed as the mainstay for the treatment of diabetics. Such agents may be the source of factitious hypoglycemia in non-diabetics; also, this may occur when they are self-administered by emotionally disturbed individuals or administered by others with a malevolent or homicidal intent. A comprehensive list of etiologies of hypoglycemia is listed in Table 22.1.

A. Etiologies of Hypoglycemia

Alcohol consumption by fasting individuals can also induce hypoglycemia. Hepatic metabolism of ethyl alcohol blunts gluconeogenesis, causing blood glucose levels to decline gradually into the symptomatic hypoglycemic range. Very high titers of insulin antibodies characterize a form of hypoglycemia that occurs either in the fasted or postprandial state. These autoantibodies arise without immunization to exogenous insulin, but their kinetic characteristics resemble those of antibodies from insulin-treated diabetics. Glucose tolerance is frequently impaired.[5,7]

Whether or not late afternoon fatigue, mood changes, depression, and anxiety—the "five o'clock dwindles"—are related to blood glucose levels has been argued in the lay press and in some medical publications. Most data does not support a correlation, but suggests that such manifestations are purely emotional in origin or are perversions of the hunger drive. In a very small number of individuals, however, glucose levels do drop to symptomatically low concentrations before the evening meal or at other times following a meal rich in carbohydrate and insulin-stimulating substrate; the term reactive hypoglycemia has been used to describe this syndrome.[6]

B. Insulin-Induced Hypoglycemia

The most common adverse reaction to insulin is hypoglycemia. This may result from an inappropriately large dose, from a mismatch between the time of peak delivery of insulin and

Table 22.1
Etiologies of Hypoglycemia

Postprandial hypoglycemia
- Idiopathic
- Alimentary
- Early type-2 diabetes mellitus
- Leucine sensitivity
- Enzyme deficiencies

Fasting hypoglycemia or underproduction of glucose
- Hormone deficiencies
  - Hypopituitarism
  - Adrenal insufficiency
  - Catecholamine deficiency
  - Glucagon deficiency
  - Counter regulatory hormone deficiency in diabetes mellitus
- Enzyme defects
  - Glycogen storage disease
  - Gluconeogenesis enzyme deficiency
- Substrate deficiency
  - Ketotic hypoglycemia of infancy
  - Severe malnutrition
  - Exercise
  - Uremia
  - Pregnancy

Acquired liver disease
- Hepatic congestion (congestive heart failure)
- Hepatitis, hepatic necrosis
- Cirrhosis
- Drug-induced disease
- Inhibition of glycogenolysis of β-blockers

Fasting hypoglycemia or overuse of glucose
- Hyperinsulinism
  - Insulinoma
  - Exogenous insulin administration
  - Administration of sulfonylureas
  - Immune disease with insulin antibodies
  - Abrupt discontinuation of total parenteral nutrition
- Appropriate insulin levels
  - Extrapancreatic tumors
  - Cachexia with fat depletion
  - Carnitine deficiency

food intake, or from superimposition of additional factors that increase sensitivity to insulin (adrenal insufficiency, pituitary insufficiency) or that increase insulin-independent glucose uptake (exercise). The more vigorous the attempt to achieve euglycemia (normal blood sugar), the more frequent the episodes of hypoglycemia. Milder, but significant, hypoglycemic episodes are much more common than severe reactions, and their frequency also increases with intensive therapy. Hypoglycemia is the major risk that must be weighed against any benefits of intensive therapy. Careful investigation of a patient's insulin therapy is necessary to ensure insulin preparations have not been mistakenly taken and/or incorrectly filled by the pharmacy, as there are many different insulin preparations available for patient therapy.[6]

22.6 Pathophysiology and Clinical Symptoms of Hypoglycemia

Since brain tissue depends on glucose as its primary fuel, hypoglycemia, or a low blood glucose level, has a marked impact on brain metabolism. Alterations of brain function are responsible for the characteristic symptoms of hypoglycemia. As glucose levels fall, prodromal signs and symptoms may appear. Such manifestations include hunger, salivation, an overall ill-at-ease feeling, or even nausea. The sympathetic (adrenaline-like) response to hypoglycemia is more pronounced and is manifested by tachycardia, coldness of the skin, piloerection, sweating, and anxiety. As glucose levels decline further, cerebration may become impaired, leading to confusion, abnormalities in decision-making processes, the appearance of a glassy-eyed stare, aberrant behavior, and occasionally even overt hostility. If glucose levels fall gradually, as in a diabetic patient who is receiving a long-acting insulin, the prodromal syndrome may be lacking; the patient is thus unaware of any problem and may instead progress directly into confusion and then unconsciousness. If the hypoglycemia is severe and prolonged, irreversible brain damage and even death may ensue.[8–10]

The most frequent symptoms of hypoglycemia include sweating, tremor, blurred vision, weakness, hunger, confusion, altered behavior, and loss of consciousness. Hypoglycemia may lead to convulsions resulting in brain damage as well as serious musculoskeletal injuries. The essential biochemical event is a blood sugar level of less than 25–30 mg/100 ml, lasting one to two hours, and leading to exhaustion of the store of cerebral glucose and glycogen. Within this brief span of time, as cerebral oxidation proceeds without exogenous glucose, the structural component of neurons, that is, lipid and protein substances, are metabolized, and irreversible damage occurs. The cerebral cortex suffers major damage; cortical nerve cells degenerate and are replaced by microgliacytes and astrocytes.[11–13] In a reported autopsy following three months in coma, the pathologist described the brain tissue as follows:

> Outer layers of the cortex in the frontal and temporal areas appeared somewhat spongy with a slight loss of neurons and secondary fibrous gliosis. In the deeper layers, some of the neurons were triangular, often eosinophilic. The periventricular and perivascular areas in the caudate nucleus also appeared spongy with prominent astrocytes, some gemistocytic. However, no frank necrosis was observed. In the putamen, similar perivascular sponginess and gliosis was noted, but the other basal nuclei showed no major alteration. In the subcortical white matter, there was a slight, diffuse increase of gemistocytic astrocytes.[8]

In normal volunteers given infusions of insulin, hypoglycemic symptoms occur when the glucose falls to about 45 mg/dl (2.5 mM); however, symptoms may occur at higher glucose concentrations, depending on the rate and magnitude of the change.

22.7 Incidence

Clinically-documented hypoglycemia occurs most frequently in the insulin-requiring diabetic; other organic causes of hypoglycemia such as islet cell tumors and excessive alcohol intake also deserve consideration in the symptomatic individual. Several authors discuss the issue of animal versus human insulin-induced hypoglycemic reactions, and argue for the continued availability of beef and porcine insulin.[9] The American Diabetes Association states that human insulin has a more rapid onset and shorter duration of activity than pork insulin, whereas beef insulin has the slowest onset and longest duration of activity.[10] The ADA recommends that changing insulin species may affect blood glucose control and should only be done under the supervision of a health professional with expertise in diabetes. Pharmacists should not interchange insulin preparations without the approval of the prescribing physician or without informing the patient of the type of insulin change being made.[10]

There has been a running controversy in the literature on the effect of human insulins in decreasing the awareness of hypoglycemia in users compared to non-human insulin types. Egger et al. investigated the influence of human insulin on symptoms and awareness of hypoglycemia in a randomized double blind crossover trial. They found that insulin doses and blood glucose, glycosalated hemoglobin

A1c, and fructosamine concentrations were similar during the two treatment periods. Analyzing the results of questionnaires on hypoglycemia (234-human insulin, 259-porcine insulin), the human insulin patients were more likely to report lack of concentration and restlessness and less likely to report hunger than during treatment with porcine insulin. The authors concluded that the pattern of symptoms associated with human insulin could impair patients' ability to take appropriate steps to avoid severe hypoglycemia. They recommended caution should be exercised when transferring patients from animal insulin to human insulin.[11]

Several others dispute these findings, and suggested that a larger, more carefully designed prospective study is still required to establish the prevalence and nature of the unawareness syndrome as it can be attributed to a particular insulin type.[11] It was suggested that as diabetics got older, they lost much of their ability to tell when they were experiencing hypoglycemia. Many of the diabetics in the study may have just happened to notice this change shortly after they switched to human insulin. Follow-up studies showed the change was mainly in their own metabolism, not in their insulin.[9,12]

22.8 Pathophysiology and Biochemistry of Hypoglycemia

Glucose normally furnishes 98–100 percent of the brain's energy needs. The minimum glucose level needed to maintain glucose transport across the blood-brain barrier and into brain cells is undefined. Some individuals adapt to ambient blood glucose levels as low as 30–40 mg/100 ml.[4,5,7] Conversely, an insulin-dependent diabetic could experience a severe hypoglycemic reaction at a value of 100 mg/100 ml if the blood glucose had been rapidly lowered from a previous level of 300 mg/100 ml. Thus, the level of circulating glucose is imprecisely correlated with the brain's substrate requirements. Consequently, it is often difficult to assess the significance of symptoms in many subjects, especially those with alleged reactive hypoglycemia. Insulin-dependent diabetics may have defective counter regulatory mechanisms, and thus may be exceptionally vulnerable to hypoglycemia.[7]

22.9 Adverse Experiences with Hypoglycemia

Clinically, one of the most common situations in which severe hypoglycemia develops is accidental or deliberate overdose of insulin. The following cases demonstrate this type of occurrence.

A. Case Report: Insulin-Related Malpractice—Sliding Scale and Urine Sugars Result in Cardiac Arrest

A New Jersey woman suffered a cardiopulmonary arrest and "stopped breathing" at 1:15 P.M., preceded by labored and difficult breathing and a measured blood pressure of 40. The patient was on a peripheral parenteral nutrition solution containing 5 percent dextrose, and a sliding scale insulin based on urine sugars was in effect. She was given 20 units of insulin subcutaneously at 6:00 A.M. on the morning of the arrest. Analysis of the case was made to determine the contribution of the insulin to the cardiopulmonary arrest, as well as the use of urine glucose tests to determine the status of blood glucose and as a basis for administration of insulin.

This patient did not present with the classical manifestation of insulin reaction (shock, hypoglycemia), usually manifest with agitation, fainting, anxiety, hunger, warmth, tremulousness, weakness, confusion, emotional labiality, palpitation, pallor, abnormal behavior, fatigue, parenthesis and hyperesthesia of the lips, nose, or fingers. She did, however, present with labored difficult breathing, a hypotensive episode which preceded her cardiopulmonary arrest. In severe hypoglycemia (low serum glucose), profound cerebro-cortical dysfunction may occur. Autonomic signs and symptoms may result from the rate of decrease in blood glucose, and central nervous system effects are related to the absolute blood glucose concentration. Therefore, if glucose levels decrease slowly, which probably occurred in this patient, autonomic symptoms (the classical case—sweating, agitation palpitation, abnormal behavior, and so on) may not precede central nervous system effects.[14] Severe hypoglycemia will result in a low brain glucose, causing a shift to anaerobic (no oxygen) neural cell metabolism, brain cell anoxia, and cerebral damage. A neurologist in the case opined that this was the mechanism for the arrest.

Urine tests for presence of sugar are a gross, antiquated, obsolete, imprecise testing method, only recommended for the stable ambulatory patient who has a need for some type of gross testing, does not have the resources for glucometer equipment, or has an aversion to finger pricks for obtaining blood samples. Stated another way, fractional urine glucose levels are undependable, and should only be used when blood glucose cannot be done. Standards for monitoring serum glucose in hospitalized patients, including diabetics or others requiring glucose monitoring (such as patients receiving parenteral nutrition solutions), as early as 1985, would clearly have required a glucometer device for stat or frequent routine measures, verified periodically by laboratory analysis of serum glucose through multichannel automated analyzers (SMA-12).

Reliance on urine glucose determinations is potentially dangerous, particularly because this method is subject to interpretation errors; and particularly, in the higher 4+ range, the interpretation is open ended, and the actual level of hyperglycemia is indeterminate. If this imprecise method is used, it should only be used for screening, and not for the administration of "high" doses of insulin, which occurred in this case. "Regular" or prompt acting insulin was administered in this case. The dose was given at 6 A.M. The "peak effect," meaning the time at which the insulin level would be the highest, would occur one to two hours later. The insulin would still be "working" at the time of the arrest. This is explained by the duration of action, that is, the time over which the insulin would have a glucose lowering effect. The "lowest" level of blood glucose, in response to the insulin, is not necessarily at the peak, but when the available glucose was exhausted. The available glucose would include the blood glucose, the exogenous glucose (from the 5-percent glucose peripheral nutrition solution), and glucose stored in glycogen. The insulin would facilitate the removal of glucose from the blood; it facilitates the uptake into cells. Two references familiar to all pharmacists are Goodman and Gilman's *Pharmacological Basis of Therapeutics* and the *APHA Handbook of Non-Prescription Drugs,* and these are authoritative sources of drug information. Only after all available glucose is taken up into cells, within the period of the duration of effect (eight hours), would the glucose level fall to sufficiently low levels to precipitate signs of hypoglycemia. This scenario is consistent with a prolonged, slow rate of glucose level lowering, and thus explains the lack of a precipitous drop (which might be seen with an intravenous bolus of insulin). As mentioned above, the "absolute" level of hypoglycemia is the causative agent for cerebral effects of hypoglycemia.

The woman's family settled the lawsuit against the hospital and her treating physicians for an undisclosed sum shortly before trial in the case.[15]

B. Insulin Damages Baby's Brain; Pharmacist Error Suggested

In this case, a hospital pharmacist and technicians violated their own policies and procedures regarding operations in the laminar flow hood and IV additive room. As a result of the pharmacist's negligence in preparing sterile admixtures, a Fairfax, Virginia baby (Peterson) became brain damaged following insulin-induced hypoglycemic encephalopathy. After several seizures, the child's physicians suspected hypoglycemia and searched for a cause, initially suspecting that insulin was added to the total parenteral nutrition (TPN) bag by the pharmacist. Although none was ordered, insulin was assayed in the suspect TPN bag, confirming the suspicion of insulin-induced hypoglycemia. Others in the hospital, including the risk manager and the pharmacists involved, insisted that the insulin was not added in the pharmacy. The police were called in to look for an interloper. Hospital spokesmen argued that someone must have added the insulin to the bag while it was hanging at the patient's incubator's side in the busy ICU. Shades of Claus von Bulow! The child suffered irreversible brain damage, and is now living in a home for brain-damaged children. Glucose levels as low as 14 mg-percent were detected during periods of seizure, tremulousness, hypotonia, and pallor, all classical signs of hypoglycemia and insulin shock.

In the opinion of the pharmacist expert in the case, a former hyperalimentation pharmacist specialist (this author), the insulin was accidentally added to the baby's TPN bags while in the pharmacy, resulting in severe hypoglycemia and irreversible brain damage. Negligence was apparent in the pharmacy, policies and procedures were ignored, and this was the most probable cause for the accident to happen. Opportunities for risk were ignored or overlooked! After a series of legal battles, and unfavorable rulings regarding document requests by a malpractice panel and trial judge, the Fairfax hospital settled the Peterson case for the statutory limit of $1 million[16,17] shortly before trial was scheduled to begin. Coincidentally, on the same day the Peterson child suffered hypoglycemic-induced seizures, another child received an overdose of insulin in a neonatal TPN bag in the neonatal ICU. The other neonate, Brittany Smith, died following a severe brain-damaging insulin hypoglycemic reaction. The Smith family also filed a medical malpractice suit that was resolved.

Shortly after the settlement, the Peterson family sued the Fairfax hospital, its insurance company, and its lawyers requesting $60 million in compensatory and punitive damages.[22] The plaintiffs charge that the Fairfax Hospital breached its duty to the parents to honestly and expeditiously communicate to the parents all relevant information pertaining to Matthew Peterson's health care, including all relevant information.

According to the complaint that was filed in court, at the time the neonates were treated, it was known to the hospital that another patient at a prior time had received unauthorized administration of insulin, causing that patient's death. The lawsuit charges that the defendants engaged in a deliberate cover up and a pattern of withholding information, which was motivated by a fear of negative publicity and a potential loss of revenue. The defendant placed these considerations ahead of the hospital's duty to the Peterson's to communicate honestly and fully the circumstances of the injury.

After the hypoglycemic incidents occurred, an investigative team composed of the hospital risk manager and legal affairs director immediately interviewed pharmacists, nurses, physicians and others involved in the care of the Peterson and Smith babies. They caused testing to be made of the contents of the infants' TPN bags, and notified the police about the incidents. The police interviewed several individuals, but they were never invited to interview the pharmacists involved in the preparation of the TPNs. The plaintiffs charged that key investigative information concerning the problems uncovered in the pharmacy was not provided to the police. One defense expert who concluded that the error occurred in the pharmacy was told to tear up his notes! The matter was not referred to a regular morbidity and mortality committee or similar peer review committee as would normally be done for such a medical misadventure. The investigation quickly disclosed that the insulin was in the two babies' TPN bags, which would not be possible under ordinary clinical circumstances (insulin, if used in NICU, was diluted first, and then only added to the infants Buretrol, never the IV bag). Both infants' bags were supposed to contain heparin; neither did, a fact concealed in the investigation and subsequent litigation discovery, until the risk manager admitted this fact close to the time of trial. This was a critical point, since it explains how the insulin could have been placed in the bags, accidentally replacing the ordered heparin.

At the time following the Peterson injury, the family was not informed of the similar insulin toxicity experienced by the Smith child, nor of the previous insulin death. They were informed that both the hospital and the police investigation had determined that the injury was conclusively the result of an unknown third party's intentional act and not any fault on the part of the hospital.

The lawsuit charges that the defendants, in order to deflect liability for the hospital's malfeasance, concocted the explanation that a third party interloper entered the NICU without being seen, entered two different rooms and injected insulin into the IV bags of both infants, an explanation which is contradicted by the findings of the hospital's own investigation. When contacted, the public relations department of the Fairfax Hospital declined to discuss any changes implemented by the pharmacy at Fairfax Hospital, stating to the effect that to admit that changes had taken place was tantamount to admission that the errors had occurred, and the hospital maintains that the insulin was placed in the bag(s) by a criminal interloper, not negligently by the pharmacy. The hospital representative hastened to add that the settlement in the underlying suit does not assume an admission of guilt or liability. According to Philip Hirschkop, the Alexandria, Virginia plaintiff's attorney, all of the defendants (hospital, attorneys, and insurance company) have refused to answer any discovery in the case pending outcome of demurrers that say that the complaint does not as a matter of law state sufficient claims upon which claims can be granted. The trial judge in the case forced the defense to turn over work product notes.[18]

C. Another Interloper?

Another insulin poisoning occurred in a suburban Chicago hospital. There, a 50-year-old man was to receive an intramuscular injection of quinidine at midnight. He developed an unexplained hypoglycemic reaction, and his serum was analyzed to contain substantial amounts of exogenous insulin (same analyzing chemist that was used in the Claus von Bulow story). The hospital suggested that someone in his family was trying to "do him in." The pharmacist expert (O'Donnell) at deposition suggested that the nurse did not read the label on the insulin bottle, which incidentally is shaped like quinidine, because it was late at night, the lights were low, and so forth. The hospital settled the case before trial. The patient survived with brain damage.[19]

22.10 End Product Testing Recommended

In a related case with a newborn, Hospital Pharmacy Report correspondent Gebhart reports that the Good Samaritan Hospital of West Palm Beach, Florida, agreed to a $1.5 million settlement in what appeared to be a pharmacy error in which a hyperalimentation bag contained no glucose. After nearly a week on hyperalimentation, the child suddenly went into seizures. Medical staff suspected infection, but no evidence of sepsis could be found. They did notice, however, that bolus doses of glucose seemed to calm the seizures. It took several hours to discover that the real problem was hypoglycemia. The resulting hypoglycemia caused irreversible brain damage to the neonate. The mother of the infant, an intensive care nurse, is now campaigning for a change in pharmacy and nursing practice standards to prevent a recurrence, calling for testing of all hyperalimentation solutions before administration in order to detect such errors.[20] This plea for absolute certainty has also come from within pharmacy editorial circles. Neil Davis, a recognized medication error specialist, in an editorial, suggests a final check of admixtures formulated with automatic compounders using a refractometer, providing an instantaneous reading of the approximate concentration of dextrose present.[21] Some compounders are now manufactured with such refractometers; however, the device is optional. A reference to the use of such a simple test can be found in Meyer, AJHP.[22]

22.11 Insulin Murders

Murder using insulin is not new to either the scientific, forensic, or lay press. In the first edition of this book, *Drug Injury* (2000), the Claus von Bulow story was described. It was first publicized widely as a criminal trial, then a book, then a made-for-TV movie, in which the husband is accused of criminally administering insulin shots to his wife, attempting her murder, resulting in her lapsing into a prolonged coma.

Since the time insulin was introduced in 1921, its potential dangers have been well-recognized. Deaths were well known early to have occurred in patients as a result of accidental overdosage with insulin. A literature account by Birkinshaw et al. describes the medical and scientific investigation in a case (*Regina v. Barlow*) in which a man was convicted of murdering his wife by injecting her with insulin. This was the first occasion on which such a charge was substantiated and the first in which insulin was demonstrated in human tissue, other than the pancreas, after death. In this case, the victim was found drowned in her bath. The postmortem examination and the findings at the scene where the body was found suggested that prior to her death the woman was unconscious. The absence of common poisons in the tissues of the body, the presence of vomited food on the bedclothes and in the bath, the sweat-soaked pajamas, and the grossly dilated pupils suggested that the woman was hypoglycemic. The subsequent finding of injection marks on her buttocks led to a search for insulin in the underlying tissues. A large amount of unabsorbed insulin was found in the subcutaneous tissues. The woman's husband, a male nurse, was arrested and convicted for his wife's murder, and insulin was the weapon.

Considering the potential for permanent injury, death, suicide, and murder, perhaps insulin should be added to the "extreme caution" list like potassium chloride and lidocaine! In fact, many hospitals require stringent security precautions be taken with insulin.

22.12 Hypoglycemia from the Sulfonylurea Derivatives

Early sulfa drugs used to treat soldiers in France were serendipitously discovered to lower blood sugar, some with serious and fatal results. Some sulfa substances, specifically the sulfonylureas, were subsequently proved effective in treating some diabetic patients. Although carbutamide later was withdrawn because it caused bone marrow depression, it was the precursor of today's sulfonylureas. The use of sulfonylurea in conjunction with a diet and exercise regimen continues to be a treatment modality for type 2 diabetics in the U.S. These agents work to lower plasma glucose by several proposed mechanisms. Hypoglycemia is a common and predictable adverse reaction seen with the sulfonylureas.[23]

22.13 Adverse Effects of the Sulfonylureas

The risk of adverse reactions with sulfonylurea has been described in Koda-Kimball, a pharmacists' drug therapy textbook, as an overall incidence of 5 percent of patients taking these drug will experience a side effect. Less than 2 percent of patients on these agents need to discontinue because of side effects.[24] Adverse reactions to sulfonylurea range from relatively mild complaints of gastrointestinal upset to life-threatening hypoglycemia. Hypoglycemia is reported with all sulfonylureas and can pose a significant threat to the patient. Seltzer reported a series and noted that hypoglycemic reactions from sulfonylureas had a morbidity rate of 3 percent and were lethal in 10 percent of patients reporting this side effect.[23] Factors that predispose patients to hypoglycemia include the use of high doses, age greater than 60 years old, decreased renal function, decreased hepatic function, dehydration, and decreased food intake. Oral sulfonylureas that pose the greatest threat include those with the longer half-lives (e.g., chlorpropamide, glyburide).

Hypoglycemia is a predictable adverse effect of the sulfonylureas because they stimulate insulin secretion when given acutely. In normal subjects who take sulfonylureas to cause deliberate self-harm, or who are given them inadvertently (a prescription error), high concentrations of drug lead to inappropriately high serum concentrations of insulin and may cause prolonged and recurrent hypoglycemia. Campbell and Dahlen describe that in diabetic patients, symptomatic hypoglycemia caused by sulfonylurea is common and many patients will have transient episodes that are relieved by food.[24,25] Some patients, however, develop profound, refractory, and sometimes fatal hypoglycemia from sulfonylureas. Coma may occur. Hypoglycemic episodes may last for several days, so that prolonged or repeated intravenous glucose administration is required.[4,5,7] Reactions have occurred after one dose, after several days of treatment, or after months of drug administration. Most reactions are observed in patients over 50 years of age, and they are more likely to occur in patients with impaired hepatic or renal function. Overdose or inadequate/irregular food intake may initiate hypoglycemia.

The Druggist Mutual Insurance Company, which specializes in insuring pharmacies, reports oral hypoglycemics (anti-diabetic agents) among the top-ten drug class most frequently involved in litigation, usually resulting from some prescription error, and serious injury or death. The American Society for Pharmacy Law related a hypoglycemic reaction report that was almost verbatim from a report by in the *White Sheet*. The case was originally reported by Scala-Barnett in 1986.[26]

On discharge from the hospital, a prescription was written for a patient for acetaminophen with codeine #3, one to two every four hours as needed for pain. The patient had the prescription filled as a community pharmacy. In a diary she kept, it was documented that she took the medication as directed but experienced no relief. A grocery delivery boy who saw the patient during this time related that she was stumbling in what appeared to be a drunken stupor. On the third day following discharge, concerned neighbors forced their way into her apartment and found her unconscious. Near her unconscious body were found two vials of medicine labeled Tylenol #3 and Panadol. Eight days later she died. Although initially thought to be suicide, it was discovered that the pharmacist accidentally filled her prescription with chlorpropamide (Diabenese, Pfizer, New York) instead of the prescribed acetaminophen with codeine #3. The error was discovered by emergency room personnel. They found that one of the medicine vials by the patient's body contained blue, D-shaped chlorpropamide tablets—distinctly different than the round, white acetaminophen with codeine #3 for which the vial was labeled.

Another case of hypoglycemia-induced brain injury is reported by Kalimo. While at a small local hospital as a convalescent after an infection, the patient, due to an accidental exchange of medicine, received 10 mg gliben-clamide and 50 mg phenformin at 4 P.M. one day. The following night the patient became comatose because of severe hypoglycemia. He received repeated injections of glucose intravenously starting at about 6 A.M. He awoke somewhat, but after a seizure became comatose again and the blood glucose was not measurable at 2:15 P.M., almost 24 hours after the medication error. The patient was transferred to a larger hospital where his blood glucose was normalized. On arrival, the patient's skin was cold and clammy, and he did not react to any stimuli. The patient remained unresponsive until he died three months later with signs of pulmonary edema and bronchopneumonia.

Several examples come to mind in the author's own consulting experience (O'Donnell). A 60-year-old Michigan woman was erroneously dispensed a prescription for Dymelor (acetohexamide) in place of Dynapen, an antibiotic, resulting in coma and some residual neurologic sequelae. A 65-year-old Hawaiian woman was erroneously given Dymelor in place of a prescription for Diamox, resulting in a coma, deterioration of her general health, and death shortly thereafter. The pharmacy company in Hawaii settled the wrongful death case for $400,000.

While the sulfonylureas have not been reported in criminal activities, they clearly make up the majority of community pharmacy-related hypoglycemia adverse events, and therefore should command the respect and diligence of each pharmacist handling and dispensing these products.[27]

22.14 Drug Interactions with Sulfonylureas

Besides insulin and sulfonylureas, which are given to therapeutically lower blood sugar, a large number of drugs can cause hypoglycemia or hyperglycemia or may alter the response of diabetic patients to their existing therapeutic regimens. Commonly used drugs may precipitate hypoglycemia. The antiarrhythmic agent disopyramide, which has quinidine-like actions, has been implicated in fasting hypoglycemia. Beta-adrenergic blocking agents may aggravate the defective counter-regulatory mechanisms of insulin-dependent diabetics. Other drugs that may increase the risk of hypoglycemia from sulfonylureas include other hypoglycemic agents, sulfonamides, salicylates, phenylbutazone, probenecid, dicumarol, Indomethacin, naproxen, clofibrate, angiotensin converting enzymes, theophylline, pentamidine, chloramphenicol, monoamine oxidase inhibitors, and alcohol.[24]

Drug interactions with the sulfonylureas, as with all drugs, can be characterized as being either pharmacokinetic or pharmacodynamic in nature. Pharmacokinetic interactions are those drug interactions that affect the absorption, distribution, metabolism, or excretion of a drug. Pharmacodynamic drug interactions either directly or indirectly affect the pharmacologic effect of the drug. Primary examples of pharmacokinetic interactions with the sulfonylureas include displacement interactions, as well as induced or inhibited hepatic clearance. Drugs that have pharmacodynamic interactions with the sulfonylureas include all medications that may increase or decrease blood glucose. The most common of these includes the glucocorticoids and thiazides. Pharmacodynamic interactions are also listed on Table 22.2. Included in these drug interaction tables are some nonprescription product ingredients that should also be screened for in the diabetic patient who is having difficulty in controlling her blood glucose.

22.15 Rezulin for Type 2 Diabetes

A new class of drugs was introduced in the late 1990s for treatment of diabetes. The first drug of the class, Rezulin

Table 22.2
Drug Interactions with the Sulfonylurea Agents

Decrease Blood Glucose	Increase Blood Glucose
Pharmacokinetic	
Displacement from plasma binding sites	**Enzyme induction**
Clofibrate Phenylbutazone salicylates sulfonamides	
Decrease hepatic clearance	
Dicumarol Chloramphenicol Cimetidine MAO inhibitors Methyldopa Phenylbutazone	alcohol (chronic use) Phenobarbital Rifampin
Decreased excretion	
Probenecid Phenylbutazone salicylates sulfonamides	
Pharmacodynamic	
Increase hypoglycemic effect:	**Impair insulin/increase hepatic glucose production:**
alcohol anabolic steroids Disopyramide Guanethidine Propranolol salicylates Indomethacin Lithium Pentamidine Propranolol	L-Asparaginase caffeine corticosteroids Diazoxide diuretics estrogens Isoniazid nicotinic acid (high doses) phenytoin sympathomimetics

(Troglitazone, Parke Davis), was marketed as an agent to increase the sensitivity of insulin. Shortly after the market introduction, there were reports of liver toxicity. The FDA convened an advisory hearing addressing the safety of the drug, and whether or not the drug should remain on the market. The manufacturer prepared a "Dear Doctor" letter. Several additional hepatotoxicity reports had been issued and several lawsuits had been filed; the litigation is now concluded. The "Dear Doctor" letter is reproduced below. The Advisory Committee hearing gives a good history of the adverse reaction experiences that resulted in the warnings changes. In 2000, Rezulin was withdrawn from the market because of reports of patients developing liver failure, some deaths, and several transplants. Since that time, there have been dozens of lawsuits against the manufacturer. Rezulin litigation is discussed in Section 24.7.E in Chapter 24, *Drug-Induced Liver Disease.*

22.16 Thiazolidinediones and Cardiovascular Complications

Another drug class used to treat type 2 diabetes are the thiazolidinediones. This class is used as adjunct therapy for glucose management. The mechanism of action of the drug class involves the stimulation of peroxisome proliferator activated receptors (PPAR's) to improve insulin sensitivity. In addition, these drugs also affect the kidney's sodium (Na) channels, which results in an increase in the absorption of salt and water. The end result of the effect on the kidney has now been linked to cardiovascular death from heart failure and complications. The drugs differ on the effects of the kidney, for example rosiglitazone is better than pioglitazone, and therefore there are different reports of this complication for specific drugs within the class of medications. Routine monitoring by both the endocrinologist and cardiologist can ensure that such an adverse event can be less likely to occur. In addition, the FDA has also recognized this adverse drug reaction and has issued a warning to prescribing clinicians.[28–30]

22.17 Summary and Conclusions

Clearly, the insulins and oral sulfonylureas, while providing life-sustaining therapeutic effects, frequently cause serious, severe, and sometimes permanent and fatal adverse outcomes. A thorough understanding of their proper indications, requisite monitoring, patient education, and avoidance of interactive risks provide caregivers with a clinical challenge each time these agents are used by their patients. Attorneys dealing with a case of wrongful death or injury should determine a cause for injury or death early on, preserve evidence (such as needles, IV bags and drug containers) and consult a knowledgeable expert as soon as possible.

Endnotes

1. Banting, F.G. et al. "Pancreatic extracts in the treatment of diabetes mellitus," *Can. Med. Assoc. J.* 12:141–146 (1922).

2. Schwinghammer, Terry L. "Diabetes Mellitus." In *Pharmacotherapy handbook,* Barbara Wells et al., 7th ed. New York: McGraw-Hill Medical Pub. Division, 2009;19:210-227.

3. Miyahara, R.K. "Pharmacotherapy of oral hypoglycemic agents," *Journal of Pharmacy Practice* V(5):271–279 (1992).

4. Cryer PE, Davis SN, and Shamoon H. Hypoglycemia In Diabetes. *Diabetes Care.* 2003; 26:1902-1912

5. Kearney T and Dang C. Diabetic and endocrine emergencies. *Postgrad Med J.* 2007; 83:79-86

6. Castro W, Jarvis J, Khunti K, and Davies MJ. New insulins and new insulin regimens: a review of their role in improving glycaemic control in patients with diabetes. *Postgrad Med J.* 2009; 85:257-267

7. Kwon KT and Tsai VW. Metabolic Emergencies. *Emerg Med Clin N Am.* 2007; 25:1041-1060

8. Kalimo, H. and Y. Olsson. "Effects of severe hypoglycemia on the human brain: Neuropathological case reports," *Act Neurol. Scandinav.* 62:345–356 (1980).

9. Teuscher, A. and W.G. Berger. "Hypoglycemia unawareness in diabetics transferred from beef/porcine insulin to human insulin," *Lancet,* August 15, 1987, pp. 382–385.

10. American Diabetes Association (ADA). "Insulin administration: "Position statement," *Diabetes Care* 14, Suppl 2:30 (1991).

11. Hepburn, D.A. and B.M. Frier. "Hypoglycemic unawareness and human insulin" (letter), *Lancet,* June 17, 1989, page 1393.

12. Cahill, G.F., R.A. Arky and A.J. Perlman. "Diabetes mellitus in metabolism," in *Scientific American Medicine* (NY: Scientific American, 1987).

13. Powers, Alvin C. "Diabetes Mellitus." In *Harrison's principles of internal medicine editors,* Anthony S. Fauci et al. 17th ed. New York: McGraw-Hill Medical, 2008; 338.

14. *Brauer v. Rahway Hospital,* New Jersey State Court .

15. Jellin, J.M., ed. "David G. Groves vs ER Squibb & Sons Inc., et al., Defendants. In the Circuit Court of the 11th Judicial Circuit in and for Dade County, Florida, General Jurisdiction Division Case N.:91-10473 CA 27)," *Pharm. Letter* 6:34 (1990).

16. American Medical Association (AMA). Parenteral and enteral nutrition chapter update, in *Drug Evaluations Annual 1992* (Chicago: American Medical Association, 1991), p. 2045.

17. O'Donnell, J.T. "Pharmacist error suggested in baby's brain damage," *Drug Top. Suppl. Hospital Pharmacy Report*, September, 1991, p 1, 26–27.

18. *Mark and Linda Peterson v. Fairfax Hospital et al.,* Fairfax Circuit Court. Fairfax County, VA 111-888.

19. *Edmondson v. Severino et al.,* Cook County, Illinois, No.83 L 1452.

20. Gebhart, F. "Test hyperal solutions? Fla. mom says yes," *Drug Topics Suppl. Hospital Pharmacy Report*, February 1992, p. 35.

21. Davis, N.M. "Unprecedented procedural safeguards needed with the use of automated IV compounders" (editorial), *Hospital Pharmacy* 27:488 (1992).

22. Meyer, G.E., K.A Novelli and J.E. Smith. "Use of a refractive index measurement for quality assurance of pediatric parenteral nutrient solutions," *Am. J. Hosp. Pharm.* 44:1617–1620.

23. Seltzer, H.S. "Severe drug-induced hypoglycemia: A review," *Comp. Ther.* 5:21–29 (1979)

24. Campbell, I.W. "Metformin and the sulfonylureas: Comparative risks," *Horm. Metab. Res.* 15(Suppl): 105–111, (1985).

25. Dahlen, M. et al. "Epidemiology of hypoglycemia on oral antidiabetic drugs in the island of Gotlan, Sweden," *Acta Endocrinol.* (Suppl) 263:Abstract 21 (1984).

26. Scala-Barnett, D.M. and E.R. Donoghue. "Dispensing error causing fatal chlorpropamide intoxication in a nondiabetic," *Journal of Forensic Sciences* 31(1):293–5 (1986).

27. O'Donnell, J.T. "Hypoglycemic injuries," *Legal Medicine*, November, 1994.

28. FDA MedWatch. Avandia (rosiglitazone): Ongoing Review of Cardiovascular Safety. February 2010.

29. Juurlink DN, Gomes T, Lipscombe LL, et al. Adverse cardiovascular events during treatment with pioglitazone and rosiglitazone: population based cohort study. BMJ. 2009; 1-6 [online first]

30. Khanderia U, Pop-Busui R, and Eagle KA. Thiazolidinedione In Type 2 Diabetes: A Cardiology Perspective. *Ann Pharmacother.* 2008; 42:1466-1474

Chapter 23

Nephrotoxic Drugs

Domenic A. Sica, M.D. and Todd W.B. Gehr, M.D.

23.1 Introduction

Nephrotoxicity is a non-specific term that implies the occurrence of some form of kidney damage. The term "nephrotoxicity" does not in any way specify the cause of renal damage; thus, in a strict sense this term has come to be used to describe any of a number of forms of renal injury. When nephrotoxicity occurs, it can be expected to involve both kidneys. A nephrotoxic reaction can proceed at a slow pace and be present for months or years. This pattern often goes undetected even by the most perceptive clinician. Alternatively, nephrotoxicity can emerge suddenly, progress rapidly, and reach a stage such that some form of dialysis is needed within a matter of weeks to months. This latter pattern is one which calls for prompt diagnostic and therapeutic attention.

Nephrotoxicity can be idiosyncratic, as when it occurs when an antibiotic—such as a sulfa drug—damages the kidneys in what might be viewed as an allergic reaction. In other instances, it can have a direct cause-and-effect relationship to an excess amount of drug having been administered, as might be the case with the antibiotic gentamicin. Nephrotoxicity can occur in isolation—without any organ

systems other than the kidney involved—or it can be part of a more generalized disturbance involving heart, liver, and skin, amongst other organ systems. Such a generalized disturbance is what marks a hypersensitivity reaction to the drug allopurinol, which is commonly used in the treatment of gout.

The chronic kidney disease (CKD) patient receives many medications in the hopes of slowing the progression of renal disease. Two such medication classes routinely given to the patient with CKD are angiotensin-converting enzyme (ACE) inhibitors and angiotensin receptor blockers (ARBs). Both of these drug classes provide nephroprotection through unique mechanisms—both blood pressure (BP)-dependent and BP-independent; however, the use of these medication classes is not without risk. The major such risk with these medications is in the patient with advanced CKD where a potentially life-threatening increase in serum potassium (hyperkalemia) can occur. It remains to be determined whether the failure to use these medications in the CKD patient with progressive disease represents a departure from the standard of care.

23.2 Framework of the Problem

The way in which nephrotoxicity presents (Table 23.1) can be quite varied. A systematic approach to the patient with nephrotoxicity is of the utmost importance. The elements of such an analysis include an understanding of why the kidney is susceptible to adverse drug effects and what patient type is most vulnerable. Since pre-existing renal disease sets the stage for additional side effects in organs other than the kidney, it is important to recognize the considerable and growing numbers of patients in the United States who now have end-stage renal disease (ESRD). There are now close to 500,000 patients receiving hemodialysis or peritoneal dialysis and/or who have undergone a renal transplant. The numbers of patients with CKD who do not yet require dialysis or transplantation are substantially higher. An additional important consideration is how damage is best assessed once

Table 23.1
Scenarios of Nephrotoxicity and Adverse Effects Linked to the Kidney

Scenario	Example
Direct damage to the kidney arising from excessive exposure to a known nephrotoxin	Gentamicin
Secondary damage to the kidney as the result of medication-related muscle cell damage	Simvastatin (Zocor ®)
Direct but idiosyncratic damage to the kidney as in the case of an allergic reaction	Sulfa drugs Allopurinol
Reversible damage to the kidney	Non-steroidal anti-inflammatory drugs
Damage to organ systems other than the kidney when drug doses have not been appropriately adjusted for level of renal function in the patient with chronic kidney disease	Antiarrhythmics
Inadequate treatment of hypertension or chronic kidney disease	Failure to identify the scope of the problem and/or to select appropriate therapies
Inadequate treatment of side-effects from medications used in the treatment of renal disease	Inadequate treatment of ACE inhibitor related angioedema

it has occurred and as it advances. Finally, the list of known nephrotoxins is sizable, so this chapter provides examples of these drugs and their accompanying patterns of damage. The discussion of drug nephrotoxicity patterns will include a description of where mistakes are most commonly made either in patient assessment or treatment.

23.3 Basis for the Kidney Being Susceptible to Damage

While the kidneys make up only 0.4 percent of body weight, on a minute-by-minute basis they receive roughly 25 percent of the cardiac output. Thus, the kidneys are routinely exposed to more blood-borne drugs/toxins than any organ, other than the lung. From this blood flow a filtrate is derived as blood sieves through multiple small pores located in glomeruli of which there are several million in both kid-

neys. The collective sieving potential of these glomeruli is large: on average 125-cc of filtrate is produced each minute. This value of 125-cc is conventionally termed the glomerular filtration rate (GFR).The kidney not only filters blood-borne substances, it also processes the filtrate in a manner that conserves important substances—such as sodium and potassium—and disposes of waste products, such as creatinine and urea nitrogen. In addition, the kidney is responsible for a number of specialized physiologic functions, which are easily disturbed by medications. These characteristics lend themselves to both immunological and non-immunologically-mediated injury such as alterations in renal blood flow, intrarenal drug metabolism, and tubular transport processes.

23.4 Patient Groups Most Susceptible to Nephrotoxicity

Glomeruli can be easily damaged by direct exposure to environmental toxins or drugs; however, the effect of environmental toxins or drugs on the kidney can be quite subtle and often go unappreciated even by the most astute clinician. Irrespective of the cause, a reduction in renal function increases the future risk of developing nephrotoxicity. Chronic kidney disease can predispose to nephrotoxicity in three ways: (1) CKD limits the clearance from the body of a number of medications, which can result in systemic drug accumulation and therein the potential for concentration-dependent renal side-effects (unless the medication dose has been adjusted according to the reduced level of renal function). (2) In CKD, the already-damaged kidney is, in many instances, unable to cope with further metabolic and toxic change, as may be imposed on it with drug exposure. (3) CKD is a condition that often co-exists with other disease states, including diabetes, hypertension, coronary artery disease, and heart failure. With such a grouping of diseases, it is inevitable that "polypharmacy" becomes the norm. Whenever multiple medications are being given, the risk of drug-drug toxic interactions increases. The kidney can then become the object of such interactions. Finally, the elderly are a patient group particularly predisposed to drug-related nephrotoxicity. This greater risk of nephrotoxicity in the aged relates to the slowed disposal of drugs by both the senescent liver and kidney, which, not unexpectedly, allows blood levels for many medications to increase.

23.5 Demographics of Chronic Kidney Disease

Chronic kidney disease is globally prevalent, and over the last decade has increasingly been recognized as a health care problem of some considerable significance in the United

States. In the United States, the incidence and prevalence of kidney failure has steadily increased in the past decade. More than 10 percent of people—over 20 million, aged 20 years or older—have CKD in the United States. About 110,000 patients in the United States started treatment for ESRD in 2007, with the leading causes of ESRD being diabetes and hypertension. In 2006, seven out of 10 new cases of ESRD in the United States had diabetes or hypertension listed as the primary cause. The incidence of ESRD is greater among adults older than 65 years. African Americans are nearly four times more likely to develop ESRD than Caucasians, a disparity that has been decreasing over the last decade.[1]

Chronic kidney disease is associated with poor outcomes and high costs, especially in the elderly. Dialysis treatment costs Medicare almost $72,000 per patient per year. Total outlays for patients in kidney failure were $23 billion in 2006, 6.4 percent of Medicare's total budget. Overall, CKD and its complications account for over $49 billion, or about 25 percent of all annual Medicare expenditures. Chronic kidney disease is defined by either kidney damage, as manifested by the presence of an abnormal urinalysis, protein or blood in the urine, or a glomerular filtration rate of less than 60 ml per minute per 1.73 m² for three months or more. The most recent reporting of CKD prevalence in the United States finds an increased prevalence of all stages, which is at least, in part, explained by a rise in the prevalence of obesity, diagnosed diabetes, and treated hypertension. The primary causes of CKD remain diabetes and hypertension.[2] In an effort to better define this large group of patients, the National Kidney Foundation has developed a new classification system for CKD (Table 23.2). This system assigns patients a stage based on their GFR, which can be estimated from the serum creatinine (see discussion below).[3] This staging system has been in place for almost a decade and, with time, will be further refined to reflect the changing demographic of renal disease in the United States.

Table 23.2
Stages of Chronic Kidney Disease

Stage	Description	GFR (mL/min)
1	Chronic kidney damage with normal or increased GFR	>90
2	Mild	60-89
3	Moderate	30-59
4	Severe	15-29
5	Kidney failure	<15 or requiring dialysis

23.6 Methods to Assess Renal Function and/or Damage

The commonly available measures to test for nephrotoxicity are fairly insensitive, so damage can go unnoticed for some time. Serum creatinine measurements remain one of the most widely used tests for gauging renal function since elevated levels, when indexed for muscle mass, are indicative of kidney disease. Creatinine is a product of creatine metabolism in muscle, and its daily production correlates closely with muscle mass; thus, the greater the muscle mass, the higher the "normal" serum creatinine. For example, in a heavily muscled male, a serum creatinine value of 1.4 mg/dL might be considered normal, though such a value may be considered grossly abnormal in an individual with less muscle mass, such as a frail elderly female. Furthermore, as CKD progresses, the interpretation of an increasing serum creatinine value becomes even more problematic in that serum creatinine changes poorly correlate with actual GFR changes.[4]

Normal serum creatinine concentrations for a typical adult population range from 0.5-1.3 mg/dL (40-110 μmol/L) in males to 0.5-1.1 mg/dL (40-100 μmol/L) in females. Although a serum creatinine may fall within these established ranges it does not automatically follow that renal function is normal, since a specific serum creatinine value can be associated with a wide range of GFR values. For example, an individual with low muscle mass—such as an elderly female—with normal renal function might be expected to have a serum creatinine value close to 0.5 mg/dL. If this individual presents with a serum creatinine of 1.0 mg/dL, although this value is in the normal "population range," it represents a significant departure from the expected norm for this individual. Since the percent of renal function is reciprocally related to a change in serum creatinine concentrations, this doubling of her serum creatinine value corresponds to a halving of renal function.

Because of the aforementioned limitations of utilizing serum creatinine to estimate kidney function, more reliance on utilizing the estimated GFR has become standard medical practice. Most laboratories now report an estimated GFR for African Americans and non-African Americans based on the serum creatinine and the demographics of the patient. Most estimations of GFR utilize combinations of the serum creatinine, age, race, sex, and body size. One of these equations, the MDRD (Modification of Diet in Renal Disease) Study equation, has become the most widely used of these equations and most laboratories use this equation to estimate GFR when a serum creatinine is ordered for a particular patient. Because this equation was developed in a patient population with CKD, the accuracy of the equation is a major limitation, especially at GFR values over 60 ml/min. Because of these limitations the estimated GFR is not reported precisely for individuals with GFR values over 60 ml/min. A newly devised equation, the CKD-EPI equation, has been developed to overcome the limitations of the MDRD equation and appears to be more accurate at higher GFR values.[5] This equation or its variation will likely replace the MDRD equation for the estimation of GFR values for individual patients, although there will continue to be a distinction made between African Americans and non-African Americans. Suffice it to say, the GFR value has replaced the serum creatinine for the determination of CKD in individual patients. Failure to recognize this would now be considered a breach in the standard of care.

Thus, one of the most common errors on the part of a healthcare provider is the failure to recognize the limited sensitivity of a serum creatinine value to detect acute functional change, as well as the inability to monitor progressive disease. In the setting of progressive kidney disease it is not uncommon for considerable loss of kidney function to have occurred before referral to a kidney specialist. The exact timing of such referral remains a matter of substantial debate. Alternatively, if an acute process is at play—be it nephrotoxic or otherwise—referral should occur within a matter of days to weeks. Failure to refer to a kidney specialist in a timely fashion can be viewed as a deviation from the standard of care.

23.7 Level of Renal Function at which Drug Accumulation Occurs

The total body clearance (TBC) of a compound is the summed value of individual organ clearances including the liver and kidney amongst other organs such as skin, intestine, and muscle. Renal clearance is an important contributor to the TBC of several compounds including ACE inhibitors, certain β-blockers, most diuretics, and a number of antibiotics, antiarrhythmics, and pain medications. To be clinically important, the renal clearance of a drug need not be high in absolute terms, as long as the fractional contribution to the TBC is >50 percent. Renally cleared compounds begin to accumulate at function levels <60 percent of normal, although the precise level of renal function at which clinically relevant changes in drug clearance occur is compound-specific. It is at GFR values <30 percent of normal that the issue of drug accumulation legitimately surfaces though as stated previously significant drug accumulation can occur even at higher levels of function.[6]

Drug accumulation is pertinent in a number of ways for CVR compounds. First, if the compound administered has a narrow therapeutic window, any accumulation can result in excessive drug blood levels with sometimes hazardous consequences. For instance, excessive systemic accumulation of an antihypertensive compound can lead to a prolonged drop in BP. If the GFR falls as the result of such a BP drop, the renal clearance of a compound can be further reduced with additional drug accumulation. Second, if an administered compound has well-established concentration-related side-effects, they will occur more often and with greater severity when a drug accumulates. This is the case with renally-cleared β-blockers and the side-effect of sedation. Finally, drug accumulation increases the risk of drug-drug interactions, and thereby produces a risk from concurrent therapy that otherwise would be absent.

23.8 Nephrotoxic Drugs

The clinician should have a good working knowledge of the elimination profile of individual medications and any adverse effects that might be attributable to drug accumulation.

Prompt clinical action in the face of nephrotoxicity means identifying the offending medication/toxin and withdrawing it. Discontinuation of the medication is but the first step that needs to be taken. Of equal importance is the establishment of the rate of progression of the renal injury. This typically requires serial assessment of renal function (e.g., serum creatinine measurements), implementation of any of several recognized treatments that are reaction-specific, and discussion between the primary-care physician and the specialist evaluating the patient. As previously mentioned, nephrotoxicity can be sudden or it can be slowly-to-moderately progressive. It is the former that can prove life-threatening, and—if not quickly identified—permanent renal damage, if not death, can ensue. It is the latter that can present the greatest diagnostic challenge to the clinician. This is the area where judgment errors occur.

23.9 Nephrotoxicity Scenarios

Several medications have the potential to be nephrotoxic. Medication-related renal damage is oftentimes slow moving with pre-existent CKD increasing the risk of injury.

A. Lithium Toxicity

A 48-year-old Caucasian male with bipolar disorder has received lithium for over 20 years. His lithium levels have been sporadically checked, in part, because of poor appointment compliance. His lithium levels have been high when measured. His lithium dose was not changed since he was symptom free beyond urinary frequency, and his bipolar disorder was "stable." Recently, his lithium dose was reduced because of symptoms of lithium toxicity. A review of his laboratory studies shows that he has had a slowly rising serum creatinine value over the last several years. Five years previously, he had 70 percent of his expected renal function. A more recent measurement now shows him to have 40 percent of expected kidney function. The patient was never informed of his having lost over 50 percent of his renal function and files suit.

Discussion: Renal failure is a not uncommon complication of long-term lithium therapy, which can only be recognized with routine monitoring of renal function.[7] Once renal failure is diagnosed in a lithium-treated patient (oftentimes it is a diagnosis of exclusion for a lithium-related etiology) a treatment plan should be established. Any such treatment plan should involve the patient in a decision on the advisability of continuing therapy, particularly if the renal failure is at an advanced stage. Failure to do so can be construed to represent a departure from the standard of care. In a patient such as this, where factual recall can be called into question, any discussion of long-term treatment options should be witnessed. Moderately advanced lithium-related renal failure may go unrecognized if the parties treating such patients are unfamiliar with the importance of small changes in serum creatinine as a marker of progressive renal failure. This may be the case for psychiatrists who assume a de facto primary-care role for a patient.

B. Gentamicin Toxicity

A 70-year-old female weighing 60 kg was admitted to the hospital with osteomyelitis in her foot. Physicians prescribed her the antibiotics nafcillin and gentamicin. Nafcillin was given at a dose of 1 gram intravenously every 4 hours and gentamicin was prescribed at a dose of 5 mg/kg (300 mg) intravenously once daily. Routine admission labs reveal normal electrolytes and a serum creatinine concentration of 1.4 mg/dL. One week later, the patient showed clinical improvement. However, her serum creatinine rose to 1.7 mg/dL. She was discharged and arrangements were made for her to receive gentamicin at home. Her gentamicin was continued, without dosage adjustment, for an additional week. There was no further assessment of renal function, and gentamicin levels were not obtained over the ensuing week. At the end of the second week of treatment, the patient complained of dizziness and an inability to walk without assistance. Laboratory evaluation revealed a serum creatinine of 5.8 mg/dL and a consultation was obtained for acute kidney injury. The gentamicin was stopped and her acute kidney injury gradually resolved over several days. However, her dizziness persisted and she had considerable difficulty ambulating. Six months later she was diagnosed with vestibular toxicity from the gentamicin.

She filed suit against the treating physician and the home health agency.

Discussion: Antibiotics can cause acute kidney injury. In this case, either nafcillin (causing allergic interstitial nephritis) or the aminoglycoside antibiotic gentamicin (causing acute tubular necrosis) were possible culprits that may have caused acute kidney injury (although gentamicin toxicity is a more likely etiology). Aminoglycoside antibiotics are widely prescribed for serious infections and are drugs extensively eliminated by the kidneys; therefore, dosage adjustment is necessary to avoid excessively high levels in patients with pre-existing or developed renal failure. This patient had a serum creatinine of 1.4 mg/dL, which was a value in the normal population range; however, it reflected her having at baseline but 35 percent of normal renal function. Early on, the gentamicin dosage given should have reflected this significant reduction in her level of renal function.

The monitoring of plasma gentamicin concentrations is of some importance in the accurate dosing of this medication in a patient with pre-existing renal disease.[8] In this case, therapeutic drug-level monitoring for gentamicin should have been performed in conjunction with its administration. Aminoglycoside antibiotics cause both acute kidney injury and vestibular toxicity (dizziness and imbalance), side effects which are dependent on dose, duration of therapy, age and the level of kidney function.[9] However, the latter has a less defined relationship with elevated blood levels and is best avoided by keeping treatment to the absolute minimum amount of time.[10] This scenario represented a breach in the standard of care. Although gentamicin toxicity may be unavoidable in certain situations (owing to the nature of the infection and, sometimes, a need for a lengthy duration of therapy), careful monitoring of gentamicin blood levels can minimize its risk. When a lengthy course of treatment with gentamicin is anticipated, it is clearly the responsibility of the physician to warn the patient of the possible occurrence of these disabling and potentially life-threatening toxicities. Moreover, the patient should be routinely questioned as to the beginning signs of vestibular toxicity, since its early identification affords the opportunity to immediately discontinue gentamicin, thereby lessening the risk of additional vestibular toxicity.

The treatment modalities used in the management of ESRD themselves can carry risk. An adverse outcome within a dialysis facility can have multiple potential causes, as well as a considerable diffusion of blame.

C. Dialysis-Related Issues

A 40-year-old hemodialysis patient was asleep during a routine dialysis procedure. He was covered in a blanket and his vital signs were normal at the start of dialysis. He had been on hemodialysis for five years, had well-controlled hypertension and was gainfully employed at a local bank. Three hours into his dialysis session, a pressure alarm sounded from his dialysis machine. The technician caring for him did not disturb him and simply reset the alarm. Ten minutes later, a BP alarm signaled low BP. The technician attempted to arouse the patient, but was unsuccessful. A futile attempt was made to resuscitate the patient. A large pool of blood was noted under and behind the patient's chair during the resuscitation attempt.

Discussion: With such a technical procedure being performed an average of three times per week, it is surprising that mistakes are not more frequent. This patient had a partially dislodged venous dialysis needle, which resulted in his exsanguination.[11,12] A number of avoidable mishaps can occur in the dialysis unit, some of which are listed in Table 23.3.[13] These mishaps can be the responsibility of the technician/ nurse tending to the patient or, on occasion, can be the result of physician error. Physicians are not routinely in attendance for the entirety of a dialysis session and therefore must rely on the hemodialysis staff for the timely and accurate reporting of patient problems. Judgment errors on the part of the treating physician can occur if hemodialysis staff miscommunicate their "sense" of a patient's clinical condition.

Failure to appreciate the need to avoid certain drugs and/or to lower medication doses in CKD can prove fatal. The ultimate responsibility for appropriate drug therapy in CKD rests in the hands of the primary treating physician. Consultants experienced in the management of the patient with CKD should be used early and often when hospitalization occurs.

D. Drug Clearance in Relationship to Renal Failure

A 32-year-old dialysis patient was in a severe vehicle accident and was admitted to the hospital with multiple fractures. Since he had been dialyzed that day, the dialysis service was not notified of his admission, presuming that it would be a couple of days before he would need to undergo dialysis again. Because of severe pain, physicians prescribed the administration of meperidine (Demerol ®) 75 mg, given intramuscularly every four hours. Two days after he began meperidine, he experienced twitching, tremors, and muscle spasms. This was reported to the surgery team primarily responsible for this patient's care. The nursing staff was asked to observe the patient carefully and to notify the dialysis service. Shortly thereafter, the patient experienced several seizures, aspirates, and died shortly thereafter. A suit was filed by the patient's family against the surgery team, nursing staff, and hospital pharmacy services.

Table 23.3
Mishaps Related to Hemodialysis

Dialysate problems:
- Endotoxin exposure
- Chloramine exposure
- Fluoride exposure

Dialyzer reactions:
- First use syndromes
- Reuse related problems, infection transmission
- Anaphylactoid reactions to ACE inhibitors

Process-related problems:
- Hypotension/hypertension
- Hemolysis
- Blood loss
- Access infections
- Air embolus

Discussion: Renally-cleared drugs and/or their metabolites systemically accumulate in patients with CKD, unless the medication dose is lowered. In many instances, such drug buildup is unimportant. In other cases, when small changes in drug levels carry significant risk (narrow therapeutic index), life-threatening complications may arise.[6] The case outlined above illustrates this issue. Meperidine is metabolized to an active metabolite, normeperidine, which gradually accumulates in the CKD patient and lowers the threshold for seizures.[14] The breach in the standard of care in this patient went beyond simply failing to adjust the dose of this medication. The breach in this case arose from having even prescribed this compound without first understanding the risks inherent to its use in advanced stage renal failure. Moreover, physicians familiar with drug-dosing in renal failure were not consulted in a timely manner. If such had occurred, this medication would have been discontinued, dialysis instituted, and death averted.

In another case, a 70-year-old patient had an acute myocardial infarction complicated by ventricular tachycardia—a potentially life-threatening rhythm disturbance. Treating clinicians administered an antiarrhythmic—procainamide— via IV. As a result, the patient's ventricular tachycardia was brought under control. His serum creatinine at the time of admission was 4.5 mg/dL, indicative of approximately 25 percent of normal renal function. He is placed on a standard maintenance dose of oral procainamide in an amount not adjusted for his level of renal failure. Two days later, in the afternoon, he developed a fatal arrhythmia. Serum procainamide concentrations obtained the morning of the event were twice the upper limit of normal. Serum concentrations of the active metabolite of procainamide N-acetylprocainamide were four times the upper limit of normal.

Discussion: Excessive increases in the blood levels of renally cleared compounds can be avoided in patients with renal failure by administering lower doses with the same interval between doses, or longer intervals between doses (without adjustment of the actual dose amount). This antiarrhythmic and its active metabolite are both cleared from the body by the renal route and will accumulate in the renal-failure patient, unless the standard dose is reduced.[15] The breach in the standard of care in this instance was glaring, involving an inadequate understanding of the narrow therapeutic index in patients with advanced-stage renal failure. Moreover, there was a lapse in reporting the blood levels of procainamide and its metabolite to the treating physician. Without this critical information, the physician of record was unable to take the necessary steps to avert this catastrophe.

Therapies in common use in renal failure can cause distinctive side effects. Physicians should be familiar with the manner of presentation for such side effects as well as what would be considered best care treatment.

E. Angioedema with an ACE Inhibitor

A 45-year-old African-American male was evaluated for hypertension and CKD. His blood pressure was measured at 150/105 during a routine office visit. In light of his having CKD, he was started on the ACE inhibitor lisinopril and scheduled for follow-up in two weeks. Two days after beginning lisinopril, he developed swelling of his lower lip, which subsided over several hours without treatment. The next day, he experienced the same symptom—but this time, his tongue was swollen. He went to the emergency department and was treated with an antihistamine, as well as with epinephrine and intravenous steroids. His symptoms abated over the next 12 hours and he was discharged for follow-up with his treating physician. He was given no instructions at the time of discharge from the emergency department (the discharging physician differed from the admitting physician). The next day, the patient took another dose of his lisinopril. Shortly thereafter, he experienced profound swelling of his lips and tongue. By the time the rescue squad arrived, he was in full arrest and could not be resuscitated. His wife filed suit against the emergency department physician.

Discussion: ACE inhibitor-related angioedema (life-threatening lip and tongue swelling with the potential for airway occlusion) is two to three times more common in African Americans than in Caucasians. Once it has occurred, the risk of a subsequent episode (oftentimes more severe) rises significantly. Although the emergency department management was reasonable, there was a breach in the standard of care at discharge. Failure to advise the patient to stop his ACE inhibitor was a significant oversight. Once the ACE inhibitor angioedema is administered, subsequent use of any of the several compounds in this class is absolutely contraindicated (and the patient should be so informed). Management errors at the time of the episode can also become the basis for filing suit in the case of ACE-inhibitor angioedema. Adverse outcomes in an angioedema patient occur frequently in the several-hour time span shortly after admission. Errors are typically made in the floor monitoring of newly admitted patients, as well as in the transition of responsibility for care from the emergency-department physician to the admitting physician. It is often difficult to identify where the line of responsibility falls at the time of an adverse outcome in an angioedema patient.[16]

Hyperkalemia is becoming a much more common occurrence in renal failure patients with the growing use of reno- and cardioprotective therapies that decrease renal elimination of potassium.

F. Fatal Hyperkalemia with Medications

A 65-year-old male with a history of heart failure was being treated with standard therapy consisting of the ACE inhibitor enalapril, the beta-blocker metoprolol, digoxin, furosemide, and supplemental potassium chloride. His serum creatinine was 1.4 mg/dL ($\approx$ 60 percent of normal renal function) and he weighed 65 kg. He was clinically stable, until he presented to the emergency department of a local hospital with an acute myocardial infarction. After a short hospitalization, he was discharged on his pre-admission medication regimen (other than for the addition of the potassium-sparing diuretic spironolactone). His serum creatinine at discharge was 2.0 mg/dL ($\approx$ 40 percent of normal renal function) and his serum potassium was 4.8 mEq/L (normal range—3.5 to 5.0 mEq/L). Once discharged, he developed a gastrointestinal illness, and with it, increasing weakness, which continued for several days. On Friday, staff called his family physician, and the patient was instructed to come into the office on Monday if his symptoms did not improve. Shortly thereafter, he presented to a local emergency department with profound lower-extremity weakness and was found to have a serum potassium value of 7.5 mEq/L and a serum creatinine concentration of 4.5 mg/dL ($\approx$ 15 percent of normal renal function). His blood pressure was 70/40-mmHg and an electrocardiogram showed a "sine wave" pattern (classic pattern for advanced cardiotoxicity with hyperkalemia). Before the hyperkalemia could be initiated, the patient experienced a cardiopulmonary arrest. Although successfully resuscitated, he suffered anoxic brain damage and thereafter required permanent nursing home-care. A suit was filed against the primary care and emergency department physicians.

Discussion: Patients with complex cardiac disorders often require multiple medical therapies; therefore, the medications used in this particular patient represented standard therapies. However, as the patient's clinical condition deteriorated, it was essential that his prescription regimen be adjusted. When a patient is receiving multiple therapies capable of increasing serum potassium values, it is incumbent upon a healthcare provider to be mindful of circumstances where serum potassium values might further rise. Failure to do so can result in serious elevations in serum potassium going undetected with potentially disastrous consequences (as was the case for this patient). At the time of call-in with complaints of an undercurrent illness, steps were not taken to immediately have the patient seen. The breach in the standard of care herein was reflected in the failure to appreciate the risk of life-threatening hyperkalemia in this patient. The risk of a life-threatening elevation in serum potassium should have been anticipated for three reasons: (1) At the time of discharge following his myocardial infarction he already had a high-normal serum-potassium value, (2) discharge medications included supplemental potassium, as well as two compounds with known potassium-conserving properties—enalapril and spironolactone, and (3) an intercurrent illness leading to dehydration and an additional reduction in renal function is one of the main reasons that severe hyperkalemia develops in a patient multiply-medicated in this fashion. Careful attention to patient instruction (such as advising the patient that if significant dehydration develops for any reason [as gauged by weight loss] to contact his physician immediately) is imperative. An earlier physician visit or simply obtaining some measurement of serum potassium would have reduced the chances of this patient experiencing a cardiopulmonary arrest.[17]

Certain drugs, such as statins, can cause acute renal failure arising from muscle cell damage. An understanding of the manner in which this form of renal damage presents should be common knowledge based on the widespread use of these cholesterol-lowering agents.

G. Statin Therapy and the Development of Myopathy

A 70-year-old male with diabetes and hypertension developed hypercholesterolemia and hypertriglyceridemia, and therapy was begun with a statin for his lipid abnormalities. At first, he tolerated the medication, and the statin dose was gradually increased. With dose escalation, he developed mild muscle weakness and pain, which he attributed to his having a viral syndrome. These symptoms gradually subsided and were mentioned to his treating physician at the next office visit. The physician charted the symptoms, and in further management of the lipid abnormalities, gemfibrozil was added to his regimen. Two weeks later, he developed muscle pain and weakness, which gradually increased over several days. He spoke with staff in the office of his internist, who advised him to "stick it out," believing that he had a viral illness. Ultimately, he was brought to the emergency department, where he was diagnosed as having severe muscle damage (rhabdomyolysis) and related acute kidney injury. He required hemodialysis. Four weeks after his episode of rhabdomyolysis, he was still undergoing routine-maintenance hemodialysis. He filed suit against his internist and pharmacist.

Discussion: Statins (3-hydroxy-3-methylglutaryl coenzyme A reductase inhibitors) are associated with a range of skeletal muscle complaints and enzyme findings, including myositis and rhabdomyolysis, serum creatine kinase (CK) elevations, myalgia with and without elevated CK levels, muscle weakness, muscle cramps, and persistent myalgia and CK elevations—even with statin withdrawal. The risk of rhabdomyolysis and other adverse effects with statin use can be increased by several factors and especially concomitant medications. Medications such as the fibrate gemfibrozil alter statin metabolism and increase statin plasma concentration and noticeably increase the risk of rhabdomyolysis. Currently, no screening test is available to determine who is at risk for myopathy with a statin; therefore, patients should be advised to watch for generalized muscle pain or weakness, and if it occurs, to stop these medications, even as symptoms are being reported. The breach in the standard of care in this case was in the failure to recognize that the pre-gemfibrozil symptoms in this patient were likely secondary to statin-linked muscle toxicity. In such patients, subsequent statin-fibrate combination therapy must be undertaken cautiously and only after a careful risk-benefit assessment. Patient counseling on the risks and warning signs of myopathy is critical, but did not occur in this case. Forced to make a decision on his own, this patient believed that this second wave of symptoms would lessen as they had done before. Earlier detection, discontinuation of the culprit medications, and directed treatment would likely have favorably changed the outcome in this case.[17]

23.10 Conclusions

Chronic kidney disease is becoming more prevalent in the United States. As the patient numbers with this disease grow, the chance for adverse medication-related and/or device outcomes is following suit. The timing of CKD recognition and the management instituted can have legal consequences. The standard of care for the patient with CKD is evolving at a steady pace. Physicians must be knowledgeable on the recommended strategies to slow the rate of progression of CKD. In addition, they should be cognizant of the important role the kidney plays in drug elimination. Furthermore, the kidney is an organ liable to being injured by a wide range of medications and environmental substances. In most cases, evolving kidney disease is asymptomatic; thus, detecting progressive medication-related renal disease calls for keen interpretive skills of renal function measures.

Endnotes

1. National Kidney Foundation. *K/DOQI clinical practice guidelines for chronic kidney disease: evaluation, classification, and stratification.* Am. J. Kidney Dis. 2002; 39(2 Suppl 1): S1-S266.

2. A.F. Castro, J. Coresh. *CKD surveillance using laboratory data from the population-based national health and nutrition examination survey (NHANES).* Am. J. Kidney Dis. 2009; 53 (Supplement 3): S46-S55.

3. National Kidney Foundation. *What is chronic kidney disease?* Available at: www.kidney.org/kidneydisease. Accessed July 15, 2010.

4. D. A. Sica. *Complications of hypertension: kidney.* In: Cardiology: Crawford MH, DiMarco JP (Eds) (2nd edition) Mosby, London, England. 2004: 501-510.

5. A.S. Levy, L.A. Stevens, C.H. Shmid, et. Al. *A new equation to estimate glomerular filtration rate.* Ann. Int. Med. 2009; 150:604-612.

6. D.A. Sica. *Drug dosing in renal disease.* In The Kidney and Hypertension, Bakris G (Ed) (1st edition), Martin Dunitz, London. England. 2003: 127-138.

7. M. Gitlin. *Lithium and the kidney: an updated review.* Drug Saf. 1999; 20: 231-243.

8. C. Bartal, A. Danon, F. Schlaeffer, et al. *Pharmacokinetic dosing of aminoglycosides: a controlled trial.* Am. J. Med. 2003; 114: 194-198.

9. C.M. Lu, S.H. James, Y.H. Lien. *Acute massive gentamicin intoxication in a patient with end-stage renal disease.* Am. J. Kidney Dis. 1996; 28: 767-771.

10. R.E. Ariano, S.A. Zelenitsky, D.A. Kassum. *Aminoglycoside-induced vestibular injury: maintaining a sense of balance.* Ann. Pharmacother. 2008; 42:1282-1289.

11. T. Roy. *Patients' safety and haemodialysis devices.* Nephrol. Dial. Transplant. 2001; 16: 2138-2142.

12. J.P. Van Waeleghem, M. Chamney, E.J. Lindley, et al. *Venous needle dislodgement: how to minimize the risks.* J. Ren. Care. 2008; 34:163-168.

13. X. Bosch. *Medical devices firm offers answer to unexplained haemodialysis deaths.* Lancet. 2001; 358: 1622.

14. K.O. Hagmeyer, L.S. Mauro, V.F. Mauro. *Meperidine-related seizures associated with patient-controlled analgesia pumps.* Ann. Pharmacother. 1993; 27: 29-32.

15. J.A. Reiffel, G. Appel. *Importance of QT interval determination and renal function assessment during antiarrhythmic drug therapy.* J. Cardiovasc. Pharmacol. Ther. 2001; 6: 111-9.

16. D.A. Sica, H.R. Black. *Current concepts of pharmacotherapy in hypertension: ACE inhibitor-related angioedema: can angiotensin-receptor blockers be safely used?* J. Clin. Hypertens. (Greenwich). 2002; 4: 375-380.

17. D.A. Sica, T.W.B. Gehr. *HMG-CoA reductase inhibitors and rhabdomyolysis: considerations in the renal failure patient.* Curr. Opin. Nephrol. Hypertens. 2002; 11: 123-133.

Chapter 24

Drug-Induced Liver Disease

Donald H. Marks, M.D., Ph.D. and James T. O'Donnell, Pharm.D., MS, FCP

24.1 Introduction: The Problem of Drug-Induced Liver Disease

No discussion of gastrointestinal pathology would be complete without consideration and examination of drug-induced hepatotoxicity, also referred to as drug-induced liver disease (DILD) or drug-induced liver injury (DILI). Given the complexity and importance of the liver's drug-metabolizing systems, the fact that drugs and chemicals can poison the liver is or should be of utmost concern to pharmacists and physicians.

An exposition of the metabolic processes promotes understanding of how certain drug interactions occur and what to do about those interactions. A discussion of toxic mechanisms and specific drug-related hepatotoxicity is also important. As contrasted to prescribing physicians, pharmacists may be able to do comparatively little to prevent that toxicity, other than to recognize patients at risk, to understand the meanings and values of certain liver tests and interpretations, to recommend to patients when and why liver-function testing is important, and to inform the patient what drugs to avoid, why alcohol may make other drugs toxic, and so forth.

Injury to the liver is a common complication of drug therapy. Almost the entire spectrum of hepatic diseases can be mimicked by injury related to drug administration, including cholestatic conditions, granulomas, various forms of hepatitis, vascular disease and tumors. When confronted with a patient with liver disease, the treating physician must consider the possibility of drug-induced hepatic injury.

24.2 History of Adverse Drug Reactions

Following a major increase in the 1960s, the incidence of drug-induced liver disease has continued to rise. A larger number of agents now appear to contribute to the total burden of drug-induced liver disease, but the incidence of hepatotoxicity for most drugs is still very low. Several of the best known hepatotoxic drugs have been abandoned, or their use is diminishing. Paracetamol, halothane, isoniazid, and anticancer drugs are among the agents that continue to cause concern.

Drugs are an uncommon cause of most types of liver disease. However, in comparison to similar disorders resulting from other etiologies, drug-induced disorders tend to be more severe. This, together with the diversity of hepatic lesions that drug reactions may produce, are reasons why drug-induced liver disease assumes an importance that is disproportionate to its low incidence.

The modern era of chemotherapeutics was introduced by the use of sulfonamides, penicillin, agents that correct hormonal disturbances, antituberculous drugs, and eventually cytostatic antileukemic drugs. Thus, reports of hepatic injury and jaundice due to sulfonamides, antithyroid drugs, anabolic steroids, and methotrexate gradually appeared during the 1940s and early 1950s. Many of the drugs used during the first 70 years of the twentieth century carried a hepatotoxic potential that was not recognized for many years. One of the most spectacular examples was oxyphenisatin, a component of many popular laxatives, including Carter's Little Liver Pills. This agent was used for 40 years before Reynolds et al. (1971) identified it as the cause of "puzzling cases" of acute or chronic hepatitis.[1]

During the last 50 years, there has been an exponential increase in the quantity and diversity of therapeutic substances introduced into medical practice. For most of these, hepatotoxicity (or more usually, an adverse hepatic drug reaction) is an exceedingly rare complication; typical levels of risk are one to ten per 100,000 of those exposed. It is, therefore, not surprising that recognition that a new drug can cause liver disease is often delayed until many years after the commencement of marketing. There may then be a further delay before there is widespread awareness of that drug's potential to cause a hepatic drug reaction. Typical examples are alpha-methyldopa, isoniazid, and erythromycin esters. Alternatively, some physicians may initially refuse to accept that an otherwise useful and safe drug is really the causative agent for liver disease that has been ascribed to it. The prototypical example is the controversy that surrounded halothane as a possible cause of postoperative jaundice. Failure to accept that a drug can cause liver disease will retard efforts to reduce the frequency of the reaction.

The entire spectrum of liver injury associated with viral hepatitis, both morphologic and clinical, can result from drug administration. The assumption that a disease resembling viral hepatitis is actually produced by a drug will continue to rest on evidence provided by historical and epidemiologic data.

Hepatitic reactions can be unpredictable and, with few exceptions, are not produced in animals. In contrast to cholestatic drug reactions, which are common and relatively benign, hepatocellular reactions are uncommon, but are associated with significant mortality.

Examples of hepatotoxic drugs include halothane, isoniazid, phenytoin and carbamazepine. The presence of eosinophilia is occasionally helpful in suggesting drug-induced hepatitis, but this finding in the blood occurs in fewer than half the patients. Upon withdrawal of the offending agent, patients generally recover without sequelae. However, a second exposure, as in the case of halothane, may precipitate massive hepatic necrosis.

24.3 Overview of DILD Pathogenesis, Risk Factors, Presentation and Organization

The ability of a wide range of medications to cause DILD is well-known to the medical community. Familiar examples include acetaminophen, methotrexate, and statins. The liver is one of the principal sites of drug metabolism and detoxification in the body. Many medications pass through the liver and remain concentrated there, leading to local higher concentrations of potentially hepatotoxic medications. People are genetically diverse, which affects the way each of us metabolizes drugs and other chemicals. Liver toxicity of medication should be taken in the context of the increasing number of different medications available, the rising number of medications individual patients are concurrently taking, the complexity of drug-drug interactions, and the toxicity of drug metabolites.

According to a guidance issued by the FDA in August 2009 (updating a 2007 report on the same topic), DILI "has been the most frequent single cause of safety-related drug marketing withdrawals for the past 50 years (e.g., iproniazid), continuing to the present (e.g., ticrynafen, benoxaprofen, bromfenac, troglitazone, nefazodone). Hepatotoxicity discovered after approval for marketing also has limited the use of many drugs....Several drugs have not been approved in the United States because European marketing experience revealed their hepatotoxicity (e.g., ibufenac, perhexiline, alpidem). Finally, some drugs were not approved in the United States because premarketing experience provided evidence of the potential for severe DILI (e.g., dilevalol, tasosartan, ximelagatran)."[2]

The FDA report was designed to describe ways to distinguish drugs which have potential hepatotoxicity from those that do not. "Evidence of hepatocellular injury is...a necessary, but not sufficient, signal of the potential to cause severe DILI."[2]

A more specific signal of such potential is a higher rate of more marked peak AT elevations (10×-, 15×ULN), with cases of increases to >1,000 U/L causing increased concern. The single clearest (most specific) predictor found to date of a drug's potential for severe hepatotoxicity, however, is the occurrence of a small number of cases of hepatocellular injury (aminotransferase elevation) accompanied by increased serum total bilirubin (TBL), not explained by any other cause, such as viral hepatitis or exposure to other hepatotoxins, and without evidence of cholestasis, together with an increased incidence of AT elevations in the overall trial population compared to control. Increased plasma prothrombin time, or its international normalized ratio (INR), a consequence of reduced hepatic production of Vitamin K-dependent clotting factors, is another potentially useful measure of liver function that might suggest the potential for severe liver injury.

DILD is a relatively uncommon, but severe, cause of idiosyncratic liver damage that requires special consideration as a safety problem. There are approximately 2,000 cases of acute liver failure each year in the U.S., with medications accounting for perhaps 25 to 50 percent of these. Thirty-nine percent are due to acetaminophen, and 13 percent are idiosyncratic reactions due to other medications. DILD accounts for 2 to 5 percent of cases of patients hospitalized with jaundice, approximately 10 percent of all cases of acute hepatitis, and up to a quarter of all cases of chronic hepatitis. DILD has become the leading cause of acute liver failure among patients presenting for evaluation at liver-transplant centers in the United States, and the leading single cause for having to remove approved drugs from the market. Following are some interesting facts concerning drug-induced liver disease (DILD):

- DILD may be unaffected or exacerbated by any pre-existing liver diseases.
- Symptoms can be non-specific, such as nausea, fever, and rash.
- On aggravation of symptoms, it can be very difficult to differentiate between the deterioration or complication of underlying liver disease and new or worsening DILD.
- Our understanding at any given time of the potential for new drugs to cause liver toxicity is based upon limited data from licensing trials. It is best advised that new drugs be used under careful observation until patient data is available for large populations.

A. Risk Factors

Risk factors for DILD can be grouped in terms of specific medications that are known to have increased risk for hepatotoxicity, depending on factors such as sex, age, nutritional state, body-mass index, presence of underlying diseases (diabetes, renal failure, infection with HIV or hepatitis virus), and preexisting liver disease.

There are many different ways in which to combine, split, organize, or categorize DILD, such as:

- By risk factors (see next paragraph)
- By what is known about specific medications
- By whether the reaction is symptomatic
- By pathologic (liver biopsy) presentation
- By whether the presentation was predictable (dose-related) or unpredictable

- By whether there are extrahepatic/systemic manifestations

The following are the most well-known risk factors for drug-induced liver injury:[3]

- **Gender**: DILD is more common in females, although the cause for this is unknown.
- **Race** can influence the ability of various drugs to be hepatotoxic. Isoniazid (INH), for example, may be more hepatotoxic in African Americans and Hispanics.
- **Age**: Liver toxicity is uncommon in children, although acetaminophen toxicity is a familiar exception. Decreased clearance in the liver, drug interactions, diminished hepatic blood flow, and several other factors seem to account for increasing hepatotoxicity with increased age.
- **Alcohol** itself is a hepatotoxin. It can change drug metabolism, deplete glutathione, and can, therefore, leave a person more susceptible to DILD. A thorough alcohol use history should always be taken when evaluating possible DILD, and consideration should be given to the wisdom of treating some causes of liver disease (for example hepatitis B or C) if alcohol use or abuse is ongoing.
- **Pre-existing liver disease**: Although patients with chronic liver disease are not always at an increased risk of DILD, their total cytochrome P450 capacity may be reduced. Medication prescribers should check the metabolic pathway in the prescribing information, and heed suggestions for dosing adjustments in the presence of liver disease.
- **Co-infection of HIV with hepatitis B or C** can leave patients at increased risk for hepatotoxic effects when treated with antiretroviral therapy. Patients with cirrhosis have poor tolerance for hepatotoxic drugs.
- **Expression of genes** involved in the metabolism of medications can have a profound and idiosyncratic influence on DILD.
- **Drug formulation**: Because of their persistence, long-acting or delayed-release drug formulations may cause more injury than shorter-acting drugs.

B. Histopathology

DILD does not usually present with a characteristic histopathologic picture, regardless of the causative medication. Although there are a number of distinctive pathologic categories of DILD,[4] rarely is it possible to diagnose DILD from the histopathologic pattern, although causes sometimes can be ruled out. DILD can present with one of several pathologic categories:

1) Impaired liver function
2) Acute hepatocyte necrosis
3) Fatty liver
4) Granulomatous change
5) Acute cholestasis
6) Cholestatic type
7) Chronic parenchymal injury
8) Vascular change
9) Liver tumor

Knowing the distinctive pathologic category may or may not help in identifying a cause of liver disease, in that one drug can present with different pathologic states, and no pathologic picture seems to be pathognomic for a particular drug or toxin. In the presence of suspected DILD, the pathologic picture may help confirm the diagnosis.

It is clear that cirrhosis can follow a number of insults produced by drug intake. The drugs involved are those that lead to types of liver disease that in other circumstances also may progress to cirrhosis. Cirrhosis may be the end result of the prolonged administration of drugs that presumably act as direct toxins, such as methotrexate and isoniazid, or those that may be mediated by hypersensitivity, such as oxyphenisatin and methyldopa.[5] Cirrhosis is most commonly caused by chronic, excessive alcohol use or abuse.

C. Predictability
DILD can present in either a predictable (dose-related) or unpredictable manner.

Individuals with a history of adverse drug reactions are more likely to experience a reaction to another agent. This could be explained on the basis of genetic predisposition to immunoallergic responses, such as penicillin or sulfonamide allergy. Alternatively, prior sensitization to one agent may confer an increased risk of liver injury after exposure to a chemically related compound. Examples of such cross-sensitivity include halothane with methoxyflurane and enflurane and the phenothiazines.

DILD that presents in a predictable manner usually: is due to direct hepatotoxicity, is reproducible in animals, tends to damage hepatic lobules, and can be induced by drug metabolites. Acetaminophen is an example of a drug that can cause predictable liver damage.

DILD presenting in an unpredictable/idiosyncratic manner (not related to dosage) is typically not reproducible in animals. Examples of drugs known to cause unpre-

dictable DILD include erythromycin, INH, halothane, and chlorpromazine. Unpredictable/idiosyncratic DILD can be either a hypersensitivity or immunoallergic reaction or a metabolic-idiosyncratic reaction.

Hypersensitivity immune-related responses, as is seen for phenytoin, have a short latency, and are characterized by fever, rash, and eosinophilia. A metabolic-idiosyncratic reaction, as is seen for INH, is caused by indirect metabolites of the offending drug. The response can occur within a week of exposure to the offending drug, but can also take up to one year to manifest.

D. Clinical Manifestations
DILD does not always manifest by nausea, right upper quadrant abdominal pain and elevated liver enzymes. In fact, DILD can have a widely varied clinical presentation, including the following associated extrahepatic/systemic manifestations:

- **Fever, rash, eosinophilia**: chlorpromazine, halogenated anesthetic agents, sulindac, Dapsone (Sulfone syndrome), and anticonvulsants (anticonvulsant hypersensitivity syndrome)
- **Obstructive jaundice**: chlorpromazine, erythromycin, amoxicillin-clavulanic acid
- **Serum sickness**: para-amino salicylate, phenytoin, sulfonamides
- **Muscular syndrome** (myalgia, stiffness, weakness, elevated creatine kinase level): clofibrate
- **Antinuclear antibodies**: procainamide
- **Bone-marrow injury**: ribavirin, gold salts, propylthiouracil, chlorpromazine, chloramphenicol
- **Associated pulmonary injury**: amiodarone, nitrofurantoin
- **Associated renal injury**: Gold salts, methoxyflurane, penicillamine, NSAIDs
- **Fatty liver of pregnancy**: tetracycline
- **Bland jaundice (pure cholestatis)**: contraceptive and anabolic steroids, rifampin
- **Reye's syndrome (acute encephalopathy, cerebral edema, fatty infiltration of liver)**: aspirin
- **Reye's-like syndrome**: sodium valproate

DILD can be asymptomatic, with only mild elevations of liver enzymes. Some helpful generalities concerning aspartate transaminase (AST) and alanine transaminase (ALT) in DILD are:

- In *hepatocellular DILD*, ALT levels are increased >2 × ULN, and alkaline phosphatase (alk phos) levels are within the reference range or are minimally elevated.

- Elevation of AST > ALT, especially if more than two times greater, suggests *alcoholic hepatitis*.
- Elevation of AST < ALT is often observed in persons with *viral hepatitis*.
- In both viral and drug-induced hepatitis, the AST and ALT levels steadily increase and can peak in the low thousands range within 7-14 days of injury.
- Some medications can cause marked increases in AST. In acetaminophen toxicity, for example, transaminase levels greater than 10,000 IU/L can occur.
- Normalization of mild liver enzyme elevation has been reported with continued use of some medicines, including NSAIDs and statins.

E. Hyperbilirubinemia

Some helpful generalities concerning *bilirubin* levels in DILD include:

- Elevated aminotransferase, accompanied by elevated bilirubin, is suggestive of subfulminant or fulminant hepatic necrosis.
- With increasing hepatocellular injury, bilirubin levels are invariably increased, suggesting a worse prognosis.
- Normally, the total bilirubin level is less than 1.1 mg/dL and approximately 70 percent is indirect (unconjugated) bilirubin.
  - **Unconjugated hyperbilirubinemia** (>80 percent of the total bilirubin is indirect) suggests hemolysis or Gilbert syndrome.
  - **Conjugated hyperbilirubinemia** (>50 percent of the total bilirubin is direct) suggests hepatocellular dysfunction or cholestasis.
  - Total bilirubin >25-30 mg/dL suggests that extrahepatic cholestasis is an unlikely diagnosis. The predominantly conjugated bilirubin is water soluble, and is easily excreted by the kidney in extrahepatic cholestasis.
- **Subfulminant hepatic failure** most commonly results from acetaminophen, halothane, methoxyflurane, enflurane, trovafloxacin, troglitazone, ketoconazole, dihydralazine, tacrine, mushroom poisoning, ferrous sulfate poisoning, phosphorus poisoning or cocaine toxicity.
- **Massive hepatic necrosis**: consider PTU, INH, phenytoin, phenelzine, sertraline, naproxen, diclofenac, Kava Kava, or ecstasy.

F. Cholestatis

Acute intrahepatic cholestasis is divisible into two broad categories:

1. **Cholestasis without hepatocellular injury** (bland jaundice or pure cholestasis)
2. **Cholestasis with variable hepatocyte injury**

The most common biochemical abnormality with *acute cholestatic injury* is elevation of the alkaline phosphatase, usually without hyperbilirubinemia.

- Men and older patients are more prone to these adverse effects.
- The interval of developments is usually less than 4 weeks and may be as long as 8 weeks after exposure to toxins.
- *Fever, rash, and eosinophilia* may be observed in as many as 30 percent of individuals, but these findings do not define the disorder.

Medications commonly associated with cholestatic injury include chlorpromazine, floxins, cimetidine, phenytoin, naproxen, captopril, erythromycin and azithromycin, dicloxacillin, and amoxicillin-clavulanic acid. Sulindac or octreotide can lead to extrahepatic cholestasis secondary to biliary sludge or calculi.

An obstructive cholestasis can result from *vanishing bile-duct syndrome,*[6] which has been associated with chlorpromazine, flucloxacillin, amitriptyline and trimethoprim-sulfamethoxazone.

24.4 Hepatic Drug Metabolism

Human metabolism must deal with a variety of substances that, in excess, can cause disease. Most of the liver's detoxification is performed on substances that are fat soluble, including drugs, certain vitamins, carcinogens, pesticides, and other environmental pollutants. Many endogenous chemicals, such as fatty acids, prostaglandins, and sex hormones, are themselves fat soluble and are metabolized by the liver. The duration of the physiological or toxicological action of these lipophilic substances depends on how long they reside intact in the liver. Other substances that are not fat soluble are also metabolized by the liver after a conversion reaction that renders the chemicals into a fat soluble state on which the liver can act. The cytochrome P450 (CYP450) system of enzymes is of primary importance in this capacity. Hepatic microsomal P450s are the mixed-function oxidases (MFOs) that activate oxygen for incorporation into lipophilic substrates. Oxidized substrates are then either eliminated from the organism or are metabolized further by the allied hepatic enzyme system.

A. Cytochrome P450

This is the collective term for the family of hemoproteins that is found in the hepatic endo-plasmic reticulum. Each individual P450 exhibits a characteristic range of turnover numbers with specific substrates.[7] Several hundred isoenzymes of CYP450 have been identified, and this is a very active area of research with significant relevance to drug metabolism.

B. Induction Processes Increasing Hepatotoxicity in Humans

Induction of drug metabolism has been reported to occur in humans. Enzyme induction processes may lead to drug-induced hepatotoxicity. Ethanol, phenytoin, barbiturates, and components of cigarette smoke increase the capacity of the liver to metabolize certain drugs. In view of the importance of the liver in the elimination of most therapeutic agents, it is not surprising that induction of P450 and conjugative enzymes should have a pronounced effect on drug disposition.[7]

C. Nutritional Effects on Drug Metabolism

A person's nutritional state can exert a major influence on his capacity to metabolize and eliminate drugs and foreign compounds. Chronic alcohol abuse or malnutrition and starvation may lead to a deficiency of glutathione, a substrate necessary for inactivating hepatic toxic substances. Fasting enhances activity of P450 2E1 and reduces hepatic levels of glutathione, which may influence the body's ability to detoxify acetaminophen. The extent to which each of these factors contributes to the increased risk of paracetamol-induced hepatotoxicity among alcoholics remains unclear.

24.5 Biochemical Mechanisms

Drugs and toxins can produce liver damage by at least four general types of mechanisms. These include the following:

- The drug directly impairs the structural and functional integrity of the liver.
- Metabolism of the drug produces a metabolite, usually an oxidizing or alkylating species, that alters hepatocellular structure and function.
- A drug metabolite binds to hepatic proteins to produce new antigenic determinants that become the targets of specific immune responses.
- The drug initiates a systemic hypersensitivity response (drug allergy) that damages the liver.

The drugs that are currently important causes of drug-induced liver injury tend to be widely prescribed and have a high margin of safety. They include agents such as non-steroidal anti-inflammatory drugs (NSAIDs), antibiotics, anticonvulsants, newer antihypertensive drugs, H2-receptor blockers, and psychotropic agents. For these types of drugs, the absolute incidence is in the order of one adverse hepatic drug reaction per 100,000 person years of exposure. Because of the very large number of prescriptions filled for these medications, they are among the most common causes of drug-induced liver disease. Acetaminophen continues to be a drug with widespread prescription and OTC use; however, it continues to present challenges to the toxicological community. Dose-related toxicity leads to fatal hepatic failure, and the drug continues to be widely used in suicides.

24.6 FDA and DILD

FDA approval does not ensure that a drug is not hepatotoxic, or that DILD will not occur. Registration trials for pharmaceuticals focus on efficacy. Safety is a secondary endpoint. Study sample sizes are typically small, and if the incidence of DILD is low, then it may not become apparent until post-licensure, often collected by spontaneously reported postmarketing data. Some drugs in current or recent use, including many familiar examples, but certainly not all drugs capable of causing DILD, have been discussed in this review. The FDA has taken a number of well-publicized actions concerning hepatotoxic medications in recent years, including strengthening of warnings, restrictions on use, and removal from marketing. Examples include glimepiride, interferon beta 1a, trimethoprim sulfamethoxazone, pemoline, bromfenac, duloxetine, felbamate, Kava Kava, troglitazone, tolcapone, trovafloxacin, and zileuton.

When the hepatotoxicity of a new drug is particularly common or severe, the agent may be withdrawn by the manufacturer; benoxaprofen, bromfenac, and oxyphenisatin (in most countries) are examples. Other drugs, such as chlorpromazine, are still used because their favorable qualities continue to outweigh the small risk of drug-induced liver disease.

24.7 Specific DILD Product Areas and Case Discussions

Case reports have shown hepatotoxicity by acetaminophen in combination with phenytoin, fulminant hepatitis from clarithromycin, Rezulin (trogliatazone) and liver failure, NSAID use and hepatotoxicity, isoniazid-induced hepatotoxicity, and methotrexate-induced hepatotoxicity.

Several mechanisms of drug-induced toxicity have been discussed, most of which demonstrate different toxic mechanisms, involve special age groups, and may have resulted in removal or threats of removal of drugs from the market. This is certainly demonstrative of the serious nature of drug-induced liver toxicity. Many case series of DILD have involved litigation, following some serious injury or fatality related to a drug exposure.

A. NSAID Use and Hepatotoxicity

Strategies for minimizing risks of adverse drug reactions (ADRs) of NSAID are discussed in this section. An emphasis is placed on using minimal analgesic, rather than anti-inflammatory, doses of short-acting NSAIDs and, where possible, avoiding their use in high-risk patients.[8]

Recent emphasis on NSAID-associated hepatic injury blurs differences between specific NSAIDs. In the case of Sulindac, injury involves females more than males, and can lead to cholestatic or hepatocellular injury, most often because of immunological idiosyncrasy. In some patients, metabolic idiosyncrasy may be the mechanism.[9]

Non-narcotic analgesics can produce a variety of hepatic lesions, but clinically significant liver damage is uncommon with normal therapeutic use. The pattern of hepatotoxicity caused by the salicylates, nonsteroidal anti-inflammatory drugs (NSAIDs), paracetamol (acetaminophen), and the pyrazolones differs, but many of these drugs can cause generalized reactions that involve the liver. Depending on the drugs in question, the risk of liver injury may be conditioned by factors such as age, sex, dose, and duration of treatment. NSAIDs have been associated with rare adverse reactions in the liver, including fulminant hepatitis and cholestasis.[10] These reactions are idiosyncratic, mostly independent of the dose administered, and are host-dependent. Among the NSAIDs (excluding acetaminophen), a rank order of relative risk cannot be established, and the incidence in relation to use is not known.[11] Of the marketed NSAIDs, diclofenac has been identified to have a greater potential for hepatotoxicity.

B. Isoniazid-Induced Hepatotoxicity

1. Introduction

Isoniazid is an important hepatotoxin, especially with the resurgence of tuberculosis, and the public health clinics' protocols for prophylactic use in exposed persons. Close monitoring of patients for liver enzymes and signs of fatigue and jaundice can detect liver toxicities and save the patient from an end-stage liver disease.

When isoniazid (isonicotinic acid hydrazide) was introduced in 1952, it represented a major advance in the treatment of tuberculosis. It has remained the mainstay of an-

tituberculous chemotherapy ever since. Isoniazid is potent, bactericidal, and has good clinical efficacy. In addition, it is cheap and can be given by mouth. Initially, isoniazid was thought to have a low incidence of side effects. This apparent safety, together with the high level of patient acceptability, led to isoniazid becoming extremely popular during the 1960s. This included its use as a chemoprophylactic agent for tuberculin-reactive individuals, such as household contacts of patients with recently diagnosed tuberculosis, who were thought to be at heightened risk of active tuberculosis.

The USPHS and other studies showed that between 10 and 36 percent of patients have asymptomatic elevations of ALT levels during isoniazid therapy. In most patients, these abnormalities occur within 10 weeks, are relatively minor, and resolve spontaneously. They are often associated with trivial histological changes in the liver. The frequency of clinically significant hepatotoxicity is about 1 percent of all patients exposed. There is, however, a striking age dependence, with isoniazid hepatitis being rare in childhood and occurring in more than 2 percent of adults over the age of 50. Several observations indicate that the longer the period of isoniazid treatment prior to the recognition of hepatotoxicity, the more severe the liver injury at the time of diagnosis. Isoniazid hepatitis appears to be more severe in African-American women, in those who habitually and excessively drink alcohol, and in those treated with combined therapy with rifampicin.

Deaths still occur from isoniazid-induced liver injury. Most, if not all, deaths due to isoniazid-induced liver injury could be prevented by immediate interruption of isoniazid treatment at the onset of the first symptoms of hepatotoxicity. The role of monitoring liver enzymes during the first three months of isoniazid therapy is less clear, although it may indirectly serve a useful function by keeping the specter of dangerous hepatotoxicity in the minds of prescribers and recipients of isoniazid.

2. Clinical features and laboratory findings

a. Presenting symptoms

These typically resemble viral hepatitis. About one-third of patients present with a prodrome characterized by malaise and fatigue; this is often attributed by the patient to a "viral illness." Gastrointestinal symptoms are also present in about half of these cases. About 10 percent of patients present with jaundice alone. The remainder present with predominantly digestive complaints, such as anorexia, nausea, vomiting, and abdominal pain. Fever, arthralgia, and rash are noted in less than 10 percent of patients with isoniazid-induced hepatitis.

b. Physical signs

Hepatomegaly—with or without hepatic tenderness—is found in one-third of patients admitted to the hospital with isoniazid-induced liver injury. Jaundice is usual in severe cases, but splenomegaly and signs of chronic liver disease are rare.

c. Liver tests

These resemble acute viral hepatitis, except that in about half of the reported patients, the level of AST exceeds the ALT. Values over 500 U/L are common, and they may exceed 2,000 U/L, but the level of AT abnormality does not appear to reflect prognosis. SAP is also elevated in most patients, and about 10 percent of patients have a biochemical "mixed" hepatocellular-cholestatic hepatitis by liver-test criteria. However, this does not usually correlate with a clinical syndrome of cholestasis.

The serum bilirubin concentration is typically increased. Values greater than 250 pmol/L are common and indicate a poor prognosis. Prolongation of the PT is present in one-third of cases; in one series, 60 percent of individuals with this indicator of severe liver injury died.

d. Mechanism

Isoniazid-induced hepatotoxicity is an idiosyncratic form of drug-induced liver injury. It is independent of the total or incremental dose of isoniazid, and several studies have shown no relationship to isoniazid blood levels. Drug allergy is unlikely to be involved. Thus, the onset of the reaction tends to be later than the usual interval for drug-induced allergic reactions (fever, rash, arthralgia, and eosinophilia are uncommon), and drug-induced antibodies or autoantibodies have not been found.[12]

C. Acetaminophen/Phenytoin Interaction Leading to Fulminant Liver Failure

"I want you to publish my case. I don't want another person to go through what I've been through." "We had a freight train crash into our lives." These are quotes from two married pharmacists. The husband, a 46-year-old community pharmacist, was being treated with Dilantin for a seizure disorder. After suffering from a flu-like illness for a few days, he returned to his pharmacy on a Monday morning, feeling a tension headache coming on, took two tablets of Isocet (butalbital, acetaminophen, caffeine). Two days later, he was in the Baylor Medical Center in fulminant hepatic failure, being evaluated for a liver transplant, and fighting for his life. The report that follows was prepared by this author in support of a lawsuit filed by the pharmacist and his family against the manufacturers of Dilantin and Isocet for

failing to warn of the interaction between Dilantin, as an inducer of cytochrome P450, enhancing the metabolism of acetaminophen, including a shunt into the toxic metabolic pathway that causes severe necrosis of the liver. The case went to heated litigation. Liver specialists, pathologists, pharmacokineticists, and pharmacologists on both sides of the case scoured the literature and case reports. Some of that information is included in the ensuing report. To be fair, experts for the companies disagree with some of the opinions expressed herein; these are expressed as opinions.

Incidentally, another epileptic man being treated with Dilantin who consumed acetaminophen (Tylenol) for flu and cold symptoms was taken ill with fulminant liver failure, had his liver transplanted, and survived, and subsequently sued the manufacturers of Tylenol and Dilantin, as well as various physicians and hospitals for malpractice.[13]

1. Case report: acetaminophen/phenytoin interaction

The following is an expert report filed by the author in the case of the married pharmacists described in the previous section.

Case Summary

This case involves a 46-year-old male pharmacist who had a history of headaches and who had been diagnosed and treated for a temporal-lobe seizure disorder. He developed zonal liver necrosis/acute hepatic failure diagnosed as being caused by acetaminophen used in combination with phenytoin, with the interaction further enhanced by butalbital. His prior medication history included several sources of acetaminophen; he developed the liver toxicity after the phenytoin (Dilantin, Parke Davis) was used in conjunction with Isocet, a generic Fioricet product containing butalbital, acetaminophen, and caffeine. He was diagnosed as having fulminant hepatic failure by a hepatologist, believed to be entering hepatorenal syndrome. The hepatologist noted:

> Etiology of his acute hepatic failure is not clear. The impression that I have is that this is toxic in origin....Dilantin is the only potentially hepatotoxic medication that he has on board and it is possible that this is a result of that drug. A viral process is also possible.... He will require the facilities at a liver transplant center so that he can be supported....

The Baylor University Medical Center Discharge Summary by a liver specialist notes as follows:

It was unclear as to whether this was drug-induced vs. overwhelming sepsis....Hepatic failure work-up included a full liver transplant evaluation....Shortly after admission, multiple consultations were obtained including renal consult as the patient was in frank renal failure. Transjugular liver biopsy was obtained by interventional radiology, and a stat interpretation was that he had about a 30 percent central zonal necrosis, and it was felt, based on the biopsy, that there was a good likelihood that the patient might recover from this subfulminant failure.

The anatomic pathology report notes "Zone 3 hepatic necrosis is seen with halogenated hydrocarbons and *acetaminophen*." (emphasis added)

The Baylor Restorative Care summary notes: "...transferred from Baylor University Medical Center after a protracted hospitalization for hepatic failure, *possibly due to tylenol and anticonvulsant medication*." (emphasis added)

Opinions

1. The package insert and labeling for phenytoin[13] is inadequate, and therefore the product is defective. The warning does not mention the interactive risk between phenytoin and acetaminophen, and it should. The interaction, through an enhancement of the metabolism of acetaminophen, pushes acetaminophen into a toxic metabolism (cytochrome P450 2E1), resulting in a toxic metabolite (NAPQI), which carries a risk of hepatic necrosis. The interaction has been reported in a variety of sources, such as textbooks, journal articles,[14] and interaction handbooks. The warning needs to be included in the package insert in order for it to be promulgated fully. By not including the warning in the product insert, physicians, pharmacists, and patients would not have the benefit of the knowledge. A reasonable and prudent physician heeds warnings. With a warning of the interactive risk between phenytoin and acetaminophen, the physician can advise the patient to avoid acetaminophen products, both in prescription drugs and also, more importantly, for the OTC acetaminophen sources.

2. The warning for Isocet (Rugby), a product comprised of butalbital, acetaminophen, and caffeine, is inadequate, and, therefore, the product is defective. The warning does not mention the interactive risk between phenytoin and acetaminophen, and it should. Further, there are reports of an enhancement of the metabolism of acetaminophen by barbiturates (butalbital), leading to a potential similar toxicity.

3. Plaintiff's hepatic failure was proximately caused by an interaction between the phenytoin and the acetaminophen of the Isocet. The contribution to the interaction by the butalbital must be considered.

Bases for Opinions

1. The biopsy diagnosis of the plaintiff's liver toxicity clearly identifies acetaminophen as the most probable cause. He had no other hepatotoxins. The interaction between phenytoin and acetaminophen is the most probable cause. The medical notes point to this as the most likely cause.

2. Drug master plus interaction report:[15]

Acetaminophen (oral) and phenytoin
Clinical Significance: Moderate
Action: Studies show that phenytoin may increase the hepatic metabolism and decrease the oral bioavailability of acetaminophen. Acetaminophen-related hepatotoxicity might be increased, while the analgesic and antipyretic effectiveness may be decreased.
Recommendations: Although no special precautions are generally necessary, this interaction should be kept in mind if patients taking phenytoin are also taking large doses of acetaminophen or are on prolonged therapy.

3. Linden and Rumack describe the interaction between phenytoin and acetaminophen:

Prior exposure to drugs that stimulate the hepatic microsomal P-450 mixed function oxidase enzyme system (including phenytoin) may enhance acetaminophen toxicity.[16]

The chronic use of drugs such as antihistamines, phenytoin, barbiturates, and other sedatives that stimulate the P-450 MFO system may enhance APAP toxicity.[17]

4. Martindale, the extra pharmacopeis (para-ce-tamol/acetaminophen interactions: review of drug interactions involving paracetamol): Gastrointesti-nal absorption may be delayed by drugs, such as anticholinergic agents or opioid analgesics, that decrease gastric emptying. The likelihood of tox-icity may be increased by the concomitant use of enzyme-inducing agents, such as alcohol or an-ti-epileptic drugs.[18]

5. Drug interaction facts:[19] This issue was elevated from a possible warning in 1986 to a suspected warning in 1990, which says hydantoins alter ac-etaminophen metabolism, and several references are provided in the handbook monograph. One reference reports that in six patients on chronic-administration therapy, acetaminophen clearance was 46 percent higher and its half-life was 28 per-cent shorter in the group receiving anticonvulsants when compared to six controls. Other studies have confirmed this observation.

6. In most laboratory-animal species, the hepato-toxicity of paracetamol is increased by pretreat-ment with microsomal-enzyme inducers, such as phenobarbitone and ethanol. There had been reports of liver damage following the therapeutic use of paracetamol in chronic alcoholics, and after overdosage, the severity of liver damage appears to be greater in chronic alcoholics and patients who have previously been taking drugs likely to cause induction (such as phenytoin). The observation suggests that microsomal enzyme induction might increase the production of the reactive metabolite of paracetamol and thus enhance its hepatotoxic-ity.[20] This report appeared in the literature as far back as 1981.

7. Drugs, such as phenytoin and phenobarbitone (butalbital), which induce the cytochrome P450 en-zyme system, could lower the threshold for hepatic damage by increasing the production of the toxic metabolite and the utilization of glutathione. In-creased susceptibility to paracetamol-induced liver damage has been reported in patients taking drugs that induce hepatic enzymes or in chronic alcohol ingestion, which may even cause hepatotoxicity with therapeutic doses of paracetamol.[21]

8. 21 CFR Parts 310, 343, and 369. Internal Anal-gesic, Antipyretic, and Antirheumatic Drug Prod-ucts for Over the Counter Human Use: Tentative Final Monograph; Notice of Proposed rulemaking, comment 27 at page 46217 (1988):

Several comments cited data to express con-cern that certain drugs that induce microsomal enzyme activity (e.g. alcohol and barbiturates) may increase the potential for acetamino-phen-induced hepatotoxicity. The comments recommended that warnings such as the fol-lowing be required on the labeling of all prod-ucts containing acetaminophen:

"Do not take this product if you use alcohol or barbiturates, unless directed by a physician. Caution: do not take this product if you are pres-ently taking a prescription drug for epilepsy, barbiturates, or ethacryinic acid except under the advice and supervision of a physician...."

10. Acetaminophen's effects may be reduced by long-term use of large doses of barbiturate drugs: Carbamazepine, phenytoin (and similar drugs), ri-fampin, and sulfinpyrazone. These drugs may also increase the chances of liver toxicity if taken with acetaminophen.[22]

11. Depletion of glutathione (GSH) by starvation, alcohol ingestion, or other drugs may be important. Interestingly, chronic alcohol ingestion appears to selectively deplete mitochondrial GSH, which may contribute to increased susceptibility to acetamino-phen toxicity.[23]

These citations and sources are a representa-tive sampling of the literature and other available information sources describing the interaction risk, consequences of the interaction, and the biological mechanisms of the interaction. These materials were obtained retrospectively by this expert and others in order to prove a point and support opinions: A drug manufacturer has a duty to prospectively monitor this literature and warn users of potential and proven dangers. A drug manufacturer would employ an in-dividual with sufficient credentials and experience to perform this prospective task. Failure to do so is a departure from the standard of care of a reasonable and prudent manufacturer.

Summary

Plaintiff's liver failure and subsequent morbidity was caused by acetaminophen induction by phenytoin and butalbital. Parke Davis & Co., the manufacturer of Dilantin, and Rugby, the manufacturer of Isocet, were negligent and departed from the standard of care of reasonable and prudent pharmaceutical companies by not warning of the interaction. This departure from the standard of care and inadequate labeling rendered the drugs Dilantin and Isocet defective.

2. Therapeutic Research Center's warning, and FDA report

In a strong warning issued by the "Pharmacist's Letter," published by the Therapeutic Research Center in July 2009,[24] the dangers of acetaminophen and its toxic effects upon the liver were exposed in a report published by an FDA committee in late June 2009. The committee was convened to study the problem of acetaminophen-induced hepatotoxicity.

The guidance acknowledges that acetaminophen (paracetamol) is one of the most commonly used medications for treating pain and fever. It states that it is also combined with over-the-counter medicines (often for cold and flu), as well as with commonly prescribed painkillers, such as hydrocodone. It then identified acetaminophen as the largest cause of acute liver failure in the United States, The report states that in 2005, there were more than 28 billion doses of acetaminophen-containing products purchased by U.S. consumers, who tend to view it as a benign, safe medication—one that does not cause the gastrointestinal symptoms associated with non-steroidal anti-inflammatories, such as ibuprofen. The following is an excerpt from this committee's reported findings:

Acetaminophen is hepatically metabolized. In general, more than 90 percent of the acetaminophen dose is metabolized to sulfate and glucuronide conjugates, which are water soluble and eliminated in the urine. However. a small amount is metabolized by the cytochrome P450 (CYP450) system to N-acetyl-benzoquinoneimine (NAPOI), a metabolite which is hepatotoxic. Normally, glutathione binds NAPOI enabling the excretion of nontoxic mercapturate conjugates. However, with misuse or overdose, glutathione stores are depleted, and NAPOI Is not detoxified. This metabolite then covalently binds to hepatocytes, causing hepatotoxicity. Glutathione stores are replaced by sulfhydryl compounds from the diet (e.g.fruits and vegetables) or

from drugs, such as the antidote for acetaminophen overdose, N-acetylcystelne or NAC.

According to the letter, five surveillance systems approximated 56,000 emergency-room visits, 26,000 hospitalizations and 456 deaths between 1990 and 1996 in the United States, mostly due to unintentional overdose or concurrent usage with alcohol. Among the labeling changes the committee proposed was to emphasize that the maximum dose should be less than that recommended for people who consume three or more alcoholic beverages per day.

The report also detailed overdoses in children, due to confusion over the concentrations of acetaminophen in infant drops, versus children's preparations. It proposed removing over-the-counter (and possibly prescription) products containing acetaminophen. If not removed from prescription preparations, it recommended an emphatic warning about the liver dangers incurred by the drug, The committee proposed that the maximum single dose of acetaminophen should be 650 mg (rather than the current recommendation of 1,000 mg) for adults, and 3,250 mg per day. For those imbibing more than three alcoholic drinks each day, the dosage should be sharply reduced. In general, the committee concluded, acetaminophen has a very narrow therapeutic range—so narrow that it is easily surpassed, causing great dangers to those who ingest it.

3. Two acetaminophen cases

A $2.7 million settlement was recently reached in Cook County, Illinois (00L01842) on behalf of a 38-year-old woman who suffered liver failure secondary to acetaminophen toxicity and died on November 19, 1999. She had been taking two Vicodin ES tablets every 4 hours after undergoing an outpatient bunionectomy on November 12. The prescription provided by the defendant surgeon directed her to take "one to two tablets every 4 to 6 hours as needed for pain" which allowed the patient to ingest a lethal dose of acetaminophen.[25]

Examination of the contents of the drug product demonstrate the following:

- *400 mg/5 mg tablets:* The usual adult dosage is 1-2 tablets every 4-6 hours as needed for pain. The total 24-hour dose should not exceed 8 tablets.
- *400 mg/7.5 mg tablets:* The usual adult dosage is 1 tablet every 4-6 hours as needed for pain. The total 24-hour dose should not exceed 5 tablets.
- *400 mg/10 mg tablets:* The usual adult dosage is 1 tablet every 4-6 hours as needed for pain. The total daily dosage should not exceed 6 tablets.

As can be seen, the amount of hydrocodone, the synthetic narcotic analgesic, varies in each available dosage strength. A maximum dose of 60 mg is set, even though the maximum safe acetaminophen dose is not. The amount of acetaminophen is fixed. There is an advisement that the "total daily dosage should not exceed 5, 6, or 8 tablets," which would limit the acetaminophen exposure to 2,400–3,200 mg per day (2.4–3.2 g).

The overdosage section of the prescribing information states:

> In acute acetaminophen overdosage, dose-dependent, potentially fatal hepatic necrosis is the most serious adverse effect. Renal tubular necrosis, hypoglycemic coma, and thrombocytopenia may also occur. Early symptoms following a potentially hepatotoxic overdose may include: nausea, vomiting, diaphoresis, and general malaise. Clinical and laboratory evidence of hepatic toxicity may not be apparent until 48-72 hours post-ingestion. In adults, hepatic toxicity has rarely been reported with acute overdoses of <10 g and fatalities with <15 g. There is no mention of risk using the drug in PRN doses conventional with this product.

The above paragraph represents class labeling, and can be found in other oral narcotic/non-narcotic analgesic combination products (e.g., Tylenol W Codeine 4).

A similar case was set for trial in March 2003 (*Schmidt v. Walgreens et al.*, Cook County, IL). A 35-year-old man saw an orthopedic surgeon for some chronic back pain following an automobile accident. Tylenol with Codeine 60 mg was prescribed, "two tablets every 4 hours for pain," allowing 12 tablets per day, exceeding the upper limit of Codeine (360 mg) and providing a total acetaminophen of 3600 mg acetaminophen per day. The man was found dead on the sidewalk with toxic levels of codeine in his blood. Low levels of alcohol were also found, but not considered to be of any consequence to the death. The surgeon testified that he told the patient to take the tablets "PRN," or as needed, and did not intend the patient to take the full two tablets every four hours around the clock. The pharmacist testified that she relied on the physician, and did not usually consider the toxic effect of therapeutic doses. The pharmacist was dismissed by the court early in the litigation.

D. Biaxin (Clarithromycin)-Induced Fulminant Hepatic Failure

A 63-year-old man was treated prophylactically to eradicate H. pylori with Biaxin (Clarithromycin, Abbott). The patient was hospitalized and treated for gastric ulcer and was prescribed Biaxin 500 mg TID (three times a day) for two weeks. Helicobacter pylori was identified following a Giemsa stain. Initially, the patient's gastroenterologist had recommended Prilosec 20 mg two times daily for seven days, Biaxin 250 mg two times daily (500 mg/day) for seven days, and Flagyl 500 mg two times daily for treatment of the H. pylori. The patient's internist, however, prescribed Biaxin 500 mg TID (three times daily) for two weeks. In addition, the patient was also taking 60 mg of Procardia, 30 mg of Prevacid, and 20 mg of Mevacor per day. He was admitted to the hospital with increasing abdominal pain and ashen color. The patient had mild abdominal pain for three days, but it significantly worsened in the preceding 24 to 48 hours. He became hypotensive on ward, was transferred to ICU, coded, and was found to be profoundly acidotic, probably secondary to sepsis-WBC 19,000 range. No source for the sepsis was noted. He rapidly decompensated in the hospital, required transfer to the Intensive Care Unit and was intubated. A surgical note indicates that the patient started on Biaxin for H. pylori. The patient was discharged from the hospital a few days earlier after treatment for gastric ulcer, was placed on Biaxin, apparently, with active bleeding. The surgeons described the following: "At surgery, the liver seemed somewhat tense and firm. Wedge biopsy of the liver was procured. A pathologist's report for the liver biopsy report indicated 'severe central lobular necrosis and hemorrhage'....The possibility of shock or cardiovascular failure is mentioned. In addition, the possibility of DIC, sepsis, drugs or toxins is mentioned. These findings should be correlated clinically." The patient's pretreatment liver function tests were normal, and a pre-Biaxin CT of the abdomen did not demonstrate any abnormal liver findings. The death certificate lists the cause of death as hepatic failure, drug reaction (Biaxin).

A published article by Wallace et al.[26] and publications that followed warned about high-dose risk in the elderly and suggested caution. A December 1995 FDA Advisory Committee recommendation for a 1,500 mg/day dosage of Biaxin for treatment of H. pylori would predictably increase the use of Biaxin.

An FDA Anti-Infective Drug and Gastrointestinal Drugs Advisory Committee recommendation was as follows:

> ...a combination therapy of the antisecretory medication Prilosec and the antibiotic Biaxin be approved for the treatment of Helicobacter pylori (H. pylori) infected patients with active duodenal ulcer to eradicate H. pylori, the bacteria now believed to

cause approximately 89 percent of peptic ulcers.... The recommended dosage of eradicating H. pylori is Prilosec 40 mg once daily and Biaxin 500 mg three times daily for the first 14 days....

This FDA Advisory Committee recommendation would predictably increase the use and the dosage of Biaxin.

Literature describing the dose-related phenomenon of hepatotoxicity preceded the patient's Biaxin death. Brown et al.,[27] and previously Wallace et al.,[26] described abnormal liver-enzyme levels during high-dose clarithromycin monotherapy for Mycobacterium avium complex or Mycobacterium abscesses. Portions of the original 1993 article by Wallace et al. are reproduced here for discussion:

The elevation in enzyme levels was seen in five (36 percent) of 14 elderly patients receiving clarithromycin at a dose of 2,000 mg/day, and it was associated with unexpectedly high serum drug levels. In all five patients, both the transaminases and the alkaline phosphatases were elevated. With discontinuation of the high dose, the GOT and/or the SGPT in the five patients fell by at least 50 percent with all values 100 IU/liter or less by the next enzyme determination (one or two weeks). The alkaline phosphatase and GGT were slower to decline, and three of five patients remained at approximately the same level for at least four weeks.

Healthy, elderly volunteers have been noted to have higher peak and trough levels of both the parent drug and its major metabolite compared with younger volunteers.

This drug dose (1,000 mg/day) should be used with caution in any patient over age 55 (emphasis added). This strongly suggests that clinical trials of mycobacterial lung disease in older age populations should use no more than 1,000 mg per day except under special circumstances, with attention being paid to body mass and renal function, to minimize side effects.[26]

Brown et al. continue:

In addition, since these data were published, we have noted two other HIV-seronegative patients who developed abnormal liver enzyme levels during clarithromycin therapy....The patients who develop these signs of hepatotoxicity are typically elderly or have reduced body mass, are receiving clarithromycin doses of 2,000 mg/day, and are of-

ten asymptomatic....The ability of patients to tolerate lower doses of clarithromycin (four of four tested strongly suggest that this is a toxicity that is serum-level-related and not due to hypersensitivity.[27]

The authors recommend "reductions in doses may be required in patients with reduced renal function and/or reduced body mass to prevent hepatic or gastrointestinal toxicity." The elderly fall in both of these categories as a result of their elevated age (normal aging process reduces lean body mass and deceases renal function as a function of age).

Central zonal necrosis is an imminent liver toxic sign, frequently associated with a few drugs acting like liver toxins (i.e., acetaminophen). Biaxin was the only drug being taken by the patient discussed in this case at the time of his fatal liver toxicity that has had central zonal necrosis associated with its use.

Conventional knowledge describes macrolide toxicities, including clarithromycin, to be associated with occasional abnormalities in liver tests, and occasional cholestatic jaundice, considered idiosyncratic, and therefore not dose-related. Most are described as mild and transient. Shaheen and Grimm[28] described a 25-year-old man who developed fulminant hepatic failure following clarithromycin use; he subsequently required liver transplantation. The authors wrote, "the potential for severe liver injury associated with clarithromycin is of growing concern in the light of recent reports to the FDA. We believe that this case, although not proof of causation, supports a true association."

The Food and Drug Administration Spontaneous Reporting System (MedWatch) includes more than 132 out of a total of 325 reported cases of liver toxicity (including a few cases of pancreatitis), greater than one-third of which are in patients 50 years and over. Some of the case reports do not include the age of the patient; these have been counted in the under-50 group, and therefore the over-50 group could be higher. The age of 50 is chosen as an age marker, since 50 years of age is classically selected as the threshold for the beginning of age-related deterioration in drug metabolism (liver) and clearance (kidney) functions. Clearly, there is a disproportionate preponderance of liver toxicities in patients over the age of 50.

E. Rezulin Hepatotoxicity

This hypoglycemic agent was launched in 1997, and it was recognized pre-approval that the drug had a hepatotoxic risk. Special precautions were included in the labeling calling for close monitoring and frequent liver function tests. A number of lawsuits have been filed against physicians who fail to monitor, pharmacists who fail to counsel patients of the need to monitor, and the company, Parke Davis, for failure to adequately warn about the product.

1. Case report

The following is a case report by the author about a woman who developed Rezulin-associated cirrhosis and is now a candidate for a liver transplant.

Rezulin therapy initiated on 12-10-97

Rezulin discontinued October 1998

Glynase was changed to Amaryl because of uncontrolled blood glucose. Dr. Physician's New Patient Evaluation of 11/19/97 was as follows: "In regard to the diabetes, patient does do self glucose monitors 4 times a day. She mentioned in the morning it is 126-140 and after lunch sometimes it can drop down to 40-50 and sometimes up to 200, and this happens 2-3 times a week."

Amaryl was then changed to Rezulin. Physician's note of 12-10-97 was as follows: "The patient relates that she is still having some problems with hypoglycemia with Amaryl." PLAN: "My plan is to stop the Amaryl. We will try some Rezulin 200 mg daily for two weeks and then increasing to 400 mg daily."

The lab results for LFT show elevated LFT enzymes as early as 12-24-97. There is a rise in ALT in April 1998 that persists through July 1998. The Rezulin is discontinued in October 1998 "because of elevated liver enzymes." The October 1998 lab results list AST as 33 and ALT as 35. There is no record of the LDH or GGT for October 98; ALK PHO is 99.

In the 10/30/98 visit with a second physician, the following is recorded:

Assessment: Did have some elevation of liver enzymes last visit. Will stop Rezulin. Start Glucophage 500 mg, on bid for two weeks; if sugars drop below 120, cut insulin in half. If they remain below 120 will stop insulin. If one bid does not result in this, go up to two bid. Recheck in two weeks.

This change was apparently prompted by the July 3 and July 8 LFTs that showed AST 62 and ALT 69 on both dates (two separate, dated reports). Almost four months passed before these tests got action to discontinue the Rezulin. July 3-Oct 30.

Examination of the LFTs for the patient shows a progressive and continuous elevation of the LFTs. Subsequently, she developed a chronic hepatitis condition.

2. Discussion

The catastrophic idiosyncratic liver damage did not appear as an acute fulminant hepatitis, but rather as a chronic active hepatitis.

The purpose of frequent LFTs was to observe the onset of liver enzyme release as a result of the Rezulin exposure. With the exception of a single borderline lab study, or in the absence of an alternative treatment for diabetes, two LFTs in the abnormal range raised an alarm and caused the Rezulin to be discontinued. Since the damage may be asymptomatic, the tests were the patient's only protection from slowly evolving liver damage, perhaps from some mildly toxic metabolite of Rezulin.

The FDA advisory committee discussed monitoring LFT in Rezulin therapy. There was testimony to the fact that the liver damage was not an allergic reaction, but an idiosyncratic reaction. ALT is described as a poor measure of liver damage, but the best available. Liver damage can be estimated by monitoring a rise above normal limits. The elevation of these LFTs can be marginal, but one and one-half to three times normal is unmistakable.

Dr. Seeff, a member of the FDA panel discussing Rezulin, however, stated that the purpose of the tests was to identify the unlucky patient who was experiencing hepatic damage and that more frequent testing and prompt discontinuation was the best bet.

The testimony by Dr. Graham, FDA Epidemiology, suggested that the mean time of injury after starting Rezulin therapy was about six months; and that by one year, most patients who had not suffered the idiosyncratic injury were not likely to do so in the future.

It therefore appeared that the first four-to-six months of therapy were crucial to monitor for elevation of LFT and to discontinue Rezulin in the face of AST numbers above normal, unless no alternative therapy was available to treat diabetes. An interesting editorial in the October 1999 issue of Pharmacy Today by its editor, Daniel A. Hussar, called for the withdrawal of Rezulin.[29]

The inescapable conclusion was that Rezulin should be withdrawn from the market and that if the FDA chose to permit the continued marketing of Rezulin, its use should have been restricted to those patients who were already taking it and tolerating it satisfactorily. Most would have been better served if they were switched from Rezulin to Avandia or Actox (other agents with similar activity in treating diabetes). Since the withdrawal of Rezulin, there have been only a few reports of liver failure with these two alternate drugs, and strengthening of the package insert warnings has followed. However, both Avandia and Actox were found to have significant cardiac risks, leading to congestive heart failure, and their use has been sharply curtailed and limited by the FDA and practicing physicians.

Despite the actions of the company to defend its blockbuster drug and keep it on the market, the drug was withdrawn, and there has been extensive litigation associated with Rezulin.

F. Methotrexate Hepatotoxicity

1. Introduction

Methotrexate (MTX) is a folic-acid antagonist and is used as a cell-proliferation inhibitor in the treatment of a variety of diseases including neoplasms (especially juvenile leukemia), psoriasis (for over 20 years), rheumatoid arthritis (RA) and other immune-mediated diseases. The risk of developing hepatotoxicity in psoriasis patients treated with MTX has long been recognized. In 1988, the FDA granted approval for the use of MTX in the treatment of RA. One of the most significant potential long-term side effects of low-dose MTX is liver fibrosis and cirrhosis. Liver biopsy is currently the only reliable method for diagnosing liver fibrosis. Biochemical abnormalities of the liver may be helpful in screening RA patients who are at high risk for the development of significant liver fibrosis. Hepatotoxicity is a major adverse reaction that can occur during methotrexate treatment of the rheumatic diseases. The pathologic lesions are nonspecific, and the pathogenesis is poorly understood. Early studies in psoriasis clearly established a relationship between hepatic injury and several risk factors, particularly alcohol use. Methotrexate hepatotoxicity occurs less frequently in rheumatoid arthritis than previously reported in psoriasis patients.[30]

Risk factors which increase the probability of MTX therapy to induce liver damage include alcohol use and, possibly, the cumulative dose of MTX. Other possible risk factors include diabetes mellitus (DM), obesity, pre-existing liver disease, advanced age at start of MTX therapy, and MTX administration every second or third day.[31]

Guidelines for monitoring for hepatotoxicity in MTX-treated psoriasis patients were established in 1982 and revised in 1988 by the Psoriatic Task Force (PTF). The "gold standard" for determining whether patients being treated with MTX have developed liver damage was and remains liver biopsy, an invasive and expensive means of monitoring. Rheumatologists adopted these guidelines in 1988 when MTX was approved for use in treating RA. Later, the American College of Rheumatology (ACR) established guidelines to monitor RA patients in order to minimize the need for liver biopsy. Patients with known risk factors or persistent elevation of liver-associated enzymes could be identified as being at risk for liver fibrosis. These new guidelines were tested and found to be predictive and are 80 percent sensitive. However, this also means that one in five patients not identified to be at higher risk and without overt clinical signs nonetheless show liver fibrosis when evaluated by liver biopsy.[32]

The ACR considers that the frequency of clinically significant liver disease in RA, even with long-term MTX use, is quite low and the need for liver biopsy is rare. Judicious screening prior to MTX institution, laboratory monitoring and appropriate clinical care are the most cost effective and advantageous to the RA patient receiving MTX therapy.[33]

The ACR recommended obtaining liver blood tests (alanine aminotransferase [ALT], aspartate aminotransferase [AST], alkaline phosphatase, albumin, bilirubin), hepatitis B and C serologic studies, and other standard tests, including complete blood-cell count and serum creatinine tests prior to starting treatment with MTX. A pretreatment liver biopsy should be considered only for patients with a history of prior excessive alcohol consumption, persistently abnormal baseline AST values, or chronic hepatitis B or C infection. At intervals of every four to eight weeks the AST, ALT, and albumin levels should be monitored. Routine surveillance liver biopsies are not recommended for RA patients receiving traditional doses of MTX. However, a biopsy should be performed if a patient develops persistent abnormalities on liver blood tests. These are defined as elevations (above the upper limit of laboratory normal) in the AST in five of nine determinations within a given 12-month interval (six of 12 if tests are performed monthly) or a decrease in serum albumin below the normal range. The recommendations for monitoring and selection of patients for liver biopsy identify patients at potential risk for CSLD, and thus significantly reduce the number or patients who would be exposed to this procedure. Close monitoring is essential to reduce the risk of unrecognized serious liver disease. These recommendations should be revised as necessary to reflect new and compelling information.[34]

Before starting low-dose methotrexate therapy in patients with RA, a full blood count, liver function tests, renal function tests, and chest radiography should be performed. Blood counts and liver function tests should be repeated at regular intervals. Therapeutic drug monitoring of methotrexate has also been suggested as a means of limiting toxicity. Patients with RA usually respond very favorably to low-dose methotrexate therapy, and the probability of patients continuing their treatment beyond five years is greater than for other slow-acting antirheumatic drugs. Thus, given its sustained clinical utility and relatively predictable toxicity profile, low-dose methotrexate is a useful addition to the therapy of RA.[35]

2. Clinical features and laboratory findings

a. Presenting symptoms
MTX-induced hepatic injury and liver-enzyme elevations have been demonstrated after treatment of leukemia, gestational disease and during treatment of psoriasis and rheumatoid arthritis. A 40-year-old man with a long-standing history of rheumatoid arthritis was treated with MTX over a six-month period and developed an overwhelming hepatic necrosis. He was successfully transplanted.[36]

b. Screening for higher risk
In a retrospective Canadian study evaluating MTX hepatotoxicity in psoriatics, the incidence of severe hepatotoxicity was shown to be high: 23.1 percent (24 of 104 patients). This study showed diabetic patients to be at particular increased risk of MTX hepatotoxicity. Occasional alcohol consumption was not associated with increased risk. Three patients who developed cirrhosis over two years of standard MTX therapy may represent a subset of psoriatics with increased hepatic susceptibility to MTX. Another three patients whose severe hepatic fibrosis had regressed upon discontinuation of MTX, but who developed accelerated recurrence of the severe hepatic fibrosis upon resumption of MTX therapy, suggests the possibility of unusual sensitivity to the drug. These cases reemphasize the need for continuing surveillance, with regular liver biopsies, of psoriatic patients on MTX.[37]

c. Liver function tests
Serial measurement of liver enzymes is useful to detect liver toxicity due to methotrexate in patients with rheumatoid arthritis or other rheumatic diseases. A Spanish series of 141 adult patients treated with methotrexate were studied retrospectively from 1988 to 1991. The more common diagnoses included rheumatoid arthritis (120 cases) and psoriatic ar-

thritis (12 cases). In periodic studies carried out every two to three months, a transient increase in transaminase values associated with methotrexate in 13 patients (9.2 percent) was observed. Two patients developed a viral infection during therapy, one due to cytomegalovirus and the other due to the Epstein-Barr virus. Both patients had a favorable outcome once methotrexate was withdrawn.[38]

In using liver enzymes as a means of monitoring for liver damage, AST values that were abnormal <49 percent of the time had a 97 percent specificity for a normal biopsy grade. Regular AST measurements are useful markers of hepatic histologic outcome, within the range of mostly normal histology, in patients with RA receiving long-term weekly MTX.[39]

The value of dynamic hepatic scintigraphy (DHS) and serum aminoterminal propeptide of type III procollagen (PIIINP) were investigated as screening methods for early detection of MTX-induced hepatic damage in 25 patients. These relatively non-invasive procedures were compared with the liver-biopsy classification. DHS appeared to be very promising as a screening test to differentiate between the presence or absence of MTX-induced hepatic damage, but appeared unsuitable to grade the severity of hepatic damage. Although a global relationship was demonstrated between serum PIIINP concentration and hepatic damage, single measurements in individual patients were not reliable. The combination of PIIINP measurements with DHS had only a limited additional value above DHS alone. The present study indicates that DHS has great promise for the detection of early MTX-induced hepatic damage. These results reinforce the need for regular liver biopsies to ensure the safe prolonged use of MTX in psoriasis patients.[40]

d. Mechanism of damage
The mechanism by which MTX causes liver damage is unknown. Methotrexate is eliminated almost entirely by the kidneys. The risk of methotrexate toxicity is therefore increased in patients with poor renal function, most likely as a result of drug accumulation. Declining renal function with age may thus be an important predictor of toxicity to methotrexate. Up to 60 percent of all patients who receive methotrexate for rheumatoid arthritis (RA) discontinue taking it because of adverse effects, most of which occur during the first year of therapy. Gastrointestinal complications are the most common adverse effects of methotrexate, but hepatotoxicity, hematological toxicity, pulmonary toxicity, lymphoproliferative disorders and exacerbation of rheumatic nodules have all been reported. Decreased renal function as a result of disease and/or aging appears to be an important determinant of hepatic, lymphoproli ferative, and hemato-

logical toxicity. Concomitant use of low doses of folic acid has been recommended as an approach to limiting toxicity. Interactions between methotrexate and several nonsteroidal anti-inflammatory drugs have been reported, but they may not be clinically significant. However, caution is advised in the use of such combinations in patients with reduced renal function.[35]

24.8 Summary and Conclusions

The liver is a vital organ for life, and is vital for metabolism of drugs and other substances consumed by patients. When the drugs consumed for a variety of therapeutic purposes cause injury to the patient, it creates a quandary for the therapist. Special monitoring and evaluation of continued benefit over risk may lead to selection of an alternative but less-toxic agent. Sometimes, the FDA and the manufacturer must make the difficult choice to not bring the product to market, restrict its use after release, or eventually withdraw the product from the market.

Endnotes

1. I.R. Mackay. *Chapter 3. The immunological mediation of drug reactions affecting the liver in Farrell GC: Drug-Induced Liver Disease.* Churchill Livingstone, Edinburgh London. (1994) :69.

2. U.S. Department of Health and Human Services. Food and Drug Administration. Center for Drug Evaluation and Research (CDER). Center for Biologics Evaluation and Research (CBER). *Guidance for Industry Drug-Induced Liver Injury: Premarketing Clinical Evaluation.* October 2007. Available at www.fda.gov/downloads/drugs/guidancecomplianceregulatoryinformation/guidances/ucm072278.pdf. Accessed May 10, 2012.

3. Rubin E. Iatrogenic hepatic injury. Human Pathology. 11(4): 312-31, Jul 1980

4. G.C. Kanel GC, J. Korula. *Liver Biopsy Evaluation. Histologic Diagnosis and Clinical Correlations.* W.B. Saunders. (2000)

5. Black M, Mitchell JR, Zimmerman HJ, Ishak KG, Epler GR. Isoniazid-associated hepatitis in 114 patients. Gastroenterology 1975; 69:289–302.

6. D.H. Marks. "Case Report: Drug Toxicity Leading to Vanishing Bile Duct Syndrome and Cholestatic Jaundice." *Internet Journal of Gastroenterology* [Peer-reviewed online serial.] (2009).

7. M. Murray. *Chapter 1. Role of the Liver in Drug Metabolism in Farrell GC: Drug-Induced Liver Disease.* Churchill Livingstone, Edinburgh London. (1994) b:13.

8. G. Nuk. *Pain control and the use of non-steroidal analgesic anti-inflammatory drugs.* British Medical Bulletin (1990) Jan;46(1): 262-278.

9. E.M. Tarazi, J.G. Harter, H.J. Zimmerman, et al. *Sulindac-associated hepatic injury: analysis of 91 cases reported to the Food and Drug Administration.* Gastroenterology (1993) Feb;104(2): 569-574.

10. U.A. Boelsterli, H.J. Zimmerman HJ, and A. Kretz-Rommel. *Idiosyncratic liver toxicity of nonsteroidal anti-inflammatory drugs: molecular mechanisms and pathology.* Crit Rev Toxicol. (1995) ;25(3):207-235.

11. L.F. Prescott. *Liver damage with non-narcotic analgesics.* Med Toxicol (1986) ;1 Suppl 1:44,56.

12. G.C. Farrell. *Drug-Induced Liver Disease: Chapter 12. Drug-Induced acute hepatitis.* Churchill Livingstone, Edinburgh London. (1994) :248-269.

13. *Michael Colley v. Parke Davis & Company et al.,* No. 96-530040-NH, State of Michigan in the Circuit Court for the County of Oakland.

14. W.M. Lee. *Drug Induce Hepatotoxicity.* New Engl J Med, Vol 233, No. 17. (Oct 26, 1995) 1118-1127.

15. Rapha Group Software, Inc. 1996.

16. Linden CH and Rumack BH. Acetaminophen Overdose, Emergency Medicine Clinics of North America, Vol. 2, No. 1. (February 1984) 103-119.

17. C.H. Linden, and B.H. Rumack. *Acetaminophen Poisoning.* In Tintinalli JE, Krome RL and Ruiz E. eds. Emergency Medicine, A Comprehensive Study Guide, McGraw-Hill, New York, 1992.

18. J.E.F. Reynolds, ed. Martindale, *The Extra Pharmacopoeis,* 29th Ed. (1989) p. 32.

19. *Facts and Comparisons Drug Information.* St. Louis, MO: Facts and Comparisons, 1986. Print.

20. L.F. Prescott, J.A.J.H. Critchley, M. Balali-Mood, and B. Pentland. *Effects of Microsomal Enzyme Induction on Paracetamol Metabolism in Man.* Br. J. Clin Pharmc. (1981) 12, 149-153.

21. N.A. Minton, A. Henry and R.J. Frankel. *Fatal Paracetamol Poisoning in an Epileptic. Human Toxico.*, (1988) 7, 33-34.

22. H.M. Silverman, ed. *The Pill Book, 7th Edition.* Bantam Books, New York. (1996)

23. N. Kaplowitz. *Drug Metabolism and Hepatotoxicity.* (1992)

24. "New warnings and proposed changes to acetaminophen." Pharmacist's *Letter/Prescriber's Letter 2009;25(7):250701*

25. Cook County Jury Verdict Reporter, Illinois Jury Verdict Reporter-Urban Ring Edition, Law Bulletin Publishing Company, February 2003

26. R.J. Wallace, B.A. Brown, and D.E. Griffith. *Drug intolerance to high-dose clarithromycin among elderly patients.* Diagn Microbiol Infect Dis. (1993) Mar-Apr;16(3): 215-221.

27. B.A. Brown, R.J. Wallace Jr,, D.E. Griffith and W. Girard. *Clarithromycin-induced hepatotoxicity.* Clin Infect Dis. (1995) Apr;20(4): 1073-1074.

28. N. Shaheen and I.S. Grimm. *Fulminant Hepatic Failure Associated with Clarithromycin.* American Journal Gastroenterology, Vol. 91, No. 2, (1996) 394-395.

29. D.A. Hussar. *They may call it an "express," but it is on the wrong track* (Call for Rezulin Market Withdrawal). Editorial. Pharmacy Today. (October 1999) American Pharmaceutical Association.

30. West SG. *Methotrexate hepatotoxicity.* Rheum Dis Clin North Am. 1997;23:883–915

31. Hashkes, P.J., W.F. Balistreri, K.E. Bove, E.T. Ballard and M.H. Passo, 1999. *The relationship of hepatotoxic risk factors and liver histology in methotrexate therapy for juvenile rheumatoid arthritis.* J. Pediatr., 134: 47-52.

32. Erickson, A. R., Reddy, V., Vogelgesang, S. A. and West, S. G. (1995), *Usefulness of the american college of rheumatology recommendations for liver biopsy in methotrexate-treated rheumatoid arthritis patients.* Arthritis & Rheumatism, 38: 1115–1119.

33. Newman, ED., and Scott, DW. "The Use of Low-dose Oral Methotrexate in the Treatment of Polymyositis and Dermatomyositis" *Journal of Clinical Rheumatology*, 1995 Apr;1(2):99-102. Print

34. Kremer JM, Alarcon GS, Lightfoot RW Jr, et al. *Methotrexate for rheumatoid arthritis: Suggested guidelines for monitoring liver toxicity.* Arthritis Rheum 1994;37:316-28.

35. Tett, SE and Triggs, EJ (1996) *Use of methotrexate in older patients—A risk-benefit assessment.* Drugs & Aging, 9 6: 458-471.

36. Hakim AJ, Machin SJ, Isenberg DA. *Autoimmune thrombocytopenia in primary antiphospholid syndrome and systemic lupus erythematosus: the response to splenectomy.* Semin Arthritis Rheum 1998;28:20–5.

37. Malatjalian DA, Ross JB, Williams CN, Colwell SJ, Eastwood BJ. *Methotrexate hepatotoxicity in psoriatics: report of 104 patients from Nova Scotia, with analysis of risks from obesity, diabetes and alcohol consumption during long term follow-up.* Can J Gastroenterol. 1996 Oct;10(6):369-75.

38. Montilla, Morales C. *Hypertransaminemia and Methotrexate: Not Always a Toxic Effect?.* Rev Clin Esp. 1998 Dec;198(12):822-4. Print.

39. Kremer JM, Furst DE, Weinblatt ME, Blotner SD. *Significant changes in serum AST across hepatic histological biopsy grades: prospective analysis of 3 cohorts receiving methotrexate therapy for rheumatoid arthritis.* J Rheumatol 1996; 23:459

40. vanDooren-Greebe, P. C. M., et al. (1996) *The value of dynamic hepatic scintigraphy and serum aminoterminal propeptide of type III procollagen for early detection of methotrexate-induced hepatic damage in psoriasis patients.* British Journal of Dermatology, 134: 481–487.

Chapter 25

Anticoagulants: Therapeutics, Risks, and Toxicity—Special Focus on Heparin-Induced Thrombocytopenia

James T. O'Donnell, Pharm.D., MS, FCP

25.1 Introduction

The purpose of this chapter is to provide the reader with the mechanisms of action, requisite clinical and laboratory monitoring, toxicities, and examples of errors and complications leading to litigation involving pharmacists and other healthcare providers. A secondary objective is to address the current knowledge on heparin-induced thrombocytopenia (HIT), a serious, life-threatening complication that is recognized but not well understood.

Consider the following serious consequences of too much or too little anticoagulant:

1. Pharmacist dispenses 2 mg warfarin instead of 5 mg; patient's routine INR (International Normalized Ratio) is non-therapeutic. Hospital notification system fails. Woman has stroke and is permanently disabled.

2. Pharmacist dispenses warfarin instead of Cogentin; technician testifies pharmacist does not check her prescriptions. Patient dies of intra-cerebral bleed (this case is described in full detail later in this chapter).

3. Nursery infants administered 50× overdose of heparin for catheter flush (the Dennis Quaid case). Babies develop bleeding. California Boards of Nursing and Pharmacy investigate hospital practices. Floor stocking with 5,000 unit/mL vials instead of 10 unit/mL or 100 unit/mL discovered.

4. Texas hospital reports heparin overdoses in several infants. Heparin syringes compounded in hospital pharmacy contained excessive amounts of heparin. Some infants died of heparin overdose.

5. Doctor mistakenly writes 10 mg instead of 1 mg dose of warfarin. Pharmacist does not question the very high (almost never chronic) dose. Patient bleeds intracranially and dies.

6. Patient transferred from one hospital to another with heparin infusion. First hospital uses 25,000

Note: For purposes of full disclosure, Dr. O'Donnell has consulted and testified in numerous heparin and oral anticoagulant injury claims, many involving pharmacists' error and malpractice. He has also served as an expert for a plaintiff in a lawsuit against several pharmaceutical companies related to Heparin Induced Thrombocytopenia (HIT) units in 500 mL and the receiving hospital infuses a more concentrated infusion at first hospital's infusion rate, resulting in massive hematoma, allegedly leading to sciatic nerve injury.

7. A pregnant woman with a history of pulmonary emboli is non-compliant for enoxaparin treatment. Baby born with low birth weight. Placenta 25 percent infarcted. OBGYN sued—defense of non-compliance by patient.

25.2 Summary of Anticoagulant Therapy[1]
A. Definition
An anticoagulant is a substance that prevents coagulation; that is, it stops blood from clotting. A group of pharmaceuticals called anticoagulants can be used in vivo as a medication for thrombotic disorders.

B. Use

1. Treatment of coronary heart disease
Morbidity and mortality associated with an arterial or venous thrombotic event is extremely high. In 1999, there were 529,659 deaths caused by coronary heart disease and 167,366 caused by stroke. Anticoagulants are used for the prevention and treatment of cardio embolic events as well as of venous thrombosis. Anticoagulant use has increased in the management of cardiovascular disease states due to heightened awareness of the mechanism of thromboembolism.

2. Warfarin and dabigatran
The oral anticoagulant most commonly used, warfarin, certainly does not fit the image of an ideal medicine. With a narrow therapeutic index, routine monitoring, and the risk of bleeding, warfarin therapy can be time-consuming for the healthcare professional as well as for the patient. The ideal oral anticoagulant would be an agent taken only once daily with limited or no drug interactions, low risk of bleeding, no routine laboratory monitoring, and minimal side effects. A recent market addition of the oral anticoagulant dabigatran provides some benefits not achievable by warfarin (standard twice daily dose, without the need of INR tests and constant dosage adjustment). It is currently indicated for patients with atrial fibrillation not caused by a heart valve problem.[2]

The target for many of the newer oral therapies under development for prevention and treatment of embolic events is thrombin. Inhibition of thrombin generation or its activity is an area of focus because it unites the extrinsic and intrinsic pathways for coagulation.

3. Treatment of thrombogenesis
Arterial thrombosis, the most common cause of myocardial infarction, stroke, and peripheral arterial disease, is caused mainly by platelet aggregation and fibrin, which stabilizes the thrombus. Initially, an atherosclerotic plaque ruptures, exposing tissue factor (TF) to the blood. Once the site is exposed, platelets attach to the subendothelium, where they are activated and aggregate. Platelet and fibrin deposition can form an occlusive thrombus that blocks blood flow to the coronary, carotid, or peripheral arteries. Venous thrombosis, which can lead to pulmonary embolism, occurs under low shear states, and usually consists of fibrin and red blood cells. The origin of venous thrombi is typically the muscular veins of the calf as well as the valve cusp pockets of the deep calf veins. Vascular trauma in addition to venous stasis is the usual source for coagulation in the veins. After vessel wall injury occurs, exposure of TF activates the coagulation cascade, leading to thrombin generation (Figure 25.1). Platelets adhere to the injured areas of the vessel walls by platelet glycoprotein (GP) Ib/IX on the platelet membrane binding with von Willebrand factor. Once activated, platelet aggregation occurs by several mechanisms. Storage granules on activated platelets release adenosine diphosphate (ADP), which stimulates adjacent platelets. Clotting factors gather on the surface of activated platelets and further thrombin formation, which enhances platelet activation and coagulation. In addition, platelets are also stimulated by the release of thromboxane A2 from activated platelets. Thrombin plays a key role in several stages of thrombus formation. Thrombin promotes platelet aggregation, cleavage of fibrinogen to fibrin to form the fibrin clot, and activation of factors that stabilize fibrin clots. Through feedback mechanisms, thrombin can also activate its own production, furthering the coagulation process. For these reasons, inhibition of thrombin generation or activity is the focus of many investigational treatment strategies.

25.3 Limitations of Current Therapy
All anticoagulants and fibrinolytic drugs have an increased bleeding risk as their principle toxicity, with intracranial hemorrhage (ICH) as the most severe example. Particularly serious episodes involve sites where irreversible damage may result from compression of vital structures, such as the pericardial, nerve sheath, or spinal cord, as well as massive internal blood loss that may not be diagnosed rapidly: gastrointestinal, intraperitoneal, or retroperitoneal.

A. Heparin
Unfractionated heparin (UFH), while commonly used intravenously, is not orally bioavailable. UFH must be monitored

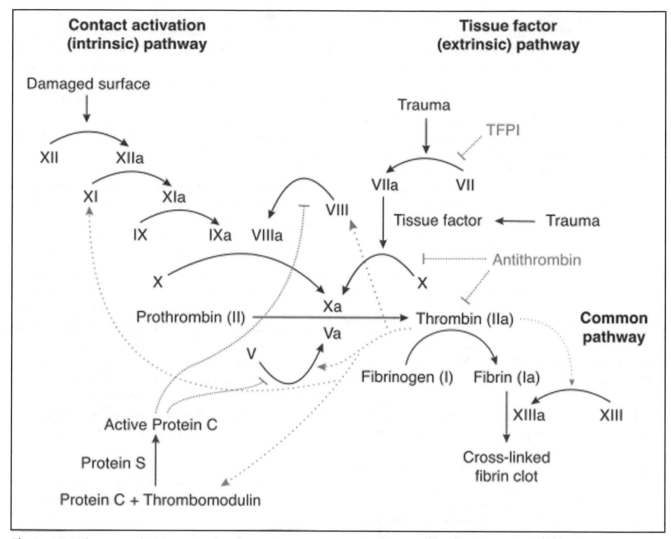

Figure 25.1 *The coagulation cascade of secondary hemostasis. Source: http://en.wikipedia.org/wiki/coagulation.*

closely due to the narrow therapeutic window, and has a significant risk of bleeding. This risk can be decreased by scrupulous patient selection, careful control of dosage, and close monitoring. Heparin, an indirect thrombin inhibitor, increases endogenous antithrombin activity. Antithrombin normally inhibits thrombin and factor Xa. Thrombin has three binding sites: an active site and two exosites. The first exosite is used for binding substrates such as fibrinogen in the correct orientation for cleavage to fibrin. Thrombin converts fibrinogen to fibrin, then remains bound to fibrin while continuing to activate platelets, enhancing thrombus formation. The second exosite (exosite 2) is used as the heparin binding site. To inactivate thrombin, heparin must bind to antithrombin and exosite 2 on thrombin. If heparin binds to fibrin and exosite 2, thrombin is resistant to inactivation by the antithrombin/heparin complex, which enhances the thrombin/fibrin interaction and may lead to further thrombus formation. Once thrombin and fibrin are bound, heparin cannot inactivate thrombin.

Limitations of heparin use include heparin-induced thrombocytopenia (HIT). While studies show that HIT affects between 1 to 5 percent of patients receiving heparin, with up to 600,000 cases occurring yearly. It is important to recognize that HIT is generally under-diagnosed in patients with myeloproliferative syndromes because of high baseline platelet counts (8). Heparin can cause two types of HIT. Type 1, heparin-associated thrombocytopenia (HAT), occurs early (within 48 to 72 hours of administration), is a non-immune cause of the disorder, and does not confer an increased risk of thrombosis. Platelet counts do not typically fall below 100,000 platelets per microliter (mcL), and return to normal limits within a few days, even with continued administration. Type 2, or HIT II, occurs within five to ten days after initial heparin administration, with the platelet count usually falling to less than 100,000 platelets per microliter (mcL). Unlike HAT, HIT is associated with immune response and activation of platelets and has a high risk of thromboembolic events.

Patients with HIT cannot receive heparin or low molecular weight heparin (LMWH). HIT patients need to be anticoagulated with agents such as direct thrombin inhibitors (DTI) to prevent thrombosis. DTIs should be continued until a sufficient number of platelets have been replenished.

B. Low Molecular Weight Heparin (LMWH)

Anticoagulant effects of LMWH are produced by activation of antithrombin as well as inactivation of factor Xa. Because LMWH is composed of smaller fragments than UFH, these fragments do not bind to antithrombin or thrombin. LMWH does not require routine monitoring like UFH and has a more predictable anticoagulant effect. Although LMWH can be used in the outpatient setting due to the lack of monitoring needed, its use is still restricted because of subcutaneous administration. Monitoring is, however, necessary for patients with obesity or renal failure. Pregnant patients requiring anticoagulation cannot use warfarin; LMWH is commonly used in this population instead of UFH. The incidence of HIT is lower with LMWH (less than 1 percent). However, the same problem exists with LMWH as with UFH; it cannot inactivate thrombin bound to fibrin.

C. Heparin-Induced Thrombocytopenia (HIT)

According to Priziola et al., anywhere from 15 to 58 percent of intensive care unit (ICU) patients are thought to experience thrombocytopenia, with an estimated 10 million persons per year having a drug-induced form of the disease.[3] Functionally, HIT occurs through bone marrow suppression, increased platelet destruction, or platelet sequestration, and should not be confused with pseudothrombocytopenia—an in vitro clumping of platelets that does not carry the same clinical consequences.

Early descriptions of the clinical HIT syndrome delineated its emergence after 5 to 12 days of continuing heparin exposure, defining the disease in terms of a platelet count drop of around 50 percent.[2] This is the classic presentation, but in a patient exposed to heparin within the preceding three months, a preformed circulating antibody can lead to a rapid onset of HIT within hours or even minutes of re-exposure. Some patients experience anaphylactic-like cardiorespiratory collapse upon re-exposure.[4]

HIT is caused by an autoimmune reaction leading to the formation of antibodies directed against platelet factor 4.[5] Conditions favoring the development of anti-platelet factor 4/heparin antibodies differ from those required for the formation of macromolecular ternary complexes (HIT antibody/platelet factor 4/heparin), which are able to activate platelets and induce clinical HIT. HIT can be diagnosed by combining its pretest probability with the quantitative re-

sult of rapid HIT-antibody assays. Treatment of acute HIT requires inhibition of thrombin generation by means of alternative non-heparin anticoagulant drugs. As HIT antibodies are transient, HIT patients can be re-exposed to heparin, provided that previous heparin treatment is remote and that anti-platelet factor 4/heparin antibodies are undetectable. Likewise, not all patients who develop antibodies against PF4/heparin complexes experience the platelet drop-off that would define them as having HIT.[4]

1. Pathogenesis of the autoimmune response

HIT is caused by the development of immunoglobulin G (IgG) antibodies that recognize a "self" protein, platelet factor 4 (PF4), bound to polyanions, forming PF4/heparin complexes.[6] PF4 is a positively charged protein of 70 amino acids belonging to the CXC subfamily of chemokines. It is synthesized by megakaryocytes and stored in α-granules, in which it self-associates to form tetramers of approximately 31 kDa complexed with chondroitin sulfate. Upon platelet activation, PF4 is released, dissociates from chondroitin sulfate, and binds more anionic glycosaminoglycans (GAG) on cell surfaces, such as heparin sulfate. Unlike other cytokines that have clearly defined receptors, PF4 appears to function by this high-affinity cell-surface binding. It has been proposed that PF4 may be involved in several biological processes, such as angiogenesis, immune response, thrombosis, and megakaryopoiesis.

Recent work has further investigated the molecular structure of PF4/heparin complexes, showing that conditions favoring the generation of anti-PF4/heparin antibodies differ from those required for intense platelet activation. Conceptually, the current working model of HIT immune pathogenesis implies the following aspects:

1. PF4 bound to anionic GAG expresses at least two immunogenic neoepitopes.
2. In-vivo PF4 bound to physiologic GAG forms antigenic complexes on cell surfaces.
3. Infusion of the more anionic heparin displaces PF4 from physiologic GAG, leading to the formation of PF4/heparin complexes.
4. PF4/heparin complexes carrying a net positive charge (i.e., those with a molar excess of PF4) are most immunogenic.
5. PF4/heparin complexes expressing neutral charges (i.e., those with a PF4–heparin molar ratio of about 1:1) are able to form the largest macromolecular complexes (more than 670 kDa), which are the most potent in mediating binding of HIT antibodies possibly by close approximation of PF4 tetramers

and the inducement of heparin-dependent platelet activation.

6. Disruption of the PF4/heparin complexes by infusion of excess heparin or protamine sulfate impairs their ability to bind anti-PF4/heparin antibodies and activate platelets.

This model, showing that PF4 bound in vivo to cell-surface GAG is immunogenic, could explain why healthy individuals are found to be positive for anti-PF4/heparin antibodies and why in HIT patients anti-PF4/heparin antibodies of the IgG class are already detectable as early as five days after initiation of heparin treatment. A second implication of this model, based on the different stoichiometries of PF4/heparin complexes, is that patients with higher degrees of surface-bound and circulating PF4 and lower (prophylactic) heparin concentrations would carry the highest risk of developing HIT. In fact, the incidence of HIT is higher among surgical than medical patients; among surgical patients it is higher in those with "traumatic" surgery, such as orthopedics or cardiopulmonary bypass; among medical patients it is higher in those with peripheral arterial disease, cancer, or other inflammatory conditions promoting platelet activation and PF4 release. Moreover, the dissociation of conditions favoring the immune response from those necessary for platelet activation would explain why only a subset of patients who have developed anti-PF4/heparin antibodies progress to full-blown HIT.

Finally, it has been shown that PF4 is a modulator of T-cell activation, with opposite effects on regulatory versus non-regulatory T-cells, and that generation of anti-PF4/heparin antibodies is a T-cell-dependent process. Future research will have to delineate how PF4/heparin complexes initiate antigen presentation and modulate T-cell responses.

2. Pathogenesis of the prothrombotic state

Ternary HIT-IgG/PF4/heparin complexes bind to cell surfaces. On platelets, the IgG Fc regions cross-link the low-affinity receptor for immune complexes, FcγRIIa (CD32), leading to platelet activation and development of platelet-procoagulant activity. At the same time, HIT-IgG/PF4/heparin complexes are able to induce synthesis and expression of tissue factor on endothelial cells and monocytes.[5] All these events contribute to the development of unbalanced thrombin generation, which is central to the severe prothrombotic state peculiar to HIT.

In addition to the pro-coagulant state, other factors may increase the thrombotic risk in HIT. HIT antibodies may promote thrombosis through platelet adhesion to the vessel wall and formation of platelet-leukocyte aggregates.

3. Clinical presentation of HIT[6]

HIT is indicated by a severe decrease of platelet count (more than 50 percent drop or more than 150,000), sometimes with associated venous, arterial, and/or cutaneous thrombosis a week or two after the introduction of heparin (referred to as "typical onset"). Among patients who have previously been exposed to anti-PF4/heparin antibodies, HIT can present within hours after receiving heparin, with a drop of the platelet count, thrombosis, and symptoms such as flushing, hypotension, tachycardia, and dyspnea (this is referred to as "rapid-onset" HIT).[7] Finally, HIT can be diagnosed several days after heparin has been stopped ("delayed-onset" HIT). It is thus necessary to consider delayed-onset HIT as a possibility in order to be able to recognize and diagnose it. Warkentin and Kelton (2001) found that "the presence of heparin-dependent antibodies in the blood was usually transient and did not always recur with subsequent heparin therapy."[9] This leads them to conclude that those with a history of heparin-induced thrombocytopenia should be re-exposed to heparin only in extreme cases such as cardiac or vascular surgery, and then only if heparin-dependent antibodies cannot be detected.

A protocol useful for HIT detection includes:

1. Pre-op ELISA screening for all cardiac surgery patients.
2. Elimination of all unnecessary sources of heparin and availability of heparin-free products for all HIT-positive patients.
3. HIT precautions and testing for any cardiac surgery with thrombocytopenia.
4. Anticoagulant management of all post-op ventricular assist device patients with direct thrombin inhibitors.
5. Utilization of citrate for hemodialysis and CVVH.

While such practices do involve a minor increase in associated costs, this is more than made up for in the fact that it reduces those costs associated with the failure to detect HIT.[10]

4. Diagnosis

It is common practice to institute alternative (i.e., non-heparin) anticoagulant treatment as soon as HIT is suspected as a possibility, as not doing so carries a far greater risk. However, alternative anticoagulants are extremely costly (estimated at $800–$1,000 per day) with life-threatening potential side effects, such as major bleeding or anaphylactic reactions.[11] This suggests the need for the development of a rapid HIT diagnosis method to ensure proper action.

a. Dismissing HIT

The chance of a given patient having HIT can be approximated through a clinical scoring system known as the "4T," in which patients are marked as having a low, intermediate, or high risk for the disease. Patients are scored between zero and eight, with scores less than three indicating a high negative predictive value for HIT. While this test does appear to be a reliable strategy to rule out HIT, combining pre-test clinical probability with rapid immunoassay results remains the most effective for excluding HIT.[7] Priziola et al. (2010) also indicate "this scoring system has not been validated in an ICU population."[12] Figure 25.2 demonstrates the "4 T's" scoring method for predicting HIT.

b. Diagnosing HIT

HIT cannot be diagnosed solely through clinical methods, but must include a positive laboratory testing in the appropriate context, and as such it will be critical here to consult a hematologist.

Tests for HIT antibodies include both immunological assays that detect PF4/heparin antibodies and functional platelet activation assays—such as the serotonin release assay—that work by detecting heparin-dependent antibodies. Functional assays have the advantage of very high specificity, but are also technically demanding, have a long turn-around time, and are conducted by only a small fraction of laboratories. If a correctly performed functional assay produces positive results, then HIT can be definitively diagnosed up to 99 percent certainty.[13] Unfortunately, platelet activation assays are not widely available for emergency testing, and it is possible that a patient may have HIT without testing positively.

The second group of methods for detecting HIT antibodies is immunoassays. Presently, there are three commercial enzyme-linked immunosorbent assays (ELISAs) (Asserachrom HPIA, GTI-PF4, Zymutest HIA) and a PaGIA (in-vitro diagnostic) called ID-Heparin/PF4–PaGIA that are available to detect PF4 antibodies. All of these assays can

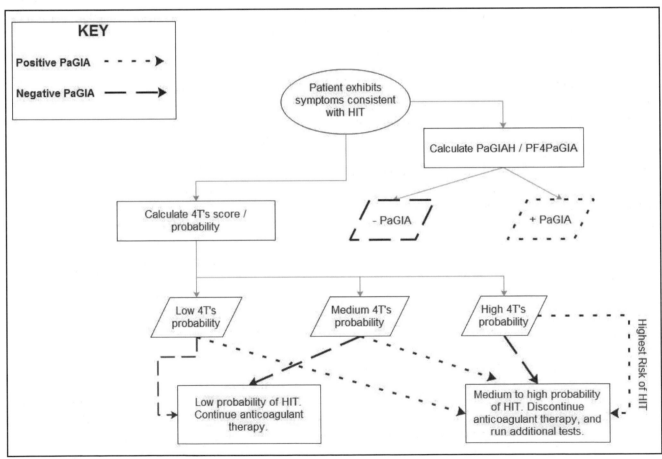

Figure 25.2 *Use of the 4T's scoring system and results of PaGIA in the diagnosis of heparin-induced thrombocytopenia. Adapted from C. Pouplard, P. Gueret, M. Fouassier et al. Prospective evaluation of the 4T's score and particle gel immunoassay specific to heparin/PF4 for the diagnosis of heparin-induced thrombocytopenia. J Thromb Haemost 2007;5:1373-1379.*

detect IgG, IgM, and IgA antibodies and have a very high sensitivity, with a slightly better performance than the Pa-GIA, found to have operating characteristics in-between the ELISA and functional assays. The drawback of these immunoassays is their relatively low specificity for pathogenic HIT antibodies, which in turn provides a risk of over-diagnosing HIT. This is especially problematic for the cardiovascular surgery population, in which assay testing suggests 25 to 50 percent of patients have heparin antibodies while platelet activating antibodies are actually found only in 15 to 20 percent of patients.[14]

c. Two approaches: class and titer

One method against over-diagnosis uses immunoassays that only detect HIT antibodies of the IgG class. A second way to approach this problem is to consider the extent of the immunoassay result. Alberio (1998) has shown that "the absolute optical density values of two commercial ELISAs strongly correlate with the antibody titer obtained by the ID-H/PF4–PaGIA, and that the antibody titer independently correlates with a retrospective likelihood score for HIT, a positive functional platelet aggregation test, the prevalence of thromboembolic events during treatment with heparin, and the concentration of prothrombin fragments F1+2, thrombin–antithrombin complexes, and D-dimers."[15]

It is also worth noting that antigens besides PF4 may be a relevant factor in HIT pathogenesis, including interleukin 8 (IL-8) or neutrophil-activating peptide 2 (NAP-2), two PF4-related CXC chemokines with high affinity for heparin. A reasonable "gold standard" suggested by Alberio for diagnosing HIT is "either a positive functional assay or high-titer anti-PF4/heparin antibodies in the presence of a clinically-likely HIT."[15] Both plasma from sodium citrate or EDTA tubes and serum can be employed for detecting HIT antibodies by immunoassay.

5. Treatment of HIT

For patients suspected or known to have HIT, all heparin should be stopped without exception, replaced with alternative anticoagulation method by means of the direct thrombin inhibitors (DTIs) lepirudin (half-life 69 minutes; renal excretion; immunogenic, with antibodies increasing the anticoagulant effect and anaphylactic reactions) or argatroban (half-life 45 minutes; hepatic metabolism; nonimmunogenic). The DTI danaparoid is not yet available in the United States.

HIT patients with or without thromboembolic complications require therapeutic anticoagulation. Platelet transfusions must also be discontinued, as they have been observed to potentiate thrombosis.[16]

Vitamin K antagonists (VKA), such as warfarin, are ill-suited for cases of acute HIT because they fail to inhibit the marked hypercoagulability state of HIT, while at the same time they can cause severe depletion of the vitamin K-dependent natural anticoagulant, protein C,[8] and VKAs increase the risk of micro vascular thrombosis, especially venous limb gangrene.

a. Fondaparinux

Fondaparinux is a synthetic "pentasaccharide" anticoagulant, modeled after the antithrombin-binding sequence of heparin molecules. Interestingly, patients treated with fondaparinux develop anti-PF4/heparin antibodies with a similar frequency as those treated with low molecular weight heparin (LMWH), but fondaparinux-induced HIT appears to be exquisitely rare, although documented. This may be explained by the inability of fondaparinux to form large complexes with PF4, thus failing to activate platelets.[9] Recently, a few reports have suggested that fondaparinux may be useful in patients with acute HIT. This is an interesting option; however, prospective clinical studies should verify whether fondaparinux is able to control the strong procoagulant state of acute HIT. Moreover, several "unstable" HIT patients, such as those in ICU or those requiring surgical interventions, are not suited for treatment with a renally-excreted anticoagulant with a long half-life and no antidote available. Finally, as fondaparinux can induce the formation of anti-PF4/heparin antibodies, one still has to be aware that a subsequent treatment with unfractionated heparin (UFH) or LMWH may precipitate HIT. The author's institution occasionally employs fondaparinux for prolonged anticoagulation after successful acute treatment with lepirudin in those HIT patients who cannot be switched to VKA.

b. Re-exposure with heparin

There is a good rationale for short-term heparin re-exposure of patients with a history of HIT in order to permit surgery. In fact, HIT antibodies are transient, generally disappearing within four months, and patients with "rapid-onset" HIT have been shown to have circulating HIT antibodies. The feasibility of this option has been demonstrated for cardiovascular surgery. These publications clearly indicate that there is no anamnestic immune response in HIT. Moreover, the recent data on the stoichiometric requirements for the formation of immunogenic and platelet-activating PF4/heparin complexes would speak against an elevated recurrence risk as well.

6. Conclusion HIT and HITT

Despite decreasing use of UFH in favor of LMWH

and fondaparinux, HIT still constitutes a clinically relevant challenge, based on difficulty in diagnoses, ubiquitous presence of heparin, high costs of alternative DTIs, and the life-threatening risk of HIT and HITT. In recent years, there has been a continuing elucidation of pathogenic and clinically relevant issues, which are intellectually rewarding to follow and should enable us to offer a steadily improving treatment to the patients in our charge.[7]

D. Warfarin[10]

Warfarin is currently the standard for providing long-term oral anticoagulation for atrial fibrillation, prosthetic heart valves, venous thrombosis, and pulmonary embolism. Warfarin is an antagonist of vitamin K and interferes with hepatic synthesis of coagulation factors II, VII, IX and X. Inhibition of the hepatic vitamin K conversion cycle causes production of clotting factors with reduced coagulant activity. There are several shortcomings to warfarin therapy. Frequent therapeutic monitoring is required due to the narrow therapeutic range and risk of bleeding associated with warfarin. Monitoring can be difficult because of changes in dietary vitamin K consumption as well as numerous drug interactions.[11] Dosing must be specifically modified for the individual patient to avoid thromboembolic events caused by subtherapeutic levels as well as supertherapeutic levels, which lead to increased risk of bleeding. A therapeutic response to warfarin is not achieved for the first 12 hours after introduction, and often takes between two to seven days to become effective. When rapid anticoagulant effect is needed, an additional form of anticoagulation such as heparin should be used, and warfarin should not be prescribed unless a patient's platelet count is above a minimum sustainable threshold. Finally, warfarin must *never* be administered during pregnancy (contraindicated: Pregnancy Category X) as it crosses the placenta readily and can cause a hemorrhagic disorder in the fetus.

If an excessive anticoagulant effect without bleeding occurs, cessation of the drug responsible can often be enough. In the setting of severe bleeding, however, the warfarin effect can be rapidly reversed with the administration of prothrombin complex or rFVIIa coupled with intravenous vitamin K (though this carries a risk of anaphylaxis). It is important to note that due to the long half-life of warfarin, a single dose of vitamin K or rFVIIa may not be sufficient.[12]

Current therapy for prevention and treatment of thrombosis has been hindered by lack of oral anticoagulants that are easily managed. More effective anticoagulation treatments are needed with simplified dosing schedules, less monitoring, and less risk of bleeding complications to replace warfarin. Consistent oral bioavailability appears to be the key in developing the next oral anticoagulant. The new agents must be as effective as warfarin yet easier to monitor and, hopefully, safer, such as dabigatran discussed below.

25.4 Monitoring Oral Anticoagulation

The number of indications for, as well as the number of patients on, oral anticoagulation (OAC) therapy has increased significantly. Primary indications for OAC therapy include venous thromboembolism, atrial fibrillation, cerebrovascular disease, heart valve prosthesis, peripheral vascular disease, and myocardial infarction. Evidence shows an exponential increase in the risk of thrombosis when international normalized ratio (INR) values fall below 2.0, and the risk of hemorrhage increases when INR values rise above 4.5. Thus, maintenance of a close target therapeutic range is a critical component of successful OAC therapy. Several drug- and patient-related factors make this task difficult to achieve, including a narrow therapeutic index of the drug, numerous drug-drug and drug-food interactions, and individual differences in dose-response to warfarin sodium. The above challenges make regular monitoring of patients' INR values and dosage adjustments an essential part of OAC therapy. The standard test is the plasma-based PT test, which was traditionally done in a laboratory. Point of Care (POC) testing eliminates the need of transporting blood specimen and enables the clinician to immediately assess the results and adjust the dosing of OAC therapy, if necessary. It has been suggested that the use of portable prothrombin time (PPT) monitors allows more convenient and thus more frequent testing, which may be translated to better control of OAC therapy. Patients requiring long-term anticoagulant therapy are recommended to have their PT measured every 1 to 4 weeks. However, as PT values are dependent on the sensitivity of the thromboplastin reagent, INR is a better scale of measurement because it adjusts for this factor:

$$INR = (patient\ PT \div mean\ normal\ PT) \times ISI$$

Where ISI is the international sensitivity index. Close supervision by a health professional remains an integral part of anticoagulant therapy.[16]

25.5 Alternatives to Warfarin[17]
A. Pradaxa (Dabigatran) vs. Warfarin

Pradaxa (dabigatran) is a new medication designed to prevent clots that can be caused by atrial fibrillation. This drug has a few benefits not conferred by warfarin (Coumadin), including that it does not require frequent INR testing. Furthermore, dabigatranis is less likely to adversely interact with other medications or with foods containing vitamin K (as warfarin does).

Warfarin still holds some advantages over Pradaxa, including its price, which is about one-third of the new drug. Also, warfarin requires only once-daily dosing, as opposed to dabigatran (twice daily dosing).

Pradaxa may cause gastrointestinal side effects, especially when taken on an empty stomach.[13]

25.6 Conclusion

The double-edged sword caution applicable to any medication is exemplified in anticoagulant therapy. These absolutely essential medications must be used for a variety of medical conditions; there are no substitutes. Pharmacists can better contribute to these patients' care by a thorough understanding of the clinical pharmacology, indications, toxicity, and selection of anticoagulants to limit such toxicity. These efforts will predictably decrease claims of legal tort against pharmacists and other health workers (no injury/no suit).

Endnotes

1. (Chapter 118 contributor) Antiplatelet, Anticoagulant, and Fibrinolytic Drugs, In Fauci AS, Braunwald E, Kasper DL, Hauser SL, Oongo DL, et al. *Harrison's Principles of Internal Medicine*, 18th Ed. www.access-medicine.com/content.aspx?aid=9101027.

2. www.pradaxa.com (official prescribing information).

3. Priziola JL, Smythe MA, and Dager WE. Drug-Induced Thrombocytopenia in Critically Ill Patients.Drit Care med. 2010 Jun;38(6 Suppl): S145-54.

4. Warkentin TE. Clinical Picture of Heparin-Induced Thrombocytopenia. Chapter 2, In Wakkentin TE and Greinacher A, Eds. Heparin-Induced Thrombocytopenia, 4th Edition, Informa Healthcare, NY, 2007 at p. 26.

5. Warkentin TE. Clinical Picture of Heparin-Induced Thrombocytopenia. Chapter 2, In Wakkentin TE and Greinacher A, Eds. Heparin-Induced Thrombocytopenia, 4th Edition, Informa Healthcare, NY, 2007 at p. 21.

6. Alban S and Greinqacher A. Role of Sulfated Polysacchariedes in the Pathogenesis of Heparin-Induced Thrombocytopenia. Chapter 7, In Wakkentin TE and Greinacher A, Eds. Heparin-Induced Thrombocytopenia, 4th Edition, Informa Healthcare, NY, 2007 at p.172.

7. Pouplard C, Gueret P, Foussier M, Ternisien C, Trosssaert M, Regina S, and Gruel Y. Prospective evaluation of the '4Ts' score and particle gel immunoassay specific to heparin/PF4 for the diagnosis of heparin-induced thrombocytopenia. J Thromb. And Haemostasis. Vol 5, No 7, 1373-1379, July 2007.

8. Greinacher A and Warkentin TE.Treatment of Heparin-Induced Thrombocytopenia: An Overview. Chapter 12, In Wakkentin TE and Greinacher A, Eds. Heparin-Induced Thrombocytopenia, 4th Edition, Informa Healthcare, NY, 2007 at p. 296.

9. Bradner JE and Eikkelboom JW. Emerging Anticoagulants and Heparin-Induced Thrombocytopenia: Indirect and Direct Factor Xa Inhibitors and oral Thrombin Inhibitors., Chapter 17, In Wakkentin TE and Greinacher A, Eds. Heparin-Induced Thrombocytopenia, 4th Edition, Informa Healthcare, NY, 2007 at p.444.

10. (Chapter 112 contributor) Antiplatelet, Anticoagulant, and Fibrinolytic Drugs, In Fauci AS, Braunwald E, Kasper DL, Hauser SL, Oongo DL, et al. *Harrison's Principles of Internal Medicine, Seventeenth Edition.*

11. Zehender, J.L. "Drugs Used in Disorders of Coagulation." *In* Katung, B.G., Masters, S.B., and Trevor, A.J. (eds.) *Basic and Clinical Pharmacology, Twelfth Edition* (2012). McGraw Hill, New York.

12. NovoSeven®is recombinant human coagulation Factor VIIa (rFVIIa), intended for promoting hemostasis by activating the extrinsic pathway of the coagulation cascade. 1 NovoSeven (coagulation factor via recombinant) is a vitamin K-dependent glycoprotein consisting of 406 amino acid residues (MW 50 K Dalton). NovoSeven (coagulation factor via recombinant) is structurally similar to human plasma-derived Factor VIIa.

13. www.pradaxa.com (official prescribing information).

14. Arepally, Gowthami M., and Thomas L. Ortel. "Heparin-Induced Thrombocytopenia." *New England Journal of Medicine* 355.24 (2006): 2598-599. Print.

15. Alberio L. "Heparin-induced thrombocytopenia: some working hypotheses on pathogenesis, diagnostic strategies and treatment." *Curr Opin Hematol.* 2008;15(5):456–64.

16. Refaai, Majed A., Richard P. Phipps, Sherry L. Spinelli, and Neil Blumberg. "Platelet Transfusions: Impact on Hemostasis, Thrombosis, Inflammation and Clinical Outcomes." *Thrombosis Research* 127.4 (2011): 287-91. Print.

17. Connolly SJ, Ezekowitz MD, Yusuf S, et al; RE-LY Steering Committee and Investigators. Dabigatran versus warfarin in patients with atrial fibrillation. N Engl J Med. 2009;361:1139-1151.

Chapter 26

Drug-Induced Movement Disorders

Jadwiga Najib, Pharm.D.

26.1 Introduction

Drug-induced movement disorders (DIMDs) represent a variety of iatrogenic and clinically distinct movement disorders and are a major problem in clinical neuropsychiatry and medicine. DIMDs refer to a variety of treatment-emergent, involuntary motor symptoms including dystonia, dyskinesia, akathisia, parkinsonism, tremor, asterixis, chorea, and serotonin syndrome. DIMDs were first described in the 1950s shortly following the introduction of antipsychotic agents, and more recently have been described with other psychotropic agents and central nervous system medications. Metoclopramide, used for gastrointestinal motor dysfunction and as an antiemetic, is now a recognized major cause of DIMDs. Although most of the offending agents are primarily characterized as dopamine receptor-blocking agents (DRBAs), which primarily block D2 receptors, various other agents including central nervous system stimulants, anticonvulsants, antidepressants, H2-receptor antagonists, antiemetics, hormones, antiarrhythmics and calcium channel blockers can affect motor behavior and cause movement disorders.

To highlight that neuroleptics are one of the most important causes of DIMDs, *Diagnostic and Statistical Manual of Mental Disorders*, fourth edition, text-revised (DSM-IV-TR) published by the American Psychiatric Association (APA) contains a separate category involving medication-induced movement disorders, including Neuroleptic-Induced parkinsonism, Neuroleptic Malignant Syndrome, Neuroleptic-Induced Acute Dystonia, Neuroleptic-Induced Acute Akathisia, Neuroleptic-Induced Tardive Dyskinesia, and Medication-Induced Postural Tremor.[1] The addition of the category, Medication-Induced Movement Disorder Not Otherwise Specified, acknowledges that agents other than neuroleptics (e.g., antidepressants, stimulants, and so on) can produce comparable movement disorders. Various drugs may either cause a new movement disorder in a normal brain or convert a covert vulnerability to an overexpression of involuntary movements by potentially activating an underlying susceptibility from a sub-clinical degenerative process or insult such as a brain injury. How best to manage DIMDs remains controversial including using the lowest effective dosage of the agent, treating the reactions with medications, and changing the neuroleptic to one with a lower potential for inducing DIMDs.

26.2 Presentation

DIMDs are divided into three main categories reflecting time periods: 1) acute and intermediate, which occur shortly following exposure to the offending agent, usually within 2 to 5 days, and quickly reach maximal severity and intensity; 2) continuous, which are non-acute syndromes that appear after variable exposure to the offending agent and last as long as the agent is administered; and 3) tardive, which appear following long-term exposure (usually greater than three months) to the offending agent and continue even after the causative agent is discontinued.[2]

The symptomatology of DIMD is often indistinguishable from that of idiopathic movement disorders, hence the diagnosis of DIMDs requires a careful observation and description of symptoms, a thorough medication history, as well as a neurologic and general physical examination.[3] Recognition of the abnormal movement, as well as identification of the temporal relationship between initiation of therapy with a DRBA (acute onset) or exposure to such an agent within the previous three months (tardive) and the onset of the abnormal movement is important in diagnosing DIMDs. The etiology of movement disorders is more likely to be drug-induced when the patient has movements which are both hypokinetic (paucity of movements which are slow and stiff) and hyperkinetic (excessive or abnormal movements) occurring simultaneously; when certain patterns are present that may be more typical of tardive dyskinesia (e.g., axial distribution dystonia); when the DIMD occurs in conjunction with facial dyskinesia; or a when a patient may present with a subacute onset of parkinsonism.[4]

26.3 Agents Associated with Drug-Induced Movement Disorders

Since various medications may induce movement disorders, the estimated rates of DIMDs have been inconsistent and difficult to quantify. However, DRBAs account for most cases of DIMDs, with neuroleptics (also referred to as antipsychotics) accounting for majority of the reported cases of DIMDs. Neuroleptics are utilized in clinical practice not only for the treatment of schizophrenia, or psychosis, but for conditions such as various anxiety and mood disorders, including bipolar and depressive disorders. Some reports note that approximately 60 to 75 percent of patients who receive

acute treatment with neuroleptic agents develop clinically significant DIMDs in one form or another, with some patients developing more than one form at the same time.[5-7] One study noted that nearly two-thirds (62 percent) of institutionalized chronic schizophrenic patients were known to suffer neuroleptic-induced movement disorders from conventional neuroleptics: approximately one-quarter had parkinsonism, one-third had tardive dyskinesia and another one-third reported akathisia.[8]

The typical neuroleptics, also referred to as conventional or first-generation antipsychotics (FGAs) have a narrow range between the therapeutic dose and toxicity. The milligram potency is highly correlated with the type of adverse effects noted with conventional neuroleptics. High-milligram, low potency agents such as chlorpromazine and thioridazine, which have weak activity at dopamine receptors and strong activity at anticholinergic sites, produce fewer extrapyramidal side effects (EPS) but more anticholinergic adverse effects, sedation and hypotension. Low-milligram, high potency neuroleptics such as haloperidol and trifluoperazine produce more EPS but fewer anticholinergic adverse effects due to their strong activity at dopamine receptors. Atypical neuroleptics, also referred to as second generation antipsychotics (SGAs), have a broader range between the dose that controls symptoms and the one that produces EPS.

Antipsychotics work primarily by blocking dopamine neurotransmission in the brain. However, dopamine blockade is also related to EPS and the degree of blockade is associated with the incidence of EPS. Typical antipsychotics exhibit a higher degree of dopamine blockade than the atypical antipsychotics, and patients treated with conventional antipsychotics have been known to exhibit a higher incidence of EPS. Such variations are associated with each drug's unique pharmacology, as noted by their different degree of blockade of specific receptors, leading to differences in their potential for DIMDs. Generally speaking, clozapine and quetiapine, both atypical antipsychotics, exhibit a broad degree of separation between efficacy and induction of EPS, and hence are associated with a low risk of EPS across their entire clinical dosage range; whereas the incidence of movement disorders for risperidone, paliperidone, olanzapine and ziprasidone appears to be dose-related as they have a narrower separation between antipsychotic effect and EPS. Thus, EPS effects may be masked at low doses, and be more pronounced at the higher dosage range.[9,10] For instance, the level of EPS observed with risperidone at 16 mg/day was shown to be comparable to that observed with haloperidol at 10 mg/day.[11]

Antipsychotic-induced movement disorders are estimated to occur in 19 percent and 42 percent of patients receiving atypical and typical antipsychotic drugs, respectively.[12] Generally, the SGAs or atypical antipsychotics are associated with a lower risk for DIMDs than the conventional or typical high potency neuroleptics (e.g., haloperidol).[13,14] The reduced risk of DIMDs associated with the atypical antipsychotics, when compared with the low potency neuroleptics (e.g., chlorpromazine), appears to be less robust, with the exception of clozapine.[15] Although as a class, atypical neuroleptics [i.e. clozapine (Clozaril®), risperidone (Risperdal®), quetiapine (Seroquel®), olanzapine (Zyprexa®), ziprasidone (Geodon®), aripiprazole (Abilify®), paliperidone (Invega®), iloperidone (Fanapt®)] are associated with a lower risk of treatment-emergent EPS, data shows that the ease and consistency with which atypicals achieve this benefit may be varied.[16–18] A meta-analysis of randomized controlled trials comparing effects of FGAs and SGAs in patients with schizophrenia noted that all the SGAs were associated with much fewer EPS than haloperidol, and most of them even when haloperidol was used at doses less than 7.5 mg/day. The relative risk for EPS among the SGAs compared to haloperidol was as follows (from least risk to highest risk): clozapine, sertindole, olanzapine, quetiapine, aripiprazole, ziprasidone, amisulpride, zotepine, and risperidone.[19] (Sertindole, amisulpride, and zotepine are not commercially available in the United States.) It should be noted that the generally recommended dose for risperidone is up to 6 mg/day, with the drug losing its EPS advantage at higher doses. Generally, clinicians should exercise caution when comparing data regarding the use of the novel atypical agents, and until long-term data becomes available they should administer the newer agents at doses below the EPS producing reaction.[20] Some investigators have found the SGAs to be superior to the FGAs regarding quality of life issues.[21,22] However, some clinicians have noted that atypical neuroleptics did not improve quality of life more so than the typical neuroleptics.[23]

Data from the Clinical Antipsychotic Trials of Intervention Effectiveness (CATIE) showed that patients treated with perphenazine, a conventional typical high-potency agent, had the highest rate of drug discontinuation due to EPS (8.4 percent), than those receiving any of the atypical antipsychotics.[24] However, a secondary analysis noted no significant differences in incidence or change in rating scales for akathisia, dystonia, parkinsonism, or tardive dyskinesia when comparing the atypical antipsychotics with perphenazine or comparing between atypical antipsychotics. Thus these findings show that atypical antipsychotics appear less advantageous then they initially did, especially when compared to a typical antipsychotic (perphenazine) that is less potent than haloperidol.[25] Recently, a meta-analysis noted that the atypical antipsychotics do not necessarily have greater efficacy than their typical counterparts, with haloperidol being the predominant comparator, and that improvements in efficacy are selective at best, with all atypicals inducing EPS.[19]

Clozapine, an atypical neuroleptic utilized at doses of 150 to 900 mg/day, produces low levels of EPS; however it is associated with an increased incidence of anticholinergic adverse effects, weight gain and metabolic effects, seizures, sedation, orthostatic hypotension, drooling, myocarditis, and other cardiovascular and respiratory effects. Agranulocytosis, a life-threatening blood disorder, is a major treatment problem and hence stringent blood monitoring is warranted. Clozapine, like quetiapine, can be used to effectively treat drug-induced psychosis in patients with Parkinson's disease without potentially worsening their symptoms. Clozapine appears to be the least likely to produce tardive dyskinesia and has been shown to significantly reduce dyskinetic movements in patients with tardive dyskinesia. Thus in some instances it has been invoked in patients with tardive dyskinesia from exposure to other antipsychotics but who still require treatment with a neuroleptic.

Most antipsychotics and antidepressants lower the seizure threshold and may cause seizures. The risk is greater with clozapine than with most other atypical antipsychotics, and greater with the tricyclic antidepressants (TCAs) than with the selective serotonin reuptake inhibitors (SSRIs).[13] A retrospective cohort study of cases involving acute toxic ingestion of FGAs and SGAs noted that the odds of a major adverse outcome or death were significantly greater for the SGAs than the FGAs. The odds of respiratory depression, coma, and hypotension were higher in patients who ingested the SGAs, whereas the odds of dystonia and rigidity were higher in patients who ingested the FGAs, suggesting that the SGAs appear no safer than FGAs in acute overdose.[26]

A variety of other drugs have been associated with hyperkinetic movement disorders. DRBAs such as metoclopramide and prochlorperazine, commonly prescribed for nausea and vertigo, have been associated with various DIMDs. It is estimated that 1 in 500 people who take metoclopramide will likely develop EPS, with the risk being highest in the pediatric patient population and adults younger than 30 years of age. The length of exposure and total cumulative exposure to metoclopramide also increases the risk of developing EPS or tardive dyskinesia.[27]

The antiepileptic drug phenytoin has been associated with chorea, dystonia, tremor and myoclonus. Carbamazepine, another antiepileptic drug, has been associated with tics and dystonias. Adrenergics, stimulants, lithium, lamotrigine, theophylline, and TCAs may cause postural tremor, a rhythmic alteration in movement. The prevalence of lithium-induced tremor is about 40 percent and may take the form of twitching in the arms and legs. TCAs and SS-RIs have been reported to cause myoclonus. Buspirone has been noted to cause akathisia, myoclonus and dyskinesias. Dyskinesias have also been reported with oral contraceptives, fentanyl, digoxin, cimetidine, diazoxide, lithium, TCAs, and methadone.[28–30] Amiodarone, an antiarrhythmic agent, is associated with various neurologic adverse effects including tremor, ataxia and peripheral neuropathy, with the incidence of neurotoxicity reportedly varying from 3.2 to 74 percent.[31,32] Clindamycin, an antibiotic known to have neuromuscular effects and to prolong the activity of neuromuscular blockade drugs, has been implicated in causing abnormal movements which consisted of hic-cough-like or twitch-like abdominal movements, and progressed to shoulder and jaw-jutting movements in a girl with autism who was receiving ongoing treatment with risperidone.[33]

Anticholinergic toxicity can occur from therapeutic or toxic doses of various medications with anticholinergic properties, including antihistamines (e.g., diphenhydramine), atropine, benztropine (commonly used with neuroleptics to prevent/manage DIMDs, and in patients with Parkinson's disease), oxybutynin (medication used for overactive bladder), low potency antipsychotics, TCAs, quinidine, and disopyramide. Additionally, anticholinergic toxicity may occur when diphenhydramine, benztropine, phenylpropanolamine, salicylate or lysergic acid (LSD) are added to illegal drugs. Toxicity from anticholinergic drugs causes both central (confusion, tremor, myoclonus, agitation, seizures, coma) and peripheral effects (dry mouth, blurry vision, urinary retention, increased heart rate). Hyperthermia associated with anticholinergic toxicity may occur due to muscular rigidity secondary to agitation and seizures.[34]

Tremor can occasionally be caused by corticosteroids and preexistent tremor is usually enhanced by steroid medications. The tremor produced by steroid therapy may respond to dosage reduction or the use of beta-adrenergic blockers.[35] Similarly, midazolam, a short-acting benzodiazepine used for induction and maintenance of general anesthesia and as an adjunct to regional anesthesia, has been noted to induce muscle tremor, athetoid movements, and tonic clonic movements.[36] Clonazepam has been implicated in suppressing a variety of abnormal movements, including myoclonus, dystonias, paroxysmal dystonic choreoathetosis and various forms of tremor.[37]

DRBAs, dopamine depleting drugs (e.g., reserpine, tetrabenazine), or drugs that act as dopamine "false" transmitters (e.g., alpha-methyldopa), may be associated with drug-induced parkinsonism. SPECT imaging of the dopamine transporter may aid in determining whether the neuroleptic-induced parkinsonism is entirely drug-induced or an exacerbation of subclinical Parkinson's disease.[38]

Although SSRI-induced movement disorders are less common, they may occur, and with the continued increasing use of SSRIs, the clinician should be attuned to this complication. EPS induced by antidepressants and neuroleptics are identical in manifestation and response to treatment. In fact, the only difference between the two is that antidepressant-induced extrapyramidal symptoms are relatively rare and thus often underdiagnosed/misdiagnosed. Risk factors associated with antidepressant-induced EPS appear to be similar to those risk factors associated with neuroleptic-induced EPS, which include advanced age, females, patients with Parkinson's disease, patients concurrently treated with certain psychotropics and patients with a history of affective disorders.[39–42]

26.4 Risk Factors

Although not all DRBAs carry the same risk for DIMDs, various populations have been determined to be at increased risk for developing DIMDs.[43] Patients with bipolar depression are at an increased risk of acute antipsychotic-induced movement disorders. Generally, the elderly have a decreased functional reserve and may be susceptible to neuronal loss that may render them vulnerable to the effects of the DRBAs. Additionally, advanced age may reduce the capacity for metabolizing medications, increasing the risk for EPS by increasing levels of exposure to the offending agents. Many DRBAs can produce hyperprolactinemia, which may lead to decreased estrogen and amenorrhea, potentially increasing the risk for DIMDs in women. Patients with phenyletonuria have increased phenylalanine levels which may predispose them to DIMDs. Diabetic patients, independent of their use of DRBAs, are at a high risk for developing DIMDs, although the risk increases with the use of these agents due to impaired glucose metabolism. Also, chronic exposure to a DRBA for more than three months puts patients at an increased risk for DIMDs. Children and adolescents, compared to adults, are more sensitive to the development of DIMDs when treated with typical antipsychotics.[44] Generally, young males are more susceptible to dystonic reactions, older patients are more likely to develop drug-induced parkinsonian symptoms, and older females are more susceptible to develop tardive dyskinesia. The duration of medication exposure and total cumulative dose of the psychotropic agents utilized seem to increase the risk of emergence of tardive dyskinesia.[45] DIMDs occur more frequently with parenteral agents than oral agents, and more than half of patients receiving long-acting depot antipsychotic medications have been noted to show drug-induced EPS.[46] Smoking may also increase the risk for tardive dyskinesia.[47] One report found that 58 percent of patients treated with classical antipsychotics will develop treatment-emergent tardive dyskinesia after 10 to 15 years of treatment; however, the rates of emergence of tardive dyskinesia are still not clear regarding the more recent atypical agents as there has not been an opportunity to assess rates of tardive dyskinesia longitudinally.[48]

26.5 Sequelae of Drug-Induced Movement Disorders

Symptoms of DIMDs involve abnormalities in the coordination and integration of body movements and can be both painful and disfiguring. Both drug-induced dystonias and dyskinesias can be very noticeable and set patients apart socially, and add to the stigma of psychiatric illness. Patients with DIMDs may experience difficulty with social functioning, interpersonal communication, performance of motor tasks and activities of daily living. The DIMDs can cause patients distress, impair quality of life, and in severe cases lead to secondary morbidity and even death. For example, severe drug-induced parkinsonism may impair dexterity and impinge on occupational and social activities. Additionally, the festinating gait associated with that DIMD may lead to falls and injuries, such as hip fractures in the elderly.[13] Higher rates of mortality and increased rates of respiratory tract infection are observed in patients with tardive dyskinesia.[49] Akinesia is known to produce depression, fatigue, and psychomotor retardation, while akathisia has been associated with inducing anxiety, psychomotor agitation, aggression, and insomnia.[50] Anecdotal reports have linked drug-induced akathisia to violence and suicide attempts, although it is not possible to categorically prove either association.[51] Patients with DIMDs may also be less likely to adhere to a medication regimen, increasing the risk of relapse and rehospitalization.[52] Additionally, neuroleptic-induced movement disorders are an important cause of psychiatric malpractice lawsuits.[53,54]

26.6 Theories of Causation

The extrapyramidal system contains multisynaptic neurons which are involved in controlling and integrating motor and cognitive function, contributing to the unconscious stability of movement and balance, and providing coordination of gait, posture, and voluntary movement. The pathophysiology of DIMDs is complex and multifactorial, and not clearly understood. It is likely related to a combination of genetic predisposition, dopaminergic system hypersensitivity, overactivation of the cholinergic system, and decreased

function reserve. Various other hypotheses have been proposed including a dysfunction in gamma-aminobutyric acid (GABA) neurons and oxidative stress resulting in neurotoxicity. Since use of DRBAs increases the turnover of neurotransmitters, the overproduction of free radicals created as a byproduct of catecholamine metabolism may participate in the genesis of tardive dyskinesia.

The risk for drug-induced parkinsonism with neuroleptics appears to directly correlate to occupancy at nigrostriatal dopamine receptors. Compared to the conventional antipsychotics, the atypical antipsychotics possess lower affinities for nigrostriatal dopaminergic receptors, and more rapidly dissociate from the D2 receptors. Dopamine blockade in the mesocortical dopamine pathway and involvement of adrenergic neurotransmitters systems, with relative excess of serotonergic activity, has been hypothesized as the underlying cause of akathisia. Support for this model is noted as akathisia is observed with the use of central acting DRBAs and serotonergic agents such as the selective serotonin reuptake inhibitors (SSRIs). Some primary dystonias appear to be caused by specific genetic mutations, affecting dopamine D3 allele, and further research involving the genetic basis of primary dystonias will assist in understanding the pathophysiology of dystonic movements and potentially aid in suggesting effective means for treatment.[55,56]

The cytochrome P450 2D6 enzyme (CYP 2D6) is responsible for the metabolism of various antidepressants and neuroleptics, and many medications that are substrates for the CYP 2D6 (i.e. are metabolized by the enzyme) are themselves strong inhibitors of the enzyme. Medications which inhibit CYP 2D6, or individuals with poor metabolizer status, may have increased serum concentrations of medications which require the enzyme for proper metabolism, and make them more susceptible to EPS. CYP 2D6 is responsible for the metabolism of MPTP, a dopamine neurotoxin, which together with its metabolite MPP+, have the ability to produce symptoms of parkinsonism. Inhibition of CYP 2D6 by psychotropic agents may cause accumulation of these neurotoxins and increase the possibility of DIMDs. All SSRIs to some extent are inhibitors of CYP 2D6; however, paroxetine, fluoxetine and its active metabolite, norfluoxetine, are potent inhibitors of this isoenzyme. Citalopram and sertraline also inhibit this enzyme but to a lesser extent. Bupropion and duloxetine, two different antidepressants, are noted to be moderate inhibitors of CYP 2D6. Medications whose major metabolic pathway involves metabolism with CYP 2D6 include beta-blockers, antidepressants, antipsychotics (especially risperidone), opioids, dextromethorphan (a common antitussive agent), and Class I antiarrhythmics. Concomitant use of these substrates with medications which are potent CYP 2D6 inhibitors may result in increased levels of the substrates, exposing the patient to an increased risk of adverse effects.[57] Interestingly, most of the non-psychotropic agents that are CYP 2D6 isoenzyme inhibitors induce EPS: quinidine induces psychosis and hallucinations; quinine induces ataxia and restlessness; quinolone antibiotics may cause restlessness; captopril may induce hallucinations; lidocaine may cause psychosis and tremors; cimetidine may cause EPS and hallucinations; and dextromethorphan may induce hallucinations.[58] Ethnicity is a factor in the phenotypical variability of CYP 2D6. The prevalence of CYP 2D6 poor metabolizers is approximately 6 to 10 percent amongst Caucasians, higher in African-Americans, and lowest in most other ethnic groups such as Asians. However, the occurrence of CYP 2D6 ultrarapid metabolizers appears to be greater amongst individuals of North African and Middle Eastern descent.

26.7 Drug-Induced Movement Disorders in Children and Adolescents

In recent years, there has been a remarkable increase in prescription rates of psychoactive medications used in children and adolescents by both general practitioners and child psychiatrists.[59] Stimulants, antidepressants, antipsychotics, mood-stabilizing medications including anticonvulsants, and benzodiazepines are the most commonly prescribed psychoactive medications in this patient population. A retrospective cohort study noted that the proportion of children who became new users of antipsychotics nearly doubled from 1996 to 2001, mainly for use in managing non-psychotic conditions, attributed to the widespread use of the atypical antipsychotics.[60] Although most antipsychotics are used to treat psychotic symptoms and schizophrenia spectrum disorders, their use extends to various nonpsychotic disorders, including nonspecific treatment for conduct disorders associated with a variety of neuropsychiatric disorders, as well as intellectual and developmental disabilities.[59]

Since safety and tolerability profiles of psychoactive medications have not been thoroughly assessed in the younger patient population, much of the current data on prevalence of movement disorders in children and adolescents treated with neuroleptics is unsatisfying, and is mainly based on data from adults or on unsystematic clinical experience.[61,62] Some studies have noted that youth treated with antipsychotic medications may be more sensitive to EPS.[63] One European study examined the prevalence of DIMDs, namely akathisia, parkinsonism, and tardive dyskinesia in an adolescent population with schizophrenia and in relationship to predominantly atypical antipsychotic treatment. The number of patients treated with atypical, typical, or a com-

bination of atypical/typical antipsychotics was 76, 10 and 7, respectively. Movement disorder symptoms were noted in 37 out of the 93 patients (40 percent), fulfilling strict/subthreshold criteria for akathisia ($^1/_{12}$ percent), parkinsonism ($^2/_{26}$ percent), or tardive dyskinesia ($^5/_{12}$ percent).[64] These prevalence rates are similar with results from other studies, noting that symptoms of movement disorders are less prevalent and less pronounced under treatment with atypical antipsychotics than with typical antipsychotics. However, some former studies have reported higher prevalence rates, namely for tardive dyskinesia, most likely because of treatment with predominately typical antipsychotics, different assessment methods, and heterogeneous patient populations which included patients suffering from mental retardation or autism.[64]

Another concern in children exposed to the long-term use of antipsychotics, specifically the atypicals, is the risk of development of metabolic and endocrine dysfunction. Weight gain, hyperglycemia, and dyslipidemia (including hypercholesterolemia and hypertriglyceridemia) are associated with the use of atypical antipsychotics as well as with schizophrenic disorders.[65–67] Chronic exposure to these agents may pose a higher risk of cardiovascular morbidity and mortality in adult life. Elevated prolactin levels, often seen with typical antipsychotics and risperidone, and their possible long-term repercussions on reduced bone mineral density, hypogonadism, and sexual dysfunction, remain uncertain.[68,69]

EPS are very rare in neonates but have been reported in babies born to mothers who received antipsychotic drugs for extended periods during pregnancy. Although metoclopramide administered to mothers in labor usually has no significant effects on newborns, a case of dystonia in a newborn due to placental transfer of metoclopramide following a single standard dose has been reported.[70]

Since DIMDs may be a result of individual vulnerability, some patients may be more susceptible for symptoms of movement disorders, just as some patients may be more susceptible for body weight gain from atypical neuroleptics. In view of the fact that the long-term safety of psychoactive medications on the developing brain needs to be clarified, the risk and benefit of the treatment needs to be assessed in each patient. It may be best to avoid using these agents to treat conditions in the pediatric patient population that can be adequately treated with medications presenting less risk of serious adverse effects.

26.8 Drug-Induced Movement Disorders in the Elderly

The elderly tend to have more co-morbidities and consume

more drugs, including medications bought over-the-counter, than any other age group. They have compromised renal and/or hepatic function and this may affect how a particular medication is metabolized (by the liver) or eliminated (by the kidney). Additionally, patients with compromised mental capacity may not adhere to their medication regimen and will usually require aids to improve their compliance. All these factors may make the elderly patient more prone to side effects and drug interactions that may adversely affect them.

Sedation from medications, in combination with unsteadiness, may make elderly patients more prone to falls and other aspects of motor incoordination. Medications with strong anticholinergic properties may lead to confusion in the geriatric patient population and complicate delirium or dementia. Patients with Parkinson's disease may have their disease state aggravated with the use of DRBAs which may exacerbate the symptoms of parkinsonism. Debilitated patients may be at an increased risk for neuroleptic malignant syndrome.[71] Older patients are often at risk for developing serious side effects from DRBAs, particularly from antipsychotic medications. DIMDs, especially tardive dyskinesia, are more persistent in the elderly than in younger patients.

The association of typical antipsychotics with sudden cardiac death is well established.[72,73] However, recently a study noted that atypical agents were associated with a comparable risk of sudden cardiac death.[74] Antipsychotics are not approved for the treatment of dementia-related psychosis, yet many elderly patients receive typical and atypical antipsychotics to manage the behavioral disturbances associated with dementia. Recently the U.S. Food and Drug Administration (FDA) and Health Canada have issued warnings that treatment with typical and atypical antipsychotics in elderly patients with dementia may be associated with increased mortality.[75] Their off-label use in elderly patients with dementia has led to deaths from heart-related events, such as heart failure, or infections, chiefly pneumonia, and will require drug manufacturers to label the drugs with a black box warning against such off-label use.[76,77]

26.9 Acute/Intermediate Drug-Induced Movement Disorders

These DIMDs usually occur shortly after exposure to the drug and are of such rapid evolution reaching maximal severity that patients may present to the emergency room necessitating hospitalization. Failure to accurately diagnose them and treat them appropriately may result in unnecessary pain and distress, increased morbidity, and in severe cases, even death.[78]

A. Dystonia

1. Presentation

Acute dystonic reactions are manifested by an abrupt onset of sustained, often painful muscular spasms producing twisting movements and abnormal postures of the muscles of the eyes, face, neck and throat. The symptoms are often distressing and frightening for the patient and may interfere with ambulation, respiration, vision, speaking, and swallowing. Dystonic movements may interfere with motor performance by superimposing an unwanted posture on parts in use causing discomfort and anxiety in affected patients. The involuntary movements include rigid contractions and arching of the back muscles, called opisthotonos; a spasm in which the eye(s) turns upward called oculogyric crisis; a spasm of the neck in which the head is turned backward or sideways, called retrocollis or torticollis, respectively; forced opening of the mouth and jaw clenching called trismus; and tongue protrusion, swelling of the tongue, which may cause slurred speech due to hypertonic tongue called dysarthria and macroglossia.[79,80] Laryngospasm with compromise of the airway, which is the most severe acute dystonic reaction, may lead to stridor, dyspnea, and choking, and may create a medical emergency.[81] Sustained muscle contractions may lead to aching pain and even rhabdomyolysis. These acute dystonic reactions are terrifying to the patient who has no prior experience with these problems or knowledge of this adverse effect. When a dystonic reaction does occur in a psychotic patient, the fragile trust developed between psychiatrist and patient may be irrevocably harmed, leading to a deteriorating compliance with the neuroleptic agents and further diminishing the patient's willingness to take the medications.[82] Malpractice suits are frequently based on dystonic reactions that persist. Occupational or task-specific dystonias once thought to be psychogenic in origin are now considered to be organic in nature.[83]

The signs or symptoms of acute dystonic reactions develop within seven days of initiating therapy or rapidly raising the dose of a neuroleptic agent or reducing a medication being used to treat or prevent acute EPS, that is, an anticholinergic agent. Over 50 percent of acute dystonic reactions occur within 48 hours, and 90 percent within five days, following exposure to DRBAs.[84] The risk of an acute dystonic reaction dramatically decreases with the duration of therapy and is minimal beyond one month after initial therapy or dose increase. Acute dystonic reactions may also develop in the third to seventh day following each depot neuroleptic injection.

Acute dystonic reactions last anywhere from a few seconds to several hours, and may present with a diurnal variation with the symptoms being markedly worse in the afternoon and evening. Dystonic movements may occur anywhere in the body and may fluctuate and spread over time to involve other parts of the body. Dystonias generally intensify during voluntary movements, excitement, nervousness, and psychological stress; they decrease during periods of relaxation, and disappear during sleep. They can also occur as bursts with return to normal function between attacks, hence "paroxysmal dystonias."

Drug-induced Pisa syndrome is a rare form of dystonia characterized by sustained truncal lateroflexion and has been associated with prolonged treatment with typical and atypical antipsychotics. However, it has also been reported in patients who received cholinesterase inhibitors and antiemetics. It may occur following the addition of another neuroleptic to an established regimen of neuroleptics, or it may subtly occur in neuroleptic treated patients. It may be acute or tardive and develops predominately in females and older patients with organic brain disorder.[85–87] Acute dystonic reactions differ from tardive dystonias in that the former are sudden in onset, cause acute discomfort and stress to the patient, and are rapidly resolved following the administration of anticholinergic agents.

2. Implicated agents

The reported prevalence of acute dystonic reactions in patients exposed to neuroleptics has varied with estimates ranging from a low of 2.3 percent to high of 94 percent.[80,84,88] The discrepancies are most likely due to differences in the examined patient population including age and gender, concurrent treatment with other medications, the design of the study, and the type of neuroleptic drug and dosage utilized. Generally, the increased incidence of acute dystonic reactions is attributed to the more frequent use of high-potency antipsychotics and the use of higher doses. The atypical antipsychotic agents, clozapine, risperidone, olanzapine, quetiapine, aripiprazole, ziprasidone, paliperidone, and most recently iloperidone, are less likely to induce acute dystonic reactions than their typical antipsychotic counterparts at clinically effective dosages. The risk of dystonias and other extrapyramidal adverse effects associated with risperidone therapy appear to be dose-related and generally observed with doses above 6 mg/day. Following abrupt clozapine withdrawal, worsening of movement disorders has been reported to occur within one week of discontinuing the neuroleptic, with resolution of symptoms observed within two weeks.[89]

The relationship between dose and risk of a dystonic reaction is less clear, however, lower dosages appear to produce fewer extrapyramidal side effects than moderate dosages, and moderate dosages appear to produce more extrapyramidal ad-

verse effects than very high doses.[90] An inverted U-shaped curve function between the prevalence of dystonia and neuroleptic dose appears to exist. Thus, most dystonia occurs with moderate to high doses of neuroleptics, while the very low doses and the very high doses of neuroleptics (approximately over 2,000 mg/day of chlorpromazine equivalence) produce the least dystonia.[91] Dystonic reactions usually begin reversing after a few hours and tend to disappear 24 to 48 hours after the antipsychotic agent is withdrawn.[92]

Dopamine agonists such as levodopa, and dopamine stimulating agents such as amphetamines and cocaine, may induce acute dystonic reactions. Paroxysmal dystonias have also been reported following ingestion of amphetamines and related compounds. A wide range of abnormal movements including choreiform movements, multifocal tics, dystonias, akathisia, parkinsonism, and opsoclonus-myoclonus have been reported in patients abusing cocaine and other central nervous system stimulants and depressants.[93,94]

Antiemetic compounds, with dopamine receptor blocking activity, such as metoclopramide, prochlorperazine, promethazine, trimethobenzamide, and thiethylperazine, are well-recognized for their dystonia-producing capacity. A profound acute dystonic reaction may occur after only one or two doses of a dopamine-blocking antiemetic.[95] This is particularly common in children, young adults and adolescents. In pediatric patients, metoclopramide-induced dystonia may present as encephalitis.[96] Patients with AIDS on metoclopramide may be at an increased risk for developing EPS than others receiving the same therapies.[97] Droperidol, also a dopamine receptor antagonist, is used as a pre-anesthetic anxiolytic agent and precipitates acute dystonic reactions.[98] There are a handful of reports implicating type-2 histamine antagonists (H2 antagonists) as causative agents of dystonias and other EPS. Cimetidine, one such agent, utilized widely for peptic ulcer disease as well as acid reflux, has been noted to induce dystonic reactions. Predisposing factors for such reactions included advanced age, renal and hepatic impairment, higher doses, pre-existing psychiatric illness, and concurrent use of psychotropic medications.[99]

Antidepressants have also been implicated in causing dystonic reactions. A review of published reports of SSRI-induced dystonic reactions noted that the time to onset of symptoms was 1.5 days to 8 months following the initiation of SSRI therapy, with a mean of 70 days. Managing the reactions included dosage reduction, or discontinuing the SSRI, or the coadministration of a benzodiazepine, anticholinergic agent, or botulinum toxin with partial to complete resolution observed within one day to six months.[100] An acute dystonic reaction resulting in jaw and neck rigidity with trazodone at a dose of 50 mg has been cited in an adolescent already receiving fluvoxamine. The synergistic potentiation may have caused the dystonic reaction.[101] A case of acute dystonia induced by bupropion is cited consisting of neck stiffness, trismus (clenched jaw), and unilateral temporomandibular joint (TMJ) pain and subluxation.[102] The long half-life of fluoxetine and its active metabolite, norfluoxetine, may be implicated in delaying the appearance of extrapyramidal adverse effects associated with the antidepressant. As serum levels slowly rise to steady state, there may be a delay in acute dystonic reactions and the movements may represent a delayed acute reaction rather than tardive dyskinesia, an important distinction since the latter effect implies irreversibility.[103] Amoxapine, an antidepressant with dopamine receptor blocking properties, may cause acute dystonias, other extrapyramidal adverse effects and tardive dyskinesias. Although TCAs are not reported to affect dopamine metabolism, they have been noted to produce dystonic reactions in patients. Since the TCAs are implicated in the production of parkinsonism as well as tardive dyskinesia, their role in dystonias is not surprising.[104]

Other agents that have been implicated in producing acute dystonic reactions include buspirone, bupropion, disulfiram, carbamazepine, erythromycin, flecanide, bethanechol, reserpine, ergotamine, and monoamine oxidase inhibitors.[95,104-106] Dystonia secondary to carbamazepine therapy has been associated with abnormal movements restricted to the tongue.[107]

3. Other causes of dystonia

Dystonias caused by physical agents have been described as an occupational hazard in users of lasers and in survivors of the Chernobyl nuclear accident in Russian literature. The pathogenesis is unclear but appears to be attributed to radiation-induced lesions of small blood vessels in the brain. Exposure to toxic environmental agents such as manganese, copper, methyl alcohol, and cyanide have also been implicated in producing dystonic reactions.[108,109] Blepharospasm, oculogyric crisis, and cervical dystonia have been reported with manganese neurotoxicity from occupational exposure in mining, smelting, and workers using permanganate-containing fungicides.[110] Ergotism from plant derivatives have been associated with focal and generalized dystonia, epilepsy, stroke and peripheral ischemia in limbs while mildewed sugar cane poisoning has been noted to produce encephalopathy and dystonia in the developing world.[111,112]

4. Risks

Risk factors for developing acute dystonic reactions include male gender, young age, a primary psychotic disorder,

history of electroconvulsive therapy, mental retardation, use of potent DRBDs without concomitant anticholinergic prophylaxis, and a past history of dystonias.[113] The frequency of acute dystonic reactions is more commonly associated with the high potency neuroleptics in the butyrophenone class (e.g., haloperidol), as compared with the lower potency neuroleptics in the phenothiazine class (chlorpromazine, thioridazine).[114] Electrolyte or metabolic disorders such as hypocalcemia, hyperthyroidism, and hyperparathyroidism have been reported as risk factors in several cases.[4] Concurrent use of cocaine or ecstasy with a DRBA appears to predispose patients to acute dystonic reactions and can also cause this DIMD when used alone.[115] If acute dystonia is encountered as a recurring problem with stable neuroleptic treatment, then one should have a high index of suspicion and search for alternate explanations. Perhaps the patient has ingested a larger neuroleptic dose than prescribed, has combined her neuroleptic with other neuroleptics or alcohol, or has suddenly discontinued anticholinergic or antihistaminic medications. Alcohol ingestion may trigger dystonia in patients receiving neuroleptics who have not previously experienced dystonic episodes.[98] Or perhaps the patient is demonstrating signs of tardive dystonia or has a separate underlying etiology of dystonia. Children and adolescents are at risk for acute dystonic reactions not only from prescribed DRBAs, but also from various scenarios leading to inadvertent ingestion of agents which may cause these DIMDs. For example, acute dystonic reactions have been reported following ingestion of "street Xanax" tablets that actually contained haloperidol.[116]

5. Management

Patients initiating therapy with antipsychotics should be warned about the possible occurrence of acute dystonic reactions, to avoid panic reactions, and should receive instructions on how to deal with these adverse events adequately. Management of acute dystonias includes administration of intravenous or intramuscular antimuscarinic drugs with anticholinergic (e.g., benztropine) or antihistaminic (e.g., diphenhydramine) properties. These agents are very effective and rapid in managing the dystonic reaction and a prompt therapeutic response to either parenteral agent is virtually diagnostic of acute dystonic reactions. Other agents which may be utilized in managing a dystonic reaction include a benzodiazepine (e.g., lorazepam, diazepam, clonazepam), a dopaminergic agent (amantadine), or a beta-blocker (e.g., propranolol, metoprolol). If anticholinergics are ineffective or not tolerable, then benzodiazepines may be administered intravenously. Since antipsychotic agents have long half-lives and duration of action, and all anticholinergic drugs given parenterally will wear off after several hours, additional oral anticholinergic drugs (e.g., diphenhydramine, benztropine, biperiden, procyclidine, or trihexyphenidyl) should be continued for prophylaxis at least two to four weeks after the dystonic reaction has resolved, especially if a long acting DRBA was used or if therapy with a DRBA will need to be continued.[92] Alternative strategies include lowering the psychotropic dosage or switching to a psychotropic from a different class with a lower potential for dystonic reactions. There is an inverse relationship between the incidence of drug-induced acute dsytonias and age, and also the efficacy of anticholinergic agents for prophylaxis appears to be inversely related to the patient's age.[117] Thus the use of prophylactic anticholinergic agents in older patients for primary prevention of acute dystonias is not favored, and should be utilized in patients at high risk for developing this DIMD.[28]

The American Psychiatric Association (APA) guidelines suggest that the use of prophylactic anticholinergics may be considered especially for those patients receiving high potency agents with a prior history of experiencing acute EPS, patients who prefer preventive treatment to avoid discomfort or distress, or patients for whom the occurrence of adverse effects would lead to poor compliance and adversely affect their disease state.[118] A consensus statement issued by the World Health Organization recommends prophylactic use of antimuscarinic agents in the first few weeks of treatment to prevent acute dystonic reactions, and the need for their continued use should be reevaluated after their discontinuation or after a decrease in the antipsychotic dose.[119]

In all patients, the benefit of using prophylactic antimuscarinic agents should be weighed against the potential for adverse effects. As a class, antimuscarinic agents are associated with tachycardia, urinary retention, constipation, and mydriasis, and should be used with caution in patients with heart disease, prostatic disease, ileus, and glaucoma. They may also impair cognitive function in elderly patients, worsen the severity of tardive dyskinesia, and exacerbate existing psychosis. Additionally, anticholinergics may mask some EPS, an indicator for the future development of tardive dyskinesia in some susceptible patients.

B. Ataxia

Ataxia refers to the unsteady gait and coordination usually associated with cerebellar dysfunction and is marked by the inability to maintain normal postures and perform normal movements. Ataxia may affect any part of the body, and the movements are jerky and uncoordinated, without the smooth flow of normal motion. Symptoms are quite variable and may include postural instability, swaying while standing, a wide-based gait sometimes likened to a "drunken reeling," and an uneven gait with steps of various uneven lengths and lateral deviations. Additionally, patients may present with dysarthric speech and nystagmus. Many different conditions may cause ataxia including cerebellar injury (stroke), multiple sclerosis, infections, vitamin E deficiency, vitamin B12 deficiency, alcoholism, and exposure to toxins such as lead. Medications that may cause ataxia include aminoglycosides, benzodiazepines, sedatives, and anticonvulsants (e.g., phenytoin, carbamazepine).[120]

C. Bruxism

Bruxism is the involuntary grinding or gnashing of teeth and clenching of the jaw that can occur during daytime or at night. Medications reported to cause bruxism include the SSRIs, selective norepinephrine reuptake inhibitors (SNRIs), amphetamines, flecanide, flunarizine, haloperidol, and levodopa/carbidopa. Of all these medications, the most frequently cited cause is the use of SSRIs, with the DIMD detected as early as one day to as late as eleven months following the start of therapy. Most reports of drug-induced bruxism have resolved either with dose adjustment of the offending medication or the use of buspirone or gabapentin. Bruxism may also occur due to drug interactions, and two reports in literature cite bruxism in children within hours following concomitant valproic acid for seizure disorder and methylphenidate for attention-deficit hyperactivity disorder.[121,122]

D. Neuroleptic Malignant Syndrome

Neuroleptic malignant syndrome (NMS) is a rare idiosyncratic adverse drug reaction which may occur from the use of medications that involve the central dopaminergic system. Neuroleptic agents are by far the biggest culprits in NMS, although the disorder may occur with other dopamine depleting agents such as metoclopramide or after withdrawal from levodopa therapy. Antidepressants, including TCAs, SSRIs, and lithium, either alone or in combination, have been implicated in causing a syndrome resembling NMS.[123] Likewise, a similar syndrome has been reported in patients using cocaine.[115] Although the incidence of this adverse effect is low, with a reported prevalence ranging from 0.07 percent to 2.2 percent of patients receiving neuroleptics, the morbidity and mortality associated with this reaction is quite high, with death reported in 20 percent to 40 percent of cases.[123]

The disorder may occur hours to months after the initial dose and the syndrome usually lasts five to ten days after the oral antipsychotic is discontinued and two to three times longer upon withdrawal of depot medications.[124,125] NMS develops acutely and the essential feature is hyperpyrexia which occurs in conjunction with or shortly after the onset of muscular rigidity. Temperatures of 101°F (38.3°C) to 103°F (39.4°C) typically occur, and in some cases, may rise above 107°F (41.6°C).[4] The muscular hypertonicity is usually described as a "lead pipe" rigidity and may be associated with dyskinetic or choreiform movements. The symptomatology may also consist of diaphoresis, dysphagia, tremor, incontinence, mental status changes that may range from confusion to coma, mutism, tachycardia, elevated or labile blood pressure, leukocytosis and elevated creatine phosphokinase (CPK).[124,126] CPK levels increase as a result of muscular activity and myonecrosis from intense and sustained muscle contractions. Myoglobinuria may occur due to severe myonecrosis and this may lead to acute renal failure. Metabolic acidosis may occur and liver function tests may be elevated suggesting acute fatty acid changes in the liver secondary to hyperthermia.[125–127] Other sequelae may include respiratory complications such as pneumonia and pulmonary embolism, and cardiovascular complications such as cardiac arrest and arrhythmias.[4] Even among patients who recover from NMS, persistent symptoms such as residual catatonia may occur in a small percentage of patients.[128]

Certain antipsychotics have been implicated more than others in this disorder, which may reflect their frequency of usage or potency. Haloperidol, a high potency neuroleptic, either as monotherapy or with other agents, has been cited as a causative agent in 49 percent to 65 percent of NMS cases. This high incidence may reflect its use in rapid neuroleptization and its relatively high dopamine blockade.[125] The atypical neuroleptics including aripiprazole, clozapine, olanzapine, quetiapine, risperidone, and ziprasidone, also have been implicated as causative agents in NMS.[13,16,129,130]

Potential risk factors include male sex, dehydration, severe agitation, mood disorder, high drug dosage, and intramuscular administration of the drug. Patients with pre-existing Parkinson's disease may even be at an increased risk of this disorder since further depletion of dopamine occurs secondary to the neuroleptic. Mentally retarded patients and those with preexisting brain disease also appear to be at a greater risk for NMS.[127] Catatonia may also be a risk factor for development of NMS.[131]

Treatment of NMS depends on recognition and immediate withdrawal of the offending neuroleptic agent. General medical supportive measures should be initiated including hydration, fever reduction and treatment of any intercurrent infection. Pharmacologic agents such as bromocriptine will reduce parkinsonian symptoms, and benzodiazepines may facilitate muscle relaxation. Symptoms of peripheral muscular rigidity may be decreased using dantrolene, which is also effective in reducing the fever.[13]

Once an episode of NMS is treated, at least two weeks should pass before restarting neuroleptics in patients who absolutely require such agents. Guidelines for restarting neuroleptics have been proposed by clinicians. A higher occurrence rate of NMS is observed in patients rechallenged with a high potency agent than in those administered lower potency agents. Upon rechallenge, the occurrence of NMS may be as high as 83 percent in patients who receive a neuroleptic of the same potency as the initial offending drug. The rate may be as low as 10 percent when lower-potency neuroleptics are used in such patients.[132,133] The low potency or atypical neuroleptics should be utilized while avoiding the long-acting depot agents. Therapy should be initiated with the lowest possible dose and patients should be monitored for any signs of the disorder upon rechallenge with neuroleptics.[134,135]

E. Serotonin Syndrome

Drugs that block serotonin reuptake or have serotonin-like activity may induce a rare, but potentially lethal, serotonin syndrome. This syndrome is characterized by cognitive and behavioral changes (e.g., confusion, elevated mood, agitation, insomnia, coma), autonomic symptoms (e.g., increased heart rate, fever, labile blood pressure), and neurological symptoms (e.g., myoclonus, rigidity, hyperreflexia, tremor, ataxia, akathisia).[123,136]

Symptoms of serotonin syndrome usually appear very rapidly, and in a review of published cases, approximately 60 percent of patients presented with symptoms within 6 hours of the causative medication initiation, change in dose, or overdose.[137] Serotonin syndrome may occur with a single serotonergic drug, but is more severe when two or more drugs with serotonergic properties are co-prescribed. It has also been reported to occur following the administration of a single dose of a serotonergic drug.[138,139] Drugs that increase serotonin transmission include antidepressants [monoamine oxidase inhibitors (MAOIs), selective serotonin/norepinephrine reuptake inhibitors (SNRIs), selective serotonin reuptake inhibitors (SSRIs), tricyclic antidepressants (TCAs)], migraine medications (e.g., triptans and ergotamines), dietary supplements (St. John's wort, ginseng), and drugs of abuse (e.g., cocaine, LSD, MDMA or "ecstasy"). Other medications include tramadol, tryptophan, meperidine, buspirone, lithium, amphetamines, linezolid, selegiline, sibutramine and dextromethorphan (a cough suppressant found in many over-the-counter cough preparations). Metoclopramide as well as the atypical antipsychotics have been shown to cause serotonin syndrome when prescribed in combination with SSRIs.[123,140] The U.S. Food and Drug Administration (FDA) noted that there is the potential for life-threatening serotonin syndrome in patients taking 5-hydroxytryptamine receptor agonists (triptans) and SSRIs or SSRIs/SNRIs concomitantly. In 2006, the FDA issued an alert, "Potentially Life-Threatening Serotonin Syndrome with Combined Use of SSRIs or SNRIs and Triptan Medications," and later added an update including sibutramine.[141,142]

Management of serotonin syndrome includes discontinuing the causative drug(s). Depending on the severity of symptoms, patients may require supportive care. Complications may include renal failure from muscle breakdown, and benzodiazepines may help control the agitation and limit the excessive muscle activity.[13] Patients may also be managed with cyproheptadine, propranolol, chlorpromazine, diphenhydramine, and methysergide.[2]

26.10 Continuous Drug-Induced Movement Disorders

Continuous DIMDs are non-acute syndromes that persist only while the offending agent is being administered and remit when the offending agent is discontinued. Various medications may produce single movement disorders such as tremor, myoclonus, or chorea and are considered simple side effects. Drug-induced akathisia and parkinsonism are of intermediate-onset, usually occurring within the first three months of initiation of therapy with the causative agent, and represent more complex syndromes.

A. Akathisia

1. Presentation

The most poorly understood of all extrapyramidal side effects and the most challenging to manage is akathisia. It is reported to occur in 8 to 76 percent of patients treated with neuroleptics with 20 to 30 percent being a conservative estimate.[143] The disorder is classified into acute, chronic, tardive and withdrawal subtypes based on the epidemiology and presentation of this movement disorder. The disorder is characterized by a subjective inner feeling of anxiety, restlessness, and an irresistible urge to be in motion to satisfy the urge to move. Objective signs of motor activity are manifested as pacing, fidgety movements or swinging of the legs, crossing and uncrossing one's legs, "walking on the spot" while standing, hand wringing, rocking back and forth, or some other purposeless repetitive motions where patients have an inner urge to move various parts of their bodies. Although akathisia literally means inability to remain seated, most patients describe that the condition worsens when they

are standing still.[143,144] Unlike most movement disorders that are involuntary, movements associated with akathisia are voluntary and due to the subjective feeling of restlessness.[145]

Onset of acute akathisia is associated within days to weeks of drug initiation, with most symptoms occurring within 6 weeks of initiating neuroleptic medication. However, it may occur within the first few hours of increase of dose of neuroleptic medication or reduction of medication used to treat (or prevent) acute EPS. Tardive akathisia starts during long-term neuroleptic treatment and is not related to a change in the medication or dose. Withdrawal akathisia refers to akathisia that begins after the neuroleptic agent is reduced in dose or discontinued.[146] Regardless of the onset—whether acute, tardive, or withdrawal—akathisia may persist and is then termed chronic akathisia. No major differences in the motor phenomena of acute and chronic akathisia are observed; however, patients with chronic akathisia may have a less intense subjective sense of restlessness.[13]

A common problem with assessing patients with akathisia is distinguishing it from psychomotor agitation associated with the psychoses. This poses a clinical challenge since mistaking akathisia for psychotic agitation may worsen akathisia, if the dose of the neuroleptic is increased. Since drug-induced akathisia is often clinically indistinguishable from medical conditions associated with restlessness (e.g., restless leg syndrome, iron deficiency anemia, parkinsonism), it should be suspected if symptoms occur soon after the implicated drug is initiated in the absence of such other conditions. Although it has been reported that mild akathisia may be difficult to differentiate from generalized anxiety,[82,147] it has been noted that complaints concerning the legs discriminate most effectively between mild akathisia and restlessness due to an underlying psychiatric disorder.[144]

Symptoms of akathisia can cause severe distress for affected patients and if left untreated, may lead to serious complications including aggression, medication non-adherence, dysphoria, and worsening of psychosis.[148–150] A patient may experience significant mental distress if asked not to move or is restrained from moving, and if the akathisia occurs early in treatment or after increases in doses, it may be more troublesome and distressing for the patient.[151] Akathisia has also been associated with depressive mood, suicidal or assaultive ideation, depersonalization, and severe agitation.[152] Given the implications of untreated akathisia, it is important to recognize early signs since one of the gravest consequences of this movement disorder is its reported association with suicide. Several reports have looked at the relationship between suicidal ideation and akathisia, and it is thought that sudden suicidal ideation emerges as a response to the intolerable feelings of restlessness.[145,153]

2. Case study, akathisia

A 58-year-old male with bipolar disorder was hospitalized for a recurrent depressive episode. At the time of admission, the patient described depressed mood, feelings of hopelessness, guilt and insomnia. It was noted that the patient's past depressive episodes were characterized by profound anergia and psychomotor retardation; however at the present time his primary complaints were of restlessness and dysphoria. The restlessness was associated with a marked inability to sit still for more than a few moments and the inability to find a comfortable position to fall asleep, hence, insomnia. His medical history was noncontributory. For at least one year prior to this episode, the patient was maintained on lithium carbonate with a plasma level of 0.8 mEq/L and trazodone 200 mg/day. However, just prior to the onset of his decompensation, the patient's daily dose of trazodone was increased to 300 mg. The antidepressant was tapered and subsequently discontinued, while the lithium was maintained. Within a few days the patient's symptoms improved regarding his motor restlessness and anxiety and completely remitted by the tenth day after discontinuation of trazodone.

In this case we see a neuroleptic-naive patient exhibit motor restlessness clinically indistinguishable from either the idiopathic or neuroleptic-induced forms of akathisia. The development of akathisia is associated with the use of trazodone, however similar reports have been cited in the literature involving numerous other antidepressants.

3. Implicated agents

Medications commonly associated with acute akathisia include typical and atypical neuroleptics, and phenothiazine antiemetics, with the majority of tardive akathisia cases involving the neuroleptic agents.[154] Additionally, many medications used in the palliative care setting, including antiemetics (metoclopramide, prochlorperazine) and antidepressants (tricyclic, SSRIs, venlafaxine), may cause significant akathisia.[123]

Although atypical antipsychotics may induce akathisia, they do so at a much lower rate compared with the conventional antipsychotics.[155,156] A pooled analysis of four 6-week studies reported akathisia in 2.4 percent of patients treated with olanzapine (dose range from 5 to 20 mg/day) compared with 10 percent in patients treated with chlorpromazine (dose range from 200 to 800 mg/day).[157] Another study noted the point prevalences of akathisia associated with conventional neuroleptics, risperidone, and clozapine to be 24 percent,

13 percent and 7 percent, respectively.[158] The CATIE study showed that akathisia is still a problem and occurred at a frequency of 5 percent in patients treated with olanzapine or quetiapine, 7 percent for patients who received risperidone or perphenazine (a typical antipsychotic), and 9 percent for patients treated with ziprasidone. Akathisia is the main EPS reported in patients with schizophrenia and mania who are taking aripiprazole.

Since clozapine is not used as a first line agent in managing psychosis but rather when treatment with other agents fails, a caveat in relation to clozapine studies is that patients have previously received other antipsychotic medications and some may have persistent akathisia as a result of exposure to the earlier agents.[159] Recently, a rare case of acute nocturnal akathisia induced by clozapine has been reported in a 43-year-old male with schizophrenia that was successfully treated with propranolol 40 mg/day while the patient continued on clozapine at a dose of 350 mg/day.[160]

Discontinuation of SGAs may be associated with sudden EPS and sudden emergence of akathisia has been reported in four female patients with bipolar disorder following sudden ziprasidone dose reduction.[161] The newer SGA, iloperidone, when compared to zipasidone, was shown to be associated with lower incidence of EPS, particularly akathisia.[162] Four randomized placebo-controlled double-blind trials evaluated the prevalence of EPSE and akathisia in quetiapine-treated bipolar manic patients and concluded that quetiapine treatment was similar to placebo in terms of occurrence of akathisia in such patients.[163,164] Additionally, another study noted significant reduction in parkinsonism and akathisia when patients with schizophrenia and pre-existing EPS were switched from previous antipsychotics to quetiapine.[164] Reports also note that severe akathisia has been associated after the initiation of a low-dose quetiapine regimen for the management of insomnia.[165]

Aripiprazole, recently approved by the FDA as an adjunct for the treatment of major depressive disorder in patients taking antidepressants, has been associated with treatment-related akathisia. One study noted that akathisia occurred in 4.5 percent of patients who received an antidepressant and adjunct placebo, compared with 23 percent of those who took an antidepressant and adjunct aripiprazole. Similarly, another study using aripiprazole in refractory bipolar depression noted that 42 percent of patients had treatment-related akathisia, suggesting that SGAs in combination with other psychotropic medications may increase the risk of developing akathisia.[166,167]

The SSRIs are also implicated in acute akathisia, but rarely in tardive akathisia. As more and more non-psychiatrists prescribe SSRIs for various psychiatric conditions, there is the potential for akathisia to be misdiagnosed, further complicating the patient's condition. This is illustrated in a case involving a 21-year-old male prescribed sertraline for depression who developed akathisia, which was misdiagnosed as an anxiety disorder. The prescriber doubled the patient's dose but the symptoms got worse, and then his sertraline was changed to paroxetine with no improvement in symptoms. After being referred to a psychiatrist who properly diagnosed the patient as having drug-induced akathisia, the patient's akathisia resolved following discontinuation of paroxetine.[168]

SSRI-induced akathisia appears to occur in at least 4.5 percent of exposed patients.[169] More reports of SSRI-induced movement disorders have been cited in women than men; however, this may be due to gender bias since epidemiologic studies indicate a two-fold greater incidence of depression in females than males causing more women to be likely to be prescribed an SSRI. There is an interpatient variability regarding the development of akathisia in response to exposure time. The onset of akathisia has been reported from half a day to three months after initiating therapy with the SSRI, with a mean of two weeks, and in some cases, symptoms were noted after a dose increase. Most cases resolve within two weeks of discontinuing therapy or decreasing the dose of the SSRI, adding a benzodiazepine (e.g., lorazepam) or beta-blocker (propranolol).[100]

Since many treatment emergent adverse effects associated with SSRIs include agitation, anxiety, and restlessness, it is possible that a subset of these patients may be experiencing akathisia. Several patient case reports have noted suicide attempts may be a means to end the restlessness that akathisia provokes. For example, a patient on sertraline for three weeks developed akathisia and attempted suicide "to escape from the profound discomfort and restlessness."[170] An 83-year-old male with SSRI-induced akathisia described it as a "restless nightmare" that if it would not stop, he would "rather be dead."[171] Another case report noted a female as having a good mood, but being afraid that "she would kill herself because of these restless and out-of-control feelings."[149] Following a dose increase of fluoxetine, a 22-year old female experienced akathisia and had an "elaborate suicidal ideation revolving around her own violent death."[172] It has been hypothesized that the suicidal ideation at times observed in patients treated with an SSRI may, at least in part, be attributable to akathisia.[173–175]

Metoclopramide is a DRBA that is not used as an antipsychotic, but is an antiemetic and gastroprokinetic agent associated with numerous reports of drug-induced akathisia.[176–180] Its uses include management of severe nausea, diabetic gastroparesis, esophageal reflux, dyspepsia, neu-rogenic bladder, orthostatic hypotension, hiccups, and non-prolactinemic amenorrhea among others. Following a single dose of intravenous metoclopramide as pulmonary aspiration prophylaxis prior to endoscopic sinus surgery, akathisia accompanied by motor restlessness, flushing and diaphoresis, was noted to occur in a male patient who experienced occasional gastro-esophageal reflux.[181] Likewise, in 25 percent of healthy volunteers, a 10 mg intravenous bolus dose of metoclopramide produced complaints of akathisia, usually within 15 to 30 minutes, and the effect lasted for three to four hours.[182]

4. Other drugs

Although akathisia is generally not considered to be an adverse effect of heterocyclic antidepressants, a few case reports have cited this effect.[183–185] Amoxapine, a dibenzoxapine antidepressant with intrinsic neuroleptic activity used in managing patients with psychotic depression, has been associated with producing akathisia.[186–189] Mirtazapine, a tetracyclic antidepressant, has been cited as a cause of akathisia four hours after the first dose was administered.[190] Droperidol, a dopamine antagonist with some histamine and serotonin antagonist activity used for post-operative nausea and vomiting, has been noted to produce acute akathisia within 90 minutes following oral administration.[191] Several case reports have also cited serotonin antagonists such as cyproheptadine, methysergide, and buspirone in inducing akathisia in patients treated with such agents.[192–195] Additionally, calcium channel blockers (cinnarizine, flunarizine, diltiazem [the former two are not available in the U.S.]), carbamazepine, ethosuximide, and methysergide may occasionally be associated with akathisia.[143,196] Levodopa and dopamine agonists have the potential to produce akathisia paradoxically, especially in patients with Parkinson's disease.[124]

5. Risks

Risk factors for drug-induced akathisia include drug dosage, rate of dosage increment, and drug potency.[144] Other risk factors not well delineated include advanced age, female gender, cognitive impairment, iron deficiency, mental retardation, and history of affective disorder.[28]

Also, use of multiple akathisia-inducing drugs may increase the risk of drug-induced akathisa. Simultaneous use of an SSRI has been shown to increase the number of cases of akathisia in patients who receive FGAs either as oral or as depot injections.[197] Patients with bipolar mood disorders, especially bipolar depression, are at an increased risk of developing akathisia with both FGAs and SGAs.[198] This is relevant to practice since several atypical antipsychotics are currently used in managing bipolar disorders. Akathisia may be mistaken for agitated psychosis, leading to an increase in the dose of the antipsychotic drug, which could further worsen the restlessness. Some clinicians have suggested that drugs with greater anticholinergic properties may reduce the risk for developing akathisia, since anticholinergics may be used in managing akathisia.[199] Worsening of akathisia has been associated with atypical neuroleptics other than clozapine, thus atypicals, especially risperidone at doses greater than 6 mg/day, continue to carry notable risks for akathisia, and unfortunately this DIMD may be overlooked as an adverse effect of second-generation antipsychotics.[200]

6. Management

The optimal pharmacologic management for neuroleptic-induced akathisia is yet to be determined, and the most effective treatment for acute akathisia is to discontinue the offending drug. Alternatively, a clinician may lower the dosage of the offending agent, or if a neuroleptic is the causative agent, change it to a lower potency agent with higher anticholinergic properties. Although the treatment of choice is to lower the antipsychotic dose or switch to a different antipsychotic, this may lead to worsening psychosis or relapse, and various adjunctive medications to treat akathisia may be the best treatment option for some patients.

Various agents including benzodiazepines, lipophilic beta-blockers, anticholinergic agents, cyproheptadine, and clonidine, have been utilized in the management of neuroleptic-induced akathisia. Some clinicians hypothesize that beta-blockers act peripherally to relieve the somatic manifestations of akathisia via their action on beta-adrenergic receptors located in the muscle, while the subjective signs of akathisia are ameliorated with either beta-blockers or benzodiazepines.[201] Benzodiazepines, most commonly lorazepam at a dose of 1.5–3.0 mg/day in divided doses or clonazepam 0.5 mg once daily are also used; however most benzodiazepines may be beneficial in managing this disorder.[202] Centrally acting (lipophilic) beta-blockers are regarded by some as the most effective treatment for akathisia,[203] and propranolol is the most common agent administered at a dose of 30 to 120 mg/day titrated to produce clinical response while monitoring blood pressure and pulse rate.[183,204] Generally benzodiazepines or beta-blockers are preferred for patients who do not have symptoms of Parkinson's disease and anticholinergics may be used in patients with Parkinson's. Although a recent Cochrane review concluded that there was insufficient data based on good quality research to support the use of anticholinergics in neuroleptic-induced akathisia, anticholinergics should not be abandoned in the treatment of akathisia as some patients may be responsive

to this adjunctive treatment.[205] Alternative agents that have been equivocally shown to be effective include amantadine, opiates, and buspirone.[206,207] Amelioration of akathisia has been associated with current clozapine therapy.[200] Recently, the role of mitrazapine in the treatment of antipsychotic-induced akathisia has been evaluated and it may be useful for patients with contraindications or intolerability to beta-blockers and for those patients with comorbid depression or negative symptoms associated with schizophrenia.[208]

B. Parkinsonism

1. Presentation

Drug-induced parkinsonism (DIP) presents very similarly to the symptom complex associated with idiopathic Parkinson's disease (PD). The constellation of akinesia, tremor, bradykinesia, and rigidity which impair balance and coordination, constitute parkinsonism. Akinesia is defined as poverty of movement, secondary to impaired movement initiation. The patient may complain of feeling listless, lacking spontaneity or oversleeping, and normal everyday activities such as grooming are reduced. This global slowing and slowness in initiating movements is the most common presenting symptom. Bradykinesia refers to slowness of movement while rigidity is increased resistance to passive stretch. This may be associated with decreased arm swinging, decreased eye blinking, a mask-like face, and drooling. Parkinsonian muscular rigidity involves excessive firmness and tensing of resting muscles. It may affect all skeletal muscles or only discrete muscular areas. Two kinds of rigidity may occur: continuous or "lead-pipe" rigidity in which the limb or joint resists movement and feels locked in place, and cogwheel rigidity which involves the muscle stretched around a joint to cause a rhythmic resistance that interrupts the usual smooth motion of the joint. Parkinsonian tremor consists of low frequency oscillations occurring mainly at rest and looks as if the patient is rolling a pill between their fingers and thumb. The incidence of this rest tremor has been reported to be as high as 50 percent in DIP, while the incidence is much higher in PD. Although resting tremor may be less prominent, it can be as vigorous as in PD. Additionally, in PD an asymmetrical presentation is more common, while drug or toxin-induced tremors tend to be bilateral as they represent an exacerbation of physiologic tremor. A highly characteristic although not pathognomonic sign of DIP is a low frequency perioral high amplitude tremor known as the rabbit syndrome.[2]

In the majority of cases, symptoms of DIP often appear in the first month after the offending agent has been started, and most symptoms will resolve within one to two months after the implicated agent has been discontinued. However, some patients may require up to one year for complete resolution of symptoms. Although tremor is the most visible feature of DIP, it is generally the least disabling. Bradykinesia is associated with much of the difficulty observed in carrying out activities of daily living. Even mild symptoms of DIP may cause muscle aches and weakness and severe symptoms may lead to impaired dexterity which may impinge on occupational and social tasks. Functional impairment can lead to increased caregiver burden and significant reductions in quality of life.[13] In the institutionalized elderly population, DIP was reported at a prevalence rate of 0.5 percent to 3 percent, with essential tremor being the most common movement disorder observed in that population.[209,210]

2. Case study, dyskinesia with parkinsonian features

A 52-year-old woman complained of depression, manifested by tearfulness, decreased energy level, insomnia, delusions and anhedonia for over one year which worsened over the last few months. She was treated with amoxapine 200 mg/day and titrated to 300 mg/day for her depression. After three months of therapy, treatment was discontinued however, it was reinstated after her depression returned. Approximately two months into her second course of therapy with amoxapine, the patient developed a resting tremor in her right hand and amoxapine was discontinued. Since her depression worsened, amoxapine therapy was resumed and the tremor reappeared. Some four months later, the patient noted chewing and sucking movements in addition to her tremor and amoxapine was discontinued. Phenelzine, a monoamine oxidase inhibitor, at a dose of 15 mg twice a day was started and the tremor relaxed; however, the chewing and sucking movements persisted. Upon examination the patient was not depressed, but mild facial masking, axial rigidity, and asymmetric resting tremor of both hands, right more than left, was noted. At this time definite oral-buccal-facial-lingual-masticatory dyskinesia was present. For the next six months the patient was maintained on the same dose of phenelzine with good control. Over nine months the parkinsonian features and facial dyskinesia resolved completely. This case demonstrates dyskinesia with parkinsonian features in a patient who had no prior exposure to amoxapine and was never treated with neuroleptics. Again, such movement disorders occurred and were indistinguishable from those induced by antipsychotic agents.

Another case involved a patient treated with gentamicin, an aminoglycoside antibiotic, who developed severe bilateral vestibular dysfunction resulting in imbalance and other movement disorders secondary to ototoxicity from the drug. The patient was given two doses of 240 mg of gentamicin by his physician and subsequently was given a prescription for 5,040 mg of gentamicin with directions to self-administer 240 mg daily for 21 days. The pharmacist dispensed 8 grams of gentamicin, nearly 3 grams more than what was ordered on the prescription. Subsequently, the patient self-administered another seven unauthorized doses of the very potent antimicrobial agent believing she was to finish the full amount of the antibiotic that was dispensed. A jury awarded the patient just over $5.7 million in damages citing the physician 85 percent at fault, the pharmacist 10 percent at fault and the patient 5 percent at fault. The trial court reduced the award reflecting a legal ceiling on malpractice in Louisiana. On appeal the award was upheld and according to the court, the physician should have had the drug administered and monitored by a home health nurse while the pharmacist's act of "dispensing additional doses clearly fell below the standard of care."[211]

3. Implicated agents

DIP may be due to drugs that deplete dopamine from intraneuronal storage sites (e.g., reserpine), drugs that act as dopamine "false neurotransmitters" (e.g., alpha-methyldopa), or drugs that block striatal dopamine receptors (e.g., neuroleptics and metoclopramide) resulting in an imbalance of dopamine and acetylcholine in the nigrostriatum.

The prevalence of DIP associated with typical neuroleptics ranges from 20 percent to 66 percent, while the prevalence with atypical neuroleptics is thought to be much lower, although this has not been well documented.[8,212] A retrospective cohort study of adults 66 years and older noted that the risk of development of DIP was similar among those patients who received a high-dose atypical antipsychotic and those patients who received a higher-potency typical antipsychotic. Thus, when potency and dose of antipsychotics is considered, atypical antipsychotics are not necessarily safer than typical antipsychotics in relation to DIP.[213]

The atypical neuroleptics, olanzapine and risperidone may cause DIP, and have been shown to worsen the primary motor manifestations of the disease, especially at high doses. Generally, clozapine has a low incidence of EPS, including parkinsonism. Clozapine produces sialorrhea, due to an increase in salivary flow, which is independent of EPS, and this is in contrast to conventional antipsychotics which typically cause hypersalivation due to bradykinesia of the swallowing muscles.[214] Quetiapine and ziprasidone appear to be associated with a low incidence of DIP. Quetiapine has not been shown to significantly cause or exacerbate parkinsonism, even at relatively higher doses, and like clozapine, has been shown to effectively reduce psychotic symptoms in

PD patients without worsening the primary motor manifestations of the disease.[215]

A review of SSRI-induced parkinsonism suggests that SSRIs may have the potential to worsen symptoms in patients with PD; however, establishing a definitive role is difficult. Since the disease is slow and subtle, any worsening of symptoms thought to be drug related may be attributed directly to the progression of the disease. A review of published reports of SSRI-induced movement disorders noted that patients experienced cogwheel rigidity, resting tremor, bradykinesia, akinesia or gait disturbances. The time of onset of symptoms was found to be from three days to four months after initiating therapy with the SSRI.[179] Although the majority of cases were attributed to fluoxetine, all SSRIs have the potential for DIP. One patient developed irreversible DIP within two months of initiating treatment with sertraline. Even with the discontinuation of the SSRI, the patient steadily over the next three years progressed with symptoms of gait disturbance, tremor, rigidity, and cognitive deficits.[216]

Chronic treatment with valproate, an antiepileptic agent utilized for seizures and mood disorders, has been associated with parkinsonism.[217] Dopamine-blocking antiemetic agents, including prochloperazine and metoclopramide, may induce reversible parkinsonism when these agents are used at therapeutic doses for nausea.[218]

4. Other drugs

Calcium channel blockers, such as diltiazem, verapamil, flunarizine and cinnarizine, have also been implicated in DIP; however, the latter two agents are relatively potent dopamine blockers that are not marketed in the United States, but are prescribed in Europe and Latin America for various disorders, including vertigo, migraine, and tinnitus.[219,220]

DIP has been reported in four patients with schizophrenia exposed to high doses of diazepam (> 100 mg/day).[221] Cisapride, a parsympathomimetic and gastroprokinetic agent no longer marketed in the U.S. (voluntarily removed from the U.S. market in 2000 due to concerns of QT prolongation), has also been associated with DIP. Other medications known to cause or worsen parkinsonism include amphotericin B, amiodarone, bethanechol, captopril, lovastatin, meperidine, methyldopa, phenelzine, phenytoin, and procaine. Lithium, a mood stabilizer, commonly produces a postural tremor; however, it is not firmly established if it can induce parkinsonism.[222]

5. Other causes of parkinsonism

In the early 1990s, it was discovered that the mitochondrial toxin, the pyridine 1-methyl-4-phenyl-1,2,3,6-tetrahydropyridine (MPTP), can cause clinical and experimental parkinsonism. Although it is unlikely that this compound is environmentally present in sufficient quantities to be a causative agent for most cases of PD, other compounds may be more contributory. Environmental exposure and risk of PD has been suggested with farming, rural residence, herbicide/pesticide and heavy metal exposure, and employment in industries manufacturing chemicals and wood pulp and paper, as well as iron mining and steel.

Parkinsonism secondary to environmental or occupational exposure has been associated with increased exposure to manganese, cyanide, mercury, and petroleum products. Chronic occupational exposure to manganese from welding is associated with a progressive course of parkinsonism and a poor response to levodopa.[110,223] Many Latin American countries are world leaders in manganese production, and parkinsonian symptoms with dystonic features are prevalent in miners from these countries. Exposure to manganese-containing fungicides, industrial component N-hexane, organophosphate insecticides, and consumption of derivatives of plants of the Annonaceae family have also been associated with inducing parkinsonism in patients.[224]

Individuals with a vitamin B12 deficiency may present with myelopathy and peripheral neuropathy, which may lead to weakness and spasticity. Elderly patients may not even present with anemia but exhibit ataxia and abnormal gait upon examination. Less commonly, folate deficiency may also lead to a myelopathy and neuropathy associated gait disorder which like the vitamin B12 deficiency disorder is treatable.[225]

6. Risks

Factors that increase the risk of DIP include patients with advanced age, dementia, pre-existing parkinsonism, exposure to DRBAs, exposure to higher doses of neuroleptics, and female gender (twice as common in women than men).[226,227] Patients with basal ganglia dysfunction may also be at risk and some individuals may be more susceptible to DIP due to a pre-existing deficiency of nigrostriatal dopamine.[228] DIP has a significantly higher incidence in patients with AIDS psychosis who are receiving DRBA, and one study noted that the likelihood of developing EPS was 2.4 times higher in psychotic patients with AIDS compared to psychotic patients without AIDS.[229] Other proposed risk factors include trauma, infection, premorbid personality, and emotional stress. An inverse association between cigarette smoking and Parkinson's disease has been noted to be present in the majority of case-control studies.[230–234]

7. Management

The most effective management of DIP involves discontinuation of the offending agent, and symptoms will usually resolve within one to two months. Rarely, however, some patients may require up to one year for complete resolution of symptoms. Some patients may never recover and this raises the question as to whether they had subclinical PD that was uncovered by the use of DRBA. Autopsy findings of typical histologic features of PD in patients with a past history of DIP supports this concept, and thus concomitant PD should be kept in mind if parkinsonism persists after the implicated agents are discontinued.[235]

If discontinuing the agent is not feasible, or if discontinuing the agent does not improve symptoms, then management of symptoms of DIP involves lowering the dosage of the offending agent to the lowest effective dosage or adding an antiparkinsonian medication. Switching to a neuroleptic that is a low-potency agent with anticholinergic properties, or an atypical antipsychotic such as quetiapine, may also be helpful. The most common drug treatment modalities for neuroleptic-induced pseudoparkinsonism are anticholinergics and the indirect dopamine agonist amantadine.

Anticholinergic agents currently available for managing pseudoparkinsonism are all effective but differ somewhat in adverse effects and duration of action. These include diphenhydramine, benztropine, trihexphenidyl, biperiden and procyclidine. Diphenhydramine is the most sedating while trihexphenidyl is the least. All of the anticholinergics need to be administered two to four times a day except benztropine which may be administered once daily due to its long duration of action. Amantadine may be used as an alternative to anticholinergics due to its indirect dopaminergic properties. Advantages of amantadine over anticholinergics are that it may be better tolerated, it does not adversely affect memory and may be an alternative in patients for whom anticholinergics are contraindicated, such as in patients with narrow angle glaucoma or benign prostatic hypertrophy.[236–238] Amantadine is administered in doses of 100 to 400 mg daily in divided doses with dosage adjustments required in renal dysfunction. Although the incidence of adverse effects is low, some patients may experience dizziness, nervousness, insomnia, anxiety and impaired concentration during treatment. Livedo reticularis, a skin discoloration which is reversible upon discontinuation of amantadine has also been noted in some patients especially those in colder climates. Rarely, hallucinations and abnormal dreams may also occur in patients treated with amantadine. Levodopa, which is generally utilized in managing idiopathic PD, is generally not utilized for neuroleptic-induced parkinsonism due to insufficient efficacy and increased risk of exacerbating an underlying psychiatric disorder.

The use of clozapine in the management of drug-induced psychosis in patients with Parkinson's disease has become increasingly popular.[239] Numerous open trials have demonstrated improvement in psychosis in more than 80 percent of patients with Parkinson's disease who received clozapine. Clozapine will not worsen Parkinson's disease and a surprising effect has been improvement of motor features, notably tremor in such patients. It appears to improve tremor in a majority of patients with Parkinson's disease, and completely ameliorates Parkinson's disease tremor in some cases.[240–242] Additionally, the use of clozapine in treating psychosis in patients with Parkinson's disease has been associated with dramatic improvements in facial and truncal dystonias.[243,244]

C. Myoclonus, Tremor, Tics, Asterixis

Other continuous DIMDs, including tremor, chorea, and myoclonus, may be associated with various medications, and a dose reduction or discontinuation of the offending medication will typically relieve the symptoms.

Myoclonus is defined as sudden, brief, shock-like or lightning-like involuntary movements caused by muscular contractions. Although various disorders—including neurodegenerative, systemic metabolic disorders—and infections may cause myoclonus, this involuntary movement may also be drug-induced. Evidence is available to indicate that levodopa, bismuth salts, and cyclic antidepressants alone or in combination with lithium, may induce reversible myoclonus. SSRIs can also induce myoclonus, although this DIMD is most frequently associated with serotonin syndrome. Other drugs that have been reported to induce myoclonus include typical and atypical antipsychotics, MAOIs, metoclopramide, anticonvulsants (valproic acid, carbamazepine, phenytoin, gabapentin, lamotrigine), opiates (morphine, fentanyl, methadone, hydrocodone), general anesthetics (propofol, enflurane, etomidate), antineoplastics (chlorambucil, prednimustine, ifosfamide), cardiovascular drugs (propafenone, flecainide, diltiazem, nifedipine), and anti-infectives (penicillins, cephalosporins, imipenem, quinolones, isoniazid, and acyclovir). Anxiolytics, such as buspirone, carisoprodol, and benzodiazepines have also been implicated in myoclonus. High doses of morphine and meperidine and opioids have been implicated as causative agents of myoclonus; however, these studies usually cite concomitant factors such as malignancies, renal failure treated with hemodialysis, and exposure to neuroleptics.[245,246] Withdrawal from benzodiazepine treatment may also induce drug-induced myoclonus. Withdrawal of the offending drug usually leads to gradual resolution of the drug-induced myoclonus, although some cases may require treatment with serotonin antagonists such as methysergide and cyproheptadine.[247]

Tremor is rhythmic and usually monomorphic, and unlike myoclonus it does not unpredictably and chaotically change in direction. Tremor is a recognized complication of antidepressant therapy, and it is estimated that up to 10 percent of patients on a tricyclic antidepressant, such as imipramine, may experience it. The mechanism may be enhancement of physiologic tremor since propranolol ameliorates the tremor. However, generalized choreoathetoid movements may be a manifestation of tricyclic antidepressant poisoning.[248] The relatively recent recognition of the serotonin syndrome has been associated with the use of serotonin reuptake inhibitors, tricyclic antidepressants, monoamine oxidase inhibitors and other agents known to increase the biologic activity of serotonin. Symptoms associated with serotonin syndrome include myoclonus, ataxia, agitation, altered mental status, shivering and hyperreflexia.[249]

Occasional tremor has been reported with phenytoin and carbamazepine. Amiodarone, a cardiac antiarrhythmic agent, may produce a tremor, typically of the postural type, and may also cause ataxia. Cyclosporine-A, an immunosuppressive agent utilized in organ transplantation, may produce a tremor of low amplitude and high frequency.[31,250] Alcohol use or withdrawal may be associated with tremor, ataxia, myoclonus, parkinsonism, and orolingual dyskinesias. Drugs used in the management of asthma can often produce tremor as an adverse effect. Agents known to cause this effect include isoproterenol, aminophylline, theophylline, terbutaline and other beta agonists utilized in the management of asthma. Lithium, utilized for the prophylaxis and management of manic depressive disorders, is known to produce enhancement of physiological tremor. The incidence is from 33 to 65 percent and the occurrence increases with increasing lithium levels and is seen in 100 percent of lithium toxicity cases. Valproic acid is the most common tremor inducing agent among the antiepileptic drugs. Approximately 25 percent of patients receiving chronic valproic acid therapy will experience tremor which is generally postural. Alcohol ingestion may lead to improvement in some primary movement disorders including essential tremor and myoclonic dystonia.[251] Tranquilizers, including benzodiazepines are often utilized in the management of tremor; however, tremor may occur during benzodiazepine withdrawal. Additionally, many medications that are renally eliminated may produce disturbances in the central nervous system when utilized in individuals with some degree of renal impairment.

Abnormal involuntary choreiform movements have been reported in an elderly male on chronic maintenance hemodialysis who received valacyclovir and famciclovir.[252] Stimulants such as cocaine, even in small doses, can exacerbate or cause the recurrence of motor tics in patients with different movement disorders, including Tourette's syndrome and tardive dyskinesia. Some clinicians have concluded that cocaine addiction is a predisposing factor for the development of tics and dystonias upon exposure to neuroleptics. Since over 30 million Americans have used cocaine and over 5 million use it regularly, it may be regarded as an important cause or trigger of hyperkinetic movement disorders, especially if there is a sudden onset or an acute exacerbation.[253,254] Amphetamines may also lead to movement disorders commonly described as stereotypies.[255]

Asterixis is a movement disorder characterized by intermittent loss of muscle tone, resulting in a coarse "flapping tremor." It appears as an involuntary jerk superimposed on a postural or intentional movement and is also referred to as "negative myoclonus." The symptoms are most obvious when the patient stands still with outstretched arms and dorsiflexed wrists and the extremities are usually asynchronously affected. Although metabolic disorders and hepatic encephalopathy are the most common causes for asterixis, some anticonvulsants medications and mood stabilizers such as carbamazepine, gabapentin and lithium have been associated with this disorder.[256–259] In most patients, a cessation or reduction of the medication has led to cessation of asterixis.

26.11 Persistent/Tardive Drug-Induced Movement Disorders

DIMDs may also be persistent and tardive, appearing during long-term exposure to the offending agent, hence the term "tardive" meaning "late-onset." These DIMDs are patterned and periodic, and persist beyond discontinuation of the causative agent.

A. Tardive Dyskinesia

1. Presentation

Originally, tardive dyskinesia (TD) referred to the classical rhythmic oral-facial movements but is now renamed as tardive stereotypies and is the most common type of TD, followed by tardive dystonia, akathisia, tremor, chorea, and myoclonus.[260] TD is a syndrome characterized by repetitive muscle movements that are purposeless in nature and can impair the patient's ability to function socially and, rarely, physiologically. Most movements are rapid unsustained movements variously described as choreic or stereotypic, with the former referring to movements that are unpredictable, rapid and flow from one body region to another, while the latter are rhythmic, reproducible and regular, remaining generally restricted in their anatomic distribution. Athetoid movements may also occur and these are slow, sinuous and continual. Any body area may be affected, but the orofacial area is commonly involved, affecting more than 75 percent of patients with TD.

Symptoms include lip-smacking and puckering, tongue protrusion, chewing, sucking, grimacing, blinking, puffing of cheeks and frowning. Other abnormal movements involve the extremities and trunk and are observed in 50 percent and 25 percent of patients, respectively. Symptoms manifested include shoulder shrugging, rocking, incessant flexion-extension movements, wrist flexion or torsion, ankle flexion or rotation, or ballistic movements. In the elderly patient population, orofacial dyskinesias are more common whereas limb or truncal dyskinesias without orofacial involvement are more commonly observed in younger patients.

Over the past 20 years, the prevalence of TD has doubled. This may be because more patients are receiving DRBAs, patients may be starting medication at an earlier age and taking them longer, the doses are higher, and drug holidays are more likely.[212] To fit the definition of TD, patients must have a history of at least three months of total cumulative exposure to at least one DRBA with exposure being continuous or intermittent. In patients over the age of 60, the history of neuroleptic use should be for at least one month. The signs or symptoms of TD develop during exposure to neuroleptic or within four weeks of withdrawal from an oral neuroleptic agent. In the case of depot, the time of withdrawal is extended to eight weeks.[261]

The symptoms of TD tend to be worsened also by stimulants and may be transiently worsened by emotional arousal, stress, and distraction during voluntary movements in unaffected parts of the body. The abnormal body movements are transiently reduced by relaxation and are generally absent during sleep. Symptoms of TD may appear during neuroleptic treatment, after dosage reduction, or after discontinuation of the neuroleptic agent. Upon neuroleptic withdrawal, symptoms of this disorder may appear to be aggravated; however, with time their severity usually subsides. TD may be irreversible, and improvement of TD after drug withdrawal is variable in reported studies, with remission rates reported lower in the elderly. One study noted that only 2 percent of patients who withdrew from neuroleptics had a significant recovery, and another 20 percent reported some level of improvement within one year.[262]

In severe cases, TD may be associated with medical problems such as ulcers in cheeks and tongue, ill-fitting dentures, loss of teeth, macroglossia, difficulty in walking, swallowing, or breathing, weight loss, depression, and suicidal ideation. Although most cases of TD are of minor functional significance, the disorder is cosmetically and socially disfiguring and by the very nature of these constant odd movements, patients may be hindered from fully participating and functioning successfully within the community setting.[263–266]

Spontaneous dyskinesias may resemble TD and have been observed in patients with schizophrenia long before the discovery of antipsychotics. Their reported rate has been as high as 53 percent. However, the development of dyskinesias has also been associated with normal aging, with 4 to 8 percent of healthy elderly males experiencing them.[267,268]

2. Implicated agents

Neuroleptics are by far the biggest culprits in causing the symptoms of TD. Increased risk of TD has been associated with the cumulative amount of neuroleptic agent, the number of interruptions in neuroleptic treatment as well as the cumulative amount of anticholinergic agents. Generally, if treatment with neuroleptics is required, then treatment should not be given intermittently, since the risk of TD is three times as great for patients with more than two interruptions as for patients with two or less interruptions in treatment.[269] The incidence of persistent TD was noted to increase with longer duration of treatment in a study of antipsychotic-naïve patients with first-episode schizophrenia. The cumulative incidence of TD after 1 year, 2 years, and 4 years was reported at 4.8 percent, 7.2 percent, and 15.6 percent, respectively.[270] A review in 2008 noted that the annualized TD incidence was 3.9 percent for atypical antipsychotics and 5.5 percent for typical antipsychotics.[271] Stratified by age, annual TD incidence rates were 0.35 percent with atypical antipsychotics in children, 2.98 percent with atypical antipsychotics versus 7.7 percent with typical antipsychotics in adults, and 5.2 percent with typical antipsychotics in the elderly. TD in four adult studies noted TD prevalence rates were 13.1 percent for atypical antipsychotics, 15.6 percent for antipsychotic-free patients, and 32.4 percent for typical antipsychotics.[271]

The expectation that the atypicals would reduce the threat of TD has received considerable support in reviews and several clinical trials, although some of the latter have been industry sponsored. Although a substantial number of clinical studies do note a beneficial effect, all of the atypicals, with the exception of paliperidone and iloperidone, due to lack of relevant reports to date, have been implicated in causing, or failing to relieve, tardive dyskinesia. Reports of TD associated with the use of atypical antipsychotics are increasing, as more patients are exposed to these agents for longer time periods. For example, risperidone demonstrated a lower incidence of acute EPS during initial clinical trials; however, postmarketing data indicates that EPS liability is dose dependent. In the absence of longer-term data, the limited evidence available indicates that the atypical antipsychotics have a decreased liability of TD, approximately 1 percent compared with 5 percent for typical antipsychotics annually.[272] The apparent incidence of TD with risperidone is between 0.03 and 2.4 percent; the risk of EPS increases when risperidone is dosed above 6 mg/day. Cases have been reported demonstrating a relationship between this atypical neuroleptic and TD,[273–277] and in one trial, a jury awarded a 45-year-old female $6.7 million who was on risperidone and developed TD over a 15-month period.[278] Although quetiapine has been associated with a lower risk of inducing EPS, it has been reported to precipitate TD in patients never exposed to typical neuroleptics.[279,280] The incidence of TD with olanzapine is 0.5 to 1 percent compared with 4.5 to 7.5 percent for haloperidol, and some reports cite that the rate of TD with quetiapine is similar to olanzapine and significantly less than that associated with haloperidol in all age groups.[281] Ziprasidone has been reported to induce TD in a patient with a long history of treatment with traditional antipsychotics.[282] Aripiprazole has been implicated in causing TD in a patient following 18 months of treatment for refractory depression and in a patient following 9 months of treatment for schizophrenia.[283,284] However, aripiprazole has also been noted to improve symptoms of TD in a patient who developed TD while on quetiapine and later on ziprasidone.[285] Clozapine, although less likely to cause EPS, may also induce TD in care cases.[286]

The relationship between initiating therapy with either a typical or atypical antipsychotic agent and subsequent new diagnosis of a DIMD other than parkinsonism in older patients with dementia was evaluated. In the one year follow-up period it was noted that the risk of developing TD or another DIMD other than parkinsonism, while being treated with an atypical agent, was not statistically different from that with a typical antipsychotic.[43] More recently, a records-based case control study did not find a significant difference in the risk of TD between atypical and typical antipsychotic medication users in adult patients at the Veterans Administration Puget Sound Health Care System after adjusting for age, race, gender, schizophrenia, schizoaffective disorder, depression, and anti-parkinsonian drugs.[287] Thus, the relative risk for TD may be smaller with the atypicals; however, they cannot be said to have an absolute advantage over the typical antipsychotics.

Reports also show that low doses of clozapine are effective in the management of neuroleptic-induced EPS (TD, DIP, and chronic akathisia) in neuroleptic-resistant chronic schizophrenic patients.[288] A few case reports note the onset of TD following clozapine treatment; however, in all those cases, patients had exposure to other antipsychotic drugs and the dyskinesia can be considered an idiosyncratic reaction to clozapine.[289–291] Since clozapine is utilized in patients who have previously been exposed to neuroleptics, as this is not a first-line agent, but one reserved for patients who are treatment resistant or cannot tolerate any of the other neuroleptics, such patients may already have been sensitized to develop TD as a result of their exposure to various other neuroleptics.[292] However, more recent reports have noted that there is no association between the development of TD and therapy with neuroleptics of any class, including clozapine.[200]

Metoclopramide, a dopaminergic receptor blocker, is also implicated in causing TD. It is used in the treatment of diabetic gastroparesis, esophageal reflux, and as an antiemetic. It may cause or exacerbate TD and the course of the disorder is similar to that observed with neuroleptic usage. Symptoms of the movement disorder may disappear following drug withdrawal or they may be irreversible. The majority of the cases reported with metoclopramide as a causative factor in TD are in elderly women.[293–295] One study noted a higher incidence of TD in diabetic patients treated with metoclopramide than in nondiabetics treated with the agent.[105] Although metoclopramide has been available for over twenty years, the manufacturers did not adequately study the long-term safety of this drug and grossly underestimated the risk of TD and other related movement disorders associated with its use. Analyses published recently have cited metoclopramide as the most common cause of DIMDs, and exposure greater than 12 weeks was evident in a majority of those reports.[296,297] The FDA now requires manufacturers of metoclopramide to add a boxed warning to the drug's labeling advising of the risk of TD associated with long-term, high-dose use and to implement a risk evaluation and mitigation strategy, or REMS, so patients are provided a guide addressing the risk.[298]

Oral facial dyskinesias, described as persistent involuntary movements of the face and mouth, have been linked to extended use of antihistaminic decongestants.[299] Amiodarone, an antiarrhythmic agent, is associated with various neurologic adverse effects including severe cases of dyskinesia.[31,32] Choreoathetotic movements as well as facial dyskinesia have been reported with gabapentin, an anticonvulsant, utilized for seizure disorders, pain management, and as a mood stabilizer.[300]

SSRI-induced movement disorders have been reported as involuntary movements of the face, limbs, or trunk as well as facial grimaces. Dyskinesias were noted to occur within one day to two months of initiating therapy with the offending SSRIs, while the latent dyskinesias (i.e. TD) were noted to occur within six months to four years of initiating the antidepressant. A majority of the patients were receiving a neuroleptic concurrently or had done so in the past.[100] Most of the cases involved fluoxetine, used alone and in conjunction with neuroleptics, and several dozen spontaneous reports of TD have been recorded by the manufacturer.[301] TD has been associated with most classes of antidepressant agents and, in contrast to neuroleptics, dyskinesia associated with antidepressant treatment appears to be typically rapid in onset and disappears rapidly after withdrawal of the offending antidepressant.[302–304]

3. Risks

Advanced age has always been cited as a major risk factor for TD, and elderly patients have a greater likelihood that the TD may be more severe or more generalized with continued neuroleptic usage compared to younger patients.[305] Other risk factors for TD have cited female gender, duration and cumulative amount of antipsychotic medication, organic brain damage, alcohol abuse, recent drug-free intervals, a diagnosis of affective disorder and subsequent adjunctive neuroleptic use for such disorders other than their use in schizophrenia or schizoaffective disorders, and early development of EPS, particularly DIP.[47,306] Diabetic patients have been noted to have an increased risk of spontaneous dyskinetic movements and TD compared to non-diabetics.[307] Genetic factors responsible for differences in inter-individual vulnerability have also been implicated.[308] Alcohol and/or drug abuse has been found to increase the risk of TD by threefold, particularly the orofacial subtype involving the head and upper extremities in patients with a long history of alcohol abuse or dependence.[306,309–311] Recently, a preeminent association was noted between the level of cigarette consumption and the current severity of TD, and requires further exploration considering the high prevalence of smoking in psychiatric patients.[47] Since smoking induces hepatic enzymes and accelerates the metabolism of antipsychotics, patients may require higher doses of prescribed neuroleptics which may contribute to the increased prevalence of TD in smokers.

The perception has existed that patients treated with conventional neuroleptic medications may be at increased risk of developing a diagnosis for TD compared to patients treated with atypical neuroleptics.[214,312] The purported TD suppressing and TD preventive effects of atypical neuroleptics cannot be endorsed, as recent data has shown that compared to typical neuroleptics, atypical neuroleptics do not have a reduced risk of causing TD nor do they have an ability to suppress pre-existing TD.[200] Additionally, among patients with a diagnosis of TD, the same incidence of use of atypical neuroleptics as typical neuroleptics was noted, even after adjustments were made for age, gender, race, diagnosis, and anti-parkinsonian drugs. Thus there was no significant difference in risk of TD between patients who received atypical and typical neuroleptics.[313] According to a multivariate analysis, the only variable for the long-term evolution of tardive dyskinesia was dependent on illness duration, independent of age.[200]

4. Management

Various agents have been utilized for managing symptoms of TD; however there is no consistently effective and satisfactory treatment of this movement disorder, hence prevention of its development must be the cornerstone of therapy. The continued need for chronic neuroleptic treatment needs to be regularly assessed and their use should be discontinued when their efficacy is uncertain or when alternative agents can be used instead.[261]

Treatment of TD primarily consists of discontinuing the causative agent, although abrupt cessation of a neuroleptic should be avoided as acute withdrawal may induce transient worsening of symptoms. Palliative treatment with benzodiazepines (e.g., clonazepam) may be used during the period when symptoms of TD may be worsened by neuroleptic withdrawal. Presynaptic dopamine blockade by reserpine or tetrabenazine may be used to control the symptoms of TD in more severe or disabling cases following neuroleptic withdrawal. Tetrabenazine, available in the U.S. as an orphan drug to treat chorea associated with Huntington's disease, is the solely licensed treatment of TD available in the United Kingdom. Both reserpine and tetrabenazine have been associated with producing symptoms of depression.[314] Other agents that have been associated with a reduction in the magnitude of symptoms include baclofen, valproic acid, vitamin E, vitamin B6, melatonin, branch-chain amino acids, and essential fatty acids. However, there is no convincing evidence that any of these pharmacologic interventions or dietary supplements are successful treatment options, as their success rate is low.[13,315] It is also recommended that anticholinergics be discontinued since these agents may at times worsen TD. Case reports cite possible improvement in neuroleptic-induced TD after changing to the atypical antipsychotic aripirazole.[316,317] Clozapine has been shown to be the most effective drug in managing tardive syndrome and noted not to be associated with worsening of any tardive syndrome.[318]

Due to no adequate therapy available for managing TD, it is important to minimize exposure to DRBAs in an attempt to prevent the occurrence of this movement disorder. Periodic evaluations of patients on long-term neuroleptics should be undertaken, and patients should be examined regularly, at least every three to six months, for dyskinesia as well as other types of neurological disorders. The nature and severity of the movement disorder should be noted to serve as a baseline for ongoing evaluations. The Abnormal Involuntary Movement Scale (AIMS) is the most widely recommended and utilized tool for evaluating TD in clinical practice.[319,320] In recent years, malpractice suits have resulted in substantial judgments for the plaintiffs over the development of TD in psychiatric patients. Plaintiffs are successful in approximately 50 percent of all TD-related malpractice cases, compared with only about 10 to 20 percent of all medical malpractice suits. The lawsuits have cited improper administration of neuroleptic agents including the misdiagnosis of a medical condition that did not warrant therapy with a DRBA. Physicians have been known to either fail to monitor patients or poorly monitor patients' body movements while under treatment.[321] It is essential that periodic assessment of abnormal movements be undertaken for the early detection of TD. Additionally, proper documentation of the indication of drug therapy and obtaining an informed consent are equally important in avoiding liability. Hospital policies and state law mandate that patients be informed of the potential benefits and risks of psychotropic agents, and it has been recommended that informed consent be obtained every six months due to the fluctuating mental competence of patients with schizophrenia and other chronic mental illnesses.[322–328] Additionally, another prevalent recovery theory under which TD malpractice claims are brought cite the drug manufacturer and the doctor (as the manufacturer's agent) as having produced a medication with defective design, testing, or warning information (product liability).[321]

B. Tardive Akathisia

Chronic, tardive and withdrawal akathisia commonly are reported with long-term use of neuroleptic agents. Reported rates for tardive akathisia are approximately 30 percent, similar to the 20 to 30 percent reported for acute akathisia.[329] The incidence with atypical antipsychotics appears to be lower compared to the typical antipsychotics; however no systematic data are currently available and studies are limited.[146,330]

Although the temporal criteria for tardive akathisia are debatable, symptoms of tardive akathisia may occur after three months on a stable medication regimen or several months after drug withdrawal or dose reduction. The term chronic akathisia refers to the duration of akathisia, irrespective of whether the type of onset is acute, tardive or withdrawal. Withdrawal akathisia, however, is restricted to akathisia which may develop when the dose of a neuroleptic is withdrawn or reduced.[331,332] Risk factors for the development of chronic and tardive akathisia are poorly understood, but female gender, old age, iron deficiency, negative symptoms, cognitive dysfunction and affective disorder

may increase the risk of tardive or chronic akathisia.[146,333,334] In contrast to acute akathisia which may improve with anticholinergic agents, propranolol, and clonazepam, tardive akathisia responds best to monoamine-depleting drugs, such as reserpine.[335]

Management strategies for tardive akathisia are very similar to those used for acute akathisia and include beta-blockers, antimuscarinic agents, and benzodiazepines, although improvement may be equivocal.[28] Recently, a case of aripiprazole-induced tardive akathisia responding to the dopamine agonist ropinirole has been reported.[336] Chronic akathisia due to risperidone has been cited as a reason for a patient to become extremely irritable, easily agitated, and at times violent.[146]

C. Tardive Dystonia

Tardive dystonia may occur as a result of chronic neuroleptic exposure with preferential involvement of axial muscles and characteristic rocking movements of the trunk and pelvis. Facial dystonia can present as blepharospasm or facial grimacing, while involvement of the mandible may present in tonic deviation, protrusion, bruxism, or sustained opening or closing of the jaw. Tardive dystonia appears to be most prominent in younger adults and in males. This DIMD frequently persists even after discontinuation of the causative agent and patients are often refractory to medical management. It is important to exclude neurological causes of dystonia (e.g., Wilson's disease, multiple sclerosis) while making the diagnosis. Most reports of tardive dystonias have been associated with typical neuroleptics; however, cases have been reported with atypical agents including olanzapine, risperidone, and aripiprazole.[13] Many tardive dystonias involve the cranio-cervical region which constitutes the most common and most severely affected region. Botulism toxin injection may be beneficial for certain forms of focal movements affecting the tongue, jaw muscles, or cervical musculature.

D. Other Tardive Variants

Other tardive variants less commonly reported in literature include tardive myoclonus, tardive tics, tardive Tourette's syndrome, tardive parkinsonism and tardive tremor.[2] Tardive gait has also been reported and may be part of the TD spectrum. Patients with tardive gait present with different gait abnormalities, including "unsteadiness," "pelvic thrust," stiffness," "dancing gait," and a "duck-like" gait. This type of heterogeneous neurological disorder has been noted to occur in patients who had taken DRBAs such as prochloperazine, metoclopramide, as well as antipsychotics for a number of years.[337]

26.12 Drugs Used for Movement Disorders

Restless leg syndrome (RLS) is characterized by an irresistible urge to move, usually the legs, to stop an uncontrollable sensation. If affects women twice as often as men. RLS may be primary, where the pathophysiology is not established, although impaired iron metabolism and abnormal dopaminergic neurotransmission have been proposed. Secondary causes of RLS include iron deficiency anemia, folate deficiency, chronic kidney disease, diabetes mellitus, pregnancy, peripheral neuropathy, and drug-induced causes. Medications which have been reported as causative agents in drug-induced RLS include analgesics (NSAIDS), anti-epileptic agents (phenytoin, topiramate, zonisamide), antidepressants (SSRIs, TCAs, trazodone, mirtazapine, venlafaxine), atypical antipsychotics (clozapine, olanzapine, quetiapine, risperidone), donepezil, lithium, metoclopramide, interferon-alfa, anesthetics, nicotine, caffeine, and thyroid harmones.[338] Generally, antidepressants are the drugs most commonly implicated in secondary RLS and symptoms occur shortly, usually within one week, after drug initiation or dose increase. With regard to other drug-induced RLS, the onset of symptoms varies widely. Symptoms have been shown to occur 1 to 5 days following drug initiation or dose increase with antipsychotics, while symptoms following supplementation with thyroid hormones may take 2 months to appear.[339]

Dopamine agonists are an effective treatment option for managing symptoms of RLS and PD. Their use in PD is associated with fewer motor complications, including wearing-off phenomenon or dyskinesias compared to levodopa. However, hallucinations, somnolence and dizziness are adverse effects observed with dopamine agonists.[340] One such dopamine agonist, pergolide (PermaxTM), was removed from the market in 2007 since it was associated with raising the risk of heart valve damage, or cardiac valvulopathy, a life-threatening condition in which the heart valves leak. Additionally, numerous pathologic behaviors and impulse control disorders such as compulsive gambling, hypersexuality, compulsive eating, excessive shopping or spending have been highly associated with use of dopamine agonists. A retrospective study noted that among patients with PD, new-onset compulsive gambling or hypersexuality occurred in 18.4 percent of patients taking therapeutic doses of dopamine agonists (e.g., pramipexole [MirapexTM], ropinirole [RequipTM]) but was not found among untreated patients, those taking sub-therapeutic doses or those taking carbidopa/levodopa (SinemetTM) alone. After dose reduction or discontinuation of the causative agents, the pathologic behaviors abated.[341]

Long-term treatment with levodopa for PD may lead to levodopa-induced abnormal movements in patients with PD. Monophasic dyskinesia occurs at the time of maximal clinical improvement and is usually of the choreic type commonly referred to as "peak-dose" dyskinesia, whereas diphasic dyskinesia is of the dystonic or ballistic type and is referred to as the "onset" or "end-dose" dyskinesia. Discontinuing selegiline (deprenyl) may reduce dyskinesias, and reducing the dose of or discontinuing treatment with a dopamine agonist may also be beneficial.[342]

26.13 Monitoring

Patients receiving DRBAs should be examined regularly for DIMDs as a component of a regular evaluation of extrapyramidal symptoms (EPS). Hence documentation of informed consent is critical in reducing liability, and consent forms have been developed to aid in providing appropriate documentation of the risk of TD and the benefits of antipsychotic medications.[343] The Mount Sinai guidelines on the pharmacotherapy of schizophrenia represent a minimal level of monitoring and recommend that patients be evaluated for EPS and tardive dyskinesia prior to starting on new medications, and every three to six months for patients who receive typical antipsychotics and every 12 months for patients who receive an atypical antipsychotic agent. Additionally, the guidelines call for more frequent monitoring for patients who are at a higher risk for EPS.[344] Examination of EPS can be performed easily by clinicians trained to recognize the various manifestations and movements associated with DIMDs.[345] These DIMDs are assessed formally in clinical trials using several different standardized rating scales such as the Barnes Akathisia Scale, Simpson Angus Scale, Extrapyramidal Symptom Rating Scale and the Abnormal Involuntary Movement Scale which detect and quantify these movement disorders.[346–350]

26.14 Clinical and Legal Issues in Psychiatry

Unfortunately DIMDs may be undiagnosed, misdiagnosed, and untreated even among psychiatrists and neurologists.[351] In one study of 25 representative schizophrenic patients who underwent a standardized neurological examination to detect EPS, two-thirds were prescribed an atypical neuroleptic, and 18 of the 25 had EPS. Upon review of the clinician's notes for the past 12 months, it was noted that only half of the patients had documented evidence of a management plan addressing the EPS. However, only one patient of the 25 during that time period had a documented physical examination recording the presence or absence of EPS.[352] Likewise, a review of medical records of 204 hospitalized patients showed a high rate of failure to document the assessment and course of EPS.[353] These findings suggest that clinicians do not recognize the importance of documentation of these significant adverse effects, and it highlights the fact that although screening for EPS is recommended by the APA, it may not be routine. Possible reasons for this may be that clinicians may lack the knowledge and skills to accurately diagnose and appropriately manage EPS, they may underestimate the distress the neuroleptic may produce, or they may simply lack the time to address this aspect of patient care. Additionally, lack of understanding of DIMDs, complacency among prescribers of DRBAs, and the increased use of DRBAs in populations that had never previously been exposed to such agents (e.g., children, adolescents, elderly) and wider use in the adult population, may increase the number of cases of DIMDs.[354]

From a legal standpoint, the greater the risk of any treatment, the greater is the duty to warn, monitor, or look for other alternatives.[355] However, there is evidence that the fear of litigation may influence treatment methods to a greater degree than sound medical evidence and best practice guidelines. A report in 2005 noted that up to 93 percent of physicians in high-liability specialties report practicing defensive medicine.[356] To avoid this counterproductive trend, physicians should be concerned first with safety and efficacy, and should manage the risk of malpractice liability by following the traditional golden standards of medicine of informed consent, use of evidence-based medicine, integration of specialized medicine, and thorough patient follow-up care.[357]

Prevention and early recognition of the symptoms compromise the best method of managing DIMDs. First patients, and if appropriate their family members, need to be informed of the risks of DIMDs and benefits of treatment before starting therapy with a DRBA. Second, the use of the DRBAs should be restricted to only those patients for whom no alternative treatment is available. Third, the exposure should be limited by keeping the dose of the DRBA to the lowest possible effective level. Fourth, the patient should be assessed every three months, and the patient's need for continued treatment with a DRBA should be reassessed. Fifth, whenever possible, the patient's medication should be switched to one that has limited antagonism of dopamine receptors (e.g., use an antiemetic such as ondansetron instead of metoclopramide or compazine). And last, but not least, every patient who is taking a DRBA should be examined every three months for symptoms of DIMDs.

The plaintiff in a medical malpractice suit must prove by a preponderance of the evidence that the physician was negligent. What is sometimes referred to as " the four D's" must be established: the physician had a duty to care for the patient, the physician derelictly breached that duty, the injuries caused were the direct and proximate result of the physician's breach, and the injuries suffered by the plaintiff are compensable damages resulting from the physician's malpractice.[358–361] The prescription of psychotropics exposes the clinician to significant professional liability claims and the psychiatrist's prescription liability pertains largely to two areas: negligence and informed consent.[362–364] A patient may claim malpractice liability based on the intentional tort of battery or on grounds of negligence for unwarranted use of medications without the patient's meaningful consent to the treatment course. Prescribing psychiatrists risk negligence liability in various areas such as: failure to obtain an adequate medical and psychiatric history; failure to obtain an adequate physical examination; failure to obtain adequate laboratory tests; lack of indication for a prescribed medication; contraindication to a prescription; prescription of an improper dosage; prescription for an improper duration; failure to recognize, monitor, and treat medication side effects; failure to abate drug reactions and interactions; and failure to consult with other physicians.[365] Negligence may also be claimed if the prescriber misdiagnosed the patent's condition, or if the patient was subjected to an excessive dosage or duration of treatment. Prescribers who misdiagnose patients and treat them with psychotropics may be held liable for negligent malpractice when a patient develops a DIMD. A forensic non-treating expert may express an opinion that a different diagnosis would have been more accurate than the one provided by the treating prescriber, and the correct diagnosis would not have required treatment with the psychotropic in question. A patient may also bring suit against the drug manufacturer on product liability grounds associated with defective design, testing or warning information relating to the medication that may have caused the DIMD. In many states, products liability law holds every person who transmits a defectively made drug product from manufacture to the injured patient liable without fault for administering the drug. Patients who are committed to a state or federal governmental agency (e.g., the Department of Veterans Affairs, a state mental hospital, or a state detention center) may also claim that their civil rights under the Eighth and Fourteenth Amendments to the Constitution were violated by the physician treating them if the patient is under some type of legal restraint at the time of treatment such as confinement to prison, a pretrial detention center, a mental institution or a psychiatric ward in any hospital. The allegation is that the treating physician under the Civil Rights Act (42 USC 1983) violated the patient's civil rights since the patient was under the control of the state. A patient treated in prison or in a state mental institution who develops a DIMD may also claim that the prescriber was "deliberately indifferent" to the patient's condition, a separate "Constitutional Tort" that permits recovery of damages for pain, suffering, impairment of functioning and loss of earnings. State-created medical malpractice claims based on negligence may be joined to a Federal Civil Rights Act suit.

With the advent of managed care and the dramatic changes in health care produced by it, more and more managed care organizations are increasingly named as defendants in malpractice suits. Such malpractice suits against managed care organizations have focused mainly on the negligent selection of unqualified panel clinicians, inappropriate medication usage evaluations seen as substandard medical care, and negligent provision of care usually for staff model health maintenance organizations in which the physicians are "supervised" employees.[366,367] Since medical records are legal as well as clinical documents, record keeping is as much a part of providing health care as the underlying care activity itself. In addition to an initial evaluation and examination before diagnosing a patient, clinical consultations may be necessary and appropriate before and/or during treatment. The clinician requesting the consultation should document any discussion especially if the consultant is not likely to keep notes. Permission should be obtained from the consultant to record his name, and if a formal consultation is requested, the consultant should write a note in the chart or treatment record, especially if the consultant has seen the patient or is seeking reimbursement for his intervention.[368]

Physicians since the beginning of the twentieth century have been required to obtain the consent of their patients before undertaking a proposed procedure or treatment. However, for the past several decades, physicians have also been legally required to provide information to patients about the proposed intervention prior to proceeding. Together, consent and disclosure of information help promote the increased recognition of autonomy and the variety of medical treatment options available regarding decisions in health care. Additionally adequate informed consent can aid to maximize patient compliance with treatment and improve the psychiatrist-patient relationship.[369-371]

Elements of informed consent in medical care are threefold: information, competency and voluntariness of decision making. According to the legal doctrine of informed consent, sufficient information is needed to make an adequate consent, since accepting a consent based on insufficient information may constitute malpractice.[372] This applies to diagnostic evaluation procedures as well as treatment. The question for physicians is how much and what information is needed for a patient to make an informed choice.[373] It appears that the most common answer is what a "reasonable person" would want to know to accept or reject treatment such as: the nature or diagnosis of the patient's condition;

the nature of the proposed intervention; the purpose of the proposed intervention; the benefits of the proposed intervention; the risks of the proposed intervention, including incidence, severity, and significance; the possible alternatives to the proposed intervention, including no treatment; the benefits of the alternative interventions; and the risks of the alternative interventions, including incidence, severity, and significance.[374] With regard to information about the risks of treatment, disclosure is warranted when the risks are frequent, significant, severe or life-threatening. Since package inserts for antipsychotics clearly state TD is a possible side effect, the issue of informed consent is crucial. Obtaining informed consent for antipsychotics, however, poses difficulty to psychiatrists due to their potential for severe adverse effects and the impaired judgment and potential incompetence of acutely psychotic patients for whom those agents are usually prescribed.[323,375]

Voluntariness, the second component of informed consent, requires the patient to give consent freely, without coercion. The last component, competency, is a legal concept not yet defined in a consistent or clinically instructive manner. It generally refers to the ability to understand and manipulate relevant information in a rational way regarding the informed consent provided. Four components in considering competency include: understanding the information, appreciating its relevance for the person's particular situation, expressing a consistent choice, and rationally manipulating the relevant information in the final decision-making process. Competency is dependent on time and context and varies with the patient's changing status.[376,377] Once a patient is said to be incompetent, a substitute decision maker is appointed to make any treatment choices. This decision maker may be the physician, a guardian, a neutral third party, or the judge.[378] Generally, an involuntarily committed patient is presumed competent unless legally adjudicated otherwise. Additionally both voluntary and involuntary patients have the right to accept or reject proposed treatment with medications.[379] The courts recognize four exceptional situations in which the usual requirements of informed consent do not apply: medical emergencies, waivers, therapeutic privileges and incompetence.[380]

The difference between battery and negligent failure to disclose is outlined in *Lackey v. Bressler*,[381] a combined negligent medical malpractice, assault and battery, breach of contract for the use of antipsychotics which caused the patient to develop TD. The court provided the following explanation of the difference between negligent failure, negligent failure to warn and intentional battery: "Where a medical procedure is completely unauthorized, it constitutes an assault and battery, i.e., trespass to the person....If, however, the procedure is authorized, but the patient claims a failure to disclose the risks involved, the cause of action is bottomed on negligence."

Numerous suits have been brought against nonpsychiatric physicians, psychiatrists, hospitals and manufacturers regarding cases of DIMDs. Pharmaceutical reference guides, package inserts, and regulations of the U.S. Food and Drug Administration are valuable sources in malpractice litigations.[355] Since only legal cases constituting those that have been tried and then appealed by the losing party are published in the legal literature, many that are settled out of court are sealed from disclosure by the settlement agreement. As TD is neither too infrequent nor too insignificant a risk of treatment to avoid disclosure, informative discussions regarding movement disorders should occur as soon as clinically feasible. Failure to detect early signs of TD and to intervene early once it occurs and is diagnosed has been a significant area of malpractice litigation.[324,364] The doctrine of *res ipsa loquitur* ("the thing speaks for itself") does not apply to cases with TD in establishing fault, since TD may occur in the absence of negligence.[355] The following cases demonstrate patient-plaintiff allegations of psychiatrist's failures to properly prescribe and monitor treatment outcomes with neuroleptic agents and make a timely diagnosis of a DIMD.

In *Collins v. Cushner*, a 56-year-old housewife sought treatment for anxiety from a family practitioner. She was diagnosed by the physician with "spastic colon" and prescribed low doses of trifluoperazine for a period of six years. For almost 2.5 years the patient received phone renewals on her antipsychotic without being seen by the defendant physician. She subsequently developed abnormal movements in her arms and hands and the defendant discontinued the antipsychotic for two months, but reinstated it and doubled the dose. Six months later the defendant prescribed benztropine to treat the patient's involuntary movements of the face. In the lawsuit, the plaintiff stated that the defendant continued to prescribe the antipsychotic despite product information warnings stating its use in anxiety and potential for TD in long-term treatment of females in the patient's age group. This case combines the elements of negligence, failure to warn of side effects and failure to monitor. The plaintiff also stated that the anticholinergic, benztropine, further aggravated her condition and the litigation was settled for $125,000.[382]

In another case, *Clites v. Iowa*, the parents of a mentally retarded male at a state residential facility sued the state for negligence and for treatment without adequate informed consent. The patient was institutionalized since age 11 and from the age of 18 to 23, the patient was treated with various neuroleptics for "aggressive behavior" under the auspices of several physicians. The patient received medications for five years before TD was diagnosed of the face and extremities. The trial court noted that the severe aggression and self-destructive behavior justifying the use of antipsychotics argued by the defendant was lacking and that the medications were used inappropriately for the staff's convenience and not for the patient's treatment. In addition, the court cited that the patient was improperly monitored because he was not "regularly visited" by a physician and for a period of three years no physical examinations were conducted. It further cited that staff at the facility "ignored the known risks of uninterrupted use of major tranquilizers," and the medical staff failed to react to the patient's symptoms of TD and change the drug management program accordingly. Also, the court stated that polypharmacy was not warranted in this case nor the use of the particular agents involved. Furthermore, the attending physician not familiar with TD failed to obtain consultation. The trial court also noted that the patient's parents, his legal guardians, "were never informed of the potential side effects of the use, and prolonged use, of major tranquilizers, nor was consent to their use obtained" and thus violated the "standard that requires some form of informed consent prior to the administration of major tranquilizers." The trial court ruled for the plaintiff and awarded $385,165 for future medical expenses and $375,000 for past and future pain and suffering.[383] Two years later the district court's ruling was subsequently upheld in the Iowa Court of Appeals.[384] The judge in the case commented that "although the evidence may have justified a higher award, such is not controlling. The determinative question posed is whether on the record, giving the jury its right to accept or reject whatever portions of the conflicting evidence it chose, the verdict effects substantial justice between the parties."

In *Hedin v. United States*, another case involving TD, the plaintiff was treated with thioridazine and later chlorpromazine as an outpatient following a two month psychiatric hospitalization for alcohol abuse. He continued to take 600 mg of chlorpromazine daily for almost four years before his physicians noted his movement disorder and subsequently discontinued his drug therapy. The movements involved the face, mouth, trunk, and extremities, and the patient stated he had been aware of these movements but that he was not aware that they were due to the medication. The defendant, the U.S. Veterans Administration, admitted that it was negligent in prescribing the neuroleptics in excessive amounts for prolonged periods without proper supervision. The plaintiff who had become functionally disabled due to the TD was awarded damages of nearly $2.2 million.[385]

In *Barclay v. Campbell*,[386] the defendant psychiatrist admitted to not disclosing the risks of TD to a young schizophrenic patient. The court sided with the psychiatrist, and the decision was upheld on appeal, on the basis that he was justified in not disclosing this risk because it was not "medically feasible" to do so and that the patient was not a "reasonable person." This was reversed on appeal to the Texas Supreme Court in 1986 on the grounds that the psychiatrist could not use the therapeutic-privilege exception to the informed-consent disclosure requirement. It was also cited that although the patient's young age posed a small risk for TD, it did not negate the psychiatrist's duty to disclose this movement disorder. At trial the jury found the defendant had not informed the patient of the risk of TD; however, the patient would have consented to the treatment anyway. Subsequently the case was settled out of court.[387]

In the case *Ronald Bloom v. Will Creed, M.D.*, Dr. Bloom allegedly called in a prescription for an antipsychotic medication while covering for a colleague.[388] Dr. Bloom had never met nor treated Mr. Creed, and Mr. Creed did not know Dr. Bloom. The patient contended that the physician failed to warn him of side effects or to monitor his condition while using antipsychotic medication. The Supreme Court of Mississippi ruled 7-2 in favor of Dr. Bloom. Since many physicians provide coverage for one another frequently without access to full medical records, this case suggests a duty to provide informed consent when a prescription is filled for a patient treated by a colleague prescriber.

Psychiatrists and the members of the mental health treatment team have many means and opportunities to provide information about neuroleptic agents and TD to patients. Medication counseling can be provided by pharmacists as well as psychiatrists as a matter of sound clinical practice.[389] Additionally, pharmacists may provide a warning label regarding involuntary movements on prescription bottles as well as instructions to the patient on how to recognize movement disorders and report such to the psychiatrist.[390] The Task Force Report of the American Psychiatric Association on TD makes the following recommendations for the prevention and management of TD: to review the reasons why neuroleptics are chosen and consider alternative treatments if available; to educate patients and family members regarding the benefits and risks and obtain informed consent for long-term treatment, with documentation provided in the medical record; to establish objective evidence of the benefit of antipsychotic medications, and review it periodically, at least every three to six months, in order to assess ongoing need and benefit; to administer the lowest effective dosage for chronic management; to exercise particular caution with children, elderly patients and those with affective disorders; to examine patients regularly for early signs of dyskinesia and note such in the medical record; to consider alternative

neurologic diagnosis if dyskinesia does occur; to reevaluate the indications for continued neuroleptic treatment and obtain informed consent from patients regarding continuing or discontinuing antipsychotic therapy if presumptive TD is present; to attempt to decrease the dosage if a neuroleptic is continued; to consider discontinuing the neuroleptic or switching to an atypical neuroleptic if dyskinesia worsens; to utilize more benign agents first such as benzodiazepines, or vitamin E, if treatment for TD is indicated and to keep abreast of new treatment developments; to consider obtaining a second opinion if movement disorder is severe or disabling.[261]

The legal aspects of psychiatric practice continue to evolve dramatically with changes observed in the healthcare system and vary from state to state. Obtaining informed consent, disclosing adverse effects, and proper management of such adverse effects along with documentation are all activities the clinician needs to undertake while treating patients with neuroleptic agents.

26.15 Conclusion

Movement disorders occur as a heterogeneous group of conditions in which abnormalities in the form and velocity of movements of the body predominate. DIMDs have gradually emerged as a major problem in clinical psychiatry and medicine. A number of various types of movement disorders have been identified and associated with different dopamine receptor blockers, namely DRBAs. The clinical spectrum of these movement disorders ranges from slight embarrassment or discomfort to life-threatening conditions such as neuroleptic malignant syndrome and other potentially detrimental disorders. DIMDs are among the most common iatrogenic disorders to result in malpractice suits and continue to remain among the most distressing of all drug-induced disorders. The potential for medications to induce movement disorders has to be balanced against their benefits. Simple measures such as ensuring that the lowest effective dose of medication is used, that dosages are titrated gradually, that the potential for drug interactions is considered, and that unnecessary polypharmacy is avoided may reduce the risk of DIMDs. It is imperative for clinicians to continuously monitor for the emergence of DIMDs and to treat them, so that patients are not distressed or uncomfortable, and to facilitate medication adherence with proper therapy management.

The risk of DIMDs is observed with both typical and atypical neuroleptics. Some of the initial superiority of atypical neuroleptics compared with conventional neuroleptics may be biased by the use of inappropriately high doses of the latter agents. Now as the doses of atypical antipsychotics used in clinical practice are increasing, the EPS advantage of these agents narrows with the continuous frequent use of these higher doses. Thus DIMDs remain a significant concern for patients despite the introduction of atypical antipsychotic drugs.

Endnotes

1. Diagnostic and Statistical Manual of Mental Disorders, Fourth Edition, Text Revision (DSM-IV-TR). Washington, DC: American Psychiatric Association; 2000.

2. Rodnitzky RL: Drug-induced movement disorders. Clin Neuropharmacol. 2002; 25:142-152.

3. Anouti A, Koller WC: Diagnostic testing in movement disorders. Neurologic Clinics. 1996;14:169-182.

4. Sachdev PS: Neuroleptic-induced movement disorders: an overview. Psychiatr Clin North Am. 2005;28:255-274.

5. Casey DE: Neuroleptic drug induced extrapyramidal syndromes and tardive dyskinesia. Schizophr Res. 1991;4:109-120 .

6. Cunningham Owens DG, Johnstone EC: Spontaneous involuntary disorders of movement. Arch Gen Psychiat. 1982;39:452-461.

7. Ebadi M, Srinivasan SK: Pathogenesis, prevention, and treatment of neuroleptic-induced movement disorders. Pharmacol Rev. 1995;47:575-604.

8. Janno S, Holi M, Tuisku K, Wahlbeck K: Prevalence of neuroleptic-induced movement disorders in chronic schizophrenia inpatients. Am J Psychiatry. 2004;161:160-163.

9. Anonymous: The scourge of EPS: have atypical antipsychotics solved the problem? J Clin Psychiatry. 2000;61:955-961.

10. Gerlach J: The continuing problem of extrapyramidal symptoms: strategies for avoidance and effective treatment. J Clin Psychiatry. 1999;60(supplement 23):20-24.

11. Conley RR. Risperidone side effects. J Clin Psychiatry. 2000;61(supplement 8):20-23.

12. de Leon J: The effect of atypical versus typical antipsychotics on tardive dyskinesia: a naturalistic study. Eur Arch Psychiatry Clin Neurosci. 2007;257:169-172.

13. Haddad PM, Dursun SM: Neurological complications of psychiatric drugs: clinical features and management. Human Psychopharmacol. 2008;23:15-26.

14. Correll CU, Leucht S, Kane JM: Lower risk for tardive dyskinesia associated with second-generation antipsychtoics: a systematic review of 1-year studies. Am J Psychiatry. 2004:161:414-425.

15. Leucht S, Wahlbeck K, Hamann J, Kissling W: New generation antipsychtoics versus low-potency conventional antipsychtoics: a systematic review and meta-analysis. Lancet. 2003:361:1581-1589.

16. Caroff SN, Mann SC, Campbell EC, Sullivan KA: Movement disorders associated with atypical antipsychotic drugs. J Clin Psychiatry. 2002:63(supplement 4):12-19.

17. Beasley CM, Tollefson GD, Tran PV: Safety of olanzapine. J Clin Psychiatry. 1997;58(supplement 10):13-17.

18. Schillevoort I, de Boer A, Herings RMC, Ross RAC, Jansen PAF, Leufkens HGM: Risk of extrapyramidal syndromes with haloperidol, risperidone, or olanzapine. Ann Pharmacother. 2001;35:1517-1522.

19. Leucht S, Corves C, Arbter D, Engel RR, Li C, Davis JM: Second-generation versus first-generation antipsychotic drugs for schizophrenia: a meta-analysis. The Lancet. 2009;373:31-41.

20. Casey DE: Side effect profiles of new antipsychotic agents. J Clin Psychiatry. 1996:57 (suppl 11):40-45.

21. Ritsner M, Bibel A, Perelroyzen B, Kurs R, Jabarin M, et al: Quality of life outcomes of resperidone, olanzapine, and typical antipsychotics among schizophrenia patients treated in routine clinical practice. J Clin Psychopharmacol. 2004;24:582-591.

22. Mortimer AM, Al-Abib, A.O.A: Quality of life in schizophrenia on conventional versus atypical antipsychotic medication: a comparative cross-sectional study. Int J Soc Psychiatry. 2007;53:99-107.

23. Kilian R, Dietrich S, Toumi M, Angermeyer MC: Quality of life in persons with schizophrenia in outpatient treatment with first-of second-generation antipsychotics. Acta Psychiatr Scand. 2004;110:108-118.

24. Lieberman JA, Stroup TS, McEvoy JP, et al: Effectiveness of antipsychotic drugs in patients with chronic schizophrenia. N Engl J Med. 2005; 353:1209-1223.

25. Miller DD, Caroff SN, Davis SM, et al for the Clinical Antipsychotic Trials of Intervention Effectiveness (CATIE) Investigators: Extrapyramidal side effects of antipsychotics in a randomized trial. Br J Psychiatry. 2008;193:279-288.

26. Ciranni MA, Kearney TE, Olson KR: Comparing acute toxicity of first-and second-generation antipsychotic drugs: a 10-year, retrospective cohort study. J Clin Psychiatry. 2009;70:122-129.

27. Kennedy C, Hunter C, Davidson A: Metoclopramide, an increasingly recognized cause of tardive dyskinesia. J Clin Pharamcol. 2008;48:379-384.

28. Claxton KL, Chen JJ, Swope DM: Drug-induced movement disorders. Journal of Pharmacy Practice. 2007;20:415-429.

29. Detweiler MB, Kalafat N, Kim KY: Drug-induced movement disorders in older adults: an overview for clinical practioners. Consult Pharm. 2007;22:149-165.

30. Tarsy D: Chapter 17: Miscellaneous Drug-induced Movement Disorders. In: Drug Induced Movement Disorders. Edited by Factor, Lang and Weiner. 2nd edition. Blackwell-Futura Publishing. 2005;430-441.

31. Charness ME, Morady F, Scheinman MM: Frequent neurologic toxicity associated with amiodarone therapy. Neurology. 1994;34:669-671.

32. Palakurthy, PR, Iyer V, Meckler RJ: Unusual neurotoxicity associated with amiodarone therapy. Arch Intern Med. 1987;147:881-884.

33. Malone RP, Harvey JA: Abnormal movements with the addition of clindamycin to risperidone in a girl with autism. J Child Adol Pychop. 2008;18:221-222.

34. Stotter Cuddy ML: The effects of drugs on thermoregulation. AACN Clinical Issues: Advanced Practice in Acute and Critical Care. 2004;15:238-253.

35. Vincent FM: The neuropsychiatric complications of corticosteroid therapy. Compr Ther. 1995;21:524-528.

36. Vorsanger GJ, Roberts JT. Midazolam-induced athetoid movements of the lower extremities during epidural anesthesia reversed by physostigmine. J Clin Anesth. 1993;5:494-496.

37. Davis TL, Charles PD, Burns S: Clonazepam-sensitive intermittent dystonic tremor. South Med J. 1995;88:1069-1071.

38. Lorberboym M, Treves TA, Melamed E, et al: [123I]-FP/CIT SPECT imaging for distinguishing drug-induced parkinsonism from Parkinson's disease. Mov Disord. 2006;21:510-514.

39. Blair DT, Dauner A: Nonneuroleptic etiologies of extrapyramidal symptoms. Clin Nurse Spec. 1993;7:225-231.

40. Caley CF: Extrapyramidal reactions and the selective serotonin-reuptake inhibitors. Ann Pharmacother. 1997;31:1481-1489.

41. Leo RJ: Movement disorders associated with the serotonin selective reuptake inhibitors. J Clin Psychiatry. 1996;57:449-454.

42. Najib, J: Tardive dyskinesia: a review and current treatment options. Am J Ther. 1999;6:51-60.

43. Lee P, Sykora K, Gill SS, Mamdani M, et al: Antipsychotic medications and drug-induced movement disorders other than parkinsonism: a population-based cohort study in older adults. J Am Geriatr Soc. 2005;53:1374-1379.

44. McConville BJ, Sorter MT: Treatment challenges and safety considerations for antipsychotic use in children and adolescents with psychoses. J Clin Psychiatry. 2004; 65(Suppl 6):20-29.

45. Kane JM: Tardive dyskinesia rates with atypical antipsychotics in adults: prevalence and incidence. J Clin Psychiatry. 2004;(suppl 9):16-20.

46. Luft B, Berent E: Prevalence of extrapyramidal side effects in patients receiving depot antipsychotic medication. Euro Psychiat. [Abstract] 2009;24 (supple 1): S1011.

47. Diehl A, Reinhard I, Schmitt A, Mann K: Does the degree of smoking effect the severity of tardive dyskinesia? A longitudinal clinical trial. Euro Psychiat. 2009;24:33-40.

48. Chouinard G, Annable L, Ross-Chouinard A, Mercier P: A 5-year prospective longitudinal study of tardive dyskinesia: factors predicting appearance of new cases. J Clin Psychopharmacol. 1988;8(suppl):S21-S26.

49. Youssef HA, Waddington JL: Morbidity and mortality in tardive dyskinesia: associations in chronic schizophrenia. Acta Psychiatr Scand. 1987;75:74-77.

50. Chouinard G, Chouinard V: Atypical antipsychotics: CATIE study, drug-induced movement disorder and resulting iatrogenic psychiatric-like symptoms, supersensitivity rebound psychosis and withdrawal discontinuation syndromes. Psychother Psychosom. 2008;77:69-77.

51. Hansen L: A critical review of akathisia, and its possible association with suicidal behaviour. Hum Psychopharmacol. 2001;15:139-141.

52. Hummer MF, Fleischhacker WW: Compliance and outcome in patients treated with antipsychotics: the impact of extrapyramidal syndromes. CNS Drugs. 1996;5:13-20.

53. Shriqui CL, Bradwejn J, Jones BD: Tardive dyskinesia: legal and preventive aspects. Can J Psychiatry. 1990;35:576-580.

54. Slovenko R: Update on legal issues associated with tardive dyskinesia. J Clin Psychiatry. 2000;61;45-57.

55. Gasser T: Advances in the genetics of movement disorders: implications for molecular diagnosis. Curr Opin Neruol. 1997;244:341-348.

56. Casey D: Pathophysiology of antipsychotic drug-induced movement disorders. J Clin Psychiatry. 2004;65(suppl 9):25-28.

57. de Leon J, Susce MT, Pan RM, et al: The CYP2D6 poor metabolizer phenotype may be associated with risperidone adverse drug reactions and discontinuation. J Clin Psychiatry. 2005;66:15-27.

58. Vandel P, Bonin B, Vandel S, Sechter D, et al: CYP 2D6 phenotype hypothesis of antidepressant extrapyramidal side-effects. Medical Hypotheses 1996;47:439-442.

59. Olfson M, Blanco C, Liu L, et al: National trends in the outpatient treatment of children and adolescents with antipsychotic drugs. Arch Gen Psychiatry. 2006; 63:679-685.

60. Cooper WO, Hickson GB, Fuchs C, Arbogast PG, Ray WA: New users of antipsychotic medications among children enrolled in TennCare. Arch Pediatr Adolesc Med. 2004;158:753-759.

61. Vitello B, Jensen MD: Medication development and testing in children and adolescents. Arch Gen Psychiatry. 1997;54:871-876.

62. Stigler KA, Potenza NM, McDougle CJ: Tolerability profile of atypical antipsychotics in children and adolescents. Pediatr Drugs. 2001;3:927-942.

63. McConville BJ, Sorter MT: Treatment challenges and safety considerations for antipsychotic use in children and adolescents with psychoses. J Clin Psychiatry. 2004;65:20-29.

64. Gebhardt S, Hartling F, Hanke M, Mittendor M, Theisen FM, et al: Prevalence of movement disorders in adolescent patients with schizophrenia and in relationship to predominantly atypical antipsychotic treatment. Eur Child Adolesc Psychiatry. 2006;15:371-382.

65. Newcomer JW: Second-generation (atypical) antipsychotics and metabolic effects: a comprehensive literature review. CNS Drugs. 2005;19(Suppl 1):1-93.

66. Fedorowicz VJ: Metabolic side effects of atypical antipsychotics in children: a literature review. J Psychopharmacol. 2005;19:533-550.

67. Patel J, Buckley PF, Woolson S et al: Metabolic profiles of second-generation antipsychotics in early psychosis: findings from the CAFE study. Schizophr Res. 2009;111:9-16.

68. Pappagallo M, Silva R: The effect of atypical antipsychotic agents on prolactin levels in children and adolescents. J Child Adolesc Psychopharmacol. 2004;14:359-371.

69. Laita P, Cifuentes A, Doll A, Llorente C, Cortes I, et al: Antipsychotic-related abnormal involuntary movements and metabolic and endocrine side effects in children and adolescents. J Child Adolesc Psychopharmacol. 2007;17:487-501.

70. Gokhale SG, Panchakshari MB. Maternal medication causing drug dystonia in a newborn: placental transfer of drugs. J Matern-Fetal Neo Med. 2004;16:215-217.

71. Cancelli, I, Beltrame M, Gigli GL et al: Drugs with anticholinergic properties: cognitive and neuropsychiatric-side effects in elderly patients. Neurol Sci. 2009;30:87-92.

72. Ray WA, Meredith S, Thapa PB, et al: Antipsychotics and the risk of sudden cardiac death. Arch Gen Psychiatry. 2001;58:1161-1167.

73. Strauss SM, Bleumink GS, Dieleman JP, et al: Antipsychotics and the risk of sudden cardiac death. Arch Intern Med. 2004;164:1293-1297.

74. Ray WA, Chung CP, Murray KT, et al: Antipsychotics and the risk of sudden cardiac death. N Engl J Med. 2009;360:225-235.

75. Yan J: FDA Extends Black-Box Warning to All Antipsychotics. *Psychiatry News* July 18, 2008;43:1. http://psychnews.psychiatryonline.org.

76. Gill SS, Bronskill SE, Normand SLT, et al: Antipsychotic drug use and mortality in older adults with dementia. Ann Intern Med. 2007;146:775-786.

77. Schneeweiss S, Setoguchi S, Brookhart A, et al: Risk of death associated with the use of conventional versus atypical antipsychotic drugs among elderly patients. CMAJ. 2007;176:627-632.

78. Rodnitzky RL: Drug-induced movement disorders. Clin Neuropharmacol. 2002;25:142-152.

79. Casey DE: Neuroleptic-induced acute extrapyramidal syndromes and tardive dyskinesia. Pscyhiatr Clin North Am. 1993;16:589-610.

80. Tarsy D: Neuroleptic-induced extrapyramidal reactions: classification, description, and diagnosis. Clin Neuropharmacol. 1983;6(suppl):S9-S26.

81. Russell SA, Hennes HM, Herson KJ, et al: Upper airway compromise in acute chlorpromazine ingestion. Am J Emerg Med. 1996;14:467-468.

82. Van Putten T: Why do schizophrenic patients refuse to take their drugs? Arch Gen Psychiatry. 1974;31:67-72.

83. Sheehy MP, Marsden CD: Writer's cramp -- a focal dystonia. Brain. 1982;105:461-480.

84. Grebb JA: Medication-induced movement disorders. In: Kaplan HI, Sadock BJ, eds. Comprehensive Textbook of Psychiatry. 6th ed. Baltimore: Williams & Wilkins; 1995:1909-1915.

85. Suzuki T, Matsuzuka H: Drug-induced Pisa syndrome (pleurothotonus): epidemiology and management. CNS Drugs 2002; 16:165–174.

86. Ziegenbein M, Schomerus G, Kropp S: Ziprasidone-induced Pisa Syndrome after clozapine treatment. J Neuropsychiatrty Clin Neurosci. 2003;15:458-459.

87. Nishimura, K, Mikami Y, Tsuchibuchi S, Horikawa N: Pisa syndrome resolved after switching to olanzapine. J Neuropsychiatry Clin Neurosci. 2007;19:202-203.

88. Boyer WF, Bakalar NH, Lake CR: Anticholinergic prophylaixis of acute haloperidol-induced acute dystonic reactions. J Clin Psychopharmacol. 1987;7:164-166.

89. Ahmed S, Chengappa KNR, Naidu VR, Baker RW, Parepally H, Schooler NR: Clozapine withdrawal-emergent dystonias and dyskinesias: a case series. J Clin Psychiatry. 1998;59:472-477.

90. Keepers GA, Clappison VJ, Casey DE: Initial anticholinergic prophylaxis for neuroleptic-induced extrapyramidal syndromes. Arch Gen Psychiatry. 1983;40:1113-1117.

91. Keepers GA, Casey DE: Clinical management of acute neuroleptic-induced extrapyramidal syndromes. In: Current Psychiatric Therapies, Masserman JH, ed. New York, Grune & Stratton, 1986:139-157.

92. Van Kammen DP, Marder SR: Dopamine receptor antagonists. In: Kaplan HI, Sadock BJ eds. Comprehensive Textbook of Psychiatry, 6th ed. Baltimore: Williams & Wilkins; 1995:1988-2022.

93. Daras M, Koppel BS, Atos-Radzion E: Cocaine-induced choreoathetoid movements ("crack dancing"). Neurology. 1994;44:751-752.

94. Weiner WJ, Rabinstein A, Levin B, Weiner C, Shulman LML Cocaine-induced persistent dyskinesias. Neurology. 2001;56:964-965.

95. Paulson GW, Reider CR: Movement disorders in childhood. In: Watts RL, Koller WC, eds. Movement Disorders - neurologic principles and practice. New York: McGraw Hill 1997:661-672.

96. Incecik F, Onlen Y, Ozer C, et al: Metoclopramide induced acute dystonic reaction: two case reports. Marmara Medical Journal. 2008;21:159-161.

97. Van der Kleij FGH, de Vries PAM, Stassen PM, et al: Acute dystonia due to metoclopramide: increased risk in AIDS (letter). Arch Intern Med. 2002;162:358-359.

98. Freed E: Alcohol-triggered neuroleptic induced tremor, rigidity and dystonia. Med J Aust. 1981;2:44-45.

99. Peiris RS, Peckler BF: Cimetidine-induced dystonic reaction. J Emerg Med. 2001;21:27-29.

100. Gerber PE, Lynd LD: Selective serotonin-reuptake inhibitor-induced movement disorders. Ann Pharmacother. 1998;32:692-698.

101. Tesler-Mabe CS: Acute dystonic reaction with trazodone. Can J Psychiat. 1998;43:1053. (letter).

102. Detweiler MB, Harpold GJ: Bupropion-induced acute dystonia. Ann Pharmacother. 2002;36:251-254.

103. Coulter DM, Pillans PI: Fluoxetine and extrapyramidal side effects. Am J Psychiatry. 1995;152:122-125.

104. Garcia de Yebenes J, Sanchez Pernaute R, Tabernero C: Symptomatic dystonias. In: Watts RL, Koller WC, eds. Movement Disorders-neurologic principles and practice. New York: McGraw Hill 1997:455-475.

105. Ganzini L, Casey D, Hoffman W, McCall A: Prevalence of metoclopramide-induced tardive dyskinesia and acute extrapyramidal movement disorders. Arch Intern Med. 1993;153:1469-1475.

106. Detweiler MB, Harpold GJ: Bupropion-induced acute dystonia. Ann Pharmacother. 2002;36:251-254.

107. Scully C, Bagan JV: Adverse drug reactions in the orofacial region. Crit Rev Oral Biol Med. 2004;15:221-239.

108. Danks DM: Copper-induced dystonia secondary to cholestatic liver disease. Lancet. 1990;335:410.

109. Ross: Methanol induced dystonia. Can J Neurol Sci. 1990;97:155-162.

110. Kumar A: Movement disorders in the tropics. Parkinsonism & Related Disorders. 2002;9:69-75.

111. Quinn NP: Dystonia in epidemic ergotism. Neurology. 1983;33:1267.

112. Spencer PS, Ludolph AC, Kisby GE: Neurologic diseases associated with use of plant components with toxic potential. Environ Res. 1993;62:106-113.

113. Ballerini M, Bellini S, Niccolai C, Pieroni V, Ferrara M: Neuroleptic-induced dystonia: incidence and risk factors. Eur Psychiatry. 2002;17:366-368.

114. Spina E, Sturiale V, Valvo S, et al: Prevalence of acute dystonic reactions associated with neuroleptic treatment with and without anticholinergic prophylaxis. Int Clin Psychopharmacol. 1993;8:21-24.

115. Fines RE, Brady WJ, DeBehnke DJ: Cocaine-associated dystonic reaction. Am J Emerg Med. 1997;15:513-515.

116. Hendrickson RG, Morocco AP, Greenberg MI: Acute dystonic reactions to "street Xanax". N Engl J Med. 2002;346:1753.

117. Raja M: Managing antipsychotic-induced acute and tardive dystonia. Drug Safety Concept. 1998;19: 57-72.

118. American Psychiatric Assocation: Practice guideline for the treatment of patients with schizophrenia. Am J Psychiatry. 1997;154(suppl 4):1-63.

119. World Health Organization Heads of Centres Collaborating in WHO co-ordinated studies on biological aspects of mental illness. Prophylactic use of anticholinergics in patients on long-term neurolpetic treatment. Br J Psychiatry. 1990;156:412.

120. Chapron DJ: Chapter 10: Adverse effects of medications on gait and mobility in the elderly. In: Evaluation and Management of Gait Disorders. Edited by Spivak. Taylor & Francis, Inc.,New York 1995: 223-242.

121. Pearson NL: A grinding issue: drug-induced bruxism. CPJ/RPC. 2008;141:300-301.

122. Ranjan S, Chandra PS, Prabhu S: Antidepressant-induced bruxism: need for buspirone? International Journal of Neuropsychopharmacoloy. 2006;9:485-487.

123. Jackson N, Doherty J, Coulter S. Neuropsychiatric complications of commonly used palliative care drugs. Postgrad Med J. 2008; 84:121-126.

124. Velamoor VR, Norman RM, Caroff SN et al: Progression of symptoms in neuroleptic malignant syndrome. J Nerv Ment Dis 1994;182:168-173.

125. Dickey W: The neuroleptic malignant syndrome. Prog Nuerobiol. 1991;36:425-436.

126. Kornhuber J, Weller M: Neuroleptic malignant syndrome. Curr Opin Neurol. 1994;7:353-357.

127. Najib, J: Neuroleptic malignant syndrome: a case report and review of treatment. Hosp Pharm. 1997;32:512-518.

128. Caroff SN, Mann SC, Keck PE Jr, et al: Residual catatonic state following neuroleptic malignant syndrome. J Clin Psychopharmacol. 2000;20:257-259.

129. NMS case reports associated with SGAs. Available at: www.currentpsychiatry.com/pdf/0608CP_Article5-upt1.pdf.

130. Accessed August 13, 2009.

131. Ananth J, Parameswaran S, Gunatilake S, et al: Neruoleptic malignant syndrome and atypical antipsychotic drugs. J Clin Psychiatry. 2004;65:464-470.

132. White DAC, Robins AH: Catatonia: harbinger of the neuroleptic malignant syndrome. Brit J Psychiatr. 1991;158:419-421.

133. Caroff SN, Mann SC: Neuroleptic malignant syndrome. Psychopharmac Bull. 1988;24:25-29.

134. Shalev A, Munitz H: The neuroleptic malignant syndrome: agent and host interaction. Acta Psychiat Scand. 1986;73:337-347.

135. Rosebush P, Stewart TD, Glenberg AJ: Twenty neuroleptic challenges after neuroleptic malignant syndrome in 15 patients. J Clin Psychiatry. 1989;50:295-298.

136. Slack T, Stoudemire A: Reinstitution of neuroleptic treatment with molindone in a patient with a history of neuroleptic malignant syndrome. Gen Hops Psychiat. 1989;11:365-367.

137. Evans CE, Sebastian J: Serotonin syndrome. Emerg Med J. 2007;24:e20Mason PJ, Morris VA, Balcezak TJ: Serotonin syndrome: presentation of 2 cases and review of the literature. Med (Baltimore). 2000;79:201-209.

138. Phan H, Casavant MJ, Crockett S, et al: Serotonin syndrome following a single 50 mg dose of sertraline in a child. Clin Toxicol. 2008;46:845-849.

139. Isenberg D, Wong SC, Curtis JA: Serotonin syndrome triggered by a single dose of suboxone. Am J Emerg Med. 2008;26:840.

140. Boyer EW, Shannon M: The serotonin syndrome. N Engl J Med. 2005;352:112-1120.

141. US Food and Drug Administration. Information for healthcare professionals. Selective serotonin reuptake inhibitors (SSRIs), selective serotonin-norepinephrine reuptake inhibitors (SNRIs), 5-hydroxytryptamine receptor agonists (triptans). July 19, 2006. Available at: www.fda.gov/Drugs/DrugSafety/PostmarketDrugSafetyInformationforPatientsandProviders/DrugSafetyInformationforHeathcareProfessionals/ucm085845.htm. Accessed April 16, 2012.

142. US Food and Drug Administration. FDA public health advisory. Combined use of 5-hydroxytryptamine receptor agonists (triptans), selective serotonin reuptake inhibitors (SSRIs) or selective serotonin/norepinephrine reuptake inhibitors (SNRIs) may result in life-threatening serotonin syndrome. November 24, 2006. Available at: www.fda.gov/Drugs/DrugSafety/PostmarketDrugSafetyInformationforPatientsandProviders/DrugSafetyInformationforHeathcareProfessionals/PublicHealthAdvisories/ucm124349.htm. Accessed April 16, 2012.

143. Sachdev P: The epidemiology of Drug-Induced Akathisia: Part 1. Acute akathisia. Schizophrenia Bull. 1995;21(3):431-449.

144. Braude WM, Barnes TRE, Gore S: Clinical characteristics of akathisia: A systematic investigation of acute psychiatric inpatient admissions. Brit J Psychiat. 1983;143:139-150.

145. Chung WSD, Chiu HFK: Drug-induced akathisia revisited. Brit J Clin Pract. 1996;50:270-278.

146. Bratti IM, Kane JM, Marder SR. Chronic restlessness with antipsychotics. Am J Psychiatry. 2007; 164:1648-1654.

147. Raskin DE: Akathisia: a side effect to be remembered. Am J Psychiatry. 1972:129:345 347.

148. Gupta S: Media or fluoxetine induced akathisia {letter}? Am J Psychiatry. 1993;150:532.

149. Hamilton MS, Opler LA: Akathisia, suicidality, and fluoxetine. J Clin Psychiatry. 1992;53:401- 406.

150. Kalda R: Media or fluoxetine induced akathisia {letter}? Am J Psychiatry. 1993;150:531-532.

151. Hansen L, Kingdom D. Akathisia as a risk factor for suicide. Br J Psychiatry. 2006; 188:192.

152. Atbasoglu EC, Schultz SK, Andreasen NC: The relationship of akathisia with suicidality and depersonalization among patients with schizophrenia. J Neuropsychiatry Clin Neurosci. 2001;13:336-341.

153. Iqbal N, Lambert T, Massand P. Akathisia: problem of history or concern of today. CNS Spectr. 2007;12(9 Suppl 14):1-13.

154. Kane JM, Fleischhacker WW, Hansen L et al. Akathisia: an updated review focusing on second-generation antipsychotics. J Clin Psychiatry. 2009;70:627-643.

155. Bagnall AM, Jones L, Ginnelly L, et al: A systematic review of atypical antipsychotic drugs in schizophrenia. Health Technol Assess. 2003; 6:1-193.

156. Geddes J, Freemantle N, Harrison P, et al: Atypical antipsychotics in the treatment of schizophrenia: systematic overview and meta-regression analysis. Brit Med J. 2000; 321:1371-2137.

157. Dossenbach M, Treuer T, Kryzhanovskaya L, et al: Olanzapine versus chlorpromazine in the treatment of schizophrenia: a pooled analysis of four 6-week, randomized, open-label studies in the Middle East and North Africa. J Clin Psychopharmacol. 2007; 27:329-337.

158. Miller CH, Mohr F, Umbricht D, Woerner M, Fleischhacker WW, Lieberman JA: The prevalence of acute extrapyramidal signs and symptoms in patients treated with clozapine, risperidone, and conventional antipsychotics. J Clin Psychiatry. 1998;59:69-75.

159. Kumar R, Sachdev PS: Akathisia and second-generation antipsychotic drugs. Curr Opin Psychiatry. 2009;22:293-299.

160. Sahoo S, Ameen S. Acute nocturnal akathisia induced by clozapine. J Clin Psychopharmacol. 2007; 27:205.

161. Oral ET, Altinbas K, Demirkiran S. Sudden akathisia after a ziprasidone dose reduction. Am J Psychiatry. 2006; 163:546.

162. Cutler AJ, Kalali AH, Weiden PJ, et al: Four-week, double-blind, placebo- and ziprasidone-controlled trial of iloperidone in patients with acute exacerbations of schizophrenia. J Clin Psychopharmacol. 2008; 28:S20-S28.

163. Nasrallah HA, Brecher M, Paulsson B. Placebo-level incidence of extrapyramidal symptoms (EPS) with quetiapine in controlled studies of patients with bipolar mania. Bipolar Disord. 2006; 8:467-474.

164. Cortese L, Caligiuri MP, Williams R, et al: Reduction in neuroleptic-induced movement disorders after a switch to quetiapine in patients with schizophrenia. J Clin Psychopharmacol. 2008; 28:69-73.

165. Catalano G, Grace JW, Catalano MC, et al: Acute akathisia associated with quetiapine use. Psychosomatics. 2005;46:291-301.

166. Berman RM, Marcus RN, Swanink R, et al:The efficacy and safety of aripiprazole as adjunctive therapy in major depressive disorder: a multicenter, randomized, double-blind, placebo-controlled study. J Clin Psychiatry. 2007; 68:843-853.

167. Kemp DE, Gilmer WS, Fleck J, et al: Aripiprazole augmentation in treatment resistant bipolar depression: early response and development of akathisia. Prog Neuropsychopharmacol Biol Psychiatry. 2007; 31:574-577.

168. Walker L: Sertraline-induced akathisia and dystonia misinterpreted as a panic attack. Psychiatr Serv. 2002;53:1477-1478.

169. Baldassano CF, Truman CJ, Nierenberg A, Ghaemi SN, Sachs GS: Akathisia: a review and case report following paroxetine treatment. Compr Psychiatry. 1996;37:122-124.

170. Settle EC: Akathisia and sertraline. J Clin Psychiatry. 1993;54:321.

171. Hansen L, Wilkinson DG: Drug induced akathisia, suicidal ideation and its treatment in the elderly. Int J Geriatr Psychiatry. 2001;16:231-232.

172. Hansen L: Fluoxetine dose-increment related akathisia in depression: implications for clinical care, recognition and management of selective serotonin reuptake inhibitor-induced akathisia. J Psychopharmacol. 2003;17:451-452.

173. Opler LA: Akathisia and suicide. Am J Psychiatry. 1991;148:1259.

174. Wirshing WC, Van Putten, Rosenberg J, et al: Fluoxetine, akathisia, and suicidality: Is there a causal connection?. Arch Gen Psychiatry. 1992;49:580-581.

175. Koliscak LP, Makela EH: Selective serotonin reuptake inhibitor-induced akathisia. J Am Pharm Assoc. 2009;49:e28-e38.

176. Allen JC, Gralla R, Reilly L et al: Metoclopramide: Dose related toxicity and preliminary antiemetic studies in children receiving cancer chemotherapy. J Clin Oncol. 1985;3:1136.

177. Bui NB, Marit G, Albin H, et al: High dose metoclopramide during cancer chemotherapy: Phase II study in 80 consecutive patients. Bulletin du Cancer. 1982;69:330-335.

178. Graham Pole J, Weare J, Engel S, et al: Antiemetics in children receiving chemotherapy: a double blind prospective randomized study comparing metoclopramide with chlorpromazine. J Clin Oncol. 1986;4:1110-1113.

179. Miller LG, Jankovic J: Metoclopramide induced movement disorders: Clinical findings with a review of the literature. Arch Intern Med. 1989;149:2486 2492.

180. Richards PD, Flaum MA, Bateman M: The anti emetic efficacy of secobarbital and chlorpromazine compared to metoclopramide, diphenhydramine, and dexamethasone. Cancer. 1986;58:959 962.

181. Moos DD, Hansen DJ: Metoclopramide and extrapyramdial symptoms: a case report. J Peri Anesthesia Nurs. 2008;23:292-299.

182. Jungmann E, Schoffling K: Akathisia and metoclopramide. Lancet. 1982;2:221.

183. Zubenko GS, Cohen BM, Lipinski JF,Jr: Antidepressant-related akathisia. J Clin Psychopharmacol. 1987;7:254-257.

184. Pohl R, Yeragani VK, Balon R, et al: The jitteriness syndrome in panic disorder patients with antidepressants. J Clin Psychiatry. 1988;49:100-104.

185. Zitrin, CM, Klein DF, Woerner MG: Behavior therapy, supportive psychotherapy, imipramine and phobias. Arch Gen Psychiatry. 1978;35:307-316.

186. Barton JL: Amoxapine-induced agitation among bipolar depressed patients (letter). Am J Psychiatry. 1982;139:87.

187. Hullet FJ, Levy AB: Amoxapine-induced akathisia. (letter) Am J Psychiatry. 1983;140(6):820.

188. Ross DR, Walker JL, Patterson J: Akathisia induced by amoxapine. Am J Psychiatry. 1983;140:115-116.

189. Shen WW: Alcohol, amoxapine, and akathisia. Biol Psychiat. 1984;19:929-930.

190. Gulsun M, Doruk A. Mirtazapine-induced akathisia. J Clin Psychopharmacol. 2008;28:467.

191. Barnes TRE, Braude WM, Hill DJ: Acute akathisia after oral droperidol and metoclopramide preoperative medication. Lancet. 1982;2:48-49.

192. Bernick C: Methysergide-induced akathisia. Clin Neuropharmacol. 1988;11:87-89.

193. Calmels JP, Sorbette F, Montastruc JL, et al: Iatrogenic hyperkinetic syndrome caused by an antihistaminic. (letter) Nouvelle Presse Medicale. 1982;11(30):2296-2297.

194. Patterson, JF: Akathisia associated with buspirone. J Clin Psychopharmacol. 1988;8:296-297.

195. Ritchie EC, Bridenbaugh RH, Jabbari B: Acute generalized myoclonus following buspirone administration. J Clin Psychiatry. 1988;49:242-243.

196. Blaisdell GD: Akathisia a comprehensive review and treatment summary. Pharmacopsychiatry. 1994;27:139-146.

197. Markkula J, Helenius H, Lauerma H: On the relationship of atypical and low-dose conventional antipsychotics with akathisia in a clinical patient population. Nord J Psychiatry. 2007;61:152.157.

198. Gao K, Kemp DE, Ganocy SJ, et al: Antipsychotic-induced extrapyramidal side effects in bipolar disorder and schizophrenia: a systematic review. J Clin Psychopharmacol. 2008; 28:203-209.

199. Bauer M, Hellweg R, Baumgartner A: Fluoxetine-induced akathisia does not reappear after switch to paroxetine. J Clin Pscyhiatry. 1996;57:593-594.

200. Modestin J, Wehrli MV, Stephan PL, Agarwalla P: Evolution of neuroleptic-induced extrapyramidal syndromes under long-term neurolpetic treatment. Schizophr Res. 2008;100:97-107.

201. Ratey JJ, Sorgi P, Polakoff S. Nadolol as a treatment for akathisia. Am J Psychiatry. 1985;142:640 642.

202. Bartels M, Heide K, Mann K, et al. Treatment of akathisia with lorazepam: an open clinical trial. Pharmacopsychiatry. 1987;20:51-53.

203. Fleischhacker WW, Roth SD, Kane JM: The pharmacologic treatment of neuroleptic induced akathisia. J Clin Psychopharmacol. 1990;10:12-21.

204. Derom C, Elink W, Buylaert W, Van Der Straeten M: Which beta blocker for the restless leg? Lancet. 1984;1:857.

205. Rathbone J, Soares-Weiser K: Anticholinergics for neuroleptic-induced acute akathisia. Cochrane Database Syst Rev 2006:CD003727. doi: 10.1002/14651858. CD003727.pub3.

206. Fleischhacker WW, Roth SD, Kane JM: The pharmacologic treatment of neuroleptic-induced akathisia. J Clin Psychopharmacol. 1990;10:12-21.

207. Miller CH, Fleischhacker WW: Managing antipsychotic-induced acute and chronic akathisia. Drug Safety. 2000;22:73-81.

208. Hieber R, Dellenbaugh T, Nelson LA: Role of mirtazapine in the treatment of antipsychotic-induced akathisia. Ann Pharmacother. 2008;42:841-846.

209. Moghal S, Rajput AH, Meleth R, D'Arcy C, Rajput R: Prevalence of movement disorders in institutionalized elderly. Neuroepidemiology. 1995;14:297-300.

210. Tse W, Libow LS, Neufeld R, Lesser G, Frank J, Dolan S, et al: Prevalence of movement disorders in an elderly nursing home population. Arch Gerontol Geriat. 2008;46:359-366.

211. *Hall v. Brookshire Brothers*, 2002 La.App. LEXIS (August 21,2002).

212. Halliday J, Farrington S, MacDonald S, MacEwan T, Sharkey V, McCreadie R: Nithsdale Schizophrenia Surveys 23: movement disorders: 20-year review. Br J Psychaitry. 2002;181:422-427.

213. Rochon PA, Stukel TA, Sykora K, Gill S, Garfinkel S, et al: Atypical antipsychotics and Parkinsonism. Arch Intern Med. 2005;165:1882-1888.

214. Pierre JM: Extrapyramidal symptoms with atypical antipsychotics. Incidence, prevention and management. Drug Safety. 2005;28:191-208.

215. Targum SD, Abbot JL: Efficacy of quetiapine in Parkinson's patients with psychosis.J Clin Psychopharmacol. 2000;20:54-60.

216. Gregory RJ, White JF: Can sertraline induce parkinson's disease? Psychosomatics. 2001;42:163-164.

217. Armon C, Shin C, Miller P, Carwile S, Brown E, Edinger JD, Paul RG: Reversible parkinsonism and cognitive impairment with chronic valproate use. Neurology. 1996;47:626-635.

218. Masmoudi K, Gras-Champel V, Douadi Y, Masson H, Andrejak M. Parkinsonism and/or cognitive impairment with valproic acid therapy: a report of ten cases. Pharmacopsychiatry. 2006;39:9-12.

219. Jamora D, Lim SH, Pan A, et al: Valproate-induced Parkinsonism in epilepsy patients. Mov Disord. 2007;22:130-133.

220. Mena MA, de Yebenes JG: Drug-induced parkinsonism. Expert Opin Drug Saf. 2006;5:759-771.

221. Suranyi-Cadotte BE, Nestoros JN, Nair NPV, et al: Parkinsonism induced by high doses of diazepam. Biol Psychiatry. 1985;20:451-460.

222. Hubble JP: Chapter 24: Drug-Induced Parkinsonism. In: Movement Disorders: Neurologic Principles & Practice, 2nd edition. Edited by Watts R, Koller W. McGraw Hill. 2004:395-402.

223. Wyckoff J, McBride M. Manganese exposure from welding: an emerging liability risk. Environmental Claim J. 2004;16:117-134.

224. Triano AR, Micheli FE, Alarcon F, Teive H: Movement disorders in Latin America. Parkinsonism Related Disord. 2006;12:125-138.

225. Alexander, NB: Gait disorders in older adults. J Am Geriatr Soc. 1996;44:434-451.

226. Marsden CD, Jenner P: The pathophysiology of extrapyramidal side effects of neuroleptic drugs. Psychol Med. 1980;10:55 72.

227. Marder SR, Ames D, Wirshing WC et al: Schizophrenia. Psychiatr Clin North Am. 1993;16:567-587.

228. Nordstrom AL, Farde L, Wiesel FA, et al: Central D2-dopamine receptor occupancy in relation to antipsychotic drug effects: a double-blind PET study of schizophrenic patients. Biol Psychiatry. 1993;33:227-235.

229. Hriso E, Kuhn T, Masdeu JC, Grundman M: Extrapyramidal symptoms due to dopamine-blocking agents in patients with AIDS encephalopathy. Am J Psychiatry. 1991;148:1558-1561.

230. Baron JA: Cigarette smoking and Parkinson's disease. Neurology. 1986;36:1490-1496.

231. Koller W, Vetere-Overfield B, Gray C et al: Environmental risk factors in Parkinson's disease. Neurology 1990;40:1218-1221.

232. Montgomery EB Jr: Heavy metals and the etiology of Parkinson's disease and other movement disorders. Toxicology. 1995;97:3-9.

233. Tanner CM: The role of environmental toxins in the etiology of Parkinson's disease. Trends Neurosci. 1989;12:49-54.

234. Zayed J, Ducic S, Campanella G, et al: Environmental factors in the etiology of Parkinson's disease. Can J Neurol Sci. 1990;17:286-291.

235. Rajput A, Rozdilsky B, Hornykienicz O, et al: Reversible drug-induced parkinsonism, clinicopathologic study of two cases. Neurology. 1982;39:644-646.

236. Fayen M, Goldman MB, Moulthrop MA et al: Differential memory function with dopaminergic versus anticholinergic treatment of drug induced extrapyramidal symptoms. Am J Psychiatry. 1988;145:483-486.

237. Koller WC: Pharmacologic treatment of parkinsonian tremor. Arch Neurol. 1987;44:921-923.

238. McEvoy JP: A double-blind crossover comparison of antiparkinson drug therapy; amantadine versus anticholinergics in 90 normal volunteers, with an emphasis on differential effects on memory function. J Clin Psychiatry. 1987;48(9suppl1):20-23.

239. Factor SA, Friedman JH: The emerging role of clozapine in the treatment of movement disorders. Mov Disord. 1997;12;4:483-496.

240. Bonuccelli U, Ceravolo R, Salvetti S, et al: Clozapine in Parkinson's disease tremor: Effects of acute and chronic administration. Neurology. 1997;49:1587-1590.

241. Koller WC, Pahwa R, Lyons K, et al: Low dose clozapine in the treatment of levodopa induced psychosis(Abstract). Mov Disord. 1994;9(supple 1):64.

242. Obeso JA: Therapy of myoclonus. Clinical Neuroscience. 1996;3:253-257.

243. Factor SA, Brown D: Clozapine prevents recurrence of psychosis in Parkinson's disease. Mov Disord. 1992;7:125-131.

244. Friedman JH, Lannon MC: Clozapine in the treatment of psychosis in Parkinson's disease. Neurology. 1989;39:1219-1221.

245. Cardoso F, Jankovic J: Movement disorders. Neurologic Clinics. 1993b;11:625-638.

246. Mercadante S:Pathophysiology and treatment of opioid-related myoclonus in cancer patients. Pain. 1998;74:5-9.

247. Jimenez-Jimenez FJ, Puertas I, de Toledo-Heras M: Drug-induced myoclonus. Frequency, mechanisms and management. CNS Drugs. 2004;18:93-104.

248. Kronfol Z, Greden JF, Zis AP: Imipramine-induced tremor: effect of a beta-adrenergic blocking agent. J Clin Psychiatry. 1983;44:225-226.

249. LoCurto M: The serotonin syndrome. Neurologic emergencies. Emerg Med Clin North Am. 1997;15:665-675.

250. Manyam BV: Uncommon forms of tremor. In: Watts RL, Koller WC. eds. Movement Disorders, Neurologic Principles and Practice. New York: McGraw-Hill,1997:387-403.

251. Lou JS, Jankovic J: Essential tremor: clinical correlates in 350 patients. Neurology. 1991;41:234-238.

252. Maru MC, Fialkow RZ, Haria DM: Choreiform movements in dialysis patient taking valacyclovir and famciclovir. Southern Med J. 2001;94:655.

253. Cardoso FEC, Jankovic J: Cocaine related movement disorders. Mov Disord. 1993a;8:175-178.

254. Hegerty AM, Lipton RB, Merriam AE, et al: Cocaine as a risk factor for acute dystonic reactions. Neurology 1991;41:1670.

255. Lopez W, Jeste DV: Movement disorders and substance abuse. Psychiatric Services. 1997;48:634-637.

256. Rittmannsberger H, Leblhuber F. Asterixis induced by carbamazepine therapy. Biol Psychiatry. 1992;32:364-368.

257. Sechi GP, Murgia B, Sau GF et al. Asterixis and toxic encephalopathy induced by gabapentin. Progress in Neuro-Psychopharmacology & Biological Psychiatry. 2004;28:195-199.

258. Stubblefield BM, Herklotz M, Hand M. Asterixis related to gabapentin as a cause of falls. Am J Phys Med Rehabil. 2005;84:136-140.

259. Rittmansberger H. Asterixis induced by psychotropic drug treatment. Clin Neuropharmacol. 1996;19:349-355.

260. Stacy M, Cardoso F, Jankovic J: Tardive stereotypy and other movement disorders in tardive dyskinesias. Neurology. 1993;43:937-941.

261. Kane JM, Jeste DV, et al., (eds): American Psychiatric Association Task Force Report on Tardive Dyskinesia. American Psychiatric Press, Washington, DC, 1992.

262. Glazer WM, Morgenstern H, Schooler N, et al: Predictors of improvement in tardive dyskinesia following discontinuation of neuroleptic medication. Br J Psychiatry. 1990;157:585-595.

263. Fetner DE, Hertzman M: Progress in the treatment of tardive dyskinesia; theory and practice. Hosp Community Psychiatry 1993;1:25-34.

264. Kane JM, Jeste DV, Barnes TRE, et al. editors. American Psychiatric Association Task Force Report on Tardive Dyskinesia: A task force report, 1992, Washington DC: American Psychiatric Press Inc.

265. Latimer PR: Tardive dyskinesia: a review. Can J Psychiatry 1995;40(suppl 2):49S-54S.

266. Rifkin A, Doddi S, Karajgi B, et al: Dosage of haloperidol for schizophrenia. Archives of General Psychiatry 1991;48:166-170.

267. Kane JM, Weinhold P, Kinon B, et al: Prevalence of abnormal involuntary movements ("spontaneous dyskinesias") in the normal elderly. Psychopharmacology. 1982;77:105-108.

268. Klawans HL, Barr A. Prevalence of spontaneous lingual-facial-buccal dyskinesias in the elderly. Neurology. 1982;32:558-559.

269. Van Harten PN, Hoek HW, Matroos GE, Koeter M, Kahn RS: Intermittent neuroleptic treatment and risk for tardive dyskinesia: curacao extrapyramidal syndromes study III. American Journal of Psychiatry 1998;155:565-567.

270. Chakos MH, Alvir JM, Woerner MG et al: Incidence and correlates of tardive dyskinesia in first episode of schizophrenia. Arch Gen Psychiatry. 1996;53:313-319.

271. Correll CU, Schenk EM. Tardive dyskinesia and new antipsychotics. Curr Opin Psychiatry 2008. 21:151-156.

272. Remington G. Tardive dyskinesia: eliminated, forgotten, or overshadowed? Curr Opin Psychiatry. 2007;20:131-137.

273. Buzan R: Risperidone-induced tardive dyskinesia. Am J Psychiatry 1996;153:734-735.

274. Jeste DV, Lacro JP, Bailey A, Rockwell E, Harris MJ, Caligiuri MP: Lower incidence of tardive dyskinesia with risperidone compared with haloperidol in older patients. Journal of the American Geriatric Society 1999;47:716-719.

275. Marder SR, Meibach RC: Risperidone in the treatment of schizophrenia. Am J Psychiatry 1994;151:825-835.

276. Addington DE, Toews JA, Addington JM: Risperidone and tardive dyskinesia: a case report. (letter). Journal of Clinical Psychiatry 1995;56:484-485.

277. Thomas N, Swamidhas P, Russell S, et al: Tardive dyksinesia following risperidone treatment in Tourette's syndrome. Neurology India. 2009;57:94.

278. White A. Woman whose face is disfigured by drugs awarded $6.7 million. The Legal Intelligencer (Philadelphia, Pa.). 2000;222:104.

279. Ghaemi SN, Ko JY: Quetiapine-related tardive dyskinesia. (Letter). American Journal of Psychiatry 2001;158:1737.

280. Tollefson G, Beasley C, Tamura, R: Blind, controlled, long term study of the comparative incidence of treatment emergent tardive dyskinesia with olanzapine or haloperidol. Am J Psychiatry. 1997;154:1248-1254Glazer WM, Morgenstern H, Pultz JA, et al: Incidence of tardive dyskinesia is lower with quetiapine treatment than with typical antipsychotics in patients with schizophrenia and schizoaffective disorder. Schizophrenia Resource 2000;41:206-207.

281. Rosenquist KJ, Walker SS, Gjhaemi SN: Tardive dyskinesia and ziprasidone. (letter). American Journal of Psychiatry 2002;159:1436.

282. Maytal G, Ostacher M, Stern TA: Aripiprazole-related tardive dyskinesia. CNS Spect. 2006;6:435-439.

283. Abbasian C, Power P: A case of aripirazole and tardive dyskinesia. Journal of Psychopharmacology. 2009;23:214-215.

284. Rizos E, Douzenis A, Gournellis R, et al. Tardive dyskinesia in a patient treated with quetiapine. The World Journal of Biological Psychiatry. 2009;10:54-57.

285. Bruscas MJ, Gonzalez F, Santos JL, et al. Tardive dyskinesia associated with clozapine treatment. [Letter]. Progress in Neuro-Psychopharmacology & Biological Psychiatry. 2007;31:963-964.

286. Marshall DL, Hazlet TK, Gardner JS: Neuroleptic drug exposure and incidence of tardive dyskinesia: a records-based case-control study. J Man Care Pharm. 2002;8:259-265.

287. Spivak B, Mester R, Abesgaus J, Wittenberg N, Adlersberg S, Gonen N, Weizman A: Clozapine treatment for neuroleptic-induced tardive dyskinesia, parkinsonism, and chronic akathisia in schizophrenic patients. Journal of Clinical Psychiatry 1997;58:318-322.

288. Ertugrul A, Demir B: Clozapine-induced tardive dyskinesia: a case report. Prog Neuropsychopharm Biol Psychiatry. 2005;29:633-635.

289. Duggal HS, Mendhekar DN: Clozapine-induced tardive dystonia (blepharospasm). J Neruopsych Clin Neurosci. 2007;19:86-87.

290. Uzun O, Doruk A: Tardive oculogyric crisis during treatment with clozapine: report of three cases. Clin Drug Investig. 2007;27:861-864.

291. Kumet R, Freeman MP: Clozapine and tardive dyskinesia. (letter). Journal of Clinical Psychiatry 2002;63:167-168.

292. Beauclair L, Fontaine R: Tardive dyskinesia associated with metoclopramide. Can Med Assoc J 1986;134:613-614.

293. Modrego PP, Perez TJM: Acute dyskinesia after metoclopramide withdrawal. J Am Geriatric Soc 1997;45(4):536.

294. Wiholm BE, Mortimer O, Boethus G, et al: Tardive dyskinesia associated with metoclopramide. Br Med J 1984;288:545-547.

295. Kenney C, Hunter C, Davidson A, Jankovic J. Metoclopramide, an increasingly recognized cause of tardive dyskinesia. J Clin Pharmacol 2008; 48:379-384.

296. Pasricha PJ, Pehlivanov N, Sugumar A, and Jankovic J. Drug Insight: from disturbed motility to disordered movement – a review of the clinical benefits and medicolegal risks of metoclopramide. Nat Clin Pract Gastroenterol Hepatol 2006 Mar; 3(3):138-148.

297. FDA Requires Boxed Warning and Risk Mitigation Strategy for Metoclopramide-Containing Drugs. Agency warns against chronic use of these products to treat gastrointestinal disorders. Available at:. 298. www.fda.gov/NewsEvents/Newsroom/PressAnnouncements/ucm149533.htm. Accessed April 16, 2012.

298. See note 297.

299. Thach BT, Chase TN, Bosma JF: Oral facial dyskinesia associated with prolonged use of antihistaminic decongestants. The New England Journal of Medicine 1975;293:486-487.

300. Buetefisch CM, Gutierrez A, Gutmann L: Choreathetotic movements: a possible side effect of gabapentin. (Letter) Neurology 1996:851.

301. Sandler NH: Tardive dyskinesia associated with fluoxetine. J Clin Psychiatry 1996;57:91.

302. Arya DK: Extrapyramidal symptoms with selective serotonin re-uptake inhibitors. Br J Psychiatry 1994;165:728-733.

303. Fishbain DA, Dominguez M, Goldberg, Olsen E, et al: Dyskinesia associated with fluoxetine use. Neuropsychiatry, Neuropsychology, Behavioral Neurology 1992;5:97-100.

304. Yassa R, Camille Y, Belzile L: Tardive dyskinesia in the course of antidepressant therapy: a prevalence study and review of the literature. J Clin Psychopharmacol 1987;7:243-246.

305. Kane J, Honigfeld G, Singer J, et al: Clozapine for the treatment resistant schizophrenic. Arch Gen Psychiatry 1988;45:789-796 .

306. Dixon L, Weiden PJ, Hass G, et al: Increased tardive dyskinesia in alcohol abusing schizophrenic patients. Compr Psychiatry 1992;33:121-122.

307. Ganzini L, Heintz RT, Hoffman WF, et al: The prevalence of tardive dyskinesia in neuroleptic-treated diabetics. Arch Gen Psychiatry. 1991;48:259-263.

308. Rosengarten H, Schweitzer JW, Friedhoff AJ: Possible genetic factors underlying the pathophysiology of tardive dyskinesia. Pharmacol Biochem Behav. 1994;49:663-667.

309. van Os J, Fahy T, Jones P, et al: Tardive dyskinesia: who is at risk? Acta Psychiatr Scand. 1997;6:206-216.

310. Lucey JL, Dinan TG: Orofacial dyskinesia and the alcohol dependence syndrome. Psychological Medicine 1992;22:79-83.

311. Olivera AA, Kiefer MW, Manley NK: Tardive dyskinesia in psychiatric patients with substance use disorders. American Journal of Drug and Alcohol Abuse 1990;16:57-66.

312. Friedman JH: Historical perspective on movement disorders. J Clin Psychiatry. 2004;65(suppl 9):3-8.

313. Marshall, DL, Hazlet TK, Gardner JS, Blough DK: Neuroleptic Drug Exposure and Incidence of Tardive Dyskinesia: A Records-based Case-Control Study. J Man Care Pharm. 2002:(8)4:259-65.

314. de Leon J, Greenlee B, Barber J, et al: Practical guidelines for the use of new generation antipsychotics (except clozapine) in adult individuals with intellectual disabilities. Research in Developmental Disabilities. 2009;30:613-669.

315. Margolese HC, Chouinard G, Kolivakis T, et al: Tardive dyskinesia in the era of typical and atypical antipsychotics. Part 2: Incidence and management strategies in patients with schizophrenia. Can J Psychiatry.2005;50:703-713.

316. Grant MJ, Baldessarini RJ: Possible improvement of neuroleptic-associated tardive dyskinesia during treatment with aripiprazole. The Annals of Pharmacotherapy. 2005;39:1953.

317. Caykoylu A, Ekinci O, Yilmaz E. Resolution of risperidone-induced tardive dyskinesia with a switch to aripiprazole monotherapy. Progress in Neuro-Psychopharmacology & Biological Psychiatry. 2009;33:571-572.

318. Factor SA, Friedman JH: The emerging role of clozapine in the treatment of movement disorders. Mov Disord. 1997;12:483-496.

319. Guy W (ed): ECDEU Assessment Manual for Psychopharmacology, revised. Rockville,Md:National Institute of Mental Health;1976:534-537. Psychopharmacology Research Branch, National Institute of Mental Health. Publication ADM 76-338. Washington, DC, US Department of Health, Education, and Welfare.

320. Munetz MR, Benjamin S: Who should perform the AIMS examination. Hosp Community Psychiatry 1990;41:912-915.

321. Kaye NS, Reed TJ. Tardive dyskinesia: tremors in law and medicine. J Am Acad Psychiatry Law. 1999;27:315-333.

322. Heaton H: Plaintiffs win half of suits involving tardive dyskinesia. Clinical Psychiatry News 1990:18:12-17.

323. Mills MJ, Eth S: Legal liability with psychotropic drug use: extrapyramidal syndromes and tardive dyskinesia. J Clin Psychiatry 1987;48(Suppl 9):28-33.

324. Mills MJ, Norquiest GS, Shelton RC, et al: Consent and liability with neuroleptics: the problem of tardive dyskiensia. International Journal of Law and Psychiatry 1986;8:243-252.

325. Rinck C, Guidry J, Calkins CF: Review of states' practices on the use of psychotropic medication. Am J Ment Retard 1989;93:657-668.

326. Schwartz HI: Legal and ethical issues in neuroleptic noncompliance. Psychiatr Ann 1986;16:588-595.

327. Wetttstein RM: Informed consent and tardive dyskinesia J Clin Psychopharmacol 1988;8(suppl 4):65S-70S.

328. Sprague RL, Kalachnik JE, Shaw KM: Psychometric properties of the Dyskinesia Identification System: Condensed User Scale (DISCUS). Ment Retard 1989;27:141-148.

329. Sachdev P: The epidemiology of drug-induced akathisia: II: chronic, tardive, withdrawal akathisias. Schizophr Bull. 1995;21:451-461.

330. Kyriakos D, Bozikas VP, Garyfallos G et al. Tardive nocturnal akathisia due to clozapine treatment. Int'l J Psychiatry in Medicine. 2005;35:207-211.

331. Stone RK, Alvarez WF, Ellman G: Lifetime antipsychotic-drug exposure, dyskinesia, and related movement disorders in the developmentally disabled. Pharmacology, Biochemistry, and Behavior 1989a;34:759-763.

332. Stone RK, May JE, Alvarez WF et al.: Prevalence of dyskinesia and related movement disorders in developmentally disabled population. Journal of Mental Deficiency Research 1989b;33:41-53.

333. Sachdev P: Neuroleptic-induced movement disorders and body iron status. Prog Neuropsychopharmacol Biol Psychiatry 1992; 16:647-653.

334. Sachdev P: The epidemiology of drug-induced akathisia: Part II. Chronic, tardive, and withdrawal akathisias. Schizophrenia Bulletin 1995b;21(3):451-461.

335. Jankovic J: Tardive syndromes and other drug-induced movement disorders. Clinical Neuropharmacology 1995;18:197-214.

336. Hettema JM, Ross DE. A case of aripiprazole-related tardive akathisia and its treatment with ropinirole. J Clin Psychiatry. 2007; 68:1814-1815.

337. Kuo SH, Jankovic J: Tardive gait. Clinical Neurology and Neurosurgery. 2008;110:198-201.

338. Giudice M: Drug-induced restless leg syndrome. CPJ/RPC. 2009;142:41-42.

339. Harris MK, Shneyder N, Borazanci A, et al: Movement disorders. Med Clin N Am. 2009;93:371-388.

340. Baker WL, Silver D, White CM et al: Dopamine agonists in the treatment of early Parkinson's disease: a meta-analysis. Parkinsonism and Related Disorders.2009;15:287-294.

341. Bostwick JM, Hecksel KA, Stevens SR, et al: Frequency of new-onset pathologic compulsive gambling or hypersexuality after drug treatment of idiopathic Parkinson Disease. May Clin Proc. 2009;84:310-316.

342. Durif F: Treating and preventing levodopa-induced dyskinesias. Drugs & Aging. 1999;14:337-345.

343. Gupta S, Frank B, Madhusoodanan S. Tardive dyskinesia: legal issues and consent. Psychiatric Annals. 2002;32:245-248.

344. Marder SR, Essock SM, Miller AL, Buchanan RW, Davis JM, Kane JM, Lieberman J, Schooler NR: The Mount Siani conference on the pharmacotherapy of schizophrenia. Schizophr Bull. 2002;28:5-16.

345. Loonen AJM, van Praag HM. Measuring movement disorders in antipsychotic drug trials. The need to define a new standard. Journal of Clinical Psychopharmacology. 2007;27:423-430.

346. Barnes TR: A rating scale for drug-induced akathisia. Br J Psychiatry. 1989;154:672-676.

347. Simpson GM, Angus JW: A rating scale for extrapyramidal side effects. Acta Psychiatr Scand. 1970(suppl);212:11-19.

348. Chouinard G, Ross-Chouinard A, Annable L, et al: Extrapyramidal Symptom Rating Scale [abstract]. Can J Neurol Sci. 1980;7:233.

349. Chouinard G, Margolese HC: Manual for the Extrapyramidal Symptom Rating Scale (ESRS). Schizophrenia Research. 2005;76:247-265.

350. Lane RD, Glazer WM, Hansen TE, et al: Assessment of tardive dyskinesia using the Abnormal Involuntary Movement Scale. J Nerv Ment Dis. 1985;173:353-357.

351. Dixon L, Weiden P, Frances AJ, Rapkin. Management of neuroleptic-induced movement disorders: effects of physician training. Am J Psychiatry. 1989;146:104106.

352. Mitra S, Haddad PM: Documentation of extrapyramidal symptoms. Psychiatr Bull. 2007;31:76-77.

353. Cortese L, Jog M, McAuley TJ et al. Assessing and monitoring antipsychotic-induced movment disorders in hospitalized patients: a cautionary study. Can J Psychiatry. 2004;49:31-36.

354. Day JC, Kinderman P, Bentall R: A comparison of patients' and prescribers' beliefs about neuroleptic side-effects: prevalence, distress and causation. Acta Psychiatr Scand. 1998;97:93-97.

355. Slovenko R. Update on legal issues associated with tardive dyskinesia. Journal of Clinical Psychiatry. 2006;61(suppl 4):45-57.

356. Studdert DM, Mello MM, Sage WM et al. Defensive medicine among high-risk specialist physicians in a volatile malpractice environment. JAMA 2005;293:2609-2617.

357. Bailey RK, Adams JB, Unger DM. Atypical antipsychotics: a case study in new era risk management. Journal of Psychiatric Practice. 2006;12:253-258.

358. Bonnie R: Professional liability and the quality of mental health care. Law Med Health Care 1988;16:229-240.

359. Klein JI, Glover SI: Psychiatric malpractice. Int J Law Psychiatry 1983;6:131-157.

360. Simon RI, Sadoff RL: Psychiatric malpractice: causes and comments for clinicians, 1992, Washington, DC: American Psychiatric Press.

361. Meyer DJ. Psychiatry malpractice and administrative inquiries of alleged physician misconduct. Psychiatr Clin N Am. 2006;29:615-628.

362. Brackins LW: The liability of physicians, pharmacists, and hospitals for adverse drug reactions. Defense Law Journal 1985;34:273-344.

363. Dukes MNG, Swartz B: Responsibility for drug-induced injury. Amsterdam, Elsevier 1988.

364. Wettstein RM: Legal aspects of neuroleptic-induced movement disorders. In: Legal Medicine 1985, edited by: Wecht CH, New York, Praeger:117-179.

365. Wettstein RM: Tardive dyskinesia and malpractice. Behavioral Sciences and the Law 1983;1:85-107.

366. Applebaum PS: Legal liability and managed care. Am Psychol 1993;48:251-257.

367. Applebaum PS: Managed care and the next generation of mental health law. Psychiatr Services 1996;47:27-28.

368. Garrick TR, Weinstock R: Liability of psychiatric consultants. Psychosomatics 1994;35:474-484.

369. Applebaum PS, Lidz CW, Meisel A: Informed consent: legal theory and clinical practice.1987, New York:Oxford University Press.

370. Faden RF, Beauchamp TL: A history and theory of informed consent. New York, 1986, Oxford University Press.

371. Tietz GF: Informed consent in the prescription drug context: the special case. Washington Law Review 1986;61:367-417.

372. Munetz MR, Roth LH: Informing patients about tardive dyskinesia. Arch Gen Psychiatry 1985;42:866-871.

373. Laugharne J, Davies A, Arcelus J et al. Informing patients about tardive dyskinesia: a survey of clinicians' attitudes in three countries. International Journal of Law and Psychiatry. 2004;27:101-108.

374. Rozovsky F: Consent to treatment: a practical guide, 2nd ed., Boston, MA, 1990, Little Brown.

375. Applebaum PS, Schaffner K, Meisel A: Responsibility and compensation for tardive dyskinesia. Am J Psychiatry 1985;142:806-810.

376. Applebaum PS, Grisso T: Assessing patients' capacities to consent to treatment. N Eng J Med 1988;319:1635-1638.

377. Grisso T, Applebaum PS: Comparison of standards for assessing patient's capacities to make treatment decisions. Am J Psychiatry 1995;152:1033-1037.

378. Gutheil TG, Bursztajn HJ: Clinician's guidelines for assessing and presenting subtle forms of patient incompetence in legal settings. Am J Psychiatry 1986;143:1020-1023.

379. Applebaum PS: The right to refuse treatment with antipsychotic medication: retrospect and prospect. Am J Psychiatry 1988;145:413-419.

380. Applebaum PS, Gutheil TG: Clinical handbook of psychiatry and the law. 2nd ed. 1991, Baltimore: Williams & Wilkins.

381. *Lackey v. Bressler*, 358 S.E. 2d 560 (Court of Appeals of North Carolina 1987).

382. *Collins v. Cushner Montgomery County Maryland*, Circuit Court, Number 48751, (October 20, 1980).

383. *Clites v. Iowa*, Law #46274 Iowa District Court, Pottawattamie County (August 7, 1980).

384. *Clites v. State of Iowa*, 322 N.W. 2d 917 (Court of Appeals of Iowa 1982).

385. *Hedin v. U.S.*, Number 5-83 CIV 3 (D. Minn.) (1985).

386. *Barclay v. Campbell*, 683 SW2d 498, Texas (1984).

387. *Barclay v. Campbell*, 704 S.W. 2d 8 (Supreme Court of Texas 1986).

388. *Ronald Bloom v. Will Creed, M.D.*, 724 So. 2d 357 (Supreme Court of Mississippi 1998).

389. Eng K, Emlet CA: Srx: a regional approach to geriatric medication education. Gerontologist 1990;30:408-410.

390. Brown CS, Solovitz BL, Bryant SG, et al: Short-and long-term effects of auxiliary labels on patient knowledge of precautionary drug information. Drug Intelligence and Clinical Pharmacy 1988;22:470-474

Chapter 27

Dangers of Opioids

James T. O'Donnell, Pharm.D., M.S., FCP, ABCP, FACN, R.Ph.

27.1 Introduction
A. Definition

Opioids are pain-relieving drugs which include the classic opiates produced directly from the poppy plant (e.g., morphine and codeine, see Figure 27.1), compounds semi-synthesized from opium (e.g., heroin, hydromorphone, and oxycodone), and compounds fully synthesized to achieve similar effects (e.g., meperidine, propoxyphene, diphenoxylate, fentanyl, buprenorphine, methadone, and pentazocine).[1] Found in a variety of forms including powders, liquids, tablets, syrups, and capsules, they are central nervous system depressants with a high potential for abuse.[2]

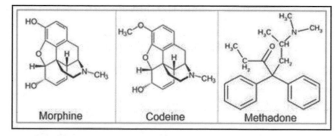

Figure 27.1 *Chemical composition of common opioids.*

B. History
See Table 27.1.[3]

C. Cultivation

Cultivation of opium poppy plants, or Papaver Somniferum, primarily occurs in South East Asia, West Asia, and Latin America, with an average Indian acreage yielding 25-30 kg of raw opium.[4]

27.2 Pharmacology of Opioids
A. Effects

Effects of opioids include analgesia, drowsiness, mood changes, respiratory depression, nausea, vomiting, reduced gastrointestinal motility, and alteration of endocrine and autonomic nerve systems.[5]

Table 27.1
Brief History of One of the Most Ancient
and Powerful Drugs Known to Humankind[3]

Date	Event
3400 B.C.	The opium poppy is cultivated in lower Mesopotamia. The Sumerians refer to it as Hul Gil, the "joy plant."
1300 B.C.	Opium poppies are grown by ancient Egyptians in the capital city of Thebes.
460 B.C.	Acknowledged by Hippocrates, "the father of medicine."
1527 A.D.	Paracelsus recommends laudanum, or black pills made from opium, as a pain killer in European medical literature.
1753	Linnaeus, the father of botany, first classifies the poppy, Papaver Somniferum, as "sleep-inducing," in his book *Genera Plantarum*.
1803	Friedrich Sertürner of Paderborn, Germany, discovers morphine, by dissolving opium in acid then neutralizing it with ammonia.
1827	E. Merck & Company of Darmstadt, Germany, begins commercial manufacturing of morphine.
1874	Heroin first synthesized by English researcher, C.R. Wright.
1895	The Bayer Company of Elberfeld, Germany, begins commercial manufacturing of heroin.

B. Opioid Neural Receptors

1. Central nervous system (CNS) receptors

CNS receptors and effects include the following:[6]

1. Mu (μ): Analgesia, Euphoria, Respiratory Depression, Miosis
2. Kappa (κ): Analgesia, Sedation, Respiratory Depression, Miosis
3. Sigma (σ): Dysphoria, Psychosis
4. Delta (δ): Euphoria, Seizures

2. Peripheral nervous system (PNS) receptors

PNS receptors, the most likely cause of gastrointestinal (GI) effects, are present in the musculoskeletal system, in autonomic ganglia, in the submucosal and myenteric plexus of the GI tract, and in the adrenal medulla.[7]

C. Routes of Administration[8]

1. Oral

Oral opioids undergo first-pass metabolism. Because one of the effects is suppression of gastric emptying, initial onset is delayed. Fortunately, this is offset by the high absorption of morphine in the GI tract.

2. Intramuscular

Although this route presents less of an initial delay than oral administration, unpredictability of absorption and short peak effect restricts its use to nurses and midwives in countries such as the UK.

3. Subcutaneous

Small volume opiates, such as diamorphine and buprenorphine, are the best candidates for this method, which has better systemic update than the intramuscular route.

4. Intravenous

This includes bolus injection, continuous infusion, and patient-controlled analgesia: the greater absorption and predictability of this route (compared to those previously mentioned) is offset by a greater risk of sudden allergic reaction and respiratory depression.

5. Transdermal

Represented by the fentanyl patch, the advantages of sustained constant release and ease of application are offset by a long initial delay to steady state (~15 hours), and a long half-life after removal (~21 hours). This slow decay exacerbates the risk of respiratory depression.

6. Sublingual and buccal

A new "lozenger under the tongue" approach to administering fentanyl, this method avoids the first pass metabolism drawback of the oral route.

7. Neuroaxial

This route, which includes epidural and intrathecal administration, has the advantage of strong effect and long duration with a relatively small dose. Caution must be exercised to avoid synergistic effects with other opioids and drugs.

D. Excretion

In healthy patients, opioids are metabolized by hepatic conjugation, and then excreted in the urine. Liver disease or impaired renal function can interfere with this process, leading to accumulation and toxicity.[9]

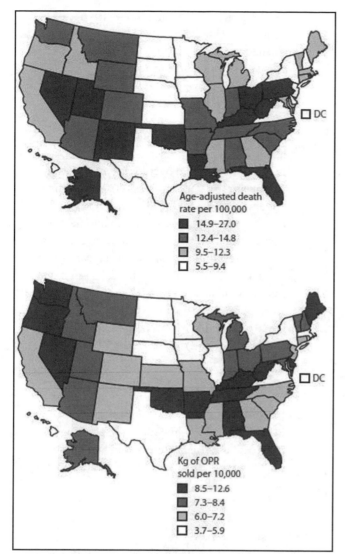

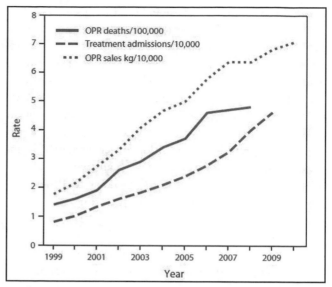

Figure 27.3 *Rates of opioid pain reliever (OPR) overdose death, OPR treatment admissions, and kilograms of OPR sold—United States, 1999–2010. Age-adjusted rates per 100,000 population for OPR deaths, crude rates per 10,000 population for OPR abuse treatment admissions, and crude rates per 10,000 population for kilograms of OPR sold.*

- respiratory depression
- altered mental states
- severe perspiration
- shock
- pulmonary edema
- unresponsiveness

Figure 27.2 *Drug overdose death rate in 2008 and rate of kilograms (kg) of opioid pain relievers (OPR) sold in 2010—United States.*

27.3 Toxicity of Opioids
A. Respiratory Depression

Respiratory depression, a potentially fatal condition, results from the presence of μ-opiate receptors in the ventrolateral medulla, including on neurons in the region of the ventral respiratory column.[10]

Opioid-induced hypoxia, or lack of oxygen, is characterized by pulmonary congestion, increased permeability of the lung capillaries, edema and hemorrhages.[5]

B. Symptoms of Overdose

Symptoms of opioid overdose include the following:[11]

- coma
- pinpoint pupils

C. Opioid Deaths

A recent study released by the Center for Disease Control and Prevention has shown an alarming trend in opioid-related overdoses within the U.S. (Figures 27.2 and 27.3).[12]

27.4 Case Reports: Opioid Toxicity Causing Respiratory Arrest, Brain Damage, and Death

Several case reports follow that discuss the clinical course, drug treatment, toxicity, morbidity, and sometimes mortality following the clinical use of opioids.

A. Case Report: Respiratory Arrest and Brain Damage Following Morphine Overdose in the Hospital

The following case report describes an overdose in a clinical setting; a very high dose of morphine administered with a very short frequency, with no special monitoring by the nurses, in a patient with extra pulmonary risk factors, which resulted in a respiratory arrest and brain damage.

This case involves the administration of morphine to Ms. Patient, and an evaluation of excessive dosage leading to acute respiratory failure and subsequent anoxic brain damage. Ms. Patient's height and weight were recorded as 5'4" and 263 lbs. This is morbidly obese (greater than 100 percent over ideal body weight of 120 lbs), which is in itself an increased risk for respiratory depression, thus exacerbating the risk from morphine. Electroencephalographic impression showed diffuse slowing (of brain waves)—indicative of severe toxic metabolic encephalopathy. Patient was described to be in decerebrate posturing.

Opinions

In my opinion, with reasonable pharmacological certainty, Ms. Patient was prescribed and administered morphine sulfate at excessive dosages and insufficient time intervals. She had inadequate monitoring, diagnosis and treatment of her obvious respiratory depression (08:20 A.M.). Furthermore, the combination of overdosage, inadequate monitoring, and non-recognition of the severity of morphine toxicity was a proximate cause of her anoxic brain damage and permanent neurological deficits.

Finally, in my opinion, aggressive reversal of morphine at the first sign of overdose (8:00 A.M.) would have prevented any permanent injury to this young lady. Pulse oximetry, arterial blood gases, and intensive monitoring should have been executed at this point. When Narcan (an opioid antidote) was finally prescribed (10:20 A.M.), inadequate doses were administered. Adequate and responsive Narcan administration would have shortened the time that this patient was experiencing narcosis and hypoxia. The following recitation of facts and background information regarding morphine pharmacology, toxicology, and requisite monitoring will serve as the bases for my opinions.

Bases for opinions

The following physician orders, drug administration records, and patient chart notes are relevant in this case evaluation:

- Restoril 15 mg HS PRN
- Demerol 25 mg IV q 3 hour PRN severe pain
- Lopressor 50 mg PO HS
- Phenergan 25 mg IV 1 6 hour PRN nausea One dose at 0210 A.M.
- Morphine sulfate 10 mg IV q 4-6 hours PRN Pain

- 1810 10 mg, 2210 10 mg, 0030 10 mg, 0215 10 mg
- Change morphine 20 mg q 2 hour IV PRN pain (given at 5 A.M. and 7 A.M.) (*On the PRN chart, there is a strike out, changing q2 to q3-4*)
- Life Flight note "A20 mg MS at 0700"
- 0835 decrease morphine to 20 mg IV q 3-4 hours as needed. (Responsive only to pain, thought to be in mild overdose of narcotics, no signs of respiratory depression) Pt. sleeping, not able to arouse, Had 40 mg MS in last 2-3 hours. Hold next dose until patient is awake. The nurses notes for 0830 note a focus on shallow respirations, and what appears to be a strike over originally written as 34/min and finally written at 24/min. (*These are clearly signs of respiratory distress.*)
- 10:20 called to room, peripheral cyanosis, (nailbed cyanosis) pulse oximetry 30, decerebrate posturing, poor response to 0.4 mg Narcan. Pupils were pinpoint and fixed bilaterally (these signs were actually 09:55, according to the nurse's notes).
- 8 A.M. Clinical Progress note: Pt. sleeping, not able to arouse. Had 40 mg MS in last 2-3 hours
- 10:20 A.M. Pulse ox ~30%, Narcan—no response
- 10:50 A.M. Blood draw for arterial blood gases.

Case discussion/facts

The patient was admitted to the Memorial Hospital for severe headache, was administered several doses of morphine and a single dose of Phenergan and a single dose of Restoril. Diagnoses recorded at the subsequent hospital for the 11/1/97 admission include: anoxic brain damage, respiratory failure, hypothyroidism, obesity, hypertension, and tobacco-use. An admission note of a possible iatrogenic morphine overdose is recorded. The history/present illness is relevant for the following entry: During the hospitalization, a total dose of 50 mg of morphine plus Phenergan (a phenothiazine tranquilizer used to relieve nausea) was administered. Early this morning, the patient became unresponsive and apneic. Upon arrival to the emergency room, 8 mg of Narcan was administered and the patient became quite violent and agitated. (A later chart note indicates the patient received 60 mg of morphine sulfate within eight hours IV overnight. Actually, the 60 mg of morphine was given between 0030 and

0655, precisely 6 hours and 25 minutes.) The final diagnostic impression of J. Physician MD is iatrogenic morphine overdose.

This patient had a number of factors that compromised her respiratory system. First, she had morbidly obese apnea. She had 60 mg of morphine administered in a little more than 6 hours. It is likely that obesity, the very large doses of morphine and the lack of adequate monitoring and treatment measures contributed to respiratory arrest in this patient.

The physician and hospital settled the case with the patient's guardian, thus avoiding the need for a trial.

B. Case Report: Fentanyl Epidural Respiratory Arrest

This case went to trial in the summer of 2002. The interesting part of this case is that the hospital had a policy requiring continuous pulse oximetry for all fentanyl (a synthetic opioid 100 times the potency of morphine) epidural patients. Unfortunately, the labor and delivery nursing staff elected not to follow the safety policy: "We don't do that (pulse oximetry) in L&D." The hospital settled the case during trial for $8 million. The pharmacologist case report (with fictitious names) is provided as follows:

December 10, 2001

James Esquire
Attorney at Law
RE: PATIENT v. Doctor

Mr. Esquire:

I reviewed the following materials in this matter:
1. Complaint at Law
2. Medical records comprised of 70 alphabetized file folders
3. Glasgow Coma Record Synopsis
4. 24 Hour Flowsheet Synopsis
5. Thirteen medical personnel depositions (Dr. Moore, Dr. Basara, Dr. Perreault, Dr. Asfaha, Nurse Jones, Dr. Laukka, Dr. Swift, Dr. Welch, Nurse Miller, Nurse Karala, Nurse Nowakowski, Nurse Bence, Dr. Entwistle)
6. Authoritative texts (Harrison's Internal Medicine On-Line, 2001, Goodman and Gilman, The Pharmacological Basis of Therapeutics, McGraw Hill, New York, 1995), and manufacturers' prescribing information (package inserts) describing the pharmacology and toxicology of fentanyl, Ativan, Stelazine Tegretol, Wellbutrin, and related drugs.

Facts of the case and summary of testimony

Ms. Patient was admitted to St. Jude Hospital for a scheduled elective C-section and a tubal ligation. Her previous deliveries had been accompanied by postpartum depression and she had been receiving psychiatric care for depression and bi-polar disorder. She had also been seen by a postpartum depression group as an outpatient. Nurse Karala, RN, was her coordinator for the postpartum depression counseling clinic. Dr. Kadlec was the previous prescribing physician for the psychiatric medications. Dr. Laukka was the psychiatrist at St. Jude; Kadlec did not have authority to prescribe at St. Jude Hospital. The patient asked for and received a referral for an obstetrician, Dr. Basara, who admitted her for elective C-section on April 17, 1998.

On April 17, 1998 the patient was received at the birthing room at St. Jude Hospital at 6:00 A.M., entered the birth-center operating room at 7:30 A.M., had the epidural fentanyl anesthesia started at 7:35 A.M., and had the incision for the C-section at 8:25 A.M. Surgery ended at 9:20 A.M. and Ms. Patient left the operating room at 9:25 A.M. (per the birth center data record), a live baby boy was delivered at 8:31 A.M. (anesthesia record). Her anesthesiologist, Dr. Moore, wrote the following orders for post-op continuous epidural infusion:

Moore post-op orders: Fentanyl, 1,000mcg in 100 ml normal saline, final concentration fentanyl 10 mcg per ml. Initial dose: none. Infusion: start at 6 cc per hour and increase in increments of 2 cc up to maximum of 14 cc per hour. Dr. Moore also wrote routine orders for Benadryl for severe itching and for Narcan as an antidote along with an Ambu bag and oxygen set up.
Dr. Moore also wrote: No. 7 RR and sedation scale every hour when patient asleep and/or bed rest. Also: continuous pulse oximetry for 24 hours and for 24 hours after any increase in dose.

Dr. Moore recalls that a nurse called (Miller) who said that the patient was not relieved with 14 cc (fentanyl) so "I asked her to give her some Delgan." 16:30: Post anesthesia note: "Patient being very well and comfortable with CLE and Delgan."

Although this patient was described as being in no acute distress, she also was described as drowsy, and wheezing was heard in both lungs. Her history included smoking, sleep apnea, and postpartum depression. Prescriptions originated by Dr. Ralph Kadlec, continued by Dr. Laukka, and ordered by Dr. Basara include Tegretol, Ativan, Wellbutrin, and Stelazine.

The patient's psychotropic drugs, namely 2 milligrams of Stelazine, 2 milligrams of Ativan, 150 milligrams of Wellbutrin, and 200 milligrams of Tegertol, per Dr. Laukka's recommendation and Dr. Basara's post-operative major gynecology orders were added to the patient's post-op medications and given at 22:00 on April 18. It should be noted that although Dr. Basara states in her deposition that she ordered the 2 mg dose because that is what Ms. Patient was taking, her adult health history done on 4/9/98 and her pre-natal flow sheet (the last page of it) have Ms. Patient only taking a one 1 mg dose at a time. This differs from the birth center data, which appears to have a change in the dosage amount and time. At this time, the patient was receiving fentanyl at 14 cc per hour and had received Delgan at 16:30. Nurse Bence's shift began at 23:00 and she received the patient from Nurse Jones who gave her a verbal report: Bence recalls that Jones told her the patient was post-C-section with a history of PP depression, that she had a CEA and IV and the basics of her medical condition. The first time that Nurse Bence checked on the patient, she found her at 23:54. "Patient found in bed unresponsive to verbal and tactile stimuli. Patient found lying on right side in supine position. Color, cyanotic. Unable to obtain pulse. No respirations. Code blue call. CPR in progress."

Although the post-anesthesiology orders required pulse oximeter monitoring for this patient (and other patients), according to testimony of the nurses, these orders were routinely ignored per their training and no pulse oximeters were on the postpartum floor. The same post-anesthesiology orders called for frequent vital signs and evaluations which were admittedly not followed as well. The orders read as follows:

Monitor the patient and notify the anesthesiologist if any of these symptomatology occur such as respiratory rate less than 10 respirations per minute, pulse oximetry, that the oxygen level in the blood is less than 90, evidence of obstruction of the airway. Patient is drowsy, excessively somnolent or unable to arouse. Pain relief is deemed inadequate.

It was routine to ignore, per the nurses training, this post-anesthesia order regarding pulse oximeter monitoring on 4-17-98. Nurse Miller says that standard operating procedure for a floor admission post-C-section was a measurement of vital signs on admission, at two hours, then every four hours for 48 hours. This practice is contrary to Dr. Moore's orders recorded in the chart and the policy and procedures for that floor.

The patient's history of sleep apnea was not considered in evaluating fentanyl and other drug-induced respiratory depression. The patient had some wheezing and was listed as 245 pounds but these were mistakenly considered normal for a term pregnancy.

Dr. Perreault, a board certified pulmonologist, was consulted on the night of the respiratory arrest. The arrest occurred around midnight 4-17 to 4-18. Dr. Perreault arrived around 3:00 A.M. on 4-18. She charted around 7:00 A.M.: cardiorespiratory arrest followed by seizures. Impression: history of postpartum depression and bipolar disorder; left lower lobe pneumonia; sleep apnea; history of smoking. Respiratory arrest may have been caused from a combination of obstructive sleep apnea with upper airway obstruction, combined with the use of epidural fentanyl and possible drug interaction with psychiatric medications.

Laboratory toxicology samples were sent to outside laboratories—National Medical in Pennsylvania and MedTox in Minnesota. Neither fentanyl nor lorazepam (Ativan) were reported in these toxicology tests.

Opinions

I hold the following opinions with reasonable pharmacological certainty:

1. Ms. Patient suffered a respiratory arrest leading to a cardiac arrest as a result of the combined effects and interactions of fentanyl, Ativan, Stelazine, Wellbutrin, and Tegretol. There is a strong temporal relationship between the administration of the psychotropic medications and the

carotid endarterectomy anesthesia (CEA) Fentanyl. The interactive and synergistic toxicity of these medications with fentanyl (and other opioid analgesics) is well known and cautioned in product information for all the drugs involved, as well as in authoritative literature. For purposes of this report and my opinions, fentanyl, Stelazine, and Ativan will be discussed. Compared to Wellbutrin and Tegretol, Stelazine and Ativan have the greatest effect on the central nervous system, thus exacerbating the respiratory depression of fentanyl.

2. The labor and delivery nurses were negligent in adequate monitoring and failure to follow the orders of the anesthesiologist, specifically failure to monitor the oxygenation of the patient's hemoglobin through pulse oximetry. Narcan, although ordered, was not administered, and should have been. These nurses should have considered the dangerous interactive potential of the CEA fentanyl and the psychotropic drugs which were prescribed. Systematically ignoring the safety policy, they demonstrated reckless disregard for the welfare of their patients.

3. The St. Jude Hospital nursing and hospital administration was negligent for failure to uniformly implement the safety policies for labor and delivery patients as it applies to the use of pulse oximetry for CEA patients on opioids such as fentanyl.

4. The postpartum psychiatric medications should not have been administered to this patient receiving the CEA fentanyl. Nurse Karala, Dr. Basara, Dr. Moore, and Dr. Laukka should have considered the dangerous interactive potential of the CEA fentanyl and the psychotropic drugs which were prescribed.

5. Use of the pulse oximeter would have detected a drug-induced respiratory depression and oxygen deprivation, and prevented the cardiorespiratory arrest. The pulse oximetry alarm, appropriate oxygenation, establishment of an airway, and reversal of opioids with Narcan would have precluded the hypoxic injury to Ms. Patient's brain.

6. The toxicology tests are limited by their design. Fentanyl was not detected; it was probably not part of the panel screen of the test, so therefore, it would not be reported. The clinical record supports that fentanyl was administered, and

had a proper test been administered, it would have been detected. Benzodiazepines were negative. Since Ativan (lorazepam) was charted, it would be expected to be detected in the sample. Either the test result is erroneous (since it should be there), or the specific screen was not designed to detect the specific benzodiazepine lorazepam. Further investigation will be needed to fully address these toxicology testing issues.

The drugs: opioids (fentanyl) and respiratory depression, with and without additional central nervous system (CNS) depressants.

Fentanyl

Fentanyl is a synthetic opioid, 100 times more potent than morphine. It is used as an anesthetic and analgesic, both intravenously and epidurally. It is a very short-acting analgesic, but it also demonstrates a bi-phasic kinetic profile, which has been reported to result in late toxicities (rebound) after the infusion is stopped. The following text is taken directly from the Fentanyl manufacturer's package insert:

Fentanyl citrate is a narcotic analgesic. A dose of 100 mcg (0.1 mg) (2 ml) is approximately equivalent in analgesic activity to 10 mg of morphine or 75 mg of meperidine. The principal actions of therapeutic value are analgesia and sedation. Alterations in respiratory rate and alveolar ventilation, associated with narcotic analgesics, may last longer than the analgesic effect. As the dose of narcotic is increased, the decrease in pulmonary exchange becomes greater. Large doses may produce apnea. Fentanyl appears to have less emetic activity than either morphine or meperidine. Histamine assays and skin wheal testing in man indicate that clinically significant histamine release rarely occurs with fentanyl. Recent assays in man show no clinically significant histamine release in dosages up to 50 mg/kg (0.05 mg/kg) (1 ml/kg). Fentanyl preserves cardiac stability and blunts stress-related hormonal changes at higher doses.

The pharmacokinetics of fentanyl can be described as a three-compartment model, with a distribution time of 1.7 minutes, redistribution of 13 minutes and a terminal elimination half-life of 219 minutes. The volume of distribution for fentanyl is 4 L/kg.

The onset of action of fentanyl is almost immediate when the drug is given intravenously; however, the maximal analgesic and respiratory depressant effect may not be noted for several minutes. The usual duration of action of the analgesic effect is 30 to 60 minutes after a single intravenous dose of up to 100 mg (0.1 mg) (2 ml). Following intramuscular administration, the onset of action is from seven to eight minutes, and the duration of action is one to two hours. As with longer acting narcotic analgesics, the duration of the respiratory depressant effect of fentanyl may be longer than the analgesic effect. The following observations have been reported concerning altered respiratory response to carbon dioxide (CO_2) stimulation following the administration of fentanyl citrate:

Diminished sensitivity to CO_2 stimulation may persist longer than depression of respiratory rate. (Altered sensitivity to CO_2 stimulation has been demonstrated for up to four hours following a single dose of 600 mg (0.6 g) (12 ml) fentanyl to healthy volunteers.) Fentanyl frequently slows the respiratory rate, duration and degree of respiratory depression being dose-related. The peak respiratory depressant effect of a single intravenous dose of fentanyl citrate is noted 5 to 15 minutes following injection. See also WARNINGS and PRECAUTIONS concerning respiratory depression.

Serious respiratory depression can occur, even with proper doses, in vulnerable individuals. As with other potent anesthetic agents, fentanyl has been associated with cases of serious respiratory depression in individuals with respiratory disorders, cases of excessive or improper dosage, individuals with unsuspected abnormalities of absorption or metabolism of the drug, and in rare cases where no specific etiology can be identified. Fentanyl should be administered only in specifically monitored settings and by persons specifically trained in the use of anesthetics and the management of the respiratory effects of potent opioids, including establishment and maintenance of a patent airway and assisted ventilation (see also BOXED WARNING and PRECAUTIONS).

Respiratory depression caused by opioid analgesics can be reversed by opioid antagonists such as naloxone, also known as Narcan. Because the duration of respiratory depression produced by fentanyl may last longer than the duration of the opioid antagonist action, appropriate surveillance should be maintained. As with all potent opioids, profound analgesia is accompanied by respiratory depression and diminished sensitivity to CO_2 stimulation, which may persist into or recur in the postoperative period.

Impaired Respiration: Fentanyl should be used with caution in patients with chronic obstructive pulmonary disease, patients with decreased respiratory reserve, and others with potentially compromised respiration. In such patients, narcotics may additionally decrease respiratory drive and increase airway resistance. During anesthesia, this can be managed by assisted or controlled respiration.

Because of the risk of hypoventilation, the lowest effective dose of oral fentanyl should be used, and it should be administered only in monitored settings and by persons specifically trained in the use of anesthetics and the management of the respiratory effects of potent opioids, including the establishment and maintenance of a patent airway and assisted ventilation.

Drug Interactions: Other CNS depressant drugs (e.g., barbiturates, tranquilizers, narcotics and general anesthetics) will have additive or potentiating effects with fentanyl. When patients have received such drugs, the dose of fentanyl required will be less than usual. Following the administration of fentanyl citrate, the dose of other CNS depressant drugs should be reduced.

Stelazine

Selected text, relevant to this case, is excerpted from the manufacturer's prescribing information for Stelazine, a potent phenothiazine antipsychotic:

If agents such as sedatives, narcotics, anesthetics, tranquilizers or alcohol are used either simultaneously or successively with the drug, the possibility of an undesirable additive depressant effect should be considered.

Ativan

The following is an excerpt from the manufacturer's prescribing information:

Ativan (lorazepam) is an anti-anxiety drug, and a member of the benzodiazepine class. It is classed as a CNS depressant. Lorazepam is indicated for the management of anxiety disorders or for the short-term relief of the symptoms of anxiety or anxiety-associated with depressive symptoms. Anxiety or tension associated with the stress of everyday life usually does not require treatment with an anxiolytic.

Lorazepam is not recommended for use in patients with a primary depressive disorder or psychosis. As with all patients on CNS-acting drugs, patients receiving lorazepam should be warned not to operate dangerous machinery or motor vehicles and that their tolerance for alcohol and other CNS depressants will be diminished.

Clinically significant drug interactions: The benzodiazepines, including lorazepam, produce CNS-depressant effects when administered with such medications as barbiturates or alcohol.

Lorazepam produces depression of the central nervous system when administered with ethyl alcohol, phenothiazines, barbiturates, MAO inhibitors, and other antidepressants. Doses of other injectable central nervous system depressant drugs should ordinarily be reduced (see PRECAUTIONS).

Obesity-hypoventilation syndrome

Ms. Patient had additional risk factors for respiratory depression in addition to the combination of fentanyl and other CNS depressant drugs (Stelazine, Ativan, Tegretol, Wellbutrin). These risk factors include wheezing and dyspnea as noted in Dr. Abass' anesthesia evaluation and obesity.

Summary and conclusions

In my opinion, Ms. Patient's respiratory arrest was caused by the fentanyl and other medications she was administered. The gross negligence of the la-

bor and delivery nursing staff at St. Jude Hospital allowed this tragedy to occur, which would have been prevented had the staff exercised reasonable and prudent judgment and care, and followed the policies and procedures which were in place to protect patients undergoing therapy with predictably dangerous analgesics (Fentanyl). The use of the psychotropics for postpartum depression enhanced the fentanyl respiratory toxicity and must therefore be considered at least additive, and probably were not needed/should have been avoided until the patient was off the fentanyl. The resuscitation efforts, once the patient was discovered as unresponsive (Code Blue) were inadequate, in that Narcan was not administered and the ambu bag giving the patient oxygen was not administered until 7 minutes after Ms. Patient was found.

C. Case Report: Duragesic (Fentanyl) Death in Discharged Patient

I reviewed the Medical Center records, the death certificate, autopsy, and toxicology reports, and the Certificate of Merit by Dr. Larson. I also reviewed authoritative pharmacology, toxicology, and prescribing information for fentanyl.

Mr. Decedent had ear nose and throat surgery related to tonsilar cancer by Dr. ENT Surgeon on February 23, 1999 and discharged home on March 5, 1999. He died the next day. An autopsy toxicology report found elevated tissue liver levels of fentanyl, a synthetic opioid, the active ingredient in the Duragesic patch. In addition to Duragesic, he was also discharged on Vicodin (hydrocodone/acetaminophen—also a synthetic opioid) tablets crushed through a feeding gastroscopy tube.

While recovering from surgery, Mr. Decedent was treated with Morphine PCA (patient-controlled analgesia) pump as well as single Morphine IV doses through 3/4/99 ("D/C IV MS in 12 hours. May continue Vicodin II QID per G tube"). On 2/28, Vicodin was initiated. Duragesic 75mcg/hour was prescribed on 3/4/99. Mr. Decedent experienced significant respiratory depression. The following excerpts from the medical record are instructive:

Rec'd pt Lethargic pale w/d. Respo 16-18 with stidorous/congested respirations noted. Responds quickly to verbal/ tactile stimuli but drifts back to sleep within a few seconds. Lips pink w/d; vss; D. Hehn made aware of above. Suctioned with thick dark beige sputum noted. Respo. Clear...PO2—<60-70s 0900 Dr. Surgeon paged by D. Nurse made aware of above. Rec'd order for Narcan 0.4 mg in titrated doses. Narcan 0.13 mg IVP given—Pt. alert and responding verbally to questions within 1" of Narcan administered. Pt. then became alert and responded appropriately to questions and pulse ox(imetry) increased to 88%. Removed fentanyl 75mcg. Successful reversal of narcotic effect. D. Nurse RN (Oncology CNS Note) and Narcan (naloxone-narcotic antagonist/antidote) was prescribed/administered (09:25 and 11:15) to reverse the effect of the Duragesic/ fentanyl ("remove Fentanyl patch").

Inexplicably, "change Fentanyl (sp) dose to 100mcg d/t (due to) narcotic effect," a higher dose of fentanyl, was prescribed for home use. Oxygen was also prescribed for home use.

Fentanyl (duragesic)

The prescribing information (package insert) for Duragesic states:

Serious respiratory depression can occur, even with proper doses, in vulnerable individuals as with other potent anesthetic agents, fentanyl has been associated with cases of serious respiratory depression in individuals with respiratory disorders, cases of excessive or improper dosage, in individuals with unsuspected abnormalities of absorption or metabolism of the drug, and in rare cases where no specific etiology can be identified. Fentanyl should be administered only in specifically monitored settings and by persons specifically trained in the use of anesthetics and the management of the respiratory effects of potent opioids, including establishment and maintenance of a patent airway and assisted ventilation (see also BOXED WARNING and PRECAUTIONS).

Hypoventilation (respiratory depression): Hypoventilation may occur at any time during the use of fentanyl. Because significant amounts of fentanyl are absorbed from the skin for 17 hours or more after the system is removed, hypoventilation may persist beyond the removal of fentanyl. Consequently, patients with hypoventilation should be carefully observed for degree of sedation and their respiratory rate monitored until respiration has stabilized.

The use of concomitant CNS active drugs requires special patient care and observation. See WARNINGS.

Dosage and administration

With all opioids, the safety of patients using the products is dependent on healthcare practitioners prescribing them in strict conformity with their approved labeling with respect to patient selection, dosing, and proper conditions for use.

As with all opioids, dosage should be individualized. The most important factor to be considered in determining the appropriate dose is the extent of preexisting opioid tolerance. (See BOXED WARNING and CONTRAINDICATIONS.) Initial doses should be reduced in elderly or debilitated patients (see PRECAUTIONS).

Dose selection

Doses must be individualized based upon the status of each patient and should be assessed at regular intervals after fentanyl application. Reduced doses of fentanyl are suggested for the elderly and other groups discussed in precautions.

Opinions

1. Mr. Decedent died from the respiratory toxicity of fentanyl, which may or may not have been used in combination with Vicodin.

2. Mr. Decedent experienced significant respiratory toxicity from fentanyl in the hospital (3/5/99), hours prior to his discharge, following an attempt to treat his pain with Duragesic 75mcg/hour patch. He had been treated with morphine 4 mg/hour as well as vicodin. The clinical record clearly shows that the Duragesic dose of 75mcg was too much for him, as evidenced by the administration of Narcan to reverse narcotic effects.

3. Once started on Duragesic patch, the patient should be monitored for at least 24 hours in a controlled environment to determine the

patient's ability to tolerate the "patch." This delay is necessary because it takes some time for the patch to reach peak efficacy, and early release may occur before the peak, therefore leaving the patient at risk.

4. Mr. Decedent was clearly toxic on 75 mcg/hour dose strength patch. It is inexplicable why a higher dose, i.e., 100mcg/hour patch was ordered, in view of this known and demonstrated toxicity.

5. In my opinion, the prescribing physicians, attending nurses, and home-health nurses demonstrated incompetence and ignorance in their negligent use of the Duragesic patch, resulting in the death of Mr. Decedent from acute fentanyl overdose. The inappropriate prescribing, administering, and monitoring represents a departure from the standard of reasonable care upheld by health care professionals in the United States.

6. In this matter, the standard of care would have prevented the escalation of the dose of the Duragesic patch (fentanyl) from 75mcg/H to 100mcg/H in the face of fentanyl toxicity. The standard of care would have dictated that Mr. Decedent would have been safely stabilized on an effective analgesic before being discharged home.

D. Case Report: High Dose Fentanyl Patch Prescribed in Opiate-Naïve Patient—Death

Facts of the case

Ralph Rodgers, a 42-year-old man with severe heart disease, implanted with an implantable cardioverter defibrillator (ICD), and a candidate for a orthoptic heart transplant, complained to Dr. David Houston of pain. On August 3, 2005, Dr. Houston prescribed Fentanyl Transdermal System (FTS) patches, 100mcg/hour patches, #5, apply one patch to chest wall every 72 hours. The prescription was picked up by Mr. Rodgers's sister-in-law, Carrie Hughes, at Dr. Houston's office and taken to a local pharmacy where it was filled. The completed prescription was picked up by Mr. Rodgers's wife, Elizabeth Williams. A single patch was applied to Mr. Rodgers's chest that evening. The next morning, August 4, 2005, Ms. Williams noted that Mr. Rodgers was still sleeping, and indeed, was snoring. Mr. Rodgers was found dead in bed later that day. 911 was called, EMS arrived, and determined that CPR was futile, he was cold, stiff, and unresponsive. An autopsy was conducted; toxicology tests were ordered, but the toxicology test results were lost in the chaos associated with Hurricane Katrina.

Dr. Houston testified at his deposition that he considered Ralph Rodgers a drug user, dependent, and opioid tolerant, and he ordered the highest dose out of "compassionate care," admittedly ignoring the dosing guidelines described in the prescribing information (package insert) for the FTS. Dr. Houston denied prescribing based on a phone call and insisted that Rodgers came to his office and was despondent, crying, and felt like he was dying.

The records described multiple prescription medications current in August 2005. The most recent opiate prescription was for 60 Darvocet 100 mg, prescribed in June 2005. A history of Meperidine and hydrocodone/acetaminophen is noted earlier in May and June 2004.

Opinions and bases of opinions

All of the following opinions are expressed with reasonable pharmacological certainty and by a preponderance of the evidence.

- Mr. Rodgers's death was caused by an overdose of fentanyl, a potent synthetic opiate, 100 times more potent than morphine. Mr. Rodgers's heart condition increased his risk to succumbing to the fentanyl overdose, but he would have died absent any cardiac disease. While Mr. Rodgers did have serious heart disease, his death was not imminent (testimony of Dr. Houston).

- The dose prescribed, 100mcg/hour, is the equivalent of ~360 mg oral morphine (package insert).

- The onset of action and time to peak actions are consistent with the onset of sleep, the appearance of snoring (respiratory depression), and his death.

- Mr. Rodgers was not opiate tolerant; indeed, even if he were still consuming the prescribed amounts of Darvocet, he was still not a candidate for the highest dose of FTS, i.e., 100mcg/hour. The use of meperidine and hydrocodone/acetaminophen 15 months earlier would not render Rodgers opiate-tolerant or dependent.

- The use of FTS at any dose in Rodgers in August 2005 was contraindicated. Contraindication, as noted in the black box warning for the FTS, means that the FTS should not have been used. FTS is indicated for opioid tolerant patients requiring continuous high dose opiates for a prolonged period of time. The high dose of FTS would only be justified by a titration up from lower doses. The lowest dose of FTS is 25mcg/hour. The use of the 25mcg FTS would also have been contraindicated in Rodgers.

- The FDA and manufacturers of FTS have frequently issued warnings and guidelines for the safe use of fentanyl patches. The following was issued shortly (July 2005) before Mr. Rodgers's death:

> FDA Public Health Advisory: Safety Warnings Regarding Use of Fentanyl Transdermal (Skin) Patches
> FDA is investigating reports of death and other serious side effects from overdoses of fentanyl in patients using fentanyl transdermal (skin) patches for pain control. Deaths and overdoses have occurred in patients using both the brand name product Duragesic and the generic product. The directions for using the fentanyl skin patch must be followed exactly to prevent death or other serious side effects from overdosing with fentanyl. These directions are provided in the product label and patient package insert.

MedWatch—The FDA Safety Information and Adverse Event Reporting Program issued an update that highlights important information on appropriate prescribing, dose selection, and the safe use of the fentanyl transdermal system (patch). The FDA previously issued a Public Health Advisory and Information for Healthcare Professionals in July 2005 regarding the appropriate and safe use of the transdermal system. However, the Agency continues to receive reports of death and life-threatening adverse events related to fentanyl overdose that have occurred when the fentanyl patch was used to treat pain in opioid-naïve patients and when opioid-tolerant patients have applied more patches

than prescribed, changed the patch too frequently, or exposed the patch to a heat source. The fentanyl patch is only indicated for use in patients with persistent, moderate to severe chronic pain who have been taking a regular, daily, around-the-clock narcotic pain medicine for longer than a week and are considered to be opioid-tolerant. Patients must avoid exposing the patch to excessive heat as this promotes the release of fentanyl from the patch and increases the absorption of fentanyl through the skin which can result in fatal overdose. Directions for prescribing and using the fentanyl patch must be followed exactly to prevent death or other serious side effects from fentanyl overdose. Read the complete 2007 MedWatch Safety Summary including a link to the FDA Public Health Advisory and Information for Healthcare Professionals Sheet regarding this issue at: www.fda.gov/medwatch/safety/2007/safety07.htm#Fentanyl.

- Dr. Houston denies prescribing based on a phone call. The FTS would have been contraindicated even if Dr. Houston had seen Rodgers in his office on August 3, 2005.

- The use of FTS 100mcg/hour would caused death in any opioid naïve or slightly tolerant person.

Summary and conclusion

Ralph Rodgers died as a result of the use of the prescribed Fentanyl Transdermal System, 100mcg/hour patch. The prescription of the patch, considering the facts of the case, was contraindicated, and should not have occurred.

E. Case Report: Heroin and Other Opiates

Widespread abuse of heroin and other opiates (e.g., OxyContin) predictably will result in criminal and civil litigants "under the influence" or at least charged as being so, as a result of evidence of opiate use (see Chapter 44, *Forensic Issues in Recreational Drugs,* Section 44.11.D).

The following report was filed in civil cases where the issue of heroin use was considered.

Facts of the case

The defendant was observed by Miami Police Officers on the evening of December 5, 2000, at a "drug house" on the West Side of Miami. As the defendant drove away, he was followed by police officers, who executed a stop, at which time, the defendant fled the police. During the "chase," the defendant narrowly missed colliding head-on with another CPD vehicle, the crash was avoided by the officer, and then he crashed the 1995 Mustang into a viaduct on Elm street. An ambulance was called at the time of the crash, the officer anticipated that there would be injuries. The defendant exited his vehicle and resisted several officers who were attempting to arrest him, and he was handcuffed. Shortly after he was subdued and handcuffed, he complained of difficulty breathing. The police officers took the handcuffs off and again requested an ambulance. When the paramedics arrived, the defendant was in full arrest. He was taken to El Camino Hospital where he was pronounced dead.

The family and friends reported that the defendant was taking multiple medications for heart disease and blood pressure, which caused the defendant to be drowsy. The defendant's wife reported that he did not abuse alcohol or drugs.

The toxicology report identified morphine, 70 nanograms (ng)/ml in the postmortem testing. The postmortem examination noted a weight of 322 pounds. The medical examiner indicated that opiate intoxication contributed to the defendant's death.

A police dog examined the Mustang for the presence of drugs. The dog sensed drugs, but none were found.

Opinions

In my opinion, within a reasonable degree of pharmacological certainty, the defendant used heroin shortly before he was observed by the police and the pursuit began. A blood test of 70 nanograms/ml of morphine indicates recent and high dose of an opiate. Based on the defendant's weight and height, I estimate that he consumed a dose of ~15–20 mg of heroin. The opiates responsible include heroin and morphine, as heroin is rapidly metabolized to morphine in the blood. Since morphine is generally not available on the street, and heroin is, it is probable that heroin was used by the defendant within a period of an hour or two before the crash. His subsequent actions and behavior, in my opinion, were impaired by heroin. He acted erratically and with poor judgment (fleeing police; attempting to collide with another police car; resisting arrest). After he was subdued, he complained of difficulty breathing and chest pain. In my opinion, the pres-

ence and actions of heroin on the respiratory center (breathing) probably contributed to the defendant's breathing difficulty, which preceded his cardiac arrest and death.

The records and statements indicate that the defendant was diagnosed with multiple medical conditions, and treated for those conditions with multiple medications. Those same statements indicate a concern that his medications caused drowsiness. Many medications may interact with and increase the toxicity of heroin and morphine.

Bases for opinions

Intoxication and impairments by heroin, an illegal narcotic (opiate) central nervous system (CNS) depressant, causes brain and behavioral toxicity, including lethargy, euphoria, dysphoria, mental clouding, hallucinations, depression, cognitive impairment and paranoia.

Morphine and related opioids produce their major effects on the CNS. The effects are remarkably diverse and include analgesia, drowsiness, changes in mood, respiratory depression, decreased gastrointestinal motility, nausea, vomiting, and alterations of the endocrine and autonomic nervous systems.

Morphine-like opioids depress respiration, at least in part by virtue of a direct effect on the brainstem respiratory centers. The respiratory depression is discernible even with doses too small to disturb consciousness, and increases progressively as the dose is increased. In human beings, death from morphine poisoning is nearly always due to respiratory arrest. Therapeutic doses of morphine depress all phases of respiratory activity (rate, minute volume, and tidal exchange) and may also produce irregular breathing. The diminished respiratory volume is due primarily to a slower rate of breathing, and with toxic amounts the rate may fall to three or four breaths per minute. Although respiratory effects can be documented readily with standard doses of morphine, respiratory depression is rarely a problem clinically in the absence of underlying pulmonary dysfunction. However, the combination of opiates with other medications, such as general anesthetics, tranquilizers, alcohol, or sedative-hypnotics, may present a greater risk of respiratory depression.

Maximal respiratory depression occurs within five to ten minutes after intravenous administration of morphine or within 30 to 90 minutes following intramuscular or subcutaneous administration, respectively. Maximal depressant effects occur more rapidly with more lipid-soluble agents. Following therapeutic doses, respiratory minute volume may be reduced for as long as four to five hours.

The primary mechanism of respiratory depression by opioids involves a reduction in the responsiveness of the brainstem respiratory centers to carbon dioxide. Opioids also depress the pontine and medullary centers involved in regulating respiratory rhythmicity and the responsiveness of medullary respiratory centers to electrical stimulation.

Conclusion

The defendant, the decedent, was intoxicated and impaired by heroin when he resisted arrest and fought with the police, and the presence, action, and toxicity of the heroin probably impaired his ability to breath. The toxicity of heroin and morphine is greater in a naïve or occasional user. (His wife told police that her husband did not abuse drugs.) The peak action of heroin/morphine is 10–15 minutes. Respiratory depression can occur at therapeutic doses without significant mental and motor depression. This intoxication and impairment is also consistent with the abnormal behavior manifested by the decedent.

F. Case Report: Dilaudid Respiratory Arrest

Relevant facts of the case

Ruth Tighe was an elderly woman admitted to O'Connor Hospital from the emergency room (ER) on January 18, 2005 for a complaint of left flank pain radiating down to the left lower abdomen. She was found to have a kidney stone. In the ER, Ms. Tighe's oxygen saturation initially was 98% on room air. In the ER, she received two injections of Dilaudid, 2 mg IV (intravenous) at 7:00 P.M. on 1/17/05 and at 2:00 A.M. and 11:00 A.M. on 1/18/05. Shortly thereafter, she was admitted to the 4th floor and was treated by staff nurses and nurse's aides. At 12:25, she had a nursing assessment that revealed a respiratory rate of 24, pulse 114, and her oxygen saturation was 81% on room air. Oxygen by nasal cannula was administered, and her oxygen saturation went up to 95%. An arterial blood gas (ABG) was ordered and performed at 1 P.M. on January 18 that revealed a pH of 7.29, pC02 = 53, pO2 175.

HCO3 26. The blood gas showed an acute respiratory acidosis. Later that day, Ms. Tighe's oxygen was removed when she was eating, and her oxygen saturation deteriorated to below 88%. Nurse notations indicate that her pupils were constricted. Other than the standard vital sign (VS) equipment and pulse oximetry, no cardiac monitoring with telemetry was available on this floor and the nurses observed standard assessments once per shift.

A pulmonary consult was ordered for SOB (shortness of breath). The pulmonary consultant, Dr. Cunningham, saw the patient and ordered a bronchodilator treatment as needed; he did not note any concern or relationship to her abnormal oxygen and blood gas status to the Dilaudid, either in the chart or in his deposition.

At 1:35 P.M. on January 18, 2005, a routine pharmacy note reduced the Levaquin antibiotic order from 500 mg to 250 mg, due to a decreased GFR (glomerular filtration rate—a measure of kidney perfusion and function affecting the clearance of medications from the body), per hospital protocol.

Dr. Anderson testified that the hypoventilation was secondary to pain, not respiratory depression due to Dilaudid. Ms. Tighe received an additional 2 mg of Dilaudid at 4:00 A.M. on 1/19/05. When Dr. Anderson first saw Ms. Tighe before 7:30 A.M. on January 19, she was complaining of nausea and vomiting with liquids and he questioned whether this was due to her kidney stone or the Dilaudid. Toradol was ordered as an additional pain medication, in the hope of reducing the Dilaudid or not increasing it. He did, however, increase the frequency of the Dilaudid from 2 mg every four hours to 2 mg every two hours. Later on January 19, 2005, she received 2 mg of Dilaudid at 11:15 A.M., 5 P.M. and 9:45 P.M. On January 19, 2005 at 9:50 A.M., she complained of urinary incontinence.

Several of the nurses who treated this patient have testified that they were not aware of the risk of giving Dilaudid at all. Some did not know that it had a risk of causing respiratory depression and did not know the risk was greater in the elderly. Nurse Jackson covered this patient during the night shift of January 19-20 from 11:00 P.M. to 7:00 A.M. After listening to the tape-recorded nursing report she assessed the patient around midnight but did not record her assessment until 3:30 A.M. She was medicated with Dilaudid 2 mg IV by the RN (Sherry Blevins) at 1:25 A.M.

Nurse Jackson states that she would usually check on each patient hourly, but would not awaken them if sleeping comfortably. She had no recollection of these checks. She has no recollection of finding the patient in any distress until 6:15 A.M. when the patient was unresponsive and without a pulse. A code was called. The patient expired at 6:50 A.M. No autopsy was done; no toxicology was tested.

Opinions

In my opinion, with reasonable pharmacological certainty, Ruth Tighe suffered a respiratory arrest that progressed to a cardiac arrest directly resulting from the effect of Dilaudid. Any pre-existing cardiac disease would increase her risk from hydromorphone respiratory depression.

Bases for opinions

1. Ms. Tighe was a small woman with a GFR, who had two documented episodes of decreased oxygen saturation following the initiation of Dilaudid, a potent respiratory depressant. The respiratory toxicity was further documented by arterial blood gas analysis indicating respiratory acidosis and hypercapnia (elevated CO_2), which is evidence of narcosis-induced respiratory depression. These documented respiratory warnings are compelling.

2. Her clinical signs are consistent with Dilaudid effects and toxicity:
   • constricted pupils
   • pain relieved
   • urinary incontinence
   • shortness of breath
   • nausea and vomiting
   • unresponsiveness

3. Opiates cause respiratory depression at therapeutic doses.

4. The defense experts suggest that the timing of the Dilaudid administration and Ms. Tighe's death makes it unlikely that respiratory issues contributed to her death. I disagree. The elderly are particularly sensitive to the effects of opiates, especially respiratory depression. Clearance of opiates may be decreased in geriatric patients, resulting in longer duration of action. Care should be exercised, and appropriate dosage adjustments (e.g., lower initial doses, longer dosing intervals) should be considered.

Dilaudid (hydromorphone) is a particularly potent opiate, seven times more potent than morphine. The half-life and thus the blood levels and toxicity are enhanced with decreased renal function. The half-life of Dilaudid in the elderly is up to four hours, bringing the maximum effects (in the first half-life) after the 1:25 A.M. dose during the period in which no vital signs were taken. She was only observed as resting comfortably. Nurse's observations would not be able to discern compromised breathing function, changes in respiratory rate or depth of respirations, and increasing risk of narcosis—until she was noted to be unresponsive at ~6:15 A.M.

5. Renal function is depressed by opioids. It is believed that in humans this is chiefly due to a decreased renal plasma flow. Opioids can decrease systemic blood pressure and glomerular filtration rate. Opiate agonists (hydromorphone) may have a prolonged duration and cumulative effect in patients with hepatic or renal dysfunction. Care should be exercised and the initial dosage of the opiate should be reduced in patients who have renal insufficiency. Recall that the calculated GFR in Ms. Tighe was low, precipitating a reduction of dose of the Levaquin.

6. The half-life of hydromorphone is 1.5–3.8 hours. The metabolite, hydromorphone-3- glucoronide, appears to have significant pharmacological activity, and lasts longer than the active ingredient, contributing to cumulative and prolonged activity. The use of hydromorphone may result in muscle flaccidity (urinary incontinence).

7. The defense experts suggest that because Ms. Tighe did not have obvious changes in mental status on January 18 and January 19, Dilaudid did not contribute to her demise. I disagree. Standard methods for assessing level of consciousness may not detect respiratory depression. Even though patients can be aroused for a brief period of time and may in fact be able to speak, they may immediately fall back into a state of over sedation when the stimulus is removed. In addition, an overly sedated patient's respiratory rate may improve with stimulation but quickly decreases when the stimulation is removed.

27.5 Methadone Special Kinetics and Case Report

Methadone is in a class of medication called opiate analgesics and was first presented by the Eli Lilly and Company in 1947. Its suggested use was for the withdrawal symptoms of heroin, termed methadone maintenance. This, in turn, sparked the acceleration of its use in the 1970s. Currently, there is a new realization for its utility in pain treatment and management in relation to a number of chronic disorders.[13]

A. Methadone Use and Treating Chronic Pain

Methadone is a long-lasting opioid analgesic. Its effects are very similar to other opioid agents such as heroin and morphine. This congruity causes methadone to have similar effects and durations. The use of methadone was once restricted to only treat narcotic addicts who willingly underwent the detoxification process.

Opiate addiction is a significant problem for affected patients, their families and society in general. In 2002, it was estimated that approximately 980,000 people in the United States were addicted to heroin and other opiates such as OxyContin and hydrocone. The risks of such addiction often result in premature death or the contraction of HIV, hepatitis B/C, sexually transmitted diseases (STDs) and other physical/mental problems. Between 5,000 and 10,000 injection drug users die of an overdose every year.[14]

Methadone is a drug agent that functions by binding to brain receptor sites called opioid receptors. The receptor sites are affected by a number of other opiates including heroin. When an opiate binds to the opioid receptor, two effects are produced: pain relief and pleasure (reward). When a person injects or administers heroin, the drug travels quickly from the blood stream to the brain and is then converted to morphine. The morphine then activates the opioid receptors involved in the reward system of the brain. Stimulation of these receptors result in feelings of reward and activates the pleasure pathways due to greater amounts of dopamine. This induces a potent euphoric experience, or rush. The large amounts of dopamine and reward system stimulation can lead to addiction seen in heroin drug users.[15]

Methadone is a useful agent in heroin addiction because it acts on the very same receptors that are affected by heroin and other opiates. Methadone blocks the euphoria and pain relief attributed to the use of heroin and other opiates. It also suppresses the intense craving for opiates that are a significant factor in opiate relapse (withdrawal). The serious symptoms of withdrawal are more of an incentive for a heroin user to keep using heroin.[15]

Within the past 20 years, methadone has been utilized especially in the treatment of chronic pain relief. Methadone's distinct pharmacological characteristics necessitate higher precautionary measures than the other opioid therapies. It has both a slow onset of action and a long elimination half-life. The elimination half-life of methadone is broad—between 8-59 hours—and is longer than its duration of analgesic action (4-8 hours).[16] The pharmacodynamics and pharmacokinetics of methadone demand careful dosing management. For chronic pain, specialized team evaluation and treatment plans are mandatory in implementing effective analgesia in various levels of severity.

Methadone is not the opioid drug of choice for chronic pain. Morphine sulfate (MS) is the most effective and one of the strongest opioids used. However, if patients do not gain suitable pain relief from increased administration of morphine sulfate, or have idiopathic reactions to MS, methadone is the second line therapy of choice. Methadone is also the only long duration opioid that can be taken orally. The risk of respiratory depression and death are a significant concern in using methadone for the treatment of chronic pain.

Opiates, in general, can also act on the respiratory center within the brainstem, where they cause a decrease in activity which induce a decrease in breathing rate. Large amounts of an opiate, such as heroin, can cause a toxic effect which shuts down breathing altogether (respiratory depression). An overdose of heroin can therefore cause a person to stop breathing and die.

Therapeutic levels of methadone can normalize patients by appeasing the opioid withdrawal syndrome. Higher doses of methadone antagonize the euphoria associated with heroin, morphine and other opioids. The methadone replacement therapy, also known as Methadone Maintenance Treatment (MMT) decreases the illegal use of pertinent opiates and encourages improvement of health and social behavior.

An added benefit of MMT is the indirect prevention of the transmission of infectious diseases associated with the opiate injection process. The injection of illicit drugs increases the likelihood of the transmission of hepatitis and HIV. The suppression of narcotic craving, the relief of withdrawal pains and blockage of narcotic opiate euphoria certainly decreases the pursuit of said disease-hazardous injections.

Methadone is also acceptable for pregnant opiate addicts with the proper dosing regimen.

As mentioned previously, methadone has a slow onset and therefore lacks the "rush" of heroin. MMT is limited to specialized licensed clinics which employ specific methods to promote safe and highly effective dosing schedules, which aim to detoxify without acute withdrawal. Professionals who are not licensed are unable to treat addicts. The only exception would involve an MMT patient that requires acute medical care, and would undergo a serious medical complication (withdrawal).

The above scenario is quite common in acute care hospitals in which the admission of addicted patients necessitates the treatment for both pain and withdrawal prevention.

B. Adverse Effects of Methadone

Deaths due to cardiac and respiratory threats from methadone have been reported during initiation (onset of treatment) and conversion of chronic pain patients to methadone treatment from treatment with other opiates such as OxyContin. It is important to comprehend the pharmacokinetics and pharmacodynamics of methadone before converting patients from other opioids to methadone. A degree of vigilance needs to be in place before the onset of treatment conversion.[17]

C. Respiratory Depression

Any opiate use will acutely or chronically cause a risk of respiratory depression. Methadone in particular has a greater risk of respiratory depression due to its unique kinetics (long half-life) and efficacy (longer duration of analgesic action). This means that at the beginning of methadone therapy, methadone can stay present in the body for 15 to 30 hours, and the patient may be taking the drug up to three times a day. In some fatal cases, significant respiratory depression occurred within 48 hours. Methadone also has a large volume of distribution (V_d), which means that it is distributed to many areas of the body such as lung, brain and fat stores. The accumulation in fat stores may cause inadequate analgesia. As progression of dosing is taken for further pain relief, more methadone is trapped in the fat. Once the analgesia wears off, methadone is released from the fat stores and can induce a toxic reaction to the brain's respiratory center, thereby causing respiratory depression.[17]

D. Equianalgesia

When converting from morphine or oxycodone to methadone, it is likely to underestimate methadone's potency. The usual equianalgesic dosing tables are only a guideline. Previous use of ineffective high doses of morphine sulfate may lead to overestimating the correct replacement dose of methadone. There is a broad variation in individual responses to a change over to methadone so that each patient must be evaluated separately. The starting dose should be conservative and dose increments should not be made frequently. Until a stable pattern of effective dosing has been established, frequent monitoring of each patient undergoing a change to methadone is of vital importance.

E. Drug Interactions

The pharmacology of methadone differs greatly from person to person. The idiosyncrasies of a human system may result in a pharmacological effect that is too small, too strong or too prolonged after the administration of the same dose of methadone. Methadone is mostly metabolized in the liver by Cytochrome P450 3A4 (CYP3A4) into an inactive metabolite. The idiosyncratic effects mentioned above apply to the activity of CYP3A4 in which varied CYP450 efficacy results in differences in methadone bioavailability. CYP2D6 and CYP1A2 also take part in methadone metabolism.

During MMT, other treatments/drugs may be necessary to treat the comorbities of drug addicts and chronic pain patients. These supplemental treatments include: psychotropic drugs, antibiotics, anticonvulsants and antiretroviral drugs, which are also CYP3A4 inducers. These drugs can also reduce the levels of methadone, thereby causing additive withdrawal symptoms. Buprenorphine, for example, is a partial opiate agonist and, in the presence of methadone, will act as an antagonist. In turn, this causes the emergence of withdrawal effects.[18]

Patients taking combined drug treatments must therefore be carefully monitored. For MMT patients, the drug-drug interactions of methadone have minimal life-threatening consequences, but they usually induce a reduction in a drug's concentration and efficacy, which results in withdrawal symptoms and risk of falling prey to heroin abuse again.[19] Drug interactions, however, have caused increased morbidity and mortality in chronic pain patients. Thus, in the non-chronic pain patient population, other medications that share the same intracellular metabolic pathway may antagonize methadone's metabolism, thereby leading to increased methadone levels and toxicity. These other medications include anti-depressant SSRIs (selective serotonin reuptake inhibitors) such as Prozac and antifungals such as fluconazole.

Other than antagonistic drug interactions, methadone's additive drug interactions result in an increased CNS depressive effect with drugs such as sedatives, tranquilizers and alcohol. These interactions result in respiratory depression and sedation. Because methadone can potentiate the effects of alcohol, the two drugs should never be co-administered.[18]

F. Cardiovascular Effects

Patient cases of QT interval prolongation and cardiac arrhythmias (torsades de pointes) have been evident during methadone treatment. Co-administration with other drugs such as albuterol, tricyclic antidepressants (TCA) and fluconazole can increase the risk of these abnormal cardiac occurrences and cause sudden cardiac death. Many of these cases include chronic pain patients being treated with large, multiple doses per day; however some cases involve pa-

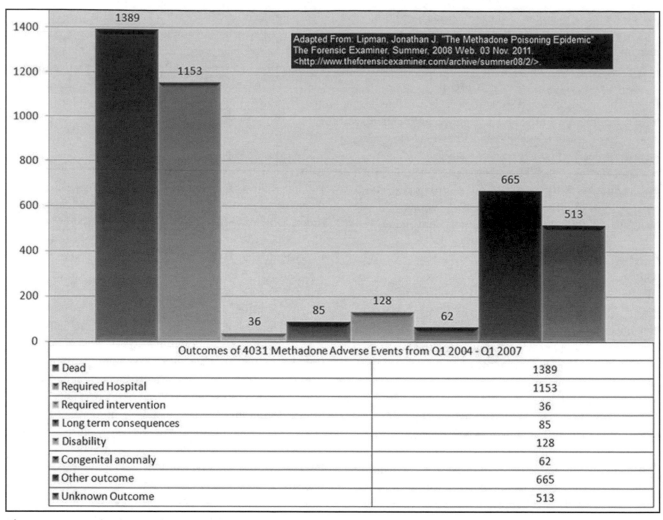

Figure 27.4 Methadone adverse events and outcomes Q1 2004 through Q1 2007.

tients undergoing treatment for opioid addiction.[17] The FDA has recently reviewed a number of reports of death and serious side effects such as slowed breathing and dangerous alterations in heart beat. This may be due to the buildup of methadone to a toxic level in the body if methadone is taken too often. High doses range between 400 mg and 1000 mg. In these patients, the QT prolongation can occur without any co-administered interacting drugs.[16]

G. Problem of Not Knowing How Dangerous Methadone is and Case Law Examples

There are well-established sources of knowledge presenting the adverse implications in methadone use. Figure 27.4, compiled with data extracted from the FDA MedWatch database, presents the outcomes of 4,031 methadone adverse events from Q1 2004 through Q1 2007.

According to the U.S. National Center for Health Statistics,[20] medical examiners listed methadone in contribution to 3,849 deaths in 2004. That number was up from 790 in

1999. Approximately 82 percent of those were accidental deaths, and most deaths involved adverse drug interactions with methadone, especially benzodiazepines.

On November 29, 2006, the U.S. Food and Drug Administration (FDA) issued a Public Health Advisory about methadone titled "Methadone Use for Pain Control May Result in Death and Life-Threatening Changes in Breathing and Heart Beat." The advisory went on to explain that the FDA had received a number of reports of death and serious side effects of patients taking methadone, and that they occurred in patients beginning methadone for pain and in patients that had switched to methadone after other potent narcotic pain relievers. The Agency justifiably vocalized caution directed at physicians who are prescribing methadone to patients that are not used to the drug and that methadone be taken exactly as directed.[21] In many cases, the patient will err the dosing regimen or may simply react poorly to the medication with proper doses. Therefore, as with any strong medication with the potential to be fatal in large doses, methadone must be taken properly and with due care. The accumulation of methadone could potentially reach a level of toxicity if the dose is too high or if the patient's metabolism of the drug is too slow (i.e. impaired CYP3A4). A patient who reacted normally after the first few doses could reach high, toxic levels of the drug in her body while taking no more than what was prescribed. For this reason, it is essential to ensure that when sent home, patients and their families are educated with the symptoms characteristic of opiate overdose.

H. Methadone Legal Case Examples Involving Patient Demise

Patient 1: A 35-year-old mother of two was being treated by a pain management physician in a midwestern state. She had a long history of low back pain and a laminectomy a few years earlier, which did not seem to improve her condition. Her pain was maintained with OxyContin 20 mg every 12 hours. She complained to her physician that her husband lost his job and they no longer had health insurance. Her physician then prescribed methadone, 10–15 mg every 8 hours and the OxyContin was discontinued. The woman and her husband went to a local chain pharmacy to fill the prescription for methadone. He does not recall counseling about the danger of taking methadone and the risk of respiratory depression. She took three tablets (15 mg) that night, two tablets (10 mg) in the morning, two mid-day, and three tablets at bedtime. The husband found her unresponsive on the laundry room floor the following morning. EMS was called and she was declared dead at the scene.

Patient 2: A 35-year-old divorced male school teacher and wrestling coach in a southwestern state was seen by a sports medicine specialist. He had complained of chronic low back pain, and he had been taking hydrocodone/acetaminophen for the pain. The sports specialist was concerned about acetaminophen toxicity, and prescribed "low dose" methadone, 10 mg twice daily, and discontinued the hydrocodone/acetaminophen. The next day, he stayed at his parent's home. He was very drowsy, sleeping on and off most of the day, and went to bed early. In the late morning of the third day, his mother was unable to awaken him. He was declared dead by EMS.

Findings from autopsy and toxicology studies conducted on both patients 1 and 2 found toxic levels of methadone. Methadone intoxication was noted by the medical examiners to be the cause of death in both cases.

Both physicians (and their practices—one a local hospital, the other a specialty group) were sued for wrongful death of these patients. Both testified that the dose of methadone used was "equivalent" to the prior opiates. They also

considered the patients to be opiate tolerant, and the methadone prescriptions to be safe. Neither physician was aware of the unusual (and cumulative) kinetics of methadone, nor the need to start with a low dose, gradually discontinue existing opiates, and re-assess the patient's tolerance to the methadone.

I. Summary: Applying Lessons Learned and Action for Institutional Committees

Methadone is a medication that probably should be made available to practitioners. It is used to bridge treatment for MMT patients, and it provides a low-cost option for chronic pain patients, especially those who have lost their prescription drug health insurance. Its use, however, should be governed by well-written and promulgated prescription guidelines, informing physicians, pharmacists and especially patients on safe and effective use of methadone.

Clear warnings and usage data including adverse events are readily available for use in prescribing guideline development and in clinical staff member (physicians, nurses, pharmacists, etc.) education of the risk management components of their clinical care.

Medical care delivery organizations (hospitals, clinics or medical groups) and their clinical staff are not only on the forefront of patient care, but also readily exposed to various malpractice claims creating significant financial as well as negative reputation exposure for all parties in a legal suit. Individual practitioners along with key institutional operating committees, such as P&T and Quality Improvement, share a need to protect both their patients and their organization from causing avoidable errors.[22]

27.6 Conclusion

Any potent opioid has the potential to cause respiratory depression and arrest. The risk is increased when other CNS depressant drugs are used, when the patient is obese, has sleep apnea, and is not closely monitored. In this author's opinion, all patients on strong opioids should have periodic pulse oximetry monitoring. Patients with additional risk factors should probably have continuous pulse oximetry. The noninvasive nature and relatively low costs associated with such monitoring are resources well used.

Endnotes

1. From Braunwald, Fauci, Kasper, Hauser, Longo, and Jameson (Eds): *Harrison's Principles of Internal Medicine*, Fifteenth Edition, CD-ROM, 2001 Chapter 388. OPIOID DRUG ABUSE AND DEPENDENCE—Marc A. Schuckit, David S. Segal

2. Florida Alcohol & Drug Abuse Association Resource Center. *What Are Psychoactive Drugs.* Available at: www.fadaa.org/resource_center/just_the_facts/PSY-CHO1.pdf. Accessed April 2, 2012.

3. *Opium: A History.* by Martin Booth. Simon & Schuster, Ltd., 1996

4. Presentation School of Chemical Sciences, University of Illinois at Urbana-Champaign *Synthesis of Morphine Alkaloids.* Sept. 2011. www.scs.illinois.edu/denmark/presentations/2006/gm-2006-01n31.pdf

5. H. Ağın, S. Çalkavur, D. Özdemir & M. Bak : A Case Of Opium Intoxication Mimicking Nephrotic Syndrome. *The Internet Journal of Toxicology.* 2003 Volume 1 Number 1

6. Chisholm CD: Opioid poisoning. In Harwood-Nuss A, editor: The clinical practice of emergency medicine, Philadelphia, 1991, JB Lippincott

7. North, R.A.; T.M. Egan: Actions and distributions of opioid peptides in peripheral tissues. Brit. Med. Bull. 39 (1983) 71-7523 (s)

8. P. Lierz & S. Punsmann : Opioids In Pain Therapy . *The Internet Journal of Pharmacology.* 2000 Volume 1 Number 1

9. Everett Stephens, MD "Toxicity, Opioids." *Medscape Reference: Drugs, Disease, and Procedures* (November, 2010)

10. McCrimmon DR, Alheid GF. : On the opiate trail of respiratory depression. *American Journal of Physiology Regulatory, Integrative and Comparative Physiology.* 2003 285:R1274–R1275.

11. Stead, LG; Stead, SM; Kaufman, MS (2006). *First Aid for the Emergency Medicine Clerkship* (2nd ed.). Mc-Graw-Hill. pp. 395–6.

12. "Vital Signs: Overdoses of Prescription Opioid Pain Relievers—United States, 1999–2008." *Centers for Disease Control and Prevention.* Web. 02 Nov. 2011. http://www.cdc.gov/mmwr/preview/mmwrhtml/mm6043a4.htm?s_cid=mm6043a4_w.

13. "Methadone—PubMed Health." *National Center for Biotechnology Information.* N.p., n.d. Web. 25 Oct. 2011. www.ncbi.nlm.nih.gov/pubmedhealth/PMH0000591.

14. "Methadone Maintenance Treatment" *Centers for Disease Control and Prevention.* N.p., n.d. Web. 25 Oct. 2011. www.cdc.gov/idu/facts/MethadoneFin.pdf.

15. "Opiate." *Rapid Detox Treatment from Opiate Addiction Under Sedation—Waismann Method.* N.p., n.d. Web. 25 Oct. 2011. www.opiates.com/opiates.

16. "Methadone Hydrochloride (marketed as Dolophine) Information." *U S Food and Drug Administration Home Page.* N.p., n.d. Web. 25 Oct. 2011. www.fda.gov/Drugs/DrugSafety/PostmarketDrugSafetyInformationforPatientsandProviders/ucm142827.htm.

17. "Dolophine (Methadone) Drug Information: Dosage, Side Effects, Drug Interactions and User Reviews at RxList." *RxList.com.* N.p., n.d. Web. 25 Oct. 2011. www.rxlist.com/dolophine-drug.htm.

18. "Drugs and Human Performance FACT SHEETS - Methadone." *Home | National Highway Traffic Safety Administration (NHTSA).* N.p., n.d. Web. 25 Oct. 2011. www.nhtsa.gov/people/injury/research/job185drugs/methadone.htm.

19. Ferrari A, Coccia CP, Bertolini A, Sternieri E. Methadone-metabolism, pharmacokinetics and interactions. Pharmacol Res. 2004 Dec: 50(6): 55 1-9.

20. Fingerhut LA. "Increases in methadone-related deaths: 1999–2004." *Health E-Stats. Hyattsville, MD: National Center for Health Statistics;* 2006. N.p., n.d. Web. 25 Oct. 2011. www.cdc.gov/nchs/data/hestat/poisoning/poisoning.htm.

21. "MedWatch Safety Alerts for Human Medical Products." U S Food and Drug Administration Home Page. N.p., n.d. Web. 25 Oct. 2011. www.fda.gov/medwatch/safety/2006/safety06.htm#Methadone.

22. O'Donnell JT. Strategies for Risk Management with Methadone. *Pharmacy and Therapeutics Journal.* 2012, *in press.*

Chapter 28

Acute Adverse Drug Events in Critical Care: Emergency Department and Intensive Care Units

Gourang Patel, B.S. Chem, Pharm.D., MSc, BCPS

28.1 Background
A. Epidemiology

The critical-care area of medical practice is fast-paced and replete with changes in the management in patient care. Adverse drug events (ADEs) have a significant impact on morbidity and mortality. In the United States, ADEs account for approximately $150 billion in costs annually.[1] The Institute of Medicine's (IOM) 1999 report "To Err is Human" reported approximately 100,000 deaths each year as a result of medical errors. This number is steadily increasing.[1] Generally, there are five categories of ADE: (1) adverse drug reactions, (2) medication errors, (3) therapeutic failures, (4) adverse drug withdrawal events, and (5) overdoses.[2] A medication error is defined as a preventable event that occurs as a result of inappropriate use by a healthcare professional. The advent of hundreds of new medications to the market each year has resulted in an increase in the occurrence of untoward outcomes attributable to these errors.

The IOM describes the need to further improve safety within the healthcare system.[1] Since the reduction of medication errors is a priority for patient safety, the IOM published another report specifically addressing this topic.[1] It indicated that a hospitalized patient is subjected to at least one medication error per day. In the intensive-care unit, the median error rate is approximately 106 per 1,000 patient days (range=1.2 to 947 per 1,000 patient days).[3] Due to the large number of medications prescribed for patients in the emergency department (ED) and ICU—as well as the acuity and severity of the patient population—it is necessary to focus resources in areas where there is a high risk and high potential benefit from prevention efforts. The Joint Commission (formerly the Joint Commission on Accreditation of Healthcare Organizations, or JCAHO) has focused its efforts on providing standards for healthcare institutions. One of its areas of specialization is the utilization of medications in the ED and ICU. The Joint Commission provides oversight to medical institutions through the process of accreditation. That process includes the establishment of numerous patient-safety goals developed to ensure consistent evaluations among evaluators. Several patient safety goals focus on medication utilization. In addition, the Joint Commission provides the rationale, strategies, and recommendations for the implementation of these patient-safety goals.[4]

The Joint Commission has several goals addressing components of medication safety. The National Patient Safety Goals, which are updated annually, focus on areas of improved care (e.g., patient identification, safety of medication use, medication reconciliation, and reducing patient fall risk). These goals are a constructive and consistent way to evaluate a patient's condition. They also include components of clinician education.[4]

B. Environment

One tool developed for such a task is provided by the Institute for Safe Medication Practices (ISMP). ISMP is currently organized to aid healthcare institutions around the world in establishing safe medication practices. It has developed a list of "high-alert" medications to serve as a reference and starting point for ICU and ED clinicians.[2,5] The medications on this list include the following medication classes: vasoactive agents, intravenous sedation and analgesia, anticoagulants, insulin, total parenteral nutrition, intravenous electrolytes, epidurals, and chemotherapeutic agents. The purpose of intense surveillance over these medication classes is because of their potential to cause significant morbidity and mortality when they are used incorrectly.

Medication errors can occur during any stage of the process—prescription, distribution/operations, administration, or monitoring. The first stage, prescribing, describes how the original order for a medication was obtained. Many institutions have not yet developed a process for computerized prescription order entry (CPOE). Often, the process of medication ordering and transcription is still a manual one. As a result, the probability of error increases. Administration errors occur the most frequently compared to other stages of the medication-use process. The utilization of automation—including bar-coding and advanced infusion pumps—reduces the occurrence of these errors and, therefore, improves patient safety.[5]

The final stage in which medication errors occur is within the monitoring process.[3] For example, clinicians need to be aware that when patients are receiving anticoagulation with unfractionated heparin (UFH) infusion, aPTT needs to be monitored to avoid supra or sub-therapeutic levels of the anticoagulant. Monitoring errors are reported to occur the least frequently compared to other stages. Rather than an indication of positive performance, however, this statistic most likely points to a deficient error detection mechanism.

28.2 High-Risk Medication-Related Events

The ISMP has provided a guide to direct our attention to a group of medications that—if prescribed, distributed, administered, and/or monitored inappropriately—can result in temporary or permanent harm.[2] In fact, in some cases, these events and reactions can result in fatality.

A. Hypersensitivity Reactions

Hypersensitivity reactions can encompass a variety of clinical presentations. In this section, there will be particular focus on the following types of life-threatening hypersensitivity reactions: anaphylaxis, angioedema, and dermatologic manifestations (i.e., Steven-Johnsons Syndrome [SJS] and Toxic Epidermal Necrolysis [TENS]). (See Chapter 14, *Adverse Drug Reactions: Focus on Drug Allergy*, for more information on dermatologic manifestations from medications.) In summary, the dermatologic reactions of SJS and TEN often involve an immune reaction in the body in response to a drug. Often the drugs implicated in SJS and TENS are similar and can include any of the following: sulfonamides, phenytoin, penicillin (and its associated derivatives), barbiturates, phenothiazines, thiazides, and NSAIDs. Both SJS and TENS can have devastating outcomes for a patient; however the distinguishing factor between TENS and SJS is the percentage of skin detachment.[6,7] The treatment for SJS and TENS is to identify and remove the offending agent and provide supportive care in a specialized unit that is prepared to treat severely burnt patients, as the physiology and infection risk are similar between these two patient groups.

Anaphylaxis is a rare reaction to a drug, but carries devastating consequences if unrecognized. (See Chapter 21, *Drugs for Asthma, Allergies, and Anaphylaxis*, for further detail.) In summary, anaphylaxis is a severe allergic reaction to a food or drug. The reaction can turn fatal once the respiratory and/or circulatory systems are affected. The reaction has an onset of minutes. The main cellular mediator of this reaction is histamine. Histamine affects changes in blood-vessel permeability. The result of changes in vessel permeability can manifest either in edema of the airway—leading to respiratory compromise—and/or vasodilation of blood vessels (which manifests as a clinical presentation of hypotension, low blood pressure).[8] The treatment of anaphylactic reactions involves the administration of intravenous, intramuscular, or oral antihistamine (i.e., diphenhydramine) and/or epinephrine via a subcutaneous or intra-muscular route, depending on the severity of the reaction. Drugs that have been more widely documented to cause this type of reaction are antibiotics, sulfa drugs, opioids, chemotherapy, and immune therapies used in rheumatoid arthritis or gastrointestinal disorders (e.g., infliximab).

Angioedema is a reaction that involves respiratory complications as a result of stimulation of upper airway-edema (i.e., tongue and larynx) that can result in impaired carbon dioxide and oxygen exchange. This can potentially be fatal. (See Chapter 21, *Drugs for Asthma, Allergies, and Anaphylaxis*.) Angioedema typically occurs with the administration of an anti-hypertension drug class called angiotensin inhibitors or angiotensin receptor blockers. There are many drugs in this class, although the reaction is more likely to occur in African-Americans. It does not have a time-onset, although the majority of these reactions are thought to occur within the first few weeks of therapy.[9] The treatment for these types of reactions can include an antihistamine, epinephrine, and/or an H2 antagonist.[8] As with the other types of hypersensitivity reactions, it is imperative that such a hypersensitivity be documented in patients' medical records. The patient's pharmacy should also be notified, in order to avoid an unwanted encounter in the future. In the same respect, it is very important for clinicians to evaluate for drug allergies prior to the prescription, dispensing, and administration of medications, as the consequences of any of these reactions can be fatal. The treatment of these reactions does vary; however with anaphylaxis and angioedema, the use of an antihistamine (i.e., diphenhydramine), H2 receptor antagonist (i.e., ranitidine or famotidine), and epinephrine 0.3 mg (pediatric) or 0.5 mg (adults) are given either subcutaneously or via intramuscular route. Intravenous administration of epinephrine is not advised, as the systemic adverse event (i.e., ventricular arrhythmias) is more likely to occur.

B. Cardiovascular Reactions

Cardiovascular reactions can have a variety of presentations as either a change in blood pressure (BP), heart rate (HR), and/or heart rhythm. The cardiovascular changes can be classified as either minor, moderate, or severe. The degree of the cardiovascular compromise dictates the relative changes in BP, HR, or heart rhythm.

1. Blood pressure (BP)

Blood pressure is primarily regulated via the selective constriction or dilation of arteries and veins. Therefore, drugs that can affect the degree of artery resistance or venous capacitance greatly affect the degree of blood-pressure control. The reactions that affect BP are generally accidental or iatrogenic (i.e., caused by healthcare provider). An iatrogenic reaction with anti-hypertensive medications often occurs when multiple providers are prescribing drugs to lower a patient's blood pressure. Often, one prescriber is unaware that another is prescribing a similar medication at a different dose. The blood pressure has a vital role in determining the amount of oxygen carried by the red-blood cell to vital organs such as the brain and heart. The two categories of blood pressure that are concerning are those readings that are very high (i.e., SBP >180 mmHg or DBP >110 mmHg) or those that are very low (i.e., a decrease of 40 mmHg from baseline BP or SBP <90 mmHg). The blood-pressure readings reported as high are secondary to patient-related factors (i.e., non-adherence to medication) and generally present in the ED or post-operatively. These situations are best handled via intravenous or oral medication administration, depending on the degree of end-organ damage. End-organ damage is defined as clinical evidence of damage to the brain

(i.e., stroke), heart (i.e., heart attack), eyes (i.e., evidence of palpilaedema), and kidney (i.e., evidence or kidney failure). The evidence of end-organ damage requires administration of intravenous medication to lower blood pressure.[10] On the other-hand, low blood pressure can also be accidental or iatrogenic. When patients are admitted to the hospital or examined in the ED, they may be prescribed additional anti-hypertensive therapy if the prescriber is unaware of the patient's current medications. Another scenario involves the titration upward of medication that may be too rapid for a patient's BP, which can result in overmedication or harm.

2. Heart rate (HR)

Heart rate is a component of cardiovascular function and determines the ability of the body to have a blood pressure and appropriate blood flow. Heart rates that are often high (i.e., greater than 100) or low (i.e., less than 60) are often benign unless associated with a particular disease state or symptoms the patient may be complaining of. High heart rates are often experienced by many who exercise or have stress. High heart rates can be problematic in conjunction with patients with a cardiac history and/or prior stroke. Clinically relevant low heart rate is defined as HR less than 40 beats per minute (BPM). However, if a patient has subjective complaints (i.e., syncope or shortness of breath) with a heart rate of less than 60 BPM, this warrants investigation. The vast majority of these reactions are (again) mediated by anti-hypertensive or anti-angina medications. If a high or low heart rate goes untreated, it may lead to cardiac arrest.

3. Arrhythmias

The American Heart Association (AHA) describes heart rhythms that have been identified as incompatible with life. The heart rhythms of ventricular tachycardia (VT), pulseless electrical activity (PEA), and asystole carry a high rate of mortality. They require prompt medical attention or may cause fatality. The treatment of VT, PEA, or asystole requires the use of an Advanced Cardiac Life Support (ACLS) in order to increase the chance of reversal of the acute situation.[11] The initiation of ACLS is key, as minutes are critical to a patient's neurological and physical outcomes. The incidence of VT is highest for people outside a medical facility, which is why there are often automated external defibrillators (AEDs) placed in public facilities such as shopping malls, airports, schools, and universities, as well as in medical facilities that serve patients in remote areas of a hospital campus.

C. Nephrotoxicity

Kidney damage, or nephrotoxicity, has a variety of definitions. The implications are that some types are permanent (requiring life-long dialysis), and other types are reversible over a short time period. The following section will address two anti-infective drug classes: amino glycosides and amphotericin B. The reader is also referred to Chapter 23, *Nephrotoxic Drugs*.

1. Amino glycosides

The amino glycosides are a class of antibiotics that are utilized for a variety of gram-negative and gram-positive bacteria infections. Although drugs in this class are effective in killing bacteria, they carry the risk of ototoxicity (hearing loss) and nephrotoxicity (decreased kidney function). The nephrotoxicity of the amino glycosides has been described in the order of greater to least: neomycin > tobramycin > gentamicin > amikacin.[12] The functionality of a patient's renal system is monitored by measuring urine output and serum creatinine throughout the course of treatment. The onset of kidney damage is variable, with elderly individuals (age >65) exhibiting a higher susceptibility. Prompt recognition is often accomplished by routine monitoring of the renal function, but also the drug levels (i.e., trough) of the amino glycoside are utilized in this regard. Successful reduction of nephrotoxic incidents, and improved patient care, are therefore accomplished through the collaboration of the dedicated pharmacist and the prescribing clinician.

2. Amphotericin B

Polyenes or amphotericin B (ampho B) are a class of anti-infectives used to treat fungal infections most often associated with patients who are immuno-compromised (i.e. HIV, cancer, or steroid use). Ampho B has several different formulations, including deoxycholate, colloidal dispersion, lipid complex, and liposomal. All the formulations can cause nephrotoxicity (deoxycholate > colloidal dispersion > lipid complex > liposomal); however the liposomal formulation carries the lowest risk. Ampho B also requires frequent renal-function monitoring (i.e., urine output and serum creatinine) in order to detect nephrotoxicity from drug therapy. Inadequate monitoring of ampho B therapy can result in life-long dialysis from irreversible injury to the kidney tubules. In addition to nephrotoxicity, infusion-related reactions, countered by antihistamine and acetaminophen, pose a risk for patients who are prescribed drugs in this class. For the prevention of nephrotoxicity, an intravenous hydration infusion of normal saline (osmolarity = 0.9%) or sodium bicarbonate ($NaHCO_3^-$) is administered prior to amphotericin B.[13]

3. Intravenous contrast

Intravenous (IV) contrast is associated with three main types of reactions: anaphylaxis, tissue extravasations (skin injury), and nephrotoxicity (kidney damage). IV contrast is useful in several diagnostic procedures for detection of blood clots in the lung (pulmonary embolism) and for cardiac procedures (percutaneous coronary intervention in cath-lab). The use of IV contrast is widespread; therefore, monitoring for one of the three types of reactions during this diagnostic therapy is warranted.

The anaphylaxis presentation is similar to what has already been described in this chapter. The presentation is within minutes of the infused contrast and results in shortness of breath and tongue swelling. The treatment includes prompt administration of an antihistamine and epinephrine as described above.

Tissue injury (extravasations) resulting from IV contrast administration depends on the osmolarity of the solution (available in forms ranging from hyper-osmolar to iso-osmolar), and the site of infusion (the type of line access the patient has for the infusion). Management of tissue extravasation includes supportive care, and consultation with a plastic surgeon to determine if surgery is necessary.

The other type of event to monitor with IV contrast is the occurrence of nephrotoxicity. The occurrence of kidney injury can be prevented by the administration of normal saline (osmolarity = 0.9%), sodium bicarbonate infusion, or N-acetylcystine therapy prior to the patient receiving IV contrast. Kidney injury is more likely to occur in the elderly, and patients who are already receiving nephrotoxic drugs (aminoglycosides or amphotericin B). Management includes hydration and the monitoring of urine output. In the worst cases, temporary dialysis is required until the kidney recovers physiologic function.[14]

D. Hypoglycemic Events

The utilization of insulin and/or oral medication to effectively control a patient's blood sugar while they are admitted to a hospital is increasing. The one untoward consequence of using either an insulin preparation or oral hypoglycemic agent (glyburide, glimeperide, etc.) is hypoglycemia. The blood sugar used to define hypoglycemia is variable, since patients may experience signs and/or symptoms (such as perspiration, fast heart rate, tremor, and so on) of hypoglycemia without having a blood sugar that may be low. Low blood sugar can be defined as blood sugar less than 60 mg/dL or what is commonly used in clinical trials within the medical literature which is a blood sugar less than 40 mg/dL. The reader is also referred to Chapter 22, *Adverse Effects of Diabetic Drugs*, which describes adverse events with diabetic therapy. The emphasis for the management of hypoglycemia revolves around the premise of prevention and appropriate monitoring of a patient while on therapy.

For example, the prevention of hypoglycemia requires an analytical review of blood-sugar protocols for drug therapy and developing criteria for selecting an insulin regimen based on organ function (i.e., kidney and liver). In addition, the development of appropriate criteria for monitoring patients receiving insulin or oral diabetic therapy is critical for safe and effective blood sugar management.

E. Infusion-Related Reactions

1. Extravasations

Intravenous infusions of catecholamine may be required to increase a patient's blood pressure in order to maintain perfusion to the brain and heart. The vasoactive infusions (i.e., dopamine, norepinephrine, epinephrine, and so on) are utilized to attain this goal. The intravenous infusions described have the capability to migrate outside the vein and cause tissue necrosis and extravasations. The extravasations more often occur when a peripheral line (as opposed to a central line access) is utilized for drug administration. The management of extravasations secondary to catecholamine infusions is the use of phentolamine intravenous and/or subcutaneous injections around the site of injury. Phentolamine provides a reversal effect (i.e., alpha antagonist activity) of the catecholamines, so that the vein can stay patent and so that there is minimal progression of tissue necrosis. Prevention of extravasations requires appropriate monitoring by nursing staff each time there is an infusion started in order to detect subtle changes in the patient's physical exam and line site.[15] Extravasation can also occur secondarily to a diluent in the intravenous drug. One example is with lorazepam, which contains propylene glycol. Several extravasations secondary to drugs require supportive care which may include raising the affected limb or applying compression to increase the process of drug diffusion from the affected tissue site.

2. Propofol-related infusion syndrome (PRIS)

Propofol-related infusion reactions (PRIS) is described as a cascade of events leading to cardiovascular collapse and death. The triad of events which center around PRIS include metabolic acidosis, hypotension, bradycardia, and hyper-triglyceridemia. PRIS is more likely to be prominent in patients receiving higher dosing of propofol (i.e., 4 mg/kg/hr) for greater than 48 hours.[16,17] The supportive evidence of the events related to propofol infusion center around the pharmacology that propofol is composed of a commercial preparation which is 10 percent lipid emulsion which can predispose to hypertriglyceridemia. Propofol can also inhibit beta-receptors on the heart, and calcium receptors on the

blood vessels, which can lead to bradycardia and hypotension, respectively. The progression to metabolic acidosis is secondary to the ability of propofol to inhibit mitochondrial activity and increase anaerobic metabolism, consequently leading to the formation of lactic acid.[16,17] Propofol-infusion syndrome can be prevented with appropriate monitoring by clinicians to ensure that the dose and duration of drug infusion are tailored to patient requirements. In the event that PRIS does occur, there is not a specific treatment for this reaction. The management of PRIS is supportive care by keeping the organ systems from failing to a catastrophic, fatal level.

3. Intravenous N-acetylcystine (NAC)

Intravenous NAC can be used for prevention of contrast-induced nephropathy, treatment of acetaminophen toxicity, and drug-induced liver injury. Currently, there are two preparations of NAC, one that has an FDA-approved indication for intravenous administration (i.e., Acetadote®), and another preparation—NAC solution—which can be administered orally. Prior to the NAC solution, Acetadote was also given via intravenous infusion via an infusion filter.[18,19] The occurrence of infusion reactions is minimal; however, the reactions most commonly reported include anaphylaxis (as described earlier), itching, and flushing. The patient can be pre-treated for the non-anaphylaxis type of reactions; however, clinicians need to be aware that these reactions are more likely to occur when given via the intravenous route and used in the treatment of acetaminophen toxicity or drug-induced liver injury in which the dosing (mg/kg) and frequency (number of doses) required are significantly higher.[18,19]

F. Reversal Agents

The management of patients in an emergency department or a critical-care area often require the administration of anticoagulants for the management of a blood clot, opioids for the management of pain, or benzodiazepines for the management of anxiety. All of these conditions require a careful approach, as excessive dosing and/or frequency can have untoward effects leading to patient harm and even death.

1. Protamine

Protamine is by nature a basic compound used to neutralize the effects of a parenteral anticoagulant unfractionated heparin (UFH) or low-molecular weight heparin (LMWH), which are both acidic compounds. Either UFH or LMWH can be used to treat patients with suspected or documented blood clots in the lower extremity or lung (i.e., venous thromboembolism) or acute coronary syndrome (heart attack).[20,21] Protamine intravenous infusion requires prompt administration and must be monitored for infusion-related reactions as well. The infusion of protamine can cause decreased blood pressure, heart rate, and flushing.[20,21] Therefore, the decision to prescribe and administer protamine requires careful consideration in relation to the time of the administration of UFH or LMWH to ensure that the medication will continue to be safe and effective after administration.

2. Vitamin K

A form of anticoagulation which patients may be on at home or in the hospital for blood clots (pulmonary or deep venous thromboembolism) is a vitamin K antagonist, such as warfarin. Warfarin is used as an anticoagulant for a variety of blood coagulation disorders. Generally, the medication may be started in the hospital and then patients are followed up on an out-patient basis to ensure that the drug is effective (in the appropriate INR range) and safe (without evidence of over-anticoagulation or bleeding). Warfarin is an oral vitamin-K antagonist that possesses anticoagulant activity via inhibition of vitamin K clotting factors (Factors II, VII, IX, and X) via inhibition of the carboxylation of glutamic residues. The drug is monitored via an INR blood test. Over-anticoagulation can occur when patients are at home and they may present to the ED. The other instance is a patient receives over-anticoagulation in the hospital and presents to the ICU. Either scenario may require the administration of vitamin K. Vitamin K is adjunct therapy, which means often the patient is also receiving blood products for a high INR or active bleeding. Vitamin K is available as an oral tablet that can be given to patients with no evidence of active bleeding with an INR greater than 9.[20,22] Vitamin K is also a parenteral product that can be administered either subcutaneously or via intravenous infusion. The subcutaneous route is not recommended for patients with or without active bleeding as the drug absorption, activity, and effectiveness are questionable, at best. The preferred route of administration of vitamin K in a patient with an elevated INR with active bleeding is intravenous infusion. The intravenous push route is no longer recommended secondary to infusion hypersensitivity reactions and cardiovascular manifestations; therefore, the infusion is not the selected route. In patients requiring vitamin K for INR reversal, the routes of administration would be either oral tablet (slow onset) or intravenous infusion (fast onset) in combination with adjunct therapy (blood-product administration).[20,22] The dosing for vitamin K is dependent on the INR and the clinical scenario of the patient presentation.

3. Naloxone

Naloxone is an opioid antagonist generally used for opioid reversal. Naloxone is given via intravenous push administration at a dose of 0.4 mg for opioid naive patients. Naloxone has a short half-life, and can be given repeated times. In some cases a continuous infusion may be required for patients having difficulty eliminating opioid metabolites, drug interactions, or who have long-acting opioid preparations. The actions of opioids are primarily on the mu receptor. The activity of opioids on the mu1 receptor is for analgesia and pain relief. The activity of the opioids on the mu2 receptor is responsible for the adverse effects that are observed with respiratory depression and gastrointestinal complications of therapy.[23,24] Naloxone is also not to be confused with naltrexone, which is the oral preparation of the medication.

4. Flumazenil

Flumazenil is a GABA-antagonist used to reverse the side effects of sedation and disorientation from GABA agonist activity or benzodiazepines. Flumazenil is generally dosed at 0.2 mg intravenous push. The main monitoring effect from flumazenil administration is seizures. The science behind why seizures may develop is that often when GABA activity is reversed too quickly, it lowers the seizure threshold. The concept is similar to when patients with a large alcohol history abruptly stop drinking. The consequence is the development of seizure activity; therefore, the decision to administer flumazenil should be carefully reviewed in order to prevent this side effect.[23,24]

28.3 Summary

The use of medications in the emergency department (ED) and critical care (ICU) areas can often improve patient care. However, clinicians should maintain careful vigilance and monitoring to ensure patient safety and to avoid unnecessary harm or risk. Clinicians in the ED and ICU need to be aware of clinical data that helps make the selection of a therapy more effective. However, a balance must be weighed to provide safe medication therapy. In addition, consideration of all aspects of the medication process—prescribing, distribution, administration, and monitoring—are recommended in order to achieve this balance.

Endnotes

1. L.T. Kohn, J.M. Corrigan, M.S. Donaldson. *To Err is Human: Building a Safer Health-System. Institute of Medicine.* Washington, DC: National Academy of Press, 1999.

2. Institute of Safe Medication Practices (ISMP) High Alert Medications. www.ismp.org/Tools/highAlert-Medications.asp, retrieved 04/02/2012.

3. S. Kane-Gill and R.J. Weber RJ. *Principles and Practices of Medication Safety in the ICU*. Crit. Care Clin. 2006; 22:273-290.

4. Joint Commission. www.jointcommission.org, retrieved 04/02/2012.

5. G.P. Patel and S. *Kane-Gill. Medication Error Analysis: A systematic approach*. Curr. Drug Saf. 2010; 5:2-5.

6. M. Mockenhaupt. *Severe drug-induced skin reactions: clinical pattern, diagnostics and therapy*. J. Detsch Dermatol. Ges. 2009;7:142-162.

7. L. French. *Toxic Epidermal Necrolysis and Steven-Johnson Syndrome: Our Current Understanding*. Allergol. Int. 2006; 55:9-16.

8. B. Schnyder. *Approach to a patient with Drug Allergy*. Immunol. Allergy Clin. N. Am. 2009; 405-418.

9. B.G. Katzung. *Basic and Clinical Pharmacology*. 11th edition. 2009.

10. J. Varon. *The diagnosis and treatment of hypertensive crises*. Postgrad. Med. 2009;121:5-13.

11. *Advanced Cardiac Life Support*. Circulation. 2005;112: Supplement 1-209.

12. P.K. Kiel, M. Lo, D. Stockwell, G.P. Patel. *An evaluation of Amikacin Nephrotoxicity in the Hematology/Oncology population*. Am. J. Ther. 2008;15:131-136.

13. A. Lemke, A.F. Kiderlen, O. Kayser. *Amphotericin B*. Appl. Microbiol. Biotechno. 2005;68:151-162.

14. R.W. Katzberg and R. Lamba. *Contrast-Induced Nephropathy after intravenous administration: Fact or Fiction?* Radiol. Clin. N. Am. 2009; 47:789-800.

15. R.A. Phillips, P. Andrades, J.H. Grant, P.D. Ray. *Deep dopamine extravasation injury: a case report*. J. Plast. Reconstr. Aesthet. Surg. 2009:62:222-4.

16. J. Orsini, A. Nadkarnia, J. Chen, N. Cohen. *Propofol Infusion Syndrome: case report and literature review*. Am. J. Health. Syst. Pharm. 2009; 66:908-915.

17. A. Fudickar and B. Bein. *Propofol Infusion Syndrome: update of clinical manifestations and pathophysiology*. Minerva Anestesiol. 2009; 75:339-344.

18. A.J. Whyte, T. Kehrl, D.E. Brooke, K.D. Katz, D. Sokolowski. *Safety and Effectiveness of Acetadote for Acetaminophen toxicity*. J. Emerg. Med. 2008; Nov 18 [E-pub ahead of print].

19. M. Kanter. *Comparison of oral and i.v. acetylcysteine in the treatment of acetaminophen poisoning*. Am. J. Health. Syst. Pharm. 2006; 63:1821-1827.

20. *American College of Chest Physicians (ACCP) Guidelines on Antithrombotic Therapy*. Chest. August, 2008. Supplement:1-793.

21. M. Levi. *Emergency reversal of antithrombotic treatment*. Intern Emerg. Med. 2009; 4:137-145.

22. A. Lubetsky, H. Yonath, D. Olchovsky, R. Loebstein, H. Halkin, D. Ezra. *Comparison of oral vs. intravenous phytonadione (vitamin K1) in patients with excessive anticoagulation*. Arch. Intern. Med. 2003; 163:2469-2473.

23. L Brunton, J Lazo, and K Parker. *Goodman and Gilman's the Pharmacological Basis of Therapeutics*. 11th edition. 2006.

24. *American Hospital Formulary Service (AHFS)*. 2010.

Chapter 29

Hemophilia Holocaust Litigation Related to Blood Factor VIII and IX Products and AIDS Transmission

Charles R. Kozak, J.D.

29.1 Introduction

Hemophilia is an inherited condition that causes uncontrolled bleeding or hemorrhaging, usually into an internal organ, joint, or muscle. There are two types of hemophilia—hemophilia A, which results from a deficiency of the Factor VIII protein, and hemophilia B, which results from a deficiency of Factor IX protein. Approximately three-fourths of all cases are hemophilia A. In 1982, estimates suggested there were from 14,000 to 20,000 hemophiliacs residing in the United States. All populations throughout the world have the same rates of hemophilia. One in 10,000 people have type A and one in 40,000 type B. By 1980, the standard of care in most of the advanced countries of the world involved the treatment of the disease in patients over four years of age with blood derivatives called factor concentrates.

Blood derivatives such as Factor VIII and IX are prescription biologicals, subject to federal regulation as both "biological products" and "drugs." By the time the last hemophiliac patient dies from viral infection transmitted through "intermediate purity, nonpasteurized" factor concentrates, the two drugs will have killed between 40,000 and 70,000 hemophiliacs worldwide.[1] In the United States

alone, the Centers for Disease Control and Prevention (CDC) estimates that almost one-half of the nation's 14,000 hemophiliacs who used the drugs as regular therapy between 1974 and 1984 will have succumbed to the HIV and hepatitis C (HCV) viruses transmitted by these products.[2] Remarkably, hundreds of hemophiliacs and their spouses who were infected in the early to mid-1980s continue to survive in various countries throughout the world where these products were distributed. No one knows their eventual fate. They continue to live lives of quiet desperation. In many countries, the fear of being identified as HIV-positive or as a person with AIDS has reinforced their anonymity. Most have lost many friends and family members who died without receiving any compensation from injuries inflicted by the drugs. Some of the victims are doing remarkably well, and do not have AIDS after over 20 years of HIV infection. To these people, the most imminent danger is the threat of liver destruction from years of exposure to hepatitis C.

Will advanced drug therapies used to treat HIV infection, such as highly active antiretroviral therapy, succeed in postponing fatal immune-system collapse indefinitely in these survivors? Will pegulated-interferon therapies or liver transplants succeed in avoiding liver failure in these patients? Will new therapies arrive in time to allow these unfortunate individuals to live normal life spans? These questions regarding the "Hemophilia Holocaust" will have to wait for the next decade for answers. If the past is any indication of their future, the answers may, indeed, be grim.

It is unlikely that a complete history of these two drugs will ever be written, due to the secretive and collusive nature of the handful of companies who commercially manufacture these therapies worldwide.

In addition, the United States Food and Drug Administration's (FDA) Bureau of Biologics (BOB), has taken a

491

decidedly defensive posture with regard to providing factual disclosures. This is, no doubt, due to the extremely high mortality and morbidity rate of the drugs, intertwined with the documented inadequacies of the agencies in responding to the contamination of the nation's blood supply with HIV.[3]

29.2 Challenges of Factor VIII and IX Litigation

Since 70,000 deaths are the equivalent of a fully loaded 747 crashing every day, for 200 straight days, it is remarkable that more public outrage was not forthcoming as the hemophilia death statistics started accumulating in the late 1980s in the CDC's *Morbidity and Mortality Weekly Report*. Initial attempts to litigate against the drug's four manufacturers in the U.S. were sporadic and unsuccessful, with the defendants winning all but one case at the trial level. The manufacturers, known in the litigation as the "fractionators," had anticipated these lawsuits many years before hemophiliacs had even a vague perception of the conduct that caused them to contract AIDS. Hundreds, if not thousands, of hemophiliacs, died without ever knowing what caused their untimely demise through the use of these drugs.

Eventually, an awakening occurred in the hemophilia community through the work of activist organizations such as the Committee of Ten Thousand. A class-action lawsuit was filed on behalf of all hemophiliacs infected with HIV in the Northern District of Illinois in September 1993. It was not until 1996 that an Indiana jury decided a case against Cutter Biological Corporation in the death of a teenager from AIDS. The jury awarded the surviving family $2 million. Also, in 1996, a class-action settlement was negotiated in the Seventh Circuit of the Federal District Court in Chicago, which resulted in payments to 6,000 victims of $100,000 per claimant, for a total sum of $600 million. Several hundred claimants opted out of the class, and eventually received amounts several times that of the class members. Fewer than ten claims remain active in the United States.

Recently a class action suit was filed in San Francisco federal court on behalf of thousands of hemophiliacs worldwide. They were infected with HIV, HCV, or both, through the use of factor concentrates manufactured by the same fractionators named in the U.S. class action.

Litigating a Factor VIII or IX case presents challenging, scientific, and factual issues requiring intensive preparation for even the most skillful trial lawyer. Presentation of the case requires experts in the fields of virology, protein chemistry, and drug regulation. The fractionators have assembled a stable of experts in the fields of blood banking, biological statistics, fractionation, and federal regulation to assist them

in presenting their defense. Depending on the facts of the particular case, the fractionators rely upon one or more of the following common defense theories:

- A statistical analysis prepared by Dr. Barbara Kroner in her doctoral thesis, supported by a retrospective testing of serum samples taken from hemophiliacs at major treatment centers, demonstrated that over 50 percent of all type A severe hemophiliacs had been infected with HIV by November 1981. Since HIV was not identified until April 1984, and no test was commercially available to test donors until May 1985, the fractionators cannot be held liable for cases of AIDS in hemophiliacs that did not develop until years later.

- In order to hold a company liable, the plaintiff must identify which particular company's product caused the plaintiff's infection with the HIV virus. It is virtually impossible to determine which of the four companies' products caused the HIV infection, because most hemophiliacs used different brands over the course of their treatments. Therefore, no company should pay damages to a plaintiff.

- In treating physicians as "learned intermediaries," we are compelled to prescribe factor concentrates for their patients, despite what was known about AIDS transmission through factor concentrates in 1982. There was no viable alternative treatment for severe type A or B hemophiliacs at the time. The benefits of therapy outweighed the risks because internal cranial bleeds or bleeds into vital areas of the body can be fatal, and factor concentrates are the only effective safeguard against these risks.

- The fractionators had no duty to amend their warning labels to include an AIDS warning until they obtained permission to do so from the FDA's Bureau of Biologics. The FDA refused to approve such a warning until December 1983, at which time all companies included virtually identical AIDS warnings in their package inserts.

- The statute of limitations has run out on most hemophilia claims because suits should have been filed within one or two years from the date the hemophiliac learned that he was HIV positive as a result of infusing the product. The vast majority of hemophiliacs were tested for HIV and informed of the results in 1985 and 1986.

Initially, virtually all trial judges and juries found these arguments convincing. However, as persistent investigation was conducted by some trial lawyers, these arguments began to fall away.

29.3 Development of Factor VIII and IX

To understand why this is so, one must go back to the initial years of the drug's development. Factor VIII was invented by Dr. Ed Shanbrom and Dr. Harold Fekete in 1968 at Hyland Therapeutics, located in Glendale, California. Factor IX was developed by Cutter Biological at about the same time in Emeryville, California. These companies had the technology to pool thousands of paid commercial donors' plasma, extract the Factor VIII and IX proteins from the pools and lyophilize, or freeze dry, the proteins in a vacuum. The remaining powder was bottled and could be kept under refrigeration and reconstituted with saline solution when infusion was required by the patient. With a little training, the hemophiliac could self-administer the product. Factor VIII could be stored for two years without losing its therapeutic properties. Before factor concentrates, hemophiliacs were required to go to emergency-treatment facilities whenever they suffered a spontaneous or traumatic bleed. There they would receive a transfusion of cryoprecipitate.

Cryoprecipitate was obtained from volunteer blood donor's plasma. The plasma would be separated from the red cells and platelets and frozen in plastic bags until needed. Hemophiliacs, their families, and those who treated them were enthusiastic supporters of factor-concentrate therapy because of the independence and convenience it gave them. Families could take vacations together without the need to have a treatment center nearby. Patients could obtain gainful employment with confidence that they could fulfill their commitments. Treaters had a new "wonder drug" they could prescribe to worried parents who were informed that they had a hemophiliac baby or child. The National Hemophiliac Foundation (NHF), the leading hemophilia advocate organization in the world, began promoting use of the drugs. The NHF was instrumental in getting Congress to pass the Hemophilia Comprehensive Treatment Act (HCTA) in 1975. This act established approximately 22 comprehensive treatment centers in the United States. At these centers, the hemophiliac could receive yearly checkups, dental services, family counseling, and orthopedic surgery. Government-subsidized Factor VIII and IX drug therapy was available for those who had no means to pay.

By 1974, four companies were engaged in intensive marketing activities for licensed Factor VIII and IX blood products—Cutter Biological (later the Bayer Company of Germany), Hyland/Travenol (later Baxter Healthcare, an American company), Armour Pharmaceutical (later acquired by Rhone-Polenc Therapeutic Co., a French company), and Abbott Laboratories (later spun off as Alpha Therapeutics and sold to Green Cross Corporation, a Japanese company).

Treating physicians began serving on the local NHF boards of directors in many regions. Promotional devices, such as summer camps for kids and comic-book-type publications were distributed to parents for use by children in promoting widespread use of the drugs. In many instances, children were introduced to factor concentrates for the first time at these summer camps.

The treatment centers began to see profits from sales of factor concentrates at their pharmacies. The government became supporters of the drugs because hemophiliacs became self-sufficient taxpayers and useful members of society. Treaters were held in utmost respect and patients and their families were even in awe of them, almost to the point of cult-like adoration. These treaters began to acquire increased prestige and influence at their medical centers as a result of the increased income from increasing patient participation. The treaters also began to develop close ties to the fractionators, due to aggressive sales programs utilized by the companies. All of these events set the stage for the tragedy that was about to occur in the worldwide hemophilia community.

29.4 Sources of Plasma Donors and Transmission of Hepatitis C

Dr. Shanbrom, Baxter's head of scientific development in 1968, used plasma from prisoners at Angola State Prison in Louisiana to prepare the initial batches of Factor VIII concentrate for Baxter's first clinical trials. Almost immediately after administering the initial doses to his patients, Dr. Shanbrom observed episodes of acute, short incubation hepatitis in the subjects. Because the patients had been previously exposed to the hepatitis B virus through cryoprecipitate infusions, he was suspicious that a new viral agent was causing this infection. He informed Hyland's CEO of his findings, and strongly recommended that Angola prisoners be discontinued as a source for Hyland's plasma. In Dr. Shanbrom's opinion, this recommendation caused him to be dismissed by Baxter within the next few weeks.[4]

The existence of this new virus, although not isolated in the laboratory, was so sufficiently recognized that it resulted in the National Blood Policy of 1973. The virus would eventually be named hepatitis C, but was then referred to as "nonA-nonB." The objective of the policy was to eliminate all commercial blood and plasma donors as soon as possible. Studies had indicated that paid donors were up to six times more likely to transmit nonA-nonB hepatitis than volunteer donors.[5]

NonA-NonB virus transmission could be detected by measuring the level of liver enzymes present in the donor or recipient (in the absence of the usual symptoms of the disease, such as nausea, jaundice, and discolored urine or stools). Most cases of transmission were asymptomatic. The long-term implications for infected hemophiliacs or blood-transfusion recipients were unknown. No enhanced warnings were implemented regarding this new virus—not by blood banks or by blood-product manufacturers—even after the National Blood Policy was announced.

By 1974, certain subgroups within the population of commercial donors had been identified as being more at risk for hepatitis transmission than others. These groups included impoverished inner-city inhabitants, IV drug users, and prisoners. In 1975, the National Transfusion Transmitted Virus Study (TTV) was launched, with the goal of determining whether there were means available to eliminate or reduce donors at high risk for viral transmissions from the blood supply.[6]

Most of the higher-risk groups had been developed as sources of plasma by the fractionators since the introduction of the drugs in the early 1970s. These sources included prisons located in Mississippi, Alabama, Florida, Louisiana, Arkansas, Nevada, and Arizona. Central American sources were located in Nicaragua, Belize, and Haiti. Numerous plasma centers were situated on the Mexican border in Texas to exploit sources in Mexico and Central America. Plasma centers were situated in urban centers inhabited by those characterized as the "underclass," by the head of the TTV Study, Dr. James Mosley. Donors were largely alcohol and drug dependent. They were in desperate need of the $8 to $10 payment they could receive for twice-weekly plasma donations. All of these sources of plasma had been described in the medical and scientific literature as extremely high-risk populations for nonA-nonB and hepatitis B transmission by 1975.[7]

With the exception of the Belize center, which was in operation well into the 1980s, the shipments from Central America largely ceased in 1975 because of the Somoza revolution. The editor of the leading Nicaragua newspaper was assassinated because of his exposé regarding the over-bleeding of poverty-stricken people at the center. This event sparked the citizens to take to the streets and end the Somoza regime in Nicaragua.

29.5 Response to Reported Side Effects of Factor VIII and IX

By 1976, the reported side effects from use of Factor VIII and IX had accumulated to such an extent that the National Heart Lung and Blood Institute called a special meeting to discuss possible responses.

The conference was entitled "Unsolved Problems in Hemophilia Therapy." Many of the side effects were caused by repeated infusions of foreign proteins in massive amounts, as well as in infections from viruses contained in the products. The body's immune system responded to the foreign proteins and viruses by forming immune complexes. The hemophiliac's body was in a constant state of antigenic stimulation as a result. The long-term effects of antigenic stimulation and NonA-NonB viral infection were unknown.

Other disorders discussed included liver dysfunction, splenomegaly (enlarged spleen), hepatitis B and nonA-nonB hepatitis infection, lymphocytopenia (loss of white blood cells), thrombocytopenia (loss of platelets), renal failure, and high blood pressure, which was caused by deposits of immune complexes on artery walls. The leading hemophiliac treater in Massachusetts, Dr. Peter Levine, commented, "One wonders whether our patients are suffering a sort of immune complex disease as a result of intensive bombardment with foreign antigens...." Dr. Jeffrey Shapiro, a leading treater in Philadelphia warned of the possibility that "a new spectrum of disease may be seen in this population" and urged that it "behooves us to follow the suggested findings very closely over the coming years." Dr. Seeff concurred, "It is evident that continued surveillance of the hemophiliac population is mandatory."[8]

None of these disturbing side effects found their way on to any fractionator's warning label for the products. The fractionators' package inserts were required to disclose adverse reactions pursuant to federal and state regulations and applicable standards of care.

Although the companies' inserts mentioned a risk that plasma may contain the causative agent of hepatitis, the warning was seriously deficient, in that the companies failed to disclose that the risk of hepatitis was essentially 100 percent, due to the practices of using high-risk donors and, specifically, because donors with a high risk for both hepatitis B and nonA-nonB hepatitis were recruited. Hepatitis simply means inflammation of the liver. Often, it is a relatively benign, temporary condition. The companies failed to warn that some forms of hepatitis were believed to present a considerable risk of severe liver damage, cirrhosis, and significantly elevated risk of cancer. The companies misleadingly stated that the source of plasma used in preparation of the product had been found to be non-reactive for hepatitis B surface antigen. This implied that no hepatitis was present in the plasma. They falsely stated that available methods were not sensitive enough to detect all units of potentially infectious plasma. The companies failed to disclose that they had refused to implement more sophisticated tests that would have excluded essentially all plasma contaminated by hepatitis B. The companies' labeling stated that the product was made from large pools of fresh human plasma, but failed to disclose that paid donors increased the risk of disease, and that the particular groups of paid donors targeted by the companies were known to be the highest-risk groups available.[9]

By 1977, as the demand for factor concentrates was rapidly increasing, liver biopsies were performed on hemophiliacs at two treatment centers. Reports were published indicating severe liver damage from heavy use of Factor VIII and IX. The investigators, who were also treaters, called for the implementation of manufacturing technologies to virally inactivate factor concentrates. These reports failed to motivate any U.S. fractionator to initiate serious efforts to implement such technologies.[10,11]

By 1978, Cutter, Alpha, and Baxter had developed other products that were manufactured from the same starting plasma pools used to manufacture factor concentrates. Among these products were intravenous immunoglobulins (IVIG) and hepatitis B immunoglobulins (HBIG). These are antigen-specific therapies manufactured by the process of "fractionating" plasma into various elements or proteins. After the plasma used to manufacture factor concentrates is removed from the pool, the remaining liquid is subjected to the Cohn fractionation method. The Cohn method involves using a series of precipitating chemicals to isolate and extract from the remaining supernatant liquid, proteins used to make HBIG and IVIG. In order to ensure an adequate amount of specific antibodies in the later stages of the fractionation process (where immunoglobulin manufacture takes place), it is necessary to have sufficient numbers of antibodies to the hepatitis B virus in the starting plasma pool.[12]

29.6 Identifying Hepatitis

Identification and recruitment of donors with previous exposure to the hepatitis B virus became a necessity in order to ensure a sufficiently high titer of antibody level to pass FDA requirements. These donors were identified by testing their plasma for the presence of antibody to the core, HBc or the surface, HBs, protein of the hepatitis B virus. HBc is present in the donor's plasma long after the donor has recovered from hepatitis B infection.

Abbott Laboratories obtained FDA approval of the HBc and HBs tests as a class III medical device in 1979. The test was developed to address the need to accurately diagnose a previous hepatitis B infection. Federal regulations prohibit the use of donors "with a history of viral hepatitis." The fractionators now had an objective test that would enable them to adhere to the regulations with increased accuracy. They no longer had to rely on a donor's understanding of

her medical history, which may be unreliable. Another advantage of the HBc test was its ability to identify hepatitis B carrier donors. These donors could not be identified by using only the FDA-mandated HBsAg test.[13] However, the need to maximize profits through single-pool manufacture of factor concentrates and immunoglobulins provided substantial disincentives to implement HBc testing.

According to a National Heart Lung and Blood Institute (NHLBI) report, by the late 1970s, at least 17 different components of blood were manufactured by the process of fractionating plasma into its various elements. The NHLBI Report noted that "as the costs of fractionating plasma" increased, fractionators produced as many products as possible from a liter of plasma. The report further noted that plasma with a very high titer, or antibody level, for a corresponding antigen is "very expensive." In addition, the FDA requires a minimum of 1,000 donors in a given lot of immunoglobulin. The report stated specifically, however, that "plasma collected for high antibody titer cannot be used for fractionation into therapeutic products, such as factor concentrates." However, in the minds of the fractionator executives, the increased profitability from manufacturing all products from the same original starting material justified the increased risk to hemophiliacs of exposure to multiple high-risk donors.[14]

The alanine aminotransferase test (ALT) had been available since the mid-1970s. This test measures increased levels of specific enzymes produced in the liver. Increased enzyme production, above 45 Icteric Units, in the blood stream is an indication of liver pathology. The ALT test was eventually implemented in 1986, but could have been used a decade earlier to substantially reduce the number of NonA-NonB infected donors in the plasma pool.[15]

By 1978, many donor centers, either owned by the fractionators or under contract with them, were using the HBc or HBs tests as a screening device to identify donors who had previously been infected with hepatitis B. However, the testing was for the purpose of including, rather than excluding, the donor who tested positive for the antibody. By 1980, advertisements intended to attract male homosexuals to plasma centers began to appear in various publications aimed at the homosexual communities in urban areas. Throughout 1981 and into 1983, publications such as the *Advocate*, the *Blade*, *Guess What Mom?* and others, were running advertisements for donor centers in Florida, Washington, D.C., Los Angeles, and San Francisco. Advertisements also appeared in the yellow pages of gay telephone directories in cities such as San Francisco, which had large gay neighborhoods.[16]

By the end of 1981, the prudence of targeting HBc positive donors, to whom hemophiliacs would ultimately be exposed through single-pool source manufacture of plasma products, was a risky enterprise, at best. Hepatitis investigators had established in the mid-1970s that hepatitis B was transmissible by blood. Dr. Wolf Smuzness, principal investigator for the New York Blood Center (NYBC), had published several studies linking male homosexual practices with transmission of hepatitis B and other sexually transmitted diseases, such as gonorrhea. In 1975, Dr. Smuzness publicly recommended that urban gay males be discouraged from making blood donations.[17] The NYBC put this policy into practice in the late 1970s.[18]

By 1980, numerous investigators had suggested a strong correlation between hepatitis B core positive donors and nonA-nonB hepatitis transmission.[15] Data from the Transfusion Transmitted Virus Study indicated that almost one-third of nonA-nonB carriers could be eliminated through HBc testing.[19]

Other studies indicated similar results could be obtained using the ALT test. Fortuitously, because the two tests screened out different groups of donors, using the two tests together would have identified almost two-thirds of all nonA-nonB carriers. However, despite the existence of the supporting data, the Transfusion Transmitted Virus Committee of the American Association of Blood Banks declined to recommend the implementation of either test. Likewise, because the FDA allowed the American Association of Blood Banks, the blood bank trade association, to set its own standards in the FDA regulatory scheme, it did not recommend use of the two tests either. Two blood banks in the U.S., the Blood Bank of Hawaii and the Blood Bank of the National Institutes of Health (NIH), did begin to use the ALT test as a surrogate test for nonA-nonB hepatitis in 1981. Interestingly, the NIH blood bank was directed by Dr. Paul Holland, who recommended against use of the HBc or ALT test as a member of the TTV committee. In 1986, Dr. Holland changed his recommendation, along with his fellow members of the TTV committee and the Blood Products Advisory Committee. They agreed that the HBc test should be implemented as a surrogate test for nonA-nonB hepatitis. His change of opinion was based on his re-examination of serum samples collected in the TTV study from 1975 to 1979. Upon retesting the samples he observed a 30 to 40 percent correlation between HBc-positive donors and nonA-nonB transmission.[20] Despite his strong opposition to the use of paid donors, Dr. Holland has remained a staunch defender of the fractionators' conduct in the late 1970s and early 1980s. He has served as an expert on their behalf in numerous hemophilia-related AIDS cases in the United States. He also became a paid consultant to Baxter Healthcare.

Implementation of the HBc and ALT tests at fractionator donor centers would have sharply curtailed the use of prisoners as plasma donors. Prisoners were associated with ALT levels of over 60 IUs per milliliter, a level that increases the risk of HCV transmission by a factor of six. Many prisons used as plasma sources by the companies had HBc rates over 25 percent. In addition, by 1978, studies had reported that so-called "carrier donors," donors who could pass the standard HBsAg test and still transmit hepatitis B, were strongly HBc positive. Despite all of this published information, the fractionators failed to implement ALT or HBc, except for purposes of inclusion, testing as a screening device to make their products safer by lowering the viral load.[21]

The companies continued the simultaneous manufacture of high-titer immunoglobulins and factor concentrates as standard industry practice, even after *Morbidity and Mortality Weekly Reports* (*MMWR*) reported an epidemic of the fatal immunosuppressive disease in the homosexual population.

29.7 AIDS Epidemic and Treatment of Hemophilia

On June 5, 1981, the United States Centers for Disease Control reported in their *Morbidity and Mortality Weekly Report* that five homosexual men had unusual and similar immunosuppressive disorders.

On July 3, 1981, the CDC reported similar diseases in 26 homosexuals, noting that cases of hepatitis B "were commonly reported" in this patient cohort. The CDC warned doctors to be alert for "opportunistic infections associated with immune suppression in homosexual men."

By August 28, 1981, less than two months later, the reported figure had grown to 108 cases of the mysterious disorder and 40 percent fatalities. Ninety-one percent of the 101 males were homosexual or bisexual. In December, 1981, the CDC published Dr. Michael Gottlieb's "Orange County Cluster" study, which contained data strongly suggesting patient-to-patient transmission of AIDS in his homosexual patient cohort. All of Dr. Gottlieb's patients were HBc positive.

On June 11, 1982, the CDC reported that 281 homosexual men and 33 IV drug users had been diagnosed with similar immune suppression and opportunistic infections, with a 43-percent fatality rate. Based on this information and the high prevalence of hepatitis in the same population, the companies knew, or should have known, by the summer of 1981, that urban homosexual males were not "suitable donors" within the meaning of the federal regulations.

In June 1982, the *MMWR* reported the existence of cases of severe immune dysfunction in intravenous drug users. Dr. Donald Francis, one of the CDC's investigators, has testified that hemophiliacs were being closely observed in anticipation of further cases, since all three groups had one thing in common. They had all been previously exposed to hepatitis B through sexual contact or blood.[22]

An internal memo from Dr. Henry Kingdon, Baxter's medical director, indicated that Baxter had also been "closely monitoring" the new occurrences of immunosuppressive disease in the homosexual population since December 1981.[23]

The CDC reported the first three cases of opportunistic infections among individuals with hemophilia on July 16, 1982. All three were reported to be heterosexual males. The CDC reported that the clinical and immunologic features of the three patients were strikingly similar to those recently observed among homosexual males and heterosexual IV drug users. While noting that the hemophilia patients did not share the latter two group's risk factors, the CDC stated, "Although the cause of the severe immune dysfunction is unknown, the occurrence among the three hemophiliac cases suggests the possible transmission of an agent through blood products." This suggestion was reinforced by the common denominator of previous hepatitis B exposure in all three groups.

On July 27, 1982, in response to the three hemophilia cases, a meeting was held at FDA headquarters in Bethesda, Maryland. Present were the Director of the Bureau of Biologics, Dr. Harry Meyer, and the assistant director, Dr. Dennis Donohue. Also present were the responsible heads of the four companies, the medical co-director of the NHF, Dr. Lou Aledort, Dr. Donald Francis, Dr. Jeffrey Koplin, and Dr. Ed Foegge from the CDC. The first item on the agenda was an attempt by the CDC to determine whether or not there was any connection between the sources of plasma used to make factor concentrates and the AIDS epidemic occurring in the homosexual community.

Dr. Michael Rodell, the responsible head for Baxter, spoke as the representative for the Biologic Section of the Pharmaceutical Manufactures Association (of which all four companies were members). Dr. Rodell made no mention of the fact that three of the companies were targeting HBs-positive donors and donors from predominantly homosexual donor centers, for plasma used in the manufacture of Factor VIII and IX. Dr. Francis has later testified that had this information been made available to the CDC at the meeting, it is highly probable that the course of the AIDS epidemic in the hemophilia community in America would have taken a different course. Dr. Francis is convinced that the CDC would have insisted on immediate recall and warnings to physicians and patients.[24]

After the meeting, Dr. Donohue informed Dr. Rodell that it might be necessary for the companies to discontinue the use of plasma collected from predominantly homosexual donor centers in the manufacture of factor concentrates.[25]

In fact, within 30 days, Cutter was informed that a donor from its Trimar Center had contracted AIDS. Trimar had centers located in Hollywood, San Diego, and Sacramento, California. All of these centers advertised in gay publications to attract male homosexual donors who were HBs-positive.[26]

Internal "alpha" documents revealed that Dr. Meyer and Dr. Donohue exerted immediate pressure upon the companies to stop the practice, without alerting the hemophilia community. Dr. Meyer sent out written demands to the companies stating that use of HBs-positive homosexuals violated FDA standards with regard to "history of hepatitis" prohibitions in the regulations.[27,28]

The FDA also attempted to persuade the companies to cease plasma collections from prisons and AIDS hotspots, such as Los Angeles, San Francisco, and New York. Dr. Donohue specifically mentioned that use of recovered plasma from Irwin Memorial Blood Bank (in San Francisco's famously gay Castro District) would not meet FDA standards. Eventually, on December 13, 1982, Dr. Donohue obtained what he thought was a binding "gentleman's agreement" that plasma from the aforementioned sources would not be used in the manufacture of factor concentrates.[29] It was not until October 20, 1983, that he discovered that Baxter had ignored the agreement and continued collections from various prisons. Baxter also continued collections from its donor center in Hollywood, California, until March 31, 1983, when the contract expired. Collections at its Polk Street Center in San Francisco continued into February 1983.

Baxter continued collections at two other plasma centers in Los Angeles throughout the entire AIDS epidemic. Lots that contained plasma from Baxter's San Francisco and Hollywood centers and prisons were released and sold into 1983 and 1984 with no enhanced warnings to the consumer.[30,31]

The full extent of contamination of lots manufactured by Cutter and Baxter with plasma collected from known male homosexuals will probably never be fully revealed. Cutter claims that it is extremely difficult, if not impossible, to trace HBIG donors into factor concentrate lots without reviewing HBIG manufacturing records. Cutter reported to the Class Action Steering Committee in 1996 that its HBIG manufacturing records were inexplicably destroyed. In addition, Cutter and Baxter employed the manufacturing technique known as "scrap filling." This meant that when excess plasma from batches used to fill the final containers was left over, it was used to fill any deficiency in subsequently manufactured lots. Therefore, it was entirely possible that plasma from predominantly homosexual donor centers would wind up in several lots, even if only one lot was originally scheduled to be manufactured with a lot of HBIG.

By December 1982, it was obvious that factor concentrates had been contaminated with an agent that was causing fatal immunosuppressive disease in the hemophilia community. Dr. Bruce Evatt informed the fractionators of the developing AIDS epidemic at an American Blood Resources Association (ABRA) meeting in Anaheim California on November 10, 1983. The next day, Cutter's representative at the meeting, Robert Barden, reported to Cutter officials that the company was "just seeing the tip of this iceberg."[32]

On December 3, 1982, Dr. Evatt repeated the grim epidemiological evidence to the fractionators at a BPAC meeting. There were now eight confirmed cases of AIDS in hemophiliacs. The number of AIDS cases was doubling every six months and there were now over 400 cases in the gay community. Dr. Evatt reaffirmed the CDC's belief that AIDS was caused by a transmissible agent through sexual contact and blood and that hemophiliacs were the next group to be exposed to the agent through the use of factor concentrate. It was reported at the meeting that studies had been completed at two treatment centers. Investigators tested hemophiliacs for signs of t-cell abnormalities like those found in homosexuals with asymptomatic, pre-AIDS conditions. Similar, severe t-cell abnormalities were detected in heavy users of factor concentrates, but not in hemophiliacs treated with cryoprecipitate.[33]

The American Red Cross sent out a communiqué to their blood banks, instructing them to begin preparations for increased demands from hemophilia treaters switching patients to cryoprecipitate.[34]

In December 1982, the CDC sent out notice to the fractionators that a confirmed case of transfusion-transmitted AIDS had been reported in a San Francisco infant and recommended that warnings be sent out to physicians and patients about this new disease.[35]

In that same month, Cutter's General Counsel, Ed Cutter, sent a memorandum to Cutter executives, advising them to revise their package insert and send out letters to physicians immediately, in response to the emerging risk of AIDS transmission through factor-concentrate use.[36] His advice was ignored. Instead, Cutter hired the public relations firm of Hill and Knowlton to enhance Cutter's public perception that it was doing its best to confront the growing threat of AIDS transmission through its factor concentrate products, and that the risk of transmission was extremely low.

At a meeting at CDC headquarters in Atlanta in January 1983, fractionators were advised by the CDC investigators that hemophiliacs were now considered at risk for contract-

ing AIDS through infusions of factor concentrates. It was suggested that high-risk groups be precluded from donating at all plasma centers and that use of the HBc test would exclude approximately 88 percent of these donors. The fractionators were told, once again, that a substantial percentage of hemophiliacs who used factor concentrates heavily were exhibiting pre-AIDS symptoms, such as t-cell abnormalities. However, cryoprecipitate users were not exhibiting abnormalities or pre-AIDS symptoms.[37]

Two days later the four companies' responsible heads met at the Pharmaceutical Manufacturing Association headquarters in Washington D.C. At the meeting, agreements were reached between the fractionators that no AIDS-warning enhancements would be made without prior consultation with the other companies. The wording would be similar if, and when, label amendments were eventually made. No further laboratory tests, such as HBc, would be done, and donor screening would be limited to placards being placed at the plasma centers along with questionnaires to be filled out by the donor, concerning membership in a high-risk AIDS group. Over the course of the next several years, the same representatives would meet to form joint positions with regard to AIDS transmission through their products, including prevention of recalls, stonewalling improved testing, limiting "look backs" on AIDS donors, and other matters affecting the safety of factor-concentrate blood products.[38,39]

One of the most egregious incidents is described in a Cutter-documented meeting held on December 15, 1983. The fractionators anticipated a recommendation by Dr. Donohue at the next day's BPAC meeting to implement HBc testing at all commercial plasma centers. Despite acknowledging that "the time had come" for HBc testing, the fractionators conspired to propose a "delaying tactic." They successfully stalled the FDA recommendation by proposing a "study committee," with themselves as members, to investigate the wisdom of implementing the test. The strategy was successful. Dr. Donohue agreed to the "study committee" proposal. HBc testing was never recommended by the FDA in plasma-collection centers. This enabled the fractionators to continue simultaneous manufacture of immune globulins and factor concentrates from the same plasma pools.[40]

By February 1983, the FDA still had made no recommendation for a general recall of factor concentrates. The NHF, speaking largely through its co-medical director Dr. Lou Aledort, continued to take the position that the benefits of the products outweighed the risks of AIDS transmission. Treaters at the HCTs had significantly advanced their careers by prescribing the products. They had developed close and beneficial relationships with the fractionators. Nevertheless, some members of the BPAC were raising questions about continued unabated use of the products without any enhanced warnings or viral-inactivation techniques. Even the NHF had sent out a patient and medical advisory in December 1982 stating that patients and parents should be notified of the risk of AIDS transmission.[41] Years later, the Institute of Medicine (IOM) investigation would comment that the FDA failed to exercise leadership by not recommending a general recall of stocks of factor concentrates that had been manufactured prior to February 1983 from unscreened plasma.[42]

A closed session of the BPAC was held on February 7, 1983, to discuss some of these issues. Dr. Donohue assured the committee that he had an agreement with the fractionators that they were no longer collecting plasma from prisons, homosexuals, or areas with large populations of AIDS cases, such as New York, Los Angeles, San Francisco, Miami, or Houston.

He reported there were only three plasma centers dedicated to collecting plasma from homosexuals. In fact, there were at least 22 such centers. As he spoke, Baxter was either collecting or manufacturing factor concentrates from plasma collected at some or all of these sources.

Later in the meeting, Dr. James Mosley questioned why any responsible fractionator or blood bank would target male homosexual donors—even before the AIDS epidemic—given their history of transmitting numerous infectious agents.[43] In depositions years later, Dr. Meyer would admit that recruiting known homosexuals in fast-track gay publications was a violation of Current Good Manufacturing Practices.[44] Dr. David Aronson, head of the FDA's coagulation laboratory, admitted that after the beginning of 1982 donors from known gay neighborhoods in urban areas were not "suitable" under the regulations.[45] Upon retirement from the FDA, Dr. Aronson became a paid consultant and expert witness for Cutter Biologics in hemophilia-AIDS cases.

Dr. Bruce Evatt again visited the fractionators at an ABRA meeting, this time in Las Vegas in March of 1983. He informed them that the CDC continued to recommend use of HBc testing to screen out donors who had a high risk of AIDS. He also informed them that the CDC expected half of the hemophiliac community to come down with full-blown AIDS. This was because most heavy concentrate users were displaying t-cell abnormalities, and the cases were continuing to increase. Dr. Evatt predicted approximately 5,000 full-blown AIDS cases in hemophiliacs before the epidemic was brought under control.[46] Baxter's internal documents reveal that Baxter had done its own investigation with regard to implementing the HBc test. Its laboratory reported that by combining the HBc and Staff Binding Assay (SBA) tests, Baxter could "eliminate virtually all AIDS" transmis-

sions through its products. Nevertheless, Baxter continued to delay implementing either test.[47]

No general recalls of factor concentrates were ever carried out by the companies, even as the number of cases continued to increase. They had also been informed by the CDC at the March 1983 ABRA meeting that over 5,000 hemophiliacs would probably progress to full-blown AIDS. No letters were ever sent out to the treaters. It was as if the companies realized that their past violations of the regulations and abuses of common sense in their donor-recruitment practices had sealed the doom of hemophiliacs who had used their products before July 16, 1982. This collective mindset was further confirmed when the CDC reported in its October 28, 1984, *MMWR* that 70 percent of all severe type-A hemophiliacs had been infected with the HTLV-III virus. Forty percent of all type-B hemophiliacs had been infected.[48]

Despite these terrifying statistics, which established beyond any argument that the companies' Factor VIII and Factor IX blood products were contaminated with a deadly virus, it was business as usual. No general recalls were initiated anywhere in the world. In fact, at least one company, Cutter, continued to sell nonvirally inactivated product to countries in the Far East.[49]

The fractionators did have a response to the reports from the CDC that the majority of hemophiliacs were HIV-positive. Cutter published information to the effect that being HIV positive did not necessarily mean the hemophiliac would go on to develop full-blown AIDS. Treaters such as Dr. Lou Aledort and Dr. Margret Hilgartner from New York took this position publicly. Dr. Hilgartner stated in the Cutter publication, *Echo Magazine*, in September 1985, that "a positive test result does not mean that the person will actually get AIDS" and that "there is no evidence to warrant changing the current use of Factor VIII or IX."[50] Dr. Aledort would later become a paid consultant to Armour and an expert witness for the fractionators in scores of hemophilia-AIDS cases.

The NHF also took the position that being HIV positive did not necessarily mean progression to full-blown AIDS. It went a step further and opined that being HIV positive might mean the hemophiliac had developed an immunity to protect them from AIDS.[51]

29.8 Litigation Strategies

Contrary to the information being disseminated by Cutter and the NHF, internal memos from Cutter indicate that based on the information it received from the CDC's Dr. Bruce Evatt in March 1983, it began formulating a litigation strategy by the summer of 1983. Meetings headed by

Dr. D. Buchner, a risk-management specialist sent from the German parent company, Bayer A G, were conducted under the name of "AIDS Scenarios." In those meetings Cutter correctly predicted that one realistic scenario was the death of over 5,000 hemophiliacs from full-blown AIDS. Various personnel within the company were assigned specific tasks calculated to give the fractionators an overwhelming advantage in the inevitable litigation. Part of the plan was to prevent the hemophilia community from becoming aware of the fact that they had been infected with a deadly virus that would eventually prove fatal over time. Other measures included:

- A public-relations campaign to influence the general public favorably towards the fractionators' position, before the other side could be publicized or understood.
- The creation of a common defense plan with the other fractionators.
- Retaining experts to support the common defense.
- Providing input into scientific studies that supported their theories of defense.[52,53]

These actions may well have postponed awareness within the hemophilia community as to the devastating injuries that had been inflicted upon them until widespread mortality began in 1988. However, many hemophiliacs were convinced by their treaters, whom they were used to turning to for advice, that there was no fault with the companies' conduct.

Treaters such as Dr. Levine and Dr. Aledort told their patients there was nothing that could have been done to prevent the unforeseeable and unpredictable HIV virus from infecting hemophiliacs before its existence was suspected.[54] Dr. Aledort had previously informed hemophiliacs in Cutter's May 1983 issue of *Echo Magazine*, that "there is no evidence to support that AIDS is transmitted in either cryoprecipitate or concentrate, although it is possible."[55] Dr. Aledort had recommended no extraordinary measures to the leadership of the NHF regarding AIDS by rationalizing that if it was caused by a transmissible agent, most hemophiliacs would already be infected.[56]

The NHF published material in its mailings of "Chapter Advisories" and "Medical Bulletins" that took the positions similar to the fractionator publications regarding AIDS and hemophilia. The NHF took an active role in discouraging a number of class actions filed in various parts of the country. At the request of Cutter's legal counsel, the board of directors provided an affidavit that was filed in opposition by Cutter to class action certification motions in California,

Washington, and Hawaii.[57] A class action that could toll the statute of limitations was not in the best interests of the fractionators.

Eventually, in September 1993, a class action was filed and partially certified in Chicago's Federal District Court. By then, however, sufficient time had elapsed to allow the companies to implement their strategy of using the threat of the statute-of-limitations defense. This succeeded in keeping most claimants from opting out of the class action settlement in 1996.

29.9 Viral Inactivation

Questions have been raised as to why the FDA would license a drug for sale that transmitted hepatitis B and nonA-nonB hepatitis. At least it could be expected that the FDA would closely track the product and pressure the companies to develop viral inactivation methods as soon as the technology could be reasonably implemented. This was required by any rational interpretation of the Current Good Manufacturing Practices statute. Although some justification for licensing was defensible in 1974 (due to the serious nature of hemophilia in its most severe form), by 1976, the reported side effects had been sufficiently reported to require regulatory action of some sort. Dr. Prince recently testified before the Irish government's Lindsay investigative tribunal that creating products from small pools of donors would drastically reduce the risk of infection from nonA-nonB hepatitis. He further stated that a change to cryoprecipitate should have been made the day it was realized that untreated Factor VIII pool preparations were highly infectious.[58] However, the fractionators, in the absence of any regulatory action, continued to ignore the problems. At a minimum, they should have applied to the FDA for permission to include the serious side effects discussed at the 1976 NHBLI meeting on their warning labels.

With regard to viral inactivation, the companies took the position that the state of the art prevented the products from being virally inactivated. The industry's consistent rationalization was that the Factor VIII and IX proteins were "labile" and, therefore, heat would destroy the ability of the Factor VIII and IX proteins to perform their functions in the coagulation cascade. However, by 1986, after the AIDS epidemic had provided the incentive to develop viral inactivation methods, it became clear that these methods were available a decade earlier and that they could have been implemented then, with a reasonable effort. The Institute of Medicine, a panel of experts convened by the National Academy of Sciences, reported in 1995 that there were no significant scientific obstacles that should have prevented implementation of effective viral inactivation obstacles by

1980.[59] There is no doubt that, had the companies started on these techniques in the early 1970s, the AIDS epidemic would not have occurred in the hemophiliac population. The methods that were eventually implemented included solvent and detergent, steam vapor, pasteurization, and dry heat.[60]

The companies have hotly disputed the conclusions of the IOM committee. A fair analysis of the evidence in the litigation has demonstrated the following scenario: In 1972, Cutter made brief attempts to heat Factor IX in the laboratory, but abandoned the efforts after only a few days. The scientist who conducted these efforts believes that given more time and resources, he could have solved the problem.[61] Little was done by any American company until 1977. By this time, word was leaking out that a German company called Behringwerke had succeeded in purifying Factor VIII in solution by heating the solution in the presence of a sucrose stabilizer, without destroying the Factor VIII protein's ability to remain active. A substantial loss of yield was a trade-off with this process. Nevertheless, the Behringwerke product constituted a sufficient threat to the American companies' expansion into European markets. Armour, Baxter, and Cutter attempted to duplicate the Behringwerke results. Baxter also began to do some work on a dry-heat process. However, none of the companies assigned a top priority to the project, and all were hampered by insufficient personnel and funding.

By 1981, Behringwerke had obtained a license in Germany for the sale of its pasteurized Factor VIII product. In a way, the Behringwerke success was unfortunate, because as it turned out, the most effective and simplest method for virally inactivating Factor VIII was the solvent-detergent process. This process was investigated by Dr. Ed Shanbrom in the mid- to late-1970s.[62] However, publications regarding the utility of using solvents to disrupt the lipid coat of viral agents had been available since 1972.[63,64] The U.S. fractionators were caught flat-footed by the news that Behringwerke, a company much smaller than Baxter, had made substantial inroads towards solving the problem. Consequently, they stampeded hastily down the heat-treatment path, without investigating the solvent-detergent alternative.

Although Dr. Shanbrom approached all of the companies about his solvent process sometime in the late 1970s, they were committed to the heat-treatment approach by their in-house research people.[63] The "NIH" (not invented here) philosophy prevailed.

The solvent process successfully avoids three of the major impediments to applying heat to the Factor VIII protein. First, it does not affect the yield or the ability of the protein to retain its activity after the treatment. Second, it does not denature the protein or change its configuration.

Denaturation causes concern that the body will develop antibodies to the Factor VIII protein, known as inhibitors, and reject the protein in the future. This is a serious matter for a severe hemophiliac, because it precludes future treatment with factor-concentrate therapy. Third, the solvent kills all lipid viruses. HIV, HCV, and hepatitis B are lipid viruses.[65]

Dr. Shanbrom filed his patent application in 1980. A Baxter executive acknowledged being approached by Shanbrom in that same year. Shanbrom has stated that he made his process available to all of the companies around that time but was uniformly rejected. He describes the implementation of his process as "easy as washing your hands."[66,67]

Eventually the New York Blood Center was granted an FDA license for a solvent-detergent process in June 1985. The process was implemented by the NYBC by 1986 through the work of Dr. Horowitz and Dr. Prince. Dr. Shanbrom sued the NYBC in a patent-infringement action, which was eventually settled. Dr. Shanbrom received a percentage of the royalties generated by the NYBC process. The NYBC took the position that the technology required to remove the solvent was a difficult obstacle to overcome, and that Dr. Shanbrom had not described a method for this step in his patent. Dr. Shanbrom argued that this is not a difficult step and was, in fact, so perfunctory that he did not see the need to include it in the patent description. Regardless of the merits of either argument, it seems reasonable to conclude that motivated fractionators could have investigated and implemented a solvent-detergent process well before 1980.[65]

Baxter, Cutter, and Alpha adopted the NYBC technology and, by 1988, all but Armour were using it to virally inactivate their Factor VIII blood products.

Factor IX presented a different set of problems. The Factor IX protein was more stable than the Factor VIII protein when heated. The fear was that denaturation would activate the prothrombin complex and trigger clotting, which would lead to thrombosis in the patient. According to Dr. Milan Wickerhauser, former head of the Plasma Fractionation Division of the American Red Cross Blood Research Laboratory, this problem was surmountable by the mid to late 1970s.

After 1978, stabilizers such as heparin or antithrombin III became available through the Red Cross Blood Research Laboratory. These materials could be used as stabilizers, which would allow heating at higher temperatures without activation of the Factor IX protein. In addition, the heating step could be applied in the final container, reducing the risk of contamination after the application of heat. This technology could have been implemented within a year, and would have completely solved the denaturation problem, while at the same time killing all lipid viruses. The solvent-detergent process was a viable alternative for Factor IX also. Both Dr. Shanbrom and NYBC describe the process as applicable to the Factor IX protein.[65] An FDA license was granted to apply the solvent-detergent process to Factor IX in 1987.

Given these facts, the question arises as to why the FDA was not following up with the companies in the 1970s to ensure that they were working diligently to resolve the viral-transmission problem.

The litigation discovery and interviews with former employees of the FDA have revealed that the Bureau of Biologics took a protective, rather than a coercive, stance regarding enforcement issues involving biologic drug manufacturers.[68] Many FDA employees went to work for the biologic drug industry upon leaving the FDA. Dr. Harry Meyer took the position of president of American Cyanamid. Dr. Donohue became a consultant to the American Red Cross.

Dr. Meyer once stated to his director of compliance, Sammie Young, that he viewed the fractionating companies as a "fragile" industry. Dr. Meyer was formerly head of the Bureau of Biologic's predecessor organization, the Department of Biological Statistics (DBS). The DBS was formerly a section within the National Institutes of Health (NIH). The DBS was removed from the NIH to the FDA. This was mandated by Congress, after certain revelations surfaced in the "Ribicoff Hearings" related to DBS malfeasance in overseeing the polio vaccine defectively manufactured by Cutter Biological.

The intent was to make the DBS more effective as a regulatory agency, utilizing the coercive tools of the FDA. Unfortunately, the new Bureau of Biologics retained much of its autonomy and continued to take a tolerant stance towards industry practices in the fractionation area. For instance, Dr. Meyer insisted that the BOB conduct a substantial portion of the industry's plasma center inspections, as an extension of BOB's licensing authority. This meant that advance notice would be sent to the center, allowing it to correct or conceal discrepancies that unannounced inspections might disclose. Instead of having trained inspectors from the FDA local District Offices conduct the inspections, only BOB employees were allowed to perform this function. It was not uncommon for Dr. Meyer or his wife to personally inspect centers themselves. This resulted in less-rigid enforcement of the safety regulations that applied to the plasma centers. There was a decidedly more informal, relaxed approach to plasma-center inspections that were conducted by BOB personnel.

Dr. Meyer adopted a policy that allowed fractionator executives and responsible heads virtually unlimited access to his office at any time. He implemented an unwritten directive within the agency that issues regarding inappropriate conduct by a biological pharmaceutical company were not

to be memorialized in writing.[69] A striking example of this policy was demonstrated in internal Cutter documents regarding the continued shipments of non-virally inactivated product after October 1984. Dr. Meyer had understandably assumed that the companies had terminated distribution of untreated factor concentrates after they had obtained their expedited heat-treatment licenses in February 1984. Certainly by October 1984, when the CDC had published in its MMWR that hemophiliacs had been infected with the HIV in the products, and that Cutter's heat-treatment process killed the HTLV-III virus, Dr. Meyer assumed no shipments of unheated factor concentrates were still taking place. When Dr. Meyer discovered that such shipments were ongoing, he hastily called a meeting with the companies on May 20, 1985. He advised the fractionators that he wanted them to surrender their licenses for further manufacture of unheated concentrates because "no one in the world should be exposed to contaminated product" at this point in time. Further, he stated he wanted the problem handled "quietly, without alerting the Congress, the medical community or the public." No official FDA document has been produced that would give any indication of what actually transpired at this meeting. Dr. Meyer's philosophy of regulation was to form a consensus with industry through consultation and cooperation, rather than through coercion.[70]

This philosophy led to some curious interpretations of important regulations by the BOB. For instance, the regulations clearly required permanent rejection of any plasma donor with a history of viral hepatitis, or anyone who was in close contact with someone who had hepatitis within the last six months, or anyone who had been previously tested and found positive to the HBsAg test, a test for hepatitis B surface antigen.[71]

29.10 History of Hepatitis Regulation

By the mid-1970s, it was undisputed scientific fact that the presence of antibodies to the surface protein (HBs) or the core protein (HBc) of the hepatitis B virus meant that the donor had been previously infected by the hepatitis B virus. In addition, the presence of either of these antibodies meant that the donor would have tested positive for hepatitis B surface antigen at some time in the past. The only reason the donor had escaped permanent deferral was the timing of the donation. If, by the time the donor entered the plasma center or blood bank, the live virus had been neutralized by HBs or HBc antibody, the donor could pass the HBsAg test. However, to allow that donor to make a donation was clearly contrary to the intent expressed in the plain language of the regulation. The intent behind the "history of hepatitis" regulation was to eliminate donors whose behaviors had lead to hepatitis infection, as well as the risk of hepatitis transmission itself.[72,73]

Another useful fact that a positive HBc antibody test reveals about donors is that they are capable of transmitting the hepatitis B virus, even though they pass the HBsAg test. These are known as carrier donors. These donors are chronically infected, and never completely clear the live virus from their systems. However, the level of circulating Hepatitis Surface Antigen is too low to be detected using the standard HBsAg test. In 1979, after the licensing of the HBc test as a medical device, the fractionators had the means to comply with the letter of the "history of hepatitis" regulation, by eliminating these donors.[74]

Simply stated, a positive HBc test result meant unequivocally that the donor had previously had HBsAg circulating in his blood. However, because he did not happen to walk into the donor center at the particular time when his HBsAg was detectable, he was allowed to donate his plasma. At the time he presented himself at the plasma center, the HBsAg antigen had been neutralized by an HBc and/or HBs antibody.

The blood banks and the fractionators had similar motives for not implementing HBc testing. The blood banks were not anxious to disqualify HBs- or HBc-positive donors, because they had become dependent upon gay men for repeat blood donations. By 1978, blood banks were receiving 10–15 percent of their blood donations from gay donors, particularly in large, metropolitan blood centers located in Los Angeles and San Francisco.[75] These blood centers were also supplying plasma, referred to as "recovered plasma," to the fractionators for the dual manufacture of factor concentrates and immunoglobulins. Approximately 20 percent of the plasma used by the fractionators came in the form of recovered plasma from voluntary blood donors.

Consistent with Dr. Meyer's and the BOB's "protective" regulatory philosophy, the BOB found a way to interpret the regulations that allowed HBc- and HBs-positive donors to donate, despite their laboratory-confirmed "history of hepatitis." Without this interpretation, the fractionators would have been forced to change their manufacturing methods. They would have had to find a way to manufacture factor concentrates and immunoglobulins without intermingling the starting pools of plasma. Rather than have the industry devise new manufacturing methods, the BOB accommodated the economic interests of the blood industry by defining "history of hepatitis" as being a "clinical" history that a patient might give orally to a treating physician, as opposed to a laboratory-test result. Therefore, if a donor denied that he had ever been told by a physician that he had been diagnosed with viral hepatitis, he would be allowed to

donate. This policy ignored the issue of a paid donor's disincentive to be completely candid, or his bad memory (due to possible substance abuse). The use of a laboratory test, which did not rely upon the memory of the donor, would seem to be the safer course of action. It was only through this tortured, illogical interpretation of the "history of hepatitis" regulation that the industry was allowed to continue accepting high-risk donors who had been previously infected with the hepatitis B virus. The end result was that the donors and, consequently, its plasma pools, became increasingly infectious with hepatitis B and C and eventually HIV.

The voluntary blood banks eventually came into compliance with the "history of hepatitis" regulation in 1987. In 1986, the Blood Products Advisory Committee recommended implementation of the HBc and ALT tests as surrogate tests for nonA-nonB hepatitis. Despite the BPAC recommendation, the FDA did not issue guidelines formally requiring the HBc test until 1989. The guideline stated that the test was required as a means to eliminate carrier donors for the hepatitis B virus. The fact that HBc-positive donors were known carrier donors for the hepatitis B virus had been published in peer-reviewed medical literature since 1978.[76–78] However, it took ten years for the FDA to finally acknowledge the ability of the HBc test to eliminate hepatitis B-carrier donors from the blood supply.

Unlike blood banks, the fractionators did not implement the HBc test in 1986, despite the BPAC recommendation. Many blood banks had implemented HBc and ALT testing prior to the 1986 BPAC recommendation. Some blood bankers reported at the 1986 BPAC meeting that both hepatitis B and nonA-nonB transmissions had been substantially reduced in the United States after the tests were implemented. It is worth noting that despite the fact that the fractionators were virally inactivating their factor concentrates with heat by 1986, those techniques had been demonstrated to be unreliable with regard to nonA-nonB hepatitis. In fact, factor concentrates inactivated only with heat have been reported to have caused hepatitis C transmission to hemophiliacs as recently as 1994.[79]

In 1993, the FDA published guidelines specifically exempting the fractionators from doing HBc testing, despite requiring the blood banks to test each donor for the HBc antibody. Thus, two different standards were established for blood bankers and for fractionators. No scientific justification is set forth in the regulation guideline for the two standards.[80,29]

By publishing this guideline, the FDA's Bureau of Biologics accommodated the fractionator position that to prosper economically, the industry must be allowed to manufacture all of its products out of a single plasma pool. The fractionators must have HBc- and HBs-positive donors to make the broad range of blood products coming out of the Cohn fractionation process from a single pool of starting material.

29.11 Defending Factor VIII and IX

Despite the fact that Factor VIII and IX drugs will arguably kill more people than any drug in history, it has clearly defined, vehement defenders. The defenders consist of three groups of "experts" who played prominent roles in the events leading up to the high mortality rate among hemophiliacs from AIDS. These are the same people whom the victims relied upon to protect them from harm. Many of them are scientists who were employed by the fractionators. They rationalize, in court testimony, that nothing more could have been done to virally inactivate the products, until it was finally accomplished in 1984.

Another group consists of the U.S. BOB regulators, who failed to require the fractionators to comply with Good Manufacturing Practices until the AIDS epidemic was so far along that no amount of regulation could save the hemophilia community from the ravages of HIV and HCV. The third group is comprised of the hemophilia treaters who championed the product to their patients, but allowed their loyalties to their patients to be influenced by their relationships to the fractionators. These physicians were heads of large treatment centers that profited from the sales of the product and from the participation of their patients at the HCTs. As a result, their advice to the patients lacked the required objectivity when the risk was potential death from AIDS, versus the temporary inconvenience of using alternative treatments, such as cryoprecipitate. In many cases, these treaters accepted expert-witness fees of several hundred dollars per hour to serve as experts for the fractionators in the ensuing hemophilia litigation.

It is remarkable that despite the misconduct and conflict of interest by influential people in these groups, sufficient facts have emerged about these drugs to allow some measure of compensation to hemophiliacs and their families. However, as a result, an accurate and satisfactorily complete history of Factor VIII and Factor IX blood products will probably never be written.

Endnotes

1. Author. Personal communications with participants at Kobe AIDS conference: Kobe, Japan, November 2–3, 1996.

2. Chorba, TL, et al. "Effects of HIV infection on age and cause of death in persons with hemophilia in the U.S.," *Am. J. Hematol.* 66:229–240 (2001).

3. "HIV and the blood supply: A crisis in decision making. Executive summary," *IOM Report* 3–16 (1995).

4. *Schulten v. Cutter et al.*, October, 2002.

5. Dr. Ed Shanbrom. Deposition in *Schulten v. Cutter et al.*, October 30, 2002.

6. Francis K. Wipman, ed. *Technical Manual of the American Association of Blood Banks* (Basel, Switzerland: Karger, 1981).

7. Dr. James Mosley. Personal communication with author, March, 2003.

8. Dr. James Mosely. Deposition in *Wadleigh v. Armour et al.*, 1996.

9. *Proceedings of a Workshop on Unsolved Therapeutic Problems in Hemophilia* (publication no. 77–1089) J. Fratatoni and D. Aronson, eds. (Washington, DC: NIH, 1976), pp. 15–22.

10. "Warning label factor VIII and factor IX blood products," Cutter Biological, Alpha Therapeutic, Armour Pharmaceutical, and Baxter Healthcare, 1976.

11. "Chronic hepatitis in hemophilia," *Ann. Intern. Med.* 86:818–820 (1997). J.A. Spero et al. "Asymptomatic structural liver disease in hemophilia," *N. Engl. J. Med.* 298:1373–1378.

12. Dr. Michael Rodell. Deposition in *Wadleigh v. Armour, MDL* 986:1996.

13. David Link. Letter to Abbott approving HBc as medical device, January 19, 1979.

14. U.S. Department of Health, Education, and Welfare. 1977. *Study to evaluate the supply-demand relationships for AHF and PTC through 1980* (publication no. 77-1274) (Washington, DC: U.S. Department of Health, Education, and Welfare, 1977).

15. R.D. Ach et al. "Serum alanine aminotransferase of donors in relation to the risk of non-A, non-B hepatitis in recipients," *N. Engl. J. Med.* 304(17): 989–994 (1981). *Krever Commission Report: The Report of the Commission of Inquiry on the Blood System in Canada* (Ottawa: Canadian Government Publishing, 1997).

16. Bill Horn. Personal communication with author, March 2003.

17. W. Smuzness et al. 1975. "On the role of sexual behavior in the spread of hepatitis B infection," *Ann. Intern. Med.* 83:489–495.

18. Dr. Louis Aledort. Deposition in *Osborn v. Irwin Memorial Blood Bank*, 1988.

19. Supra, 15.

20. C.E. Stephens. "Hepatitis B virus antibody in donors and occurrence of nonA–nonB hepatitis in transfusion recipients," *Ann. Intern. Med.* 101:733–738 (1984).

21. D.E. Koziol et al. "Antibody to hepatitis B core antigen as a paradoxical marker for nonA–nonB hepatitis agents in donated blood," *Ann. Intern. Med.* 104:488–495 (1986).

22. J. Hoofnagle et al. "Type B hepatitis after transfusion with blood containing antibody to hepatitis B core antigen," *New Engl. J. Med.* 298:1379–1383 (1978).

23. Centers for Disease Control. 1981–1985. *Morbidity and Mortality Weekly Report.* Vol. 30–34.

24. H. Kingdon. Baxter memorandum to A. Northrup, January 5, 198

25. Dr. Donald Francis. Trial testimony in *Dowling v. Cutter et al.*, 2003.

26. P. Kaufman. Memorandum to Dr. Michael Rodell, August 3, 1982.

27. FDA. August 20, 1982. Minutes of meeting with Cutter representatives re plasma from a donor with Kaposi's Sarcoma.

28. P. Carr. Alpha memorandum to Colton, August 27, 1982.

29. H. Meyer. Letter to Penny Carr, August 20, 1982.

30. *Krever Commission Report,* supra, 15.

31. John Bacich and Richard Srigley. Testimony in *Dowling v. Cutter Biological*, 2003, and *Alverado v. Cutter Biological et al.,* 1994.

32. R. Barden. Memorandum to Cutter executives, November 11, 1982.

33. Minutes of December 3–4 Blood Products Advisory Committee Meeting, Bethesda, MD.

34. Letter from Blood Service Advisory of the American Red Cross, December 20, 1982.

35. Curran and Evatt (CDC). Letter to Heinrichs at Cutter Biological, December 3, 1982.

36. E. Cutter. Memorandum to Cutter executives, December 29, 1982.

37. Johnson. Armour memorandum to Ethical Products Division, January 12, 1983.

38. Dr. Stephen Ojala. Deposition in *Doe v. Cutter Hawaii*, November 14, 1988, and *Jane Doe v. Miles Maryland*, September 17, 1987.

39. Dr. Stephen Ojala. Cutter memorandum to Schaeffler et al., December 19, 1983.

40. NHF. *Chapter Advisory # 4*, December 9, 1982.

41. "HIV and the blood supply: A crisis in decision making. executive summary," *IOM Report* 3–16 (1995).

42. FDA. Minutes of Blood Products Advisory Committee closed session, February 7, 1983.

43. Dr. Harry Meyer. Deposition, April, 1998. "Factor VIII or IX concentrate blood products" Products Liability Litigation. MDL 986.

44. Dr. David Aronson. Deposition in *Cross v. Cutter et al.*, 1993.

45. Hink. Cutter memorandum to Ojala, March 13, 1983.

46. Slimak. Baxter memorandum to Castaldi, June 27, 1983.

47. Centers for Disease Control. *Morbidity and Mortality Weekly Report,* October 28, 1984.

48. W. Bogdanich E. Koli. "Two paths of Bayer drug in 80s: Riskier type went overseas," *The N.Y. Times*, May 22, 2003.

49. M. Hilgartner. "Cutter Biologic: questions and answers," *Echo Magazine* 3:6–11 (1985).

50. NHF. *Chapter Advisory #17, Medical Bulletin #12*, July 31, 1984.

51. Cutter memorandum, "AIDS scenarios," September, 1983.

52. Cutter memorandum, "AIDS Roadmap," undated.

53. Dr. Peter Levine. Affidavit in *Wadleigh v. Armour et al.*, 1999.

54. L. Alieport. "Puts AIDS disease in perspective," *Echo Magazine* 4(1) (1983)

55. Donold Goldman. Deposition in *Wadleigh v. Armour et al.*, 1996.

56. NHF. Resolution of Board of Directors, October 31, 1985.

57. Dr. Prince. Testimony in Lindsay tribunal, Dublin, Ireland, June 27, 2001.

58. "HIV and the blood supply: A crisis in decision making. Executive summary," *IOM Report* 3–16 (1995).

59. Dr. Milan Wickerhauser. Testimony in *Dowling v. Cutter et al.*

60. Sohachi Wada. Deposition, "Factor VIII or IX concentrate blood products," *Products Liability Litigation,* MDL 986.

61. Dr. Ed Shanbrom. Deposition in *Dowling v. Cutter et al.,* 2003.

62. Dr. William Robinson. Testimony in *Dowling v. Cutter et al.,* 2003; also, B.C. Evatt, "Risk factors for infection with HBV and HCV in a large cohort of hemophiliac males," *Transfusion* 41:(2001).

63. Dr. Ed Shanbrom. Speech at Kobe AIDS Conference, Kobe, Japan, November 2, 1996

64. Dr. Milan Wickerhauser. Testimony in *Dowling v. Cutter et al.,* 2003.

65. Dr. Ed Shanbrom. Testimony in *Dowling v. Baxter et al.*; deposition in *Morrison v. Baxter Healthcare,* April 25, 2000.

66. Shanbrom. Supra, 63.

67. Shanbrom. Supra, 63.

68. Sammy Young. Personal communications with author, March, 2003.

69. Dr. Stephen Ojala.Cutter memorandum to BSU, May 30, 1985.

70. FDA. "Additional standards for human blood and blood products: Suitability of donor." 2003. 21 C.F.R. § 640.63. pp. 99–100.

71. Dr. Donald P. Francis. Affidavit in *Adney v. Cutter,* 1996.

72. Minority Report of Committee on HBc Testing, March 1984.

73. Cutter press release announcing HBc testing, April 4, 1984.

74. A. Katz. Speech to American Red Cross National Convention, May 24, 1983.

75. Cutter press release announcing HBc testing, April 4, 1984.

76. Dr. Donald Francis. Affidavit in *Adney v Cutter,* 1996.

77. Minority Report of Committee on HBc testing, March, 1984.

78. Cutter draft position paper advocating the implementation of anti-core testing, undated.

79. J.M. Soucie et al. "Risk factors for infection with HBV and HCV in a large cohort of hemophiliac males." *Transfusion* 41:338–343 (2001).

80. *Krever Commission Report. Supra, 15.*

Chapter 30

HIV Pharmacotherapy and Its Complications

Vincent Idemyor, Pharm.D.

30.1 Epidemic Overview

In June 1981, the United States Centers for Disease Control and Prevention (CDC) reported an unusual outbreak of Pneumocystis pneumonia (PCP) among men that have sex with men (MSM). This disease had previously affected only people with severely compromised immune systems.

In 1982, the CDC determined that the disease responsible for this was found in blood. Public health professionals started noticing the occurrence of opportunistic infections (OIs) among MSM and they called it "Acquired Immune Deficiency Syndrome," or AIDS.

In 1984, the virus that is responsible for the development of AIDS—Human Immunodeficiency Virus (HIV)—was isolated and discovered. By 1984, almost 5,000 cases of AIDS in the United States had already been identified and more than 2,000 Americans had died from its complications. By 2009, about 33 million individuals worldwide were living with HIV and more than 2 million were infected with the virus during 2008.[1]

30.2 Use of Antiretroviral Therapy

Significant progress has been made in the development of antiretroviral therapy (ART). ART can successfully delay destruction of the immune system, reduce severity and frequency of opportunistic infections, and consequently delay AIDS progression. During the last decade, highly active antiretroviral therapy (HAART) has revolutionized the care of HIV-infected individuals. As of January 2010, more than 23 individual antiretroviral agents had been approved by the Food and Drug Administration (FDA) for use in treatment. These agents are designed to attack HIV by interfering with the processes necessary for HIV infection and replication. The agents fall into these six categories:

- Nucleoside Reverse Transcriptase Inhibitors (NRTIs)
- Non-Nucleoside Reverse Transcriptase Inhibitors (NNRTIs)
- Protease Inhibitors (PIs)
- Fusion Inhibitors
- Chemokine binding receptor (CCR5) antagonists
- Integrase Inhibitors

The classification of antiretroviral agents is based on where the drug acts in the replication cycle of the virus. The NRTI named Zidovudine was the first agent approved specifically for the treatment of HIV disease in 1987. Subsequently, other NRTIs were developed. In 1996, the first NNRTI and PI were introduced. In 2003, a new agent in the fusion-inhibitor category was introduced, and in 2007, two other agents were approved in the CCR5 and integrase-inhibitor categories, respectively.

The introduction of HAART, consisting of a combination of nucleoside/nucleotide reverse transcriptase inhibitors (NRTIs), non-nucleoside reverse transcriptase inhibitors (NNRTIs), and/or protease inhibitors (PIs), can reduce viral load to below detectable levels in patient plasma, resulting in improved patient health and lifespan.[2-4] However, the virus is suppressed, rather than eradicated, by HAART. On HAART regimens, multiple drug therapies can lead to increased adverse effects and toxicities due to long-term use and drug-drug interactions.[5,6]

There are several goals of therapy in treating HIV-infected individuals. The main goals of therapy are clinical, virologic, immunologic, and epidemiologic.

- Clinical goal: Extend life expectancy and quality of life in the infected individuals.
- Virologic goal: Reduce the viral load to the lowest possible level, so as to prevent disease progression and limit development of resistance to the antiretroviral agents.
- Immunologic goal: Preserve the immunologic function of the respective organ system.
- Epidemiologic goal: Reduce transmission of HIV.

Many factors influence the ability to sustain suppression of viral replication in HIV disease, such as the pharmacokinetic and pharmacodynamics of the combination regimen, cellular penetration, tolerability of the regimen, adherence and antiretroviral resistance due to development or preexisting presence of the resistant viral mutants. See Table 30.1.

Table 30.1
Antiretroviral Drugs for Use in the United States, as of January 2010

Year Approved	Generic Name	Class
1987	Zidovudine	NRTI
1991	Didanosine	NRTI
1992	Zalcitabine	NRTI
1994	Stavudine	NRTI
1995	Saquinavir	PI
1995	Lamivudine	NRTI
1996	Indinavir	PI
1996	Ritonavir	PI
1996	Nevirapine	NNRTI
1997	Delavirdine	NNRTI
1997	Nelfinavir	PI
1998	Efavirenz	NNRTI
1998	Abacavir	NRTI
1999	Amprenavir	NRTI
2000	Lopinavir/ritonavir	PI
2001	Tenofovir DF	nucleotide RTI
2003	Atazanavir	PI
2003	Emtricitabine	NRTI
2003	Enfuvirtide	Fusion inhibitor
2004	Fos-amprenavir	PI
2005	Tipranavir	PI
2006	Darunavir	PI
2007	Maraviroc	CCR5 antagonist
2007	Raltegravir	Integrase Inhibitor
2007	Etravirine	NNRTI

A. NRTIs

The NRTIs were the first set of medications approved by the United States FDA based on demonstrable survival benefits in AIDS patients. They work by binding to HIV-1 reverse transcriptase. They are not active as parent compounds and must be phosphorylated to their active intracellular forms. The nucleoside analogs generally have the potential for toxicity due to interaction with human DNA polymerases.

- Zidovudine—The first antiretroviral agent approved for use against HIV infection. It is an important component of fix-dose combination therapy. Toxicities such as anemia and neutropenia are known side effects.
- Didanosine—Efficacy has been demonstrated in large-scale clinical trials involving adults and children at various stages of HIV disease progression. The major toxicities are pancreatitis and peripheral neuropathy, which, if recognized early, are often reversible upon discontinuation of the medication.
- Zalcitabine—This nucleoside analog is rarely used in antiretroviral treatment, since there are more potent and less toxic drugs that are currently available in the management of HIV disease.
- Stavudine—Like other nucleoside analogs, stavudine must be phosphorylated to the active intracellular form. Its long-term toxicities limit its use in routine clinical settings. Because of the increased risk of lipoatrophy, it is generally considered a less desirable alternative to other preferred regimens.
- Lamivudine—Because of its ease of administration and favorable oral bioavailability, lack of frequent toxicity and lack of frequent drug interactions, lamivudine has become an important component of combination antiretroviral therapy.
- Emtricitabine—This pyrimidine nucleoside analog is similar to lamivudine, with mild toxicity usually not leading to discontinuation of therapy.
- Abacavir—This agent is a carbocyclic nucleoside analog with potent and selective activity against HIV-1. The single most important treatment-limiting condition in the usage of the drug is severe hypersensitivity reaction in some of the patients. The hypersensitivity syndrome, characterized by fever, nausea and rash usually occurs during the first month of therapy. In some parts of the world, testing for HLA-B*5701 is performed before the usage of the medication.
- Tenofovir DF—This compound is a nucleotide analog designed to circumvent the first phosphoryla-

tion step necessary for activation of nucleoside analogs, such as zidovudine, didanosine, zalcitabine, stavudine, lamivudine, and abacavir.[7] The safety of tenofovir DF has been studied in several hundred HIV-infected individuals in clinical trials and many more in routine clinical care, and the drug is generally well tolerated. However, there continues to be much interest in defining the long-term safety of tenofovir DF and renal function.

B. NNRTIs

The NNRTIs inhibit reverse transcriptase by binding to a hydrophobic subunit of the HIV-1 reverse transcriptase near the catalytic site of the enzyme.

- Delavirdine is rarely used today in the treatment of HIV disease, because of issues of dosing frequency, cross-resistance to other NNRTIs, and the potential for unexpected pharmacokinetic interactions.
- Nevirapine—The effectiveness of nevirapine has been demonstrated in both treatment-naïve and treatment-experienced patients, as well as in pediatric patients. Because serious and life-threatening hepatotoxicity has been observed in adults with high pretreatment CD4+ T-cell counts, nevirapine should not be initiated in women with pretreatment CD4+ T-cell counts exceeding 250/mm^3 or in men with CD4+ T-cell counts exceeding 400/mm^3 unless the benefits outweigh the risks.
- Efavirenz activity is mediated predominantly by noncompetitive inhibition of HIV-1 reverse transcriptase. Efavirenz was one of the first agents to be included in once-daily regimen because of its favorable pharmacokinetics for daily dosing. The most common adverse events noted during efavirenz therapy are rash and central nervous system symptoms, such as dizziness, insomnia, impaired concentration, somnolence, abnormal dreams, and hallucinations.
- Etravirine—This agent is the most recent of the NNRTIs. It was approved by the FDA in 2007. Etravirine has a higher genetic barrier to resistance in vitro than currently available NNRTIs and requires the accumulation of multiple mutations before its activity is substantially impaired.[8]

C. PIs

Mapping of the HIV genome revealed the existence of the virus-specific protease, and this became a target for HIV drug discovery starting in the 1990s and continuing into the present. Computer technology was also applied to design some of the compounds based on crystallographic structure of the target enzyme.[9,10] This approach is different from the traditional drug development, which relies on mass screening of thousands of potential compounds.[9,10]

The PIs work by inhibiting protease enzyme encoded by HIV-1. PIs are largely responsible for the improvement of health witnessed during the last decade in HIV-infected individuals with continuous access to therapy and are now an integral part of HIV-disease drug therapy. The advent of PIs in combination with two NRTIs led to the coining of the concept known today as HAART.[11,12] Their use as a component of HAART has shown to result in durable virologic suppression and improvement in the morbidity and mortality of those infected with HIV-1.[13,14] The currently available PIs approved as of January 2012 are; saquinavir, indinavir, ritonavir, nelfinavir, amprenavir, lopinavir/ritonavir, atazanavir, fos-amprenavir, tipranavir, and darunavir.

The earlier generation PIs had limitations, such as high pill burden, severe or life-threatening toxicities, pharmacokinetic interactions with other drugs, food, and cross resistance.

The modern generation PIs are more potent than the earlier generation PIs, with a much more favorable adherence, tolerability, pharmacokinetic, and resistance profiles. The strategy of boosting PI plasma drug concentration with a low-dose of ritonavir has enabled further pharmacokinetic improvements such as once or twice daily administration and better enhancement of the PI resistance barrier. Recently developed PIs have been associated with fewer side effects than earlier medications and it is anticipated that the PIs in development will also have a favorable tolerability profile.

The process of HIV entry into target cells is complex and can be divided into three phases: attachment, co-receptor binding and membrane fusion.

The first step in the HIV-1 life cycle is viral attachment to the CD4+ T-cell surface. The next step is viral entry that involves the cascade of molecular interactions between the viral envelope glycoprotein and two T-cell surface receptors—a primary receptor and a co-receptor. The glycoprotein (gp) 120 subunit of HIV enveloped protein first binds to CD4+ T-cell, the primary receptor. This induces a conformational change in the gp 120 that allows it to bind to the co-receptor.

Co-receptor binding then triggers conformational changes in the viral transmembrane glycoprotein (gp41) subunit, leading to the insertion of its N-terminal fusion peptide into the host cell membrane. Fusion results in the release of the viral genome into the cytoplasm.

The molecular nature of gp41 consists of heptad repeat sequences in two regions. The regions of gp41 form a helical bundle structure that is critical for membrane fusion to occur. Enfuvirtide works on the third phase involving fusion of the membrane when enfuvirtide competitively binds to one of the heptad repeat regions when gp41 is in its extended conformation and prevents the structure from folding back onto itself.

Enfuvirtide is a valuable addition to the antiretroviral armamentarium, but the compound also has its limitations: there is no oral formulation of the drug, there are difficulties in drug administration, and there is a limited barrier to resistance.

D. CR5 Antagonist

As mentioned above, there are multiple stages to the process by which HIV attaches to and fuses with target cells, the different stages being susceptible to intervention by different compounds. The second phase of viral entry is co-receptor binding. HIV uses CCR5 as a co-receptor during the binding of the gp 120 envelope protein to CD4 on the target cell. Most transmitted strains of HIV-1 use the CCR5 co-receptor for entry into CD4+ cells.

When a CCR5 inhibitor is present, binding of the CCR5 N-terminus and second extracellular loop with the V3 stem of gp120 is blocked, resulting in inhibition of viral entry.[15] The strategies to block CCR5 co-receptor binding include modified non-agonistic CCR5 chemokine natural ligands, CCR5 antibodies, and CCR5 small-molecule antagonists.

Maraviroc is a selective CCR5 antagonist with potent antiviral activity against all CCR5-tropic HIV-1 viruses at low nanomolar concentrations.[16] The compound was obtained by medicinal chemistry optimization of a high throughput screening lead, the imidazopyridine derivative.

Maraviroc was the first agent in the class of chemokine co-receptor antagonists to be approved by the FDA. It binds to CCR5, one of two possible coreceptors used by HIV to enter CD4+ cells, thus blocking entry of CCR5-tropic HIV into these cells. As with all antiretroviral medications, maraviroc should be used only in combination regimens so as to optimize its treatment efficacy. Maraviroc is a substrate of the cytochrome P450 enzyme system (CYP3A) and p-glycoprotein, and has therapeutically significant interactions with many medications, including other antiretroviral agents.

E. Integrase Inhibitors

The integration of HIV-1 genetic material into host DNA is necessary for HIV infection. This process is catalyzed by the viral enzyme, integrase, which is a 288 amino acid protein, derived from the 3-end of the HIV polymerase gene. Integration of viral cDNA into host chromosomes is a multi-step process.[17]

Integration follows reverse transcription, which synthesizes double-stranded DNA copies of HIV-1 RNA after infection. Integrase catalyses the processing of the 3-ends of the viral DNA (3-processing); integrase then remains bound in a complex with the viral DNA ends in the pre-integration complex (PIC). After the PIC enters the host nucleus, integrase catalyzes the insertion (strand-transfer) of the viral DNA ends into host chromosomes.[17]

Raltegravir is the first agent in the class of integrase inhibitors to be approved by the FDA. It inhibits integration of reverse-transcribed HIV DNA into the chromosomes of host cells. Raltegravir is indicated in combination with other antiretroviral agents for the treatment of HIV-infection in adult patients. Raltegravir interacts synergistically and sometimes deleteriously with several medications, including other antiretroviral agents. Raltegravir does not interact with the hepatic cytochrome P450 enzyme system. It is metabolized primarily by glucuronidation, particularly by uridine diphosphate glucuronosyltransferase (UGT) 1A1.

30.3 Complications of Anti-Retroviral Therapy

The discovery of antiretroviral agents for the treatment of HIV disease occurred in the context of an urgency to prevent death from the devastating illness. Some of these compounds received accelerated approval in the 1990s and 2000s from the United States FDA, based on 24-week results from two randomized, placebo-controlled Phase III studies. Some deleterious adverse events observed later were not observed during the period of the trials. When minor toxicities were noticed—such as gastrointestinal symptoms, rash, and elevation of liver enzymes—they were considered to be of secondary importance when compared to the consequences resulting from HIV disease. At present, HIV-infected individuals are placed on HAART for years (based on guidelines) to prolong patients' lives. However, a certain proportion of the individuals on treatment are also exposed to adverse events from HAART.

Some of the adverse events from HAART include: antiretroviral therapy-related lipodystrophy; glucose and insulin resistance; ART-induced lipid alterations and cardiovascular events; hepatotoxicity; renal consequences of ART; osteopenia; and osteoporosis. Some specifics on each of these follows:

- Antiretroviral therapy-related lipodystrophy: An association between HIV therapy and development of lipodystrophy was first noticed in the late 1990s.

It was observed that HIV-infected individuals on HAART had a remarkably increased risk of subcutaneous fat loss and metabolic syndrome, including visceral fat gain, mixed hyperlipidemia, and insulin resistance.[18,19] Since the first clinically noticed cases of lipodystrophy occurred after the introduction of PIs, this class of compounds was considered responsible for the fat loss.

The first-generation PIs can affect the differentiation and survival of adipose cells, consistent with their potential role in peripheral fat loss.[20] Lipoatrophy preferentially affecting the limbs and face are probably the most visible body composition changes in this population. The duration of therapy with selected NRTIs were reported to be the predominant risk factor.[19-22] Stavudine and zidovudine directly target adipocytes by interfering with the production of mtDNA and inducing organelle dysfunction, leading to the death of adipocytes.[23-25]

Several lines of evidence now suggest that the PIs play a lesser role in the development of lipoatrophy than the NRTIs.

- Glucose and insulin resistance: The increased prevalence of diabetes in HIV-infected individuals was first noticed in the 1990s,[26] when it was speculated that PIs may have a role in its causality. Studies are now available showing the deleterious impact of some PIs, as evidenced in health controls given the medications for a few weeks.[27,28] The new PIs appear to have a milder insulin-resistant effect; however, its prevalence still remains higher than the general population within the same age range. A variety of factors and mechanisms are likely to contribute to the pathogenesis of insulin resistance that may be observed in some of these HIV-infected individuals.[29]

- ART-induced lipid alterations and cardiovascular events: HIV infection is known to cause changes in lipid metabolism. Its treatment and several other factors can also upset lipid metabolism. Although the use of medications from each of the three major classes (NRTIs, NNRTIs and the PIs) have been associated with dyslipidemia, the most noticeable effects have been observed after exposure to PIs. The Data Collection on Adverse Events of Anti-HIV Drugs (D:A:D) investigators found the highest level of lipids in individuals taking two PIs or a ritonavir-boosted PI.[30] The D:A:D found that each extra year of antiretroviral therapy, adjusted to relative rate of

exposure, raised the risk of myocardial infarction or any ischemic vascular event by a factor of 1.26.[31,32] As with any observational study, these findings must be interpreted with caution and in the context of the benefits that these medications provide. According to Patrick W.G. Mallon's published review, "Protease inhibitors have been shown to affect several molecular pathways important for lipid metabolism, including intranuclear transcription factors and the nuclear proteasome."[33]

- Hepatotoxicity: Since the advent of HAART, the overall life expectancy of HIV-infected individuals has increased tremendously.[4,34] Although the precise mechanisms of toxicities of most antiretroviral medications are unknown, virtually all of them can exert toxic effects on the hepatocyte. They can cause liver injury through a variety of mechanisms. The NRTIs' main toxicity is caused by inhibiting the human mitochondrial DNA polymerase gamma, an enzyme needed for mtDNA replication. NRTI-induced depletion of mtDNA can lead to the impairment of fatty acid oxidation and steatosis of the liver.[35,36] The current clinical observations do not demonstrate an excess risk of hepatosteatosis in individuals on HAART; however, the long-term impact of HAART on the liver remains unknown.

- Renal consequences of ART: HIV infection and its treatment are a risk factor for renal disease. There continues to be much interest in defining the long-term safety of antiretroviral drugs, including the relationship between the NRTI tenofovir and renal function. The impact of antiretroviral therapy and host factors on changes in renal function remain active areas of investigation.

  As the optimal care of HIV-infected individuals becomes increasingly complex as a result of co-morbidities, efforts must be made to detect a decline in the glomerular filtration rate in order to provide optimized medication-therapy management. In a retrospective study covering a one-year period and 209 admissions, antiretroviral medication errors were analyzed showing that HAART-treated HIV-infected patients are at high risk of prescription errors at the time of hospitalization.[37] The most common errors were related to dosage and frequency of the regimen, with almost half the errors attributed to inappropriate renal function-adjusted dosage.[37]

- Osteopenia and osteoporosis: The scientific community continues to explore antiretroviral therapy,

HIV disease, and host factors contributing to the decrease of bone density in HIV-infected individuals. It is widely appreciated that both HIV infection and its treatment contribute to the high rates of demineralization and osteoporosis in HIV-infected individuals on HAART,[38] especially in those on NRTI and PI-containing regimen.[38,39] As of the date of this writing, the mechanism underlying the initiation and progression of this condition is unclear. Also, these studies failed to demonstrate whether or not there were greater degrees of bone loss with HAART after treatment has been established, as compared to the progressive loss that would have occurred in the untreated individuals over time.

30.4 Concluding Remarks

This chapter demonstrates the progress that has been made in our understanding of the usage of antiretroviral drugs in the management of HIV disease and the complications that have emerged from essentially all classes of pharmaceuticals currently employed. The scientific community continues to explore how antiretroviral therapy, HIV disease, and host factors contribute cardiovascular events and loss of bone density in HIV-infected individuals. Researchers are also investigating the impact of antiretroviral agents on changes in renal function and the other disease states discussed above that are currently believed to sometimes be promoted by the administration of HAART or ART.

Patients will have different degrees of adverse effects to different medications. Physicians and other clinicians must therefore determine not only which medications are best from the HIV treatment perspective, but also from the perspective of balancing benefits with adverse effects. When then considering resistance issues, the prescribed regimens must balance HIV viral load reduction, as well as adverse effects, resistance issues, and benefits. These factors can pose complex treatment issues and can have significant treatment implications regarding patients in all settings. These complexities will pose very dynamic challenges in resource-limited settings in which laboratory test assistance may be limited or absent.

It is hoped that the readers of this chapter can expand their knowledge today and in the future about HIV pharmacotherapy and its complications. For more detailed information on specific subject matter, the reader may consult the references below, all of which have been published in peer-reviewed literature.

Endnotes

1. UNAIDS/WHO AIDS Epidemic Update: December, 2008. Retrieved from www.unaids.org.

2. D.D. Ho, A.U. Neumann, A.S. Perelson, et al. *Rapid turnover of plasma virions and CD4 lymphocytes in HIV-1 infection.* Nature (1995) 373 (6510):123-126.

3. S.M. Hammer, M.S. Saag, M. Schechter, et al. *Treatment of adult HIV infection: 2006 recommendations of the International AIDS Society –USA panel.* JAMA (2006) 296:827-843.

4. F.J. Palella, K.M. Delaney, A.C. Moorman, et al. *Declining morbidity and mortality among patients with advanced human immunodeficiency virus infection.* N. Engl. J. Med. (1998) 338: 853-860.

5. S.C. Piscitelli, C. Flexner, J.R. Minor, et al. *Drug interactions in patients with human immunodeficiency virus.* Clin. Infect. Dis. (1996) 23(4):685-693.

6. M. Louie, M. Markowitz. *Goals and milestones during treatment of HIV-1 infection with antiretroviral therapy: A pathogenesis-based perspective.* Antiviral Res. (2002) 55(1):15–25.

7. L. Naesens, R. Snocek, G. Andrei. *HPMC (cidofovir), PMEA (adefovir), and related acyclic nucleoside phosphonate analogues: a review of their pharmacology and clinical potential in the treatment of viral infections.* Antivir. Chem. Chemother. (1997) 8:1.

8. J. Vingerhoets, H. Azijn, E. Fransen, et al. *TMC125 displays a high genetic barrier to the development of resistance: evidence from in vitro selection experiments.* J. Virol. (2005) 79: 12773-82.

9. M.A. Navia, P.M. Fitzgerald, B.M. McKeever, et al. *Three-dimensional structure of aspartyl protease from human immunodeficiency virus HIV-1.* Nature (1989) 337:615-620.

10. N.A. Roberts, J.A. Martin, D. Kinchington, et al. *Rational design of peptide-based HIV proteinase inhibitors.* Science (1990) 248:358-361.

11. S.M. Hammer, K.E. Squires, M.D. Hughes, et al. *The AIDS Clinical Trials Group 320 Study Team. A controlled trial of two nucleoside analogues plus indinavir in persons with human immunodeficiency virus infection and CD4 cell counts of 200 per cubic millimeter or less.* N. Engl. J. Med. (1997) 337:725-733.

12. R.M. Gulick, J.W. Mellors, D. Havlir, et al. *Treatment with indinavir, zidovudine, and lamivudine in adults with human immunodeficiency virus infection and prior antiretroviral therapy.* N. Engl. J. Med. (1997) 337:734-739.

13. F.J. Palella Jr., K.M. Delaney, A.C. Moorman, et al. *Declining morbidity and mortality among patients with advanced human immunodeficiency virus infection. HIV Outpatient Study Investigators.* N. Engl. J. Med. (1998) 338: 853-860.

14. R.M. Gulick. *Assessing the benefits of antiretroviral therapy.* Ann. Intern. Med. (2000) 133: 471-473.

15. K. Vermeire, D. Schol, T.W. Bell. *CD4 down-modulating compounds with potent anti-HIV activity.* Curr. Pharm. Des. (2004) 10(15):1795–1803.

16. P. Dorr, M. Westby, S. Dobbs, et al. *Maraviroc (UK-427,857), a potent, orally bioavailable, and selective small-molecule inhibitor of chemokine receptor CCR5 with broad-spectrum anti-human immunodeficiency virus type 1 activity.* Antimicrob. Agents Chemother. 2005; 49(11): 4721-4732.

17. Y. Pommier, A.A. Johnson, C. Marchand. *Integrase inhibitors to treat HIV/AIDS.* Nat. Rev. Drug Discov. (2005) 4: 236-48.

18. M. John D. Nolan, S. Mallal . *Antiretroviral therapy and the lipodystrophy syndrome.* Antivir. Ther. (2001) 6: 9-20.

19. D. Nolan, M. John, S. Mallal. *Antiretroviral therapy and the lipodystrophy syndrome, part 2: concepts in aetiopathogenesis.* Antivir. Ther. (2001) 6: 145-160.

20. M. Caron, C. Vigouroux, J.P. Bastard, J. Capeau. *Adipocyte dysfunction in response to antiretroviral therapy: clinical, tissue and in-vitro studies.* Curr. Opin. HIV AIDS. (2007) 2:268-273.

21. J. Amin, A. Moore, A. Carr, et al. *Combined analysis of two-year follow-up from two open-label randomized trials comparing efficacy of three nucleoside reverse transcriptase inhibitor backbones for previously untreated HIV-1 infection: OzCombo 1 and 2.* HIV Clin. Trials (2003) 4: 252-261.

22. M. Law, R. Puls, A.K. Cheng, et al. *Evaluation of the HIV lipodystrophy case definition in a placebo-controlled, 144-week study in antiretroviral-naïve adults.* Antivir. Ther. (2006) 11: 179-186.

23. D. Nolan, E. Hammond, A. Martin, et al. *Mitochondrial DNA depletion and morphologic changes in adipocytes associated with nucleoside reverse transcriptase inhibitor therapy.* AIDS (2003) 17: 1329-1338.

24. E. Hammond, D. Nolan, I. James, et al. *Reduction of mitochondrial DNA content and respiratory chain activity occurs in adipocytes within 6-12 months of commencing nucleoside reverse transcriptase inhibitor therapy.* AIDS (2004) 18:815-817.

25. M. Buffet, M. Schwarzinger, B. Amellal, et al. *Mitochondrial DNA depletion in adipose tissue of HIV-infected patients with peripheral lipoatrophy.* J. Clin. Virol. (2005) 33:60-64.

26. C. Vigouroux, S. Gharakhanian, Y. Salhi, et al. *Diabetes, insulin resistance and dyslipidemia in lipodystrophic HIV-infected patients on highly active antiretroviral therapy (HAART).* Diabetes Metab. (1999) 25: 225-232.

27. M. Schambelan, C.A. Benson, A. Carr, et al. *Management of metabolic complications associated with antiretroviral therapy for HIV-1 infection: recommendations of an International AIDS Society-USA panel.* J. Acquir. Immune. Defic. Syndr. (2002) 31: 257-275.

28. M.A. Noor, O.P. Flint, F. Maa, et al. *Effects of atazanavir/ritonavir and lopinavir/ritonavir on glucose uptake and insulin sensitivity: demonstrable differences in vitro and clinically.* AIDS (2006) 20: 1813-1821.

29. S. Grinspoon. *Mechanisms and strategies for insulin resistance in acquired immune deficiency syndrome.* Clin. Infect. Dis. (2003) 37:S85-S90.

30. E. Fontas, F. van Leth, C.A. Sabin, et al. *Lipid profiles in HIV-infected patients receiving combination antiretroviral therapy: are different antiretroviral drugs associated with different lipid profiles?* J. Infect. Dis. (2004) 189: 1056-1074.

31. N. Friis-Moler, C.A. Sabin, R. Weber, et al. *Combination antiretroviral therapy and the risk of myocardial infarction* [see comment]. N. Engl. J. Med. (2003) 349: 1993-2003 [erratum appears in N Engl J Med 2004; 350:955].

32. S.W. Worm, C. Sabin, R. Weber, et al. *Risk of myocardial infarction in patients with HIV infection exposed to specific individual antiretroviral drugs from the 3 major drug classes: the data collection on adverse events of anti-HIV drugs (D:A:D) study.* J. Infect. Dis. (2010) 201(3):318-330.

33. P.W.G. Mallon. *Antiretroviral therapy-induced lipid alterations: in-vitro, animal and human studies.* Curr. Opin. HIV AIDS (2007) 2: 282-292.

34. A. Mocroft, B. Ledergerber, C. Katlama, et al. *Decline in the AIDS and death rates in the EuroSIDA study: an observational study.* Lancet (2003) 362: 22-29.

35. S.J. Clark, S. Creighton, B. Portmann, et al. *Acute liver failure associated with antiretroviral treatment for HIV: a report of six cases.* J. Hepatol. (2002) 36: 295-301.

36. M. Puoti, C. Torti, D. Ripamonti, et al. *Severe hepatotoxicity during combination antiretroviral treatment: incidence, liver histology, and outcome.* J. Acquir. Immune Defic. Syndr. (2003) 32: 259-267.

37. D.A. Rastegar, A.M. Knight, J.S. Monolakis. *Antiretroviral medication errors among hospitalized patients with HIV infection.* Clin. Infect. Dis. (2006) 43: 933-938.

38. P. Tebas, W.G. Powderly, S. Claxton, et al. *Accelerated bone mineral loss in HIV-infected patients receiving potent antiretroviral therapy.* AIDS (2000) 14: F63-F67.

39. T.T. Brown, R.B. Qaqish. *Antiretroviral therapy and the prevalence of osteopenia and osteoporosis: a meta-analytic review.* AIDS (2006) 20: 2165-2174.

Chapter 31

Fetal Drug Exposure

Damani Parran, Ph.D., DABT

31.1 Introduction

The term *developmental toxicology* covers any detrimental effect produced by exposure to agents or conditions during embryonic and fetal stages that lead to abnormal development. Such lesions can be either irreversible or reversible including structural malformations, growth retardation, functional impairment and death of the organism.[1] Conditions that result in the death of the conceptus (embryolethal) result in resorption, spontaneous abortion or stillbirth. In the situation where the offspring survives, irreversible lesions may result in structural or functional abnormalities and are referred to as *teratogenic*. Persistent lesions that cause overall growth retardation or delayed growth of specific organ systems are generally referred to as *embryotoxic*. In order for an agent to be labeled a teratogen, it must significantly increase the occurrence of structural or functional abnormalities in offspring after it is administered to either the parent before conception, to the female during pregnancy or directly to the developing organism.

Birth defects have been depicted throughout time. As far back as 6500 B.C., a sculpture from the southern regions of Turkey depicts conjoined twins.[2] In around 3000 B.C., Egyptian wall paintings depicting cleft palate and achondropasia were documented. By 300 B.C., early theories that maternal stress can lead to deleterious effects on the developing organism started to emerge.[3] This theory was expanded in 1649 by Ambrois Pare who stated that narrowness of the uterus, faulty posture of the pregnant woman and physical trauma could lead to birth defects. Around this time, the early age of biological science emerged giving rise to scientifically based theories on the causes of birth defects including the theory of developmental arrest.[4] This theory states that malformations result from incomplete development of an organ or structure. The theory of developmental arrest was solidified in the early twentieth century with several experiments showing that by chemical and physical manipulation of the growth medium, developmental malformation of minnow embryos was produced.[5] In addition, the nature of the malformation depended on the developmental stage and was explained that all non-hereditary malformations stem from developmental arrest. From the early nineteenth century through the middle of the twentieth century, a variety of environmental conditions (temperature, microbial toxins, drugs) and physical trauma (jarring, inversion, pricking) were found to perturb development in several animal species, including avian, reptile, fish and amphibians.[4] The first documentation of birth defects in mammals as a result of nutritional stress was published in 1935.[6] As a result of maternal nutritional deficiency of vitamin A, swine offspring showed such malformations as anophthalmia and cleft palates. Numerous studies by Warkany and coworkers demonstrated that, in addition to maternal dietary deficiencies,[7] chemical and physical agents such as nitrogen mustard, trypan blue, hormones, alkylating agents and X-rays were clearly shown to cause malformations in mammals.[7]

The first truly documented human malformation epidemic occurred in the early 1940s, where a link between rubella viral infection and elevated incidences of eye, heart and ear malformations along with mental retardation was established.[8] Infection with the rubella virus in the first two months of pregnancy was associated with malformations in the heart and eye. By the third month, if infection occurs, elevated occurrences of hearing and speech defects and mental retardation were observed. In 1960 and 1961, a sharp increase of newborns born with exceedingly rare limb malformations was evident. The affected newborns had amelia (absence of the limbs) or various degrees of phocomelia (reduction of the long bones of the limbs), usually affecting the arms more than the legs and usually involving both the left and right sides, although to differing degrees. The unusual nature of the malformations was a key to unraveling the epidemic and in 1961, two separate research groups identified the sedative thalidomide as the causative agent.[9]

By this time, Wilson (1959) proposed the basic principles of abnormal development, which have stood the test of time and remain an excellent guideline.[10] Wilson stated that:

- Susceptibility to abnormal development depends on the genotype of the conceptus and the manner in which its genetic composition interacts with the environment.
- Agents that cause abnormal development vary with the developmental stage at the time of exposure.
- Teratogenic agents act in specific ways (mechanism) on developing cells and tissues to initiate abnormal embryogenesis (pathogenesis).
- The final manifestations of abnormal development are death, malformation, growth retardation and functional disorders.
- The access of adverse environmental influences to developing tissues depends on the nature of the influences (agents).
- Manifestations of deviant development increase in degree as dosage increases, from no effect to the totally lethal effect.

Many studies have validated these principles, with malformations as gross structural deficits being the main focus.[11] It has been demonstrated that any agent administered under appropriate dosing conditions and during specific developmental timepoints will lead to lesions in embryonic development.

31.2 Critical Periods of Human Development and Susceptibility

As Wilson mentioned in his basic principles of abnormal development, the effect of an agent varies greatly depend-

ing on the developmental time of exposure (Wilson, 1959). Periods of human development are measured in trimesters, each being about three months. The most sensitive period for teratogenesis, the production of congenital defects, is during organogenesis (first trimester) in the embryonic stage.[12] Later during the fetal stage, the environment provided by the mother affects the baby's size, behavior, intelligence and health, rather than the formation of organs and limbs.[13] The timing of some key developmental events in human development is presented in Table 31.1. It should be made clear, however, that development is a continuum and that these stages are used for descriptive purposes and do not necessarily represent discrete developmental events.

Table 31.1
Timing of Key Developmental Events in Humans

Developmental Event	Developmental Age (Days of Gestation)
Blastocyst formation	4-6
Implantation	6-7
Primitive streak	16-18
Neural plate	18-20
First somite	20-21
First pharyngeal arch	20
Organogenesis	21-56
Ten somites	25-26
Upper limb buds	29-30
Lower limb buds	31-32
Forepaw rays	35
Testes differentiation	43
Heart septation	46-47
Palate closure	56-58
Length of gestation	267

Now we will discuss each stage of human development in more detail and the possible outcomes following toxicological insult.

Following fertilization, the zygote undergoes cleavage, a series of mitotic divisions without accompanying cell growth and cavitation of the embryo to form fluid-filled blastocoels. While traversing the oviduct toward the uterus, the conceptus is surrounded by the zona pellucid, an acellular, polysaccharide-containing coating that prevents premature implantation.

Exposure to toxicants immediately after fertilization has been demonstrated to result in malformed fetuses for a number of agents including ethylene oxide, ethylmethane sulfonate, ethylnitrosourea and triethylene melamine.[14]

The conceptus enters the uterus at gestational day 3-4, when it has developed into a solid cluster of 16 cells called a marula. The marula becomes a blastocyst by growing up to over 100 cells and developing a fluid-filled cavity between gestational day 4 and 5. The blastocyte contains two major types of cells: the inner cell mass and the trophoblast. The inner cell mass develops into the embryo, while the trophoblast makes up the outer layer of cells which develops into the chorion and the placenta. The fates of the cells in the early embryo stage are not completely determined at this stage. The relatively undifferentiated preimplantation embryo has great restorative growth potential.[15] This was exemplified by an experiment where 8-cell rabbit embryos were capable of producing normal offspring.[16] By gestational day 5, the blastocyte leaves the zona pellucid and can now directly interact with the endometrium. This begins the implantation stage of development.

Toxicity during preimplantation is largely thought to result in no effect or a slight effect on growth due to regulative growth. Death of the preimplanted embryo is another result if it is overwhelmed by damage or fails to implant. Agents including DDT, nicotine and methylmethane sulfonate can cause defects in body and brain weights and embryo death in the absence of malformations.[17] Other agents including methylnitrosourea,[18] cyproterone acetate and medroxyprogesterone acetate,[19] when administered at specific gestational timepoints, can induce fetal malformations, specifically neural tube defects and cleft palate. It is expected that agents that target DNA synthesis or microtubule assembly will be particularly toxic due to the rapid mitoses that occur during the preimplantation period.

Implantation occurs between 6 and 7 days after fertilization in humans. At this point, the embryo undergoes gastrulation, where the three primary germ layers start to form: the ectoderm, mesoderm and endoderm. The ectoderm becomes the central nervous system. The mesoderm becomes the muscles, skeleton, circulatory system and internal organs. The endoderm becomes the digestive system, lungs, urinary tract and glands. The outer membrane of the blastocyte becomes the amnion, which encloses the developing zygote in amniotic fluid. The foundation for the human uteroplacental circulation system starts to develop at gestation day 9, when vacuoles called trophoblastic lacunae emerge with the syncytiotrophoblast and maternal capillaries expand to form maternal sinusoids that anastomose with the trophoblastic lacunae.[20] Anastomosis is the connection between the blood vessels or between other tubular structures.[21,162] By gestational day 16, the extraembryonic mesoderm proliferates and invades the centers of the primary stem villi, forming secondary stem villi. By gestational day 21, the mesodermal tissue differentiates into connective tissue and blood vessels, forming the tertiary stem villi. Therefore, materials diffusing between maternal and fetal tissues must pass from maternal blood in the lacunae, through the trophoblast layer, the connective tissue in the core of the villus and endothelium of the embryonic villus capillaries.[20] It is well-known that toxic agents given during gastrulation can produce malformations in the eye, brain and face. This is indicative of damage to the anterior neural plate.

The formation of the neural plate in the ectoderm marks the onset of organogenesis, where most of the body structures and organs are established. Individual organ systems possess highly specific periods of susceptibility to teratogenic damage during organogensis. Table 31.2 depicts the sensitive periods of the major human embryonic body systems and structures. At gestational day 21, the human conceptus is in most ways indistinguishable from other vertebrate embryos. By gestational day 56, the conceptus, which can now be termed a fetus, has a form clearly recognizable as human. The rapid changes of organogenesis require cell proliferation, cell migration, cell-cell interactions and morphogenetic tissue remodeling. These processes are exemplified by the neural crest cells, which originate at the border of the neural plate and migrate to form a wide variety of embryonic structures. Within organogenesis, there are periods of maximum susceptibility for each organ system and structure. Several animal studies demonstrated that malformations observed, following carefully timed developmental exposures, coincide with the timing of key developmental events in these structures.[21–23]

Table 31.2
Sensitive Periods of Body Systems During Human Embryonic Development

Body System	Especially Sensitive	Development up to...
Central nervous system/Brain	4th to 8th weeks	Postnatal, through to adulthood
Heart	5th to 9th weeks	12th week
Upper limbs	6th to 10th weeks	12th week
Eyes	6th to 10th weeks	Term
Lower limbs	6th to 10th weeks	12th week
Teeth	9th to 11th weeks	Term
Palate	9th to 11th weeks	16th week
External genitalia	9th to 11th weeks	Term
Ears	6th to 11th weeks	13th week

The end of organogenesis marks the beginning of the fetal period (gestation day 56-58), which is characterized by palate closure, tissue differentiation, growth and physiological maturation. This does not mean that development of the organs is complete. However, most of the organs are present and grossly recognizable. Further maturation of organs occurs, including fine structural morphogenesis and biochemical maturation.

Insult at this relatively late stage of development leads to a broad spectrum of effects that generally manifest as growth retardation or as functional disorders and transplacental carcinogenesis. The fetus is more resistant to lethal effects than is the embryo, but the incidence of stillbirth is still measurable. The functional manifestations are not immediately apparent prenatally and require very precise postnatal observation, testing and biomonitoring.[24] Such postnatal functional manifestations can be sensitive indicators of in utero toxicity, and recent reviews of the postnatal effects of the immune system,[25] the respiratory system,[26] the reproductive system,[27] the central nervous system,[28] and heart and endocrine glands[29] are available. Major structural alterations can occur during the fetal period, but these changes generally result from deformations, which are disruptions of previously normal structures versus malformations. Development does not stop at birth and special susceptibilities exist in the neonatal, childhood and adolescent years.[30]

31.3 Special Considerations of Drug Exposure during Pregnancy

A pregnant mother's exposure to toxic agents and external insult represents a unique scenario both in managing a potential poisoning of the mother and direct or indirect effects on the developing embryo/fetus. The maternal, placental and embryonic compartments constitute independent yet interacting systems that undergo profound changes throughout the course of pregnancy. As a normal pregnancy progresses, specific hemodynamic and cardiovascular changes occur in the mother. The following general physiological changes are observed during normal pregnancy:[31]

A. Cardiac output can increase as much as 40 percent above normal nonpregnant levels during the first trimester and thus can be considered a natural state of volume overload. In a third trimester pregnant female, approximately 10 percent of cardiac output goes to the uteroplacental unit. Normally, uterine blood flow is directly related to maternal cardiac output. As pregnancy progresses, other adjustments occur that are necessary for fetal development. Cardiac output is increased largely because of an increase in stroke volume, with a normal or slightly increased heart rate. The altered hemodynamic status of the pregnant woman is often not recognized because of the large cardiovascular reserve found in the normal healthy system.

B. Increased tidal volume, resulting in a resting pCO_2 lower than normal.

C. Increased potential for regurgitation and aspiration, due to pressure on hollow abdominal viscera.

D. Inability to concentrate urine.

E. Decreased serum albumin.

F. Relative anemia.

G. Changes in absorption due to decreased gut motility, changes in hepatic metabolism, or changes in excretion due to increased glomerular filtration rate.

Some of the physiological changes that occur in the mother during the course of pregnancy are summarized in Table 31.3.

For practical purposes, the fetus is exposed to most of the chemicals to which the mother is exposed, and the greater the dosage to the mother, the greater will be the exposure for the fetus. Although the placenta is a barrier for many purposes, it should not be considered a toxicological barrier with respect to many common drugs in use. The lipid membranes of the placenta are relatively permeable to substances having a molecular weight less than 1,000 daltons, although several large molecules have been identified as reaching the fetus. The passage of substances across the placenta increases with increased placental blood flow. A role for metabolism by the placenta has not been identified. However, due to differences in fetal circulation and metabolism at different stages of development, toxic exposure in a fetus may exhibit different levels of that agent during the exposure, equilibration and elimination phases of its kinetics.

Factors such as (but not limited to) variations in pH gradients between maternal and conceptual compartments, differences in maternal and conceptual fluid protein binding of chemicals and active transporters in the placenta may play important roles in regulating embryonic drug exposure.[32] The pH gradients between maternal blood and the embryonic fluid/cells influence the disposition of basic and acidic compounds from maternal blood to the embryo. This difference in pH may lead to accumulation of some acidic or basic compounds in embryos due to ion trapping.[33,34] Ion trapping involves the diffusion of protonated weak acids into a compartment with a relatively higher pH. Weak acids become ionized and can no longer diffuse back across the compartment membrane. This has been documented in

Table 31.3
Physiological Changes During Pregnancy

	Nonpregnant	Pregnant		
		1st Trimester	2nd Trimester	3rd Trimester
Cardiac output (l/min)	4-6	Increasing	6-7	6-7
Heart Rate (beats/min)	60-80	Increasing	Increasing	80-95
Systolic BP (mm Hg)	90-120	Decreasing 0-15	Decreasing 0-15	Normal
Diastolic BP (mm Hg)	60-90	Decreasing 10-20	Decreasing 10-20	Normal
HCT (%)	37-47	38	34-39	34-39
Peripheral WBC (m3)	4.7-10.6	5-12	12-18	12-18
Polymorphonuclears	55	66	69	60
Sed. Rate (mm/hr)	20	Increasing	Increasing	Increasing
Fibrinogen (mg/dl)	200-400	200-286	286-315	353-410
BUN (mg/dl)	10-16	7-10	7-10	7-10
Creatinine (mg/dl)	0.5-1.5	0.4-0.8	0.4-0.8	0.4-0.8
Systemic vascular resistance (dynes/cm3)	1743	979	1277	1224
Blood volume (ml)	2600	3150	3850	3950

a number of animal studies, with compounds including valproic acid, methoxyacetic acid, butyric acid, propionic acid and glycolic acid.[32,35] In these studies, embryonic and/or exocoelomic fluid concentrations of the agents were two to four times higher than those of maternal blood. In humans, the pH of the coelomic fluid is 0.2 pH units lower than that of maternal blood, while amniotic fluid pH is similar to maternal pH until 10 weeks of gestation, but then decreases between gestation weeks 11-14.[36] If embryonic dosimetry were based solely on these pH gradients, one would expect weak bases to accumulate in early human embryos. However, many other factors that influence embryo dosimetry are in play and may be more influential than ion trapping.

Another factor is protein binding. Extensive protein binding in the maternal circulation would decrease the amount of unbound, free chemical from crossing the placenta and thus decrease embryonic exposure. In general, plasma protein binding occurs to a lesser extent in experimental animal models than in humans. The total protein concentration of maternal blood tends to decrease with advancing gestation. Factors that may influence the extent of protein binding include coadministration of other drugs, hormones and nutrition and stress.[33] In humans, the concentration of protein coelomic fluid is reportedly 18-fold lower than in maternal blood.[36]

An additional means of crossing the placenta is through active transport by carrier systems for pyrimidine, amino acids and other nutrients. Active transport is the movement of material against the concentration gradient and requires energy. Active transport is also governed by the laws of competitive inhibition. Besides essential materials, there are a number of drugs that are actively transported into cells including fluorouracil and alpha-methyldopa.[37] The presence or absence of a particular transporter could influence the bioavailability and perhaps the toxicity of particular chemicals to the embryo.

31.4 Historical Human Developmental Toxicants

It has been estimated that more than 3,300 agents have been tested for teratogenic potential.[38] Approximately 63 percent were not considered a teratogen, 7 percent were teratogenic in more than one species, 21 percent were teratogenic in most species tested and 9 percent producing equivocal experiment results. The following are several human developmental toxicants, which provides both a historical view of the field of development toxicology and an illustration of Wilson's[39] key principles of teratology.

A. Thalidomide

Thalidomide was introduced in 1956 by Chemie Grunenthal as a sedative/hypnotic and was used through the world as a sleep aid. In addition, thalidomide was used to ameliorate nausea and vomiting during pregnancy. It had no apparent toxicity or addictive properties in humans or adult animals at therapeutic doses (50 to 200 mg/day). In 1960, a significant increase in newborns with extremely rare limb malformations started to emerge. The affected individuals had an absence of limbs (amelia) or various degrees of long bone reduction (phocomelia), which usually affected the arms more than the legs and involved both the left and right sides. Limb reduction anomalies of this nature are exceedingly rare. For example, there were no cases of phocomelia in Germany before 1959.[40] In 1959, there was one case and the following year, there were 30 cases, while in 1961 there were 154 cases of phocomelia. In addition to the limb malformations, congenital heart disease, ocular, intestinal, external ear and renal anomalies were observed. The unusual nature of the malformations was a key to solving this epidemic. Two separate research teams determined that this sedative/sleep aid was the causative agent.[41–43] Once this association was established, thalidomide was removed from the market and case reports ended in mid-1962. Over 5,800 malformed infants were born worldwide.[44] As a result of this catastrophe, many countries began developing regulations requiring the evaluation of the effects of drugs on pregnancy outcomes.

B. Ethanol

The developmental toxicity of ethanol has been recognized throughout time but it was not until the early 1970s when Jones and Smith described fetal alcohol syndrome (FAS) that a clear pattern of its developmental effect was accepted.[45] FAS refers to a distinct cluster of congenital abnormalities observed in the offspring of alcoholic mothers.[46] Prolonged exposure to ethanol during gestation and lactation is correlated with a pattern of abnormal development in newborns. The spectrum of alcohol's teratogenic effects spans a wide continuum that includes central nervous system dysfunction, optical abnormalities, craniofacial anomalies, growth deficiency and pathologic organ and skeletal conditions. The mechanisms by which ethanol exerts its teratogenic effects are not understood, but excess cell death in sensitive cell populations appears to be a common finding.[47]

Dittmer and Lentz-Kapua[48] describe the following neurodevelopmental abnormalities associated with FAS: microcephaly, corpus collasum agenesis or hypoplasia, developmental delay, intellectual impairment (mild to moderate retardation), low intelligence quotient (IQ 65-70), hypotonia, poor coordination, cognitive impairment, irritability in infancy and hyperactivity in childhood or attention deficit/hyperactivity disorder (ADHD), language impairment, sleep/wake cycle disturbances, seizure disorder, delayed or deficient myelination, electroencephalogram hypersynchrony, echolalia, and cerebral palsy. Several aspects of the developmental program are involved in the alcohol-induced malformations of the brain.[49] Among them, the most striking abnormalities appear to involve the impairment of neuronal cell migration.[50,51] FAS patients at different ages have shown a wide spectrum of neuroanatomical abnormalities, including white matter lesions.[52–56] These white matter abnormalities have been described in corpus callosum, cerebellar vermis, optic nerves, hippocampus, basal ganglia and temporal, parietal and occipital white matter. Lesions in the temporal, parietal and occipital white matter were described by Archibald et al.[54] where a decrease in white matter volume in these structures was observed in the brains of children with a history of prenatal alcohol exposure. A common abnormality was a leptomeningeal neurological neuroglial[57] eterotopias that assumes the form of a sheet of aberrant neuronal and glial cells covering portions of the cerebral, cerebellar and brainstem surfaces.[58] Aberrations of brainstem and cerebellar development have also been especially frequent along with the migrational disturbances of schizencephaly and polymicrogyria.[59] Disordered midline prosencephalic formation (e.g., agenesis of the corpus callosum, septo-optic dysplasia and incomplete holoprosencephaly) has also been documented.[60] Thus it appears that multiple aspects of central nervous system development can be affected, including neurulation, canalization and retrogressive differentiation, prosencephalic development, neuronal proliferation, neuronal migration and neuronal differentiation and synapse formation.[61] Several animal studies have also demonstrated that even a single administration of a high level of alcohol during a period of pregnancy can cause serious effects on the migration of immature neurons.[61] Microcephaly is also present in nearly all cases, and this reflection of disturbed brain growth is accompanied by delayed neurologic development in approximately 90 percent of cases.[62]

The eyes and vision have also been shown to be damaged by maternal alcohol misuse during pregnancy.[63–66] Up to 90 percent of the children whose mothers have misused alcohol in pregnancy may show ocular manifestations.[66] Several studies revealed that one of the greatest areas of white matter lesions was in the optic radiation. Clinically, the majority of FAS patients are known to exhibit ocular and visual anomalies, with up to 76 percent showing optic nerve hypoplasia.[66] All parts of the eye can be affected, from the periocular facial region to the intraocular structures and the optic nerve. Children with FAS may show a spectrum of eye abnormalities, ranging from extensive malformations, such as microphthalmus, buphthalmus (enlarged eye), coloboma of the iris and uvea (abnormal closure of choroidal embryonic eye fissure), persistent hyperplastic primary vitreous body or a severely malformed retina, to minor anomalies.[66,67] Microphthalmia has frequently been observed among children with FAS[66,67] and was included in the criteria for a diagnosis of FAS set by the Fetal Alcohol Study Group of the U.S. Research Society on Alcoholism.[68] The retinal fundus abnormalities in FAS range from discrete lesions of the optic disc and retinal vessels to severe malformations of both the retina and the optic nerve. The most frequent abnormalities are optic nerve hypoplasia and increased tortuosity of the retinal vessels.[66,67,69] Hypoplasia of the optic nerve head is characterized by subnormal vision and a subnormal number of optic nerve axons, showing morphological signs such as small size, pallor, irregular margins and an abnormal retinal vascular pattern of the optic disk. Optic nerve hypoplasia was found in a group of children with FAS, and morphometrically assessed by a specially designed method for digital analysis of retinal fundus photographs. The analysis results showed that 48 percent of the optic discs were hypoplastic in these patients.[66]

C. Diethylstilbestrol

Diethylstilbestrol (DES) is a synthetic nonsteroidal estrogen that was first synthesized in 1938 and was made available in the 1940s through the 1970s in the United States as a drug to prevent miscarriages. DES gained notoriety in 1971 when several young women between the ages of 14 and 22 were diagnosed with clear cell adenocarcinoma of the vagina. This type of tumor had never before been seen in patients under the age of 30. Following an epidemiological study, an association between DES exposure during the first trimester and the development of clear cell adenocarcinoma was established.[70] Specifically, DES exposure before gestation day 126 appeared to increase the risk of developing this tumor by 40-fold. DES is considered an established human carcinogen and is the only transplacental carcinogen known in humans. In addition to clear cell adenocarcinoma, developmental DES exposure was also linked to other abnormalities of the reproductive tract, including vaginal epithelial changes, increased cervical transformation zone and uterine abnormalities. In male offspring of exposed pregnancies, a high incidence of epididymal cysts, hypotrophic testes and capsular induration were observed.[71]

D. Retinoids

The retinoids are a class of chemical compounds that are related to vitamin A. When taken in excess, retinoids can induce widespread developmental effects, including malformations of the face, limbs, heart, central nervous system and skeleton. All trans-retinoic acids and the 13-cis isomer produce congenital malformations in all mammalian species tests, with varying ranges of sensitivity. The 13-cis retinoid acid is an active ingredient in the recalcitrant cystic acne

drug Accutane. Despite clear warnings against the use of Accutane during pregnancy on the label of this prescription drug, an extensive physician and patient education program and restrictive requirements for prescription to women of childbearing age, infants with malformations of the ears, heart, brain and thymus began to be reported.[72,73] It has also been shown that risk of premature delivery doubles if the developing embryo is exposed to the 13-cis retinoic isomer during the first trimester.[73]

E. Cocaine

Cocaine, a plant alkaloid derived from coca, is a local anesthetic with vasoconstrictor properties. Pharmacologically, cocaine disrupts neural transmission by blocking fast sodium channels and blocks neuronal uptake of catecholamines and 5-hydroxytryptamine.[74-76] Researchers have studied women who 1) use cocaine only; 2) use cocaine plus other narcotics; 3) used narcotics in the past and were maintained on methadone during pregnancy; and 4) are drug-free. Cocaine-using women had a significantly higher rate of spontaneous abortion. Infants that were exposed to cocaine during development had depression of interactive behavior with poor organization response to environmental stimuli. This observation was similar to that found in infants delivered to methadone-maintained women,[74] and women addicted to pentazocine, tripelennamine and phencyclidine during pregnancy.[75,77] Increased fetal activity and premature labor were observed within minutes of using cocaine. A variety of other adverse effects have been reported, including abruption placentae, premature delivery, microcephaly, altered prosencephalic development, decreased birth weight, abnormal sleep, tremor, poor feeding, irritability, occasional seizures and sudden infant death syndrome. Congenital malformations of the genitourinary tract have also been reported.[78] Both vasoconstriction, which could inhibit placental transport and function, and the pharmacological effect have been implicated as causes of altered embryo development.

31.5 Developmental Toxicity of Prescription Drugs

Ideally, the pregnant woman should not take any medications during pregnancy, other than those associated with routine prenatal care. However, there are situations that may require active pharmaceutical intervention including seizures, thrombic disorders and anxiety. The pathophysiological consequences of maternal seizures are a major risk for the fetus. Maternal grand mal seizures associated with apnea can cause transient hypoxia and acidosis in the fetus.[79] Prompt control of breakthrough seizure activity is of utmost importance to minimize the effects of oxygen deprivation on the fetus. Obstruction of blood flow through the circulatory system, specifically to the fetus, can also pose a major concern and may require pharmaceutical intervention with the use of anticoagulants. The mental well-being of the pregnant mother may require the need to prescribe sedative and antipsychotic drugs. Maternal disorders and the following treatment of these disorders during pregnancy may present an increased risk to the fetus and the newborn infant. The long-term cognitive function of offspring of pregnant women taking the following prescription drugs is also a concern.

A. Valproic Acid

Valproic acid (2-propylpentanoic acid) was approved in 1978 in the United States for the treatment of epilepsy. In 1982, a surveillance study in Lyon, France, revealed that in 146 cases of spina bifida aperta, nine of the mothers had taken valproate during the first trimester.[80,81] The estimated risk of a valproate-exposed woman having a child with spina bifida was calculated to be about 1.2 percent. This risk level was similar to that for a woman whose previous child was born with a neural tube defect.[82] More recent cohort studies of more than 1,700 babies exposed to monotherapy with valproic acid showed an associative relative risk of 2.59 for major malformations (95 percent confidence interval [CI] 2.11 to 3.17) when compared with monotherapy using other anticonvulsant drugs.[83–92] When compared to untreated epileptic patients, the relative risk was 3.16 (95 percent CI 2.17 to 4.60).[85–87,90,91,93,94] When compared to the general population of healthy control subjects the relative risk of major congenital malformations among patients receiving monotherapy with valproic acid was 3.77 (95 percent CI 2.18 to 6.52).[95] This means that women exposed to valproic acid monotherapy during embryogenesis have more than 2.5 times the risk of having babies with malformations and that this trend is highly significant (p <0.001).[96]

When valproic acid was administered as part of an anticonvulsant polytherapy, the relative risk also increased significantly over that of other anticonvulsant drugs (1.84 [95 percent CI] 1.34 to 2.52), untreated epilepsy (3.24 [95 percent CI] 2.06 to 5.08) and healthy control subjects (3.35 [95 percent CI] 1.87 to 6.01).[86–91,97–99]

The experimental animal work by Nau et al. was very important in establishing that valproic acid caused the development of neural tube defects.[33,100] These authors introduced the relationship between teratogenicity and embryonic pH, where 8 of 11 chemicals known to produce congenital anomalies in humans were acids and none were bases. They also noted that valpronide produced only one exencephalic fetus among 116 implants in mice compared to 61 affected fetuses among 136 implants after exposure to the more

acidic sodium valproate.[33] Valproic acid concentrations in the mouse embryo were at least twice as high as in maternal plasma, whereas valpromide concentrations were similar in the two compartments. This is consistent with the theory that ion trapping would be greater for more acidic compounds. Even though valproic acid concentrations were higher in the umbilical cord blood than maternal plasma concentrations, the theory of ion trapping may not completely explain this difference in humans and other mammalian models. The fetal pH is lower than maternal pH in humans[101] and sheep.[102] The differences in maternal and fetal concentrations are better explained by the extent of protein bind for valproic acid. As gestation advances, fetal albumin concentration increases and free valproic acid decreases.[103]

B. Phenytoin

Phenytoin was first introduced for the treatment of partial and generalized tonic-clonic seizures in 1938. Rapidly it became one of the most commonly used drugs for the control of epileptic seizures because it had no sedative side effects.[104] A number of antiepileptic drugs, including phenytoin, interfere with maternal folate metabolism.[105,106] Patients taking phenytoin may therefore become deficient in folate, leading to the development of macrocytic anemia and possible complications during pregnancy. It has become widely accepted that maternal deficiency in folate is associated with neural tube defects in the fetus.[107] Because the neural tube develops between 18 and 30 days after conception, many women do not know that they are pregnant when these defects are occurring. Research indicates that phenytoin causes a decreased plasma concentration of folate by depleting total hepatic folate.[107] Therapy recommendations suggest that women begin taking folic acid supplements throughout the first trimester to reduce the risk of neural tube defects. Additionally, phenytoin therapy may increase the metabolism of vitamin D, leading to a decrease in vitamin D levels that can in turn cause alterations in calcium homeostasis.[108]

Fetal hydantoin syndrome is a rare disorder that is caused by exposure to phenytoin. Major signs of this disorder include abnormalities of the skull and facial features, growth deficiencies and underdeveloped nails on the fingers and toes. The full-blown syndrome is estimated to occur in approximately 5 to 10 percent of newborns exposed to phenytoin in utero.[109] The teratogenic mechanism of phenytoin may also be related to an accumulation of epoxides, which are highly reactive oxidative metabolites of phenytoin.[110]

Phenytoin was the most commonly implicated antiepilepsy drug in several large-scale studies.[110,111] In these studies, approximately 2 percent of infants born to women with epilepsy who were taking antiepilepsy drugs experienced congenital heart disease and/or had cleft lip or cleft palate. These rates are four-fold greater than the rates in the general population for congenital heart disease and ten-fold greater than the rates for cleft lip or cleft palate.[108]

The effect of maternal epilepsy on cognitive function in the offspring has been the subject of several studies. Small head size can occur in neonates prenatally exposed to antiepilepsy drugs.[109] Infants with fetal hydantoin syndrome may have cognitive impairments, but whether these impairments are permanent or disappear over time is unclear.[112] There is evidence that small head size is a common observation in infants prenatally exposed to multiple antiepilepsy drugs versus a single antiepileptical exposure. Persistent learning disorders in approximately 12 percent of phenytoin-exposed infants were also observed compared to only 1 percent of the general population.[113]

C. Warfarin

Warfarin is an oral anticoagulant that inhibits synthesis of vitamin K-dependent clotting factors including factors II, VII, IX and X and the anticoagulant proteins C and S.[114] Warfarin is a synthetic derivative of dicoumarol, a 4-hydroxycoumarin-derived mycotoxin and coagulant found in spoiled clover-based animal feeds. Coumarin-derivative exposure in the first trimester of pregnancy results in a specific malformation syndrome know as warfarin embryopathy, which is characterized by nasal hypoplasia and punctuate stippled calcifications of the laryngeal cartilage, head of the ribs, transverse process of the vertebrae or epiphyses.[115–118] Ophthalmologic abnormalities are frequently observed[116] and include optic atrophy, microphthalmia, lens opacities and large prominent eyes. Also, use of warfarin during the second and third trimesters has been associated sporadically with central nervous system abnormalities, including mental retardation, microcephaly, and blindness.[119–122] Overall risk of central nervous system defects is about 3 percent.

In the late third trimester, exposure to coumarin anticoagulants may result in late prenatal, perinatal or postnatal hemorrhages.[123,124]

One study reported on 418 cases of warfarin exposure from conception to 38 weeks after birth.[125] About 16 percent of all pregnancies ended in spontaneous abortions or stillbirths, and another 15 percent resulted in babies with abnormalities at birth. The abnormalities included skeletal malformations (e.g., stippling of cervical vertebrae, sacrum, and femurs; kyphoscoliosis; and nasal hypoplasia), bilateral optic atrophy leading to blindness, deafness, focal cerebral atrophy, respiratory distress, and seizures.

In another study, a report on 128 babies exposed to warfarin therapy from 0 to 38 weeks gestation observed that about 8 percent of the 38 live-born infants displayed teratogenic effects of warfarin at birth, including nasal hypoplasia, choanal stenosis, and stippled epiphyses.[126] When compared with 68 pregnancies where women's warfarin therapy had been replaced with 1 g of acetylsalicylic acid and 400 mg of dipyridamole daily at the onset of pregnancy, it was clear that the rate of spontaneous abortions was significantly higher in the warfarin group (28 percent vs. 10 percent). The rate of neonatal deaths was also higher in the warfarin group (2.3 percent vs. 0). The rate of stillbirths was approximately 7 percent in both groups. Warfarin dose was adjusted for a target prothrombin time of 2 to 2.5 times control in most women.

In summary, coumarin-derivative use or abuse by mothers during gestation results in one-sixth of pregnancies ending with abnormal liveborn infants, one-sixth ending in abortion or stillbirth, and about two-thirds ending with a relatively normal outcome.

D. Benzodiazepines

Benzodiazepines are psychoactive drugs whose core chemical structure is the fusion of a benzene ring and a diazepine ring. There are numerous benzodiazepines marketed in the United States, and they differ primarily in their pharmacokinetic properties.[127] Exposure to benzodiazepines, assessed by calls to U.S. poison control centers, represents half of all exposures to sedative-hypnotic and antipsychotic drugs. Benzodiazepines are among the drugs most frequently prescribed to women of reproductive age and to pregnant women for reducing anxiety and managing preeclampsia or eclampsia in the latter part of pregnancy.[128]

Benzodiazepines are divided into three categories on the basis of elimination half-life (t ½): 1) short-acting (t ½ <10 hours); 2) intermediate-acting (t ½ 10-24 hours); and 3) long-acting (t ½ >24 hours). The following are common short-, intermediate- and long-acting benzodiazepines:

- Short-acting: Midazolam (Versed), Temazepam (Restoril), Triazolam (Halcion)
- Intermediate-acting: Alprazolam (Xanax), Lorazepam (Ativan), Oxazepam (Serax)
- Long-acting: Diazepam (Valium), Chlordiazepoxide (Librium), Chlorazepate (Tranxene), Flurazepam (Dalmane), Prazepam (Centrex)

Short- and intermediate-acting benzodiazepines are generally used to treat insomnia, while long-acting benzodiazepines are used to treat anxiety. In general, benzodiazepines are relatively safe drugs even in overdose because of the rapid body adaptations to high blood levels. There is controversy concerning the safety of benzodiazepines in pregnancy, specifically their association with cleft palate and neurobehavioural disorders as a result of prenatal exposure.[129] The FDA classifies benzodiazepines as either a D or X category drug, which means that the potential for harm in the newborn has been demonstrated.[130]

All major classes of benzodiazepine compounds can be assumed to be excreted into the breast milk and diffuse readily across the placenta to the fetus. This depends on the characteristics of the particular drug-plasma protein binding, ionization, the degree of lipophilicity, molecular weight, half-life, maternal blood concentrations, oral bioavailability and pharmacokinetics.[131] Among anxiolytic agents, only diazepam has been systematically studied among pregnant women. Until the early 1980s, diazepam was the most prescribed benzodiazepine in the United States and worldwide. Diazepam and its major metabolite, N-desmethyldiazepam, which are both pharmacologically active, freely cross the human placenta during early pregnancy as a result of their high lipid solubility.[132–139] Natural processes during pregnancy have been shown to facilitate the transport of diazepam across the placenta, and both diazepam and N-desmethyldiazepam extensively bind more to fetal plasma proteins than maternal plasma proteins.[140–142] Available data from various epidemiological studies are inconsistent in showing the risk of congenital malformations among children born to women who took diazepam during pregnancy. Several studies found that the use of diazepam during the first trimester of pregnancy was significantly greater among mothers of children born with oral clefts. Aarskog found that 6.3 percent of 30 infants born with cleft palate in the United States between 1967 and 1971 had been exposed to diazepam in the first trimester, compared with 1.1 percent of control infants.[143] This rate of exposure to diazepam (6.2 percent) among the children with cleft palate was similar to another study.[144] Safra and Oakley reported that mothers of infants with cleft lip, cleft palate, or both had used diazepam four times more frequently than mothers of control infants.[145] However, in another article these same authors pointed out that a fourfold increase in oral clefts, if confirmed, imply only a 0.4 percent risk of cleft lip with or without cleft palate and a 0.2 percent risk of cleft palate.[145] A review of 599 oral clefts by Saxen and Saxen showed a significant association (p<.05) between oral clefts and ingestion of anxiolytics, mostly diazepam, during the first trimester of pregnancy.[146] Many other epidemiological studies have shown an association between the use of diazepam in the first trimester and oral clefts.[147–151] However, these studies were followed by prospective and retrospective studies that did not show a greater risk of congenital malformations.[147,151–155] Also, there has been a large

increase in the use of diazepam over the past several years, without a concomitant increase in the occurrence of cleft lip or cleft palate.

Chlordiazepoxide, another long-acting benzodiazepine, has been associated with congenital malformations following exposure during early pregnancy.[156] An analysis of over 19,000 live births revealed that several congenital anomalies were present including spastic diplegia, microcephaly, duodenal atresia and mental deficiency. These anomalies were more prevalent among infants of mothers who took chlordiazepoxide during the first 42 days of pregnancy than among infants of mothers who took other drugs or no drugs (11.4 per 100 compared with 4.6 per 100 and 2.6 per 100, respectively). Fetal death rates were also higher in the chlordiazepoxide group. In another study of more than 50,000 pregnancies, malformations were identified in approximately 6.5 percent of the offspring before their first birthday.[157]

31.6 Additional Prenatal Environmental Influences

A. Malnutrition

Women who begin pregnancy underweight, eat poorly during pregnancy, and consequently do not gain at least 3-4 pounds per month in the second and third trimesters run a much higher risk of having low birth weight babies.[158] Research indicates that obese women should gain 15 to 24 pounds during pregnancy; normal-weight women 24 to 35 pounds; and underweight women even more. Beyond overall weight, certain nutrients defend against low birth weight, including zinc, iron, and folic acid. Indeed, malnutrition (not age) is the primary reason young teenagers tend to have small babies. They tend to eat sporadically and unhealthily; and because their own bodies are still developing, their diet is inadequate to support the growth of two. If the baby is malnourished, there is serious damage to the CNS, seen in lower brain weight. It will also affect other organ system development, especially the immune system, resulting in frequent illness. Lack of folic acid particularly affects neural tube formation, presenting as anencephaly or spina bifida.

B. Poverty

Compared with women of higher socioeconomic status, pregnant women at the bottom of the economic ladder are more likely to be ill, malnourished, teenaged, and stressed.[159] They often receive late or inadequate prenatal care, breathe polluted air, live in overcrowded conditions, move from place to place and ingest unhealthy substances. Poor women have less access to family planning services, and they live in communities that encourage higher birth rates, partly because these communities have higher death rates. In this way, the social context may underlie many of the biological causes of low birth weight.

- Of the more than 25 million low birth weight infants born worldwide each year, the overwhelming majority are in developing countries.
- Developing countries in the same geographic region, with similar ethnic populations, have markedly different low birth weight rates when they have different average incomes.
- Within nations, differences in low birth weight rates among ethnic groups follow socioeconomic differences among those groups.
- Within the United States, low birth rates in the poorest states are almost twice those in wealthier states.

C. Emotional State

The mother's stress can be transmitted to the fetus. When a pregnant woman experiences intense fears, anxieties and other emotions, physiological changes occur in the fetus. These include changes in respiration and glandular secretions. For example, producing adrenaline in response to fear restricts blood flow to the uterine area and may deprive the fetus of adequate oxygen. Also, reassuring the mother of fetal well-being has positive outcomes for the infants in the study.[159] Stress also relates to miscarriage, prematurity, low birth weight, baby irritability, and GI tract problems. In addition, stress is related to cleft palate and pyloric stenosis, which affects nutritional intake.

D. Mother's Age

Two time periods are of special interest: adolescence and the thirties and beyond. Infants born to adolescents are often premature. The mortality rate of infants born to adolescent mothers is double that of infants born to mothers in their twenties. Down syndrome, a form of mental retardation, is related to the mother's age. By age 40, the probability is slightly over 1 in 100. By age 50, it is almost 1 in 10. The risk is also higher before age 18. Women also have more difficulty in becoming pregnant after the age of 30.[159]

E. Infections and Diseases

Maternal diseases and infections can produce defects by crossing the placental barrier. For example, the greatest damage to the fetus from the mother contracting German measles occurs during the third and fourth weeks of pregnancy. Syphilis is more damaging later in prenatal development, four months or more after conception. Rather than affecting organ development as Rubella does, syphilis dam-

ages organs after they have formed. The importance of the mother's health to the health of her offspring is nowhere better exemplified than when the mother is infected with HIV.[159] HIV and AIDS is passed to a fetus 20 to 30 percent of the time. It causes weight loss, diarrhea, respiratory illness, and brain damage. Most babies survive only 5–8 months once symptoms appear. If the mother uses AZT, it reduces transmission to the baby 95 percent of the time.

31.7 Pregnancy Categories for Prescription Drug Labeling

More than 80 percent of all drugs approved and on the market are not officially approved by the Food and Drug Administration (FDA) for use during pregnancy.[160] Although there is much animal and human research given to determine teratogenicity, an FDA statement that a substance is safe for use during pregnancy is usually won after long empiric experience and is not often granted. The prescription drug labeling for newly approved drugs now contains one of five required pregnancy categories (A, B, C, D, and X) as one of the items in the "Precautions" section of the package insert and other labeling. This follows an FDA regulation that became effective on December 26, 1979.[160] All prescription drugs absorbed systemically or known to have a potential for harm to the fetus came under this rule as part of the FDA labeling revision on November 1, 1980.

- Category A: Controlled studies in women failed to demonstrate a risk to the fetus in the first trimester and there is no evidence of a risk in later trimesters. The possibility of fetal harm appears remote.
- Category B: Either studies of animal reproduction have not demonstrated a fetal risk but there are no controlled studies in pregnant women, or studies of animal reproduction have shown an adverse effect (other than a decrease in fertility) that was not confirmed in controlled studies in women in the first trimester (and there is no evidence of a risk in later trimesters).
- Category C: Either studies in animals have revealed adverse effects on the fetus (teratogenic or embryocidal effects or other) and there are no controlled studies in women, or studies in women and animals are not available. Drugs should be given only if the potential benefit justifies the potential risk to the fetus.
- Category D: There is positive evidence of human fetal risk, but the benefits from use in pregnant women may be acceptable despite the risk (e.g., if the drug is needed in a life-threatening situation or

for a serious disease for which safer drugs cannot be used or are ineffective). There will be an appropriate statement in the "Warnings" section of the labeling.

- Category X: Studies in animals or humans have demonstrated fetal abnormalities or there is evidence of fetal risk based on human experience, or both, and the risk of the use of the drug in pregnant women clearly outweighs any possible benefit. The drug is contraindicated in women who are or may become pregnant. There will be an appropriate statement in the "Contraindications" section of the labeling.

Labeling for drugs with a recognized use during labor delivery, whether or not the use is stated in the "Indications" section of the labeling, will describe the available information about the effect of the drug on the mother and the fetus.

Endnotes

1. R.D. Hood *Developmental and reproductive toxicology, a practical approach, 2nd ed.* Boca (2006) Raton: Taylor & Francis.

2. J. Warkany. *Teratology: Spectrum of a Science,* In Kalter H (ed). Issues and Reviews in Teratology. New York: Plenum Press, 1983, vol 1, pp 19-31.

3. N. Chernoff, J.M. Rogers, A.J. Alles, et al. *Cell cycle alterations and cell death in cyclophosphamide teratogenesis.* (1989) Teratogenesis Carcino Mutagen 9: 199-209.

4. J.M. Rogers and R.J. Kavlock. *Developmental Toxicology.* In Klaassen CD (ed): Toxicology: The Basic Science of Poisons 5th Edition. New York, NY: McGraw-Hill, (1996) pp 301-331.

5. C. R. Stockard. *Developmental rate and structural expression: An experimental study of twins, "double monsters," and single deformities, and the interaction among embryonic organs during their origin and development.* (1921) Am J Anat 28: 115-277.

6. F. Hale. *Pigs born without eyeballs.* J Hered (1935) 27: 105-106.

7. J. Warkany, R.C. Nelson. *Appearance of skeletal abnormalities in the offspring of rats reared on a deficient diet.* Science (1940) 92: 383-384.

8. N.M. Gregg. *Congenital cataract following German measles in the mother.* Tr Ophthalmol Soc (1941) Aust 3: 35-40.

9. W.G. McBride. *Thalidomide and congenital anomalies.* Lancet (1961) 2: 1358.

10. J.G. Wilson. *Experimental studies on congenital malformations.* J Chronic Dis (1959) 10: 111-130.

11. T.W. Sadler and E.S. Hunter. *Principles of abnormal development: Past, present and future.* In Kimmel CA, Buelke-Sam J (eds): Developmental Toxicology 2nd ed. New York: Raven Press, (1994) pp. 53-63.

12. W. Lenz. *Time plan of human organogenesis as a standard in the assessment of teratogenic effects.* Fortschr Med (1969) 87: 520-526.

13. D. Bernstein and P. Nash. *Human Development.* In Bernstein D and Nash P (eds): Essentials of Psychology 2nd ed. Boston: Houghton Mifflin Company. (2008) pp 341-388.

14. W.M. Generoso, J.C. Rutledge, K.T. Cain et al. *Exposure of female mice to ethylene oxide within hours after mating leads to fetal malformations and death.* Mutat Res (1987) 176: 269-274; and W.M. Generoso, J.C. Rutledge, K.T. Cain et al. *Mutagen-induced fetal anomalies and death following treatment of females within hours after mating.* Mut Res (1988) 199: 175-181.

15. M.H. Snow and P.P. Tam. *Is compensatory growth a complicating factor in mouse teratology?* Nature (1979) 3: 461-480.

16. N.W. Moore, C.E. Adams, and L.E. Rowson. *Development potential of single blastomeres of the rabbit egg.* J Reprod Fertil (1968)17: 527-531.

17. S. Fabro. *Passage of drugs and other chemicals into the uterine fluids and preimplantation blastocyst.* In Boreus L (ed): *Fetal Pharmacology.* New York: Raven Press, (1973) pp 443-461; and S. Fabro, J.A. McLachlan, and N.M. Dames. *Chemical exposure of embryos during the preimplantation stages of pregnancy: Mortality rate and intrauterine development.* Am J Obstet Gynecol (1984)148: 929-938.

18. I.K. Takeuchi. *Teratogenic effects of methylnitrosourea on pregnant mice before implantation.* Experienta (1984)40: 879-881.

19. H.G. Eibs, H. Speilman, and M. Hagele. *Teratogenic effects of cyproterone acetate and medroxyprogesterone treatment during the pre- and postimplantation period of mouse embryos.* Teratology (1982) 25: 27-36.

20. A.C. Enders. *Anatomy of the placenta and its relationship to function.* Mead Johnson Symp Perinat Dev Med (1981)18: 3-7.

21. R.E. Shenefelt. *Morphogenesis of malformations in hamsters caused by retinoic acid: Relation to dose and stage of treatment.* Teratology (1972) 5: 103-118.

22. J.M. Rogers, B.D. Barbee BD, B.F. Rehnberg. *Critical periods of sensitivity for the developmental toxicity of inhaled methanol.* Teratology (1993) 47: 395.

23. D. Neubert, P. Zens, A. Rothenwallner, H-J. Merker. *A survey of the embryotoxic effects of TCDD in mammalian species.* Environ Health Perspect (1973) 5: 63-79.

24. L.L. Needham, A.M. Calafat, D.B. Barr. *Assessing the developmental toxicant exposures via biomonitoring.* Basic and Clinical Pharmacology and Toxicology (2008) 102: 100-108.

25. S.D. Holladay, Smialowicz. *Development of the murine and human immune system: Differential effects of immunotoxicants depend on time of exposure.* Environ Health Perspect (2000) 108(Suppl 3): 463-475.

26. K.E. Pinkerton, J.P. Joad. *The mammalian respiratory system and critical windows of exposure for children's health.* Environ Health Perspect (2000) 108(Suppl 3): 457-462.

27. J.L. Pryor, C. Hughes, W. Foster, B.F. Hales, B. Robaire. *Critical Windows of Exposure for Children's Health: The Reproductive System in Animals and Humans.* Environ Health Perspect (2000) 108(Suppl 3): 491-504.

28. D. Rice, S. Barone Jr. *Critical periods of vulnerability for the developing nervous system: evidence from human and animal models.* Environ Health Perspect (2000) 108(Suppl 3):511-33.

29. T.W. Sadler. *Susceptible Periods during Embryogenesis of the Heart and Endocrine Glands.* Environ Health Perspect (2000) 108(Suppl 3): 555-562.

30. P.S. Guzelian, C.J. Henry, S.S. Olin SS (eds). *Similarities and Differences between Children and Dults: Implications for Risk Assessment.* Washington DC: ILSI Press, (1992).

31. J.L. Margulies. (1993) "Special Considerations in Pregnancy," In Viccellio P (ed). *Handbook of Medical Toxicology.* Boston: Little, Brown and Company, 1993, pp 128-135.

32. E.W. Carney, A.B. Liberacki, B. Tornesi et al. *Ethylene glycol kinetics in pregnant rats; Differences between slow and fast dose-rate exposures.* Toxicologist (2002) 66 (Suppl 1): 139.

33. H. Nau, W.J. Scott Jr. *Weak acids my act as teratogens by accumulating in the basic milieu of the early mammalian embryo.* Nature (1986) 323: 276-278.

34. M. Srivastava, M.D. Collins, W.J. Scott Jr et al. *Transplacental distribution of weak acids in mice: Accumulation in compartments of high pH.* Teratology (1991) 43: 325-329.

35. N. Brown. *Teratogenicity of carboxylic acids: Distribution studies in whole embryo culture.* In Nau H, Scott WJ Jr (eds). *Pharmacokinetics in teratogenesis. Vol II.* Boca Raton: CRC Press, (1987) pp 154-163.

36. E. Jauniaux, B. Gulbis. *Fluid compartments of the embryonic environment.* Hum Reprod (2000) 6: 268-278.

37. H.P. Kuemmerle. *The diaplacental kinetics of drugs.* Int J Clin Pharmacol (1974) 9: 298-304.

38. J.L. Schardein. *Chemically induced birth defects, 2nd ed.* New York: Marcel Dekker. (1993)

39. J.G. Wilson. *Experimental studies on congenital malformations.* J Chronic Dis (1959) 10: 111-130.

40. H.B. Taussig. *A study of the German outbreak of phocomelia: The thalidomide syndrome.* JAMA (1962) 180: 1106.

41. W.G. McBride. *Thalidomide and congenital anomalies.* Lancet (1961) 2: 1358.

42. W. Lenz. *Kindliche Missbildungen nach Medikament-Einnahme während der gravidität?* Dtsch Med Wochenschr (1961) 86: 2555-2556.

43. W. Lenz. *Das thalidomide-syndrom.* Fortschr Med (1963) 81: 148-153

44. W. Lenz. *A short history of thalidomide embryopathy.* Teratology (1988) 38: 203-215.

45. K.L. Jones, Smith. *Recognition of the fetal alcohol syndrome in early infancy.* Lancet (1973) 2: 999-1001.

46. H.L. Rosett, L. Weiner. *Alcohol and the fetus: a clinical perspective.* New York: Oxford University Press. (1984)

47. L.E. Kotch, K.K. Sulik. *Experimental fetal alcohol syndrome: proposed pathogenic basis for a variety of associated facial and brain anomalies.* Am. J. Med. Genet (1992) 44: 168-176.

48. C.D. Dittmer, S.L. Lentz-Kapua. *Fetal alcohol syndrome.* www.emedicine.com/PED/topic767.htm (2006)

49. C. Guerri. *Mechanisms involved in central nervous system dysfunction induced by prenatal ethanol exposure.* Neurotox Res (2002) 4: 327-335.

50. M.W. Miller. *Effects of alcohol on the generation and migration of cerebral cortical neurons.* Science (1986) 233: 1308-1311.

51. M.W. Miller. *Migration of cortical neurons is altered by gestational exposure to ethanol.* Alcohol Clin. Exp. Res. (1993) 17: 304-314.

52. T.M. Roebuck, S.N. Mattison, E.P. Riley. *A review of the neuroanatomical findings in children with fetal alcohol syndrome or prenatal exposure to alcohol.* Alcohol Clin. Exp Res (1998) 22: 339-344.

53. E.R. Sowell, P.M. Thompson, S.N. Mattison, K.D. Tessner, T.L. Jernigan, E.P. Riley, A.W. Toga. *Voxel-based morphometric analyses of the brain in children and adolescents prenatally exposed to alcohol.* Neuroreport (2001) 12: 515-523.

54. S.L. Archibald, C. Fennema-Notestine, A. Gamst, E.P. Riley, S.N. Mattison, T.L. Jernigan. *Brain dysmorphology in individuals with severe prenatal alcohol exposure.* Dev Med Child Neurol (2001) 43: 148-154.

55. National Institute on Alcohol Abuse and Alcoholism. *Prenatal exposure to alcohol.* Alcohol Re Health (2000) 24: 32-41.

56. S.K. Clarren, E.C. Alvord Jr., S.M. Sumi, A.P. Streissguth, D.W. Smith. *Brain malformations related to prenatal exposure to ethanol.* J. Pediatr (1978) 92: 64-67.

57. E.R. Sowell, P.M. Thompson, S.N. Mattison, K.D. Tessner, T.L. Jernigan, E.P. Riley, A.W. Toga. *Voxel-based morphometric analyses of the brain in children and adolescents prenatally exposed to alcohol.* Neuroreport (2001) 12: 515-523.

58. S.K. Clarren, E.C. Alvord Jr., S.M. Sumi, A.P. Streissguth, D.W. Smith. *Brain malformations related to prenatal exposure to ethanol.* J. Pediatr (1978) 92: 64-67.

59. J. Peiffer, F. Majewski, H. Fishbach, J.R. Bierich, B. Volk. *Alcohol embryo and fetopathy.* J. Neurol Sci (1979) 41: 125-137

60. C.L. Coulter, R.W. Leech, G.B. Schaefer, B.W. Scheithauer, R.A. Brumback. *Midline cerebral dysgenesis, dysfunction of the hypothalamic-pituitary axid and fetal alcohol effects.* Arch Neurol (1993) 50: 771-775.

61. T. Kumada, Y. Jiang, D.B. Cameron, H. Komuro. *How does alcohol impair neuronal migration?* J Neurosci Res. (2007) 85: 465-470.

62. J.C. Marcus. *Neurological findings in the fetal alcohol syndrome.* Neuropediatrics (1987) 18: 158-160.

63. B. Altman. *Fetal alcohol syndrome.* J. Pediatric Ophthal. (1976) 13: 255-258.

64. T. Chan, R. Bowell, M. O'Keefe, B. Lanigan. *Ocular manifestations in fetal alcohol syndrome.* British Journal of Ophthal. (1991) 75: 524-526.

65. M.T. Miller, J. Israel, J. Cuttone. *Fetal alcohol syndrome.* Journal of Ped. Opththal. (1981) 18: 6-15.

66. K. Stromland. *Ocular abnormalities in the fetal alcohol syndrome.* Acta Ophthalmologica Scandinavica (1985) 63 (Suppl 171): 369-392.

67. T. Chan, R. Bowell, M. O'Keefe, B. Lanigan. *Ocular manifestations in fetal alcohol syndrome.* British Journal of Ophthal. (1991) 75: 524-526.

68. H. Rosett. *Guest editorial. A clinical perspective of fetal alcohol syndrome.* Alcoholism: Clinical and Experimental Research (1980) 4: 119-122.

69. K. Stromland. *Ocular abnormalities in the fetal alcohol syndrome.* Acta Ophthalmologica Scandinavica (1985) 63 (Suppl 171): 369-392.

70. A.L. Herbst, P. Cole, T. Colton et al. *Age-incidence and risk of diethylstilbestrol-related clear cell adenocarcinoma of the vagina and cervix.* Am J Obstet Gynecol (1977) 128: 43-50.

71. M. Bibbo, W. Gill, F. Aziz et al. *Follow-up study of male and female offspring of DES-exposed mothers.* Obstet Gynecol (1977) 49: 1-8.

72. F.W. Rosa. *Teratogenicity of isotretinoin.* Lancet (1983) 2: 513.

73. E.J. Lamner, D.T. Chen, R.M. Hoar et al. *Retinoic acid induced embryopathy.* New Engl J Med (1985) 313: 837-841.

74. I.J. Chasnoff, R.P. Hatcher, W.J. Burns. *Polydrug and methadone addicted newborns: A continuum of impairment?* Pediatrics (1982) 70: 210-213.

75. I.J. Chasnoff, R.P. Hatcher, W.J. Burns, S.H. Schnoll. *Pentazocine and tripelennamine ("t's and blue's") effects on the fetus and neonate.* Dev Pharmacol Ther (1983a) 6: 162-169; and . I.J. Chasnoff, W.J. Burns, R.P. Hatcher, K.A. Burns. *Phencyclidine effects on the fetus and neonate.* Dev Pharmacol Ther (1983b) 6: 404-408.

76. I.J. Chasnoff, W.J. Burns, S.H. Schnoll, K.A. Burns. *Cocaine use in pregnancy.* New Engl J Med (1985) 313: 666-669.

77. I.J. Chasnoff, W.J. Burns, R.P. Hatcher, K.A. Burns. *Phencyclidine effects on the fetus and neonate.* Dev Pharmacol Ther (1983b) 6: 404-408.

78. B. Lutiger B, K. Graham, T.R. Einarson, G. Koren. *Relationship between gestational cocaine use and pregnancy outcome: A meta-analysis.* Teratology (1991) 44: 405-414.

79. J.O. Donaldson. *Neurologic complications.* In: Burrow GN, Duffy TP, eds. *Medical Complications During Pregnancy*, 5th ed. Philadelphia, PA: WB Saunders Co; (1999) pp 410-412.

80. D. Lindhout, D. Schmidt. *In Utero Exposure to Valproate and Neural Tube Defects.* Lancet: (1986)1: 1392-1393.

81. Centers for Disease Control. *Valproic acid and spina bifida: A preliminary report—France.* MMWR (1982) 31 (42): 565-566.

82. Centers for Disease Control. *Valproate: A new cause of birth defects—Report from Italy and follow up from France.* MMWR (1983) 32 (33): 438-439.

83. E.B. Samren, C.M. van Duijn, S. Koch, V.K. Hiiesmaa, H. Klepel, A.H. Bardy et al. *Maternal use of antiepileptic drugs and the risk of major congenital malformations: a joint European prospective study of human teratogenesis associated with maternal epilepsy.* Epilepsia (1997) 38: 981-90

84. E.B. Samren, C.M. van Duijn, G.C. Christiaens, A Hofman, D. Lindhout. *Antiepileptic drug regimens and major congenital abnormalities in the offspring.* Ann Neurol (1999) 46:739-46.

85. R. Canger, D. Battino, M.P. Canevini, C. Fumarola, L. Guidolin, A. Vignoli et al. *Malformations in offspring of women with epilepsy: a prospective study.* Epilepsia (1999) 40:1231-1236.

86. S. Kaneko, D. Battino, E. Andermann, K. Wada, R. Kan, A. Takeda A, et al. *Congenital malformations due to antiepileptic drugs.* Epilepsy Res (1999) 33:145-58.

87. G. Mawer, J. Clayton-Smith, H. Coyle, U. Kini. *Outcome of pregnancy in women attending an outpatient epilepsy clinic: adverse features associated with higher doses of sodium valproate.* Seizure (2002) 11:512-8.

88. R. Meischenguiser, C.H. D'Giano, S.M. Ferraro. *Oxcarbazepine in pregnancy: clinical experience in Argentina.* Epilepsy Behav (2004) 5:163-7.

89. K. Wide, B. Winbladh, B. Kallen. *Major malformations in infants exposed to antiepileptic drugs in utero, with emphasis on carbamazepine and valproic acid: a nationwide, population-based register study.* Acta Paediatr (2004) 93:174-176.

90. M. Artama, A. Auvinen, T. Raudaskoski, I. Isojarvi, J. Isojarvi. *Antiepileptic drug use of women with epilepsy and congenital malformations in offspring.* Neurology (2005) 64:1874-1878.

91. J. Morrow, A. Russell, E. Guthrie, L. Parsons, I. Robertson, R. Waddell et al. *Malformation risks of antiepileptic drugs in pregnancy: a prospective study from the UK Epilepsy and Pregnancy Register.* J Neurol Neurosurg Psychiatry (2006) 77:193-198.

92. D.F. Wyszynski, M. Nambisan, T. Surve, R.M. Alsdorf, C.R. Smith, L.B. Holmes. *Increased rate of major malformations in offspring exposed to valproate during pregnancy.* Neurology (2005) 64:961-965.

93. E. Kaaja, R. Kaaja, V. Hiilesmaa. *Major malformations in offspring of women with epilepsy.* Neurology (2003) 60:575-579.

94. N. Adab, U. Kini, J. Vinten, J. Ayres, G. Baker, J. Clayton-Smith, et al. *The longer term outcome of children born to mothers with epilepsy.* J Neurol Neurosurg Psychiatry (2004) 75:1575-1583.

95. E.B. Samren, C.M. van Duijn, S. Koch, V.K. Hiiles-maa, H. Klepel, A.H. Bardy et al. *Maternal use of anti-epileptic drugs and the risk of major congenital malfor-mations: a joint European prospective study of human teratogenesis associated with maternal epilepsy.* Epilepsia (1997) 38: 981-90

96. G. Koren, A.A. Nava-Ocampo, M.E. Moretti, R. Suss-man, I. Nulman. *Motherisk Update: Major malforma-tions with valproic acid.* Canadian Family Physician (2006) 52: 441-447.

97. P. Tanganelli, G. Regesta. *Epilepsy, pregnancy, and major birth anomalies: An Italian prospective, con-trolled study.* Neurology (1992) 42(4 Suppl 5):89-93.

98. E.B. Samren, C.M. van Duijn, G.C. Christiaens, A Hof-man, D. Lindhout. *Antiepileptic drug regimens and major congenital abnormalities in the offspring.* Ann Neurol (1999) 46:739-46.

99. S. Kaneko, D. Battino, E. Andermann, K. Wada, R. Kan, A. Takeda, et al. *Congenital malformations due to antiepileptic drugs.* Epilepsy Res (1999) 33:145-58.

100. H. Nau, R. Zierer, H. Spielmann, D. Neubert, C.A. Gansau. *A new model for embryotoxicity testing: Teratogenicity and pharmacokinetics of valproic acid following constant-rate administration in the mouse using human therapeutic drug and metabolite con-centrations.* Life Science (1981) 29: 2803-2814.

101. D.W. Fowler, M.J. Eadie, R.G. Dickinson. *Trans-placental transfer and biotransformation studies of valproic acid and its glucuronide(s) in the perfused human placenta.* J. Pharmacol Exp Ther (1989) 249: 318-323.

102. S. Kumar, H. Wong H, S.A. Yeung et al. *Disposi-tion of valproic acid in maternal, fetal and new born sheep. I: Placental transfer; plasma protein bind and clearance.* Drug Metab. Dispos. (2000) 28: 845-856.

103. H. Nau, B Krauer. *Serum protein binding of valproic acid in fetus-mother pairs throughout pregnancy: Correlation with oxytocin administration and albu-min and free fatty acid concentrations.* J. Clin. Phar-macol (1986) 26: 215-221.

104. B.K. Alldredge (2000). "Seizure disorders," In: Her-findal ET, Gourley DR, eds. *Textbook of Therapeu-tics: Drug and Disease Management. 7th ed.* Phila-delphia, PA: Lippincott Williams & Wilkins: pp. 1118-11120.

105. M.L. Netzloff, R.R. Streiff, J.L. Frias, O.M. Rennert. *Folate antagonism following teratogenic exposure to diphenylhydantoin.* Teratology (1979) 19: 45-50.

106. D.K. Hansen, R.E. Billings. *Phenytoin teratogenicity and effects on embryonic and maternal folate metabo-lism.* Teratology (1985) 31: 363-371.

107. American Academy of Pediatrics Committee (AAPC) on Genetics. *Folic acid for the prevention of neural tube defects.* Pediatrics (1999) 104: 325-327.

108. J.M. Brewer, P.A. Wattman. *Epilepsy and Preg-nancy: Maternal and fetal effects of phenytoin.* Crit. Care Nurse (2003) 23: 93-98.

109. J.J. Volpe (2001). "Teratogenic effects of drugs and passive addiction." In: *Neurology of the Newborn, 4th ed.* Philadelphia, PA: WB Saunders Co: pp. 859-898.

110. R.H. Finnell, B.A. Buchler, B.M. Kerr, P.L. Ager, R.H. Levy. *Clinical and experimental studies linking oxidative metabolism to phenytoin-induced terato-genesis.* Neurology (1992) 42 (4th suppl): 25-31.

111. M. Ogun, L. Dansky, E. Andermann, A. Sherwin, F. Andermann. *Improved pregnancy outcome in epilep-tic women in the last decade: Relationship of mater-nal anticonvulsant therapy.* Brain Dev. (1992) 14: 371-380.

112. M.S. Yerby, A. Leavitt, D.M. Erickson et al. *Antiepi-leptics and the development of congenital anomalies.* Neurology (1992) 42: 132-140.

113. A.B. Dessens, P.T. Cohen-Kettenis, G.J. Mellenbergh, J.G. Koppe, N.E. van De Poll, K. Boer. *Association of prenatal Phenobarbital and phenytoin exposure with small head size at birth and with learning problems.* Acta Paediatr. (2000) 89: 533-554.

114. J. Koch-Wesser, E.M. Sellers. *Drug interactions with coumarin anticoagulants.* New England Journal of Medicine (1971) 285: 487-498.

115. P.J Disaia. *Pregnancy and delivery of a patient with a Starr-Edwards mitral valve prosthesis.* Obste Gyne-col (1966) 28: 469-472.

116. W.L. Shaul, J.G. Hall. *Multiple congenital anomalies associated with oral anticoagulants.* Am J Obstet Gy-necol (1977) 127: 191-198.

117. R.M. Pauli, J.G. Hal, K.M. Wilson. *Risks of anticoagulation during pregnancy.* Am Heart J, (1980) 100: 761-762.

118. M.J. Robinson, J. Pash, J. Grimwade et al. *Fetal warfarin syndrome.* Med J Aust (1978) 1: 157.

119. W. Holzgreve, J.C. Carey, B.D. Hall. *Warfarin-induced fetal abnormalities.* Lancet (1976) 2:914-915.

120. D. Born, E.E. Martinez, P.A. Almeida, D.V. Santos, A.C. Carvalho, A.F. Moron et al. *Pregnancy in patients with prosthetic heart valves: the effects of anticoagulation on mother, fetus, and neonate.* Am Heart J (1992) 124:413-417.

121. P. Sareli, M.J. England, M.R. Berk, R.H. Marcus, M. Epstein, J. Driscoll et al. *Maternal and fetal sequelae of anticoagulation during pregnancy in patients with mechanical heart valve prosthesis.* Am J Cardiol (1989) 63:1462-5.

122. P.I. Pillans, E.J. Coetzee. *Anticoagulation during pregnancy.* S Afr Med J (1986) 69:469.

123. G. Quenneville, B. Barton, E. McDevitt et al. *The use of anticoagulants for thrombo-phlebitis during pregnancy.* Am J Obstet Gynecol (1959) 77: 1135-1149.

124. U. Villasanta. *Thromboembolic disease in pregnancy.* Am J. Obstet Gynecol (1965) 93: 142-160.

125. J.G. Hall, R.M. Pauli, K.M. Wilson. *Maternal and fetal sequelae of anticoagulation during pregnancy.* Am J Med (1980) 68:122-140.

126. E. Salazar, A. Zajamas, N. Gutierrez, I. Hurbe. *The problem of cardiac valve prostheses, anticoagulants, and pregnancy.* Circulation (1984) 70(Suppl 1):169-177.

127. N. Sussman. *The benzodiapines: Selection and use in treating anxiety insomnia and other disorders.* Hosp Formul (1984) 20: 298-305.

128. M.B. Bracken, T.R. Holford. *Exposure to prescribed drugs in pregnancy and association with congenital malformations.* Obstetrics and Gynecology (1981) 58: 336-344.

129. American College of Obstetricians and Gynecologist Committee on Practice Buletins—Obstetrics. ACOG Practice Bulletin no. 92: "Use of psychiatric medications during pregnancy and lactation" Obstet Gynecol (2008) 111 (4): 1001-1020.

130. S.S. Roach, S.M. Ford (2006). "Sedatives and hypnotics." Introductory Clinical Pharmacology (8th ed.). Lippincott Williams & Wilkens. pp. 236.

131. M.M. Iqgal, T. Sobhan, T. Ryals. *Effects of commonly used benzodiazepines on the fetus, the neonate and the nursing infants.* Psychiatric Services (2002) 53: 39-49.

132. W. Kuhnz, H. Nau. *Differences in in vitro binding of diazepam and N-desmethyldiazepam to maternal and fetal plasma proteins at birth: relation to free fatty acid concentration and other parameters.* Clinical Pharmacology and Therapeutics (1983) 34:220– 226.

133. M. Mandelli, P.L. Morselli, S. Nordio et al. *Placental transfer of diazepam and its disposition in the newborn.* Clinical Pharmacology and Therapeutics (1975) 17:564–572.

134. O.M. Bakke, K. Haram, T. Lygre et al. *Comparison of the placental transfer of thiopental and diazepam in caesarian section.* European Journal of Clinical Pharmacology (1981) 21:221–227.

135. C. Gillberg. *"Floppy infant syndrome" and maternal diazepam.* Lancet (1977) 2:244.

136. E. Mazzi. *Possible neonatal diazepam withdrawal: a case report.* American Journal of Obstetrics and Gynecology (1977) 129:586–587.

137. J.E. Cree, J. Meyer, D.M. Hailey. *Diazepam in labour: its metabolism and effect on the clinical condition and thermogenesis of the newborn.* British Medical Journal (1973) 4:251–255.

138. R.W. Shannon, G.P. Fraser, R.G. Aitken et al. *Diazepam in preeclamptic toxemia with special reference to its effect on the newborn infant.* British Journal of Clinical Practice (1972) 26:271–275.

139. E. Van der Kleijn. *Protein binding and lipophilic nature of ataractics of the metrobamate and diazapime group.* Archives Internationales de Pharmacodynamie et de Therapie (1969) 179:225–250.

140. M.D. Allen, D.J. Greenblatt. *Comparative protein binding of diazepam and desmethyldiazepam.* Journal of Clinical Pharmacology (1981) 21:219–223.

141. W.A. Colburn, M. Gibaldi. *Plasma protein binding of diazepam after a single dose of sodium oleate.* Journal of Pharmaceutical Sciences (1978) 67:891–892.

142. J. Krasner, S.J. Yaffe (1975). *Drug-protein binding in the neonate, in Basic and Therapeutic Aspects of Perinatal Pharmacology.* Morselli PL, Garattini S, Sereni F (eds). New York, Raven.

143. D. Aarskog. *Association between maternal intake of diazepam and oral clefts [letter].* Lancet (1975) 2: 921.

144. I. Saxen. *Associations between oral clefts and drugs taken during pregnancy.* International Journal of Epidemiology (1975) 4:37–44.

145. M.D. Safra, G.P. Oakley. *Association between cleft lip with or without cleft palate and prenatal exposure to diazepam.* Lancet (1975) 2: 478–480.

146. I. Saxen, L. Saxen. *Association between maternal intake of diazepam and oral clefts.* Lancet (1975) 2:498.

147. L. Rosenberg, A.A. Mitchell, J.L. Parsells et al. *Lack of relation of oral clefts to diazepam use during pregnancy.* New England Journal of Medicine (1983) 309:1282–1285.

148. S.S. Entman, W.K. Vaughn. *Lack of relation of oral clefts to diazepam use in pregnancy [letter].* New England Journal of Medicine (1984) 310:1121–1122.

149. A. Czeizel. *Diazepam, phenytoin, and aetiology of cleft lip and/or cleft palate [letter].* Lancet (1976) 1:810.

150. I. Saxen. *Epidemiology of cleft lip and palate: an attempt to rule out chance correlations.* British Journal of Preventive and Social Medicine (1975) 29:103–110.

151. A. Czeizel, A. Lendvay. *In utero exposure to benzodiazepines [letter].* Lancet (1987) 1:628.

152. P.H. Shino, J.L. Mills. *Oral clefts and diazepam use during pregnancy.* New England Journal of Medicine (1984) 311:919–920.

153. A. Czeizel (1986). "Endpoints of reproductive dysfunction in an experimental epidemiological model: self-poisoned pregnant women," in Chambers PL, Gehring P, Sakai F (eds). *New Concepts and Developments in Toxicology.* Amsterdam, Elsevier, pp. 34.

154. A. Czeizel, A. Pazsy, J. Pusztai et al. *Aetiological monitor of congenital abnormalities: a case-control surveillance system.* Acta Paediatrica Hungarica (1983) 24:91–99.

155. A.J. Gelenberg. *Diazepam: not a teratogen?* Massachusetts General Hospital Newsletter (1984) 7(2).

156. L. Milkovich, B.J. Van den Berg. *Effects of prenatal meprobamate and chlordiazepoxide hydrochloride on human embryonic and fetal development.* New England Journal of Medicine (1974) 291:1268–1271.

157. S.C. Hartz, O.P. Heinonen, S. Shapiro et al. *Antenatal exposure to meprobamate and chlordiazepoxide in relation to malformations, mental development, and childhood mortality.* New England Journal of Medicine (1975) 292:726–728.

158. C.L. Keen, A. Bendich, C.C. Willhite (eds): *Maternal Nutrition and Pergnancy Outcome.* Ann NY Acad. Sci 678: 1-372. (1993).

159. Santrock, JW (ed): *Life-span development.* McGraw-Hill College, New York 652 pages (1999).

160. J.L. Margulies (1993). "Special Considerations in Pregnancy," In Viccellio P (ed). *Handbook of Medical Toxicology.* Boston: Little, Brown and Company, 1993, pp 128-135.

161. Barbara A Gylys and Mary Ellen Wedding. *Medical Terminology Systems*, F.A. Davis Company, 2005.

Chapter 32

Nonscientific Uses and Illegal Marketing of Drugs and Dietary Supplements

Stephen Barrett, M.D. and Robert S. Baratz, M.D., DDS, Ph.D.

32.1 Overview

Drugs and dietary supplements are associated with three types of harm: direct, indirect, and financial. Direct harm can be caused by inherent toxicity, overdose, and adverse drug/drug, drug/supplement, and supplement/supplement interactions. Indirect harm occurs when appropriate treatment is delayed because an unscientific practitioner fails to make an adequate diagnosis or when an ineffective modality is used instead of effective treatment.

The products discussed in this chapter can be divided into six categories: (1) prescription drugs, (2) over-the-counter (OTC) drugs, (3) vitamins and minerals with known dietary needs, (4) other substances marketed as dietary supplements, (5) herbs, and (6) homeopathic products. Prescription and standard OTC drugs are closely regulated and almost always live up to their advertised claims. Dietary supplements and herbs are much less regulated; and many involve unsubstantiated claims, insufficiently tested ingredients, and poor quality control. The FDA generally ignores homeopathic products unless they are marketed as vaccine substitutes or as cures for serious diseases. They are presumed safe, but there is no logical reason to use them. Table 32.1 compares the six product categories.

32.2 Prescription Drugs

Prescription drugs must have Food and Drug Administration (FDA) approval as safe and effective for their intended purposes and are tightly regulated. To gain approval, they must undergo laboratory tests and well-designed clinical trials that demonstrate safety and effectiveness. The testing and approval of a new drug is very expensive and takes many years.

Before a new drug can be approved and marketed, the manufacturer generally must take the following steps:

- The drug must be subjected to laboratory and animal tests, which must indicate that it can be safely tested in humans.
- Before the drug is given to people, the sponsor must submit a "Notice of Claimed Investigational Exemption for a New Drug," which is commonly referred to as an "investigation new drug" (IND). The application must describe the composition of the substance, the results of the animal studies, the design (protocol) of the proposed clinical trial, the measures that will protect the experimental subjects, and the training and experience of the investigators. Testing proceeds under FDA supervision, which requires that studies be approved and monitored by Investigational Review Boards for the Protection of Human Subjects (IRBs) as required by 21 CFR 50 and 21 CFR 56.
- Approved clinical investigations follow three phases. In Phase 1, about 100–200 people are exposed to the drug to determine the tolerance, absorption. excretion, half-life, and other pharmacologic

Table 32.1
Regulatory Status of Drugs and Dietary Supplements

	Prescription drugs	OTC drugs	Vitamins and minerals	Other nutritional supplements	Herbal products	OTC homeopathic products
Permissible claims	Must be generally recognized by experts as safe and effective for their intended purposes	Must be generally recognized by experts as safe and effective for their intended purposes	"Structure-function" claims permitted, but drug claims require premarket approval	"Structure-function" claims permitted, but drug claims require premarket approval	"Structure-function" claims permitted, but drug claims require premarket approval	Can be marketed for treatment of self-limiting ailments readily diagnosable by consumers
Labeling	Must provide ingredient amounts and adequate directions for use, including warnings	Must provide ingredient amounts and adequate directions for use, including warnings	Must list serving size, ingredients, and quantities of vitamin/mineral ingredients; no warnings are required	Must list serving size, ingredients, and quantities of vitamin/mineral ingredients; no warnings are required	Must list ingredients but not quantities; no warnings are required	Must identify ingredients and provide directions for use; products are assumed to be nontoxic
FDA approval	New Drug Application (NDA) must be approved	Must conform to OTC monographs	Not required for truthful structure-function claims	Not required for truthful structure-function claims	Not required for truthful structure-function claims	Not required for use of ingredients listed in the U.S. Homeopathic Pharmacopeia
Advertising regulation	FDA (stringent regulation; violative claims are uncommon)	FTC (violative claims are rare)	FDA/FTC (enforcement actions are uncommon)	FDA/FTC (violations greatly exceed regulatory resources)	FDA/FTC (violations greatly exceed regulatory resources)	FDA/FTC (minimal regulation)
Adverse event reporting	Required	Required	Required	Required	Required	Required
GMP required	Yes	Yes	Yes	Yes	Yes	Yes
Product quality	Generally good	Generally good	Generally good	Inconsistent	Poor; most products have not been standardized	No data exist
Recommended legislative and regulatory reforms	None needed	None needed	FDA should be authorized to limit dosages	Should be regulated as least as stringently as OTC drugs; penalties for violations should be increased	Should be regulated as least as stringently as OTC drugs; penalties for violations should be increased	Public warning or ban should be implemented

reactions; the preferred route of administration; and the safe dosage. In Phase 2, initial trials are conducted on 500–1,000 patients to assess the treatment or prevention of the specific disease. Additional animal studies to indicate safety may be conducted concurrently. If these preliminary studies demonstrate sufficient promise, Phase 3 clinical trials are performed with several thousand patients.

- The manufacturer submits a new drug application (NDA) that includes the experimental data, a sample package insert, and the proposed label.
- The FDA either approves the NDA after Phase 3, asks for further evidence, or rejects the application.

Phase 3 clinical trials compare people who receive the treatment being tested with a control group of people who receive a different treatment or no treatment. For example, the experimental group may receive tablets with active ingredients, whereas the control group receives another treatment, an inert substance (placebo), or no treatment. In "double-blind" trials, neither the experimenters nor the patients know who gets what. Controlled studies are necessary to distinguish between drug effects, placebo effects, and the natural course of the ailment. A placebo effect is a beneficial response to a substance, device, or procedure that cannot be accounted for on the basis of pharmacologic or other direct, physical action. Feeling better when the physician walks into the room is a common example.

After a drug is approved, additional studies (Phase 4 or postmarket surveillance studies) may be done to gather additional information about use of the product in much larger patient populations.

After marketing begins, manufacturers must report adverse effects. If a drug produces unexpected side effects or is found to be less effective than expected, approval can be withdrawn, which happens from time to time.

Whereas the FDA regulates the sale and labeling of drugs in interstate commerce, the prescribing of drugs is regulated by individual state laws and regulations. Off-label use for rational purposes is permissible (see Chapter 11, *Important Code of Federal Regulations Applicable to Drug Product Liability Suits*), but practitioners who violate standards of care can be disciplined by licensing boards. Some irrationally prescribed drugs are obtained through ordinary commercial channels, through prescriptions that patients fill at ordinary pharmacies. Others are prepared by compounding pharmacies that sell them to practitioners, patients, or both.

32.3 Irrational Use of Legal Drugs

The irrational uses of legal drugs include chelation therapy for cardiovascular disease and autism; long-term antibiotic treatment for Lyme disease, and human growth hormone for "anti-aging" purposes. "Bioidentical" hormones may have the same active ingredients as their standard counterparts but are marketed as though they do not.

A. Unwarranted Chelation Therapy

Chelation therapy, as used by fringe practitioners, involves a series of pills, intravenous infusions, or intramuscular injections of drugs that increase the excretion of heavy metals. The infusions usually include various vitamins and minerals in addition to the chelating agent.

Proponents typically assert that heavy metal toxicity is a major underlying cause of disease and that "detoxification" with chelation therapy is beneficial. For cardiovascular disease, they commonly claim that chelation blocks production of free radicals involved in a chain of reactions that result in atherosclerosis. This theory has no scientific support. Some chelationists claim that autism is caused by the accumulation of mercury from thimerosal (a preservative formerly used in several multidose vaccines), dental fillings, or environmental fallout from coal-fired power plants. However, many national and international studies have found no association between vaccination for any disease and autism. Moreover, autism prevalence and incidence have not dropped even though thimerosal was eliminated from childhood vaccines (except for multiuse vial flu) many years ago. Similarly, no association between dental fillings and autism has been demonstrated.

Because lead and mercury are ubiquitous in the environment, all individuals contain some in their body and regularly absorb some from food and water and excrete some in their feces and urine. Normal reference ranges for lead and mercury are well established for both blood and urine. Despite this, chelation promoters conduct tests purported to detect abnormal levels of lead, mercury, and other heavy metals. The most common is a urine test in which the specimen is collected six hours after a chelating drug is administered. This procedure—called "provoked testing" or "challenge testing"—temporarily raises the urine levels by forcing the harmlessly circulating amounts to be excreted faster. The collaborating lab then incorrectly compares the forced excretory levels to normal ones and reports the expected increase in levels as "elevated" or "very elevated" which the chelationist interprets as "heavy metal toxicity" for which detoxification is necessary.[1]

The name "EDTA" (ethylene diamine tetra-acetic acid) is commonly used to refer to two separate drugs: Disodium EDTA (edetate disodium, also known as endrate and generic versions) and calcium disodium EDTA (also known as calcium disodium EDTA and versenate). These drugs have significantly different effects and legal status.

Edetate disodium was approved many years ago only as an emergency treatment for certain patients with dangerously elevated blood calcium levels or a heart-rhythm disturbance due to digitalis toxicity. However, safer methods and drugs are now available for these purposes. Improper intravenous administration can cause fatal decreases in blood calcium levels. In 2008, after two such deaths were reported, the FDA issued a public warning, the only two licensed manufacturers withdrew their NDAs and the drug disappeared from the FDA list of approved drugs (*Orange Book*). Despite this, compounding pharmacies that cater to chelationists still prepare and sell it. Edetate disodium was never approved for heavy metal intoxication of any kind.

Calcium disodium edetate (CaEDTA, versenate) was approved many years ago to treat severe lead poisoning. It is still used for this purpose today, but few cases of lead exposure require it, and other agents are available. Calcium disodium EDTA must be used with caution as it can mobilize lead and lead to kidney damage. When required, it is safest if given intramuscularly. Intravenous use should be scrupulously monitored in a hospital setting with cardiac monitors and controlled drip pumps to assure slow instillation. CaEDTA is not approved for mercury intoxication.

No diagnosis of lead or mercury toxicity should be made unless the patient has symptoms of heavy-metal poisoning as well as a high non-provoked level (blood for lead and urine for mercury). Even if the blood level is above the normal range—as might occur in an unsafe workplace or by eating lead-containing paint—all that is usually needed is to avoid further exposure. Chelation therapy is rarely necessary and should be used only for acute exposure with severe symptoms. Real intoxications with mercury or other inorganic heavy metals are extremely rare and can be confirmed with nerve conduction velocity studies that show conduction delayed by the toxic agent. In most cases, the body will naturally excrete the agent, so removal from the source is the only treatment needed.

The protocols used by chelationists differ greatly from standard protocols for treating true lead poisoning. Whereas standard therapy is guided by clinical disappearance of symptoms and by blood levels and is usually completed within a few weeks, chelation for unsubstantiated uses may be administered over many months or even years.

No well-designed clinical trial has found any benefit of chelation therapy for atherosclerosis, autism, or any serious chronic disease. Four well-designed trials involving cardiovascular disease have been negative, one for ischemic heart disease and three for intermittent claudication. Fatalities have been reported among patients who relied on chelation rather than standard treatment for coronary heart disease.[2]

Chelation therapists sometimes use DMSA or DMPS instead of disodium or calcium EDTA. DMSA is an FDA-approved oral agent for treating metal poisoning. DMPS lacks approval in the United States but is prepared and distributed by compounding pharmacies who cater to chelationists. DMPS can cause serious adverse effects.

Patients with iron overload conditions are legitimately treated with other approved chelating agents such as desferoxamine. Although this treatment is referred to as "chelation therapy," the term is more commonly used to refer to irresponsible use of chelation agents as noted above.

B. Excessive Antibiotic Usage for Alleged "Chronic Lyme Disease"

Lyme disease is a deer tick-borne spirochetal infection that is easily cured with oral antibiotics if diagnosed within a few months after the infection begins. Mainstream physicians have shown that the infectious agent can be eradicated with two-round weeks of antibiotic treatment. The most common regimen is for oral doxycycline to be given twice daily for three weeks. Thus, after a normal course of antibiotic therapy the organism is killed. If treatment is not timely, neurologic, cardiac, or joint abnormalities may follow. Because such symptoms are common to many other diseases and conditions, when Lyme disease is suspected, the patient should be diagnosed using the U.S. Centers for Disease Control and Prevention (CDC) criteria for Lyme disease.[3]

These criteria call for initial ELISA and then specific confirmatory Western Blot DNA testing.

Most exposures to deer ticks do not result in Lyme disease. Most such ticks do not carry the Lyme spirochete, and transmission takes more than 24 hours of tick contact with the patient. Other tick-borne diseases can be confused with Lyme disease. Even when Lyme is correctly diagnosed, many of these later symptoms are not due to the presence of the organism, but are rheumatologic in nature. Despite any evidence of persistent organisms, a small network of so-called "Lyme-literate" physicians and patients believe that Lyme frequently becomes chronic and requires months or even years of antibiotic treatment. In many cases, these patients never had Lyme disease and, if truly sick, have another illness or condition.

The long-term intravenous antibiotic therapy administered to Lyme patients can have disastrous results. During the early 1990s, for example, the CDC described 25 cases of antibiotic-associated biliary complications among persons with suspected disseminated Lyme disease. All patients had received intravenous ceftriaxone for an average of 28 days for suspected Lyme disease. (Ceftriaxone can form precipitates in the presence of bile salts. The resulting "sludge" can block the bile duct.) Twelve patients subsequently developed gallstones. Fourteen underwent cholecystectomy to correct bile blockage. Twenty-two developed catheter-associated bloodstream infections. Yet most of the patients lacked documented evidence of disseminated Lyme disease or even antibodies to the Lyme spirochete.[4]

A 1993 report concluded that for most patients with a positive Lyme antibody titer and only symptoms of fatigue or nonspecific muscle pains, the risks and costs of intravenous antibiotic therapy exceed the benefits. Two more recent trials of patients claiming to suffer from chronic Lyme disease found that treatment with intravenous and oral antibiotics for 90 days did not improve symptoms more than placebo.[5]

In 2006, the Infectious Diseases Society of America (IDSA) published guidelines for effective intravenous (and oral) antibiotic regimens to treat various manifestations of Lyme disease. Under pressure by the Connecticut Attorney General, the IDSA appointed a new guideline committee, but there is no reason to believe the guidelines will be significantly modified. The European Concerted Action on Lyme Borreliosis (EUCALB) has also published recommendations for treating Lyme disease with various oral and intravenous antibiotics. In 2007, the ad hoc International Lyme Disease Study Group concluded:

> Chronic Lyme disease is the latest in a series of syndromes that have been postulated in an attempt to attribute medically unexplained symptoms to particular infections. Other examples that have now lost credibility are "chronic candida syndrome" and "chronic Epstein-Barr virus infection." The assumption that chronic, subjective symptoms are caused by persistent infection with *B. burgdorferi* is not supported by carefully conducted laboratory studies or by controlled laboratory studies or by controlled treatment trials. Chronic Lyme disease, which is equated with chronic *B. burgdorferi* infection, is a misnomer, and the use of prolonged dangerous, and expensive antibiotic treatments for it is not warranted.[6]

C. Human Growth Hormone for "Anti-Aging" Purposes

Human growth hormone (HGH)—also called somatotropin—which is secreted by the pituitary gland, promotes growth during childhood and adolescence. Growth hormone acts on the liver and other tissues to stimulate production of insulin-like growth factor I (IGF-I), which is responsible for the hormone's growth-promoting effects and also reflects the amount produced. Blood levels of circulating IGF-I tend to decrease as people age or become obese. Many marketers claim falsely that boosting HGH blood levels can reduce body fat; build muscle; improve sex life, sleep quality, vision and memory; restore hair growth and color; strengthen the immune system; normalize blood sugar; increase energy; and "turn back your body's biological clock."

In 1990, *The New England Journal of Medicine* published a study that attracted mainstream media attention. The study involved 12 men, aged 61 to 81, who were apparently healthy but had IGF-I levels below those found in normal young men. The men were given growth hormone injections three times a week for six months and compared with nine men who received no treatment. The treatment resulted in a decrease in fatty tissue and increases in muscle mass and lumbar spine density.[7] An accompanying editorial warned that some of the subjects had experienced side effects and that the long-range effects of administering HGH to healthy adults were unknown. It also warned that the hormone shots were expensive and that the study had not examined whether the men who received the hormone had substantially improved their muscle strength, mobility, or quality of life.[8] Despite the warning, the study inspired many offbeat physicians to market themselves as "anti-aging specialists." Many such physicians offer expensive tests that supposedly determine the patient's "biological age," which they promise to lower with expensive hormone shots and dietary supplements. Studies that have followed the 1990 NEJM report confirm the effects of growth hormone on body composition but do not show improvement in function.[9] In contrast, resistance training improves muscle strength and function, indicating that real effort is beneficial.

HGH is useful for treating growth hormone deficiency in children and adults and has several other proven (FDA-approved) uses. But the American Association of Clinical Endocrinologists has warned against using growth hormone as an anti-aging treatment or for patients with ordinary obesity.[9]

Although growth hormone levels decline with age, it has not been proven that trying to maintain the levels that exist in young persons is beneficial. Age-related hormonal changes might serve as useful markers of physiological aging. However, this has not been demonstrated experimentally for either humans or animals. Although hormone-replacement trials have yielded some positive short-term results, it is clear that negative side effects can occur in the form of increased risk for cancer, cardiovascular disease, and behavior changes. Considering the high cost, significant side effects, and lack of proven effectiveness, HGH shots appear to be a very poor investment.

It is illegal to sell HGH without a prescription. So-called "growth-hormone releasers," oral "growth hormone," and "homeopathic HGH" products are fakes.

In 2007, the College Pharmacy of Colorado Springs, Colorado, its owner (pharmacist Thomas Bader) and two salesmen were indicted by a federal grand jury for illegally importing and distributing HGH from China. The indictment charged that the defendants obtained Chinese-manufactured HGH that lacked FDA approval and repackaged and sold it to physicians throughout the United States. In response to the indictment, the Colorado Board of Pharmacy revoked Bader's license. In 2008, the U.S. government and the pharmacy owners reached a civil agreement under which $3.5 million (representing the proceeds from illegal importation and sale of HGH) was forfeited.

D. "Bioidentical Hormones"

"Bioidentical hormone" is a marketing term meant to imply that some substance is biologically identical to a human hormone. There is no proof that this is true. The term is commonly applied to mixtures of plant-derived hormones that compounding pharmacists prepare and label as drugs. The products are claimed to be biochemically similar or identical to those produced by human ovaries. However, the relevant chemicals (steroids) in plants are not identical to those in humans. To make products that work in humans, raw materials from the plants must be synthetically converted to human hormones. More often than not, the substances promoted as "bioidentical" are not chemically identical, but are hormones in the same class. Promoters assume that they perform identically to known human hormones, but this has not been substantiated. To the extent that they are potent in any way, the so-called "bioidentical" products would pose the same risks as those of standard hormones—plus whatever problems might be introduced during compounding.

For many years, the evidence-based scientific medical community believed that hormone replacement therapy (HRT) at any age would reduce the risk of heart attack and stroke. This hope was dashed when the Women's Health Initiative Study found that taking estrogen plus progestin for more than five years places postmenopausal women at risk for heart attacks, strokes, and several other serious problems. HRT (using low doses of an estrogen such as estradiol) is now mainly prescribed for the short-term treatment of postmenopausal symptoms that interfere with the woman's ability to function. Because of risks of ovarian and breast cancer from end-organ stimulation by estrogen and estrogen-like compounds, the use of HRT is discouraged for long-term or routine use.

The risk involved in prescribing a hormonal product depends on its chemical composition and biochemical properties, not on how it was made. However, many offbeat physicians are prescribing compounded "bioidentical" products as though they are safer than standard prescription drug products. In 2005, the American College of Obstetricians and Gynecologists warned against these products and the saliva tests typically used by those who prescribe them.[10]

In 2008, the FDA ordered seven compounding pharmacies to stop making illegal claims about "bioidentical hormone replacement therapy (BHRT)" products. The companies were told that the FDA regards "bioidentical" as a marketing term that implies a benefit for which there is no medical or scientific basis. Some were also making unsupportable claims that their drugs are better than FDA-approved menopausal hormone therapy drugs and can be used to prevent and treat serious diseases such as Alzheimer's disease, stroke, and various forms of cancer. Some products contained estriol as well as progesterone and estrogen. No drug product containing estriol is FDA-approved, and its safety and effectiveness are unknown.

32.4 OTC Drugs

OTC drugs must be generally regarded by experts as safe and effective and suitable for self-use by consumers. In 1972, the FDA began an extensive evaluation to ensure the effectiveness and safety of OTC drugs. Rather than attempting to evaluate hundreds of thousands of individual products, it divided the ingredients into categories and appointed expert advisory panels to evaluate the categories. The first phase of the review spanned about 10 years and covered 722 ingredients. After advisory panels concluded that only one-third of these ingredients were safe and effective, manufacturers reformulated many products by removing unsafe and ineffective ingredients or by adding others. In addition, some prescription-drug ingredients were approved for use in OTC drugs, generally in lower dosages. Today, except for homeopathic products, the vast majority of OTC drugs are backed by scientific evidence that they are safe and effective for their intended purposes.

32.5 Vitamins, Minerals, and Other Dietary Supplements

The *Federal Food, Drug, and Cosmetic Act* defines a "drug" as any article (except devices) "intended for use in the diagnosis, cure, mitigation, treatment, or prevention of disease" and "articles (other than food) intended to affect the structure or function of the body." Drugs that are not "generally recognized as safe and effective by experts" are "new drugs" that cannot be legally marketed without FDA approval. The pertinent laws and regulations permit the FDA to stop the marketing of "dietary supplements" with unsubstantiated "drug" claims on their labels.

To evade the law's intent, sellers use many channels to ensure that the public learns of "medicinal" uses that are not stated on product labels. This is done mainly by promoting the ingredients of the products in books, magazines, newsletters, booklets, lectures, radio and television broadcasts, oral claims by retailers, and communication through the Internet. Although these communications assert that various substances can function like drugs, the FDA lacks jurisdiction unless the claims are made directly in the labeling or advertising of the products.

Passage of the *Dietary Supplement Health and Education Act of 1994* (DSHEA) worsened this situation by increasing the amount of misinformation that can be *directly* transmitted to prospective customers. It also expanded the types of products that could be marketed as "supplements." The most logical definition of "dietary supplement" would be something that supplies one or more essential nutrients missing from the diet. DSHEA went far beyond this to include under the term "supplement" any substance that contains vitamins, minerals, herbs or other botanicals, amino acids, or other dietary substances to supplement the diet by increasing dietary intake, and/or any concentrate, metabolite, constituent, extract, or combination of any such ingredients. Although many such products (particularly herbs) are marketed for their alleged preventive or therapeutic effects, DSHEA has made it difficult or impossible for the FDA to regulate them as drugs. Since DSHEA's passage, even chelating agents (DMSA) and hormones, such as dehydroepiandrosterone (DHEA), human growth hormone (HGH), and melatonin, have been hawked as supplements. The law does not require "dietary supplements" to be proven effective before marketing. Technically, under DSHEA, they are considered foods.

DSHEA also prohibits the FDA from banning dubious supplement ingredients as "unapproved food additives." During the 1980s, the FDA considered this strategy more efficient than taking action against individual manufacturers that made illegal drug claims. Because of the passage of DSHEA, the only way to banish an ingredient is to prove it is unsafe. Ingredients that are useless but harmless are protected.

The marketplace would be safer if the FDA could regulate the upper dosage limits of vitamins and minerals and could hold other nutritional supplements to at least the same standards as those for OTC drugs. However, DSHEA prevents the FDA from doing this unless a product poses an imminent hazard.

Because manufacturers are not required to submit safety information before marketing "dietary supplements," the FDA must rely on adverse event reports, product sampling, information in the scientific literature, and other sources for evidence of danger. Because the FDA is unable to monitor and regulate thousands of individual products, the public is virtually unprotected against supplements and herbs that are unsafe.

The agency is permitted to restrict substances that pose a "significant and unreasonable risk" under the conditions of use on the label or as commonly consumed. The FDA has the burden of proof and cannot act until substantial harm occurs to consumers.

The Dietary Supplement and Nonprescription Drug Consumer Protection Act, which took effect in December 2007, requires manufacturers of OTC drugs and dietary supplements to notify the FDA when serious adverse events are reported to them by consumers or healthcare professionals. However, even when harm is obvious, instituting a ban can take years. For example, even though thousands of consumers appeared to have been harmed by ephedra-containing products, it took the FDA more than five years and a lengthy court battle to go through the procedures needed to ban its use in doses above 10 mg per pill.

32.6 "Nutritional Support" Statements

DSHEA allows dietary supplements to bear "statements of support" that (1) claim a benefit related to classical nutrient-deficiency disease, (2) describe how ingredients affect the structure or function of the human body, (3) characterize the documented mechanism by which the ingredients act to maintain the body's structure or function, and (4) describe general well-being from consumption of the ingredients. To be legal under DSHEA, a "nutritional support" statement must not be a "drug" claim. In other words, it should not suggest that the product or ingredient is intended for the prevention or treatment of disease. However, the marketplace has been flooded by statements related to organs (such as "supports the eyes" or "supports the cardiovascular system") that deliver an equivalent message.

Actually, few statements about the biochemical or physiologic properties of nutrients have practical value for consumers. By definition, every essential nutrient is important to proper body function. Simple statements about nutrient function are more likely to be misleading than helpful. A statement such as "vitamin A is essential to good eye function" could suggest that (1) people need to take special steps to be sure they get enough, (2) extra vitamin A may enhance eyesight, and (3) common eye problems may be caused by vitamin A deficiency or remedied by taking supplements. A "nutritional support" statement about vitamin A, to be entirely true, would have to counter all three of these misconceptions and indicate that people eating sensibly do not need to worry about whether their vitamin A intake is adequate. In other words, truthful statements about nutrient supplements would have to indicate who does *not* need them. No vitamin manufacturer has ever done this or ever will. Because herbs are not nutrients, the concept of "nutritional support" statements for herbs is absurd. Yet thousands of herbal products are marketed with claims that they support various body functions.

Under DSHEA, manufacturers who make statements of "nutritional support" are supposed to have substantiation that such statements are truthful and not misleading. The law also requires that the Secretary of Health and Human Services (HHS) be notified no later than 30 days after the first marketing of a supplement for which the statement is being made. DSHEA does not define substantiation.

Historically, the FDA has considered literature used directly in connection with the sale of a product to be "labeling" for the product. DSHEA exempts publications from "labeling" if they (1) are not false or misleading, (2) do not promote a particular manufacturer or brand, (3) present a balanced view of pertinent scientific information, and (4) are physically separated from the items discussed. However, because substantial percentages of "dietary supplements" are useless, irrationally formulated, or overpriced, the supplement industry has little reason to provide literature that is not misleading. In addition, the FDA does not have the resources to police the huge numbers of "support" statements to ensure that they are appropriately "balanced."

The passage of DSHEA was spearheaded by an avalanche of communication to Congress from people who expressed fears that without special protection, consumers would lose their freedom to buy vitamins. These fears were unfounded, but many congressional representatives concluded that the FDA should be restrained.[11]

Ironically, by the time DSHEA was enacted, the OTC drug review had rid the marketplace of nearly all of the standard OTC products that had been marketed with unsubstantiated claims. In contrast, few "dietary supplements" promoted with disease-related claims can live up to such claims. In 1999, a review of 964 herbs and dietary supplement products listed in the Natural Medicines Comprehensive Database found that only 15 percent had been proven safe, and only 11 percent had been proven effective for the indications for which they were advocated.[12] These numbers may have been overly optimistic, however, because "effective" products can be impractical because they are less effective or cost-effective than proven drug products.

A 2001 Roper survey of 1,480 persons age 50 or older found that about 75 percent of the respondents wanted the government to review safety data and approve dietary supplements before sale and to verify all health-related claims before they can be included in advertisements and on product labels.[13] This is just the opposite of what DSHEA permits, but there is little hope that Congress will modify its provisions. (For a complete review of DSHEA, see Chapter 2, *Dietary Supplement and Health Education Act of 1994*.)

32.7 Herbal Problems

Many herbs contain hundreds or even thousands of chemicals that have not been completely characterized or cataloged. Some of these chemicals may turn out to be useful as therapeutic agents, but others could prove harmful. No legal standards exist for the processing, harvesting, or packaging of medicinal herbs, and the FDA does not require herbal products to adhere to any standards of identity or dosage. Many investigations have found that the amounts of the ingredients listed on herbal product labels are inaccurate. Moreover, many practitioners who recommend, dispense, or sell herbal products are non-physicians who are not qualified to make appropriate diagnoses or to determine how herbs compare with proven drugs. Thus, even if a substance is potentially useful, consumers cannot be certain what is in them or how to use them.

Herbs in their natural state can vary greatly from batch to batch and often contain chemicals that cause side effects but provide no benefit. Surveys conducted in the United States have found that the ingredients and doses of various products vary considerably from brand to brand and even between lots of the same product.[14] For example, researchers at the University of Arkansas tested 20 "supplement" products containing ephedra (ma huang) and found that half the products exhibited discrepancies of 20 percent or more between the label claim and the actual content, and one product contained no ephedra alkaloids. Ephedra products are marketed as "energy boosters" or "thermogenic" diet aids, even though no published clinical trials substantiate that they are safe or effective for these purposes. The researchers also noted that hundreds of such products are marketed and that their number exceeds that of conventional prescription and non-prescription ephedra products, which are FDA-approved as decongestants.[15] Studies have also found that the recommended dosage can vary greatly from product to product.

OTC combinations of ephedrine and caffeine were removed from the market in the 1980s by the FDA due to hundreds of reports of adverse events—tachycardia, arrhythmias, heart attacks, psychoses, strokes, and other serious medical events. Nevertheless, some ephedra marketers have spiked "natural" ephedra products with high doses of caffeine to increase their product's pharmacologic effect. Once FDA regulatory action against ephedra/cola nut products was taken, supplement sellers were quick to substitute similar agents in redesigned products.

Many herbal products have been found to contain known toxic substances. Extracts of kava, for example, have been implicated in liver-related injuries including hepatitis, cirrhosis, and liver failure leading to death.

To make a rational decision about an herbal product, it would be necessary to know what it contains, whether it is safe, how it interacts with drugs or other herbs, and whether it has been demonstrated to be as good, or better, than pharmaceutical products available for the same purpose. For most herbal ingredients, this information is incomplete or unavailable.

The FDA could improve this situation by establishing a special category of OTC drugs called "traditional herbal remedies." These products could then be marketed with less-than-standard proof of effectiveness provided that (1) reasonable evidence exists that they are safe and effective, (2) labels identify the name and quantity of each active ingredient, (3) indications are restricted to non-serious, self-limiting conditions, (4) labels contain adequate directions for use, including a warning about inappropriate self-treatment, and (5) adverse reactions are reported.

Products should also be produced by good manufacturing processes (GMP) and checked regularly for purity and consistency of ingredients. These standards are similar to the current OTC standards. However, even if the products were improved, only a few herbs have been studied enough to conclude that they might be effective, and even fewer have been studied enough to determine whether their use is practical.

Garlic provides an example of research-based support that does not necessarily make its use practical. Although some garlic preparations have been demonstrated to lower cholesterol, prescription drugs are more potent for this purpose, and garlic's anticoagulant properties could pose a significant risk. No data are available to quantify the risk of combining garlic with other widely used products (vitamin E, Ginkgo, fish oil, or aspirin, for instance) that can interfere with blood clotting.

Adulteration, which can be accidental or deliberate, is another problem. Many herbal products have been found to contain prescription or OTC drugs and dangerous heavy metals. In 1998, for example, the California Department of Health reported that 32 percent of Asian herbal medicines sold in that state contained undeclared pharmaceuticals or heavy metals.[16] A subsequent study of more than 500 Chinese herbal medicines found that about 10 percent of them contained undeclared drugs or toxic levels of metals.[17] The FDA and other investigators have also detected sildenafil, colchicine, adrenal steroids, alprazolam, and other prescription-drug ingredients in many products claimed to contain only natural ingredients.

Products that contained ephedrine alkaloids or steroid precursors have caused several prominent athletes to be disqualified after their urine tested positive for banned substances.

Although drugs are subject to rigorous quality control to ensure the nature, potency, and safety of their ingredients, dietary supplements and herbs are not. In 2007, the FDA issued regulations to require current good manufacturing practices (CGMPs) for dietary supplements. The requirements include provisions related to (1) the design and construction of physical plants that facilitate maintenance, (2) cleaning, (3) proper manufacturing operations, (4) quality-control procedures, (5) testing final product or incoming and in-process materials, (6) handling consumer complaints, and (7) maintaining records. These regulations may reduce safety problems introduced during manufacturing but do not address the risk of using the products that are ineffective.

Consumer Lab (www.consumerlab.com), which has tested over 2,600 products since November 1999, reported in March 2010 that 19 percent of the vitamins and minerals, 22 percent of the other supplements, and 47 percent of the herbals failed their evaluations. The most common reason for the failure was too little or none of the main ingredient. The other problems included too much active ingredient; the wrong ingredient; potentially dangerous or illegal ingredients; contamination with heavy metals, pesticides, or pathogens; "spiking" with unexpected ingredients; poor disintegration (which affects absorption); and misleading or incomplete product information.

The entry of drug companies into the herbal marketplace could result in dosage standardization for some products, and public and professional interest in herbs are likely to stimulate more research. However, with safe and effective medicines available, treatment with herbs rarely makes sense, and many of the conditions for which herbs are recommended are not suitable for self-treatment.

32.8 Homeopathic Products

Homeopathy dates back to the late 1700s, when a German physician named Samuel Hahnemann began formulating its basic principles. Proponents postulate that (1) diseases represent a disturbance in the body's ability to heal itself, (2) only a small stimulus is needed to begin the healing process,

(3) substances that produce symptoms in healthy people can cure similar symptoms in sick people ("law of similars"), and (4) remedies become more potent with greater dilution. The word "homeopathy" is derived from the Greek words *homoios* (similar) and *pathos* (suffering or disease).

Homeopathic products are derived from minerals, botanical substances, zoological substances, microorganisms, and several other sources. Soluble sources are serially diluted with distilled water or alcohol. Insoluble sources are pulverized and mixed with milk sugar. One part of the diluted mixture is diluted again, and the process is repeated to reach the desired concentration. Serial dilutions of 1:10 are designated by the Roman numeral "X" (for example, 1X = 1/10, 3X = 1/1,000, and 6X = 1/1,000,000). Serial dilutions of 1:100 are expressed with the Roman numeral "C" (1C = 1/100, 3C = 1/1,000,000, and so on.) Most products range from 6X to 30C, but some carry designations as high as 1,000X.

Dilution beyond Avogadro's number (6.022×10^{23}), will lose the original substance altogether. This limit corresponds to 12C or 24X potencies (one part in 10^{24}). But proponents claim that vigorous shaking ("succussion") or pulverizing between dilutions would leave behind a spirit-like essence that cures by reviving the body's "vital force." Proponents also postulate that the solute retains a "memory" of the substance. If this were true, every substance encountered by a molecule of water, alcohol, or milk sugar might imprint an "essence" that could exert powerful and unpredictable medicinal effects.

Many proponents allege that homeopathic products resemble vaccines because both provide a small stimulus that triggers an immune response. This comparison is not valid. The amounts of active ingredients in vaccines are much greater and are measurable. Immunizations produce measurable antibodies, but ultradilute homeopathic products have no measurable active ingredients and produce no measurable response. In addition, vaccines are used preventively, not for curing symptoms.

Homeopathy was given legal status by the 1938 *Federal Food, Drug, and Cosmetic Act*, whose chief sponsor, Senator Royal Copeland, was also a homeopathic physician.[18] One provision of this law recognizes as drugs all substances included in the *Homœopathic Pharmacopœia of the United States*. The current (ninth) edition of this book[19] provides protocols for preparing more than 1,200 substances for homeopathic use but says nothing about how those substances should be used. Manufacturers and practitioners decide that.

The basis for formulating homeopathic products is not clinical testing but homeopathic "provings," during which substances are administered to healthy people who record their thoughts and physical sensations over various periods of time. The reported symptoms have been compiled into lengthy reference books, called *materia medica*, which proponents regard as gospel and use to match the patient's symptoms to "corresponding" products. However, most of the provings were done between 100 and 200 years ago, when medical science was in its infancy. Very little was known about the nature of health and disease or about how to conduct experiments that separate cause and effect from coincidence.

"Classical" homeopaths purport to tailor their prescriptions to the individual patient based on a detailed history. Some practitioners maintain that certain people have special affinity to a particular remedy (called their "constitutional remedy") to which they will respond for a variety of ailments. However, most practitioners prescribe products targeted at symptoms rather than at the individual's "constitution." Some practitioners select remedies with the help of a galvanometer purported to measure "electromagnetic energy imbalances" responsible for disease.[20]

The fact that a symptom occurs after taking a substance can have several explanations. During a typical day, most people experience occasional unpleasant thoughts and bodily sensations. To determine whether a substance actually causes a symptom, it would be necessary to compare people who receive the substance with people who receive a control substance. To guard against bias, neither the experimenters nor the test subjects should know who received which.

The provings used to compile *materia medica* were not conducted in that way. There were wide variations in the amounts of substances administered, the timing of the administrations, the way in which data were recorded, and the length of the studies—and there were no controls.[21] Thus, it is impossible to know whether the reported symptoms were actually related to the administration of the test substances. In addition, many symptoms may have resulted from the suggestibility of the test subjects. In most cases, participants have known which substances were administered. Potencies have ranged from the undiluted original substance to dilutions as high as 200C. Provings also constitute the basis for inclusion in the *Homœopathic Pharmacopœia*.

A Dictionary of Practical Materia Medica, a widely used three-volume set authored by John Henry Clarke, M.D., illustrates the foolishness involved in provings.[22] The book contains about 2,500 pages that describe the symptoms that supposedly were reported following administration of about 1,200 substances. Most descriptive pages contain more than 100 claims, which means that the total number of symptoms exceeds 200,000. The book does not indicate when or how the original "provings" were done or who reported most of the specific findings. Thus, it would be impossible to examine whether the studies were properly done, who did them, and whether the findings were accurately reported.

Many of the listed symptoms are odd. *Lac felinum* includes "cannot bear the smell of clams, of which she is naturally fond." *Latrodectus mactans* includes "screams fearfully, exclaiming that she would lose her breath and die." *Magnesia sulphurica* includes "stupidity." *Oleum animale* includes "singing, tinkling, and buzzing in ears." *Natrum carbonicum* includes "hurries out of bed in the morning." Some listings include symptoms that occur predominantly on one side of the body, such as "sickening sensation in left testicle." All are supposedly useful in determining whether the patient might "fit" a particular remedy.

Even if the proving reports were consistent, there is no logical reason why substances that could produce symptoms should cure such symptoms. Nor is there evidence from appropriately designed studies that the "law of similars" actually operates. The real way to test whether something works is to test whether it helps sick people. This requires clinical trials in which people who receive the test substance are compared with people who do not. No research has demonstrated that homeopathic products offer any practical benefit.[23] No homeopathic product has ever been proven effective; and the vast majority of products have never even been clinically tested.

Even if results could be consistently produced, the most that the study of a single remedy for a single disease could prove is that the remedy is effective against that disease. It would not validate homeopathy's basic theories or prove that homeopathic treatment is useful for other diseases. *The Medical Letter on Drugs and Therapeutics* has concluded that, "The chemical content of homeopathic products is often undefined, and some are so diluted that they are unlikely to contain any of the original material. These products have not been proven effective for any clinical condition. There is no good reason to use them."[24]

Some proponents rationalize that homeopathic remedies are not testable like standard drugs because treatment must be individualized. However, most OTC homeopathic products are mixtures marketed directly to consumers.

Sanum therapy—used by a small network of misguided practitioners—is based upon the medically disputed concept of pleomorphism, which holds that microorganisms can shift from one form to another in response to environmental influences. It was developed by Günther Enderlein (1872-1968), who theorized that tiny microorganisms called "protits" normally circulate harmlessly throughout the body but can change into disease-producing bacteria or fungi if exposed

to various internal or environmental triggers. Sanum remedies are dilutions of bacteria or fungi that are said to work homeopathically against more than 300 diseases. Given by injection, these products have serious potential for indirect harm when prescribed instead of standard treatment. State dental boards have taken action against four dentists who included Sanum remedies in their practice.

Although the FDA could insist that homeopathic products be proven effective by scientific testing to remain marketable, it has not chosen to do so. Its regulations merely state that homeopathic drugs cannot be offered without prescription for such serious conditions as cancer, AIDS, or any other requiring diagnosis and treatment by a licensed practitioner. Non-prescription homeopathics may be sold only for self-limiting conditions recognizable by consumers.[25] No homeopathic product has FDA approval as a result of having an NDA approved. Products offered for conditions not amenable to OTC use can be marketed as prescription products, the labels of which generally make no claims. The FDA database of warning letters indicates that between 2002 and 2009 the agency ordered 18 manufacturers to stop making illegal claims, mostly for products falsely claimed to be as effective as or better than standard vaccines. However, it has ignored the vast majority of complaints about homeopathic products brought to its attention.

If the FDA required homeopathic remedies to be proven effective in order to remain marketable—the standard it applies to other categories of drugs—homeopathy would face extinction in the United States. However, there is no indication that the agency is considering this. FDA officials regard homeopathy as relatively benign (compared, for example, to unsubstantiated products marketed for cancer and AIDS) and believe that other problems should get enforcement priority. If the FDA attacks homeopathy too vigorously, its proponents might even persuade a lobby-susceptible Congress to rescue them.

In 1994, 42 prominent critics of quackery and pseudoscience asked the agency to curb the sale of homeopathic products.[26] The petition urged the FDA to initiate a rulemaking procedure to require that all OTC homeopathic drugs meet the same standards of safety and effectiveness as non-homeopathic OTC drugs. It also asked for a public warning that although the FDA has permitted homeopathic remedies to be sold, it does not recognize them as effective. The FDA did not officially respond to the petition. However, in 1998, at a symposium sponsored by *Good Housekeeping* magazine, former FDA Commissioner David A. Kessler, M.D., J.D., acknowledged that homeopathic remedies do not work but that he did not attempt to ban them because he felt that Congress would not support a ban. Although regulations require the FDA to respond within 180 days, it failed to do so.

32.9 Deceptive "Informed Consent" and Illicit Research

Chelation therapists and similar fringe providers commonly ask patients to sign consent forms designed to protect themselves rather than their patients. They may, for example, state that a treatment has not been substantiated but fail to indicate that it lacks a scientifically plausible rationale and is therefore senseless to use. They may say that the treatment is "believed to be effective" by many doctors, but fail to indicate that the proponents represent a tiny minority of physicians. Some consent forms pretend that the treatment is part of a legitimate research study when it is not. Some forms provide blanket consent for "alternative and complementary" medical treatment without specifying what will be used. Many acknowledge that the patient has been told the risks but agrees to hold the provider harmless if trouble occurs. However, public policy does not permit people to sign away their right to be protected against fraud or negligence. Thus, although injured patients might believe they have no redress, contracts of this type are unlikely to stand up in court.

Some provider networks have even formed sham institutional review boards so that their treatment has a veneer of legitimate research.

32.10 Government Jurisdiction

The FDA has jurisdiction over advertising of prescription drugs and labeling of all drug and biological products. To combat wrongdoing, the agency can issue warning letters, initiate seizures or criminal prosecution, and issue alerts to block importation of products from other countries.

The Federal Trade Commission (FTC) has jurisdiction over the advertising of non-prescription products that are marketed in interstate commerce. Although the FTC has a very powerful law, the agency can handle only a small percentage of the violations it detects. The U.S. Postal Service has overlapping jurisdiction over products sold by mail. It also has a strong law, but has not pursued falsely advertised health products since the early 1990s.

State Attorneys General have jurisdiction over business conduct that affects the citizens within their own state. If a marketer is headquartered within the state, an Attorney General's action can have nationwide impact. Coordinated multi-state actions can also have nationwide impact. However, state Attorney General actions involving dietary supplement claims or dangers are rare.

Licensed practitioners are regulated by their respective state licensing boards. Unlicensed practitioners are subject to regulation by their state Attorney General.

32.11 Recommended Reforms

Government agencies have never had sufficient resources to cope with the enormous amount of deception in the marketing of herbs, dietary supplements, and homeopathic products. DSHEA made the problem worse. Without an adequate law, the FDA cannot curb the deceptive marketing of what DSHEA calls "dietary supplements." Regulators have the power to ban homeopathic remedies but have shown no interest in doing so.

In matters of health, there should be no tolerance for wrongdoing. In line with that philosophy, the following measures are needed:

- DSHEA should be repealed.
- The FDA should be authorized to set safe upper limits for vitamin dosage.
- Other dietary supplements and herbal remedies should be held to regulatory standards that are at least as stringent as those for OTC drug products. At the very least, active ingredients should be required to meet standards for purity, content, safety, and some level of effectiveness before they can be marketed.
- Chelation therapists, other fringe practitioners, and the compounding pharmacies that supply them should be more closely regulated.
- Homeopathic products should be banned. If that is not politically feasible, the FDA should issue a public warning that none of them has been proven effective.
- At present, marketers who make unsubstantiated health claims are not penalized when the FDA warns them to stop. The FDA should be permitted to generate civil penalties in connection with warning letters.
- The effectiveness of state Attorneys General could be greatly increased by permitting them to seek federal-court injunctions that would apply throughout the U.S.

32.12 Recommended Information Sources

Several sources provide reliable information on dietary supplements, herbs, and homeopathic products. Some recommended information sources include the following:

- The *Natural Medicines Comprehensive Database* provides information about more than 1,400 herbal and dietary supplement ingredients. It is available online or in print for $92 per year (or $132 for both versions).[27]

- *AboutHerbs*, a project of Memorial Sloan-Kettering Cancer Center (New York, New York), evaluates more than 300 herbs, dietary supplements, and "alternative" cancer treatments.[28] Both "professional" and consumer versions are provided, but most of the professional information is readily understandable by laypeople. The articles are shorter than their counterparts in the *Natural Medicines* database, but they are researched and written quite well.

- *ConsumerLab.com*, which has moderately priced subscriptions for more detailed information, posts product evaluations that include the results of laboratory tests of ingredient levels.

- *Herbal Medicines: A Guide for Healthcare Professionals* (Third Edition) contains 152 detailed herbal monographs.[29]

- *Snake Oil Science: The Truth about Complementary and Alternative Medicine* describes how research is done and examines the evidence related to dietary supplements, herbal and homeopathic products, and other controversial products and practices.[30]

- *Basic and Clinical Pharmacology* includes an excellent review of dietary supplements and herbals.[31]

Endnotes

1. S. Barrett. *How the "urine toxic metals" test is used to defraud patients.* Quackwatch website. Last retrieved March 5, 2010, from www.quackwatch.org/t.

2. K. Atwood, et al. *Why the NIH Trial to Assess Chelation Therapy (TACT) should be abandoned.* Medscape Journal of Medicine. (2008) 10(5):115. Last retrieved from www.ncbi.nlm.nih.gov/pmc/articles/PMC2438277.

3. *Lyme disease diagnosis.* CDC Web site. Last retrieved from www.cdc.gov/ncidod/dvbid/lyme/ld_humandisease_diagnosis.htm.

4. P.J. Ettestad, et al. *Biliary complications in the treatment of uncomplicated Lyme disease.* J. Infectious Dis.(1995)171:356-361.

5. R.W. Lightfoot, Jr., et al. *Empiric parenteral antibiotic treatment of patients with fibromyalgia and fatigue and a positive serologic result for Lyme disease. A cost-effectiveness analysis.* Ann. Int. Med. (1993)119:503-9.

6. H.M. Feder, et al. *A critical appraisal of "chronic Lyme disease.* N.E.J.M., (2007) 357:1422-30.

7. D. Rudman, et al. *Effects of human growth hormone on men over 60 years old.* N.E.J.M., (1990) 323:1-6.

8. M.L. Vance. *Growth hormone for the elderly?* N.E.J.M. (1990) 323:52-4.

9. J.M. Drazen. *Inappropriate advertising of dietary supplements.* N.E.J.M. (2003;348:777-8.

10. *ACOG reiterates stance on so-called "bioidentical" hormones.* American College of Obstetricians and Gynecologists press release. (Feb 3, 2009)

11. S. Barrett, and V. Herber. *The vitamin pushers: how the health food industry is selling america a bill of goods.* (1994) Amherst N.Y.: Prometheus Books.

12. A.T. Marty. *Natural medicines comprehensive database.* JAMA (2000) 283:2992.

13. Prevention Magazine staff. *Survey of consumer use of dietary supplements.* (1999) Emmaus, Pennsylvania: Rodale Press.

14. S. Barrett. *The herbal minefield, Quackwatch website.* Retrieved Jan 26, 2009 from www.quackwatch.org/01QuackeryRelatedTopics/herbs.html.

15. B.J. Gurley, et al. *Content versus label claims in ephedra-containing dietary supplements.* A. J. Health Sys. Pharm. (2000) 57,:963-5.

16. R.J. Ko. *Adulterants in Asian patent medicines.* NEJM. (1998) 339, 847.

17. A.M. Au, et al. *Screening methods for drugs and heavy metals in Chinese patent medicines.* Bull. Environ. Contam. Toxicol. (2000) 65:112.

18. S. W. Sjunod. *An alternative perspective: Homeopathic drugs, Royal Copeland, and federal drug regulation.* Pharmacy in History. (2000)42:13. Retrieved from www.homeowatch.org/history/reghx.html.

19. Homeopathic Pharmacopœia Revision Service, *Homeopathic Pharmacopœia Convention of the United States (HPCUS).*Homœopathic Pharmacopœia of the United States. (1988) Southeastern, P.A., 94.

20. S. Barrett. *"Electrodiagnostic" devices.* Quackwatch website, revised February 13, 2004. Retrieved from www.quackwatch.org/01QuackeryRelatedTopics/electro.html.

21. J.Y. Sherr. *The Dynamics and Methodology of Provings.* (1994) West Malvern, England Dynamis Books.

22. J.H. Clarke. *A dictionary of practical Materia Medica.* (1921) New Delhi, India: B. Jain Publishers. (Reprinted 2000)

23. E. Ernst. *Trick or treatment: the undeniable facts about alternative medicine.* (2008) New York: W.W. Norton. pp 91-143.

24. *Homeopathic products.* Med. Lett. Drug. Ther. (1999) 41(1047), 20–21.

25. Office of Regulatory Affairs. *Conditions Under Which Homeopathic Drugs May Be Marketed.* CPG 7132.15, Sec. 400.400, FDA, Rockville, M.D., Revised March 1995.

26. S. Barrett, et al. *Petition regarding homeopathic drugs.* Docket # 94P-0316/CP 1, Filed August 29, 1994.

27. Therapeutic Research Faculty. *Natural Medicines Comprehensive Database.* Retrieved from www.naturaldatabase.com.

28. Memorial Sloan-Kettering Cancer Center, Information Resource. *About Herbs, Botanicals, and Other Products.* Retrieved from: www.mskcc.org/mskcc/html/11570.cfm.

29. J. Barnes, L.A. Anderson, and J.D. Phillipson. *Herbal medicines: a guide for healthcare professionals.* (2007) London, UK: Pharmaceutical Press.

30. R. B. Bausell. *Snake oil science: the truth about complementary and alternative medicine.* (2007) New York: Oxford University Press.

31. C.E. Dennehy, C. Tsourounis. *Dietary supplements and herbal medications.* In B.G. Katzung, et al., Eds. (2009) *Basic and Clinical Pharmacology*, 11th Ed. New York: McGraw Hill/Lange.

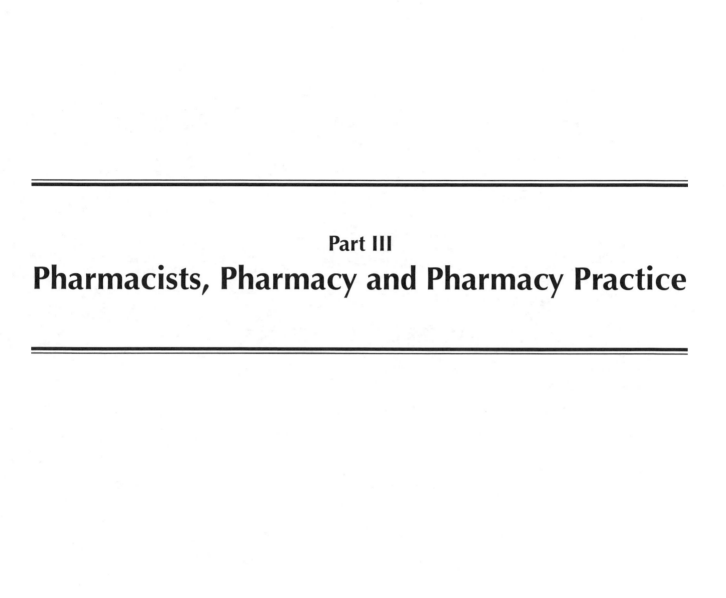

Part III
Pharmacists, Pharmacy and Pharmacy Practice

Chapter 33

Regulation of Pharmacy Practice

Ned Milenkovich, Pharm.D., J.D.

33.1 Introduction

The pharmacy profession, pharmacies, and supporting personnel—such as pharmacy technicians—are typically governed by the Pharmacy Practice Act (PPA) of a particular state. In turn, the PPA provides the state's Board of Pharmacy with the authority to promulgate regulations pursuant to the PPA and enforce statutory and regulatory provisions that govern the practice of pharmacy. Some states provide that a governing board of pharmacy has ultimate authority over the profession of pharmacy, while other states have reduced the role of the pharmacy board to that of an advisory panel to a greater state government entity.

Ultimately, the pharmaceutical profession and pharmacists licensed to practice in the profession are overseen by a governmental body charged with the task of protecting the public health by regulating the profession. This is achieved through (1) holding public meetings to address various issues affecting the profession and the public, (2) enforcement of the profession by carrying disciplinary hearings and adjudication when appropriate, and (3) promulgation of new regulations and making old regulations obsolete.

33.2 Board of Pharmacy Practice

Each state PPA describes how many state pharmacy board members will exist, how long the term will be for, how such an appointment takes place, and what the requirements are to be eligible for a board position. The PPA can be amended in any way by an act of the state legislature, along with a state governor signing the PPA into law (for any purpose). This is the only method by which such a provision can be changed.

Typically, a pharmacy board consists of a majority of licensed pharmacists with a few public members who are non-pharmacists. Some PPAs and pharmacy regulations require that each of the major sub-divisions of the profession be represented. For example, there might be a board member from retail pharmacy, hospital pharmacy, long-term care pharmacy, and the like.

In most states, a board member serves the state governor. In most PPAs, the governor is required to appoint the board member. Some states require the board member to run a campaign and be elected by the citizens of the state, but it is far more typical that the PPA calls for appointment by a governor. Some state PPAs require input from interest groups such as state pharmacy associations. While some state PPAs require each pharmacy professional segment be represented, many states do not have such a provision. This has been criticized by some pharmacy stakeholders not represented on a state board of pharmacy, who believe that a lack of knowledge of the intricacies of the particular professional segment leads to the development of laws and regulations that do not take into account the needs of that segment.

Once a board member obtains membership on a state board of pharmacy, there are many opportunities for being involved in the governance of the pharmacy profession. Typically, several public meetings are held throughout the course of a year, in which issues affecting the public are discussed. During these public meetings, a multitude of issues are addressed that may range from a limited impact on a particular and specific pharmaceutical entity to the entire profession and beyond. Often, stakeholders are present at these public meetings to provide input and knowledge to the pharmacy board. In particular, representatives from state pharmacy associations are invariably present, as well as major stakeholders from representative pharmacies who are interested in tracking regulatory developments.

In addition, state pharmacy board members are often faced with dealing with disciplinary challenges in regard to pharmacy, pharmacist, and pharmacy technician violations of laws or regulations. Hearings before a pharmacy board are common and range in the form of licensure issues, theft of drugs, drug diversion, drug abuse, and other broad-ranging violations of the PPA and regulatory construct. Pharmacy board members, in concert with state prosecutors, typically hold informal hearings and offer settlement opportunities prior to escalation of the adjudicatory process to an administrative judge or the judicial system.

33.3 Licensure Process to Practice Pharmacy

The process of becoming a licensed pharmacist begins with enrollment in an accredited pharmacy school. In addition to obtaining the standard curriculum from the accredited school, most states require the student pharmacist to obtain a minimum number of experiential work hours. This typically involves working at an approved pharmacy site to gain practical experience in the workplace. In order to qualify those work hours properly, the training site must be approved by the state and the proper documentation must be submitted in support of those hours. These hours worked must be attained prior to sitting for any licensure examination to be a registered pharmacist. The time invested at the pharmacy must be certified by an overseeing pharmacy preceptor who takes responsibility for the development of the student pharmacist.

Upon graduation from a properly accredited pharmacy school, the graduate pharmacist must pass the NAPLEX licensure examination to practice pharmacy, as well as the appropriate state MPJE law licensure examination. The NAPLEX examination tests the graduate pharmacist in the substantive areas of pharmacy practice and is a standardized test administered nationally. The MPJE portion of the examination is intended to test the graduate pharmacist's ability to comprehend the pharmacy laws that govern the pharmacy profession. Although pharmacy laws tend to be uniform from state to state, there are unique nuances as well. As a result, each state has MPJE questions unique to its own state legal construct. Only after passing these exams may the graduate pharmacist obtain state licensure to practice pharmacy and become a registered pharmacist fit to practice pharmacy and serve the general public.

Once licensed as a registered pharmacist, the PPA and regulations of a given state provide that the pharmacist licensee must meet continuing education requirements in order to renew the pharmacy license and continue to practice in the profession. Opportunities for continuing education in the profession are widespread. These may consist of written materials followed by examination, webinars, webcasts, and live conferences.

A failure to properly maintain the minimum required continuing education credit hours will result in the suspension and eventual revocation of a pharmacist's license to practice pharmacy. Each pharmacist must report to the board of pharmacy and demonstrate — upon request — fulfillment of the hours through production of a certificate, upon request from the licensing board of pharmacy.

33.4 Categories of Pharmacy Licensure

The PPA, pharmacy regulations, and pharmacy boards typically oversee licensure for many different categories of licensed pharmacy practice. In general, such licensure could include that of the pharmacist, the pharmacy technician, and the pharmacy. Some states now specifically require that pharmacy technicians be certified to practice in a pharmacy and may be subject to continuing technician education credits similar to what a pharmacist may be required to do.

Licensure categories for a pharmacy may be further sub-divided into sub-practice areas. For example, some states may have licensure categories specific to a retail pharmacy, institutional pharmacy (such as a hospital), long-term care pharmacy, mail-order pharmacy, or specialty pharmacy, among others. Additionally, some state laws could require additional state licensure for controlled substances in addition to any federally-mandated requirements by the Drug Enforcement Administration (DEA). Although these licenses are typically independent from any Drug Enforcement Administration registration requirements, they are issued by a state that would have independent jurisdiction over the pharmacy in addition to any other federal laws that must be followed by the pharmacy.

A. Practice Focus on Licensure

Increasingly, pharmacies are becoming involved with new business opportunities that go beyond the traditional dispensing of drugs to patients. As technology and professional innovation both evolve, the profession is moving forward into areas of patient treatment that involve complex compounding methods, specialty pharmaceutical drugs and related supply-chain issues, as well as new types of practitioner-administered medications.

An area of significant legal concern for any dispensing pharmacy in activity that goes beyond its licensure mandate is whether it possesses the required license for any expanded business activity in which it is engaged. One example would be where a pharmacy is engaging in wholesale distribution activities and would require a separate licensure in such case.

Because drug supply-chain dispensing/distribution activities are typically driven by state law, a state-specific legal analysis must be undertaken for the state in question, in order to determine the licensure requirements for the business activity being undertaken. If drug supply-chain activities are crossing state lines, the laws and regulations of each state in question should be analyzed to ensure that full compliance with the law is being achieved. In some cases, depending on the nature of the business activity, federal law should also be reviewed.

The failure to achieve full licensure compliance could result in a state board of pharmacy (or other enforcement body) taking an enforcement action in response to the unauthorized practice of pharmacy or wholesale distribution of drug. The result of such a disciplinary action might involve monetary penalties and possibly suspension or revocation of existing licenses, depending on the severity of the unauthorized activity. At a minimum, any such business activity will be prohibited until proper licensure is obtained or until a successful challenge can be brought by the business entity.

33.5 Federal Drug Laws

In addition to state PPA and board of pharmacy-imposed regulatory requirements on a pharmacist and pharmacy, there are federal requirements that may need to be met. Although the federal Food & Drug Administration (FDA) does not have jurisdiction over pharmacy practice matters, when certain activity rises to the level of perceived drug manufacturing, the FDA can invoke its authority.

A. Pharmacy Compounding

While the FDA regulates drug manufacturing, state laws and regulations govern pharmacy compounding. Nevertheless, legal tension arises when pharmacy compounding is alleged by the FDA to rise to the level of manufacturing. The law continues to evolve with respect to pharmacy compounding and has undergone multiple court battles leading to the FDA issuance of a Compliance Policy Guide that reflects the FDA's current enforcement scheme respecting human drug compounding. In the guide, the FDA recognizes that traditional "pharmacy compounding" exists, and has made some qualifying statements where pharmacies are exempt from FDA registration requirements, inspection provisions, and misbranding provisions.

However, the exemption applies only to those pharmacies that operate in accordance with state law and dispense drugs upon prescriptions written by prescribing practitioners for an identifiable patient. Moreover, pharmacies may not manufacture, prepare, propagate, compound, or process drugs or devices for sale other than in the regular course of their business of dispensing or selling drugs or devices at retail. The FDA further stated that traditional compounding was not the subject of its enforcement focus. Rather, the focus is on a pharmacy's activity that raises the types of concerns associated with a drug manufacturer and that re-

sults in violations of new drug, adulteration or misbranding provisions such that the FDA would consider enforcement action against such a pharmacy.

B. FDA REMS

REMS stands for Risk Evaluation and Mitigation Strategies. It originated in 2007 federal legislation and provides the FDA with the authority to require REMS for certain drugs and biological products, to ensure that the benefits of such products outweighed the risks.

In short, REMS is an FDA risk-management plan that applies to prescription drugs and biologicals, and requires use of tools beyond the routine labeling and dispensing of prescriptions. The type of REMS implementation requirement is addressed by the FDA on a drug-specific basis and is described either pre-approval or post-approval of a particular drug.

REMS ultimately can affect how pharmacies dispense medication, even though the FDA has no regulatory authority beyond manufacturers. However, if a manufacturer does not comply with REMS requirements, the FDA can: (1) prohibit the drug from being introduced into the market, (2) find the drug to be misbranded, and (3) impose civil penalties. As a result, through regulations of manufacturers, REMS might affect prescribers and pharmacists at the level of professional practice.

C. DEA

Another federal enforcement body is the Drug Enforcement Agency (DEA). In addition to being governed by any PPA and state board of pharmacy requirements, a pharmacy may not dispense any controlled substances unless it is registered with the DEA and in good standing regarding the same. The Controlled Substances Act of 1970 (CSA) is federal law that provides for this construct. Additionally, the DEA has promulgated a myriad of regulations further refining the CSA and providing additional laws respecting the purchase, control, storage, security, dispensing, and disposal of controlled substances.

33.6 Progressive and Miscellaneous Areas of Pharmacy Law

The day-to-day practice of pharmacy is governed by the PPA and supporting regulations. In general, these laws and regulations are wide ranging. However, a common theme can be gleaned from all of them in many respects. For example, prescriptions dispensed for outpatient patients and medication orders in the in-patient setting must be written for legitimate medical purposes by an authorized prescriber in the usual course of professional practice.

Additionally, prescription drugs must be prepared, compounded, filled, labeled, stored, and dispensed by pharmacy personnel in accordance with applicable federal and/or state statutes governing the practice of pharmacy. Pharmacy staff must also ensure that all necessary components—which may include, but not be limited to, patient name, address, date of birth, sex, weight, allergies/idiosyncrasies, drug name and strength, directions for use, quantity, refills, and proper prescriber identifiers—are obtained prior to entering a prescription or medication into a patient's medical profile.

The law may mandate that medication orders be documented manually or transmitted electronically into a patient's medical record or chart in a clinical setting by an authorized prescriber or their agent, pursuant to a computerized process commonly referred to as a Computerized Prescriber Order Entry.

Invariably, state laws will require that prescriptions be accepted by a pharmacy in hardcopy form or by a prescriber (or their designated agent) via telephone, facsimile, or through electronic prescription, via a secure computer-to-computer transmission. After the pertinent data is entered into the patient profile or chart, most states require that a pharmacist perform Drug Utilization Review (DUR) prior to dispensing all new prescriptions or medication orders. The DUR process ensures that a vaccine, device, biological, or drug is proper for the age, weight and disease state and that the therapy does not interact with the patient's other medication or nutritional intake.

After fulfilling and labeling a prescription order, state laws typically require that a pharmacist must undertake visual product verification to further ensure that the correct drug product is being dispensed. Most states will mandate that the initials or unique identifiers of the pharmacist and/or technician, who completed each component function of the prescription or medication order, be recorded on a patient profile and that this information be readily retrievable. This is commonly referred to as an audit trail. Pharmacy workflows and practice settings may vary, however the component functions may include data entry, data verification, drug utilization review, product fulfillment, final product validation and consultation. Each of the component functions may be completed by one or more pharmacist and/or technician, depending on how the workflow is constructed.

After a medication order is checked and dispensed, it is usually required by law to be administered to the in-patient by another healthcare provider in the institutional setting. In the retail setting, most states require that prior to prescriptions being dispensed to patients or their representatives, a consultation, or offer to counsel, must be made and documented. In the mail-order setting, most states require printed materials and a toll-free telephone number with access to a pharmacist in the event a patient should have a question about her medication.

States have recognized that technology has evolved and are accommodating new methods of managing workflows through changes in the law. As prescription volumes increase and profit margins decrease, stakeholders in all sectors of pharmacy are increasingly relying on technology and automation to facilitate patient demands. Examples of technology that have been implemented through legal change include prescription image routing, remote data entry, automated dispensing systems, bar code scanning devices, central fill facilities, common electronic files, and automated prescription drug pick-up kiosks. Each of these technology advances have enabled pharmacists and pharmacies to more efficiently complete data entry, undertake product fulfillment, finalize product validation, and complete distribution components of the filling process. States have moved to make changes to their laws and regulations in some respects to support technological advances; however, technological advances move at excessive speed, and typically state laws trail progressive technological advances, and change in the laws and regulations are always at issue.

Quality assurance regulations are yet another area in which states have an impact on the practice of pharmacy. These regulations vary from state to state. Some states require a comprehensive peer review program, continuous quality improvement initiatives, and/or a mandatory drug error reporting, while other states mandate only that an audit trail be maintained for every prescription. The disparity is so great that one state may require remediation through additional course work in the form of continuing education, while another state may fine a pharmacist and even suspend or revoke the pharmacist's license for a period of time or indefinitely. Although pharmacies in every state need access to a coordinated and extensive set of tools designed to prevent medication errors, most pharmacies will only take a process-driven, system-based approach to addressing quality assurance when mandated by state statute or regulation.

33.7 HIPAA and State Privacy Laws

The federal Health Insurance Portability and Accountability Act of 1996, as amended, including regulations promulgated relating to privacy, security, and transaction code sets, now requires pharmacies as a "covered entity" to adhere to additional safeguards that will protect patient health information. Additionally, state laws may further embellish federal requirements, thereby creating additional privacy obligations on the pharmacy and pharmacist. Full policy and procedures, implementation processes that protect all electronic information, as well as business agreements with pharmacy business partners are just some of the additional requirements to which the pharmacist professional must adhere.

Chapter 34

Pharmacy Case Law Update: October 2009 through October 2010

Roger Morris, R.Ph., J.D. and William J. Stilling, R.Ph., M.S., J.D.

Note: Presented at the American Society for Pharmacy Law Developments in Pharmacy Law Seminar XXI in La Quinta, California, November 21, 2010.

34.1 Antitrust
A. Mergers and Acquisitions

1. *Golden Gate Pharmacy Services, Inc. v. Pfizer, Inc.*, 2010 WL 1541257 (N.D. Cal.) (April 16, 2010)

Relief sought: Plaintiffs, a group of pharmacies, asserted a claim against defendants, Pfizer Inc. and Wyeth, under Section 7 of the Clayton Act and Section 1 of the Sherman Act, alleging that the effect of their merger in October 2009 was to "lessen competition or to tend to create a monopoly, and has already lessened competition and tended to create a monopoly in numerous markets and submarkets...."

Issue: Did the plaintiffs sufficiently allege in their amended complaint that the product market of the defendants was reasonably interchangeable or that the products and their substitutes had cross-elasticity of demand?

Facts and procedural history

- In October 2009, Pfizer announced that the purchase of Wyeth was complete.
- Plaintiffs alleged that the merger has or will have "anticompetitive effects" in the "pharmaceutical market" and in submarkets because each of the companies considers the prices charged by the other, whether their products are substitutes or not.

Reasoning

- Antitrust law requires an allegation of a product market, the outer boundaries of which "are determined by the reasonable interchangeability of use or the cross-elasticity of demand between the product itself and substitutes for it." Interchangeability implies that one product is roughly equivalent to another for the use for which it is intended. Cross-elasticity is a measure of substitutability of products from the buyer's point of view.
- Plaintiffs failed to allege that all the commodities sold by the defendants are reasonably interchangeable with one another. Court was unwilling to assume that if the price for "a prescription drug used to treat osteoporosis rises, consumers react by switching to a prescription drug used to treat Alzheimer's disease."
- Although the court accepted the plaintiffs' proposition that the price charged by one company would affect the price charged by another company, regardless of whether the products were substitutes for one another, the plaintiffs failed to show that such pricing consideration has any effect on consumer behavior. It is unlikely that a consumer would substitute one drug for another unless they are direct substitutes.

Holding: Plaintiffs failed to sufficiently allege the existence of a cognizable product market because they did not allege that any of the identified markets or submarkets consisted of products that were reasonably interchangeable by consumers. Court granted defendants' motion to dismiss the complaint.

B. Monopolization

1. *In re Flonase Antitrust Litigation*, 692 F. Supp. 2d 524 (E.D. Pa. 2010) (January 21, 2010)

Relief sought: Plaintiffs, indirect purchasers of Flonase, sought relief for their claims brought under several states laws, including: monopolization under the laws of Arizona, Iowa, North Carolina, and Wisconsin; unfair and deceptive trade practices under the laws of Arizona, Florida, Illinois, Iowa, Massachusetts, and North Carolina; and unjust enrichment under the laws of Arizona, Florida, Illinois, Iowa, Massachusetts, North Carolina, and Wisconsin. Plaintiffs claimed they sustained injury when they purchased and/or provided reimbursement for Flonase in the respective states.

Issue: Could plaintiffs' claims survive the defendant's motion to dismiss based on their allegation that GlaxoSmithKline (GSK) filed sham citizen petitions with the Food and Drug Administration (FDA) in an effort to delay the entry of a generic version of Flonase?

Facts and procedural history
- Manufacturer of a new drug who obtains FDA approval enjoys a period of market exclusivity during which their patent is protected. Once this period expires, other (generic) manufacturers may market and sell the drug. Prospective manufacturers of a generic drug must file an Abbreviated New Drug Application (ANDA) with the FDA.
- While an ANDA is pending, "citizen petitions" may be filed with the FDA to express legitimate concerns regarding a product and to request that the FDA take, or refrain from taking, administrative action. These citizen petitions can delay a generic drug's approval and are open to abuse by pharmaceutical companies attempting to prolong their monopoly in the market.
- Plaintiffs alleged GSK filed sham citizen petitions to delay entry of generic versions of Flonase.
- GSK filed a motion to dismiss.

Reasoning
- Regarding the issue of standing:
  - Plaintiffs experienced an injury by paying too much for Flonase in states where they are located, in states where they purchased Flonase, and in states where they reimbursed members for purchases of Flonase.

- Defendants allegedly caused this injury by wrongfully filing citizens' petitions, thereby unfairly extending its monopoly on the market by preventing the entry of generic versions of Flonase.
- Injury was likely to be redressed by a favorable court decision.
- Court deferred the question of whether the plaintiffs could represent a nationwide class until the time of class certification.
- Regarding the monopolization claims:
  - Under North Carolina law, plaintiffs' monopolization claims could fall under two provisions of North Carolina General Statutes but plaintiffs did not specify under which provision they make their monopolization claim. Plaintiffs alleged facts that support a claim under the first provision. Defendant did not apparently move to dismiss any claim under the second provision.
  - Under Wisconsin law, defendant argued that plaintiffs had not alleged that the conduct complained of "substantially affects" the people of Wisconsin as required by Wisconsin's antitrust statute. The court found that the plaintiffs' allegations meet this standard as the defendant's conduct caused plaintiffs and many others to pay higher prices for the drug in many states, including Wisconsin, even though the conduct itself may have occurred outside the state.
- Regarding the unfair and deceptive trade practice claims:
  - In Arizona, defendant argued that under the Arizona Consumer Fraud Act (ACFA), deception is required. Plaintiffs countered that ACFA should be construed similarly to the Federal Trade Commission Act (the FTC Act), under which deception is not required. The court found that the plain terms of the ACFA lack a prohibition on unfair acts or methods of competition and that courts do not have to find that all allegations that would violate the FTC Act necessarily violate ACFA. Rather, allegations of deception, and not merely of unfair acts, are required to state a claim under the ACFA. Plaintiffs' allegations were insufficient to support a conclusion that defendant made a false promise or misrepresentation.
  - The court found that the Florida Deceptive and Unfair Trade Practices Act (FDUTPA) allows

claims made by out-of-state plaintiffs as there was no plain language limiting it to in-state consumers. Also, the court found no language in the statute that would require injuries to take place entirely within the state. Plaintiffs alleged some injury in the State of Florida, even if not all the offending conduct allegedly took place in Florida. This was sufficient to state a claim under FDUTPA.

- Illinois law does not allow plaintiffs to state a cause of action that was a typical antitrust allegation under the Illinois Consumer Fraud and Deceptive Business Practices Act (ICFA), where the legislature has declined to include such a cause of action under the Illinois Antitrust Act. Plaintiffs were prohibited from making claims under the Illinois Antitrust Act because the Act does not provide relief to indirect purchasers through class actions. Because their claims were precluded under the Illinois Antitrust Act, they could not be brought under the ICFA.

- Plaintiffs conceded there was no private right of action under the Iowa Consumer Fraud Act.

- Under Massachusetts General Law Chapter 93A, Regulation of Business practice for Consumer Protection, a plaintiff must generally send a written demand for relief to a prospective defendant at least 30 days before filing a complaint. Massachusetts courts apply the demand requirement strictly. Plaintiffs failed to send such a demand letter to defendants.

- To state a claim under the North Carolina Unfair and Deceptive Trade Practices Act (NCUDTPA), plaintiffs must allege that (1) defendant committed an unfair or deceptive act or practice, (2) in or affecting commerce, and (3) plaintiffs were injured as a result. Plaintiffs sufficiently alleged these elements. Plaintiffs alleged that defendant maintains two large development and production facilities in North Carolina and sold large amounts of Flonase within the state, including to plaintiffs, at artificially inflated prices.

- Regarding the unjust enrichment claims:
  - Elements necessary to state an unjust enrichment claim vary by state, but almost all states require, at a minimum, that plaintiffs allege that they conferred a benefit upon defendant and that it would be inequitable or unjust for defendant to accept and retain the benefit.

- In *Illinois Brick v. Illinois*, 431 U.S. 720 (1977), the Supreme Court held that any benefit gained by the defendant manufacturer through anti-competitive conduct which violated the federal antitrust laws was to be taken away solely by the direct purchaser. It follows that indirect purchasers are not permitted to claim that the injury suffered by direct purchasers, for example overpaying, was passed to them.

- Some states have adopted *Illinois Brick* and deny indirect purchaser plaintiffs recovery under their state antitrust statutes. Where state antitrust law would preclude recovery, a plaintiff cannot circumvent the statutory framework by recasting their claim as unjust enrichment.

- Illinois has adopted the logic of *Illinois Brick*. Arizona, Florida, Iowa, Massachusetts, North Carolina, and Wisconsin have at least partially rejected it. However, Florida and North Carolina require, for a claim of unjust enrichment, that the plaintiffs confer a benefit directly upon a defendant.

Holding

- Plaintiffs had standing in all states where they resided, purchased Flonase, or were reimbursed for purchases of Flonase. Therefore, they had standing in Arizona, Florida, Illinois, Iowa, Massachusetts, North Carolina, and Wisconsin.

- Motion to dismiss was denied in regards to plaintiffs' monopolization claims under Arizona and Wisconsin law.

- With regard to the unfair and deceptive trade practice claims, the motion to dismiss the Illinois and Iowa claims was granted; motion to dismiss the Massachusetts and Arizona claims was granted without prejudice; and motion to dismiss the Florida and North Carolina claims was denied.

- Motion to dismiss the plaintiffs' unjust enrichment claims under Florida, Illinois, and North Carolina law was granted; under Arizona, Iowa, Massachusetts, and Wisconsin law it was denied.

C. Predatory Pricing

1. *Safeway, Inc. et al. v. Abbott Laboratories*, 2010 WL 147988 (N.D. Cal. 2010) (January 12, 2010)

Relief sought: Abbott sought summary judgment against various parties alleging antitrust claims.

Issues: Did plaintiffs sufficiently allege claims for predatory pricing, bundling, and failure to deal?

Facts and procedural history

- In 1996, Abbott introduced Novir (ritonavir) as a stand-alone protease inhibitor to treat AIDS (dose: 12 × 1,000 mg capsules per day (about $18/day)).
- Later, it was learned Novir could be used as a booster for other PIs in smaller doses (1 to 4 capsules per day). By 2003, the daily price of Novir therefore dropped to about $1.71/day.
- In 2000, Abbott introduced Kaletra (lopinovir/ritonavir), but it had significant side effects.
- In 2003, Bristol-Meyers Squibb introduced Reyataz and Kaletra's market share fell more than expected.
- Studies then showed Novir could be used in even smaller booster doses (1 capsule/day).
- In December 2003, Abbott raised the price of Novir 400 percent because of the drug's "enormous clinical value."
- Plaintiffs claimed this increase was intended for an anticompetitive purpose in the "boosted market" for drugs like Reyataz, Lexiva, and Kaletra.
- Direct purchasers claimed Abbott engaged in predatory pricing of a bundled product (Kaletra) and violated its duty to deal in the boosting market (Novir).
- GlaxoSmithKline (GSK), which sold Lexiva, claimed Abbott violated its duty to deal in the boosting market.

Reasoning: Abbott's main argument was that the plaintiffs' claims for predatory pricing should fail because in *John Doe v. Abbott Laboratories,* 571 F.3d 930 (9th Cir. 2009), the court required plaintiffs to allege below-cost pricing and dangerous probability of recoupment in the boosted market. The court explained that the *Doe* case was limited to monopoly leveraging claims. The court distinguished plaintiffs' claims in this case (discounting a bundled product to drive purchasers from the boosted market and duty to deal) from the monopoly leveraging claims in *Doe*.

Holding: The court denied Abbott's motion for summary judgment.

D. Price Fixing

1. *Clayworth et al. v. Pfizer, Inc. et al.,* 233 P.3d 1066 (Cal. 2010) (July 12, 2010)

Relief sought: Plaintiffs, retail pharmacies located in California, sought treble damages, restitution and injunctive relief. They alleged that defendants, brand-name pharmaceutical manufacturers and distributors, unlawfully conspired to fix the prices of their brand-name pharmaceuticals in the U.S. market.

Issue: Were the plaintiffs' claims barred because the plaintiffs passed on any alleged overcharge to third parties and, therefore, suffered no compensable injury?

Facts and procedural history

- Plaintiffs filed suit under section 1 of the Cartwright Act and the Unfair Competition law (UCL), alleging defendants had unlawfully conspired to fix the prices of their brand-name pharmaceuticals in the United States market, including California. The complaint alleged that the defendants had agreed to set artificially high prices for their products, and had acted in concert to restrain re-importation of their lower-priced foreign drugs into the United States and to restrict price competition from generics.
- Defendants asserted, as an affirmative defense, that the plaintiffs' claims were barred on the ground that they had passed on any alleged overcharge to third parties and, therefore, did not suffer a compensable injury. Defendants filed for summary judgment arguing that under the plain language of the Cartwright Act, a pass-on defense was available.
- The trial court granted the summary judgment motion and held that the pass-on defense was available under the Cartwright Act. The plaintiffs had passed on all of the defendants' overcharges to consumers and had thus sustained no damages.
- The Court of Appeals affirmed the trial court decision.

Reasoning

- In *Hanover Shoe v. United Shoe Machinery*, the United States Supreme Court held that when a buyer could show that the price paid by him is illegally high, and show the amount of the overcharge, he has made out a prima facie case of injury under section 4 of the Clayton Act. Damage has occurred to the buyer even if the buyer is allowed to pass on the overcharge to others.
- The text of the Cartwright Act, referring to "damages sustained" is ambiguous, as evidenced by the diametrically opposite conclusions of the Court of Appeals in this case, and that of the U.S. Supreme Court in *Hanover Shoe* when it interpreted essentially identical language in the Clayton Act.

- Every indication available from the legislature demonstrated that, given a choice, it would prefer an enforcement regime in which *Hanover Shoe* is the law.
- Allowing a pass-on defense would plunge parties and courts into mini-trials attempting to trace where every penny of an initial overcharge goes, as well as seeking to measure the further ramifications that an overcharge might have in the form of lost sales and other tertiary consequences.

Holding: For state antitrust purposes, the *Hanover Shoe* rule should apply in California; therefore a pass-on defense by the defendants could not be asserted. Summary judgment for the defendants was reversed.

34.2 Consumer Fraud
A. Consumer Protection Acts

1. *Zapata v. Walgreen Company*, 2009 WL 3644897 (D. Minn. 2009) (November 2, 2009)
Relief sought: Plaintiff sued Walgreens based on three consumer fraud statutes claiming she suffered corneal burns from using a contact lens solution.

Issues: Was defendant liable under state consumer fraud statutes or common law negligence?

Facts and procedural history: Plaintiff bought contact lens cleaning and disinfecting solution marked as "75% off" that was in a "tattered" box. The box was a sample that was not intended for sale. Plaintiff did not read the warning "DON'T PUT IN YOUR EYES" in black letters on top of the bottle. She put the solution in her eye and suffered a corneal burn.

- She sued for negligence and for claims under three Minnesota statutes: (i) Deceptive Trade Practices Act; (ii) False Statement in Advertising Act; and (iii) Prevention of Consumer Fraud Act.
- Her claim under the statutes was based on: (i) an ad that Walgreens "is the pharmacy you can trust;" and (ii) that the 75 percent sign falsely represented the product was for sale.

Reasoning
- Consumer fraud claims were dismissed because there was no evidence of "fraud, false advertisement, or deceptive act."
- "Pharmacy you can trust" was puffery and not actionable.
- Walgreens did not falsely imply the product was for sale because an implied, unspoken message cannot

be grounds for consumer fraud. Furthermore, the message was not false because the solution was for sale.
- A duty exists if the court determines the harm is foreseeable. It was not reasonably foreseeable that the plaintiff would ignore the warning not to use the product in the eye. Moreover, even if Walgreens had a duty, its breach could not have been the proximate cause. Rather, plaintiff's failure to read and heed the warning caused her injury.

Holding: The court granted Walgreens' motion for summary judgment because there were: (i) no false or deceptive statements and (ii) no facts that could have established a duty or cause.

B. False Advertising

1. *In re WellNx Marketing and Sales Practices Litigation*, 673 F. Supp. 2d 43 (D. Mass. 2009) (December 11, 2009)
Relief sought: Consumers sought damages from inventors, retailers, and manufacturers of weight-loss products allegedly engaged in fraudulent marketing techniques.

Issue: Were the consumers' claims sufficiently pled to survive a motion to dismiss?

Facts and procedural history
- Plaintiffs, who purchased a variety of weight loss products allegedly containing *Hoodia gordonii* filed 16 cases alleging fraud-based claims against WellNx Life Sciences, Swiss Caps USA, Inc., and Robinson Pharma, Inc. (RPI), plus other defendants who produced and marketed weight-loss products including "Slimquick—the Female Fat Burner," "NV—Rapid Weight-Loss Beauty Pill," and "Liquid Hoodia."
- Cases were filed in Maryland, Massachusetts, Nevada, and New Jersey.
- WellNx was the claimed inventor of SlimQuick, NV, and Liquid Hoodia.
- Plaintiffs claimed WellNx: (i) falsely represented the ingredients of its products and (ii) fabricated consumer testimonials. Tests of product samples often demonstrated that they contained none or reduced amounts of the labeled ingredients.
- Defendants filed motions to dismiss various counts of the amended complaint as insufficiently pled.
- Swiss Caps and RPI asserted that the complaint failed to allege that any of the named plaintiffs re-

lied on the product labels in deciding to make a WellNx purchase.

- WellNx argued that the complaints do not allege reliance or causation, essential elements of both common-law and statutory consumer fraud claims.
- Defendants argued that none of the plaintiffs were alleged to have purchased NV, and only one was alleged to have purchased Liquid Hoodia.
- WellNx argued that the "economic loss doctrine" barred out-of-pocket damages for torts.

Reasoning

- In the absence of any definitive statement from the New Jersey Supreme Court recognizing an exception to the economic loss doctrine for intentional conduct, the federal court found that common-law fraud claims were barred.
- The negligence claim, which sought out-of-pocket damages for defendants' "failure to procure and/ or obtain the proper amounts of ingredients in Slimquick, NV and Liquid Hoodia and negligent failure to properly test the key ingredients in those products," was barred.
- As none of the named plaintiffs alleged they purchased NV, the claims involving NV must be dismissed.
- None of the bellwether jurisdictions requires anything more than that causation be pled. Thus, the plaintiffs plausibly pled that defendants made representations about the weight-reducing properties of their products, that plaintiffs purchased the products expecting to lose weight, and that the products did not perform as advertised.

Holding: Motions for summary judgment were granted in part and denied in part.

- Consumers pled fraud with sufficient particularity.
- Economic loss doctrine barred claims for out-of-pocket damages under New Jersey law.
- Named plaintiffs did not have standing to raise consumer fraud claims regarding products they had not purchased.
- Consumers were not required to plead causation with particularity.
- Economic loss doctrine did not bar consumers' common law fraud claims under Massachusetts and Nevada law.

2. *Ferring Pharmaceuticals, Inc. v. River's Edge Pharmaceuticals, LLC*, 2010 WL 3087419 (D. Md. 2010) (August 6, 2010)

Relief sought: Plaintiff, Ferring Pharmaceuticals, sought injunctive and monetary relief for loss of sales and damage of goodwill based on its assertion that defendant, River's Edge Pharmaceuticals, marketed its product as being a lower cost alternative to plaintiff's brand-name drug, though defendant's drug was by no means equivalent, in violation of section 43(a) of the Lanham Act.

Issues

- Does the Food, Drug, and Cosmetic Act (FDCA) preempt the Lanham Act?
- Was the plaintiff's failure to provide a statement or copy of the allegedly false advertisement insufficient to plead a cognizable claim under the Lanham Act?
- Did the plaintiff fail to state a cognizable claim due to its failure to plead the amounts of each ingredient in its drug and that there is a legally significant difference in the strengths of the ingredients in the parties' respective products?

Facts and procedural history

- Plaintiff manufactures the drug Prosed. Defendant has a purportedly similar drug called RE Methylphen. Neither drug is listed in the *Approved Drug Products with Therapeutic Equivalence Evaluations*, which is a list of drugs approved by the Food and Drug Administration (FDA).
- Plaintiff alleged that defendant marketed its product as a lower cost alternative to Prosed, but that defendant's drug was not equivalent. Such marketing included statements on its label, packaging insert, and elsewhere that RE Methylphen contains the same amounts of the five active ingredients in Prosed.
- Plaintiff contended that defendant knew its marketing was misleading because it failed to include a disclaimer in the labeling and packaging inserts of RE Methylen that states "[e]ven when a River's Edge product is labeled as containing the same active ingredients, they may be subject to different potency and dissolution specifications." Such disclaimer was included on its website. Plaintiff also claimed that it conducted laboratory testing of RE Methylphen that resulted in a finding that it did not fall within the "clinically acceptable range for a generic equivalent" because it contained higher amounts of four of the five active ingredients.

- Defendant filed a motion to dismiss based on its belief that the FDCA preempted the Lanham Act, or if it did not, that the plaintiff failed to allege sufficient information to state a cognizable claim.

Reasoning

- Section 43(a) of the Lanham Act provides that any person who "uses in commerce…any…false or misleading description of fact, or false or misleading representation of fact," which "misrepresents the nature, characteristics, or qualities…of his or her or another's person's goods…" is liable to any person alleging damage because of such false or misleading advertising. The FDCA provides that the FDA may regulate "adulterated drugs" which are drugs whose strength differs from that which it purports to possess, and misbranded drugs, which are drugs whose labeling is false or misleading. Claims requiring the interpretation or application of the FDCA are precluded from being brought by private litigants.
- Case law is relatively consistent in holding that claims that a competitor has falsely advertised its product as the generic of another drug, especially where the drugs are not subject to FDA approval, are permissible Lanham Act claims and not barred by the FDCA. Furthermore, courts have indicated that an allegation that a defendant has falsely or misleadingly marketed its product as an "alternative" to the plaintiff's product is less problematic in interfering with FDA territory than claims asserting that the products are "equivalent."
- It was sufficient for the plaintiff to describe the advertisements in its complaint, though it will eventually have to provide the materials in order to prevail on its Lanham Act claim. At this point in the litigation, it was not necessary for the plaintiff to prove its case.
- The test results attached to the complaint indicate that Prosed contains 90-110 percent of the amount listed for each ingredient, while the amount of those ingredients in RE Methylphen ranged from 120-185 percent. This was a sufficient allegation that the range of active ingredients varied between the two drugs.

Holding

- Plaintiff's claim under the Lanham Act was not precluded by the FDCA.
- Plaintiff alleged sufficient facts that, if proven to be true, would entitle plaintiff to relief under the Lanham Act.
- Motion to dismiss was denied.

34.3 Controlled Substances
A. Controlled Substance Act

1. *United States v. Birbragher*, 603 F.3d 478 (8th Cir. 2010) (April 26, 2010)

Relief sought: Criminal defendant, Birbragher, sought to set aside his indictment under the federal Controlled Substances Act (CSA), claiming that the CSA was unconstitutionally vague as applied to him.

Issue: Was the CSA unconstitutionally vague as applied to the criminal defendant in this case?

Facts and procedural history

- Defendant, Birbragher, was co-owner and operator of Pharmacom International Corporation (Pharmacom), an online distributor of prescription drugs, including Schedule III and IV controlled substances.
- Customers visiting Pharmacom's website to place orders for prescription drugs were required to complete a short health history questionnaire and provide credit card information. Pharmacom did not verify customer identities or require them to submit any medical records. Doctors who had contracted with Pharmacom would then review the prescription orders, and issue a prescription without an in-person examination, and typically without viewing any medical records.
- Defendant was indicted and charged with two counts of conspiracy: Count I alleged conspiracy to violate the CSA and Count II alleged conspiracy to launder from the drug conspiracy. Defendant entered into a plea agreement in exchange for his assistance in the prosecution of his co-defendants.

Reasoning

- To defeat a vagueness challenge, a statute must pass a two-part test: first, the statute must provide adequate notice of the proscribed conduct; and second, it must not lend itself to arbitrary enforcement.
- Defendant argued that he lacked the notice required by the first prong because at the time of his conduct, it was not clear that the CSA applied to non-registrants like him, nor was it clear that the manner in which Pharmacom distributed controlled substances was prohibited by the CSA.

- The plain language of the statute does not limit its application to just registrants and courts have repeatedly held that non-registrants can be convicted for participating in conspiracies to distribute controlled substances in violation of the CSA.
- Defendant was not indicted because Pharmacom utilized the Internet to distribute controlled substance, but rather because he was conspiring with doctors and pharmacists to violate the CSA.
- CSA used the term "usual scope of professional practice," which has an objective meaning that prevents arbitrary prosecution and conviction.

Holding: The CSA passed both prongs of the vagueness test; therefore the statute was not unconstitutionally vague as applied to the defendant's ownership and operation of Pharmacom. The court rejected defendant's appeal of indictment.

B. Drug Dealer Liability Act

1. *Whittemore et al. v. Owens Healthcare-Retail Pharmacy, Inc.*, 111 Cal.Rptr.3d 227 (Cal. 2010) (June 22, 2010)

Relief sought: Plaintiff, Melody Whittemore, sought economic and non-economic damages from the defendant, Owens Healthcare-Retail Pharmacy, Inc., as a result of her addiction to controlled substances obtained from defendant's employee. Melody's husband, Kenneth, sought damages for severe emotional distress.

Issue: Is a pharmacy liable under the Drug Dealer Liability Act for the conduct of an employee who furnished stolen prescription pills to a plaintiff?

Facts and procedural history

- Melody was treated by a doctor for a severe infection but was unable to pay for the medication the doctor prescribed. She began receiving the pain medication from Steven Correa, an employee of the defendant. Over the span of a year and a half, Melody paid Correa over $330,000 in cash for the pain pills. Her addiction was subsequently discovered, and she was hospitalized. Melody later cooperated with drug enforcement officers to expose and arrest Correa.
- Melody and her husband, Kenneth, learned that pharmacies are required by law to monitor medications in their possession and to report missing medication to the Drug Enforcement Agency and brought suit against Owens Healthcare-Retail Pharmacy, Correa's employer.

- The trial court sustained the pharmacy's demurrer without leave to amend on the ground that Melody could not recover for injuries caused by her own illegal conduct. Kenneth's claims could not survive without Melody's.

Reasoning

- The "unclean hands" doctrine was created to protect judicial integrity and to promote justice because "allowing a plaintiff with unclean hands to recover in an action creates doubts as to the justice provided by the judicial system." Conduct that renders a plaintiff's hands "unclean" does not need to include a crime or actionable tort, but could be any conduct that violates the conscience or good faith. Melody's conduct in this case was particularly egregious because she illegally acquired, possessed, and used controlled substances repeatedly over a period of 18 months.
- The purpose of the Drug Dealer Liability Act is to allow a person who was injured as a consequence of the use of an illegal controlled substance to recover damages from those who participated in the marketing of the substance, in order to shift the cost to those who illegally profit from the market.
- The Act has a scienter requirement for liability and only those who "knowingly participate in the marketing" of such substances could be held liable. The pharmacy did not knowingly participate in the marketing of the controlled substances to Melody.

Holding: Court of Appeals affirmed the judgment of the trial court. Melody was unable to recover because her "unclean" hands contributed to her injury. Nor could the pharmacy be held liable for her or her husband's injury because it did not "knowingly participate" in the marketing of the controlled substances to Melody.

34.4 Employment
A. Contracts

1. *Taylor v. Mele*, 2010 WL 3042129 (Tex. App. 2010) (August 5, 2010)

Relief sought: Terri Mele, a pharmacist, filed suit against Dr. Jill Taylor for breach of contract, *quantum meruit*, and detrimental reliance damages following the termination of her employment at Taylor's family medicine clinic.

Issue: Did the letter sent by Taylor to Mele outlining the terms of her employment, create an employment contract and alter the at-will employment relationship?

Facts and procedural history

- Taylor offered Mele, a pharmacist, a position at her family clinic. Taylor sent a letter that provided for an annual salary, a $5,000 relocation package, paid vacation in the first and second years of employment, and insurance coverage.

- Mele was subsequently terminated from her position as pharmacist at the clinic.

- Trial court granted summary judgment in favor of Mele and awarded her post-employment lost wages, relocation expenses, and attorney's fees.

Reasoning

- Employment in Texas is presumed to be at-will employment and can only be altered if the employer unequivocally indicates "a definite intent to be bound not to terminate the employee except under clearly specified circumstances." The agreement to modify the at-will relationship must be (1) expressed, not implied, and (2) clear and specific.

- The letter at issue did not contain any provision specific to the term of employment or termination. One provision concerned compensation calculated annually, and another referenced vacation. These provisions, taken separately or together, did not express an "unequivocal intent to be bound not to terminate" Mele's employment except under clearly specified circumstances.

- Though the contract may be terminated at-will, the employer may still remain contractually liable to the employee. Taylor did not dispute that Mele signed the letter and incurred expenses to move to Texas in order to work, nor did she challenge the sufficiency of the evidence to support the award for relocation expenses.

Holding: As a matter of law, the contract in dispute was an agreement for at-will employment; therefore the court modified the trial court's judgment to omit the damage award for lost wages, but affirmed the award of relocation expenses. Due to the change in the award, the court remanded for reconsideration of attorney's fees.

B. Discipline

1. *Amedson v. Washington State Board of Pharmacy*, 2010 WL 3232302 (Wash. App. 2010) (August 17, 2010)

Relief sought: Joseph Amedson appealed from the lower court's decision to affirm the Washington State De-

partment of Health (Department) decision to revoke his pharmacist license.

Issue: Was the Board's decision to revoke Amedson's license supported by the record?

Facts and procedural history

- Amedson was employed by A-Z Pharmacy. He voluntarily contacted the Department to discuss A-Z Pharmacy's prescription and billing practices and claimed that certain employees were engaging in prescription fraud schemes. Amedson did not implicate himself in these schemes, but after investigation the Department discovered that Amedson was linked to these schemes.

- Amedson voluntarily met with investigators during which he provided detailed information about his involvement in the fraudulent scheme. Investigators provided Amedson with a packet explaining the investigation, informing him of his rights, and indicating that any written statement he made could be used in disciplinary proceedings.

- At a subsequent meeting, Amedson again met with the investigators and reviewed a written summary of the statements he had previously made and requested changes. When he was satisfied with the document, Amedson signed it.

- The Department issued a statement of charges alleging unprofessional conduct by Amedson under the Uniform Disciplinary Act (UDA). Amedson refused to appear at a deposition and claimed that prosecutors had granted him immunity arising out of the criminal prosecution of A-Z Pharmacy, but he failed to produce any evidence supporting the alleged immunity agreement. The Department subsequently moved for sanctions based on Amedson's refusal to appear for the deposition.

- Amedson moved to dismiss the disciplinary case based on his alleged immunity. The presiding officer denied the motion based on lack of evidence.

- Amedson filed a motion for reconsideration of the Board's final pretrial order, within which he informed the Board that unless it reversed the order, he would protest by not attending the hearing. The Board commenced a hearing on the allegations that Amedson acted unprofessionally under the UDA. Neither Amedson nor his counsel was present. The presiding officer found Amedson in default and conducted the hearing in his absence.

- The Board issued its final decision and order revoking Amedson's license to practice pharmacy in

Washington with no right to reapply for reinstatement for 20 years. Rather than filing a motion to vacate the default order, Amedson petitioned for judicial review. The trial court affirmed the Board's decision.

Reasoning

- The UDA governs the discipline of pharmacists.
- As an agency, the Board had authority to enter a default judgment against Amedson for failing to attend or participate in the hearing. Once a default judgment was entered, Amedson was required to file a motion to vacate the default order within seven days after service of the default order. Amedson failed to do so. By this failure, Amedson waived his right to argue that the default judgment was invalid as a petitioner must exhaust all administrative remedies before judicial review is appropriate.
- There was adequate evidence that Amedson violated professional conduct rules as he voluntarily provided a statement to the Department in which he admitted to participating in a reimbursement scheme to defraud.

Holding: Amedson failed to exhaust all administrative remedies; therefore, the court declined to disturb the Board's default judgment against him. Additionally, the court found that the Department established by clear and convincing evidence that Amedson acted unprofessionally by his involvement in the fraud schemes, and the Board's decision to revoke Amedson's pharmacy license for no less than 20 years was supported by the record.

C. Discrimination

1. *Bonilla v. Freedom Pharmacy, Inc.*, 2009 WL 4782119 (D. Puerto Rico 2009) (December 7, 2009)

Relief sought: Plaintiffs, Edmarie Bonilla, Fernando Toro, and their conjugal partnership, sought damages under the Civil Rights Act, Title VII.

Issue: Did plaintiff plead facts sufficient to state a claim that her husband and the "conjugal partnership" could recover damages under Title VII?

Facts and procedural history: Plaintiffs claim that Bonilla's demotion and eventual termination by defendants, was discriminatory and based on her pregnancy. Defendants filed a motion to dismiss Toro's and the conjugal partnership's claims arguing that spouses lacked standing to sue under Title VII and Commonwealth employment statutes.

Reasoning

- The court noted that plaintiffs' complaint was devoid of any allegations regarding Toro and the conjugal partnership in the events that led to this lawsuit.
- Plaintiffs did not allege that Toro was defendant's employee. Thus Toro's only connection with this case was the fact that he is married to Bonilla.
- Courts have held that "spouses of individuals who have been victimized by employment discrimination cannot be said to fall within the class of persons Title VII was intended to protect."
- Since Toro and the conjugal partnership did not maintain an employer-employee relationship with defendants, their claims under Title VII were dismissed.

Holding: Toro's and the conjugal partnership's claims were dismissed with prejudice.

2. *Lindsey v. Walgreen Co.*, 2010 WL 3156549 (7th Cir. 2010) (August 11, 2010)

Relief sought: Plaintiff Lindsey sought damages under the Age Discrimination in Employment Act (ADEA), alleging that defendant Walgreen Co. wrongfully terminated her based on her age.

Issue: Did the decision-maker who fired plaintiff blindly rely on biased information of the manager of the store where she worked?

Facts and procedural history

- Walgreens hired Plaintiff as a pharmacist in May 1995 and she worked for the company until her termination on August 30, 2007. She was 53 years-old when she was fired.
- Plaintiff was rated "meets expectations" once or twice in her performance evaluations but in March 2006, plaintiff was rated "needs improvement."
- In early 2007, some employees complained that plaintiff was violating pharmacy policies and procedures. An investigation concluded that plaintiff had filled expired prescriptions and modified the price of certain drugs in violation of Walgreens' policies.
- After a demotion and transfer to another store, plaintiff alleged (i) her manager made remarks to her that she was "old and slow" and (ii) her district manager took no action when her co-workers called her "old, crazy and slow."
- Plaintiff filled a prescription that was in the "exception queue" that had a notation directing employ-

ees not to fill the prescription until the prescriber returned a phone call.

- Plaintiff was terminated after an investigation and she was replaced by a younger pharmacist who had just completed pharmacy school.
- District court granted defendant's motion for summary judgment, citing undisputed testimony that the decision-maker who fired plaintiff independently reviewed the incident before firing her.

Reasoning

- Plaintiff failed to show that the information the manager provided to the decision-maker was biased and defendant presented undisputed evidence that the decision-maker did not rely solely on what she learned form the manager.
- Even if the decision-maker relied on the biased information of the manager, the most plaintiff showed was that her age was a motivating factor in defendant's decision to fire her. To establish liability under the ADEA, plaintiff had to show that age was the determinative factor.
- Substantial evidence showed that plaintiff violated company policy and that was the reason for her firing.

Holding: Defendant Walgreens motion for summary judgment was affirmed.

D. Fair Labor Standards Act

1. *In re Novartis Wage and Hour Litigation*, No. 09-0437 (2nd Cir. 2010) (July 6, 2010)

Relief sought: Plaintiffs, current or former pharmaceutical sales representatives (the "Reps"), appealed the decision of the district court that denied their claims for overtime pay under the Fair Labor Standards Act of 1938 (FLSA) and state law.

Issue: Were the Reps "outside salesmen" and/or "administrative employees" who are exempt from FLSA's overtime pay requirements?

Background and procedural history

- In visits typically lasting no longer than five minutes, the Reps provide physicians with information about the benefits of particular Novartis pharmaceuticals and encourage the physicians to prescribe those products.
- Novartis gives the Reps written promotional materials developed by others within the company; the

Reps do not play any role in developing the written materials or in formulating the message given to the physicians.

- The Reps are trained to end their meeting with a physician by asking for a commitment to prescribe the Novartis product. There is no way to know whether physicians actually follow through on their commitment.
- The Reps are expected to be in the field from 8:00 A.M. to 5:00 P.M. on workdays; they eat lunch with physicians or while driving to a visit; and they attend mandatory dinner programs during evenings that Novartis requires them to hold on a periodic basis.
- District court granted summary judgment in favor of Novartis, stating that the Reps were outside salesmen and/or administrative employees, thus they were exempt from FLSA overtime requirements.

Reasoning

- Regulations provide that an "outside salesman" is one whose primary duty is to make sales. Promotional work that is done in conjunction with the employee's own outside sales is exempt work. Promotional work that is incidental to sales made by someone else is not.
  - Novartis sells its drugs to wholesalers. The Reps do not speak to the wholesalers or to the pharmacies that the wholesalers sell to, or to the patients who ultimately buy the drug. Physicians neither buy products from the Reps nor commit to buying anything from the Reps or Novartis.
  - When a representative promotes to a physician a product that may be purchased by a patient from a pharmacy if the physician—who cannot give a legally binding commitment to do so—prescribes it, the representative does not, in any sense, make the sale.
- Regulations interpret the term "administrative employee" as one whose primary duty includes the exercise of discretion and independent judgment with respect to matters of significance. This means more than simply the need to use skill in applying techniques or procedures prescribed by the employer.
  - What Novartis characterized as the Reps' exercise of discretion and independent judgment—ability to answer questions about the

product, ability to develop rapport with a physician who has a certain social style, ability to remember past conversations, and ability to recognize when a message has been persuasive—are skills gained and honed in Novartis training sessions. Furthermore, these skills are exercised within severe limits imposed by Novartis.

Holding: The Reps could not be classified as either outside salesmen or administrative employees. Therefore, they were eligible for overtime pay under FLSA and state law.

E. Pharmacy Regulation

1. *Golden Drugs Co., Inc., v. Maxwell-Jolly*, 102 Cal.Rptr.3d 446 (Cal. Ct. App. 2009) (December 9, 2009)

Relief sought: Golden Drugs Pharmacy (Pharmacy) appealed from a judgment denying its petition for a writ of mandamus, which challenged the termination of Pharmacy's Medi-Cal provisional provider licensed by defendant, the director of the state Department of Health Care Services.

Issues: Pharmacy contended (1) the court should consider extra-record evidence; (2) the evidence was insufficient to support the judgment; and (3) the Department's actions were arbitrary and capricious and denied due process.

Facts and procedural history
- The State Department of Health Care Services (the "Department") sent a letter to the Pharmacy stating that the Department was terminating the Pharmacy's Medi-Cal provisional provider status because during a field audit, an auditor and consultant observed a pharmacy technician dispensing medication intended for delivery to clients without "direct supervision and control of a pharmacist."
- An informal meeting between the Pharmacy's attorney, pharmacist-in-charge, and members of the Department's Medical Review Branch occurred, during which the pharmacist-in-charge allegedly provided documents and live testimony contradicting the Department's facts. The Department subsequently sent another letter informing the Pharmacy that its provider status was still being terminated due to the lack of supervision and control of the pharmacist.
- The letter sent by the Department informed the Pharmacy of its rights to an appeal. The Pharmacy sent a notice of appeal to the Office of Adminis-

trative Hearing and Appeals (OAHA) and stated that "pertinent documentation and other evidence for consideration" would follow. No such evidence followed.
- The Board of Pharmacy (the "Board") conducted an investigation and determined that there was insufficient evidence to determine that a violation of pharmacy law occurred. Therefore, no action on the Pharmacy's license was being taken. The Pharmacy submitted the Board's letter to the hearing officer for consideration.
- The hearing officer, based on the declarations of the auditor and consultant describing their inspection of the Pharmacy, rejected Pharmacy's appeal. It stated that the Pharmacy had not denied that the events occurred as reported by the Department, and that the only evidence submitted by the Pharmacy was the Board's letter.
- The Pharmacy filed a petition for traditional mandamus, alleging the Department based its decision on unreliable evidence and failed to consider other evidence by the Pharmacy. The Pharmacy attempted to submit declarations that had not been submitted to the OAHA. The trial court entered a judgment denying the writ petition, stating that the Department's decision was not arbitrary, capricious or wholly lacking in evidentiary support.

Reasoning
- The fact question was not merely whether the pharmacist had his eyes fixed on the technician while she filled prescriptions, but whether the pharmacist exercised adequate supervision and control to protect public welfare. This was a question within the Department's expertise.
- The court observed that the hearing officer did consider the Board's letter indicating insufficient evidence of unlicensed activity, but that it did not clear the Pharmacy of any alleged violation of pharmacy law. Rather the decision was made because it had insufficient evidence to revoke its license.
- The Department came to an adjudicatory decision dependent on the facts of the case, and the Pharmacy failed to show any reason why it should have been allowed to add extra-record evidence in the trial court. The right to appeal statute required the Pharmacy to submit the written appeal along with all documents and relevant evidence to the Department's director or to the director's designee. The OAHA was the Department's designee, and the

Pharmacy did not submit such evidence though it was aware that it was supposed to.

- There is a rational connection between a threat to public welfare and an unauthorized, unsupervised person distributing drugs into containers for delivery to customers' homes. There was no evidence of any control system to make sure the pharmacy checked the prescriptions that were filled by the technician and placed at the pick-up point for delivery.

Holding: The trial court's judgment to deny the writ of mandamus was affirmed. Pharmacy failed to show grounds for reversal.

2. *Adusumelli v. Steiner*, No. 08-6932 (S.D.N.Y. 2010) (September 30, 2010)

Relief sought: Plaintiffs sought a judgment declaring a New York statute that prohibited the licensure of aliens who have not obtained "legal permanent residence" (LPR) status as unconstitutional and permanently enjoining the defendants from enforcing it.

Issue: Did the New York statute violate the Equal Protection Clause and unconstitutionally encroach upon the federal immigration power?

Background and procedural history

- New York Education Law § 6805(1)(6) provided that to qualify for a pharmacist license, an applicant must be a United States citizen or an alien lawfully admitted for permanent residence in the United States. This excluded those aliens who have received authorization from the federal government to work in the United States temporarily.
- Plaintiffs were 26 aliens with temporary authorization from the federal government to work in the United States. They all are pharmacists. They had secured "limited licenses" to practice pharmacy under a previous version of the law. These licenses had since expired, but the court had ordered that they be extended pending the outcome of the litigation.
- Twenty-two of the plaintiffs had applied for green cards to grant them LPR status, demonstrating that most of them intend to stay in the United States.
- Defendants, the Commissioner of Education and the Chancellor of Regents, argued that such nonimmigrant aliens are transient as a class and that the statute rationally protected the public from the consequences of such transience.
- Both sides filed for summary judgment.

Reasoning

- State classifications based on alienage are subject to strict scrutiny unless a state is excluding aliens from political and governmental functions or they are denying benefits and opportunities to undocumented aliens. Defendants agreed that neither of these exceptions applied, but rather they argued that strict scrutiny should not apply because the law treated citizens and LPR aliens alike, and placed all other aliens into a disfavored class. Two circuit courts have relied on this distinction to uphold state laws that denied benefits and opportunities to only non-LPR aliens.
- Even if the court applied intermediate scrutiny, the law did not meet the standard. Under intermediate scrutiny, the government bears the burden of proving that the classification serves "important governmental objectives and that the discriminatory means are substantially related to the achievement of those objectives."
  - Defendants presented no evidence that the law met this standard. It did not show, for example, that transience among New York pharmacists threatened public health or that nonimmigrant pharmacists, as a class, are in fact more transient than LPR and citizen pharmacists. United States citizenship does not guarantee that the person will never leave the United States.
- State laws which impose discriminatory burdens upon the entrance or residence of aliens lawfully within the United States conflict with the constitutionally derived federal power to regulate immigration, and have accordingly been held invalid.
  - By declaring that plaintiffs may not practice pharmacy, New York law imposed additional burdens not contemplated by Congress, and thus unconstitutionally encroached upon the federal immigration power.

Holding: The court granted summary judgment in favor of the plaintiffs and permanently enjoined defendants from applying the New York statute against the plaintiffs.

34.5 ERISA
A. Administrative Remedies

1. *Templin v. Independence Blue Cross*, 2010 WL 2991259 (E.D. Pa. 2010) (July 27, 2010)

Relief sought: Plaintiffs, individuals and pharmacies, alleged claims arising under ERISA for wrongful denial of benefits.

Issue: Did the plaintiffs fail to exhaust their administrative remedies as required by ERISA so that judicial review at this point was inappropriate?

Facts and procedural history

- Plaintiffs were individuals and pharmacies who were beneficiaries of, or assignees of beneficiaries, of a group health insurance policy. They alleged facts that suggested a fixed policy that denied benefits for some claims. Plaintiffs also alleged facts that show defendants failed to comply with their own internal administrative procedures for other claims by failing to render a decision.
- Of the 51 disputed claims identified by the plaintiffs, over half of the claims received a decision from defendants in the form of a partial payment.
- Defendants filed motions to dismiss.

Reasoning

- Plaintiffs did not allege any facts showing an attempt to avail themselves of the remedies under the insurance policy. The partial payments constituted adverse benefit determinations that plaintiffs should have challenged through the appeal process set up by the policy.
- For the court to perform the first level of review of these claims, that is, to examine the individual claim forms, identify any individual defects, and interpret and apply the policy's terms to each claim, would contravene the purpose of ERISA and would waste judicial resources.
- Exhaustion of administrative remedies may render subsequent judicial review unnecessary because a plan's own remedial procedures will resolve many claims, and where it does not, it enables administrators to assemble a factual record that will assist a court in reviewing actions.

Holding: The court denied defendants' motions to dismiss without prejudice and stayed the proceedings in the case. The court ordered the parties to conduct an expedited administrative review of all the claims at issue.

B. Preemption

1. *Pharmaceutical Care Management Association v. District of Columbia*, 613 F.3d 179 (D.C. Cir. 2010) (July 9, 2010)

Relief sought: The District of Columbia appealed the judgment of the district court that held provisions of Title II of the Access Rx Act of 2004 were preempted by the Employee Retirement Income Security Act (ERISA).

Issue: Is Title II of the Access Rx Act of 2004 preempted by ERISA insofar as provisions apply to a pharmaceutical benefits manager (PBM) under contract with an employee benefit plan (EBP) because they "relate to" an EBP?

Facts and procedural history: Title II imposes a number of requirements upon PBMs and upon any health care plan that contracts with a PBM, thus becoming a covered entity. These requirements include:

- A PBM owes a fiduciary duty to a covered entity and shall perform its duties in accordance with the standards of conduct applicable to a fiduciary (§ 48-832.01(a) and (b)(1)(A)).
- A PBM shall notify the covered entity in writing of any conflict of interests (§ 48-832.01(b)(1)(C)).
- A PBM that receives from any drug manufacturer or labeler any payment or benefit of any kind in connection with the utilization of prescription drugs shall pass that payment on in full to the covered entity (§ 48-832.01(b)(2)).
- Upon request by a covered entity, a PBM shall disclose the quantity of drugs purchased by the covered entity and the net cost to the covered entity for the drugs (§ 48-832.01(c)(1)(A)).
- Upon request by a covered entity, a PBM shall disclose the terms and arrangements for remuneration between the PBM and a drug manufacturer or labeler (§ 48-832.01(c)(1)(B)).
- A PBM that dispenses a substitute drug that costs more than the prescribed drug shall disclose to the covered entity the cost of both drugs and any benefit or payment to the PBM as a result of the substitution (§ 48-832.01(d)(2)).
- A PBM shall transfer in full to the covered entity any benefit or payment received as the result of a prescription drug substitution (§ 48-832.01(d)(3)).

The Pharmaceutical Care Management Association (PCMA), a national trade association representing PBMs, filed suit arguing Title II is preempted by ERISA. The district court held Title II is preempted in its entirety by ERISA and granted summary judgment for the PCMA.

Reasoning

- ERISA expressly preempts "any and all state laws insofar as they...relate to any employee benefit plan." A state law "relates to" an EBP if it (1) has a connection with or (2) has a reference to such a plan. To find whether a state law has a connection with an EBP, the court must look to the objectives of the ERISA statute as a guide to the scope of the state law that Congress understood would survive, as well as to the nature of the effect of the state law on ERISA plans.

- A principal goal of ERISA is to enable employers to establish a uniform administrative scheme that provides a set of standard procedures to guide processing of claims and disbursement of benefits. The provisions of Title II regulate a PBM's administration of benefits on behalf of an EBP by requiring a PBM to follow a specific practice in administering pharmaceutical benefits on behalf of an EBP.

- The District argued Title II does not have an impermissible constraining effect upon EBPs because the statute offers clear benefits that an EBP can simply decline. This is true of §§ 48-832.01(b)(2) and (c) because they can be waived. Sections 48-832.01(a), (b)(1), and (d), however, are clearly meant to govern the relationship between a PBM and an EBP regardless of whether their contract provides otherwise. These sections bind plan administrators because the "choice" they leave an EBP between self-administration and third-party administration of pharmaceutical benefits is, in reality, no choice at all. For most EBPs, internal administration of beneficiaries' pharmaceutical benefits is a practical impossibility because it would mean forgoing the economies of scale, purchasing leverage, and network of pharmacies only a PBM can offer.

Holding: Sections 48-832.01(a), (b)(1), and (d) have a "connection with" and therefore "relate to" an EBP and are preempted by ERISA. Because an EBP may avoid the default terms of §§ 48-832.01(b)(2) and (c) by contract, and because those provisions do not make "reference to" ERISA plans or create an enforcement mechanism for the rights provided by ERISA, they are not preempted by ERISA.

2. *Feldman's Medical Center Pharmacy, Inc. v. CareFirst, Inc.*, 2010 WL 2639881 (D. Md. 2010) (June 29, 2010)

Relief sought: Feldman's Medical Center Pharmacy, Inc. (FMCP) sued CareFirst, Inc. for breach of contract, unjust enrichment and bad faith. CareFirst removed to federal court on the ground that one of FMCP's claims was completely preempted by ERISA. FMCP moved to remand back to state court.

Issue: Did FMCP's claims rely on the assignment of benefits by patients which would directly implicate ERISA?

Facts and procedural history
- FMCP is a Maryland specialty pharmacy. CareFirst is a Maryland health insurer. FMCP became a participating provider in CareFirst's network and CareFirst agreed to reimburse FMCP for "covered services rendered to CareFirst members."
- FMCP alleged that CareFirst failed to pay $1.5 million in legitimate claims submitted by FMCP involving the provision of "factor," a blood-clotting substance used in the treatment of hemophilia. FMCP sued for breach of contract, unjust enrichment and bad faith.
- CareFirst filed a third-party complaint naming FMCP patients "John Does 1 and 2" as third-party defendants and alleged that FMCP was a "non-participating provider" and any CareFirst member who obtained factor at FMCP was required to submit a claim to CareFirst, which would reimburse the member—not FMCP, thus creating potentially adverse claims between FMCP and the patients.
- CareFirst removed the claim to federal court. FMCP moved to remand based on the court lacking subject matter jurisdiction.

Reasoning
- ERISA's civil enforcement provision, § 502(a), completely preempts state law claims that come within its scope and converts these state claims into federal claims. Under § 502(a)(1)(B), a civil action may be brought by a participant or beneficiary to recover benefits due to her under the terms of her plan.
- A healthcare provider may acquire derivative standing under ERISA by obtaining a written assignment from a participant or beneficiary of her right to payment of medical payments.
- FMCP's claims relied on the patients' benefit assignments because in its complaint, it alleged that an alternative basis for its entitlement as a non-participating provider was due to the assignment.
- The patients obtained their health insurance from CareFirst through an employer-sponsored plan governed by ERISA. Thus, FMCP's claim based on the assignment of those benefits required the interpretation of ERISA.

Holding: FMCP's motion to remand was denied because the assignment of benefits by the patients required an interpretation of the patients' ERISA plans. Federal subject matter jurisdiction existed.

34.6 Fraud
A. False Claims Act

1. *Hopper v. Solvay Pharmaceuticals, Inc.*, 588 F.3d 1318 (11th Cir. 2009) (December 4, 2009)

Relief sought: Qui tam relators, James Hopper and Colin Hutto, sought recovery on behalf of the United States pursuant to the False Claims Act, 31 U.S.C. § 3729, et seq., for claims paid by government health programs as a result of a marketing campaign by Solvay Pharmaceuticals, Inc.

Issue: Did the relators plead the submission of specific false claims with particularity as required by Federal Rules of Civil Procedure Rule 9(b)?

Facts and procedural history

- Solvay employed the relators as sales representatives. One of their duties was to implement what they allege to be an illegal marketing scheme for Marinol, a prescription drug manufactured and sold by Solvay.
- Marinol was approved by the Food and Drug Administration as an appetite stimulant for AIDS patients and for the treatment of nausea and vomiting associated with cancer chemotherapy. To increase sales, the relators allege, Solvay implemented an off-label marketing campaign to encourage physicians to prescribe Marinol for appetite loss in cancer patients and for treatment of nausea in HIV patients, purposes for which Marinol was not approved.
- Relators asserted that sales generated from the marketing scheme caused the government to pay false claims through Medicaid and other programs that provide prescription drug benefits. The relators did not allege that Solvay itself submitted any false claims. The complaint did not identify any specific false claims presented to a government healthcare program or any person or entity who submitted a claim. Nor did it allege that Solvay intended that the government rely on the alleged false statements or records in deciding whether to pay claims.
- Solvay filed a motion to dismiss. The district court dismissed the relators' federal claims with prejudice.

Reasoning

- The False Claims Act makes any person liable who presents, or causes to be presented, a false or fraudulent claim. 31 U.S.C. § 3729(a)(1). Subsection (a)(2) makes liable any person who knowingly makes, uses, or causes to be made or used, a false record or statement to get a false claim paid or approved.
- Subsection (a)(1) contains a "presentment clause" that requires an allegation of an actual false claim for payment being made to the government. Although the complaint includes a statistical analysis that "renders inescapable the conclusion that a huge number of claims...resulted from Solvay's illegal marketing campaign" it did not identify a single physician, pharmacist, or state healthcare program that submitted a claim for reimbursement to the federal government.
- Subsection (a)(2) does not contain a presentment clause, but it does require that the relators show that the defendants intended for the government to rely on their false statements in deciding whether to pay a false claim. The complaint did not allege that any person or entity had knowledge of the off-label marketing campaign or that Solvay intended for that campaign to influence the government's decision to pay for those prescriptions.

Holding: The court affirmed the district court's dismissal of the relators' federal claims for failure to comply with the particularity requirements of Federal Rule of Civil Procedure 9(b). Under subsection (a)(1) of the False Claims Act, the relators failed to plead with particularity the actual presentment of a claim. Under subsection (a)(2), the complaint failed to allege that Solvay intended its false statements to play any role in the government's decision to reimburse state health programs for the cost of those prescriptions.

B. Off-Label Promotion

1. *In re Neurontin Marketing and Sales Practices and Products Liability Litigation*, 677 F. Supp. 2d 479 (D. Mass. 2010) (January 8, 2010)

Relief sought: Plaintiffs, Kaiser Foundation Health Plan, Inc., Kaiser Foundation Hospitals, Aetna, Inc. and Guardian Life Insurance Company, brought this case against Pfizer, Inc. and Warner-Lambert Company, alleging violations of the Racketeer Influenced and Corrupt Organizations Act (RICO); the California Unfair Competition Law;

the unfair competition status of other states; the Pennsylvania Insurance Fraud Statute; and requesting restitution or disgorgement for unjust enrichment related to the sales and marketing of Neurontin.

Issues: Did the plaintiffs have standing? Also, did the plaintiffs create a triable issue of fact as to the following:

- Causation;
- Whether Neurontin is ineffective for the relevant off-label uses; and
- Whether defendants misrepresented Neurontin's effectiveness with scienter?

Facts and procedural history

- Neurontin was approved by the Food and Drug Administration to treat partial seizures in adults with epilepsy and to treat pain in shingles patients. The defendants began to market the drug for off-label indications, including mood disorders, pain, and restless leg syndrome.
- Plaintiffs allege that the defendants were aware that Neurontin was no more effective than a placebo at treating these off-label conditions, but they aggressively marketed the drug to doctors anyway.
- Defendants moved for summary judgment.

Reasoning

- Pharmaceutical manufacturers, who have superior access to information about their drugs, especially in the postmarketing phase as new risks emerge, are under a special duty to investigate and report adverse effects of their drugs.
- A plaintiff third party payor must prove through individualized evidence that the misrepresentation caused specific physicians, third party payors, or consumers to rely on the fraud, and cannot rely on aggregate or statistical proof. While each of the plaintiffs could prove through aggregated proof that the fraudulent marketing campaign likely caused them injury, they could not prove which doctor's prescriptions were caused by defendants' alleged fraudulent misrepresentations or omissions and which were not.
- Kaiser's Drug Information Service (DIS) had direct communications with Pfizer both through its information-gathering activities and its Inquiry Department service for physicians and members. Kaiser alleged that, had Pfizer not made misrepresentations regarding Neurontin's effectiveness for certain off-label indications, DIS's activities

would have highlighted problems with Neurontin such that Kaiser could have responded sooner and thereby reduced its payments and reimbursements for Neurontin.

- There was no evidence in the record that Guardian or Aetna at any point relied directly on Pfizer's "half truths" communicated through its alleged manipulation and withholding of studies that suggested Neurontin's ineffectiveness for off-label indications.
- Sufficient evidence was presented to support the claim that Neurontin was ineffective for the off-label indications and that there were "cheaper and more optimal" alternatives to Neurontin.
- Abundant evidence was submitted that showed Pfizer engaged in off-label marketing for multiple indications, all while it was in possession of studies showing that Neurontin was not more effective than a placebo in treating those indications.

Holding: Defendant's motion for summary judgment was granted as to plaintiffs Guardian and Aetna. Defendant's motion for summary judgment was denied as to plaintiff Kaiser, as Kaiser presented evidence allowing a reasonable inference of causation to be drawn in its favor.

2. *In re Neurontin Marketing and Sales Practices and Products Liability Litigation*, 2010 WL 3169485 (D. Mass. 2010) (August 10, 2010)

Relief sought: Plaintiff, Mary Dorsey, brought this case against Pfizer, Inc. alleging that she was injured by defendants' drug Neurontin, and that defendants failed to adequately warn of potential adverse effects connected to the ingestion of the drug.

Issues

- Did the plaintiff have a causation expert who would testify that Neurontin specifically caused her injuries?
- Did plaintiff concede that the side effects from which she suffered were the subject of warnings on Neurontin's label?
- Does the plaintiff have any proximate cause evidence that either she or her prescribing physicians would have done anything differently if additional warning had been listed on the label?

Facts and procedural history

- Plaintiff was initially prescribed Neurontin in 1999. During 2002 and 2003, while still taking Neurontin, plaintiff began to experience more seizure-like symptoms. She was constantly lethargic and often experienced black-outs.

- Neurontin had been approved by the FDA for the treatment of epilepsy. Plaintiff claimed she was prescribed Neurontin off-label, but the record was not clear which medical condition Neurontin was prescribed to treat.
- In May 2003, plaintiff consulted a neurologist who told her she was being "over-medicated." He reduced plaintiff's medication regimen by taking her off both Neurontin and a drug called Klonopin. She experienced significant improvement.
- Defendants moved for summary judgment.

Reasoning

- Plaintiff relied on the opinions of her neurologist to show that Neurontin specifically caused her symptoms. During depositions, however, the neurologist refused to state that he believed Neurontin was the source of plaintiff's symptoms.
- Plaintiff conceded that many of her symptoms were listed in a warning on Neurontin's label during all relevant time periods. Although Neurontin's label did mention central nervous system depression as a possible side effect, it did not specifically warn that it could cause black-outs. Plaintiff did not provide any general or specific causation testimony that Neurontin caused her black-outs or fainting.
- Doctors are permitted to prescribe drugs off-label. Plaintiff failed to show that the doctors prescribed the medication as a result of a failure to warn or a misrepresentation.

Holding: Court granted the defendants' motion for summary judgment because the plaintiff failed to provide an expert who believed Neurontin was the source of her symptoms, plaintiff failed to provide any testimony that Neurontin caused symptoms that she was claiming it failed to warn about, and because the plaintiff did not present any evidence of proximate causation.

34.7 HIPAA and Privacy

A. *Liska v. United States*, 2010 WL 1038652 (D. Ariz. 2010) (March 19, 2010)

Relief sought: Liska, plaintiff, sought relief from Walgreen Arizona Drug Company for damages as a result of negligence per se due to violation of the Health Insurance Portability and Accountability Act (HIPAA).

Issues: Did Walgreens violate HIPAA or Arizona privacy laws for its disclosure of pharmacy records to a law enforcement official? As a result of the disclosure, did Walgreens intentionally inflict emotional distress upon the plaintiff?

Facts and procedural history: Plaintiff alleged the following facts, pertinent to the claims against Walgreens:

- Liska had been a registered nurse for eight years and suffered from numerous injuries, osteoporosis, elective surgery, ulcers, and dehydration, for which she had been prescribed medications by her treating physicians. Liska began having a romantic affair with Dr. Brian Gallman, one of her treating physicians. He prescribed legitimate medications for Liska while she was in recovery from her elective surgery. One of those prescriptions was for Soma. Liska subsequently ended the affair.
- Several months later, Liska attempted to obtain a refill for the Soma prescription. The Walgreens pharmacy contacted Gallman to verify the validity of the prescription, and Gallman denied knowledge of the prescription or of Liska. The pharmacy reported the matter to Defendant Lake Havasu Police Department. Officer David Dodge was assigned to investigate. The pharmacy disclosed Liska's prescription records to Dodge for his investigation.
- Dodge interrogated Liska regarding a possible claim of prescription fraud and caused her employment to be ended. He was later removed from the case.
- As a result of these events, Liska lost her job, could not work as a nurse, and lost her income for five months. She had great difficulty supporting herself and two children. Her emotional distress manifested as loss of sleep, weight loss, loss of appetite, nightmares, anxiety, and depression.
- Liska alleged that Walgreens violated HIPAA by disclosing her prescription history to Dodge, that Walgreens had a fiduciary duty to protect the privacy and confidential records of the consumers who fill their prescriptions at Walgreens, and that Walgreens intentionally inflicted emotional distress upon her.
- Defendant Walgreen Arizona Drug Company filed a motion to dismiss for the claims against it.

Reasoning

- Under HIPAA, a covered entity may disclose "to a law enforcement official protected health information that the covered entity believes in good faith constitutes evidence of criminal conduct that occurred on the premises of the covered entity." The complaint did not allege that Walgreens acted in bad faith, and the pharmacy was presumed to have acted in good faith.

- Arizona statutes require that a pharmacy keep its records of prescriptions "open for inspection at all times by...officers of the law in performance of their duties" and provides immunity for disclosure of medical records in good faith and a presumption of good faith. Walgreens apparently disclosed Liska's prescription history in a good faith belief that it was required to permit Dodge, a law enforcement officer investigating Liska's possible prescription fraud, to inspect Liska's records. The complaint did not allege otherwise.

- To state a claim for intentional infliction of emotional distress, a plaintiff must allege that the defendant "by extreme and outrageous conduct intentionally or recklessly caused severe emotional distress." Liska, however, alleged only legal conclusions, and did not specify how Walgreens behavior was "extreme and outrageous."

Holding: All claims against Walgreens were dismissed. Walgreens did not violate HIPAA or Arizona privacy statutes, as it acted in good faith when it disclosed prescription records to the Lake Havasu investigator. Nor did the plaintiff allege any behavior by Walgreens that would be considered outrageous or extreme.

34.8 Negligence
A. Learned Intermediary

1. *DiGiovanni v. Albertson's Inc.*, No. 1-09-1297 (Ill. App. Ct. 2010) (August 25, 2010)

Relief sought: Estate of decedent, Laverne DiGiovanni, filed a wrongful death suit against defendant Albertson's Inc. d/b/a Osco Drugs (Osco), and alleged that Osco failed to warn the patient of the interaction between two drugs prescribed by her doctor.

Issue: Did the trial court properly hold that the learned intermediary doctrine did not require Osco to warn the patient of a potential drug interaction?

Background and procedural history

- The patient had been prescribed lithium by her physician for a period of ten years. In January 2003, her physician also prescribed a drug called Tenoretic for her high blood pressure. The prescription was filled by Dr. Jonathan Huynh on January 20, 2003.

- When Dr. Huynh filled the prescription for Tenoretic, the pharmacy computer indicated there would be an interaction between it and the lithium. Dr. Huynh called the patient's physician and was told to fill the prescription and that the physician would monitor the patient. A note was made and placed in the patient's file.

- A refill prescription for lithium was filled by another pharmacist, John Glowacki, seven days later. Glowacki saw the note written by Dr. Huynh and did not call Laverne's physician before filling the prescription.

- Several days later, Laverne became ill and later died, allegedly from lithium toxicity.

- The trial court dismissed Osco from the case because it found the pharmacy had no duty to warn the patient under the learned intermediary doctrine.

Reasoning

- The learned intermediary doctrine provides that manufacturers of prescription drugs have a duty to warn prescribing physicians of a drug's known risks and physicians, in turn, have a duty to convey warnings to their patients.

- Previous case law has exempted pharmacies and pharmacists from giving warnings to patients. Because the propriety of a prescription depends not only on the propensities of the drug, but also on the patient's condition, to impose a duty to warn would require the pharmacist to "interject himself into the doctor-patient relationship and practice medicine without a license."

- Courts are unwilling to subject pharmacists to liability for failure to give warnings not requested by the physician. Doing so would place a greater burden on pharmacists than on drug manufacturers, as such duty to warn is placed on the physician.

Holding: Trial court properly dismissed Osco from the suit. The pharmacists were under no duty to warn the customer of the possible interaction between the two drugs under the learned intermediary doctrine.

2. *Smith v. CVS Pharmacy, Inc.*, 2009 WL 3678256 (W.D. La. 2009) (November 4, 2009)

Relief sought: Defendant filed a motion for summary judgment to dismiss because plaintiff failed to timely file an expert report.

Issues: Should the court exclude the plaintiff's expert

affidavit because it was filed late? Even if the expert affidavit is allowed, did the Learned Intermediary Doctrine (LID) preclude liability as a matter of law?

Facts and procedural history: Plaintiff claimed the pharmacy negligently filled her prescriptions for multiple diuretics, which caused renal failure. One month after the deadline for expert reports, defendant filed a motion for summary judgment on the ground that without an expert, plaintiff could not prove the elements of her case. In response, plaintiff filed an expert affidavit. Defendants subsequently filed a motion in limine to exclude the affidavit.

Reasoning

- **Motion in Limine:** Because dismissing a case is an extreme discovery sanction, a court will only do so when failure to comply with a discovery order results from willfulness or bad faith. Here, the actual plaintiff had no role in the late filing. The court denied the motion in limine, penalized plaintiff by moving the trial back and required plaintiff's counsel, Sir Clyde Lain II, to pay defendant's cost for filing its motion.
- **Motion for Summary Judgment:** The court explained "[t]he learned intermediary doctrine does not apply to absolve pharmacists of all duties to patients, though, particularly where the prescription is facially incorrect or inadequate and creates a substantial risk of harm to the patient." Plaintiff's expert averred that the computer system at CVS would have warned the pharmacist of the duplication and the pharmacist would have to override the warning. Thus, there is a question of fact for the jury to determine if the pharmacist breached a duty to the patient.

Holding: The motion in limine and motion for summary judgment were denied. Court ordered plaintiff's counsel to pay costs for the motion in limine.

B. Preemption

1. *Wimbush v. Wyeth, Inc.,* 2010 WL 3256029 (6th Cir. 2010) (August 18, 2010)

Relief sought: Plaintiff, estate of Mary Buchanan, sought economic, non-economic, and punitive damages based on claims for strict liability and common law negligence.

Issues: Did the district court err in granting summary judgment in favor of Wyeth, the defendant, on all of the plaintiff's claims?

Facts and procedural history

- Buchanan was prescribed and ingested Redux for several months in order to control her weight. She was diagnosed with primary pulmonary hypertension (PPH) in 2001. She died in 2003, allegedly as a result of taking Redux.
- Wyeth provided several warnings regarding the health risks associated with ingesting Redux. A second warning letter explained that the risk of PPH was greater than previously stated and that PPH was a serious disorder "with an estimated 4-year mortality rate of 45%."
- District court granted Wyeth's motions for summary judgment on all claims, explaining that the strict liability and negligence claims relating to Wyeth's conduct prior to the FDA's approval of Redux were preempted by the FDA's subsequent approval of the drug. The court also stated that any post-FDA approval claims, which were not preempted, failed on their merits.

Reasoning

- According to Ohio law, as long as adequate warning has been given for a pharmaceutical product, the manufacturer cannot be strictly liable for design defects. Wyeth presented substantial evidence that it had distributed information regarding risks of the drug to physicians, including the plaintiff's doctor, and that those warnings were adequate. Plaintiff did not specifically point to any evidence that would contradict Wyeth's evidence.
- Ohio statutory law has abrogated common law negligence claims for product liability, but plaintiff's complaint was filed prior to the statutory amendment that provided so. The amendment did not apply retroactively.
- Plaintiff argued that Wyeth's warnings were irrelevant because Wyeth should have known that the drug was so dangerous that no warning could make the drug acceptable. Plaintiff, however, did not point to any facts or evidence that revealed why Wyeth should have known this.
- A federal law may preempt a state law when an actual conflict between a federal and a state law exists. The court found no impossibility between complying with a state law duty to exercise reasonable care in the process leading up to placing a drug on the market and complying with the federal government's process for approving drugs. Also, case law supports the conclusion that Congress did

not intend to preempt state tort law claims when it passed the Food, Drug, and Cosmetic Act.

Holding

- Because plaintiff failed to point to any evidence creating a factual dispute as to the adequacy of warning, the strict liability design defect claim failed as a matter of law. Judgment granting summary judgment in favor of Wyeth was affirmed.
- Plaintiff failed to point to any evidence as to why Wyeth should have known its drug was too dangerous that no warning was adequate. Court affirmed summary judgment granted in favor of Wyeth.
- FDA approval does not automatically preempt state law tort claims for negligence. District court erred in granting summary judgment on plaintiff's pre-approval common law negligence claims.
- District court's mootness ruling as to punitive damages was reversed and remanded.

C. Proximate Causation

1. *Cochran v. Wyeth, Inc.*, 2010 WL 2902717 (Pa. Super. 2010) (July 27, 2010)

Relief sought: Plaintiff filed a complaint against Wyeth, asserting that the warnings accompanying the drug, Redux, were inadequate.

Issue: Can a plaintiff prove proximate causation by showing that a drug manufacturer failed to disclose a risk of injury that the plaintiff did not sustain, but can show that she sustained an injury that was warned of by the manufacturer?

Facts and procedural history

- Plaintiff, Nancy Cochran, ingested the weight-loss drug, Redux, for approximately 10 months. Redux was manufactured by defendant, Wyeth Inc.
- Wyeth informed plaintiff's doctor that Redux may cause primary pulmonary hypertension (PPH), and the doctor, in turn, warned the plaintiff of such risk prior to prescribing Redux. Plaintiff's doctor was unaware of the risk that Redux may cause valvular heart disease (VHD), and therefore never warned the plaintiff of such risk. The plaintiff was subsequently diagnosed with PPH.
- Wyeth filed a motion for summary judgment claiming that its warnings were sufficient because it informed the plaintiff's doctor of the risk of PPH and plaintiff was diagnosed with such disease.
- Trial court granted the motion for summary judg-

ment in favor of Wyeth. It concluded that because the plaintiff suffered from PPH and not VHD, she could not establish that Wyeth's failure to warn of the risk of VHD was the proximate cause of her particular injury.

Reasoning

- Proximate cause is an essential element in a failure to warn case and is defined as "a substantial contributing factor in bringing about the harm in question." A plaintiff must show that had the defendant issued a proper warning to the learned intermediary (the physician), he would have altered his behavior and the injury would have been avoided.
- The court was unable to find case law related to the issue of whether, in a failure to warn claim, a plaintiff must show the exact harm that the manufacturer failed to warn about. It did, however, analogize a failure to warn claim to that of a tort of informed consent, given their similar elements of duty, breach of duty, and causation.
- In informed consent cases, courts have held that an unrevealed risk that should have been made known must materialize, otherwise the omission is without legal consequence.
- Although the plaintiff's doctor testified in his deposition that he would not have prescribed Redux had he known of the risk of VHD, the relationship between the legal wrong (the failure to disclose the risk of VHD) and the injury (PPH) is too remote for proximate causation.

Holding: Before a plaintiff can prove that a non-disclosed risk would have altered the physician's decision to prescribe a drug, the plaintiff must first demonstrate that she suffered from the precise injury that the manufacturer allegedly failed to disclose. The plaintiff failed to do so here, because she alleged that Wyeth failed to warn of VHD, but she in fact suffered from PPH, which was adequately warned of by Wyeth. Summary judgment in favor of Wyeth was affirmed.

D. Punitive Damages

1. *Horn v. Wal-Mart Stores Inc.*, 2009 WL 4672329 (D.N.J. 2009). (December 4, 2009)

Relief sought: Plaintiff sought compensatory damages of $150,000 plus interest, costs, and punitive damages.

Issue: Could a reasonable juror find from the facts alleged by plaintiffs that the dispensing pharmacist's conduct rose to the level of willfulness or wantonness required by

New Jersey law, to justify plaintiff's claim for punitive damages?

Facts and procedural history

- A cardiologist prescribed Warfarin for the 81-year-old plaintiff in January 2008, starting at 10 mg the first day and 5 mg per day thereafter.
- The prescription was telephoned to the defendant pharmacy, where it was properly transcribed by one pharmacist and left to be filled by another pharmacist. The label on the finished prescription read "*TAKE TWO [5 MG] TABLETS BY MOUTH EVERY DAY THEN TAKE 1 TABLET IN THE EVENING.*"
- Plaintiff claimed that he took a total of 15 mg of Warfarin daily for four days in accordance with these directions, then he suffered a stroke that caused permanent injuries.
- At deposition, the dispensing pharmacist testified that he was required to know the dosage of the medications he was dispensing, that he knew the medication being dispensed was a "High Therapeutic Index" drug, meaning that even a slight dosage error could cause serious health consequences, and that he did not know the safe loading dose.
- The defendant pharmacy had a computer program that assisted in review of prescriptions, and in this case the computer system displayed a warning to the pharmacist at the time of dispensing. The pharmacist testified he was required by the warning to consult with the prescriber, but that he overrode the warning and dispensed the medication.

Reasoning

- New Jersey law provides that punitive damages may be awarded when a plaintiff can prove: (i) by clear and convincing evidence that the (ii) defendant's acts or omissions that caused harm (iii) "were actuated by actual malice or accompanied by a wanton and willful disregard of persons who foreseeably might be harmed…." (N.J.S.A. § 2A:15-5.12).
- The dispensing pharmacist testified at his deposition that he: (i) *knew* of the risks associated with overdose of Warfarin and (ii) overrode the computer warning that explicitly told him to confirm the dosage with the prescribing physician. The court would not conclude, as a matter of law, that these actions did not rise to the level of "willful and wanton conduct" as defined in the New Jersey punitive damages statute.

Holding: The defendants' motion for partial summary judgment to remove the punitive damages claim was denied.

E. Standard of Care—Design

1. *Lance v. Wyeth*, 2010 WL 2991597 (Pa. Super. 2010) (August 2, 2010)

Relief sought: Plaintiff, Administratrix for the Estate of Catherine Lance, appealed from the trial court's order granting summary judgment in favor of defendant, Wyeth. In her complaint, plaintiff alleged that Wyeth was negligent in placing an unreasonably dangerous prescription drug on the market and failing to withdraw it upon discovering that it was unsuitable for public consumption. She also asserted that Wyeth breached the standard of care in designing, developing, inspecting, testing and preparing the drug.

Issue: Did the plaintiff present a cognizable claim under Pennsylvania law?

Facts and procedural history

- Decedent, Lance, ingested Wyeth's diet drug, Redux, for approximately three months before discontinuing its use. Redux was prescribed to treat obesity.
- The Food and Drug Administration (FDA) approved Redux as "safe and effective" and continued to approve Redux after Lance stopped using it. Several months after Lance discontinued her use of the drug, Wyeth voluntarily withdrew Redux from the market.
- Seven years later, Lance was diagnosed with Primary Pulmonary Hypertension and she suspected her ingestion of diet drugs was related to the diagnosis. Lance subsequently died and the cause of her death is at issue.
- Wyeth filed a motion for summary judgment, which the trial court granted. The trial court concluded that as a matter of law, the plaintiff failed to plead a cognizable cause of action.

Reasoning

- Pennsylvania has limited the potential causes of action available to a plaintiff who alleges a strict liability claim against a drug manufacturer to the following claims: (1) a manufacturer defect claim, or (2) a failure to warn claim. Although plaintiff labeled her claim as "negligent and unreasonable marketing," her proposed cause of action duplicates a design defect claim, seeking to impose strict liability on Wyeth because Redux was unreasonably dangerous. A design defect claim for strict liability is not cognizable under Pennsylvania law when it is asserted against a manufacturer of prescription drugs.

- A strict liability design defect claim is distinct from a negligence design defect claim because strict liability examines the product itself, whereas a negligence cause of action examines the conduct of the defendant.

- The court was persuaded by the majority of jurisdictions that have decided not to impose a common law duty to recall on a manufacturer. The weighing of costs and benefits of recalls should be left to agencies. The FDA's power to withdraw approval of a prescription drug is analogous to the power to recall. During the timeframe in which plaintiff ingested Redux, Wyeth did not have a duty to withdraw Redux from the market because the FDA did not withdraw its approval of the drug.

Holding

- Plaintiff did not allege that Redux contained a manufacturing defect or inadequate warnings. The trial court, therefore, did not err in granting summary judgment in favor of Wyeth on plaintiff's "unreasonable marketing" claim because it averred a strict liability design defect claim.

- Plaintiff's negligent design claim was not precluded by Pennsylvania law, and was a valid cause of action upon which relief may be granted. The trial court erred in granting summary judgment on plaintiff's claim for negligent design of the drug.

- Given the FDA's regulatory authority and a drug manufacturer's post-sale duty to warn, court concluded that Wyeth did not have a common law duty to recall or withdraw Redux. The trial court did not err in granting summary judgment in favor of Wyeth on plaintiff's claim for negligent withdraw and/or recall.

F. Third Party Liability

1. *Sanchez ex rel. Sanchez v. Wal-Mart Stores, Inc.*, 221 P.3d 1276 (Nev. 2009) (December 24, 2009)

Relief sought: Widow and minor children of motorist sued pharmacies that filled controlled substances prescriptions after state agency warned that the patient may be abusing drugs.

Issues

- Under common-law principles, do pharmacies have a duty to act to prevent a pharmacy customer from injuring members of the general public?

- Do Nevada's pharmacy laws and regulations allow third parties to maintain a negligence *per se* claim for alleged violations concerning dispensing prescription drugs and maintenance of customers' records?

Facts and procedural history

- On June 4, 2004, Mr. Sanchez stopped on the side of the road to fix a flat tire. Appellant Robert Martinez, Sanchez's co-worker, arrived at the scene to assist Sanchez. Defendant Patricia Copening's vehicle struck and killed Sanchez and seriously injured Martinez. She was arrested for driving under the influence of controlled substances.

- Appellants filed a wrongful death and personal injury complaint against the pharmacies that filled multiple prescriptions for Copening. Sanchez's estate claimed that because the pharmacies had knowledge of the woman's prescription-filling activities, they owed Sanchez a duty not to fill those prescriptions.

- In June 2003, the Prescription Controlled Substance Abuse Prevention Task Force (Task Force) sent a letter to the pharmacies that had dispensed to, and physicians who had written prescriptions for, Copening, explaining that from May 2002 to May 2003, she had obtained approximately 4,500 hydrocodone pills at 13 different pharmacies.

- Plaintiffs alleged: (i) Copening was intoxicated by controlled substances, and (ii) pharmacies filled Copening's prescriptions after they had received the Task Force letter. The complaint did not allege: (i) any irregularities on the face of the prescriptions; (ii) the prescriptions were filled in violation of the prescriptions' language; (iii) the prescriptions were fraudulent or forged; or (iv) the prescriptions involved dosages that were potentially harmful to Copening's health.

- The pharmacies asserted defendants failed to state a claim upon which relief could be granted on the basis that no duty was owed to appellants. Subsequently, pharmacies moved the district court for summary judgment.

- The trial court concluded: (i) no statute imposed a duty on the pharmacies to take action after receiving the Task Force letter and (ii) absent a legislative duty, the case was governed by Nevada's dram-shop cases with no material difference between a bartender providing a customer alcohol and a pharmacist filling a customer's prescription. Proximate cause did not exist and the court granted summary judgment in favor of the pharmacies.

Reasoning

- The Nevada Supreme Court found the pharmacies did not owe a duty to Sanchez by dispensing drugs to Copening. They had no direct relationship with the third-party appellants who were unidentifiable members of the public who were unknown to the pharmacies.
- Nevada law does not require pharmacies to take action to protect the general public after receiving a Task Force letter. Thus, there was no duty to protect third parties.
- On the negligence *per se* claim, the court held the governing regulations were not intended for the general public's protection or to protect against any injury that the third-party appellants may have sustained. The duty owed under these statutes is to the person receiving the prescription, if there is any duty at all, but it is not for the general public's protection.
- Although various statutory and regulatory provisions may express standards of care for the practice of "pharmacology," under the circumstances of this case, those standards of care do not extend to unidentified third parties.

Holding: The Nevada Supreme Court affirmed, holding that:

- Pharmacies had no duty to third parties under the circumstances of this case.
- The statute governing Task Force notice to pharmacies of potential drug abuse did not create a duty of care to unidentified members of the general public.
- The negligence *per se* claim failed because statutes and regulations were not intended to protect the general public from the kind of injury suffered in this case.

34.9 Pharmaceutical Pricing
A. Reimbursement

1. *AstraZeneca LP v. State*, 41 So.3d 15 (Ala. 2009) (October 16, 2009)

Relief sought: Drug manufacturers appealed a jury verdict finding them liable for misrepresentation and fraudulent suppression regarding average wholesale prices (AWP).

Issue: Did the state reasonably rely on alleged assertions by drug manufacturers about AWP prices?

Facts and procedural background

- After the trial court reduced the amount of punitive damages, Astrazeneca was liable for $160 million. Judgment against Novartis and GlaxoSmithKline (GSK) was for about $114 million including punitive damages.
- On appeal of the verdicts, the court focused on whether the state presented substantial evidence that it reasonably relied on the published wholesale acquisition costs (WAC) and AWP.

Reasoning

- Throughout the relevant period (1991-2005), the state claimed it believed that the published WAC and AWP represented actual prices and that it reimbursed providers based on those prices.
- The companies argued that everyone in the industry knew AWP was a list price and did not include discounts and other deductions.
- The court reviewed extensive evidence that documented the state's knowledge about AWP. According to the court, "[T]he most irrefutable evidence of the State's actual understanding of WAC and AWP is the reimbursement methodology itself. The AMA uses WAC + 9.2% and AWP – 10.2% *to arrive at EAC [estimated acquisition cost].* The State concedes that 'EAC is not a "list" price or an "undiscounted price," but is a "price paid." ' Remarkably, the State has taken the position that AWP *also* means 'an *actual* average price' paid. If these assertions were true, then the State could merely reimburse on the basis of AWP – 0%, as it was doing in 1985. The State, however, has not reimbursed providers on the basis of an undiscounted AWP since 1985 when the DHHS threatened to cut off federal funding on account of that practice. In truth, the State—as do all the states—takes a dis-

count from AWP to compensate for the fact that AWP is *not a net figure*. The AWP discounts are meant to offset the discounts and other price concessions that are available to providers."

- Given the state's knowledge, it could not have reasonably believed, or relied on the belief, that AWP was the actual price pharmacies paid for medications.

Holding: The trial court erred by not granting defendants' motion for judgment as a matter of law. The court reversed the judgments and rendered judgment in favor of defendants.

2. *Hays v. Sebelius*, 589 F.3d 1279 (D.C. Cir. 2009) (December 22, 2009)

Relief sought: Ilene Hays, plaintiff, challenged the decision of four Medicare contractors who announced that the medical necessity of administering the two drugs combined in DuoNeb, rather than in separate doses, had not been established and that payment of the combination drug would be based on the least costly alternative policy.

Issue: May the Secretary of Health and Human Services determine that the reimbursement rate for a particular drug be only up to the price of its least costly alternative?

Facts and procedural history

- Plaintiff was a Medicare Part B beneficiary who suffered from Chronic Obstructive Pulmonary Disease and who used DuoNeb for approximately four years. DuoNeb is an inhalation drug that provides a combination of two drugs in one dose. It can be more expensive than separate doses of the two component drugs.
- 42 U.S.C. § 1395(a)(1)(A) states that "no payment may be made...for expenses incurred for items or services which...are not reasonable and necessary for the diagnosis or treatment of illness or injury...." The Secretary had instructed contractors that when determining whether a treatment is "reasonable and necessary" under this section, they may apply the so-called least costly alternative policy.
- Under the least costly alternative policy, Medicare provides reimbursement for treatments only up to the price of their "reasonably feasible and medically appropriate" least costly alternatives.
- The district court granted the plaintiff summary judgment because the Medicare Act requires that Medicare pay for covered items or services at a statutorily prescribed rate.

Reasoning

- In the relevant section, only a dependent clause separates "reasonable and necessary" from the phrase "items and services." "Expenses," by contrast, appears earlier in the sentence. Ordinarily, qualifying phrases are to be applied to the words or phrase immediately preceding and are not to be construed as extending to others that are more remote.
- Section 1395w-3a provides that for multiple source drugs like DuoNeb, "the amount of payment is" 106 percent of the average sales price of drugs within the same billing and payment code. By reimbursing DuoNeb at 106 percent of the average sales price of its two component drugs—which have different billing and payment codes—the Secretary would fundamentally alter the reimbursement scheme.

Holding: The statute unambiguously authorizes the Secretary to make only a choice: either an item or service is reasonable and necessary, in which case it may be covered at the statutory rate, or it is unreasonable or unnecessary, in which case it may not be covered at all. Decision to grant summary judgment was affirmed.

B. State Pricing Challenges

1. *Division of Medicaid v. Mississippi Independent Pharmacies Association*, 20 So.3d 1236 (Miss. 2009) (November 12, 2009)

Relief sought: Pharmacists appealed Div. of Medicaid (DOM) rule that established a State Maximum Allowable Cost (SMAC) for certain generic drugs.

Issue: Did the DOM rule violate the authorizing statute providing that reimbursement to providers could not be reduced unless authorized by an amendment to the statute?

Facts and procedural history

- The DOM proposed a rule to establish a SMAC for certain generic drugs.
- After pharmacists filed objections, DOM amended the proposed rule to merge SMAC into one of three existing estimated acquisition cost (EAC) methods.
- A chancery court agreed with the pharmacists' claim that the new pricing violated the authorizing statute because a change in reimbursement methodology must be sought through legislation.
- DOM appealed.

Reasoning

- Mississippi law stated that "payments or rates of reimbursement to [Medicaid] providers…" may not be "increased, decreased, or otherwise changed from the levels in effect on July 1, 1999, unless… authorized by an amendment to this section by the Legislature." Miss. Code Ann. § 43-13-117.
- DOM acted beyond its authority because it altered the way Medicaid providers were reimbursed without prior legislative amendment.
- Even though the legislature had given DOM discretion to define estimated acquisition cost (EAC), the prior legislative history and the DOM's own methodology for defining EAC always used average wholesale price (AWP) as the basis for reimbursement. The removal by the legislature of a provision stating a specific discount subtracted from AWP as a calculation did not give DOM the authority to change the manner in which EAC was calculated, but only gave it the discretion to change the discount subtracted from AWP. SMAC was its own method of reimbursement that required legislative amendment.

Holding: DOM exceeded the discretion provided by the legislature when it created SMAC and the new rule was void.

2. *Minnesota Pharmacists Association v. Pawlenty*, 690 F. Supp. 2d 809 (D. Minn. 2010) (February 10, 2010)

Relief sought: Plaintiffs, who were pharmacies, associations representing pharmacies, and several Medicaid recipients, sought to reverse reductions in the reimbursement rates that the State of Minnesota paid pharmacies for brand-name pharmaceutical drugs by the state's Medicaid program.

Issues

- Could plaintiffs maintain a claim under 42 U.S.C. § 1983 for violation of 42 U.S.C. § 1396(a)(30)(A) (Subsection (30)(A))?
- Could plaintiffs maintain any of their claims under the Supremacy Clause based on an alleged conflict between the state plan and federal Medicaid law?
- Could plaintiffs maintain any of their claims based on state law despite principles of state sovereign immunity?

Facts and procedural history

- Section 1396(a)(30)(A) requires that payments under a state plan be "consistent with efficiency, economy, and quality of care" and also be "sufficient to enlist enough providers" so as to provide care and services that are at least equal to that "available to the general population in the geographic area."
- Until July 2009, the actual acquisition costs (AAC) was estimated as the average wholesale price (AWP) minus 14 percent. To calculate the AAC, the state uses data from First DataBank, Inc., a private clearinghouse of pharmaceutical data. On July 1, 2009, the State changed its reimbursement rate from AWP minus 14 percent to AWP minus 15 percent, resulting in a decrease of the reimbursement amount.
- A separate reduction was taken as a result of a settlement that First DataBank entered in other litigation, in which it agreed to reduce its published AWP figures for all drug products from a 25 percent markup to a 20 percent markup.
- Defendants filed for judgment on the pleadings.

Reasoning

- The Eleventh Amendment is construed to bar suits against a state by its own citizens. This immunity extends to agencies of the state.
- To be entitled to the remedy provided by Section 1983, the underlying federal law that a plaintiff alleged was violated must have clearly conferred enforceable personal rights. Subsection 30(A) does not focus on individual rights but rather on the methods and procedures a state must employ. It reflects a policy judgment regarding the states' administration of a program with multiple disparate goals more than it creates individual rights.
- A plaintiff can challenge a state law under the Supremacy Clause when it is inconsistent with federal law. Defendants contend that no such preemption challenge is possible because the federal government has approved the State Plan Amendment, as required to obtain funds under the Medicaid Act. An agency's interpretation of a statute which it is charged with implementing is entitled to substantial deference. Plaintiffs offered no basis for questioning the approval of the State Plan, but no evidence was put forth by the defendants that showed why the reimbursement reduction complied with Subsection (30)(A).

Holding

- Subsection (30)(A) does not create any rights enforceable under Section 1983 by pharmacists, their associations, or Medicaid recipients. Therefore, the state was entitled to judgment on the plaintiffs' Section 1983 claim.

- The court deferred making a final judgment on the plaintiffs' Supremacy Clause claims until the parties had an opportunity to develop a fuller record regarding the basis for the Secretary's approval of the State Plan.

34.10 Prescriber Identifying Information
A. *IMS Health Incorporated v. Mills*, 2010 WL 3025496 (1st Cir. 2010) (August 4, 2010)

Relief sought: Plaintiffs challenged the constitutionality of a Maine law that allows prescribers licensed in Maine to choose not to make prescriber identifying information available for use in marketing prescription drugs to them.

Issues

- Is the Maine law that prohibits the use of prescriber identifying information for marketing purposes unconstitutional based on the First Amendment?
- Is the Maine law unconstitutionally vague?
- Does the Maine law regulate transactions outside of Maine in violation of the dormant Commerce Clause?

Facts and procedural history

- Pharmaceutical manufacturers use prescriber identifying data to personally market particular drugs to particular prescribers, a practice known as "detailing." With the information gathered, manufacturers can pinpoint the prescribing habits of individual prescribers in a region and target prescribers who might be persuaded to switch brands or prescribe more of a detailer's brand of products. Aggregated survey data confirms that physicians have a predominantly negative view of detailing.

- Plaintiff companies were prescription drug information intermediaries that mine specialized data. They contract with numerous pharmacies to buy their raw data. Under those contracts, the pharmacy's computer software collects data it sends to plaintiffs. Plaintiffs assemble a complete picture of individual prescribers' prescribing histories by cross-referencing prescriber names with publicly available databases. Plaintiffs then license or sell these specialized databases and reports to pharmaceutical manufacturers.

- The Maine law, section 1711-E(2-A) states that "a carrier, pharmacy or prescription drug information intermediary…may not license, use, sell, or transfer or exchange for value, for any marketing purpose, prescription drug information that identifies a prescriber who has filed for confidentiality protection." It does not prohibit detailing, nor does it purport to prohibit speech by detailers to prescribers. It only limits detailers' access to an individual prescriber's identifying data if the prescriber has affirmatively opted for this protection. The pharmacy still collects the prescriber's identifying data and may transfer it to its central data center. The pharmacies, however, may not sell, transfer, or license data for opted-in prescribers for a marketing purpose.

- Maine enacted the statute to achieve three compelling state interests: to improve the public health, to limit annual increases in the cost of health care, and to protect the privacy of prescribers in the health care system of the state.

- The district court granted plaintiffs a preliminary injunction and prohibited Maine from enforcing the statute on the basis of plaintiff's First Amendment claims.

Reasoning

- First Amendment
  - The court was bound by *IMS Health Inc. v. Ayotte*, 550 F.3d 42 (1st Cir. 2008) in which the same plaintiffs challenged a similar statute in New Hampshire. The *Ayotte* decision found that such a statute regulated conduct, not speech, thus the First Amendment does not protect plaintiffs' conduct.
  - Even if the Maine law regulates protected speech, prescribers have a privacy interest in avoiding unwanted solicitations from detailers who have used their individual prescribing data to identify and target them. Maine has a substantial interest in protecting its prescribers from unwanted solicitations based on their prescribing histories. The Supreme Court has recognized this interest in the context of "do not mail" lists.
  - Maine's opt-in confidentiality mechanism is a less restrictive means of vindicating prescribers' interests in not having their information used in detailing. Targeted prohibitions are by definition less restrictive than a categorical ban.

- Vagueness
  - The vagueness doctrine invalidates only statutes whose terms are "so uncertain that persons of average intelligence would have no choice but to guess at their meaning and modes of application." Whatever ambiguity lurks in the phrase "any marketing purpose," the law's lengthy definition of the term "marketing" provides enough of a benchmark to satisfy due process.
  - This ambiguity did not exist on the facts: plaintiffs intend for their databases and reports to facilitate detailing.
- Dormant Commerce Clause
  - The Supreme Court's current dormant Commerce Clause jurisprudence is concerned with preventing economic protectionism and inconsistent regulation, not with enforcing geographical limits on states' exercise of their police power that necessarily regulates commerce. The Supreme Court has not barred states from regulating any commercial transactions beyond their borders that involve their own citizens and create in-state harms.
  - Maine's regulation does not discriminate against out-of-state entities in favor of in-state competitors, nor does the law risk imposing regulatory obligations inconsistent with those of other states.
  - The statute targets a series of underlying transactions that cause harm to in-state prescribers, which start and end in Maine, even if all the transactions covered in order to effectuate the statute's purposes do not occur in Maine.
  - Plaintiffs did not show any disproportionate burden on interstate commerce, and the law creates substantial in-state benefits for those Maine prescribers who have affirmatively asked Maine to protect their identifying data and for Maine in its efforts to lower health care costs.

Holding: The court rejected all of plaintiffs' constitutional challenges to the Maine law. The statute regulates conduct, not speech; is not void for vagueness; and constitutionally reaches out-of-state transactions as a necessary incident of Maine's strong interest in protecting opted-in Maine prescribers from unwanted solicitations. Judgment of the district court was reversed, and the case was remanded with instructions to dismiss the case with prejudice.

34.11 Product Liability
A. Non-Manufacturing Sellers

1. *Whitener v. Pliva, Inc.*, 2010 WL 3021866 (E.D. La. 2010) (July 29, 2010)

Relief sought: Plaintiffs, Joshua and Lindsey Whitener, brought this suit for personal injuries to Lindsey and their son, Lucas, allegedly caused by Lindsey's ingestion of the drug metoclopramide.

Issue: Did the claims brought against one of the defendants, Teva, Inc., need to be limited to claims for products manufactured by Teva?

Facts and procedural history

- Plaintiffs alleged that while Lindsey was pregnant with Lucas, she was prescribed metoclopramide, a generic form of Reglan, to treat her nausea and morning sickness. They further alleged that metoclopramide was not approved by the FDA for prescription to pregnant women and such prescription was off-label.
- Defendants were pharmaceutical entities alleged to have designed, manufactured, marketed, or sold metoclopramide. Plaintiffs did not expressly allege which of the defendant entities manufactured the pills that Lindsey was prescribed or which were involved in the chain of commerce which delivered the pills to her.
- Defendant, Teva Pharmaceuticals, filed a motion to dismiss all of plaintiffs' claims against it other than those brought under the Louisiana Products Liability Act (LPLA) because claims should be limited to claims for products manufactured by Teva.

Reasoning

- The LPLA provides the exclusive theories of recovery against manufacturers of a product for damages caused by their product. Non-LPLA causes of action, such as negligence, strict liability, or breach of express warranty, are not available against the manufacturer of a product for damages caused by that product. The LPLA does not govern claims against a non-manufacturing seller of a product.
- Plaintiffs pled that Teva was either a manufacturer or a seller of the specific metoclopramide pills at issue. They allege that Teva was in the business of selling metoclopramide, and they cite published medical studies regarding the risks of prescribing the drug to pregnant women and allege that Teva had actual or constructive knowledge of those findings.

Holding: Plaintiffs adequately stated a claim under Louisiana law for their alternative theory of non-manufacturing seller liability. Teva's motion to dismiss was denied.

B. Pharmacies

1. *Winters v. Alza Corp.*, 690 F. Supp. 2d 350 (S.D.N.Y. 2010) (March 5, 2010)

Relief sought: Plaintiff, husband of the deceased patient, sought relief from the drug manufacturer and the pharmacy that dispensed a generic patch which he claimed suffered from a design defect that caused the death of his wife. Plaintiff claimed that the pharmacy sold to the decedent the inferior of two generic patches.

Issue: Could the plaintiff state a claim that DVS, the pharmacy, was negligent in filling the prescription as written and dispensing the Alza/Sandoz patch to the decedent, which he claimed was the more dangerous of two competing generic patches?

Facts and procedural history

- The decedent was given a prescription by Dr. Cash for a name-brand transdermal patch known as Duragesic, which delivers fentanyl, a pain-relieving drug, through the patient's skin. The prescription form used indicated that the prescription could be filled with a generic version of the Duragesic patch.

- A pharmacist at DVS filled the decedent's prescription with a generic patch manufactured by Alza and marketed and distributed by Sandoz (the "Alza/Sandoz patch"). Plaintiff alleges that the Alza/Sandoz patch had a design flaw that delivered a level of fentanyl above the intended and designed level and this heightened level of the medication caused decedent's death. Other patches available were designed differently so to prevent such leakage.

- Plaintiff claimed that at the time the decedent received the Alza/Sandoz patch, there had been at least one highly publicized recall of Alza/Sandoz patches due to such leaks.

Reasoning

- A pharmacist generally cannot be held liable for negligence under New York law in the absence of an allegation that he either (a) failed to fill a prescription precisely as directed or (b) was aware that the customer had a condition contraindicating the prescription of the drug at issue. New York courts

have also found pharmacists liable when there has been some "active negligence," for example, when a pharmacist erroneously switches labels on medications or sells misbranded drugs. A pharmacist does not have a duty to inspect or test a prescription drug for latent dangers.

- Plaintiff contended that DVS could be held liable because New York law imposes a duty on a pharmacist to fill a prescription with the safer of two competing products, but plaintiff failed to provide a single case in which any court has used this theory to find a pharmacy liable for negligence.

- New York law prevents lawsuits against doctors who authorize pharmacists to substitute generics for brand-name drugs. Nevertheless, the plaintiff asked the court to hold DVS liable for filling the prescription within the parameters that Dr. Cash legally set out. However, the plaintiff did not provide any argument that would support this differential result.

- By asking that pharmacies ensure the complete safety of any product that they dispense, the plaintiff would have the court place pharmacies on the same level with drug manufacturers for the purposes of tort liability.

Holding: The plaintiff did not allege that the pharmacist failed to follow the doctor's prescription or the manufacturer's prescribing information, and he conceded that the drug dispensed to the decedent was FDA-approved. Court found no reason that the pharmacy could be negligent in failing to second-guess the FDA. Defendant, DVS, was dismissed from the action.

C. Preemption—Generic Drugs

1. *Mensing v. Wyeth, Inc.*, 588 F.3d 603 (8th Cir. 2009) (November 27, 2009)

Relief sought: Plaintiff brought a failure to warn and misrepresentation case against the brand name and generic manufacturers of metoclopramide (Reglan) claiming damages for tardive dyskinesia, a severe neurological movement disorder.

Issues

- Does the Food, Drug, and Cosmetic Act preempt state failure to warn claims against generic defendants?

- Did the name-brand defendants owe a duty to warn patient?

Facts and procedural history

- Plaintiff's doctor prescribed Reglan and her pharmacist filled her prescription with the generic equivalent, metoclopramide. After taking the generic drug for four years, plaintiff developed tardive dyskinesia.

- Plaintiff argued that despite mounting evidence that long-term metolopramide use carries a risk of tardive dyskinesia far greater than indicated on the label, no metoclopramide manufacturer took steps to change the label warnings.

- Even though she did not ingest any of the brand name product, plaintiff argued the brand name manufacturer was liable under theories of misrepresentation and negligence because her doctor relied on the labeling when assessing the risks and proper use of metoclopramide.

- The district court dismissed plaintiff's claims against: (i) generic defendants on the basis of federal preemption because the failure to warn claims created an impermissible conflict with federal law that would have required generic manufacturers to deviate from the name brand drug label, and (ii) name brand manufacturers on the basis that they did not owe a duty of care to the plaintiff because she had not ingested their products.

Reasoning

- Since the district court's decision, the Supreme Court had decided in *Wyeth v. Levine* that failure to warn claims against name brand manufacturers were not preempted by federal law.

- Generic manufacturers argued the *Wyeth* decision did not apply to generic manufacturers and that federal law required their labels to comply with the brand name product. The court rejected this argument, stating that the logic of *Wyeth* applied and explained that generic manufacturers have an obligation to ensure their products are safe—and if they knew the drug was not safe, generic manufacturers could have, at least, proposed to the FDA that metoclopramide manufacturers change the label. Federal law did not require the generic drug manufacturers to passively accept the inadequacy of the labels when evidence was mounting that the risks of the drug were greater than once thought.

- Traditional products liability requires that the plaintiff show she actually consumed the defendants' products. Regardless of whether her physician re-

lied on the Reglan label, the plaintiff must show that the name brand drug manufacturers owed her a duty of care. Because plaintiff did not purchase or use the brand name brand product, there was no direct relationship between them that gave rise to a duty of care.

Holding

- Federal law did not preempt patient's failure to warn claims against generic manufacturers. Judgment in favor of the generic manufacturers was reversed.

- Name brand manufacturers did not owe duty to warn patient who did not use their product. Judgment in favor of the name brand manufacturers was affirmed.

2. *Gaeta v. Perrigo Pharmaceuticals Co.*, 672 F. Supp. 2d 1017 (N.D. Cal. 2009) (November 24, 2009)

Relief sought: Parents of a child who sustained liver failure sought damages against the manufacturer of generic over-the-counter (OTC) ibuprofen, alleging state law negligence and breach of warranty claims related to manufacturer's failure to warn of potential injury on drug label.

Issue: Did the Supreme Court's holding in *Wyeth v. Levine* apply to failure to warn claims against generic manufacturers?

Facts and procedural history: Defendant manufactured a generic form of ibuprofen. In its order granting defendant summary judgment, the court found that plaintiffs' state law causes of action were pre-empted to the extent that they allowed for liability based on a lack of adequate warning on defendant's OTC ibuprofen.

- The court's preemption finding rested on two separate grounds:
  - A generic drug manufacturer could not comply with heightened state law warning label requirements without running afoul of FDA regulations which require generic drug labels to conform to the approved labeling for the listed drug; and
  - The FDA interpreted the scope of its authority in the area of drug labeling as broad enough to pre-empt any conflicting or contrary state law.
- Following summary judgment for the manufacturer, the parents moved for reconsideration.

Reasoning: The court found that *Levine* did not address the dispositive issue in this case, namely, whether a generic drug manufacturer may use the "changes being effected" (CBE) process to make warning-label changes without prior FDA approval. Thus *Levine* does not govern whether the Court may grant summary judgment on plaintiff's state tort claims based on the defense of impossibility pre-emption.

Holding: The court denied motion for reconsideration and held that state tort law claims for inadequate labeling of a generic drug are preempted.

34.12 Securities

A. *Merck & Co., Inc. v. Reynolds*, 130 S.Ct. 1784 (2010) (April 27, 2010)

Relief sought: Plaintiff investors filed a securities fraud action on November 6, 2003, under § 10(b) of the Securities Exchange Act of 1934, alleging that petitioner Merck & Co. knowingly misrepresented the heart-attack risks associated with its drug Vioxx.

Issue: Did the plaintiffs "discover" the facts prior to November 6, 2001, so that their filing of the action would have been untimely under 28 U.S.C. § 1658(b)?

Facts and procedural history

- A securities fraud complaint is timely if filed no more than "2 years after the discovery of the facts constituting the violation" or 5 years after the violation. 28 U.S.C. § 1658(b).
- In March 2000, Merck announced the results of a study comparing Vioxx with another pain reliever, naproxen. The study showed adverse cardiovascular results for Vioxx, but suggested that it might be due to the absence of a benefit conferred by naproxen rather than a harm caused by Vioxx.
- In September 2000, the Food and Drug Administration (FDA) sent Merck a warning letter, calling its marketing of Vioxx false and misleading. The FDA acknowledged that the benefits of naproxen was a possible explanation for the study results, but that Merck did not adequately present the hypothesis that the results could also be due to Vioxx's adverse cardiovascular properties.
- District court dismissed the complaint as untimely because the plaintiffs should have been alerted to the possibility of Merck's misrepresentations prior to November 2001, more than two years before the complaint was filed. The Third Circuit reversed, holding that the pre-November 2001 events did not suggest that Merck acted with scienter, an element of a § 10(b) violation, and con-

sequently did not commence the running of the limitations period.

Reasoning

- When "discovery" is written directly into a statute, courts have typically interpreted the word to refer not only to actual discovery, but also to the hypothetical discovery of facts a reasonably diligent plaintiff would know.
- The limitations period does not begin to run until the plaintiff discovers or a reasonably diligent plaintiff would have discovered "the facts constituting the violation," including scienter. Scienter is a "fact" that is among those that constitutes the violation. Unless a § 10(b) complaint sets out facts showing that it is more likely than not that the defendant acted with the relevant intent, the claim will fail.
- Facts that tend to show a materially false or misleading statement are not necessarily sufficient to show scienter, as it could be that the speaker made an innocent mistake.
- The limitations period cannot begin at "inquiry notice," which is the point where the facts would lead a reasonably diligent plaintiff to investigate further. That is not necessarily the point at which the plaintiff would have "discovered" the facts showing scienter or other facts constituting the violation. The statute says the plaintiff's claim accrues only after the "discovery" of those facts.

Holding

- Prior to November 6, 2001, the plaintiffs did not discover, and Merck did not show that a reasonably diligent plaintiff would have discovered, "the facts constituting the violation." The FDA's warning letter showed little or nothing about the relevant scienter.
- Supreme Court affirmed the judgment of the Third Circuit.

34.13 Settlements

A. Average Wholesale Price

1. *In re Pharmaceutical Industry Average Wholesale Price Litigation*, 588 F.3d 24 (1st Cir. 2009) (November 19, 2009)

Relief sought: Consumers filed a class action seeking damages against a manufacturer claiming that they had overpaid Medicare co-payments because the manufacturer had inflated the price of drugs.

Issue: Did the court abuse its discretion in approving the settlement agreement?

Facts and procedural history

- One plaintiff appealed from an order approving a $24 million class action settlement in a multidistrict litigation, in which class members allege that AstraZeneca Pharmaceuticals LP (AstraZeneca) published artificially inflated prescription drug prices.
- The settlement was between AstraZeneca and a class of consumer plaintiffs who claimed they overpaid Medicare co-payments because Astra-Zeneca inflated the price of Zoladex, commonly used to treat prostate cancer.
- The United States District Court for the District of Massachusetts approved the settlement.
- M. Joyce Howe, one of the class representatives for the AstraZeneca consumer subclass, appealed. The other AstraZeneca subclass representative, Leroy Townsend, asked the court to uphold the settlement.
- Howe argued that the settlement be rejected on the grounds that it created a *cy-près* fund of up to $10 million rather than distributing all recovery to class members; that the settlement was not fair, reasonable, and adequate because its method for calculating and distributing class members' damages was flawed; and that the parties allegedly improperly negotiated fees simultaneously with the settlement.

Reasoning

- The district court's actions in this case were entirely congruent with the proposed draft's purposes.
- The court ultimately insisted that the settlement pay class members treble damages before any money is distributed through *cy-près*. This set the benchmark well above the American Law Institute's hope that class members might receive 100 percent recovery.
- There was nothing inherently wrong with class counsel advocating for a *cy-près* fund to benefit those class members whose recovery would go unclaimed after counsel ensured all claimants would receive more than their damages.
- The settlement formula tailored class members' recovery to their actual losses, since those who had supplemental insurance paid less out of pocket than those who did not. As the district court found, this

agreement therefore avoided under-compensating class members who lacked supplemental insurance.

Holding: The Court of Appeals affirmed, holding that the district court did not abuse its discretion in approving the settlement agreement.

B. False Claims Act

1. *United States ex rel. Kammerer v. Omnicare Inc.* (D. Mass. 2009) (November 3, 2009)

- Omnicare Inc., the nation's largest nursing home pharmacy, agreed to pay $98 million to resolve allegations that the pharmacy engaged in kickback schemes with drug manufacturers and nursing homes.
- Omnicare knowingly submitted, or caused to be submitted, drug reimbursement claims to Medicaid and Medicare that were false or fraudulent because they resulted from a $50 million payment that Omnicare paid to nursing home chains in violation of the federal anti-kickback statute. In exchange for the payment, the nursing home chains agreed to refer their nursing home patients to Omnicare for the patients' drug purchases, including drug purchases covered by Medicaid and Medicare.
- Drug manufacturer, Ivax Pharmaceuticals, also will pay the United States $14 million for allegedly receiving kickbacks from Omnicare. Omnicare agreed to purchase $50 million worth of generic drugs from Ivax and to recommend that physicians prescribe those drugs for their nursing home patients, including patients covered by Medicaid.
- Omnicare regularly paid kickbacks to nursing homes by providing consultant pharmacist services at rates below the company's cost and below the fair market value of such services in order to induce the homes to refer their patients to Omnicare for pharmacy services.

C. Off-Label Marketing

1. Allergan Inc. (September 2010)

- Allergan Inc. will pay $600 million to resolve allegations that it illegally marketed Botox Therapeutic for uses not approved by the Food and Drug Administration (FDA) and will plead guilty to criminal misdemeanor misbranding in violation of the Food, Drug, and Cosmetic Act.

- The civil lawsuits alleged that Allergan illegally promoted Botox for off-label uses such as treatment for headaches, pain, and juvenile cerebral palsy; paid physicians kickbacks to prescribe Botox; and instructed physicians on coding Botox claims so as to obtain Medicare and Medicaid reimbursement.

- According to Allergan, it has filed for FDA approval of Botox to treat chronic migraines and was expecting the agency to rule on its application in 2010.

- As part of the settlement, Allergan agreed to drop a lawsuit against the FDA asserting it has a First Amendment right to share scientific information with the medical community about unapproved uses for Botox.

2. Novartis (September 2010)

- Swiss drug manufacturer, Novartis, agreed to pay $422.5 million to settle criminal and civil investigations into off-label marketing of six of its drugs. The settlement includes a $170 million criminal fine and $15 million in criminal forfeiture.

- Federal prosecutors accused Novartis of paying illegal kickbacks to health care professionals through speaker programs, advisory boards, entertainment, travel, and meals. The company allegedly singled out psychiatrists and pain specialists who were known to use one of its drugs off-label.

- Four whistleblowers will share more than $25 million under the government program intended to encourage company insiders to report illegal activity.

- As part of the settlement, Novartis signed a five-year corporate integrity agreement with the Department of Health and Human Services, which requires the company to monitor its sales practices and report any irregularities.

Chapter 35

Pharmacist Malpractice and Liability

James T. O'Donnell, Pharm.D., M.S., FCP, ABCP, FACN, R.Ph.
and David M. Benjamin, Ph.D., FCLM, FCP

35.1 Introduction

In August 14, 2009, as the Institute for Safe Medication Practices (ISMP) reported it a week later, calling it "unfair," Ohio pharmacist Eric Cropp was sentenced to six months in prison, six months of home confinement with electronic monitoring, three years of probation, 400 hours of community service, a $5,000 fine, and payment of court costs in retribution for the part he played in the case of a fatal medication error. Cropp's mistake, which involved an overdose of sodium chloride in a custom chemotherapy solution, had resulted in the death of a child. The child developed severe hypernatremia, which led to her death. Cropp's is just one of a handful of high-profile medication-error cases that have come under media scrutiny over the last few years. A few years before, in November of 2005, television stations in Northern California (where a handful of incidents were uncovered) reported the issue as though it was a horrifying new revelation. However, as every healthcare worker (and attorney) knows, drug mishaps are nothing new. In fact, studies dating back several years[1] show that about 2 percent of hospital patients experience prevent-

able adverse drug events, although the majority are not fatal. Medication error has been cited as the cause of death for one out of every 131 outpatient deaths and one in 854 in-patient deaths. One study estimated that 6.7 percent of hospitalizations resulted in an adverse drug reaction, and 0.32 percent of cases were fatal. This extrapolates to about 2,216,000 cases annually in hospitalized patients and 106,000 deaths.[2] Of course, it does not take a lawyer to figure out that this adds up to a whopping number of potential lawsuits against medical personnel.

Although originally these lawsuits were almost always aimed at physicians and nurses, pharmacists are now increasingly becoming the target of malpractice litigation. This phenomenon, predictably, has resulted in the development of strategies to help reduce the risks of medication errors, as well as to manage pharmacist liability.

35.2 The Science of Risk Management

The risk management of pharmacist malpractice includes identifying theories of liability through the examination of case law and civil litigation. Pharmacists have an independent duty to protect their patients from harm, and must consult with prescribing physicians in a positive way so that mistakes and misunderstandings can be avoided or corrected.

35.3 Most Common Categories of Errors

Pharmacists Mutual (see Figure 35.1) has identified the most common categories of errors and omissions responsible for claims made against pharmacists for malpractice. They are, in order of frequency:

- Wrong drug
- Wrong strength of drug
- Wrong directions
- Lack of drug review (which can result in allergies or contraindicated combinations of drugs being administered)

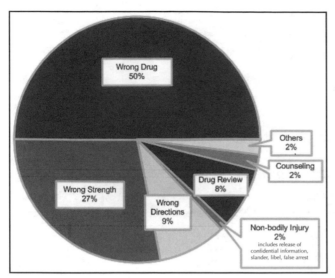

Figure 35.1 *Categories of errors and omissions most responsible for claims against pharmacists for malpractice. Reproduced by permission from Pharmacists Mutual Insurance Company, Algona, IA. © Pharmacists Mutual Insurance Company, 2011.*

- Failure to properly counsel patients on medication usage
- Non-bodily injury
- Other (miscellaneous)

A. Most Common Error: Wrong Drug

Since 1990, the number of "wrong drugs" administered has remained relatively consistent, although the reasons for these errors appear varied. In one case, the pharmacist took a prescription over the phone from a doctor's office for digoxin. The pharmacist prepared the label, counted the correct drug into the tray, and then poured it into the bottle. As he placed the bottle next to the completed label, the phone rang again, with a request for warfarin. The pharmacist filled the prescription for warfarin in the same manner, but somehow, the two labels were mixed up. The warfarin bottle received the digoxin label and was given to the wrong patient.

In another case, a technician simply took the wrong bottle from the shelf, and counted out the wrong drug. If a busy pharmacist does not catch the error when he performs his check, or does not check the technician's work, the results can be serious.

Distractions in the pharmacy are another common and unavoidable part of every workday. Label switches can result, due to a pharmacist's "multi-tasking," or filling multiple prescriptions for a single patient. A patient may have a prescription for Coumadin once a day and Lasix twice a day, for example. If the labels are switched, and the patient ends

up taking Coumadin twice a day, he may suffer a serious hemorrhage.

1. The "look-alike" problem

Sometimes drug names look alike. For example, prescriptions for Navane can be mistaken for Norvasc, Prilosec for Prozac, Lasix for Losec. Interestingly, the Lasix/Losec error precipitated a name change by the Losec manufacturer (it was renamed Prilosec). After that, Prilosec and Prozac began to be mistakenly dispensed in place of one another. This problem occurs so frequently that a special committee of the United States Pharmacopeia (USP) has been formed to look at the selection of new drug names. There is an evolving science in understanding and preventing this error of fine distinction.

2. Physician's handwriting

Physician's handwriting is another cause of pharmacist error. Often the subject of jokes, the typical physician's scrawl presents the most dangerous type of pharmacist error. There is increased interest in electronic prescribing, which would help obviate such interpretative errors between physician and pharmacist.

B. Wrong Drug Strength: Another Common Error

The second largest category of claims (24.4 percent) shown in the Pharmacists Mutual Study is "wrong strength." A common example would be receiving a prescription for digoxin 0.125 mg, and filling it in error with digoxin 0.25 mg. In fact, misplacement of a decimal point is a very common way these errors occur. Another error is picking up the wrong bottle when filling the prescription. Perhaps the drug is correct, but the dosage is wrong. Depending upon the drug prescribed, the results of selecting the wrong strength can be dangerous, even fatal. Another common outcome is a lack of efficacy. For example, if too low a dose of an anticoagulant (such as coumadin) is administered, it could fail to prevent a fatal clot.

Even old, familiar drugs are subject to this kind of error. The drugs that are filled most frequently are going to be involved in more errors, simply as a matter of statistics. For example, Haldol is used for senile dementia. It would be unusual for Haldol 5 mg to be prescribed for an ambulatory elderly patient. A more common dosage is 0.5 mg. The drugs with the greatest numbers of available dosage forms offer the greatest probability for a dosage error.

In addition to a wide range of available strengths, potential toxicity is another predictive factor for dosage error litigation. If the patient suffers some type of damage or adverse effect, even if the only consequence is an unplanned visit to the emergency room, a cause of action against the pharmacist and the pharmacy can result.

C. Third in Line: Wrong Directions

At 7.8 percent of all claims, "wrong directions" represents a significant number of the claims reported in the Pharmacists Mutual Study. These cases involve incorrectly entering the directions into the computer. For example, in one case, a pharmacist entered a new prescription for birth-control tablets into the computer and inadvertently typed, "Take two tablets daily." For nine months, this patient refilled her birth-control prescription every 15 days while following the erroneous label directions, apparently without anyone at the pharmacy noticing the discrepancy. The most dangerous "wrong-directions" claims are for children's prescriptions (and especially prescriptions for children under the age of six years).

As a preventative measure, it's recommended that the label directions are checked against the "hard-copy" prescription. Another good idea is for the pharmacist to follow a standard procedure of removing the prescription from the bag as he counsels each patient. The pharmacist should read the written directions to the patient and ask, "What did your doctor explain about how you are to take this medication?" The pharmacist can use similar words to determine whether the patient understands the directions. This serves two additional purposes: it allows the pharmacist to double-check the label directions, and, by removing the prescription from the bag, it creates the appearance of a professional service rather than merely sales of a "commodity " in a sack.

D. Lack of Drug Review

OBRA-90 (Omnibus Budget Reconciliation Act) required pharmacists to review all prescriptions prior to filling them—checking for interactions, allergies, and a list of other potential problems. Because pharmacy technicians are increasingly being used to reduce the pharmacist's workload, this category of error, previously almost unheard of, now represents about 8 percent of all claims.

Drug review was first described in The Standard of Practice of the Profession of Pharmacy.[3] The American Pharmaceutical Association (APA), in concert with the American Association of Colleges of Pharmacy (AACP), has defined standards of practice for the profession of pharmacy. Most, if not all of the requirements that were eventually legislated and mandated by OBRA-90 were already components of this standard. OBRA requires medication profiles, as well as review for therapeutic duplication, allergy, cross sensitivity, drug-induced disease, and contraindications. Failure

to provide meaningful patient drug review has resulted in claims and lawsuits that plead error of omission.

One way that a pharmacist can easily ensure that each prescription has been reviewed is to personally hand it to the patient, while counseling on its use. The pharmacist can take the prescription out of the bag and examine it while explaining to the patient how the drug should be used, the goal of therapy, contraindications, and so on. By the time the pharmacist then hands the drug to her patient face-to-face, 90 percent of the errors that occur in the filling process will have been detected.

The Supreme Court of Illinois recently reviewed a case involving Wal-Mart Pharmacy, where the patient told all of her physicians that she was allergic to aspirin. After a medical procedure, the patient was given a prescription for Toradol, a drug contraindicated for patients allergic to aspirin. She took the prescription to the Wal-Mart Pharmacy, which (appropriately) asked her if she had any drug allergies. As always, the patient responded that she was allergic to aspirin. The Wal-Mart Pharmacy filled the Toradol prescription anyway. The patient developed a life-threatening anaphylactic shock after taking the drug (although she recovered after emergency treatment). Of course, she later sued the pharmacy.

Precedent cases involving the same theory have accumulated, eliminating any doubt that the pharmacist has a duty to screen for cross-allergenicity. The standard of care requires that the pharmacist should have called the physician and informed him that his patient was allergic to aspirin. Because there is cross-sensitivity for Toradol in patients allergic to aspirin, giving Toradol was contraindicated. The pharmacist should have suggested an analgesic with no cross-allergenicity to aspirin. In any case, he should have refused to dispense this drug to a patient at risk.[4]

E. Failure to Counsel

Progressive pharmacy companies make it a standard business practice to actually counsel each patient on every new prescription, instead of merely offering a perfunctory option of obtaining counseling if they have any questions. (Rather than requiring counseling, OBRA only requires that the pharmacist *offer* to counsel the patient.) With critical-care drugs, failure to counsel leads to predictable and serious problems. Inadequate or incomplete counseling, as well as lack of documentation or proof of counseling, are omissions that can indicate that the pharmacist is providing a lower-than-standard level of care. The patient cannot be expected to understand everything in the patient package insert without professional advice and guidance from the pharmacist.

Counseling is also a growing area of claims (compared

to just a few years ago). Most of these claims are for "failure to counsel," but a few involve allegations of "inadequate" or "incorrect" counseling. Patients often report that the pharmacist failed to counsel when, in reality, they did receive counseling (but there is no record of this having taken place). This is also a growing area for boards of pharmacy to administer disciplinary actions.

In one case, when dispensing trazodone, a pharmacist printed out only the "short form" of the patient package insert (PPI) from the computer, instead of the "long form," which included the warning that this drug can cause prolonged erections, and to call a physician if this side effect occurs. The standard of care requires that pharmacists provide complete and accurate counseling, which should include printing the "long form" PPI.[5]

It is recommended that pharmacists employ some form of quick documentation (that can be later shown as evidence) that counseling took place. One practical means of doing this is to place a mark on each new prescription, such as "O/W_____ initials of RPh_____ date_____," written on the front of the prescription. This shows that the pharmacist provided oral (O) and written (W) counseling (in the form of a patient-information leaflet). Documentation must always be after the fact, so the marks must be made only after the counseling was actually given. This type of documentation is not foolproof, but it is certainly better than having no documentation at all.

F. Non-Bodily Injury

In insurance terminology, "personal injury" refers to non-bodily claims including false arrest, malicious prosecution, wrongful eviction, libel, slander, and violation of the right of privacy. Unauthorized release of confidential records, a violation of the right of privacy, accounts for approximately one-half of all non-bodily injury claims against pharmacies. This fast-growing area of litigation usually involves the pharmacist or technician, but may involve any employee with access to patient information.

The risk of being sued increases when there are confidentiality violations or breaches related to mental-health issues, sexually transmitted diseases, use of birth control, or the release of prescription records to a relative. For example, one technician filled a prescription for an AIDS drug and recognized that the man was receiving treatment for HIV. The patient's son was acquainted with the technician's own children, and the technician told her children not to associate with their friend anymore. When the patient discovered that the pharmacy had disclosed information about his HIV treatment, he brought suit against the pharmacy.

G. Miscellaneous Errors

At the end of the list of medication errors reported by Pharmacists Mutual is a category for "other." This category may include several types of miscellaneous errors responsible for a significant number of claims.

One relatively new area of claims involves utilizing proper safety caps on prescription bottles. Safety-cap claims either involve the pharmacist not following federal law, or the pharmacist being unable to prove it was the patient who requested "no safety cap." According to Pharmacist Mutual's claims, the pharmacist cannot rely on a notation in the computer, nor on the testimony, "I always use safety caps, unless the patient requests otherwise." For the pharmacist's protection, the patient or caregiver should be required to sign a written request for each new prescription ordered without a safety cap. An annual blanket release is inadequate.

Another area of miscellaneous claims involves the use of generic drugs. In these claims, the pharmacist usually believes that a generic product is equivalent to the brand-name drug, but is mistaken. Inadequate generic substitution may result in therapeutic inefficacy, adverse reactions, or allergies.

Hospital and home-care pharmacy therapy involving the preparation of intravenous (IV) solutions for treating acutely ill patients is another area where critical mistakes occur. These solutions are usually mixed in the pharmacy (called "compounding"). Close coordination between the medical staff and the compounding pharmacist is a vital necessity here. There is a greater risk for errors with this activity, and when errors occur, they tend to result in more serious outcomes from life-threatening infections. Examples include the substitution of insulin for heparin, overdoses of sodium, excessive or no glucose, and alterations and errors in almost any ingredient. Many deaths and permanent injuries have been reported as a result of compounding errors in hospital and home-care pharmacies.

One home-care pharmacist was reported to have dispensed syringes filled with potassium chloride, instead of sodium chloride, which resulted in an infant patient's sudden cardiac arrest. Profound brain damage was the result. An investigation revealed that technicians had mislabeled the refrigerator storage bags. The case was eventually settled out of court. In other case, a Springfield, Missouri, hospital inaccurately compounded a cardioplegia solution, with fatal results. The hospital was sued, and was subjected to a punitive-damage award.[6]

When it comes to compounding, pediatric patients are at the greatest risk. In one case, a child in Boston was given a 125× overdose of a drug, causing prolonged low blood pressure and serious brain damage. The family was awarded a multi-million-dollar judgment. Another child in a Wisconsin hospital received a 10-fold overdose of digoxin, due to a dosage miscalculation by a hospital pharmacist. The nurses did not detect the error. The child died. The hospital was sued, and settled the case. The State Pharmacy Board of Wisconsin learned of the lawsuit and settlement and charged the pharmacist and the hospital pharmacy director with failure to report the error (a little known regulation in Wisconsin—one that exists in only a few states).

Some classes of drugs seem to lend themselves to medication errors and adverse events. For example, the aminoglycosides, such as gentamicin, have a well-known ability to cause damage to the kidneys, as well as to both the auditory and vestibular portions of the inner ear. This toxicity is both dosage- and time-dependent, requiring careful monitoring of serum drug concentrations. Lack of monitoring can cause catastrophic kidney and ear damage to patients and liability for the pharmacist and physician. The vestibular damage can result in terrible balance problems for affected patients. In fact, there are so many patients who have suffered vestibular damage from gentamicin that they have created their own website (www.wobblers.com.).

35.4 Negligence

In a case discussed in *Pharma-Law e-News* in August 2008, the court dismissed the plaintiffs' claims for failure to provide expert testimony on a claimed duty of Walgreen's pharmacists to refrain from filling prescriptions for Vytorin and/or gemfibrozil when the patient was also taking cyclosporine. The patient developed rhabdomyolysis. Plaintiffs moved for reconsideration, arguing that the parties had agreed not to engage in discovery and the hiring of experts until the court decided the legal question of whether the defendants owed a duty to the plaintiff to refrain from filling the prescriptions in question. Walgreens disputes that such an agreement existed, and the alleged agreement was not before the court at the time its ruling was made. On reconsideration, the court noted that—as conceded by plaintiffs—Indiana does not recognize a duty to warn on the part of a pharmacist, unless the prescriber directs the pharmacist to do so.[7] However, pharmacists have a duty to cease filling a prescription under certain circumstances.

In *Hooks SuperX*, the patient was consuming the medication more frequently than ordered by the physician.[8] The Indiana Supreme Court held that 1) pharmacists possess expertise regarding dispensing of prescription drugs; 2) the relationship between pharmacist and patient is sufficiently close to justify a duty; and 3) it is foreseeable that one who consumes excessive quantities of habit-forming drugs may become addicted to them, and "such an addiction carries

with it certain reasonably foreseeable consequences." Finally, the court concluded that public policy favors preventing intentional and unintentional drug abuse. Having found a duty, the *Hooks SuperX* court found that the pharmacist must exercise the degree of care that an ordinarily prudent pharmacist would under the same or similar circumstances.

The district court then examined whether, applying similar tests, the Indiana Supreme Court would "find that pharmacists have a duty to refrain from filling a prescription that is incompatible with medication previously dispensed to the customer at a different store location." It began by noting that such a duty is not well-settled; however, the relationship test is met such that the Walgreens pharmacists do owe the plaintiff a duty. As to foreseeability, the court held that "[t]he issue is whether it is reasonably foreseeable to a pharmacist filling a valid prescription that a customer will suffer harm from an adverse drug interaction with other medications. In the absence of special circumstances placing the pharmacist on notice that the customer is taking other adverse medications, the resulting harm isn't foreseeable." Under the facts of the case, a cyclosporine prescription was filled by Walgreens in May 2004, but all additional supplies of cyclosporine were provided to the plaintiff by the University of Nebraska Medical Center. The court ruled that "nothing in the record could establish that Walgreens knew or should have known that Ms. Bobay was taking Cyclosporine in April/May 2005....The foreseeability factor weighs against imposing a duty in this case."[8]

Finally, in the absence of special circumstances, the court held that the public policy stance in *Ingram* remains in force; the interest in patient safety permits, but does not require, a pharmacist to act to refrain from filling a lawful prescription, and thus, "relying on the reasoning [in *Ingram*], this court finds that the public-policy concern of customer safety in this instance isn't paramount to the policy concern of avoiding interference with the physician-patient relationship." The court granted anew Walgreen's motion for summary judgment, albeit on new grounds.[9]

The risk management of drug malpractice includes identifying theories of liability through the examination of case law and civil litigation. Pharmacists have an independent duty to protect their patients from harm, and must consult with prescribing physicians in a positive way so that mistakes and misunderstandings can be avoided or corrected. The volume of daily work that each pharmacist must perform has created a role for pharmacy technicians to perform many of the steps in filling a prescription. Each and every prescription must still be checked and approved by a licensed pharmacist. This is mandated both by law and by professional obligation. All of these obligations are in force for all prescription drug products—but even greater scrutiny is required for investigational drugs, because of the greater risk of toxicity, and because of the possibility of adverse effects that may not yet be well understood or reported.

35.5 Mail-Order Pharmacies

The emergence of the mail-order pharmacy has created its own unique category of liability. In one case, a psychiatric patient in New Jersey called in a phone order to his Florida mail-order pharmacy. When the promised prescriptions did not arrive, the patient called the pharmacy back to inquire about the status of his pills. He was told, "They are in the mail." In reality, the pharmacy had placed the prescription on hold because the patient's insurance company was delinquent in paying the pharmacy for its mail-order prescriptions. The patient never received his drugs. After being without his required medication, his mental state deteriorated. He was admitted to a psychiatric hospital several times, and eventually committed suicide. In court, the patient's psychiatrist testified that the suicide was the result of decompensation caused by the withdrawal of effective psychotropic medication. An investigation of the case revealed that the patient was abandoned because he had fallen into some type of "insurance-hold loop." A more professional and compassionate approach would have been to call the patient and explain that he would have to do something else to obtain his medication for a short period of time, because of lack of insurance approval.[10]

35.6 Steps Toward a Better Outcome

Errors contributing to the death of a patient or causing serious harm are every pharmacist's worst nightmare. Regardless of the setting, be it a hospital, a chain pharmacy, or a community pharmacy, all run this same risk. The results can be disastrous—from the pharmacist losing his license, to huge monetary awards in court. Several studies show that the chances of such mistakes are about one in 30 in a retail pharmacy and one in 1,000 in a hospital pharmacy. According to a study conducted by Flynn et al. at the Center for Pharmacy Design at Auburn University in Alabama, dispensing errors at retail pharmacies across the nation have actually gone up (from 22 to 24 percent) between 1995 and 2009. The rate of critical injury fell 1 percent in the same time period. Even counseling rates have decreased—from 43 percent in 1995 to 27 percent in 2009, despite legislation mandates.[11] Things are getting worse, not better, despite evidence that counseling is an effective means of decreasing error. Labeling errors were also implicated by Flynn and her team.[12]

Additionally, efforts to cut costs and increase the volume of prescriptions filled seems to contribute to the problem. Jim Aichelman, RPh, a California pharmacist, reported to *Drug Topics* in July 2009 that most community/retail pharmacists fill about 250 prescriptions a day, and up to 1,300 per week. Of course, such volume increases the opportunity for errors to occur. There is also a necessity for more pharmacy techs to help out, which require more management on the part of the pharmacist. The result is less counseling, less attention to detail, and fewer breaks (tired minds make mistakes).

Aichelman's team also found that pharmacists who have to skip breaks to keep up with an ever-increasing workload were less likely to counsel or "go out of their way" to help patients. This, too, may contribute to increased error rates.

A good computer system—one that flags allergies, cross-interactions, and so on, can also help free up a pharmacist's time to help patients. It is crucial that pharmacists take advantage of all of the tools available, leaving her time free to supervise techs, check scripts, and counsel patients (not to mention taking a lunch break!). Pharmacists have been known to "override" computer warnings in the face of long lines and impatient customers. Worse, some pharmacists give override codes to their support staff (technicians), who override the alerts even before the pharmacist has considered them.

35.7 Overreliance on Technicians

One important allegation in a pharmacy malpractice case currently in litigation revolves around hospital pharmacists delegating responsibilities to technicians and not supervising or exercising follow-up or control over those activities. Excerpts from an expert report filed by this author follow:

Facts of the case

A patient presented to the Southwestern US Hospital on March 31, 2008 with chest pain. He was diagnosed with acute coronary syndrome, taken for cardiac catheterization (CABG), and recommended for coronary artery bypass graft (CABG). The surgery was performed on April 2, 2008. During the surgery, ~90,000 units of heparin was used for anticoagulation and extracorporeal pump purposes. Post-operatively, protamine 50 mg was administered to reverse/neutralize any remaining active heparin. The patient was later discharged home and shortly thereafter came back to the ER with complaints related to deep vein thrombosis and difficulty breathing. He was diagnosed with deep vein thrombosis (DVT) and saddle block pulmonary embolism, HIT, and treated with direct thrombin inhibitors. His DVT and pulmonary thrombosis was noted to be caused by (late onset) HIT.

As early as 2007, the FDA started to receive reports of severe allergic type reactions, some serious and life-threatening, and death reports associated with Baxter Heparin. The source was isolated to the Chinese raw materials heparin formulator, and eventually the probable causative agent of the severe reactions was an oversulfated chondroitin sulfate (OSCS).[a] In January 2008, Baxter issued a recall for certain lots of multiple dose heparin, allowing certain other heparin products to remain on the market until an assured supply was available for the marketplace. A total Baxter heparin product recall was issued in late February; documents referenced earlier describe the reason and urgency for the recall: that serious allergic reactions (shock) and deaths were associated with Baxter Heparin, and that use of all Baxter heparin was to be discontinued. Baxter issued instructions for acknowledgement of the recall (a standard industry practice).

Hospital clinical and billing records for drugs, initiated by Cardiovascular OR (CVOR) personnel, indicate that heparin 1,000U/ml, 10ml vials were administered to the patient and charged. The product listed on the billing statement identifies Baxter as the manufacturer of the heparin. Since the surgery was on April 2, 2008, two (2) months after all recalled heparin use was ordered discontinued, no Baxter heparin should have been in the hospital, let alone in the CVOR, where exposure/use in patients could result in life-threatening reactions or death. Returns documented by EXP, a service company that removes and provides credits for outdated and other unusable drugs, documented picking up Baxter heparin over a several month period following the February recall, indeed as late as November 2008.

a. Alban S, Greinacher A. Role of Sulfated Polysaccharides in the Pathogenesis of Heparin-Induced Thrombocytopenia. Chapter 7, in Warkentin TE and Greinacher A. Editors. Heparin-Induced Thrombocytopenia, Fourth Edition, Informa, New York, 2007, at page 167 et seq.

Pharmacists employed by the hospital, the director of pharmacy and the clinical manager, as well as a pharmacy technician (storeroom supervisor) all testified as to their usual procedures for inventory control, distribution of stocks of procedure drugs (heparin), policy and procedure for recalls, and their actions (and inactions) related to the two Baxter heparin recalls. The management pharmacists relied totally on the technician to execute the recall of the adulterated heparin. The pharmacy technician further relied on 50 other technicians to bring back any of the recalled heparin from their assigned areas of the hospital. Neither the management pharmacists nor the supervising technician executed any quality assurance checks to assure that each storage location in the hospital had been checked. For almost 6 months after the patient's surgery in April, recalled heparin was found in the hospital and returned through the return service.

An additional important factor in the litigation is that the clinical manager of the pharmacy made a conscious decision *not* to recall and sequester the heparin, fearing shortages for clinical use. Furthermore, neither the physicians nor the nurses involved in the care of patients receiving heparin were informed of his decision not to sequester the product.

This pharmacist expert author issued a report expressing the following opinions:

1. The patient probably received unusable, adulterated heparin during his CABG procedure on April 2, 2008;
2. The patient's DVT and pulmonary emboli were caused by a HIT. The risk of HIT is enhanced with OSCS-adulterated heparin, the subject of the recall.
3. The hospital pharmacists deviated from the standard of care of reasonable hospital pharmacists and were grossly negligent in how they executed their professional duties related to the heparin;
   a. Failed to follow their hospital recall policy—adulterated heparin was not removed from all hospital locations and pharmacy inventory and quarantined;
   b. Violated their state Pharmacy Practice Act regarding recalls and protection of patients from "unusable" drugs. An unusable drug would include a recalled drug product;
   c. Failed to follow American Society of Health-System Pharmacists Practice Guidelines and Standards regarding recalled pharmaceuticals;
   d. The clinical manager pharmacist consciously decided to *not* sequester recalled heparin, and in doing so, failed to involve cardiovascular physicians, and inform them that adulterated heparin was not recalled from the hospital. Further, during this period of known (and allowed) continual availability of contaminated heparin, no effort was made to identify, document, monitor, and notify treating physicians

and patients that they received recalled heparin.

e. Woefully inadequate supervision of the pharmacy technician, an inventory control technician, in searching the hospital and assuring that all Baxter heparin products were removed. This technician relied on ~50 other pharmacy technicians to "check their respective areas"; no plan was in place, no follow-up with individual technicians, no quality assurance spot checks or visits to key areas (phoresis, CVOR) was undertaken. No communication within nursing and medical staffs was promulgated by the managing pharmacists on the recall or in follow-up. In short, these managing pharmacists dropped the ball! The recall was ineffective and incomplete and placed patients at risk for exposure to a deadly heparin product. Certainly the use of technicians is widespread, but that use is reserved for tasks that do not require professional judgment. The pharmacists should not have relied totally on a technician to adequately execute the recall. The pharmacists had professional responsibilities for the safety of hospital patients that required he assure the recall was executed properly and completely. The technician certainly was not qualified or equipped to be the responsible person.

f. The clinical manager pharmacist discounted the seriousness of the recall, ignoring the obvious description of signs and symptoms of severe allergic reactions and anaphylactic shock described in the recall notice, as justification for allowing recalled products to go un-sequestered after the recall notice.

g. Failed to complete the Baxter recall acknowledgement.

35.8 Pharmacist's Responsibility Regarding Recalls

Drug use control is a term that was coined and found in the pharmacy literature decades ago. It means that the hospital pharmacist is responsible for the use of drugs *throughout* the hospital. Recalls are initiated by manufacturers, and usually influenced by the FDA and public health concerns. The pharmacist in the hospital is the one most responsible for insuring that dangerous, unusable, or recalled drug products are not available for, or used in, patients. The topic has always been addressed by practice standards/guidelines for pharmacists (American Pharmacists Association, American Society of Health-System Pharmacists), State Pharmacy Practice Acts (i.e., Texas), and Joint Commission inspections.

This "important drug recall" did not occur as it should have, and patients, including subject patient described herein, were at risk for serious life-threatening reactions as a result of that exposure.

The same principles of recall, and citation of literature describing the standards of practice, are in Chapter 19, *The Story of E-Ferol*.

35.9 Conclusion

As a pharmacy-liability consultant, I am often asked, "How can we avoid malpractice?" My response has always been "to practice at a high level." When pharmacists do their jobs well, drugs will be used more efficaciously and safely, and patients will suffer fewer drug injuries. I tell pharmacies to slow down and hire more staff—not to attempt to take on more work than can be safely done in a specified period of time. I tell them to make counseling their standard practice, supervise support staff, and to employ quality-assurance techniques wherever possible. I tell pharmacists to stay up-to-date with the pharmacy literature, and to read and circulate the "Institute for Medication Safety Practices" (www.ismp.org) newsletter.

The most important thing I tell my clients is to speak up—to communicate with physicians on a regular basis. Pharmacists cannot read physician's minds (even if they are used to reading their handwriting!). Pharmacists must have the determination to actually call and ask for help in interpreting a confusing prescription. When the pharmacist observes what appears to be an error in the physician's prescription, it is negligence to avoid calling the physician to diplomatically address the problem and offer an alternative.

Although pharmacy errors (and, thus, pharmacy malpractice) will never be completely eliminated, the entire profession must continue efforts to minimize mistakes and protect the lives of patients.

According to a 2009 report from the Institute for Safe Medication Practices (ISMP) in Horsham, Pennsylvania, "the first step in setting up an error reduction program is to establish a multidisciplinary team to improve medication use." This team, the Institute explained, must collaborate to assess medication safety and invent fool-proof systems of checks and balances to prevent errors from occurring.

Such checks should include a system for reporting errors, understanding the root causes of medication errors, and educating practitioners thoroughly about the systems in place for preventing errors. The report recommended Computerized Prescriber Order Entry (CPOE), bar-coding systems, infusion pumps with pre-programmed dose limits, automated dispensing cabinets and an integrated pharmacy order-entry system that can communicate with other computerized systems in the hospital.

Pharmacists are taught to be a "safety net" for every patient who is given a prescription. But even the best-laid plans for drug development, research, and physician diagnosis can go awry, if pharmacists give the patient the wrong drug, the wrong strength, or the wrong instructions. Even when dealing with conscientious professionals, Murphy's Law still applies—if anything can go wrong, it will. Errors and negligence can harm or even cause death. Pharmacists must consider various theories of liability when an injured patient initiates a lawsuit naming the pharmacist or his pharmacy.

Endnotes

1. Institute of Medicine (IOM), "To Err Is Human: Building a Safer Health System," 2000.

2. Lazarou J, Pomeranz BH, Corey PN. Incidence of adverse drug reactions in hospitalized patients: a meta-analysis of prospective studies. *JAMA*. April 15,1998; 279(15):1200-5.

3. Kalman and Schlegel. (1979, March). Standards of Practice for the Profession of Pharmacy. *American Pharmac*. 19, No 3.

4. *Heidi Happel v. Wal-Mart Stores, Inc.*, d/b/a Wal-Mart Pharmacy, 90482, Lexis 296 (Illinois Supreme Court 2002)

5. *Robert L. Cottam v. CVS Pharmacy*, SJC-08497, Lexis 146 (Supreme Judicial Court of Mass. 2002

6. *Lester B. Cobb Memorial Hospital, Springfield, MO v. Baxter Laboratories*, 1989.

7. *Pansey and Dennis Bobay v. Walgreen Company*, No. 1:07-CV-119 RM, N.D. Ind., 2009 U.S. Dist. LEXIS 56779, June 30, 2009.

8. *Hooks SuperX v. McLaughlin*, 642 N.E.2d 514 (Ind. Supr. Ct. 1994).

9. *Ingram v. Hook's Drugs, Inc.*, 476 N.E. 2d 881 (Ind. Ct. App. 1985)

10. O'Donnell, JT. Pharmacist Practice and Liability. *J Nursing Law*. November 4, 2005; 10(4): 201-207.

11. Flynn EA, Barker KN, Berger BA, Braxton Lloyd K, Brackett PD. Dispensing errors and counseling quality in 100 pharmacies. *J Am Pharm Assoc*. 2009; 49:171-180.

12. Flynn EA, Barker KN, Carnahan BJ. National observational study of prescription dispensing accuracy and safety in 50 pharmacies. *J Am Pharm Assoc*. 2003; 42:191-200.

Chapter 36

Specialized Services:
A Full-Service Community Pharmacy Practice:
Is this Feasible, Beneficial, and Risk-Free?

Roger S. Klotz, R.Ph., BCNSP, FASCP, FACA, CDM

36.1 Is There a Need for Community Pharmacy Practice?

The first question we must ask is: "Will there be a need for community pharmacy practice in the coming future?" The answer to this question will help us answer the questions regarding feasibility, benefits, and possible risks. Some individuals and organizations—both inside and outside of the profession—believe that the community pharmacy will be eliminated by the centralization (i.e., mail-order pharmacy, chain drug stores, food stores) of prescription dispensing or the continued expansion of managed care. If they are correct, then the discussion of the future of community pharmacy practice becomes moot. The Fourth Report of the Pew Health Professions Commission, released in December 1998, indicated that the automation and centralization of prescription dispensing would reduce pharmacy manpower requirements and that the colleges of pharmacy should reduce their enrollment. Thus, the Pew report would support a belief in the centralization of dispensing.

There is no doubt that automation can further increase the efficiency of the dispensing function, which could allow for the creation of prescription factories and thereby potentially reduce the need for community-focused pharmacy practice. This, of course, assumes that pharmacy practice in the community setting is solely a dispensing function. This also assumes that patients would accept and support the centralization of their medical care and therapy management and that patients are only looking for efficient distribution. These concepts also assume that efficient filling of massive quantities of prescriptions is a desired therapeutic outcome and that modern drug therapy is totally without risk. If all of these assumptions proved correct, then centralization of dispensing would create a more efficient—and, therefore, a more cost-effective—approach to drug distribution, leaving no need for community-focused pharmacy practice.

To be sure, cost-effective distribution does not necessarily imply clinically effective or safe drug therapy. Consumer polls also indicate that patients are not completely comfortable with centralization of pharmacy or medical care.

Unfortunately (or fortunately, depending on one's position in the healthcare-delivery system), patient care requires a very individualized focus and a deep understanding of a patient's lifestyle, nutritional habits, metabolic status, medical history, and family history. Modern drug therapy requires patient-specific dosing, as well as the avoidance of food-drug, laboratory-drug, and drug-drug interactions to achieve desired therapeutic outcomes and avoidance of adverse effects. The maximization of therapeutic benefits requires that a multifaceted healthcare team work in concert, with full understanding of the individual patient's status and needs.

In other words, individualized health care requires trained individuals to work closely with individual patients. The patient's diagnosis, nutritional status, genetics, and physiological status influence the pharmacokinetic and pharmacodynamic effects of each drug utilized in her therapy. The management of these issues in the present and in the foreseeable future cannot be automated as easily as the dispensing function. Automation of drug distribution may increase efficiency and result in more drugs being made more rapidly available; but without proper cognitive processes in place, the enhanced distribution of drugs may actually result in an increased incidence of adverse outcomes. While managed-care programs have tried to drive down the cost of prescription drugs, the treatment of drug-induced adverse outcomes is in danger of driving up the cost of patient care.

Published reports continue to appear in the medical literature regarding the increased incidence of adverse effects, including deaths, as a result of modern drug therapy. Phillips et al. examined U.S. death certificates between 1983 and 1993 and found that there was a 2.57-fold increase in deaths from medication errors.[1] Of further interest is the group's finding that outpatient medication error deaths increased 8.48 fold. This is not surprising, because during this period, outpatient visits in the U.S. increased by 75 percent, while in-patient days decreased by 21 percent. A more recent report found that 40 potentially harmful medication errors occurred daily in an average-size healthcare facility.[2]

Lazarou et al. reported on a meta-analysis of 39 prospective studies of adverse drug reactions (ADRs) in the U.S. over a period of 32 years. They found from their analysis that the incidence of serious ADRs (defined as incidents requiring hospitalization, patients who were permanently disabled, or incidents resulting in death) was 6.7 percent, and that fatal ADRs occurred at a rate of 0.32 percent. As a result of these findings, they estimated that 2,216,000 hospitalized patients in the U.S. had serious ADRs and 106,000 (76,000–137,000) patients had fatal ADRs in 1994. This frequency of fatal ADRs would put these reactions somewhere between the fourth and sixth leading causes of death in the U.S. They felt, therefore, that ADRs represented a significant clinical issue.[3] The IOM reports of 1999 and 2006 reaffirmed the significance of these findings, noting an estimated 49,000–100,000 death and a growing number of reports of ADRs in ambulatory and long-term care patients.[4,5]

Another study of adverse drug events in hospitalized patients found that there was a twofold-increased risk of death for ADRs.[6] The study, by Johnson and Bootman, found that the drug-related morbidity and mortality cost estimate was $76.6 billion in the U.S. ambulatory setting.[7] Aparasu's analysis of data abstracted from the 1992 National Hospital Ambulatory Medical Care Survey found that an estimated 367,647 (322,186–413,108) drug-related-injury visits per year were made to hospital emergency rooms in the U.S. It is interesting to note that antibiotics, hormones/synthetic substitutes, psychotropic agents, and anti-infective agents accounted for 41.5 percent of the drug-related-injury visits.[8]

It is becoming more apparent that the risks of drug therapy are increasing, particularly when multiple drugs are administered. Unfortunately, the extent of the problem has continued to grow. Dealing with this problem is going to require close cooperation between physicians and pharmacists (collaborative-practice models), in order to take advantage of the individual skills of these highly trained clinicians. Fortunately, many states have passed legislation outlining guidelines for physician/pharmacist collaborative-practice agreements, in an attempt to encourage a more cooperative approach to patient care. Collaborative-practice programs allow for integration of the individual skills of the practitioners, to better manage patient therapy and to develop disease-state management programs. It appears that society is now recognizing how important it is that each patient's total drug therapy (prescription, OTC, herbals, and nutrients) be carefully implemented, monitored, and managed by a collaborative group that includes a practitioner who is trained in diagnosis, as well as a practitioner trained in pharmacology, pharmacokinetics, and pharmacodynamics. The complexity of modern drug therapy requires a multidisciplinary approach, because the knowledge base required is so diverse. The pharmacist, particularly in the community setting, is in a good position to deal with many of these issues—especially if communications with the prescriber are complete and frequent.

The increasing complexity of treating chronic diseases—coupled by compliance issues associated with these complex therapeutic regimens—presents a therapeutic challenge. The treatment of asthma, for example, often requires the use of inhalers and oral agents. The training of patients in the use of their medications, particularly the inhalants, is critical to the safe and effective use of these therapies. The treatment of asthma also now requires the self-monitoring of peak flow to ensure that the therapy is effective and that the disease is being controlled. The treatment of diabetes requires not only appropriate drug therapy, but also the close self-monitoring of blood glucose to determine the safety and efficacy of the patient's therapy. The training and motivation of the patient is critical to the effective management of these chronic diseases and to the prevention of end-organ damage.

With the market explosion of OTC and herbal drugs, patients are also increasingly becoming "prescribers" of their own medications. Easy access to a pharmacist—for *all* "prescribers"—will become ever more critical to reducing the potential for adverse effects with increasingly powerful drugs. It is also correlated with better therapeutic outcomes. Therefore, well-trained, readily accessible healthcare professionals who are knowledgeable in the drug-therapy sciences indicated above should be available in every patient's community.

The community-focused pharmacy that provides a wide range of services and is very accessible to the patient can allow for good communications and therapy selection in co-operation with the prescribers. Knowing the patient from a medical, pharmaceutical, and social standpoint can only be done with a one-to-one relationship between the practitioners and the patients.

The incidence of chronic disease is increasing. Bronchial asthma is a major health problem affecting approximately 14 to 15 million Americans, at a cost of over $6 billion per year.[9] It is estimated that 4 to 6 million women have osteoporosis.[10] The number of patients with diabetes mellitus continues to grow—particularly the Type-2 patients. Public-health officials and the Centers for Disease Control and Prevention (CDC) have become increasingly concerned about the diabetes "epidemic." A cohort study defining all prescriptions filled for lipid-lowering drug regimens during a one-year period found a high incidence of compliance failure in all populations studied. The authors found that all of the studied populations (in the United States and Canada) who were prescribed lipid-lowering drug regimens exhibited a significant compliance problem. Over one-third of the patients did not fill their prescriptions during the study year. They also found that about half of the original cohort in the United States had stopped using lipid-lowering therapy altogether.[11] These authors also referred to a number of other studies that showed a long-term compliance rate of approximately 50 percent in patients receiving lipid-lowering therapy. In all of the cases described above, sophisticated drug therapy is required to manage chronic disease and prevent long-term complications. This therapy involves patient education, patient motivation, and ongoing monitoring to maximize therapeutic benefit. All of these require effective communication between the healthcare professionals and their patients. Again—the training, experience, and accessibility of the community-focused pharmacists put them in a good position to deal with these disease states and improve patient compliance. It is obvious that we must do a better job in preventing adverse reactions and managing chronic disease. Both of these challenges will require a readily accessible professional to deal with the drug therapy.

36.2 Collaborative Practice

Collaborative practice involves physicians and pharmacists working together to jointly manage patients—particularly those with chronic disease. Many states have passed legislation allowing pharmacists to have collaborative-practice agreements with physicians. The details of the activities/services that the pharmacy can provide to the patients referred by the physician/prescriber depend upon the specific state legislation. Generally, state laws require that the pharmacist and/or physician develop a collaborative-practice protocol that is signed by each practitioner and reviewed annually. The collaborative-practice agreement is required whenever the pharmacist is authorized to prescribe dosage changes, therapy changes, and/or laboratory services. An example of a collaborative-practice approach is the signing of a pharmacist's protocol for prescribing and administering a vaccine. In California, for example, pharmacists can order and administer vaccines to patients over 18 years of age—as long as they employ a protocol and are certified immunizers. This is required because, under this protocol, the pharmacist becomes a prescriber. Other collaborative-practice protocols are created for the purpose of cooperative disease-state management programs for chronic diseases (i.e., asthma, diabetes mellitus, osteoporosis, arthritis) or for the management of narrow therapeutic drugs (i.e., anticoagulants, aminoglycosides, digoxin).

A different approach to collaborative practice in managing patients is to have a prescriber write a prescription for a specific therapy/service for a specific patient. Some physicians are hesitant to sign a protocol because, in their minds, it is the equivalent of signing a blank check. They have significant fear of losing control or being held responsible for the actions of the pharmacist. One can be successful in getting referrals, often requested by the patient, from physicians on a patient-specific basis. An example is the administration of hepatitis-B vaccine to a patient. The pharmacist calls a physician to inform him that the patient would like to have a hepatitis series completed in the pharmacy. If the physician agrees, a verbal prescription is taken, and the vaccination is administered. On completion of the series, a copy of the progress note is sent to the physician for his records. This updates the patient's medical record and completes the communication circle with the physicians.

Regardless of the specific approach, collaborative practice forces the pharmacist and physician to communicate and share medical/therapeutic information. It also allows the physician access to a pharmacologically focused practitioner. Either approach brings significant benefit to the patient, who ends up with two experts focused on their care, instead of just one. This approach also reduces both the pharmacist's and the physician's medical-legal risk. Better care leads to significant risk reduction. The author has found that patients who receive collaborative care are more confident in their therapy and more compliant.

36.3 Centralization

Centralized dispensing cannot improve patients' understanding of their drug therapy or their compliance with prescribed regimens. Only a motivated, knowledgeable healthcare professional can accomplish these goals. As a previous *JAMA* editorial explained, "Some risks are inevitable, they can be significantly reduced, and learning more about these risks will make this possible."[12]

The risk of adverse effects can be reduced by careful management of therapy, monitoring for reactions, documenting allergy and reaction history, monitoring for adverse effects and effectiveness of therapy, evaluating dosing, and considering new additions to therapy for drug interactions. (Remember, additions to therapy can include the patient's own selection of potentially interacting products.)

A community-focused pharmacist is in a good position to reduce the incidence of adverse reactions and help in the management of drug therapy in patients with chronic disease by providing the above services—particularly if the pharmacist is in collaborative practice with prescribers. A community pharmacist is readily accessible. If the pharmacy is a full-service provider, it can be of major benefit in managing these problems.

A dispensing-only focus will not result in the maximum patient benefit. Dispensing more drugs more rapidly does not combat the obvious problems or inhibit the increasing healthcare costs associated with adverse reactions and patient-compliance failures. Increasing prescription volume only leads to a greater risk of adverse effects and treatment failures, due to the lack of collaborative care. Furthermore, dispensing of medications will not provide the economic foundation for the provision of the services required to prevent these problems. This fact is exemplified by the recent findings that the percent of prescriptions filled for non-Medicaid third-party payers fell from 54 percent (in 2000) to 53 percent (in 2001) of the total prescriptions filled for the first time in history.[13] It appears that the reduced reimbursement is beginning to drive community pharmacies away from some of the payer contracts. An additional fact is that the prescription-error rate in community pharmacy is currently about 1.56 percent per 100 prescriptions.[14] Who would want to increase that risk, just in order to increase prescription load?

A wider scope of practice must be implemented, and the community pharmacy must extend its practice into new and, in some cases, old established areas of practice. Not only will a wider scope of practice allow for better management of these problems, but it should also provide the financial base for the establishment of this wider scope of practice. The documented adverse-effects data indicate the need for the expansion of the pharmacist's practice—not the need to increase prescription volume. A total focus on drug therapy and its management is required to reduce the risks of drug therapy. The partnering of prescribers with pharmacists in collaborative-practice agreements can result in the reduction of the patient's risk of adverse reactions and therapy failures.

36.4 What is a Full-Service Community Pharmacy?

The definition of a full-service pharmacy should be influenced by an evaluation of the community's needs (market analysis). In the author's community, a full-service approach to our practice was chosen, which allows us to coordinate with our patients and their physicians. We have tried to communicate to physicians, dentists, and veterinarians that we are trying to be an extension of their practices and to partner with them in the care of their patients. Our approach to providing a full-service community pharmacy practice was chosen to provide numerous product and service offerings, including the following:

- compounding, non-sterile, and sterile dosage forms (humans and animals)
- traditional dispensing with patient counseling
- drug-information services for patients and healthcare professionals
- clinical laboratory services (CLIA certified)
- medical equipment
- OTC, herbal, and nutritional products (with counseling)
- Patient-care services:
  - "fat-loss" program
  - smoking-cessation program (in our area, though, there are very few smokers)
  - body-composition measurement, with risk assessment
  - osteoporosis risk assessment
  - immunization services
  - physical assessment (i.e., blood pressure, pulse, eye exam, temperature, chest sounds)
  - disease-state-focused patient support
- pet products, including vaccines
- therapy-review counseling for patients receiving their drugs from other pharmacies, particularly centralized filling pharmacies (i.e., mail-order, Internet, and so on), or dealing with nonprescription products (i.e., herbal, nutrients, diet aids)

The necessity of reintroducing the older service of compounding has come about to meet the growing need for specialized dosing and dosage forms, as well as to provide dye-free and preservative-free drugs. Demand is increasing for patient-specific dosing for hormonal therapy (estrogen, progesterone), combining multiple drugs into one dosage form to improve compliance, creating new dosage forms (for example, acyclovir lip balm), as well as developing new delayed-release dosage forms. There continues to be a need for sterile ophthalmic and parenteral dosage forms.

Compounding services are equipment and labor intensive; they include a need to evaluate the patient's status and special requirements, and they require a high level of professional commitment. As a result of the demands created by compounding services, this service is only available in a limited number of pharmacies. This allows for the community pharmacy to add a market-differentiating service that truly meets patients' needs. However, a number of risks are associated with this service. The risks include the responsibility for the quality assurance of the products and services produced, as well as the need to work very closely with the patient and her physician. Reimbursement is generally not provided through the payer, because there is no NDC code (since the final product is not produced by a manufacturer). Therefore, the patient is responsible for full payment of her prescription. A major problem associated with compounding is that the service requires very high staff competency to assure the quality of the compounded medications and to minimize the potential medical-legal liability.

Compounding now has become an "issue," in that some compounding pharmacies are producing bulk quantities of compounded items, which they provide to prescriber offices or other organizations. This approach makes them more akin to manufacturers, and thereby subject to Food and Drug Administration (FDA) regulation and Good Manufacturing Practices (GMP). For example, to avoid being considered a manufacturer, the pharmacist must maintain a direct and regular interaction with the patient. The pharmacist, patient, and physician "triangle" must be maintained. This also allows the compounding pharmacy to tailor the product and dosage form to meet the individual patient's needs. On its website (www.fda.gov), the FDA has published the rules for separating compounding (states' responsibility) from manufacturing (the federal government's responsibility). Community pharmacists interested in developing compounding programs should review these points before developing a compounding practice.

Because of poor reimbursement, coupled by payers' lack of understanding of the total effect on healthcare cost, traditional prescription dispensing is now considered by many community pharmacists to be a very poor financial risk. In this context, it might appear to make sense to turn this phar-maceutical function over to the centralized prescription services. However, if you plan to provide a full-service community pharmacy, and you recognize the need to reduce the high number of adverse reactions, this must be part of your practice offering (unless the centralized prescriptions are distributed through the pharmacy or the pharmacist has access to the patient's medication records). The development of the Health Insurance Portability and Accountability Act (HIPAA) regulations ultimately may help eliminate the need for local filling of prescriptions when the community-based pharmacist has access to the patient's medical and prescription records.

Patient counseling—required for the safe and effective use of drugs—has turned out to be critical to other services provided as well. We are also finding that as patients become more frustrated by our healthcare-delivery system, they become much more focused on obtaining knowledge about their therapy, and may be more willing to pay for additional services. It seems from personal observation that an increasing number of patients believes that their physicians do not really understand drug therapy and that they are at a subsequently higher risk of adverse outcomes. This is predominately the result of the fact that physicians spend less and less time with patients during an average visit. There is little time to discuss issues. This factor, ultimately, may be the biggest failure of managed care and cost-reduction programs. On the other hand, this is a significant opportunity for the pharmacist to help the physician increase customer satisfaction, while at the same time reducing the prescriber's medical-legal risk. This is particularly true if the pharmacist shows an interest in the patient's total therapy and communicates well with both patient and prescriber. The provision of traditional dispensing services allows the community pharmacist to develop and maintain relationships with his patients. This relationship allows the pharmacist to expand his service offerings to each individual. However, this can only continue if there are some changes to the current pharmaceutical care reimbursement approaches.

36.5 Drug Information

The availability of drug-information services in the community allows all of the prescribers to use resources not generally available in the prescriber's office. The complexity of modern drug therapy requires all practitioners to have access to sophisticated information in order to avoid therapy failures and adverse reactions. The multitude of drugs on the market makes it completely impossible for individual practitioners to maintain a thorough knowledge base within their memories. Therefore, ready access to a literature source is critical to avoid negative therapeutic outcomes. OTC and herbal medications further compound the issue.

At our practice site, we have chosen to build a small drug-information center (including journals, textbooks, and computerized access to the National Library of Medicine), which can also be used for training groups of patients. This provides us with the resources to do drug-therapy reviews, which are done by appointment and are billed directly to the patient. The present reimbursement systems require the patient to pay for these additional services, which creates a risk for the pharmacy (in that the services may end up being under-utilized). However, we have found that a significant number of patients or family members will readily pay for this service.

One significant source of concern is the complexity of the drug regimens of patients who mix prescribed medications with OTC and herbal drugs. Physicians and dentists are becoming increasingly worried about their lack of knowledge regarding the herbal and OTC medications used by their patients and the potential interactions that these substances may have with their prescription drugs. Adding to this concern is the increasing number of prescription drugs that are making the transition to OTC status. The community pharmacy can become a very beneficial resource to patients, physicians, and dentists—while simultaneously developing new sources of revenue.

Some pharmacists worry that by proffering therapeutic opinions they could expose themselves to medical-legal liability. The risk can be minimized by obtaining thorough information, having adequate information resources, and by providing a written consultation to the patient and physician. The written consultation should be placed in the patient's pharmaceutical care record (pharmacy medical record), since it is now considered a legal document. The consultative services provided by the pharmacist may actually become a major medical-legal risk-management program for the pharmacist and the prescriber. The avoidance of adverse reactions, and/or the assurance of appropriate therapeutic outcomes, can prevent injuries that ultimately could be litigated. Consultations can be billed to the patient's payer using the standard Form 1500, since these services are not covered by the prescription-benefit service, but will be covered by the patient's major medical plan. At present, we bill the patients and provide them with the documentation to bill the payers themselves. This approach makes the patients responsible for obtaining reimbursement from their payers. Remember, the patients are responsible for payment for all services, but they have contracts (health-insurance plans) with payers to provide coverage for some services. We choose not to bill the payer, because generally the payer does not fully understand the risks associated with modern drug therapy (and therefore sees no reason to reimburse for preventive consultative services).

36.6 Clinical Laboratory Services

We have added clinical laboratory services to our offerings in an effort to provide monitoring capabilities for a number of disease states. This approach allows the pharmacist's knowledge of pharmacodynamic effects to be augmented by the readily available clinical laboratory results, uncovering adverse effects before they become serious and enabling more rapid responses to treatment failures.

For example, monitoring a patient's international normalized ratio (INR) when she comes in for a warfarin refill allows for dosage adjustment before the refill is dispensed. The availability of INR determination allows the pharmacist to become an extension of the physician's practice, thus implementing a collaborative approach to disease-state management. Such direct communication between healthcare professionals allows for appropriate dosage modification—before the patient experiences an adverse-reaction or develops a blood clot. In another example, monitoring the lipid profile of patients on lipid-lowering agents allows for rapid response to changes in the patient's response to therapy. Likewise, a simple finger-stick test (AST) can help a pharmacist monitor for liver toxicity secondary to numerous medications.

The clinical laboratory capability also allows the pharmacist to do screenings (i.e., cholesterol, glucose, triglycerides, fructosamine) that prompt referrals to physicians when the values are questionable or elevated. The accessibility and convenience of the community pharmacy makes it more likely that the patient will readily commit to a screening procedure.

The pharmacy-based clinical laboratory is also a more cost-effective and convenient site for monitoring some of the basic clinical chemistries. The new technologies for the basic tests allow the provision of services to be more cost-effective.

The benefits of a community pharmacy's clinical laboratory services are accessibility, responsiveness, use of capillary blood sample, and coordination with the patient's drug therapy. The risk to the community pharmacy is the expense of laboratory equipment, possible reimbursement difficulties, governmental oversight requirements, and potential medical-legal liability. On the other hand, closely monitoring a patient's drug therapy for efficacy and potential adverse reactions can reduce the medical-legal liability risks to the pharmacist and physician. The laboratory equipment required to do the screening tests can be leased (and, thus, paid for over time), which will help minimize the initial investment.

We have chosen to become a CLIA-certified laboratory, with a pharmacist as the registered laboratory director. We have registered to do "waived" tests only at this time. Being registered as a laboratory allows us to obtain laboratory reimbursement, but at this time, since the costs of the tests to the patient are so reasonable, we do not bill the payers. We do give the patient a receipt, which can be used to seek reimbursement. However, most patients do not bother to do so, because the tests cost under $50. The low patient charge for the tests also makes it costly to seek reimbursement from the payers. If we did seek reimbursement, the billing costs would force us to significantly increase the cost of each test to cover the administrative expenses. The use of laboratory procedures, compliance with the quality-assurance guidelines provided by the manufacturer, and the written documentation of all test results help minimize the medical-legal liability.

To become a CLIA-certified laboratory, one must register with the Department of Health and Human Services using the Clinical Laboratory Application, which is HCFA Form 116 (8-92). The director of the laboratory must complete and submit the form. In California, the certificate of waiver application must be submitted to the Department of Health Services, which will then submit the application to the federal agency. Other states may have requirements similar to California's, so pharmacies should check with the appropriate state agency to identify any special application requirements.

Furthermore, other local health-department requirements may apply, so one must also contact the local health department. One example of local requirements occurs in California, where one must apply for a "non-diagnostic health-assessment provider permit" in certain counties. This permit allows pharmacists to provide non-diagnostic health-assessment services without a physician's order. The requirements for the permit vary by county; one must contact the county in which the service will be provided. Most county health departments will require the pharmacy to assure that its staff has been trained to minimize its exposure to blood-borne diseases, and in the proper disposal of all blood-contaminated materials.

The federal OSHA standards must be addressed as well. We chose to register as a provider of "waived" tests only, since this eliminates the need for inspections and regular submission of unknown sample results to HCFA. Our lab tests are also listed as "waived" tests by the FDA (the agency responsible for issuing the "waived" test designation). The list of "waived" tests is included with the certification form. A pharmacy can move up to moderate-level testing, but there is not usually a need to carry out these more elaborate tests, and they dramatically increase equipment costs.

Registering with HCFA under CLIA is a method of managing medical-legal risk and gaining credibility for a pharmacy's clinical laboratory services. We have found that patients are receptive to a pharmacy performing clinical laboratory services and have not shown any concern over having a pharmacist obtain a capillary sample and run the appropriate tests. We have even received physician referrals for laboratory services. Recently, a physician requested an H. pylori test, which we conducted, faxing the results to the physician's office. We have been monitoring one particular patient's INR for over two years, working collaboratively with the patient's cardiologist to modify the dose when necessary. We provide written documentation of the INR results, along with our recommendations, to the physician after each visit.

36.7 Home Medical Equipment

The availability of a home medical equipment (commonly known as HME) section within a community pharmacy further adds to its "full-service" capabilities, thus more completely addressing patients' total needs. Recently, we decided to add breast-prosthesis services to our HME offering, further expressing our "full-service" approach. We sent our pharmacy technicians and registered nurse for training to fulfill this function. (We have a nurse available on a part-time basis to provide services that pharmacists are not comfortable performing, and to provide clinical services in a more cost-effective fashion. For example, wound care requires specific products and dressings. A registered nurse is more knowledgeable in this area than most pharmacists.)

A community pharmacy deals predominately with chronic disease, which requires basic medical equipment and supplies. Convenient access to these items can definitely increase traffic in a pharmacy and provide a beneficial service to patients. Again, the major risk of adding this service to the community pharmacy is the financial risk of investing in inventory—but this can be managed by having next-day access to products and equipment, so that the pharmacy only needs to stock a few sample products. Another financial risk is incurred if the pharmacy decides to rent equipment to Medicare patients, since that requires tying up money in rental equipment (and may also present the problem of recovering the rental equipment). On the flip side, the money tied up with the rental equipment can be recouped within a reasonable period of time, and an equipment-tracking mechanism can help facilitate equipment recovery.

The community pharmacy is in the best position to handle these problems, because it is readily available to the patient and his family. Also, because most of these patients will require prescription medications, a pharmacist will be seeing the patients or their family members on a regular basis. The community pharmacist, therefore, can keep in close

contact and monitor the patient's progress (or lack of progress). This approach to providing a broad range of services
will, in the long run, produce significant patient interaction
and subsequent increases in revenue. If done well, the benefits outweigh the risks.

36.8 Herbal and OTC Medications

A full-service pharmacy should offer consultations with a
pharmacist about herbal and OTC medications, and nutrition. This service is actually an extension of our clinical and
drug-information resources capability. Access to information about the potential toxicity of, and adverse reactions to,
these agents—when used alone or combined with prescription drugs—is a major benefit to patients, their physicians,
and their dentists.

Numerous individuals and organizations are jumping
on the alternative-medicine bandwagon. Unfortunately,
many of the remedies being promoted—such as dehydroepiandrosterone (DHEA)—have unknown potential risks.
DHEA, for example, can produce significant androgen or
estrogen imbalances.[15,16] Individuals without proper medical or pharmaceutical training are promoting these remedies
because they are a good source of revenue. The community
pharmacy can become a resource for credible information
regarding the safety and efficacy of these alternative pharmacological or nutrient therapies.

Safety depends on the patient's present medical status
and medication history. Our approach is to make the pharmacist readily available to the patients purchasing OTC drugs,
herbal medications, and nutritional products. We promote
the concept that the pharmacists should spend the majority
of their time in front of the prescription counter—increasing
their accessibility to their patients.

We find that patients are willing to make appointments
with the pharmacist and pay for consultations, with the
goal of maximizing the efficacy and safety of their therapy.
Perhaps one reason is because of the increasing number of
reported illnesses and deaths due to self-administration of
nutrients and herbal and OTC remedies. For example, a case
of renal toxicity secondary to the self-administration of a
creatine supplement has been reported, as well as the deaths
of college wrestlers who were taking this supplement. All of
these athletes were taking maintenance doses of two to five
grams per day.[17]

Researchers from Beth Israel Deaconess Medical Center presented the findings of a telephone survey in *JAMA*
regarding the use of alternative therapies by 2,055 patients.
Dr. Eisenberg and his colleagues found that fewer than 40
percent of the patients had informed their physicians that
they were taking alternative therapies. The authors also

concluded that 20 percent of the patients who were taking
prescription medications were also taking herbs, high-dose
vitamin supplements, or both.[18] This report points to a significant reason why there is such a high incidence of severe
adverse reactions.

This point has been emphasized time and time again at
our pharmacy. For example, an INR patient had an INR of
4.6, which resulted in a significant bleed. When questioned,
he admitted that his bodybuilding friends had given him a
product to increase muscle mass. Unfortunately, his friends
did not know that this compound also increased the effectiveness of the warfarin he was taking. The patient had to
be admitted to the hospital for a short period. We instructed
him and his wife that he was never to take any other medications again—including herbal products—without first talking to his physician or pharmacist.

It is critical for a healthcare professional to track a patient's total therapy, in order to avoid severe adverse reactions. The community pharmacist is in the best position to
track the patient's total therapy. Therefore, it is very important that a "full-service" community pharmacy be available
to patients, since a centralized dispensing system cannot
deal with these issues. People must know their healthcare
providers to have full confidence and trust in them; this allows them to comfortably share very private information.
This type of trust can only happen when there is regular,
direct communication and interaction between people and
their healthcare providers. The new approach of training
pharmacists in physical assessment provides the pharmacist
with increased skills to closely monitor each new patient
that comes into the pharmacy. This personal contact between a trained healthcare professional and a patient greatly
enhances the quality of care and reduces the risks of therapy.
We have referred numerous patients to a physician when we
observed potential medical or pharmacological problems.
Centralized dispensing does not allow for personal, private
interaction (which results in the building of patients' trust
and confidence). Neither does centralized dispensing allow
for observation of the patient and physical assessment of the
patient's status.

36.9 Risks and Benefits

Patients' care services (i.e., services that are not associated
with a product) are a new area of benefit, responsibility,
and potential risk for the community pharmacy. They also
present the community pharmacist with significant financial
and professional opportunities. The accessibility and convenience allow the patient to obtain these very personal services through a healthcare professional that will take the time
necessary to provide the services. The benefit to patients

is the availability of health screening, drug therapy, nutritional therapy, and health-maintenance programs in a convenient community center. The benefit to physicians is that these accessible screening programs may identify high-risk patients who may be referred to them for a full diagnostic work-up. The early identification of hypertensive patients, for example, may result in earlier diagnosis and treatment, which may result in the reduced chance of end-organ damage. The risks of this approach to the patients are relatively minimal, with the possibility of a false-positive screening (which could lead to the expense of a full diagnostic work-up) as the highest risk. Obviously, this risk is worth taking, when one considers the risk to the patients of undiagnosed chronic disease.

The pharmacist faces medical-legal liability risk by providing these types of services, but these risks can be managed by obtaining proper training and certification, documenting all services performed in the patient's record, and reviewing the results. Proper documentation is critical to the risk-management program of all healthcare professionals, including the pharmacist's. This patient-focused care approach, when accompanied by proper documentation, has a more positive impact on medical-legal risk management than it does on increasing the pharmacist's and physician's risk.

The provision of some of these services could actually reduce the pharmacist's medical-legal risk, by monitoring for potential adverse effects. For example, the package insert for the appetite suppressant Meridia (sibutramine HCl) includes a warning regarding the potential for development of hypertension in patients receiving this drug. If a pharmacist refills this medication without monitoring the patient's blood pressure, the question then becomes, "could the pharmacist be held responsible for any negative outcomes when the side effect has been strongly indicated?" Many individuals would argue that monitoring this side effect is the physician/prescriber's responsibility, but drug therapy is a collaborative responsibility, because of each practitioner's particular skills. Thus, the provision of some of these services could actually reduce the pharmacist's liability risk.

There are three major benefits of identifying the occasional patient who will develop a side effect from any prescription drug: it (1) reduces the medical-legal risk of the pharmacist, (2) increases her credibility with the patients and the prescriber, and (3) reduces the cost (financial and human) of adverse reactions.

36.10 Disease-State Management
The involvement of the community pharmacist in disease-state management programs has begun to gain much interest among pharmacists and, more recently, among medical

groups. All of the previously described services, including the patient-care services, lend themselves very well to participation by the community pharmacist in disease-state management programs. The need for initial training and long-term management of patients with dyslipidemias, diabetes mellitus, hypertension, asthma, and coagulation disorders requires a healthcare team focused on meeting the ongoing needs of patients. The education of patients regarding new findings in the treatment of these diseases, the ongoing monitoring for efficacy and toxicity, as well as the patient support to assure compliance is critical to the effective management of these chronic diseases and the reduction in the cost of care. A Canadian study referred to earlier in this chapter found that patients taking lipid-lowering drugs were without agents for 40 percent of the year, even though the cost of these drugs was almost completely covered by their insurance.[11] Obviously, the cost of the medication was not the reason for noncompliance, since most patients in the studies did not fully pay for their medications.

The real fact that these studies point to is that patients are not seeing or not understanding the value of continuing a medication when they do not feel ill. This results from the patients' lack of understanding as to the true implications of long-term effects of dyslipidemia, such as heart disease and stroke. This lack of risk appreciation seems to be a result of healthcare professionals' complacency—physicians write prescriptions and pharmacists dispense the medications. We need to do more. Project Impact's published results prove that the community pharmacist can significantly improve outcomes by taking a strong role in disease-state management.[19] Pharmacists made a major impact on increasing compliance and documenting the maintenance of lower serum lipids. One study substantiated that even in elder patients (ages 70 to 82), the use of lipid-lowering medication (Pravastatin) resulted in the reduced risk of coronary disease.[20] Thus, even in the elderly group, the pharmacist can make a significant impact in improving outcomes, by supporting the management of a disease state. The simple act of contacting patients and reminding them to refill their prescriptions shows that a healthcare professional is interested in their health and believes that compliance with their therapy is very important. This does have a major effect on compliance; we actually see this occurring in our practice. This is a simple form of disease-state management, which could be enhanced—if there were some form of reimbursement for this service.

A more complex form of disease-state management can involve the pharmacist's monitoring the therapy efficacy and toxicity and, when appropriate, recommending appropriate dosage adjustments. This approach can be beneficial in managing patients on oral anticoagulant therapy, since this therapy requires intense initial and ongoing patient education, diet-history evaluation, drug-therapy evaluation (including OTC drugs, herbal preparations, prescriptions, and nutrients), and clinical monitoring.

By monitoring the patient's diet, drug utilization (including OTC drugs, herbal preparations, prescriptions, and nutrients), refill compliance, and the patient's INR every two weeks or when the patient's refills are due, the pharmacist can improve not only compliance, but reduce the risk of therapeutic failures, adverse reactions, and toxicity. It is interesting to note that a published study of patients receiving oral anticoagulation who self-managed their therapy found that there was improved accuracy of anticoagulation control and enhanced treatment-related quality-of-life measures.[21]

A number of studies evaluating management of warfarin therapy through a warfarin clinic found that patients managed through these clinics had better outcomes (fewer hospital readmissions and fewer dosing modifications) than did patients not managed through a warfarin clinic. In these studies, the pharmacist was proven to be a critical part of the team, because of the significant pharmacological and pharmacokinetic understanding required. The pharmacist-management approach has resulted in a reduced cost of patient care,[22–25] and improved patient satisfaction with therapy.[24,25]

While all of these examples of pharmacy-managed warfarin patients have occurred in hospital-based warfarin clinics, there is no reason that similar levels of care and cost reduction could not be achieved in the community pharmacy. There is no doubt that a pharmacist, with adequate training and interest, can enhance the quality of care for those patients maintained on warfarin.

The most difficult problem with a community-pharmacy-based program is the lack of physician confidence in the community-based pharmacy practitioner. We have found that it is very difficult to gain physician confidence in the pharmacy as a source of clinical laboratory results. Physicians have no difficulty accepting the pharmacists' role in monitoring diet and other drugs and educating patients. It is the pharmacy's role as a laboratory that physicians are more reluctant to accept. It will take time and aggressive marketing to gain this confidence. That said, we, in our practice, are committed to doing just that. In our experience, we have found that physicians have accepted our clinical-screening results and have become comfortable with the pharmacist's involvement. The risks with this program are the financial risks inherent in purchasing equipment and materials and the medical-legal risks associated with more direct patient-care involvement by the pharmacist. We have already taken the financial risk, and we use documentation (policies and procedures, patient's medical records, and so on) to minimize our medical-legal risk. Laboratory screening in a community pharmacy of patients on drugs with the potential for therapy failure or adverse reactions reduces the patient's clinical risk and, at the same time, reduces the pharmacist and physician's risk. Collaborative practice—at any level—is a risk-reduction program for the patient and the healthcare professionals caring for them.

36.11 Immunizations and Vaccinations

Immunization programs increasingly are becoming part of the services provided by a full-service community pharmacy. The growing concern about adult vaccinations, particularly in the senior citizen group (greater than 65 years of age), now has an even greater priority. According to the CDC, "Outbreaks of influenza in nursing homes have shown attack rates as high as 60%, with case fatality ratios as high as 30%." Reports regarding diseases that have vaccines available for prevention found that "high death rates occur despite therapy with antibiotics, and older adults are at an increased risk, from 30% to 40% in those 50 to 69 years of age and as high as 55% to 60% in those 70 years or older."[26] The author's personal experience is that the average adult, upon questioning, cannot remember when she had her last tetanus vaccination or whether she ever had a pneumococcal vaccination. All of these diseases are vaccine-preventable, but we obviously continue to have a problem.

Healthcare professionals need to focus on adult vaccinations. The CDC has chosen to support the community pharmacist as an adult-vaccination advocate and provider, in that it was instrumental in the development and presentation of the pharmacist-certificate programs. The American Pharmaceutical Association and the American Society of Health-System Pharmacists have both developed policies and training programs to enhance the pharmacist's skills in vaccine administration and infectious-disease prevention. The basic plan is to provide this resource at a convenient healthcare site. The community pharmacy provides the general public with a readily accessible healthcare professional who, with a reasonably short training program, can be an advocate and provider of vaccinations. The CDC will provide all healthcare professionals with the up-to-date recommendations for all available vaccinations. This reference provides a history of each vaccination, recommended dosing, high-risk population guidelines, guidelines on administration, contraindications, and potential adverse reactions.[26] This reference costs only $25 and is readily available to pharmacists.

The community pharmacist can be involved in the education of adults regarding the need for maintaining their vaccinations. The pharmacist can also retain a vaccination history for each patient. Thus, the community pharmacist can become a very important advocate and vaccination-information resource (even if he is not interested in learning to administer the vaccinations personally), and the community pharmacy can add adult-vaccine education programs to its full-service offerings. At our pharmacy, we have chosen to participate as an advocate, as well as the provider of the vaccine, since this offers easy access for our patients (and patients with access to convenient vaccinations are more likely to actually follow through and obtain them).

Requiring the patient to complete a vaccination form (which provides information on past allergies and vaccination history) may minimize the risk of an adverse reaction from a vaccine. This form also acts as a consent form. Another risk-management approach is to require the patient to remain in the pharmacy for 15 minutes after receiving an injection, in order to monitor for adverse reactions. Finally, the CDC's program requires that all pharmacists attending its course be certified in basic life support.

The addition of an immunization program to a community-pharmacy practice can bring the patient closer to the pharmacist and enhance the whole pharmacy's image as a community healthcare provider (as opposed to being viewed as a mere provider of products). This program also has significant financial benefits, because it is a cash business for low-risk patients and is reimbursable by the payers—including by Medicare—for high-risk patients. High-risk patients for influenza would include people 65 years of age and older, chronic diseases, pregnant females, residents of long-term care facilities, those on chronic aspirin therapy (because of the risk of Reye's Syndrome following influenza infection), and those who are immunocompromised (inactivated virus vaccine).[26]

An additional financial benefit is that the patients become aware that they pay the pharmacist a fee for professional service and the payers may learn to see the pharmacist as a care provider. As with any of the programs provided by a full-service pharmacy, there are benefits and risks that each pharmacist must evaluate. We have made the decision that the benefits to our practice and business far outweigh the risks. On the other hand, we manage our risks by documenting our activities.

36.12 Documentation

The management of any organization requires an effective documentation program, and the community pharmacy is no exception. As with any business, a community pharmacy is responsible for having guidelines and training programs for its employees in order to maintain a consistent quality of care and manage its medical-legal liability. Organized healthcare

sites have traditionally provided protocols and procedures, as well as training programs for employees. Community pharmacists can develop these kinds of programs by promoting ongoing continuing education for their staffs and sending them to specific continuing-educational programs (national and state meetings) that will develop or enhance required skills. For example, our staff (both the pharmacists and the nurse) was required to complete the American Heart Association's Basic Life-Support training program. Our pharmacists were required to attend a physical-assessment class to become competent in this area of practice. Our nurse also can help refine the pharmacists' assessment skills with direct patient observation. These are just a few of the programs that we attended prior to initiating our new pharmacy services.

While helping manage our medical-legal risk, these programs and their associated certifications also assure our patients and other healthcare professionals that we are capable of providing this full-service-pharmacy approach. Attendance at a compounding-certification program was required of all our pharmacists, as was obtaining immunization certification through a program sponsored by the state pharmaceutical association. The certifications and continuing-education certificates become documentation for the pharmacy's management, and they indicate the competence of the staff.

These continuing education and development programs not only reduce risks—they also build the pharmacists' confidence. A pharmacist may never have imagined he would be administering injections into patients' deltoid muscles, but a good and proper technique develops with time. One becomes more confident and effective with more "shots" administered. Confidence can be developed as a result of a certification program. Even compounding is much easier, more comfortable, and more efficient when one learns how to use the newer technologies and capabilities.

Although familiar to hospital and home-infusion-care pharmacists, the development of policies and procedures for many of the services provided is not a traditional approach familiar to most community pharmacists. Community pharmacists must begin to develop this expertise or find outside resources to develop the required protocols and procedures. The availability of polices and procedures is also a confidence-building factor for the pharmacy's staff, as well as for other healthcare professionals. We will readily share our procedures with the prescribers, if they are interested, and will ask for their suggested changes, if they see something with which they disagree. Remember, prescribers—particularly physicians—are very familiar with the use of protocols and procedures in the hospital environment.

The use of this approach definitely increases the credibility of patient-care programs and, at the same time, helps the community pharmacist manage her medical-legal liability. We even have a procedure on blood-pressure assessment, so that there is consistency among our staff (this also comes in handy when training students or new staff members). Other examples of protocols available at our practice site include:

- nutritional assessment,
- pediatric pharmacist assessment,
- anaphylaxis protocol,
- clinical laboratory,
- clinical laboratory monitoring,
- clinical patient monitoring,
- dyslipidemia protocol,
- warfarin protocol,
- bio-impedance protocol (used in assessing patient's weight and percent body fat),
- health-risk assessment, and
- immunization protocol.

Healthcare professionals use procedures and protocols to assure the quality and consistency of the care they provide. The basic approach to developing procedures is to first indicate the goal of the procedure. This approach is particularly advantageous if one intends to have a medical advisor, because this will allow patients to quickly understand why the service is being offered. The goal may also be useful in marketing to prescribers, in general. The second major focus of the procedure is to indicate the goals of the function or procedure. The goals should indicate the basic factors in providing the service and the desired outcomes. Next, one should outline, step-by-step, the actual procedures—including the required documentation. Finally, the references (journal publications and so on) supporting the steps in the procedure should be included.

36.13 Medical/Pharmaceutical Records and Documentation

The medical/pharmaceutical care record is another major portion of all healthcare professionals' documentation programs and, therefore, their risk-management programs. This record is the patient's database and the record of care that allows for communication between the professionals caring for the patient. The medical record allows us to track the patient's care and recall information, when needed, from this database. It also provides all healthcare professionals with a medical-legal record critical to managing their medical-legal liability and reimbursement.

Pharmacists are no exception. They, too, require this basic approach for documenting and tracking their patients' care. The patient's medical history is the initial document in the patient's medical/pharmaceutical care record, to which progress notes, medication profiles, and clinical monitoring (i.e., physical assessment, laboratory results, and physician documents) are added to complete the patient's medical/pharmaceutical care record. All progress notes should be done in the SOAP format (SOAP stands for Signs and Symptoms, Objective Findings, Assessment of Symptoms, Plan), so that any healthcare professional can follow your thought process. Progress notes are a method for documenting each intervention (visit) and its outcome. This visit record may also be documented in a paper format or on a computer system.

A full-service pharmacy providing patient-care services (i.e., immunizations, clinical laboratory services, and physical assessment) must maintain an ongoing medical record of all interventions. The community pharmacist is familiar with prescription files, but the full-service community pharmacy must add the patient's medical record to his documentation files. All of the patient's documentation can be kept manually in patient files or can be maintained on a computer system, or both. It is recommended that, even with a computer system, which is backed up daily, a paper medical record be maintained. Also, many state and federal regulations still require paper documents to be signed by the appropriate healthcare professional. Unfortunately, paper records require a great deal of storage space, which may present a problem for a community pharmacy. We use thin cardboard folders in lateral filing cabinets behind the prescription counter to maintain our patient records. We were fortunate in that the original design of our facility considered the need for a patient-records filing cabinet space as part of the design of a full-service pharmacy.

Another form of required documentation is a record of your communications with other healthcare professionals. Our standard procedure is to provide written letters notifying the patient's physician (if the patient approves) that the patient has requested a particular service and informing her what our initial findings have shown. Thus, we are creating a consultation letter to the prescriber, which provides her with documentation for her medical record. If the prescriber or patient requests a drug-therapy review, we will send a consultation letter with our findings and recommendations (remember the SOAP notes). If laboratory data is requested, we will call the prescriber and follow up with a simple written report.

Communication and documentation go hand-in-hand with providing quality care and supporting your reimbursement and marketing efforts. Remember, physicians are trained to observe, so written, professional communications present the pharmacist as a well-informed professional and give the prescribers documentation for their patients' records. We even contact the primary physician regarding the patient's full medication history when we suspect that he is unaware that his patient is receiving other medications from another prescriber. We follow up this phone communication with a printed copy of the patient's medication profile.

Communication to obtain information is critical—not only to the pharmacist, but also to the prescriber. The prescribers to whom we have marketed our services are very concerned about the drug interactions, pharmacological duplication, and, in particular, the OTC and herbal medications the patient may be taking. The community pharmacist is in the best position to see the overall drug therapy and, therefore, provide communication, information, and documentation to other healthcare professionals who are caring for the patient. This maximizes the benefits of therapy and minimizes the negative effects of therapy. The medication profile in the community pharmacy can be of great value to the other members of the patient-care team. The documentation and communication of the patient's pharmacy documentation is a critical part of the full-service community pharmacy, and it should be available to other healthcare professionals involved in the patient's care.

Remember that you must get the patient's approval to provide information to other healthcare professionals, including to her physicians. It is preferable to use a written consent form signed by the patient to document her approval. However, there are cases in which drug-interaction problems must be taken care of immediately. In those cases, the pharmacist should contact the prescriber verbally and make a note in the patient's prescription. The pharmacist must decide when a full consent is necessary and when one can safely simplify communication. We generally require a consent form when we are providing one of our patient-care services requested by the patient.

Effective April 15, 2003, all providers (including community pharmacies) of direct healthcare were required to be fully compliant with HIPAA (Health Insurance Portability and Accountability Act) requirements for patient data as they relate to electronic transactions (payment), privacy, and security. HIPAA regulations specify that PHI (protected health information) may only be used for TPO (treatment, payment, or operations) by the healthcare provider, without the specific approval of the patient. The patient must sign an "authorization" for each disclosure of PHI for non-TPO purposes. Violation of HIPAA regulations can result in significant civil penalties and, if the violation is extensive, can result in criminal penalties.

Each healthcare-provider organization must provide each patient with a "Notice of Privacy," which explains how PHI will be used for TPO and outlines who will have access to the PHI. The "Notice of Privacy" must also explain that each patient has the right to review his PHI and can ask for corrections to this record. The "Notice of Privacy" must also explain how patients' PHI is protected (secured) from inappropriate use. Each healthcare provider must have a CCO (Chief Compliance Office) to assure that the organization is meeting all of the HIPAA regulations and to oversee staff training. The federal Office for Civil Rights is responsible for monitoring compliance and overseeing compliance by providers. HIPAA requires that all providers have contracts in place with their business associates (i.e., software vendors, nursing services, and so on) who may have access to the patient's PHI. The use for marketing or marketing analysis is considered non-TPO use and requires the patient's authorization for each specific use. This authorization must be dated and may only be used for the specific purpose and the specific time period stated. All community pharmacies must have been compliant by the April 15, 2003, deadline. It is extremely important that community pharmacies and their attorneys become familiar with all of the HIPAA regulations.

36.14 Physical Assessment and Pharmacist's Diagnosis

Physical assessment is the process of monitoring the patient's vital signs (i.e., blood pressure, pulse, temperature), reflexes, skin condition, eyes, nose, ears, chest sounds, and heart sounds. The concept of the pharmacist conducting some degree of physical assessment on patients—such as with the immunization programs—is becoming increasingly acceptable in community pharmacy, particularly in full-service community pharmacies.

The addition of these services by pharmacists is designed to enhance their ability to provide patient-screening services. It also helps prevent the inappropriate use of OTC and herbal medications, and, at the same time, helps patients determine when medical intervention is required. We are not diagnosticians and have no intention of becoming diagnosticians, but the ability to find patients who require medical intervention can be very valuable. We have found patients with elevated blood pressures, patients with fasting blood glucose over 120 mg/dl (indicates diabetes mellitus), and patients wanting to purchase OTC eye preparations who, upon eye exam, appeared to have an infection. All of these patients were instructed to see a physician immediately, or their physicians were contacted directly and informed of our findings. The physician decides whether to do a full workup and determines the need for intervention, but we can help the process along by providing basic screening services. A number of the patients with suspected eye infections have returned with prescriptions for antibiotic ophthalmic drops. The self-treatment of an eye infection would obviously not be appropriate under these circumstances and a delay in diagnosis could have produced significantly negative outcomes, resulting in much more difficult and expensive treatment.

People purchasing OTC and herbal medications without having this type of service available are at increased risk of complications and adverse drug reactions. The patient with a fasting blood glucose over 120 mg/dl could have been missed — if she had not come in for a basic screening — which could have resulted in a continued delay in receiving appropriate treatment. Any diagnostician will tell you that the earlier the diagnosis, the easier (and less expensive) the treatment will be.

The ability to do basic physical assessment of patients also allows for monitoring of the effectiveness and potential adverse effects of the patient's therapy. The recent FDA recommendations for monitoring the peak-and-trough blood pressure of all patients at the beginning of antihypertensive therapy demonstrate the need for pharmacists to do physical assessments. A patient starting on a new antihypertensive therapy should have multiple blood-pressure measurements during the day and at regular intervals. Unfortunately, visiting the physician's office twice a day, every few weeks, is too impractical and expensive. On the other hand, the accessibility (and therefore the convenience) of the community pharmacy makes it very possible to meet the FDA guidelines. The hypertensive patient's blood pressure follows a circadian pattern and, obviously, will be affected by the peak-and-trough serum-drug concentrations.

This does bring up the concept of a pharmacist's diagnosis, which originally was concerning. However, with years of being in practice and seeing the effect of this type of screening, this concept has become more comfortable. The nursing profession has, for years, talked about "nursing diagnosis," as a means of delineating the patient needs that could be cared for by the nurse. Having now done physical assessment on many patients, we now recognize the need for pharmacists to carefully screen the patient who comes in for OTC and herbal medications — in order to prevent inappropriate use and prevent significant problems from going undiagnosed for an extended period. While screening and reviewing a particular patient's drug therapy, some patient complaints are found to actually be side effects or the result of effective blood concentrations of one of their prescribed medications. A "pharmacological diagnosis" was reached,

in that a significant problem was found that could be dealt with by modifying the patient's therapy. There is a place for a pharmacist's diagnosis. We may need to add "pharmacy diagnosis" and "pharmacological diagnosis" to our vocabulary.

A practicing community pharmacist with physical-assessment capabilities will be able to play a more significant role in disease-state management programs. The ability to check the feet of a diabetic or listen to the lung sounds and pulse of an asthmatic can be very beneficial to a disease-management program. This approach allows one to monitor patient compliance and, at the same time, reinforce the disease and therapy education given to the patient by the physician.

A chronic disease can result in significant complications, present compliance problems, and result in severe adverse reactions. All of these problems are known to increase morbidity, which results in increased costs of care and increased mortality. The pharmacist supporting the management of the patient's disease is more readily available than other healthcare professionals and, therefore, can often have a much closer relationship with the patient. Reinforcing the care guidelines presented to patients, and then monitoring for their compliance, can be extremely critical to disease-state management outcomes.

The provision of physical-assessment services requires minimal financial investment, but it can have a significant financial return. It also will promote the use of the community pharmacy over centralized dispensing systems. The personal relationships that are built are more likely to give patients an incentive to purchase all of their medications at your pharmacy. Again, this approach enhances the pharmacist's role as a care provider and helps the patients understand that the pharmacist, like other healthcare professionals, must charge a fee for professional services rendered.

The disease-management approach requires a total patient-care focus — not just a product orientation. If we are to truly provide disease-management services, we must be able to look beyond the dispensing of drugs to patient outcomes, which require an appreciation of patients' physical status. Centralized pharmacy services can never provide this type of hands-on patient care. Only the community pharmacy providing a full-service approach can support a true disease-management approach.

36.15 Facilities
The implementation of a full-service approach to community pharmacy requires the proper physical environment, enabling patient confidentiality, patient privacy, adequate space for medical equipment, and physical facilities for

proper control of the environment for compounding. "Proper control" includes having a space for sterile compounding (ideally, in a clean-room environment). The compounding of sterile products exposes the community pharmacist to a significant medical-legal liability. For this reason, training and the appropriate facilities are a critical part of risk-management programs. Having a clean room can also provide the business with an effective marketing angle.

The pharmacy providing disease-state management and physical assessment must provide private patient-care counseling rooms, which, in a medical environment, are known as treatment rooms. The treatment room provides a private environment, as well as a place for the appropriate equipment storage (i.e., treatment table, blood-pressure cuff, scale, stethoscope, and hazardous waste-disposal containers) required for the delivery of services.

The full-service pharmacy providing clinical laboratory services will need an environment that allows for storage of reagents (refrigerator) and the laboratory equipment, and for storage and disposal of biological hazardous waste. Non-sterile compounding space with adequate shelving for chemicals and equipment—as well as adequate counter space for compounding equipment (i.e., electronic balance, pH meter, and capsule-making machine)—is also required. Medical equipment requires enough space to display everything from support bandages to wheelchairs.

A pleasant environment, which includes carpeting and a comfortable patient-waiting area, is very valuable in getting the idea across to the patient that this is a patient-care-focused provider, not a dispensing-only pharmacy. We have added a small library and drug-information center and made it available to pharmacy staff, patients, and other healthcare professionals.

Our prescription-dispensing area has private consulting booths. The disadvantage of this approach is how much space it requires space that could be devoted to product sales. Most large pharmacy organizations would not commit the space to adequately provide these services. On the other hand, this environment provides adequate facilities to safely provide prescription services, compounding services, laboratory services, and privacy for direct patient care.

The above facility-design points are now very critical to meeting HIPAA regulations regarding the protection of PHI privacy and to assure that all PHI is kept in a secure environment. HIPAA regulations require that all PHI used for TPO be kept private—regardless of whether the PHI is accessed via computer, is kept as paper documents, or is verbally captured and relayed. Private and secure access and sharing of PHI is now a critical issue. Thus, the original design of the full-service community pharmacy resulted in

our organization's ability to easily address the privacy and security requirements of HIPAA, thereby reducing our civil and legal risk, at no additional cost.

These facilities also present a totally different picture of pharmacy practice. We have found that patients feel very comfortable in our environment and readily accept us as healthcare professionals. While the cost of space and equipment is relatively expensive, the effect, from a marketing standpoint, offsets much of this cost. This becomes an even more significant factor as patients and their other healthcare providers become more focused on HIPAA requirements. In marketing to physician groups, we can now describe how our physical environment is addressing the HIPAA regulations. Remember, other healthcare providers are highly affected by the community pharmacy's ability to protect their patients' PHI. In order to provide a full-service approach to community pharmacy, there must be a commitment to appropriate facility design. While this is one of the major financial risks in developing a full-service pharmacy, it now has proven to produce significant financial, legal, and marketing benefits.

While one must take a significant financial risk to develop the appropriate facilities, the development of adequate private areas for patient care and compounding are critical, from a risk-management and marketing standpoint. Patients want confidentiality and an appropriate environment, which allows the pharmacist or nurse to concentrate on meeting the patient's needs. Physicians are not going to support innovative pharmacy practice without assurance of patient confidentiality and adequate facilities for providing laboratory services.

There can be many distractions in a busy pharmacy, which can lead to errors (and increase your medical-legal risk). Therefore, having an appropriate environment must become part of your risk-management program. Furthermore, having private consulting rooms, well-lighted compounding areas, adequate space for medical equipment, a private area for fittings, and a clean, pleasant environment are all excellent marketing tools.

36.16 Summary

There is an obvious and well-documented need for improvement in our delivery of drug and nutrition therapy. A past consensus statement published in *JAMA* stated that "serious and widespread quality problems exist throughout American medicine."[27] The Institute of Medicine National Roundtable on Healthcare Quality stated: "These problems, which may be classified as underuse, overuse, or misuse, occur in small and large communities alike, in all parts of the country, and with approximately equal frequency in managed care and fee-for-service systems of care."[28] The paper indicated that a very large number of Americans are harmed every year as a direct result of this quality issue. The authors went on to say, "Current efforts to improve will not succeed unless we undertake a major, systematic effort to overhaul how we deliver healthcare services, educate and train clinicians, and assess and improve quality."

Pharmacists can become major contributors to improving the quality of care—particularly if they work closely with prescribers and provide a full-service pharmacy program. We found that it is feasible to develop a full-service community pharmacy, and that patients are accepting of the new role of the pharmacist as a care provider, rather than as a mere provider of products and merchandise.

Furthermore, the centralization of prescription dispensing requires community pharmacists to expand their practice into new areas, in order to enhance their survivability. Other benefits of such practice extension include improved financial well-being for the community pharmacy, and an increasing quality of healthcare in the United States. This full-service approach can also potentially lead to collaborative-practice programs in other healthcare professions.

A full-service community pharmacy can also help the pharmacist extend the practice of licensed prescribers beyond their office practices. While there are financial and medical-legal risks, they can be managed, yielding significant financial and professional benefits. The personal contact and expanded services will improve the quality of care to the patient. At the same time, it provides personalized care from a very accessible professional. This new, full-service approach to community pharmacy is feasible and is a boon for patients, healthcare professionals, and the community.

Endnotes

1. Phillips, D.P.; Christenfeld, N.; Glynn, L.M. 1998. "Increase in U.S. medication-error deaths between 1983 and 1993." *Lancet.* 351:643–644.

2. Sept. 9, 2002. "Documenting the extent of the medication error problem in community and nonaccredited hospitals and nursing homes." *Arch. Intern. Med.*

3. Lazrou, J.; Pomeranz, B.H.; Corey, P.N. 1998. "Incidence of Adverse Drug Reactions in Hospitalized Patients." *JAMA.* 279(15):1200–1205.

4. Kohn, Linda T. *To Err is Human: Building a Safer Health System.* Washington, National Academy, 1999. Print.

5. Aspden, Philip. *Preventing Medication Errors.* Washington, D.C.: National Academies, 2006. Print.

6. Classen, D.C. et al. 1997. "Adverse drug events in hospitalized patients." *JAMA.* 277(4):301–306.

7. Johnson, J.A.; Bootman, J.L. 1995. "Drug-Related morbidity and mortality." *Arch. Intern. Med.* 155:1949–1956.

8. Aparasu, R.R. 1998. "Drug-related-injury visits to hospital emergency departments." *Am. J. Health-Syst. Pharm.* 55:1158–1161.

9. Weiss, K.B.; Gergen, P.J.; Hodgson, T.A. 1992. "An economic evaluation of asthma in the United States." *N. Engl. J. Med.* 326:862–866.

10. Osteoporosis Task Force. 1996. "AACE Clinical practice guidelines for the prevention and treatment of postmenopausal osteoporosis." *J. Florida Med. Assoc.* 83:552–566.

11. Avorn, J. et al. 1998. "Persistence of use of lipid-lowering medications." *JAMA.* 279(18):1458–1462.

12. Bates, D.W. 1998. "Drugs and adverse drug reactions: How worried should we be?" *JAMA.* 279(15):1216–1217.

13. No author. Nov. 4, 2002. "Independent R.Ph. digest releases final results." *Drug Topics.* 7.

14. Nov. 4, 2002. "New study sheds light on medication errors." *Drug Topics.* 33.

15. Baulieu, E. 1996. "Dehydroepiandrosterone (DHEA): A fountain of youth?" *J. Clin. Endocrinol. Metab.* 81(9):3147–3151.

16. Ebeling, P.; Kovisto, V.A. 1994. "Physiological important of dehydroepiandrosterone." *Lancet.* 43:1479–1481.

17. Pritchard, N.R.; Kalra, P.A. 1998. "Renal Dysfunction Accompanying Oral Creatine Supplements." *Lancet.* 351:1252.

18. Eisenberg, D.M. et al. 1988. "Trends in alternative medicine use in the United States, 1990-1997: results of a follow-up national survey." *JAMA*. 280(18): 1569–75.

19. Bluml, B.M. et al. 1998. "Interim Report from Project ImPACT: Hyperlipidemia." *J. Amer. Pharm. Assoc.* 38(5):529–534.

20. Shepherd, J.; Blauw, G.J.; Murphy, M.B. 2002. "Pravastatin in elderly individuals at risk of vascular disease (PROSPER): A randomised controlled trial." *Lancet*. 360(9346):1623–1630.

21. Sawicki, P.T. 1999. "A structured teaching and self-management program for patients receiving oral anticoagulation." *JAMA*. 281(2):145–150.

22. Wilt, V.M. et al. 1995. "Outcome analysis of a pharmacist-managed anticoagulation service." *Pharmacotherapy*. 15(6):732–739.

23. Lee, Y.; Schommer, J.C. 1996. "Effect of pharmacist-managed anticoagulant clinic on warfarin-related hospital admissions." *Am. J. Health Syst. Pharm*. 53:1580–1583.

24. Calcagno, D.; Pubentz, M.; Carey, R. 1996. "Improving patient satisfaction with warfarin management." *Amer. J. Managed Care*. 2(7):804–810.

25. Wilson-Norton, J.L.; Gibson, D.L. 1996. "Establishing an outpatient anticoagulation clinic in a community hospital." *Am. J. Health-Syst. Pharm*. 53:1151–1158.

26. Atkinson, W. et al., eds. Feb. 1998. "Epidemiology and prevention of vaccine-preventable diseases." "The Pink Book" 4th Edition. United States Department of Health and Human Services.

27. Chassin, M.R.; Galwin, R.W. 1998. "National roundtable on health care quality: The urgent need to improve health care quality." *JAMA. 280(11):1000–1005.*

28. Institute of Medicine. Jan.1, 1999. "Statement on Quality of Care: National Roundtable on Health Care Quality—The Urgent Need to Improve Health Care Quality." www.nap.edu/books/NI000165/html.

Chapter 37

Pharmacy Compounding Regulations

Loyd V. Allen, Jr., B.S., M.S., Ph.D.

37.1 Introduction

Compounding is an integral part of pharmacy practice and is essential to the provision of quality healthcare. The activities involved in compounding can be simple (such as the addition of a liquid to a manufactured drug powder) or complex (such as the preparation of a sterile, multi-component parenteral-nutrition solution).

It has been important to define compounding—as it compares to manufacturing—for purposes of enforcement, especially at the state level. Compounding differs from manufacturing in that compounding involves a specific practitioner/patient/pharmacist relationship, a relatively small quantity of medication prepared, and the conditions of sale (specific prescription orders).

Pharmaceutical compounding has been central throughout the history of pharmacy (at least until the twentieth century, when the industrial revolution changed the way pharmaceuticals were prepared and made available to the public). During the first two-thirds of the twentieth century, pharmaceutical manufacturers provided a wide variety of dosage forms for their commercial products to accommodate infants, children, adults, and the elderly. However, in recent years, there has been a trend to minimize the variety of dosage forms available (to assist with cost containment and profit maximization). As a result, compounding has re-emerged.

The increase in pharmaceutical compounding began in the 1970s and continued into the 1980s. By the early and mid-1990s, it was evident that compounding was making a dramatic comeback in pharmacy practice. A number of reasons have been presented for the increase in preparing patient-specific medications, including the following:

- Many patients need drug dosages different from those that are commercially available.
- Many patients need specific dosage forms (such as suppositories, oral liquids, or topicals) that are not commercially available.
- Many patients are allergic to excipients used in the manufacture of certain commercially available products.
- Pediatric medications need to be prepared with liquids and flavored to enhance compliance. They also sometimes benefit from alternative dosage forms (such as lozenges, "gummy bears" and ice pops).
- Some medications are not very stable and require preparation and dispensing every few days; these are not really suited to being manufactured products.
- Many drugs and drug-delivery systems are reported

in the literature, but have not yet been manufactured. Pharmacists can compound these for their patients' use, even before they are commercially available.

- Many physicians desire to try products in innovative ways, and pharmacists often work with them to solve individual patient-medication problems.
- The preparation of veterinary drugs can be very complex (due to the variety and size of the patients involved); consequently, most products are not available for animals and must be compounded.
- Home healthcare and the treatment of an increasing number of patients in the home environment have resulted in the need to compound sterile products for home use.

Pharmaceutical compounding has always been an important part of pharmacy practice, and is necessary to ensure an uninterrupted flow of quality medications to patients. Individualizing patient care is at the heart of pharmaceutical compounding, and at the heart of the practice of clinical pharmacy. The thread that runs through all the guidelines and laws discussed in this chapter is the thread of quality compounding and quality patient care.

The 1990s brought up interesting issues related to the pharmacist's right to compound medications and the physician's right to prescribe medications of choice. Although pharmacists are the only health professionals formally trained in the art and science of compounding medications, the growth of compounding has produced an escalation of concern over the quality of compounded products, the expertise of those involved, and the utilization of proper facilities and equipment.

As the extent of compounding increased, it became evident that many standards-setting agencies and regulatory bodies wanted to ensure the development of high-quality compounded products. Consequently, there was considerable activity during the mid-1990s to establish guidelines for pharmaceutical compounding. Three primary organizations have responded—the Food and Drug Administration, the U.S. Pharmacopeia, and the National Association of Boards of Pharmacy. The results of their efforts are described in this chapter.

37.2 Food and Drug Administration

During the early and mid-1990s, the Food and Drug Administration district offices began investigating a number of pharmacies that were compounding very large quantities of selected drug products. Also, during this time period, an unfortunate accident was reported, where some ophthalmic products were improperly autoclaved, resulting in the loss of a patient's sight. Some other incidents were reported, and the Food and Drug Administration became active in investigating individual compounding pharmacies.

At the American Pharmaceutical Association meeting in 1993, FDA Commissioner David Kessler stated that it was not the purpose of the FDA to stop the compounding activities of pharmacists, but to stop the practice of manufacturing under the guise of compounding. However, over the next few years, the activities of the FDA inspectors and district personnel increased, resulting in some pharmacists being threatened with arrest and legal proceedings when their compounded products did not meet the requirements of manufactured products as "New Drugs." (A new drug is defined as "any drug that has not been generally recognized, among experts qualified by scientific training and experience, as safe and effective under the conditions recommended.")

The FDA was determined to require that all compounded medications meet the requirements set forth as a "New Drug," or to prohibit their dispensation to patients. Obviously, this was impossible, and seriously threatened pharmaceutical compounding.

The national pharmacy organizations were united in their efforts to protect the rights of compounding pharmacists. The National Association of Boards of Pharmacy promulgated the "Good Compounding Practices" that have been either adopted or modified and adopted by many states.[1] The U.S. Pharmacopeial Convention was already involved in compounding in preparing a chapter for the USP/NF and in establishing compounding monographs for the compendia.

In 1997, the efforts of many organizations, including the FDA, politicians, and pharmacists resulted in Section 503a of the Food and Drug Administration Modernization Act of 1997 (FDAMA97), supporting pharmacists' right to compound (with some guidelines, as detailed later). However, in April 2002, the section related to prohibiting advertising was ruled by the U.S. Supreme Court to be unconstitutional and non-severable from the rest of the section, so Section 503a was removed from FDAMA97. Regardless, it is of some value to understand some of the FDA's thinking on this topic.

37.3 Food and Drug Modernization Act of 1997 (FDAMA)

On November 21, 1997, President Clinton signed into law the Food and Drug Administration Modernization Act of 1997 (Modernization Act). Section 127 of the Modernization Act, entitled "Application of Federal Law to Practice of Pharmacy Compounding,"[2] amended the Federal Food, Drug, and Cosmetic Act (FFDCA) by adding a new section (503A) governing the practice of pharmacy compounding, to become effective one year after enactment. The effective date was postponed until November 21, 1999.

The purpose of Section 127 of Public Law 105-115 was to ensure patient access to individualized drug therapy and prevent unnecessary FDA regulation of health professional practice. This legislation exempted pharmacy compounding from several regulatory requirements, but would not exempt drug manufacturing from the Act's requirements. The legislation also set forth conditions that must be met in order to qualify for exemption from the Act's requirements. In other words, compounding, according to FDAMA, would exempt pharmacists from having to meet the "New Drug" requirements for each product compounded.

An excerpt from the Senate Labor and Human Resources Committee Report (S. Rpt. 105-43) related to the compounding provisions of the FDAMA 1997 include the following:

> Section 809 of S. 830 is intended to clarify the application of the Federal Food, Drug and Cosmetic Act to the professional practice of pharmacist compounding of drug products. States currently have the authority to license pharmacists and regulate pharmacies, including the scope of pharmacy practice. All states include compounding as a core component of the profession of pharmacy. While the Food, Drug and Cosmetic Act specifically exempts pharmacies from inspection and registration provisions of the Act, it has been the contention of the Food and Drug Administration that compounded products are not exempt from the Act's new drug provisions. The committee has found that clarification is necessary to address current concerns and uncertainty about the Food and Drug Administration's regulatory authority over pharmacy compounding.

According to Senator Tim Hutchinson, "…this legislation would ensure patient access to individualized drug therapy, and prevent unnecessary FDA regulation of health professional practice. This legislation would exempt pharmacy compounding from several regulatory requirements but would not exempt drug manufacturing from the act's requirements. The legislation also sets forth a number of conditions that would have to be met in order to qualify for the exemption from the act's requirements."

FDAMA has a number of specific requirements that will be individually addressed, according to the general outline of the section of the law, as follows:

A. General
  1. The triad
  2. Licensed pharmacist or physician
  3. Anticipatory compounding

B. Compounded Drug
  1. Substances that can be used in compounding
    a. USP/NF substances
    b. Components of approved drug products
    c. FDA-approved list of bulk drug substances
    d. FDA-registered manufacturers of bulk drug substances
    e. Certificates of analysis
    f. USP/NF standards
  2. Substances not to be used in compounding or products not to be compounded
    a. Drug products/substances withdrawn or removed because they are unsafe or ineffective
    b. Inordinate amounts of commercially available drug products
    c. Products that present demonstrable difficulties for compounding that reasonably demonstrate an adverse effect on the safety or effectiveness of that product
  3. Memorandum of understanding
    a. Distribution of inordinate amounts of compounded drug products
    b. Investigation of complaints
C. Advertising and Promotion
D. Regulations
E. Application
F. Definition

37.4 The "Triad"

The Act states that a compounded product is exempt from meeting the "New Drug" requirements if the drug product is compounded for an individual patient based on the unsolicited receipt of a valid prescription order; or a notation, approved by the prescribing practitioner, on the prescription order indicating that a compounded product is necessary for the identified patient—if the product meets certain requirements. A pharmacist may compound a drug when a prescription clearly requires compounding (because the drug is not commercially available in the form needed, or when a physician authorizes compounding). Also, a pharmacist may compound a drug if—with the physician's approval—the pharmacist determines that a compounded drug is necessary and notes that information on the prescription. This allows pharmacists to suggest therapeutic switches to a compounded drug, just as they do for other types of medications. The physician, the patient, and the pharmacist form the legal compounding "triad."

The law states that the "individual patient" must be identified on the prescription. This brings up a question of compounding for office stock. If a physician identifies the patient for whom the prescription will be used in the office setting, such compounding is clearly within the law. However, the law does not explicitly authorize the compounding of a prescription for "office stock," even if the pharmacist later obtains a list of the patients to whom the medications were administered or dispensed. Nevertheless, it is acknowledged that some office-stock compounding is appropriate. Office-stock medication has historically played a valuable role in promoting patient care. Also, some of the drugs on the FDA-initiated bulk-drug substances list proposed during the implementation of FDAMA97 are recommended for approval for office use only, which necessitates the compounding of office stock.

37.5 Licensed Pharmacist or Physician

The product must be compounded by a licensed pharmacist—in a state-licensed pharmacy or federal facility—or by a licensed physician or other licensed practitioner authorized by state law to prescribe drugs.

37.6 Anticipatory Compounding

Limited quantities of products can be compounded in advance—if there is a history of receiving valid prescription orders for the product, generated by an established relationship between the licensed pharmacist and individual patients for whom the prescriptions are provided. There must also be an established relationship with the physician or other licensed professional who wrote the prescription.

37.7 Substances that May be Used in Compounding

Substances that may be used for compounding include the following:

- Bulk drug substances that contain monographs in the USP/NF, according to the USP Chapter on Pharmacy Compounding.
- Drug substances that are components of FDA-approved drugs/drug products, including any ingredient that is contained in commercially available FDA-approved drug products.
- Bulk drug substances that appear on a list of approved bulk-drug substances developed by the FDA.
- Substances used must be manufactured by establishments registered with the FDA—including foreign establishments—and comply with standards of any monograph in the USP/NF (if a monograph exists), as well as with the USP Chapter on Pharmacy Compounding.

- Outside of FDAMA97, there is really no restriction on what can be used for compounding, except that one cannot compound (1) a drug product, or (2) with a drug substance that is included on the List of Compounding Drugs that were Withdrawn or Removed from the Market for Safety Reasons (see Appendix 37.3) or subsequently removed, or any substance that would be considered unsafe.

37.8 Substances that May Not be Used in Compounding

Compounding should not be done using substances or involving products that fall under the following categories:

- Products listed in Appendix 37.3 should not be used in compounding, because they are on the list of drug products withdrawn or removed from the market (because they have been found to be unsafe or ineffective).
- Inordinate amounts of commercially available drug products (not including drug products in which there has been a change made for an individual patient, such as omitting a dye, flavor, sweetener, preservative, or the like) to which the patient may be sensitive. According to this law, pharmacists are allowed to compound copies of commercially available drug products within the definition the FDA provides. In other words, the quantity described as "inordinate amounts" has yet to be defined. Much latitude is given to the prescribing practitioner in this area. It should be mentioned, however, that a small variation in strength, such as from 50 mg to 45 mg, would probably not be determined to be a significant difference.
- The FDA did not formally define "products that present demonstrable difficulties for compounding," but did discuss (1) metered dose inhalers using gas propellants, (2) transdermal "systems," and (3) sterile preparations. The latter were determined to be okay for compounding if done in compliance with USP General Chapter <797> Pharmacy Compounding-Sterile Preparations.

37.9 Memorandum of Understanding (MOU)

Section 503A(b) (3) (B) established that to qualify for the exemptions in section 503A, the drug product must be compounded in accordance with either of the following: (1) It was compounded in a state that had entered into an MOU with the FDA that addressed the interstate distribution of inordinate amounts of compounded drug products and provided for investigation by a state agency of complaints related to compounded drug products distributed outside such state; or (2) it was compounded in a state that had not entered into such an MOU, but the licensed pharmacist, pharmacy, or physician distributes (or causes to be distributed) compounded drug products outside of the state in which they were compounded—in quantities that did not exceed 5 percent of the total prescription orders dispensed or distributed by such pharmacy or physician.

Although never completed, the MOU was being developed by the FDA—in consultation with the National Association of Boards of Pharmacy (NABP)—related to the interstate distribution of inordinate amounts of compounded drug products and the investigation of complaints related to pharmacy compounding.

37.10 Advertising and Promotion

Pharmacies, licensed pharmacists, and licensed physicians cannot advertise or promote the compounding of any particular (1) drug, (2) class of drug, or (3) type of drug. Advertising can, however, include the promotion of the compounding service offered. Pharmacists cannot advertise, for example, "we can compound progesterone 200 mg suppositories." However, they can advertise that they offer compounding services. (Note: This was the controversial portion that resulted in Section 503a being ruled unconstitutional as a limitation on free speech.)

37.11 Definitions

For the purposes of FDAMA, the term "compounding" does not include mixing, reconstituting, or other such acts that are performed in accordance with directions contained in approved labeling provided by the product's manufacturer or other manufacturer directions consistent with that labeling. From this it is assumed, for example, that reconstituting with different volumes of water than are written on the label constitutes compounding. To clarify, it would not be compounding if an approved manufacturer's label states to add 88 mL of purified water to an antibiotic for suspension, and the pharmacist does just that. It could be considered compounding, however, if the pharmacist was directed by the physician to add 38 mL of purified water for an increased concentration per dose of the drug.

37.12 Implementation of FDAMA

This Act did remove any doubt that compounding was legal under the FDC Act and Congress has clearly recognized the importance of compounding. It also established limits on compounding and a mechanism for handling recommended changes in its implementation. The U.S. Supreme Court also clearly recognized the important role of pharmacy compounding in individualizing patient care, as detailed in their decision.

A. Organization

In the implementation of FDAMA, the FDA was required to convene and consult with an advisory committee on compounding and to develop the MOU, in consultation with the National Association of Boards of Pharmacy (NABP). The FDA Compounding Advisory Committee included representatives from NABP, USP, pharmacy, physician, and consumer organizations, as well as other experts selected by the FDA. The role of the committee was to make recommendations to the FDA—specifically in the areas of bulk-drug substances and difficult-to-compound products. The list of drugs that was not to be compounded (due to safety and efficacy), shown in Appendix 37.3, was generally straightforward. In addition, the FDA developed an internal Pharmacy Compounding Steering Committee to help organize and assist in the implementation of the compounding section of FDAMA.

B. Lists to Develop

As a result of the Federal Food and Drug Administration Modernization Act of 1997 (FDAMA) Section 503(a), the Food and Drug Administration (FDA) was charged with the development of numerous lists relating to compounding, including (1) a list of bulk-drug substances for compounding that are not already approved for compounding, (2) a list of products not to be compounded because of withdrawal from the market due to safety or efficacy concerns, and (3) a list of difficult-to-compound products.

The list of bulk-drug substances was to be constantly updated as new substances were submitted to the FDA for consideration for inclusion on this list. The general criteria used for inclusion on the approved list relates to historical use, reports in peer-reviewed medical literature, or other criteria identified by the FDA. This list is now defunct.

The list of products not to be compounded because of withdrawal from the market due to safety or efficacy concerns appeared in the October 8, 1998, Federal Register (63[195]:54083-54087). Unless otherwise noted, all drug products containing a specific ingredient have been removed. Compounding may still be permitted for other dosage forms of the product or for other indications. This list includes the items shown in Appendix 37.3.

The third list to be developed included the difficult-to-compound products but was never formalized. However, Section 37.8, above, addresses this topic.

37.13 FDA Compliance Policy Guide (CPG)

In May 2002, the FDA released "Guidance for FDA Staff and Industry, Compliance Policy Guides Manual, Sec. 460.200 Pharmacy Compounding." This document was issued to describe some of the FDA's current thinking on the issue and to request comments. It should be noted that a CPG is not enforceable and does not bind either the FDA or the public. This CPG is somewhat related to the CPG 460.200 that was issued on March 16, 1992, which remained in effect until 1997, when Congress enacted FDAMA97.

The CPG states that the FDA recognizes that pharmacists traditionally have extemporaneously compounded and manipulated reasonable quantities of human drugs upon receipt of a valid prescription for an individually identified patient from a licensed practitioner and that this traditional activity is not the subject of this CPG.

However, the FDA believes that there are a number of establishments with retail pharmacy licenses that are actually engaged in manufacturing and distributing unapproved new drugs for human use that are in violation of traditional pharmacy practice. It is their activities that comprise the focus of the CPG. In other words, the FDA believes that some pharmacists are attempting to find shelter under compounding laws (laws that are licensed and regulated by states) when, technically, they are manufacturing (licensed and regulated by the FDA, and being required to meet New Drug requirements).

The FDA has listed nine different acts they consider to be related to manufacturing and which may result in an action against the pharmacy. These acts include:

1. Compounding of drugs in anticipation of receiving prescriptions (except in very limited quantities of drugs compounded after receiving valid prescriptions)
2. Compounding drugs that have been withdrawn or removed from the market for safety reasons
3. Compounding finished drugs from bulk active ingredients that are not components of FDA-approved drugs, without an FDA sanctioned Investigational New-Drug application (IND), in accordance with 21 U.S.C. § 355(i) and 21 C.F.R. 312
4. Receiving, storing, or using drug substances without first obtaining written assurance from the supplier that each lot of the drug substance has been made in an FDA-registered facility
5. Receiving, storing, or using drug components not guaranteed or otherwise determined to meet official compendial requirements

6. Using commercial-scale manufacturing or testing equipment for compounding drug products
7. Compounding drugs for third parties reselling to individual patients or offering compounded drug products at wholesale prices to other state-licensed persons or commercial entities for resale
8. Compounding drug products that are commercially available in the marketplace or that are, essentially, copies of commercially available, FDA-approved drug products (In certain circumstances, it may be appropriate for a pharmacist to compound a small quantity of a drug that is only slightly different than an FDA-approved drug that is commercially available. In these circumstances, the FDA will consider whether there is documentation of the medical need for the particular variation of the compound for the particular patient.)
9. Failing to operate in conformance with applicable state law regulating the practice of pharmacy

The CPG goes on to state that this list of factors is not intended to be exhaustive, and that others may be appropriate for consideration in a particular case.

37.14 U.S. Pharmacopeia

In 1990, the U.S. Pharmacopeial Convention approved the appointment of a Pharmacy Compounding Practices Expert Advisory Panel. The activities of the panel initially were to (1) prepare a chapter on compounding for the USP/NF, and (2) to begin the process of preparing monographs of compounded products for inclusion in the National Formulary.

The prepared chapter, <1161>, "Pharmacy Compounding Practices," was published and became official in 1996. With the mention of this chapter in FDAMA 1997, this chapter was renumbered as chapter <795>; subsequently, its title was also changed to "Pharmaceutical Compounding—Nonsterile Preparations."[3] (It should be noted that USP chapters with numbers greater than <1000> are informational, while numbers less than <1000> are enforceable.)

The first of the compounding monographs became official in November 1998, and these monographs are being published in the U.S. Pharmacopeia section of the USP/NF. For each monograph published, a considerable amount of work is done, including a detailed, validated stability study. Some monographs that were previously published in the USP/NF are being reintroduced into the compendia.

A second chapter related to compounding in the USP/NF is Chapter <1206> "Sterile Drug Products for Home Use"; this chapter is being renumbered as <797> and re-titled as "Pharmaceutical Compounding-Sterile Preparations."[4]

Two additional chapters, Chapter <1075>, "Good Compounding Practices" and Chapter <1160>, "Pharmaceutical Calculations in Prescription Compounding," have also been added. Recently, USP Chapters <795>, Pharmacy Compounding—Nonsterile Preparations and <1075> Good Compounding Practices, were combined and expended into a new USP General Chapter <795>, Pharmacy Compounding-Nonsterile Preparations. USP Chapter <797>, Pharmacy Compounding—Sterile Preparations, has also been updated.

A. Chapter <795>: "Pharmaceutical Compounding—Nonsterile Preparations"

This is divided into discussions on the (1) Introduction, (2) Definitions, (3) Categories of Compounding, (4) Responsibilities of the Compounder, (5) Compounding Process, (6) Compounding Facilities, (7) Compounding Equipment, (8) Component Selection, Handling and Storage, (9) Stability Criteria and Beyond-Use Dating, (10) Packaging and Drug Preparation Containers, (11) Compounding Documentation, (12) Quality Control, (13) Patient Counseling, (14) Training, and (15) Compounding for Animal Patients.

The introduction to the chapter discusses the chapter's purpose, which includes information to enhance the compounder's ability to extemporaneously compound preparations that are of acceptable strength, quality and purity. The following section provides a number of definitions, including the definition of compounding and manufacturing. Three categories of compounding are described in the third section, including simple, moderate and complex.

This section details the differences between these three categories.

The fourth section describes the responsibilities of the compounder, which are detailed later in this chapter. The Compounding Process section describes 15 criteria to be followed when compounding each drug separation. The Compounding Facilities section discusses the design and maintenance of the facilities to be used and the equipment selected for compounding. It refers to other specific chapters in the USP and to other documents, including the OSHA Technical Manual-Section VI: Chapter 2, Controlling Occupational Exposure to Hazardous Drugs and the NIOSH Alert: Preventing Occupational Exposure to Antineoplastic and Other Hazardous Drugs in Health Care Settings. Section 7 on compounding equipment states that any equipment used for compounding must be of appropriate design and size for compounding and suitable for the intended use.

The section on Component Selection, Handling and Storage describes, in detail, sources for drugs and excipients that are appropriate for compounding. The discussion on Stability Criteria and Beyond-Use Dating discusses the packaging, sterility, stability criteria, and guidelines for assigning beyond-use dates for compounded preparations; the latter is detailed in Table 37.1. The chapter goes on to explain that these beyond-use date limits can be exceeded if there is supporting valid scientific stability information that is directly applicable to the product being compounded. The product must of the same drug, in a similar concentration, similar pH, similar excipients, similar vehicle, similar water content, and so on.

Table 37.1
Beyond-Use Dates (BUDs) for Extemporaneously Compounded Preparations

In the absence of stability information that is applicable to a specific drug and preparation, the following are maximum BUDs recommended for (1) nonsterile compounded drug preparations that are packaged in tight, light-resistant containers and stored at controlled room temperature, unless otherwise indicated; and for (2) sterile preparations for which a program of sterility testing is in place. Drugs or chemicals known to be labile to decomposition require shorter BUDs.

- **For Nonaqueous Formulations**—The BUD is not later than the time remaining until the earliest expiration date of any Active Pharmaceutical Ingredient or six months, whichever is earlier.

- **For Water-Containing Oral Formulations**—The BUD is not later than 14 days when stored at controlled cold temperatures.

- **For Water-Containing Topical/Dermal and Mucosal Liquid and Semisolid Formulations**—The BUD is not later than 30 days.

The BUD shall not be later than the expiration date on the container of any component.

The section on Packaging and Drug Preparation Containers relates several different USP General Chapters that are to be considered in extemporaneous compounding. As described in Section 11, Compounding Documentation, record-keeping requirements of various states must be followed, and generally include a formulation record and a compounding record. The formulation record is a file of individually compounded preparations, including the name, strength, and dosage form of the preparation compounded, all ingredients and their quantities, equipment needed to prepare the preparation (when appropriate), and mixing instructions. The formulation record must also include an assigned beyond-use date, the container used in dispensing, storage requirements, and any quality-control procedures. The compounding record contains documentation of the name and strength of the compounded preparation, the formulation record reference, and the sources and lot numbers of ingredients used in compounding. Among other items, it should also contain the results of quality-control procedures that were conducted on the lot of compounded product.

The chapter also places an emphasis on quality control and the responsibility of the pharmacist to review each procedure and observe the finished preparation. The chapter continues with the importance of patient counseling in the proper use, storage, and observation (for instability) of the dispensed product. Next, the training section states that all personnel involved in the compounding processes must be properly trained for the type of compounding conducted. Finally, the chapter ends with a short discussion on compounding for animal patients and the standards that should be considered. The overall emphasis of the chapter is to support the pharmacist in the compounding of products of acceptable strength, quality and purity.

B. Chapter <797>: "Pharmaceutical Compounding—Sterile Preparations"

In general, this chapter separates sterile products compounding into different categories, depending upon the risk levels associated with different types of compounding. For example, reconstitution and combining of commercially available sterile products is considered a low-risk-level operation, whereas compounding sterile products (CSPs) from nonsterile ingredients is a high-risk-level operation, based upon a reference to microbiological quality and the potential for contamination. The purpose of the chapter is to prevent harm and death to patients treated with CSPs. The chapter is divided into several sections, including (1) Definitions, (2) Responsibility of Compounding Personnel, (3) CSP Microbial Contamination Risk Levels, (4) Personnel Training and Evaluation in Aseptic Manipulation Skills, (5) Immediate-Use CSPs, (6) Single-Dose and Multiple-Dose Containers, (7) Hazardous Drugs as

CSPs, (8) Radiopharmaceuticals as CSPs, (9) Allergen Extracts as CSPs, (10) Verification of Compounding Accuracy and Sterility, (11) Environmental Quality and Control, (12) Suggested Standard Operating Procedures, (13) Elements of Quality Control, (14) Verification of Automated Compounding Devices for Parenteral Nutrition Compounding, 915) Finished Preparation Release Checks and Tests, (16) Storage and Beyond-Use Dating, (17) Maintaining Sterility, Purity, and Stability of Dispensed and Distributed CSPs, (18) Patient or Caregiver Training, (19) Patient Monitoring and Adverse Events Reporting, (20) Quality-Assurance Program, (21) Abbreviations and Acronyms, and four appendices.

The overall objective of the chapter is to describe conditions and practices to prevent harm, including death, to patients that could possibly result from microbial contamination, excessive bacterial endotoxins, variability in the intended strength and composition, unintended chemical and physical contaminants and ingredients of inappropriate quality in CSPs. All compounding personnel are responsible for understanding fundamental practices and precautions described within this chapter, for developing and implementing appropriate procedures, and for continually evaluating these procedures and the quality of final CSPs to prevent harm.

C. Chapter <1160>: "Pharmaceutical Calculations in Prescription Compounding"

The purpose of this chapter is to provide general information to guide and assist pharmacists in performing necessary calculations when preparing or compounding any pharmaceutical article (or when simply dispensing prescriptions).

Calculations are discussed as they relate to the amount of concentration of drug substances in each unit or dosage portion of a compounded preparation. Special emphasis is placed on calculations involving the purity and dosage portion of drugs, their salt forms, and equivalent potencies.

The chapter is generally divided into an introduction, basic mathematical concepts (significant figures, logarithms), and basic pharmaceutical calculations (calculations in compounding, buffer solutions, dosage calculations, percentage concentrations, specific gravity, dilution and concentration, use of potency units, base versus salt or ester forms of drugs, reconstitution of drugs using volumes other than those on the label, alligation alternate and algebra, molar, molal and normal concentrations, isosmotic solutions, flow rates in intravenous sets, and temperature).

D. Chapter <1163>: "Quality Assurance in Pharmaceutical Compounding"

Quality assurance is paramount in any compounding pharmacy practice. A quality-assurance program for compounding should include at least the following eight separate, but integrated, components, as detailed in this chapter. These components include (1) Training, (2) Standard Operating Procedures, (3) Documentation, (4) Verification, (5) Testing, (6) Cleaning and Disinfecting, (7) Containers, Packaging, Repackaging and Storage, and (8) Outsourcing. This chapter provides guidance for each of these topics as well as suggested compendial testing methods for bulk substances and various dosage forms. Additional information is provided on selected dosage forms. Physical, chemical and microbiological testing is discussed.

E. USP Pharmacists' Pharmacopeia

The USP was originally established to provide standards for pharmacy compounding since, in 1820, all medications were compounded. However, during the mid-1900s, the USP focus broadened to also include manufactured drug products. By the 1960s, most of the work of the USP was for manufactured products. However, with the growth of pharmacy compounding and the emphasis of the current USP-NF on manufactured products and the difficulty of requiring pharmacists to wade through all the standards to pull out those related to compounding, the USP published the first USP Pharmacists' Pharmacopoeia in 2005. It was revised and updated in 2008 and is the current pharmacopeia for pharmacy compounding. It consists of information from the official USP-NF as well as additional reference information for compounding pharmacists.

37.15 Individual Drug Monographs

The first of the compounding monographs became official in November 1998. The compounding committee developed these monographs from widely used formulations. After evaluation and optimization, various pharmacists throughout the U.S. prepare the formulas.

Validated, stability-indicating assays are used, and a stability study is developed for each formulation. In many cases, the regular, official USP/NF procedures are used, as appropriate. The pharmacists prepare the products for the study, ship them immediately to the USP, where they are properly stored, sampled, and analyzed, according to USP monograph procedures. In some cases, alternate methods are involved, due to stability problems, or the like. A beyond-use date is determined. These formulations are to be used when prescriptions are received for these official preparations, unless otherwise substantiated.

37.16 National Association of Boards of Pharmacy

The Good Compounding Practices Applicable to State-Licensed Pharmacies document developed by the National Association of Boards of Pharmacy discusses eight different recommendations. The subparts include: (A) general provisions, (B) organization and personnel, (C) drug compounding facilities, (D) equipment, (E) control of components and drug product containers and closures, (F) drug compounding controls, (G) labeling control of excess products, and (H) records and reports.

The first part, (A), "General Provisions," provides two important definitions, as follows:

1) Compounding—the preparation, mixing, assembling, packaging, or labeling of a drug or device (1) as the result of a practitioner's prescription drug order or initiative based on the practitioner/patient/ pharmacist relationship in the course of professional practice, or (2) for the purpose of, or as an incident to, research, teaching, or chemical analysis and not for sale or dispensing. Compounding also includes the preparation of drugs or devices in anticipation of prescription drug orders based on routine, regularly observed prescribing patterns.

2) Manufacturing—the production, preparation, propagation, conversion, or processing of a drug or device, either directly or indirectly, by extraction from substances of natural origin or independently by means of chemical or biological synthesis, and includes any packaging or repackaging of the substance(s) or labeling or re-labeling of its container, and the promotion and marketing of such drugs or devices. Manufacturing also includes the preparation and promotion of commercially available products from bulk compounds for resale by pharmacies, practitioners, or other persons.

The second subpart, (B), "Organization and Personnel," discusses the responsibilities of pharmacists and other personnel engaged in compounding. It also stresses that only personnel authorized by the responsible pharmacist shall be in the immediate vicinity of the drug-compounding operation. The pharmacist is the ultimate responsible individual for all the activities involved in compounding, including inspection and approval/rejection of all components, drug-product containers, closures, in-process materials, labeling, compounding records, proper maintenance, cleanliness and use of all equipment, training, protective apparel for employees, facilities, equipment, and so on.

Subpart (C), "Drug Compounding Facilities," describes the areas that should be set aside for either nonsterile or sterile compounding. Special attention is required for radiopharmaceuticals and for products requiring special precautions to minimize contamination, such as penicillins and the like. This section of the document covers appropriate space, lighting, ventilation, water supply, plumbing, washing facilities, trash disposal, and storage facilities.

The "Equipment" section, (D), states that equipment used must be of appropriate design, adequate size and suitably located to facilitate operation for its intended use and for its cleaning and maintenance. If automated, mechanical, or electronic equipment is used, controls must be in place to assure proper performance.

Subpart (E), "Components, Containers and Closures," describes the packaging requirements for compounded products. Components, drug-product containers, and closures used in compounding shall be stored off the floor so as to permit cleaning and inspection. The container and closure components shall not be reactive, additive, or absorptive in such a way that they would alter the safety, identity, strength, quality, or purity of the compounded drug. The pharmacist's responsibility also includes the selection of the final container, based upon the physicochemical properties of the compounded preparation and the container and closure.

Subpart (F), "Drug Compounding Controls," discusses the written procedures to ensure that the finished products are of the proper identity, strength, quality, and purity, as labeled. These written procedures should describe the process from beginning to end and provide documentation for quality compounding. This can be done using standard operating procedures (SOPs) that are written, followed, and periodically reviewed and updated. These controls also include validation of equipment and selected processes, such as sterilization.

Subpart (G), "Labeling Control of Excess Products," briefly discusses labeling of excess products and would be applicable to what is described as anticipatory compounding in FDAMA 1997.

Subpart (H), "Records and Reports," describes the various records and reports that are required under these guidelines. These documents must be maintained for the same period of time as the respective state requires for the retention of prescription files.

Many individual states have used this model or implemented their own versions for their specific states and situations. All pharmacists and pharmacy students should become familiar with the individual state requirements where they practice. Many states make provisions for the maintenance of records using electronic media. If this method is used, documentation is required for backup, and procedures are to be followed in case of malfunction.

It will be important as the practice of pharmacy compounding increases to ensure reasonable agreement between the national and state agencies—to balance the need for controls against the need to provide patients with important and necessary individualized medications.

37.17 Pharmacists' Responsibilities

It is evident that pharmacy compounding has grown to the level of attracting attention. Along with that attention has come enhanced regulation and practice guidelines. It is clear when reading the different standards, guidelines and laws that safety and efficacy are prime considerations in pharmacy-compounding practice. Following are a few additional comments related to the responsibilities of the compounding pharmacist.

First off, the pharmacist is responsible for compounding preparations of acceptable strength, quality, and purity—with appropriate packaging and labeling—in accordance with good pharmacy practices, official standards, and current scientific principles. Pharmacists should continually expand their compounding knowledge by participating in seminars, studying literature, and consulting colleagues.

Also, pharmacists should possess the education, training, and proficiency necessary to properly and safely perform their compounding duties at the level they practice. All pharmacists who engage in compounding of drugs should be proficient in the art and science of compounding and should maintain that proficiency through current awareness and training.

Pharmacies engaging in compounding should have a designated area with adequate space for the orderly placement of equipment and materials to be used to compound medications. The compounding area for sterile drug products should be separate and distinct from the area used for the compounding or dispensing of nonsterile drug products.

The pharmacist has the responsibility and authority to inspect and approve or reject all components, drug-product containers, closures, in-process materials, and labeling. He also has the authority to prepare and review all compounding records to assure that no errors have occurred in the compounding process. The pharmacist is also responsible for the proper maintenance, cleanliness, and use of all equipment used in prescription-compounding practice.

The pharmacist is responsible for the equipment in the compounding process. Equipment used in the compounding of drug products should be of appropriate design, of adequate size, and suitably located to facilitate operations for the dosage forms to be prepared.

Pharmacists should receive, store, and use drug substances for compounding that meet official compendial requirements. If this is not possible, then pharmacists should use their professional judgment to procure alternatives, such as analytical reagent (AR) or certified American Chemical Society (ACS) grades. A certificate of analysis should be obtained to ensure its suitability by comparison with general USP/NF standards. It is the pharmacist's responsibility to select the most appropriate quality of chemical for compounding.

The pharmacist must review each step in the compounding procedure to assure accuracy and completeness before dispensing the prescription to the patient. The steps to be reviewed include the preparatory steps, final checks, and sign-off by the compounding pharmacists. A pharmacist may also use professional judgment and discretion to complete analytical testing of the dissolution rates and concentrations of compounded medications, and to perform sterility and pyrogen testing.

Compounded preparations must be packaged in containers meeting USP standards. The container used depends upon the physical and chemical properties of the compounded preparation and the intended use of the product. Labeling must be in accordance with state and federal regulations.

SOPs should be available describing tests or examinations to be conducted on the finished product. These tests could include physical examination, pH determinations, weight, volume, and so on. The procedures are established to monitor the output of the compounding pharmacy and to validate the performance of compounding processes that may cause variability in the resultant drug product.

If large quantities of any one product are legitimately prepared, it is advisable for potency and stability assays to be conducted on the product to provide the compounding pharmacist with the assurance of product potency to the assigned beyond-use date. It is also recommended that pharmacists have a routine quality-control program, where representative samples are tested for potency, stability, and so on, and—in the case of sterile products—for sterility and non-pyrogenicity.

Lastly, compounded prescriptions provide an excellent opportunity for patient counseling and to explain to the patient that this particular prescription has been prepared especially for them. If further steps are required prior to administration, this should be explained in detail to the patient in addition to the other routine items the pharmacist would normally explain.

Endnotes

1. National Association of Boards of Pharmacy. *Model State Pharmacy Act and Model Rules of the National Association of Boards of Pharmacy*. C.1-C.5. Illinois: National Association of Boards of Pharmacy.

2. Anon. Sec. 127 of Public Law 105-115, *Application of Federal Law to Practice of Pharmacy Compounding*, (Sec. 503A), 1997.

3. <795> Pharmaceutical Compounding-Nonsterile Preparations. In *United States Pharmacopeia 33-National Formulary 28*. 2053-2057. Maryland: U.S. Pharmacopeial Convention, Inc.

4. <797> Pharmaceutical Compounding—Sterile Preparations. In *United States Pharmacopeia 33-National Formulary 28*. 2231-2247. Maryland: U.S. Pharmacopeial Convention, Inc.

Appendix 37.1

SUPREME COURT OF THE UNITED STATES
THOMPSON, SECRETARY OF HEALTH AND HUMAN SERVICES et al. v. WESTERN STATES MEDICAL CENTER et al.
CERTIORARI TO THE UNITED STATES COURT OF APPEALS FOR THE NINTH CIRCUIT

No. 01——344. Argued February 26, 2002—Decided April 29, 2002

Drug compounding is a process by which a pharmacist or doctor combines, mixes, or alters ingredients to create a medication tailored to an individual patient's needs. The Food and Drug Administration Modernization Act of 1997 (FDAMA) exempts "compounded drugs" from the Food and Drug Administration's (FDA) standard drug approval requirements under the Federal Food, Drug, and Cosmetic Act (FDCA), so long as the providers of the compounded drugs abide by several restrictions, including that the prescription be "unsolicited," 21 U.S.C. §§ 353a(a), and that the providers "not advertise or promote the compounding of any particular drug, class of drug, or type of drug," §§353a(c). Respondents, a group of licensed pharmacies that specialize in compounding drugs, sought to enjoin enforcement of the advertising and solicitation provisions, arguing that they violate the First Amendment's free-speech guarantee. The District Court agreed and granted respondents summary judgment, holding that the provisions constitute unconstitutional restrictions on commercial speech under *Central Hudson Gas & Elec. Corp. v. Public Serv. Comm'n of N. Y.*, 447 U.S. 557, 566. Affirming in relevant part, the Ninth Circuit held that the restrictions in question fail Central Hudson's test because the Government had not demonstrated that the restrictions would directly advance its interests or that alternatives less restrictive of speech were unavailable.

Held: The FDAMA's prohibitions on soliciting prescriptions for, and advertising, compounded drugs amount to unconstitutional restrictions on commercial speech. Pp. 8–19.

(a) For a commercial speech regulation to be constitutionally permissible under the Central Hudson test, the speech in question must concern lawful activity and not be misleading, the asserted governmental interest to be served by the regulation must be substantial, and the regulation must "directly advanc[e]" the governmental interest and "not [be] more extensive than is necessary to serve that interest," 447 U.S., at 566. Pp. 8-9.

(b) The Government asserts that three substantial interests underlie the FDAMA: (1) preserving the effectiveness and integrity of the FDCA's new-drug approval process and the protection of the public health it provides; (2) preserving the availability of compounded drugs for patients who, for particularized medical reasons, cannot use commercially available products approved by the FDA; and (3) achieving the proper balance between those two competing interests. Preserving the new-drug approval process is clearly an important governmental interest, as is permitting the continuation of the practice of compounding so that patients with particular needs may obtain medications suited to those needs. Because pharmacists do not make enough money from small-scale compounding to make safety and efficacy testing of their compounded drugs economically feasible, however, it would not make sense to require compounded drugs created to meet the unique needs of individual patients to undergo the entire new drug approval process. The Government therefore needs to be able to draw a line between small-scale compounding and large-scale drug manufacturing. The Government argues that the FDAMA's speech-related provisions provide just such a line: As long as pharmacists do not advertise particular compounded drugs, they may sell compounded drugs without first undergoing safety and efficacy testing and obtaining FDA approval. However, even assuming that the FDAMA's prohibition on advertising compounded drugs "directly advance[s]" the Government's asserted interests, the Government has failed to demonstrate that the speech restrictions are "not more extensive than is necessary to serve [those] interest[s]." Central Hudson, supra, at 566. If the Government can achieve its interests in a manner that does not restrict commercial speech, or that restricts less speech, the Government must do so. E.g., Rubin v. Coors Brewing Co., 514 U.S. 476, 490-491. Several non-speech-related means of drawing a line

between compounding and large-scale manufacturing might be possible here. For example, the Government could ban the use of commercial scale manufacturing or testing equipment in compounding drug products, prohibit pharmacists from compounding more drugs in anticipation of receiving prescriptions than in response to prescriptions already received, or prohibit them from offering compounded drugs at wholesale to other state licensed persons or commercial entities for resale. The Government has not offered any reason why such possibilities, alone or in combination, would be insufficient to prevent compounding from occurring on such a scale as to undermine the new drug approval process. Pp. 10-15.

(c) Even if the Government had argued (as does the dissent) that the FDAMA's speech-related restrictions were motivated by a fear that advertising compounded drugs would put people who do not need such drugs at risk by causing them to convince their doctors to prescribe the drugs anyway, that fear would fail to justify the restrictions. This concern rests on the questionable assumption that doctors would prescribe unnecessary medications and amounts to a fear that people would make bad decisions if given truthful information, a notion that the Court rejected as a justification for an advertising ban in, e.g., Virginia Bd. of Pharmacy v. Virginia Citizens Consumer Council, Inc., 425 U.S. 748, 770. Pp. 15-18.

(d) If the Government's failure to justify its decision to regulate speech were not enough to convince the Court that the FDAMA's advertising provisions were unconstitutional, the amount of beneficial speech prohibited by the FDAMA would be. Forbidding the advertisement of compounded drugs would prevent pharmacists with no interest in mass-producing medications, but who serve clienteles with special medical needs, from telling the doctors treating those clients about the alternative drugs available through compounding. For example, a pharmacist serving a children's hospital where many patients are unable to swallow pills would be prevented from telling the children's doctors about a new development in compounding that allowed a drug that was previously available only in pill form to be administered another way. The fact that the FDAMA would prohibit such seemingly useful speech even though doing so does not appear to directly further any asserted governmental objective confirms that the prohibition is unconstitutional. Pp. 18-19.238 F.3d 1090, affirmed.

O'Connor, J., delivered the opinion of the Court, in which Scalia, Kennedy, Souter, and Thomas, J., joined. Thomas, J., filed a concurring opinion. Breyer, J., filed a dissenting opinion, in which Rehnquist, C. J., and Stevens and Ginsburg, J.J., joined

Appendix 37.2
Guidance for FDA Staff and Industry Compliance Policy Guides Manual

Sec. 460.200, Pharmacy Compounding

Submit written comments regarding this guidance document to the Dockets Management Branch (HFA-305), 5630 Fishers Lane, rm.1061, Rockville, MD 20852.

Additional copies of this document may be obtained by sending a request to the Division of Compliance Policy (HFC-230), Food and Drug Administration, 5600 Fishers Lane, Rockville, MD 20857, or from the Internet at: www.fda.gov/ICECI/ComplianceManuals/CompliancePolicyGuidanceManual/ucm116791.htm.

U.S. Department of Health and Human Services
Food and Drug Administration
Office of Regulatory Affairs
Center for Drug Evaluation and Research
May 2002

Compliance Policy Guide
Compliance Policy Guidance for FDA Staff and Industry[a]
CHAPTER 4
SUB CHAPTER 460

Sec. 460.200 Pharmacy Compounding

This guidance represents the Food and Drug Administration's (FDA's) current thinking on this topic. It does not create or confer any rights for or on any person and does not operate to bind FDA or the public. An alternative approach may be used if such approach satisfies the requirements of the applicable statutes and regulations.

INTRODUCTION

This document provides guidance to drug compounders and the staff of the Food and Drug Administration (FDA) on how the Agency intends to address pharmacy compounding of human drugs in the immediate future as a result of the decision of the Supreme Court in *Thompson v. Western States Medical Center*, No. 01-344, April 29, 2002. FDA is considering the implications of that decision and determining how it intends to regulate pharmacy compounding in the long term. However, FDA recognizes the need for immediate guidance on what types of compounding might be subject to enforcement action under current law. This guidance describes FDA's current thinking on this issue.

BACKGROUND

On March 16, 1992, FDA issued a compliance policy guide (CPG), section 7132.16 (later renumbered as 460.200) to delineate FDA's enforcement policy on pharmacy compounding. That CPG remained in effect until 1997 when Congress enacted the Food and Drug Administration Modernization Act of 1997.

On November 21, 1997, the President signed the Food and Drug Administration Modernization Act of 1997 (Pub. L. 105-115) (the Modernization Act). Section 127 of the Modernization Act added section 503A to the Federal Food, Drug, and Cosmetic Act (the Act), to clarify the status of pharmacy compounding under Federal law. Under section 503A, drug products that were compounded by a pharmacist or physician on a customized basis for an individual patient were entitled to exemptions from three key provisions of the Act: (1) the adulteration provision of section 501 (a)(2)(B) (concerning the good manufacturing practice requirements); (2) the misbranding provision of section 502(f)(1) (concerning the labeling of drugs with adequate directions for use); and (3) the new drug provision of section 505 (concerning the approval of drugs under new drug or abbreviated new drug applications). To qualify for these statutory exemptions, a compounded drug product was required to satisfy several requirements, some of which were to be the subject of FDA rulemaking or other actions.

Section 503A of the Act took effect on November 21, 1998, one year after the date of the enactment of the Modernization Act. In November, 1998, the solicitation and advertising provisions of section 503A were challenged by seven compounding pharmacies as an impermissible regulation of commercial speech. The U.S. District Court for the District of Nevada ruled in the plaintiffs' favor. FDA appealed to the U.S. Court of Appeals for the Ninth Circuit. On February 6, 2001, the Court of Appeals declared section 503A invalid in its entirety (*Western States Medical Center v. Shalala*, 238 F.3rd 1090 (9th Cir. 2001)). The government petitioned for a writ of certiorari to the U.S. Supreme Court for review of the circuit court opinion. The Supreme Court granted the writ and issued its decision in the case on April 29, 2002.

The Supreme Court affirmed the 9th Circuit Court of Appeals decision that found section 503A of the Act invalid in its entirety because it contained unconstitutional restrictions on commercial speech (i.e., prohibitions on soliciting prescriptions for and advertising specific compounded drugs). The Court did not rule on, and therefore left in place, the 9th Circuit's holding that the unconstitutional restrictions on commercial speech could not be severed from the rest of section 503A. Accordingly, all of section 503A is now invalid.

FDA has therefore determined that it needs to issue guidance to the compounding industry on what factors the Agency will consider in exercising its enforcement discretion regarding pharmacy compounding.

DISCUSSION

FDA recognizes that pharmacists traditionally have extemporaneously compounded and manipulated reasonable quantities of human drugs upon receipt of a valid prescription for an individually identified patient from a licensed practitioner. This traditional activity is not the subject of this guidance.[b]

FDA believes that an increasing number of establishments with retail pharmacy licenses are engaged in manufacturing and distributing unapproved new drugs for human use in a manner that is clearly outside the bounds of traditional pharmacy practice and that violates the Act. Such establishments and their activities are the focus of this guidance. Some "pharmacies" that have sought to find shelter under and expand the scope of the exemptions applicable to traditional retail pharmacies have claimed that their manufacturing and distribution practices are only the regular course of the practice of pharmacy. Yet, the practices of many of these entities seem far more consistent with those of drug manufacturers and wholesalers than with those of retail pharmacies. For example, some firms receive and use large quantities of bulk drug substances to manufacture large quantities of unapproved drug products in advance of receiving a valid prescription for them. Moreover, some firms sell to physicians and patients with whom they have only a remote professional relationship. Pharmacies engaged in activities analogous to manufacturing and distributing drugs for human use may be held to the same provisions of the Act as manufacturers.

POLICY

Generally, FDA will continue to defer to state authorities regarding less significant violations of the Act related to pharmacy compounding of human drugs. FDA anticipates that, in such cases, cooperative efforts between the states and the Agency will result in coordinated investigations, referrals, and follow-up actions by the states.

However, when the scope and nature of a pharmacy's activities raise the kinds of concerns normally associated with a drug manufacturer and result in sig-

nificant violations of the new drug, adulteration, or misbranding provisions of the Act, FDA has determined that it should seriously consider enforcement action. In determining whether to initiate such an action, the Agency will consider whether the pharmacy engages in any of the following acts:

1. Compounding of drugs in anticipation of receiving prescriptions, except in very limited quantities in relation to the amounts of drugs compounded after receiving valid prescriptions.

2. Compounding drugs that were withdrawn or removed from the market for safety reasons. Appendix 37.3 provides a list of such drugs that will be updated in the future, as appropriate.

3. Compounding finished drugs from bulk active ingredients that are not components of FDA approved drugs without an FDA sanctioned Investigational New Drug application (IND) in accordance with 21 U.S.C. § 355(i) and 21 C.F.R 312.

4. Receiving, storing, or using drug substances without first obtaining written assurance from the supplier that each lot of the drug substance has been made in an FDA registered facility.

5. Receiving, storing, or using drug components not guaranteed or otherwise determined to meet official compendia requirements.

6. Using commercial-scale manufacturing or testing equipment for compounding drug products.

7. Compounding drugs for third parties who resell to individual patients or offering compounded drug products at wholesale to other state licensed persons or commercial entities for resale.

8. Compounding drug products that are commercially available in the marketplace or that are essentially copies of commercially available FDA-approved drug products. In certain circumstances, it may be appropriate for a pharmacist to compound a small quantity of a drug that is only slightly different than an FDA-approved drug that is commercially available. In these circumstances, FDA will consider whether there is documentation of the medical need for the particular variation of the compound for the particular patient.

9. Failing to operate in conformance with applicable state law regulating the practice of pharmacy.

The foregoing list of factors is not intended to be exhaustive. Other factors may be appropriate for consideration in a particular case.

Other FDA guidance interprets or clarifies Agency positions concerning nuclear pharmacy, hospital pharmacy, shared service operations, mail order pharmacy, and the manipulation of approved drug products.

REGULATORY ACTION GUIDANCE

District offices are encouraged to consult with state regulatory authorities to assure coherent application of this guidance to establishments that are operating outside of the traditional practice of pharmacy.

FDA-initiated regulatory action may include issuing a warning letter, seizure, injunction, and/or prosecution. Charges may include, but need not be limited to, violations of 21 U.S.C. §§ 351 (a)(2)(B), 352(a), 352(f)(1), 352(o), and 355(a) of the Act.

Issued: 3/16/1992 Reissued: 5/29/2002

Endnotes to Appendix 37.2

a. This guidance has been prepared by the Office of Regulatory Policy and the Office of Compliance in the Center for Drug Evaluation and Research (CDER) at the Food and Drug Administration.

b. With respect to such activities, 21 U.S.C. 360(g)(1) exempts retail pharmacies from the registration requirements of the Act. The exemption applies to "Pharmacies" that operate in accordance with state law and dispense drugs "upon prescriptions of practitioners licensed to administer such drugs to patients under the care of such practitioners in the course of their professional practice, and which do not manufacture, prepare, propagate, compound, or process drugs or devices for sale other than in the regular course of their business of dispensing or selling drugs or devices at retail" (emphasis added). See also 21 U.S.C. §§ 374(a)(2) (exempting pharmacies that meet the foregoing criteria from certain inspection provisions) and 353(b)(2) (exempting drugs dispensed by filling a valid prescription from certain misbranding provisions).

Appendix 37.3
List of Drugs that were Withdrawn or Removed from the Market for Safety Reasons

*   Adenosine phosphate: All drug products containing adenosine phosphate.
*   Adrenal cortex: All drug products containing adrenal cortex.
*   Aminopyrine: All drug products containing aminopyrine.
*   Astemizole: All drug products containing astemizole.
*   Azaribine: All drug products containing azaribine.
*   Benoxaprofen: All drug products containing benoxaprofen.
*   Bithionol: All drug products containing bithionol.
*   Bromfenac sodium: All drug products containing bromfenac sodium.
*   Butamben: All parenteral drug products containing butamben.
*   Camphorated oil: All drug products containing camphorated oil.
*   Carbetapentane citrate: All oral gel drug products containing carbetapentane citrate.
*   Casein, iodinated: All drug products containing iodinated casein.
*   Chlorhexidine gluconate: All tinctures of chlorhexidine gluconate formulated for use as a patient preoperative skin preparation.
*   Chlormadinone acetate. All drug products containing chlormadinone acetate.
*   Chloroform: All drug products containing chloroform.
*   Cisapride: All drug products containing cisapride.
*   Cobalt: All drug products containing cobalt salts (except radioactive forms cobalt and its salts and cobalamin and its derivatives).
*   Dexfenfluramine hydrochloride: All drug products containing dexfenfluramine hydrochloride.
*   Diamthazole dihydrochloride: All drug products containing diamthazole dihydrochloride.
*   Dibromsalan: All drug products containing dibromsalan.
*   Diethylstilbestrol: All oral and parenteral drug products containing 25 milligrams or more of diethylstilbestrol per unit dose.
*   Dihydrostreptomycin sulfate: All drug products containing dihydrostreptomycin sulfate.
*   Dipyrone: All drug products containing dipyrone.

- Encainide hydrochloride: All drug products containing encainide hydrochloride.
- Fenfluramine hydrochloride: All drug products containing fenfluramine hydrochloride.
- Flosequinan: All drug products containing flosequinan.
- Gelatin: All intravenous drug products containing gelatin.
- Glycerol, iodinated: All drug products containing iodinated glycerol.
- Gonadotropin, chorionic: All drug products containing chorionic gonadotropins of animal origin.
- Grepafloxacin: All drug products containing grepafloxacin.
- Mepazine: All drug products containing mepazine hydrochloride or mepazine acetate.
- Metabromsalan: All drug products containing metabromsalan.
- Methamphetamine hydrochloride: All parenteral drug products containing methamphetamine hydrochloride.
- Methapyrilene: All drug products containing methapyrilene.
- Methopholine: All drug products containing methopholine.
- Mibefradil dihydrochloride: All drug products containing mibefradil dihydrochloride.
- Nitrofurazone: All drug products containing nitrofurazone (except topical drug products formulated for dermatologic application).
- Nomifensine maleate: All drug products containing nomifensine maleate.
- Oxyphenisatin: All drug products containing oxyphenisatin.
- Oxyphenisatin acetate: All drug products containing oxyphenisatin acetate.
- Phenacetin: All drug products containing phenacetin.
- Phenformin hydrochloride: All drug products containing phenformin hydrochloride.
- Pipamazine: All drug products containing pipamazine.
- Potassium arsenite: All drug products containing potassium arsenite.
- Potassium chloride: All solid oral dosage form drug products containing potassium chloride that supply 100 milligrams or more of potassium per dosage unit (except for controlled-release dosage forms and those products formulated for preparation of solution prior to ingestion).
- Povidone: All intravenous drug products containing povidone.
- Reserpine: All oral dosage form drug products containing more than 1 milligram of reserpine.
- Sparteine sulfate: All drug products containing sparteine sulfate.
- Sulfadimethoxine: All drug products containing sulfadimethoxine.
- Sulfathiazole: All drug products containing sulfathiazole (except those formulated for vaginal use).
- Suprofen: All drug products containing suprofen (except ophthalmic solutions).
- Sweet spirits of nitre: All drug products containing sweet spirits of nitre.
- Temafloxacin hydrochloride: All drug products containing temafloxacin.
- Terfenadine: All drug products containing terfenadine.
- 3,3′,4′,5-tetrachlorosalicylanilide: All drug products containing 3,3′,4′,5-tetrachlorosalicylanilide.
- Tetracycline: All liquid oral drug products formulated for pediatric use containing tetracycline in a concentration greater than 25 milligrams/milliliter.
- Ticrynafen: All drug products containing ticrynafen.
- Tribromsalan: All drug products containing tribromsalan.
- Trichloroethane: All aerosol drug products intended for inhalation containing trichloroethane.
- Troglitazone: All drug products containing troglitazone.
- Urethane: All drug products containing urethane.
- Vinyl chloride: All aerosol drug products containing vinyl chloride.
- Zirconium: All aerosol drug products containing zirconium.
- Zomepirac sodium: All drug products containing zomepirac sodium.

Chapter 38

After-Hours Pharmacy Services, Medication Use and Safety in U.S. Hospitals

Christopher A. Keeys, B.S., Pharm.D., BCPS, RPh

38.1 Introduction

Diverse and intersecting perspectives exist among healthcare providers, hospital administrators, risk managers, regulators, lawmakers, and leadership organizations on the subject of after-hours medication use, patient safety and pharmacy services in U.S. hospitals. The view of the hospitalized patient (and family), however, is convincingly consistent and clear: their medication needs are to be met day or night, weekdays, weekends, and holidays—as long as the hospital is open. Many patients are willing to make allowances for special circumstances after-hours (e.g., delaying the start of their intravenous chemotherapy until morning when the oncology nurse and pharmacist are on duty). However, patients do not expect variations in the level or quality of services after-hours to reach the point where their chances of injury due to medication errors, adverse drug events, or poor treatment outcomes are increased.

Practicing pharmacists, pharmacy educators, and national pharmacy organizations have performed principal roles for many years in evaluating, designing, implementing, staffing, and monitoring the medication-use systems employed in the U.S. to fulfill the patient's medication-related needs. The sustained rise in the use of emergency rooms and hospital admissions during the evenings and night in many acute-care community, tertiary, psychiatric, rehabilitation, critical-access, and long-term acute care hospitals in regions of the country reveals the growing importance after-hours healthcare plays in medication utilization and patient safety.[1]

38.2 24/7 Healthcare: The After-Hours Pharmacy Gap

Although it is widely acknowledged that the presence of pharmacists is imperative for patient safety in hospitals, national surveys continue to reveal that a majority of hospital pharmacies operate less than 24 hours a day, seven days a week. In 1994, hospital in-patient pharmacies were estimated to operate an average of 15.6 hours a day, Monday through Friday. Only about one-third of hospital pharmacies operated around the clock.[2] Surveys conducted again in 1996, 1999, and 2003 revealed similar findings.[3-5] More than 3,000 hospitals nationwide—including acute care, rehabilitation, and psychiatric facilities—close their pharmacy departments in the evenings, at night, and/or occasionally on weekends and holidays. Thus, in many hospitals, drug distribution and medication review during the night is carried out by night nursing supervisors, nursing and allied health staff, and on-call pharmacists. The traditional on-call pharmacist service allows medical and nursing staff to contact a pharmacist in emergencies to provide pharmaceutical support by telephone or in person. In Massachusetts, 68 of the 72 (94 percent) hospitals participating in a medication-error prevention project provided on-call pharmacist services during hours when the pharmacy department was closed.[6] The absence of a pharmacist in a hospital after-hours may increase the risk of medication errors, but this issue has not been well-studied so far. Intensive efforts are now being directed towards reducing medical errors and improving patient safety within the healthcare system. The Institute of Medicine (IOM), the Institute for Safe Medication Practices (ISMP), the American Society of Health-System Pharmacists (ASHP), The Joint Commission (TJC), the United

States Pharmacopeia (USP) and many other groups and individuals have spoken forcefully on the need for greater patient safety.[7] More than 50 percent of medication errors are due to prescribing errors, followed by administration errors, transcription errors, and dispensing errors.[8-9] Strategies for systematically reducing medication errors have been described, and prospectively reviewing orders by pharmacists and preventing non-pharmacy personnel from accessing pharmacies after hours are recognized as two important measures.[10-11,17]

38.3 Scope of Pharmacy Services in U.S. Hospitals

Pharmacy services have been developed, enhanced and redesigned continuously in order to address the often complex medication-related needs of patients, family members and caregivers, and to support pharmacy, medical, and other hospital staff. Change and advances in drug therapy, medical and surgical devices, diagnostics, laboratory science, information technology, automation, public health, emergency preparedness, healthcare financing, and other conditions have elevated the requirements for pharmacy services in hospitals. The academic training, experience, and requirements of pharmacy practitioners—including pharmacists and pharmacy technicians—have evolved markedly to maintain and promote competency in the provision of distributive,

clinical, and other pharmacy services. The extent and rate at which pharmacy services are keeping up with recommended or required practices in hospitals is measured periodically by investigators working with the ASHP, ISMP, and other groups.

Key areas of pharmacy services assessed in U.S. hospitals based on daytime hours—and, to a limited extent, nighttime/weekend (after-hours)—are described in detail elsewhere.[2-5] However, some notable trends that reveal both progress and persistent limitations with the gaps between daytime and after-hours medication use and pharmacy services in hospitals are highlighted in Table 38.1. Informed observations were applied in determining the gaps between the daytime and nighttime services and practices in hospitals over the past decade.

The acute-care community hospital is the setting for the majority of in-patient hospital care provided in the U.S. and is the basis for much of the available data on pharmacy services in hospitals. However, important trends in after-hours pharmacy services should also be observed in non-acute care hospitals, including adult and pediatric facilities, as well as in rehabilitation and psychiatric hospitals.

All medications (including biologicals and contrast agents) used for therapeutic, prophylactic, or diagnostic purposes can be associated with serious errors and adverse events in patients. Several of these medications and medica-

Table 38.1
Select Trends in Medication Use/Pharmacy Services: Daytime and After-Hours Gaps

Observations	Daytime Practice	After-hours Practice
I. Progress		
A. Large quantities of high-risk medications are controlled by pharmacy staff (example: concentrated electrolytes and high doses of concentrated heparin)	Usually yes	Increasing yes
B. Prospective review of new medication orders by pharmacist prior to dispensing/administering	Usually yes	Increasing yes
C. Unit dose vs. bulk supplies of medication available on units	Usually yes	Increasing yes
D. Computer-supported patient profile for screening of allergies and drug interactions by pharmacist	Usually yes	Increasing yes
II. Persistent Limitations		
A. Pharmacist on site at hospital	Yes	Usually no except larger or tertiary care hospitals
B. Nurses and nurse supervisors required to review new med orders in lieu of a pharmacist	No, except limited settings	Usually yes
C. Hospital introduces electronic medical records with medication-safety systems supported by pharmacist	Yes	Often no

tion classes routinely utilized in hospitals have been associated with sufficient medication errors and adverse events as to have been classified by organizations as high-risk drugs. These high-risk medications principally possess a narrow therapeutic index, are inherently toxic, and require extraordinary knowledge and precautions to minimize errors and harm to the patient. Our most effective safety system and practices are employed to properly manage these agents and mitigate patient injury, as well as to prevent drug misuse and diversion. Examples of high-risk drugs include morphine and other opioids, concentrated injectable electrolytes (e.g., potassium chloride), neuromuscular blocking agents, antineoplastic drugs, as well as anticoagulants including heparin and warfarin. Most high-risk drugs are mainstays of therapy and must be utilized 24/7 in hospitals.

Polypharmacy is a consequence of many factors in modern therapeutics. It is seen in common chronic and acute conditions afflicting hospitalized patients, such as congestive heart failure, diabetes, hypertension, seizures, mood disorders, HIV/AIDS, asthma, pain, renal disease, autoimmune disorders, and transplantations. Polypharmacy—defined in part as patients taking five or more medications per day—occurs frequently in hospitalized adult patients and is seen more often in populations 65 years and older.[12] For these patients, proper care requires the support of pharmacists who are trained and equipped to appropriately dispense and perform a complete review of each non-emergency medication order for drug allergies, contraindications, dosing and administration issues, serious drug-drug interactions, pregnancy and lactation precautions, and compliance with institutional protocols and restrictions.

The outpatient medications that hospitalized patients list on admission histories must be reviewed against admission, transfer, and discharge medication orders. This review—performed by the prescriber and heavily supported by the nurse and pharmacist—is known as medication reconciliation. Designated a National Patient Safety Goal by TJC in 2006, it is an essential part of efforts in hospitals and other healthcare systems to avoid medication errors and subsequent adverse events.[13] A vast number of medications, numbering in the thousands, exists in practice. Lack of information, knowledge and/or adequate time by physicians and hospital staff can frequently cause errors of omission and commission associated with the medication admission list of patients. The average hospital pharmacy may stock 1,500 medications, some of which are various dosage forms and strengths of the same product. The number of FDA-approved medications continues to expand, with a larger percentage of these products designed for routine use by patients and clinicians outside the hospital, thereby limit-

ing the hospital formulary's ability to easily address each patient's medication needs on admission. Alternative appropriate therapies must often be established based on existing formulary policies, including direct change of order by the physician and/or hospital-approved, pharmacist-managed automatic therapeutic interchanges. Today, non-formulary interventions are the most common pharmacist-directed intervention in many hospitals. After-hours pharmacists continue the activity throughout the night when clinically necessary, especially for the newly admitted patients who present the greatest likelihood of delays or missed doses for non-formulary drug orders.

Special populations of patients are often recognized for their unique drug therapy needs and/or risk of harm from medications. Pregnant, pediatric-neonatal, obese, elderly (especially the frail elderly) patients and those with renal or hepatic disease are increasingly included in patient-safety practices and systems designed to provide additional safeguards and monitoring for medications. New FDA-approved drug-labeling information often addresses proper use and monitoring for many of these special populations. The consequences of caring for special populations in practice are significant and present challenges in the best daytime systems where emphasis is placed on clinical competency of staff, vigilance (e.g., policies and protocols), and, sometimes, restrictions on the use of medications in special populations. The loss of a pharmacist's services after-hours in some hospitals creates the potential for increased patient and institutional liability around two different standards of care with these special populations.

38.4 After-Hours Pharmacy Service Models

The dispensing of new and refill prescriptions in the community setting by law requires the services of a licensed pharmacist operating during hours when the pharmacy is open. Of course, exceptions exist for the issuing of emergency supplies or samples of medications in the doctor's office, a clinic or emergency department by the prescriber. There is no substitute for access to a 24-hour retail pharmacy when it comes to patients obtaining the medications prescribed by their physician, nurse practitioner, dentist, podiatrist, or other authorized prescriber in the community. Consistent with trends in other service sectors, the retail-pharmacy community has recognized the growing need for 24/7 access to care and has responded by markedly expanding the number of pharmacies and personnel available after-hours in the U.S.[14]

In-patient or institutional pharmacy practice providing dispensing and related clinical-pharmacy functions for hospitalized patients have, in fact, operated differently from retail pharmacies in many cases for decades. These in-patient practices are often consistent with state laws that were created to regulate hospital pharmacies. However, many of these practices may not be in the patient's best interest. As described earlier, most hospital pharmacies close at night and institutions are permitted to establish alternative after-hours models for servicing the needs of patients for new and re-ordered medications. Four primary service models for after-hours pharmacy services have been utilized in the U.S. for drug distribution and related medication-use processes (depending on the organization, its pharmacy service, and the state laws and regulations). The models, along with some associated strengths, weaknesses and budget considerations, are described in Table 38.2. There is a growing emphasis on 24/7 access to care, avoidance of medical errors, optimizing nursing support and adoption of information technology, and automation. These and other factors have driven some, but not most, private and governmental hospitals (without on-site 24-hours services) to embrace advanced after-hours pharmacy models or established 24/7 (on-site) pharmacies.

38.5 Nighttime Medication Errors

It is difficult—if not nearly impossible—to provide an adequate description of the nature of medication errors and adverse drug events encountered by patients after hours in U.S. hospitals. Very few specific studies on this topic have appeared in the published, peer-reviewed, biomedical English literature. The landmark report by the IOM "*To Err Is Human*" did not address nighttime medical or medication errors.[7] The Physician Insurance Association of America (PIAA), which has maintained surveillance for many years on the nature and scope of medical injuries resulting in malpractice claims, does not offer specific data on nighttime or after-hours medical errors. However, multiple investigations into the epidemiology of medication errors in hospitals have incorporated these events, regardless of the time of day or night of their occurrence. It may be assumed that these reports provide some perspective on after-hours medication risk.[7-9]

Keeys et al. provided original observational data from a single hospital on nighttime medication use and prescribing errors from an after-hours telepharmacy practice in 2002.[15] Most notable were findings that (1) 1,039 orders were written at night over a three-month period, (2) high-risk targeted medications (see Table 38.3) accounted for 29 percent of all orders reviewed at night by the pharmacist, and (3) clarification of the physician's orders, many due to prescribing errors, was performed by the pharmacist in 21.7 percent of the 1,039 medication orders.

Since the original publication, the practice has received over 1.3 million after-hours prescriptions from over 35 hospitals in 12 different states and in the District of Columbia. Potential prescribing errors and other order clarifications addressed by the after-hours pharmacist are referred to as the pharmacist's intervention rate. Across all these hospitals, pharmacy documentation revealed an annual mean after-hours intervention rate of 3 percent. The facilities possessing the full electronic medical record and computerized physician order entry generated a lower mean intervention rate of about 1.5 percent. A few community hospitals—operating entirely with handwritten physician orders and experiencing frequent after-hours admissions—have run intervention rates of between 8 and 10 percent. These mean rates are likely an underestimation, due to the nature of reporting during peak order processing times.

In 2006, TJC announced that all non-pharmacy personnel were banned from entering pharmacies in accredited hospitals in the U.S. Although the trend towards enforcing this restriction was already evidenced in some practices, the heightened awareness and accountability precipitated by this declaration revealed the inherent seriousness of dispensing errors and availability of viable alternate models for providing medication to patients when the pharmacy was closed. Some state regulations had already moved to ban nurses and other non-pharmacists from entering and removing medications from pharmacies after hours in order to reduce medication errors and control drug access.

A detailed accounting of prescribing, dispensing, and other medication errors observed in the after-hours telepharmacy practice is beyond the scope of this review. Actual medication errors encountered in the practice typically fall into the category of near misses—that is, errors that did not reach the patient. Examples of after-hours medication errors maintained within a pharmacy quality-assurance database and reported elsewhere are provided in Table 38.4.[15] These examples serve to illustrate the variety of patient safety issues encountered at night.

38.6 Pharmacy Technology and After-Hours Services

Hospitals and pharmacy services are increasingly supported in the care of patients via use of information technology and automation. An exciting, complex, and growing array of technology offerings have impacted the provision of after-hours pharmacy services and hold promise in promoting improved patient care. These newer technologies include the electronic medical record, computerized physician order entry, electronic prescribing (ePrescribing), pharmacy computer systems order-imaging technologies,

Table 38.2
Service Models for After-Hours Pharmacy and Medication Use in Hospitals

Features	Models			
	RN Managed without on-call RPh.	**RN Managed with on-call RPh.**	**Telepharmacy with on-call RPh.**	**Pharmacy open 24/7**
Prevalence in U.S.	Historical and declining; estimate less than 500 hospitals	Over 3,500 hospitals (approximately 60 percent of hospitals)	Newer model; number of hospitals not known but estimated about 1,000 hospitals use this model including daytime and/or after-hours services	Approximately 2,000 hospitals (approximately 30 percent)
Staffing Requirements	Lowest after-hours workload; opening pharmacy workload often heavy; inconvenient and more liability for RN	Low RPh. workload; opening pharmacy workload often heavy; inconvenient and more liability for RN	Higher RPh. workload; improved use of RPh. staff via shared service between hospitals or outsourced companies; more convenient and less liability for RN	Highest RPh. workload but may be under-utilizing staff for slower facilities; most difficult to staff with RPh.; most convenient for RN including dispensing support
Technology Requirements	Low-technology use usual; more manual processes and limited support for nurse for review of orders and drug information	Usually limited to phone consults; may have emergency remote access to pharmacy profile/labs/automated dispensing technology and computerized MD order entry	Routine access to computerized pharmacy/hospital records; work through phone, fax and Internet; can interface routinely with automated dispensing machines and CPOE; more drug information and clinical support	Maintains major technology support for pharmaceutical services 24/7; often some or all decentralized (unit) services and major clinical activities are limited based on hospital's choice after-hours
Fulfills "Best Practice" and Accreditation Standards	Not designed and unlikely to meet best practice and standards	Not designed to meet best practices and standards: no routine RPh. order review until pharmacy reopens; inconsistent support for drug information/clinical consults; supports emergencies when requested by RN only	Designed to meet best practices and standards. Routine RPh. order review before medication given; consistency for drug information/clinical consults; supports RN in proper preparation/dispensing procedures	Recognized as the original design to meet best practices and standards. Routine RPh. order review before medication given; consistency for most clinical as well as distributive pharmacy services
Estimated Annual Cost* per 8 hour shift for 7 days/week	Usually lowest cost (e.g., $0)	Usually low cost (e.g., $0-30K/yr)	Moderate cost (e.g., $40-100K/yr)	Highest cost (e.g., $150-200K/yr)

RN = Registered Nurse; RPh. = Registered Pharmacist
*Cost estimates include only RPh. staff hours or outsourced service cost. No cost included for pharmacy technician(s), which are often staffed after-hours in hospitals.

Table 38.3
Classification of High Risk and Targeted Medications

1. Anti-infective (antibiotics and antifungals)
2. Anticoagulants
3. Antiplatelet agents
4. Hematopoietic agents (e.g., epoetin alfa)
5. Hemostatic agents
6. Miscellaneous blood agents
7. Drugs for newly admitted patients
8. Drugs for patients transferred to or from critical care areas
9. Drugs with many potential interactions or contraindications
10. Drugs with a narrow therapeutic index
11. Drugs for which a test dose is required (e.g., iron dextran)
12. Drugs indicated for treating adverse drug events (e.g., naloxone)
13. Drugs identified by TJC as being associated with sentinel events, such as opiate agonists and I.V. potassium and other concentrated electrolyte solutions
14. Restricted-use drugs and agents specified in hospital-approved protocols

drug-drug interaction screening (real-time and back-end alerts), pharmacy-generated and electronic medication-administration records, electronic clinical guidelines and/or decision-support systems, bar-coding for drug preparation/dispensing and administration, smart infusion pumps, automated medication-dispensing cabinets, web cams, high-speed remote connectivity, and robotics. Careful integrating of these technologies with practice is required to optimize patient safety.

Pharmacy practice and the optimal provision of pharmaceutical care to patients is not primarily defined by IT, but rather supported by technologies. Consequently, after-hours services must be delivered in technologically advanced, as well as limited, organizations. Large and small, rural and urban, teaching and non-teaching hospitals have been classified by the American Hospital Association (AHA) for their degree of IT resources as follows: (a) just getting started (32 percent), (b) with low use (22 percent), (c) with moderate use (30 percent), and (d) with high use (16 percent).[16] Drug-distribution systems in hospitals very commonly provide for the nurses' and patients' unit-based medication supplies, at least for urgent and emergency drugs (e.g., analgesics, antipyretics, and critical drugs), via use of automated-dis-

pensing cabinets. The majority of these cabinets are electronically linked to the pharmacy department where, per regulations and laws, the pharmacist oversees the clinical and operational review and authorized use of prescribed medications. After-hours, in the absence of a pharmacist, the registered nurse and/or nursing supervisor may serve to review the orders (often in a manual fashion as nurses are rarely authorized to operate the hospital's computerized pharmacy system). Unit-based manual and/or electronic drug-information resources are available to assist them in this function. However, bypassing review of the patient's medication profile in the computerized environment—except for emergencies or when use of medication is under the direct control of a licensed independent practitioner, for example, a physician—is problematic in fulfilling professional-accreditation and regulatory requirements.[10] A growing number of hospitals have addressed this potential practice variation after-hours by outsourcing or contracting authorized telepharmacy service providers or affiliating themselves with hospitals with 24-hour pharmacy services. Through either method, technology can be employed to remotely link the pharmacist in real time to the order review, computerized order-entry process, and automated dispensing cabinet or alternative sources at the hospitals—thereby maintaining pharmacist control over the after-hours medication review and distribution systems. Two other key aspects of the medication-use process, ordering and administration, can operate differently after pharmacies close in hospitals. Computerized provider order entry (CPOE) is still significantly relied on in only about 10–17.8 percent of non-federal hospitals and has not replaced the role of the pharmacist in reviewing these orders for completeness, appropriateness, and compliance with institutional guidelines, protocols, and restrictions.[16,18] Earlier consideration by TJC to potentially permit the nurse to directly administer medication after a physician electronically prescribed it was abandoned, as experience from organizations, including the U.S. Department of Veterans Affairs, revealed that medication orders, though markedly improved by CPOE, still required pharmacist review to optimize safe systems. Other investigators have found that CPOE, depending on multiple factors, significantly reduced prescribing errors in many, but not all, studies.[19,20] Bar-code medication administration (BCMA) is a technology that combines error-reduction performance of properly designed and implemented bar-coding with the nurse's electronic medication-administration records. In order to support and optimize CPOE and BCMA, the pharmacist's computerized patient profile must be skillfully operated and maintained, along with the records of the physician and nurse. Commonly, hospitals that adopt pharmacy-gen-

Table 38.4
Summary of Selected After-Hours Medication Errors and Pharmacist Interventions

Case Description	Intervention and Rationale	Type of Intervention	High Risk Category	Resolution
An 81-year-old man with manic depressive episodes and chronic obstructive lung disease was prescribed albuterol 2 puffs q4hr– q6hr prn and Proventil 2 puffs bid prn.	The nurse was notified that Proventil is the brand name for albuterol. The nurse then contacted the physician.	Duplicate order	No	The physician verified that the order for Proventil was in error. The order was stopped.
A 24-year-old woman with nausea, vomiting, dehydration, aseptic meningitis, and acute sinusitis was prescribed acetaminophen 650 mg IV q6hr prn.	The nurse was notified, and a physician communication form was sent indicating that acetaminophen is available only for oral or rectal administration.	Route change	No	The physician changed the order to acetaminophen 650 mg po q6hr prn.
An 83-year-old woman with acute back pain was prescribed ketorolac 30 mg IM q6hr prn.	The service recommended that the ketorolac dosage be reduced to 15 mg q6hr on the basis of the patient's age. The patient was noted to have an aspirin allergy. Ketorolac is contraindicated in patients with hypersensitivity to aspirin. The nurse was notified orally and the physician in writing.	Dosage change and allergy	Yes	The ketorolac dosage was reduced to 15 mg q6hr and the aspirin allergy was noted in the patient's profile as to be clarified.
An 81-year-old man with arthritis of the right hip was prescribed enoxaparin 70 mg, SCQ 12hr after hip replacement surgery.	A physician communication form was sent since the order was not written on the preprinted standard post hip-replacement form and more information was needed about the indication. The dosage written is therapeutic, not prophylactic.	Dosage change	Yes	The physician was notified; two doses of enoxaparin were given before stopped. The patient was continued on warfarin 2.5 mg po daily.
A 69-year-old man diagnosed with renal insufficiency and agitation was prescribed meperidine 5-15 mg IV q3hr prn.	The service recommended discontinuing meperidine in a patient on dialysis given the potential for adverse effects from the normeperidine metabolite.	Adverse drug reaction	Yes	Meperidine was discontinued.
Gentamicin 80 mg IV q12hr was ordered for a 3 day old neonate. Patient's weight was 3.2kg.	The nurse was notified to not give the dose but rather 8 mg IV every 12 hours was the appropriate dose. The nurse had already removed from the unit's automated dispensing cabinet and administered the MD prescribed dose (80 mg) ten minutes earlier. The RPh. notified the MD and Poison Control Center for management and monitoring. The gentamicin order was discontinued.	Dose change and drug information for overdose	Yes	The gentamicin levels and renal function were monitored. No acute toxicity was noted. Ototoxicity studies were not done. Procedures for nurse access to adult gentamicin syringe were reviewed/ restricted at hospital.

erated medication-administration records, with or without bar-coding administration, rapidly recognize the need to establish real-time pharmacist's support 24/7, either remotely, via telepharmacy service providers, and/or with expanded on-site pharmacist staffing.

At night, hospitals experience planned and occasionally unscheduled computer down times, during which time the pharmacy, nursing, medical, and other hospital staff may delay care or, when necessary, operate on a manual or modified medication-use process.

Continuation of acceptable drug-distribution and clinical-pharmacy services must be maintained, however, in order to deliver an after-hours model that substantially delivers quality care to patients.

The fundamental prescribing document—the medication order or prescription—remains available in the after-hours service model via at least one of several means. Pharmacists and nurses receive the order manually via couriers, pneumatic tube, fax, and/or a digital image of the order, or electronically. The advent of the digital scanners and order management systems, as well as CPOE, affords the greatest means to enhance the access to and accuracy of the medication orders day or night. Ten years of personal practice in after-hours care has revealed a shift in many urban and rural hospitals from paper only with fax transmittal to either digital scanning and order management or electronic prescribing. The medication order, for many reasons, still remains a leading cause of medication errors in hospitals, with multiple opportunities for mishaps. The error may be due to one or more often-preventable causes, including missing or delayed orders, illegibility, incomplete orders (e.g., missing dose, strength, route, etc.), transcription errors, poor order interpretation, or miscommunication between clinical staff, and clinical knowledge deficits. Twenty-four hour chart check, often performed by nursing personnel, typically occurs at night and, depending on the level of health IT at the hospital, serves to detect and resolve medication errors generated inadvertently by prescribers, nurses, unit secretaries, pharmacists, and other staff throughout the previous shifts. Resolution of identified errors may require actions on the part of the nurse or, as often observed in practice, corrections or clarifications to the pharmacy profile. The strict user access and policies of the patients' electronic or manual medical records dictates that resolution of errors be properly addressed and documented in the applicable sections of the physician's, pharmacist's, nurse's, or other clinician's record. The interdependency of the nursing and medical staffs with pharmacy and health IT resources of the hospital remains a constant throughout the day and is optimized by the vigilant and competent work of each shift of personnel that cares for patients.

38.7 Standards Setting and After-Hours Service

Certainly in large part to assure patient safety, the practice of pharmacy and the requirements for medication use in hospitalized patients is heavily standardized, regulated, and monitored. Variations in standards, regulations, and laws have—in limited areas—been modified at the state and local levels in order to navigate specific needs and challenges of hospitals to care for patients after-hours.

Some major leading regulatory, professional and accreditation groups address practice and medication use requirements after-hours in U.S. hospitals. These include, but are not limited to, the state boards of pharmacy, the departments of health, ASHP, and TJC. Technical and practice standards and specifications for use of telepharmacy and remote pharmacist-order review must comply with the Health Insurance Portability and Accountability Act of 1996 (HIPAA) and the High Tech Act of 2010. Academic requirements set for pharmacy graduates in the Colleges of Pharmacy and pharmacy technician training programs in the U.S. offer no curriculum requirements specific to after-hours servicing of patients in hospitals, aside from those applicable to the pharmacy regulations, laws, and standards. General pharmacy practice residency programs accredited by the ASHP provide many post-doctor of pharmacy graduates with the experience of caring for patients in hospitals at night during their staffing rotations. However, no specific curriculum or set of learning objectives are established at the national level.

The innovations associated with use of after-hours telepharmacy services and remote order-entry services have generated new and similar standards between established service providers. In the spring of 2010, new guidelines on remote medication-order processing were made available by the ASHP, based on work completed by the Council on Pharmacy Management in collaboration with an expert panel.[21] Because remote medication-order review is an increasingly adopted model for assuring 24-hour access by hospitals to the skill and services of a pharmacist, these guidelines should be sought for guidance by both service providers and client hospitals and other healthcare facilities.

There are national organizations dedicated to medication error prevention and safe medication use, most notably ISMP. This organization is certified as a Patient Safety Organization (PSO) by the U.S. Agency for Healthcare Research and Quality. Among its offerings is the Medication Safety Self Assessment tool for hospitals.[17] This tool, endorsed by multiple major pharmacy, medical, quality and health-provider organizations, identifies key safety areas for after-hours medication use, based on best practices. Included in these best practices are drug standardization, storage and distribution recommendations; on-site or remote pharmacist access 24/7 to review medication orders and answer drug information questions; as well as prohibition of non-pharmacy personnel from entering the pharmacy when it is closed.

Pragmatic alternatives to these after-hours best practices have been proposed and permitted by TJC and other organizations. Examples of alternative approaches include double-checking the patient's order and medications by two trained on-site nurses, as well as deferring non-urgent treatment until the pharmacist is available in the daytime. However, evidence to support the effectiveness of these alternatives to prevent medication errors and optimize medication outcomes in the practice setting is needed. The American Organization of Nurse Executives, the nursing leadership group of the American Hospital Association, has not specifically established a position regarding the role of nursing in the care of hospitalized patients after-hours when the pharmacy is closed.

The need to effectively fulfill the medication needs of hospitalized patients at night and during other after-hour periods is increasingly recognized and supported by regulatory standards-setting bodies and professional associations. A greater understanding by health professionals, hospital administrators, academics, legislators, regulators and the general public should serve to strengthen and expand the training, practices, resources, laws, and regulations of after-hours pharmacy services and medication use.

38.8 Medication Use and Interdisciplinary Roles

Medication use in the hospital is a multistep, integrated, time-sensitive process. It engages the patient and many members of the healthcare team in the selection, procurement, storage, prescribing, preparation/dispensing, transcription/administration and monitoring of drugs and biologicals, as well as some nutrients and nutraceuticals. Health professionals employ these medicines in varied clinical settings, such as surgical, critical care, labor and delivery, and so on for prophylactic, therapeutic, and/or diagnostic purposes. Core knowledge, through medical terminology, is shared by the team; however, major roles are established for distinct health professionals. Licensed clinicians are responsible for prescribing, preparing/dispensing, administering and monitoring (including patient education) medication use in patients. The designated roles for key hospital staff are listed in Table 38.5.

The team provides medication use around-the-clock for patients as care is continually being initiated, modified, and monitored. No single or uniform description of changes in the roles of the team is established for the after hours. However, several frequent adjustments occur, especially in non-critical care settings and even, for some hospitals, in their intensive-care units. These after-hours adjustments in roles may include a shift from private attending physicians to hospital-based physicians, on-call physicians or house staff models. There is also reduced staffing and complementary

Table 38.5
Medication-Use Process and Common Roles of Healthcare Team* in Hospitals

Prescribing**	Preparation/Dispensing	Transcription/Administration	Monitoring/Patient Education
• **Physician (MD)** • **Podiatrist (DPM)** • **Dentist (DDS)** • **Nurse Anesthetist (CRNA)** • **Nurse Practitioner (NP)** • **Physician Assistant (PA)** • **Nurse Midwife (NM)** • Clinical Pharmacist (RPh) • Nurse • Radiology Technologist (CRT) • Respiratory Therapist (RT)	• **Pharmacist (RPh)** • **Pharmacy Technician** • Nurse Anesthetist (CRNA) • Nurse (RN) • MD/DP/DDS • Licensed Practicing Nurse (LPN) • Physicians Assistant (PA) • Nurse Practitioner • Technologist • Respiratory Therapist • Technicians • Other	• **Nurse (RN)** • **Unit Secretaries (transcription only)** • MD/DPM/DDS • (RPh) • NP • PA • NM • RT • CRT • Technologists • Pharmacy Technicians	• **MD/ DPM /DDS** • **Nurse (NP/CRNA/NM/RN/LPN)** • **RPh** • **PA** • **RT** • **Clinical Dietician** • **CRT** • **Pathologists** • **Lab Specialists** • **Case Coordinators**

*Bold denotes major or routine role. Unbolded is a supportive or occasional role.
**The prescriptive authority of non-physicians varies by jurisdiction.

specialists in nursing and other clinical personnel, assignment of senior clinical task to a night (nursing) supervisor, closing of some units (e.g., outpatient surgery and critical-care satellite pharmacy) and services (e.g., the pharmacy department, MRI studies, and the infusion center), as well as limiting or eliminating new patients or the types of new patients admitted until the next day. More subtle role changes compared with daytime operations may also occur, including (1) change in the method by which new medication orders are processed due to closure of pharmacy or computer downtimes associated with maintenance requirements, (2) modified drug-distribution systems to provide nurse supervisors access to additional and more complex medication supplies for patient, (3) altered or underuse of standard order sets (to prescribe) and medication protocols (to dose and/or convert patients to formulary equivalent products), and (4) reduced or inconsistent support for education and training. Unlike the daytime, when the healthcare team is most likely to conduct interdisciplinary patient care rounds, the after-hours staff more heavily relies on one-on-one communication between each team member to manage patients' medications. This dialogue, more than in the daytime, involves discussions between covering or on-call physicians and staff who may have less first-hand familiarity with the medication-related issues of the patient. Consequently, the proper handoff between professionals (the practice of providing necessary clinical information regarding patients to the next covering shift/staff member) and maintenance of adequate staffing, resources and systems is needed to deliver continuous quality in medication use and patient care among an array of team members after-hours.

38.9 Research and Education Needs

The paucity of research publications, public epidemiology data, as well as educational materials on after-hours medication use and patient safety in U.S. hospitals is perplexing, given the earlier findings and recommendations on medical errors in hospitals addressed in the IOM 1999 and 2001 reports.[11] After-hours pharmacists, nurses, doctors and other health professionals in hospitals may not have found sufficient resources, time and/or venues for addressing their needs, successes, and shortcomings through research and educational efforts. Academics, quality-improvement groups, accreditation organizations, governmental agencies, policymakers and professional associations, among others, are often better positioned to create the means for the after-hours experience to be better studied and taught. Others, including innovators in practice and technology, as well as patient-advocacy groups and insurers, are also in a position

to report on the risk, liability, economic cost and opportunities for improvement in after-hours medication use for patient care in U.S. hospitals.

Endnotes

1. T.C. Garcia, A.B. Bernstein, and M.A. Bush. *Emergency department visitors and visits: who used the emergency room in 2007?* NCHS Data Brief. 2010 May;(38):1-8.

2. J.P. Santell. *ASHP national survey of hospital-based pharmaceutical services- 1994.* Am. J. Health-Syst. Pharm. 1995; 52:1179-98.

3. C.E. Reede, M. Dickson, C.M. Kozma, et al. *ASHP national survey of pharmacy practice in acute care settings—1996.* Am. J. Health-Syst. Pharm. 1997; 54:653-69.

4. D.J. Ringold, J.P. Santell, P.J. Schneider. *ASHP national survey of pharmacy practice in acute care settings: dispensing and administration—1999.* Am. J. Health-Syst. Pharm. 2000; 57:1759-75.

5. C.A. Pedersen, P. Schneider, D.J. and Scheckelhoff. *ASHP national survey of pharmacy practice in hospital settings: monitoring and education—2003.* Am. J. Health- Syst. Pharm. 2004; 61:457-71.

6. *Executive summary: Massachusetts Hospital Association medication error prevention project in collaboration with the Massachusetts Coalition for the Prevention of Medical Errors.* Burlington, MA: Massachusetts Hospital Association; 2001 Feb:25-6.

7. J. Loeb. *To err is human: an interview with the Institute of Medicine's Linda Kohn.* J. Qual. Improv. 2000; Apr:227-34.

8. D.W. Bates, D. J. Cullen, L. Nan, et al. *Incidence of adverse drug events and potential adverse drug events: implications for prevention.* JAMA 1995; 274:29-34.

9. R. Kaushal, D.W. Bates, C. Landrigan, et al. *Medication errors and adverse drug events in pediatric inpatients.* JAMA 2001;285:2114-20.

10. D.S. Rich. *More on automated dispensing machines.* Hosp. Pharm. 2001; 36:220-3.

11. L.T. Kohn. *The Institute of Medicine report on medical error: overview and implications for pharmacy.* Am. J. Health-Syst. Pharm. 2001;58:63-6.

12. E.R. Hajjar, A.C. Cafiero, and J.T. Hanlon. *Polypharmacy in elderly patients*. Am. J. Geriatric Pharmacother. 2007;5:345-351.

13. American Hospital Association. *Successful practices for improving medication safety*. Retrieved April 9, 2012, from www.aha.org/advocacy-issues/tools-resources/advisory/96-06/991207-quality-adv.shtml.

14. Anon. *All-night services: 24-hour stores. Drugstore News, April 26, 1999*. Accessed June 30, 2010 at www.findarticles.com/p/articles/mi_m3374/is_7_21/ai_54563525.

15. C.A. Keeys, K. Dandurand, J. Harris, et.al. *Providing nighttime pharmaceutical services through telepharmacy*. Am. J. Health-Syst. Pharm. 2002. 59;716-21.

16. Anon. *Continued progress: Hospital use of information technology*. American Hospital Association. 2007. Chicago, IL 60606

17. Institute for Safe Medication Practices. *ISMP Medication Safety Self Assessment for Hospitals*. Accessed April 9, 2012, from www.ismp.org/survey/default.asp.

18. C.A. Pedersen and K.F. Gumpper. *ASHP national survey on informatics: Assessment of the adoption and use of pharmacy informatics in U.S. hospitals—2007*. Am. J. Health-Syst. Pharm. 2008; 65(23):2244-2264.

19. F. Van Rosse, B. Maat, C.M. Rademaker, et al. *The effect of computerized physician order entry on medication prescription errors and clinical outcome in pediatric and intensive care: a systematic review*. Pediatrics. 2009; 123(4):1184-1190.

20. M.H. Reckmann, J.I. Westbrook, Y. Koh, et al. *Does computerized provider order entry reduce prescribing errors for hospital inpatients? A systematic review*. J. Am. Med. Inform. Association. 2009; 16(5):613-213.

21. ASHP Report. *ASHP Guidelines on remote medication order processing*. Am. J. Health-Syst. Pharm. 2010; 67(8): 672-677.

Chapter 39

The Emergency Department Pharmacist

Victor Cohen, B.S., Pharm.D. and Megan Musselman, B.S., Pharm.D.

39.1 Introduction

The emergency department (ED) is a frenetic place, with overwhelmed, multi-tasking emergency-healthcare providers treating severely ill patients that demand prompt, time-critical decision-making—often based on limited patient information.[1] These stresses make for an environment at high risk for drug injury and liability.

Goldberg et al. suggest that decisions regarding treatment engage one's highest level of cognitive capacity, and that the ED's inevitable shortages of information—in addition to its heuristic biases—make this process highly fallible, particularly under conditions of stress.[2] Other factors that make the ED a high-risk environment for errors in treatment include (1) unremitting pressure to move patients through the ED, disposing the clinicians to processing errors such as premature closure and omission; (2) insufficient information for confirmation of diagnosis; and (3) limitations on the clinician's ability to effectively research, prescribe, and direct the appropriate administration of medications. One solution to this problem of treatment error is to employ a clinical pharmacy service that engages in pharmacotherapeutic decisions during acute stabilization of critically ill patients at the bedside and provides general pharmaceutical care to all patients who visit the ED.[3] This chapter is designed to illustrate the inherent risks associated with use of medications in the department of emergency medicine, and to demonstrate the impact of clinical-pharmacy services in detecting, mitigating, and preventing drug injury. The objectives of this chapter are (1) to introduce the reader to drug injury occurring in the emergency department, (2) to describe the role of a specialized, trained clinical pharmacist in mitigating the risk, and (3) to discuss the methods used for preventing drug injury.

39.2 Epidemiology of Drug Injury and Contributing Risk Factors

Multiple small-scale epidemiological studies have been published that provide a glimpse into the incidence and prevalence of drug injury in patients visiting the emergency department, but few—if any—identify the incidence or prevalence of drug injury associated with the treatment by clinicians providing emergency care. For example, in 2002, Hafner et al. reported 321 suspected adverse drug events (ADEs) identified from 13,004 ED charts. Thirteen ADEs were caused by the ED therapeutic intervention, representing 6 percent of total ADEs.[4] Herr et al. evaluated the incidence of potential adverse drug interactions (ADIs) with any new medication given in the ED.[5] They discovered that out of 199 visits, 26 percent of ED patients had been exposed

Acknowledgement: Special thanks Dr. Frank Paloucek for sharing relevant cases with the authors for this chapter.

to a potential ADI, and 3 percent had experienced clinically significant reactions, as determined by a three-member physician-review panel. Using a retrospective design, Beers et al. revealed a 10 percent rate of exposure to potential ADIs among ED patients who received at least one prescription.[6] In addition, charts failed to indicate that the prescribing clinician was aware of such a potential interaction (thus classifying the event as an error).

Another source of drug injury observed in the emergency department is due to preventable adverse events that occur out of hospital, and this contributes to the large number of patients that emergency departments must manage. Zed et al. conducted a prospective study to evaluate the frequency, severity and preventability of drug-related visits to the emergency department over a 12-week period. Of the 1,017 patients included in the study, 122 patients were identified as having drug-related visits, while 83 of these visits were deemed to be preventable. For the 122 cases detected, severity was classified as mild in 16 percent, moderate in 75 percent and severe in 10 percent. The most common drug-related visits were due to adverse drug reactions (39 percent), nonadherence (28 percent), and the utilization of the wrong drug (12 percent). Rates of hospital admission and length of stay were increased in patients presenting to the ED with a drug-related event.[7]

A. Contributing Risk Factors

Goldberg et al. reviewed ED records from two different hospital settings, examining a specific population of patients previously shown to be at high risk for ADIs.[8] Inclusion criteria specified patients on three or more medications who were 50 years or older and who were taking at least two medications. Drug regimens were analyzed for potential ADIs using the Drug Master computer-software program. Drug interactions that were moderate to high were included in the analysis. Eighty-nine out of 191 patients (49 percent) had a total of 226 potential adverse drug interactions—50 percent of which were related to ED treatment. As expected, the potential for ADIs rose dramatically with the number of medications administered. For example, 13 percent of patients taking two medications were at risk of ADE, versus 38 percent for patients taking five medications, and 82 percent for patients taking seven or more medications. Of the 226 potential drug interactions, 11 drugs accounted for 223 of them (98 percent). The significance of risk was achieved with digoxin, furosemide, theophylline, nifedipine, enalapril, ranitidine, and glyburide; but not with prednisone, prochlorperazine, dilantin, or aspirin. Goldberg et al. also reported that 44 of 205 patients (21.5 percent) had a total of 94 potential drug-disease interactions. Thirty-two (34 percent) were related to ED treatment.

The leading drug-disease interactions included patients with congestive heart failure, renal disease, hypertension, and diabetes. Based on this data and the high-risk population, the authors suggested that this population is at substantial risk of drug-drug and drug-disease interactions. The authors also suggest that half of the drug-drug or drug-disease interactions are attributable to medications administered or prescribed in the ED. Adverse drug interactions increase with the number of medications administered, from 13 to 82 percent, as the number of medications increased from two to seven. Others have found that 90 percent of potential ADIs are related to ten specific drugs: aspirin, digoxin, steroids, propranolol, phenytoin, aminophylline, prochlorperazine, quinidine, penicillin, and carbamazepine.

Although this data has significant legal implications, there is little information confirming the clinical significance of these interactions. Estimates of the rate of clinical significance of these interactions range from 1 to 23 percent.

Further supporting the potential risks of medication errors, Rothschild et al. conducted an observational, multicenter study evaluating medication errors that were recovered by ED pharmacists. The two main outcomes of the study were *mitigated adverse drug event,* defined as medication errors recovered by the pharmacist that reached the patient but before causing harm, or *ameliorated adverse drug event,* defined as a medication error caught after minimal harm to the patient but further or worsening harm was avoided. The researchers reported that pharmacists recovered 505 recovered medication errors that occurred in 6.8 percent of the patients. The overall recovered medication error rate was 7.8 percent. The majority of recovered medication errors found by the researchers were potential adverse drug reactions intercepted before reaching the patient (90.3 percent) followed by mitigated adverse drug events (3.9 percent) and ameliorated adverse drug events (0.2 percent). The potential severities of the intercepted medication errors were deemed to be either serious (47.8 percent) or significant (36.2 percent). The most common medication class associated with the recovered errors was antimicrobial agents (32.1 percent), central-nervous system agents (16.2 percent), and anticoagulant and thrombolytic agents (14.1 percent). Lastly, the most common types of errors were dosing errors, drug omission, and incorrect frequency of medications.

In summary, ADEs are not uncommon in the ED, and may represent substantial annual costs. ADEs in the ED are significant. They represent the chief complaint of the patient, are more common in elderly and in those taking multiple drugs, and are associated with treatment initiated in the ED. Therefore, they warrant scrutiny and vigilance when managing patients in the ED. An ED pharmacist can aid in prevention of potentially harmful medication errors reaching the patient.[9]

39.3 Etiology and Sources of Drug Injury in the ED

The fast pace of the ED does not permit for an accurate, detailed medication history. This situation often results in time wasted and medication errors. Rusnak et al. reported that most medication errors occurred at the interface of care—for example, at admission, transfer, or discharge.[10] The ED encompasses all three interfaces, thereby constituting a great risk for medication error.

Other challenges to safe medication use in the ED include point-of-care orders, verbal orders, incomplete medical records, multitasking with frequent interruptions and distractions and the high prevalence of information gaps for patients.[11] Moreover, some clinicians have the impression that a "stat dose," given only once, cannot cause drug injury. The "barroom" culture of the ED—where visitors are permitted and clinicians are frequently interrupted—is potentially the cause of a medical error. Patients may harbor a drug interaction during acute stabilization, but because there is a lack of accurate, essential, and believable information, a general approach to stabilization is instituted (as opposed to a more informative approach). These interventions, which are often instituted without complete information, may worsen the situation or prolong hospitalization.

Another source of drug injury in the ED is discharge prescriptions. Wingert et al. found that 33 percent of 2,213 prescriptions written by house staff in a California pediatric ED contained a dosing error, and 95 percent were incomplete (according to broader specifications, including that all prescriptions contain the medication quantity, dosage interval between doses or hours to be given, as well as any appropriate instructions).[12] Community pharmacists corrected these errors less than 10 percent of the time, and most errors made it to the patients' medicine cabinets. Johnson et al. conducted a follow-up study on written original prescriptions and discharge instructions, comparing them to instructions written on the labels of the bottles provided by the pharmacist. They found discrepancies in 12 percent of 192 pediatric patients. Half of the errors were related to the original prescription, while 3 percent were transcription errors. It was also noted that the packaging was distinctly different than what the discharge instructions assumed (increasing the risk for error and confusion).[13] In summary, all parts of the medication process—prescribing, transcribing, dispensing, procuring, administering, and monitoring—are at risk for error, due to the nature of emergency care.

39.4 Clinical Pharmacy in the ED: An Historical Perspective

Historically, the role of the clinical pharmacist in emergency medicine has been well described. R. M. Elenbaas stated that the major goal of clinical pharmacy services in the ED was to promote and assure rational pharmacotherapeutics for all aspects of healthcare offered by departments of emergency medicine.[14] The general activities of the pharmacist include practice, education, and research.

Elenbaas' initial description of the key clinical activities included:

1. Bedside consultation with physicians and nurses to design, implement, and monitor patient-specific therapeutic plans using the most cost-effective and least toxic therapies.
2. Patient education directed toward increased understanding of medication use and maximizing chances of therapeutic success.
3. Assistance in maintaining ED compliance with pharmacy procedures and developing an appropriate ED medication formulary.

Further illustration of the pharmacist's clinical role was described by Lada et al. The types of services provided by the pharmacist in the ED include drug information consultations, pharmacokinetic consultations, anticoagulation services, emergency resuscitation team participation, antimicrobial surveillance, patient recruitment for ongoing research, order entry and dispensing of medications, formulary interchange, and sample medication provision to indigent care patients.[15]

Brown et al. evaluated the frequency of medication errors in an ED before and after an ED pharmacist was assigned to review medication orders. The study investigators defined a medication error as any preventable event that may lead to inappropriate medication use or patient harm while the medication is in the control of the healthcare professional. A total of 490 medication orders written for 198 patients were examined. The researchers conducted a retrospective review of patient charts in the ED prior to pharmacist involvement in the ordering process, designated as the control group. Similarly, the researchers conducted a prospective review of patient charts in the ED once a pharmacist was involved in the ordering process, designated as the intervention group. The rate of errors in the control group was 16.09 per 100 medication orders, compared to 5.38 per 100 medication orders in the intervention group. This demonstrated that pharmacist involvement in the medication-review process decreases the rate of medication errors that can potentially occur in the ED.[16] There are historical and present accounts of pharmacists in the ED fostering the lead in assuring safe and effective medication-use practices.

Despite the well-defined historical role of the pharmacist in the ED, the presence of pharmacists in the ED is still slow-growing. The American Society of Health-Systems Pharmacy (ASHP) conducted a national survey in 2008 pertaining to pharmacy practice in the hospital setting. A stratified random sample of 1,310 general and children's hospitals in the United States were surveyed regarding pharmacy dispensing and administration of medications. The response rate to the survey was 40.2 percent. Only 6.8 percent of hospitals had pharmacists in the ED.[17]

39.5 The ED Pharmacist Plays a Dual Role at Maimonides Medical Center

The following is a description of clinical pharmacy services provided at the Department of Emergency Medicine with case-based illustrations.

The Department of Emergency Medicine at Maimonides Medical Center (MMC) is a primary teaching facility for the medical school of the State University of New York, also serving the Boro Park community of Brooklyn, New York. The department sees 80,000 patients annually, with an admission rate of 25 percent. The acute adult facility is divided into three main areas, consisting of four critical-care beds, 23 general beds (with two quiet rooms), one obstetrics-and-gynecology room, an isolation room, and an asthma-treatment area—all staffed with board-certified emergency-medicine physicians and nurses. Nurse practitioners and physician assistants staff a "fast-track" area. Board-certified pediatric emergency-medicine physicians staff the pediatric ED.

Clinical pharmacy services were offered to the department by the pharmaceutical department at Maimonides Medical Center through an affiliation with the Arnold and Marie Schwartz College of Pharmacy and Health Sciences at Long Island University in July 1998. Since the department of emergency medicine has a medical-residency program and a training program for the Fiorello H. Laguardia Community College paramedic program, a clinical pharmacist specializing in emergency medicine seemed mutually beneficial. The ED would be used as a pharmacy practice-training site for entry-level Pharm.D. students, with the goal of the specialized clinical pharmacist to establish a practice.

The pharmaceutical department provided a centralized, 24-hour distribution-support service to the department of emergency medicine. A medication room located in the ED stores most of the necessary medications. The room is able to fit five persons for procurement of medications. The central pharmacy refills the floor stock daily and sends medi-

cations that are not floor stock through the translogic CTF 30 pneumatic-tube system. Drug and poison information is provided as needed. The department of emergency medicine at Maimonides is busiest during the hours of 11 P.M. and 2 A.M. The ED pharmacist provides a dual role that includes a traditional and contemporary practice of pharmaceutical care. The ED pharmacist specializes in acute stabilization of the critically ill patient, while also providing a traditional pharmacy role with the goal of providing optimal pharmaceutical care.

39.6 The ED Pharmacist: A Sub-Specialist in Emergency Medicine
A. Training and Education

The ED pharmacist is a post-baccalaureate Pharm.D. At the time of this writing, the ED pharmacist at MMC was someone who had completed two residencies—a pharmacy-practice residency and a specialized residency in emergency medicine. The ED pharmacist has been cross-trained to do procedures, for example, phlebotomy, attaining an ECG, placing a patient on a cardiac monitor, and assisting with intubation. These procedures are all important for the team approach to acute stabilization of the patient.

B Certification

The ED pharmacist is certified in Basic Life Support, Advanced Cardiac Life Support, Pediatric Advanced Life Support, and Advanced Hazardous Materials (also called "HazMat") Life Support. The ED pharmacist is also a Certified Medical Investigator—important for detecting drug injury and providing expert testimony. These credentials are all essential to providing the immediate life-saving emergency care described by Schwerman and Schwartau in the 1970s. These authors suggested that the involvement of a pharmacist during cardiac arrest allows for the physician to focus on the diagnosis and immediate treatments needed, while the pharmacist focuses on the preparation, dosage, and appropriateness of necessary therapy—thus making this a collaborative, team-oriented activity resulting in a high rate of success.[18] The ED pharmacist provides a rapid approach upon anticipation at the bedside pharmacotherapy consultation to support the medical staff's procedures during stabilization of the patient. The ED pharmacist monitors for life-threatening dysrhythmias and recommends immediate action and intervention. The ED pharmacist also documents medications administered during a cardiac arrest. Research has demonstrated hospital mortality rates are improved as well as compliance to Advance Cardiovascular Life Support (ACLS) treatment guidelines when pharmacists participate on the resuscitation team.[19] In addition, the ED pharmacist—depending on the personnel available—may support the clinicians with intubations, chest compressions, phlebotomy, and other nontraditional roles (such as manually ventilating patients until the patient is placed on a respirator by the respiratory therapists).

However, the ED pharmacist's role is not limited to acute stabilization. The ED pharmacist also has a role in providing general pharmaceutical care for patients admitted or discharged from the ED. The generalist role of the ED pharmacist includes (1) ensuring optimal continuum of care; (2) detecting, preventing and managing drug injury; and (3) building a defense system against the risk of medication misadventures.

39.7 The ED Pharmacist as a Generalist

The generalist role of the ED pharmacist is based on a pharmaceutical-care approach applied to the ED, as described by Carter et al. The ED pharmacist conducts a drug-therapy assessment, in order to identify any problems with medication orders. The assessment includes the following nine pharmaceutical-care questions concerning the drug therapy prescribed in the ED: (1) Is there an immediate indication? (2) Are there any absolute or relative contraindications that are clinically relevant that prohibit the use of this medication? (3) Is this drug the safest and most cost-effective therapy available to facilitate the attainment of positive outcomes, or at least improve the patient's immediate quality of life? (4) Are there any untreated illnesses that require immediate therapy? (5) Is the dosing regimen correct (dose, route, and rate)? (6) Are there any immediate adverse drug reactions that would worsen the critical condition of this patient (precluding the use of this agent)? (7) Are there any drug interactions that have an immediate onset, or an unpredictable duration, or with major severity, which I must prevent from occurring? (8) Is this the most cost-effective drug? (9) What monitoring parameters must be assessed before and after therapy, and how frequently should the patient be monitored while in the ED?[20] It is not always feasible to provide answers to all of these questions—due to lack of information, higher-priority activities, and immediate transfer. However, the goal is not the quantity—but the improved quality—of care provided to the patient. This systematic approach allows the ED pharmacist to be efficient and ensure a continuum of care from the ED to the in-patient setting.

39.8 The ED Pharmacist Ensuring Optimal Continuum of Care
A. The ED Pharmacist and Infectious Diseases

At Maimonides Medical Center, the ED pharmacist is charged with solving problems, such as delays in treatment of serious infections or overutilization of antimicrobials throughout the ED. Through collaboration between pharmacy, infectious disease (ID), and emergency medicine, a clinical infectious disease "pathway" was developed. This pathway was initiated in the ED and implemented in October 1999. Information cards containing the clinical pathway were disseminated to the medical staff. A restricted antimicrobial empiric-therapy card was developed to allow ED clinicians to request the antibiotics indicated from the central pharmacy. The ED pharmacist was responsible for maintenance of this clinical service. After three months of service, 231 restricted antimicrobial cards had been sent to the pharmacy by the ED clinicians, with a 95 percent rate of compliance with the clinical infectious disease pathway recommended by the Antibiotic Surveillance Committee. The incidence of inappropriate selection was 10 percent, which was deemed an "acceptable" level (due to confounding clinical presentation). "Door-to-needle" times for treatment of serious infectious diseases improved dramatically—to less than one hour from the time of the order written by the physician. The ED pharmacist, upon follow-up of the patient, has intervened and consistently streamlined therapy on a daily basis, assuring optimal cost-effective antibiotic therapy. As part of continuous quality improvement, the Medical Director for the Department of Emergency Medicine is notified in cases of inappropriate selection (and education is provided to the prescribing physicians when necessary). For continuity, this antimicrobial guideline is used across the medical center and has gained wide acceptance.

Because of the initial success of the empiric antibiotic-approval program in the ED, they developed target quality-assurance programs to optimize treatment of the most common infectious diseases, such as community-acquired pneumonia (CAP). Pre-printed antimicrobial guides with the recommended indications were provided to the ED, via the same antimicrobial approval card. The antimicrobial approval card tagged the patient for follow-up by the ED pharmacotherapy team. ED approval was granted for 24 hours, after which the physician (in the in-patient setting) would either discontinue therapy, switch to alternative therapy, or—if a diagnosis of CAP was confirmed—order gatifloxacin, the preferred CAP therapy, through a novel computerized physician order entry (CPOE) CAP pathway. The CPOE CAP pathway required the physician to consider renal adjustments, to plan for streamlining therapy, or to make an automatic switch from IV-PO therapy (minimum time permitted was within 48 to 72 hours), and to screen for allergies or co-morbid conditions that would make gatifloxacin alone an inappropriate selection for that patient. Two years after the implementation of the integrated ED-ID approval system and the CPOE CAP pathway, the quality of patient care has improved, as demonstrated by a reduction in the average length of stay from 4.3 days to 3.34 days. This program has improved the medication-use process, enhanced the quality of patient care by reducing the average length of stay in the hospital, and enhanced the safety and effectiveness of use of antimicrobial agents in the institution.

Beyond this quantitative example, the following qualitative example demonstrates the role of the pharmacotherapist as an essential team member for providing important continuum of care in patients with infectious diseases. A patient with a brain abscess on CT scan was initially managed with ceftriaxone 2 g IV. The ED pharmacist's surveillance suggested that this patient was at risk of drug-resistant streptococcal pneumonia and anaerobic organisms. The ED pharmacist recommended metronidazole and vancomycin to assure broad-spectrum coverage. The recommendations were well accepted. Initial empiric therapy was enhanced.

ED pharmacists also take on the role of assuring appropriate selection of therapy for treated and released patients who are prescribed an antibiotic in the ED. ED pharmacists are involved in reviewing culture reports and modifying antimicrobial therapy based on the results. For example, in 2009, Randolph describes the ED pharmacist involvement in the management of patients who have a culture obtained in their ED. If the patient is not receiving appropriate therapy, a new prescription is called in to the patient's outpatient pharmacy. Patients are also contacted by the ED pharmacist regarding their culture result and to receive counseling for the new antimicrobial regimen.[21]

B. The ED Pharmacist and the Ambulatory Care Interphase

The discharge-prescription program (DPP): the ED pharmacist initiated the DPP in the ED. For this service, the ED pharmacist provides the discharge prescription, counsels the patient on use, and verifies that the patient comprehends the instructions for use of the medication prescribed before her discharge from the ED. The ED pharmacist surveys for discharge prescriptions in the ED fast track, pediatric, and acute-care areas. The ED pharmacist processes the prescriptions and conducts a therapeutic assessment (as described above), while the outpatient pharmacy procures the medication. The patient is provided with the medication at the bedside, and with demonstrations on how to use the medication (during a formal counseling session). The ED pharmacist documents the counseling sessions in the patient's medical chart.

Since the inception of the program, the ED pharmacist has referred 700 prescriptions to the outpatient pharmacy.

Future goals of this program include assessing the impact of counseling on compliance and outcomes and attaining reimbursement for counseling and follow-up (for patients who return to the same pharmacy and visit the ED pharmacist for medication management). This program is likely to prevent unwarranted visits to the ED. Examples of the DPP's impact on reducing drug injury is illustrated below:

Case #1: A 51-year-old white female was given a prescription for two weeks' worth of Ketorolac 30 mg PO every six hours. The ED pharmacist providing the discharge prescription reviewed the prescription, conducted a therapeutic assessment, and deemed that—among other things—the dose was actually an intravenous dose, the duration of therapy was too long, and the patient had a prior history of peptic ulcer disease and hypertension. The ED pharmacist intervened, recommended alternative therapy, and avoided the potential overdose and drug misadventure.

Case #2: A pediatric resident wrote a prescription for oral amoxicillin, to be administered to a child. An ED pharmacist student was called to provide the discharge prescription at the bedside. Upon review, the pharmacy student noted that the dosage on the prescription was double the recommended maximum dose. The student notified the ED pharmacist, and the dosing was corrected. The patient was discharged with a positive outcome.

Case #3: A 71-year-old male was prescribed enoxaparin 100 mg SC every 12 hours for a total of 5 days and warfarin 5 mg PO daily for an acute deep-vein thrombosis. The ED pharmacy specialty resident was paged to provide discharge counseling for the patient and his wife regarding administration technique of enoxaparin and his new medications. Enoxaparin is a weight-adjusted and renal-adjusted medication; considered a high-risk, high-alert drug by The Joint Commission and requires a safety check. Upon review of the patient's electronic medical record by the pharmacy resident, it was discovered that the most recent set of laboratory values assessing renal function for this patient was completed two years prior; understating the variation of this set of tests, the pharmacy resident wanted to assure that the current levels were not abnormal (as this would require a dose adjustment). The pharmacy resident notified the attending physician and a new set of values were ordered and completed. The new tests revealed some degree of renal impairment that subsequently required a dose adjustment for the enoxaparin, from the initially prescribed twice-a-day dosing to once-daily dosing. The prescription was clarified and re-written and the potential harm of hemorrhage and re-admission was avoided.

C. The ED Pharmacist as a Clinical Toxicology Consultant

As famously described in 1979 by Czajka et al., the pharmacist has three main functions in clinical toxicology consultations.[22] The first is assisting in obtaining the patient history and conducting a patient assessment of the toxicological problem. He next recommends a plan for management and, thirdly, counsels the patient and caregiver on poison prevention to prevent reoccurrences. The ED pharmacist at MMC is consulted for these services. This pharmacist conducts a comprehensive investigation of the patient medication history, counts pills, assesses other medication the patient may have had access to, and identifies foreign medications. He also recommends a management plan. In addition—and most importantly—the pharmacist provides bedside care during the initial supportive care of the toxicological emergency, in the form of assisting with gastric decontamination, administering activated charcoal, or gastric lavage. The ED pharmacist recommends and procures antidotes too—especially those that are not commonly used, such as the cyanide antidote kit, dantrolene, flumazenil, methylene blue, sodium bicarbonate, glucagon and ethanol infusion drip. The ED pharmacist evaluates drug levels, arterial blood gas, toxicodynamics, and toxicokinetics, to assist with disposition of the patient. In addition, ED pharmacists can also become board-certified toxicologists with the American Academy of Clinical Toxicology providing them with knowledge, experience and competence to provide toxicological expertise in emergent and non-emergent situations. The impact of the ED pharmacist is demonstrated in the following cases:

Case #1: A 24-year-old Asian male presented with an acute altered mental status. The physician requested a consult from the ED pharmacist, and requested that Ceftriaxone IV be administered for suspected bacterial meningitis. The ED pharmacist questioned the patient, and through patient assessment, noticed widely dilated pupils and a moderately confused sensorium, similar to what is seen in anticholinergic toxicity. Although the patient had difficulty remembering, the ED pharmacist was able to obtain evidence that the patient attempted suicide. The patient's family corroborated this. After further investigation, the patient admitted to taking 30 Unisom tablets (Unisom is a well-known over-the-counter sleep aid that contains diphenhydramine 50 mg). The patient was given activated charcoal and supportive care. Antimicrobial therapy was discontinued.

Case #2: A seven-year-old child treated with risperidone for aggressive behavior had a dystonic reaction in school, according to the guidance counselor. After further evaluation, the physician determined that this was an expected event. The ED pharmacist conducted a further investigation and discovered that the instruction on the medication bottle was incorrect, and that a pipette dispensing tool used to deliver the medication orally had been used inappropriately, resulting in the mother administering at least 10 times the recommended dose. Hence, this reaction was a drug misadventure due to the overdose—not necessarily an expected untoward effect of the drug. A re-challenge at normal doses was negative, permitting reinstitution of risperidone therapy, which led to a positive outcome. The ED pharmacist was trained in detecting drug errors. Without his investigation, another accidental overdose might have occurred, or the physician might have unnecessarily discontinued risperidone in a patient who had been effectively managed on this therapy.

Case #3: A 28-year-old male was brought into the ED for suspected overdose of his sister's Naprosyn prescription. He presented with the bottle and his sister who identified the medication to be her Naprosyn prescription. Upon arrival to the ED, the patient was admitted to medicine for psychiatry clearance. The clinical ED pharmacist reviewing the case prior to transfer to the floor opened the vial and noted the presence of acetaminophen 500 mg tablets rather than naproxen tablets. An acetaminophen concentration was ordered, and an occult acetaminophen overdose was identified.

Case #4: A 49-year-old patient, a frequent flier to the ED, presented with suspected alcohol-related seizures for the seventh time over the previous four months. Upon presentation, the patient had altered mental status and was unable to give an adequate medical history. Based on his admission laboratory results, it was noted the patient had an anion gap acidosis. The medical team attributed these laboratory findings to be due to a suspected seizure that occurred prior to presentation to the ED. A pharmacist reviewing the patient's progress 6 hours after initial presentation, noticed an anion gap acidosis still present and suggested toxic alcohol levels be sent to the laboratory for testing. Based upon these results, an ethylene glycol ingestion was discovered, and the patient was initiated on antidotal therapy.

D. The ED Pharmacist and the Cardiology Interface

Prior to clinical pharmacy service, the "door-to-needle" time for initiating fibrinolytic therapy for acute myocardial infarction was estimated at three hours. A primary goal of the Medical Director was to reduce this time to the standard of less than one hour. To this end, the emergency nurse specialist, medical director, and the ED pharmacist at MMC developed and implemented the first chest-pain order form. The chest-pain order form was created to assure that initial standard medications were considered and immediately requested by the treating clinician, barring any contraindications that might be listed on the form. The chest-pain order form served as a reminder of the medications recommended by the ACC/AHA guidelines for use during an acute coronary syndrome. As a result of the chest-pain order form, the "door-to-needle" time improved from three hours to less than one hour—within just three months of implementation. Interestingly, when the ED pharmacist was present, there were case reports of administration of fibrinolytic therapy within 15 minutes. This rapid approach to instituting life-saving medications improves the goal of salvaging myocardium, while assuring safe and appropriate use of the fibrinolysis. The importance of assuring appropriate procurement and administration of fibrinolysis cannot be overstated, as reported by Cannon et al., who demonstrated that mistakes with administration of fibrinolysis result in outcomes worse than in those who never received fibrinolysis.[23] To provide greater safety, fibrinolytic kits are now available in the MMC's ED, with instructions and guidelines for dosing, administration, procurement, and monitoring. A medication-use evaluation card is attached to the kits for future pharmacovigilance studies. The goal of the card is for real-time data collection on the use of fibrinolytics. The hope is that a review of the annual medical charts will indicate which strategies have been most successful in acute myocardial infarction, and provide information on the preferred fibrinolytic, and any adverse outcomes that may have resulted.

The ED pharmacist uses epidemiological tools, such as the TIMI (Thrombolysis in Myocardial Infarction) risk score, to estimate the risk of morbidity and mortality for patients presenting with symptoms of acute coronary syndromes. The TIMI risk score will compare the risk of death if the patient is left untreated with the risks incurred by treatment with antithrombotics. The ED pharmacist intervenes when the risk of antithrombotic therapy outweighs its benefits, or to avoid potential harmful dosing regimens with anticoagulants (such as heparin, enoxaparin, or glycoprotein 2B3A receptor inhibitors). The ED pharmacist also ensures appropriate and immediate preparation and administration by conducting a direct observation of therapy at the bedside.

At MMC the ED pharmacist is providing even more intense direct patient care through the management of physician-approved protocols. In 2009 the ED pharmacist has been managing the rate control of atrial fibrillation/flutter patients to assure achievement of endpoints and sustained rate control. To date 48 patients have been managed by the pharmacist. The program has been shown to be safe and effective, and has resulted in increased patient satisfaction with intense monitoring and ED physician approval through allowing the ED physician to manage the surge and enhance the throughput.

E. The ED Pharmacist and Neurological Emergencies

The ED pharmacist observes at the bedside during neurological emergencies. He provides immediate recommendations and procurement of neurological emergency pharmacotherapy. In addition, he makes a bedside assessment of contraindications, to avoid any medication-related problems with use of t-PA for stroke.

F. The ED Pharmacist and Pulmonary Emergencies

The ED pharmacist is involved in acute status asthmaticus, in procurement of medications at the bedside as requested by the physician, and consultation, as illustrated by the following case presentation. A patient (who happened to be a cardiologist) presented at the ED for acute status asthmaticus unrelieved by aggressive bronchodilator therapy. The ED physician was ready to intubate the patient, as recommended by the pulmonologist. The ED pharmacist suggested aminophylline. The pulmonologists consulting on the case disagreed and stated that aminophylline no longer had a role in status asthmaticus. However, to avoid intubation, the ED physician agreed with the pharmacist. The aminophylline infusion provided instant alertness and appeared to improve extra-pulmonary ventilation, allowing the patient to express himself (which, minutes before, he had been unable to do). Intubation was avoided and the patient was discharged a day later. The cardiologist suggested publishing this case supporting the use of aminophylline in acute status asthmaticus. This intervention prevented substantial morbidity and a prolonged length of stay in the intensive-care unit.

G. The ED Pharmacist and Public Health Services in the ED

Several public-health programs have been developed and initiated within the ED. The ED pharmacist has engaged in screening and brief intervention for smoking cessation and for preventing exposure of children to second-hand smoke from their family members. One-hundred thirty-four patients have been screened and counseled on methods for preventing second-hand smoke exposure to their children.

Between 2008 and 2010, the ED pharmacist trained hundreds of community and hospital pharmacists in administering vaccinations, and has been granted approval by the institution to administer influenza and pneumococcal vaccines to treated and released patients. Over 70,000 patients who visit the ED are treated and released. Many of these patients do not get vaccinated appropriately, so this newly granted access may improve the vaccination rates of the community. The ED pharmacist has collaborated with the Department of Health to provide vaccinations during the H1N1 pandemic at health fairs, resulting in the vaccination of hundreds of people. In 2010, the ED pharmacist screened patients for the need of vaccinations from the ED.

Additionally, the ED pharmacist conducts emergency preparedness and training of all staff for disasters and has educated the media and the population about risk and mitigating strategies in the event of a terrorist attack.

39.9 Medication Admission Notes in the ED

It has been reported that up to 27 percent of all hospital prescribing errors have been attributed to incomplete medication histories at time of admission.[24] Therefore, it is essential to attain a verified, reliable, and accurate medication history upon ED admission in order to ensure optimal continuum of care. Medication histories may unveil reasons for the patients' illnesses, such as noncompliance or adverse drug reactions. Also, patients' at-home medication regimens are often continued during and after hospitalization; however, the patient's inability to recall medications can sometimes be a limitation or a source of error. Traditionally, medications are identified in the histories taken by physicians or nurses. However, in recent clinical data, pharmacists have been shown to obtain more accurate medication-related in-

formation from patients than either of these aforementioned clinicians. Carter et al. affirmed that clinical pharmacists obtain more complete medication histories for patients upon admission. Pharmacists identified 1,096 home medications compared to 817 that were identified by ED physicians, medical students or nurses. The most common discrepancy was the omission of the dosing information (78 percent) or the omission of a home medication (25 percent).[25] Bond et al. report an annual cost savings of $7 million per hospital, as well as a reduced annual rate of deaths, for a group of 128 hospitals with pharmacists taking medication histories, compared with a control group of hospitals that did not have pharmacists on staff to take histories.[26] Currently, only 3 percent of hospitals employ pharmacists in this role, and even fewer emergency departments are equipped with this resource. Nester et al. demonstrated that pharmacist-conducted medication histories improved rates of clinical interventions, as compared to nursing-acquired medication histories (34 percent vs. 16 percent, p <0.001). The authors also suggested that, perhaps, a pharmacist could work in areas such as the emergency room or admission areas during certain hours to conduct medication histories as patients are admitted to the hospital. Nester et al. suggested targeting certain populations, such as those at high risk, the elderly, and those admitted due to drug-related morbidity. Interestingly, however, the authors reported that this clinical pharmacy service was curtailed at their institution, due to major personnel and budgetary changes—even though this service was found to reduce cost and mortality.[10] Lastly, Hayes et al. examined the effect of pharmacist-conducted medication reconciliation in the ED on compliance with The Joint Commission's National Patient Safety Goal requiring hospitals to accurately and completely reconcile medications. The medication reconciliations not conducted by pharmacists were designated as the control group, and the pharmacist-conducted medication reconciliations were designated as the study group. In the eight-week study period, a total of 117 errors were identified on the medication histories conducted by the control group compared to only two errors for the study group (p = 0.001). Also, allergy documentation was recorded for only 62 patients in the control group (79 percent) versus all 60 patients in the study group (100 percent) (p = 0.001).[27]

The ED at MMC conducts medication histories upon admission. The ED pharmacist will immediately alert the ED clinicians to the potential risks involved with mixing ED-initiated therapy with current therapies or if the pattern of care indicates a potential drug-related admission. This information may assist with the disposition and optimal management of the patient.

The ED pharmacist conducts a comprehensive medication history as an initial triage of patients entering the ED. The data collected includes:

1. Medications prior to admit
2. Medications taken right before the event
3. Over-the-counter medications used regularly
4. Herbal products taken regularly
5. Illicit drug substances used
6. Social history
7. Allergies and reactions
8. Immunization history
9. Initial vital signs and quick assessment
10. Compliance history
11. Medications needed immediately to prevent withdrawal reactions
12. Identification of foreign medications
13. Identification of medication taken in overdose
14. Adverse drug reactions

An example of the impact of attaining comprehensive medication histories is seen in the following cases:

Case #1: A 54-year-old Russian female presented in a catatonic state. After the ED pharmacist conducted an extensive medication history, it was revealed that the patient was self-administering Kavololum—a Russian tonic for anxiety—that had phenobarbital as its main ingredient. This explained the patient's initial presentation.

Case #2: A 31-year-old female taking carbamazepine for a seizure disorder was recently started on treatment for Helicobacter pylori. The private physician started the patient on a combination regimen containing clarithromycin and lansoprazole. The patient presented to the ED with a clinical presentation of dizziness, nystagmus, and ataxia, as well as an elevated level of carbamazepine. The ED pharmacist identified the drug interaction between the carbamazepines and clarithromycin and treated accordingly, by reducing the dose of carbamazepine. The patient was subsequently discharged within six hours.

39.10 Building Layers of Defense against Drug Injury
A. Detecting and Preventing Drug Injury in the ED
The department of emergency medicine at Maimonides Medical Center initiated a Division of Pharmacovigilance.

Pharmacovigilance is traditionally defined as the postmarketing surveillance for adverse drug reactions, with the ultimate goal of minimizing their occurrence. MMC has applied this definition to the ED. The Division of Pharmacovigilance conducts post-prescribing surveillance for medication errors, potential adverse drug events, and drug misadventures within the department. The goal is to minimize their occurrence.

Using the ED Information System (EDIS), MMC has created safeguards at the point of prescribing. First, they created a restricted emergency-medicine-specific drug formulary, based on the most common medications charged for, and then added this list as floor stock. Chemotherapeutic agents were omitted, because of the rarity for use in an ED setting (they placed a safeguard that includes a prior approval from an oncologist before using any of these agents).

Through the ED's computerized physician order entry system (CPOE), they created a clinical alert system that warns the clinician that the use of the medication being prescribed has been designated a high-risk medication, as described by the Institute of Safe Medication Practices. For example, a double asterisk is used to trigger clinicians to double-verify the medication order for appropriateness. Some high alerts include medications requiring dose adjustment, such as enoxaparin, as well as antibiotics and medications that should be dose-adjusted for the elderly (such as ketorolac and opiates). Alerts to the use of potassium supplements and insulin have also been developed.

The ED pharmacist is involved in constant surveillance of real-time medication orders while in the ED (or while in the office, via a unique tracking board available through the hospital-wide intranet). An electronic pill-bottle icon has been added to the tracking board screen to permit the pharmacist to quickly verify medications for appropriateness. When placing the computer cursor over the pill bottle, the medication orders appear. The pharmacist uses a paper ED screening form to document a therapeutic assessment of the prescribed order and verifies the order for appropriateness. A verification pill bottle (in yellow) on the screen notifies the physician and nurse of a modification made to an incompletely transcribed order, or simply an inappropriate order. The nurse and physician are verbally notified before the change, to ensure that they agree with it. Qualitative examples of the effectiveness of this surveillance system are illustrated in the following cases.

Case #1: A physician assistant completed orders during the shift change (at 7:30 A.M.). Upon review of the orders, the ED pharmacist noticed two discrepancies: a digoxin order was written for 1.25 mg by mouth daily, and an order for Diovan was written for 800 mg by mouth daily. The ED pharmacist noticed this discrepancy and notified the nurse to hold the order. The ED pharmacist conducted a medication history and corrected the orders.

Case #2: The ED pharmacist identified an order written for aminophylline 75 ml, to be administered over a period of 30 minutes. A concentrated dose of 75 ml would have resulted in a serious and life-threatening overdose—especially if given over a half-hour period. The prescribing physician was educated on how to properly order an aminophylline infusion. A drug misadventure was avoided.

Case #3: A patient was started on an incorrect infusion rate of tirofiban (an antithrombotic). Usually, an initial bolus dose must be administered, followed by a maintenance infusion. The nurse, who was unfamiliar with procurement, started the patient on a maintenance infusion dose, but without the bolus dose that had been ordered by the cardiology fellow. Upon survey, the ED pharmacist detected this discrepancy and adjusted the rate. He also educated the nurse.

Case #4: An oncology patient on chronic opioid therapy consisting of morphine 30 mg PO three times a day was brought to the ED with altered mental status. Upon arrival to the ED, the patient was subsequently intubated. An ED medical resident converting the patient's home oral medications to intravenous (IV) regimens ordered a 1:1 conversion of oral morphine (30 mg PO three times a day) to IV morphine (30 mg IV three times a day). The ED pharmacist reviewed the patient's medication history prior to verifying the IV morphine and noticed the three-fold error. The order was changed to morphine 10 mg IV three times daily and education was provided to the medical resident regarding conversion of morphine between oral and IV formulations.

In summary, various safeguards have been put into place at the prescribing interface to pre-empt any medication-related events.

B. The ED Pharmacist and Community Surveillance for Adverse Drug Reactions

As part of pharmacovigilance, MMC actively surveys and reports ED visits due to adverse drug reactions. Before July 1998, MMC's adverse drug event or reaction (ADER) reporting was accomplished by using an ADR "stat" line. The healthcare professional would leave a voice recording of the name and medical-record number of the patient who had experienced the ADER. Although this system is convenient for pharmacy, it has little utility in a busy ED. The presence of the ED pharmacist and students surveying the computerized tracking board and assessing for ADERs to report (but also to confirm and to assist in management) is convenient. The ED pharmacist presence is beneficial, because it allows the pharmacist to track medication-related visits and medication-related problems that occur in community, and to visit the ED. Through this surveillance, the community clinicians are notified and educated of the event.

The ED pharmacist surveys for ADER, and then records and files the reaction. An evaluation of the ADER is made using the Naranjo Algorithm. A report to MedWatch and the FDA is filed, based on the severity of the reaction. The ADER is filed for in-hospital review and TJC requirements.

Feedback of the ADER that occurred in the ED and methods of prevention are provided to the medical director and clinical staff. The following case illustrates the importance of ED pharmacist surveillance for potential ADERs. A patient presented with shortness of breath and a headache. In the past, the patient was treated with subcutaneous sumatriptan for relief of migraine headaches. Prior to laboratory evaluation, the patient was given a subcutaneous dose of 6 mg of sumatriptan. The patient immediately developed chest pain and back pain. At the time there was no cardiac monitoring. It was concluded that this adverse event, because of its temporal relation, was sumatriptan-induced. The ED pharmacist requested an electrocardiogram (ECG) to assure that there was no further ischemia. No changes were detected on the ECG. As the patient's clinical manifestations ran its course, it was clear that the initial headache was due, in part, to a urinary-tract infection—not the migraine headache. The physician was educated on the fact that sumatriptan must be used with caution and with appropriate monitoring. Acetaminophen alone might have relieved the headache associated with this patient's infection. The patient was discharged and released from the ED with antibiotics. To further educate the clinicians, case reports of sumatriptan-induced vasospasm were provided, with certain predictive risk factors that would help them be alert to the risk factors for such an event.

39.11 Pharmacy Practice in the ED: Pharmacotherapy Specialty

A clinical pharmacist may prevent drug injury through the use of consultation services. Berry et al. reported that a clinical pharmacist-consultation service yielded consultation in 3 percent of all ED cases. The service was most highly used in July for new house staff.[28] Powell et al. described a 24-hour satellite pharmacy in a 75-bed ED. From the satellite, the pharmacist mixed and distributed drugs, tracked inventory, took part in work rounds, instructed residents and students, and concurrently reviewed all medications orders. The authors describe the substantial benefits to patient care as a result of the pharmacist's clinical, distributive, and educational services.[29] Aldridge et al. established a 24-hour clinical ED pharmacy program within the Veterans Affairs San Diego Healthcare System. During the six-month implementation period, 9,568 interventions were recorded that were deemed to have high probability of preventing serious harm to the patient. After the initial implementation period, providers and nurses were asked to identify the most important and beneficial duties provided by the ED pharmacist. The three most important roles identified were consultations to the clinical staff (27 percent), patient education (26 percent), and prospective medication order review (13 percent).[30] The impact of the ED pharmacist on providing specialist consultation in the ED is demonstrated in the following case examples:

> Case #1: A patient who ingested a quart of "OOPs" latex remover presented to the ED. The patient was stable at the time. The ED pharmacist was consulted for this toxicological emergency. The ED pharmacist investigated the case and provided recommendations that ensured that the standard of care was maintained. "OOPs" is considered a hydrocarbon; therefore, supportive management was recommended. However, the ED pharmacist recognized that the patient may have been a chronic alcoholic, and raised concerns about possible alcohol withdrawal. The "OOPs" contained ethyl alcohol. After further investigation, the son stated that his mother was a chronic alcoholic. The ED pharmacist estimated the alcohol level and recommended that alcohol-withdrawal management be initiated as soon as possible, to avoid delirium tremens. The patient was admitted to the medical intensive-care unit without going into alcohol withdrawal. She recovered and was subsequently discharged from the hospital. Thus, acute suffering due to delirium tremens was prevented.

> Case #2: A stray cat bit a 61-year-old Caucasian female. The ED pharmacist was consulted to determine whether the patient, who was on warfarin, should receive intramuscular injections of rabies vaccination. After review of the CDC guidelines, and of the patient's history and the circumstances of the bite, he concluded that the recommendation for the rabies vaccination was justified. The patient was counseled and the pharmacist verified her understanding of the risk for rabies. The patient agreed to have the rabies vaccine. Because of the empathic counseling and assurances provided by the ED pharmacist, the patient sent a letter to the chairman of the department, describing the excellent care she received in the ED. In summary, the generalist role of the ED pharmacist requires a diverse knowledge of pharmacotherapy.

39.12 Conclusion

Drug injury in the ED is not uncommon, and represents a potential source of liability. Clinical pharmacists specially trained in acute stabilization—while providing general pharmaceutical care—may reduce this liability and help reduce risk by detecting, mitigating, preventing, and treating drug injury. Presently the role of the ED pharmacist is growing and becoming well-accepted and desired by emergency healthcare teams. Outcome-based studies are needed to demonstrate the operational and quality improvement associated with pharmacists practicing in the ED.

Endnotes

1. A. Karcz, R. Korn, R., M.C. Burke, et al. *Malpractice claims against emergency physicians in Massachusetts 1975-1993*. 1996; Am. J. Emerg. Med. 14:341-345.

2. R.M. Goldberg, G. Kuhn, L.B. Andrew, et al. *Coping with medical mistakes and errors in judgement*. Ann. Emerg. Med. 2002; 39(3):287-291.

3. S. Schenkel, *Promoting patient safety and preventing medical error in emergency departments*. Academic Emerg. Med. 2000; 7(11):1204-1218.

4. J.W. Hafner, S.M. Belknap, M.D. Squilante, et al. *Adverse drug events in emergency department patients*. Ann. Emerg. Med. 2002; 39(3):258-266.

5. R.D. Herr, E.M. Caravati, L.S. Tyler, et al. *Prospective evaluation of adverse drug interactions in the emergency department*. Ann. Emerg. Med. 1992; 21(11):1331-1336.

6. M.H. Beers, M. Storrie, G. Lee, G. *Potential adverse drug interactions in the emergency room*. Ann. Intern. Med. 1990; 112(1): 61-64.

7. P.J. Zed, R.B. Abu-Laban, R.M. Bale, et al. *Incidence, severity and preventability of medication-related visits to the emergency department: a prospective study.* Canadian Assn. Med. J. 2008; 178:1563-1569.

8. R. M. Goldberg, J. Mabee, L. Chan, et al. *Drug-drug and drug-diseases interactions in the ED: Analysis of a High-Risk Population.* Am. J. Emerg. Med. 1996; 14(5):447-450.

9. J.M. Rothschild, W. Churchill, A. Erickson, et al. *Medication Errors Recovered by Emergency Department Pharmacists.* Ann. Emerg. Med. 2010; 55:513-521.

10. T. M. Nester, H.S. Ladonna. *Effectiveness of a pharmacist-acquired medication history in promoting patient safety.* Am. J. Health-Syst. Pharm. 2002; 59(22):2221-2225.

11. R.A. Rusnak, T.O. Stair, K. Hansen, et al. *Litigation against the emergency physician: common features in cases of missed myocardial infarction.* Ann. Emerg. Med. 1989; 18:1029-34.

12. A. Stiell, A.J. Forster, I.G. Stiell, et al. *Prevalence of information gaps in the emergency department and the effect on patient outcomes.* Canadian Assn. Med. J. 2003; 169:1023-1028.

13. W. A. Wingert, L.S. Chan, K. Steward, et al. *A study of quality prescriptions issued in a busy pediatric emergency room.* Public Health Rep. 1975. 90:402-408.

14. R. M. Elenbass, J.F. Waeckerle, W.K. McNabey. *The clinical pharmacist in emergency medicine.* Am. J. Hosp. Pharm. 1977; 34:843-846.

15. P. Lada, G. Delgado. *Documentation of pharmacists' interventions in an emergency department and associated cost avoidance.* Am. J. Health-Syst. Pharm. 2007; 64:63-68.

16. J.N. Brown, C.L. Barnes, B. Beasley, et al. *Effect of pharmacists on medication errors in an emergency department.* Am. J. Health-Syst. Pharm. 2008; 65:330-333.

17. C.A. Pedersen, P.J. Schneider, D.J. Scheckelgoff. *ASHP national survey of pharmacy practice in hospital settings: Dispensing and administration—2008;* Am. J. Health-Syst. Pharm. 2009; 66:926-946.

18. E. Schwerman, N. Schwartau, C.O. Thompson, et al. *The Pharmacist as a member of the cardiopulmonary resuscitation team.* Drug Intell. Clin. Pharm. 1973; 7:299-308.

19. H. M. Draper, J.A. Eppert. *Association of Pharmacist Presence on Compliance with Advanced Cardiac Life Support Guidelines During In-Hospital Cardiac Arrest.* Ann. Pharmacother. 2008; 42:469-474.

20. B. Carter. *How many of us provide pharmaceutical care.* Pharmacotherapy. 1997; 17(4):845-6.

21. T. C. Randolph. *Expansion of pharmacists' responsibilities in an emergency department.* Am. J. Health-Syst. Pharm. 2009; 66:1484-1487.

22. P. A. Czajka, V.A. Skoutakis, G.C. Wood. *Clinical toxicology consultation by pharmacists.* Am. J. Hosp. Pharm. 1979; 36:1087-1089.

23. C.P. Cannon. *Thrombolysis medication errors: benefits of bolus thrombolytic agents.* Am. J. Card. 2000; 85(8A):17C-22C.

24. V.A. Tam, S.R. Knowles, P.L. Cornish, et al. *Frequency, type and clinical importance of medication history errors at admission to hospital: a systematic review.* Canadian Assn. Med. J. 2005; 173:510-515.

25. M.K. Carter, D.M. Allin, L.A. Scott, D. Grauer. *Pharmacist-acquired medication histories in a university hospital emergency department.* Am. J. Health-Syst. Pharm. 2006; 63:2500-2503.

26. C.A. Bond, C.L. Raehl, T. Franke. *Clinical pharmacy services and hospital mortality rates.* Pharmacotherapy. 1999; 19:556-564.

27. B.D. Hayes, J.L Donovan, B.S. Smith, C.A. Hartman. *Pharmacist-conducted medication reconciliation in an emergency department.* Am. J. Health-Syst. Pharm. 2007; 64:1720-1723.

28. Berry NS, Folstad JE, Bauman JL, et al. Follow-up observations on 24-hour pharmacotherapy services in the emergency department. Ann Pharmacother 1992; 26: 476–480.

29. Powell MF, Solomon DK, McEachen RA. Twenty-four hour emergency pharmaceutical services. Am J Hosp Pharm. 1985; 42:831-5.

30. V.E. Aldridge, H.K. Park, M. Bounthavong, A. Morreale. *Implementing a comprehensive, 24-hour emergency department program.* Am. J. Health-Syst. Pharm. 2009; 66:1943-1947.

Chapter 40

The NABP Model Act and Rules Initiative toward Pharmacy Technicians

Ed Sweeney, Esq. and James T. O'Donnell, Pharm.D., M.S., FCP, ABCP, FACN, R.Ph.

40.1 Introduction

"Pharmacy technicians," and, more informally, "techs," are the names generically used to describe the estimated 200,000 pharmacy-support personnel who are employed in the United States to assist pharmacists in dispensing medication.[1-3] Notwithstanding the prevalence of pharmacy technicians and their importance to safe pharmacy-dispensing practice, little has been done on a systematic basis to ensure that technicians are licensed, regulated, trained, and properly educated.[4] With some notable exceptions, the regula-tion of pharmacy technicians has often been erratic and even nonexistent by the various boards of pharmacy—the administrative agencies responsible in each state jurisdiction for regulating pharmacy practice.

The National Association of Boards of Pharmacy (NABP) recently approved important revisions of its "Model Act" provisions, which, for the first time, comprehensively address the recognition, regulation, training, and education of various levels of pharmacy technicians.[5] As the national and international umbrella organization for 68 boards of pharmacy,[31] the NABP revisions to its Model Act reflect an important consensus by a respected preeminent authority as to issues connected with the practice of pharmacy in general, and with pharmacy-support personnel in particular.

The NABP MA&R is a milestone because it, rather belatedly, treats a major class of clinical workers with the detail and seriousness their role in the workplace deserves. Most of the revisions to the NABP MA&R are noncontroversial and are beneficial to the practice of pharmacy. The revisions provide solid guidelines to ensure that technicians are recognized as professionals and are adequately educated and trained. On a larger level, the NABP revisions foreshadow a movement away from the traditional notion of practice mores and responsibility in clinical settings, which has been synonymous with the practice and responsibility of pharmacists. This shift has important implications for the analysis of the future direction of legal responsibility in clinical settings.

The NABP revisions were undoubtedly influenced by the growing consensus among many commentators that the use of pharmacy technicians in the workplace should be liberalized and regularized to allow pharmacists to concentrate on tasks that require counseling, judgment, or discretion. There are several reasons for this growing consensus, including a greater acknowledgment that technicians are a valuable asset in the pharmacy, a shortage of pharmacists, market-driven pressures to reduce pharmaceutical costs, growing attention to medical errors, and a movement by some critics to allow technicians to check technicians (TCT).

In the authors' view, the NABP initiative deserves praise, and its revisions have greatly complemented earlier provisions towards technicians that can only be considered highly inadequate. Its most present serious flaw results from trying to accommodate two major conflicting points of view as to the role of technicians in clinical settings. Many commentators desired to greatly liberalize the use of pharmacy technicians in clinical settings, even to the extent of technicians checking technicians (TCT). Other, more traditional, observers thought that moving away from past notions of pharmacist responsibility in clinical settings would be a serious mistake.

The revised NABP MA&R attempted to please both camps in the debate by not clearly delineating its position on what is, perhaps, the most critical clinical issue: the extent of pharmacist supervision required over technicians. As this is perhaps the most important issue involving techs—both as a matter of clinical practice and as a matter of legal accountability—this failure should not be understated. This is decidedly uncharacteristic of the purpose behind a MA&R, which is to provide clear notice of expectations.

This problem has been made more glaring by two actions. First, the NABP recommended that boards of pharmacy eliminate pharmacist-to-technician ratios, a position which, although not new, was made once again concurrent with the revised MA&R. Second, the NABP took a more liberal approach to defining technician tasks than currently embodied by most state boards and by current mores. Surely, these actions can be taken as a signal on how to interpret the NABP MA&R provisions regarding pharmacist supervision of technician activity. The authors believe that eliminating the pharmacist-to-technician ratio is a radical proposal with the potential to fundamentally undermine a reasonable balance between pharmacist control and technician assistance in clinical settings.

This chapter analyzes the NABP pharmacy-technician initiative—from both a legal and practice perspective—and evaluates how successful the MA&R revisions are and what they may foreshadow for the future. In evaluating the NABP MA&R initiative, the authors are cognizant that there has been little written concerning standards for pharmacy technicians. Indeed, while the use of pharmacy technicians has existed for many years, it is somewhat surprising that little has been done in the way of systematically analyzing the legal boundaries applicable to technicians in clinical settings.

40.2 The Significance of the NABP "Model Act and Model Rules" Revisions

A "Model Act and Rules" (MA&R) is an exemplar of legal requirements that are thought appropriate to govern a profession. Simply put, a MA&R is drafted by a professional organization to set forth the standards and rules that are meant to govern everyday practice. State legislatures and agencies look to a MA&R when creating or revising their internal laws or regulations.

An important point to be made about a MA&R is that its provisions are meant to be used by various jurisdictions as substantive law. Once adopted by a jurisdiction as the law applicable to that particular state, pharmacy personnel will be responsible for adhering to the provisions of the MA&R. Thus, clarity and thoroughness are significant goals of any MA&R, as personnel who violate its provisions will be subject to sanction by a state board of pharmacy, including the suspension or termination of licenses to practice pharmacy.

MA&R provisions are not always simply a statement of contemporary mores and standards. Typically, most provisions that appear in a MA&R are present because they are universally agreed to reflect current practice and legal requirements. However, Model Act provisions are often put in place by organization leaders attempting to spur change that they think is appropriate for their profession. Thus, a MA&R can advocate future change and direction for everyday practice, and it is important to take note of what provisions embody current practice and what provisions are meant to change it.

Accordingly, the year 2000 NABP MA&R revisions regarding pharmacy technicians are very important to the present and future requirements for the practice of pharmacy. In one sense, the revised MA&R is an important reflection of what consensus exists in the pharmacy community towards pharmacy technicians and the clinical practice of pharmacy. In another real sense, the revised MA&R may be a push by leaders of the NABP towards a future direction for the practice of pharmacy. As the NABP is one of the most important national and international pharmacy organizations—composed of agencies responsible for regulating pharmacy practice to protect the public—the revisions are very important to anyone interested in pharmacy practice.

40.3 The Pharmacy Technician Phenomenon

Any discussion of pharmacy technicians logically starts with a definition. "Pharmacy technicians" is a generic title used loosely to describe the pharmacy-support personnel who clinically assist a pharmacist in filling prescriptions and stocking drugs.[2,4] Much like the term "nurses" is used to describe as a whole the various levels of nursing professionals (LPNs, RNs, and so on), "pharmacy technicians" refer to the body of pharmacy-support personnel who assist in dispensing medication. Other pharmacy-support personnel who perform nondispensing activities, such as pharmacy billing or the operation of a cash register, are typically not considered pharmacy technicians.

Pharmacy technicians, depending on their experience and the laws of a particular state, can select drugs off of a shelf, count pills and place them in a prescription vial, take orders for new prescriptions, refill prescriptions over the phone, input data into a computer system, and even prepare solutions.[4,6] In short, a pharmacy technician performs many of the same clinical tasks that pharmacists perform—particularly those of a routine nature that require little or no exercise of discretion or judgment. Typically, they are paid much less than a pharmacist. Pharmacy technicians command in the range of $6 to $12 per hour, depending on education, training, and experience. This is compared to the typical pharmacist's pay of $30 to $35 per hour.[7–9]

Pharmacies throughout the United States recognize different gradations of a pharmacy technician, with the nomenclature differing from clinical setting to clinical setting or from state to state. An entry-level technician is known in many settings as a "technician-in-training," a "pharmacy assistant," a "pharmacy aide," or a "pharmacy assistant apprentice," with the term "pharmacy technician" reserved for those who later reach a certain level of proven competence through education, experience, or testing.[8] Many other settings term their entry-level personnel "pharmacy technicians," with more advanced personnel being termed "certified pharmacy technicians."

The lack of uniform terms to describe the various gradations of pharmacy-support personnel can lead to confusion and imprecision. Fortunately, the NABP recognized that definitional problems exist and made a concerted effort in its proposed Model Act to provide guidance and to recommend uniform terminology.

40.4 The History of U.S. Pharmacy Technicians in Clinical Settings

The history of pharmacy practice in the United States helps to explain the origin and current treatment of pharmacy technicians. "Pharmacy technician" is a term and profession of recent origin. It is a term that was devised to reflect a reality that gradually came to exist.

The history of pharmacy practice in the United States has been the history of the rise and growth as a profession of pharmacists. The pre-1776 European physicians who came to the New World to settle did not bring with them a concept of pharmacy as a separate profession from that of the physicians.[10] Physicians who settled our country would prepare and administer their own medications to patients. However, over time, as drugs became more complex to compound, a separate profession developed.[10] Druggists, the forerunners of pharmacists, performed their occupations largely by extemporaneously compounding medications. Their tasks were primarily product-oriented, and their expertise lay in compounding (at a physician's request) the correct medication ingredients to produce the intended result.

These druggists eventually formed local associations, where ideas of greater professionalism were promoted.[10] By the end of the nineteenth century, most states had enacted laws to regulate the practice of pharmacy.[10] State laws would later establish state boards of pharmacy, whose general mission was to ensure the safety of the public. As current mores indicated that the pharmacy practice was the practice of pharmacists, the individuals with the expertise to compound medications, state boards fulfilled their role by regulating pharmacist practice. Underlying the regulation of pharmacy practice was the notion that public safety required strict regulation, in terms of how pharmacists dispense and store medications (because medications are potentially lethal and addictive).

The widespread use of pharmacy technicians is a phenomenon that has occurred over the last 20 to 30 years. While many factors can explain the advent of pharmacy technicians, perhaps the most significant factor facilitating their use is the development of prepared medications that can be dispensed without mixing or compounding. Most medications are now pre-prepared on a mass basis in factories in pill or liquid form, and are sold in bottles or vials. In hospital settings, pills are also often purchased in individual packets know as "unit doses" which contain a single dosage and are clearly labeled. The mass production of pre-prepared medication makes clinical dispensing easier and more routine, and sets the stage for the use of pharmacy-support personnel.

The original use of pharmacy-support personnel has a somewhat clandestine origin. Given that mixing ingredients was, at one time, the major activity performed in a clinical setting, the conventional governing wisdom was that pharmacists were the only individuals competent to practice pharmacy, given their expertise in compounding medications and providing clinical advice. Indeed, the use of pharmacy-support personnel was of questionable legal validity, according to the following excerpt from the *National Association of Boards of Pharmacy Newsletter*:

If technicians were involved, they were out of sight and seldom visible even to board of pharmacy inspections. They were not legally recognized or defined by the majority of states, and, in those states where technicians were recognized, their use was tightly regulated through pharmacist to technician ratios, usually 1:1 in retail settings and 1:2 in hospital settings.[11]

Only over the last 30 to 40 years have pharmacy-support personnel grown into a regular part of pharmaceutical dispensing practice. Their growing use was reflected by organizations willing to recognize or promote their use. Over 40 years ago, the United States Army established a program for training "pharmacy specialists."[12] During the 1950s, increasing mention of the need for pharmacy-support personnel was mentioned in the literature.[12] In the 1960s, pharmacy technicians were the topic of significant discussion, with important professional and governmental organizations starting to endorse their use.[12,32] In the 1970s, the use of pharmacy technicians in hospitals became commonplace.[6] In 1974, the governing board of the American Society of Hospital Pharmacists (ASHP) supported the development of regulations for the safe use of pharmacy-support personnel.[12] In 1977, the ASHP published a "Manual for Hospital Pharmacy Technicians, A Programmed Course in Basic Skills."[12] In May 1980, the NABP recommended that supportive personnel "be trained and qualified according to the standards set by the responsible pharmacist...."[12] By the 1980s, national studies by ASHP showed that 75 percent of all hospitals responding used technicians.[12] The growth of technicians throughout this period can be characterized very much as a grassroots, "bottom-up" movement, where the demand for pharmacy-support personnel eventually overcame the reluctance of state boards to formally recognize them.

The growing reliance on technicians has not been without some tension, as there are those who strongly feel that "technicians" were being allowed to perform too many tasks, at the expense of the highly trained and educated pharmacists.[12] State boards have not been reluctant to step in and discipline pharmacies or pharmacists who permitted technicians to overstep their boundaries. In 1998, an Associated Press analysis of disciplinary records for all 50 states showed that state boards of pharmacy disciplined drug stores and druggists 75 times for letting technicians do tasks reserved for pharmacists.[4]

Commentators generally agree that there are certain activities that pharmacy-support personnel should not undertake in dispensing medication. One dividing line that is traditional and without controversy is that pharmacists, alone, are qualified to perform tasks which require judgment or discretion.[6] Thus, only pharmacists have been considered qualified to analyze the potential for drug interactions, to counsel patients, and to discuss drug therapy with physicians. Another dividing line is that the ultimate dispensing authority is solely the responsibility of the pharmacist's. While exactly what this means has become somewhat more blurred in recent years, it certainly implies that pharmacists should have supervisory responsibility over the dispensing process and perform final checks on prescriptions. There are many other tasks that rely on training and background, such as compounding mediation and taking prescriptions over the phone, where there is disagreement among practitioners as to the proper level of technician involvement.[6]

40.5 A Pharmacist-Centered Legal and Regulatory System

In regulating the practice of pharmacy, it is not surprising that, traditionally, states have focused their efforts almost exclusively toward pharmacists. Pharmacists have traditionally been seen as central to the dispensing process, with their educational experience as a prerequisite for compounding medications or for recognizing the potential for adverse drug interactions. Also, states have ensured the safety of the public by requiring that the much more rigorously trained and educated pharmacist be responsible individually to clinically dispense medications.

The common law has followed the lead of the state regulatory focus on the pharmacist in developing rules of liability for negligence. Under the common law in every jurisdiction, a pharmacist is ultimately held responsible for any errors in the dispensing of medication. "The pharmacist must maintain control over the various technical tasks and the right to determine those functions that the technician is qualified to perform.[12] Much like a captain of a ship, the negligence of subordinates is attributable to the pharmacist. Even when a technician has committed a dispensing error, the common law has viewed liability in terms of whether the pharmacist has properly supervised the technician (if so, she should have caught the dispensing error).[12]

In theory, the pharmacist's duty of care is to act with the level of education, skill, and training generally possessed by other competent pharmacists in the profession. In regard to dispensing medications, courts have been particularly sensitive to the pharmacist's responsibility for ensuring the safety of the public, confirmed by each state's pharmacy statute and regulations. The pharmacist's duty of care has been described by courts as "a high degree of care" or "great care." In practice, it is generally accepted that a pharmacist breaches the duty of care by allowing a prescription to leave a pharmacy other than the way it was ordered by a physician.[1] This sentiment led two leading authorities, Richard R. Abood and David R. Brushwood, to comment,

As a practical matter, pharmacists may be the only health care professionals who are legally required to practice in a completely-error-free manner. Pharmacists have traditionally adopted a "no mistakes" approach to practice, and legal standards have reflected this impossible-to-achieve and self-imposed standard.[1]

The rigorous notion of the necessary standard of care in pharmaceutical dispensing derives from several factors that are important to an analysis of how to appropriately regulate technicians. First of all, the product-oriented tradition of the practice of pharmacy has led to the notion that prescription drugs are highly dangerous commodities requiring rigid—if not fastidious—control. Second, as sequelae to this notion, the law and regulations promulgated in various states often require a pharmacist to dispense medications in a completely error-free manner. Courts often look to—and even adopt state statutes and regulations as evidence of—the standard of care. Lastly, there is a tradition that the standard of care is commensurate with the arduous education and training given to pharmacists and the trust placed on them as part of their monopoly on pharmaceutical dispensing.

Pharmacy-technician regulation was unknown 30 years ago, and has been a long-neglected area of pharmacy practice. Regulation of pharmacy technicians has been, in many states, an afterthought; and in the states where it existed, it was oriented towards establishing that technicians must perform their work under the direct supervision of a pharmacist. The baseline assumption that informed technician regulation has been that technicians have little or no technical competence above the average layperson.

It is not surprising that the regulation concerning pharmacy technicians has been primarily one of prohibition rather than facility. State pharmacy-practice laws are more interested in defining what technicians should not do rather than assuring they have the competence to go beyond routine tasks. Indeed, the many state pharmacy practice laws, at one time, did not always even explicitly authorize practice by technicians.[1] Rather, these states only implicitly permitted it by defining what duties a pharmacist must perform and leaving it to the discretion of the individual pharmacist concerning what pharmacy tasks the technicians would perform.[1]

A "though shall not" rather than a "thou shall" approach to pharmacy technicians made sense at one time. Ensuring that technicians were treated as professionals had little urgency if they performed minor, ministerial duties in a pharmacy and worked one-on-one with the pharmacist. More-over, given the lack of a demand for educated or trained technicians, neither the private nor public sector possessed the institutional capacity on a wide-enough scale to educate technicians or assure their competence through testing. Until recently, pharmacy education was limited to college-level private and public universities, and the only degree available was a bachelor of science and now a doctor of pharmacy (Pharm.D.). Arguably, viewing technicians as no different from the average layperson has hindered their development into a viable professional organization with different gradations of achievement (similar to the LPNs, RNs, and so on).

The authors opine that a technician's role in the current workplace calls for education and training—even where the individual is limited to performing "ministerial" tasks. With regard to technicians, the word "ministerial" should in no way imply that a pharmacy technician's role is one that does not require thought or is other than complex. There are hundreds of drugs on the market, most having both a generic name and a brand name. For the technician to perform his job safely, he must have a variety of skills. A technician must have a good memory and must be careful not to confuse drugs or dosages (many of which often sound or look alike). Computer skills are important for a technician to possess. Moreover, the ability to decipher the handwriting on a prescription or a medical chart is helpful. Finally, the technician needs to receive strong training in procedures that make clear the appropriate interaction between the technician and the pharmacist. In practice, proper accountability results from all workplace team members knowing exactly what role they play, as well as how each individual will execute her responsibilities.

40.6 Current Technician Training, Education, Licensing, and Regulation

Pharmacy-technician training, education, licensing, and regulation have always been a state (as opposed to a federal) issue. States have done a generally poor job of setting requirements to facilitate the development of technicians as professionals. Indeed, in many states, there is no requirement that the technician be trained or educated. An individual can become a pharmacy technician by simply walking into a pharmacy and applying for a position.[4] While most states do attempt to regulate the practice of technicians, this is done primarily by requiring pharmacists to prevent technicians from overreaching and performing clinical tasks reserved for pharmacists. This section looks at the current education and training, licensing, and regulation required by state boards of pharmacy.

A. Pharmacy Technician Education and Training

Pharmacy technicians have received varied treatment under the regulatory systems in each U.S. state, district and commonwealth. Twenty-six jurisdictions out of the 50 U.S. states, Puerto Rico, the District of Columbia, and Guam do not require any pharmacy-technician training.

Of the states that do require technician training, there are several different approaches taken. Most states have a decentralized approach to training. In some states, training requirements are developed by pharmacists and are subsequently approved by the state boards of pharmacy. In at least one other state, a pharmacist-in-charge is responsible for providing technicians with appropriate training.

Thus, the training requirements are minimal and typically depend on the extent of the training employed at individual pharmacies. Several states follow a variation of the pre-2000 NABP Model Act's proposed regulation, which makes each workplace responsible for devising its own training program.

Notwithstanding the lack of mandatory requirements, many technicians have attempted to further their marketability by passing a certifying examination. Of the estimated 200,000 technicians in the United States, approximately 30 percent have taken and passed the exam developed by the Pharmacy Technician Certification Board (PTCB), a voluntary accreditation program.[13]

B. Licensing, Registering, and Certifying Technicians

The issue of licensing, registration, and certification is of extreme importance to the development of pharmacy technicians as a profession.

A license allows an individual to practice in a regulated profession.[12] The benefit of a license is that it typically provides a state regulatory body with the power to withdraw or suspend the license for misconduct.[12] Registration, in comparison, is a lesser requirement which obliges an individual to file with the regulatory body certain basic information, such as name, address, and phone number.[12] Registration is typically a means by which the qualifications of an individual can be verified.[12]

Both licensing and registration are important, because both systems allow jurisdictions to monitor individuals who are incompetent, who commit theft, or are drug and alcohol abusers. This is particularly important for individuals who attempt to flee the repercussions of their actions by moving to other states. According to the 2000–2001 NABP Survey of Pharmacy Law, the only five jurisdictions that require pharmacy technicians to be licensed are Alaska, Maine,

Utah, Washington and Wyoming.[5] Fewer than half of U.S. jurisdictions even require technicians to be registered.[5]

Certification is fundamentally different in nature from licensure or registration, in that it typically involves the activity of a nongovernmental agency or association.[12] Certification is granted by the nonpublic entity to those individuals who meet specific qualifications in all practice areas encompassed by an occupation.[12] A governmental entity can require certification as a condition of practice.

Only one state, Wyoming, has passed a law that considers support personnel "technicians in training" until they pass a certifying exam. Another state, Texas, has required technicians to pass the national PTCB exam, effective January 1, 2001, although there is indication that Texas is backing away from this requirement, due to the enormity of the task.[14]

C. Regulation of Technician Clinical Tasks

The regulation of pharmacy technicians' clinical tasks has been erratic until quite recently. As late as 1991, 25 states did not even legally recognize pharmacy technicians.[15] Twenty-three of the 25 states during that year, however, acknowledged that although technicians were not legally recognized, they were currently used in pharmacy practice.[15] Since that time, only in Ohio is the use of pharmacy technicians not recognized in law or regulation.[5]

Most states have allowed pharmacy technicians to perform "ministerial" clinical tasks in the dispensing process.[6] "Ministerial" refers to routine tasks not requiring judgment or discretion.[6] Tasks generally accepted as ministerial and within the ability of experienced technicians include preparing prescription labels, entering prescriptions on the computer, retrieving medication from stock, placing medications into the container, and placing a prescription label on the container.[5,6,9]

The clinical tasks considered "ministerial" are subject to debate at the margin. Distinctions as to appropriate tasks are not always easy to draw, particularly in the areas of taking new or refill prescriptions and compounding medications. While counseling physicians and patients about medications is obviously beyond the ability of technicians, the aforementioned tasks often rely on a pharmacist's education, training, and even judgment.

There appears to be almost universal agreement among various jurisdictions that a pharmacy technician should be prohibited from accepting a prescription from a physician over the phone.[5] There are rare exceptions, and these exceptions have safeguards. One state, Tennessee, allows the practice, but requires that it be performed only by a certified pharmacy technician.[5] The majority (fewer than ten) of the other jurisdictions that allow the practice require immediate supervision or verification of the new prescription by a pharmacist.[5] Informing the majority approach appears to be a belief that taking a new prescription over the phone poses inherent risk of miscommunication. It is thought that only a pharmacist is in a position to minimize this risk to acceptable levels. The authors strongly agree with this conventional wisdom.

Interestingly, jurisdictions are much more divided as to whether technicians should be allowed to communicate with physicians regarding refill prescriptions. The overwhelming number of jurisdictions allows such contacts, but many of these jurisdictions have, at the same time, restricted the communications to circumstances where the prescription is unchanged and no counseling is necessary.[5]

A similarly balanced approach is typically taken with regard to whether technicians should be allowed to compound medication for dispensing.[5] While most jurisdictions allow technicians to compound medication, a large subset of the majority appear to require immediate supervision or verification of the technicians by a pharmacist.[5]

40.7 Expanding Reliance on Pharmacy-Support Personnel

The attempt of the NABP to comprehensively address the issue of pharmacy-support personnel is part and parcel of the expanding need for and reliance on non-pharmacists in the workplace. This appears to result, in part, from a well-publicized shortage of pharmacists, which has been described as "moderate to critical." Also, reliance on non-pharmacists appears to derive from a conscious decision by hospital and community pharmacies to cut costs.

Pharmacists are currently faced with a greatly expanding workload with shrinking numbers. According to the National Association of Chain Drug Stores, the number of prescriptions filled each year has doubled in only ten years from 1.5 billion in 1989 to 3 billion in 1999.[16] During the same time, the number of pharmacists rose only 5 percent, from 171,000 to 180,00.[16] The shortage of pharmacists is expected to become an even more serious problem. In 2004, the number of prescriptions filled is expected to jump to 4 billion a year, a 33 percent jump from the 1999 level.[16]

The dramatic increase in the use of prescription drugs has led to rapid growth for pharmacy technicians. A national study of general medical-surgical hospitals in the United States from 1989 to 1998, based in part on data from National Clinical Pharmacy Services (NCPS), indicates that there was a 15-percent increase in use of pharmacy technicians, while noting that over the same period, the increase in pharmacists was much slower.[17] And in the last seven years,

the use of pharmacists actually decreased.[17] While noting that further study was needed, the report declared that "[I]n view of the lack of growth in the number of pharmacists… it is possible that pharmacists are being replaced by less well trained pharmacy personnel."[17] The report concluded, "[t]hese trends in pharmacy staffing may have implications for pharmacy's ability to deliver pharmaceutical care."[17]

Driving the need for pharmacy technicians has also been the shrinkage of profit margins.[7] Third-party payors are imposing ever-lower reimbursement rates on pharmacies.[7] Notwithstanding pressures to cut costs, counseling requirements imposed on pharmacists by the federal government under OBRA take valuable time away from the pharmacist during the workday. The increased use of pharmacy technicians allows much of the manual labor of a pharmacist to be performed by someone who commands only one-third of the hourly rate of a pharmacist. The pharmacy technician is intended to bring relief from routine tasks, freeing up the pharmacist for supervision, cognitive tasks, and counseling patients. This allows a pharmacy to fill more prescriptions at a lower cost, which leads to increased profit.

In community pharmacies, the phenomenon of the increase in the employment of pharmacy technicians has not always been a success story, and has been critically noted.[16,18–19] In certain pharmacy settings where the bottom line (as opposed to patient safety) is stressed, the use of pharmacy technicians can increase safety problems, wherein the technicians are used as a stop-gap solution to fundamental problems with pharmacist staffing and quality.

40.8 The Tech-Check-Tech (TCT) Debate

A significant backdrop to the pharmacy-technician revisions to the NABP MA&R is the Tech-Check-Tech, or TCT, debate. There has been considerable impetus among commentators and some practitioners to have legal restrictions revoked so that technicians can check the work of technicians' filling prescriptions, particularly in a hospital setting.[6,14,20–22] The stated goal of these commentators is to free up pharmacists to perform tasks that require judgment and to counsel physicians and patients.[12]

This change would profoundly affect the current system of regulation and legal accountability by making technicians either solely or primarily responsible for dispensing. Any discussion of pharmacy-technician regulation has to address whether, and to what extent, TCT will be an accepted norm.

Under the TCT proposal, the dispensing process would be managed by technicians, who would be responsible for checking each other's work. In its most radical form, TCT does not envision supervision by a pharmacist. A more moderate version of TCT would have technicians performing all dispensing functions, including checking, up to the final check, which would be performed by a pharmacist.[23] Simply put, proponents of TCT wish to abandon the pharmacist as the primary focus of the dispensing process and rely either solely or primarily on technicians to fill prescriptions and to check their accuracy.[24]

TCT has its origin in the belief that pharmacists are over-trained for the typical tasks performed in the dispensing process. Proponents of the TCT assert that the changing role of hospital pharmacists requires their availability to participate as part of a clinical team, along with physicians and nurses. TCT frees pharmacists from the allegedly mundane tasks of filling prescriptions, and allows them to participate in judgmental, patient-oriented functions.[24] Focusing on the current shortage of pharmacists, advocates state that practice should be sufficiently liberalized so that technicians can fill the gap created by market conditions.

TCT proponents also claim that their proposal simply reflects pharmacy as it is being practiced today. Arguing that many pharmacies already bend—if not actually break—the rules regarding technicians in various states, proponents urge that relevant pharmacy law should be made current, to recognize what already goes on in many settings. According to these commentators, technicians are already filling prescriptions and checking fellow technicians' work, with little or no pharmacist oversight,[24] which would be a clear violation of the standard of care in nearly every jurisdiction—a dangerous situation for patients, in the authors' opinion.[24]

In hospital settings, particularly, it is argued that less-stringent regulatory requirements are appropriate, because hospitals typically have rigorous quality-assurance standards in the form of hospital rules, regulations, practices, and accreditation standards.[24] Typically, nurses dispense medication in a hospital setting, which provides an additional (presumably competent) layer of monitoring. Moreover, most hospitals have moved to the individualized packaging system of unit dose, which makes it easier for both pharmacy personnel and other hospital staff to recognize dispensing errors.

Although this topic has generated heated debate, TCT has not gained acceptance with state boards or rank-and-file practitioners. Only two states currently permit TCT—Minnesota and Washington. Both states permit TCT in hospital settings (as opposed to in-community pharmacies).[24] Moreover, a survey performed by *Drug Topics/Hospital Pharmacy Report* indicates that only 20 percent of community and hospital pharmacists want their state boards of pharmacy to let techs do more.[9] The survey further found that only one in five community pharmacists endorsed TCT, while a majority of hospital pharmacists are comfortable with it.[9]

From a legal standpoint, one serious deficiency with TCT is that pharmacy practice has been treated as being synonymous with the practice of pharmacists. As TCT is really about the practice of pharmacy being performed primarily by technicians, TCT would involve a fundamental change to the regulation of pharmacy practice in the United States. To achieve TCT, the public and its elected representatives would have to be persuaded that quality and standards would not decline.

Second, a serious concern is whether technicians can perform the high degree of oversight necessary to dispense medication.[9] Pharmacy practice is highly regulated, because it involves dangerous and addictive medications. Opponents warn that current experience has shown that many pharmacy technicians do their tasks mechanically, and are not nearly as proficient or knowledgeable as pharmacists.[9] Technicians simply have not been required to receive the education and training necessary to ensure public safety, and the regulation of technicians has not advanced beyond a preliminary stage.

Finally, pharmacists have significant incentive to protect their licenses, because of the investment they have placed in their careers, while technicians do not have similar incentives.[9] A simple, yet profound, point is that pharmacists have a much greater incentive to act with a high level of care to maintain a license that took five years or more study to acquire and that guarantees them a well-paying position in a respected profession. The authors of this article agree that some, but not all, of TCT arguments have a level of persuasiveness about them. The central focus of TCT is to expand the use of technicians, and this is a commendable goal, but the old adage "the devil is in the details" applies. One can concede that technicians can participate in checking other technicians' work without divorcing the pharmacist from monitoring and being professionally accountable for the dispensing process. The authors believe that absent state law to the contrary, the national standard of care is that a pharmacist should—at the very least—perform the final check, perform spot checks, and supervise the manner and method of technician performance.

The most persuasive argument for TCT is that it makes much more sense in a hospital with unit doses and a well-trained nursing staff. A modified version of TCT is acceptable in this setting, because sufficient checks and balances can be implemented to adequately safeguard the public. The authors opine that the standard of care dictates that at least "final checks" should be performed by a pharmacist.[31] To a certain extent, with adequate controls and quality control and assurance, limited TCT may be allowable in the community pharmacy setting.

Not nearly as a persuasive argument is the "reality" is that TCT already exists, and the law should reflect reality. While the authors have no doubt that pharmacies may bend state regulations at the margin, it is not normative in current practice to divorce pharmacists from checking prescriptions. Further, even if some pharmacies ignore state laws requiring pharmacist control, the authors do not see this as a reason for anything but a need for severe discipline of the pharmacists, technicians, and pharmacies involved. TCT probably does exist in some workplaces, and a modified form with a highly trained and monitored staff may provide adequate safeguards for the consuming public. However, totally divorcing a pharmacist from the dispensing process—even in a hospital setting—seems misguided.

The United States legal system has demanded standards commensurate with the potential risk of harm. Traditionally, state boards of pharmacies were created because the compounding, dispensing, and storing of potentially dangerous and addictive medications were thought necessary for public safety. It is not clear whether the commentators who support TCT fundamentally dispute that there is a high degree of danger with allowing nonpharmacists to control the dispensing process. At the root of TCT may be the inaccurate presumption that pre-prepared medication obviates the need for pharmacists to be active in the normal routine steps that make up the dispensing process.[32]

40.9 National Focus on Dispensing Errors

The NABP action on pharmacy-technician regulation comes as a backdrop to growing recognition of the importance of medical errors and error reporting to patient care. The Institute for Safe Medication Practice's (ISHP) "To Err is Human" report galvanized medical and pharmaceutical communities into greater attention to error reduction by detailing that medication errors may kill as many as 98,000 hospitalized patients a year.[25] Those reports, studies, and surveys have supported the need for greater education, training, and regulation.

In a recent report commissioned by the Virginia Assembly in 1998, the state board of pharmacy noted that pharmacists found that their technicians made an average of 6.5 errors per week,[3] in a system where pharmacists made the final check. In another study performed by U.S. Pharmacopoeia of Rockville, Maryland, half of the 314 errors found in the study were made by technicians and went undetected by pharmacists.[4]

A recent survey of the Pharmacy Technician's Educators Commission found basic agreement that the length of pharmacy-technician training should be standardized.[13] They further agreed that minimum standards should be es-

tablished for pharmacy technicians, with required examinations for certification or licensure.

Concern over the number of errors made by pharmacy-support personnel is appropriate, and should prompt the establishment of training, mandatory education, and further regulation. The current lack of controls has caused major tragedies—tragedies that might have been averted had technicians been aware of their appropriate role in the dispensing process, and by the establishment and enforcement of appropriate supervision.

For instance, in a Walgreen's pharmacy in Port Richey, Florida, a tech violated the fundamental rule that pharmacy-support personnel should not give advice concerning medication. The technician told a questioning mother to ignore a special warning regarding pediatric use of compazine on a vial, "because all children can use compazine." The child sustained a learning disability as a result of the technician's conduct, having mistakenly dispensed an adult dose of the drug.[4]

Violating the fundamental rule that a only a pharmacist may dispense medication, a Parkersburg, West Virginia, pharmacy technician mistakenly dispensed an antidepressant medication in the pharmacist's absence, fraudulently logging the pharmacist's initials into the computer. The customer was given ten times the correct dose and is now so disoriented that she cannot even dress herself.[4]

In another case, where the court allowed a punitive damage count, the plaintiff went to have a doxepin prescription refilled, but was given loxapine succinct instead. She questioned whether the drug was a generic, or whether it might have been issued in error, and asked the clerk to verify with the pharmacist that the drug was correct. The clerk pretended to check with the pharmacist (but did not) and told the patient that the pharmacist had given assurance that the medication was correct.[26]

These highly publicized tragedies—along with the reports, studies, and statistics—confirm the need for greater attention to pharmacy-technician regulation.

40.10 Previous NABP Model Act Provisions Relating to Pharmacy Technicians

The current revisions to the NABP MA&R provision relating to pharmacy technicians are vastly superior to the previous version, which can best be described as regulations in an infancy stage.

Characteristic of a traditional, pharmacist-oriented view of the dispensing process, the previous NABP MA&R stated that pharmacists were responsible for having "personal and direct" supervision over pharmacy technicians.[5] This traditional "personal and direct" requirement was found in the law or regulations of numerous states, which required "immediate," "direct," or "personal" supervision of technicians.

The previous MA&R made no attempt to define different levels of pharmacy-support personnel, simply deeming all of them "pharmacy technicians." It did not define different gradations of pharmacy technicians. Nor did it set any educational or uniform training requirements to work as a pharmacy technician.

The basic method for regulating technicians in the previous MA&R was a quality-assurance (QA) program. Under the previous MA&R provisions relating to technicians, each pharmacist-in-charge of a pharmacy was responsible for designing a technician manual with guidelines for technicians, reviewing it with technicians, and assuring the relevant state boards that the technicians understood their responsibilities.[27] The previous MA&R provisions delegated total responsibility to each individual pharmacy for technician training and control. This approach may have been dictated by the lack of an infrastructure to deal with technician issues.

In the author's view, the former NABP MA&R approach toward technician regulation met at least one basic principle one would expect of a MA&R—namely, it provided advance notice of expectations to interested individuals. Proponents might also say that its strength was a radical decentralization (because each pharmacy was to determine the most appropriate structure for its own technicians). This approach was the antithesis of a "one-size-fits-all" approach, and diverse ways of regulating and training techs have emerged as a result.

Critics of this approach usually note that a MA&R typically sets forth what a profession believes are—or should be—the standards for professional practice. In contrast, the past MA&R took a decentralized approach rather uncharacteristic of a "Model Act." One of the criticisms of this approach is that it promulgated little (if any) state regulation. Rather, it is state delegation to individual pharmacies to set their own standards, with the state (presumably) monitoring whether each pharmacy designs and follows its own standards. Since there is controversy in the several states as to what technicians can and cannot do, one could criticize the previous MA&R as failing to set forth basic standards. Furthermore, in practice, such radical decentralization would seem to make it difficult for state boards of pharmacy to monitor compliance and/or to evaluate the significance of a pharmacy's failure to implement or stick to a QA program.[33] Even though pharmacy-technician regulation was in an infancy stage, this approach to technician regulation was fundamentally flawed from a legal and accountability perspec-

tive. It turned out to be a significant failure, as proved by the ultimate test of a MA&R—few state boards of pharmacy actually implemented the approach.

40.11 Internal NABP Debate on Pharmacy Technician Regulation

The NABP engaged in an internal debate about revising the NABP Model Act and Regulations to deal more extensively with pharmacy-technician practice.[28] The goal was to delineate activities that could and could not be performed by technicians, to define the types of technicians that exist in the workforce, and to determine what sort of interaction must be required with a pharmacist. One facet of this debate is a pharmacist shortage—placing the issue of expanded roles for technicians under a spotlight. Presumably, the fact that this debate is going on is also tacit recognition that the current MA&R does not go far enough and is too decentralized in scope.

The NABP Task Force on Standardization of Technicians' Role and Competencies was responsible for reviewing, in the first instance, the issue of pharmacy-technician regulation.[28] The task force was granted a broad mandate to look at the appropriate role for pharmacy technicians, determine the need for new model regulations, examine whether minimal educational and credentialing standards should be recommended, review the barriers to expansion of technician roles, and come up with a recommendation on whether or not an expanded role was appropriate.

The task force advocated the adoption of three levels of responsibility, including "pharmacy assistant," "pharmacy technician," and "certified pharmacy technician."[28] It also recommended that the program in each pharmacy be overseen and maintained by a licensed pharmacist and that a quality-assurance (QA) plan be put in place (as a means for addressing the increased responsibility and decreased supervision of technicians).[28] The task force reiterated the NABP recommendation that state boards eliminate the pre-determined ratio of pharmacists to technicians in pharmacies with a QA plan in place. Currently, most states require that for every two technicians working in the pharmacy, there be at least one pharmacist supervising them.[28]

The recommendations of this task force regarding technicians was echoed by the NABP Task Force on Manpower Shortage, which promoted the elimination of pharmacist-to-technician ratios and endorsed the delegation of all dispensing functions to pharmacy technicians (with the exception of the final check)."[28] The NABP Task Force of Manpower Shortage further recommended that pharmacists be primarily responsible for tasks requiring judgment, such as drug-utilization review and counseling.[28]

The NABP Committee on Law Enforcement/Legislation also weighed in on technician regulation. The committee took a more conservative approach to technician regulation.[28] While the committee concurred that the roles of pharmacy-support personnel should be delineated in the NABP Model Act, it disagreed with the levels of responsibility assigned to such personnel.[28] The committee advocated NABP recognizing the "certified pharmacy technician" and the "pharmacy technician" levels of support personnel, as well as outlining the activities such personnel may not perform.[28] However, the committee did not endorse the concept of a "pharmacy assistant." The committee further strongly recommended that the pharmacist maintain responsibility for all activities within the pharmacy.[28]

40.12 Regulation of Pharmacy Technicians under the Revised NABP Model Act

The revised NABP MA&R provides, in contrast to the previous MA&R, a concerted attempt to comprehensively and uniformly address the regulation of pharmacy technicians.

The NABP adopted the suggestion of the Committee on Law Enforcement Regulation by dividing pharmacy-support personnel into two levels—pharmacy technician and certified pharmacy technician. Both appear in the definitional sections of the NABP MA&R, which clearly state the activities that each gradation of pharmacy technician is prohibited from performing.

The definition of "pharmacy technician reads" is as follows:

"Pharmacy Technician" means personnel registered with the Board as defined in Article III of this Act, and allowed, under the supervision of a Pharmacist, to perform the activities involved in the Practice of Pharmacy, except that a Pharmacy Technician may not perform the following activities: drug utilization review; clinical conflict resolution; prescriber contact concerning prescription drug order clarification or therapy modification; patient counseling; dispensing process validation; receive new Prescription Drug Orders; prescription transfer; and compounding.

The definition of "certified pharmacy technician" reads as follows:

"Certified Pharmacy Technician" means personnel registered with the Board as defined in Article III of this Act, and allowed, under the supervision of a Pharmacist, to perform the activities involved in the Practice of Pharmacy, except that a Certified Pharmacy Technician may not perform the following activities: drug utilization review; clinical conflict resolution; prescriber contact concerning prescription drug order clarification or therapy modification; patient counseling; dispensing process validation; receive new Prescription Drug Orders when communicating telephonically or electronically unless the original information is recorded so the Pharmacist may review the Prescription Drug Order as transmitted.

Thus, the revised MA&R affords technicians the ability to perform all activities of pharmacy practice except for certain prohibited tasks that are specifically set forth. The main difference between the two types of technicians is that certified technicians could receive new prescription drug orders under certain circumstances, transfer prescriptions, and compound.

The delineation of tasks by the NABP goes somewhat beyond current practice.

In most states, technicians are allowed to prepare prescription labels, enter prescriptions into a pharmacy computer, enter information into a patient's file, retrieve medication from stock, place medication into the prescription container, place the prescription label on the container, and call physicians for refill authorization. Most states, however, prohibit a technician from accepting a prescription called in from a physician's office.

One aspect to the NABP revisions that should be noted is that the personal level of pharmacist supervision required over technicians has not changed much, if any. As noted in an earlier section, the past version of the NABP MA&R defined pharmacy technicians as support personnel who operated under the "personal and direct" supervision of a pharmacist. The words "personal and direct" have been deleted in the current definitions of pharmacy technicians, so that the MA&R more generically calls for both types of technicians to work under the "supervision" of a pharmacist. While the NABP Model Act has been modified to delete the words "personal and direct," the Model Rules have not been made parallel.

The revised NABP MA&R does, however, require that each pharmacy—through its pharmacist-in-charge—set written policies and procedures specifying that both types of technicians are to be personally and directly supervised by a pharmacist. The pharmacist must be stationed within the same work area as the certified pharmacy technicians and pharmacy technicians, and must have the ability to control and be responsible for the activities of the technicians.

The Pharmacist-in-Charge shall develop and implement written policies and procedures to specify the duties to be performed by Certified Pharmacy Technicians and Pharmacy Technicians. The duties and responsibilities of these personnel shall be consistent with their training and experience. These policies and procedures shall, at a minimum, specify that Certified Pharmacy Technicians and Pharmacy Technicians are to be personally and directly supervised by a Pharmacist stationed within the same work area who has the ability to control and who is responsible for the activities of Certified Pharmacy Technicians and Pharmacy Technicians, and that Certified Pharmacy Technicians and Pharmacy Technicians are not assigned duties that may be performed only by a Pharmacist. Such policies and procedures shall also specify that Pharmacy Technicians shall not be assigned duties that may be performed only by Certified Pharmacy Technicians.

The authors note that in light of the above provision, the deletion in the definitional section in the current version of the MA&R appears not to signal a radical departure from the past.

40.13 Training, Education, Certification, Registration, and Licensing under the Revised NABP Model Act

The revised NABP Model Act makes no change for entry-level technicians. A pharmacy technician is required to complete a training program conducted pursuant to a pharmacy-technician training manual and successfully complete an objective assessment mechanism prepared in accordance with the state board of pharmacy. The NABP presumably envisions that individuals hired to be trained as technicians will be given a structured program of "on-the-job" training, after which they will be tested with an objective assessment mechanism devised by the pharmacy. The NABP MA&R's aforementioned definition of "pharmacy technician" makes much more sense, if one assumes that there will be rigorous training and testing before an individual is named a pharmacy technician. A newly hired individual is not competent to perform all the routine duties of a pharmacy technician, such as type prescription labels, count out pills, or enter information into a patient's file. To the neophyte with no prior experience of drug names, usual dosages, or the dispensing routine, pharmacy practice is often confusing and complex. In the writers' experience, until they become more experienced with the mores and customs of the workplace,

entry-level support personnel are often limited to stocking shelves, searching shelves for medications whose expiration dates have passed, and pulling prescription bottles and placing them next to the prescription for the pharmacist to fill. The process of becoming fit to practice as a technician could take several months or longer. These individuals are sometimes called "aides" or "assistants," and are not provided tasks of greater complexity until they have mastered the nomenclature, terminology, and practice of pharmacy.

The NABP MA&R, as explained earlier, eventually rejected the incorporation of the title "pharmacy assistant" for entry-level support personnel into its proposed structure for technicians. This may be more a matter of subjective preference for a means to the end of acceptable training for entry-level personnel than a rejection of the concept. Time and experience will tell if this is a mistake. Certainly, this will depend on whether pharmacies train entry-level individuals with the seriousness the NABP provisions would suggest. As the training for technicians is totally delegated to individual pharmacies, one would expect differing levels of rigor in ensuring that entry-level support personnel are completely ready to handle their roles.

It is important to remember that the technician will ordinarily be doing many of the "hands-on" tasks required in dispensing medication as part of a unified process. A mistake can occur during any task performed in the process. Thus, it is unreasonable to think that entry-level personnel who are being trained should be provided several discrete tasks at the same time. This would be below the standard of care. The risk for mistake is simply too great to allow entry-level personnel to participate in the dispensing process as coequals to pharmacists and trained technicians.

A certified pharmacy technician has the added requirement that the individual pass "an examination or examinations approved by the Board of Pharmacy." This requirement, by its nature, has to be a bit flexible. Some states have designed their own examinations. Others rely on leaders' tests put out by organizations such as the Pharmacy Technician Certification Board. The Pharmacy Technician Certification Board came into existence in 1995, and in its first five years of existence, 50,000 technicians have passed its accreditation test. The PTCB does not provide study manuals, but provides a web-based list of study aids that will be helpful in preparing for its examination. Those who pass the test may use the appellation CPhT.

Although the MA&R does not require technicians to be licensed, it requires technicians to be registered and allows, through its provisions, that technicians be subject to discipline by state boards of pharmacy.

40.14 Elimination of Pharmacist-to-Technician Ratio

The NABP has, for some time, formally advocated the elimination of the pharmacist-to-technician ratios.[3] This approach has continued in its recent MA&R revisions.

Traditionally, many states have tightly regulated the use of pharmacy-support personnel by requiring mandatory pharmacist-to-technician ratios—typically one-to-one in retail settings and two-to-one in hospital settings. While perhaps a one-to-one ratio can be criticized as too conservative, the NABP Model Act approach advocates legislation that allows each pharmacy the right to decide on an appropriate staffing ratio in the workplace. The authors opine that such ratios serve a decidedly beneficial purpose, particularly in community clinical settings. Realistically, the ability of pharmacists to self-regulate with an appropriate ratio is handicapped by the disproportionate bargaining power in a pharmacy workplace.

The NABP has performed a study showing that, generally speaking, a pharmacist should be able to effectively monitor two to four technicians.[3] The law in most states has a fixed requirement that one pharmacist can supervise no more than a set number of technicians. The typical figure is somewhere between one pharmacist to two-to-four techs (one pharmacist to two techs is normative). Nearly six out of ten pharmacists, according to one survey, are satisfied with their pharmacist-to-technician ratio.[9] More chain pharmacists (43 percent) than independents (28 percent) believe more techs per pharmacist should be allowed.[9]

In 1990, at least ten states increased their pharmacist-to-technician ratio: Alabama, Colorado, Florida, Indiana, Kansas, New Mexico, Oregon and Tennessee.[4] This was, perhaps, a reaction to the nationwide shortage of pharmacists and a growing confidence in the institutional ability to educate, test, and certify support personnel. The actions of these states also appear to confirm that there is movement away from a pharmacist-centered dispensing process.

While it is true that employers have incentive—through fear of litigation—to keep staffing ratios relatively low, they also have an opposing incentive to save money through the employment of cheaper and less well-trained technicians. There is little sound reason for the NABP not to promote mandatory, reasonable ratios of technicians to pharmacists (much less ask state boards of pharmacy to eliminate their present standards).

40.15 Legal Analysis of the NABP MA&R Initiative

The NABP approach to pharmacy-support personnel is a solid product of thoughtful deliberation, and it has improved the rather anemic efforts of the previous NABP Model Act by leaps and bounds.

The NABP has done a solid job delineating boundaries for its two levels of support personnel: "pharmacy technicians" and "certified pharmacy technicians." The proposed regulations facilitate the performance of most tasks thought to be appropriate for technicians. The authors would have the minor criticism that the NABP has gone beyond tasks considered normative of most technicians, as noted above. Many jurisdictions would not allow technicians to take phone calls from doctors' offices regarding refills (which, apparently, both types of technicians are permitted to do under NABP guidelines).[34] Most jurisdictions would prohibit all technicians from taking new prescriptions over the phone, while the NABP allows certified pharmacy technicians to take new prescriptions over the phone (although not under particularly demanding circumstances).[35] Indeed, while the NABP has restricted compounding to certified pharmacy technicians, there are not the same safeguards recommended by most states.

The standard of care for tasks prohibited for either type of technician—while open to critique—has the advantage (except in one major instance) of being clear and easy-to-follow.

One problem with the NABP revisions is the decision not to set forth an entry-level pharmacy position (e.g., pharmacy assistant). The standard of allowable tasks in the revised NABP MA&R should not be applied to entry-level personnel. As stated earlier in this chapter, personnel recently introduced to clinical practice do not have the requisite skill, knowledge, or experience to participate in the dispensing process as a whole. Until they have been properly trained, entry-level personnel should be limited to working the cash register, stocking shelves, or pulling pill bottles for the pharmacist.

The NABP is sending mixed signals regarding how pharmacists should interact with pharmacy technicians in clinical settings. The NABP was able to do this by using imprecise language that failed to specifically set forth the appropriate balance between pharmacist control and technician assistance. While ostensibly keeping pharmacist control over the dispensing process, the revised MA&R can be criticized for failing to give practitioners a clear notion of the extent of the control necessary.

The NABP revisions, at least rhetorically, seem to have maintained the pharmacist-centered model by keeping the "personal and direct" supervision requirement. Notwithstanding these, there are numerous reasons to think a more flexible approach is also supported. First, the NABP's September 2000 newsletter downplays the significance of the "personal and direct" requirement and gives the wording a more liberal interpretation than its wording suggests.[6,36] Second, technicians are prevented from performing "dispensing process validation," which the authors would submit is rather "flexible" phraseology for a MA&R and accommodates greater technician involvement in checking medication than previously afforded by mores and custom. Third and finally, the NABP has endorsed the elimination of pharmacist-to-technician ratios in its MA&R and has taken a more liberal approach to defining technician clinical tasks.

The first reason that the NABP appears to be moving away from a pharmacist-centered approach to pharmacy is the interpretation it gives to the words "personal and direct" supervision. The NABP issued a newsletter in September 2000 which spoke in a rather comprehensive fashion about the evolving nature of pharmacy-technician regulation and various NABP initiatives. The NABP claimed in that newsletter that the words "personal," "direct," and "immediate" are conceptually similar when used throughout the United States. The NABP further claimed that the "personal and direct" supervision requirement means that the pharmacist "should be stationed in the same work area and have the ability to control and be responsible for the activities of the pharmacy technician." Thus, the NABP has asserted that these words have been interpreted by the NABP with much less rigor than the natural import of the words "personal and direct" would suggest. Presumably, the NABP wishes observers to conclude that the present supervisory requirement of technicians by a pharmacist under the MA&R is something less demanding than the rather blunt words "personal and direct" might suggest. If the NABP claim is to be taken at face value, the "personal and direct" language is a rather general requirement that the pharmacist be in the workplace and have the ability to control and be responsible for the work of the technician.[37]

A MA&R must be drafted with the knowledge that its words will become legal standards, both under a board of pharmacy's regulatory scheme and under the common law. Resort cannot and will not be made to an explanatory newsletter to clarify the standard of care. The words "personal," "direct," and "immediate" are throwbacks to a conception of the use of clinical supervision that many commentators find antiquated. Whatever the nuances the NABP currently claims should be afforded its choice of words, it is relatively clear that the "personal and direct" phraseology is a continuance of a pharmacist-centered approach to pharmacy. The use of such wording by the NABP and state jurisdictions reflected considerable misgivings that pharmacy-support personnel should be acting without rigorous and direct control by pharmacists in a close relationship (one-to-one or

two-to-one). The NABP continuance of the "personal and direct" language can only be seen as an intentional signal that pharmacists should continue to be held to a high degree of accountability for supervision of technicians during the clinical dispensing process.

Second, the NABP could be thought to have made a major break from the past by stating in the revised MA&R that technicians should not perform "dispensing process validation." At first glance, this formulation might seem to be a restriction, albeit an unclear restriction, on technician activity. However, when compared to past customs and mores, it is a change in approach. Pharmacists at pharmacy schools throughout the United States have been traditionally trained in the "three-check method" or the "four-check method" in checking medications before they are dispensed. This would mean that they are personally, immediately, and directly involved in dispensing medication and supervising support personnel. In fact, the "three check" or "four check" method arguably blurs the distinction of who actually filled the prescription, as the pharmacist is so integrally involved that he is actually participating in filling the prescription and not simply supervising another's work.

The phrase "dispensing process validation" is inherently vague, and the formulation could obviously be subject to varying interpretations, from prohibition of technicians' participation in any checking of work, to prohibition of technicians performing a "final check" of the process, or to a more generic prohibition of technicians monitoring the dispensing process as a whole. The better argument is that the NABP is affording technicians the ability to perform some checks. The use of the word "process" makes clear that technicians are afforded the ability to perform validation of dispensing, but are prohibited from performing a more generic oversight, validation of a "process," which is left to pharmacists. This interpretation would draw support from the NABP's concerted reliance on QA programs to bridge the safety problems created by a more liberalized use of technicians. One could interpret "dispensing process validation" to refer to the application of QA programs.

The use of this wording in the revised NABP Model Act approach glosses over what can be a most thorny issue—does the MA&R have a relaxed view to technician supervision, or one that is pharmacist-centered? While, by implication, requiring pharmacists to validate the dispensing process, the NABP does not state the exact degree of validation necessary. Possibilities, as noted above, vary over a wide spectrum of possible conduct—including a weakening of the number of checks performed by pharmacists, the delegation of initial checks to pharmacy technicians, or the maintenance of the status quo concepts of traditional practice (with a one-to-one pharmacist-to-technician ratio).[38] A third important item to highlight is that at the same time the NABP revised its MA&R provisions towards technicians, the NABP reissued its long-standing recommendation for the state boards to eliminate the pharmacist-to-technician ratios that are present in many states and provided, in its revised rules, a more liberal approach to technician tasks than current mores permit. In practice, both decisions will affect the ability of pharmacists to supervise technicians, with supervision becoming more difficult and less extensive as the ratio grows. Together with the vagueness expressed by the wording regarding "dispensing process validation," these actions provide insight into the NABP's approach to technicians.

While not seeming to touch the "hot" issue of TCT, the NABP, perhaps, has given us its answer without clearly spelling it out. The NABP approach is best described by the adage of "rejection of, but movement towards" TCT. The call for "personal and direct" supervision is pleasing to commentators who have a traditional view of how a pharmacist should oversee technicians. But as described above, the NABP appears to be moving away—in several ways—from the natural import of this approach to supervision. While the NABP has clearly rejected the most extreme form of TCT, where the pharmacist is divorced from supervision of technicians, there are many indications that the NABP is comfortable with much less direct supervision of technicians in the workplace.

From a legal standpoint, legitimate concern exists over how practitioners should determine the standard of care under the NABP MA&R for pharmacist supervision of pharmacy dispensing practice. As noted above, there is "zero tolerance" for dispensing mistakes in clinical settings, and the pharmacist has always been held absolutely accountable for mistakes. The NABP initiative can only be said to provide very mixed signals as to what pharmacist supervision is necessary in a clinical setting.

The practical effect of modern trends in clinical practice—which is reflected in part by the NABP MA&R revisions—would be to dilute the ability of the pharmacist to maintain this high standard of care. The pharmacist, arguably, will be faced with being less involved in the dispensing process, without a commensurate re-evaluation of the standards of regulation and legal liability. This may lead to the fundamentally unfair scenario where pharmacists will continue to be held personally liable for technicians' mistakes, yet individual pharmacy employers will significantly and unrealistically increase the number of technicians to be supervised in the workplace.

The NABP approach places significant reliance on QA programs to ensure that a more expansive use of technicians

will not weaken the dispensing standards. The hope is that the QA program will set a sufficient routine that will make up for the lack of personal contact by a pharmacist. However, the authors feel this is rather optimistic. The NABP approach relies too much on the good intentions of each pharmacy for public safety, despite a growing public recognition that some pharmacies—particularly chain pharmacies—have emphasized profit margin over safety. The delegation to each pharmacy to set its own appropriate supervisory limits allows, in many circumstances, the proverbial fox to watch the hen house.

40.16 Re-Evaluation of a Pharmacy Technician's Legal Responsibility, in Light of the Proposed Changes to the NABP Model Act

With certification and regulation, the question of whether technicians or certified technicians should be accountable for negligence will be a topic that merits significant discussion. There is no reason to think that pharmacy technicians are in a position any different than nurses or other medical support professionals, who are currently—both in practice and in law—held accountable for their mistakes. The NABP MA&R may make suits filed against technicians as defendants or codefendants more prevalent. Malpractice insurance for technician conduct may become a topic of greater discussion as time goes on, particularly in relation to licensed/certified technicians.

There have been some recent legal decisions that have moved beyond the traditional notion of pharmacist responsibility for negligence in the dispensing process and, additionally, requiring pharmacies to be responsible for sufficient "institutional controls" in clinical settings.[39] The net effect of the NABP Model Act may be for courts and legal authorities to continue the growing trend to evaluate pharmacy safety, in terms of establishing and adhering to institutional controls in each workplace, in addition to evaluating safety simply as a by-product of an individual pharmacist's negligence. From a litigation standpoint, any practitioner in a civil suit involving a pharmacy mistake in a state that adopts the NABP MA&R must take a serious look at the pharmacy's QA program. The NABP approach may actually have the unintended effect of increasing the possibility for punitive damages awarded against pharmacies that intentionally or recklessly fail to establish and follow institutional controls in the workplace.[39]

40.17 Summary

The year 2000 NABP MA&R initiative regarding pharmacy technician practice is a collection of generally mainstream, but some forward-looking, provisions that are very significant for the practice of pharmacy. The NABP initiative should facilitate technicians becoming a legitimate professional group whose members are licensed, trained, and educated. The NABP revisions ostensibly retain pharmacist pre-eminence in the workplace, yet have been drafted with flexibility built in to accommodate much more significant use of technicians in the future workplace. Taken with the NABP's long-standing recommendation that state boards of pharmacy should eliminate pharmacist-to-technician ratios, one can only conclude that the NABP, as an organization, wishes to dramatically increase the use of technicians and move away from a pharmacist-centered clinical practice. Indeed, a legitimate argument could be made that the NABP approach will lead to a future climate where a technician-centered dispensing process becomes more acceptable, including technicians checking technicians. However, that day has clearly not come, nor do the authors believe the NABP wished to endorse this concept.

The NABP revisions attempt to bridge the past with the perceived future of pharmacy practice. This is not an easy thing to do, as it essentially required—to borrow a phrase from president Abraham Lincoln—the NABP to change horses in midstream (an activity Lincoln did not think advisable). Notwithstanding the difficulty of the task, as well as the enviable goal to bridge the past with the future, the authors feel that more precision was called for in the NABP MA&R, regarding the level of supervision expected of pharmacists. This was particularly true in light of its advocacy of eliminating pharmacist-to-technician ratios. A MA&R should set firm boundaries to guide conduct, as opposed to creating vague principles susceptible to multiple interpretations.

The authors feel that greater use of technicians in the pharmacy workplace is not only justified, but also necessary, given current circumstances—particularly in hospital settings. An expansion of a one-to-one or one-to-two technician ratio is a necessary corollary.[40] However, the authors also feel the elimination of ratios is precipitous. The current training and education of pharmacy technicians does not—in the least—justify an aggressive liberalization of requirements.

The authors feel that public safety mandates a rejection of pure TCT—particularly given the fact that technician education and training is in an infancy stage. The rigorous education and training provided to pharmacists helps to guarantee to the consuming public that potentially dangerous and addictive medications will be dispensed only by licensed professionals with a high level of competency, and

who have a significant investment to lose if they act without appropriate care. These factors help ensure that the pharmacist, like a naval captain, runs a "tight ship."

The ultimate winners under these new proposals may be the chain drug stores and technicians, rather than the pharmacists. It is true that pharmacists should have greater numbers of technicians to share their responsibilities on a day-to-day basis. This may, perhaps, alleviate some of the crushing workload many face. But the direction pharmacy practice appears to be going is to not use technicians to complement pharmacists in dispensing medication, but to supplant them. Without constraint on the number of technicians and the extent of supervision required, the greater use of technicians may actually increase the volume of work for pharmacists.

The current standard of care is that the pharmacist should always retain oversight over the technician's manner and method of clinical performance, should spot-check a technician's work at least once before the final check, and should conduct the final check. Dilution of the three-check or four-check methods to a final-check method is valid and, therefore, within the standard—if there is also an appropriate QA program that is being properly administered and supervised by a pharmacist.

The NABP revisions should be a first step to opening a serious debate about regulatory and legal accountability in clinical-pharmacy settings. The regulatory and legal regimes in each state jurisdiction traditionally have placed accountability squarely on the shoulders of the pharmacist. The NABP, ostensibly, has not moved from this legal paradigm, although the greater use of technicians almost requires the paradigm's re-evaluation.[41] In the future, greater attention will be paid to the responsibility of pharmacies as an institution, as well as to the responsibility of technicians for the work they perform. Legal theory and analysis must evolve to address the new realities that the market and technology have created in pharmacy clinical practice—particularly in regards to the growing importance of pharmacy technicians.

Endnotes

1. R.R. Abood and D.B. Brushwood. *Pharmacy Practice and the Law* (NY: Aspen, 1994), 243–244.

2. J. Henderson. "Pharmacy techs: Low-cost help, mixed blessings," *Amarillo Globe News*, February 15, 2000.

3. J. Levine. "Study finds mistakes by pharmacy technicians," February 23, 2000. Available online at www.webmd.com/news/20000224/study-finds-mistakes-pharmacy-technicians.

4. APBnews.Com."Untrained pharmacy techs give drugs, advice: stores criticized for cutting corners on supervision," February 15, 2000.

5. National Association of Boards of Pharmacy. *Model Pharmacy Act and Rules of the National Association of Boards of Pharmacy* (2000).

6. J.A.Molzon. "Legal and professional issues related to the use of pharmacy technicians," *Ill. J. Pharm. Prac.* 3:176 (1990).

7. A. Rock. "Prescription for trouble," *Money* 27(4):114 (1998).

8. N. Saffer. "Pharmacy: Technicians and assistants," *Occupational Outlook Quarterly* 43(1):34.

9. M.F. Conlan. "Tech's time," *Drug Topics* 143(22):60 (1999).

10. D.B. Brushwood. *Pharmacy Malpractice Law and Regulations*, 2nd ed. (Hoboken: Wiley Law, 1998).

11. National Association of Boards of Pharmacy. 2000. National Association of Boards of Pharmacy Newsletter. 29(8):109.

12. H.M. Calmes and M. Ausmus. "Pharmacy technicians historical review: Practitioners' concerns and recommendations," *J. Pharm. Pract.* 57:182 (1993).

13. K.D. Moscou. "Pharmacy technician educators' attitudes toward education and training requirements for pharmacy technicians," *J. Pharm. Tech.* 16:133–137 (2000).

14. C. Ukens. "Texas rethinks mandatory certification for technicians," *Drug Topics* 143(6):42 (1999).

15. W.L. Fitzgerald, M.D. Smalley and H. Cash. "Pharmacy technicians: Current status in the states," *American Pharmacy* 31(6):36 (1991).

16. K. MacPherson. "Pharmacists overworked and in short supply," July 2, 2000. Available online at www.postgazette.com/headlines/20000702drugs1.asp.

17. C.A Bond and C.C. Raehl. "Changes in pharmacy, nursing, and total personnel staffing in U.S. hospitals, 1989-1998," *Am. J. Health-Syst.* 57:970.

18. Consumer Affairs. "Prescription errors rising," June 10, 2000. Available online at www.consumeraffairs.com/news/pharmacy_errors.html.

19. J. Hendren. "Worked to death: Pharmacist shortage leads to fatal errors," *Amarillo Globe News*, February 13, 2000, p. 21. D. Schuman. "When pharmacies make mistakes: Mistakes at the pharmacy can damage lives forever," November 15, 1999.

20. H.E. Hess and P.E. Grauss. "Is tech-check-tech good for the profession?" *Drug Topics* 141(13):56 (1997).

21. C. Ukens. "Pharmacy boards tackling touchy technician issues," *Drug Topics* 140(3):36 (1996).

22. R.W. Anderson. "Technicians and the Future of Pharmacy," *Am. J. of Hosp. Pharm.* 44:1594 (1987).

23. F. Gebhart. "The rise of techs," *Drug Topics* 140(9):62 (1996).

24. J. Nguyen. "Regulatory agency action," *Calif. Reg. L. Rep.* 15:114 (1995).

25. A. Otto, A. "Focus on errors may bring changes to the pharmacy," *Pharmacy Today* 1:112 (2000).

26. W.L. Fitzgerald and D.B. Wilson. "Medication errors: lessons in law," *Drug Topics* 142(2) (1998).

27. National Association of Boards of Pharmacy. Model Pharmacy Act and Rules of the National Association of Boards of Pharmacy (1999).

28. National Association of Boards of Pharmacy. 2000. Task Forces and Committees' Web Report of the 96th Annual NABP Meeting in Nashville, Tennessee.

29. The NABP member boards include not only the boards in all 50 states, Puerto Rico, the District of Columbia, and Guam, but also member boards in several nations outside of the United States.

30. The American Society of Hospital Pharmacists was a moving force behind technicians, issuing a statement recognizing hospital pharmacy technician-helpers, and holding a workshop in 1969 on sub-professional personnel. The Department of Health, Education and Welfare (HEW) recommended the use of nonprofessional helpers as a condition of participation in Medicare. A HEW Task Force on Prescription Drugs found that the use of support personnel could increase the efficiency of community and hospital pharmacies.

31. The authors do not suggest that a modified version of TCT is unacceptable, when multiple pharmacy personnel participate in an overlapping series of checks with the final check reserved for the pharmacist. This occurs

in many hospitals, and is in keeping with traditional notions of a pharmacist's responsibility.

32. Proponents of TCT are misleading when they posture the choice as between whether to use pharmacists *either* for reviewing dispensing or as part of a "clinical team." One can do both. The motive behind TCT seems to be one of holding down hospital costs, rather than focusing on the predominant goal of pharmacy regulation or the protection of the consuming public.

33. For instance, one pharmacy could prohibit a certain activity in its QA program, while other pharmacies permit the same activity. It is difficult to rationally evaluate how to discipline, or decide whether to discipline, pharmacies who do not adhere to their own QA program in these circumstances.

34. This is somewhat ameliorated by the NABP's requirement that only pharmacists contact prescribers concerning prescription drug-order clarification or therapy modification.

35. A requirement that the technician record the original information does not prevent a miscommunication problem between the doctor's office and the technician.

36. One would note that different states have interpreted the same "direct and immediate" supervision requirement to mean different things. In New Mexico, the pharmacy board, at one time, held that the licensed pharmacist must be in the physical presence of the technician while he or she is performing assigned duties and that the pharmacist must provide guidance to the technician in the performance of the duties. Minnesota, on the other hand, merely required the pharmacist to be in the same work area as the technician.

37. Oddly, while the NABP did note its past requirement of "personal and direct" supervision in the September, 2000, newsletter, it did not undertake to explain the significance of the proposed deletion of this wording in some parts of its MA&R. It would later comment, in passing, that both types of technicians would work under the supervision of a pharmacist "with varying degrees of independence." However, neither the year 2000 MA&R, nor the NABP's explanatory newsletter, indicates with any specificity what degree of independence the MA&R would allow.

38. This approach continues a disconcerting feature of the prior Model Act, which promoted safety by delegating the responsibility for standards to each pharmacy individually. One rational explanation for the vagueness in the choice of the words "dispensing process validation" is that the QA program in each pharmacy will inform the meaning of these words. However, from a legal standpoint, allowing each individual pharmacy to define applicable standards is problematic. This imprecision towards boundaries is uncharacteristic of a MA&R, which is usually mostly concerned with promoting regulations to protect the public.

39. *Harco Drugs, Inc. v. Holloway*, 669 So.2d 878 (Ala. 1995) (failure to follow institutional controls for dispensing medication appropriately warrants punitive damage charge); *cf. Nelms v. Walgreen Co.*, 1999 WL 462145 (Tenn. App. 1999) (no error in failing to submit punitive damage claim to the jury despite violation of state board of pharmacy rules where no evidence that prescriptions were dispensed without a pharmacist's approval); *Murphy v. Rite Aid*, 52 Northampton 111 (July 26, 2000) (a Pennsylvania Court of Common Pleas decision which denies partial summary judgment on punitive damages where there is an averment of unsafe procedures); *see also* Roseann B. Termini et al., *Pharmacy Liability for Punitive Damages—Pennsylvania Practice Pointers, LXXI Pa. Bar Institute Q. 1, 6 (January 2000).*

40. For instance, a reasonable suggestion from one Texas pharmacy task force was to allow a ratio of 3:1, as long as one of the three technicians was certified.

41. See, for example, the NABP's continued choice of the words "personal and direct" to describe pharmacist supervision.

Appendix 40.1
APhA's letter to ACPE regarding the Dialogue with the Profession on the Education and Training of Pharmacy Technicians

December 12, 2003
Accreditation Council for Pharmacy Education
c/o Michael Rouse
20 North Clark Street, Suite 2500
Chicago, IL 60602-5109

Dear ACPE:

On behalf of the American Pharmacists Association (APhA), thank you for the opportunity to participate in the *Dialogue with the Profession on the Education and Training of Pharmacy Technicians*. APhA has a long history in the support of pharmacy technicians and the important part they play on the pharmacy team. The dialogue that the profession has started is one that is critically important for the profession as pharmacists continue to move to patient care/medication therapy management service-related roles.

Introduction
Over the last several months, APhA staff and leadership have attended many of the ACPE Open Hearings held as a part of the *Dialogue*. APhA has also held its own discussions with leadership, members, and with state pharmacy association executives at our recent Affiliated States meeting. We have heard a wide array of opinions and comments from individuals, as well as major employers of pharmacists and pharmacy technicians, and have experienced an obvious difficulty in reaching consensus on this issue that impacts pharmacy practice settings in such different ways. Considering the number of years it took the profession to reach consensus on a single entry-level degree, it is not surprising that a vision on the issues presented in the *Dialogue* is not clear after eight months of testimony. We have also heard a great deal of uneasiness with what is being perceived as a "rush" to complete this *Dialogue* and move forward to implementation of standards and accreditation program development.

This *Dialogue* is extremely important as the profession continues to examine its future place in health care. As such, we recommend that ACPE delay implementation of the published timeline for completion and continue a dialogue outside the Council's usual formal

standards development process. As one of the three founding members of ACPE, APhA recommends that the next step in a dialogue include going back to each of ACPE's three founding organizations (American Association of Colleges of Pharmacy, National Association of Boards of Pharmacy, and APhA) to determine how best for the profession to work towards consensus on this issue.

A baseline foundation for further discussions could stem from the "Vision for Pharmacy Technicians" as outlined by the Sesquicentennial Stepping Stone Summit on Pharmacy Technicians:[1]

Vision for Pharmacy Technicians in the Daily Practice of Pharmacy

(As defined by the Stepping Stone Summit 2: Pharmacy Technicians—2002)

- *Pharmacists and pharmacy technicians will work as a team to provide patient care services through the mutual recognition of their roles and responsibilities and through the responsible and efficient use of technology and resources.*
- *Patient care, public safety, and organizational (company or institution) goals will be maximized through the synergistic application of the knowledge, skills, and abilities of team members.*

The Invitation to Dialogue Questions & APhA Responses
In the spirit of the *Invitation to Dialogue*, APhA will address each of the questions posed. But because APhA firmly believes that the exploration of the issues should continue beyond the announced timeline, our responses often pose more questions for discussion than express a definitive position.

1. Definition
ACPE Question: The 2002 White Paper[1] lists the following definition: "A pharmacy technician is an individual working in a pharmacy setting who, under the supervision of a licensed pharmacist, assists in pharmacy activities that do not require the professional judgment of a pharmacist." Is this definition appropriate and adequate? How could it be improved to better define pharmacy technicians, and reflect what is happening and required in practice, both now and in the future?

The importance of a standard definition of "pharmacy technician" cannot be overstated. By our observations, however, the necessary consensus around such a definition has not yet occurred. The APhA Board of Trustees adopted the *White Paper on Pharmacy Technicians 2002: Needed Changes Can No Longer Wait* in 2002. By this adoption, it agreed with the definition of a pharmacy technician as stated in the paper. During our recent discussion, our members and others had varying viewpoints on this published definition.

Viewpoint One

Some of our members observed that the *White Paper* definition was not forward-looking enough, that it did not look forward to practice five to ten years in the future. The commenters believe that pharmacy technicians may be asked to take on additional activities as practice and patient care become more complex.

Viewpoint Two

Other members indicated that state board of pharmacy registration or licensure of all pharmacy technicians was critical and thus should be included in the definition of "pharmacy technician." Specifically, these commenters supported the pharmacy technician definition as outlined in the *NABP Model State Pharmacy Practice Act* that includes this requirement. However, even with the NABP definition, there were some who were concerned about the vagueness in the definition's phrasing of the "supervision of the pharmacy technician."

Viewpoint Three

The *Stepping Stone Summit Two: Pharmacy Technicians* (See Footnote 1) called for the profession to develop and adopt a standard pharmacy technician definition. While the Summit participants understood that the *White Paper* had outlined a definition, it had not yet been adopted by the profession as a whole as evidenced by the fact that one state's practice regulations still do not mention pharmacy technicians or any type of supportive personnel and 12 states still use the terms supportive personnel, ancillary personnel, unlicensed person, or non-pharmacist personnel. Even in this *Invitation to Dialogue* the definitions and use of terms have not been consistent, as questions are posed using the phrase "Pharmacy Support Personnel"—are we truly having a dialogue about "pharmacy support personnel" or is the dialogue supposed to be focused on "pharmacy technicians"?

Based on these differing viewpoints, APhA supports

further examination of a pharmacy technician definition that yields a profession-wide consensus.

2. Level of Pharmacy Support Personnel

ACPE Question: Should different levels of pharmacy support personnel (not including clerical, accounting and housekeeping functions) be defined? If so, what should these be? What additional definition(s) would be applicable?

The Stepping Stone Summit participants noted that there are a number of individuals in the pharmacy who are not "pharmacy technicians." They may be delivery personnel, inventory control clerks, cashiers, and customer service representatives, among others. As such, these individuals are "pharmacy support personnel" but should not be included in any level/category of pharmacy technician. We will focus on only those individuals who would have "responsibilities" assigned to a pharmacy technician.

Viewpoint One

The Stepping Stone Summit Two: Pharmacy Technicians identified three possible categories of pharmacy technicians:

Category One—Individuals performing pharmacy technician duties who are either trainees or persons who are not "certified" (i.e., who have not passed the PTCB or other state-board recognized certification examinations).

Category Two—Pharmacy Technicians who have passed the PTCB examination and are Certified Pharmacy Technicians (CPhTs) or hold other state board-recognized certification.

Category Three—Pharmacy Technicians who have been certified and work in lead positions based upon experience or in specialty areas requiring specialty training and/or experience. Compared to Categories One and Two, fewer pharmacy technicians are in this category, but they represent an important trend for the future.

Viewpoint Two

Some members who agreed with the Summit-defined categories suggested that pharmacy technicians in Category One should only be a transitional category, that pharmacy technicians should only occupy that category for a defined period of time while they are training or studying for certification. If neither of these (training/certification) is completed within that defined period of time, the individual should no longer be considered a pharmacy technician. The Summit did not define a time period for any of the categories.

Viewpoint Three

Others outlined four categories with one for training, the second for non-certified technicians (with no time limit—suggesting that there will always be a need for pharmacy technicians who do not seek certification), the third for certified pharmacy technicians, and the fourth for specialty pharmacy technicians.

While the levels of pharmacy technicians appear to be less controversial, profession-wide consensus should be developed. This cannot occur without further discussion.

3. Roles, Responsibilities, and Competencies of Pharmacy Support Personnel

ACPE Question: For each level of pharmacy support personnel identified in #2 above, describe the roles, responsibilities and required competencies.

Consensus Building

When the Council on Credentialing in Pharmacy (CCP) discussed a possible need for standards/guidelines for pharmacy technician training programs, it determined that ACPE could develop such standards through its established process, "if desired by the profession and endorsed by its three sponsors: AACP, APhA, and NABP."[2] As a result, CCP requested that ACPE undertake a dialogue to determine if the proposed type of standards/guidelines was desired by the profession. It was also recognized by CCP that a "necessary prerequisite to accreditation standards would be a profession-wide consensus around the roles of the pharmacy technician and the amount and nature of the education and training needed to prepare individuals for those roles."[3] Unfortunately, it appears from the timeline in the *Invitation to Dialogue* as presented that such a consensus building process will not take place. Consensus building is a critical step to resolving many of the questions posed in the *Invitation*.

To begin this consensus building, a resource that may be of some use in determining the roles of pharmacy technician activities is the task analysis conducted by PTCB. This task analysis was conducted as part of PTCB's due process to construct its certification examination. The 1999 task analysis measured current pharmacy technician duties within each of their practice sites. This task analysis was used to develop the PTCB certification examination's test specifications, which along with the related roles and responsibilities, is available on its Website (www.ptcb.org). It is our understanding that PTCB will be conducting a new task analysis in 2004. As a PTCB governor, I would be willing to ask PTCB to include appropriate questions on this new task analysis survey that could benefit this dialogue.

Individual State Pharmacy Practice Acts

Each state board of pharmacy in the U.S. and the District of Columbia outlines pharmacy technician/support personnel roles and responsibilities differently. It is therefore difficult to obtain feedback that is broad enough in scope to address this issue from a national perspective. For example, our members developed their responses and opinions based on their own experiences, which may be limited to one or a few states in which they are licensed. As such, their knowledge of, and contributions to, this discussion can be limited.

In a review of current state pharmacy practice acts, definitions and limitations on pharmacy technician duties are vastly different—ranging from broad activity under the purview of "whatever" a pharmacist deems necessary via a written policy and procedure to only very basic functions of answering the phone and counting medication dosage forms. Without some national consensus on these roles, developing standards and competencies is at best a difficult task.

APhA again supports additional time for consensus on the roles and responsibilities to emerge. This is absolutely critical to any further discussion of education and training of pharmacy technicians.

4. Education

ACPE Question: Education involves a deep understanding of a subject, based on explanation and reasoning, through systematic instruction and teaching. For each level of pharmacy support personnel identified in #2 above, describe the required education, including eligibility requirements and continuing education.

It is difficult to address pharmacy technician education and training requirements when the profession has not yet reached consensus on their roles and responsibilities. Education and training must be driven by what a person is expected to do on his/her job. This profession-wide consensus must be developed prior to the construction of education and training standards and/or accreditation of these programs.

Formal Education Definition

When the phrase "formal education" is used, it is confusing. Does this phrase refer only to academic-based programs such as those offered by a community college or vocational school? Does it mean a formal didactic and skills training program conducted by an employer? Does it address both? Or, does it refer to a prerequisite of a high school diploma or equivalent to work in the pharmacy? For purposes of our response, we will limit the definition of the term "education" to describe a formal academic-based pharmacy technician education program. Training will be discussed under the next section.

Formal Education Viewpoint

The notion of formal education (as defined above) for pharmacy technicians garnered the most concern and discussion in our comment-collection process. Most concerns stemmed from the fact that current economic models (for both the practice site and the individual) do not support mandatory formal education. Many pharmacy practices cannot support sending their pharmacy technicians to an academic-based education program. From the individual's perspective, if (s)he chooses to attend a formal education program, after graduation (s)he would expect to have increased his/her ability to get a job as a pharmacy technician and to be offered a higher starting salary. Based on what we have heard from our members, neither is true in practice. The way in which the *Invitation to Dialogue* was announced, and the process outlined, led individuals to the assumption that ACPE would develop standards for mandatory formal education. This assumption then led individuals to believe that eventual regulatory changes would mandate graduation from a formal education program for *all* pharmacy technicians.

Formal Education versus Accreditation Confusion

Attending a formal pharmacy technician education program and the accreditation of a formal education program are separate and distinct issues and should not be combined in the same discussion. Unfortunately, because people are more focused on mandatory formal education for pharmacy technicians, a discussion of the merits for accreditation of formal education programs has been lost. APhA does not believe that the *Dialogue* meant for this to occur. Unless the discussion of these two issues can be separated, a meaningful discussion of either is unlikely to occur.

Prerequisite Education Viewpoints—High School Diploma or Not?

During our discussions, we heard two differing viewpoints on the prerequisite level of education needed to be considered for a pharmacy technician position.

Viewpoint One

The Stepping Stone Summit determined that pharmacy technicians in all categories/levels should either be high school graduates, have a GED, or be currently enrolled in high school and making satisfactory progress toward graduation. The participants felt that it was important to recognize that there may be high school students who were enrolled in a pharmacy technician program at a vocational center.

Viewpoint Two

Others took a differing view. They believed that all pharmacy technicians should have their high school diploma or equivalent. When asked about high school students in vocational training programs, they indicated that these individuals would be titled "pharmacy technician students" or "pharmacy technicians in training" just as those in pharmacy school are titled "student pharmacists" but should not be considered pharmacy technicians while enrolled in high school.

APhA strongly supports a continuing profession-wide dialogue on appropriate education needed for defined levels and roles for pharmacy technicians.

5. Training

ACPE Question: Training involves learning through specialized instruction, repetition and practice of a task, or series of tasks, until proficiency is achieved (from White Paper). For each level of pharmacy support personnel identified in #2 above, describe the required training, including eligibility requirements.

For this discussion, it is critical to note that formal training programs may be offered in a variety of settings, including directly in pharmacy practice. These programs can range from on-the-job didactic learning and skills training conducted by the pharmacist to a company/institution-based program incorporating live, video, and/or Internet didactics and on-the-job skills training. Some employers may grant pharmacy technicians increased levels of activities based on additional testing or evaluation by the employer. Formal training programs are not the same as orientation or preparation to take a certification examination. Orientation and exam preparation could be parts of a pharmacy technician training program.

Model Curriculum Guidelines
There was some agreement within our membership that a model guideline for training programs would be beneficial if the guideline was available to a pharmacist charged with developing a program.

It was noted by the Stepping Stone Summit that the *Model Curriculum for Pharmacy Technician Training*[4] was more suited for academic-based education programs rather than typical training programs. The Summit did call for the profession to take portions of the *Model Curriculum* and develop core training modules so that individual practices could use the modules best suited for their practice. If, for example, a practice does not involve preparation or dispensing of sterile products, then its training program would not include sterile technique. If a pharmacy conducted a substantial amount of compounding, then a module specific to this area would be included in that practice's training program.

Training Program Viewpoint One
Some of our members indicated that if they were to purchase a self-contained training program for use in their practice, it would be reassuring to know that the program voluntarily followed a set of national guidelines. They were quick to add that because training programs are voluntarily conducted at practices, they did not believe that mandatory accreditation of practice-based training programs was necessary. Again, they cited that the economics (staffing and monetary resources) of pharmacy practice did not support mandatory accreditation of practice site-based training programs.

Training Program Viewpoint Two
We learned that many practices conduct structured training programs to develop a long-term pharmacy technician staff, to offer career ladders for pharmacy technicians, to enhance productivity and efficiency in their practices, and to enhance patient safety. These programs take precious resources from the pharmacy's practice in both money and staff time. Because the requirements for an accreditation process for this type of program are unclear at this time, the added burden of a formal accreditation process for these programs could be resource-prohibitive and could actually provide disincentives for conducting such programs. The lack of formal training at the practice-site could lead to a return to pharmacy technicians who begin interacting with patients after just an orientation.

APhA Proposed Policy
The timeliness of the *Dialogue* is readily apparent. The APhA Board of Trustees charged the Association's 2003-04 Policy Committee to review our current pharmacy technician policy statements—specifically looking at the education and training issues. These draft statements will be available in late January 2004 and debated by the APhA House of Delegates during our Annual Meeting March 27-30, 2004, in Seattle. At this time, APhA has no formal policy statements that specifically address pharmacy technician education and training.

6. Quality Assurance of Pharmacy Technician Education and Training
ACPE Question: For the education and training of pharmacy technicians described in #4 and #5 above, what is/are the most appropriate system(s) of quality assurance?

The quality assurance question proposed in the *Invitation to Dialogue* presumes a consensus position on education and training and is difficult to answer when issues are outlined but a consensus has not yet been reached. Our members did indicate that it was important for each pharmacy practice to have a continuous quality assurance program to assess the performance of its pharmacy technicians along with assessing the performance of its pharmacists.

Accreditation of Formal Academic-based Programs Viewpoint
Accreditation is one mechanism that could assure quality of formal education programs. APhA heard from members who operate pharmacy technician education programs at community colleges and vocational schools who support accreditation as being beneficial to their programs. These members indicated that recognition by an accrediting body would provide assurance for their students (who pay tuition) that the program was legitimate and superior to a correspondence course advertised on television or in magazines.

Continuing Education as a Means to Assure Quality?
Some of our members support a mandatory continuing education requirement for all pharmacy technicians, expanding from the current system which is limited to those who are certified. This proposal met with substantial resistance from other members who cited the arduous process of changing state pharmacy practice acts, along with the absence of any proof that continuing education is a measure of quality. Many believe that

mandatory continuing education has not worked to assure quality for pharmacists and, therefore, would have the same or little value for pharmacy technicians.

Certification as a Means to Assure Quality?
Some members believe that all pharmacy technicians should be certified by PTCB or an approved state board process. Others believe that certification should not be mandatory for all pharmacy technicians. They believe that certification only measures a level of didactic knowledge at a given point in time and it does not assure quality or a pharmacy technician's skills set. For those pharmacy technicians who opt to pursue certification, most pharmacists we spoke to strongly believe that completion of some type of training program should be a prerequisite to sitting for the pharmacy technician certification examination.

State Board Registration as a Quality Assurance Measure?
There are those in our membership who support a state board system to register all pharmacy technicians as a step to assuring quality, at least at the time of hire. However, they indicated that this registration must be more than a list. It should be a system that allows the state board to hold pharmacy technicians accountable for their actions "within the scope of their activities" and gives the board the ability to administer disciplinary action that would be reportable to future employers. This same type of state registration "with teeth" was recommended by the Stepping Stone Summit.

Conclusion
APhA is very supportive of pharmacy technicians functioning in roles that will enhance patient care and strongly recommends that more dialogue and strategic thinking occur in all areas outlined in the *Invitation to Dialogue*—especially those related to defining pharmacy technician roles and responsibilities. It is critical that a positive environment for these on-going discussions be created, that it is not biased by the trepidation of a process intended to lead to regulations that may severely impact practice and patient care.

For the reasons outlined in this letter, APhA believes that it is too early in the dialogue for the profession to

reach consensus and, therefore, the process outlined by ACPE should not move forward. The profession must continue to discuss these issues. In addition, ACPE should request that its three founding member organizations work with their constituencies to determine pharmacy technicians' roles and responsibilities and the corresponding education and training.

I have included two documents that may assist ACPE as you continue exploring these issues with the profession: 1) proceedings from The Sesquicentennial Stepping Stone Summits: Summit 2 Pharmacy Technicians and 2) current APhA Policy Statements on pharmacy technicians.

If APhA—its leadership and staff—can be of any assistance to ACPE, please do not hesitate to contact me.

Sincerely,
John A. Gans, Pharm.D.
Executive Vice President & CEO

Notes

[1] The Sesquicentennial Stepping Stone Summit Two: Pharmacy Technicians was held in the Spring of 2002. APhA along with the members of the Council on Credentialing in Pharmacy, the National Association of Chain Drug Stores, and the National Community Pharmacists Association, conducted the Summit by bringing together 25 invited participants from community and hospital practice, state boards of pharmacy, and pharmacy technician education programs to study pharmacy technicians' roles, education, training, and regulation with a goal of developing recommendations for the profession that could be implemented within three-to-five years.

[2] Taken from the Council on Credentialing in Pharmacy August 2002 Meeting Minutes.

[3] Ibid.

[4] The Model Curriculum for Pharmacy Technician Training, 2001, was developed collaboratively by the American Association of Pharmacy Technicians (AAPT), APhA, American Society of Health-System Pharmacists (ASHP), National Association of Chain Drug Stores (NACDS), and the Pharmacy Technician Educators Council (PTEC).

Part IV
Forensic and Toxicology Issues: Recreational Drugs, Drug Testing, and Pain Equipotency

Chapter 41

The Forensic Pharmacist

Peter D. Anderson, Pharm.D. and James T. O'Donnell, Pharm.D., M.S., FCP, ABCP, FACN, R.Ph.

41.1 Introduction

Dictionaries define "forensic" as the application of science to legal issues. Pharmacists are experts in medications. "Forensic pharmacy" is the application of medication sciences to legal issues.[1] Forensic pharmacists engage in professional work relating to litigation, the regulatory process, or the criminal justice system.[2] Forensic pharmacy is a broad field. The domain of forensic pharmacy overlaps with forensic medicine, forensic psychology, forensic toxicology, forensic accounting, fraud examination, forensic chemistry, forensic document examination, death investigation, forensic nursing, and accident reconstruction. Issues relevant to pharmacists include professional malpractice, patient confidentiality, drug diversion, impaired capacity, drug-induced violence, appropriate use of chemical restraints, adverse drug reactions (including drug interactions), testing for drugs of abuse, drugged and drunk driving, product tampering, medication errors, quackery and health care fraud, and poisoning.

Many pharmacists do forensic work, but we know of only one that actually had the job title "Forensic Pharmacist."[3] Most work in the profession only part-time, performing forensic work as part of their regular positions or providing services as freelance consultants. Some full-time forensic pharmacists work for the government, and others serve as forensic toxicologists.

Pharmacists hold numerous types of positions with local, state, and federal agencies.[4–7] Pharmacists with training in criminalistics have worked as criminalists for police departments and crime laboratories.[3] At the state level, pharmacists have worked as investigators and inspectors for boards of pharmacy, health departments, and narcotic bureaus. The Massachusetts Attorney's General Office employs pharmacists as investigators in its Medicaid Fraud Unit.[8] State medical examiners have pharmacists with advanced training in toxicology and analytical chemistry in the capacity of forensic toxicologists.[4] A pharmacist served as a coroner in Illinois. Many state Medicaid agencies have pharmacists as auditors, as do private insurance companies. The Drug Enforcement Administration (DEA) has employed pharmacists as special agents, as diversion investigators, and in administrative positions.[6,7] The second person to serve as the Commissioner of the Federal Bureau of Narcotics (a predecessor of DEA) was a pharmacist. The Food and Drug Administration (FDA) has pharmacists as consumer-safety officers, chemists, pharmacologists, interdisciplinary scientists, compliance officers, and in various other management and professional positions. A pharmacist was the commissioner of the FDA in the early 1980s. Qualified pharmacists can become special agents with the Federal Bureau of Investigation. Pharmacists may also provide traditional pharmacy services at state forensic psychiatric hospitals.[5] Another aspect of forensic pharmacy is providing pharmaceutical care to inmates at correctional institutions. Some forensic work done by pharmacists is part of their main job. Hospital pharmacists must have systems in place to deter, prevent and detect drug diversion. Some nuclear pharmacists serve as radiation-safety officers for their facilities. Pharmacist attorneys are lawyers who are also registered pharmacists. They practice law in the traditional settings often specializing in health care law or patent law.

The majority of forensic pharmacists work as independent consultants. Pharmacists have served on the drug-testing crews for collegiate sports and as "technical officers" for the Olympics.[9] Their work can be of great value to attorneys, paralegals, claims adjusters, and other forensic scientists. They can also be of assistance to accident-reconstruction specialists by evaluation of the role—if any—drugs or medication played as contributing factors to the accident. Pharmacists also have a role at evaluating drug use in driving accidents.[10]

Forensic pharmacists can be of assistance to fraud examiners and healthcare administrators in reducing waste and fraud—especially if complex therapeutic issues are involved. They also provide educational presentations for lawyers and law enforcement. The lead author of this chapter, Dr. Anderson, has given lectures on psychopharmacology and toxicology to investigators with the Southeastern Area of the Massachusetts Department of Mental Health Office of Investigations. Forensic pharmacists can assist with death investigations by evaluating the role of medications or toxins when these substances are believed to have contributed to the person's death.

41.2 Consultant and Expert Witness

The emphasis of this chapter is on pharmacists that provide litigation-consultation services to lawyers and serve as expert witnesses. Consulting activities may include:

1. Reviewing the case and offering an opinion
2. Identifying clinically relevant issues
3. Conducting research and literature reviews
4. Advising on issues to be pursued
5. Interpreting medical records
6. Suggesting questions for other witnesses

By providing technical evaluation of the answers given by factual and expert witnesses, forensic pharmacists can be of assistance during the deposition process. They can also suggest questions to be asked of the witnesses. A major legal difference exists between retaining a pharmacist as an expert witness, and retaining one as a consultant. Work done by a consultant to an attorney is generally protected by the attorney-client privilege. Work done by an expert witness is generally discoverable.

Pharmacists can obtain and review literature to refute the opposing parties' arguments. They assist attorneys during the discovery process by advising them on what information to request. This may include patient records, incident reports, policy and procedures manuals, training guides, and work schedules.

Pharmacists have testified as experts in two main areas: the original role of the pharmacist/expert witness was in the area of pharmacy practice.[11] In this role, pharmacists testify as to whether another pharmacist was negligent in performance of her duties. The second (newer) role of pharmacists as expert witnesses is in the area of therapeutics and human pharmacology.[12] In the 1980s, pharmacists emerged as experts in drug therapy, and this has extended to court cases.[12] Certain pharmacists have advanced education in substance abuse or environmental toxicology, and thus would be qualified to testify in those areas. Pharmacists have testified in court in matters relating to:

- Pharmacy practice
- Professional discipline/licensing
- Adverse drug reactions
- Labor relations
- Medication errors
- Divorce proceedings
- Personal injury
- Controlled substance issues
- Drug testing
- Worker's compensation
- Impaired capacity
- Driving under the influence
- Poisoning
- Product liability
- Patents
- Sexual Assault

41.3 Pharmacist Malpractice

Pharmacists have been sued for dispensing the wrong medication, committing compounding errors, failing to detect interactions, and not warning patients about side effects. Even if a given prescription is filled correctly the dispensing pharmacist can be liable if the dosage was unsafe or contraindicated due to a major drug interaction. Clinical pharmacists can end up liable for improperly monitoring drug therapy. Proving malpractice cases against pharmacists usually requires testimony from other pharmacists—except when the error is so obvious that even a layperson can understand it without expert testimony. However, in general, most lawyers will not file lawsuits against pharmacists unless an affidavit is obtained from another pharmacist expressing an opinion of negligence. The defense may also have pharmacists as expert witnesses for rebuttal testimony.

An 11-year-old boy received bupropion XL (Wellbutrin) 300 mg, three tablets daily. The indication was for Attention Deficit Hyperactivity Disorder. This dose is twice the maximum adult dosage. The prescription was correctly filled by the pharmacy. Approximately three weeks later the patient suffered a massive seizure while visiting a theme park. A week later the child died from complications of the seizure. No bupropion was found at the autopsy, as any remaining traces disappeared by the time of death. One of the authors (Anderson) reviewed the pharmacy records, a copy of the prescription, the incident report at the park, the hospital records, and the autopsy. The pharmacist expert wrote a report opining that the dispensing pharmacist demonstrated gross negligence in not contacting the prescriber and filling the prescription. He also expressed an opinion on pharmacological certainty of the reaction. The pharmacy settled before the case went to trial. Several points are instructive. One, filling a prescription exactly as written from a prescriber does not rule out negligence on the part of the pharmacist. Two, a well-written report from a forensic pharmacist can be used to negotiate a settlement. Lastly, just because no bupropion was found at the autopsy does not mean that it was not the initial cause of the fatal event.

Pharmacist consultants can be useful in many other ways to attorneys, as well. They can review documents and educate the lawyer about medication-related issues. They can, for example, review a personal-injury or malpractice case resulting from an adverse drug reaction to determine the probability that an adverse reaction actually took place. The forensic pharmacist can educate the attorney about the predictability of the reaction and offer an opinion as to whether proper monitoring and precautions were followed. They can obtain literature supporting the attorneys' arguments, and/or refuting the opposition's arguments.

The lead author of this chapter once prepared a report discussing the duties of a pharmacist to monitor gentamicin therapy. The opposing counsel retained an expert witness who testified that pharmacists did not have a responsibility to monitor gentamicin levels.

41.4 Interpreting Drug Levels

Certain drugs have a narrow therapeutic range and should be closely monitored, including testing blood levels of the drug. Such drugs include antiepileptics (e.g., phenytoin, carbamazepine), cardiac glycosides (e.g., digoxin), lithium, chloramphenicol, aminoglycosides, antiarrhythmics, theophylline, and cyclosporine A. Clinical reasons to draw blood samples for these drugs include high or borderline-high doses, signs of toxicity, a lack of a therapeutic effect, or suspected non-compliance.[13] (An additional resource for toxicologic purposes is Baselt and Cravey, *Disposition of Toxic Drugs and Chemicals in Man*, CTI, Eighth Edition). In emergency room situations, the level of certain drugs determines how the case will be treated (such as whether an antidote should be administered, for example). Toxicological analysis is a common part of the forensic autopsy.

Pharmacists may be consulted to interpret drug levels. Interpreting drug levels is much more complex than comparing it to the normal "therapeutic range." Certain individuals require levels below or above the therapeutic range. Published therapeutic levels applying to a specific disease state may not apply to other disease states. The collection time for samples may affect the results of some drugs. The equipment or analytical procedures used may also impact the results. Certain disease states or nutritional status can alter the levels of specific drugs. Numerous changes occur in drug distribution and metabolism after death.[14] Factors contributing to postmortem changes include cessation of blood flow and uneven clotting; changes in pH; release of drug from binding sites; ending of energy-dependent, drug-transport processes; and effects of putrefaction on drugs. Therefore, postmortem levels frequently cannot be directly extrapolated from published clinical levels. In addition, the presence of other medications or drugs may interfere with clinical test results. Tolerance may occur with many drugs over time. A given drug level may produce minimal effects in one individual but produce major effects in another individual who is not used to the substance.

Questions about drug concentrations the pharmacist can help answer include:

- Is the drug level high enough to produce toxicity consistent with the relevant forensic event? (For example, was the theophylline level high enough to produce seizures?)
- Did an elevated or decreased level of drug result from a drug interaction?
- Did sub-therapeutic levels of prescribed medication lead to the relevant event? (For example, is a low level of carbamazepine a contributing factor to seizures that led to an accident? Another example: Low levels of certain antidepressants may provide insight as to why a person committed suicide. Only a few antidepressants have defined therapeutic ranges.)
- Is therapeutic monitoring (blood levels, for example) normally performed for this medication?
- Does a published therapeutic range of a medication apply to the condition it was prescribed for in the individual? (For example, doses of tricyclic antidepressants are generally lower when used for pain than for depression.)
- Were the signs and symptoms of the patient consistent with the pharmacology and toxicology of the drug?

- Did the patient have any risks for the alleged adverse drug reaction? (For example many drugs are eliminated from the body by the kidney. Persons with kidney disease and the elderly often require lower doses to avoid toxicity.)

41.5 Malpractice Cases of Other Professionals

The pharmacist can be of assistance in the malpractice cases of other healthcare professionals as well. The role of the pharmacist in pharmacist malpractice is discussed earlier in this chapter and in Chapter 35, *Pharmacist Malpractice and Liability*. The pharmacist can assist in cases involving physicians and nurses. Generally, pharmacists cannot testify as to the standard of practice of other professionals. A pharmacist with extensive experience in teaching pharmacology to nurses will probably be allowed to testify on the nursing standard related to drug therapy and administration. Experts trained in chemistry and pharmacology have been allowed by the Mississippi Supreme Court to testify as to the standard of care related to a prescribing physician in that state. However, if the case involves an adverse drug reaction, the pharmacist can testify about the properties of that drug, including causation. The pharmacist can also discuss alternative therapies with lower risk. The role of the pharmacist testimony in malpractice cases is not limited to adverse drug reactions. Pharmacists can provide opinions that medications can prevent disease complications. For example, if a patient develops renal failure from diabetes or hypertension, the pharmacist can discuss medications that would have prevented kidney damage.

41.6 Criminal Cases

Pharmacists may be needed in different types of criminal cases. This includes cases where the drug or poison was used as the weapon, or where medications impair the mental capacity of the defendant or victim. Drugs as a causative factor for aggression have been used as a criminal defense. Drugs alleged to contribute to criminal activity include insulin (from hypoglycemia), ethanol, anabolic steroids, psycho stimulants, opiates, and hallucinogens (including phencyclidine—PCP). Drug-induced mental changes include aggression, depression, hallucination (a sensory experience without a corresponding sensory input), illusions (misinterpretations of sensory inputs), and delusions (mistaken but unshakable beliefs).[15] This defense is more likely to be successful if the drug is a prescribed medication rather than a substance of abuse. Information on the effects of these drugs is frequently introduced into the mitigation phase of criminal defense trials, in order to lessen the penalty or sentence of

the accused/now-convicted defendant. Diminished capacity, inability to realize the seriousness of his act, severe intoxication, impaired perceptions, drug-induced psychosis, and so on, are toxicities introduced and discussed by the pharmacist as part of the criminal case. Although these "mitigating circumstances" will not necessarily clear a defendant, they may sometimes offer proof that the offender has not fully deliberated his acts.

The effects of drugs on victims are often related to criminal cases.[16] Medications are often used as agents for suicides and suicide attempts. Drugs have been used as tools for the commission of homicide. Drugs may be administered to victims so they cannot resist an act or remember an act. The most well-known example is flunitrazepam (Rohypnol), "the date-rape drug."[17] Flunitrazepam can produce anterograde amnesia, especially when combined with ethanol. Drugs and chemicals have been a means of child abuse, including Münchausen syndrome by proxy. This condition involves mothers (or other caregivers) who cause factitious disease in a child with the intention of deceiving physicians or health professionals. Münchausen syndrome is classified as a factitious disorder and involves the individual trying to get admitted to the hospital in order to attain the attention usually garnered by those who are ill.[18] Patients sometimes ingest drugs to produce symptoms of disease (for example, taking syrup of ipecac to produce vomiting). Drugs can also lead the complainant to perceive that a criminal act was committed.[15]

Drugs also can be an issue in the capacity to stand trial. One of this chapter's authors (O'Donnell) was retained in a case regarding impaired capacity. The defendant was convicted of kidnapping and murder. Tranxene (clorazepate) was administered to this individual without the knowledge of the defendant or the defense lawyers. On appeal to the Illinois State Supreme Court, Dr. O'Donnell testified that clorazepate has cognitive diminishing effects. The defense lawyers argued that the defendant should have had a fitness hearing during the original trial since he was receiving clorazepate. The conviction was overturned and a new trial ordered.[19]

41.7 Utilization Review for Insurance Claims

Pharmacists review claims relating to medication therapy, especially where new and unusual uses of medications have been prescribed. A pharmaceutical manufacturer, before marketing of a drug, has to obtain FDA approval. The product's labeling is part of this application process. A pharmaceutical company may only market the drug for FDA-approved indications. However, healthcare providers may prescribe these medications for uses other than the FDA-approved uses. These are referred to as "unlabeled" or "off-label" uses. Patients, medical professionals, and healthcare organizations often submit claims to insurance companies seeking payment for unlabeled medications. These unlabeled uses may raise "red flags" with the insurance provider. A pharmacist can review such claims and offer an opinion as to whether the use is reasonable and common practice.

41.8 Workers' Compensation

Pharmacist Anderson provided written testimony in a worker's-compensation claim.[20]

The claimant slipped on ice at the employer's parking lot and sustained neck injuries in 1989, resulting in numerous surgeries and extensive physical therapy. The claimant had a history of panic attacks and of a suicide attempt in the 1970s. She was receiving imipramine for panic attacks from her psychiatrist at the time.

The patient was prescribed paroxetine (Paxil) for chronic pain and depression from pain by her orthopedic surgeon. Paroxetine is pharmacologically classified as a Selective Serotonin Reuptake Inhibitor (SSRI). The SSRIs increase the neurotransmitter (substances brain cells use to communicate with each other) serotonin but do not significantly increase levels of other neurotransmitters in the brain. (Common uses of SSRIs include treatment of depression, panic attacks, obsessive-compulsive disorder, and bulimia.) The claimant was seeking payment for the paroxetine from workers' compensation.

The insurance company felt paroxetine was not a common indication for chronic pain, and so refused to pay the claim. The case was taken to court. Dr. Anderson reviewed the claimant's medical records and her court testimony. He conducted a literature search on paroxetine for pain control and prepared a report. Dr. Anderson's opinion was that inadequate literature was available (at that time) to support the use of SSRIs for pain control. However, paroxetine can treat the depression and anxiety associated with chronic pain. Depression is often a major component of chronic pain. In addition, he reported that imipramine and paroxetine constitute a therapeutic duplication.

41.9 Alcohol Cases

Pharmacists apply pharmacological and pharmacokinetic principles in court cases related to alcohol. Pharmacokinetics is the quantification of the absorption, distribution, metabolism, and excretion of drugs. Pharmacokinetics can be used to estimate a level of drug (including alcohol) at a given time period. This would be helpful in driving-under-the-influence (DUI, DWI) cases where the breath analysis

or blood level was obtained awhile after the alleged incident. The forensic pharmacist is frequently used in discussions of the scientific principles related to various alcohol testing methodologies. Issues include: margin of error of the "breathalyzer," interpretation of field-sobriety tests, and description of the pharmacology of alcohol, including interactions between prescription and over-the-counter (OTC) drugs and alcohol. (See Chapter 46, *Postmortem Redistribution and Interpretation of Drug Levels*.)

Pharmacokinetic principles can also be used to estimate the dose of medication required to obtain a given blood level. (However, as discussed earlier, this can have several limitations if the level was taken postmortem.)

Pharmacists have numerous skills that are useful in DUI cases, either on behalf of the prosecutor or the defendant. They interpret blood-alcohol levels and discuss the typical effects seen with varying blood-alcohol levels. They apply pharmacokinetics to estimate the level of alcohol at the time of the alleged event. Pharmacokinetics calculations can be especially helpful if an extended time period exists between the incident and the time of sample collection. Drug interactions may also be relevant to DUI cases. Certain medications can have additive effects with ethanol (for example, lower levels of ethanol will produce greater effects). Other medications can alter the absorption or metabolism of ethanol. Certain disease states may make a person susceptible to the effects of ethanol. Pharmacists provide input about alcohol in other civil cases relating to alcohol consumption, such as personal-injury cases involving automobile or other vehicle accidents, premises liability, dram shop, or any injury involving alcohol. Since the use of alcohol substantially increases the risk of all trauma, and injury frequently leads to litigation, understandably there is a substantial amount of litigation involving alcohol and personal injury. An extensive discussion about alcohol, including specific case discussions, may be found in Chapter 44, *Forensic Issues in Recreational Drugs*.

41.10 Drug-Induced Violence and Aggression

Pharmacists can educate their patients (MedGuides for SSRIs), the general public, law enforcement officials, lawyers, and other health professionals about the dangers of violence from drugs of abuse and even prescription drugs. Many are aware of the limitations of the literature in concluding whether a given drug can or cannot cause aggression. Pharmacists may review adverse drug reaction reports involving aggression in either the clinical or medicolegal setting. The forensic pharmacist should be skeptical but open minded when reviewing a case claiming drug-induced violence.

Pharmacists may also serve as expert witnesses in criminal or civil trials where impairment for drugs is an issue. The forensic pharmacist may serve as an expert for either the defense or prosecution.

41.11 Pain Assessment

In personal injury cases, pharmacists can assist in evaluating the degree of pain by the process by reviewing the pain medications (e.g., dose and kind of medication). This is discussed fully in Chapter 45, *Pain Equipotency*.

41.12 Experience, Background, and Skills of the Forensic Pharmacist

Federal rules of evidence require that an expert have special knowledge, skill, experience, training, and/or education to be qualified as an expert in a court of law. The trial judge has wide discretion as to who may be an expert in a given case based on these guidelines. Pharmacists with their education and experience in therapeutics and pharmacology have served as expert witnesses in numerous types of civil and criminal cases.

A forensic pharmacist requires a variety of skills, depending on their particular role. The litigation-consultant pharmacist should have at least five years of practice experience. The pharmacist should also have superior communication skills (both orally and in writing), poise, the ability to think as a detective, and flexibility. The pharmacist witness must understand the big picture, and must avoid focusing on irrelevant details. Excellent communication skills are required to explain complex scientific and clinical issues to the layperson, attorney, paralegal, other forensic scientist, claims adjustor, or juror. A pharmacist involved in fraud examinations needs exceptional interviewing skills. The expert witness also needs to be objective and honest. The duty of a pharmacist as an expert witness is not to win the case, but to provide an unbiased professional/scientific opinion.

There are no specific certifications available (or needed) to become a forensic pharmacist. Many pharmacists have certifications from various organizations. These certifications provide support that a pharmacist is an expert in a given area. Many practicing pharmacists seek certification from the Board of Pharmacy Specialties (BPS: www.bpsweb.org). Pharmacists can obtain certification from BPS in pharmacotherapy, nuclear pharmacy, nutritional support, psychiatric pharmacy, and oncology. The American Society of Consultant Pharmacists has a certification program for geriatric pharmacy. Some pharmacists obtain certification in clinical pharmacology from the American Board of Clinical Pharmacology (www.ABCP.net) or clinical toxicology from the American Board of Applied Toxicology (ABAT).

The Forensic Toxicologist Certification Board offers certification in forensic toxicology. Board certification is certainly not a requirement for a pharmacist to serve as an expert witness. In fact, many specialties in pharmacy practice (e.g., pediatrics, ophthalmics, pharmacokinetics, organ transplantation, and so on) do not have specific certification programs. The American College of Forensic Examiners has the American Board of Forensic Examiners (ABFE), which offers a certification in forensic examination. Many pharmacists are diplomates of the ABFE. The American College of Forensic Examiners also offers a Certified Medical Investigator program. At least one pharmacist is a certified medical investigator. At least three pharmacists are Certified Fraud Examiners, a program run by the Association of Certified Fraud Examiners.

The only specific degree program in forensic pharmacy is a Master of Science degree offered at the University of Florida. Course work includes federal regulations, risk management, pharmaceutical crimes, forensic toxicology, drugs of abuse, and natural products. A specific degree in forensic pharmacy is not a requirement to be a great forensic pharmacist. The main consideration is experience and scientific knowledge.

41.13 Sample Forensic Pharmacist's Reports

Five affidavits follow. The first four are related to criminal proceedings wherein the cognitive impairing effects of acute morphine use are evaluated; the last affidavit addresses the effect of diabetes on an alcohol breathalyzer test in a DUI arrest matter.

Morphine and Miranda

The following is an affidavit filed by one of the authors (O'Donnell) that demonstrates the forensic application of a pharmacist's background and training in the criminal arena. The defendant was under treatment for gunshot wounds, and made statements to the police that were subsequently used against him. The defense attorney sought to squash the statements, claiming that the defendant was unable to voluntarily waive the Miranda right to remain silent.

A. Affidavit: May 2010

Mr. Gabrys was shot several times and taken to St. Joseph's Hospital. While awaiting transfer to Northwestern Memorial Hospital for advanced surgical care, he was interviewed by the police. Shortly before the interview (0340), Mr. Gabrys was administered 4 mg intravenous morphine sulfate (morphine). During the interview (which started at 0355), he gave a statement to the police, which purportedly included a Miranda waiver. He denied any memory of the Miranda warning. The Miranda waiver was not signed, as Mr. Gabrys was "unable to sign" due to his injuries.

Mr. Gabrys related that he was in severe pain due to his multiple gunshot wounds, and that the morphine did relieve his pain. He further related that the morphine made him feel "good." "Euphoric"? (I asked). "Yes." Mr. Gabrys thought that the police were there "to help him," and that they were interested in arresting the person who shot him several times. He relates that his memory is "foggy/spotty" for the time that the two detectives were with him.

- Reports of the interview by police are dated at 0355, 0420, 0535.
- Dilaudid (hydromorphone) 1 mg Intravenous, was administered to Mr. Gabrys at 0430.
- Pupils are noted at 3/2 (constricted) at 0500.
- Additional opiate (morphine) drug administration is noted as follows:
  - 0412 Morphine 4 mg IV
  - 0443 Dilaudid 1 mg IV
- For purposes of discussion, Dilaudid 1 mg is considered to 7 mg morphine.

Opinions

In my opinion, with reasonable pharmacological certainty, Mr. Gabrys was experiencing significant effects of medicinal morphine/Dilaudid during the time he was interviewed by the police detectives. The morphine/Dilaudid was administered to control his pain, in full therapeutic doses and at relatively high frequency, and the effects of morphine would cause significant impairments in his cognitive and deliberative functions. By definition, patients administered therapeutic morphine, particularly in acute and early stages, are predictably impaired, and that impairment is to be expected. In my clinical practice over a period of 20 years involved in the treatment of patients with morphine and other strong opiate analgesics, it was very common to observe patients on therapeutic morphine to be obviously intoxicated, and frequently have no memory of their interaction with the clinician at a later time in the hospitalization when off morphine. Thus, Mr. Gabrys was impaired and under the influence of strong opiate narcotics (morphine and Dilaudid) at the time he was interrogated.

As a result of the therapeutic morphine, he would be in a cognitively impaired state, unable to deliberate clearly, and unable to waive his Miranda rights.

Bases for opinions

Morphine is an opioid Controlled Substance Schedule II. It is indicated for the treatment of severe pain, and known to cause euphoria, mental clouding, and central nervous depression. There is substantial evidence and experience with morphine. Morphine has been shown to impair a variety of functions, including reaction time, tracking, information processing, attention, and memory.[a,b] This broad pattern of impairment is consistent with a sedating effect, which is also apparent from subjective reports of mental clouding, confusion, grogginess, and light-headedness.[c]

The prescribing information for morphine intravenous (PDR) lists the following relevant information which is instructive in this case (*emphasis* added):

Adverse reactions
Most Frequently Observed
Constipation, *light-headedness, dizziness, drowsiness, sedation,* nausea, vomiting, *sweating, dysphoria and euphoria.*

The less severe adverse events seen on initiation of therapy with morphine sulfate are also typical opioid side effects....They should be expected and managed as a part of opioid analgesia. The most frequent of these include *drowsiness, dizziness,* constipation and nausea. In many cases, the frequency of these events during initiation of therapy may be minimized by careful individualization of starting dosage, slow titration, and the avoidance of large rapid swings in plasma concentrations of the opioid. Many of these adverse events will cease or decrease as morphine sulfate therapy is continued and some degree of tolerance is developed, but others may be expected to remain troublesome throughout therapy.

Less Frequently Observed Reactions
Central Nervous System: *confusion,* dry mouth, anxiety, *abnormal thinking, abnormal dreams, lethargy, depression, tremor, loss of concentration,* insomnia, *amnesia,* paresthesia, agitation, vertigo, foot drop, ataxia, hypethesia, slurred speech, *hallucinations,* vasodilation, *euphoria, apathy,* seizures, myoclonus, weakness, uncoordinated muscle movements, *alterations of mood* (nervousness, apprehension, depression, floating feelings), muscle rigidity, *transient hallucinations and disorientation, visual disturbances, insomnia* and increased intracranial pressure.

Conclusion

Thus, it is clear that Mr. Gabrys was being administered therapeutic doses of morphine intravenously prior to and during the time that he was interviewed by the police detectives. It is my opinion that any statements or decisions made during that time would have to be considered to be "under the strong influence of a narcotic," and certainly not made voluntarily, by an intoxicated and impaired patient who would, in my opinion, be unable to exercise his right to waive Miranda.

Notes

a. Zacny, J.P. "A review of the effects of opioids on psychomotor and cognitive functioning in humans." *Experimental and Clinical Psychopharmacology*, 3, 432-466.

b. DiPiro et al. (eds.) *Pharmacotherapy: A Pathophysiological Approach.* New York: Elsevier, 1989. p. 700.

c. Burns, M. (ed.) *Medical Legal Aspects of Drugs.* Tucson, Arizona: Lawyers & Judges Publishing, 2003.

B. Affidavit: November 2003

Mr. Brown, a 31-year-old man incarcerated at the Cook County Jail awaiting trial, presented as a well-groomed, alert man. He was taking no medication at the time of my examination. He related a history of 5 years of heavy and daily chronic heroin abuse, which followed recovery from a gun shot wound in 1997, in addition to prior and continued chronic alcohol and marijuana abuse. His daily experiences with heroin are described as "sleepy, high, nod" (euphoria and central nervous system depression/somnolence). The statement recorded by the State's Attorney 6:40 A.M. 9/19/02) notes that the patient "is currently on pain medication, morphine, which is controlled by the Nurse and it is not affecting his judgment in any way."

On the day of the statement to ASA Murphy, Mr. Brown was hospitalized recovering from major orthopedic surgical repair the day prior and was receiving intravenous morphine via a PCA (Patient Controlled Analgesia) pump. The records indicate that Mr. Brown attempted IV injection 46 times (the pump allowed 23 injections), delivering 63 mg of morphine, according to lockout times and dose limits noted in the medical records.

Interestingly, Mr. Brown related daily heavy heroin use. He had used heroin shortly before the motor vehicle crash which caused the injuries for which he was hospitalized. During my interview, it became apparent that Mr. Brown knew that he had received a pain reliever in the hospital, but did not know the name of the drug. Given the history of daily heroin use, I asked Mr. Brown to advise me of the following:

1. Effectiveness of his intravenous pain medicine.
2. Comparison of the pain medicine to heroin's effects.
3. Any experiences of withdrawal effects from stopping the heroin (once hospitalized).

Mr. Brown related that the IV pain medicine was quite effective; when switched to oral (Vicodin), he experienced pain. The IV pain medicine (morphine) made him experience highs and he felt "knocked out all the time"—like Heroin. And he did not experience withdrawal in the hospital (while receiving morphine).

Mr. Brown was quite experienced with withdrawal: "getting sick from no heroin," "first need it when you get up." Mr. Brown remembers little of the hospitalization before his transfer to the Cermak Hospital at the Cook County Jail. He does remember being awakened by the police officer guards, who awoke him to remove and re-apply handcuffs when they changed shifts. He was also awakened by the hospital staff to be fed (mealtime), but described most of the time in the hospital as "nodding out, falling asleep, no pain." He has no memory of his interview by the state's attorney. Mr. Brown further described what appear to be visual hallucinations while in the hospital: "Thinking (seeing) I'm in park (across street from Hospital), but obviously I was in the Hospital."

On transfer to the Cermak Hospital of Cook County Jail, Mr. Brown described experiencing withdrawal from narcotics, once the intravenous morphine was stopped, and he was put on a lower dose of oral narcotic analgesic.

Opinions

In my opinion, with reasonable pharmacological certainty, Mr. Brown was experiencing significant effects of medicinal morphine during the time he made a statement to ASA Murphy. The morphine was administered to control his pain, and the effects of morphine would cause significant impairments in his cognitive and deliberative functions. By definition, patients administered therapeutic morphine, particularly in acute and early stages, are predictably impaired, and that impairment is to be expected. In my clinical practice over a period of 20 years involved in the treatment of patients with morphine and other strong opiate analgesics, it was very common to observe patients on therapeutic morphine to be obviously intoxicated, and frequently have no memory of their interaction with this clinician at a later time in the hospitalization when off morphine. Thus, Mr. Brown was impaired and under the influence of heroin at the time he was interrogated and signed the statement prepared by the state's attorney Murphy. As a result of his morphine use, he would be in a cognitively impaired state, unable to deliberate clearly, and unable to waive his Miranda rights. Mr. Brown's chronic history of use necessitates daily use; thus his withdrawal experience upon transfer to Cook County Hospital Cermak Hospital, when the intravenous morphine was replaced with oral opiate/acetaminophen combination (resulting in a pain score of 5/10) is quite understandable, and is evidence that the morphine administered in the hospital prevented withdrawal from heroin, thus essentially replacing his heroin use.

Bases for opinions

Morphine is an opioid Controlled Substance Schedule II. It is indicated for the treatment of severe pain, and known to cause euphoria, mental clouding, and central nervous depression. There is substantial evidence and experience with morphine. Morphine has been shown to impair a variety of functions, including reaction time, tracking, information processing, attention, and memory. This broad pattern of impairment is consistent with a sedating effect, which is also apparent from subjective reports of mental clouding, confusion, grogginess, and light-headedness.

The prescribing information for morphine intravenous (PDR) lists the following relevant information which is instructive in this case (emphasis added):

Adverse reactions

Most Frequently Observed

Constipation, light-headedness, dizziness, drowsiness, sedation, nausea, vomiting, sweating, dysphoria and euphoria.

The less severe adverse events seen on initiation of therapy with morphine sulfate are also typical opioid side effects. They should be expected and managed as a part of opioid analgesia. The most frequent of these include drowsiness, dizziness, constipation and nausea. In many cases, the frequency of these events during initiation of therapy may be minimized by careful individualization of starting dosage, slow titration, and the avoidance of large rapid swings in plasma concentrations of the opioid. Many of these adverse events will cease or decrease as morphine sulfate therapy is continued and some degree of tolerance is developed, but others may be expected to remain troublesome throughout therapy.

Less Frequently Observed Reactions

Central Nervous System: Confusion, dry mouth, anxiety, abnormal thinking, abnormal dreams, lethargy, depression, tremor, loss of concentration, insomnia, amnesia, paresthesia, agitation, vertigo, foot drop, ataxia, hypethesia, slurred speech, hallucinations, vasodilation, euphoria, apathy, seizures, myoclonus, weakness, uncoordinated muscle movements, alterations of mood (nervousness, apprehension, depression, floating feelings), muscle rigidity, transient hallucinations and disorientation, visual disturbances, insomnia and increased intracranial pressure.

Conclusion

Thus, it is clear that Mr. Brown was being administered therapeutic doses of morphine intravenously, clear by the medical record, clear by the ASA Murphy statement, and clear by Mr. Brown's recollection of the hospitalization ("it was just like heroin"). It is my opinion that any statements or decisions made would have to be considered to be "under the strong influence of a narcotic," and certainly not made voluntarily, by an intoxicated patient who would, in my opinion, be unable to exercise his right to waive Miranda.

C. Affidavit: June 2010

I interviewed Mr. John Mucha at the Will County Jail on Thursday morning, May 27, 2010, for approximately 60 minutes. Mr. Mucha was severely injured in a motorcycle crash shortly after midnight on 7/26/09, and he was taken urgently to the Adventist Bolingbrook Hospital where he was treated for severe orthopedic and head injuries. He was treated with morphine sulfate (morphine) during the several hours of his treatment.

```
0254 Morphine 2 mg Intravenous Push (IVP)
0435 Morphine 2 mg IVP
0554 Morphine 2 mg IVP
1430 Morphine 2 mg IVP
1833 Morphine 2 mg IVP
```

An interview of the defendant was conducted by Reporting Officer (R/O) 946, beginning at 0800 on the morning of 7/26. The officer noted that Mucha was conscious and coherent. Information was recorded in the officer's report; the arrest sequence noted that "based on all evidence accumulated, R/O established probable cause to arrest the Defendant for Driving under the Influence of Alcohol." R/O told the defendant that he was under arrest for driving under the influence of alcohol and the defendant acknowledged the arrest later that evening at 2009 hours.

Mucha has a vague memory of a police officer talking with him in the hospital. He does not remember receiving any Miranda warnings. He described feeling free of pain, a "Cloud 9" feeling, "in and out," "was there and I wasn't." "Can't remember much."

Mucha is a recovering heroin addict. He had been drug free for 19 months at the time of the crash. He had no prior experience with morphine (although heroin is a morphine derivative).

Mucha described the morphine effect, in addition to relieving his pain, as "more than heroin," "stronger than heroin."

Mucha states that he would not have made a statement to the police. "Don't talk" has always been his lawyers' advice.

Opinions

In my opinion, with reasonable pharmacological certainty, Mr. John Mucha was experiencing significant effects of medicinal morphine during the time he made was interviewed by the police detective. The morphine was administered to control his pain, in full therapeutic doses and at relatively high frequency, and the effects of morphine would cause significant impairments in his cognitive and deliberative functions. By definition, patients administered therapeutic morphine, particularly in acute and early stages, are predictably impaired, and that impairment is to be expected. In my clinical practice over a period of 20 years involved in the treatment of patients with morphine and other strong opiate analgesics, it was very common to observe patients on therapeutic morphine to be obviously intoxicated, and frequently have no memory of their interaction with the clinician at a later time in the hospitalization when off morphine. Indeed, we would never consent a patient for a procedure or surgery, and would never allow the patient to sign "important papers" while being treated with morphine.

Thus, Mr. John Mucha was impaired and under the influence of strong opiate narcotics (morphine and Dilaudid) at the time he was interrogated.

In my opinion, with pharmacological certainty, as a result of the effects of therapeutic morphine, John Mucha would have been in a cognitively impaired state, unable to deliberate clearly, and unable to waive his Miranda rights.

Bases for opinions

Morphine is an opioid Controlled Substance Schedule II. It is indicated for the treatment of severe pain, and known to cause euphoria, mental clouding, and central nervous depression. There is substantial evidence and experience with morphine. Morphine has been shown to impair a variety of functions, including reaction time, tracking, information processing, attention, and memory. This broad pattern of impairment is consistent with a sedating effect, which is also apparent from subjective reports of mental clouding, confusion, grogginess, and light-headedness.

The timing, dose, and duration of action of the morphine given to John Mucha would have been at therapeutic and thus impairing levels at the two documented times noted in the police report (0800, 2009).

The prescribing information for morphine intravenous (PDR) lists the following relevant information which is instructive in this case (emphasis added):

Adverse reactions

Most Frequently Observed

Constipation, light-headedness, dizziness, drowsiness, sedation, nausea, vomiting, sweating, dysphoria and euphoria.

The less severe adverse events seen on initiation of therapy with morphine sulfate are also typical opioid side effects. They should be expected and managed as a part of opioid analgesia. The most frequent of these include drowsiness, dizziness, constipation and nausea. In many cases, the frequency of these events during initiation of therapy may be minimized by careful individualization of starting dosage, slow titration, and the avoidance of large rapid swings in plasma concentrations of the opioid. Many of these adverse events will cease or decrease as morphine sulfate therapy is continued and some degree of tolerance is developed, but others may be expected to remain troublesome throughout therapy.

Less Frequently Observed Reactions

Central Nervous System: Confusion, dry mouth, anxiety, abnormal thinking, abnormal dreams, lethargy, depression, tremor, loss of concentration, insomnia, amnesia, paresthesia, agitation, vertigo, foot drop, ataxia, hypethesia, slurred speech, hallucinations, vasodilation, euphoria, apathy, seizures, myoclonus, weakness, uncoordinated muscle movements, alterations of mood (nervousness, apprehension, depression, floating feelings), muscle rigidity, transient hallucinations and disorientation, visual disturbances, insomnia and increased intracranial pressure.

Conclusion

Thus, it is clear that Mr. John Mucha was being administered therapeutic doses of morphine intravenously prior to the time that he was interviewed by the police detective. It is my opinion that any statements or decisions made during that time would have to be considered to be "under the strong influence of a narcotic," and certainly not made voluntarily, by an intoxicated and impaired patient who would, in my opinion, be unable to exercise his right to waive Miranda.

D. Affidavit: April 2005

County of Cook
State of Illinois
AFFIDAVIT OF JAMES THOMAS O'DONNELL
April 15, 2005

You have asked that I prepare an affidavit addressing the effects of acute intravenous morphine analgesia use and ability to voluntarily waive Miranda rights.

I reviewed portions of a transcript of Douglas Ray Weikart, M.D., wherein Dr. Weikart described Mr. Mayes' injuries, the surgery Mr. Mayes received, the level of pain experienced by Mr. Mayes, and his analgesia treatment with Morphine. Dr. Weikart described a nurse administered ("pretty significant") doses of morphine, 2–4 mg, with a dose approximately 1.5 hours before the time that Mr. Mayes provided a statement to Deputy Steve Wilson at 1:00 P.M. on April 16, 2001.

Dr. Weikart describes the following morphine doses on April 16:

- 2 mg at 2:45 A.M.
- 2 mg at 4:45 A.M.
- 4 mg at 6:45 A.M.
- 4 mg at 9:40 A.M.
- 4 mg at 11:30 A.M.
- Statement given at 1:00 P.M.
- 4 mg at 2:30 A.M.

Opinion

In my opinion, with reasonable pharmacological certainty, Mr. Shannon Mayes was experiencing significant effects of medicinal morphine during the time he made a statement to Deputy Wilson. The morphine was administered to control his pain, and the effects of morphine would be present and cause significant impairments in his cognitive and deliberative functions. By definition, patients administered therapeutic morphine, particularly in acute and early stages, are predictably impaired, and that impairment is to be expected. In my clinical practice over a period of 20 years involved in the treatment of patients with morphine and other strong opiate analgesics, it was very common to observe patients on therapeutic morphine to be obviously intoxicated, and frequently have no memory of their interaction with the clinician at a later time in the hospitalization when off morphine. Thus, Mr. Shannon Mayes was impaired and under the influence of morphine at the time he was interrogated and provided a statement. As a result of his morphine use, he would be in a cognitively impaired state, unable to deliberate clearly, and unable to waive his Miranda rights.

Bases for opinions

Morphine is an opioid Controlled Substance Schedule II. It is indicated for the treatment of severe pain, and known to cause euphoria, mental clouding, and central nervous depression. There is substantial evidence and experience with morphine. Morphine has been shown to impair a variety of functions, including reaction time, tracking, information processing, attention, and memory. This broad pattern of impairment is consistent with a sedating effect, which is also apparent from subjective reports of mental clouding, confusion, grogginess, and light-headedness.

The prescribing information for morphine intravenous (PDR) lists the following relevant information which is instructive in this case (emphasis added):

Adverse reactions

Most Frequently Observed

Constipation, light-headedness, dizziness, drowsiness, sedation, nausea, vomiting, sweating, dysphoria and euphoria.

The less severe adverse events seen on initiation of therapy with morphine sulfate are also typical opioid side effects. They should be expected and managed as a part of opioid analgesia. The most frequent of these include drowsiness, dizziness, constipation and nausea. In many cases, the frequency of these events during initiation of therapy may be minimized by careful individualization of starting dosage, slow titration, and the avoidance of large rapid swings in plasma concentrations of the opioid. Many of these adverse events will cease or decrease as morphine sulfate therapy is continued and some degree of tolerance is developed, but others may be expected to remain troublesome throughout therapy.

Less Frequently Observed Reactions

Central Nervous System: Confusion, dry mouth, anxiety, abnormal thinking, abnormal dreams, lethargy, depression, tremor, loss of concentration, insomnia, amnesia, paresthesia, agitation, vertigo, foot drop, ataxia, hypethesia, slurred speech, hallucinations, vasodilation, euphoria, apathy, seizures, myoclonus, weakness, uncoordinated muscle movements, alterations of mood (nervousness, apprehension, depression, floating feelings), muscle rigidity, transient hallucinations and disorientation, visual disturbances, insomnia and increased intracranial pressure.

Conclusion

Thus, it is clear from the testimony of Dr. Weikart that Mr. Shannon Mayes was being treated with therapeutic doses of morphine intravenously. It is my opinion that any statements or decisions made would have to be considered to be "under the strong influence of a narcotic," and certainly not made voluntarily, by an intoxicated patient who would, in my opinion, be unable to exercise his right to waive Miranda.

Summary and conclusions

Applying accepted scientific principles to the facts of this case, the description of activities, description of the defendant and the police officer, the admitted amount of drinking, the start time of drinking, and the arrival of the police officer, and assuming the defendant's description of amount consumed as accurate, the blood alcohol level could not have exceeded 0.05 gm/dl, and indeed was probably closer to 0.025 mg%. The defendant was probably experiencing a hypoglycemic reaction. Vomitus in his mouth probably contaminated the Breathalyzer, rendering the reading falsely elevated.

41.14 Conclusion

The forensic pharmacist has a large number of roles in society. Pharmacists can assist attorneys in case review, the discovery process, depositions, and in trial. Pharmacists have testified in court cases relating to malpractice, product liability, criminal defense, substance abuse, DUI, and personal-injury cases.

Endnotes

1. Anderson, P.D. 2000. An Overview of Forensic Pharmacists Practice. *J Pharm Pract.* 13 (3): 179-186.

2. Anderson, P.D. 2000. An Overview of Forensic Pharmacists Practice. http://jpp.sagepub.com/content/13/3/179. abstract.

3. From personal contact with Gamal Hussein, Pharm.D., Associate Professor of Clinical Pharmacy, Northeast Louisiana University. Former Chief Forensic Pharmacist/ Criminologist, Division of Poisons and Narcotics, Federal Crime Laboratory, Cairo, Egypt.

4. Caplan, Y.M. 1987. The toxicologist: part pharmacist, part detective. *Tomorrow's Pharmacist* 4-5.

5. Gibler, B.; Hayes, G.; Raleigh, F; Levenson, B; Heber, B; Tham, A. 1996. Forensic Psychiatric Pharmacy Practice at Atascadero State Hospital. *J Pharm Pract.* 14 (4): 222-228.

6. McCarthy, R. July, 1987. Pharmacists heads up DEA task force. *American Druggist* 90-93.

7. Rucker, T.D. 1996. Appendix: Selected Job Titles of Positions Held (or Recently Held) by Pharmacy Graduates Who Serve as Nonpractitioners, Classified by Major Area of Employment. *J Pharm Pract.* 14 (4): 281-293.

8. Spencer, E. 2000. Externship at the Massachusetts Attorney General's Office. *J Pharm Pract.* 14 (3): 199-201.

9. Ambrose, P.J. 1997. Doping control in sports- a perspective from the 1996 Olympic games. *Am J Health-System Pharmacists* 54(9):1053-1057.

10. ImObersteg, A. 2000. The Role of the Pharmacist in Evaluating Drug Use in Drivers: The Drug Evaluation and Classification Program. *J Pharm Pract.* 14(3): 202-209.

11. Fraser, G.L.; Davis, T.D. 1990. The pharmacist as expert witness. *Am J Hosp Pharm.* 47: 2082-5.

12. Brody, R. 1992. Witnesses for hire: pharmacists take the stand. *American Druggist.* 44-49.

13. Schulz M, Schmold A. Therapeutic and toxic blood concentrations of more than 500 drugs. Pharmazie1997 12: 895-911.

14. Pounder, D.J. 1993. The nightmare of postmortem drug changes. In *Legal Medicine,* ed. C.H. Wecht. 163-191.

15. Ferner, R.E. 1996. Effects of drugs on behaviour. In *Forensic Pharmacology: Medicines, Mayhem, and Malpractice.* Oxford/New York: Oxford University Press.

16. Ferner, R.E. 1996. Effects on drugs on the victims of crime. In *Forensic Pharmacology: Medicines, Mayhem, and Malpractice.* Oxford/New York: Oxford University Press.

17. Hollinger, M.A. 1997. Rohypnol: the date rape drug. *The Forensic Examiner* 6 (3&4): 15-17.

18. American Psychiatric Association 1994. Factitious Disorders. *Diagnostic and Statistical Manual of Mental Disorders* 4th Edition.

19. *The People of the State of Illinois v. Richard C. Nitz.*

20. *Herman v. Sunbury Textile Mills, Inc. and American Manufacturers Mutual Insurance Company/Kemper.*

Chapter 42

Forensic Drug Testing

Anne D. ImObersteg, M.S., J.D., MBA, B.A.,
and James T. O'Donnell, Pharm.D., M.S., FCP, ABCP, FACN, R.Ph.

42.1 Introduction

Review of this chapter will assist counsel in understanding the tests, communicating with their own experts, and cross-examining opposing experts.

In order for a scientist, toxicologist, pharmacologist, pharmacist, or pathologist to correlate drug action or effects with the drug found in the body, the concentration found in the body must be sufficient to cause the adverse reaction or be beyond the expected therapeutic dose. In addition, the type of specimen collected must be one that will properly reflect the drug concentration in the body at the time of the incident/death. For these reasons, the interpretation of the drug's reaction for the purposes of determination of cause and effect can be problematic. The method of sample analy-sis and a review of the laboratory data are of key importance. Test results have the potential for error, and may need to be critiqued by a qualified expert.

The analysis of a biological specimen can take several steps. The first step, which is sometimes bypassed, is the presumptive or screening test, which enables the analyst to identify a class of drugs that may be present in a biological specimen. This step is followed by the extraction of the drug or unknown substance from the biological matrix, followed by an analysis on a scientific instrument capable of quantifying the amount of specific drug in the specimen.

42.2 The Screening Test

Laboratory analysis of a subject's urine or blood sample is often performed in two stages. The first analysis is performed using immunoassay technology and is often called a "screening" or "presumptive" test. Most commercially available immunoassay kits are screening tests for the common drugs of abuse (cocaine, methamphetamine, marijuana, phencyclidine, morphine), although some kits are available for testing other types of drugs such as the benzodiazepines and the phenothiazines. When possible, most laboratories avail themselves of the commercial screening tests since they are generally quick and inexpensive.

Presumptive drug screening is simple to perform, but difficult to interpret. Most immunoassays are called "presumptive tests," since a positive reaction is an indication that a drug or drug class is present, yet the method does not rise to the required level of certainty. Confirmation by a second test is required. The main reason why presumptive tests are not used forensically is because there is considerable cross-reactivity with drugs other than the target drug.

Lack of specificity is a common problem with immunoassay tests. For example, an immunoassay test for "opi-

---

Note: This chapter was originally produced and written, for an earlier edition of this book, by Anne D. ImObersteg, who has since deceased. It has been revised and updated by James T. O'Donnell.

ates" will flag positive for codeine, naloxone, morphine, heroin, hydrocodone, and hydromorphone. Thus a presumptive "positive" opiates result may mean that an individual has taken Tylenol with codeine, Vicodin for pain relief, or heroin. In addition, depending on the kit used and the manufacturer of the kit, still other drugs that are not considered an "opiate" may cross-react. Moreover, sometimes the analysis will give a random "false positive," flagging a sample positive when there is no target drug present at all.

There are a variety of different types of immunoassay techniques on the market. Some immunoassay techniques are more specific to the target drug than others. However, all immunoassay techniques utilize an antibody-antigen relationship to identify a drug class in a sample. An antigen is a foreign substance, such as a drug, that has been introduced into a host body. This antigen will cause an immune response in the host's body, which, in turn, will prompt the host's B-lymphocytes and plasma cells to create an antibody protein. This antibody will then be able to identify and bind to any similar antigen that is introduced into the host.

Commercial immunoassay kits contain a substrate with an antibody to a specific class of drugs, and also the target drug that is "labeled" with a tracer. In radioimmunoassay kits, the label is radioactive iodine or carbon. In fluorescence immunoassays, the label is a fluorochrome. In enzyme immunoassays, the label is a lysozyme or other enzyme. One of the most popular enzyme immunoassay kits is the enzyme multiplied immunoassay test (EMIT) developed by Syva Corporation.

The EMIT utilizes a technique known as "competitive binding." The drug (antigen) labeled with the enzyme competes with any drug found in the subject's sample for a limited supply of antibodies. When the labeled drug in the kit is bound with the antibody, the enzyme activity is inhibited. When a sample has a measurable amount of the target drug, antibodies will not bind to some of the labeled drug, and the enzyme will be active and can give a measure of the target drug concentration in the tested sample.

More target drug in the subject's sample means that there are fewer antibodies available to bind to the kit's enzyme-labeled antigen. By measuring the magnitude of enzymatic change on a substrate, the amount of drug present in the subject's sample can be determined. For example, a subject's sample with no target drug will enable most of the kit's enzyme-labeled drug to be bound to the antibodies and will result in an inhibition of the enzyme's activity. When the enzyme activity is inhibited, the substrate in the kit, NAD, cannot be oxidized into NADH. The result is a small absorbance change at 340 nm, measured spectrometrically. Conversely, a large amount of drug in a subject's sample

will leave few antibodies to react with the kit's enzyme-labeled drug, and many enzymes will be able to convert NAD to NADH, and result in a large absorbency change. The amount of NAD produced and measured is inversely proportional to the amount of target drug in the sample.

In the past, thin-layer chromatography (TLC) was occasionally used as a confirmation test. However, with the advent of more specific instruments, such as the GC-MS, TLC is now generally used as a screening test. TLC is a simple procedure that enables the chemist to determine the number and possible identity of each compound present in a mixture. This instrument allows a mixture of two or more substances in a specimen (such as urine or a pharmaceutical pill dissolved in a volatile solvent) to distribute between a stationary phase and a mobile phase. The stationary phase is a thin layer of adsorbent (silica gel or alumina) coated on a glass, metal, or plastic plate.

The mobile phase is a solvent, into which one edge of the plate is placed. A small amount of the mixture to be analyzed is spotted on the stationary phase, near the bottom of the TLC plate. The plate is then placed in a solvent in a developing chamber so that only the very bottom of the plate is in the liquid. The chamber is capped, and the solvent, by way of capillary action, is allowed to rise up the layer of silica on the plate. For each one of the mixture's components, as the solvent moves through the spot that was applied, equilibrium is established between the molecules that have adsorbed on the solid and the molecules in solution.

Since the components in the applied mixture differ in solubility in the mobile phase and in the strength of their adsorption to the stationary phase, each component will move up the plate at a unique rate, based on its partitioning between the mobile liquid phase and the stationary phase. Highly polar organic molecules interact fairly strongly with the polar adsorbents and will tend to adsorb onto the particles of the adsorbent. In contrast, weakly polar molecules are allowed to move more freely.[1] Thus, weakly polar molecules will move through the adsorbent more rapidly than the polar species, and will been seen higher up the plate than the polar molecules. In this manner, the components of a specimen are separated and may be identified by comparison to known compounds.

When the solvent front reaches the other edge of the stationary phase, the plate is removed from the solvent reservoir and dried. When the plate is examined, the original sample will have resolved into a row of spots running up the plate, with each spot containing one of the components of the original mixture

Some substances are colored, which allows a simple visual comparison of the amount of movement up the plate the compound traveled. Generally, however, the spots are difficult to detect, and must be visualized with an ultraviolet lamp or with staining agents. When the dried plate is placed in a chamber with iodine vapor, the iodine vapor oxidizes the substances in the various spots, making them visible to the eye. Ninhydrin (0.2-percent solution) is effective for visualizing amino acid spots.[2] When sprayed on the plate, amino acids display a purple coloration. In addition, visualization can be achieved through the use of an ultraviolet lamp. In this method, the adsorbent is impregnated with a fluor (zinc sulfide), which enables the plate to fluoresce everywhere except where an organic compound is present on the plate.

The amount of movement up the plate is determined by and compared against a known standard. This "retention factor," or Rf, is defined as the distance traveled by the compound divided by the distance traveled by the solvent. If the two substances have the same Rf value, they may be the same compound. If they have different Rf values, they are definitely different compounds. Since the amount of movement up the plate also is dependent on the solvent system used, the type of adsorbent, the thickness of the adsorbent, and the amount of material spotted, Rf values will change from system to system. For this reason, a known standard must be run on the same plate as the unknown specimen (so that their relative Rf values may be compared).

There are a variety of different TLC separation techniques. TLC can be automated using forced solvent flow in a vacuum-capable chamber. The ability to program the solvent delivery makes it convenient to do multiple developments in which the solvent flows for a short period of time. This method enables a higher resolution than in a single run.[3] A two-dimensional TLC process can also be applied. After running a sample in one solvent, the TLC plate is removed, dried, rotated by 90 degrees, and run in another solvent. After this process, any of the spots from the first run that contain mixtures can now be separated.

Although TLC seems like a simple procedure, there are some potential difficulties. For example, a sample that has been too heavily applied will visualize as a streak, rather than a spot. A sample possessing a strongly acidic or basic group (such as an amine) may visualize as a smear or an upward crescent. The plate solvent front may run crookedly, which makes it harder to measure Rf values accurately. Sometimes no compound can be seen on the plate because an inadequate sample was applied; or, due to heavy sample application, components with similar Rf values may not be resolved and may appear to be one large spot.

A legal action cannot be scientifically supported solely by a screening test, since a positive result may be due to a different substance or a random error. The laboratory must perform a "confirmation" test on an instrument—such as a gas chromatograph or mass spectrometer (GC-MS)—capable of differentiating between the many drugs in a drug class and quantifying the amount of drug present in the specimen. However, a biological specimen must first be properly prepared before it can be analyzed on a GC/MS instrument.

A. Case Report: False Positive Opiate from Pastry Poppy Seed Consumption

Expert opinion

The urine test in question does not prove that Mr. Richard Silver used heroin or any illicit opiate prior to the "morphine" positive test of 2/24/11. Eating poppy seed bakery products will result in exactly the same imprecise finding that is the basis of the probation revocation action.

Materials reviewed

1. Probation office petition to revoke Mr. Silver's supervised release.
2. Acculab Toxicology Services, Inc., Acct 03150001P/18090, specimen POSITIVE—MORPHINE; CONFIRMATION CUT-OFF 150NG/ML.
3. Acculab Toxicology Services Website (www.acculabs.com);
4. US Probation and Pretrial Services, 3/1/11 POSITIVE OPIATES (875NG/ML; CUT-OFF 300NG/ML).
5. www.hhs.gov/asl/testify/t980723f.html. Testimony on Federal Workplace Drug Testing by Joseph H. Autry III, M.D. SAMSHA; 7/23/98.
6. 60 FR 51118-01; 1997 WL. 596172 (F.R.). Notices, Department of Health and Human Services, Substance Abuse and Mental Health Services Administration (SAMSHA). Mandatory Guidelines for Federal Workplace Drug Testing Programs.
7. Authoritative references in analytical toxicology documenting the false positives caused by food sources in opiate urine testing and justifying the 2,000ng/ml SAMSHA and DOD confirmation cut-off for urine morphine (absent 6-MAM, a metabolite unique to heroin).

Facts of the case

Two urine samples were taken and showed positive on preliminary screening tests by the probation department (2/24/11 and 3/1/11). The 2/24/11 test was sent to Acculab

Toxicology Laboratory for confirmation testing using the sophisticated GC/MS, and the confirmation test was confirmed using a cut-off of 150ng/ml (not quantified). The second sample had insufficient volume for Acculab to conduct a confirmation test. Since only the first test was confirmed, I will not discuss the second test on 3/1/11.

Richard Silver, a methadone maintenance patient and former heroin abuser, has tested positive for morphine in the past and admitted to "using." He adamantly denies using heroin during the time period preceding the 2/24/11 test.

GC/MS—gas chromatography/mass spectroscopy—is the gold standard for analytical toxicology. It is extremely accurate, and besides positively identifying a drug, it also has the capacity to measure the amount of drug present—that is, quantify, quantitate—usually in a ng/ml measurement that is related to some amount beyond the cut-off (established to rule out false positives). IN THIS TEST, NO QUANTITATION WAS CONDUCTED. THEREFORE, IT IS UNKNOWN AS TO HOW MUCH MORPHINE WAS PRESENT IN THE URINE. The amount is important, for consumption of common food products, specifically those using poppy seeds, are well known to contribute to morphine positive tests on urine, easily far exceeding the outdated and low cutoffs set for routine urine drug screens.

Discussion

Dr. Autry (Substance Abuse and Mental Health Services Administration) provides a regulatory documentation of the level of advanced analytical toxicology science supporting higher confirmation cutoffs for opiates to rule out "poppy seed" defenses. The current understanding of the science prompted the adoption of higher cutoffs for use for Federal Employees and Department of Defense personnel.

It is well known that poppy seeds contain morphine. In one study, ingestion of three poppy seed bagels resulted in 2797 ng/mL morphine at three hours (Struempler, R., "Excretion of Codeine and Morphine Following Ingestion of Poppy Seeds," J. Anal. Tox, 1987, 11(3):97-9). In another study, the ingestion of 25 grams of poppy seeds from four brands of poppy seeds, containing between 17 and 294 mcg of morphine per gram, resulted in urine detectability over 48 hours (Hayes, L., Krasselt, W., Mueggler, P., "Concentration of Morphine and Codeine in Serum and Urine After Ingestion of Poppy Seeds," Clin Chem, 1987, 33(6): 806-8). The vast majority of the searched literature indicates that depending on the cutoff level utilized by the laboratory, the detection of morphine in the urine does not necessarily indicate illegal drug use.

Even before the 1997 FR Notice, the federal government (Department of Health and Human Services) also rec-

ognized that a positive for morphine may be a result of the donor consuming "normal dietary amounts" of poppy seeds. The Medical Review Officer (MRO), assigned to review the analytical results prior to reporting, is directed to report the result as negative unless clinical evidence of abuse or illegal use of opiates is verified. The guidelines state the MRO "shall determine that there is clinical evidence—in addition to the urine test—of illegal use of any opium, opiate, or opium derivative…" prior to reporting the result as positive. One exception to this rule: if the specimen is negative for 6-monoacetlymorphine, the result may still be verified positive if the morphine is at 15,000 ng/mL or above ("Mandatory Guidelines for Federal Workplace Drug-testing Programs," Federal Register, Vol. 59, Number 110, pp. 29908-29931, June 9, 1994; Department of Health and Human Services, Substance Abuse and Mental Health Services Administration, "Mandatory Guidelines for Federal Workplace Testing Programs," September 1, 1994).

In this case Richard Silver is charged with violating the terms of his supervised release by "using" an illegal controlled substance based on the finding of morphine in his urine. The laboratory tests that were conducted and reported can be explained by the normal consumption of poppy seeds in the routine diet (bagels, muffins). THERE IS NO PROOF THAT HEROIN OR ANY OPIATE CONTROLLED SUBSTANCE was used.

Therefore, with reasonable pharmacological certainty, there is no evidence that Mr. Silver used any morphine or heroin, prescription or illegal. The presence of the morphine reported in the urine screening and (unquantified) confirmation tests—if you believe Mr. Silver—were probably the result of dietary consumption of poppy seeds, which is certainly not a violation of anything. If you do not believe Mr. Silver, there is still no proof!

As a final note, this confounding interpretation would be eliminated by quantifying the confirmation test, not just reporting the tests that exceed thresholds. Levels beyond 2 to 4,000 are *not* considered to be caused by food ingestion of poppy seeds.

B. Case Report: Positive Cocaine Urine Drug Test—Cause of Accident

Mr. Morrow, a 44-year-old, 120 lb, 5'10" man, was washing windows on a third floor window sill, at approximately 11 A.M. on the morning of October 13, 2001, when the window frame that he was holding onto gave way, disintegrated, causing him to fall to the ground, sustaining serious injuries.

The medical records indicate the following relevant history and laboratory data:

1. Positive urine opiate
2. Positive urine cocaine
3. Negative blood alcohol
4. Denied drug use today. Patient admitting to ethanol and cocaine use last night. Social history of alcohol and cocaine use daily
5. Morphine for pain
6. Beer 3/day pre-anesthesia evaluation
7. Glasgow Coma Scale—15 (Highest rating, fully alert)
8. Alert and oriented, pupils equal and reactive, moves all extremities

Dr. Vernon has opined that this injury would have not occurred if Mr. Morrow had not been using opioids and cocaine. He further opines that ethanol (alcohol) may have also contributed to this injury, as "the patient was likely in ethanol withdrawal at the time he fell."

Mr. Morrow has been a window washer for 28 years, and the type of work he was doing when he fell was common work for him. (Having been a commercial window washer for 5 years, I am familiar with the work and the necessary tools of the trade).

He reported an alcohol consumption of 3 to 4 beers per day, twice weekly at the time of the fall. He had a history of heavier alcohol consumption earlier in his life. At the time of the fall (41 years old) he had decreased his consumption of alcohol: he did not want it as much, his "dad frowned on it." He used it a few days a week to "take the edge off."

Mr. Morrow has used cocaine for 20 years, snort and smoke, never injected. He used it 2 to 3 times a week; never more because of the cost. He never used it before work and never used it at work. His boss would send him home if he smelled alcohol or suspected drug use.

He reported no signs, symptoms or complaints that would attribute dependency, craving, or problems to the use of alcohol or cocaine during the time preceding the fall.

He denied any use of cocaine and alcohol on the day of or before work on the day of the fall. He did use cocaine and alcohol either the night before or two nights before the day of the fall. The time of consumption was recalled as 10:30 P.M.–midnight.

Opinions

You have asked for my opinion of the effect, if any, of cocaine, opiates, and/or alcohol on Mr. Morrow at the time of the fall, and if any or all of these substances contributed to the fall.

In my opinion, none of these substances contributed in any way to the fall.

First of all, the presence of opiates is due to the morphine given to Mr. Morrow before the urine test.

Secondly, his alcohol was negative. Therefore there was none in his blood. I seriously doubt and formally opine that alcohol withdrawal would cause or contribute any impairment or contribution, based on the stated and historical amounts of alcohol used at the time.

Finally, even if the cocaine was used the night before the accident, there would be no active cocaine available, and any residual effects would have been dissipated long before the fall. Urine testing only indicates that a drug is in the system; it can never be used to determine clinical effect.

Therefore, with reasonable pharmacological certainty, none of these substances (cocaine, alcohol, or opiates) contributed in any manner to Mr. Morrow's fall. He would not have been under the influence of or experiencing any effects or any drug-induced impairments at the time of the fall.

42.3 Extraction of the Drug from the Biological Matrix

Preparation of the sample for analysis requires that the biological sample be "extracted" from the biological matrix. This is generally performed using a variety of chemicals that help eliminate possible interfering substances, and allow the drug or drug class in question to dissolve in a solvent, which can then be measured on the instrument. The traditional way of extracting a drug from a biological matrix employed the use of organic solvents for extraction, back extraction into an aqueous phase, a pH adjustment, and then a final extraction into an organic solvent. Some laboratories still use this method, even though it is more cumbersome and time-consuming than the more modern way. However, there is nothing forensically wrong with using the old method; and often, especially when dealing with an unknown substance in the biological matrix, a liquid-liquid extraction is employed.

A newer method, called SPE (solid-phase extraction), is more efficient. SPE techniques use a disposable tube containing bonded silica sorbents to trap and release components of a specimen. The efficiency and selectivity of the method depends on the type of SPE sorbent used, as well as the relative physical or chemical properties of the sorbent, the solvent used for extraction, and the group of drugs targeted. There are a variety of different commercial SPE cartridges available, such as copolymer/anion exchange, bonded or nonbonded silica, reverse phase, or anion exchange. The sole purpose of these methods is to extract out, as selectively as possible, only the specific drug or drug class to be analyzed. Once extracted, the sample may be ready for analysis, or may go to an additional step called "derivitization."

The derivitization step is often performed on a drug or drug class that may (depending on the instrument used) benefit from the addition of the attachment of the derivitizing agent to the test molecule. Derivitization often enhances the quality of the analysis and enables the identification of the drug. Once this step, if required, is performed, the sample is ready for analysis on the instrument.

42.4 The Instruments

There are a variety of laboratory instruments capable of identifying and quantifying the drugs that may be found in a biological specimen. Most procedures call for the use of mass spectrometry. Mass spectrometry separates matter by molecular and atomic mass. Mass spectrometry is arguably the most versatile technology used in analytical analysis today, in that it enables the analyst to determine chemical and structural information about the different types of molecules found in the specimen.

There are many techniques that combine the power of mass spectrometry with other instruments to achieve the goals of selectivity, specificity, and sensitivity. The most common—by far—are the instrument combinations known as the GC/MS, LC/MS, and GC/MS/MS.

A. GC/MS

The gas chromatograph/mass spectrometer (GC/MS) utilizes the gas chromatograph (GC) to separate the components (drugs) of a mixture by injecting the mixture into a metal or glass column inside the instrument. The instrument's inner capillary column is coated with a chemical and packed with sand-like, chemical-coated particles. The column is contained in a heated oven designed to liquefy the coating. When a sample is injected onto the column, the injection port is at a temperature capable of volatilizing the sample (transforming it into a gas). A carrier gas pushes the volatilized sample through the column.

The chemical makeup of each of the mixture's compounds and each component's interaction with the liquefied chemicals in the column determine how long the component will take to travel the entire length of the column. Some molecules will make a slow migration through the column, and some will travel quickly through the column relatively unhindered. In any event, each component of the mixture will travel as a group through the column. The amount of time the compound is retained in the column is called the retention time (RT) of the compound. As each compound exits the column, a detector recognizes the passing of a compound and records the event on chart paper.

A drug may be identified in a specimen by comparing the retention time of any instrumental response from the analysis of the specimen with that of a calibrator or control sample, using just a GC alone. The quantity is determined by measuring the magnitude of the response. However, with the GC/MS, the GC functions as a separating mechanism and the identification and quantification is mainly the responsibility of the MS.

The MS creates gas phase ions, separates these ions in accordance to mass or time, and measures the quantity of ions of each mass-charge ratio. Gas phase ions can be prepared by a variety of methods. Perhaps the most common methods are chemical ionization (CI) and electron impact (EI). As each component exits the GC column, it enters the MS. In CI, molecules are ionized by reaction between the analyte molecules and a reagent ion to form ions by proton or hydride transfer. The other method, EI, uses an electron beam to ionize gasphase molecules. CI is sometimes used instead of EI because it provides increased sensitivity and provides more specific molecular-weight information. However, the method is technique intensive. Hardware limitations also make EI more common.

In EI, the MS bombards the drug with electrons and shatters the structure into pieces, depending on the weak points in the drug's structure. Theoretically, since each drug structure is different, each different drug will break at different points on the molecule and thus shatter into predictable pieces. The size and quantity of the pieces form a "fingerprint" of the drug. If one looks at all the pieces and their relative size, one can identify the drug in the sample.

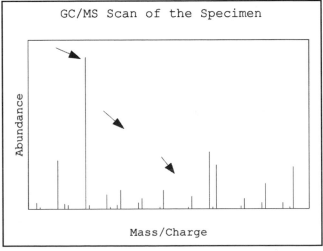

Figure 42.1 GC/MS scan of the specimen. A "scan" records all (each 0.1 amu) of the fragments created from the ionization of the molecule creating a "fingerprint" of the drug. In SIM, the analyst chooses a few relatively unique fragments to represent the identification (arrows). Each fragment must be present at an abundance relative with each other—and in correct proportion, as established by a known drug calibrator—to constitute an identification.

The data set produced by looking at all the fragmentation pieces of the molecule is called a "scan." (See Figure 42.1.) Scans are sometimes used when the identity of the molecule causing the instrument response is unknown and does not match any of the known drugs analyzed with the specimen. The fragmentation pattern of the specimen can be identified by the pattern produced, and the relative sizes of each of the fragments can be compared with one another. Identification can be performed by computation or by library match. In manual computation, the analyst must determine the chemical structure of the molecule by determining the source of the fragment. For example, a fragment with one carbon and three hydrogen atoms will have a mass of 15 (C = 12, H = 1; 12 + 3 = 15), and a fragment of 15 will be seen on the chromatogram. A trained mass spectrometrist will be able to look at an ion chromatogram, with all the ion fragments, and determine the molecular structure of the drug. An easier way, however, is to compare the pattern of the fragments with a known library match. Library databases can be purchased or created in-house. However, library matches are rarely 100 percent accurate, and most library programs will give the analyst the best match, leaving the decision up to the analyst of whether an 80 or 90 percent match constitutes an identification. Scans can be performed to identify a drug, but not to quantify the amount of drug present.

Determining the amount of drug present in the specimen is performed using selected ion monitoring (SIM). In the SIM method, the analyst selects only specific ions (rather than all the ions, as in the scan method). The benefit to using the SIM method is the ability to perform quantitations, greater instrument sensitivity, better chromatography, and better accuracy and precision. It is up to the laboratory method to decide which ions to use for identification, but they should be unique (in order to differentiate between the target drug and any similarly structured drugs).

In a typical analysis, the analyst will choose a "target" or "parent" ion for quantifying a drug and "qualifier" ions to assist in identifying the drug. These qualifier ions are two more pieces from the electron fragmentation that must be in correct proportion to the target ion in order for the identification to be made. (See Figure 42.2.) The calibrators will establish what the proportion will be for the method. When analyzing an unknown specimen, the analyst/method allows the relative sizes of the qualifier ions to the target ion to differ by about 20 percent. Thus if the qualifier ion is generally 80 percent as abundant as the target ion, a range of 64 to 96 percent is acceptable when analyzing an unknown specimen. Taken together, with the retention time as recorded by the gas chromatograph and the presence of a target ion and the qualifier ions in proper proportion, these methods can identify a drug with fairly high certainty.

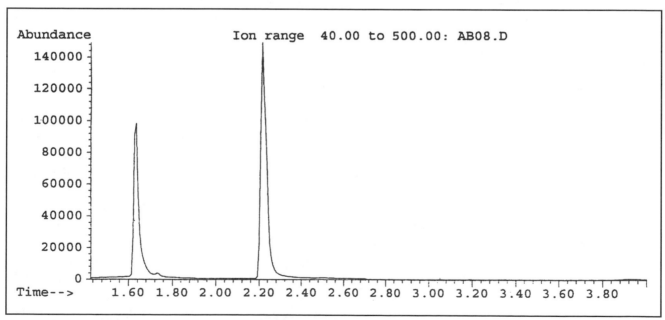

Figure 42.2 *The total ion chromatogram. Once the specific ions to be monitored are selected by the analyst via SIM, the resulting chromatograms show only the fragments selected. A total ion chromatogram (TIC) will be generated, representing the total abundances of all the selected ions at different retention times. For example, in this figure, a major compound at 12.86 minutes and another at 13.82 minutes are seen by the instrument.*

B. Quantifying a Drug Using the GC/MS

Quantifying a drug on the GC/MS is generally performed by the use of an internal standard. An internal standard is used to monitor the efficiency of the extraction procedure, or to insure that the amount detected is not due to an erroneous injection. The internal standard is usually a compound closely related in structure to the drug being sought, since it must have a retention time within a few minutes of the target drug. However, the analyst must be careful and select an internal standard that will not likely be found in the sample to be analyzed. In the GS/MS, the internal standard is usually a deuterated version of the target drug.

The internal standard is typically added at the beginning of the extraction procedure. Since the internal standard is added to an aliquot of the specimen at the beginning of the analysis, there exists from the start of the analysis a relationship of the internal standard to the drug that never changes. No matter if one drop or one cup of the extracted sample is tested, the ratio of drug to internal standard will remain constant. By plotting the ratio obtained by the instrument for a suspect's sample against a variety of standards of known drug concentrations and their respective ratios, one can determine the amount of drug present in the sample.

In order for the specimen to be quantitated, there needs to be a relationship established between the instrument response and the concentration of the specimen. To establish this relationship, a series of samples of known concentrations, called calibrators, must be created and tested. This is performed by taking a solution of the target drug and spiking the same type of biological fluid as the specimen to be tested with the drug at various concentrations. A calibrator or control without drug must also be tested. These calibrators are extracted in the same manner and around the same time as the specimen to be tested, and have the same amount of internal standard as the test specimen.

A "target" ion, generally the most abundant ion in the molecule, is chosen to be used to quantify the drug. The more abundant the target ion, the higher the concentration of the calibrator/sample. Since an internal standard is used, the ratio of the target ion of the internal standard to the target ion of the calibrator is used to help eliminate the possibility of an incomplete or overstated injection onto the GC/MS.

After the analysis of the calibrators, the relationship of the calibrator/internal standard instrument responses versus the calibrator concentration can be plotted. A straight line will be generated by the analyst or performed automatically by the computer-assisted instrument. (See Figure 42.3.)

The line generated is tested by the use of a quality control. The quality control is a sample of known concentration, which is created separately from a different solution than the calibrators. The result of the quality control, utilizing the line plotted by the calibrators, must fall within specified guidelines, generally no more than ±20 percent of the true value.

Once a relationship has been created between drug concentration versus instrument response and the line is validated by the acceptability of the quality-control result, the analyst can begin to analyze the specimen of unknown concentration. This analysis results in the determination of the instrument response, the abundance of target ions of the unknown specimen, and the target ions of the specimen's internal standard. Utilizing the line generated by the analysis of the calibrators, the analyst can then mathematically determine the concentration of the drug in the sample. (See Figure 42.4.)

C. The GC/MS/MS

The GC/MS/MS is similar to the description for the GC/MS above, but a third step is added. The initial fragmentation goes through yet another fragmentation to produce daughter fragments. This method is often used for better selectivity and specificity, but is not as common as the GC/MS because of the cost of the instrument.

D. The LC/MS

Liquid chromatography (LC) is a separation technique whereby the test specimen is forced over a chemical system contained in a column by means of a flowing solvent stream rather than via gas (as with the GC). As with a GC, the individual compounds in the mixture travel at different rates down the column, depending on the chemical interaction of the mixture with the chemical system contained in the column.

The solvent system can be of a single buffered solvent (isocratic) or be a combination of several solvent systems (gradient). The benefit of a gradient system is the versatility in analyzing a wide range of compounds, and the ability to produce a higher concentration of the drug. Gradient is most often used when the specimen contains unknown drugs. The isocratic method is faster, and thus is more attractive to laboratories that analyze large quantities of specimens.

LC can be used alone with the traditional ultraviolet, visible, fluorescence, or electrochemical detector, or coupled with a MS. Use of LC/MS is steadily increasing in the field of toxicology, partly due to the ease in sample preparations, and partly because of the instrument's simple extractions and lack of need for derivitization.

42.5 Sources of Instrumental Error

Regardless of the instrument chosen, there are many opportunities for error to be introduced into the testing process.

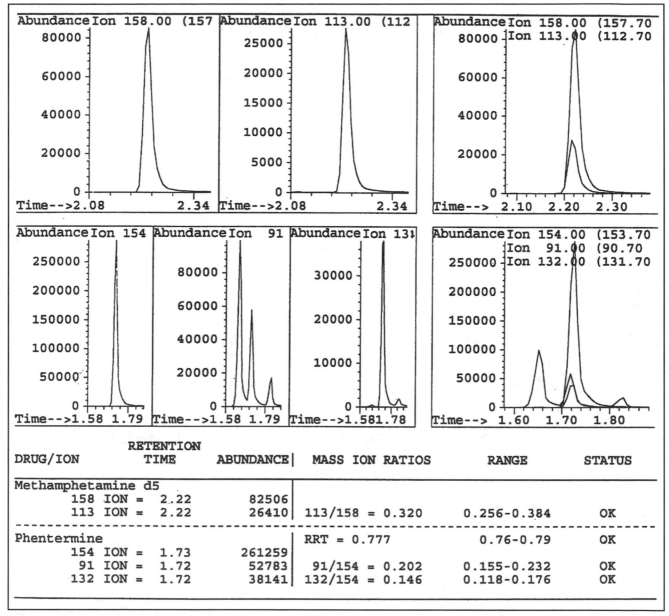

DRUG/ION	RETENTION TIME	ABUNDANCE	MASS ION RATIOS	RANGE	STATUS
Methamphetamine d5					
158 ION =	2.22	82506			
113 ION =	2.22	26410	113/158 = 0.320	0.256-0.384	OK
Phentermine			RRT = 0.777	0.76-0.79	OK
154 ION =	1.73	261259			
91 ION =	1.72	52783	91/154 = 0.202	0.155-0.232	OK
132 ION =	1.72	38141	132/154 = 0.146	0.118-0.176	OK

Figure 42.3 *Sample data sheet. The peaks seen on the TIC (Figure 42.4) chromatogram represent the instrument's response and detection of a compound with any or all of the selected ions at different retention times. On the left side of Figure 42.4, the abundances of the selected ions of the TIC peak with retention times at 13.813 and 13.833 are shown. On the right side of Figure 42.4, the deuterated (D3) morphine internal standard and the morphine in the specimen are shown. The ratio of the response (Resp) of the D3-morphine target ion (470302) and the specimen target ion response (278222) determine the resulting concentration of 0.056 ug/mL for the specimen. Note that the target ion has a ratio of 100, and the qualifier ions (432 and 199 for D3-morphine, and 429 and 196 for morphine) must be between the upper and lower established ranges to constitute an identification.*

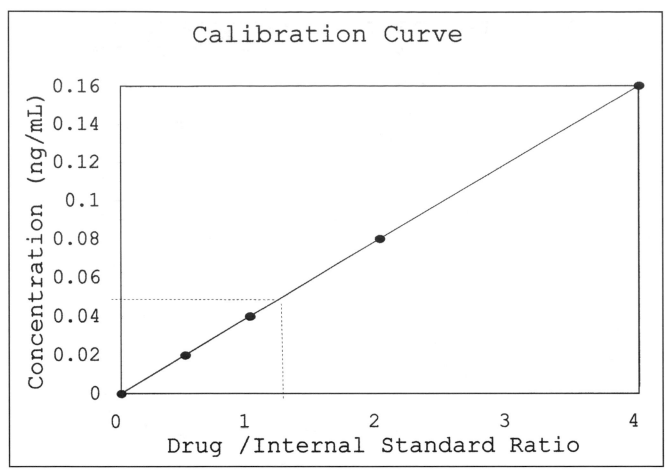

Figure 42.4 *Calibration curve figure. A relationship between 1) the concentration of the calibrator prepared by the analyst and 2) the ratio of the instrument's response of the drug—divided by the instrument's response of the internal standard—is plotted. A straight line is drawn to establish a linear relationship. The concentration of drug in the specimen can then be determined by measuring the drug/internal standard instrument response and mathematically or visually determining the corresponding concentration. In this example, a specimen with a drug/internal standard response ratio would be about 0.06 ng/mL. All modern GC or LC/MS systems are computerized to perform this function automatically.*

The magnitude of the error is dependent on the type and degree of error allowed by the analyst of the method employed. Regardless of the source, appreciable error results in uncertainty of the identification and quantitation of the drug in the specimen and may directly impact litigation.

Errors in sample preparation, including extraction, directly affect the resulting numerical result. Improperly prepared calibrations and changes in the amount of sample used for extraction introduce the greatest magnitude of error. For these reasons, the quality-control sample must always be used to ensure that the calibrators were properly made. Likewise, the internal standard must be added as soon as possible in the preparation steps.

Errors in analysis can be introduced in many ways. One way is by the improper selection of calibrators to create the concentration/instrument response relationship. The calibra-

tion line does not always travel through zero, and may not be linear at all levels. Of special concern is when the drug concentration of the unknown specimen is greater than the highest calibrator used to create the linear relationship, since the relationship can only be shown to be linear through the range of the calibrators. After the highest or lowest calibrator, the line may cease to be linear and may curve. Thus, it is important to elicit the experimental upper range of linearity from the testing laboratory. It should be noted that although the laboratory has scientifically determined this upper level in the past, only the calibrators used at the time of the test can determine the working parameters of the instrument at the time of the subject's test.

To overcome the problem of a sample being higher than the calibrators, some laboratories dilute the sample, or use less sample volume, and then multiply the calculated concentration by the dilution factor. This dilution step, unfortunately, introduces another possible source of experimental error.

Sometimes the concentration of the drug in the subject's sample is too minute for the limit of detection for the method and instrument used. Although the GC/MS is state of the art, there is a level of target molecule so low that the instrument cannot identify or consistently quantify the sample. These levels are respectively called the "limit of detection" and the "limit of quantitation."

The analyst must be careful to measure the amount of response properly so that a proper ratio can be determined. Typically, the responses should be Gaussian in shape, or much like a sharp triangle. However, when the chromatography starts to deteriorate, "shoulders" and other bumps start to distort the Gaussian peak. When this happens, area is added to the peak, and is erroneously attributed to the amount of drug.

42.6 Types of Errors

Errors can include the following:

- improper sampling of the aliquot from the sample vial,
- error in spiking calibrators from which the instrument response line will be generated,
- improper addition of the internal standard,
- poor chromatography,
- inadequate testing of other drugs to eliminate interference or misidentification,
- improper range of calibrators,
- lack of proper controls,
- lack of linearity of the concentration/instrument response curve, and
- carryover or contamination from the sample analyzed immediately preceding.

42.7 Discovery

Discovery of the proper laboratory data is essential for determining the exact quantity of drug found in a biological specimen. The following data should be discovered.

A. Sample Collection

- documentation of the time of the incident/death
- documentation of the location of the sample draw (arm, heart, femoral artery, and so on)
- postmortem: time of autopsy
- method of body storage prior to autopsy
- damage to stomach and other internal organs

B. Standard Operating Procedure

Standard operating procedure (SOP) for evaluating analysis QA/QC should include the following:

1. Testing and certification

- results of the last two proficiency tests given by an outside organization, if any
- results of in-house blind QA tests given in the last 12 months
- results of any proficiency tests given to the analyst in this case

2. Screening test

- all screening test results for the subject's specimen
- all quality controls and calibrator results for the run in which the specimen was tested
- the identification of the manufacturer of the reagent kit used in the analysis
- the manufacturer's product insert provided with the kit
- the method used by the laboratory in the analysis
- procedures used that differ from the manufacturer's method
- results of specificity tests performed by the laboratory for the drug in question

3. Confirmation

- identification of the type of instrument and detector used
- all GC, GC/MS, and/or LC/MS data (chromatograms and ion identification) of the subject's specimen
- all GC, GC/MS, and/or LC/MS data (chromatograms and ion identification) of the calibrators/controls
- the GC, GC/MS, and/or LC/MS method identifying the chromatography, RT and ion ratio acceptability
- all specificity data for the drug in question on the GC, GC/MS, LC/MS
- the extraction procedure and sample preparation method
- the run list identifying the position of the subject's sample in the order of analysis

42.8 Summary

Proper analysis of the biological specimen for drugs is crucial to the litigation of drug-related cases. The identity and quantity of the drug found in the specimen should always be critically reviewed and questioned. Whether representing a plaintiff or defendant, the data gleaned from a close review may make or break a case.

Analysis of the sample generally starts with a screening of the specimen by use of a presumptive test, followed by extraction of the drug from the biological matrix and analysis on a confirming instrument, such as the GC-MS. It is critical that each of these steps follow acceptable forensic and scientific standards to ensure the identity and integrity of the analysis.

Generally, the specimen will go through a screening or presumptive test to determine whether it contains a specific drug or drug class. The screening test must have quality controls, calibrators, and negative controls that meet the defined criteria as established by the laboratory. Ideally, the specimen should be tested in duplicate. Specimens tested in singlet have the potential of error because of incorrect sampling by the analyst, cross-reactivity with other drugs in the sample (which can cause false positives), as well as unexplained, randomly occurring errors. Thus, though specimens tested in singlet may be quick and inexpensive for the laboratory, they do not rise to the certainty required in court. The most that can be said about a result from a presumptive screening test is that there is a potential of the target drug class being present in the specimen.

The extraction of the drug from the specimen is necessary to prepare it for the confirmation step. A series of standards and controls should be extracted concurrently with the sample specimen. The use of an internal standard in the extraction procedure is the most common and recommended practice. Use of an internal standard helps eliminate extraction errors, since any error in the extraction of the target drug from the specimen will likely be reflected in an equally poor extraction of the internal standard. A poor recovery of the internal standard alerts the analyst to a possible extraction error.

After extraction, the specimen extract is analyzed on a confirmation instrument, generally a GC/MS. The GC/MS will identify and quantitate the drug in the specimen. However, the accuracy of the measurement is only as good as the method used by the laboratory. The selected method must have been rigorously validated in the laboratory prior to use to help eliminate the possibility of misidentification. Calibration standards and controls must be used in the analysis to ensure that the measurement is correct.

If the presumptive screening result and the GC/MS result are consistent, and if all standard scientific criteria are met, the specimen result is then reported. Toxicology experts then interpret the results to determine the levels of the drug and corresponding effects.

Interpretation of the results is dependent on the quality and quantity of the data given to the expert to review. The expert must be given all the screening and confirmation data from the specimen, as well as from the standards and controls used in the analysis. A copy of the laboratory's SOP should be reviewed to ensure that the proper steps were taken. The laboratory's validation data should be reviewed to ensure that the method used has the necessary level of sensitivity and accuracy for the test.

Finally—but perhaps most importantly—the identity and integrity of the specimen must be documented through each step.

Endnotes

1. Caplan, Y.A. 1981. "Analytical Techniques." Cravy, B.; and Baselt, R., Eds. *Introduction to Forensic Toxicology.* (Davis, CA: Biomedical Publications) 160.

2. Caplan, Y.H.; Levine, B. 1989. "Abbott Phencyclidine and Barbiturates Abused Drug Assays Evaluation and Comparison of ADx FPIA, TDx FPIA, EMIT, and GC/MS Methods." *J. Anal. Toxicol.* 13:289.

3. Chen, X.H.; Franke, J.P.; DeZeeuw, R.A. 1992. "Solid Phase Extraction for Systematic Toxicological Analysis." *Forensic Sci. Rev.* 4:147.

Recommended Reading

Clement, R.E. et al. 1986. "Gas Chromatography." *Analytical Chem.* 52:321.

Cody, J.T. 1990. "Cross-reactivity of Amphetamine and Analogues with Roche Abuscreen Immunoassay Reagents." *J. Anal. Toxicol.* 14:50.

Cody, J.T. 1995. "Metabolic Precursors to Amphetamine and Methamphetamine." *Forensic Sci. Rev.* 5:111.

Cone, E.J. et al. 1992. "Forensic Drug Testing for Opiates. IV Analytical Sensitivity, Specificity and Accuracy of Commercial Urine Opiates Immunoassays," *J. Anal. Toxicol.* 16:72.

Cooks, R.G.; Kalser, R.E., Jr. 1990. "Quadruple Ion Mass Spectrometry." *Acc. Of Chem. Res.* 23:213.

Crane, T.; Dawson, C.M.; Tickner, T.R. 1987. "False-Positive Results from the Syva EMIT d.a.u. Monocolonal Amphetamine Assay as a result of Antipsychotic Drug Therapy," *Clin. Chem.* 39:1080.

Dixit, V.; Dixit, V.M. May/June 1990. "A Solid-Phase Extraction Technique for Preparation of Drugs of Abuse Samples." *Amer. Clin. Lab.* 46.

Ferrara, S.D. et al. 1994. "Drug-of-Abuse Testing in Urine: Statistical Approach and Experimental Comparison of Immunochemical and Chromatographic Technique," *J. Anal. Toxicology.* 18:278.

Karasek, F.W. 1988. *Basic Gas Chromatography-Mass Spectrometry.* (N.Y.: Elsevier Press).

Liu, R.H.; Goldberger, B.A.; Eds. 1995. *Handbook of Workplace Drug Testing.* (Washington, D.C.: AACC Press).

Maurer, H.H. 1992. "Systematic Toxicological Analysis of Drugs and Their Metabolites by Gas Chromatography-Mass Spectrometry." *J. Chromatog.* 580:3.

McLafferty, F.W. 1983. *Interpretation of Mass Spectra,* 3rd Edition. (Mill Valley, CA: University Science Books).

Poklis, A. 1981. "An Evaluation of EMIT-d.a.u. Benzodiazepine metabolite Assay for Urine Drug Screening." *J. Anal. Toxicol.* 5:174.

Price, P. 1991. "Standard Definition of Terms Relating to Mass Spectrometry." *J. Am. Soc. Mass Spectrom.* 2:236.

Rouse, B.A. 1996. "Epidemiology of Illicit and Abused Drugs in the General Population, Emergency Department Drug-Related Episodes and Arrestees." *Clin. Chem.* 42:1330.

Scheurer, J.; Moore, C.M. 1992. "Solid-phase Extraction of Drugs from Biological Tissues: A Review." *L. Anal. Toxicol.* 16:264.

Suzuki, O; Seno, H.; Ishii, A. 1996. "Analytical Toxicology." *Forensic Sci. Int.* 80:65.

Weaver, M.L. et al. 1986. "Correlations of Radioimmunoassay, Fluorescence Polarization Immunoassay, and Enzyme Immunoassay of Cannabis Metabolites with Gas Chromatography/Mass Spectrometry Analysis of 11-nor-delta nine tetrahydrocannabinol-9-carboxylic Acid in Urine Specimens." *Forensic Sci. Int.* 49:43.

Appendix 42.1
Hair Test Report

December 6, 2009

At your request, I reviewed the two Psychiatric Reports RE: Mr. C of Stafford C. MD, and a report of Quest Labs regarding an October 20, 2009 hair test. I also interviewed Mr. C in your office on Wednesday, December 2, 2009.

For purposes of my consultation, at issue is the interpretation of a positive cocaine hair test. Mr. C absolutely denies any cocaine use contemporaneous with the test. Indeed, random tests for urine and hair for several months previous were negative for cocaine, consistent with cocaine abstinence.

Richard provided samples of urine and hair on October 20, 2009. Substance abuse panels on the urine and hair were conducted for the following substances:

	Hair	Urine
Amphetamines	Negative	Negative
Cocaine—metabolites		
Benzoylecgonine	Negative	Negative
Cocaine	POSITIVE (730pg/mg)	Negative
Cocaethylene	Negative	Negative
Norcocaine	Negative	Negative
Marijuana Metabolite	Negative	Negative
Opiates	Negative	Negative
Phencyclidine (PCP)	Negative	Negative
Alcohol (ethyl glucoronide)	Negative	Negative

Mr. C reported to me and to Dr. H that "my wife had a usage problem cocaine, marijuana, prescription medication and alcohol. I was finding remnants in baggies and pen caps....I saw a razor blade, rolled up dollar bills...." Mr. C further reported to me that he lived part time in his home before the October 20 "positive," sleeping in the marital bed, using a common bath, towels, sometimes the same toothbrush. He further noted that he and his wife "always had sex," and was intimately exposed to mouth and genital bodily fluids.

Dr. H opines that "there is evidence that Mr. C had within the summer of 2009 self-administered cocaine and alcohol. Dr. H discounts Mr. C's denial of cocaine use and adopts the positive cocaine hair test "as Quest Laboratories and all other reputable laboratories have an elaborate, *scientifically-proven* washing procedure prior to specimens undergoing analysis (GC/MS). This washing procedure is designed to specifically remove external contaminants and *decrease the likelihood* of false positives. It is further clinically significant that the method of laboratory analysis involves assessing for cocaine that has been ingested and incorporated into the hair follicle....Further, the qualitative laboratory value was found to be 730 picograms/milligram, more than twice the cutoff value of 300 pg/mg."

Opinions

I have the following opinions with pharmacological certainty:

1. I disagree with psychiatrist. There is insufficient evidence to conclude that Mr. C ingested cocaine sometime between the last hair and urine test in the summer and several days before October 20, 2009. In fact, careful consideration of the test results rule out consumption in favor of environmental or passive exposure to cocaine.

Bases for opinions

1. There is no dispute as to Mr. C's wife's substance abuse, including cocaine.
2. Use of cocaine by a household member in and out of the house can and does result in detectable cocaine in residents of the same household. There is no dispute as to this scientific fact.
3. "Elaborate and scientifically proven" washing methods do NOT *always* (and completely) remove environmental (passive) cocaine contamination of hair. The toxicology literature, including SAMHSA conference proceedings, caution against misinterpretation of hair testing results, due the known passive exposure in and inability to "wash" all environmental sources from the tested hair. (Christine Moore, PhD, SAMHSA 1997)
4. Consumed cocaine results in both COCAINE (COC) and the BENZOYLECGONINE (BE) METABOLITE in the hair shaft, with a preponderance of the COC. Environmental exposure results in findings of COC alone, no BE. Mr. Sklare's 10/20/09 hair test was NEGATIVE for the Cocaine metabolite (BE).
5. A 730pg/mg Cocaine is not a high level. Indeed, some laboratories use 500pg/mg as a cutoff, and one reported a cutoff of 1,250pg/mg (Reuschel SA. Smith FP. *Journal of Forensic Sciences.* 36(4):1179-85, 1991 Jul.). Further, there is very little correlation be-

tween cocaine levels in hair and dose or frequency of cocaine use.

6. In general, hair test data have been judged to be variable and unreliable in military court-martials and data have usually not been admitted when urine results are positive and hair results are negative. Hair test data have been admitted more frequently when used to substantiate other positive test results.(Huestis MA. Chapter 1: Technical and Legal Aspects of Drugs of Abuse Testing in Hair.)

7. Unresolved scientific, forensic, and ethical issues may have a greater effect on the weight applied to hair test evidence rather than its admissibility in future court proceedings. (Huestis MA. Judicial Acceptance of Hair Tests for Substances of Abuse in the United States courts: Scientific, Forensic and Ethical Aspects. *Therapeutic Drug Monitoring.* 18; 456–459. 1996)

Literature extracts

An extraction of the Moore statements from a SAMHSA symposium, as well as abstracts from several toxicology references and journals are appended to this report for the edification of the reader.

Summary and conclusion

There is INSUFFICIENT evidence of clinical use of cocaine—that is consumption—by Mr. C. The only reasonable, scientifically sound evidence based conclusion that can be drawn from the 10/20/09 positive cocaine hair test is that Mr. C was environmentally exposed to cocaine, which no one disputes.

Very truly yours,

James O'Donnell, Pharm.D., MS, FCP, ABCP, FACN, CNS. R.Ph.
Diplomate-American Board of Clinical Pharmacology
Associate Professor of Pharmacology
Rush University Medical Center—Rush Medical College

Relevant literature

Excerpts and abstracts are presented and annotated (emphasis added). Full text articles have been ordered and will be supplemented.

1. Substance Abuse and Mental Health Services Administration (SAMHSA) Scientific Meeting on: Drug Testing of Alternative Specimens and Technologies (Part II), Transcript - Day 2.

Christine Moore Ph.D.: "In June in this meeting in Strasbourg, the European Society decided that they would have no further discussion of meaningful cutoff levels for hair, which is very interesting. The acceptance of cutoffs above which would mean use and below which would mean exposure, to my mind, for hair, is nonsense. I think that I am in a bit of a unique position to say that. The vast majority of our samples that we look at—and I will get to that in a moment—come from children in households who have been exposed to drugs, where the parents are users and these children are exposed. I see levels all the time above these proposed cutoff levels, from individuals who have been exposed, not users. I guess you could say, how do you know these children don't use drugs. Well, I don't. I wasn't in the house.

Dr. Smith and I think Dr. Kidwell published some work from Alabama where they looked at hair, skin swabs, saliva and urine from children in this situation. With some outliers, predominantly they found the urine and saliva to be negative and the skin swabs and the hair to be positive, which would suggest that there is exposure and not use by the children. What we do is, we don't have cutoffs. We have limits of detection. This is the level to which we can reliably take our technology on a daily basis.

2. Despite the fact that hair is considered an important—if not the most important—non-conventional biological sample and despite the bulk literature that exists on hair analysis, the interpretation of hair analysis results, in many cases, still remains a debated question among the scientific community.

To date, an unequivocal decontamination procedure, widely accepted for hair analysis for all substances, does not exist, as it was mentioned in the relevant section in this review. Relevant studies have reported that the application of an effective washing procedure could result in grater than 90 percent removal of the contaminated substance. However, it still remains the most critical point: the successful identification of those samples that possibly exceed the cutoff levels as false positives, due to the remaining portion of contaminating drug (<10 percent) that has not been removed by the washing procedure. (Boumba VA, Ziavron KS, and Vougiouklakis T. Hair as a Biological Indicator of Drug Use, Drug Abuse or Chronic Exposure to Environmental Toxicants. *International Journal of Toxicology* 25:165–163, 2006, at page 154.)

3. Abstract Only
Unique Identifier: 8138216
Status: MEDLINE
Authors: Blank DL. Kidwell DA.
Authors Full Name: Blank, D L. Kidwell, D A.
Institution: Bureau of Naval Personnel, Navy Drug and Alcohol Program, Washington, DC 20370.
Title: External contamination of hair by cocaine: an issue in forensic interpretation.
Source: *Forensic Science International.* 63(1-3):145-56; discussion 157-60, 1993 Dec.

Abstract: This paper explores the variables by which hair samples may become contaminated with cocaine and thereby generate false positives during analysis of hair samples. A novel method for following the incorporation and removal of cocaine from hair was developed. This method allowed a large number of specimens to be analyzed under a variety of conditions with high precision. The quantity of cocaine was carefully followed in each step of a published procedure. Regardless of washing technique, a substantial amount of cocaine could still be found in the final hair digest. Very few of our externally contaminated samples could be identified as externally contaminated by previously published criteria and washing procedures. Attempts to further decontaminate this hair were without success. Our data strongly suggest that external contamination of hair by drugs of abuse may make the interpretation of forensic results problematical. Abstract Full Text PDF Online for $32 or member of ACCP.

4. Unique Identifier: 1640006
Status: MEDLINE
Authors: Koren G. Klein J. Forman R. Graham K.
Authors Full Name: Koren, G. Klein, J. Forman, R. Graham, K.
Institution: Department of Pediatrics, Hospital for Sick Children, Toronto, Ontario.
Title: Hair analysis of cocaine: differentiation between systemic exposure and external contamination.
Source: *Journal of Clinical Pharmacology.* 32(7):671-5, 1992 Jul.

Abstract: Cocaine has been shown to accumulate in the hair of admitted users. Before using this test to verify cocaine use, however, it is crucial to differentiate between systemic exposure and external contamination from being in contact with crack smoke. In the present studies, the authors document that pyrolysis of crack results in hair accumulation of cocaine, but not its benzoylecgonine metabolite, whereas after admitted cocaine use both species are detectable in hair. External contamination with crack smoke is washable, whereas systemic exposure is not. The authors suggest these two criteria to distinguish systemic exposure from external contamination.

5. Abstract Only
Unique Identifier: 1537640
Status: MEDLINE
Authors: Magura S. Freeman RC. Siddiqi Q. Lipton DS.
Authors Full Name: Magura, S. Freeman, R C. Siddiqi, Q. Lipton, D S.
Institution: Narcotic and Drug Research, Inc., New York, New York 10013.
Title: The validity of hair analysis for detecting cocaine and heroin use among addicts.
Source: *International Journal of the Addictions.* 27(1):51-69, 1992 Jan.

Abstract: Radioimmunoassay of hair (RIAH) was compared with two criterion measures, confidential EMIT urinalysis and self-reporting of cocaine/heroin use, for a purposive sample of 134 persons in methadone treatment. Positive or negative RIAH was "confirmed" by urinalysis and/or self-report in 87 and 84 percent of the cases for cocaine and heroin (morphine), respectively. Corroborative evidence indicated that "excess" RIAH positives were attributable to the narrow window of detection for urinalysis (2 days), failure to admit drug use even to researchers, and/or inadvertent ingestion of small amounts of drug. A global self-report of cocaine use intensity was related to amount in the hair.

6. Abstract Only
Unique Identifier: 8336486
Status: MEDLINE
Authors: Martinez F. Poet TS. Pillai R. Erickson J. Estrada AL. Watson RR.
Authors Full Name: Martinez, F. Poet, T S. Pillai, R. Erickson, J. Estrada, A L. Watson, R. R.
Institution: Department of Family and Community Medicine, University of Arizona, Arizona Health Sciences Center, Tucson 85724.
Title: Cocaine metabolite (benzoylecgonine) in hair and urine of drug users.
Source: *Journal of Analytical Toxicology.* 17(3):138-42, 1993 May-Jun.

Abstract: Two methods of drug detection, urinalysis and hair analysis, were compared with respect to the efficiency of identification of drug use in a population of men living on the Arizona-Mexico border. The standard curve of cannabinoids in urine was linear to 20 ng/mL. The GC/MS levels for all cannabinoids combined in urine were very similar to that obtained by radioimmunoassay (RIA), 91 percent concordance. Similar results were obtained from samples analyzed dually for the cocaine metabolite benzoylecgonine (BE) after spiking. As determined by RIA of urine, 74 percent of the subjects were positive for cannabinoids. The majority were in the range of 100-1000 ng/mg creatinine. The pattern of excretion of THC metabolites with respect to the verbally reported time of first use was fairly normal, with the peak rate of elimination 13-24 hours following the last reported use. Washed hair samples were extracted by overnight acid hydrolysis. Urine samples and neutralized hair extracts were analyzed for cocaine and BE by RIA. Of the hair samples, 55 percent contained cocaine/BE, as compared with only 4.3 percent of the urine samples. Most hair samples contained cocaine/BE in the range of 25-100 ng/sample (100 mg hair). All hair samples testing negative for cocaine/BE by RIA also tested negative by GC/MS, and four samples containing the highest amounts of cocaine and BE by RIA were similarly found to contain the highest amounts by GC/MS. Hair analysis, therefore, gives a wider window of detection of drug use than does urinalysis and shows merit in the confirmation of cocaine use in small clinical research studies.

7. Abstract Only
9042714
Status: MEDLINE
Authors: Mieczkowski T.
Authors Full Name: Mieczkowski, T.
Institution: Department of Criminology, University of South Florida, USA.
Title: Distinguishing passive contamination from active cocaine consumption: assessing the occupational exposure of narcotics officers to cocaine. [Review] [47 refs]
Source: *Forensic Science International.* 84(1-3):87-111, 1997 Jan 17.

Abstract: Hair analysis has been used in probationary and parole populations to monitor for cocaine use, but only in very limited settings or circumstances. Its wider adoption has been limited by questions regarding the ability to distinguish environmental contamination of hair via casual contact from actual ingestion. To evaluate this capability we sought to identify persons routinely exposed to cocaine, who were not cocaine users. Undercover narcotics officers engaged in cocaine-centered enforcement activities and evidence room clerks who have no history of cocaine use were identified as an appropriate example population. Thirty-six active undercover officers and four evidence technicians were asked to voluntarily submit hair samples for analysis. Additionally two cocaine contaminated (aqueous soaked), three negative control samples, and hair from a self-reported crack smoker were also blindly submitted to the testing laboratory. The hair samples were washed and after washing, enzyme digested. The wash solutions and hair digest were each analyzed for the presence of cocaine. The results indicate that nearly every person had trace amounts of cocaine contamination in the wash fraction, and one person had cocaine present in his hair digest. That person, when retested, was a negative. The laboratory correctly identified and characterized the contaminated, negative, and positive controls. The study concludes that the findings support the capability of hair analysis to distinguish cocaine use from exposure under normal field conditions. The study results indicate that cocaine-abstinent persons who are in chronic, casual environmental contact with cocaine are not likely to test hair positive for cocaine using the analysis protocols followed in this project. The study also indicates that passive microingestion of cocaine needs to be considered when examining persons who are in cocaine intensive environments. [References: 47]

8. Abstract Only
Unique Identifier: 8138220
Status: MEDLINE
Authors: Moeller MR. Fey P. Wennig R.
Authors Full Name: Moeller, M R. Fey, P. Wennig, R.
Institution: Institute of Legal Medicine, University of the Saarland, Homburg, Germany.
Title: Simultaneous determination of drugs of abuse (opiates, cocaine and amphetamine) in human hair by GC/MS and its application to a methadone treatment program.
Source: Forensic Science International. 63(1-3):185-206, 1993 Dec.

Abstract: A new method was developed for the simultaneous detection and quantitation of 6-acetyl-morphine (MAM), amphetamine, benzoylecgonine (BZE), cocaine, codeine, dihydrocodeine, EDDP (methadone metabolite), methadone and morphine in hair. The hair samples were washed, cut into 2-cm segments, pulverized, incubated with phosphate buffer and beta-glucuronidase/aryl-sulfatase. After solid phase extraction and derivatization with pentafluoropropionic anhydride/pentafluoropropanol, the drugs were identified

and measured by gas chromatography/mass spectrometry using their deuterated analogues as internal standards. The method is reproducible with detection limits under 0.1 ng/mg hair for almost all substances tested. Fifteen hair samples from five subjects of a methadone treatment program were collected in a 6-month period. The hair samples were segmented and examined for methadone, its main metabolite EDDP, and drugs of abuse. Of the 96 segments analyzed, 95 percent were positive for methadone (mean value, 10.9 ng/mg), 76 percent for the metabolite EDDP (mean value, 1.2 ng/mg), 69 percent for opiates (mean values, MAM, 7.3 ng/mg; morphine, 2.9 ng/mg; codeine, 1.0 ng/mg) and 43 percent for cocaine (mean values, cocaine, 2.6 ng/mg; BZE, 1.1 ng/mg). A correlation of 0.63 was found between administered methadone dosages and concentrations measured by hair analysis. Further investigation is needed to clarify interindividual differences.

9. Abstract Only
Unique Identifier: 1294835
Status: MEDLINE
Authors: Moller MR. Fey P. Rimbach S.
Authors Full Name: Moller, M R. Fey, P. Rimbach, S.
Institution: Institute of Legal Medicine, State University of Saarland, Homburg, Germany.
Title: Identification and quantitation of cocaine and its metabolites, benzoylecgonine and ecgonine methyl ester, in hair of Bolivian coca chewers by gas chromatography/mass spectrometry.
Source: Journal of Analytical Toxicology. 16(5):291-6, 1992 Sep-Oct.

Abstract: Twenty hair samples obtained from Bolivian mine workers who chewed 3-8 g of coca leaves daily for several years were analyzed for cocaine and its main metabolites, benzoylecgonine (BZE) and ecgonine methyl ester (EME). A new method was developed for the detection and quantitation of cocaine and its metabolites, BZE and EME, from hair in a single procedure. The hair samples were washed, cut into 56 segments (2-cm length), pulverized, and incubated with phosphate buffer and the enzyme beta-glucuronidase-arylsulfatase. After solid phase extraction and derivatization with pentafluoropropionic anhydride/pentafluoropropanol, the drugs were identified and measured by gas chromatography/mass spectrometry (GC/MS) using deuterated cocaine, BZE, and EME as internal standards. The method is reproducible (cocaine, CV = 8 percent; BZE, CV = 14 percent) and the detection limit for cocaine and BZE was 0.1 ng/mg, for EME 1 ng/mg. In the different hair segments, cocaine was found to be present in concentrations between 1.4 to 50.6 ng/mg, benzoylecgonine from 0.4 to 17.6 ng/mg, and ecgonine methyl ester traces below the calibration curve of approximately 12.9 ng/mg. In 95 percent of the cases cocaine exceeded BZE and EME in concentration.

10. Abstract Only
Unique Identifier: 9042708
Status: MEDLINE
Authors: Pepin G. Gaillard Y.
Authors Full Name: Pepin, G. Gaillard, Y.
Institution: Laboratoire d'Expertises Toxlab, Paris, France.
Title: Concordance between self-reported drug use and findings in hair about cocaine and heroin.
Source: Forensic Science International. 84(1-3):37-41, 1997 Jan 17.
    Abstract: We have presented the results concerning 135 judicial expert opinions over a 3-year period. We have compared the measured levels in hair of 6-acetylmorphine (6-AM) and of cocaine with the habitual use declared by the consumers. This allows us to propose three levels (low, medium, high) of consumption in relation to the level of the 6-AM marker found in hair for the consumption of heroin, and the level of cocaine as a marker for the cocaine intake.

11. Abstract Only
Unique Identifier: 1919477
Status: MEDLINE
Authors: Reuschel SA. Smith FP.
Authors Full Name: Reuschel, S A. Smith, F P.
Institution: Department of Criminal Justice, University of Alabama, Birmingham.
Title: Benzoylecgonine (cocaine metabolite) detection in hair samples of jail detainees using radioimmunoassay (RIA) and gas chromatography/mass spectrometry (GC/MS).
Source: Journal of Forensic Sciences. 36(4):1179-85, 1991 Jul.
    Abstract: Benzoylecgonine (BE) was detected in hair samples using nonproprietary extraction methodology and modifications of well-established radioimmunoassay (RIA) screening/quantitative gas chromatography/mass spectrometry (GC/MS) confirmation procedures. Samples collected anonymously from a population of 48 jail detainees weighed between 5.3 and 61.2 mg. All of the 22 hair samples which had RIA results indicating the presence of BE or immunologically similar substances above a cutoff amount of 1.25 ng/sample (50 ng/mL) were confirmed by GC/MS. Several varieties of hair color and texture were tested, although in each general category there were samples which contained BE as well as other samples which did not reveal detectable amounts of BE. The range of concentrations in 22 hair extracts that screened positive were 0.26 to 18 ng/ mg hair as determined by GC/MS. In comparison with other reports of cocaine-related substances in hair, these data show consistent concentrations.

12. Abstract Only
Unique Identifier: 7860027
Status: MEDLINE
Authors: Selavka CM. Rieders F.
Authors Full Name: Selavka, C M. Rieders, F.
Institution: National Medical Services, Incorporated, Willow Grove, PA 19090-0437.
Title: The determination of cocaine in hair: a review. [Review] [66 refs]
Source: Forensic Science International. 70(1-3):155-64, 1995 Jan 5.
    Abstract: The explosion of literature related to the analysis of hair for cocaine and its products is reviewed. In the commonly accepted applications of hair testing for cocaine, those related to criminal or civil investigations and pharmacotoxicologic studies occupy most of the relevant published work. This review uses detailed, "binary" (yes/no) tables to demonstrate trends in the literature, and allows researchers and caseworkers quick access to the literature most important for answering a variety of questions. [References: 66]

13. Abstract Only
9032952
Status: MEDLINE
Authors: Smith FP. Kidwell DA.
Authors Full Name: Smith, F P. Kidwell, D A.
Institution: Department of Justice Sciences, University of Alabama at Birmingham 35294-2060, USA. smith@sbs.sbs.uab.edu
Title: Cocaine in hair, saliva, skin swabs, and urine of cocaine users' children.
Source: Forensic Science International. 83(3):179-89, 1996 Dec 27.
    Abstract: The concentrations of cocaine and benzoylecgonine (BE) in the hair, saliva, skin secretions, and urine samples of cocaine-using mothers, their children, and other adults living in the same environment were compared. Subjects were screened from urban cocaine

dependence treatment patients. Drug-using adults had mean hair concentrations of 2.4 ng cocaine/mg hair (range = 0-12.2, sigma = 3.1, 15/16 positive) and 0.39 ng BE/mg hair (range = 0-1.9, sigma = 0.62), compared with children's mean hair concentrations of 2.4 ng cocaine/mg of hair (range = 0-14.4, sigma = 3.8, 22/24 positive) and 0.74 ng benzoylecgonine/mg hair (range = 0-5.4 sigma = 1.3). None of the children's urine specimens (0/22) were positive above 300 ng BE/ml. In contrast, 3/16 adult urine specimens were positive, even though they were enrolled in drug treatment. Saliva had detectable levels of BE for only one child (1/17) and one adult (1/17). Forehead swabs contained measurable quantities of cocaine for most children (19/26) and adults (15/17) and BE for children (7/26) and adults (7/17). Unlike urine results, overall hair cocaine concentrations for adults paralleled those of children and a clear cut-off concentration could not be established to differentiate these two groups.

14. Abstract Only
Unique Identifier: 3783101
Status: MEDLINE
Authors: Smith FP. Liu RH.
Authors Full Name: Smith, F P. Liu, R H.
Title: Detection of cocaine metabolite in perspiration stain, menstrual bloodstain, and hair.
Source: Journal of Forensic Sciences. 31(4):1269-73, 1986 Oct.

Abstract: Low nanogram and picogram quantities of cocaine metabolite equivalents were detected in extracts from perspiration stains, menstrual bloodstains, and hair using radioimmunoassay. The theory of drug inclusion in hair and its significance are discussed.

15. Abstract Only
Unique Identifier: 8138227
Status: MEDLINE
Authors: Springfield AC. Cartmell LW. Aufderheide AC. Buikstra J. Ho J.
Authors Full Name: Springfield, A C. Cartmell, L W. Aufderheide, A C. Buikstra, J. Ho, J.
Institution: Department of Pathology, University of North Texas Health Science Centre, Fort Worth.
Title: Cocaine and metabolites in the hair of ancient Peruvian coca leaf chewers.
Source: Forensic Science International. 63(1-3):269-75, 1993 Dec.

Abstract: Cocaine and its metabolites, benzoylecgonine (BZE) and ecgonine methylester (EME), were found in hair samples from ancient Peruvian coca-leaf chewers dating back to AD 1000. Hair was analyzed by gas chromatography/mass spectrometry (GC/MS) to quantitate the concentrations. The two metabolites were found in higher concentration than the parent drug. The metabolite levels appear to be below that of modern cocaine abusers. Gender does not appear to be a factor in the incorporation of drug into hair.

16. Abstract Only
Unique Identifier: 7860035
Status: MEDLINE
Authors: Wang WL. Cone EJ.
Authors Full Name: Wang, W L. Cone, E J.
Institution: Addiction Research Center, National Institute on Drug Abuse, National Institutes of Health, Baltimore, MD 21224.
Title: Testing human hair for drugs of abuse. IV. Environmental cocaine contamination and washing effects.
Source: Forensic Science International. 70(1-3):39-51, 1995 Jan 5.

Abstract: Active cocaine use results in sequestration of parent drug in hair. In addition, hair has unique physicochemical properties that permit absorption of cocaine from the environment. When hair is tested for evidence of cocaine, it is important to consider whether the positive test resulted from active drug use or environmental contamination. In a series of laboratory experiments, it was found that exposure of "cut" hair to cocaine vapor ("crack" smoke) and to aqueous solutions of cocaine hydrochloride resulted in significant contamination of hair samples. Similar results were obtained with two subjects who were exposed to cocaine vapor in an unventilated room. The amount of contamination adsorbed by hair depended upon both time and extent of exposure. Washing the hair samples with methanol removed >70 percent of the cocaine contaminant after cocaine vapor exposure, but was less effective (<50 percent) following contamination with aqueous cocaine. Shampoo treatment cycles (overnight soaking) progressively removed increasing amounts of cocaine from the contaminated hair, but residual cocaine remained after 10 cycles. Studies were also performed to determine the usefulness of benzoylecgonine as a marker of active cocaine administration. Small amounts of benzoylecgonine (ca. 1 ng/mg) were formed in hair as a result of environmental contamination with cocaine. Also, it was found that benzoylecgonine could be adsorbed from illicit cocaine contaminated with benzoylecgonine. It was concluded that positive hair test results should be interpreted cautiously due to the possibility of environmental contamination from cocaine and related constituents.

Chapter 43

Drug Testing in the Workplace

Anne D. ImObersteg, M.S., J.D., MBA, B.A.,
and James T. O'Donnell, Pharm.D., M.S., FCP, ABCP, FACN, R.Ph.

43.1 Introduction

Illegal drug use has increased at an alarming rate. In the period between 1955 and 1980, the United States experienced a twentyfold increase in the use of illegal drugs. The highest drug-use rates are among persons aged 16 to 25—the emerging workforce in America. In a 2000 federal survey, about 14 million Americans were determined to have used illegal drugs within one month of the survey.[1]

Abuse of drugs and alcohol are two of the most costly activities to the American society. In 1993, the societal cost reached $400 billion.[2] The corporate world incurs a large share of this cost in the form of lost productivity, untimely deaths, and illnesses associated with drug use, to the tune of almost $81.6 billion a year.[3] Increased absenteeism, workplace accidents, workers' compensation claims, medical costs, and decreased productivity all negatively affect the economy and American businesses.[4]

A survey by the Hazelden Foundation determined that more than 60 percent of adult Americans know individuals who have gone to their place of business under the influence of either drugs or alcohol.[5] In fact, it is estimated that 70 percent of all illegal drug users are currently employed and affecting the efficiency of the workplace.[6] Drug-impaired employees are not only costly to the business owner and industry, they also can pose a substantial safety risk to themselves, to their co-workers, and to the general public. As an apparent response to these alarming statistics, over 80 percent of American companies now conduct some type of workplace testing.[7]

43.2 Non-Regulated Testing

The interest of an employer in the productivity and welfare of her employees is not a new concept. As early as 1914, industry attempted to regulate the "sobriety" of their employees. In the 1940s, accidents and absenteeism in the Kaiser shipyards were so prevalent that Kaiser created an in-house healthcare system, financed by payroll deductions. These

Note: This chapter was originally produced and written, for an earlier edition of this book, by Anne D. ImObersteg, who has since deceased. It has been revised and updated by James T. O'Donnell.

early attempts of identifying drug-use risk factors and drug-testing by industry leaders, however, were fundamentally flawed—the plans were unregulated, lacked clear policy statements, and had no standards of performance.

43.3 Regulated Testing

In 1983, the Department of Transportation (DOT), in conjunction with the National Institute on Drug Abuse (NIDA), drafted a drug program for regulated testing. This program was initiated in response to concerns of the National Traffic Safety Board over the increase in drug- and alcohol-related accidents in that industry.[8] However, it was not until 1986, when President Reagan's Commission on Organized Crime released a report connecting drug use with trafficking and organized crime, that regulated testing got into full swing.[9] In the report, the commission called upon the president to issue a policy statement expressing the unacceptability of drug use among federal employees, and to outline the measures necessary to achieve the commission's goals.

In response, on September 15, 1986, President Reagan signed Executive Order 12564, the first step towards the ultimate goal of a "Drug-Free Federal Workplace." The order recognized the impact of drug use in the workplace, and established the unprecedented rule of prohibiting federal employees from using illegal drugs on- or off-duty. The order states, in part,

> The Federal Government, as the largest employer in the Nation, can and should show the way towards achieving drug-free workplaces through a program designed to offer drug users a helping hand and, at the same time, demonstrating to drug users and potential drug users that drugs will not be tolerated in the Federal workplace....[10]

On July 11, 1987, Congress passed legislation affecting the implementation of the order. Congress' goals were to establish uniformity among the drug-testing plans of the various agencies, ensure reliable and accurate drug testing, allow employees access to drug-testing records, provide confidentiality of drug-testing results, and centralize oversight of the drug-testing program.[11] This legislation was made under Section 503 of the Supplemental Appropriations Act of 1987.[12]

The act placed the burden of providing mandatory guidelines on the Department of Health Services (HHS). The HHS was directed to establish "comprehensive standards for all aspects of laboratory drug-testing and laboratory procedures to be applied in carrying out Executive Order Numbered 12564, including standards which require

the use of the best available technology for enduring the full reliability and accuracy of drug tests and strict procedures governing the chain of custody of specimens collected for drug-testing."[13] The Secretary of the HHS was required to set the mandatory standards for all aspects of laboratory drug testing, including who would be tested, when the tests would be conducted, what drugs would be covered, and how the tests would be conducted. Testing was authorized for applicants, random testing of employees in designated "sensitive" positions, reasonable-suspicion testing, accident or unsafe-practice testing, voluntary testing, and testing as part of or as a follow-up to counseling or rehabilitation.

In 1988, the first guidelines were published by the U.S. Department of Health and Human Services Administration (HHS) in the document titled "Guidelines for Federal Workplace Drug-testing Programs." In 1994, the guidelines were revised and republished.[14] They established the testing criteria, the allowable specimen matrix, and the limited number of drugs that may be tested in the specimen.[15] The following entities are mandated to follow the guidelines:

- Executive agencies, as defined in 5 U.S.C. § 105.
- Uniformed services, as defined in 5 U.S.C. § 2101(3), except for the armed forces, as defined in 5 U.S.C. § 2101(2).
- Any other employing unit of the federal government, except for the U.S. Postal Service, the Postal Rate Commission, and employing units of the judicial and legislative branches.
- Laboratories that possess or seek certification to perform urine drug testing for federal agencies under a drug-testing program conducted under Executive Order 12564.
- The intelligence community, as defined by Executive Order 12333, to the extent agreed to by the head of the affected agency.

HHS established the National Laboratory Certification Program (NLCP) to certify laboratories before they are permitted to test specimens collected for federal agency drug-testing programs. The DOT, the Department of Energy (DOE), and the Nuclear Regulatory Commission (NRC) also require the industries they regulate to use these certified laboratories for their workplace drug-testing programs. The DOT, in particular, has followed the guidelines very closely in its drug-testing program. The DOT's program was codified in the Federal Register (49 C.F.R. Part 40) and became applicable nationwide in the passage of the Omnibus Transportation Employee Testing Act of 1991.[16]

43.4 Voluntary Programs

Many private companies perform functions that do not require mandatory adherence to the federal HHS guidelines, yet still have a regulated internal program. One such voluntary program, administered by the College of American Pathologists, is called the Forensic Urine Drug Testing program (FUDT). The FUDT program establishes the minimum criteria for reliable urine drug-testing procedures, which parallel the general consensus of the scientific community. While participation in the FUDT program is voluntary, many laboratories have an interest in being accredited by FUDT, since the program is one of the few non-governmental programs available to forensic laboratories.

Lack of formal regulation has some benefits and drawbacks. The most notable drawback is the possible development of a workplace drug-testing program that lacks procedural oversight and mandatory adherence to basic forensic-testing standards. Lack of adherence to scientifically accepted standards in a company's policies and procedures could increase employee-based legal challenges to any enforcement and sanctions incurred through the administration of the program. However, non-regulated testing allows employers to conduct more extensive testing of an employee's biological sample. For example, regulated testing may narrow the groups of drugs to be tested to five major drugs of abuse: cocaine, phencyclidine, opiates, amphetamines, and cannabinoids. Regulated testing often limits the sample matrix to urine, and dictates the methods of testing. Non-regulated testing may allow testing for a multitude of drugs, including prescription drugs, in a variety of testing matrices such as blood, hair, sweat, urine, or saliva.

Regardless of whether the private company chooses to follow the federal program, a private program, or its own program, certain program guidelines should be followed. Only by establishing a comprehensive program, can an effective program be created.

43.5 Establishment of a Workplace Program

The decision to develop and implement a drug-free workplace program begins with the establishment of policies guiding the program to the ultimate goal of increased safety and productivity in the workplace. Guidance for the components of a complete program can be found in Section 503 of the Supplemental Appropriations Act of 1987 (Section 503). Section 503 requires that all agencies establish a reliable workplace drug program containing five major components: a written policy statement, provision for supervisor training, provision for employee education, provision for employee assistance, and the guidelines for drug testing.[17]

All five steps are not necessary in non-regulated testing, but establishment of all five steps make the policy clear, and may minimize legal ramifications on any employer-based action taken when an employee violates the program.

A. Written Policy

A written policy statement provides the basis for an agency or company's program. Thus, an obvious starting point for the establishment of an effective program is a written policy documenting the requirements of the employer, program-adherence expectations, and ramifications of non-compliance with the policy. For federal programs, the act requires the agency to state why the drug-free program is being implemented, provide a clear description of what behaviors are prohibited, and provide a thorough explanation of the consequences of violating the policy. Regardless of whether the employer is or is not mandated to follow the steps established by the act, the following program components must be included:

- The rationale for the establishment of a policy
- A clear description of the prohibited substances and behaviors
- The type of required drug testing, and the circumstances (random, post-accident, reasonable cause, etcetera) prompting drug-testing
- Procedures for the determination of a policy violation
- The consequences for the violation of the policy (and any available appeals processes)
- A statement of when the policy will be enforced
- The documentation of what types of employees will be covered by the policy (safety-sensitive employees, contractors, pre-employment, all employees, and so forth)
- The treatment and rehabilitation services available to the employee
- Issues of employee confidentiality

B. Employee Assistance Programs

Employee Assistance Programs (EAPs) provide drug-abuse education to company managers and counseling for employees seeking assistance for drug or alcohol abuse problems. An EAP program is a benefit to the employer, in that it allows managers to become educated in drug-abuse issues while keeping them separated from the actual counseling process. An EAP is also an excellent benefit to the employee, since it often becomes an alternative to dismissal, and can provide resources for treatment facilities and counseling.

An EAP is a necessary component of any effective program, and is a requirement in HHS-regulated testing. The act states that an agency must provide an EAP to help resolve poor work performance due to alcohol or drugs, as well as for personal problems. A successful EAP must provide treatment and rehabilitation to employees who have tested positive on a drug test or who have referred themselves for assistance. In addition, an EAP should disseminate knowledge on drug abuse and effects, and reinforce the impact of drug use in the workplace. Above all, any effective EAP program must assure the employee that all functions provided by the EAP, including test results and medical treatment, will be conducted with confidentiality.

C. Employee Awareness Training

Policies that are established and enforced in a draconian manner are often not financially beneficial to the employer. Legal consequences and the cost of training and hiring new employees make the establishment of an employee-education program beneficial. Aside from educating the employee on the contents of the program and the new company policy, basic information on alcohol and drug abuse in the workplace is recommended. The act requires that the EAP administrator provide employee education to all federal employees. A model program under the act would include education on the types and effects of drugs, symptoms of drug use, effects of drugs on performance, the role of the EAP, treatments available, and confidentiality issues. Employee awareness programs should also include the recognition of substance abuse in the family or coworkers, the safety hazards of drug abuse in the workplace, and the available resources for addiction assistance in the company and community.

D. Supervisor Training

Supervisors provide the first line of drug detection in employees. The act requires that federal agencies provide and implement training to assist their supervisors in recognizing illegal drug use.[18] In addition, an agency must develop a training package or course covering the following issues:

- Employee problems with drugs and alcohol
- The role of EAP and the EAP supervisor
- Recognition of employees with drug or alcohol problems
- Documentation of performance or behavior problems
- Skills in confronting employees
- Agency procedures regarding referral to the EAP
- Disciplinary action and removal from safety-sensitive positions (Section 5 of the Executive Order)
- Reintegration of the employee into the workforce
- Written materials for the supervisor

Supervisors should be trained to recognize and understand drug-abuse and job-performance issues. The monitoring of job performance, rather than the diagnosis of drug abuse or drug-abuse counseling, is the main purview of the supervisor. Documentation of performance problems will prompt the employee's referral to the available assistance. The act requires the supervisor's training to include the organization's policy, the supervisor's specific responsibilities, and how to deal with employees who have performance problems. In addition, the supervisor should be trained on how to monitor employee job performance, document performance issues, enforce the policy, and make referrals for testing based on reasonable suspicion.

E. Drug Testing

A standard drug-free workplace program must allow for drug testing, since any sanctions against an employee for mere suspicion of drug use or influence may not stand up to legal review. Drug testing may take place prior to hiring, upon reasonable suspicion, for cause, post-accident, randomly, periodically, or post-rehabilitation. Executive Order 12564 defines illegal drugs as any drug on Schedule I or II of the Controlled Substance Act. Since it is impractical to test for all the drugs listed in these schedules, the guidelines require that random drug-testing programs shall test urine for marijuana and cocaine, at a minimum. The agency may add to the minimum list by also testing for opiates, amphetamines, and phencyclidine; or request a waiver from the HHS to routinely test drugs other than the five listed. However, when testing for reasonable suspicion, accident, or unsafe practice testing, other drugs in Schedule I or II may be tested.[19]

In nonregulated testing, the employer and the testing laboratory have wide discretion in choosing the methods used and the drugs tested in a biological specimen. HHS restricts the matrix to urine. However, non-regulated programs may allow for testing of an unlimited number of drugs in a variety of matrices, including sweat, saliva, and hair.

43.6 The Drug-Testing Process

A vital part of any drug-free workplace program is the collection of the chosen biological matrix, the analytical testing of the matrix for a series of illegal drugs, and the accurate reporting of the results. Non-regulated testing laboratories are not limited to testing only urine, and may use any method for testing. Their only oversight is the opinion in the relevant scientific community. Regulated testing, on the other hand, may take the form of the private CAP-FUDT program or the HHS guidelines.

Federal agencies of the executive branch must comply with Executive Order 12564 (1986), which establishes the on and off-duty abstinence from illegal drugs a condition for employment in a federal job. Federal grantees and contractors with contracts valued at $100,000 or more must comply with the Drug-Free Workplace Act of 1988. In addition, laboratories that perform testing on federal employees must be certified by the NLCP under the HHS. In the transportation industry (DOT), employers must comply with the Omnibus Transportation Employee Testing Act of 1991 by establishing an alcohol and drug program for safety-sensitive employees. The NRC has established standards for nuclear-power producers, and employers with Department of Defense (DOD) contracts must also establish a drug-free program for employees in "sensitive" jobs.

Private programs and the federal programs have some similarities—they are dedicated to maintaining a high analytical standard. All programs must require the laboratory to have in place a Standard Operating Procedure (SOP) manual that includes a description of the laboratory's chain-of-custody procedures, analytical testing procedures, quality control and quality-assurance programs, equipment and maintenance, accessioning and security, personnel qualifications and training, and reporting procedures. The laboratory must also be subject to inspections by the administering program, which must send proficiency samples to the laboratory on a regular basis.

The following drug-testing guidelines contain the basic scientific concepts of the testing process and provide some examples of the basic requirements of different programs. However, the complete guidelines for the College of American Pathologists Forensic Urine Drug Testing program (CAP-FUDT), the federal program as outlined in the federal mandatory guidelines, and the DOT program will not be provided here. Drug-testing programs are always subject to change with increasing needs and technology. Therefore, for a more thorough list of requirements, clarification on each activity, and new changes, the latest revision of the original documents should be consulted.

A. Collection

The collection of the specimen is a vital part of the workplace testing process. It is the foundation of the process, and can affect the reliability and effectiveness of the entire program. During the entire drug-testing process the integrity and identity of the specimen must be maintained—from the collection of the specimen to the reporting of the specimen results. The manner in which the specimen is collected, the safeguards against specimen tampering during the collection of the specimen, the correct identification of the specimen, and the accompanying chain of custody are all factors impacting the identity and integrity of the specimen.

A chain of custody must be maintained to document the location of the specimen at all times. In order to maintain the integrity of the specimen, the chain of possession of the specimen must remain intact and must not be broken at any time. The common acceptable chain-of-custody formation is generally called the "Z" formation. A "Z" formation (representing a "Z" character when the chain-of-custody documentation form has two entries per line) takes the following form: A to B, B to C, C to D, and so on. The following represents an unacceptable chain of custody: A to B, C to D, etcetera. In the latter example, there is no documentation of where "B" placed the specimen and from where "C" received the specimen—the chain has been broken. The HHS requires that its standardized Custody Control Form (CCF) be used and that the control and accountability of specimens be maintained at all times. Every individual in the chain must be identified, and documentation of the individual handling the specimen—as well as the date and purpose for access to the specimen—must be contained on the chain-of-custody document.[20]

The integrity of a urine drug test hinges on the proper collection of the specimen. The DOT has set into place strict requirements for the collection of specimens. All procedures for Department of Transportation (DOT) collection must be performed as per 49 C.F.R. Part 40.21 The correct collection procedure must be followed, a proper chain-of-custody form must be used at all times (CCF), the identity and integrity of the sample must always be maintained, and the collector must meet the training requirements of Section 40.33 of Part 40.

The DOT's collector training requirements are extensive and thorough. As of August 1, 2001, the collector must be trained in a series of procedures and must meet the requirements of 40.33 of Part 40. The collector must show knowledge and compliance in the following areas:

- Knowledgeable about the current "DOT Urine Specimen Collection Procedures Guidelines" published by the DOT
- Qualification training in the proper collection procedures, completion of the CCF, procedures in solving problem collections (e.g., "shy bladder"), correction of correctable flaws and identification of fatal flaws (for example, the specimen ID on the donor's bottle does not match the CCF or the seal is broken) during collection
- Demonstration of collection proficiency by completing five consecutive error-free mock collections by a qualified collector
- Attendance of a refresher training at least every five years

- Attendance of a refresher course within 30 days if an error in a collection results in the cancellation of a test (fatal or uncorrected flaws)
- Maintenance of documentation showing compliance with the requirements in § 40.33 of Part 40

Each agency or company must have designated collection sites. These sites must be secure, accessible only to designated personnel, and have the proper procedures in place to ensure the integrity and identity of the urine specimen. Such procedures include the deterrence of possible dilution of the sample by the donor, the presentation of a photo-identification card by the donor upon arrival, the removal of any clothing that may conceal adulteration materials, the washing of the donor's hands prior to urination, the elimination of access of the donor to water during the physical voiding of the bladder, and the collector's observation of the donor prior to urination. All collections must be performed in accordance with applicable regulations and must ensure the privacy of the donor by the use of a donor number rather than the donor's name.

Many programs require or allow the collection of "split specimens." Split specimens allow a portion of the collected sample to be poured into an additional container for independent testing or to preserve the specimen in the event that the original or first container becomes destroyed or contaminated. An example of a split collection procedure can be found in the DOT agency drug-testing requirements. In the DOT program, all specimens must be split-specimen collections. At least 45 mL of urine must be collected; 30 mL must be poured by the collector into Bottle "A," the primary testing bottle, and at least 15 mL must be poured into Bottle "B." The donor may urinate into a specimen container or a designated Bottle "A." The collection site person then pours the urine into two specimen bottles that are labeled Bottle "A" and Bottle "B" or, if Bottle "A" was used to collect the specimen, pours an appropriate amount into Bottle "B."

During the physical collection of the specimen, the donor is given a clean specimen bottle and allowed privacy to complete the voiding of the bladder. On receiving the voided specimen from the donor, the collector must ascertain that a sufficient amount of urine has been voided. The specimen temperature should always be checked immediately. A urine temperature less than 90–100°F indicates that dilution or substitution of the specimen may have occurred. If not enough urine has been voided, and the urine temperature is within range, most programs allow the donor to drink fluids and attempt another collection in the same manner as described above. All specimens—even those suspected of being adulterated or diluted—are considered evidence, and must be sent to the laboratory for testing.

After collection, the specimen is checked for color and any signs of contaminants. Any signs inconsistent with a valid sample must be noted on the chain-of-custody collection form. The specimen bottle is sealed with tamper-evident tape by placing the tape over the cap and down the sides of the bottle. An identification label containing the date, the donor's specimen number, and other identifying information (other than the donor's name) is placed on the bottle. The donor then signs the chain-of-custody form, verifying the collection process.

The privacy of the donor during collection is maintained unless certain criteria are met. Under certain circumstances, direct observation of the actual collection may be allowed. For example, employers may specify a direct collection when it is determined that there is no valid medical reason for the specimen to have been considered "invalid," when the donor's test is a return-to-duty test, or a follow-up test. The collector must conduct a direct observation of urine collection if the specimen temperature is out of range, or there is evidence of specimen tampering or adulteration.

B. Accessioning

The accessioning procedure is the gateway to the laboratory testing process. The biological specimen must arrive at the laboratory with the shipping package intact, a proper chain-of-custody form, and the specimen correctly identified. Broken specimen containers or seals or gaps in the chain of custody all call into question the integrity of the specimen. Specimens without all the indicia of reliability should not be tested.

When the specimen is received, laboratory personnel must inspect the package for evidence of possible tampering, and must compare information on specimen bottles to the information on the accompanying CCF. Most drug-testing programs have requirements in place for the acceptance or rejection of specimens during the accessioning process. Some flaws are not considered "fatal" and may be easily corrected by affidavit from the collector. At present, HHS is reviewing its policies and has proposed a list of minor issues that may appear on the CCF that do not need to be corrected by affidavit. The DOT requires that certified laboratories follow the requirements in Section 40.83 of 49 C.F.R., Part 40, in receiving and processing the sample for testing. The laboratory must inspect the CCF and the specimen and note if there are "fatal" or correctable flaws. Some types of identified fatal flaws are:

- The specimen ID numbers on the specimen bottle and CCF do not match.
- The specimen Bottle "A" seal is broken or shows evidence of tampering. Exceptions are when split specimens can be redesignated as Bottle "A."

Table 43.1

Drug or Metabolite	Initial test (ng/mL)	Confirmation tests (ng/mL)
Marijuana metabolites Deltra-9-tetrahydrocannabinol-9-carboxylic acid	50	15
Cocaine metabolites Benzoylecgonine	300	150

Phencyclidine
Amphetamines:
  ∞ amphetamine
  ∞ methamphetamine
	25
	100
		25
		500
		500
		(With amphetamine present at
		a concentration ≥ 200)

Opiate metabolites:
  ∞ codeine
  ∞ morphine
  ∞ 6-acetylmorphine
	2000	2000
		2000
		10
		(Only tested if morphine ≥ 2000 ng/mL)

- The collector's printed name and signature is omitted from the CCF.
- Specimen bottle "A" has insufficient urine. Exceptions are when split specimens can be redesignated as Bottle "A."

Fatal flaws are not correctable, and the specimen must be rejected for testing.[21] Nonfatal flaws can be corrected within five days by affidavit.

Since the accessioning area receives and maintains the urine specimens, the area must be secure and limited to authorized individuals. Entry and exit from the area must be documented. Authorized visitors are allowed in the accessioning area, but must be escorted at all times.

C. Drugs to Be Tested

Non-regulated testing has no restriction on which drugs or drug classes that a laboratory may test in a specimen. Generally, in regulated testing, only five classes of drugs are covered: phencyclidine, opiates, amphetamines, cocaine, and cannabinoids. The HHS requires that an "Agency requesting the authorization to include other drugs shall submit to the Secretary in writing the agency's proposed confirmatory test methods, testing levels, and proposed performance test program."

When performing an analysis for a particular drug or drug class, a laboratory must clearly establish the criteria for the determination of a positive or negative result, including a proper "cutoff point," below which the specimen result must be reported as "negative." In nonregulated testing, the laboratory has a broad discretion in determining what cutoff level will be used and how the ultimate result will be

reported. A nonregulated laboratory may allow the cutoff to be determined by the lower limit of detection of the instruments used, or may allow the reported result to be worded in vague terminology such as "possible presence" or "indicated." In regulated testing, however, cutoffs for screening and confirmation are mandatory (Table 43.1).

D. Initial Test/Immunoassay Testing

Laboratory analysis of a donor's urine sample is performed in two separate stages. The first analysis is generally called an "initial test," "screening," or "presumptive" test. Nonregulated programs may allow a laboratory to use thin-layer chromatography or similar technology to screen the urine specimen. HHS and DOT guidelines mandate that immunoassay techniques be employed. The requirements do not specify which initial immunoassay product to use, as long as the product meets all the requirements of the Food and Drug Administration for commercial distribution.

Most commercially available immunoassay kits have initial tests for the drugs typically covered by the regulated programs. Immunoassays are useful in separating out the negative specimens from those that may be positive for a particular drug or drug class. The technology does not yet rise to the certainty standard as required by a confirmation test, mainly because there is considerable cross-reactivity with drugs other than the target drug.

There are a variety of different types of immunoassay techniques on the market. Some common technologies utilized are radioimmunoassay (RIA), enzyme immunoassay (EIA), kinetic interaction of microparticles in a solution (KIMS), and fluorescence-polarization immunoassay (FPIA). Some immunoassay techniques are more specific to a specific target drug than others. However, all immunoassay techniques use an antibody-antigen relationship to identify a drug class in a sample.

B-lymphocytes and plasma cells create an antibody protein in an immune response to an introduced antigen. This created antibody is able to identify and bind to any similar antigen that is introduced into the host. Commercial immunoassay kits contain a substrate with antibody to a specific class of drugs, and the target drug, which is "labeled" with a tracer. In radioimmunoassay kits the label is radioactive iodine or carbon. In fluorescence immunoassays, the label is a fluorchrome, and in enzyme immunoassays the label is a lysozyme or other enzyme. One of the most popular enzyme immunoassay kits used by many NLCP laboratories is the enzyme multiplied immunoassay test (EMIT) developed by Syva Corporation.

The EMIT uses a technique known as competitive binding. The drug (antigen) labeled with the enzyme competes with any drug found in the subject's sample for a limited supply of antibodies. When the labeled drug in the kit is bound with the antibody, the enzyme activity is inhibited. The more drug in the subject's sample, the less antibodies available to bind to the kit's enzyme-labeled antigen. By measuring the magnitude of enzymatic change on a substrate, the amount of drug in the donor's sample can be determined. For example, a donor's sample with no target drug will enable most of the kit's enzyme-labeled drug to be bound to the antibodies and result in an inhibition of the enzyme's activity. When the enzyme activity is inhibited, the substrate in the kit, NAD, cannot be oxidized into NADH. The result is a small absorbance change of 340 nm, measured spectrometrically. Conversely, a large amount of drug in a subject's sample will leave few antibodies for the kit's enzyme-labeled drug, and many enzymes will be able to convert NAD to NADH and result in a large absorbance change.

Using the initial cutoffs as outlined in Table 43.1, specimens that test below the cutoff level on all initial tests will be signed out as negative, with no further testing permitted on the specimen. For positive test results, multiple re-screening may be an option, as long as quality-control and guideline cutoffs are used. Some laboratories use a second initial test that is more specific for the drug in question, thus eliminating a possible false positive on the broader, first initial test. For example, if a particular assay tends to flag positive for structural amphetamine analogues, a more specific second immunoassay test may be performed.

When conducting an initial test, every batch is required to contain an appropriate number of calibrators, negative urine samples, controls, and blind samples to ensure the accuracy of test results, along with the donor specimens. Results lower than the cutoff are considered "negative" and are not tested any further; positive results are sent on for confirmation. The laboratory must perform a "confirmation" test on a gas chromatograph (GC), gas chromatograph/mass spectrometer (GC/MS), or an equivalent instrument, to identify what substance has caused the positive initial test result.

E. Confirmation Tests

Once an initial screen indicates that the specimen may be positive for a particular drug or drug class, a confirmation test is performed. Only those specimens confirmed positive by a test utilizing an analytical technology different from the screening test may be reported as positive. Non-regulated testing has the option of using a variety of confirmation methods, some of which may not be considered acceptable with the scientific community majority. Under regulated testing, laboratories must use gas chromatography/mass spectrometry (GC/MS) for the confirmation method.

The GC/MS is, in effect, the combination of two instruments. The gas chromatograph (GC) separates the components (drugs) of a mixture by injecting the mixture into a column inside the instrument. The column contains chemicals, which slow the migration of some of the compounds, and allows other compounds to travel relatively unhindered. The chemical makeup of each of the mixture's compounds and their interactions with the chemicals in the column determines how long the component will take to travel the entire length of the column. As each compound or drug exits the column, it enters the mass spectrometer (MS).

The MS bombards the drug with electrons and shatters the structure into pieces, depending on the weak points in the drug's structure. Theoretically, since each drug structure is different, each different drug will break at different points on the molecule, and, thus, shatter into predictable pieces. The size and quantity of the pieces form a "fingerprint" of the drug. A proficient scientist can reconstruct the structure of the molecule merely by evaluating the totality of the ions produced by the electron bombardment. For quantitation, a laboratory does not look at the entire scope of ions that are produced by the molecule, but rather chooses several unique ions to represent an identification. The abundance of one ion, generally the "target" or "quantifying ion," is measured to determine the amount of drug in the specimen. The measured relative abundance of two other ions ("qualifier ions") is chosen to help assure the proper identification of the drug. Using both the retention time as recorded by the gas chromatograph and the presence of a target ion and the qualifier ions, a drug can be identified to a fairly high certainty.

As with any instrument, the quality and worth of the data achieved through the GC/MS is a function of how the instrument is maintained and operated. Confirmation methods must be validated to ensure the reliable analysis of specimens. Validation of the method includes the determination of carryover, linearity, precision, specificity, accuracy, limit of quantitation, and limit of detection of the method. Confirmations must be by quantitative analysis, and fall within the linear region of the standard curve. Tests that exceed the linear range must be documented in the laboratory record as "exceeds the linear range of the test." Periodic procedure re-validations should also be performed.

The calibrators that establish the quantitation of the result and the controls that check the proper results of the calibrators must be used in the analytical run and fall within acceptable ranges of accuracy. The appropriate number of calibrators, negative urine samples and controls must be used. Some laboratories establish a three-point calibration curve with each batch analysis. However, some laboratories use a single-point calibration and check a stored, historical calibration curve with the appropriate quality-control samples. Quality-control requirements for a confirmation test include certified negative urine samples, positive calibrators, controls containing the specific drug to be tested, and at least one control at or near the cutoff.

F. Reporting and Storage of Samples

After analysis, the final test result must be reviewed and approved by a person authorized to review the analytical data for accuracy. In regulated programs, this duty is assigned to a "certifying scientist." The certifying scientist reviews all the data of the initial and confirmation test and chain of custody and determines if the result is justified. This initial review is then sent to the MRO within an average of five working days after the laboratory receives the specimen. The completed CCF is sent by fax, mail, or courier, or electronically to a MRO—not to the employer. The laboratory may transmit results to the MRO by facsimile or computer, although this must be done in a manner designed to ensure confidentiality of the information.

Confidentiality of records is protected under the Privacy Act, 5 U.S.C. § 552a et. seq. and Section 503(e) of the act. Results may not be disclosed without written permission of the employee, unless the disclosure is to the MRO, the EAP administrator who is providing counseling to the employee, a supervisory or management official in the agency, or pursuant to a court order. An applicant for employment is not entitled to the results of the drug test, but an employee may obtain information by written request.

Results may not be provided verbally over the tele-phone. Quantitative results are not routinely sent, except for when the sample is positive for morphine or codeine at a level of 15,000 ng/mL or above. All other reports for quantitation require a letter from the MRO asking for the quantitation results. All confirmed positive specimens must be maintained in long-term frozen storage for a minimum of one year. All records must be maintained for two years.

43.7 Additional Program Aspects
A. The Medical Review Officer (MRO)

The DOT and Federal Mandatory Guidelines require that a medical review officer (MRO) review positive results. A MRO is a licensed physician, responsible for receiving laboratory results generated by an agency's drug-testing program, with knowledge of substance-abuse disorders, and appropriate medical training to interpret and evaluate an individual's positive test result. The MRO is typically a licensed physician (doctor of medicine or osteopathy) who has been specially trained to review and evaluate the laboratory's implementation of the relevant program's testing of urine samples and controlled substance-abuse disorders. The MRO must not have a conflict of interest with the employer's laboratory.

The DOT program requires that when a positive result is reported, the MRO use due diligence to contact the employee directly and confidentially to determine whether the employee wishes to discuss the result. After three unsuccessful attempts to contact the employee, the MRO requests that the designated employer representative (DER) contact the employee and have the employee call the MRO. Positive results can be verified without interviewing the employee if more than ten days have passed since the reported result and there has been no success in contacting the employee. Interviews are also not required when more than 72 hours have passed since the employee was told to contact the MRO, or if the employee refuses to speak with the MRO.

The MRO verifies a confirmed positive test for PCP, cocaine, amphetamines, and marijuana, unless a legitimate medical explanation exists for the presence of the drug in the employee's urine. If the employee can present proof of a legitimate explanation for the positive test, the test will be deemed negative. However, the MRO may still raise fitness for duty issues with the employer. If the sample contained 6-acetylmorphine (6-AM), the test is verified positive. If, however, the test is negative for 6-AM, the result will still be verified positive if the morphine or codeine is at 15,000 ng/mL or above. All other opiate positive tests must be accompanied by clinical evidence of unauthorized use of opiate or opium derivatives. Adulterated or substituted test results are treated as a verified positive if, after interviewing the employee, there is no medical reason for the result.

B. Public Interest Exclusions (PIE)

To help protect the public against service agents that fail to meet the DOT regulations, the federal government has instituted a PIE proceeding policy. PIE proceeding may be initiated against a MRO, a laboratory, a SAP, a collector, or any service agent that is non-compliant with the program's provisions. The issuing party has the burden of proving by a preponderance of the evidence that the agent was in serious non-compliance of the regulations. The duration of a PIE can last about one to five years.

C. Blind Performance Testing

Blind quality-control specimens are used as a test of the entire testing process. The current guidelines require each federal agency to ensure that a minimum of 3 percent blind quality-control samples is submitted with the donor specimens. An employer may provide blind samples to the collector, who submits the quality-control sample as if it were a donor specimen. The collector will generate a fictitious social security number or employee identification number, complete a CCF, and properly label a specimen bottle. Only the MRO's copy of the CCF, copy four, will have the designation "Quality Control Sample" in the donor's name section. The MRO is to determine whether the laboratory reported the correct result when the second copy of the CCF is received from the laboratory after the laboratory's analysis. If the laboratory reports a result different from the one expected, the MRO must contact the laboratory to determine if there is a reason why the laboratory did not report the correct result. The MRO may request that the laboratory retest the specimen or have an aliquot sent to another certified laboratory for confirmatory testing. If the retest result does not confirm the original result, the laboratory likely made an error.

A false negative result is not considered as serious as a false positive. If the retest result has confirmed that a false positive was reported by the laboratory on a blind quality-control sample, the employer and the regulatory office will be contacted, so that an investigation can be conducted. If a specific cause for the false positive is identified, the laboratory will be required to take corrective action to prevent the recurrence of the error.

D. Alcohol Testing

Not all drug-testing programs allow for the testing of ethyl alcohol. By a 1994 amendment to 49 C.F.R. Part 40, alcohol testing for the DOT is now mandated. These are separate regulations from the drug-testing requirements, and a MRO review is not required. Alcohol testing may be done in four situations: post-accident, reasonable suspicion, random testing, return-to-duty, and follow up. At this time, pre-employment testing is not required. Alcohol screening tests may be performed on breath or saliva. If the alcohol concentration result is greater than 0.02 percent (g/100mL), a confirmation test must be performed on a specified breath-alcohol testing device within 30 minutes of the screening test. Specially trained screening test technicians (SSTs) or breath alcohol technicians (BATs) may perform breath-alcohol testing procedures. Only a qualified BAT may conduct a confirmation test. A confirmation test device must be on the NHTSA conforming products list (CPL) for evidential testers. The screen test may be on the CPL list for evidential and non-evidential devices.

All confirmation results must be printed in triplicate, and the printed record must include the printed results, date and time, a sequential test number, and the name and serial number of the EBT. Confirmation tests on an evidential breath tester (EBT) must be performed after a 15-minute observation period, to ensure that alcohol in the oral cavity does not contaminate the breath test. Before beginning the test, an air blank must be conducted on the EBT.

A positive result is any confirmation test that is a 0.04 percent or higher. Employees who have a positive test must be removed from safety-sensitive duty and referred to a substance abuse professional (SAP). A test result between 0.02–0.039 percent is considered neither positive nor negative. Employees at this level must be removed from safety sensitive functions until they are below a 0.02 percent, or their next duty period (at least eight hours). Below 0.019 percent, the test is considered negative and the employee may return to work.

43.8 Special Drug-Testing Issues
A. Type of Matrix

Determining what matrix to use to detect the use or presence of drugs depends on the concentration of the drug used, route of administration, distribution in tissues, and metabolism and excretion of the drug. Drug distribution in interstitial and cellular fluids is dependent on physiological and physicochemical properties of the drug. For example, lipid-insoluble drugs cannot permeate cell membranes easily, and thus are restricted in their distribution and sites of action. Some drugs bind to plasma proteins, such as the binding of acidic drugs to plasma albumin or the binding of basic drugs to α-1 acid glycoprotein. Lipid-soluble drugs, such as cannabinoids, accumulate in tissues and fat cells, which act as a reservoir, prolonging drug action and subsequent elimination from the body. These factors, and many more, affect the concentration and detection levels of various drugs in different matrices.

Generally, the purpose for the testing and the information desired often dictates the type of sample preferred. If the employer wishes to test an employee "for cause" or post-accident, a blood sample may be far superior to a hair or urine sample, provided the employee is available close to the time of the accident or occurrence. However, if the employer wishes to determine if the employee or hiring candidate has a long-term history of drug use, a hair sample might be the best option.

The following is an overview of the benefits and drawbacks of different sample matrices for the presence of drugs of abuse in workplace testing.

1. Hair testing

Hair serves as a repository for drugs, drug metabolites, vitamins and minerals and other substances, which are delivered to the hair root by the blood supply. Most of the drug is deposited in the central part of the hair, called the cortex.[22] It takes approximately three to five days for the hair to extrude from the scalp to enable it to be cut for collection. The amount of sample required for testing varies, but generally 60 to 360 hairs are required, depending on the length of the hair and the testing technology used. Hair testing can be performed by the analysis of the whole shaft of hair, or segmented to assist in the determination of the dates of ingestion. Segmentation is not very useful, since not all individuals grow hair at the same rate and not all hair on one person's head is in the growth cycle phase at the same time.

A major benefit of using hair as a drug-testing sample is the ability to determine long-term drug abuse. Unlike urine or blood, hair represents a more lengthy record of drug exposure. The amount of hair growth per month depends on the health and sex of the individual and the anatomical location of the hair. In general, the average rate of growth for head hair is about 1 centimeter (0.4 inch) per month.[23] For example, if a 2-inch length of hair is tested, it may represent drug use over the past five months. While it may be possible for an employee to maintain sobriety for a short period of time in order to test negative in an anticipated urine test, it would be more difficult for an employee to abstain for several months.

Drugs become incorporated into hair from three major sources—the blood supply, the sweat and sebum, and from passive exposure to the smoke or solid form of the drug.[23] In general, hair testing is less susceptible to intentional adulteration or substitution by the donor; the donor is always in sight of the collector. However, there have been other contentions of contamination of the hair from external sources: environmental drug contamination from exposure to methamphetamine or cocaine smoke has been shown to be present in children exposed to drug smoke in the home environment.[24]

Studies have shown that despite a washing procedure prior to testing, environmental contamination of the hair may still cause a false-positive test result.[25] Smith and Kidwell performed a study where cocaine-using adults and their non-using children were tested for drug use and exposure. Hair from the adult subjects showed cocaine in 92 percent of the cases and hair from the children was positive in 88 percent of the cases.[26] In addition, hair is continuously in contact with body sweat. Sweat also contains drugs, which may be incorporated into the hair matrix after the hair has extruded from the skin. One study demonstrated that deuterated cocaine may be found in previously drug-free hair when volunteers, who were administered deuterated cocaine, held the hair in their hands for 30 minutes.[28] This positive result persisted even after the standard pre-test washing procedure.

Other issues in the hair-testing arena are the different amounts of uptake in the hair depending on ethnicity, and hair color.[27] Studies by Henderson et al. have shown a bias in ethnic hair types to the incorporation of the hair to cocaine vapor. The order of the degree of incorporation was largest for Asian hair, followed by African hair, and finally Caucasian hair.[28] Hair color bias was also demonstrated in a study by Reid et al., in which binding of benzoylecgonine was different for black, brown and blond hair types.[29]

Hair testing has enjoyed some popularity in a variety of arenas, including family law, insurance cases, custody cases, pre-employment, law enforcement, and the military. In workplace testing, hair is most often used for pre-employment testing only, since it best represents a history of drug use over a long period of time. If a company's goal is to determine long-term drug use, a hair sample may be the best matrix.

a. Case Report: Cocaine in hair sample

August 3, 2009

Gary Esquire
Attorney at Law

RE: Rickie Harper

Mr. Esquire:

I, James O'Donnell, earned Bachelor's and Doctorate degrees in Pharmacy from the Universities of Illinois and Michigan, respectively, and earned a Master's degree in

Clinical nutrition from the Rush University. I completed a residency in Clinical Pharmacy at the University of Illinois Research Hospitals. I currently am an Associate Professor of Pharmacology at the Rush University Medical Center, and a Lecturer in the Department of Medicine at the University of Illinois College of Medicine–Rockford. I have been a pharmacologist consultant to the State of Illinois Department of Public Health, consultant to several public defender and states attorney's offices, the Illinois Attorney General, the Department of Justice (DEA) and several U.S. attorney offices, all in the areas of pharmacology, drug and alcohol effects and drug use. I am a Diplomate of the American Board of Clinical Pharmacology, a Diplomate of the Board of Nutritional Specialties, and a Fellow in the American College of Clinical Pharmacology, and member of several professional societies. A copy of my curriculum vita is enclosed.

Materials reviewed

1. ChemTestHair Analysis Drug Test Results 12/19/2007 115545569: Cocaine 8.2ng/10mg, Benzoylecgonine 2.9ng/10mg
2. MediTest Urine Test—12/19/2007 Negative
3. ChemTestHair Analysis Drug Test Results 3/22/2008: Cocaine 24.2ng/10mg, Benzoylecgonine 2.6ng/10mg
4. MediTest Urine Test—3/22/2008 Negative
5. Acculab Diagnostics 3/28/2008 Results Hair: Cocaine 1236pg/mg, Benzoylecgonine Negative
6. Authoritative books and references regarding drug testing in hair

I also interviewed Mr. Oliver Harper on several occasions on the telephone and once in person.

Facts of the case

In April 2007, Mr. Oliver Harper had an accident at the auto plant, and he had a mandatory urine test, which was positive for cocaine. According to Mr. Harper, he was required to go to Serenity for an outpatient drug treatment program for 21 days. While there, he tested positive again (urine test). This was May 2007. He had hair tests "every three months," and his December 2007 hair test was positive (#2 above—8.3ng/10mg cocaine; 2.9ng/10mg benzoylecgonine—BE); a Med-iTest test on 12/19/2007 was negative. At this time he was told he had one "last chance"—one more time and he is out. On March 22, 2008, he was tested for hair (positive Cocaine 24.2ng/10mg; BE 2.6ng/10mg). A urine test by MediTest was negative. On his own initiative, Mr. Harper had his hair

sampled and tested by Acculab Laboratories on March 29, and the report came back cocaine positive 1236pg/mg.

Opinions

In my opinion, the March 22, 2008 and the March 29, 2008 positives are likely due to residual cocaine in the hair, which can stay for several months. That is, these tests in March are identifying the same cocaine and metabolite found in the December 2007 test. The quantities measured are miniscule, and, put in perspective, considering that billionths of a gram (pg = picogram) are being measured, do not vary substantially. Further, variance in sampling from time to time and location to location is well described. In my opinion, the "positive" tests conducted in March 2008 do not provide evidence of re-use of cocaine; thus, there is no evidence supporting a "last chance" violation.

Bases for opinions

There are many shortcomings with hair testing for drugs, one of which is the imprecision of determining when the exposure occurs, and the possibility that subsequent positives (like the March 2008 tests) are not really caused by re-use, but rather, the cocaine staying in the hair shaft until the hair is cut off or falls off the scalp. Extensive discussions of this phenomenon, the variability between samples taken from different locations on the scalp and samples taken at different times, the increased binding of cocaine in African-American hair are discussed at length in the following text discussion.

2. Saliva testing

Saliva is an oral liquid composed of water (90 percent) and various other substances, such as mucins and enzymes. Saliva testing is simple to perform, and the easiest noninvasive method available. Saliva is a substance that most reliably can be correlated to blood concentrations for certain drugs.[30] Additionally, saliva differs from urine in that saliva contains higher concentrations of the parent drug than inactive metabolites. However, there are a variety of factors that affect the concentration of drugs in the saliva.

It is well known that an increase in saliva pH can alter the partitioning of certain drugs from the blood into the saliva.[31] Many drugs are weak acids or bases. The distribution of a weak electrolyte is determined by its pKa and the pH gradient across the membrane. For drugs with a pKa less than 5.5, saliva concentrations are not pH dependent and the concentration will correlate with the plasma portion of the blood. However, drugs with a pKa greater than 5.5 are highly pH dependent. For example, cocaine (pKa 8.6) concentration in saliva may change by a factor of 12 if the saliva pH changes from 6.5 to 7.6.[32]

Saliva is a good matrix for the determination of drug use during a 12 to 24 hour period of time.[33] As compared to hair, saliva would not be useful for determination of a historical drug use pattern, but may be useful for testing employees prior to their engagement in safety-sensitive functions.[33]

3. Sweat testing

Sweat is a body fluid that was not, until recently, fully utilized in the drug-testing arena. Sweat is mainly produced by eccrine in the transdermal layer of the skin surface or apocrine glands in specific regional areas in the body. Sweat is about 99 percent water and 1 percent sodium chloride and other trace materials. Researchers have known since 1911 that drugs are excreted in the sweat.[34]

Over the years, there have been several devices that have been used to collect sweat. However, many of these devices consisted of a pad covered by an occlusive membrane, which would trap both water and solute. This type of patch design could not always eliminate bacterial growth under the patch or allow the skin under the patch to remain healthy for long-term application. However, more recent technological developments have enabled the invention of an absorbent pad covered by a non-occlusive membrane, which facilitates comfort to the wearer by allowing oxygen, water, and carbon dioxide to pass through the patch.[35] The invention of a "sweat patch" collection device developed by Sudormed™ and marketed by PharmChem™ Laboratories under the trade name Pharm-Chek™ is such a device. After approval by the Food and Drug Administration, the patch was introduced in the drug-detection and testing arena.

The Pharm-Chek patch is left on the subject for about a week, at which time it is removed. The removed patch is placed in a vial with elution buffer to extract the drug from the patch. Testing is performed in the conventional immunoassay screening procedure and confirmation of positive results is completed with a GC/MS procedure. Benefits of sweat testing are that it is non-invasive, and that it can detect use—even a one-time use—for a longer period of time than can urine.[36] Other benefits include the detection of parent compounds rather than the more polar metabolites, and the tamper-evident membrane that will likely tear if there is an attempt to tamper with the patch after it is applied. These facts have made the device popular in the drug-treatment field, as well as in custody cases, probation, parole, and in the social-service arena.

While the use of sweat as a testing matrix may be suitable for pre-employment testing, the sweat patch would likely be unsuitable in "for cause" or in post-accident testing. Concentration of the drug in the sweat patches is expressed as ng/mL of buffer eluate. This convention of reporting makes it difficult to interpret or correlate the concentration with blood levels or to determine the degree of "under the influence." In addition, certain drugs tend to deposit in adipose tissue, making an issue of "recent use" more difficult to interpret.[37]

The manufacturer claims that the "patch is carefully designed so that contaminants from the environment can not penetrate the adhesive barrier from the outside, and therefore the patch can be worn during most normal activities (bathing and swimming, for example) without affecting the integrity of the test."[38] Several scientific articles have mirrored that opinion in stating that the molecular pore structure of the plastic membrane will exclude substances greater in molecular size than vapor-phase isopropanol.[39] However, there have been questions of contamination of the patch, during application and removal of the patch, or external contamination. Early studies indicate that the cleaning solution used (70 percent isopropanol) on the skin prior to the application of the patch does not adequately clean external contaminants from the skin.[40] A 1999 study by the Naval Research Laboratory concluded that "the potential for external contamination of the skin (CFWI) as well as contamination of the patch membrane (CFWO) can occur and generate false results."[41]

4. Blood

Blood is a valuable matrix, especially for post-accident drug-use determinations. A 1985 DOT study evaluated existing data on the concentrations of a variety of drugs in drivers to assess the ability of different matrices to detect drug impairment. The study concluded that urine testing would be suitable for establishing the need to obtain and analyze blood specimens for THC (the active ingredient in marijuana), and that blood is the only body fluid that can relate drug levels to impairment albeit limitedly.[42] A blood sample showing presence of a significant concentration of a drug that impairs the safe operation of large machinery can be beneficial to the ultimate determination of impairment. Other factors that may affect the ultimate determination of impairment are whether the blood is drawn from the employee during the expected timeframe of active drug action, and whether the employee exhibits consistent signs of the expected effects. Another benefit is the plethora of studies and literature delineating therapeutic versus toxic concentrations of drugs in whole blood or plasma.

The major disadvantage to blood testing is the invasiveness of the collection process, the increased hazardous exposure of the collector to possible virulent blood, and the lower concentration of drugs found in the blood, as compared to urine.

5. Urine

HHS currently mandates that only urine may be tested. However, even in non-regulated testing, urine appears to be most popular. Since most workplace testing is either random testing or pre-employment, recent use (not drug impairment) is the information sought. Urine is suitable for the determination of recent use, especially during the past 72 hours. The time frame in which a drug may be detected depends on several factors, including the amount of drug initially consumed, the frequency of drug use, the lipid-solubility of the drug in question, and the half-life (T1/2) of the drug. For example, some drugs, such as the cannabinoids, can be detected for over a month, if the donor is a frequent user. Another benefit to using urine for drug testing is that drug concentration in urine is ten to 100 times more concentrated than in the blood, making detection easier using conventional drug-testing instruments.

In urine collection, the substitution of another substance as urine, the addition of chemicals to the urine, or the dilution of the specimen with water are common methods of tampering with the specimen during collection. Adulteration of urine samples to mask drug use or cause a false-negative result when tested can be achieved in vivo or in vitro. In-vivo adulteration is caused by the consumption of some substance that will dilute the urine or change the amount of drug excreted into the urine of drugs. Consumption of large amounts of water or the use of diuretics will increase the amount of urine produced and will cause the drug concentration in the urine to be lowered. Consumption of a substance that makes the pH more alkaline will slow down the excretion of amphetamines and result in a lower amount in the urine per unit time. Both of these methods will effectively lower the concentration in the urine and may result in the drug concentration falling below the cutoff value of the test.

The addition of chemicals directly into a specimen may create a false negative in an otherwise positive specimen. Chemicals may interfere with the screening kit's reagents, causing the test to report the specimen as negative when it is truly positive. Some common chemicals used include detergents, vinegar, and bleach. The addition of plain water to the sample cup dilutes the specimen and lowers the concentration of the drugs in the specimen. The dilution may be so great that the specimen may test below the laboratory's cutoff concentration for determining which specimens are to be considered positive. The substitution of another substance, or another person's urine, results in the false specimen being negative for drugs.

When choosing a program or laboratory, the employer must evaluate the safeguards in place at the collection site and the testing laboratory. During the actual voiding of the specimen, the employee must not have access to water to dilute the specimen. Turning the water line to the sink off during voiding, or having the employee void where no sink is accessible is necessary. The placement of bluing agent in the toilet enables the collector to check the color of the sample to make sure the specimen was not diluted with water from the toilet. A temperature indicator on the specimen cup allows the collector to check the temperature of the specimen immediately after the voiding to ascertain if the temperature is consistent with body temperature. The HHS guidelines call for the collector to check the temperature of the urine within four minutes of collection. The temperature of the urine must be within 90–100°F. Despite these precautions, a negative urine specimen may be heated to body temperature by the concealment on or in the donor and substituted for the donor's urine at the time of collection. The collector's evaluation of specimen temperature, color, or smell during the collection process may still not be sufficient to detect donor adulteration. The laboratory, then, has to determine the adulteration of a specimen.

In an effort to ascertain whether a specimen has been tampered with during collection, the laboratory should test the urine for creatinine levels, specific gravity, nitrites and/or pH. If the specimen falls outside the normal ranges expected for normal urine, the integrity of the specimen might have been compromised. Unregulated laboratories often do not have criteria in place for the determination of an adulterated or dilute specimen. However, regulated programs have addressed this issue. The DOT requires specimen validity testing, and the HHS program strongly encourages the practice, through its publication of Program Document #35 for reporting urine specimen validity test results.[43] The publication discusses the issues of adulterated, diluted, and substituted urine specimens. Under the reporting guidelines, a specimen is considered "substituted" if the urine creatinine concentration is <5 mg/dL and the urine specific gravity is <1.001 or >1.020. A specimen is considered dilute if the creatinine is less than 20 mg/dL and the specific gravity is less than 1.003. A sample is considered adulterated if the pH is less than or equal to 3 or greater than or equal to 11, or if it contains exogenous substances, such as nitrites.

Natural polyuria can occur in medical conditions such as diabetes insipidus or nephrogenic diabetes.[44] However, scientific research of medical conditions resulting in severe overhydration (polyuria) and water-loading studies has indicated that guidelines can be established to enable a laboratory to detect a specimen condition that is not consistent with normal human urine. Analytical criteria for laboratories testing federal and federally regulated specimens are outlined in

Program Document #37.[45] To report a specimen as "substituted," creatinine must be quantitatively measured on two different aliquots, both using a cutoff of 5 mg/dL, with the results reported to the first decimal place. Specific gravity must be determined by refractometry on at least one of these aliquots, using cutoffs of 1.001 or 1.020, and reported to the third decimal place.

Occasionally, the donor may have trouble urinating because of what is termed "shy bladder," or merely be unable to provide a sufficient amount of urine for the test. If this is the case, the specimen must be discarded and the collector must attempt another collection. Consumption of copious amounts of water may encourage the production and collection of sufficient urine. The DOT guidelines direct the donor to consume approximately 40 ounces of fluid during a three-hour period following the unsuccessful collection. However, an employee's decision not to drink fluids in a "shy bladder" situation will not be regarded as a refusal to test. If the employee still cannot provide a specimen, the procedure is halted and the collector must make a notation on the CCF and notify the DER and MRO within 24 hours. The DER must then direct the employee to obtain a medical evaluation from a licensed physician within five days to explain the medical condition that would have precluded the employee from providing an adequate specimen. If a medical condition does exist, the MRO must determine whether there is clinical evidence that the employee is an illicit drug user. Evidence of a dilute specimen allows the employer to ask the employee to take another test immediately. Positive specimens that are determined to be dilute are treated as a valid positive test.

B. Alternate Sources of Drug Exposure

The main focus of drug-testing programs is to detect illegal drug use by the employee. However, some positive urine drug tests may have their origins in the use of a legal substance, rather than in the use of an illegal substance or in the unintentional exposure to substances used by another. Passive inhalation of smoked drugs, dermal absorption, foodstuff ingestion, or a laboratory's technical inability may be just a few of the other reasons for a positive urine test.[46] Thus, it is imperative that the employer or MRO be versed in the alternative explanations for positive drug-test results, prior to the imposition of any sanctions.

Use of certain beauty products, health oils, and food products are typical routes of drug exposure. The use of hemp products, such as hemp-seed oil or tea, has shown to cause a positive urine test for cannabinoids.[47] In one study, a 49-year-old man consumed a total of 30mL of cold pressed hemp-seed oil a day for four days. Urine samples were collected periodically from the start of the first ingestion through 177 hours. Urine specimens from collections between hours 45 through 142 were determined to contain THCCOOH from 12–68 ng/mL.[48,49]

In the 1980s, health food stores sold a tea under the trade name "Health Inca Tea." Health Inca Tea, containing about 1.87 mg of cocaine per cup, was found to produce positive benzoylecgonine screening results 21 and 26 hours after ingestion.[49] This tea no longer contains cocaine, since the FDA banned the importation of any tea containing residual cocaine into the United States.

The ingestion of poppy seeds can cause a positive urine test for opiates. The type of poppy seeds used, the concentration of morphine and codeine per gram of seeds, and the amount of seeds ingested play an important role in the amount of morphine ultimately found in the urine. Numerous studies have been undertaken to determine whether poppy seeds can cause a positive urinalysis result. In one study, ingestion of three poppy seed bagels resulted in 214 ng/mL codeine and 2797 ng/mL morphine at three hours.[50] In another study, the ingestion of 25 grams of poppy seeds from four brands of poppy seeds, containing between 17 and 294 mcg of morphine per gram, resulted in serum levels of up to 131 ng/mL and urine detectability over 48 hours.[51] The vast majority of the searched literature indicates that depending on the cutoff level utilized by the laboratory, the detection of morphine in the urine does not necessarily indicate an illegal drug use.

The HHS also recognizes that a positive for codeine or morphine may be a result of the donor consuming "normal dietary amounts" of poppy seeds. The MRO is directed to report the result as negative unless clinical evidence of abuse or illegal use of opiates is verified. The guidelines state the MRO "shall determine that there is clinical evidence—in addition to the urine test—of illegal use of any opium, opiate, or opium derivative…." Since 6-acetyl-morphine metabolite comes only from heroin, its presence confirms the illegal use of heroin, not the legal consumption of poppy seeds. In addition, the guidelines permit an MRO to have a blanket written request on file at the laboratory to routinely receive the quantitative values associated with a positive codeine and morphine result, or request quantitative information on the presence of codeine below the cutoff for specimens that have been reported positive for morphine only.

Passive inhalation or absorption of drugs can also occur. Secondary smoke contains active ingredients and pyrolysis products of the burning substance. The lungs have a large surface area and an abundant blood flow, enabling the drug to pass readily into the blood stream. Passive inhalation can occur with any smoked substance—marijuana, PCP, cocaine, methamphetamine, and so on. The level of drug ultimately found in the bystander from the smoke depends on the proximity of the subject to the smoke, the ventilation in the confined area, the amount of smoke, the concentration of the substance smoked, and the chemical nature of the substance.

The combustion of cannabis results in the conversion of various chemical precursors to form the active constituent of marijuana, THC. Most of the dose enters the smoker's lungs during inhalation, but a small amount is released into the environmental air. The concentration of THC in the air is directly related to the THC concentration in the cigarette and the size of the room where the smoke is released. The amount of THC absorbed by the passive inhaler depends on several factors. Not only is the size of the room in which the smoke is confined important, but also the number of "joints" smoked, and the number of hours exposed to the smoke. It is shown that a casual contact with marijuana smoke in a room containing approximately four smoking cigarettes may result in the passive inhaler testing positive for marijuana use by urine analysis. In a study by Cone et al. several volunteers were subjected to two differing concentrations of THC smoke in a confined room.[52] The study took place over six days, and the exposure time was limited to one hour per day. Individuals exposed to concentrations of THC smoke from 16 cigarettes reached RIA levels of up to 100 ng/mL, and up to 87 ng/mL on the GC/MS.[52] A subject confined to a medical ward tested positive for marijuana metabolites due to passive inhalation and tested positive for marijuana in the urine in concentrations up to 260 ng/mL.[53] The detection of cannabinoids in the blood and urine were also found by Morland et al., eliciting the conclusion that "the demonstration of cannabinoids in blood or urine is no unequivocal proof of active cannabis smoking."[54] HHS recognizes that passive inhalation of marijuana smoke does occur and can result in detectable levels of THC and its metabolites in urine. However, HHS also takes the position that it is unlikely that a nonsmoking individual could unknowingly passively inhale smoke that results in a drug concentration in urine at or over the cutoff levels used in the federal program. As such, HHS directs the MRO to report the result as "positive" for cannabinoids.

Passive exposure is not limited to the cannabinoids. There are numerous articles citing incidences of passive exposure by children and infants exposed to cocaine (crack) vapor which resulted in a positive urine test for benzoylecgonine.[55] A study conducted at NIDA's Addiction Research Center has demonstrated that individuals passively exposed to "crack" smoke did not produce a urine positive for cocaine using the guidelines' established testing levels.[56]

In another unrelated study, a 73-kilogram man exposed to vapors produced by the volatilization of 200 mg of cocaine "free-base" for 30 minutes prompted the authors to conclude that "passive exposure to free-base cocaine vapor can produce low-positive results..." and that is was "probable that a longer exposure period, larger cocaine dose, or a more efficient (lower) vaporization temperature would lead to higher urinary benzoylecgonine concentrations."[57]

Accidental exposure of police officers to cocaine in work-related situations led the authors to conclude that "passive microingestion of cocaine needs to be considered when examining persons who are in cocaine intensive environments."[58] Passive exposure of crime-lab personnel to cocaine during processing and analysis was also discovered by Le et al., prompting the authors to emphasize the use of protective equipment and short exposure times.[59]

The issue of passive exposure to phencyclidine (PCP) has not been studied extensively in the literature. However, there have been numerous laboratory studies determining levels of animal exposure to PCP pyrolysis products. In addition, the literature cites a few instances of accidental or occupational exposure to PCP. A woman living above an illegal PCP synthesis laboratory developed psychiatric manifestations of PCP exposure and levels of PCP in her blood.[60] In another study, law-enforcement personnel handling illegal PCP have been shown to have PCP in their blood and urine for at least six months after their last-known occupational exposure.[61]

It is clear that when reviewing a case for the possibility of a positive result due to passive exposure that the circumstances around the exposure be carefully evaluated. Casual contact in a social setting, or a one-time exposure, may yield only a low positive test. However, individuals exposed to either large amounts of smoke, smoke with a high concentration of drug, or lower amounts on a daily basis for a long period of time, may result in higher results. Lipid-soluble drugs pose a special problem in that daily exposure of even low amounts of smoke over a long period of time may result in the accumulation of drug in the body and result in a highly positive test.

C. Amphetamine Testing Issues

Analysis of the phenethylamines, or amphetamines, has always posed a challenging problem to toxicologists and drug-testing personnel. A positive amphetamine test result could occur because of a medical use of amphetamines, use of a legal drug that metabolizes to an amphetamine or methamphetamine, identification of enantiomers of methamphetamine, and the conversion of ephedrine or pseudoephedrine to methamphetamine during the GC/MS testing process.

Conversion of ephedrine to methamphetamine during the testing process has been shown to occur. In 1990, a certified laboratory reported a false-positive result in the analysis of a proficiency sample. Further investigation by the HHS of the laboratory and the NLCP revealed that the misidentification was analytical in nature. Specimens reported positive by the affected laboratory were sent to other laboratories and found not to contain methamphetamine. The culprit in the false identification appeared to be the presence of high levels of ephedrine or pseudoephedrine. Other factors included the use of high injection port temperatures in the GC/MS, and the use of derivitizing agents such as 4-carbethoxyhexa-fluorobuturyl chloride (CB), heptafluorobutyric anhydride (HFBA), N-trifluoro acetcy-l-propyl chloride (TPC), or pentafluoropropionic anhydride (PFPA).

In an attempt to eliminate further similar problems, the NLCP now requires that for the laboratory to report a specimen positive for methamphetamine, the specimen must also contain the metabolite, amphetamine, at a concentration equal to or greater than 200 ng/mL. If this criterion is not met, the specimen must be reported negative for amphetamines. Another way to virtually eliminate the problem is for the laboratory to incorporate an extraction procedure utilizing periodate. Periodate oxidizes primary amines, by reacting with –OH and –NH on adjacent carbon atoms. The result is a change in the molecule such that the ion fragments will not be similar to methamphetamine.

Once methamphetamine is identified, the structural form should be elicited. Methamphetamine and amphetamine exist in two structural forms known as enantiomers. Enantiomers are non-superimposable mirror images. The two isomers of each substance are designated as d- (dextro) and l- (levo), indicating the direction in which they rotate a beam of polarized light. The d- isomer of each substance has a strong central-nervous system stimulant effect while the l- isomer of each substance has primarily a peripheral action. A Vicks Inhaler® contains l-methamphetamine, affording the possibility that a laboratory positive result could be reported for l-methamphetamine and/or l-amphetamine. Selegiline, a monoamine oxidase inhibitor used in the treatment of Parkinson's disease, is metabolized to l-methamphetamine and l-amphetamine.

HHS dictates that the MRO should request the laboratory to perform a d-, l- isomer differentiation. Following Vicks Inhaler use, there will be close to 100 percent l-methamphetamine with perhaps a small amount of d-methamphetamine present as a contaminant inhaler. When isomer differentiation is conducted and there is greater than 80 percent l-methamphetamine, the results are considered to be consistent with Vicks Inhaler use.

D. Medical Use of Drugs

Not all drugs found in the urine are the product of illegal use. Some drugs can be directly prescribed by a medical professional (see Table 43.2), or can be present as a metabolite of a prescribed substance (see Table 43.3). In certain medical conditions, the use of drugs that are usually illegal may be permitted. Over-the-counter (OTC) preparations may contain drugs that may interfere or be misidentified as the illegal substance. The MRO has the burden of interpreting the results found by a laboratory. As such, the MRO should request the donor to submit a copy of his medical record, or evidence of medications taken during the period around the time of the drug test.

Methamphetamine is a sympathomimetic amine legally prescribed for medical conditions such as obesity, narcolepsy, and attention-deficit disorder.[62] Methamphetamine or amphetamine can be metabolically produced by the ingestion of prescribed drugs as well. Some common drugs that metabolize to amphetamine are found in Table 43.3. Some of these drugs, such as dimethylamphetamine, ethylamphetamine and fenrthylline, are Schedule I drugs in the United States and have no recognized medical usage.[63] However, these drugs may be found in other countries.

During the analysis of a urine specimen, the main laboratory focus is to accurately identify methamphetamine or amphetamine in the specimen. However, the MRO must consider any alternative origins for these drugs. The identification of the legal parent drug, when present, will assist in the determination of the source of the illegal substance. Some of the drugs listed in Table 43.3, such as famprofazone or fenforex, undergo extensive metabolism in the body resulting in very little, if any, parent drug found in the urine specimen. However, if the parent drug is not present, other metabolic products of the drug may be found. For example, deprenyl will metabolize to methamphetamine, amphetamine, and desmethyldeprenyl. Presence of demethyldeprenyl may indicate deprenyl as the source. Other considerations include evidence of a valid prescription by the donor, and the possible concurrent use of legal drug and illegal amphetamines.

Dronabinol is chemically synthesized delta-9-tetrahydrocannabinol (THC). It is sold under the trade name Marinol® in gelatin capsules for oral administration. Marinol is used for stimulating appetite and preventing weight loss in patients with confirmed diagnoses of AIDS, for treating nausea and vomiting associated with cancer chemotherapy, and in the management of glaucoma. The MRO should request that the donor submit a copy of her medical record or court order authorizing the legal use of Marinol or marijuana.

Table 43.2

Product	Drug Present
Marinol®	Cannabinoids
Astramorph PF® Duramorph® MSIR® MS Contin Tablets® Roxanol® Amogel PG® Diabismul® Donnagel-PG® Infantol Pink® Kaodene with Paregoric® ParegoricQuiagel PG®	Morphine
Actifed with Codeine Cough Syrup® Codimal PH® SyrupDimetane-DC Cough Syrup® Phenaphen with Codeine® Robitussin A-C® Triaminic Expectorant with Codeine® Tylenol with Codeine(#1, 2, 3, or 4)® Kaodene with Codeine®	Codeine
Desoxyn® (Gradumet®)	d-methamphetamine
Adderall® Benzedrine® Biphetamine® Dexedrine® Durophet® Obetrol®	d-amphetamine or racemic d,l-amphetamine
Vicks Inhaler®	l-methamphetamine

Table 43.3

Product	Metabolizes to
Amphetaminil Clobenzorex (Dinintel®, Finedal®) Ethylamphetamine Fenethylline (Captagon®) Fenproporex (Tegisec®) Mefenorex (Pondinil®) Mesocarb Prenylamine	Amphetamine
Benzphetamine (Didrex®) Dimethylamphetamine Famprofazone Fencamine Furfenorex Selegiline (Deprenyl, Eldepryl®)	Methamphetamine (and amphetamine)

There is a variety of prescription and nonprescription drugs that contain morphine, codeine, or the by-products of opium. As mentioned earlier, though, the use of heroin can be differentiated from these other drugs in that the 6-acetyl-morphine metabolite comes only from heroin. Its presence in the urine confirms the illegal use of heroin.

43.9 Legal Aspects of Workplace Drug-Testing

The implementation and enforcement of a workplace drug-testing program is always subject to lawsuits by affected employees or state and federal legal guidelines. The development of a program must consider the potential legal ramifications. Legal basis for a workplace program review and criticism may come from several sources, including constitutionality issues (right to privacy, freedom from unreasonable searches, due process), negligence or libel and slander, contract law, and discrimination. Constitutional issues generally arise in the public sector, but may apply to private sector employers under specific circumstances. However, the other three areas are applicable to all employers.

A. Constitutional Issues

Opponents of workplace drug testing often argue the fundamental right to privacy and the intrusiveness of the drug-collection procedure. The Fourth Amendment to the Constitution affords an individual the right to be free from an unreasonable search and seizure by the government. Any unreasonable intrusion must be justified by the law. This amendment, in addition to the Fourteenth Amendment's allowance for due process, is the two major constitutional arguments cited in workplace drug-testing litigation.[64]

By implication, the Fourth Amendment affords an individual the right to privacy. The concept of an individual's right for a constitutional-based "zone of privacy" was recognized in the 1965 case *Griswold v. Connecticut* (381 U.S. 479).[65] In the *Griswold* case, citizens were accorded a "zone of privacy" free of government intrusion, and recognized an individual's right to be "let alone." The United States Supreme Court unanimously held that mandatory drug testing is a "search," under the Fourth Amendment in the case of *Samuel K. Skinner v. Railway Labor Executives' Association* (489 U.S. 602). However, the court also held that when drug testing was performed within an employment context, the intrusion was justifiable and did not unnecessarily infringe on privacy interests (*Samuel K. Skinner v. Railway Labor Executives' Association*, 489 U.S. 602, p. 625). Proponents of workplace drug testing argue that this and other court rulings are not "adequate for describing the employee's claim to privacy in an essentially social and coopera-

tive setting like the workplace."[66] To date, it appears that the prevalent view in the workforce is that workplace drug testing is not an undue intrusion of privacy rights when the standards for employment are clearly communicated to the prospective employee and there is a subsequent contractual basis for reasonable continued performance monitoring.

The due process provision of the Fourteenth Amendment prohibits states from denying federal constitutional rights, and does not generally apply to private citizens or entities.[67] The authority of Congress to enforce the Fourteenth Amendment, Section 1983 of Title 42 of the United States Code, prohibits interference with federal rights under color of state law. In fact, in 1966, the Supreme Court stated "In cases under Section 1983, 'under color' of law has consistently been treated as the same thing as 'state action' required under the Fourteenth Amendment."[68] Therefore, a private employer's action of drug testing, or discharge due to a "dirty" test, can been seen as state action in some circumstances. According to case law, a private employer's action may be considered "state action" and thus regulated under the Fourteenth Amendment if any of the following four are true:[69]

- The employer derives his income from the government.
- The employer is controlled by "extensive and detailed" regulation by the state.
- The function of the employer is "traditionally the exclusive prerogative" of the state.
- There is a "symbiotic relationship" between the employer and the government.

Similarly, the Fourth Amendment applies to government actions and generally is not applicable to private-sector drug testing. A warrant is generally required for a search to be considered reasonable under the Fourth Amendment.[70] However, in regulated industries, an exception to the warrant requirement was developed for searches of premises pursuant to an administrative inspection scheme.[71] There are two requirements that justify the unwarranted administrative search exception. One is a strong state interest in conducting an unannounced search. Additionally, the pervasive regulation of the industry has reduced the justifiable privacy expectation of the subject of the search.

B. State and Federal Mandates

An employer must be aware of the myriad state and federal mandates that affect the company's workplace drug-testing policy and implementation of the program. The DOT regulations and the Federal Workplace Act of 1988 have already been briefly discussed. The following are additional mandates to consider:

- The National Labor Relations Act
- Title VII of the Civil Rights Act of 1964
- The Americans with Disabilities Act of 1990
- The Rehabilitation Act of 1973
- State drug-testing laws and city ordinances

Title VII of the Civil Rights Act of 1964 applies to all private-sector employees with 15 or more employees and prohibits the discrimination against applicants or employees based on race, religion, sex, or national origin.[72] Disparities in sanctions or reasonable-cause testing, or a drug-testing policy that unfairly impacts a protested class, may prompt a Title VII charge. Thus, applying policies evenly and without bias is critical to the successful implementation of a drug-free workplace program.

State drug-testing laws may also place restrictions on an employer's right to implement random drug testing, or to require certain aspects of a program to be in place. For example, the California Department of Health Services prohibits drug tests performed by anyone other than a certified laboratory or licensed physician.[73] California also requires that employers with 25 or more employees must accommodate employees who wish to participate in a substance-abuse treatment program, provided the accommodation does not place an undue hardship on the employer.[74] On the other hand, Rhode Island only allows drug testing when "the employer has reasonable grounds to believe based on specific aspects of the employee's job performance and on specific contemporaneous observations, capable of being articulated, concerning the employee's appearance, behavior or speech that the employee's use of controlled substances is impairing his or her ability to perform his or her job."[75]

The confidentiality of medical records and communications in a doctor-patient relationship is generally upheld. A cause of action may be charged and damages may be awarded when there is an improper disclosure of confidential records or information. State statutes regarding unemployment compensation should also be considered, since a positive drug test may be considered "misconduct" and render a discharged employee ineligible for unemployment compensation. For these reasons, it is highly recommended that employers have a legal professional review the proposed program and policies for compliance with the relevant state and local regulations.

The Americans with Disabilities Act of 1990 (ADA) is applicable to employers with 15 or more employees.[76] Title I of the ADA prohibits employment discrimination against a "qualified individual with a disability." Among other "qualified individuals," a person who is currently not using drugs and who is participating in or has completed a supervised drug-rehabilitation program may also qualify.[77] The ADA specifically permits employers to adopt drug-testing policies, and expressly excludes drug testing as part of the prohibition against medical inquiries of a "qualified individual's" disability. In fact, a "qualified individual" expressly does not include an individual who is currently engaged in the use of illegal drugs.[78] The Rehabilitation Act of 1973 is similar to the ADA but protests a narrower class of individuals—"handicapped" persons—from certain types of discrimination by the federal government, federal contractors, and federal grantees.[79] A "handicapped" person may include an employee who is an "addict" and who has sought treatment voluntarily.[80] However, occasional users are not considered handicapped and are therefore not protected. Here, as with the ADA of 1990, employers are not prohibited from testing employees.[81]

The 1982 National Labor Relations Act (NLRA) was developed to promote, among other things, the flow of commerce and establish legitimate rights of both employers and employees.[82] Employee drug-testing issues were addressed in this updated version of the 1947 Labor Management Relations Act. Case law has established that drug testing of current employees, not applicants, is a mandatory subject of collective bargaining agreements and union contracts.[83]

Employers who hire workers who belong to a union or collective-bargaining unit need to consult with union representatives or union bylaws. Incorporation of workplace drug-testing policies that are acceptable to collective-bargaining agreements is the first step towards running a smooth company program.

Clinical Laboratory Improvement Amendments of 1988 (CLIA '88) was created to establish uniform testing standards in the clinical field. Laboratories that are HHS-certified under the NLCP are specifically exempt from the requirements set forth under CLIA '88. The exemption is limited to the certified laboratories' immunoassay and GC/MS confirmatory testing processes for the five drug classes (HHS-5) stated in the guidelines. Certified laboratories that perform tests with procedures not in accordance with the guidelines or by methods not certified by HHS are subject to the technical and regulatory requirements of CLIA '88.

43.10 Discovery: The "Litigation Package"

By the time cases are filed, specimens may get lost or become unsuitable for re-testing. In these instances, the litigation package—all of the documents pertaining to the case—is the only evidence that can be used to evaluate the reliability of the analysis. The litigation package must include:

1. The CCF. The CCF documents the circumstances around the sample collection, including the identity of the specimen, the condition of the specimen, and the chain of custody. On this form, as well, any irregularities surrounding the collection (for example, the need for an affidavit of correction) or discrepancies in labeling are noted.

2. The preliminary screening data. The screening data will include the results of the calibrators (low/high) and controls (blank/quality control) and the results of the cases in question. Also included should be evidence of integrity testing, such as creatinine, nitrates, or specific gravity. Also recommended are the following:
   - The standard-operating procedure (SOP), including criteria for acceptance of the data for the calibrators, controls and case, and specificity testing (evaluation of other drugs which may cause a false positive).
   - The manufacturer's assay kit insert describing the required procedure and cross-reactivities of other drugs with the assay.

3. The confirmation data. Confirmation is performed with GC/MS. Data should include the spectrograms for the calibrators and controls as well as the case. Some laboratories use a historical (established monthly etc.) calibration curve, and one calibrator and control. Also recommended for evaluation are the following:
   - The standard-operating procedure (SOP), including the extraction method (chemical preparation of the specimen prior to testing on the GC/MS); criteria for acceptance of the data for the calibrators, controls and case; criteria for acceptable chromatography; specificity (evaluation of other drugs which may cause a false positive) testing; and data establishing of the limit of detection and limit of quantitation.
   - Maintenance and standard tune (evaluation of the working parameters of the machine for the day) data for the GC/MS.

4. Results of proficiency tests (SAMHSA and others) for two years prior and after the case in question. This should include any reports of non-compliance or errors in identification or quantity found.

43.11 Conclusions

The effectiveness of a workplace drug-testing program is evident. It is estimated that between $5 and $16 are saved for every $1 employers invest in an EAP.[84] There are scores of statistics that support the benefits of a drug-free workplace program for both the employer and the employee. A contractor firm in Florida saved $100,000 on workers' compensation premiums in 1990, experienced increased productivity, and reduced absenteeism.[85]

Employers reap the benefits of a drug-free workplace through increased employee morale, customer satisfaction, and public image. Accidents, production error, absenteeism, employee theft, employee turnover, and legal expenses all decrease. Employees benefit through increased security, productivity, coworker relations, health, and safety. A thorough drug-free workplace program also gives an employee who may be struggling with substance abuse the resources and assistance to achieve and maintain sobriety and achieve greater career success.

Workplace drug-testing programs need continual revisions to keep up with the advances in technology. Drugs outside the DHHS-5 and the inclusion of matrices other than urine are likely to be considered in the near future. New analytical methods will likely be more specific and sensitive, allowing for more accurate and reliable testing. As the concept of workplace drug testing matures, formal policies and the scope of programs will change. Even at this writing, DHHS and DOT are making or considering changes. The following are program issues that will likely be addressed or implemented in coming years:

- Alternative matrices (sweat patch and saliva, at minimum)
- Mandatory collection of split specimens
- Mandatory testing of the five major drug classes
- Testing for other drugs, such as MDMA
- "Point-of-collection" analysis
- Initial testing facilities that perform validity testing and screening only
- Changes in cutoff levels
- Increased validity testing
- Uniform guidelines encompassing all federal agencies
- Increased training and certification requirements for MROs, SAPs, and collectors

Regardless of the program implemented, voluntary or mandatory, the employer must have all of the basic aspects of a program in place, including a written policy statement, provisions for supervisor training, employee education and assistance, and guidelines for drug testing. Inclusion of all these steps will increase the effectiveness of any program and help to achieve the goal for American commerce and the welfare of the workforce—a drug-free workplace.

Endnotes

1. Substance Abuse and Mental Health Services Administration. 2000. Summary of Findings From the 2000 National Household Survey on Drug Abuse. United States Department of Health and Human Services.

2. Center on Addiction And Substance Abuse. 1993. The Cost of Substance Abuse to America's Health Care System, Report 1; Medical Hospital Costs. Columbia University.

3. Substance Abuse and Mental Health Services Administration. May, 1995. Substance Abuse and Mental Health Statistics Sourcebook. United States Department of Health and Human Services.

4. August, 1998. National Household Survey on Drug Abuse.U.S. Department of Health and Human Services.

5. October 22, 1996. Addiction in the Workplace Survey. Center City, Minnesota: Hazelden Foundation.

6. National Institute on Drug Abuse. 1991. National Household survey on Drug Abuse. United States Department of Health and Human Services.

7. 1996 AMA Survey Workplace Drug-testing and Drug Abuse Policies Summary of Key Findings. 1996. New York: American Management Association. 1–8.

8. Walsh, Michael J. 1998. Development and Scope of Regulated Testing, in Drug Abuse Handbook. CRC Press. 730.

9. President's Commission on Organized Crime. 1986. Report to the President-and Attorney General: America's Habit; Drug Abuse, Drug Trafficking, and Organized Crime. Washington, DC: United States Government Printing Office.

10. Executive Order 12564. September 15, 1986. Federal Register. Vol. 51, No. 180.

11. 1990. Modal Plan for a Comprehensive Drug-Free Workplace Program. United States Department of Health and Human Services. Publication No. (ADM) 90-1635.

12. Supplemental Appropriations Act of 1987, Section 503, Pub. L. 100-71, July 11, 1987, 101 Stat. 391, 468–471, codified at 5 U.S.C. Section 7301

13. Supplemental Appropriations Act of 1987, Section 503(a)(1)(A)(ii)(I), Pub. L. 100-71, July 11, 1987. 101 Stat. 468, codified at 5 U.S.C. Section 7301

14. June 9, 1994. "Mandatory Guidelines for Federal Workplace Drug-testing Programs," Federal Register. Vol. 59, Number 110. 29908–29931.

15. Substance Abuse and Mental Health Services Administration. September 1, 1994. Mandatory Guidelines for Federal Workplace Testing Programs. United States Department of Health and Human Services.

16. Omnibus Transportation Employee Testing Act of 1991; Public Law 102-143, Title V.

17. Working Partners, Small Business Workplace Kit: Steps to a Drug-Free Workplace. www.dol.gov/workingpartners. United States Department of Labor.

18. 1990. Modal Plan for a Comprehensive Drug-Free Workplace Program. United States Department of Health and Human Services. Publication No. (ADM) 90-1635.

19. Substance Abuse and Mental Health Services Administration. September 1, 1994. Mandatory Guidelines for Federal Workplace Testing Programs. United States Department of Health and Human Services. Subpart B, Section 2.1.

20. Substance Abuse and Mental Health Services Administration. Mandatory Guidelines for Federal Workplace Testing Programs. United States Department of Health and Human Services. Subpart B, Section 2.4.

21. Department of Transportation. December 19, 2000. Federal Register 49 C.F.R. 40.

22. P. Kintz, ed. *Drug Testing in Hair* (Boca Raton, FL: CRC Press, 1996).

23. W. Montagna and E.J. Van Scott. "The anatomy of the hair follicle," in *The Biology of Hair Growth*, R.A. Ellis, ed. (NY: New York Academic Press, 1958), p. 39.

24. D. Lewis et al. "Determination of drug exposure using hair; application to child protective cases," *Forensic Sci. Int.* 84(1–3):123–8 (1997).

25. D.A. Kidwell. June 6–10, 1988. "Analysis of Drugs of Abuse in Hair by Tandem Mass Spectrometry," Proceedings of the 36th American Society of Mass Spectrometry Conference on Mass Spectrometry and Allied

Topics. American Society of Mass Spectrometry, San Francisco. 1364-1365. Also D.A. Kidwell and D.L. Blank. May 26, 1990. "Deposition of Drugs of Abuse in Human Hair." Society of Forensic Toxicology Conference on Hair Analysis. Washington, D.C.

26. F.P. Smith and D.A. Kidwell. 1997. "Environmental Contamination Causes Positive Hair Analysis Results," The International Association of Forensic Toxicologists, XXXV Annual Meeting.

27. G.L Henderson, M.R. Harkey and R. Jones. September, 1993. "Hair Analysis for Drugs of Abuse." Final Report on Grant Number NIL 90-NIJ-CX-0012 to National Institutes of Justice. Also Kidwell, D.A.; and Blank, D.L. 1994. "Mechanisms of incorporation of Drugs into Hair and the Interpretation of Hair Analysis Data," Research Monograph. Edited by E.J. Cone and M. Welch, National Institute of Drug Abuse.

28. G.L Henderson, M.R. Harkey and R. Jones. September, 1993. "Hair Analysis for Drugs of Abuse." Final Report on Grant Number NIL 90-NIJ-CX-0012 to National Institutes of Justice.

29. W. Reid, F. O'Connor and J. Crayton. "The in vitro binding of benzoylecgonine to pigmented human hair samples," *Clin. Toxicol.* 32:405 (1994).

30. E.J. Cone et al. "Correlation of saliva cocaine levels with plasma levels and with pharmacologic effects after intravenous cocaine administration in human subjects," *J. Anal. Tox.* 12:200–206 (1998).

31. K. Kato et al. "Cocaine and metabolite excretion if saliva under stimulated and nonstimulated conditions," *J. Anal. Tox.* 17:338–341.

32. L.K. Thompsom et al. "Confirmation of cocaine in human saliva after intravenous use," *J. Anal. Tox.* 11:36–38 (1987).

33. M. Huestis and E. Cone. "Alternative testing matrices," in S. Karch, ed., *Drug Abuse Handbook* (Boca Raton, FL: CRC Press, 1998), p. 804.

34. W. Schramm et al. "Drugs of abuse in saliva: A review," *J. Anal. Toxicol.* 16:1–9 (1992).

35. P. Kintz. "Drug-testing in addicts: A comparison between urine, sweat, and hair," *Therapeutic Drug Monitoring* 18:450–455 (1996).

36. M. Burns and R. Baselt. "Monitoring drug use with a sweat patch: An experiment with cocaine," *J. Anal. Toxicol.* 17:41–48 (1995).

37. J.A. Levisky et al. "Drug deposition in adipose tissue and skin: Evidence for an alternative source of positive sweat path tests," *Forensic Sci. Int.* 110(1):3–46 (2000).

38. N. Fortner (Vice-President, PharmChem, Inc.) June 5, 1988. Prepared statement before the House Committee on Government Reform and Oversight Subcommittee on National Security, International Affairs and Criminal Justice. Federal Information Systems Corporation Federal News Service.

39. V. Spiehler et al. "Enzyme immunoassay validation for qualitative detection of cocaine in sweat," *Clin. Chem.* 42(1):34–38 (1996).

40. D. Kidwell, M. Blanco and F. Smith. "Cocaine detection in a university population by hair analysis and skin swab testing," *Forensic Sci. Int.* 84:65–86 (1997).

41. D. Kidwell and F. Smith. 1999. "Susceptibility of PharmChek™ Drugs of Abuse Patch to Environment Contamination," Publication Number NRL/MR/6170-99-8414. Washington, DC: Naval Research Laboratory. 1–20.

42. September 1985. "Drugs Feasibility Assessment of Chemical Testing for Drug Impairment." United States Department of Transportation. HS 806 920.

43. September 28,1998. "Guidance for Reporting Specimen Validity Test Results." Program Document (PD) 35. Notice to the National Laboratory Certification Program (NLCP) Inspectors and HHS Certified Laboratories.

44. Also K.B. Kern and H.W. Meislin. "Diabetes insipidus: Occurrence after minor head trauma." *J. Trauma.* 24:69–72 (1984). Also A. Buridi, L. Corman and R. Redinger. "Hypokalemic nephropathy and nephrogenic diabetes insipidus due to excessive consumption of a soft drink," *S. Med. J.* 91:1079–1082 (1998).

45. July 28, 1999. "General Guidance/Criteria for Specimen Validity Testing" Program Document (PD) 37. Notice to the National Laboratory Certification Program (NLCP) Inspectors and HHS Certified Laboratories.

46. M. ElSohly and A. Jones "Drug-testing in the workplace: Could a Positive test for one of the mandated drugs be for reasons other than illicit use of the drug?" *J. Anal Tox.* 19(6):450–8 (1995).

47. G. Steinagle and M. Upfal. "Concentration of marijuana metabolites in the urine after ingestion of hemp seed tea," *J. Occup. Environ. Med.* 41(6):510–3 (1999).

48. R. Struempler, G. Nelson and F. Urry. "A positive cannabinoids workplace drug test following the ingestion of commercially available hemp seed oil," *A. Anal. Tox.* 21(4):283–285 (1997).

49. G. Jackson, J. Sooday and A. Poklis. "Urinary excretion of nemzoylecgonine following ingestion of Health Inca Tea," *F. Sci. Int.* 49(1):57–64 (1991).

50. R. Struempler. "Excretion of codeine and morphine following ingestion of poppy seeds," *J. Anal. Tox.* 11(3): 97–9 (1987).

51. L. Hayes, W. Krasselt and P. Mueggler. "Concentration for morphine and codeine in serum and urine after ingestion of poppy seeds," *Clin. Chem.* 33(6):806–8 (1987).

52. E. Cone et al. 1987. "Passive inhalation of marijuana smoke: urinalysis and room air levels of delta-9-tetra-hydrocannibinol," *J. Anal. Tox.* 11:89–96 (1987).

53. P. Zeidenberg, R. Bourdon, and G. Nahas. "Marijuana intoxication by passive inhalation: Documentation by detection of urinary metabolites," *Am. J. Psychiatry* 134(1):76–78 (1977).

54. J. Morland et al. "Cannabinoids in blood and urine after passive inhalation of cannabis smoke," *JJFSCA* 30(4): 997–1002 (1985).

55. S. Heidemann and M. Gietting. "Passive inhalation of cocaine by infants," *Henry Ford Hosp. Med. J.* 38(4): 252–4 (1990).

56. E.J. Cone et al. "Passive inhalation of cocaine," *J. Anal. Toxicol.* 19:399–411 (1995).

57. R. Baselt, D. Yoshikawa and J. Chang. "Passive inhalation of cocaine," *Clin. Chem.* 37(12):2160–2161 (1991).

58. T. Mieczkowski. "Distinguishing passive contamination from active cocaine consumption: Assessing the occupational exposure of narcotics officers to cocaine," *Forensic Sci. Int.* 84(1–3):87–111 (1997).

59. S. Le et al. "Occupational exposure to cocaine involving crime lab personnel," *J. For. Sci.* 37(4):959–968 (1992).

60. O. Aniline et al. "Incidental intoxication with phencylidine," *J. Clin. Psychiatry* 41(11): 393–4 (1980).

61. F. Pitts et al. "Occupational intoxication and long-term persistence of phencyclidine (PCP) in law enforcement personnel," *Clin. Toxicol.* (9):1015–20 (1981).

62. Medical Economics Staff. *Physicians Desk Reference*, 55th ed. (Montvale, NJ: Medical Economics Company, 2001), p. 438.

63. J.T. Cody. "Metabolic precursors to amphetamine and methamphetamine," *Forensic Sci. Rev.* 5:109 (1993).

64. S.M. Fogel et al. "Survey of the law on employee drug-testing," *U. Miami L. Rev.* 42:553 (1988).

65. *Griswold v. Connecticut*, 381 U.S. 479

66. M. Cranford. "Drug-testing and the right to privacy: Arguing the ethics of workplace drug-testing," *Journal of Business Ethics* 17:1805–1815 (1988).

67. *Shelly v. Kraemer*, 334 U.S. 1, 13 (1948).

68. *United States v. Price*, 383 U.S. 787, 794, n. 7 (1966).

69. *Rendell-Baker v. Kohn*, 457 U.S. 830 (1982).

70. *Payton v. New York*, 445 U.S. 573, 1980.

71. *Donovan v. Dewey*, 452 U.S. 594, 602–605, 1981.

72. Title VII of the Civil Rights Act of 1964, 42. U.S.C. § 2000c et. seq.

73. Cal. Bus. & Prof. Code § 1206, Supp. 1999.

74. Cal. Lab. Code § 1025 et. seq.

75. Rhode Island Chapter 136. R.I. Gen. Laws § 28-6.5-1 and § 28-6.5-2 (Supp. 1997).

76. The Americans with Disabilities Act of 1990, PL 101-336, § 108.

77. The Americans with Disabilities Act of 1990, PL 101-336, ¶ 104(a).

78. The Americans with Disabilities Act of 1990, PL 101-336, § 104 d1.

79. The Rehabilitation Act of 1973, 29 U.S.C. §§ 701–796 (1982).

80. *Nispero v. Buck*, 720 F. Supp. 1424, 1427 (N.D. Cal 1989).

81. *Heron v. McGuire*, 803 F. 2d 67, 68 (2d Circuit 1986).

82. Labor Management Relations Act, 1947, 29 U.S.C § 141.

83. Johnson-Bateman Co., 295 NLRB No. 26, 1331 L.R.R.M. Cas. (BNA) 1391 (1989); Labor Management Relations Act, 1947, 29 U.S.C § 141, 8(d)).

84. 1991. United States Department of Transportation.

85. M. Delancy. *Does Drug Testing Work? (Washington, DC: Institute for a Drug-Free Workplace, 1994).*

Chapter 44

Forensic Issues in Recreational Drugs: Alcohol, Cocaine and Marijuana

James T. O'Donnell, Pharm.D., M.S., FCP, ABCP, FACN, R.Ph.

44.1 Introduction

The United States experienced a widespread increase in illicit drug use in the late 1960s, when it was hallmarked as a symbol of social protest and political change.[1] Between 2002 and 2009, the percent of the U.S. population 12 and over who used an illegal drug within the past month rose from 8.3 to 8.7 percent, mostly due to an increase in the number of marijuana users (see Figure 44.1).[2]

Although these statistics present a negative implication from a public health point of view, a far more pressing concern is the impact on public safety from the increased number of impaired drivers. In 2007, the National Highway Traffic Safety Administration (NHTSA) released a study indicating that the proportion of drivers using psychoactive drugs (14 percent) was greater than those using alcohol (12 percent).[3] This unexpected finding has led a number of states to pass harsh new "zero tolerance" laws, which can be used to upgrade misdemeanor vehicular manslaughter charges to felonies when any amount of illegal drug is found in the system. For example, in May 2011, prosecutors in DuPage County, Illinois used just such a ruling by the State Supreme Court to upgrade charges against a driver who admitted taking "one or two" hits of marijuana the night before he was involved in a fatal collision with a motorcyclist. The driver now faces up to 14 years in prison instead of one year in jail.[4]

Increased risk is further evidenced by a recent study published by the *Journal of Studies on Alcohol and Drugs*, which found that among 44,000 U.S. drivers involved in fatal single-vehicle car crashes between 1998 and 2009, 25 percent tested positive for drug use.[5] The most common drugs were cannabinoids (marijuana, tetrahydrocannabinol [THC], and other cannabinoids) and stimulants (cocaine, amphetamines, benzphetamines, methamphetamines, and other stimulants) (see Figure 44.2).[6]

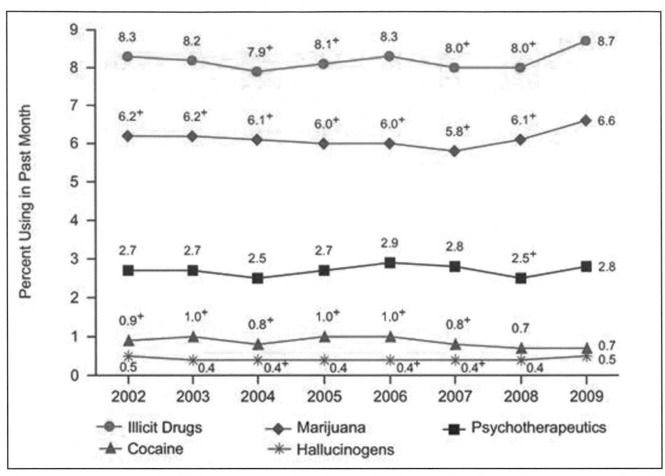

Figure 44.1 Percent of U.S. population using an illicit drug in the past month. Adapted from: Romano, Eduardo, and Voas B. Robert. "Drug and Alcohol Involvement in Four Types of Fatal Crashes." Journal of Studies on Alcohol and Drugs (2011): 567-76. Print.

44.2 Alcohol: A Major Contributor to Injury

Alcohol is a major factor in the causation of all types of accidental trauma. Motor vehicle accidents, pedestrian injuries, boating accidents, domestic violence, premises liability, and driving while intoxicated are all cases which require an attorney to evaluate the role of alcohol use and potential intoxication.

The knowledge available on the role of alcohol as a primary cause of accidental injury is largely sufficient to permit the formulation of information programs and of scientifically based control measures. On the other hand, the risk of accidents associated with taking drugs, whether obtained by prescription, over-the-counter or illicitly, while widely recognized, is difficult to assess in terms of its magnitude and impact on society and public health. The primary contribution of social epidemiological surveys to our understanding of alcohol and drug-related accidents is the determination of the population at risk. Adequate data exists to say that

far too many accidents occur in which the participants were using alcohol (see Figure 44.3). According to NHTSA:

In 2009, 10,839 people were killed in alcohol-impaired-driving crashes. These alcohol-impaired-driving fatalities accounted for 32 percent of the total motor vehicle traffic fatalities in the United States.

Traffic fatalities in alcohol-impaired-driving crashes decreased by 7.4 percent from 11,711 in 2008 to 10,839 in 2009. The alcohol-impaired-driving fatality rate per 100 million vehicle miles traveled (VMT) decreased to 0.36 in 2009 from 0.39 in 2008.

An average of one alcohol-impaired-driving fatality occurred every 48 minutes in 2009.

In 2009, all 50 states, the District of Columbia, and Puerto Rico had by law created a threshold making it illegal per se to drive with a BAC of .08

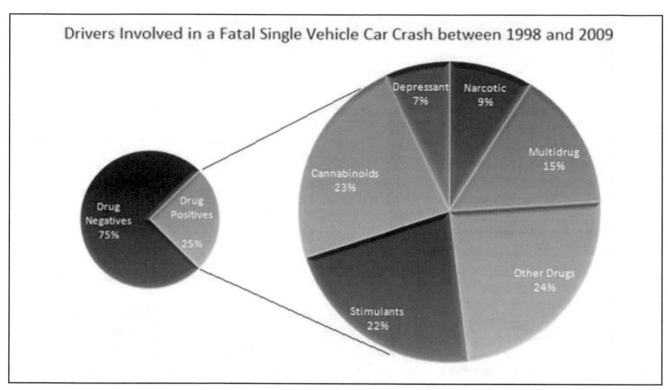

Figure 44.2 *Reproduced from: Substance Abuse and Mental Health Services Administration (2010). Results from the 2009 National Survey on Drug Use and Health: Volume I. Summary of National Findings (Office of Applied Studies, NSDUH Series H-38A, HHS Publication No. SMA 10-4856 Findings). Rockville, MD.*

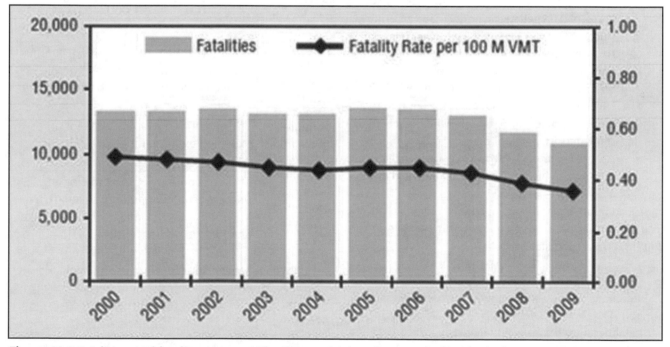

Figure 44.3 *Fatalities and fatality rate per 100 million vehicle miles traveled in alcohol-impaired-driving crashes, 2000–2009. Reproduced from: National Highway Traffic Safety Administration. Department of Transportation. "Traffic Safety Facts 2009 Data" Alcohol-Impaired Driving. DOT HS 811 385.*

or higher. Of the 10,839 people who died in alcohol-impaired-driving crashes in 2009, 7,281 (67%) were drivers with a BAC of .08 or higher. The remaining fatalities consisted of 2,891 (27%) motor vehicle occupants and 667 (6%) nonoccupants.[7]

44.3 Impairment and Intoxication by Alcohol

Although the effect of alcohol is usually described as impairment, there are several aspects of the relationship between alcohol and injuries that suggest a more complex causal pattern. Table 44.1 correlates blood alcohol levels with impairments of neurologic, cognitive, and physical functions, combined with corresponding effects on driving.

44.4 Motor Vehicles

In April 2000, NHTSA released a large scale review of the literature (112 articles from 1981 to 1997) on the effects of alcohol on driving-related skills including divided attention, drowsiness, vigilance tasks, tracking, perception, visual functions, cognitive tasks, psychomotor skills, choice reaction time, simple reaction time, and critical flicker fusion (see Table 44.2).[8] An excerpt from the abstract follows:

- Alcohol impairs some driving skills beginning with any significant departure from zero BAC. By BACs of 0.05 g/dl, the majority of the experimental studies examined reported significant impairment. By 0.08 g/dl, more than 94 percent of the studies reviewed exhibited skills impairment.
- Specific performance skills are differentially affected by alcohol. Some skills are significantly impaired by BACs of 0.01 g/dl, while others do not show impairment until BACs of 0.06 g/dl.
- All drivers are expected to experience impairment in some driving-related skills by 0.08 g/dl or less.

In addition to automobile operators, motorcyclists also face increased risk from alcohol consumption. An April 2007 NHTSA report states:

In 2004, 4,008 motorcyclists were killed and an additional 76,000 were injured in traffic crashes (NHTSA Traffic Safety Facts, 2004). Motorcyclist fatalities have been steadily increasing since 1997, when 2,116 fatalities were recorded.

It is apparent that alcohol use continues to be a significant problem in motorcycle crashes. In fatal crashes in 2004, motorcycle operators had higher blood alcohol concentration (BAC) levels (.08

grams per deciliter [g/dL] or higher) as compared to other types of motor-vehicle operators. The percentages for vehicle operators involved in fatal crashes were 27 percent for motorcycles, 22 percent for passenger cars, 21 percent for light trucks, and 1 percent for large trucks.

In 2004, there were 1,264 motorcycle operators killed who had been drinking (BAC .01+), of whom 1,025 (81%) were intoxicated (BAC .08+).[9]

44.5 Reaction Time[10]

Considering the epidemiological associations, as well as the above impairments to cognitive, psychomotor, emotional, and fine and gross motor functions described in Tables 44.1 and 44.2, the discussion now turns to the neurological and physiological considerations as to why alcohol impairs driving functions.

Successfully navigating a vehicle through any major metropolitan city requires a huge amount of information processing. One generally accepted theory divides driving maneuvers (e.g., stopping when a ball rolls out into the street) into three stages: perception (seeing the ball), decision (deciding to stop because kids often follow balls), and reaction (hitting the brakes). Together, these stages represent the driver information-processing model. Using this model, researchers have defined the following terms to explicate reaction time:

Perception Reaction Time	The interval between the visual stimulus (ball), and the beginning of a muscle movement to illicit a response from the vehicle (press the brake pedal).
Simple Reaction Time	The perception reaction time for an expected event (hit the gas when the light turns green).
Complex Reaction Time	The perception reaction time for an unexpected event in a novel situation (a large rock in the roadway forces a brake and swerve maneuver).

Psychomotor impairment increases simple reaction time and is resistant to alcohol, while central-processing impairment increases complex reaction time, and is susceptible to alcohol.

44.6 Other Non-Motor Vehicle Injuries Related to Alcohol[11]

Thus far, all attention has been focused on drunk driving, despite the fact that drunk walking, drunk arguing, or even drunk sleeping, given fire and smoke hazards, are also dan-

Table 44.1
Impairing Effects of Alcohol

Blood Alcohol Concentration (BAC)*	Typical Effects	Predictable Effects on Driving
.02%	• Some loss of judgment • Relaxation • Slight body warmth • Altered mood	• Decline in visual functions (rapid tracking of a moving target) • Decline in ability to perform two tasks at the same time (divided attention)
.05%	• Exaggerated behavior • May have loss of small-muscle control (e.g., focusing your eyes) • Impaired judgment • Usually good feeling • Lowered alertness • Release of inhibition	• Reduced coordination • Reduced ability to track moving objects • Difficulty steering • Reduced response to emergency driving situations
.08%	• Muscle coordination becomes poor (e.g., balance, speech, vision, reaction time, and hearing) • Harder to detect danger • Judgment, self-control, reasoning, and memory are impaired	• Concentration • Short-term memory loss • Speed control • Reduced information processing capability (e.g., signal detection, visual search) • Impaired perception
.10%	• Clear deterioration of reaction time and control • Slurred speech, poor coordination, and slowed thinking	• Reduced ability to maintain lane position and brake appropriately
.15%	• Far less muscle control than normal • Vomiting may occur (unless this level is reached slowly or a person has developed a tolerance for alcohol) • Major loss of balance	• Substantial impairment in vehicle control, attention to driving task, and in necessary visual and auditory information processing

*Information in this table shows the BAC level at which the effect usually is first observed, and has been gathered from a variety of sources including the National Highway Traffic Safety Administration, the National Institute on Alcohol Abuse and Alcoholism, the American Medical Association, the National Commission Against Drunk Driving, and www.webMD.com.

Reproduced from: "CDC—Impaired Driving: Effects of BAC—Motor Vehicle Safety—Injury Center." Centers for Disease Control and Prevention. Web. 12 Dec. 2011. www.cdc.gov/Motorvehiclesafety/Impaired_Driving/index. html.

Table 44.2
BAC and Impairment, by Behavioral Area

BAC (g/dl)	By lowest BAC at which impairment was found	By first BAC at which 50 percent or more of behavioral tests indicated consistent impairment
0.100	Critical Flicker Fusion	Simple Reaction Time, Critical Flicker Fusion
0.090-0.099		
0.080-0.089		
0.070-0.079		
0.060-0.069		Cognitive Tasks, Psychomotor Skills, Choice Reaction Time
0.050-0.059		Tracking
0.040-0.049	Simple Reaction Time	Perception, Visual Functions
0.030-0.039	Vigilance, Perception	Vigilance
0.020-0.029	Choice Reaction Time, Visual Functions	
0.010-0.019	Drowsiness, Psychomotor Skills, Cognitive Tasks, Tracking	Drowsiness
0.001-0.009	Driving, Flying, Divided Attention	Driving, Flying, Divided Attention

Adapted from: Moskowitz, H., and D. Fiorentino . "A Review of the Literature on the Effects of Low Doses of Alcohol on Driving-Related Skills." National Highway Traffic Safety Administration (NHTSA). Department of Transportation. DOT HS 809 028, n.d. Web. 12 Dec. 2011. www.nhtsa.gov/people/injury/research/pub/hs809028/DocPage.htm.

gerous. Contrary to popular belief, most alcohol-related injuries are due to violence, not driving.

Overall, alcohol is involved in 43 percent of all unintentional deaths from injury. On weekend evenings, close to 50 percent of emergency room patients admitted for injury have a measurable BAC. Of all non-fatal injuries occurring in the home, alcohol intoxication is responsible for 22 to 30 percent. It is further implicated in 21 to 48 percent of all lethal falls, and 50 percent of all lethal burns. Finally, alcoholics face a 3 to 16 times greater risk of accidental death than non-alcoholics.

In conclusion, if the anti-alcohol-driving programs are successful in reducing driving while intoxicated without reducing general ethanol ingestion, there is no guarantee that the overall severe injury rate will be reduced.

44.7 Adaptation Effects of Alcohol in the Central Nervous System—Tolerance

He holds his liquor better than most.

The tolerant (alcoholic) drinker is less impaired, but still experiences impairment. One decreases the BAC by 70–100 mg%.

—Alcohol expert

The old expression is common knowledge in describing individual responses to a given quantity of alcohol. Development of tolerance to the effects of various foreign agents is a general biological phenomenon of obvious adaptive significance. One aspect of differences in tolerance is seen in variation among individuals in the functional impairment caused by a particular concentration of ethanol in the blood. An important and often difficult task is to distinguish between psychological compensatory mechanisms and true "tissue tolerance." The former implies learning to function more efficiently during the influence of alcohol, the latter a change in the nervous system leading to improvement of physiological functioning in the presence of a given concentration of alcohol. This phenomenon has been described for the past 70 years since Mellanby.[12] Emergency room physicians see patients with BACs as high as 0.73 gm/dl. Walk-in patients with BACs between 0.4 and 0.5 gm/dl (coma and lethal levels) are common.[13]

The development of tolerance in humans, after prolonged exposure to alcohol, has generally been tested by comparing acute alcohol effects on people with different drinking habits. One of the first and most important studies was by Goldberg in 1943.[14] His subjects, classified as abstainers, moderate drinkers and heavy drinkers, gave clear evidence for difference between the groups in tests for sensory, motor and psychological function. Alcohol caused slightly more disturbance of EEG and ECG, and more pronounced ataxia in hospital attendants than in alcoholic patients in a study comparing the two groups. An electromyography study showed the response to disappear at blood alcohol levels of 0.012–0.082 percent in 12 virtual nondrinkers, 0.0720–0.120 percent in 11 "moderate drinkers" and 0.131–0.139 percent in three "heavy drinkers." These studies on subjects with different experience of drinking give strong evidence for tolerance but the objection can always be raised that they may represent samples of the population with differences existing prior to drinking.

Consensus among toxicologists and pharmacologists working in forensic matters is that the effect of tolerance "lowers" the effect of the alcohol level. This consensus opinion is consistent with Goldberg cited above. Alcohol abusers develop tolerance to some of the impairing effects, that is, to a degree, the impairment is less, but still exists.

Alcohol increases the risk of trauma and injury. Acute alcohol intoxication, which is common in both social drinkers and alcoholics, profoundly impairs cognitive function and motor skills, often while paradoxically enhancing the drinker's sense of mastery.[15] A large scale review of the experimental literature on alcohol's effect on skills has been reported.[16] This review considered 177 citations drawn from the literature and explored reaction time, tracking, concentrated attention, divided attention, performance, information processing capabilities, visual function, perception, and psychomotor performance.

The association of alcohol with injuries has been known since some of the earliest recorded history.[28] Alcohol intoxication increases the risk of all types of trauma.[16–18] A high percentage of seriously injured trauma center patients are at risk of having current psychoactive substance use (including alcohol) disorders (PSUD).[19] Available evidence implicates alcohol consumption as a major risk factor for almost every type of injury.

44.8 Sample Report: Extreme Alcohol Levels/Tolerance

Facts of the case
The hospital record notes:

- Security guard, fell from four feet at work (unwitnessed)
- Positive loss of consciousness
- Fractured his orbit and suffered a frontal brain contusion
- Chronic (alcoholic) ischemic changes of the brain are noted on the CT.

- "+ETOH," "smells of ETOH," "fall under ETOH"; Alcohol abuse (chronic alcoholism) Hx (history) of falls secondary to alcohol, history of loss of consciousness apparently from alcohol intoxication, no memory of the incidence of the falls
- "Drunk again?" per family
- Alcohol test 349 mg/dl (0.349 gm/dl) at 1655 on 7/26/00
- 74.4 kg (163 lb)
- Past medical history significant for alcohol intoxication/dependence

Opinions
1. There does not appear to be an ambulance report for transportation from the scene of the fall to the hospital. Since the first note at the hospital, and the blood was tested at 1655, an elapsed time of 120 minutes is assigned from the time of the unwitnessed fall to the time of the test. Medical Center tests serum, not whole blood. A blood test of 349 mg% on serum must be lowered by 18 percent to accommodate between whole blood and serum. This lowering results in a new test level of 286 mg%. Using an above average metabolic rate of elimination of alcohol (higher in alcoholics) of 20 mg% per hour, 120 minutes (2.00 hours) would indicate that 40 mg% of alcohol would be eliminated between the time of the test and the accident. This is a substantially high blood alcohol content, almost 2.5 times the presumptive level of intoxication (80 mg%) defined by the Illinois Motor Vehicle Code. Thus, for purposes of this report, a final blood alcohol concentration of 326 mg% (286 + 40 = 326 mg%) is used.

2. In my opinion, Mr. Intoxicated Plaintiff was intoxicated and impaired by alcohol at the time of the accident. Intoxication with blood levels of 326 mg% causes a loss of critical judgment, impairment in memory, release of inhibitions, increased risk taking, impairment in vision (peripheral and depth), and severe motor impairments, including delayed reflexes and balance.[10] This is the "falling down drunk" region for blood alcohol concentrations. Intoxicated pedestrians are at greater risk than sober individuals for serious injury and death from motor vehicle accidents. This is a substantially high blood alcohol content, slightly more than four times the presumptive level of intoxication (80 mg%) defined by the Illinois Motor Vehicle Code.

3. The blood alcohol level of 326 mg% would indicate presence of the equivalent of 14 drinks (glasses of one or mixed drinks with one ounce of 100-proof whiskey) in Mr. Intoxicated Plaintiff's blood at the time of the fall. Drinking over an extended period, during work or before work would ne-

cessitate additional alcohol consumption in order to replace the amount of alcohol metabolized and excreted over the drinking period or time from drinking cessation to the time of the fall. In order to calculate the amount of alcohol consumed by Mr. Intoxicated Plaintiff, I have considered the following criteria:

- Time of the accident (~ 3 P.M.)
- 163 lb weight
- Male sex
- Time of the blood test (4:55 P.M.)

The physicians noted alcohol use and alcohol presence.

The blood alcohol test provides definitive proof of the level of alcohol present, which allows a reference to the alcohol literature, which describes the type and extent of intoxication at specific alcohol levels.

4. Given the facts of the accident, Mr. Intoxicated Plaintiff's alcohol intoxication must be considered as a significant contributing cause of the fall. Further, it is my opinion that Mr. Intoxicated Plaintiff would have been too intoxicated and impaired to perform his job as a security guard.

Alcohol tolerance is dispositional and functional. Dispositional tolerance is defined as a diminution of a drug effect after a period of administration of that drug. The drug becomes less effective after chronic use because there is less of it at its site of action. The rate of metabolic inactivation of the drug is increased after chronic administration; thus, a particular dose produces lower and shorter-lasting blood levels. Functional tolerance or tissue tolerance denotes an actual change in the sensitivity of the brain to a given concentration of the drug. Included in this definition are some types of behaviorally augmented or conditioned tolerance. The various forms of tolerance have different mechanisms and presumably different sites, time course, and dose relations, even though all have the same ultimate effect in that the subject appears less intoxicated after chronic alcohol administration. In experiments documenting tolerance, heavy drinkers were less affected than moderate drinkers, and abstainers were the most sensitive to the effects of alcohol at equivalent doses.

Conclusion

Mr. Intoxicated Plaintiff was significantly intoxicated by alcohol, and in a cognitive and motor function impaired state at the time of his accident. 349 mg% is a significantly high blood alcohol level, even for a chronic alcohol abuser. This significantly high alcohol level is the most likely cause of his fall and subsequent head injury. This opinion is supported by a history of falls associated with alcohol intoxication.

44.9 Sample Expert Reports: Alcohol

RE: Bicyclist, Uninsured Motorist-bicycle fall, Alcohol

I have now reviewed the deposition of the bicyclist, the Hoffman Estates Medical Center (HEMC) Emergency Department (ED), acute hospitalization following the accident (2:15 A.M., 8/17/91), and also follow-up care medical records.

I understand that the bicyclist, a 19-year-old at the time, was riding a bicycle home from a party and narrowly missed contact with an automobile on Schaumburg Road. He was injured, taken by paramedic ambulance personnel, and treated urgently and admitted to the intensive care unit at HEMC.

The paramedic records describe "apparent ETOH (alcohol) intake, refused to identify himself and refused, to answer questions, loud abusive."

The various hospital caregivers describe the bicyclist as abusive, using foul language, amnesic to the events of the accident, having a history of drinking heavily before the accident, having admitted marijuana use at the party prior to the accident, "allegedly under influence of alcohol," and "quite intoxicated in the emergency room."

Among several other tests ordered in the ED, a blood sample was taken for alcohol at 2:55 A.M., and reported at 5:00 A.M. The blood alcohol test indicated a blood alcohol concentration of 200 mg% (0.200 gm/dl).

In my opinion, the bicyclist was intoxicated and impaired by alcohol at the time his bicycle and he struck the pavement. Intoxication at this level (twice the 0.1 gm/dl presumptive intoxication level of the Illinois Motor Vehicle Code) impairs cognitive and motor functions. The intoxicated person is disoriented, confused, and disinhibited, takes risks, and suffers from perceptual disturbances (depth and peripheral vision). The ability of the brain to react to stimuli (danger) and take action (avoidance/correction) is slowed. Stated otherwise, reactions are slowed, and when reaction is attempted, it is frequently erratic, abrupt, and clumsy.

Recall of events may be impaired by the intoxication.

The bicyclist admitted to his caregivers to drinking several beers at a party before the accident. In his deposition, he admitted to six or seven beers between 2:00 P.M. and 8:00 P.M., with no alcoholic beverages between 8:00 P.M. and 2:00 A.M. His weight recorded in the medical records is 169 pounds. Based on this weight, Mr. Mason had the alcohol equivalent of nine to ten 12-ounce beers in his body at the time of the accident. In my opinion, it is scientifically impossible for a blood alcohol test of 200 mg% based on a consumption of six to seven beers between 2:00 P.M. and

8:00 P.M. on the afternoon and evening before the injury.

RE: *Motorcyclist v. Motorist*

The motorcyclist was taken by ambulance to the Our Lady of Resurrection hospital, arriving at 2355. Blood was taken for a variety of clinical tests, including a sample for blood ethanol (ETOH), the collection occurring at 0015 (12:14 A.M.). The result of the blood alcohol test is 174 mg% (0.0174 gm/dl). Extrapolating to the time of the accident will raise the blood alcohol level to approximately 185 mg%.

Some of the witnesses to the motorcyclist's activities prior to the accident have stated that he had consumed alcohol, and the motorcyclist, in his deposition, testified that he consumed two beers shortly after 9:30 P.M. at a bar, and had no other alcohol that evening.

In my opinion, the motorcyclist was intoxicated and impaired by alcohol at the time of the accident. Intoxication at a level of 185 causes impairment in judgment, release of inhibitions, increased risk taking, impairment in vision (peripheral and depth), and motor impairments, including delayed reflexes and balance.[10] The risk of an accident occurring increases twenty-five-fold.

The motorcyclist was 200 pounds and six feet tall at the time of the accident. An adult male of his weight would require consuming the equivalent of ten 12-ounce beers before the accident in order for a 174 mg% to be measured at 12:15 A.M. In order to calculate the amount of alcohol consumed by the motorcycle passenger, I have considered the following criteria:

- time of the accident (8:00 P.M.)
- assumption of 200-pound average weight
- sex of the individual
- time of the blood test

In my opinion, assuming that the hospital test is accurate, it is scientifically impossible to achieve the blood alcohol concentration recorded with consumption of only two beers.

In summary, in my opinion, with reasonable pharmacologic certainty, the motorcyclist was intoxicated and he was experiencing the impairing effects of alcohol at the time of the accident.

Please call if you have any questions regarding this report.

Note: This case settled on the eve of trial. Testimony of the alcohol expert affected the outcome and ability to settle the case without having to go to trial.

RE: *Motorcyclist v. Motorist*

I reviewed Holy Cross Hospital records which include treatment for traumatic orthopedic injury following an accident wherein the motorcyclist fell off his motorcycle. You have advised me that the motorcyclist testified that he is 5' 11", 180 pounds, and his alcohol consumption on the day of the accident started at 2:00 P.M. with one beer, and that he might have had four to five beers between 3:30 and 8:30 P.M.

The motorcyclist denied being intoxicated.

He was admitted to the hospital through the emergency shortly before midnight. His blood was tested for alcohol (among numerous other clinical tests) and reported at 0006 (six minutes after midnight) at 222 mg% (0.222 gm/dl). The medical records note a strong odor of alcohol (EtOH) on his breath, and that "he does consume a fair amount of alcohol."

In my opinion, the motorcyclist was intoxicated and impaired by alcohol at the time of the accident (2335). Impairments at the level tested include cognitive and gross motor. Thinking is clouded, judgment is compromised, inhibitions are released, risk taking increases, emotions have a great potential for liability. Vision, both peripheral and depth, is impaired. Perceptions are distorted. Motor function and the ability to perform divided attention tasks (operation of a motor vehicle) are severely impaired.[10] Reaction time, the ability to recognize, judge, and then execute a complex task, is increased.[6] The probability of an accident occurring is greater than 25× at even lower blood alcohol levels than those measured in the motorcyclist's blood.[32,33] The motorcyclist would be considered an unsafe driver.

The motorcyclist testified that he consumed five to six beers between 2 P.M. and 8:30 P.M. It is scientifically impossible for him to have consumed only five to six beers in that period and have a 222 mg% measured at 12:00 midnight. In order for a 222 mg% blood alcohol concentration (BAC), the motorcyclist would have had to consume the equivalent of 20 12-ounce beers during the 2:00 to 8:30 P.M. period, almost three to four times the quantity he described.

44.10 An Unusual Case of Alcohol Hypersensitivity Reaction, in Combination with Marijuana, Leads to Apparent Psychotic Reaction

Senior Supervising Attorney
City of Chicago, Department of Law
30 N. LaSalle St. 14th Floor
Chicago, Il 60602

RE: *Plaintiff v. City of Chicago*

Mr. Defense Attorney:

I reviewed the following materials in this file:

Background, facts, and deposition summaries
The decedent played football for a Big Ten university until he injured his shoulder. He was a big man whose natural weight was around 250 but rose to around 300 pounds during football training. He was in a house with several other players and there were supplements in the house but no testimony has been made about steroids. The decedent would drink on occasion and consume a six pack of Miller beer. His family (and his girlfriend) described him as an occasional/social drinker, never excessive, and had no knowledge of his use of marijuana or mushrooms.

On the night of the shooting, the decedent was involved in an altercation with an Evanston family, a family with whom he had no previous contact. He was standing on the roof of a garage. When asked to come down, the decedent jumped from the garage roof down onto the roof of the victim's car. The decedent "mowed over" a male resident of the apartment and walked to the street. When the male resident said something as the decedent was walking away, the decedent ran back and "scooped the resident off his feet, causing both men to fall to the ground." The decedent bit the male resident on the back seven or eight times, while the victim and another male resident tried to get the decedent to release the man. In response to those efforts, the decedent let the first man go and chased the other male resident. The police arrived and the decedent slammed the first police officer into his squad car and onto the ground. Eventually, several police officers were able to handcuff the decedent. During this entire altercation, the decedent did not speak; instead, the decedent growled.

The decedent was taken by police to the hospital where he was diagnosed and treated for substance-induced psychosis. His blood alcohol was noted to be 71 mg%. His blood test was negative for cannabis.

Diagnoses and impressions included:

- organic psychotic disorder, psychotic break accompanied by violence and agitation,
- marijuana intoxication,
- visibly intoxicated; occasional alcohol binges,
- paranoid ideation,
- adjustment disorder with mixed emotional feature,
- alcohol abuse seems possible beyond this incident of intoxication and violence
- left ulnar fracture

The decedent was transferred to General Hospital (LGH). There, the decedent was described as delusional. He told the emergency doctor that "you are the Devil" and that he was hearing "inner voices" (auditory hallucinations). He was considered unsuitable for informal admission for the following reason:

- aggressive/violent—danger to self/others

An addendum note test result at the Lutheran General Hospital noted that the decedent's urine was positive for cannabis and opiates. He was treated with opiates, which would explain the positive opiates. At the General Hospital, he gave a history of consumption of 12 beers and two marijuana cigarettes.

Psychiatrist, MD, testified as follows:

- a differential diagnosis of Acute psychosis versus psychotic depression, versus organic psychosis secondary to possible drug ingestion,
- was under the influence of a drug,
- acting like a lunatic,
- he had a psychotic reaction to the marijuana, plus or minus the drinking,
- at least one episode where he took hallucinogenic mushrooms and he had a similar experience (acute drug-induced psychosis).
- I put organic psychotic disorder, which is basically the clinical name for what I just described to you, that he had this psychotic episode in response to smoking pot and/or drinking.

He later was treated in an outpatient Mental Health Center with a diagnosis of paranoia.

Several months later, the decedent spent the night at the house he shared in Evanston and left around midnight to "go south" to perhaps play basketball in his hometown of Calumet City. On his way south on Lake Shore Drive he was observed by a police officer to make an unsafe lane change and almost strike two motorcycles near Buckingham Fountain. The officer put on his lights to signal the decedent and traffic that he was making a traffic stop but the decedent ignored the Mars lights, though he continued to stop at red lights. At one of these red lights, the officer got out and knocked on the window of the decedent's car but the decedent did not respond, and drove off. The officer followed and called in a pursuit. An off-duty county sheriff's deputy observed this in his private car and followed the decedent and officer. Two police cars joined the chase, and after the decedent swerved and hit a patrol car three times, the decedent's car spun and was enclosed by the interstate off-ramp wall and the police cars. After coming to a stop, the decedent moved his car forward and struck the officer's car head-on from about 5 feet away.

Police officers all gave verbal commands with no response. The decedent held his hands between his legs despite being told to show his hands. The car had dark tinted windows. CPD broke the driver's side rear window with a tire iron and shouted verbal orders again. Then the decedent turned around suddenly and grabbed and pulled CPD's gun and hands into the car and was shot through the hand and chest. He was removed from the car and handcuffed. When they rolled him over the police saw that he had a fatal chest wound.

The medical examiner's report noted a weight of 273 pounds, and the toxicology report indicated a blood alcohol level of 34 mg% (0.034 gm/dl). No other drugs or intoxicants are reported in the autopsy toxicology.

Discussion

Intoxication with alcohol causes an emotional instability, impairment of perception, memory and comprehension, decreased sensory response, disorientation, mental confusion, and exaggerated emotional states (fear, rage, sorrow, etc.),[34] which are all associated with alcohol intoxication.

Marijuana is a central nervous system (CNS) depressant, usually associated with pleasant, sensual experiences. The drug rarely causes psychosis; when it does, it is usually an exacerbation of some underlying psychopathology.

Opinions

My opinions are expressed hereafter with reasonable pharmacological certainty.

1. Hospital tests serum, not whole blood, for blood alcohol tests. The test result of 71 mg% is a serum test, which is lowered to 60 mg% when converted to whole blood. Serum alcohol content is 18 percent higher than a simultaneously sampled whole blood specimen, due to the increased water content of serum, and the hydrophilic property of alcohol.[35]

2. Since the blood test at the hospital was negative for marijuana, despite a positive urine test finding at GH, the decedent was not intoxicated by marijuana on the evening of October 18. A negative blood test indicates no recent use; a positive urine test indicates use within several weeks. Therefore, any substance intoxication must have been due to alcohol alone. Based on the negative blood marijuana test, it is probable that no marijuana was smoked on the night of the Evanston incident.

3. In my opinion, the decedent's behavior is consistent with a hypersensitivity to alcohol which was evident in the Evan-

ston incident. With his previous history of substance (alcohol) induced agitation, violent psychotic reaction, where he had a relatively low serum BAC of 71 (corrected to 60 whole blood alcohol), coupled with his BAC of 34 mg% and erratic behavior of June 4–5, the decedent must have been particularly hypersensitive to the disinhibiting and central nervous system toxicity of CNS active alcohol. Hypersensitivity or hyperactivity means that a person is particularly sensitive to doses which would not be expected to have a significant effect in a majority of the population. In that hospitalization, he was noted to have two aunts with schizophrenia, and he reported auditory hallucinations.

The decedent was extremely violent and aggressive in both incidents. In both incidents he exhibited extremely poor judgment, aggression, violence, and erratic behavior (fighting with, running from, or attacking strangers and police). Alcohol intoxication makes some people more prone to aggression, violence, and impulsivity.

4. Alcohol, at very low levels, acts as a disinhibitor, by releasing the inhibiting controls on behavior in the higher levels of the brain. While a blood alcohol level of 34 mg% is usually not considered "intoxicating," with the decedent's history, he was hypersensitive to this disinhibiting effect, and the disinhibition, and any other psychopathology present, led to his obviously erratic behavior on both occasions.

44.11 Testing: Alcohol and Recreational Drugs

The reader is likely very familiar with alcohol blood testing and the breathalyzer tests which serve the basis for most DUI offenses across the country. The accuracy of the hospital blood test is rarely successfully questioned, and the physiological variation of the breathalyzer, in comparison to the blood test, is beyond the scope of this chapter. When hospital tests are run, it should be noted that they almost universally analyze serum, not whole blood. An alcohol test on serum must be lowered by 18 percent to accommodate the difference between whole blood and serum. What is important, however, is that blood and blood-equivalent tests for alcohol have benefitted from nearly 90 years of experiments, observation, and correlation between tests results and effects of the subject. Tables 44.1, 44.2, and 44.3 illustrate types of impairment correlated to ranges of alcohol in the blood. No such correlations exist for other drugs, most notably cocaine and marijuana, the subject of the remainder of this chapter. When blood tests are performed on samples, correlation can be made to the estimated time of use, given known and well-demonstrated kinetics (half-life, length of time present). However, tests on urine have severe limitations, and the reader is cautioned not to jump to conclusions about drug impairment from their results alone. As stated above, the remainder of this chapter will address cocaine and marijuana, the other recreational drugs, which, following alcohol, are most often associated with motor vehicle crashes, and thus deserve the most attention from a pharmacologic and toxicologic point of view.

A. Urine Testing

The most significant drawback to urine testing is that, in general, drug use testing as currently practiced, when urine is the tested biological specimen, does not provide information about past or present patterns of drug use, abuse, or drug dependence, or about drug-related mental or physical impairment, or other effects, at any time.

Urine tests do not tell us anything about impairment because whatever the entry route of a drug, it is carried by the blood stream to the brain, liver, kidney and other organs and the process of metabolism and excretion begins. Metabolism or bioconversion of most drugs changes them, at least partly, to conjugated forms, which are more water-soluble than the parent drug and hence excreted primarily through the kidneys into the urine. That process is controlled by various pharmacological, biochemical, and physiological factors, including the chemical nature of the metabolites and conjugates as well as the pH of the urine and other factors, including the drug concentration in plasma. Because bladder urine is a pooled specimen, accumulated over time, and because the kidneys in effect concentrate urine with respect to many constituents including most drugs, the concentration of most drugs excreted in urine is higher than in other accessible biological fluids at the same time.

B. Confirmation Testing of Urine Samples

It is not true that the requirement for a confirmation test in a two-test system is necessarily derived from inaccuracy of the initial test. This is a fallacy based mostly on a faulty understanding of the distinction between accuracy and the notions of reliability and degree of confidence. A two-test system can enhance the degree of confidence in a positive result whether or not it contributes to the accuracy that can be achieved by the initial test alone. If one makes two fundamentally different measurements of the same thing and gets the same answer, the confidence in that answer is greater than it would be on the basis of a single measurement despite the accuracy of that measurement.[20]

The reason for the scope of false positives of screening tests has been described in an affidavit by Dr. Arthur J. McBay, filed in *National Treasury Employees Union v. Von Raab*.

Table 44.3
Impairing Effects of Alcohol

Sign or Symptom	Approximate Blood Alcohol
Alcohol and Perception	
Dynamic visual acuity	0.02%
Light-dark adaptation	0.09%
Peripheral vision (multi-tasking)	0.05%
Tasking of great difficulty (above 0.08% peripheral events ignored)	0.017%
Eye blink frequency and blink closure (color discrimination very variable)	0.07%
Oculomotor Function	
Depth perception	0.015–0.04%
Sacchadic eye movements	0.05–0.10%
Nystagmus of various types	0.03–0.09%
Tracking Tasks	
With angular acceleration	0.07%
added multi-tasking	0.03–0.06%
about 90 percent of subjects affected at	0.10%
Division of Attention	
Vigilance (multi-tasking)	0.15%
Fixation time (foveal focusing)	0.10%
Mood and Emotions	
Increased drowsiness and decreased Clear headedness (attentiveness)	0.03%
Memory	
Short-term input or recall spans	0.05–0.10%

Reprinted with permission (Bederka, 1993).

The EMIT screen suffers from limitations in its reliability. This test will give a positive result to the tested drug when other prescription and over-the-counter drugs have been ingested, and may react to food and other substances, including enzymes produced by the body itself. This is because of a phenomenon known as "crossreactivity." The legitimate drugs that have triggered a positive result for marijuana, for example, include the anti-inflammatory drugs Ibuprofen, fenoprofen and Naproxen, some of the most widely used drugs in this country. They are sold under the brand names Advil, Motrin, Nuprin, Rufen, Anaprox, Naproxen,

Naproxyn, and Nalfon. A number of drugs that are closely related in chemical structure to amphetamines will also test positive, mainly diet and cold preparations containing ephedrine and phenylpropanolamine. These include Nyquil, Contact, and other brand names. In addition, the immunoassay tests cannot distinguish between codeine, a legal drug, and heroin. Both are classified as opiates.

Some of the false positives caused by cross-reactivity have been eliminated by reformulating the assays. In April 1986, after reformulation of some assays, the Syva Company notified its customers that ibuprofen, fenoprofen, and naxopren "had been found capable of affecting EMIT cannabinoid assays using maleate dehydrogenase (MDH) as the enzyme label, but not the G6PDH enzyme...." The letter also noted that fenoprofen could also yield false positive results with the EMIT assays for amphetamines, barbiturates, benzodiazepines, and methaqualone. Steroids have also been reported to create false positive results for cannabinoids.

Regardless of their accuracy, since most informed toxicologists and pharmacologists, as well as the manufacturers of the screening tests themselves, recommend that confirmatory tests be conducted before acting upon the results where a person's job or reputation is at stake, it would be unconscionable for employers to refuse to hire or fire employees based solely upon an unconfirmed positive result from a screening test.[21]

Occasionally, because of some positive urine and positive blood alcohol results, counsel will have to prove, through the use of a consulting toxicologist or pharmacologist, that the injured party (or a criminal defendant or any party) is not intoxicated or not under the influence.

C. Sample Case Report: Urine Drug Testing

RE: Marijuana urine test; low alcohol levels/not drunk

You have asked me to comment on the toxicology reports on tests of your client which indicated a blood alcohol test of 32 mg% and a urine test positive for THC (marijuana) metabolites. Specifically, you asked whether these tests are indicative of impairment in your client, and if so, to what degree.

Marijuana when consumed by smoking or ingestion is metabolized to several metabolites, and 11-hydroxytetra-hydrocannibol is a common metabolite. The methodology used to detect the presence of THC metabolites requires a certain threshold level in order for the test to register as positive. Levels of THC metabolites necessary to exceed the mini-

mum detection threshold may exist for prolonged periods following the consumption of marijuana, periods commonly of seven days, prolonged under special circumstances up to two to four weeks.[22] Thus, a positive urine test indicates that the marijuana was consumed at some time prior to the test, and there is no way to predict when that consumption occurred. Therefore, it is not unusual to find caveats in the drug testing literature cautioning the reader not to attempt to infer any clinical effect (impairment) from marijuana based on a urine test. Stated alternatively, there is no scientific basis for inferring marijuana effects, including impairment, from a urine test.

In summary, the alcohol level tested is too low to suggest any impairment, and the positive urine test, since one does not know when the marijuana was consumed, cannot be used to infer any impairment. Therefore, a reasonable scientist would not have sufficient evidence upon which to opine any impairment in this individual.

D. "Poppy Seed" Opiate False Positives

Urine drug testing, as described above, is used in a wide variety of settings. An expert report follows wherein the subject's urine tested positive for opiates after involvement in a fatal pedestrian-motor vehicle accident. The levels were substantially below a new federal drug testing threshold of 2,000 ng/ml, but the criminal and civil litigation proceeded as if the tests were valid, ignoring the contribution of poppy seeds, a common attribute of bakery goods, consumed with regularity by a large percentage of the population, with total ignorance to the far reaching legal consequences if their urine is tested while consuming "poppy seed" foods.

RE: Teen Criminal Defendant/Reckless Homicide

Facts of the case
A 14-year-old was struck and killed by the driver's vehicle. Driver #1 lost control of his vehicle after he signaled to the defendant to make a U-turn in front of him, and apparently lost control (Driver #1) of his vehicle as a result of accidentally stepping on the accelerator instead of the brake. His vehicle had been modified to accommodate for his "dropped foot." It is unclear whether the defendant's vehicle made any contact with the Driver #1 vehicle.

The defendant was interviewed extensively by the police following the accident. No indications of any effects or impairment by alcohol or drugs are noted in any of the records. The defendant denied the use of any alcohol, drugs (including any prescription drugs), or intoxicating substances. As a matter of routine, since there was a fatality, the defendant was requested to submit to drug and alcohol testing, which he submitted. A positive opiate screen finding was noted, which eventually resulted in the defendant being charged.

Opinions and discussion

I have reviewed the laboratory's analytical data for the urine analysis of the defendant. The laboratory received two blood specimens and two urine specimens, all in unsealed containers. The blood was negative for ethanol, and a urine specimen was positive for morphine (an opiate).

The screening test (ADx) indicates an opiates positive result for a specimen designated as 102, yet a negative opiates screen for 202. The presumptive positive urine was tested via a GC/MS to reveal the presence of morphine in the specimen. No 6-monoacetylmorphine was detected, and no quantization of the morphine found was performed.

Presence of 6-monoacetylmorphine is a specific metabolite of heroin. Had this substance been found, the source of the morphine could have been traced back to heroin use. However, in this case, there is no positive evidence of heroin use. As such, alternative sources of the morphine must be considered.

It is well-known that poppy seeds contain morphine. In one study, ingestion of three poppy seed bagels resulted in 2797 ng/mL morphine at three hours.[23] In another study, the ingestion of 25 grams of poppy seeds from four brands of poppy seeds, containing between 17 and 294 mcg of morphine per gram, resulted in urine detectability over 48 hours.[24] The vast majority of the searched literature indicates that depending on the cutoff level utilized by the laboratory, the detection of morphine in the urine does not necessarily indicate an illegal drug use.

The federal government (Department of Health and Human Services) also recognizes that a positive for morphine may be a result of the donor consuming "normal dietary amounts" of poppy seeds. The Medical Review Officer (MRO), assigned to review the analytical results prior to reporting, is directed to report the result as negative unless clinical evidence of abuse or illegal use of opiates is verified. The guidelines state the MRO "shall determine that there is clinical evidence-in addition to the urine test-of illegal use of any opium, opiate, or opium derivative..." prior to reporting the result as positive. One exception to this rule is, if the specimen is negative for 6-monoacetlymorphine, the result may still be verified positive if the morphine is at 15,000 ng/mL or above.[25]

In this case, in which the defendant is charged with operating a vehicle with illegal substances in his system, there is no such clinical evidence, and the laboratory tests that have been conducted and reported can be explained by the normal consumption of poppy seeds in the routine diet (bagels).

Therefore, with reasonable pharmacological certainty, there is no evidence that the defendant consumed any morphine, prescription or illegal, and there is certainly no evidence of any impairment which could be considered to be contributory to the accident and subsequent death of the victim. The presence of the opiates in the urine screening test was probably the result of dietary consumption of poppy seeds, which certainly have no impairing effect on anything or anyone. (The defendant driver was acquitted by a jury after hearing evidence regarding the false positive opiate test caused by consuming poppy seeds in food.)

44.12 Cocaine

Substantial evidence exists to suggest that use of cocaine almost invariably occurs subsequent to use of marijuana and that marijuana is, for all intents and purposes, a necessary condition for use of cocaine. There is a linear increase in the percentage of persons reporting use of cocaine as the extent of use of marijuana increases, regardless of sex or age group. It is clear from the "total" percentages that use of cocaine is most extensive in the two baby boom age groups and is a rare occurrence in the youth and the older adult groups. Given the overall prevalence of cocaine use in the 18- to 34-year-old age groups, cocaine is the drug that has the highest probability, after alcohol and marijuana, of being implicated in drug-related accidents. Another commonly accepted fact is that cocaine is almost never used alone; the user will drink alcohol or smoke marijuana to control or overcome the irritating and unpleasant stimulating effects of cocaine which continue on beyond the limited euphoric/rush period.

Cocaine is one of the most potent of the naturally occurring central nervous system stimulants. The compound is found in the leaves of *Erythroxylon coca*, a South American shrub, in amounts of up to 2 percent by weight. It was first isolated in pure form in 1855, and has been widely utilized in medicine as a local anesthetic and increasingly by drug abusers for its stimulant properties. For anesthetic uses, cocaine is administered topically as the hydrochloride in 1–4 percent solutions for opthalmological procedures and in 10–20 percent solutions for the membranes of the nose and throat. When self-administered, it is commonly taken as the hydrochloride by nasal insufflation or intravenous injection or as the free base by smoking, in doses of 10–120 mg.

A. Blood Concentrations

The chewing of powdered coca leaves containing 17–48 mg of cocaine produced peak plasma concentrations of 0.011–0.149 mg/L within 0.4–2 hours in six volunteers. A 2 mg/

kg (140 mg/70 kg) intranasal application of cocaine to four subjects yielded an average peak plasma concentration of 0.161 mg/L after one hour; an equivalent oral dose given to the same volunteers produced an average peak concentration of 0.210 mg/L at one hour, declining with an average half-life of 0.9 hours. The intravenous injection of 32 mg of cocaine resulted in an average peak plasma concentration of 0.308 mg/L after five minutes. Following the nasal topical application of 1.5 mg/kg (105 mg/70kg) of cocaine to surgical patients, plasma concentration of the drug reached an average peak of 0.308 mg/L (range 0.120–0.474) at one hour and declined to 0.206 mg/L by three hours. Nasal insufflation of 106 mg of the drug by six subjects produced average peak plasma concentrations of 0.220 mg/L for cocaine at one-half hour and 0.611 mg/L for benzoylecgonine at three hours. Smoking of 50 mg of the drug in six subjects resulted in average peak plasma concentrations of 0.203 mg/L for cocaine at 0.08 hours and 0.151 mg/L for benzoylecgonine at 1.5 hours. The blood/plasma concentration ratio for cocaine averages 1.0.

Chronic cocaine abusers given free access to cigarettes containing 75 mg each of cocaine paste developed and maintained plasma concentrations of 0.253–0.932 mg/L over a 90-minute smoking period, during which they smoked eight to ten cigarettes.

B. Metabolism and Excretion

Cocaine is rapidly inactivated in man by the hydrolysis of one or both of the ester linkages. Even in water, at pH values greater than neutrality, the drug is readily hydrolyzed to benzoylecgonine. In blood or plasma, cocaine is hydrolyzed to ecgonine methyl ester by cholinesterase; the reaction rate is highly dependent on drug concentrations and may be inhibited by freezing or by the addition of fluoride or cholinesterase inhibitors. With storage at 4°C., blood containing 1 mg/L of cocaine lost 100 percent of the drug in 21 days, whereas with 0.5-percent sodium fluoride 70 percent of the cocaine was still intact. A similar rate of decline was observed in stored postmortem tissues. Benzoylecgonine and ecgonine methyl ester are relatively stable in fluoridated whole blood for one month at 4°C, but exhibit losses of 25 percent and 50 percent, respectively, when stored at 25°C.

Benzoylecgonine is believed to arise spontaneously in vivo, since neither liver nor serum esterases produce this compound from cocaine. The further production of ecgonine from benzoylecgonine, however, may be the result of enzymatic hydrolysis. Each of these metabolites is highly polar and, when formed outside the central nervous system, is without pharmacological activity. Norcaine, an active metabolite, has not been detected in plasma after therapeutic ad-

ministration but is found in trace amounts in urine. Phenolic hydroxylation has been shown to produce a series of minor cocaine metabolites in humans. Ecgonidine, methylecgonidine and methylnorecgonidine have also been reported as minor metabolites. Cocaethylene, a substance formed when cocaine and ethanol are co-administered, is pharmacologically active and accounts for 0.7 percent of a cocaine dose in the 24-hour urine test.

C. Toxicity

Overdose has resulted in a relatively small number of serious intoxications, considering its popularity as a recreational drug. The symptoms of acute toxicity are similar to those for amphetamine, although it is believed that a direct cardiotoxic effect may be a contributory factor in cocaine-induced deaths. Myocardial infarction, ventricular tachycardia and fibrillation, cerebrovascular accident and pulmonary dysfunction may occur with acute or chronic abuse and even with medical usage. Control of seizure activity with diazepam, correction of acidosis to stabilize heart rhythm and administration of a calcium-channel blocker such as nitrendipine has been recommended as treatment for acute toxic reactions. One case was reported in which the unintentional rupture in the stomach of a 5-g packet of cocaine produced unconsciousness and massive convulsions; a maximal blood concentration of 5.2 mg/L was observed, but with treatment the patient survived.

D. Cocaine Psychoses

Cocaine euphoria was initially described by Freud as ingestion of 50–100 mg of cocaine hydrochloride and is accompanied by a profound sense of elation, increased mental agility, and physical endurance.

Cocaine's mood-elevating properties have been lauded by the Inca Indians in the 1600s and the drug culture of the 1970s, and 1980s, by which it was heralded the euphoriant of choice—"king cocaine." However, clear-cut mood elevation was not demonstrated when cocaine was administered orally in doses recommended by Freud to ten moderately to severely depressed patients hospitalized at the National Institute of Mental Health (NIMH), although one patient did have brief periods of hypomania during cocaine administration.

1. Case Report: Cocaine psychoses allegations of police misconduct

Facts of the case

Joy Forest was arrested following a traffic stop and altercation/resisting arrest with officers from the Oakland Police

Department on the a summer evening. A traffic stop was made at approximately midnight at 10th Street and Martin Luther King Drive. Notations in the police report include:

- "Jumped out of the vehicle and began to run towards me yelling, 'Don't you f—ing shoot me?'"
- "Very irate and disorientated"
- "Began to yell and jump around in circles"
- "Pepper maced Forest in attempt to gain control over her when she continued to fight and try to run away"
- "appeared to be on some type of drugs and yelled for the police several times to help her. I repeatedly advised Forest that I was the police and that I could help her if she would calm down"
- "…and began to kick swing her fist at Sgt. White and Ofc. Greene. I then pepper-maced Forest in attempt to stop her from fighting when she continued to fight and try to run away from the location"

A crack pipe was found in Ms. Forest's automobile.

Ms. Forest was taken to the St. Jude's Hospital for emergency treatment and observation. The following clinical notations are noted:

- "Psychotic episode"
- "Chief complaint: Psychotic Behavior"; "psychotic and combative"
- "Denies Etoh (alcohol) or Drug Use"
- "…in a state of stupor and agitation"; "Pt Agitated and unable to think clearly and remember instructions"
- "Pt exhibiting bizarre behavior," "was attacked by police officer and was subsequently sprayed with Mace. Combative with EMS"
- "The patient is said to have been very bizarre and very violent at the scene and to have been sprayed with a copious amount of pepper spray to subdue her prior to being arrested and then brought to the emergency department."
- "The patient was very uncooperative and would not expand on the history"
- "The patient was very restless, very uncooperative and extremely anxious upon arrival in the emergency department."
- "Diagnosis: Cocaine & Marijuana abuse"
- "…no recollection of what she did prior to the arrest by the police officers"
- "Patient displaying a lot of emotional instability with occasional crying and was indicating that she

did not know what she did to deserve the physical injuries that she sustained."
- "Thought process altered due to drugs in her system"
- "Explained to patient that pain meds would be at a minimum till drugs are out of her system and no s/s of head injury noted."

Blood alcohol, urine drug screens, and other clinical tests were ordered and biological specimens taken. Laboratory results indicated the presence of cocaine and marijuana in the patient's urine. She was admitted to the hospital for evaluation of her injuries and observed due to her injuries and drug abuse (cocaine and marijuana). A psychiatric consultation was ordered. She left the hospital later that day and went to Mercy Hospital where she was admitted.

Opinions

In my opinion, with reasonable pharmacological certainty, Ms. Joy Forest was intoxicated by cocaine and experiencing cocaine-induced psychosis and paranoid behavior at the time of the traffic stop by the Oakland Police Department. In my opinion, with reasonable pharmacokinetic certainty, Ms. Forest probably inhaled/smoked crack cocaine within no more than a few hours prior to the traffic stop. In my opinion, with reasonable pharmacological certainty, Ms. Forest's cocaine-induced psychosis caused her to act in a violent, aggressive, bizarre, and dangerous manner.

Bases for opinions

Experienced police officers described Ms. Forest as "on drugs," "violent and combative, bizarre behaviour." Clinicians at the St. Jude's Hospital further described Ms. Forest as psychotic, and (as noted above) unable to think clearly due to drugs in her system. Analgesic (pain relieving therapy) was held to a minimum until drugs were out of her system and no signs or symptoms of head injury were noted. The Hospital clinicians corroborate the observations of the police.

Ordinarily, a urine drug screen (alone) cannot be used to infer intoxication[i]; however, since there is such detailed and multiple observations describing behavior consistent with cocaine intoxication, the positive cocaine test was probably caused by use within at most a few hours of the altercation. Cocaine is well known to be a CNS stimulant intoxicant. Psychosis and paranoid behavior has been commonly associated with the use of cocaine, especially when "crack" cocaine is used. My opinions are based on my education, training and experience, and I am relying on the published literature. A listing of literature sources for text and journal publications describing cocaine intoxication is appended to this report. Full text copies of the references relied upon for my opinions are also appended to this report.

Endnotes

i.   O'Donnell JT. Recreational Drugs: Alcohol, Cocaine, and Marijuana. In O'Donnell JT. Ed. Drug Injury: Liability, Analysis and Prevention, Second Edition, 2005, L&J Publications, Tucson AZ.

E. Cocaine Dysphoria

When cocaine is abused chronically, a paranoid psychosis that is almost indistinguishable from acute paranoid schizophrenia can result. After acute intravenous cocaine administration, the development of a paranoid psychotic state (referred to by users as the "bull horrors" because of intense fear of police) can occur even more rapidly than after amphetamine administration. After chronic cocaine administration, delusions of persecution may be vague or systematized and may be accompanied by auditory, visual, or olfactory hallucinations. The user has a clear sensorium and is not confused or disoriented as in a toxic psychosis or delirium, which can also occur after an overdose, but is of less theoretical interest. A peculiar but infrequent aspect of the cocaine psychosis is the delusion of parasitosis and sensations of insects under the skin (formication) which may lead addicts to repetitively pick at their skin. Addicts may even probe their skin with needles for "cocaine bugs."

F. Violent Behavior

Violent behavior may be prominent during the height of the cocaine psychosis, apparently triggered by paranoid trends. Stereotyped compulsive behavior analogous to that seen in experimental animals can develop. Addicts may repetitively pursue the same task and be endlessly absorbed by minutiae, as depicted in the case of Sherlock Holmes. Hallucinations usually stop when use of cocaine ceases, but delusions may persist.[26]

G. Cocaine Use as a Cause of Death

Cocaine intoxication can lead to fatal cardiovascular and cerebrovascular events. In addition, the neurobehavioral effects of cocaine may increase the likelihood that a user will receive violent fatal injuries. Cocaine use, as measured by the detection of the metabolite benzylecgonine in urine or blood, was found in 26.7 percent of all New York City residents receiving fatal injuries; free cocaine was detected in 18.3 percent. Approximately one-third of deaths after cocaine use were the result of drug intoxication, but two-thirds

involved traumatic injuries resulting from homicides, suicides, traffic accidents, and falls.

It is possible that cocaine, like ethanol, increases the risk of injury by inducing states of drug intoxication (e.g., agitation, aggression, and distorted perception) or drug withdrawal (e.g., distractibility, somnolence, and depression). In addition, cocaine users frequently use other drugs, such as ethanol or opiates, simultaneously, either to modify cocaine's psychological effects or to blunt unpleasant side effects. Ethanol, for instance, was detected in 45 percent of the cases in which cocaine was detected. Thus cocaine may influence the risk of injury because it is used concurrently with other psychoactive drugs.[27]

H. Effect of Cocaine on Driving

There have been few, if any, scientific studies on the effects of cocaine on driving performance. Three main effects of cocaine relevant to driving have been studied. The effects of cocaine on vision appear to be paramount. Forty-three percent of inhaled or intranasal cocaine users reported increased sensitivity to light, halos around bright objects, and difficulty focusing. Chronic mydriasis observed in these individuals may have been contributing. Lapses of attention were also commonly reported, from ignoring changes in traffic signals to forgetting to replace gas caps at service stations. Over 34 percent of cocaine smokers reported blurred vision, often accompanied by glare problems. Hallucinations were reported by 50 percent of cocaine smokers and 18 percent of intranasal cocaine users. "Snow lights," flashes or movements of light in the peripheral field of vision, was the most commonly reported hallucination. Reaction to "snow lights" included moving in their direction or trying to avoid or evade them.

The euphoric effects of cocaine during acute intoxication may give a driver the feeling of increased mental and physical abilities. This results in the claim by users that cocaine improves their driving ability. This optimism may result in increased risk-taking behavior and perhaps increased probability of accidents, particularly in conjunction with ethanol use. While it has been shown that moderate doses of stimulants (amphetamines or cocaine) may acutely enhance performance of simple tasks, these effects decrease considerably as the complexity of the task increases. Cocaine-induced hyperexcitability has resulted in rapid steering or braking reactions due to sudden sounds such as horns or sirens. Since the effects of cocaine are brief, the fatigue or "crash" which follows cocaine use may be a particularly dangerous time for driving. Four cocaine smokers have reported being involved in collisions resulting in major injuries on the way to a cocaine treatment center.

Finally, cocaine's effect on thinking may adversely affect driving. Sixty-two percent of cocaine smokers have reported symptoms of suspiciousness, distrust and paranoia. These effects have resulted in high-speed chases with police.[28]

1. Case Report: Cocaine cause of motor vehicle accident

Facts of the case

Castle (driver), Latorre and Thibodaux (passengers) went to a party after working at a restaurant on the evening prior to the accident. After leaving the party at approximately 0251, the wheels of a truck driven by Harold Durham struck the Castle vehicle, causing the Castle vehicle to leave the road. Castle, Latorre and Thibodaux were taken by ambulance to the Medical Center and treated for their injuries. While hospitalized, the following drug and alcohol tests were conducted/reported for the automobile occupants:

	Alcohol (Blood)	Cocaine (Urine)	Cannabinoids (Urine)
Castle	0.019gm/dl	8,060 ng/ml	322 ng/ml
Latorre	0.108gm/dl	2,280 ng/ml	70ng/ml
Thibodaux	0.102gm/dl	>2000	

In the hospital notes, all three admitted to drinking alcohol at the party. In deposition, when asked about cocaine (all three) and cannabinoid (Castle and Latorre) use, each deponent took the Fifth Amendment, declining to answer questions admitting or denying illegal drug use. Testimony indicated that there was drug use (cocaine and marijuana) in addition to alcohol consumption at the party. Records for Latorre and Castle indicated that two large bore intravenous solutions, 2×1000ml, were administered, started in the field, before alcohol was tested approximately one hour after the accident.

Mr. Durham, the driver of the truck, tested positive for cannabinoids with a urine drug screen.

Opinions

I hold the following opinions with reasonable pharmacologic certainty:

1. Latorre and Thibodaux were intoxicated by alcohol at the time of the accident.
2. Latorre and Castle used cocaine and marijuana sometime before the accident. Since it is unlikely that these illegal drugs were consumed at or before work, and these illegal drugs were described as being used by other party goers, it is more likely than not that Latorre and Castle used cocaine and marijuana at the party, and therefore were intoxicated by and impaired by cocaine and marijuana use at the time of the accident.
3. Castle was probably experiencing impairments from alcohol at the time of the accident. The impairments at his extrapolated blood alcohol level ($\sim$ 40–50 mg%) include disinhibition, impaired judgment, and delayed reaction time. These impairments would have decreased Mr. Castle's ability to recognize the danger of the approaching truck, to react in time and take some avoidance action (move out of the way). Driving under the influence of alcohol, cocaine, and marijuana creates an unsafe driver, is illegal, and is never justified. The combination of the three drugs impair judgment; a sign of impairment is to take control of an automobile whereas a sober and unimpaired person knows not to drive while intoxicated and under the influence.
4. Angela Thibodaux probably used cocaine at the party (see explanation in #2 above). The combination of cocaine and alcohol intoxication and impairments must be considered.
5. Wilson Latorre and Angela Thibodaux, intoxicated and impaired by the substances indicated in the foregoing, exhibited poor judgment by getting into an automobile driven by Mr. Castle, who was drinking alcohol and using other drugs that evening. One of the primary impairments associated with these mind-altering substances is to impair judgment.
6. Mr. Durham's positive urine drug screen, given his actions and company in the immediate period preceding the accident, must be interpreted as distant (more than 24 hours) use and/or exposure, and thus do not support any impairment by cannabinoids in Mr. Durham, the truck driver.

Discussion of the drugs

Alcohol

Discussed in Sections 44.2 through 44.9 of this chapter.

Cocaine

Cocaine, like ethanol, increases the risk of injury by inducing states of drug intoxication (e.g., agitation, aggression, and distorted perception) or drug withdrawal (e.g., distractibility, somnolence, and depression). In addition, cocaine users frequently use other drugs, such as ethanol or opiates, simultaneously, either to modify cocaine's psychological effects or to blunt unpleasant side effects. Ethanol, for instance, was detected in 45 percent of the cases in which cocaine was detected. Thus cocaine may influence the risk of injury because it is used concurrently with other psychoactive drugs.

There have been few, if any, scientific studies on the effects of cocaine on driving performance. Three main effects of cocaine relevant to driving have been studied. The effects of cocaine on vision appear to be paramount. Forty-three percent of INCOC (inhaled cocaine) users reported increased sensitivity to light, halos around bright objects, and difficulty focusing. Chronic mydriasis observed in these individuals may have been contributing. Lapses of attention were also commonly reported, from ignoring changes in traffic signals to forgetting to replace gas caps at service stations. Over 34 percent of cocaine smokers reported blurred vision, often accompanied by glare problems. Hallucinations were reported by 50 percent of cocaine smokers and 18 percent of intranasal users. "Snow lights," flashes or movements of light in the peripheral field of vision, was the most commonly reported hallucination. Reaction to "snow lights" included moving in their direction or trying to avoid or evade them.

The euphoric effects of cocaine during acute intoxication may give a driver the feeling of increased mental and physical abilities. This results in the claim by users that cocaine improves their driving ability. This optimism may result in increased risk-taking behavior and perhaps increased probability of accidents, particularly in conjunction with ethanol use. While it has been shown that moderate doses of stimulants (amphetamines or cocaine) may acutely enhance performance of simple tasks, these effects decrease considerably as the complexity of the task increases. Cocaine-induced hyperexcitability has resulted in rapid steering or braking reactions due to sudden sounds such as horns or sirens. Since the effects of cocaine are brief, the fatigue or "crash" which follows cocaine use may be a particularly dangerous time for driving. Four cocaine smokers have reported being involved in collisions resulting in major injuries on the way to a cocaine treatment center.

Finally, cocaine's effect on thinking may adversely affect driving. Sixty-two percent of cocaine's smokers have reported symptoms of suspiciousness, distrust and paranoia. These effects have resulted in high-speed chases with police.

2. Case Report: Cocaine vehicular homicide

Facts of the case

Mr. Summerlin's vehicle veered off the roadway (Highway 49) at 4:51 P.M. on July 22, 2004, striking pedestrian Mr. Dillard, causing fatal injuries. Mr. Summerlin was taken into custody at the scene, and later blood and urine samples were taken for testing for alcohol and intoxicating substances. The blood sample was negative for alcohol, negative for cocaine, and positive for benzylecgonine (BE), an inactive metabolite of cocaine, with a quantitation of 446 ng/ml.

Mr. Summerlin advised me of the following:

1. He had worked as a carpenter from ~7 A.M. to 3:30 P.M. It was hot (90-95°F), he was exhausted and very tired. His work involves complicated balance work, sheeting, working on top of construction walls. He had no problem at work that day.

2. He was driving home from work. He stopped at a Lake Tahoe gas station, purchased a six pack of beer, and "chugged" 1 to 1.5 12-oz cans of beer shortly before the accident.

3. The evening before the accident, he insufflated ("snorted" into his nose) two (2) "lines" of cocaine, with some friends, at about 8 P.M. He went to bed at 11:30 P.M.; he had no difficulty getting to sleep. He slept from 11:30 P.M. to 5:30 A.M., got up, left the house for work at ~6:00 A.M.

4. He is not sure if he "fell asleep" or "dozed off," because he thinks he remembers the accident, however eyewitnesses who spoke with Mr. Summerlin at the scene reported to the police that Mr. Summerlin made that statement.

Michael Criten, Ph.D., the Director of the Acculab laboratory (which performed the toxicology test), opined that:

…at the time of the accident Mr. Summerlin was under the influence and significantly impaired due to his recent use of Cocaine prior to the accident… his actions at the time of the accident as documented by the information contained in the Supplemental Traffic Accident Report are consistent with and supportive of my opinion that the Post Stimulant Depressant effects of Cocaine was a major causative factor of the accident.

…Based on a this study and on the Laboratory Report demonstrating that Mr. Summerlin Blood contained 446 ng/ml of BE, it is my opinion that Mr. Summerlin minimally ingested approximately 150 mg or more of Cocaine within 1.5 hours prior to the time of the blood Collection.

Opinions

In my opinion, with reasonable pharmacological certainty:

1. Mr. Summerlin was not under the influence of cocaine, and not experiencing a post stimulant depressant effects.

2. BE has a serum T1/2 (half-life) of 5–9 hours; the 446ng/ml BE was probably a result of Mr. Summerlin's cocaine use the evening 20 hours before the accident.

3. Since the accident occurred at 4:51 P.M., and the blood sample could not have been taken until some time after the accident, (~6 P.M.), if cocaine had been used, all of the effects would have been stimulant, not depressant. Any cocaine used the evening before, in an acute one-time use, would not cause post stimulant depressant effects 21 hours later.

4. The half-life of cocaine, a stimulant, is ~ 0.7–1.5 hours. If, as Dr. Criten opines, the cocaine was used within 1.5 hours prior to the time of the blood collection, this would place the time of use (and peak effects of the cocaine) shortly before the time of the accident.

5. Scientific literature does not support Dr. Criten's opinion but does support the level of BE found to be consistent with distant use of the cocaine; distant use (the night before) cannot cause impairment the next afternoon.

Summary and conclusion

Based on the laboratory testing, there is no evidence supporting acute cocaine use "within 1.5 hours of the blood collection time," or, indeed, on the day of the accident. Mr. Summerlin, in my opinion was not under the influence of cocaine and not impaired by cocaine; and therefore cocaine use or its effects cannot be considered as any contributing cause to the fatal accident that occurred.

44.13 Marijuana

Cannabis, in some form or another, is used by 300 million people, about 10 percent of the world population. The plant *Cannabis sativa* has been in common use in the Middle and Far East for many hundreds of years. It was extensively sought after as a source of fiber for the manufacture of ropes and sailcloth; indeed, the word "canvas" derives from "cannabis." It was this need for reliable chandlery that prompted the British colonial authorities to encourage widespread planting in the southern states of the United States in the eighteenth century. Its use as a pleasure-giving drug only gave rise to concern amongst the Western nations in the late nineteenth century, and its use by Caucasians, as opposed to Asians and Blacks, only came into prominence in the 1920s.

Cannabis is consumed as a drug in various forms, and has various popular names. Marijuana (or marihuana) is the common North American and European preparation. It was originally imported from Mexico, and consists of the dried crushed leaves and fruiting heads. It is smoked in pipes as well as a hand-rolled cigarette. A typical "joint" contains 0.5–2.0 g of marijuana.

A. Effects of Cannabis

The vast majority of published work on the effects of cannabis is anecdotal, and in many reports the bias of the observer, either for or against "decriminalization," is very obvious. Even more recent work, carried out under carefully controlled conditions, is bedevilled by the great variation in cannabinoid content between samples—even from the same area—and the enormously wide range of individual subjective response to an apparently similar dose.[29] The subjective effects are modified by the expectations of the user, by the company (or lack of it) in which the drug is consumed, and by the surroundings in which subsequent observations are made.

1. Euphoria

In laboratory experiments, experienced cannabis users claim euphoria after a dose of marijuana equivalent to 25–50 mg/kg of 1-THC. They suffer no impairment of coordination. Novitiate smokers, in similar conditions, complain of severely impaired coordination, but gain little or no euphoria. When smoked in a social group, there is marked hilarity, increased garrulity, and introverted subjects become gregarious.

2. Perceptual changes

These begin to appear when five to ten times the above dose (i.e., more than 250 mg/kg) are taken. Temporal and spatial disorientation of varying degrees of severity are reported. Some subjects described an apparent slowing in the passage of time after doses in excess of 100 mg/kg. The description given below is particularly helpful.[30]

The usual, most noticeable effect is intensification of sensation and increased clarity of perception. Visually, colors are brighter, scenes have more depth, patterns are more evident, and figure ground relations are more distinct and more easily reversible. Other senses do not have the variety of visual stimuli, but all seem to be intensified. Sounds become more distinct, and the user becomes aware of sounds she otherwise might not have noticed. Music, recorded and live, is heard with increased fidelity and dimension, as though there were less distance between the source and the listener. Taste and smell are also enhanced under marijuana.

Skin receptors are also affected. Heat, cold and pressure receptors become more sensitive. Pain produces paradoxical effects. If attention is not on the area of pain, there is reduced sensitivity to the hurt; but awareness of pain from a lesion, such as a burn or cut, will often persist for a longer period than usual, even allowing for the changed perception of time under marijuana.

Awareness of proprioceptive responses is enhanced. The person using marijuana may become aware of usually automatic, non-conscious muscle tensions, small movements, feedback and control processes, and feelings of comfort and discomfort. These can be perceived with great clarity and directness.

When very high doses (in excess of 250 mg/kg) are smoked, hallucinations, similar to those described by users of LSD (q.v.), may occur. These are not experienced by all subjects. In many cases, sedation alone occurs. A few smokers become dysphoric rather than euphoric, and experience unpleasant sensations, fear and panic.[31] There appears to be a strong placebo effect in studies of marijuana. ("That which you expect, you will experience.") Rarely, a "flashback" effect has been described. In these cases, heavy smokers may suddenly revert to a hallucinated state at any time for several weeks after discontinuing the drug. This phenomenon, which has been well-documented in relation to the hallucinogens,[32] is also known as the "Jekyll and Hyde" effect, after Robert Louis Stevenson's unfortunate medical experimenter.

The psychopharmacology of the effects of cannabis is not clearly understood. It reduces aggression in well-fed rhesus monkeys and rats, but starved rats become more aggressive, possibly because of its appetite-stimulating effects. It appears to produce transient changes in 5-hydroxytryptamine and catecholamine levels in the brain, but the significance of these is not understood.

3. Psychiatric complications

Under some circumstances, cannabis will produce an acute toxic delirium, characterized by clouding of mental processes, disorientation, confusion, and memory impairment. It occurs most commonly with high doses, and is not unlike toxic delirium produced by other psychoactive agents. Patients who develop delirium in response to marijuana complain of feeling apprehensive, fearful, and paranoid. They may have poorly organized delusions as well as illusions and hallucinations. Toxic delirium are relatively rare with commonly available marijuana preparations, but are more likely to occur with hashish and related products containing higher concentrations of THC.

Acute panic reactions similar to non-drug-induced panic anxiety are the most common psychiatric complications

of marijuana use. Panic reactions occur most frequently in experienced users and in persons using more potent preparations. During a panic reaction the individual may feel that he is becoming psychotic; he may have pronounced paranoid ideation with impaired reality testing. Preexisting personality disorder or psychiatric illness, particularly previous psychotic states, appear to increase the risk of marijuana-associated panic reactions.

4. Other effects

Cannabis produces tachycardia, with occasional palpitations. It stimulates the appetite and has weak antiemetic properties. Recent clinical trials in the U.S. have shown improved appetite, with associated weight gain, and the nausea associated with cancer and other cacechtic illnesses and the administration of opioids was alleviated. The mild euphoriant effect was beneficial, and there was a reduced demand for major analgesic drugs. There is a transient rise in blood pressure (both systolic and diastolic) after low smoked doses, but high doses, in the hallucinogenic range, produce hypotension, as does a low dose administered intravenously.

5. Ophthalmic effects

Cannabis smokers develop red eyes. The conjunctival and scleral congestion is not merely the result of irritations by smoke; those who receive cannabis by mouth or intravenously also become "bloodshot." The diameter of the pupils is unaffected by the administration of pure 1-THC. The dilatation of the pupils reported by earlier workers is now thought to be due to impurities in the ordinary preparations, mainly alkaloids with weak-atropine-like effects. Ptosis has been described, but is merely a consequence of general muscular weakness. The intraocular pressure is reduced, especially by pure 6-THC.

6. Psychological and neurological effects

In the acute state, it appears that the mood-altering effects of marijuana are in fact dose-dependent. Intoxicated individuals who consume low to moderate dosages of the drug generally report a feeling of well-being or euphoria, a dreamlike state, a state of pleasant relaxation, an alteration of time and space perception, and a heightening of their senses—for example, better oflaction, clearer perception of music. In addition, they may experience a loss of short-term memory and an inability to perform complex psychologic or motor tasks. In some users, or in users who inadvertently take too large a dose, one can see symptoms ranging from mild anxiety to paranoid behavior to acute psychosis, with problems in dealing with reality, and obsessional thought content characterized by delusions, hallucinations, illusions, and bizarre behavior.

Cognitive functions, such as speaking and problem-solving, also seem to be affected by marijuana use. It appears that these cognitive changes are related not only to the dosage of the drug, but also to the complexity of the tasks or the problem to be solved as well as the individual's familiarity with the given tasks.

7. Psychopathology

Marijuana, an illegal controlled substance schedule I, may produce a variety of pharmacological effects including sedation, euphoria, hallucinations, and temporal distortion. It is described as a psychoactive drug. The primary effect is sedation. Many smoke marijuana for relaxation, as others might use alcohol. The experienced user usually indicates a feeling of inner joy that is described as being high. The drug produces a state of intoxication that is characterized by euphoria, time and space distortion, and motor impairment.[33] Psychological symptoms are remarkably variable and depend on the dose, the route of administration, the personality of the individual, previous experience with the drug, personal expectations, and the environmental and social setting in which the drug is used. During intoxication, perceptions of sounds, colors, tastes, textures, and patterns are commonly altered. Ideas may flow rapidly in a disconnected manner and be altered in emphasis and importance. Individuals may become withdrawn or more talkative. Mood changes vary profoundly; a mild euphoria may be experienced, although anxiety and depression also may occur. Problems may be experienced as either more or less pressing. Drowsiness or hyperactivity and hilarity may be noted. Time is experienced as passing slowly, with little activity needed and no sense of boredom. People often spend long periods of time listening to music or reading. As with the hallucinogens, cannabis-intoxicated subjects describe the unique ability to be able to observe their own intoxication, including dysphoric effects. Individuals who use cannabis intermittently or occasionally are attempting to facilitate concentration at a concert or movie or to enhance sensitivity in sensual situations. Adverse reactions are more likely to occur in naive users who are unfamiliar with the drug's effects and who take it in an unfamiliar or threatening setting. They are quite variable in intensity and characteristics and range from mild discomfort to frank hysteria, sometimes associated with the sensation of being unable to move or breathe or of an impending heart attack. It is likely that psychologically predisposed people are more susceptible to these reactions and may be vulnerable to the persistence of symptoms, the development of a cannabis-induced psychotic disorder, or even the development of a psychotic reaction.[34]

Plasma samples are positive for cannabinol metabolites within minutes and remain positive for several hours.[35] Metabolites of marijuana (cannabinoids) can be found in the urine for several weeks.

The most common adverse psychologic reaction of marijuana use represents an exaggeration of the more usual marijuana response in which the individual loses perspective (i.e., the realization that what she is experiencing is a transient drug-induced distortion of reality) and becomes acutely anxious. This reaction appears to be more common in relatively inexperienced users, although unexpectedly higher doses of the drug (e.g., a more potent variety of marijuana) can cause such a response even in the more experienced user. An acute brain syndrome associated with cannabis intoxication, including such features as clouding of mental processes, disorientation, confusion, and marked memory impairment, has been reported. It is thought to be dose-related (much more likely at unusually high doses) and to be determined more by the size of the dose than by preexisting personality.

8. Case Report: Marijuana in Urine Cause of Accident

Opinion

In my opinion, with reasonable pharmacological certainty, Mr. Eric Daughtry was not intoxicated or impaired, or under the influence of any drugs or substances, including THC or any of its metabolites, at the time of the motor vehicle crash on Monday evening, November 26, 2008. It is my opinion, stated with reasonable pharmacological certainty, that there is no proximate cause between the finding of marijuana (THC metabolites) and the crash.

Bases of opinions

1. The state has produced no expert report from the Acculab Laboratory (or any other scientist) opining that the Acculab Lab results are a proximate cause of the accident, to wit, that the THC metabolites detected would have any effect on Mr. Eric Daughtry that would or could in any way have impaired his ability to operate a motor vehicle on Monday, November 26, 2008.

2. The urine values must be disregarded outright for use in determining impairment. Urine tests cannot be inferred to any clinical effect or impairment. The literature is dogmatic and emphatic on this point. A more complete discussion of this opinion will follow later in the report.

3. The finding of urinary metabolites of THC is consistent with the smoking of marijuana twenty-two (22) hours before the crash.

4. No scientific information or evidence exists in this matter that would support a proximate cause between Eric Daughtry's use of THC and the crash. No reasonable scientist would be able to provide such an opinion with the available evidence.

Discussion and support for opinions

The intoxicating and impairing effects of marijuana are usually dissipated within a few hours. Some authors state up to 8 hours (*Barnett, Heishman*). No authors describe any risk for driving impairment beyond 12 hours, and certainly none at 24 hours or longer.

The most significant drawback to urine testing is that, in general, it does not provide information about past or present patterns of drug use, abuse, or drug dependence, or about drug-related mental or physical impairment, or other effects, at any time.

Urine tests do not tell us anything about impairment because whatever the entry route of a drug, it is carried by the blood stream to the brain, liver, kidney and other organs and the process of metabolism and excretion begins. Metabolism or bio-conversion of most drugs changes them (to metabolites), at least partly, to conjugated forms which are more water soluble than the parent drug and hence excreted primarily through the kidneys into the urine. That process is controlled by various pharmacological, biochemical, and physiological factors, including the chemical nature of the metabolites and conjugates as well as the pH of the urine and other factors, including the drug concentration in plasma. Because bladder urine is a pooled specimen, accumulated over time, and because the kidneys in effect concentrate urine with respect to many constituents including most drugs, the concentration of most drugs excreted in urine is higher than in other accessible biological fluids at the same time. Stated simply, a positive test in the urine simply means that the person was exposed to that drug during the period that the drug and/or its metabolites are circulated in and stored in the body.

It takes the active ingredient of the consumed drug, in the case of THC, the active delta 9 THC, to cause any intoxicating and impairing effects in the brain. Metabolites of THC are for the most part inactive; one metabolite is known to have slight psychotropic effects, but any substance, active or metabolite, has to be in the blood in sufficient amounts for that substance to have any impairing effect on the brain.

Several pharmacology and toxicology references support my opinions with respect to lack of impairing inference related to the finding of THC metabolites in the urine. [i,ii,iii] Karch, Handbook of Abusable Drugs, at page 401-2

states, "Delta 9 THC is the only psychoactive compound [in THC]." This sentence is important, as it implies that Delta-9-THC amounts would have to be detected in order to have a finding of impairment due to THC effect.[iv]

Cone and Heustis, both acknowledged THC experts at the National Institute on Drug Abuse (NIDA), published an article "Relating Blood Concentrations of Tetrahydrocannabinol and Metabolites to Pharmacologic Effects and Time of Marijuana Usage."[v] It is particularly telling that these renowned scientists make no mention of any metabolites of THC (11-hydroxy THC or 11-norhydroxy THC or the COOH—carboxylic acid) in their review paper on the topic. Several additional articles by Huestis, Cone and other coauthors have been reviewed. None of these articles suggests that THC metabolites detected in the urine can be related to a finding of impairment at a specific time.

The impairing substance of marijuana is Delta-9-THC, which was negative urine. THC metabolite (unspecified) was not measured/quantified. Even if there was quantification, adequate information on correlations of body fluid concentration of drugs with measurements of behavioral impairment are rare.[vi]

Summary and conclusion

Based on the above facts in this case, the laboratory reports, and the scientific literature referenced above, as well as my own background, education and training, it is my opinion, with reasonable pharmacologic certainty, that the marijuana metabolite detected in Mr. Daughtry's urine would not in any way have caused or contributed to any impairment at the time of the accident. Further, no reasonable scientist would or could provide testimony supporting impairment and/or proximate cause.

Endnotes

i.   Mason AP and McBay AJ. Cannabis: Pharmacology and Interpretation of Effects. J. Forensic Sciences, JF-SCA Vol 30, No. 3, July 1985, pp 615-631.

ii. Peat MA. Distribution of Delta 9 Tetrahydrocannabinol and Its metabolites. Advances in Analytical Toxicology, Vol II, 1989. Randall C. Baselt, ed. Yearbook Medical Publishers, Chicago.

iii. O'Donnell JT. Recreational Drugs, in O'Donnell JT. Drug Injury: Liability, Analysis and Prevention, 2nd Edition, L & J Publishing Co., Tucson, AZ. 2005.

iv. Karch SB. Drug Abuse Handbook. CRC Press, New York, 1998.

v.   Cone A and Heustis M. Relating Blood Concentrations of Tetrahydrocannabinol and Metabolites to Pharmacologic Effects and Time of Marijuana Usage Therapeutic Drug Monitoring 15:527-532, 1993.

vi. Consensus Development Panel. Drug Concentrations and Driving Impairment. J. American Medical Association, November 8, 1985, Vol. 254, No. 18, 2618-2621.

B. Marijuana in Combination with Alcohol and Other Drugs

Only limited studies of the combined use of amphetamines and marijuana in humans thus far have been done. One study found that simultaneous use, compared to use of either alone, resulted in greater intensity and duration of the subjective high.

C. Passive Exposure: I Never Smoked It!

Five healthy men were passively exposed under pre- and post-placebo controlled conditions to sidestream smoke from 4 and 16 standard marijuana cigarettes for one hour each day for six consecutive days. Subjective effects produced by the 16-cigarette exposure conditions were similar to those observed after active smoking of one 2.8-percent Delta-9-THC marijuana cigarette. Effects after the four-cigarette condition were less pronounced. Concurrent physiologic measurements showed no clear trends or effects of smoke exposure for either condition. Daily mean plasma levels of Delta-9-THC ranged from 2.4–7.4 ng/ml with an individual high of 18.8 ng/ml for the 16-cigarette condition. With the use of EMIT cannabinoid assays with 20 ng/ml (EMIT 20) and 100 ng/ml (EMIT 100) cutoffs, urines positive per subject under the four and 16-cigarette passive exposure conditions were 4.6 and 2.2, and 35.2 and 3.8, respectively, for the EMIT 20 and 0.0, and 1.0 and 0.8, respectively, for the EMIT 100 assay. From the results of these studies, caution is clearly indicated for individuals who might be substantially exposed to heavy marijuana cigarette smoke environments and for those interpreting marijuana screening data.

This study's results demonstrated that passive inhalation of a substantial amount of sidestream marijuana smoke can produce subjective effects, plasma levels of Delta-9-THC, and urinary cannabinoid metabolites in subjects similar to those found after the active smoking of marijuana.[36]

44.14 Conclusion

Alcohol is by far the world's most abused drug, and marijuana use is quite common. Cocaine continues to enjoy popularity. These psychoactive substances will appear in litigated matters, necessitating the lawyer's continuing need for assessment of the contribution, if any, to injury as a result of use. Interpretation of marijuana and cocaine, in contrast to alcohol, tests is complex. The attorney is cautioned to consult with a qualified expert to interpret the testing results and advise of the drug's contribution to the case.

Endnotes

1. "Thirty Years of America's Drug War | Drug Wars | FRONTLINE | PBS." *PBS: Public Broadcasting Service*. N.p., n.d. Web. 20 Nov. 2011. www.pbs.org/wgbh/pages/frontline/shows/drugs/cron.

2. Substance Abuse and Mental Health Services Administration. (2010). *Results from the 2009 National Survey on Drug Use and Health: Volume I. Summary of National Findings* (Office of Applied Studies, NSDUH Series H-38A, HHS Publication No. SMA 10-4856 Findings). Rockville, MD.

3. Lacey, J. H., et al. (2009). 2007 National Roadside Survey of Alcohol and Drug Use by Drivers: Drug Results (DOT HS 811 249). Washington, DC: National Highway Traffic Safety Administration.

4. Gutowski, Christy. "A question of fairness: Did Illinois Supreme Court go too far in promising harsh penalties for motorists with even the slightest trace of drugs in their system? Chicago Tribune." *Featured Articles From The Chicago Tribune*. N.p., n.d. Web. 11 Dec. 2011. http://articles.chicagotribune.com/2011-07-31/news/ct-met-drug-court-opinion-20110728_1_fatal-crash-illegal-drug-illicit-drugs.

5. Melnick, Meredith. "Drugged Driving: A Quarter of Fatal Car Crashes Involve Drugs—TIME Healthland." *TIME Healthland—A healthy balance of the mind, body and spirit*. N.p., n.d. Web. 11 Dec. 2011. <http://healthland.time.com/2011/06/24/drugged-driving-a-quarter-of-fatal-car-crashes-involve-drugs/>.

6. Romano, Eduardo, and Voas B. Robert. "Drug and Alcohol Involvement in Four Types of Fatal Crashes." *Journal of Studies on Alcohol and Drugs* (2011): 567-76. Print.

7. United States. National Highway Traffic Safety Administration. Department of Transportation. "Traffic Safety Facts 2009 Data" *Alcohol-Impaired Driving*. DOT HS 811 385.

8. Moskowitz, H., and D. Fiorentino . "A Review of the Literature on the Effects of Low Doses of Alcohol on Driving-Related Skills." *Home | National Highway Traffic Safety Administration (NHTSA)*. Department of Transportation. DOT HS 809 028, n.d. Web. 12 Dec. 2011. www.nhtsa.gov/people/injury/research/pub/hs809028/DocPage.htm.

9. Voas, Robert, Scott McKnight, David Thom, Terry Smith, Hugh Hurt Jr., Patricia Waller, and John Zellner. "Methodology for Determining Motorcycle Operator Crash Risk and Alcohol Impairment Volume 1: Synthesis Report on Alternative Approaches With Priorities for Research DOT HS 810 761." *Home | National Highway Traffic Safety Administration (NHTSA)*. Department of Transportation. DOT HS 809 028., n.d. Web. 12 Dec. 2011. www.nhtsa.gov/reports/HS810761/pages/TRD. htm.

10. Lococo, Kathy, and Renee Tyree. "Module 1: Functional Abilities and Safe Driving." *Medscape Education Pharmacists* (2010). *Medscape Education*. Medscape, LLC. Web. 12 Dec. 2011. www.medscape.org/viewarticle/725015.

11. Carson-DeWitt, Rosalyn. "Accidents and Injuries from Alcohol." *Drugs, Alcohol, and Tobacco: Learning about Addictive Behavior*. New York: Macmillan Reference USA, 2003. Print.

12. Mellanby, Dr. E. "Section of Therapeutics and Pharmacology." *Discussion on the Value of Alcohol as a Therapeutic Agent*. By Henry H. Dale. Vol. 13. London: John Bale, Sons, & Danielsson, 1920. 31-36. Print.

13. J.T. O'Donnell. "Alcohol: Gastrointestinal and other toxicities," *J. Pharm. Prac.* Vol VII(4):196–208 (1994).

14. Goldberg, Leonard. *Quantitative Studies on Alcohol Tolerance in Man*. Stockholm, 1943. Print.

15. P.D. Blanc, M. Saxena and K.R. Olson. Drug detection and trauma cause: A Case control study of fatal injuries," *Clinical Toxicology* 32(2):137–145 (1994).

16. G.S. Smith. "Alcohol and residential, recreational, and occupational injuries: A review of the epidemiologic evidence," *Ann. Rev. Public Health* 9:88–121 (1988).

17. B.G. Fahy and C.A. Soderstrom. "Alcohol, trauma, and anesthesia," *Problems in Anesthesia* 4(3):541–548 (1990).

18. C.A. Soderstrom et al. "Psychoactive substance use disorders among seriously injured trauma center patients," *JAMA* 277(22):1769–1774 (1997).

19. M.C. Dufour and H. Moskowitz. "The epidemiology of injury," *Alcohol Health and Research World*, summer, 1985, 7–10.

20. Kelly, K.L. "The accuracy and reliability of tests for drugs of abuse in urine samples," *Pharmacotherapy* 8(5): 263–275 (1988).

21. O'Donnell JT. "Recreational drugs," in J.T. O'Donnell, ed. *Drug Injury: Liability, Analysis and Prevention First Edition* (Tucson: Lawyers & Judges Publishing, 2000).

22. Leiken, J.B. and F.P. Paloucek. *Poisoning and Toxicology Handbook 1995–1996* (Cleveland: Lexi-Comp, 1995b), 871–872, 1155, 1157.

23. Struempler, R., "Excretion of Codeine and Morphine Following Ingestion of Poppy Seeds," *J. Anal. Tox*, 1987, 11(3):97-99.

24. Hayes, L., Krasselt, W., Mueggler, P., "Concentration of Morphine and Codeine in Serum and Urine After Ingestion of Poppy Seeds," *Clin Chem*, 1987, 33(6): 806-808.

25. *Mandatory Guidelines for Federal Workplace Drug-testing Programs*, Federal Register, Vol. 59, Number 110, pp. 29908-29931, June 9, 1994; Department of Health and Human Services, Substance Abuse and Mental Health Services Administration, *Mandatory Guidelines for Federal Workplace Testing Programs*, September 1, 1994)

26. Post, R.M. "Cocaine psychoses: A continuum model," *Am. J. of Psychiatry* 132(3):225–234 (1975).

27. Marzuk, P.M. et al. "Fatal injuries after cocaine use as a leading cause of death among young adults in New York City," *New England J. of Med.* 332:1753–7 (1995).

28. Isenchmid, D.S., "Toxicology of Cocaine," *Proceedings*. (Falls Church: Armed Forces Institute of Forensic Pathology, 1994).

29. Brill, N.Q., E. Crumpton and H.M. Grayson. *Arch. Gen. Psychiat.* 24:163–165 (1971).

30. Tart, C.T. *Altered States of Consciousness* (NY: Wiley and Sons, 1969), p. 575.

31. "Cannabis psychosis" (leading article), *Br. Med. J.* 2:1092–3 (1976).

32. Hatrick, J.K. *Lancet* ii:742–4 (1970).

33. K. Blum. *Handbook of Abusable Drugs* (NY: Gardner Press, 1984), 474.

34. M. Galanter and H.D. Kleber. *Textbook of Substance Abuse Treatment* (Washington DC: American Psychiatric Press, 1993), 97.

35. E.J. Cone and M.A. Huestis. "Relating blood concentrations of tetrahydrocannabinol and metabolites to pharmacologic effects and time of marijuana usage," *Therapeutic Drug Monitoring* 15(6):527–532 (1993).

36. Cone, E.J. and R.E. Johnson. "Contact highs and urinary cannabinoid excretion after passive exposure to marijuana smoke," *Clin. Pharmacol. Ther.* 40:247–56 (1986).

Recommended Reading

Alcohol involvement in highway crashes: A review of the epidemiologic evidence," *Clin. Plas. Surg.* 2:11–34 (1975a).

Ambre. J. "The urinary excretion of cocaine and metabolites in humans: A kinetic analysis of published data," *J. Analytical Toxicology*, November–December, 1985. 241–245.

Angell, M. and J.P. Kassirer. "Alcohol and other drugs: Toward a more rational and consistent policy" (editorial), *N. Eng. J. Med.* 331(8):537–539 (1994).

Baselt, R.C. and R.H. Cravey. *Disposition of Toxic Drugs and Chemicals in Man*, 3rd ed. (Chicago: Year Book Medical Publishers, 1989).

Bederka, J.P. "Under the influence of alcohol," *Triodyne Safety Brief* 89(9) (1993).

Bettinger, J. "Cocaine intoxication: Massive oral overdose," *Ann. Emerg. Med.* 9:429–430 (1980).

Blum, K. *Handbook of Abusable Drugs* (NY: Gardner Press, 1984), 333.

Brewer, R.D. et al. "The risk of dying in alcohol-related automobile crashes among habitual drunk drivers," *N. Engl. J. Med.* 331(8):513–517 (1994).

Clayton, R. Drinking, drug use and accidents: An epidemiological perspective: Social epidemiological surveys of alcohol and drug use: Some common characteristics," *Alcohol, Drugs, and Driving* 1(1–2) (1985).

"Cocaine," in M.J. Ellenhorn and D.G. Baceloux, eds., *Medical Toxicology: Diagnosis and Treatment of Human Poisoning* (NY: Elsevier, 1988).

Cornish, C.M. *Drugs and Alcohol in the Workplace: Testing and Privacy* (Wilmette, IL: Callaghan & Company, 1988).

Dubowski, K.M. and R.S. Tuggle, III. *Drug-Use Testing in the Workplace: Law and Science* (Eau Claire, WI: PESI Legal Publishing, 1990).

Ellis, G.M. et al. "Excretion patterns of cannabinoid metabolites after last use in a group of chronic users," *Clinical Pharmacology & Therapeutics* 38(5):572–578 (1985).

Free, A.H. and H.M.Free. *Urinalysis in Clinical Laboratory Practice* (Cleveland: CRC Press, 1975), 172.

Haddon, W. et al. "A controlled investigation of the characteristics of adult pedestrians fatally injured by motor vehicles in Manhattan." *J. Chron. Dis.* 14(6):656–678 (1961).

Harwood, H.J. et al. *Economic Costs to Society of Alcohol and Drug Abuse and Mental Illness* (Research Triangle, NC: Research Triangle Institute, 1980).

International conference on research methodology for roadside surveys of drinking-driving, Paris, France, 1974. "International conference on research methodology for roadside surveys of drinking-driving: Alcohol countermeasures workshop" (DOT HS 801-220) (Washington, DC: U.S. Dept. of Transportation, National Highway Traffic Safety Administration, 1974).

Jekel, J.F. et al. "Epidemic free-base cocaine abuse," *Lancet* 1:459–462 (1986).

Johansson, E. and M.M. Halidin. "Urinary excretion half-life of delta-l-tetrahydrocannabinol-7-oic acid in heavy marijuana users after smoking," *J. Analytical Toxicology* 13:218–223 (1989).

Ketli, C.V. and D.P. Fishbain."Cocaine-induced psychosis and sudden death in recreational cocaine users," *J. For. Sci.* 30:873–880 (1985).

Lesko, L.M. et al. "Iatrogenic cocaine psychosis," *N. Engl. J. Med.* 307:1153 (1982).

Mattila, M.S., vol. ed. Alcohol, Drugs and Driving: Satellite Symposium of the 6th International Congress of Pharmacology on Alcohol, Drugs and Driving, Helsinki, July 26–27, 1975 (Basel; NY: S. Karger, 1976)

O'Donnell, J.T. "Alcohol: Gastrointestinal and other toxicities," *J. of Pharmacy Practice* VII(4):196–208 (1994).

Oyler, J. et al. "Cocaine disposition in meconium in new-borns of cocaine-abusing mothers and urine of adult drug users," *J. Analytical. Toxicology* 20:453–462 (1996).

Perez-Reyes, M. et al. "Free base cocaine smoking," *Clin. Pharmacol. Ther.* 32:459 –465 (1982).

Perine, M.W. Alcohol experiments and driving related behavior: a review of the 1972–73 literature Alcohol Countermeasures Literature Review. NHTSA, Technical Report. DOT HS801 266, 1974b.

Post, R.M. "Cocaine psychosis: A continuum model," *Am. J. Psychiatry* 132:225–231 (1975).

Rolnick, M.A. and S. Szara."Marijuana," in J.F. Winchester and L.M. Haddad, eds., Clinical Management of Poisoning and Drug Overdose (Philadelphia: W.B. Saunders Company, 1983), pp. 434–447.

Smirnow, D. and B.K. Logan. "Analysis of ecgonine and other cocaine biotransformation products in postmortem whole blood by protein precipitation-extractive alkylation and GCMS," *J. Analytical Toxicology* 20:463–467 (1996).

Zylman, R. "Accidents, alcohol and single-cause explanations," in D.B. Goldstein, *Pharmacology of Alcohol* (NY: Oxford University Press, 1983).

Chapter 45

Pain Equipotency

James T. O'Donnell, Pharm.D., M.S., FCP, ABCP, FACN, R.Ph.

45.1 Treatment of Chronic Nonmalignant Pain

Although advances in knowledge about the pathophysiology of pain have been impressive in recent years, high-quality clinical research in patients with chronic pain has not been abundant. Because chronic pain often leads to profound changes in psychological state, level of functioning, and interpersonal relationships, treatment requires attention not only to the pathophysiologic cause of the pain (if one can be found) but also to the psychological and social consequences (and antecedents). For many such patients, opioid analgesics either are relatively ineffective (e.g., for neuropathic pain) or have a risk of abuse that usually outweighs their potential benefits. Even though it has been demonstrated in several studies that some patients with chronic pain can use opioid analgesics for years without problems of abuse, opioid analgesics should not be considered a permanent component of the treatment of nonmalignant pain. For patients with non-malignant chronic pain who have a history of drug abuse, the use of opioid analgesics is almost never advisable.

Because of the first component, a patient's report of the nature, intensity, and location of pain may give clues to the diagnosis of the pathologic process that is causing the pain. Because of its affective component, pain interrupts ongoing behaviors and demands attention; its aversive nature makes it a great motivator of learning by suppressing the behaviors that caused it. These affective aspects of pain are of critical survival value; but when pain becomes chronic, such characteristics make it a serious clinical problem.

When pain does not respond to treatment of the presumed injury or illness, it may lead to chronic disability, fear, and depression. As successive diagnostic tests fail to reveal an adequate pathophysiologic explanation for the severity of the pain, mounting frustration on the part of the physician and desperation on the part of the patient can lead to a premature end to their cooperation. The negative affective and cognitive concomitants of the pain experience are often summarized by the term *suffering*. In addition to the immediate reactions to pain, suffering may involve such components as shame, resentment, and fears of disability, inability to fulfill life roles, financial ruin, and death.

Some patients with chronic pain manifest so-called pain behavior, which is a collection of misdirected activities that are superficially linked to pain but are, often unconsciously, directed at ends other than pain relief. Such activities include exaggerating symptoms to get narcotics to which the patient is addicted, remaining disabled to retain a spouse's attention, or malingering to get compensation. Successful treatment of such patients requires a multidisciplinary approach based on the findings of current anatomic, physiologic, pharmacologic, and psychological research.

A. Diagnostic Evaluation of Pain

A thorough diagnostic evaluation of pain provides the cornerstone for treatment. It is important to obtain a careful history, including the nature, localization, severity, time course (e.g., always present, occurs in bouts, or worse at night), and radiation of pain. Factors that reduce or exacerbate the pain should be elicited, and it should be determined whether associated symptoms, such as nausea, weakness, or numbness, are present. A thorough psychiatric and social assessment is important, with special attention given to the presence of depression or anxiety. The patient's cultural background, job, and customary leisure activities will affect his attitude toward pain and rehabilitation. The impact of the patient's pain on the family should also be determined. Litigation or occupational injuries should always be noted.

For clinical purposes, pain can be categorized into the following three groups: (1) acute pain, in which a specific noxious stimulus of limited duration can be identified (e.g., postoperative pain, renal colic, or a fractured bone); (2) continuous pain in terminally ill patients (most often caused by cancer); and (3) other forms of chronic pain. The source of the pain is easiest to identify for the first two categories and most elusive in the evaluation of chronic pain of non-malignant origin. An additional distinction that is relevant to chronic pain is the difference between pain caused by a tissue-damaging process that excites nociceptive afferents (e.g., arthritis or cancer) and pain caused by pathologic changes in nociceptive neurons (neuropathic pain). Neuropathic pain typically persists and may even have its onset long after the original noxious stimulus has been removed.

B. Evaluation of Chronic Pain

Three guides to the diagnostic examination that provide helpful anchors in this sea of detail are the following: (1) determination of whether the pain corresponds to a physiologic pattern, such as a dermatomal pattern or the innervation pattern of a peripheral nerve; (2) identification of neuropathic pain; and (3) the assessment of suffering and pain behavior components.

C. Neuropathic Pain

Neuropathic pain may develop in response to an injury to peripheral or central sensory afferents. Because of damage to the nociceptive pathways, there is generally some loss of normal pain sensation (hypalgesia), but severe pain may occur after a delay. This type of pain is termed neuropathic, or deafferentation, pain. Such pain may be produced by amputation, nerve avulsion, cordotomy, or peripheral neuropathy. Phantom limb pain, causalgia, postherpetic neuralgia, and thalamic pain are all forms of neuropathic pain.

The symptoms of neuropathic pain often include persistent burning with unprovoked paroxysms of lancinating pain referred to the deafferented region. Patients may also describe dysesthesias—for example, pins and needles,

numbness, tingling, or formication (i.e., the sensation of ants crawling on the skin). In addition, mildly noxious stimuli may provoke severe pain in the region (hyperpathia), and even innocuous stimuli applied to this region may produce perverted sensations or severe pain (allodynia). Because neuropathic pain often responds poorly to currently known therapies, patients with such pain should be referred to a pain specialist or a multidisciplinary pain clinic.

D. Suffering and Pain Behavior

Adding to the difficulties and problems of chronic pain is the frustrating, complex, anti-therapeutic series of behaviors often called pain behavior. The core problem in such cases is that the patient has a reason not to get well. The physician, acting on the assumption that the patient has come for diagnosis and treatment, tries to eliminate the pain. The patient's goal is to keep the pain at all costs because it is the means to another end. The scene is set for prolonged mutual antagonism. It is further complicated because the patient is rarely aware of the ulterior motive.

In general, the secret of success with chronic pain patients is in the identification of suffering or pain behavior components that compound their symptoms. Patients with chronic pain have lived with their malady for months or years. Narcotic trials of varying duration, and perhaps even surgical interventions, have failed to relieve their symptoms. Repeated efforts to diagnose a structural abnormality that can be corrected have not been productive. Often, pathophysiologic abnormalities exist, but they are insufficient to account for the pain complaints.

Attention to psychiatric co-morbidity is important. Although many cases of depression and alcohol abuse appeared to be secondary to the pain syndrome, 43 percent of the patients had a history of major depression before the onset of pain. More than half of the patients who abused alcohol began this behavior before the onset of pain, and 59.5 percent had at least one first-degree relative with chronic pain. All patients with chronic pain should be considered for evidence of depression. Anxiety is another common psychiatric problem that may augment pain, even in acute situations.

45.2 Pain Equipotency

In my opinion, Mr. Jones suffered the pain equivalent of 388 heart attacks and 183 molar tooth extractions.

—Trial testimony of plaintiff's expert pharmacologist

A. Introduction

This chapter on pain medications is included in this book because it addresses the use of drugs to treat pain following injuries. There is no issue about liabilities for the use of drugs, although the issues of analgesic-induced ADR's and dependency following narcotic pain relieving drug use are real. Rather, it is included because litigants who address drug-related cases will frequently find themselves presented with a myriad variety of drugs to treat pain from various injuries, not just malpractice. The Pain Equipotency analysis has been employed by this author in approximately 40 cases. It is usually employed in a settlement brochure, as a video report, and is sometimes offered for deposition and trial testimony. Only twice has this testimony been given in trial. In one trial experience, the pharmacologist expert reviewed the painful conditions of the burned patient/plaintiff, and explained the use of analgesics and how the various pain killing drugs compared to one another. The defense in the case argued unsuccessfully in a motion in limine that the "pain equipotency" discussion was junk science, and that the jury did not need an expert to discuss the pain killing drug use. The judge denied the motion and allowed the testimony. The jury was asked to award the plaintiff $1.5 million for pain and suffering; the jury awarded $1.75 million! (*Machajewski v. Wisconsin Natural Gas Company*, 93 CV 001530, State of Wisconsin, Circuit Court, Milwaukee County.)

This section is designed to describe various types of pain, and compare pain of various types to a common denominator amount of pain; that is, that those types of pain which have been fully described in the literature, as well as those types of pain which have served as models for clinical pharmacology studies designed to test efficacy and safety of new drugs used to treat pain (analgesics). The common denominator for *equipotency* will be the pain medication used for analgesia, pain relief. The final purpose is to provide the reader with a method of expressing or quantifying pain in a description which translates to accepted, common pain types, for which a well agreed-upon dosage amount of medication is used for analgesia. This will help the lay reader understand the level of pain and suffering experienced by the injured person requiring pain relief.

The objective is to quantify the use of analgesic drugs beyond simply listing the dosages and number of drug administrations. The common and quantified painful experiences of a heart attack (MI—myocardial infarction), pain from labor experiences, and pain from extraction of a molar tooth are selected as comparisons for the pain experiences. These will be related and compared to the amount and types of drugs used to treat/relieve a patient's pain to that amount reported to relieve these commonly recognized types (MI, labor, dental).

Pain and pain management literature describe clinical pain and its measurement, and research in pain assessment, measurement, and investigation are addressed and referenced.

> Pain is an unpleasant sensory and emotional experience associated with actual or potential tissue damage or described in terms of such damage.[1]

One of the most critical aspects in the investigation of pain is the question of its quantitative documentation. Pain is a subjective experience and, because of its large emotional components, is quite dependent upon the circumstances of the person being affected. But pain is also a consequence of the activation of nociceptive (pain) afferent nerves, which of course can be measured with the methods usually applied in sensory physiology in humans. The basic expression of pain is a verbal report, and various methods are available to scale subjective pain experience.

Pain relief and analgesia are not synonyms and have no necessary relationship. They derive from two different approaches to the measurement of human suffering: clinical assessment and laboratory studies. Pain relief, however, must be measured in terms of the three dimensions of clinical pain: intensity, quality, and evaluation. It is far more than the lack of a response to a known stimulus. Analgesia is defined as "the absence of pain in response to stimulation which would normally be painful." This should better be described as hypalgesia: a partial or diminished sensibility to noxious stimulation. Pain relief is defined as behavior on the part of the animal or human which indicates a reduction in the noxiousness of an externally applied stimulus, or in humans, the report of or behavior indicating that an unobservable internal event is less noxious. It is obvious that there are degrees of pain relief, and that the patient's verbal report and behaviors are our only methods of assessing pain relief. Even though we can quantify pain behaviors and measure pain relief by such an evaluation, we measure the behaviors, not the perceptions or affects of the patients.[2]

B. Experimental and Clinical Pain

Experimentally induced pain in the laboratory environment differs from pain as seen by the physician in the clinic. The experimental pain stimulus applied to the healthy subject can always be interrupted or definitely stopped. These facts emphasize the rational component in the laboratory pain experiment, and what we do measure is primarily the sensory discriminative component of pain. In contrast, patients' pain is essentially characterized by an aversive, emotional component, causing a feeling of severe illness and forcing the individual to visit the doctor. This component is particularly accompanied by vegetative responses, such as changes in blood pressure, circulation, heart beat and transpiration. Both components of pain do interact and influence each other; as such, it might be possible to estimate the degree of clinical pain or to evaluate the efficacy of any pain-reducing treatment by measuring pain reactions to defined noxious stimuli in healthy volunteers.

Pain is a subjective experience, and we have to give credence to the pain report of the individual. But the subjective report is not only a function of the sensory input activated; it is also influenced by psychological, social, cultural and economic factors. To differentiate between pathophysiological factors and other sources as modulators of pain, it seems necessary to measure, in addition to the verbal report, pain related physiological variables. Similar problems arise if the success of any analgesic treatment is to be verified.

C. Clinical Pain

Clinical pain is often persistent, unbearable, beyond the patient's control, and accompanied by high levels of anxiety. It is not surprising, therefore, that there are marked differences in drug and placebo effects on clinical and laboratory-produced pain.[3]

Further, Beecher classifies pain with the use of words such as "mild," "moderate" and "severe," and subjects are asked to choose the word that best describes the intensity of their pain. A method consists of a 5 point scale which ranges from 1 "mild" to 5 "unbearable pain," and subjects are asked to choose the most appropriate number. Clearly, then, it is desirable to study pain in patients who are suffering it for a variety of reasons—acute injury, arthritis, surgical incision, cancer, and so forth.

Most clinical pain problems are acute. Acute pain appears, it lessens over a period of hours to days to weeks, and it resolves. Such pain can be treated easily in most cases with symptomatic medications as needed (PRN). If acute pain is not treated adequately, however, it can result in a chronic pain syndrome characterized by excessive medication usage, mood changes, multiple surgeries and inability to carry out normal activities of daily living.[4]

D. Pain Studies

Chronic pain often presents as a symptom complex.[5] Successful treatment of all symptoms is usually not possible without inducing an unacceptably high risk of side effects. Pain and anxiety are key to breaking the complex. Most currently available analgesics are effective drugs. However, they may not work in many chronic pain patients unless the principal causes of the patients' anxiety also are addressed.

If an effective analgesic with a duration of action of four hours is administered every six hours, or only after the pain has become firmly reestablished, anxiety about the continual return of pain commonly occurs. This anxiety lowers the patients's pain threshold resulting in an increased perception of pain. Therefore, to establish initial pain control for patients with agonizing, chronic pain, medications should be administered on a regular schedule, that is, a time contingent basis, according to the duration of useful analgesic activity. This regular schedule should be continued until the patient's anxiety about return of pain has abated, usually several days to weeks.

E. Therapeutic Trials

Methods employed in the clinical evaluation of analgesics and problems encountered in these studies because of the complex nature of the subjective variables of pain and pain relief, have been reviewed extensively. The choice of a pain model requires careful consideration in any clinical evaluation of analgesics. The most sensitive assays of analgesic efficacy are single dose studies in patients with acute pain, while multiple dose studies in patients with acute or chronic pain provide information on the general clinical acceptability and safety of the analgesic. Some painful conditions, such as oral surgical pain (Dental Pain Model), episiotomy pain and acute orthopedic pain, have proved to be particularly suitable models for analgesic efficacy studies, as the source of pain is understood, the duration of pain is fairly predictable, and a relatively homogeneous population of otherwise healthy subjects may be selected. Instances in which acute pain is likely to be more variable, but which represent important uses of analgesics, include headache and postoperative pain.

F. Treatment of Pain

For acute pain, analgesics and other symptomatic medications are the only treatment needed. Initially severe pain usually becomes moderate, then mild, then resolves. Drug therapy may be adjusted as shown in Figure 45.1.

For advanced pain, the opioid analgesics (like morphine and oxycodone) remain the drugs of choice in most cases. There is little difference in the efficacy of the various schedule II controlled substance opioid analgesics when the drugs are administered in equianalgesic doses according to their durations of action.

Opiate agonists (drugs from opium, such as morphine, codeine, Percocet) are generally used to provide temporary analgesia in the symptomatic treatment of moderate to severe pain such as that associated with acute and some chronic medical disorders including renal or biliary colic,

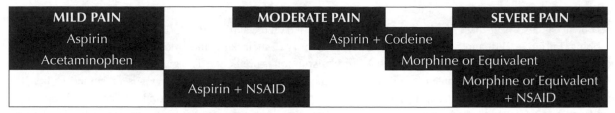

Figure 45.1 *Levels of acute pain and drug therapy.*

myocardial infarction, acute trauma, postoperative pain, and terminal cancer. The drugs may also be used to provide analgesia during diagnostic and orthopedic procedures, dressing changes, and labor. The drugs are also used to provide preoperative sedation and as a supplement to anesthesia. Although most of the opiates produce similar analgesia in equianalgesic doses, such factors as oral effectiveness, duration of action, other CNS effects such as euphoria or sedation, degree of action on smooth muscle, and individual variation in patient response should be considered in the selection of a specific drug. In patients with chronic pain who do not have a terminal illness, opiates should be used only if the patient is not afforded relief by non-opiate analgesics. If opiates must be used, the following procedures have been recommended to delay the development of tolerance and to assure the patient maximum comfort over a prolonged period of time. For initial therapy, a mild, oral opiate such as codeine should be used. Parenteral dosage forms (IV or IM) should be reserved for use if needed in the latter stages of therapy, if oral dosage forms are ineffective.

In the management of severe, chronic pain associated with terminal illness such as cancer, the principal goal of analgesic therapy is to make the patient relatively pain-free while maintaining as good a quality of life as possible. Analgesic therapy must be individualized and titrated according to patient response and tolerance. When non-opiate (Motrin, Naprosyn, Tramadol) or combinations of opiate analgesics (Tylenol with Codeine) are ineffective, oral administration of an opiate on a regular schedule generally will provide adequate relief of severe, chronic pain and the fear of its recurrence.

G. Goodman and Gilman Discussion of Morphine[6]

In man, morphine produces analgesia, drowsiness, changes in mood, and mental clouding. A significant feature of analgesia is that it occurs without loss of consciousness. When therapeutic doses of morphine are given to patients with pain, they report that the pain is less intense, less discomforting, or entirely gone. Nausea is common, and vomiting may also occur. Feelings of drowsiness and inability to concentrate, difficulty in mentation, apathy, lessened physical activity, reduced visual acuity, and lethargy may ensue. As the dose is increased, subjective effects become more pronounced; there is increased drowsiness that leads to sleep. In individuals who experience euphoria, the euphoric effect is accentuated. Patients with severe pain that is not adequately relieved by smaller doses of morphine are usually relieved by larger doses (15 to 20 mg). The incidence of nausea and vomiting is also increased, and respiratory depression, the major toxic effect of morphine-like drugs, may become pronounced.

H. Analgesia

The relief of pain by morphine and its surrogates (Fentanyl, Dilaudid, Nubain) is relatively selective, in that other sensory modalities (touch, vibration, vision, hearing, etc.) are not obtunded. Patients frequently report that the pain is still present but that they feel more comfortable. Continuous dull pain is relieved more effectively than sharp intermittent pain, but with sufficient amounts of morphine it is possible to relieve even the severe pain associated with renal colic.

I. Types of Pain

1. Myocardial infarction (heart attack) crushing pain of chest/arm

In its most characteristic form the clinical picture of acute coronary occlusion with myocardial infarction is dominated by severe and prolonged pain in the region of the sternum (breastbone), the precordium or the upper abdomen....The victim is stricken while at rest or at work, when awake or asleep, with or without the dubious benefit of premonitory pain. The pain either may begin as a relatively mild but persistent discomfort which becomes increasingly severe, or it may strike with sudden terrifying intensity. The pain of acute myocardial infarction has the same quality of constriction, oppression or compression that characterizes angina pectoris, But as a rule it is more crushing in intensity and becomes intolerable because of its prolonged duration. Usually the pain is characterized as squeezing, constricting, choking, viselike, or like a heavy weight, but it has also been described as expanding, stabbing, knifelike, dull and boring or burning in quality....Like the pain of angina pectoris, that of acute myocardial infarction radiates frequently to the shoulders and both upper extremities, to the neck and jaw and to the interscapular region. Radiation of the pain to the neck is often described as causing clutching or choking sensation. The pain in the upper extremities, more often in the left, may either extend continuously from the shoulder to the fingers, or reach only to the arms, or skip directly to the forearms or wrist....The pain persists in varying degree for at least an hour, but often for several hours, and occasionally as a milder soreness for 1 to 3 days....The duration of the pain is abbreviated frequently by the administration of *morphine*, but occasionally even opiates may hardly diminish the pain or at best leave a persistent dull ache or pressure.[7] *(emphasis added)*

2. Headache pain

Any clinician who assesses a chronic pain sufferer is aware of the complex changes that have occurred in the sufferer's emotional state, cognition, and behavior patterns. These changes are not incidental but form an integral part of the sufferer's pain problem and may even contribute to its self-perpetuation.[8] When acute injury occurs, the resultant tissue damage is associated with anxiety and pain. The pain appears to serve an important function, motivating a whole set of behaviors that promote tissue healing and recuperation (i.e., not using the body for fear of pain, further damage, exhaustion from the effort). The individual rests, sleeps, withdraws from her normal routines, and appears disinterested in her environment. These behaviors motivated by pain can thus be seen as serving a rather special function. They actively influence recovery and are associated over time with pain diminution. A somewhat different situation is evident in an individual with a chronic pain problem such as headache, backache, or facial pains. The same types of behaviors can be detected, but in this case they persist and are elaborated extensively, even though no tissue damage is evident. But more importantly, the pain recovery system appears to be disordered, in that the behaviors occur without any pain decrease. There is no recuperation, and pain does not gradually reduce. Over longer periods, these behaviors increasingly replace and disrupt normal activities so that the behavior can be seen only as unadaptive and may actively delay recovery. It has long been thought that the behavior of those in pain is simply and directly a result of the intensity of

their subjective experience. Thus, clinical assessments have focused on the subjective reports of sufferers concerning the severity of their pain, and from this the extent of behavioral disruption is predicted. The greater the pain experienced, the more extensive this pain behavior is presumed to be. It is important to assess the behavioral aspect of a chronic pain problem in its own right in order to establish the extent of the behavioral incapacities. In the past, this has been done by obtaining a count of the rate of medication use for pain. This single behavioral measure has been particularly popular in the headache treatment literature and has been used as the valid spokesman of the myriad pain behaviors that in fact occurs. Unfortunately, pharmacological aids are used only by sufferers with certain attitudes to drugs—attitudes that are often independent of the severity of their pain. Thus, this measure has proved a blunt and inadequate single measure of pain behavior. (In other words, the pain can be greater than it appears based only on headache drug use.)

The most important measure of pain in people is the verbal report. Only humans are able to verbalize their sensations, and this makes experiments in people indispensable in pain research. Meanwhile, many pain rating scales have been proposed, and an extensive section of the literature deals with the quantification of the different components of pain perception, the application of multidimensional scaling procedures, and abilities to discriminate between analgesic treatments. In the category scale, pain is classified by a set of given descriptors such as faint, mild, moderate, and strong pain, as shown in Figure 45.2.

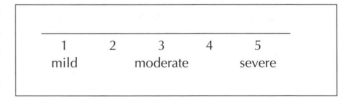

Figure 45.2 *Visual pain analog scale.*

Certain assumptions and conversions also need to be defined. They are:

1. Morphine is the reference analgesic, and all other drugs used are compared to morphine. Morphine is recognized as the standard, the most effective drug against which all other analgesics are measured and compared.

2. The route of administration will affect the potency of any drug administered. IV is the most potent, other parenteral forms (Intramuscular or IM, Subcutaneous or SQ) are less potent, and the oral route is the least potent. This means that it takes less mil-

ligrams of morphine IV compared to IM; put another way, IV morphine is 2 to 3 times as potent as IM. IV morphine is up to 6 times more potent than oral.

4 mg (IV) = 10 mg (IM) = 25 mg (ORAL)

Parenteral administration (IM, IV, SQ) of narcotics becomes the route of choice when high doses or oral drugs provide less effective control of pain or when patients have gastrointestinal alterations, in contrast to MI pain, which resolves at the end of the heart attack, and the labor pain, which resolves with the birth of the baby, and is also quantifiable by the amount, frequency, amplitude, and duration of the uterine contractions which cause the pain.

Other comparisons to be used are:

Morphine 4 mg IV	=	Pain relief of myocardial infarction	=	Pain relief of 2–4 hours of labor
Morphine 10 mg IM	=	Pain relief of myocardial infarction	=	Pain relief of 2–4 hours of labor

J. Sample Report

This report compares a quantification of intensity of pain, not precisely the same type of pain. Pain description varies with the individual, the culture, the experience, and so on. The only thing that is being compared (i.e., equipotency) is that the analgesic drug use in a particular patient compared to how much drug would be used to relieve pain in short-term, time-limited events (i.e. MI and labor), or quantifiable/measurable repeating/daily drug use to relieve terminal cancer pain, or the pain relieved by standard oral analgesics (e.g., Tylenol #3 etc.) when measured by qualified investigators, and submitted to the Food and Drug Administration in support for efficacy and safety claims for the various products tested (MS Contin).

Clinical and research literature describe certain types of medical injuries, or certain types of common surgeries or health experiences, and further describe the common types and amounts and effectiveness (efficacy) of various drugs used to relieve any acute pain associated with these occurrences, conditions, surgeries, etc. For instance, the heart attack is described as an excruciating, debilitating, crushing pain in the left chest over the sternum and radiating down the left arm. Morphine is usually considered the most effective drug of choice in relieving the pain of myocardial infarction.[9,10] To relieve pain of myocardial infarction, clinicians report an IV dose of 2-4 mg, and texts report parenteral

doses as high as 8-15 mg,[11] which would include SQ and IM dosing figures, which convert to 1/3 to 1/2 the potency of an intravenous administration.

For purposes of our pain level comparison, 4 mg morphine is assessed as the amount of morphine used to relieve the pain of a heart attack.

Morphine is the principal alkaloid of the opiate family, derived from the poppy. A number of synthetic opioid drugs have been manufactured and are in clinical use (see Table 45.1). Opioid drugs are generally used to provide temporary analgesia in the symptomatic treatment of moderate to severe pain such as that associated with acute and some chronic medical disorders, including renal or biliary colic, myocardial infarction, labor, acute trauma, postoperative pain, and terminal cancer.

Labor pain averaged among a large population of women, ranks among the severest forms of pain recorded with the McGill Pain Questionnaire (MPQ).[12] This is not to be confused with the pain of a single "bearable" uterine contraction. Rather, it refers to the intractable, unbearable severe labor contraction pain experience, for which 10 mg morphine intramuscular (or equivalent opiate parenteral narcotic) would be given to relieve the labor experience of 2-4 hours, the duration of pain relief provided by this morphine analgesia. This is described, to be conservative, as the relief for a period of 2-4 hours of severe labor pain. It is possible to compare labor pain with other pains on the basis of a Pain Rating Index (PRI). Recognizing that labor pain is greater with primiparas (first-time mothers) than with multiparas, labor pain was ranked, in descending order of pain intensity, more intense than:

- back pain,
- cancer pain,
- phantom limb,
- post herpetic neuralgia,
- toothache, and
- arthritis.

Many single dose analgesic efficacy studies use toothache/oral surgery pain as an assessment of efficacy, that is, Non-Steroidal Anti-inflammatory Drugs (NSAIDs), such as Motrin, Naprosyn, Feldene, Anaprox, Meclomen, etc. (see Table 45.2 for a complete listing of NSAIDs). Thus, it is reasonable to conclude that labor pain is of a higher intensity and more severe than the above commonly recognized/reported pains.

To provide analgesia during severe labor, 10 mg morphine sulfate is usually administered SQ or IM. (This is equivalent to an IV dose of 4 mg IV.)

Table 45.1
Opioid Drugs

Codeine	Methadone
Morphine	Fentanyl
Opium preparations	Hydrocodone
Oxycodone	Hydromorphone
Oxymorphone	Levorphanol
Porpoxyphene	Meperidine
	Sufentanil

Table 45.2
NSAIDs

Aspirin	Acetaminophen
Meclofenamate	Choline salicylate
Mefenamic acid	Magnesium salicylate
Naproxen	Salsalate
Diflunisal	Fenoprofen
Piroxicam	Ibuprofen
Sulindac	Indomethacin
Tolmetin	Ketoralac
Miscellaneous analgesic	Ketoprofen
Phenylbutazone/	
oxyphenbutazone	

Partial Opiate Agonists
Buprenorphine
Nalbuphine
Butorphanol
Pentazocine

For purposes of our pain level comparison, 4 mg IV morphine is assessed as the amount of morphine used to relieve the pain of 2-4 hours of severe labor.

Using 4 mg of IV morphine for the relief of pain of a heart attack as well as labor, as a comparison, we can now examine the amount, daily quantity, and frequency of use of the analgesics which were administered to our sample patient.

Mr. Jones (a pseudonym) was struck by an automobile and pinned against a van. He suffered bone and muscle crushing injuries, requiring seven weeks hospitalization, multiple reparative and reconstructive surgeries, debridement, traction, and received almost 1,400 milligrams of morphine sulfate during his hospitalization. Recalling the conversion factor for morphine to amounts used in common clinical painful conditions, it is apparent that Mr. Jones received the amount of morphine used during this initial hospital stay is the pain equivalent of 348 heart attacks or 696–1,392 hours of severe labor pains.

Mr. Jones also received other medications for pain. The other medications were oral tablets of Percocet (oxycodone and acetaminophen).

Assuming that one Percocet contains 4.88 mg oxycodone = 30 mg codeine, and 120 mg codeine = 10 mg IM morphine = 4 mg IV morphine, then 4 tabs of Percocet = 4 mg IV morphine = pain relief equivalent for heart attack = pain relief equivalent for four hours of severe labor pain experience.

Based on these assumptions, the pain relieved by the Percocet in Mr. Jones was the pain equivalent of 40 heart attacks or 80-160 hours of severe labor pains which can be attributed to the Percocet use.

K. Oral Analgesic Medication Studies

Morley describes the clinical pharmacology research in proving the analgesic efficacy of Zomepirac (Zomax, McNeill, since removed from the market). This is an important article, since it compares the new drug Zomax against the more standard and older analgesics for the effectiveness in treating common painful conditions, including:

- dental molar extractions
- post operative pain
- laparoscopic sterilization
- muscle contraction headache
- episiotomy pain
- acute orthopedic pain
- oral surgical pain
- cancer pain

Medications which are compared include the following:

- APC† 2 capsules
- APC with codeine 30 mg/capsule
- Acetaminophen
- Acetaminophen with codeine 30 mg (2 capsules)
- Aspirin 650 mg
- Aspirin 650 mg with codeine 60 mg[13]

†APC = Aspirin phenacetin caffeine. Phenacetin was ordered removed from the market in 1982 because it caused severe kidney disease, including interstitial nephritis and kidney cancer.

Several studies are evaluated in the literature which use dental pain model to evaluate the efficacy of analgesics, including ASA/Acetaminophen-Codeine, NSAIDs, etc. Most studies consider standard NSAID drugs as well as the Acetaminophen 300/codeine 30 mg effective for relieving at least two-thirds of the pain associated with a molar tooth extraction for a period of 6 hours. Therefore, for purposes of equilibrating the oral solid analgesic medication periods following hospitalization in which

- Tylenol #3 (Norco, Lurtab, Vicodin),
- Naprosyn,
- Darvocet N 100 (removed from market),
- Percocet, or
- equivalent drugs

were used, equivalent doses of these medications will be evaluated and converted to the equivalent medication to relieve six hours of oral surgery/dental-molar extraction pain.

References in the medical, dental, and clinical pharmacology literature which are cited to support the use of the Dental Pain Model as well suited for determining the minimally effective dose and defining the linear part of the dose effect curve for peripherally acting analgesics.[14-22]

L. Dental Extraction Pain Equivalence

The Dental Pain model, the equivalent pain medication needed to relieve the pain which follows extraction of a molar tooth for a period of six hours, is selected for comparison for the ambulatory periods in which Darvocet N-100 (propoxyphene with acetaminophen), Tylenol #3 (Acetaminophen 325 mg with codeine 30 mg), and Naprosyn 375 mg (a non-steroidal anti-inflammatory agent similar to ibuprofen, Motrin, Indocin) are used.

Turning now to the analgesics used for moderate pain relieved in Mr. Jones by the administration of the following medications:

Tylenol #3	650 tablets
Darvocet N 100	250 tablets
Naprosyn 375 mg	180 tablets
Total	**1080 tablets**

He received these for an 18-month period following the hospitalization, and applying the dose equivalent of two tablets of the above three medications equivalent to the pain relieved in a dental pain molar-tooth extraction for a 6-hour period, we can now add the following additional pain equivalent experiences of *1080 molar extractions*.

The cumulative totals for all *analgesic pain equivalents*, for the in-patient hospitalization and the outpatient

treatment which followed, are as follows: 388 heart attacks or 776–1,552 hours labor pains or 52.7 days terminal cancer pain plus 1080 molar extractions.

Restated simply, Mr. Jones received the amount of medication which would have relieved the pain of the above conditions.

Review of the medical charts for the sample patient indicates a substantial period of approximately seven weeks following the accident in which the patient required morphine for the lessening of his pain. Analgesics lessen, not eliminate, pain. The normal duration for the use of morphine post-operatively is two to three days, followed by a switch to oral opiate/NSAID-APAP products. This prolonged necessity for morphine is a further documentation of Mr. Jones' excessive level of suffering. The causes for his pain are described, and should be readily understood. No one can deny that bone-crushing injury, with the attendant soft tissue, muscle, cartilage, and tendon injury is a serious cause for pain.

Further insult to injury is the necessary, repetitive, predictable, excruciatingly painful debridement, dressing changes, and re-operations. This frequent procedure, as well as the unending pain, injects an emotional and anxiolytic component to the pain experience support. Once the pain is experienced, there is an increased degree of anticipation, anxiety, and suffering which the patient experiences once the pain is again present. Chronic pain often presents as a symptom complex.[5] Successful treatment of all symptoms is usually not possible without inducing an unacceptably high risk of side effects. Pain and anxiety are key to breaking the complex. This anxiety lowers the patients's pain threshold, resulting in an increased perception of pain; thus, the need and explanation for the frequent use of Valium (diazepam-benzodiazepine) during Mr. Jones' hospitalization.

It is clear that the treating physicians and nurses recognized the excruciating agony which the crushing injuries were having on Mr. Jones, and his analgesic orders reflect this recognition.

M. Conclusion

This pain equipotency attempts to show the reader a means of assessing and measuring analgesic medications used to relieve a variety of severe types of pain into commonly recognized pain, comprehendible to the average person.

Endnotes

1. Merskey H. Pain terms: a list with definitions and notes on usage. Pain 1979;6:249-252.

2. Loeser John D. Chapter 13 in Issues in Pain Measurement. Chapman CR and Loeser JD. Raven Press, New York, 1989

3. Beecher HK (1959) Measurement of Subjective Responses. Oxford University Press. New York.

4. Melzack R and Wall PD: The Challenge of Pain. Basic Books, Inc., New York, 1982.

5. Lipman AG. Drug Therapy in Cancer pain. Cancer Nurs 1980; 3:39-46

6. Jaffe HH and Martin WR. Opioid Analgesics and Antagonists. Chapter 22, 494-534. In The Pharmacological Basis of Therapeutics, Sixth Edition, Gilman AG, Goodman LS and Gilman A, eds. Macmillan, NY, NY, 1980.

7. Friedberg CK. Diseases of the Heart., Chapter 21, Acute Coronary Occlusion and Myocardial Infarction. P 798. WB Saunders, Philadelphia, 1969

8. Sternback RA. (1978) The Psychology of Pain . Raven Press, New York.

9. Drug Information, American Hospital Formulary Service. ASHP. Bethesda, Md. 1986 at p 914

10. Ross RS. Ischemic Heart Disease. Chapter 240, p 203, in Harrison's Principles of Internal Medicine, Seventh Edition, Wintrobe MM, Thorn GW, Adams RD, Braunwald E, Isselbacher KJ and Pertersdorf RG, eds., McGraw Hill, New York 1974

11. Drug Information, American Hospital Formulary Service. ASHP. Bethesda, Md. 1986 at p 899

12. Melzack R: Measurement of the Dimensions of Pain Experience. Chapter 23 in, Pain Measurement in Man. Neurophysiological Correlates of Pain, Bromm, B, ed. Elsevier, New York. 1984.

13. Morley PA, Brogden RN, Carmine AA, Heel RC, Speight TM, and Avery GS.zomepirac: a review of its pharmacological properties and analgesic efficacy. Australasion Drug Information Services, Auckland. DRUGS 23: 250-275,(1982)

14. Cooper SA, Needle SE, Kruger GO: An analgesic relative potency assay comparing aspirin, ibuprofen and placebo. J. Oral Surg 35:898,1977.

15. Cooper SA, Reynolds DC, Kruger GO, et al. An analgesic relative potency assay comparing zomepirac sodium and aspirin. Clin Pharmacol 20-98, 1980.

16. Cooper SA, Wagenberg B, Zissu J et al. The analgesic efficacy of Suprofen in Periodontal and oral surgical pain. Pharmacotherapy 1986;6(5)267-276).

17. Forbes JA, Calderazzo JP, Bowser MW et al. A 12 hour evaluation of the Analgesic Efficacy of Diflunisal, Aspirin, and Placebo in Postoperative Dental pain. J. Clin Pharmacol. 1982; 22:89-96.

18. Forbes JA, Foor VM, Bowser MW et al. A 12 hour evaluation of the analgesic efficacy of diflunisal, propoxyphene, a propoxyphene-acetaminophen combination, and a placebo in postoperative oral surgery pain. Pharmacotherapy Vol 2, no 1, Jan/Feb 1982.

19. Forbes JA, Jones KF, King Smith W and Gongloff CM. Analgesic effect of an aspirin-codeine-butalbital-caffeine combination and an acetaminophen—codeine combination in postoperative oral surgery pain. Pharmacotherapy 6;(5), Sept/Oct 1986 240-246.

20. Forbes JA, Butterworth GA, Burchfield WH et al. Evaluation of flurbiprofen, acetaminophen, and acetaminophen-codeine combination, and placebo in postoperative oral surgery pain. Pharmacotherapy 1989;9(5):322-330).

21. Jain AK, Ryan JR, McMahon FG et al. Analgesic Efficacy of Low dose Ibuprofen in Dental Extraction Pain. Pharmacotherapy Vol 6, No. 6, Nov/Dec 1986.

22. Mardirossian G and Cooper S. Comparison of the Analgesic Efficacy of Flurbiporfen and aspirin for Postsurgical Dental Pain.J Oral Maxillofac Surg 43:106-109, 1985.

Chapter 46

Postmortem Redistribution and Interpretation of Drug Levels

Gourang Patel, B.S. Chem, Pharm.D., MSc, BCPS

46.1 Abstract

Determining the etiology, or cause of an event, in forensic cases often creates many theories. One piece of additional information which may be helpful in cases involving a drug or medication is concentration or serum level. Because many confounders can affect the interpretation of the drug level, it is imperative to also relate the data to the clinical scenario presented. Drug levels can be highly variable, depending on the sample time and location. Postmortem drugs levels often do not reflect the blood levels before death. A drug level can be elevated exclusively because of postmortem distribution. This may result in a conclusion of a poisoning as the cause of death when in fact the death resulted from nonpharmacologic or nontoxicologic causes. We advise against making any conclusions based solely on the drug level; rather an in-depth review of the clinical scenario, reference literature, and drug characteristics are required.

46.2 Introduction

The area of death investigation involves meticulous retrieval of information from a physical location, a subject, or both. During the course of the analysis of a medication or drug-related event, a routine part of the investigation centers around medication levels. Often these medication levels are drawn from the body during an autopsy. Factors to consider when deciding which tests should be ordered from the lab include the decedent's prescriptions, illicit drug(s) of choice, and any toxic substances he may have been exposed to. A common question in forensic pharmacology is whether the given toxicant caused or contributed to the death. Ideally, drug levels are most helpful if they are obtained immediately prior to and after a death. However, this is generally not the case. Autopsies and thus blood samples may not take place for days, weeks or longer after the person died. The goal of this brief review is to discuss the variables associated with interpretation of postmortem drug (medication) levels and how to determine if one or more drugs played a role in the etiology of an event in question.

46.3 Review of a Case File

The initial steps of an investigation require a careful review of the subject's case file. Prior to any interpretation of a drug level, there are several variables which need to be addressed. One such variable is the subject's medical history. The medical history can often provide vital information in regard to the patient's medication history (or evidence of prior exposure), and laboratory values, which all need to be integrated in order for a conclusion or opinion of the investigator to be formed.[1,2]

The concept of a patient being naïve (or non-tolerant) to a medication is often very helpful, as reaction and side effects can be quite different for a subject without previous exposure, versus one with a long history.[1] There are several types of information gathered during the investigation which can be grouped into either qualitative or quantitative data. Qualitative data can provide information about exposure; however, no further details on the extent of exposure can be gathered.[2] In the case of quantitative data, a drug level from a site in the subject's body (e.g., blood, organs, etc) can provide additional information with regard to the degree of exposure in many cases. In both scenarios, the investigator is cautioned about false-positive and false-negative results which may alter the perception, conclusion or opinion from a case review.

The analytical procedure of choice for most substances is gas chromatography / mass spectrometry (GC/MS), which carries a minimal risk of false positives in comparison to antibody-based tests. An additional piece of information that needs to be researched is whether the measured drug concentration falls within the acceptable safe range, as given by a standard reference.[3–5] The reference text provides factual information. What it does not provide, however, is an etiology or circumstances leading up to an event, so it cannot be solely relied upon to draw legally binding conclusions. An investigator should also consider specific autopsy findings that may indicate toxicity with a certain agent. For example, pulmonary edema is usually found in conjunction with a fatal opioid overdose.

46.4 Postmortem Considerations

The alterations and changes that occur to a medication after ingestion during life are grouped under pharmacokinetics. The concept of pharmacokinetics described the transformation of a drug via absorption, distribution, metabolism, and elimination that occurs during the process.[1,6] Postmortem redistribution (PMR) is a term used to describe the changes that may occur after death in the human body and relates it to alterations in chemistry and pharmacology which need to be considered. Changes that occur in drug levels due to redistribution after death is also termed necrokinetics. The concept of necrokinetics is critical when interpreting the postmortem drug level. Postmortem redistribution can be divided into categories: physiologic changes in the body after death (macro level and cellular level), and drug characteristics.[1,2] The quest for research into the drug changes which occur during PMR in humans are inherently difficult to construct and incomplete for obvious reasons; therefore, a fair amount of data is available from animal models as well.

A. Physiologic Changes in the Body After Death

At a cellular level there are several changes to incorporate into an investigation. The main variables affected after death are cell membranes, respiration, synthesis of proteins, and preservation of deoxyribonucleic acid (DNA). All of these are affected after death and need to be considered. For example, a cell's death can result in a release of its contents and/or create an environment of acidosis secondary to anaerobic metabolism that occurs. In addition, blood potassium (K) levels are increased postmortem secondary to cessation of the sodium/potassium (Na/K) ATPase pump function.[7] Drugs also have the capability to diffuse from organs/tissues in the body and back into circulation, as this process is passive. In addition, body decomposition or putrefaction can create an environment in which either bacteria can facilitate further metabolism of the drug, or in some instances substances can be produced

during putrefaction. For example, alcohol can be produced secondary to the process of putrefaction which begins shortly after the time of death.[8] In addition, the main substrate for ethanol production is glucose; therefore after death, the liver, lungs, and heart can be sites where it is generated and detected. The major sites of drug deposition are lungs, heart, liver, and gastrointestinal tract (GI). Depending on the drug characteristics, medications are able to facilitate movement from these areas and translate into either lower or higher than normal blood levels.[9] For example, alcohol has been well-known to diffuse from the GI tract into circulation after death.[10] In addition, certain organs (e.g., the lungs) facilitate the process due to their enriched blood supply, vascular access to the body, and membrane thinness. The liver appears more complicated, as the drug can diffuse via hepatic circulation and/or directly into adjacent organs. The heart is also more complex, in the respect that drugs may concentrate into the organ initially while a subject is alive; however, after death the right or left chamber can serve as a sampling site postmortem.[11–13]

B. Drug Characteristics

The drug characteristics that are involved in PMR are the following: absorption, distribution, metabolism, and elimination. Absorption can be affected by the integrity of the cell membrane and the pH of the medium. Movement of the drug can also be affected by the lipophilic solubility and the ionic state (i.e. pKa) of the drug. Drugs that possess lipophilic properties are able to concentrate in major organs (i.e., heart, lungs, and liver).[1,6] In addition, after death the cellular medium becomes more aqueous and acidic; therefore, movement of basic drugs becomes more likely. Distribution of drugs can also be altered after death.[12,13] In general, drugs that are more lipophilic will tend to have further redistribution after death and can translate into increased movement from tissues/organs into circulation where these are measured (see Table 46.1).[2] The volume of distribution (Vd) refers to the total volume into which the total amount of drug would be

Table 46.1
Variables that Support PMR and Drug Level Variance[4,14,16]

- Drug characteristics (e.g., pKa, Vd, lipophilicity)
- Putrefaction
- Drug interactions (e.g., inhibition, induction, protein binding-displacement)
- Site (e.g., arterial, venous, heart, etc.) of drug level sample
- Diffusion from stomach to other organs
- Body position and movement postmortem

distributed in order to reach the plasma. According to several experts, a Vd of greater than 3-4 L/kg can be indicative of PMR changes and increasing serum concentration after death.[2,14] However, this not an absolute rule. Drugs which are highly protein-bound generally will not have a high or extensive Vd; however drugs which are not heavily bound to plasma proteins are able to undergo PMR changes. For example, morphine is a drug that undergoes extensive metabolism, and its glucuronide byproducts can be detected after death. Additional examples are included within Table 46.2.[15] There are also characteristics which drugs can have which would make them more likely to stay within the plasma or even increase after death. Characteristics which are notable are polar compounds and medications with a low Vd (e.g., valproic acid, antibiotics, and furosemide).[1,16] Metabolism is also affected during PMR. Metabolism can persist for several hours after death has occurred and can include the breakdown of a drug into metabolites and byproducts. Obtaining both a drug and drug-metabolite level is helpful in determining the true effect of PMR on the metabolism process. Elimination of drugs occurs mainly via the hepatic and renal routes. Both processes are affected shortly after death and can result in accumulation of drug/metabolite(s) which may later be detected via laboratory analysis. The main factors regarding drug characteristics which are known to affect PMR include lipophilic nature, pKa, and Vd.[16,17]

Table 46.2
Drugs and Toxins that May Undergo PMR[2,4,16]

- Alprazolam
- Amitriptyline
- Amphetamine
- Cocaine
- Dextromethorphan
- Diazepam
- Flecanide
- Gammahydroxybutarate
- Haloperidol
- Ketamine
- Lidocaine
- Morphine
- Nicotine
- Phencyclidine
- Propafenone
- Remifentanyl
- Sufentanil
- Venlafaxine
- Zolpidem

46.5 Analysis of Drug Level Information

An investigator needs to have several concepts at the base of her practice when beginning the analysis of all the information and data available. Integrating the subject's clinical scenario with past medical history, medication profile (recent and past), and laboratory information (where applicable), is the key factor. This series of steps can provide the guidance needed to formulate the appropriate conclusion or opinion. One step that would be helpful in the drug level analysis would be the central to peripheral blood compartment ratio (C/P). The C/P ratios are generally the highest for basic compounds with a large Vd.[2,18] A caution about C/P ratio is that there is still active research as to whether or not these are able to be correlated to therapeutic, toxic, or fatal drugs levels; therefore, the interpretation and true utility of these is still debated. An additional factor that needs to be determined is the timing and location of the sample postmortem.[12,19,20] The drug level at the time of the autopsy will not reflect the drug level at the time of death. Autopsies may be performed after death: hours, days, weeks or even months later. The time interval between death and autopsy can translate into changes in concentrations of a drug and/or its metabolite(s) as well. Generally, the drug is less likely to be altered in the peripheral compartment immediately after death; however, the central compartment (blood from the heart) can reflect a higher drug level secondary to diffusion and translocation of the drug from other compartments (e.g., lungs) especially those with a high Vd.[19,20] In addition, there are inherent challenges with postmortem drug levels. Newly introduced drugs by the Food and Drug Administration (FDA) often may not have therapeutic defined serum reference levels or a standard assay to which to measure them. In clinical practice, blood samples taken for drug level analysis are typically obtained from a peripheral vein in the arm. During an autopsy, a blood sample may be obtained from the femoral artery or the heart chamber.

Another technique when reviewing postmortem drug levels is to review the subject's medical records that note the patient's condition before death. Did the subject exhibit classical signs and symptoms of the toxicity of the suspected agent? For example, a person overdosing on bupropion would have convulsions. When the suspect is treated in a hospital, ambulance, or other clinical situation just prior to death, the relevant records should be reviewed as part of the forensic investigation. Unfortunately, a common scenario is that the decedent is found in the home after an apparent sudden death.

46.6 Summary

An investigator has several important concepts to incorporate during the analysis of postmortem drug levels. Integrating the subject's case with past and current medical and medication history and laboratory values is vital in determining a plausible scenario. The information recorded above will allow the investigator to proceed with the next steps in determining time and the location in the body that the postmortem drug levels were obtained. As autopsies may not be performed the same day as a subject's death, PMR may have a significant role on drug levels, depending on the drug(s) in question. Finally, the investigator needs to concentrate on several drug properties which can alter the drug level postmortem which include, but are not limited to, the lipophilic nature, pKa, and Vd of the drug.[14,16] A careful analysis of the subject's case, autopsy report, and a review of the drug's characteristics, allows the investigator to form a more sustainable conclusion or opinion for a forensic case involving a postmortem drug level.[19]

Endnotes

1. Roberts DM and Buckley NA. Pharmacokinetic Considerations in Clinical Toxicology. *Clin Pharmacokinet.* 2007;46: 897-939.

2. Ferner RE. Post-mortem clinical pharmacology. *Br J Clin Pharmacol.* 2008;66: 430-443.

3. Winek CL, Wahba WW, Winek CL, et al. Drug and chemical blood-level data 2001. *Foren Sci Int.* 2001;122: 107-123.

4. Baselt, Randall. *Disposition of Toxic Drugs and Chemicals in Man.* 8th Edition. 2008.

5. Wennig R. Threshold values in toxicology- useful or not? Forensic Sci Int. 2000;113: 323-40.

6. Goodman and Gilmans Pharmacologic Basis of Therapeutics. 11th edition. Brunton LL, Chabner BA, and Knollmann BC. Chapter 2 *Pharmacokinetics.* Buxton IL and Benet LZ. Chapter 3 *Pharmacodynamics.* Blumenthal DK and Garrison JC. Chapter 4. *Drug Toxicity and Poisoning.* Osterhoudt KC and Penning TM. 2006.

7. Pelissier-Alicot AL, Gaulier JM, Champsaur P, et al. Mechanisms Underlying Postmortem Redistribution of Drugs: A Review. *J Anal Toxicol.* 2003;27: 533-544.

8. Robertson MD, Drummer OH. Post-mortem metabolism by bacteria. J Forensic Sci. 1995;40: 382-6.

9. Pounder DJ, Adams E, Fuke C, et al. Site to site variability of postmortem drug concentrations in liver and lung. J Forensic Sci. 1996;41: 927-32.

10. Pounder DJ, Smith DRW. Postmortem diffusion of alcohol from the stomach. Am J Forensic Sci. 1995;16: 89-96.

11. Flanagan RJ, Connally G. Interpretation of analytical toxicology results in life and at postmortem. Toxicol Rev. 2005;24: 51-6.

12. Skopp G. Preanalytic aspects in postmortem toxicology. Forensic Sci Int. 2004;142: 75-100.

13. Jones GR, Pounder DJ. Site dependence of drug concentrations in postmortem blood-a case study. J Anal Toxicol. 1987;11: 186-190.

14. Yarema MC and Becker CE. Key Concepts in Postmortem Drug Redistribution. *Clin Toxicol.* 2005;43: 235-241.

15. Gerostamoulos J, Drummer OH. Postmortem redistribution of morphine and its metabolites. J Forensic Sci. 2000;45: 843-845.

16. Leikin JB and Watson WA. Post-mortem Toxicology: What the Dead Can and Cannot Tell Us. *Clin Toxicol.* 2003;41: 47-56.

17. Drummer OH. Postmortem toxicology of drugs of abuse. *Forensic Sci Int.* 2004;142: 101-113.

18. Kennedy MC. Post-mortem drug concentrations. *Int Med J.* 2010;40: 183-187.

19. Drummer OH. Forensic toxicology. *Molecular, Clinical, and Environmental Toxicology.* 2010;100: 579-603.

20. Maurer HH. Analytical toxicology. *Molecular, Clinical, and Environmental Toxicology* 2010; 100: 317-37.

Chapter 47

Guideline for Injectable Medications

Saifi Vohra, Pharm.D., RPh, MBA, FASHP, FASCP

47.1 Introduction

Navigating the hundreds of injectable drugs available on the current pharmaceutical market can present a challenge to even the most seasoned healthcare professional. This chapter lists the antibiotics, antineoplastics, vaccines, cardiac medications, and newly released biotech drugs available to the prescribing physician.

In today's era of skyrocketing medical costs, pharmacists and nurses play an increasingly critical role — especially in regards to the administration and preparation of injectable drugs and delivery systems. In recent years, medication errors and patient safety issues have received increasing concern. With patient-focused pharmaceutical care in mind, it is important that the pharmacist have a broad depth of knowledge or at least a readily accessible resource. Other professional staff constantly challenge pharmacists in regards to intravenous preparations and infusion related issues.[1-5] Administration, preparation, infusion, storage, and stability related questions are frequently asked to pharmacists in every nursing unit of every hospital and clinic. Whether working as part of a healthcare team or in a decentralized capacity, pharmacists become drug information resources and educators to doctors, nurses, and patients alike. Due to the rapid growth of new drug therapies, and an increasing awareness of adverse effects, it becomes essential to maintain a current knowledge of injectable drug guidelines. To meet the challenge of educating and sharing information to pharmacists and other professional staff, the following information has been prepared and presented.

47.2 Intramuscular Injections

Intramuscular injections (IM) are very common despite the complex techniques required to deliver medication deep inside the large muscles of the body. More than 12 billion IM injections are administered annually throughout the world. However, it is not a benign procedure, and unsafe injection practices are estimated to have significant impacts on patient morbidity and mortality and to result in millions of dollars in direct medical costs on an annual basis.[9]

47.3 Intravenous Medication

Intravenous medication (IV), especially antibiotics, should be infused in a timely fashion, with appropriate fluid to provide minimal irritation to the vessel, with the least chance of infiltration, and without causing fluid overload. In recent years, medications were not consistently being prepared and administered within the appropriate fluids and timeframes (usually 30 to 60 minutes). Consequently, the risk of fluid overload loomed high.[10]

In addition to fluid and time concerns, drug stability and compatibility are also critical elements in the accurate and appropriate administration of IV medication. Both the therapeutic adequacy and safety of a drug can be adversely affected by instability, incompatibility and incorrect methods of preparation. The term instability is usually applied to chemical reactions that are incessant, irreversible, and result in distinctly different entities that can be both therapeutically inactive and metabolically toxic. Incompatibility generally refers to physiochemical phenomena such as concentration-dependent precipitation and acid-base reactions that result in a change of physical state.[12]

Intravenous drug preparation consumes a significant portion of resources in critical care areas such as anesthesia (especially in complex cases)[11] and intensive care. When heavy patient loads and hectic schedules demand quick decisions, a readily available IV drug preparation guideline is an invaluable asset.

47.4 Conclusion

Table 47.1 is designed to provide information about more than 475 commercially available injectable drugs in hospital settings. Drug information is arranged alphabetically according to generic names followed by proprietary (trade) names. This table includes the name of the drug product, package size, route of administration, dosage range, dilution and preparation instructions, time of infusion, stability of different forms including intravenous piggyback (IVPB), syringe, and vial and any text contained in a precaution, notes, or comment section. The author has made every effort to condense the most relevant information into this table. It is our hope that it will be a useful resource and helpful guide to nurses and pharmacists alike in a variety of clinical settings.

Endnotes

1. *Micromedex.* www.micromedex.com. Accessed November 7, 2011.

2. Trissel, Lawrence A. *Handbook on Injectable Drugs, Sixteenth Edition.* American Society of Health-Systems Pharmacists, 2010.

3. King, James C. *King Guide to Parenteral Admixtures.* King Guide Publications, Inc., 2003.

4. Gahart, Betty L. *Intravenous Medications 2003.* Mosby, 2002.

5. *Drug Facts and Comparisons 2009 (Drug Facts & Comparisons).* Lippincott Williams & Wilkins, 2009.

6. Drug package inserts.

7. Vohra, S., R. Patel, and P. Do. "Guideline for injectable Medications: For Intramuscular &/or Intravenous Use—1998," *Journal of Pharmacy Practice*, August 1998, 9: p. 4.

8. Kirschenbaum, B. E. and C. J. Latiolis. "The stability of injectable Medication after reconstitution and/or Further dilution," *Parenteral,* Special Issue 1986, 4(5a): 1.

9. Nicoll, L. H. and A. Hesby. "Intramuscular injection: an integrative research review and guideline for evidence-based practice," *Applied Nursing Research*, August 2002, 15(3): 149-62.

10. Axton, S. E. and B. Hall. "An innovative method of administering I.V. medications to children," *Pediatric Nursing* 1994 Jul-Aug, 20(4): 341-44, 355.

11. Fraind, D. B., J. M. Slagle, V. A. Tubbesing, S. A. Hughes, and M. B. Weinger. "Reengineering intravenous drug and fluid administration processes in the operating room," *Anesthesiology,* July 2002, 97(1): 139-47.

12. Newton, D. W. "Physicochemical determinants of incompatibility and instability of drugs for injection and infusion." *American Journal of Hospital Pharmacy*, 1978, 35: 1213-22.

13. Centers for Disease Control and Prevention. "Vaccines: HOME page for Vaccines and Immunizations site." Accessed November 7, 2011. www.cdc.gov/vaccines.

Table 47.1
Guideline For Injectable Medication—2009

This table is designed to provide information about number of many injecatble drugs in hospital settting. The information includes name of the drug, package size, route of administeration, dosage range, dilution and preparation, time of infusion, stability of different form including IVPB, syringe and vial and also specific precaution in notes / comment sections.

Drug Name	Package Size	Routes of Administration			Injectable Preparation		IVPB Preparation			Stability			Notes/ Comments
		IVP	IM	SC	Dilute with	Conc.	Dose	Solutions	Administration rate	Reconstituted in vial	In a syringe	In Piggy bag	
Abciximab (Reopro)	10 mg/5 mL vial	2 mg/mL over 1 min (Dose = 0.25 mg/kg)	Not advised	N/A	Dilute w NS / D5W	2 mg/mL	9 mg/4.5 mL	250 mL NS or D5W	Cont. infusion: 0.125 mcg/kg/min—up to 80 kg—see protocol	Single Use Vial	12 hrs RF	24 hrs	Filter using a 0.22 micron filter. Infuse through a low protein binding filter. Avoid shaking vials. Vials in Refrigerator.
Abatacept (Orencia)	250 mg vial single use	IVPB	No	No	Dilute w 1 mL SWFI	25 mg/mL	500-1000 mg	100 mL NS	30 min	single use	N/A	RT 24 hrs	Must be used within 24 hrs of reconstitution.
ADALIMUMAB (Humira)	20 and 40 mg syringe	No	No	Yes	N/A	All doses	40-160 mg	N/A	SQ only	till expiration date	N/A	RF	discard unused portion.
Acetazolamide (Diamox)	500 mg vial (powder for reconstitution)	100 mg/ mL at 250 mg/min	Not advised	N/A	5 mL SW	100 mg/mL	Not recommended			12 hrs RT; 3 d RF	12 hrs RT; 3 d RF	N/A	Single Dose Vial
Acyclovir (Zovirax)	500 mg vial (powder for reconstitution)	Not advised	Not advised	N/A	5 mL SW, D5W, NS	100 mg/mL	0-700 mg; >700 mg	100 mL D5W or NS; 250 mL D5W or NS	100 mL/hr (Over 1 hr); 250 mL/hr (Over 1 hr)	12 hrs RT	Not advised	72 hrs RT	Do not Refrigerate; Max Dose 30 mg/kg
Adenosine (Adenocard, Adenoscan)	6 mg / 2 mL vials	6 mg over 2 seconds Conc. = 3 mg/mL	Not advised	N/A	N/A	3 mg/mL	IV Push Preferred (Can make 0.75 mg/mL in 0.9% normal saline); 140 mcg/kg/min x 6 min			Single Use Vial	Send Vials	72 hrs at RT	Follow each dose with a saline flush; Do not Refrigerate. Central line preffered
Albumin	5% 250 mL and 25% 50 mL, 100 mL	5-10 mL/ min of 5% solution	Not advised	N/A	N/A	5% and 25%	May dilute with normal saline, May be given thru buretrol over 30-120 min			4 hrs once vial opened	N/A	4 hrs	Do not Refrigerate
Aldeslukin	22mu	N/A	N/A	N/A	N/A		22mu in SWFI 1.2 mL	D5W	Final conc 18u/mL		14 D at RF		Incompatible with NS
Alfentanil	500mcg/mL 1 or 2 mL amp	N/A	Yes	Yes	Diluted	.5 mg/mL		D5W, NS, & LR	May be given as CIVI	Stable at RT	16 wks 5% D, 24 hr-NS	N/A	Dose depends on duration of surgical procedure
Alprostadil (Prostin)	500 mcg / 1 mL Ampules	Must Dilute before administering	Not advised	N/A	N/A	500 mcg/ mL	500 mcg; 500 mcg	25 mL NS or D5W; 250 mL NS or D5W	Cont. Infusion: 0.05-0.1 mcg/kg/min (0.25-6.7 mcg/min)	Single use amps	72 hrs in RF	24 hrs at RT	Keep In Refrigerate

Drug Name	Package Size	Routes of Administration			Injectable Preparation		IVPB Preparation			Stability			Notes/Comments
		IVP	IM	SC	Dilute with	Conc.	Dose	Solutions	Administration rate	Reconstituted in vial	In a syringe	In Piggy bag	
Alteplase (Activase, Cathflo)	2 mg vial (powder for reconstitution); 50 mg vial (Powder for reconstitution); 100 mg vial (Powder for reconstitution)	15 mg bolus at a conc. of 1 mg/mL over 2 min; May give 2 mg for Cath Care	Not advised—IV Only	N/A	2.2 mL SW; 50 mL SW provided; 100 mL SW provided	1 mg/mL	0.75 mg/kg (max 50 mg) infused over 30 min, then 0.5 mg/kg (max 35 mg) infused over 60 min. Conc. of 0.5–1 mg/mL diluted in NS or D5W (do not dilute less than 0.5 mg/mL; may precipitate)			8 hrs at RT or RF	8 hrs at RT or RF	8 hrs at RT or RF	May be frozen with a 6 month expiration; Flush line with 50 mL or NS after each dose. IV use only
Aminocaproic Acid (Amicar)	5 gm / 20 mL Vial	Not advised	Not advised	N/A	N/A	250 mg/mL	All Doses	100 mL NS or D5W	100 mL/hr (Over 1 hr); Cont Infusion 1-1.25 gm/hr	MDV	72 hr	72 hrs RT or RF	Max dose 4-5 gm (16-20 mL)
Aminophylline (theophylline Ethylene Diamine)	250 mg / 10 mL and 500 mg / 20 mL vial	Not advised	Not advised	N/A	N/A	25 mg/mL	0-500 mg / 1 gm	50 mL D5W or NS / 500 mL D5W	100 mL/hr (Over 30 min) / Cont. Infusion	SDV	N/A	48 hrs at RT	Do Not Refrigerate. Protect From Light.
Amiodarone (Cordarone IV)	150 mg / 3 mL Ampules	6 mg/mL given at a rate of 15 mg/min (over 3-5 min)	Not advised	N/A	N/A	50 mg/mL	150 mg / 450 mg	100 mL D5W / 250 mL D5W (GLASS)	600 mL/hr (Over 10 min) / Cont. Infusion	Single Dose Amps	Use Immediately	2 hrs in PVC bag, 72 hrs in Glass; Store at RT	Make in a glass bottle. Use 0.22 micron filter, Do not refrigerate
Amifostine (Ethylol)	500 mg vial	N/A	N/A	N/A	500 mg	50 mg/mL	500 mg	NS 50-100 mL	Infuse over 7-15 min	5 hrs RT	24 hrs RF		Do not mix except NS
Amitriptyline (Elavil)	10 mg/mL vial	No	IM	N/A	diluted	10 mg/mL	Not recommended			N/A	N/A	Vial store at RT	Protect from light
Amonium Chloride	5 mEq/mL 20 mL vial	Slow IV	N/A	N/A	diluted	5mEq/mL	100 mEq	D5W, NS, LR .5-1L	over 3 hrs	N/A	N/A	N/A	Monitor Sod Bicarb level and adjust dose. Store at RT.
Amobarbital (Amytal)	250 mg or 500 mg vial	Slow IV	Deep IM	N/A	5 mL NS, D5, D10, D20%	100 mg/mL	65-500 mg	NS, D5, D10, D20%	Do not exceed rate 50 mg/min	30 min after reconstitution	N/A	RT	Do not shake, IV is restricted use only
Amphotericin B (Fungizone)	50 mg vial (Powder for reconstitution)	Not advised	Not advised	N/A	10 mL SW	5 mg/mL	0-25 mg / 26-50 mg	250 mL D5W / 500 mL D5W	Over 2-6 hrs	24 hrs RT; 7 D RF; Undiluted vials stable for 2 weeks at RT	24 hrs RT; 7 d RF	3 d at RT; 7 d RF	Protect from light; Premeds 15-30 m prior to infusion; DO NOT FILTER;

Drug Name	Package Size	Routes of Administration			Injectable Preparation		IVPB Preparation			Stability			Notes/Comments
		IVP	IM	SC	Dilute with	Conc.	Dose	Solutions	Administration rate	Reconstituted in vial	In a syringe	In Piggy bag	
Ampicillin (Amcill, Omnipen-N)	125 mg vial (Powder for reconstitution)	Over 10-15 min	Yes: See Below	N/A	1.2 mL NS	125 mg/mL	See Below			4 hrs RF	Send Vial	8 hrs at RT, 72 hrs RF	Max dose 150-200 mg/kg/day; Dilute only with NS (Increases Stability)
	250 mg Vial (powder)				2.3 mL NS	100 mg/mL							
	500 mg vial (Powder)		IM/Buretrol Prep.: Dilute 125 mg vial with 1.2 mL yielding 125 mg/mL; 250 mg vial with 1 mL, 500 mg vial with 2 mL, 1 gm vial with 4 mL, and 2 gm vial with 8 mL—all yielding 250 mg/mL		4.8 mL NS	100 mg/mL							
	1 gm Vial (Powder)				9.6 mL NS	100 mg/mL	0-1 gm	50 mL NS	200 mL/hr (Over 15 min)				
	2 gm Vial (Powder)				19.2 mL NS	100 mg/mL	1001 mg-2 gm	100 mL NS	200 mL/hr (Over 30 min)				
Ampicillin & Sulbactam (Unasyn)	1.5 gm Vial (Powder for reconstitution)	Not advised; may be given over 10-15 min	Yes: see below	N/A	6.5 mL SW	200 mg/mL	0-1.5 gm	50 mL NS	100 mL/hr (Over 30 min)	8 hrs at RT or RF (200 mg/mL) 1 hr at 375 mg/mL	One hr—IM injection at conc. of 375 mg/mL	8 hrs in NS at RT; 72 hrs Refrig	Dilute only with NS (Increases Stability)
	3 gm Vial (Powder for reconstitution)		IM/Buretrol Prep.: Dilute each 1.5 gm w/3.2 mL lidocaine or SW to give 375 mg/mL		13 mL SW	200 mg/mL	1.5-3 gm	100 mL NS	200 mL/hr (Over 30 min)				
Amrinone Premixed (Inamrinone)	300 mg / 250 mL	Not advised	Not advised	N/A	Already Prepared	1.2 mg/mL	300 mg	250 mL NS	CIVI at 5-10 mcg/kg/min	N/A	N/A	RT	High alert drug. Avoid long term intermittent use
Antihemophilic factor (Xyntha)	250 IU, 500IU 1000 IU, 2000IU powder	IVP	No	No	4 mL NS diluent included	62.5-200IU/mL	all doses	diluent given with drug	over 5-15 mins	3 hrs	3 hrs	Use within 3 hrs	Keep RF, may store RT at 3 months
Alfentanil (Alfenta)	500mcg/mL	CIVI	Yes	Yes	D5W, NS, LR	25-80mcg/mL	varying dosing	D5W, NS, LR	start 0.3-5mcg/min upto 75mcg/kg as needed	N/A	N/A	Controlled RT	Dose varies depened on case by case
Anthrax vaccine (Biothrax)	0.5 mL	No	IM only	No	N/A	0.5 mL	5doses of 0.5 mL at 0 and 4 wks, then 6, 12, and 18 months	N/A	IM only	RF	N/A	N/A	Primary immunization q 2weeks x 3 doses or post exposure immediately then 2 & 4 wks DO NOT FREEZ
Antithymocyte Globulin (ATGAM)	50 mg/mL	No	No	No	NS, D51/4NS, D51/2NSl	1 mg/mL	10-20 mg/kg/day	1/4, 1/2 or NS 1L	Over 4-8 hrs	N/A	N/A	24 hrs RF	Test dose:0.1 mL of 1:1000 dilution, Do not use Dextrose, Do not shake vial
Aportinin (Trasylol)	10,000 Kiu/mL (1.4 mg) 100 or 200 mL vial	No	No	No	Diluted	1.4 mg/mL	CIVI at 50 mL/hr after test dose of 1 mL over 10 min			N/A	N/A	N/A	Central line only Surgical setting w complex regimine

Drug Name	Package Size	Routes of Administration			Injectable Preparation		IVPB Preparation				Stability			Notes/Comments
		IVP	IM	SC	Dilute with	Conc.	Dose	Solutions	Administration rate	Reconstituted in vial	In a syringe	In Piggy bag		
Ariprazol (abilify)	single dose, 5.25 mg / 0.7 mL 15 mg /2 mL	Do not give IV	IM only	No	N/A	all doses	5.25-15 mg/day	N/A	IM only	N/A	N/A	RT	slow, deep into muscle mass
Arginine	Diluted solution	IV only	No	No	D5W, D10W	N/A	6-30 gm/d	300 mL	over 30 min	RT	N/A	N/A	Hypertonic Solution, IV use only
Argotroban	250-500 mg premix bag	IVPB	No	No	NS, D5W or LR	1 mg/mL	varying dosing	250-500 mL NS	2mcg/kg/min	24 hrs RT, 48 hrs RF	24 hrs RT, 48 hrs RF	24 hrs RT, 48 hrs RF	do not exceed 10mcg/kg/min
Arsenic Trioxide	10 mg/10 mL amp	No	No	No	diluted	1 mg/mL	0.15-0.25 mg/kg/day	100-250 mL D5W or NS	IV over 1-2 hrs upto 4 hr	N/A	24 hrs Rt, 48 hrs RF	RT	Do not Freez
Asparaginase (Elspar)	10000 u	Yes, 2000u/mL over 5-10 min	Yes, 10000 u/mL	No	NS	10000 u/mL or 2000u/mL	1000 units/kg/day IV	NS 1L	over 30 min	N/A	8 hrs RT, 7 d RF	8 hrs RF	give test dose, Do not use if cloudy
Atenolol (Tenormin IV)	5 mg/10 mL vial	5 mg over 5 min at 1 mg/min	Not advised	N/A	N/A	0.5 mg/mL	5 mg	50 mg D5W or NS	200 mL/hr (Over 15 min)	Single Dose Amps	Send Amps	48 hrs at RT	Do not refrigerate
Atracurium Besylate (Tracrium)	10 mL vial (10 mg/mL)	Adm Rapidly; May give undiluted if needed; conc. 10 mg/mL	Not advised	N/A	N/A	10 mg/mL	100 mg / 200 mg	50 mL NS or D5W / 100 mL NS or D5W	2-30mcg/kg/min	14 days at RT; Single use vial	72 hrs RT or RF	24 hrs RT or RF	Vials are refrigerated
Atropine	0.4 mg / 0.5 mL Amps; 1 mg / 10 mL Syringe; 8 mg / 20 mL Vial	For bradycardia conc. = 0.1 mg/mL; rate = 1 mg/min followed by saline flush	Yes; 0.3-1.2 mg	Yes; 0.3-1.2 mg	N/A	0.4 and 0.1 mg/mL	Not recommended			Single Dose Amps and MDVs	Send Amps (Single Dose); MDV = 30 days	N/A	ACLS min dose = 0.5 mg; Max dose (cumulative) = 2 mg; Protect from Direct Light
Atropine & Edrophonium	10 mg/0.14 mg per 15 mL vials	0.05-0.1 mL/kg over 1 min	Not advised	N/A	N/A	0.66 & 0.01 mg/mL	Not recommended			MDV	30 days RT or RF	N/A	
Azathioprine (Imuran)	100 mg vial	Yes	No	No	SWFI 10 mL	!0 mg/mL	50-100 mg	NS, D5W 50-100 mL	Over 30-60 min	24 hrs RT or RF	24 hrs RT or RF	24 hrs RT	protect from light
Azithromycin (Zithromax)	500 mg vial (powder for reconstitution)	Not advised	Not advised	N/A	4.8 mL SW	100 mg/mL	0-250 mg / 251-500 mg	125 mL D5W or NS / 250 mL D5W or NS	125 mL/hr (Over 1 hr) / 250 mL/hr (Over 1 hr)	24 hrs RT or RF	24 hrs RT or RF	24 hrs RT; 7 D RF	Max dose = 500 mg/day

Drug Name	Package Size	Routes of Administration			Injectable Preparation		IVPB Preparation			Stability			Notes/ Comments
		IVP	IM	SC	Dilute with	Conc.	Dose	Solutions	Administration rate	Reconstituted in vial	In a syringe	In Piggy bag	
Azlocillin	3 gm, 4 gm	N/A	not advised	N/A	NS, D5W, 1/2 NS or LR	10, 50 & 100 mg/mL	2-5 gm q 8 hrs	D5W 50-100 mL	over 30 min	N/A	N/A	N/A	Frozen PB
Aztreonam (Azactam FrozenPB*)	1 gm Vial (Powder for reconstitution)	Not advised (200 mg/mL; 1 gm over 3-5 min)	Yes; dilute w/ about 3 mL per gm of NS or SW	N/A	9.6 mL SW	100 mg/mL	0-1 gm	50 mL NS	100 mL/hr (Over 30 min)	48 hrs RT; 7 d RF	48 hrs RT; 7 D RF	48 hrs RT; 7 d RF	Max dose = 8 gm/day; dilute w/ NS to prolong expiration, frozen PB
							1001 mg-2 gm	100 mL NS	100 mL/hr (Over 1 hr)				
BCG (bacillus of Calmette & Guerine) Vaccine (Therasys)	Various products Dry powder (81 mg)	Yes	No	Yes	1 amp in 3 mL SWFI			Preservative free NS 50 mL	check protocol	mix prior to use	2 hrs in RF		Avoid inhalation bladder cancer: intravesically/wk x 6 wks then 3, 6, 12, 18 and 24 months, bladder irrigation
Bendamustine (Treanda)	100 mg vial powder	IVPB	no	no	20 mL SWFI	5 mg/mL	90-120 mg/m2	500 mL NS	over 30-60 min	30 min	N/A	24 hrs RF, 3 hrs at RT	Adequate hydration is required
Benztropine (Cogentin)	2 mg/2 mL amps	1-4 mg; rarely given	Yes; 1-4 mg BID	N/A	N/A	1 mg/mL	See IM or IV administration			Single Use	72 hrs RT or RF	N/A	IM/IV time to onset the same
Betamethasone Sodium Phosphate and Acetate (Celestone)	30 mg / 5 mL vials	Not advised	Up to 9 mg/day	N/A	N/A	6 mg/mL	Not recommended—only give IM			MDV	30 D RT or RF	N/A	IM contraindicated in thrombocytopenic purpura
Bethanechol (Urecholine)	5 mg	No	No	Yes	N/A	N/A	N/A			N/A	N/A	N/A	SC only
Bevacizumab (Avastin)	25 mg/mL in 4 mL or 16 mL vials	IVPB	No	No	100 mL NS	0.25 mg/mL	5-15 mg/kg	100 mL NS	over 90 mins	N/A	N/A	8 hrs RF	Do not mix with dextrose containing solution.
Bivalirudin (Angiomax)	250 mg powder	CIVI	No	No	5 mL SWFI	5 mg/mL	varying dosing	SWFI or NS or NS	Continueos infusion	N/A	N/A	24 hrs RT	continous infusion 1.75 mg/kg/hr
Bleomycin (Blenoxane)	15u(15 mg) vial	Yes	Yes	Yes	BNS/NS 6 mL or 10 mL	2.5 u/mL or 1 mg/mL	various	In 250-1000 mL NS	IV push over 10 min, CIVI varies		24 hrs RT, 30 D in RF (BNS)	24 hrs	Can administer Intra arterial and IP, intrapleural
Brettylium (Bretylol)	500 mg syringe, 10 mL amp	Yes	Yes	No	diluted	50 mg/mL	various	D5W or NS 250-500 mL	1-2 mg/kg/min over >8 min, CIVI	N/A	N/A	24 hrs	May be frozen with a 6 month expiration; Flush line with 50 mL or NS after each dose. IV use only
Bumetanide (Bumex)	0.5 mg / 2 mL and 1 mg / 4 mL vials	<3 mg give over 1-2 min	Yes	N/A	N/A	0.25 mg/mL	>3 mg	50 mL NS or D5W	100 mL/hr (Over 30 min)	SDVs and MDVs	72 hrs from SDV; 30 days from MDV	24 hrs in NS; 72 hrs in D5W at RT	Protect vial from light. Store at Room Temp
							12 mg	500 mL D5W	Cont Inf. of 38 mL/hr				
Bupivacaine (Marcaine)	various Preservative free	Yes	Yes	Yes	NS	various	various, slow IV			MDV	N/A	RT	may administer Epdural, intradermal, intratheical

Drug Name	Package Size	Routes of Administration			Injectable Preparation		IVPB Preparation			Stability			Notes/Comments
		IVP	IM	SC	Dilute with	Conc.	Dose	Solutions	Administration rate	Reconstituted in vial	In a syringe	In Piggy bag	
Bupivacaine with Epinephrine	Various	Not advised	Not advised	N/A	N/A	various	Various—see protocols (in NS for epidural use)			SDVs and MDVs	N/A	72 hrs RT or RF	Do not use 0.75% for OB epidurals
Buprenorphine (Buprenex)	0.3 mg/1 mL amps	Given slowly over 3-5 min	Yes	N/A	N/A	0.3 mg/mL	0.9 mg	30 mL NS	PCA: Conc. is 0.03 mg/mL	72 hrs RT or RF	72 hrs RT or RF	72 hrs RT or RF	Protect from light and excessive heat
Butorphanol (Stadol)	2 mg/mL; 1 mL vial	2 mg over 3-5 min	2-8 mg q 4-8 hr	N/A	N/A	2 mg/mL	Not recommended			SDV	Send Vial	N/A	Store at RT and protect from light
Caffeine and Sodium Benzoate	0.5gm/2 mL amps	Emergency only; 250 mg over 1 min	Yes	N/A	N/A	0.25 mg/mL	See IV push or IM administration				Send Amp	N/A	max 2.5 gm / 24 hr
Calcitonin Salmon (Calcimar)	400 Units/2 mL vial	Not advised	100-200 IU daily	100-200 IU daily	N/A	200 Intl Units/mL	For IM or SQ use.			MDV	14 days	N/A	Refrigerate
Calcitriol (Calcijex)	1 mcg/1 mL amps	1-2 mcg, rapid IVP in Hemo Dialysis	Not advised	2 mcg into abd.	N/A	1 and 2 mcg/mL	See IV push or SQ administration			N/A	8 hrs RT	N/A	Protect from light; Store at RT
Calcium Chloride	1000 mg / 10 mL (10%)	50 mg/min, cardiac monitoring; 0.5-1 mL over 1 min	Not advised	N/A	N/A	100 mg/mL; 1.36 mEq/mL	0-1 gm / 1001 mg-2 gm	100 mL NS or D5W / 250 mL NS or D5W	Max rate of 50 mg/min; (max 14 mEq/min) (over 1 hr)	24 hr vial stability (SDV)	N/A	24 hrs RT or RF	CIVI preferred. Do not give IV push if patient is on Digoxin
Calcium Disodium Versenate (Edetate Calcium Disodium)	1000 mg / 5 mL Amps	Not advised	Yes; Dilute with Lidocaine	N/A	N/A	200 mg/mL	1 gm/m2/d	250-500 mL D5W or NS	over 8-24 hrs	Single Dose Amps	Send Amps	24 hrs RT or RF	monitor urine output closely. Can cause nephrotoxicity.
Calcium Gluconate	1000 mg / 10 mL; 10 mL vial	0.5-2 mL/min of a 10% solution; Max 200 mg/min	Yes, but not recommended	N/A	N/A	100 mg/mL (0.465 mEq/mL	1 gm / 1001 mg-2 gm	100 mL NS or D5W / 250 mL NS or D5W	Max rate of 200 mg/min of CaGluc (Over 1 hr)	24 hr vial stability (SDV)	24 hrs	24 hrs RT or RF	Do not give IV push if patient is on Digoxin
Carboplatinum (paraplatinum)	50, 150 & 450 mg vilas	No	No	No	NS, D5W or SWFI	10 mg/mL	Any dose	150-250 mL D5W or NS	over 30-60 min		24 hrs RT/RF in D5W	8 hrs RT/RF in NS	Protect from light
Carmustine (BCNU)	100 mg	No	No	No	w 3 mL diluent (alcohol) plus 27 mL SWFI	3.3 mg/mL	various	250-500 mL D5 W	over 1-2 hrs	N/A	8 hrs RT 48 hrs RF		Glass bottle; protect from light; avoid skin contact

Drug Name	Package Size	Routes of Administration			Injectable Preparation		IVPB Preparation			Stability			Notes/Comments
		IVP	IM	SC	Dilute with	Conc.	Dose	Solutions	Administration rate	Reconstituted in vial	In a syringe	In Piggy bag	
Carboprost (Hemabate)	250 mcg / 1 mL amp	Not advised	Yes; 250 mcg	N/A	N/A	250 mcg/mL	Not recommended—give IM			Single Dose Ampules	Send Amps	N/A	dilute immediately prior to administration
Cefazolin (Keizol/Ancef)	1 gm Vial (Powder for reconstitution)	Not advised; 100 mg/mL; 1 gm over 3-5 min.	Yes; See Below	N/A	9.6 mL SW	100 mg/mL	0-1.5 gm	50 mL D5W or NS	100 mL/hr (Over 30 min)	24 hrs RT; 4 D RF	24 hrs RT; 4 D RF	4 D RT; 10 D RF	Max Dose = 12 gm/day; Refrigerate, Frozen PB
			IM/Buretrol Prep.: dilute 500 mg vial w/ 2 mL SW or NS to yield 225 mg/mL or dilute 1 gm vial with 2.5 mL to yield 330 mg/mL		45 mL SW	200 mg/mL	>1.5 gm	100 mL D5W or NS	200 mL/hr (Over 30 min)				
Cefepime (Maxipime)	2 gm Vial (Powder for reconstitution)	Not advised	Yes—0.5-1 gm	N/A	20 mL	100 mg/mL	1 gm	50 mL NS	100 mL/hr (over 30 min)	24 hrs RT; 7 D RF	24 hrs RT; 7 D RF	24 hrs RT; 7 D RF	Protect from light
							2 gm	100 mL NS	200 mL/hr (over 60 min)				
Cefotaxime (Claforan)	1 gm Vial (Powder for reconstitution)	Not advised; conc. 100 mg/mL; 1 gm over 5 min	Yes; See Below	N/A	9.6 mL SW	100 mg/mL	0-1 gm	50 mL D5W or NS	100 mL/hr (Over 30 min)	12 hrs at IM conc., 24 hrs IV conc. at RT; 7 D RF	24 hrs RT; 7 D RF	24 hrs RT; 10 D RF	Max Dose = 12 gm/day Frozen PB
			IM Prep: Dilute 1 gm w/ 3 mL = 300 mg/mL				1001 mg-2 gm	100 mL D5W or NS	200 mL/hr (Over 30 min)				
Cefotetan (Cefotan)	1 gm Vial (Powder for reconstitution)	Not advised; Conc. 100 mg/mL; 1 gm over 3-5 min	Not advised	N/A	9.6 mL SW	100 mg/mL	1 gm	50 mL D5W or NS	100 mL/hr (Over 30 min)	24 hrs RT; 4 D RF	24 hrs RT; 4 D RF	24 hrs at RT; 4 D RF	Max dose = 6 gm/day refrigerate
	2 gm Vial (Powder for reconstitution)	Not advised; conc. 100 mg/mL; 1 gm given over 5 min	IM/Buretrol Prep.: Dilute w/ NS, SW, or Lidocaine; 1 gm w/ 2 mL = 400 mg/mL, 2 gm w/ 3 mL = 500 mg/mL				2 gm	100 mL D5W or NS	200 mL/hr (Over 30 min)				
Cefotetan (Cefotan) FrozenPB	1 gm / 50 mL Premixed	Not advised	Not advised	N/A	Already Prepared; Pre-mixed bag	Already Prepared; Pre-mixed bag	All Doses	Already Prepared	100 mL/hr (Over 30 min)	N/A	N/A	48 hrs RT; 21 D RF	
Cefoxitin (Mefoxin)	1 gm Vial (Powder for reconstitution)	Not advised; 100 mg/mL, 1 gm given over 5 min	Not advised	N/A	9 mL SW	100 mg/mL	All Doses	50 mL D5W or NS	100 mL/hr (Over 30 min)	48 hrs RT; 7 D RF	48 hrs RT; 7 D RF	24 hrs RT; 7 D RF	Refrigerate. IV Push causes Thrombophlebitis
Ceftazidime (Fortaz, Tazicef)	1 gm Vial (Powder for reconstitution)	Conc. 100 mg/mL; 1 gm given over 3-5 min	Yes	N/A	9.6 mL SW	100 mg/mL	0-1 gm	50 mL D5W or NS	100 mL/hr (Over 30 min)	24 hrs RT; 7 D RF. 8 hrs RT, 4 D RF at 280 mg/mL	24 hrs RT; D RF	24 hrs at RT; 7 D RF	Max dose = 6 gm/day Frozen PB available
			IM Prep: Dilute 1 gm w/ 3 mL NS or Lidocaine = 280 mg/mL				1001 mg-2 gm	100 mL D5W or NS	200 mL/hr (Over 30 min)				

Drug Name	Package Size	Routes of Administration			Injectable Preparation		IVPB Preparation				Stability			Notes/ Comments
		IVP	IM	SC	Dilute with	Conc.	Dose	Solutions	Administration rate		Reconstituted in vial	In a syringe	In Piggy bag	
Ceftizoxime (Cefizox)	1 & 2 gm	Not advised	Yes	N/A	SWFI 10 mL	95 mg/mL	1–2 gm	50-100 mL NS or D5W	over 30 min		N/A	24 hrs RT 96 hrs RF	24 hrs RT 96 hrs RF	May be administer IM for gonorrhea
Ceftriaxone (Rocephin)	250 mg Vial (powder); 500 mg vial (powder); 1 gm vial (Powder for reconstitution)	Not advised	Yes; See Below; IM/Buretrol Prep: Dilute 250 mg vial w/ 0.9 mL to yield 250 mg/mL; Dilute 500 mg w/ 1 mL; 1 gm vial w/ 2.1 mL; 2 gm vial with 4.2 mL lidocaine	N/A	2.4 mL NS; 4.8 mL NS; 9.6 mL NS	100 mg/mL; 100 mg/mL; 100 mg/mL	All Doses	50 mL D5W or NS	100 mL/hr (Over 30 min)		3 D RT; 10 D RF(100 mg/mL); 24 hrs RT; 3 D RF(250-350 mg/mL)	3 D RT; 10 D RF(100 mg/mL); 24 hrs RT; 3 D RF (250-350 mg/mL)	3 Days RT; 10 D RF	Max dose = 4 gm/day Frozen PB available
Cefuroxime (Zinacef)	750 mg vial (Powder for reconstitution)	Not advised; Conc. 100 mg/mL; 250 mg over 1 min	Yes; See Below; IM Prep: Dilute 750 mg w/ 3 mL SW = 220 mg/mL	N/A	7.2 mL SW	100 mg/mL	0-1 gm; 1001 mg, 1.5 gm	50 mL D5W or NS; 100 mL D5W or NS	100 mL/hr (Over 30 min); 200 mL/hr (Over 30 min)		24 hrs RT; 48 hrs RF	24 hrs RT; 48 hrs RF	24 hrs at RT; 7 D RF	Max dose 9 gm/day Fozen pre mixed bag available
Certolizumab pegol (Cimzia)	200 mg vial powder	No	No	Sq	1 mL SWFI	200 mg/mL	400 mg/ month	1 mL SWFI	SQ only		2 hrs RT 24 hrs RF	N/A	RF use mfg expiration date	may take 30 min to fully reconstitute
cidofovir (visitide)	75 mg/mL 5 mL vial	IVPB	No	No	Dilute in NS100 mL	Prescribe dose/100 mL NS	5 mg/kg	100 mL NS	Over 60 mins		N/A	N/A	RF expired in 24 hrs	Stable in D5W, NS.
Chloramphenicol (Chloromycetin)	1 gm	over 1 min central line	Yes	N/A	10 mL	100 mg/mL	1-2gm	50-100 m1 NS/ D5W	Over 30 min		N/A	24 hrs RT	24 hrs RT	use in VRSA
Chlordiazepoxide (Librium)	50 mg powder w diluent	over 1 min Central line	Yes	N/A	special diluent	20 mg/mL	50-100 mg	NS for IV bolus	Over 1 min		single dose	prepare immediately	N/A	prepare prior to use
Chlorpromazine (Thorazine)	50 mg/2 mL amps	Conc. 1 mg/mL; 1 mg over 1-2 min	10-50 mg IM	N/A	N/A	25 mg/mL	<50 mg	50 mL NS	100 mL/hr (over 30 min)		N/A	Send Amps	72 hrs RT or RF	Protect from light
Chlorothiazide (Diuril)	500 mg vial (powder for reconstitution)	May give 28 mg/mL over 3-5 min	N/A	N/A	18 mL SW	28 mg/mL	0-1 gm	50 mL NS or D5W	200 mL/hr (Over 15 min)		24 hrs at RT	N/A	24 hrs RT or RF	Single use only. Protect from freezing.
Cilastatin & Imipenem (primaxin)							See Imipenem/Cilastin (Primaxin).							
Chymopapan (chymodiactin)	4nKat units powder w 2 mL diluent	N/A	Intra discal	N/A	2 mL SWFI	4nKat/2mL		Not recommended			N/A	2 hrs	2 hrs	pre treat w H2 blocker do not use BSWFI

Drug Name	Package Size	Routes of Administration			Injectable Preparation		IVPB Preparation			Stability			Notes/Comments
		IVP	IM	SC	Dilute with	Conc.	Dose	Solutions	Administration rate	Reconstituted in vial	In a syringe	In Piggy bag	
Cimetidine (Tagamet)	300 mg/2 mL	Yes, over 5 min	Yes, 300 mg q 6 hrs		NS or D5W	150 mg/mL	300 mg q 6-8 hrs	NS D5W 50 mL	Over 15-30 min cont. infusion at 37.5 mg/hr	SDV & MDVs	48 hrs RT when mixed w IV	14 days RT, 42 days RF	pre mixed bag available
Ciprofloxacin (Cipro)	200 mg/20 mL vial	Not advised	Not advised	N/A	N/A	10 mg/mL	200 mg	100 mL D5W or NS	100 mL/hr (Over 1 hr)	N/A	14 days RT or RF	14 days RT or RF	Max dose = 400 mg q 8 hrs, Pre mixed bag
							400 mg	250 mL D5W or NS	250 mL/hr (Over 1 hr)				
Cisatracurium Besylate (Nimbex)	10 mg / 5 mL vial	Administer Rapidly (10 mg/mL)	Not advised	N/A	N/A	2 mg/mL	200 mg	100 mL D5W or NS	0.5-10 mcg/kg/min	Stable 21 days at RT; SDV	Send Vial	72 hrs RT or RF	Vials are refrigerated
Cisplatinum (Platinol)	50 and 100 mg	No	No	No	SWFI	1 mg/mL	less than 50 mg: 100 mL NS	greater than 50: 250 mL	IP in 100 mL or more	30 days in vial	72 hrs RF post dilution		Protect from light; verify over 120 mg/m2 doses
Cladribine (Leustatin)	10 mg	No	No	No	500 mL NS	1 mg/mL	NS 250–500 mL	CIVI for 7 days Use BNS	over 24 hrs	RF	8 hr: RF in vial	7 d: RT after diluted W/ BNS	I : D5W
Clavulanate Potassium and Ticarcillin (Timentin)	3.1 gm vial (Powder for reconstitution)	Not advised	Not advised	N/A	13 mL SW or NS	200 mg/mL	0-3.1 gm	100 mL NS	200 mL/hr (Over 30 min)	6 hrs RT; 72 hrs RF	6 hrs RT; 72 hrs RF	24 hrs RT; 7 D Rf	Max dose = 300 mg/kg (Ticarcillin)
Clauvulate Potassium and Ticarcillin Frozen PB (Timentin)	3.1 gm / 100 mL	Not advised	Not advised	N/A	Already Prepared; Pre-mixed bag		Already Prepared		200 mL/hr (Over 30 min)	N/A	N/A	24 hrs RT; 7 days RF	
Clevidipine (Cleviprex)	50-100 mL emulsion single dose vial	IVPB	No	No	do not dilute	N/A	1-2 mg/hr CI	N/A	Continuoues infusion	Sinlge use vial	N/A	store in RF,	may keep at RT for 2 months
Clindamycin (Cleocin)	300 mg/2 mL and 600 mg/4 mL vials (150 mg/mL)	Not advised	Not advised	N/A	N/A	150 mg/mL	0-900 mg	50 mL D5W or NS	100 mL/hr (Over 30 min)	Single use vial	72 hrs RT	14 days RT or RF	Max dose = 4800 mg/day
							1200 mg	200 mL D5W or NS	200 mL/hr (Over 45 min)				
Clindamycin Premixed PB (Cleocin)	300, 600, 900 mg / 50 mL premixed	Not advised	Not advised	N/A	Already Prepared; Pre-mixed bag		Already Prepared		100 mL/hr (Over 30 min)	N/A	N/A	Exp Date on Package	

Drug Name	Package Size	Routes of Administration			Injectable Preparation		IVPB Preparation			Stability			Notes/ Comments
		IVP	IM	SC	Dilute with	Conc.	Dose	Solutions	Administration rate	Reconstituted in vial	In a syringe	In Piggy bag	
Colchicine (Acetycol, Cosalide)	1 mg/2 mL Vials	0.5-2 mg over 2-5 min	Not advised	N/A	N/A	0.5 mg/mL	Not recommended			SDV	Send Vial	N/A	Recall Intravenous colchicine on 2/8/2008
Conivaptan (Vaprisol)	5 mg/mL ampule, 20 mg/100 mL premixed	IVPB	No	No	dilute 4 mL in 250 mL D5W	2 mg/mL	20-40 mg	100-250 mL D5W	loading dose over 30 mins then 20-40 mg over 24 hrs	N/A	N/A	RT 24 hrs	Incompatible with NS or LR. should not exceed 40 mg/day x 4 day
Conjugated Estrogens (Premarin)	25 mg vial (Powder for reconstitution)	5 mg/min at 5 mg/mL conc.	Not advised	N/A	5 mL SW (Diluent Provided)	5 mg/mL	Not recommended			60 d RF, once diluted. Vials stable for 90 d RT	Send Vial and diluent	N/A	Slow infusion rate if flushing occurs; Keep in the Refrigerator. Protect from light.
Colistin	150 mg powder	Yes	Yes	No	2 mL SWFI	75 mg/mL	2.5-5 mg/kg	SWFI or NS	intermittent infusion over 10-30 min	24 hrs RT	24 hrs RT	24 hrs RT	required renal dosing
Corticotropin (ACTH, Acthar gel)	40 mg, 80 mg	No	Yes	Yes	D5W	10-25 units/500 mL	Varying dosing	D5W 500 mL-1L	over 8 hrs continuous infusion	N/A	N/A	N/A	IV use only for diagnostic reason
Cosyntropin (Cortrosyn)	0.25 mg (25 IU/vial) (Powder for reconstitution)	Dilute in 2-5 mL NS and give over 2 min	0.25-0.75 mg	N/A	1.1 mL NS diluent provided	25 IU/mL (25mcg/mL)	250 mcg (0.25 mg)	250 mL NS or D5W	over 4-8 hrs (20-40 mcg/hr)	24 hrs RT; 7 d RF; Undiluted vials stable for 2 wks RT	24 hrs RT	12 hrs at RT	check plasma cortisol level right before and 30 min after administration
Cyanocobalamin (Vit B12)	1000 mcg / 1 mL	Not advised	100-1000 mcg	Yes	N/A	1000 mcg/mL	Not recommended			MDV	30 days RT	N/A	Protect from light. Do not refrigerate
Cyclophosphamide (Cytoxan)	100, 200, 500 mg, and 1gm, 2gm	slow IVP	No	No	SWFI or BSWFI	20 mg/mL	>800 mg / >2gm	150 mL NS / 250-500 NS or D5W	over 1-24 hrs / over 30-60 min	48 RT, 6 d RF w/BSWFI	48 RT, 6 d RF w/BSWFI	48 RT, 6 d RF w/BSWFI	hydration should be start 4 hrs before and continue 12 hrs after cytoxan administration
Cyclosporin	100 mg	Yes, infusion only	No	No	NS, D5W	0.5 mg/mL	2-7.5 mg/kg/day	D5W or NS 100 mL	over 2-6 hrs	N/A	24 hrs in RF w D5W, 12 hrs w NS	24 hrs in RF w D5W, 12 hrs w NS	Do not filter or Referigerate protect from light
Cytarabine (ARA-C, Cytosar)	100, 500 mg & 1, 2 gm	Yes	No	Yes	D5LR, D51/4NS, D5NS, D10NS, NS, LR	100-200 mg/mL	Varying dosing	250-1000 mL NS or D5W	over 30-60 min	RT only	48 hrs RT (SWFI) 8 d RT (BSWFI)	48 hrs RT (SWFI) 8 d RT (BSWFI)	Store syringes at RT
Dacarbazine (DTIC)	100 and 200 mg	No	No	No	SWFI 4 mL	50 mg/mL	Varying dosing	250-500 mL NS or D5W	over 1-2 hrs	24 hrs RT 96 hrs RF	24 hrs RT 96 hrs RF	24 hrs RT 96 hrs RF	Protect from light Keep in Referigerator

Drug Name	Package Size	Routes of Administration			Injectable Preparation		IVPB Preparation			Stability			Notes/ Comments
		IVP	IM	SC	Dilute with	Conc.	Dose	Solutions	Administration rate	Reconstituted in vial	In a syringe	In Piggy bag	
Dactinomycin (Cosmegen)	500mcg	Yes	No	No	SWFI 1.1 mL	0.5 mg/mL	15mcg/kg/day for 5 days	50 mL NS	IVP 1-3 min in running IV; IVPB: over 20–30 min	N/A	8 hrs RT 24 hrs RF	8 hrs RT 24 hrs RF	Protect from light
Dalteparin (Fragmin)	10,000 IU/mL; 9.5 mL vial	2,500 unit bolus	Not advised	Yes	N/A	N/A	15,000 units	250-500 mL NS	Over 24 hrs for 5 days continuous infusion	MDV	30 d RT or RF	48 hrs RT or RF	monitor anti-Xa level if Crcl<30 mL/min
Dantrolene (Dantrium)	20 mg vial (Powder for reconstitution)	1 mg/kg; 1st dose given rapidly, subsequent doses over 2-3 min	Not advised	N/A	60 mL SW	0.33 mg/mL	2.5 mg/Kg	None (use straight out of the diluted vial)	Over 1 hr	6 hrs at RT or RF	6 hrs RT or RF	6 hrs RT or RF	Protect from light
Daptomycin (Cubicin)	500 mg powder	4-6 mg/kg/d	No	No	NS 50 mL	N/A	4-6 mg/kg/day	50 mL	30 min	12 hrs RT 48 hrs RF	12 hrs RT 48 hrs RF	12 hrs RT 48 hrs RF	Not compatible with dextrose
Darbopoetin (aranesp)	25, 40, 60, 100, 200,300 mg vials or syringe	Yes	No	Yes	Prefilled syring	N/A	Varying dosing			N/A	N/A	RF	Do not dilute or administer with other solutions
Daunorubicin (Cerubidine)	20 mg	Yes	No	No	SWFI 4 mL	5 mg/mL	30-60 mg/m2	100–250 mL NS or D5W	over 30 min	N/A	24 hrs RT, 48 hrs RF	24 hrs RT, 48 hrs RF	Protect from light
Daunorubicin (liposomal) Dauno Xome	50 mg/25 mL	Yes	No	No	D5W ONLY	1 mg/mL	40 mg/m2	D5W 100–250 mL	over 1 hr	N/A	6 hrs RF	6 hrs RF (diluted)	do not mix with other drugs or with NS
Degarelix	120 mg powder	No	No	Yes	dilute 120 mg in 3 mL and 80 mg in 4.2 mL SW	20-40 mg/mL	80-240 mg	3-4.2 mL sterile water	infuse SQ	Within 1 hr of reconstitution	Within 1 hr of reconstitution	Within 1 hr of reconstitution	Not for IV use.
Deferoxamine (Desferal)	500 mg vial (powder for reconstitution)	Not advised	Yes; Dissolve in 2 mL SW	Slow SQ Infusion	5 mL SW (May mix with 2 mL to give 250 mg/mL)	100 mg/mL	All Doses	250 mL NS or D5W	Max Rate 15 mg/kg/hr	Dilute w/ SW = 7 days at RT	7 days at RT	7 days at RT. Do not RF	Protect from light. Have epinephrine 1:1000 ready in for allergic reaction; Not more than 6 gm/24 hrs
Desmopressin (DDAVP)	4 mcg/1 mL amp	over 1 min for diabetes insipidus	Not advised	Yes; 2-4 mcg	N/A	4 mcg/mL	0.3 mcg/kg	50 mL NS	100 mL/hr (Over 30 min)	Single Dose	Send Amps	24 hrs RF	Refrigerate vials

Drug Name	Package Size	Routes of Administration			Injectable Preparation		IVPB Preparation			Stability			Notes/ Comments
		IVP	IM	SC	Dilute with	Conc.	Dose	Solutions	Administration rate	Reconstituted in vial	In a syringe	In Piggy bag	
Dexamethasone (Decadron)	4 mg / 1 mL; 20 mg / 5 mL; 120 mg / 30 mL; 10 mg / 1 mL; and 100 mg / 10 mL	<10 mg over 1-2 min	Not advised	N/A	N/A	4 and 10 mg/mL	>10 mg	50 mL NS or D5W	over 30 min	MDV	30 days RT or RF	72 hrs RT or RF	Protect from light.
Dextrazoxane (Zinecard)	250 & 500 mg with diluent	Yes	No	No	N lactate Diluent	10 mg/mL		NS or D5W	IVPB: 1.3–5 mg/mL over 7-15 min	6 hrs RT or RF	6 hrs RT or RF	6 hrs RT or RF	do not use if discolored
Dextroxe 50%	25 gm / 50 mL	25 gm/ 5 min	Not advised	N/A	N/A	0.5 gm/mL		Give IV Push		SDVs	Send Vials	N/A	not for subQ or I.M. administration
Dezocaine (Dalgan)	5 mg, 10 mg and 15 mg/mL in 2 mL vials	Yes	Yes	Not recommended		various		N/A	over 3-5 min IV push		RT		protect from light
Diazepam (Valium)	10 mg / 2 mL ampule; 10 mg/2 mL syringes; 50 mg / 10 mL vials	conc. 1-5 mg/mL; 2-5 mg/min; over 3-5 min	2-10 mg	N/A	N/A	5 mg/mL	IV push preferred—dilution may cause precipitation; may dilute 50 mg in 500 mL D5W (Glass)			Single Dose and MDV's	Send Vials	24 hrs at RT	Use glass. Protect from light. Will bind to PVC tubing
Diazoxide (Hyperstat IV)	300 mg/20 mL amps	15 mg/mL given rapidly for emergency treatment of HTN	Not advised	N/A	N/A	15 mg/mL	Not recommended			Single Dose	Send Amps	N/A	Protect from light and freezing
Dicyclomine (Bemote, Bentyl, Antispas)	20 mg / 2 mL Amps	Not advised	20 mg QID	N/A	N/A	10 mg/mL	Not recommended			Single Dose	Send Amps	N/A	Only use for 1-2 days
Diethylstelbesrol (Stilphostrol)	500 mg			N/A			500 mg	NS or D5W 250 mL	over 1 hr				1-2 mL/min for 1st 10-15 min then over 1 hr
Digoxin (Lanoxin)	0.5 mg/2 mL amps; and 0.125 and 0.25 mg syringes	Over 5 min	Not advised; very painful	N/A	N/A	0.25 mg/mL	Not recommended; give IV push			Multi-Dose Amps	30 days	N/A	Protect injection from light.
Digoxin Immune FAB (Digibind)	38 mg Vial (Powder for reconstitution)	EMER-GENCY ONLY. Give dose over 5 min at conc. of 10 mg/mL.	Not advised	N/A	4 mL SW	9.5 mg/mL	Any Dose	50 mL NS	100 mL/hr (Over 30 min) Infuse through a 0.22 micron filter	Use reconstituted products promptly; stable for 4 hrs in refrig			Use a 0.22 micron filter for administration

Drug Name	Package Size	Routes of Administration			Injectable Preparation		IVPB Preparation			Stability			Notes/Comments
		IVP	IM	SC	Dilute with	Conc.	Dose	Solutions	Administration rate	Reconstituted in vial	In a syringe	In Piggy bag	
Dihydroergotamene Mesylate (DHE-45)	1 mg / 1 mL amps	Over 1 min	Preferred	N/A	N/A	1 mg/mL		Not recommended		Single Dose	Send Amps	N/A	Protect from light; max of 2 doses per 24 hrs
Diltiazem (Cardizem)	25 mg / 5 mL and 125 mg / 25 mL vials	Conc.: 5 mg/mL, at a rate of 10 mg/min	Not advised	N/A	N/A	5 mg/mL	125 mg (25 mL)	100 mL NS (Total Volume 125 mL)	5-15 mg/hr (Drip Conc. 1 mg/mL)	24 hrs once reconstituted; vials are stable for 30 days at RT; SDVs	24 hrs	24 hrs RT or RF	Store Vials in Refrig; Bolus Dosing: Initial= 0.25 mg/kg; Second Dose= 0.35 mg/kg
Dimercaprol (BAL in Oil)	100 mg/mL; 3 mL amps	Not advised	mix with procaine	N/A	N/A	100 mg/mL		Not recommended		N/A	N/A	N/A	Store at RT. keep urine alkline to protect renal function
Diphenhydramine (Benadryl)	50 mg / 1 mL vial	Slowly over 2 min (25 mg/min)	10-100 mg ok	N/A	N/A	50 mg/mL	IV push preferred—may dilute in 50 mL D5W at 100 mL/hr			SDV	72 hrs RT or RF	72 hrs RT or RF	Protect from light. Max single dose = 100 mg; Max dose/day = 400 mg
Diphthera and Tetnus Toxoids and acellular Pertussis vaccine (Pentacel)	0.5 mL	No	IM only	No	N/A	0.5 mL	0.5 mL at 2,4,6,&15 months	N/A	IM only	RF	N/A	N/A	Do not freeze
Diptheria Tetnus Pertussis (Tdap)	0.5 mL	No	IM only	No	N/A	N/A	25mcg/0.5 mL	N/A	N/A	N/A	N/A	RF	Do not freeze.
Dipyridamole (Persantine)	50 mg/10 mL vial and 10 mg/2 mL vial	Dilute to a total volume of 30 mL in D5W; give over 4 min	Not advised	N/A	N/A	5 mg/mL	0.57 mg/kg	QS to 30 mL in a syringe (D5W)	over 4 min	SDVs	24 hrs RT or RF	24 hrs RT or RF	Max dose = 60 mg/dose; IV Push = dilute to 20-50 mL in NS or D5W and give over a max of 4 min
Dobutamine (Dobutrex)	250 mg/5 mL vial	No-Must dilute in a IVPB			N/A	50 mg/mL	max conc. = 5 mg/mL	NS or D5W (Max conc. 250 mg/50 mL)	2-40 mcg/kg/min	SDV	N/A	48 hrs RT or RF	max dose = 40 mcg/kg/min
Dobutamine Pre-mixed (Dobutrex)	250 mg/250 mL D5W / 500 mg/250 mL D5W (Double Strength)					1 mg/mL / 2 mg/mL	Already Prepared / Already Prepared			N/A	N/A	30 days outside of wrapper	
Docetaxel (Taxotere)	20 mg & 80 mg w diluent	No	No	No	special diluent	10 mg/mL	NS 250 mL, may use D5W		over 1 hr	N/A	N/A	8 hrs Rt or RF	Let stand 10 min before mixing, mix vial gently

Drug Name	Package Size	Routes of Administration			Injectable Preparation		IVPB Preparation			Stability			Notes/ Comments
		IVP	IM	SC	Dilute with	Conc.	Dose	Solutions	Administration rate	Reconstituted in vial	In a syringe	In Piggy bag	
Dopamine (Intropin, Dopastat)	200 mg/5 mL vial (40 mg/mL)	No-Must dilute in a IVPB			N/A	40 mg/mL	max conc. = 4 mg/mL	D5W	2-50 mcg/kg/min	SDVs	N/A	48 hrs RT or RF	max dose = 50 mcg/kg/min
Dopamine Pre-mixed (Intropin, Dopastat)	400 mg/250 mL					1.6 mg (1600 mcg/mL)	Pre mixed	Pre mixed		N/A	N/A	30 days outside of wrapper	
Doripenem (Doribax)	500 mg	500 mg in 100 mL NS	No	No	10 mL SWFI NS	5 mg/mL	500 mg q 8 hrs	250 mg/ 50 mL NS	over 1 hr	N/A	N/A	NS 8 hrs, D5W 4 hrs, RF 24 hrs	Crcl <50 required dose adjustment
Doxacurium (Nuromax)	1 mg/mL 5 mL vial	IV use only	No	No	D5W, NS, LR	1:10 with D5W, NS	0.05-0.08 mg/kg	25 mg in D5W 250 mL	N/A	N/A	N/A	N/A	intibution dose 0.05g/kg
Doxapram (Dopram)	20 mg /mL 20 mL vial	Yes	No	No	NS, D5W, D10W	1 mg/mL	varying dosing	D5W or NS 250 mL	2 mg/kg for 1-2 hrs		RT only		1-5 mg/kg/min x < hrs
Doxorubicin (Adriamycin)	10, 20, 50,100 & 200 mg liquid	Yes	No	No	NS, D5W	2 mg/mL	varying dosing	NS for IVPB or CIVI, use appropriate volume	IVP over 1-5 min	N/A	24 RT, 30 d RF	N/A	Protect from light
Doxorubicin Liposomal (Doxil)	20 mg/ 10 mL	No	No	No	Diluted	2 mg/mL	<90 mg	D5W 250 mL, 500 mL for higher dose	over 30 min, higher dose over 60 min	N/A	N/A	24 hrs RF diluted	Short term freezing (<1 month)
Doxycycline (Vibramycin)	100 mg vial (Powder for reconstitution)	Not advised—must dilute	Not advised	N/A	10 mL SW	10 mg/mL	0-100 mg / 100-200 mg	100 mL D5W or NS / 250 mL D5W or NS	100 mL/hr (Over 1 hr) / 125 mL/hr (Over 2 hrs)	3 days RF	3 days RF	48 hrs RT, 72 hrs RF	protect from light; Max dose = 300 mg/day; may dilute in 250 mL if irritates tissue
Droperidol (Inapsine)	5 mg / 2 mL	2.5 mg/min; conc. 2.5 mg/mL	0.625-5 mg every 3-4 hrs	N/A	N/A	2.5 mg/mL	1 mg	50 mL D5W or NS	over 15 min	SDVs	72 hrs RT or Rf	72 hrs RT or Rf	Protect from light
Drotrecogin alfa (Xigris)	5 mg or 20 mg vial	IV via infusion pump	No	No	dilutes 5 mg vial with 2.5 mL SWFI	100-1000mcg/ mL	24mcg/ kg/hr	further diluted w NS	24mcg/kg/hrs x 96 hrs	use within 12 hrs	N/A	use within 12 hrs	Do not shake, keep refrigerate Infuse over 96 hrs
Dtap +hepB+IPV (Pediatrix0)	0.5 mL	No	IM only	No	N/A	0.5 mL	0.5 mL		N/A	N/A	N/A	RF	
DtaP+ HiB (Trihibit)	0.5 mL	No	IM only	No	N/A	0.5 mL	0.5 mL	N/A	IM only	30 min after reconstitution	N/A	N/A	Do not freeze.

Drug Name	Package Size	Routes of Administration			Injectable Preparation		IVPB Preparation			Stability			Notes/Comments
		IVP	IM	SC	Dilute with	Conc.	Dose	Solutions	Administration rate	Reconstituted in vial	In a syringe	In Piggy bag	
Eculizumab (soliris)	300 mg single dose vial	IVPB over 35 min	No	No	Dilute in NS /D5W	Final conc. 5 mg/mL	600-900 mg/wk	120-180 mL NS or D5W	Over 35 mins	N/A	N/A	diluted soln 24 hrs RF or RT	Do not freeze or shake.Protect from light.
Edetate Calcium Disodium (EDTA)	150 mg/mL 20 mL vial	Yes	Yes with Procaine	No	NS, D5W	<5 mg/mL	25-75 mg/kg/day	D5W or NS 500 mL	Over 3 hrs	N/A	N/A	RT	50 mg/kg upto 3 gm/day
Edrophonium Chloride (Enlon, Reversol, Tensilon)	10 mg/mL; 15 mL vials	2 mg over 30-45 seconds	10 mg IM	N/A	N/A	10 mg/mL	300 mg	100 mL D5W or NS	Cont. Infusion (0.25-2 mg/min) Conc. = 3 mg/mL	MDV	30 days RT or RF	24 hrs RT or RF	Max 40 mg.
Enalaprilat (Vasotec IV)	1.25 mg / 1 mL, 2.5 mg / 2 mL	1.25 mg/mL slowly over 3-5 min	Not advised	N/A	D5W, NS	1.25 mg/mL	All Doses	50 mL NS or D5W	100 mL/hr (Over 30 min)	MDV	30 days RT or RF	24 hrs at RT; 48 hrs in RF	Inspect for particulate matter and discoloration
Enoxaparin Sodium (Lovenox)	30 mg/0.3 mL amps (100 mg/mL) (also comes in 150 mg/mL)	0.5 mg/kg bolus	Not advised	Yes	N/A	N/A	2-3 mg/kg/day	250 mL NS	Continuous infusion	MDV	30 days RT or RF	48 hrs RT or RF	Only given SQ Solution?
Ephedrine sulfate	50 mg / 1 mL amp	Slowly at 25 mg/min	25-50 mg	25-50 mg	N/A	50 mg/mL	Not recommended			SDVs	72 hrs RT or RF	N/A	
Epinephrine (Adrenalin, Susphrine)	1 mg/mL; and in dilutions… etc?	1 mg over 1 min; more rapidly if cardiac arrest	Yes	Yes	N/A	various	1 mg	250 mL NS or D5W(4 mcg/mL)	1-10 mcg/min	Single Dose Amps and Syringes	72 hrs RT or RF	24 hrs at RT or RF	Protect from light
Ergonovine Maleate (Ergotrate)	0.2 mg/mL	IV for emergency use only	Yes	No	N/A	N/A	N/A				N/A		Protect from light
Ertapenem (Invanz)	1gm powder	15 mg/kg twice/day	15 mg/kg twice/day	N/A	50 mL NS	20 mg/mL	15 mg/kg q 12 hrs	NS or Lidocaine 1%	Infuse over 30 min	6 hrs RT; 24 hrs RF	6 hrs RT; 24 hrs RF	6 hrs RT; 24 hrs RF	Not to exceed 1g/day
Erythromycin Lactobionate (Erythrocin IV)	500 mg vial (powder for reconstitution)	Not advised	Not advised	N/A	10 mL SW only	50 mg/mL	501 mg-1gm / 0-500 mg	250 mL NS / 100 mL NS	125 mL/hr (Over 2 hrs) / 100 mL/hr (Over 1 hr)	24 hrs RT; 14 days RF	24 hrs RT; 72 hrs RF	8 hrs RT; 24 hrs RF	Max dose = 4gm/day; slow infusion if vein irritation occurs

Drug Name	Package Size	Routes of Administration			Injectable Preparation		IVPB Preparation			Stability			Notes/Comments
		IVP	IM	SC	Dilute with	Conc.	Dose	Solutions	Administration rate	Reconstituted in vial	In a syringe	In Piggy bag	
Erythropoietin (Procrit; Epogen)	20 Thousand units / 2 mL multidose vial; 40 Thousand units/mL; 1 mL single dose vial	Over 1 min (10,000 units/min)	Not advised	ok	N/A	10,000 units/mL and 40,000 units/mL	Not recommended; give IV push or SQ			28 D once opened; Vials stable for 14 D RT; 14 d RT (Unopened SDV's)	Send SDV; 28 d RF from MDV	N/A	Do not shake vigorously and protect from light
Esmolol (Brevibloc)	100 mg / 10 mL vial; and 2500 mg/10 mL amps	Conc. 10 mg/mL; all doses given over 1 min	Not advised	N/A	N/A	10 mg/mL and 100 mg/mL	5 gm	500 mL NS or D5W?	50-200 mcg/kg/min	SDV and Amps	72 hrs RT or RF	48 hrs RT; 72 hrs RF	Protect from freezing and avoid excessive heat
Esmolol Pre-mixed (Brevibloc)	2.5 gm/250 mL NS	(Loading dose = 500mcg/kg)				10 mg/mL	Already Prepared		50-200 mcg/kg/min	N/A	N/A	24 hrs outside wrapper	
Esomeprazole (Nexium)	20-40 mg vial	IVPB	No	No	Dilute with 5 mL NS	50 mL	40 mg	50 mL	10-30 min	N/A	N/A	RT, NS, LR 12-D5W 6 hrs	do not refergerate
Estradiol Valerate (Delestrogen)	200 mg/5 mL vial (40 mg/mL)	Not advised	10-20 mg every 4 weeks	N/A	N/A	40 mg/mL	Not recommended—give IM			MDV	30 d RT or RF	N/A	For IM use.
Estrogens, Conjugated							See Conjugated Estrogens						
Ethacrynate Sod (Edecrin)	50 mg powder	slow IV over several min	No	No	D5NS, D5W, NS, LR	1 mg/mL	0.5-1 mg/kg/dose	NS 50 mL	over 20-30 min	N/A	N/A	24 hrs RT	single IV dose do not exceed 100 mg
Etidronate Disod (Didroneal)	300 mg/6 mL	No	No	No	diluted	50 mg/mL	No	NS 250 mL	over 2 hrs	N/A	N/A	RT	7.5 mg/kg/day x 3 days
Etomidate (Amidate)	40 mg / 20 mL abboject	0.3 mg/kg over 15-30 seconds	Not advised	N/A	N/A	2 mg/mL	Not advised; see IV push			Single Dose	Send Syringe	N/A	
Etoposide (Vepesid)	100 mg/ 5 mL 500 mg/25 mL	via syring pump	No	No	NS, D5W, LR	20 mg/mL	varying dosing	NS 150,250, 500 mL, may use D5W	over 45-60 min, for syring pump over 4 hrs	N/A	Conc. Dependent	2 hrs RT at (1 mg/mL) 8 hrs at 0.6 mg/mL 24 hrs RT at 0.4 mg/mL	do not refergerate
Exenatide (Byetta)	5 mg /dose or 10mcg/dose	No	No	Sub q	No	No	No	N/A	Administer slowly by SQ route	N/A	30 days after first use	30 days after first use	Do not freeze.Protect from light.

Drug Name	Package Size	Routes of Administration			Injectable Preparation		IVPB Preparation			Stability			Notes/ Comments
		IVP	IM	SC	Dilute with	Conc.	Dose	Solutions	Administration rate	Reconstituted in vial	In a syringe	In Piggy bag	
Famotidine (Pepcid)	10 mg / 1 mL vial	10 mg/mL over min; Dilute w 5-10 mL NS or D5W	Not advised	N/A	N/A	10 mg/mL	20-40 mg	50 mL D5W or NS	100 mL/hr (Over 30 min)	SDV; Vial stable for 180 Days at RT	72 hrs RT or RF	72 hrs RT or RF	Pre mix IVPB available
Fat Emulsion (Intralipid)	10 & 20 % 500 mL	Yes	No	No	diluted	10-30%	varying dosing	D/amino acid	over 4-6 hrs	N/A	N/A	RT	monitor verious organism growth.
Fenoldopam (Corlopam)	20 mg/2 mL vial (10 mg/mL)	Not advised	Not advised	N/A	N/A	10 mg/mL	10 mg	250 NS (Conc. = 40 mcg/mL)	0.05-1.6 mcg/kg/min	SDV	N/A	24 hrs RT or RF	must be diluted beore infusion.
Fentanyl (Sublimaze)	50 mcg/mL amps/vials	2-150 mcg/kg slowly over 1-2 min for anesthesia	50-100 mcg IM for Pain	Yes	N/A	50 mcg/ mL	300 mcg / 750 mcg	300 mL NS (Conc. = 10 mcg/mL) / 30 mL NS PCA	20-60 mcg/hr	SDV and Amps	Send Amps or Vials	72 hrs RT or RF	Protect from light, freezing and moisture
Ferric Gluconate Complex (Ferrlecit)	62.5 mg/5 mL amp	Yes; undiluted at 12.5 mg/min	N/A	N/A	N/A	12.5 mg/mL	25 mg test dose / 125 mg (10 mL)	50 mL NS / 100 mL NS	50 mL/hr (Over 1 hr) / 100 mL/hr (Over 1 hr)	Single Use Amps	72 hrs RT	24 hrs RT	Max Dose = 125 mg
Filgrastim (Neupogen)	300 mcg / 1 m or 480 mcg/1.6 mL	Not advised	Not advised	Yes	N/A	300 mcg/ mL	10 mcg/ kg/day	10-50 mL D5W (Conc. 15 mcg/mL)	over 15-30 min (Min Conc. = 2mcg/mL)	Single Use vial	72 hrs RT or RF	72 hrs RT or RF	Do Not dilute with NS
Floxuridine (FUDR)	500 mg	NO	No	No	SWFI 5 mL	100 mg/mL		NS or D5W 100-250 mL	continueos infusion	2 wks RF	N/A	24 hrs RT 14 d RF 28 d in PUMP	Infuseaid pump
Fluconazole (Diflucan)	200 mg/100 mL (2 mg/mL)	Not advised	Not advised	N/A	N/A	2 mg/mL	Pre mixed		100 mL/hr (Over 60 min)	N/A	N/A	Exp. Date on Package	Do not rerigerate
Fludarabine (Fludara)	50 mg	N/A	N/A	N/A	SWFI 2 mL	25 mg/mL		D5W 50 mL, may use NS	over 30 min	16 days RT or RF	N/A	24 hrs RF	Recommend to use within 8 hrs
Flumazenil (Romazicon)	0.5 mg/5 mL and 1 mg / 10 mL vials	Give over 10-30 seconds w/ running IV	Not advised	N/A	N/A	0.1 mg/mL	Give IV push			MDV	24 hrs at RT	N/A	reversal agent
Fluorouracil (5-FU)	500 mg / 10 mL	Slow IVP	No	No	Diluted	50 mg/mL	Varying dosing	Dilute with D5W, NS	over 1-5 min	do not RF	N/A	48 hrs diluted	IVPB or CIVI diluted or undiluted, protect from light

Drug Name	Package Size	Routes of Administration			Injectable Preparation		IVPB Preparation			Stability			Notes/Comments
		IVP	IM	SC	Dilute with	Conc.	Dose	Solutions	Administration rate	Reconstituted in vial	In a syringe	In Piggy bag	
Folic Acid (Folvite)	50 mg/10 mL	Give over 2 min	Yes	Yes	N/A	5 mg/mL	<5 mg	50 mL D5W or NS	over 30 min	MDV	30 Days RF	72 hrs RT or RF	Protect from light
Foscarnet Sod (Foscavir)	24 mg/mL 250 mL	No	NO	No	diluted	Max conc 24 mg/mL		D5W or NS	over 2 hrs	MDV	N/A	RT	Rate needs to controlled by Pump
Fosphenytoin (Cerebyx)	100 mg/2 mL vial; 500 mg / 10 mL vial	150 mg PE/min; undiluted	Yes, undiluted	N/A	N/A	50 mg/mL	0-1 gm / 1001 mg, 2 gm	50 mL NS or D5W / 100 mL NS or D5W	200 mL/hr (over 15 min) / 200 mL/hr (over 30 min)	Single Use; Vials are stable for 48 hrs at RT	72 hrs RT or RF	72 hrs RT or RF	Vials are refrigerated
Fondaxaprin (arixtra)	2.5 mg, 5 mg, 7.5 mg, 10 mg single dose perfilled	Yes	No	Yes	N/A	2.5-10 mg/0.4-0.8 mL	varying dosing	N/A	N/A	has expiration date	has expiration date	has expiration date	Contraindicated if Crcl<30 mL/min
Furosemide (Lasix)	10 mg / 1 mL, 40 mg / 4 mL; 100 mg / 10 mL vials	<100 mg at 10 mg/min	20-40 mg every 2 hrs	N/A	N/A	10 mg/mL	0-100 mg / 101-200 mg	100 mL NS or D5W / 250 mL NS or D5W	Over 30 min / 250 mL/hr (Over 60 min)	Single Use Vial	24 hrs at RT	24 hrs at RT or RF	Protect from light. Do not refrigerate vials. Max conc. is 2 mg/mL for fluid restricted
Gallium Nitrate (Ganite)	25 mg/mL 20 mL vial	No	No	No	diluted	25 mg/1L NS/D5W	200 mg/m2/day	D5W or NS 1L	over 24 hrs	MDV	N/A	48 hrs RT 7days RF	Rapid infusion can cause Nausea vomiting
Gancyclovir (Cytovene)	500 mg powder	No	No	No	SWFI 10 mL	10 mg/mL	5-6 mg/kg	D5W or NS or LR 100 mL	over 1 hr	12 hrs RT	N/A	24 hrs	do not refrigerate
Gatifloxacin (Tequin)	400 mg/40 mL	Not advised	Not advised	N/A	N/A	10 mg/mL	200 mg / 400 mg	100 mL D5W / 250 mL D5W	100 mL/hr (Over 1 hr) / 250 mL/hr (Over 1 hr)	SDV	N/A	14 days w/or w/out RF	Max dose = 400 mg/day taken out of market
Gemcitabine (Gemzar)	200 mg, 1 gm	N/A	N/A	N/A	NS 5 mL	38 mg/mL		NS 250 mL	over not more than 30 min	35 days protect from light	N/A	24 hrs RT	Do not RF
Gentamicin (Garamycin)	80 mg/2 mL; 20 mg/2 mL	Not advised	Not advised	N/A	N/A	40 mg/mL and 10 mg/mL	all doses	100 mL D5W or NS	100 mL/hr (Over 1 hr)	MDV	48 hrs RT or RF	48 hrs RT; 7 days RF	Required renal dosing
Glucagon	1 mg vial	1 mg/mL at a rate of 1 mg/min	0.5-1 mg	0.5-1 mg	1 mL SW; diluent provided	1 mg (unit) per mL	Not recommended			Use Immediately	N/A	N/A	Inspect for particulate matter and discoloration
Glycopyrrolate (Robinul)	0.4 mg/2 mL vial	0.2 mg/min	Yes	N/A	N/A	200 mcg/mL (0.2 mg/mL)	Not recommended			SDV	Send Vials	N/A	Administer at a rate of 0.2 mg over 1-2 min
Granisteron (Kytril)	2 mg/2 mL	Yes	No	No	diluted	1 mg/mL		D5W or NS	over 5 min	SDV preservative freesdv	N/A	24 hrs RT	Protect from light do not freeze

Drug Name	Package Size	Routes of Administration			Injectable Preparation		IVPB Preparation			Reconstituted in vial	Stability		Notes/ Comments
		IVP	IM	SC	Dilute with	Conc.	Dose	Solutions	Administration rate		In a syringe	In Piggy bag	
Haloperidol lactate (Haldol)	5 mg / 1 mL Ampules	2.5 mg/min; conc. 2.5 mg/mL	2-5 mg every hr	N/A	N/A	5 mg/mL	0-125 mg	50 mL D5W	Over 15-60 min (max 40 mg/hr)—Cont. infusion OK	SDV	Send Vials	72 hrs RT or RF	Protect from light. Do not refrigerate.
Haloperidol Decanoate (Haldol Decanoate)	50 mg / 1 mL	Not advised	Max 450 mg per Month	N/A	N/A	50 mg/mL	Not recommended—only give IM			Multi-Dose Amps	Send Amps	N/A	Do not refrigerate and protect from light
H1N1 swine flu vaccine							*Coming soon.						
Heparin	various	Over 2 min; max. conc. 10,000 units/mL	Do Not give IM	Yes	N/A	various	All doses	50 mL D5W or NS	over 15 min	SDVs and MDV	72 hrs RT or RF	72 hrs RT or RF	pre mix bag
Hib+ Hep B Comvax	0.5 mL	No	IM only	No	N/A	0.5 mL	0.5 mL	N/A	IM only	RF	N/A	N/A	Do not freeze.
HEPA +Hep B(twinrix)	≥18 yrs: 1.0 mL	No	IM only	No	N/A	1.0 mL	3 doses of 1 mL at 0,1&6 months	N/A	IM only	RF	N/A	N/A	Do not freeze.
Heamophilius Influenza (HiB)	0.5 mL	No	IM only	No	N/A	0.5 mL	0.5 mL x 3 doses at 2 months interval	N/A	IM only	RF	N/A	N/A	Do not freeze
Hepatitis B Immune Globulin (H-BIG)	0.5 mL syringe (neonate) and 5 mL vial (adults)	Not advised	0.06 mL/kg (3-5 mL)	N/A	N/A	N/A	Not recommended—Give IM			SDV	N/A	N/A	Refrigerate Not for IV use.
Hep B	0.5 mL 1 mL	No	IM only	No	N/A	N/A	10-20 mcg/mL	N/A	N/A	N/A	N/A	RF	Do not freeze.discard if product has been frozen.
Hepatitis B Vaccine (Heptavax-B)	0.5 mL/10 mcg dose	Not advised	5-20 mcg	N/A	N	20 mcg/mL	Not recommended—give IM			SDV	N/A	N/A	Shake Well. For IM Use. Refrigerate
Hetastarch (Hespan)	6% in 500 mL	No	No	No	diluted bag	6gm, 100 mL	20-50 mL/kg/d	NS	max 20 mg/kg/hr	SD bag	N/A	RT	premix bag
Hyaluronidase (Wydase)	150 u/vial—powder or solution	No	Yes	Yes	NS 1 mL	150 u/mL	varying dosing	N/A	N/A	SDV & MDV	N/A	Solution must be RF	May be administer as intradermally
Hydralazine (Apresoline)	20 mg/1 mL Vial	Conc. 20 mg/mL at a rate of 5 mg/min	Yes—5-40 mg	N/A	N/A	20 mg/mL	0-25 mg / 26-50 mg	50 mL NS / 100 mL NS	200 mL/hr (over 15 min) / 200 mL/hr (over 30 min)	SDV	N/A	72 hrs RT	Do not refrigerate.

Drug Name	Package Size	Routes of Administration			Injectable Preparation		IVPB Preparation			Stability			Notes/Comments
		IVP	IM	SC	Dilute with	Conc.	Dose	Solutions	Administration rate	Reconstituted in vial	In a syringe	In Piggy bag	
Hydrocortisone Sodium Succinate (Solution Cortef)	100 mg/2 mL vial; 250 mg/2 mL vials	100 mg/min	15-240 MG	N/A	N/A (Activate Vial)	50 mg/mL and 125 mg/mL	All Doses	50 mL D5W or NS	over 15 min	72 hrs RT or RF	72 hrs RT or RF	24 hrs RT or RF	Protect from light.
Hydromorphone (Dilaudid)	2 mg/1 mL Carpujects and	Slow over 2-3 min	Yes	Yes	N/A	2 mg/mL	15 mg	30 mL NS	Conc. = 0.5 mg/mL; 0.25-1 mg/hr	Single Dose Carpujects; Mdv	N/A	72 hrs RT or RF (30 d if diluted w/ BNS)	IVP must be given over 2-3 min to avoid side effects
Hydroxyzine (Vistaril)	25 & 50 mg/mL vials; 1 and 10 mL	Not advised	Yes	N/A	N/A	25 and 50 mg/mL	Not recommended			SDVs and MDV	N/A	N/A	Protect from light. For IM use.
Ibutilide Fumarate (Corvert)	1 mg/10 mL	Give over 10 min	Not advised	N/A	N/A	0.1 mg/mL	1 mg-2 mg	50 mL NS or D5W	300 mL/hr (over 10 min) (max conc. 0.1 mg/mL)	SDVs	N/A	24 hrs RT; 48 hrs RF	Administer undiluted or diluted with D5W/NS
Idarubicin (Idamycin)	5, 10 mg	Yes	No	No	NS 5 mL	1 mg/mL	varying dosing	NS or D5W	over 10-15 min	N/A	72 hrs RT 7 D RF	72 hrs RT 7 D RF	protect from light
Ifosfamide (IFEX)	1 gm	N/A	N/A	N/A	SWFI 20 mL	50 mg/mL		NS 250 mL, for CIVI NS 1-2 L	over 30-60 min for CIVI over 24 hrs	N/A	N/A	7 d RT 21 d RF	Administer w MESNA
Imipenem & Cilastatin (Primaxin)	500 mg vial (powder for reconstitution)	Not advised	Yes	N/A	10 mL SWFI	50 mg/mL or 100 mg/5 mL for IM	0-500 mg / 501 mg -1 gm	100 mL NS / 250 mL NS	200 mL/hr (Over 30 min) / 250 mL/hr (Over 1 hr)	4 hrs RT; 24 hrs RF	4 hrs RT; 24 hrs RF	8 hrs RT; 48 hrs RF	Max dose = 4 gm/day
Immune globulin (Privigen)	5g, 10gm, 20g, soln	IVPB	No	No	D5W, NS, SWFI	50-100 mg/mL	200-800 mg/kg	D5W, NS, SWFI	N/A	N/A	N/A	24 month at RT	can flus line w D5W/NS infuse seperately from other meds
Immune Serum Globulin (Gamimune)	5 gm/50 mL; 10 gm/100 mL; 20 gm/200 mL	Not advised	Not advised	N/A	N	100 mg/mL (10%)	0.01-0.02 mL/kg/min for 30 min and may increase to a max. of 0.08 mL/kg/min. (less in renal dysfunction)			SDVs	N/A	24 hrs in a piggyback	Vials are kept in Refrigerator
Indigotindi sulfonate sodium (Indigo Carmine)	0.80%	5-10 mL/min of 5% solution	Rare—40 mg or more	N/A	N/A	8 mg/mL	Not recommended			SDV	Send Vials	N/A	For Diagnostic Procedures
Insulin Detemir (Levemir)	100u/mL	No	No	sub q	N/A	N/A	varying dosing	N/A	Administer slowly by SQ route	opened vial good for 42 d RT or RF	opened vial good for 42 d RT or RF	opened vial good for 42 d RT or RF	Do not mix with other insulin. Not for IV or IM use.
Infliximab (Remicade)	100 mg vial (Powder for reconstitution)	Not advised	Not advised	N/A	10 mL SW	10 mg/mL	All doses	250 mL NS	125 mL/hr (Over 2 hrs)	24 hrs at RT	N/A	24 hrs at RT	Use inline filter for administration, do not shake vial, flush line with NS before and after administration.

Drug Name	Package Size	Routes of Administration			Injectable Preparation		IVPB Preparation			Stability			Notes/ Comments
		IVP	IM	SC	Dilute with	Conc.	Dose	Solutions	Administration rate	Reconstituted in vial	In a syringe	In Piggy bag	
Influenza Virus vaccine H5N1 (avian Flu)	0.2, 0.25, 0.5, 5 mL	No	IM only	No	N/A	all doses	2doses of 1 mL at 28days apart	N/A	IM only	RF	N/A	N/A	Protect from light and freezing
Influenza Trivalent (TIV)	6-35 months: 0.5 mL; >3 yrs: 0.5 mL	No	IM only	No	N/A	N/A	N/A	N/A	N/A	N/A	N/A	RF	Do not freeze.discard if product has been frozen.
Insulin—Regular (Humulin-R or Novolin-R)	1000 units / 10 mL vial	Over 15-30 seconds; regular insulin only	Not advised	Yes	N/A	100 units/ mL	100 units (1 mL)	500 mL 0.45% NS	Cont. Infusion	Good for 28 days once vial opened at RT or RF	14 days in RF	24 hrs in RF or at RT	Only Regular insulin may be administered IV.
							100 Units	100 mL NS	Cont. Infusion (for fluid restricted patients)				
							250 units	250 mL NS					
Interferon alfa—2b recombinant (Intron A)	5 million units (Powder for reconstitution)	Not advised	Yes	Yes	1 mL diluent provided	5 million units/mL	<10 million units	50 mL NS (at least 1 million units/10 mL)	Over 15-20 min	28 d RF, 2 d RT if diluted, (28 d undiluted vial at RT)	Send Kit	24 hr	Do not freez
							>10 million units	100 mL NS					
Irinotecan (Camptosar)	100 mg/ 5 mL	Yes	N/A	N/A	diluted	20 mg/mL		D5W 500 mL, may use NS	over 90 min	N/A	N/A	24 RT 48 hrs RF	Monitor Diarrhea
Iron Dextran (DexFerrum)	100 mg / 2 mL	25 mg / 0.5 mL test dose over 5 min (may dilute in 10 mL NS)	Yes—special technique, see PI	N/A	N/A	50 mg/mL	0-100 mg	100 mL NS	over 30-60 min	Single Dose	24 hrs	24 hrs	Give Infusion 1 hr after test dose (See Policy)
Isoniazide	100 mg/mL in 10 mL vial	No	Yes	No	purified water U.S.P, SORBITOL	100 mg/mL	varying dosing	Purified water	Continuous administration with chemotherapy regimen	N/A	N/A	24 hrs	max 300 mg IM

Drug Name	Package Size	Routes of Administration: IVP	IM	SC	Injectable Preparation: Dilute with	Conc.	IVPB Preparation: Dose	Solutions	Administration rate	Stability: Reconstituted in vial	In a syringe	In Piggy bag	Notes/Comments
Isoproterenol (Isuprel)	0.2 mg / 1 mL amps	dilute 1 mL in 10 mL at a rate of 20mcg/min over 1 min	0.02-1 mg IM	0.15-2 mg SC	N/A	0.2 mg/mL	200 mcg (0.2 mg) / 1000 mcg (1 mg)	100 mL NS or D5W / 500 mL NS or D5W (2 mcg/mL)	start at 30 mL/hr (1 mcg/min) (titrate per tilt table protocol) / 2-10 mcg/min	Single Dose Amps	Send Amps	24 hrs at RT	Follow with a 20 mL saline flush
Kanamycin (Kantrex)	1 gm/3 mL vial	Not advised	Yes	N/A	N/A	333 mg/mL	each 500 mg	100 mL D5W or NS	Over 1 hr	48 hrs for opened bottles (SDVs)	24 hrs	24 hrs RT or RF	Must be diluted beore IV infusion.
Ketamine (Ketalar)	500 mg/5 mL	must dilute first	Yes—6.5-13 mg	N/A	N/A	100 mg/mL	1-2 mg/kg	dilute to 1-2 mg/mL in D5W or NS	0.5 mg/kg/min	SDV	Send Vials	24 hrs	Infusion solution concentration should be<2 mg/mL
Ketorolac (Toradol)	15; 30; and 60 mg / 1 mL vials	Over 1-2 min	Yes	N/A	N/A	15, 30, and 60 mg/mL	Not recommended			SDVs	Send Vials	N/A	Protect from light
Labetalol (Normodyne, Trandate)	100 mg / 20 mL vials	Undiluted; all doses over 2 min	Not advised	N/A	N/A	5 mg/mL	400 mg	200 mL D5W (2 mg/mL)	2 mg/min and titrate to desired BP	MDv	30 Days	72 hrs RT or RF	Do not freez. Protect from light
Lansoprazol (prevacid)	30 mg powder	IVPB	No	No	diluate with 5 mL NS	30 mg/5 mL	30 mg	NS, LR D5W	30 min	N/A	8 hrs RT or 14 hrs RF	RT, NS, LR 24 D5W 12 hrs	do not refrigerate, inline filter must be used
Lepirudin (Refludan)	50 mg vial (Powder for reconstitution)	0.4 mg/kg bolus; Dilute to 10 mL	Not advised	N/A	1 mL NS or SW, D5W	50 mg/mL	0.4 mg/kg 100 mg	250 mL NS (0.4 mg/mL)	0.15 mg/kg/hr x 72 hrs	Use Immediately; 24 hrs RT	24 hrs RT	24 hrs RT	Administer only intravenously required renal dosing
Leucovorin	50,100, 350 mg	Yes	Yes	N/A	BSWFI	10 or 20 mg/mL	>100 mg/m2	NS 250-500 mL	IVP over 1-3 min; IVPB over 15-30 min	N/A	7 D RT or RF	24 hrs RT and 4days RF	Protect from light
Leuprolide Acetate (Lupride)	5 mg/mL	No	Yes	Yes	diluent	see package insert	N/A	N/A	N/A	N/A	RT	N/A	Do not freeze. Protect from light.
leupolide depot	3.75, 7.5,11.25, 15, 22.5, & 30 mg	No	Yes	No	N/A	see package insert	N/A	N/A	pre-mixed syringe	N/A	RT	N/A	pre mix syringes
Levarterenol Bititrate (levophed)	4 mg/mL amp	Slow IV push	No	No	dilute	1 mg/mL	0.5-30 mcg/min	NS or D5W 250 mL to 1L	CIVI	N/A	RT	RT 24 hrs	Protect from light

Drug Name	Package Size	Routes of Administration			Injectable Preparation		IVPB Preparation			Stability			Notes/Comments
		IVP	IM	SC	Dilute with	Conc.	Dose	Solutions	Administration rate	Reconstituted in vial	In a syringe	In Piggy bag	
Levetiracetam (keppra)	500 mg/5 mL	Yes	No	No	NS, D5W, LR	5-15 mg/mL	NS, D5W	100 mL	15 min	N/A	N/A	RT 24 hrs	Must dilute dose in 100 mL NS or D5W or LR
Levocarnitine (Carnitor)	1 gm/5 mL	undiluted over 2-3 min (10-50 mg/kg)	Not advised	N/A	N/A	200 mg/mL	50-300 mg/kg/day	conc. of 0.5-8 mg/mL in NS	give over 15 or more min	Single Dose Amps	72 hrs RT or RF	24 hrs RT	Stable in PVC bag for 24 hrs
Levorthanol Tartrate (Levo-Dromran)	2 mg/mL in 1 & 10 mL vial	Yes	Yes	Yes	Diluted	2 mg/mL	1 mg q6-8 hrs		over 3-5 min	N/A	N/A	RT	Do not freeze
Levofloxacin (Levaquin)	500 mg/20 mL vial	Not advised	Not advised	N/A	N/A	25 mg/mL	250 mg / 500 mg	50 mL D5W / 100 mL D5W	100 mL/hr (Over 30 min) / 100 mL/hr (Over 1 hr)	72 hrs for Opened vial at RT	7 days RF	3 days at RT; 7 days in RF	Protect from light
Levothyroxine (Synthroid)	200 mcg Vial (Powder)	Over 2 min	Yes—50% of oral dose	N/A	4 mL SW	50 mg/mL	Not recommended; Give IV push			Single use (use immediately)	2 hrs	N/A	IV dose = 1/2 of oral dose
Lidocaine (Xylocaine, Nervocaine)	various	conc. 20 mg/mL at a rate of 50 mg/min (May give 50-100 mg)	Yes	Yes	N/A	0.5, 1, 2, 4%	2 gm	500 mL D5W	Not to Exceed 4 mg/min (Max conc. 8 mg/mL)	SDVs and MDv	Send Vials	72 hrs RT or RF	pre mix bag available
Linozolid (Zyvox)	400 mg to 600 mg	IVPB	No	No	premix	2 mg/mL	600 mg q 12 hrs	300 mL	30-120 min	N/A	N/A	RT	overwrap until ready for infusion, protect from freezing
Lorazepam (Ativan)	2 mg / 1 mL and 20 mg / 10 mL vial	Dilute w/ equal vol. NS, D5W, or SW—give over 2-5 min	0.05 mg/kg (up to 4 mg)	N/A	N/A	2 mg/mL	40 mg	250 mL D5W or NS (Conc. 0.16 mg/mL)	0.5-4 mg/hr	Unopened Vial stable for 60 days at RT; Single and MDv	Send SDVs; 30 days from MDv	48 hrs RT or RF	Glass Bottle only; Protect vial from light.
Magnesium Sulfate	1 gm/2 mL; 5 gm/10 mL	For Eclampsia = 1 gm/min; otherwise give IVPB	Yes	N/A	N/A	500 mg/mL	0-2 gm / 2001 mg-5 gm / 20 gm / 40 gm / 80 gm	100 mL NS or D5W / 250 mL NS or D5W / 1000 mL D5LR / 1000 mL D5W / 1000 mL D5W	200 mL/hr (Over 30 min) / 250 mL/hr (Over 1 hr) / Cont. Infusion; 1-4 gm/hr	SDVs	N/A	72 hrs RT or RF	Incompatible with 10% fat emulsion

Drug Name	Package Size	Routes of Administration			Injectable Preparation		IVPB Preparation			Stability			Notes/Comments
		IVP	IM	SC	Dilute with	Conc.	Dose	Solutions	Administration rate	Reconstituted in vial	In a syringe	In Piggy bag	
Mannitol (Osmitrol)	100 gm per 1000 mL; 100 gm per 500 mL	12.5 gm/5 min at conc. of 12.5 gm/50 mL	Not advised	N/A	N/A	0.1 gm and 0.2 gm per mL	Comes as a 10% solution in 1 Liter (100gm/liter)			SDVs	Do Not Draw Up	N/A	Examine solution for crystals. Do not refrigerate; Administer through a filter
Mechlorethamine (mustargen)	10 mg/mL	Yes	No	No	NS or SWFI 10 mL	1 mg/mL	0.4 mg/kg	NS or SWFI	over 1-3 min	N/A	8 hrs RT or RF(NS only)	60 min after dilution	intercavity administration has been used consult labeling & protocol
Medroxy progesterone (Depo Provera)	150 mg / 1 mL Vials	Not advised	150 mg	N/A	N/A	150 mg/mL		Give IM		SDVs	Send Vials	N/A	Shake Well. For IM Use Only
MMR	0.5 mL	No	No	Sub Q	Diluent included	0.5 mL	0.5 mL	diluent included	SQ only	SDV	SDV	SDV	Do not freeze. Protect from light.
MMR +Var (proquad)	≤12 yrs: 0.5 mL	No	No	Sub q	N/A	0.5 mL	0.5 mL	N/A	SQ only	72 hrs before constitution RF, 30 min after reconstitution	N/A	N/A	Live vaccine.
Mennigococcal Dipphthera Toxoid Conj vaccine (Menactra)	0.5 mL	No	IM only	No	N/A	0.5 mL	0.5 mL	N/A	IM only	RF	N/A	N/A	Do not freeze. Do not mix with other vaccins.
Meningococcal Polysaccride (MPSV4)	0.5 mL	No	IM only	Sub Q	N/A	0.5 mL	0.5 mL	N/A	IM only	RF	RF	N/A	Do not freeze. Protect from light.
Meningococcal Cong MCV4	0.5 mL	No	IM only	No	N/A	0.5 mL	0.5 mL	N/A	IM only	RF	N/A	N/A	Do not freeze. Do not mix with other vaccins.
Meperidine (Demeral)	various	dilute w 5 mL NS, over 3-5 min	Yes	Yes	N/A	25, 50, 75, 100 mg/mL	300 mg	30 mL NS	For PCA use	SDVs and MDv	72 hrs from SDV; 30 days from MDV	72 hrs RT or RF (30 days if diluted w/ BNS)	
Meropenem (Merrem IV)	1 gm vial (Powder for reconstitution)	Not advised, but can give over 3-5 min	Not advised	N/A	20 mL SW	50 mg/mL	1 gm	50 mL NS	100 mL/hr (Over 30 min)	2 hrs RT; 12 hrs RF	2 hrs RT; 12 hrs RF	24 hrs RT, 48 hrs RF	Do not mix with other drugs.
Mesna	1gm/ 10 mL	Yes, Dilute <20 mg/mL	N/A	N/A	D5W, NS	100 mg/mL	20% of ifosphamide dose	NS 50-100 mL	IVP—over 3-5 min; IVPB over 15-30 min	N/A	N/A	24 hrs RT or RF	Protect from light, may be given as Oral
Methadone	10 mg	No	Yes	Yes	diluted	10 mg/mL	N/A	N/A	N/A	RT	RT	N/A	detox use
Methohexital (Brevital)	500 mg powder	Yes	No	No	SWFI 50 mL	10 mg/mL		D5W or NS	3 mL/min, CIVI use in anesthesia	24 hrs RT	N/A	24 hrs RT	Do not dilute with solution containing bacteriostatic agents

Drug Name	Package Size	Routes of Administration			Injectable Preparation		IVPB Preparation			Stability			Notes/Comments
		IVP	IM	SC	Dilute with	Conc.	Dose	Solutions	Administration rate	Reconstituted in vial	In a syringe	In Piggy bag	
Methyldopate HCl (Aldomet)	250 mg / 5 mL	Not advised	Not advised	N/A	D5W	50 mg/mL	0-500 mg	50 mL D5W	100 mL/hr (Over 30 min)	N/A	N/A	24 hrs RT or RF	Maximum IV dose-1g q6 hrs
Methylene Blue (Urolene Blue)	10 mg / 1 mL (1%)	1-2 mg/kg over 5 min	Not advised	N/A	N/A	10 mg/mL	Not recommended			SDV	Send Vial	N/A	Administer undiluted intravenously over several minutes
Methylergonovine (Methergine)	0.2 mg / 1 mL amps	0.2 mg over 1 min (Dilute in 5 mL NS)	0.2 mg IM	N/A	N/A	0.2 mg/mL	Not recommended			SDA	Send Amps	N/A	IM preferred; Protect from light
Methylprednisolone Sodium Succinate (Solution Medrol)	40 mg / 1 mL, 125 mg / 2 mL, 500 mg / 4 mL, and 1 gm / 8 mL vials	50 mg/ min; Max conc. 62.5 mg/mL; 500 mg over 2-3 min	Yes	N/A	N/A (Activate Vial)	40, 62.5, and 100 mg/mL	all doses	50 mL NS or D5W	100 mL/hr (over 30 min)	48 hrs once activated	48 hrs RT or RF	48 hrs RT or RF	Only sodium succinate formulation should be given IV.Acetate salt should not be given IV.
Methylprednisolone Acetate (Depo Medrol)	40 mg / 1 mL and 80 mg / 1 mL vials	Not advised	Yes; Daily or Weekly	N/A	N/A	40 and 80 mg/mL	Not recommended—for IM use only			MDV	30 days RT or RF	N/A	Shake Well. Not For IV Use.
Metoclopramide (Reglan)	10 mg / 2 mL vial	<11 mg only; at a rate of 5 mg/min	Not advised	Via CIVI	N/A	5 mg/mL	0-250 mg / 251-500 mg	50 mL NS or D5W / NS or D5W 100 mL	200 mL/hr (Over 15 min) / 200 mL/hr (Over 30 min)	SDV	72 hrs RT or RF	24 hrs in Normal Light at RT; 48 hrs in RF	Protect from light
Metoprolol (Lopressor)	5 mg / 5 mL amps	Conc. 1 mg/mL; at 5 mg/min	Not advised	N/A	N/A	1 mg/mL	IV push Preferred			Single Dose Amps	Send Amps	N/A	Administer undiluted
Metronidazole (Flagyl)	500 mg vial (powder for reconstitution)	Not advised; Must Dilute	Not advised	N/A	4.4 mL SW or NS	100 mg/mL	250 mg / 500 mg / 1 gm	50 mL NS / 100 mL NS / 200 mL NS	100 mL/hr (Over 1 hr)	4 days RT	4 days RT	24 hrs at RT	Do Not Refrigerate, Pre mixed
Mezlocillin (Mezlin)	1, 2, 3 & 4 gm	Yes, over 3-5 min	Yes over 12-15 sec	N/A	SWFI 10 mL	100 mg/mL		D5W or NS 100 mL	over 30 min	N/A	48 hrs RT 7 d RF	48 hrs RT 7 d RF	stable 28 days frozen
Miconazole (Monistat)	10 mg/mL 20 mL amp	no	no	no	diluted	10 mg/mL	N/A	D5W or NS 200 mL	60-120 min	N/A	N/A	RT	bladder instillation use, intrathecal use

Drug Name	Package Size	Routes of Administration			Injectable Preparation		IVPB Preparation			Stability			Notes/ Comments
		IVP	IM	SC	Dilute with	Conc.	Dose	Solutions	Administration rate	Reconstituted in vial	In a syringe	In Piggy bag	
Micafungin (mycamine)	treatment 150 mg/day	IV	No	No	Add 5 mL NS then add 100 mL NS in 50-150 mg micafungin	0.5-1.5 mg/mL	50-150 mg daily	100 mL NS or D5W	infuse over 1 hrs	N/A	N/A	24 hrs RT	rapid infusion may result in histamine mediated reaction
Midazolam (Versed)	2 mg/2 mL, 5 mg/5 mL, 10 mg/2 mL, 100 mg/10 mL vials	Conc. 5 mg/mL; 1-2.5 mg over 2-3 min. May titrate.	0.07-0.1 mg/kg	N/A	N/A	1 mg/mL and 5 mg/mL	25 mg	250 mL D5W or NS	0.5-10 mg/hr	MDV	30 days; Send Vials	72 hrs at RT or RF	not for epidural or intrathecal injection
Milrinone (Primacor)	10 mg/10 mL vials	Conc. 10 mg/mL; any dose over 10 min	Not advised	N/A	N/A	1 mg/mL	20 mg / 40 mg (DS)	100 mL D5W (Premix) / 100 mL NS or D5W	0.25-1 mcg/kg/min	SDV	72 hr	72 hrs at RT or RF	Avoid freezing
Mitomycin C (Mutamycin)	5, 20 mg	Yes	No	No	SWFI 10 mL	0.5 mg/mL	varying dosing	NS 100-250 mL	over 5-30 min	N/A	N/A	24 hrs RT (diluted) 7 D RT, 14 D RF 1 hr frozen	do not shake vial, Intravesical or intra opthalmic use
Mitoxantrone (Novatrone)	2 mg base per mL in 10, 15 mL vial	No	No	No	D5W, NS	35mcg/mL	12 mg/m2	D5W or NS 50 mL	over 3 min	use immediately	N/A	Use immediately	do not freeze
Micacurium (Mivacron)	2 mg/mL 5 mL & 10 mL vial	Yes, over 5-15 sec	No	No	diluted	2 mg/mL		D5W or NS	CIVI at 10mcg/kg/min	RT	N/A	24 hrs RT	CIVI to maintain neuromuscular block pre mix solution
Morphine (Astramorph, Duramorph)	various	15 mg / 5 min undiluted	Yes	Yes	N/A	various	30 mg / 300 mg / 50 mg	30 mL / 30 mL NS / 250 mL NS or D5W (Premix)	Standard PCA / Concentrated PCA / 2-5 mg/hr initially, then increase (0.8-80 mg/hr maintenance)	SDVs and mdv	Send vials/ syringes	72 hrs RT or RF (30 d if diluted w/ BNS)	binds to plastic
Multi-vitamin (M.V.I.-12)	various	Yes	No	No	NS, D5W, LR	Various	varying dosing	diluted in 500 mL	over few hrs	4 hrs RF	N/A	Use immediately	Must be diluted prior to administration
Muromonab CD3 Orthoclone-OKT3	5 mg/5 mL	Yes	No	No	Diluted	1 mg/mL	N/A		rapid IV infusion, <1 min	N/A	RF	16 hrs RT or RF	do not shake use .2micron filter

Drug Name	Package Size	Routes of Administration			Injectable Preparation		IVPB Preparation			Stability			Notes/ Comments
		IVP	IM	SC	Dilute with	Conc.	Dose	Solutions	Administration rate	Reconstituted in vial	In a syringe	In Piggy bag	
Nafcillin (Nafcil, Unipen, Nallpen)	500 mg vial (powder for reconstitution)	33 mg/mL over 3-5 Min	Yes; See Below	N/A	4.8 mL SW or NS	100 mg/mL	0-1.5 gm	50 mL D5W or NS	100 mL/hr (Over 30 min)	3 Days RT; 7 Days RF	3 Days RT; 7 Days RF	24 hrs RT; 4 Days in the RF	Refrigerate
	1 gm vial (Powder for reconstitution)	IM/Buretrol Prep.: Dilute 500 mg with 1.8 mL SW or NS = 250 mg/mL; 1 gm vial w/ 3.4 mL, 2 gm w/ 6.6 mL			9.6 mL SW or NS	100 mg/mL							
	2 gm Vial (Powder for reconstitution)				19.2 mL SW or NS	100 mg/mL	>1.5 gm	100 mL D5W or NS	100 mL/hr (Over 60 min)				
Nafcillin Frozen PB (Nafcil, Unipen, Nallpen)	1 gm / 50 mL and 2 gm / 100 mL Premixed	Not advised	Not advised	N/A	Already Prepared; Pre-mixed bag	Already Prepared; Pre-mixed bag	Already Prepared	Already Prepared	100 mL/hr (1 gm over 30 min; 2 gm over 1 hr)	N/A	N/A	21 days in the RF; 72 hrs RT	Refrigerate
Nalbuphine (Nubain)	10 mg / 1 mL amps and 100 mg / 10 mL MDV	10 mg over 3-5 min	Yes (10 mg)	Yes (10 mg)	N/A	10 mg/mL	Give IV Push			Single dose amps and Mdv	Send amps	N/A	Protect vial from excessive light.
Naloxone (Narcan)	0.4 mg / 1 mL; 4 mg / 10 mL	All doses over 2 min	0.4-2 mg	0.4-2 mg	N/A	400 mcg/ mL (0.4 mg/mL)	2 mg	500 mL NS or D5W	Titrate—continuous infusion	SDVs and Mdv	Send SDVs; 30 days from Mdv	24 hrs RT or RF	
Nelaravbine (Arranon)	5 mg/mL in 50 mL vial	Yes	No	No	1/2 NS; reconstitution not required.	2-8 mcg/ mL	1500 mg/m2	N/A	Infuse over 1 hr in children and 2 hrs in adult	8 hrs RT	8 hrs RT	8 hrs RT	Stable in PVC nags or glass container.
Neostigmine (Prostigmine)	10 mg / 10 mL Vial (1:1000)	0.5 mg/min for myasthenia gravis (15-375 mg/D)	Yes; 0.25-0.5 mg	Yes 0.25-0.5 mg	N/A	1 mg/mL	Not recommended			MDV	30 days RT or RF	N/A	Protect from light.
Nesiritide (Natrecor)	1.5 mg vial (Powder for reconstitution)	Bolus— withdraw from infusion bag—give over 60 sec	Not advised	N/A	5 mL Diluted in NS or D5W	0.3 mg/mL (Approx.)	1.5 mg	250 mL D5W or NS	0.01 mcg/kg/ min (0.1 mL/ kg/hr) Conc.: 6 mcg/mL	24 hrs RT or RF	24 hrs RT or RF	24 hrs RT or RF	Do Not Shake Vial
Nicardipine (Cardene)	25 mg/10 mL amps	Not advised	Not advised	N/A	N/A	2.5 mg/mL	25 mg	250 mL NS or D5W	0.5-15 mg/hr (0.1 mg/mL)	Single dose amps	N/A	24 hrs RT	premixed bag available w 0.1 mg/mL

Drug Name	Package Size	Routes of Administration			Injectable Preparation		IVPB Preparation			Stability			Notes/ Comments
		IVP	IM	SC	Dilute with	Conc.	Dose	Solutions	Administration rate	Reconstituted in vial	In a syringe	In Piggy bag	
Nitroglycerin (Nitrostat IV)	25 mg / 5 mL Vials	Not advised	Not advised	N/A	N/A	5 mg/mL	50 mg	250 mL D5W or NS (Glass) (DS)	5 mcg/min and titrate to response	SDV	N/A	48 hrs RT; 72 hrs RF	Use only glass bottles; (Max conc. 400 mcg/mL)
Nitroglycerin Pre-mixed	25 mg/250 mL	Not advised		N/A	N/A	0.1 mg/mL	Already prepared			N/A	N/A	Exp. Date on Package	
Nitroprusside (Nipride, Nitropress)	50 mg (Powder for reconstitution)	Not advised	Not advised	N/A	2-3 mL D5W or SW	various	50 mg	250 mL D5W (Max conc. 400 mcg/mL)	0.3-10 mcg/kg/min	24 hrs in D5W in RF	N/A	24 hrs in D5W in the RF or RT	Protect from light from Opaque Wraps (Amber bags do not work)
Norepinephrine Bitarate (Levophed)	4 mg/4 mL amps	Not advised	Not advised	N/A	N/A	1 mg/mL	4 mg	250 mL D5W	2-12 mcg/min, max conc 32mcg/mL	Single Dose Amps	N/A	24 hrs at RT	Must be diluted prior to use
Octreotide (Sandostatin)	0.5 mg / 1 mL Ampules	Give over 3 min	No (LAR Depot okay)	Yes	N/A	0.5 mg/mL	All doses / 500 mcg	50 mL NS / 250 mL NS	200 mL/hr (Over 15 Min) / Cont. Infusion (25 mcg/hr)	Single dose Amps; 14 days at RT	72 hrs RT or RF	48 hrs RT	In RF; protect amps from light
Ofloxacin (Floxin)	400 mg	IV infusion	no	no	NS or D5W	4 mg/mL		NS or D5W 100 mL	over 60 min	N/A	24 hrs RT	24 hrs RT	Pre mix bag available
Olanzapine (Zyprexa)	10 mg vial	No	IM	No	N/A	5 mg/mL	10-15 mg qdaily	2.1 mL SWFI or NS	N/A	N/A	N/A	N/A	Deep in muscle mass, repeat 3doses in 2-4 hrs apart
Ondansetron (Zofran)	4 mg/2 mL; and 40 mg/20 mL vials	2 mg/min (doses <or = 4 mg)	Yes, 4 mg only	N/A	N/A	2 mg/mL	>4 mg	50 mL D5W or NS	200 mL/hr (Over 15 min)	SDVs and Mdv	Send SDVs; 30 days from Mdv	72 hrs RT or RF	protect from light??
Oprelvekin (Neumega)	5 mg vial (Powder for reconstitution)	Not advised	Not advised	50 mcg/kg	1 mL SW	5 mg/mL	Not recommended			3 hrs RT or RF	3 hrs RT or RF	N/A	Vials are kept in Refrigerator
Oxacillin	1gm & 2 gm	Slowly over 10 min	Yes	No	SWFI 10 mL	100 mg/mL	1-2gm q4-6 hrs	NS 50-100 mL	over 30 min	N/A	6 hrs RT 24 hrs RF	6 hrs RT	IM deep in gluteal mass
Oxaliplatin (eloxatin)	50 mg & 100 mg	No	No	No	D5W	5 mg/mL	85 mg/m2	D5W 500 mL	over 2-6 hrs	N/A	6 hrs RT 24 hrs RF	6 hrs RT 24 hrs RF	Incompatible with solution containing chloride.
Oxytocin (Pitocin)	100 units / 1 mL vials	Not advised	3-10 units	N/A	N/A	100 units/mL	10-40 units	1000 mL D5LR, D5W, NS, or LR	0.5-2 miliunits/min; titrate up as needed	SDV	Send Vial	24 hrs RT or RF	Infusion pump required for administration

Drug Name	Package Size	Routes of Administration			Injectable Preparation		IVPB Preparation			Stability			Notes/Comments
		IVP	IM	SC	Dilute with	Conc.	Dose	Solutions	Administration rate	Reconstituted in vial	In a syringe	In Piggy bag	
Paclitaxel (Taxol)	30 mg/5 mL 100 mg/16.7 mL	No	No	No	Diluted	6 mg/mL		NS 250-500 mL or D5W	over 1-3 hrs	N/A	72 hrs RT or RF	72 hrs RT or RF	Dispense either with glass or non-PVC container
Pamidronate Disodium (Aredia)	30, 90 mg vial (Powder for reconstitution)	Not advised	Not advised	N/A	10 mL SW	3 mg/mL	30-90 mg	250 or 500 mL NS	over 2-3 hrs	24 hrs RT or RF	N/A	24 hrs RT	Pre-Hydrate
Pancuronium Bromide (Pavulon)	10 mg/10 mL vials	Conc. 2 mg/mL, rapid over 1 min (0.1 mg/kg)	Not advised	N/A	N/A	1 mg/mL	100 mg	150 mL NS or D5W	1-1.6 mcg/kg/min	6 months at RT; MDV	30 days RT or RF	48 hrs RT or RF	May be administered undiluted by rapid IV
Paclitaxel (abraxane)	100 mg vial (Powder for reconstitution)	IVPB only	No	No	20 mL NS 5 mg/mL	50-250 mg/m2	20 mL NS	Over 30 min	Single use	N/A	8 hrs RF	3 days RT	Protect from light
Pantoprazole (Protonix)	40 mg vial (Powder for reconstitution)	Not advised	Not advised	N/A	10 mL NS	4 mg/mL	40 mg	100 mL D5W or NS	400 mL/hr (Over 15 min)	2 hrs at RT or RF	N/A	12 hrs RT or RF	Dispense with inline filter provided
							80 mg	250-500 mL D5W or NS	Cont. Infusion over 8-12 hrs				
Papaverine (Pavabid, Cerespan)	60 mg/2 mL vials	30 mg over 2 min	preferred	N/A	N/A	30 mg/mL	Not recommended			SDV	Send Vials	N/A	Do not Refrigerate
Papillomavirus Qudrivalent vaccine (Gardasil)	0.5 mL	No	IM only	No	N/A	0.5 mL	0.5 mL followed by 0.5 mL at 2,6 months	N/A	IM only	RF	N/A	N/A	Do not freeze and protect from light.
Paricalcitrol (Zemplar)	5 mg/1 mL vials	Yes; can give during dialysis	Not advised	N/A	N/A	5 mg/mL	Not recommended			SDV	Send Vial	N/A	Should not be given more frequently than every other day
Pegaspargase (Oncaspar)	3750 u/5 mL	No	Yes; no >2 mL/syr		Diluted	750 u/mL	2500unit/m2 over 1-2 hrs via IV infusion			N/A	24 hrs RT	24 hrs RT	dilute in 100 mL NS or D5W
Pegfilgrastim (Neulasta, G-CSF)	6 mg/0.6 mL	Not advised	Not advised	Yes	N/A	10 mg/mL	Not recommended			48 hrs RT	Send Syringe	48 hrs RT	RF; Protect from light

Drug Name	Package Size	Routes of Administration			Injectable Preparation		IVPB Preparation			Stability			Notes/ Comments
		IVP	IM	SC	Dilute with	Conc.	Dose	Solutions	Administration rate	Reconstituted in vial	In a syringe	In Piggy bag	
Penicillin G (Pfizepen)	5 Million unit vial (Powder for reconstitution)	Not advised; must dilute	See package insert for dilution	N/A	8.2 mL SW	500,000 units/mL	0-3 million units	50 mL D5W or NS	100 mL/hr (Over 30 min)	7 days in RF	7 days in RF	24 hrs RT; 7 days RF	Follow directions on vial for reconstitution. Refrigerate
							>3 million units	100 mL D5W or NS	100 mL/hr (Over 60 min)				
Penicillin G Frozen PB (Pfizepen)	2 and 3 million units / 50 mL piggy bag				Already prepared; pre-mixed bag		Already prepared		100 mL/hr (Over 30 min)	N/A	N/A	24 hrs RT; 14 days RF	Inactivated in acidic or alkaline solution
Pentamidine (pentam)	300 mg	Yes	Yes	No	D5W	1-2.5 mg/mL	4 mg/kg/day	D5W 100-200 mL	over 60 min	48 hrs RT	N/A	24 hrs RT	Do not use NS as a diluant
Pentobarbital (Nembutal)	1 gm / 20 mL vial	Give slowly at 50 mg/min max.	Yes	N/A	N/A	50 mg/mL	2000 mg	250 mL NS	1-3 mg/kg/hr maint. Coma=10 mg/kg load over 60 min	MDV	30 Days	24 hrs RT	Avoid rapid IV administration than 50 mg/min
Phenobarbital (Luminal)	130 mg / 1 mL; 65 mg / 1 mL	60 mg/mL over 3-5 min	Yes	N/A	N/A	65 and 130 mg/mL	15 mg/kg	100 mL NS	given over 30 min	SDV	72 hr	24 hrs RT; 72 hrs RF	Avoid rapid IV administration than 60 mg/min
Phentolamine mesylate (Ora Verse)	0.4 mg/1.7 mL x 3 cartridge	N/A	N/A	N/A	N/A	0.2-0.8 mg / 0.8-2.5 mL	0.2, 0.4, 0.8 mg	NS	Submucosal route only	48 hrs RT, 7 d RF	48 hrs RT, 7 d RF	48 hrs RT, 7 d RF	Compatible with NS
Phentolamine (Regitine)	5 mg vial (Powder for reconstitution)	5 mg in 10 mL NS over 1 min	Yes	5-10 mg	1 mL SW	5 mg/mL		Not recommended		48 hrs RT; 72 hrs RF	48 hrs RT; 72 hrs RF	N/A	Stable in NS
Phenylephrine (Neo-Synephrine)	10 mg / 1 mL vial	1 mg/mL (Dilute with NS) 0.1-0.5 mg, slowly over 3-4 min	2-10 mg	2-10 mg	N/A	10 mg/mL	10 mg	250 mL NS (40 mcg/mL)	40-60 mcg/min	SDV	Send Vial	24 hrs at RT	Protect From Light
Phenytoin (Dilantin)	100 mg / 2 mL and 250 mg / 5 mL vial	Not to exceed 50 mg/min; 25 mg/min in elderly	100-200 mg	N/A	N/A	50 mg/mL	0-500 mg	Prefer IV Push / 50 mL NS only	200 mL/hr (Over 15 min)	Single Use Vials	4 hrs RT; Do Not RF	4 hrs RT; Do Not RF	Administer with an inline filter (0.22 micron). Use NS only; flush IV line w/ NS before and after administration
							500 mg-1 gm	100 mL NS	200 mL/hr (Over 30 min)				

Drug Name	Package Size	Routes of Administration			Injectable Preparation		IVPB Preparation			Stability			Notes/Comments
		IVP	IM	SC	Dilute with	Conc.	Dose	Solutions	Administration rate	Reconstituted in vial	In a syringe	In Piggy bag	
Phosphate (sodium or potassium)	3 mmole phosphate and 4.4 mEq K or 4 mEq Na per mL	Not advised		N/A	N/A	3 mmole phosphate and 4.4 mEq K or 4 mEq Na per mL	0-10 mM	250 mL NS or D5W	Over 6-10 hrs (max. 0.2 mM phosphate/kg/hr) Kphos is limited to 20 mEq K per hr	Single Dose Vials	N/A	24 hrs	Incompatible with LR
							11-20 mM	500 mL NS or D5W					
							21-30 mM	1000 mL NS or D5W					
Physostigime Salicylate (Antilirium)	2 mg / 2 mL Ampules	1 mg over 1-3 min	Not advised	N/A	N/A	1 mg/mL	2 mg	100 mL NS or D5W	1-10 mg/hr	Multi-Dose Amps	Send Amps	N/A	check rate?
Phytonadione (Aqua Mephyton)	10 mg / 1 mL amps; 0.5 mg / 0.5 mL	Not advised; MD only; Max rate = 1 mg/min; Dilute w/ 10 mL D5W or NS	2.5-25 mg	2.5-25 mg (Preferred)	N/A	10 mg/mL and 1 mg/mL	Not recommended 0-25 mg	50 mL D5W or NS	100 mL/hr (Over 30 min)	Single Dose Amps	Send Amps	Use immediately	Protect from light. Do not filter; SC preferred
							Not recommended 26-50 mg	100 mL D5W or NS	100 mL/hr (Over 60 min)				
Piperacillin and Tazobactam (Zosyn)	2.25 gm vial (Powder for reconstitution)	Not advised, but can go 150 mg/min; conc. of 90 mg/mL	Not advised	N/A	10 mL SW	225 mg/mL	2.25 gm	50 mL D5W or NS	100 mL/hr (Over 30 min)	24 hrs RT or 48 hrs RF	24 hrs RT; 7 days RF	24 hrs RT; 7 days RF	Avoid concurrent aminoglycoside
Piperacillin and Tazobactam (Zosyn)	3.375 gm vial (powder for reconstitution)		Not advised	N/A	15 mL SW	225 mg/mL	3.375-4.5 gm	100 mL D5W or NS	200 mL/hr (Over 30 min)				
Piperacillin and Tazobactam (Zosyn) Premixed Bags—Frozen	3.375 gm	Not advised	Not advised	N/A	Already Prepared; Pre-mixed bag		Already prepared		200 mL/hr (Over 30 min)	N/A	N/A	24 hrs RT; 14 days RF	Do not refreeze after thawing
Pipercillin (Pipercil)	2,3 & 4 gm	No	Yes	N/A	10 mL SWFI	20 mg/mL	2-6 gm q 4-6 hrs	D5W or NS	over 30 min	N/A	24 hrs RT	24 hrs RT	Should not be mix with aminoglycoside
Plicamycin (Mithracin)	2.5 mg	Not advised	No	No	SWFI 4.9 mL	0.5 mg/mL	varying dosing	D5W 250 mL—1 L	over 30 min or more	N/A	N/A	24 hrs RT 48 hrs RF	
Pneumococcal Polyaccride (PPV)	0.5 mL	no	IM only	sub q	N/A	N/A	N/A	N/A	N/A	N/A	N/A	RF	Always refrigerate
Polymyxin B (Neosporin)	500,000 Units (Powder for reconstitution)	Not advised	Not advised	N/A	10 mL D5W	50,000 units/mL	500,000 units	500 mL D5W	Cont. Infusion	72 hrs RF	72 hrs RF	72 hrs RF	Infuse IV over 60-90 min

Drug Name	Package Size	Routes of Administration			Injectable Preparation		IVPB Preparation			Stability			Notes/Comments
		IVP	IM	SC	Dilute with	Conc.	Dose	Solutions	Administration rate	Reconstituted in vial	In a syringe	In Piggy bag	
Potassium Chloride	10 mEq / 5 mL and 20 mEq / 10 mL vials	Not advised	Not advised	N/A	N/A		20 mEq	100 mL D5W or NS	100 mL/hr (Over 1 hr)	SDVs	N/A	72 hrs RT or RF	Monitor electrolytes
						2 mEq/mL	If vein irritation occurs, infuse over two hrs, or add 20 mg of lidocaine per bag						
Potassium Chloride Premixed Bags	20 mEq / 100 mL						Maximum recommended dose is 20 mEq/hr (Per P&T committee)			N/A	N/A	30 days outside of wrapper	
Potassium Phosphate						See Phosphate (sodium or potassium).							
Pralidoxime Chloride (Protopam Chloride)	1 gm vial (Powder for reconstitution)	give 50 mg/mL over 5 min	Not advised	N/A	20 mL SW	50 mg/mL	1-2 gm	100 mL NS	over 15-30 min	SDV	Send Vials	Use immediately	IVPB administration preferred
Prednisolone		Yes over 3-5 min	Yes	N/A	D5W or NS			D5W or NS 100 mL					Protect from moisture
Pramlinitide (Symlin)	60 & 120 peninjector or 5 mL vial	No	No	sub Q	N/A	N/A	varying dosing	N/A	administer slowly	unopen vial till expiration date	N/A	open vial 30 day RT	used with insulin, but given seperately & should not be mixed
Procainamide (Pronestyl)	100 mg/mL; 10 mL vial	Dilute 100 mg with 5 -10 mL D5W, administer at 25-50 mg/min	Yes	N/A	N/A	100 mg/mL	1 gm	250 mL D5W	1-6 mg/min	MDV	30 Days	24 hrs in RF	Protect from light
Prochloroperazine (Compazine)	5 mg/mL vials	Give at 5 mg/min; max. 10 mg/dose	Yes	N/A	N/A	5 mg/mL	All doses	50 mL NS	over 15 min	Single Use Vials	Send Vials	24 hrs RT or RF	Protect from light.
Promethazine (Phenergan)	25 mg / 1 mL and 50 mg / 1 mL Ampules	25 mg/mL at 25 mg/min	Preferred	N/A	N/A	25 and 50 mg/mL	Not recommended—IM preferred			Single Dose Ampules	Send Amps	N/A	Protect from light.
Propofol (Diprivan)	200 mg / 20 mL	MD presence required; 20 mg over 10 seconds	Not advised	N/A	N/A	10 mg/mL	Already Prepared		6-12 mg/ kg/hr	SDVs; Discard after 12 hrs	6 hrs at RT	N/A (12 hrs once IV Hanging)	Do Not Filter; Shake well before administration

Drug Name	Package Size	Routes of Administration			Injectable Preparation		IVPB Preparation			Stability			Notes/ Comments
		IVP	IM	SC	Dilute with	Conc.	Dose	Solutions	Administration rate	Reconstituted in vial	In a syringe	In Piggy bag	
Propranolol (Inderal)	1 mg / 1 mL amps	Conc. 1 mg/mL given at 1 mg/min	Not advised	N/A	N/A	1 mg/mL	All doses	50 mL NS	over 15 min	Single Dose Amps	Send Amps	24 hrs at RT	Monitor HR and BP closely
Protamin Sulfate	250 mg	Yes	N/A	N/A	Steril water or NS or D5W	1-2 mg/mL	1 mg per 100unit heparin	D5W or NS 250 mL	loading 25-50 mg then over 8-16 hrs	N/A	N/A	2wk RT	Monitor Aptt and bleeding closely
Protirelin (Relefact) Thyroid releasing hormone	500mcg	Yes over 15-30 sec	No	No									diagnostic use
Protin C concentate (Ceprotin)	500 IU and 1000IU Powder	IV in 3 hrs	No	No	Supplied diluent of SWFI w product	100 IU/mL	SDV	5-10 mL sterile water	Initial 100-120 IU/kg, followed by 60-80 IU/kg q 6 hrs, then 45-60 q 6-12 hrs	N/A	N/A	RF 2-8C administered in 3 hrs	protect from light, avoid freezing No preservative follow instruction for mixing
Pyridostigmine (Mestinon)	5 mg/mL 2 mL amp	Yes, over 5-10 min	Yes	No	diluted		Varying dosing			N/A	N/A	N/A	large doses sholud be accompnied by Atropine or Robinul
Pyridoxine (Hexa Betalin, vitamin B6)	100 mg / 1 mL	50 mg/min; conc. 100 mg/mL	Yes	Yes	N/A	100 mg/mL	0-5 gm	50 mL NS	Over 30 min	MDV	72 hr	72 hr	Protect from light.
quinupristin 150 mg /dalfospin 350 mg (Synercid)	500 mg vial	IVPB	No	No	5 mL SWFI or D5W 100 mL	100 mg/mL	7.5 mg/kg q8-12 hrs	250 mL D5W	Over 60 min	N/A	N/A	RT 5 hrs, RF 54 hrs	7.5 mg/kg q8-12 hrs do not shake
Quinidine Gluconate	80 mg/mL (50 mg Equvi) in 10 mL vial	Yes	Yes	No	N/A	16 mg/mL	Varying dosing	250 mL D5W	Over 1 mL/min	N/A	N/A	N/A	use pump to infuse, under close supervision
Rabies vaccine (Rabavert, Imovax Rabies)	2.5 units/mL vial, powder for reconstitution (kit)	Not advised	1 mL given x 2-5 doses (See PI)	N/A	Diluent Prov-ided	2.5 units/mL	Not recommended			Single use Vials	Send kit	N/A	Kept in the Refrigerator
Rabies Immune Globulin (Imogram Rabies, Bayrab, Hyperab)	1500 units / 10 mL vial	Infiltrate full dose (20 units/kg) around the wound and if any dose remains, administer IM			N/A	150 units/ mL.	Not recommended—see IM administration			SDV	N/A	N/A	Vials are in the Refrigerator

Drug Name	Package Size	Routes of Administration			Injectable Preparation		IVPB Preparation			Stability			Notes/ Comments
		IVP	IM	SC	Dilute with	Conc.	Dose	Solutions	Administration rate	Reconstituted in vial	In a syringe	In Piggy bag	
Ranitidine (Zantac)	50 mg/2 mL; 150 mg/6 mL	Dilute 50 mg in 20 mL of NS or D5W and give over 5 min	50 mg every 6-8 hrs	N/A	N/A	25 mg/mL	0-50 mg / 150 mg	50 mL D5W or NS / 500 mL NS or D5W	100 mL/hr (Over 30 min) / continuously over 24 hrs	2 mL vial is Single Dose; 6 mL vial is Multi-Dose	Send SDV; 30 days from MDV	72 hrs RT or RF	Pre mix bag available
Regadenoson (Lexiscan)	0.4 mg /5 mL prefill syringe and vial	IVP	No	No	Premixed	No	Premix	Premix	over 10-20 seconds	N/A	N/A	store a RT use mfg expiration	10 sec IV push
Recombinant antithrombin (Atryn)	1750 IU vial powder	IVPB	No	No	10 mL SWFI	100 IU/mL	varying dosing	NS	over 20 mins	N/A	N/A	3 hrs RT	Do not refrigerate reconstituted product.
Recombinant thrombin (Recothrom)	5000 IU prefilled syr, 20000 iu vial	topical use only			NS	N/A	100-1000unit/mL	NS	topical use only	N/A	N/A	24 hrs RT	*TOPICAL USE ONLY*
Reteplase (Retavase)	10 units (Powder for reconstitution)	10 unit bolus over 2 min x 2, 30 min apart	Not advised	N/A	10 mL SW (provided)	1 unit/mL	10 units	NS or D5W	normally IV push	4 hrs at RT	Send Kit	4 hrs	Do not Shake; flush line with 30-50 mL NS or D5W before and after admin.
Rifamptin (Rimactano, Rifadin)	600 mg vial (Powder for reconstitution)	Not advised	Not advised	N/A	10 mL SW	60 mg/mL	All doses	500 mL of NS	over 3 hrs	24 hrs at RT	N/A	24 hrs at RT	Protect undiluted vial from Light
Ritodrine (Yutopar)	10 mg/mL in 5 mL 15 mg/mL in 10 mL	No	No	No	diluted	0.3 mg/mL	50mcg/min	500 mL D5W	CIVI, at 0.15-.35 mg/min	N/A	N/A	48 hrs RT	Protect from excessive heat
Rituximab (Rituxan)	100 mg & 500 mg vial	Not advised	No	No	diluted	10 mg/mL		NS or D5W at 1 mg/mL	start 50 mg/hr, increase by 50 mg/hr every 30 min max. 400 mg/hr	N/A	N/A	12 hrs RT 24 hrs RF	Fmax. Conc. Up to 4 mg/mL for renal patient
Rocuronium Bromide (Zemuron)	100 mg/10 mL vials	0.45-1.2 mg/kg	Not advised	N/A	N/A	10 mg/mL	100 mg	100 mL D5W or NS	4-16 mcg/kg/min	mdv; Exp. 60 days out of RF, 30 d w opened vial	72 hrs	24 hrs RT or RF	Do not freeze
Romiplostim (Nplate)	250mcg, 500mcg powder	no	no	Sub Q	0.72 mL SWFI (250mcg) 1.2 mL (500mcg)	500mcg/mL	1mcg/kg/wk	SWFI to conc 500mcg/mL	SQ only	N/A	N/A	24 hrs RT or RF	Protect from light

Drug Name	Package Size	Routes of Administration			Injectable Preparation		IVPB Preparation			Reconstituted in vial	Stability		Notes/Comments
		IVP	IM	SC	Dilute with	Conc.	Dose	Solutions	Administration rate		In a syringe	In Piggy bag	
Ropivicaine (Naropin)	Various	Given as an epidural			N/A	2 mg/mL (0.2%) and 5 mg/mL (0.5%)	100 mg in 200 mL NS	200 mL NS	8-30 mg/hr; given as an epidural	SDVs	24 hrs	24 hrs	Given Epidurally
Scopolamine	0.3, 0.4, 0.86 & 1 mg/mL	Yes	Yes	Yes	w SWFI	0.4-1 mg/mL	0.3-0.65 mg	Equal volume SW	Inject over 2-3 min	N/A	RT	RT	May give IV after dilution w SWFI
Secobarbital (Seconal)	50 mg/mL tubex	Yes	Yes: deep	No	N/A	N/A		not applicable		N/A	RT	N/A	Restricted use For IV
Sincalide Kinevac	5 mcg powder	Yes	No	No	SWFI 5 mL	1mcg/mL	0.02-0.04 mcg/kg	SFWI or NS	over 30-60 sec	N/A	24 hrs RT	24 hrs RT	Discard any unused portion after reconstitution
Sodium Acetate	40 mEq/20 mL	No—must dilute prior to admin.	Not advised	N/A	N/A	2 mEq/mL	For use in large volume parentals			SDVs; discard 4 hrs after entry	N/A	72 hrs in RT or RF	Protect from light, heat and freezing
Sodium Bicarbonate	50 mEq/50 mL vial (8.4% solution) and 5 mEq/10 mL (4.2% pediatric)	all doses over 1-2 min	Not advised	Yes, if diluted to isotonicity	N/A	1 mEq/mL (adult) and 0.5 mEq/mL (ped)	Not recommended; give IV push; May use in LVP's			SDVs	Send Pre-packed syringes	72 hrs RT or RF	Protect from heat and freezing. Use only clear solution.
Sodium Phosphates	See "Phosphate (Sodium or Potassium)"												
Sodium Thiosulfate (Cyanide Antidote)	1000 mg/10 mL vial	12.5 gm over 10 min	Not advised	N/A	N/A	100 mg/mL	See IV Push Administration			SDV	Send Vials	N/A	Rapid infusion may cause hypotension.
Streptokinase	250,000 units 750,000 units 1,500,000 units/vial	Yes	No	No	D5W or NS 5 mL	125,000 u/mL	varying dosing	D5W or NS	1.5 mu over 60 min; for MI 100,000 u/hr for DVT/PE	RT	Prepare just before use	8 hrs in RF	dose &duration depends on indication, cath clearance use
Streptozocin (Zanosar)	1 gm powder	Yes	No	No	NS 9.5 mL	100 mg/mL	varying dosing	D5W or NS 100-250 mL	over 30-60 min	12 hrs once diluted in vial	12 hrs	48 hrs RT 95 hrs RF	Extend infusion if venous irritation
Succinylcholine Chloride (Quelicin, Anectine)	200 mg/10 mL vial	0.3-1.1 mg/kg initially followed by 0.04-0.07 mg/kg	Max of 150 mg administered IM (3-4 mg/kg)	N/A	N/A	20 mg/mL	200 mg	100 mL NS or D5W (2 mg/mL)	0.5-10 mg/min continuous infusion	MDV; Exp. in 14 days at RT	14 days RT; 30 Days RF	24 hrs in RF	Vials are kept in Refrigerator

Drug Name	Package Size	Routes of Administration			Injectable Preparation		IVPB Preparation			Stability			Notes/Comments
		IVP	IM	SC	Dilute with	Conc.	Dose	Solutions	Administration rate	Reconstituted in vial	In a syringe	In Piggy bag	
Sulfentanil (sufenta)	50mc/mL 1,2 and 5 mL amp	Yes	No	No	diluted	slow infusion	10-25mcg	diluted	slow or continue infusion or IV push	single dose amp	RT	N/A	Administer w nitrous oxide/oxygen
Sulfamethoxazole and Trimethoprim (Bactrim)	160 mg TMP/800 mg SMZ per 10 mL vials	Not advised	Not advised	N/A	N/A	16 mg/mL TMP; 80 mg/mL of SMZ	5 mL / 10 mL	125 mL D5W / 250 mL D5W	125 mL/hr (Over 1 hr) / 250 mL/hr (Over 1 hr)	SDVs	48 hrs	2–6 hrs	Do not refrigerate; flush line w/ D5W before and after administration
Somatropin Sq (Accertropin)	5 mg/mL solution	No	No	sub Q	diluent provided	1-5 mg/mL	varying dosing	diluent provided	SQ only	N/A	21 days RF	21 days RF	do not give IV, discard 14 days after first use
Sumatriptan Succinate (Imitrex)	6 mg/0.5 mL vials	Not advised	Not advised	Max 6 mg	N/A	12 mg/mL	Not recommended—give SC			SDV	Send Vials	N/A	Max of 12 mg/24 hrs
Tacrolimus (Prograf)	5 mg/mL	IV infusion only	No	No	NS, D5W	0.004-0.02 mg/mL	0.01-0.05 mg/kg/d	D5W or NS	CIVI, over 24 hrs, 0.05 to 0.1 mg/kg/day	N/A	N/A	24 hrs RT	Prepare & store in GLASS
Temozolomide (Temodar)	100 mg powder	IVPB	No	No	41 mL NS	2.5 mg/mL conc	100-200 mg/m2/day	41 mL NS	Over 90 min	14 hrs RT	N/A	14 hrs RT or RF	use within 14 hrs of reconstitute include infusion time
Tenecteplase (TNKase)	50 mg kit	over 5 seconds	Not advised	N/A	10 mL SW (provided)	5 mg/mL	Give via IV push			8 hrs in RF	Send Kit	N/A	Incompatible with dextrose solution.
Teniposide (VU/MON) VM26	50 mg/5 mL	Yes	No	No	diluted	10 mg/mL	50-180 mg/m2	NS 250-500 mL	over 1-2 hr	24 hrs RT	N/A	<0.4 mg 24 hrs 1 mg/mL 4 hrs RT	DO not RF
Terbutaline (Brethine)	1 mg/1 mL amps	See IVPB administration	Not advised	0.25 mg/dose; 0.5 mg max. / 4 hrs	N/A	1 mg/mL	5 mg	500 mL D5W	Cont. Infusion; max. rate of 10 mcg/min	Single Use Amps	Send Amps	72 hrs at RT	Do not refrigerate. Use extreme caution when administering IV
Tetnus toxoid, reduced Diphtheria and Acelluar Pertussis vaccine (Adacel, Boostrix)	0.5 mL	No	IM only	No	N/A	N/A	N/A	N/A	N/A	N/A	N/A	N/A	
Tetnus Diphtheria (TD)	0.5 mL	No	IM only	No	N/A	N/A	N/A	N/A	N/A	N/A	N/A	RF	Shake well before use.Do not freeze.
Theophylline	400 mg in 100 mL, 800 mg in 250,500 & 1L	No	No	No	diluted	10mcg/mL	varying dosing	800 mg in D5W 500 mL	No faster than 20 mg/min	N/A	N/A	RT	use loading dose

Drug Name	Package Size	Routes of Administration			Injectable Preparation		IVPB Preparation			Stability			Notes/ Comments
		IVP	IM	SC	Dilute with	Conc.	Dose	Solutions	Administration rate	Reconstituted in vial	In a syringe	In Piggy bag	
Thiamine HCl (Vitamin B1)	200 mg / 2 mL vial	25 mg/min; conc. 100 mg/mL	Yes—50-100 mg	N/A	N/A	100 mg/mL	All Doses	100 mL NS	Over 30 min	MDV	30 days (protect from light)	24 hrs	Protect from light.
Thiethylperazine (Torecan)	10 mg/2 mL amp	Not advised	10 mg Deep	N/A	N/A	5 mg/mL	Not recommended			Single Use Amps	Send Amps	N/A	Protect from light
Thiopental	500 mg syr	Not advised	Not advised	N/A	NS,1/2NS, D5W	2-50 mg/mL	varying dosing	D5W or NS	slow infusion 0.2-0.4% solution	N/A	5d RT 45 d RF	3d RT 7 d RF	Incompatible with lactate ringer solution.
Thiotepa (Thioplex)	15 mg vial	Yes, at <1 mg/mL conc.	Yes	Yes	for IV SWFi (1.5 mL), for IT use NS	10 mg/mL	varying dosing	D5W or NS	IVP over 3-8 min and IVPB	N/A	24 hrs RT 5d RF	3d RT 14 d RF	Intravesical diluted w 20-60 mL NS, For BMT high dose use D5W at 5 mg/mL conc.
Ticarcillin (Ticar)	1, 2, 3 & 4 gm vial	IV infusion only	Yes	No	SWFi 4 mL	200 mg/mL	all doses	NS 100 mL	over 30-60 min	N/A	72 hrs Rt 14 d RF	72 hrs RT 14 d RF	Darkening of drug indicates loss of potency.
Ticarcillin Clavulanate (Timentin)	3.1gm	Yes	Yes	No	NS or D5W	0-2.5 gm/50-100 mL	3.1gm q4-6 hrs	NS 100 mL	30-60 min	6 hrs RT, 72 hrs RF	D5W hrs, NS hrs	3d RT 7d RF	Darkening of drug indicates loss of potency.
Tirofiban (Aggrastat) Premix	12.5 mg / 250 mL NS	10 mcg/kg bolus over 3 min	Not advised	N/A	N/A	50 mcg/mL	Already prepared		0.1-0.4 mcg/kg/min	N/A	N/A	24 hrs once removed from outer package	Do not freeze and protect from light.
Tobramycin (Nebcin)	80 mg / 2 mL, 2000 mg / 50 mL vials; and 1.2 gm vials (Powder for reconstitution)	Not advised	1-2 mg/kg q 8 hrs	N/A	Dilute the Powder vial with 30 mL SW	40 mg/mL	All Doses	100 mL D5W or NS	100 mL/hr (Over 60 min)	MDV; reconstituted powder is stable for 24 hrs	48 hrs RT; 4 days in RF	48 hrs RT; 4 days in RF	Incompatible with heparin.
Topotecan (Hycamtin)	4 mg vial	No	No	No	SWFi or BSWFi 4 mL	1 mg/mL	varying dosing	D5W 100 mL or NS	over 30 min	N/A	7 d RT (BSWFI)	24 hrs RT 7d RF	CIVI qs to 50-60 mL over 5-7 days
TPN (Hyperal)	various	Not advised	Not advised	N/A	N/A	N/A	Not Applicable; Various			N/A	N/A	24 hrs w MVI; 7 d in RF w/out	For IV administration only
Torsemide (Demadex)	10 mg / 1 mL amps	Over 2 min	No	N/A	N/A	10 mg/mL	100 mg	250 mL NS or D5W	Continuous infusion	Single use Amps	Send Amps	24 hrs at RT in NS; 72 hrs at RT in D5W	Flush line with NS before and after administration
Trimetrexate (Neutrexin)	25 mg vial	No	No	No	SWFi 2 mL	12.5 mg/mL	varying dosing	D5W 50-100 mL	Over 60 min	N/A	N/A	24 hrs RT or RF	45 mg/m2 daily
Triamcinolone (Kenalog)	40 mg / 1 mL vial	Not advised	40-80 mg	N/A	N/A	40 mg/mL	Not recommended; IM only			MDV	30 Days	N/A	Inject IM dose in large muscle mass, avoid deltoid.

Drug Name	Package Size	Routes of Administration			Injectable Preparation		IVPB Preparation				Stability			Notes/Comments
		IVP	IM	SC	Dilute with	Conc.	Dose	Solutions	Administration rate		Reconstituted in vial	In a syringe	In Piggy bag	
Trifluoperazine (Stelazine)	2 mg/mL	No	Yes, deep	N/A	N/A			Give IM only			N/A	N/A	N/A	Protect from light and freezing
Trimethobenzamide (Tigan)	200 mg/2 mL ampoule	Not advised	200 mg TID-QID	N/A	N/A	100 mg/mL		Give IM			Single use Amps	Send Amps	N/A	Please Inject IM dose in upper outer quadrant
Tygacillin (Tygacil)	50 mg powder	Yes	No	No	N/A	50 mg /50 mL	100 mg, then 50 mg q 12 hrs	NS, LR, D5W	Over 30-60 min every 12 hrs		6 hrs RT	N/A	24 hrs RT 48 hrs RF	Initial dose 100 mg
Urokinase Abbokinase	25000 u/vial in powder	Yes	No	N/A	SWFI 5 mL	5000 u/mL	4400 unit/kg	NS or D5W	CIVI for PE		single use	single use	single use	Discard any unused portion after reconstitution
Valproate (Depakene)	500 mg/5 mL vial	Not advised	Not advised	N/A	N/A	100 mg/mL	2-4 mg/kg	50 mL NS	Over 1 hr		Single Use Vial	24 hrs at RT	24 hrs at RT	Do not refrigerate
Vancomycin (Vancocin, Vancoled)	500 mg vials (powder for reconstitution)	No—must dilute	Not advised	N/A	4.8 mL	100 mg/mL	0-500 mg / 501 mg-1 gm	100 mL D5W or NS / 250 mL D5W or NS	100 mL/hr (Over 1 hr) / 250 mL/hr (Over 1 hr)		14 D w or w/out RF	14 D RF; 7 D RT	14 D RF; 7 D RT	Max conc. is 5 mg/mL Frozen bag available
Varicella zoster	0.5 mL	No	No	Sub q	N/A	0.5 mL	0.5 mL	N/A	SQ only		RF	N/A	N/A	Live vaccine.
Vasopressin (Pitressin)	20 units/1 mL vial	See IVPB admin.-istration	5-10 units ever 3-4 hrs	5-10 units every 3-4 hrs	N/A	20 units/mL	100 units	100 mL NS or D5W (conc. = 1 unit/mL)	0.2 units/min starting and may increase to 2 units/min		MDV	72 hrs	72 hrs	Dosage >0.04 u/min may lead cardiac arrest.
Voricanazole (V-Fend)	200 mg vial powder	IVPB	No	No	Dilute with 19 mL SWFI	0.5-5 mg/mL	200 mg	NS, D5W/ NS	3 mg/kg/hr infuse 1-2 hrs		N/A	N/A	24 hrs RF	reconstitue soln must be used immidiately
Vecuronium Bromide (Norcuron)	10 mg vial (Powder for reconstitution)	Rapid IV injection ok; 0.04-0.14 mg/kg	Not advised	N/A	10 mL SW	1 mg/mL	10 mg	100 mL D5W or NS (0.1 mg/mL)	0.8-1.2 mcg/kg/min		24 hrs RF (5 D w/ BSWFI)	24 hrs in RF (5 d w/ BSWFI)	24 hrs	Protect from light. Store at room temperature
Verapamil (Isoptin, Calan, Verlan)	5 mg/2 mL vial	5-10 mg bolus over 2 min (over 3 min in elderly)	Not advised	N/A	N/A	2.5 mg/mL	50 mg	250 mL NS (0.2 mg/mL)	5 mg/hr		SDV	N/A	24 hrs at RT	Protect from light
Velcade (bortizomib)	3.5 mg powder	IV bolus 3-5 sec	No	No	diluted in 3.5 mL NS	1 mg/mL	varying dosing	3.5 mL NS	IVP over 3-5 sec		N/A	Reconst syring in 8 hrs	Use within 8 hrs	reconstitute product must be clear and colorless
Vinblastin (Velban)	10 mg	Yes at 1 mg/mL	No	No	NS 10 mL	1 mg/mL	varying dosing	NS	IV infusion over 5-15 mins		N/A	30 d RF	28 d RF	May give as IVB or CIVI

Drug Name	Package Size	Routes of Administration			Injectable Preparation		IVPB Preparation			Stability			Notes/Comments
		IVP	IM	SC	Dilute with	Conc.	Dose	Solutions	Administration rate	Reconstituted in vial	In a syringe	In Piggy bag	
Vincristin (Oncovin)	1 mg/mL, 2 mg/2 mL	Yes over 1 min	No	No	diluted	1 mg/mL	varying dosing	NS, D5W, LR	IV infusion over 10-15 mins	N/A	7 d RT, 8.5 d RF (diluted)	2 d RT, 7 d RF	Harmful if given intrathecally
Vinorelbine (Navelbine)	10 mg/mL 50 mg/5 mL	Yes, <2 mg/mL push over 6-10 min	No	No	diluted	10 mg/mL	varying dosing	NS 50–100 mL	over 10 min	N/A	24 RT	24 hrs RT	Vesicant
VIGIV small pox vaccine (Vaccinia)	50 mg/mL	CIVI 2 mL/kg	No	No	dilute w NS or D5W	50 mg/mL	100-200 mg/kg	1:2 concentration	1 mL/kg/hr x 30 min and increase rate upto 3 mL/kg as tolerate	N/A	N/A	RT 36-46 C	do not shake, use 0.22 micron filter, 100 mg/kg start but do not exceed to 400 mg/kg
Zoledronic acid (Zometa)	4 mg	IVPB over 15-30 min	No	No	Dilute with 150-500 mL	4 mg/150 mL	4 mg		0ver15-30 min	24 hrs	N/A	RF	Invcompitable with LR
Zoledronic acid (Reclast)	5 mg	IVPB over 15 min	No	No	NS	5 mg/250 mL	5 mg	100 mL NS or D5W	over 15 min	24 hrs RF	N/A	Store at RF 24 hrs after opening	Incompatible with LR.

Key:
RF = Refrigerated
RT= Room temperature
I = Incompatible
SDV = Single dose vial
SDA = Single dose ampoule
BSWFI = Bacteriostatic SWFI
SWFI = Sterile water for inj.
BNS = Bacteriostatic normal saline
CIVI = Continuous intravenous infusion
IVPB = Intravenous piggy bag
IT = Intrathical

Disclaimer: The drug information presented in this article was compiled from published reference sources and drug package inserts. Every efforts was made to ensure that informations presented are accurate. One should not use this article as a sole source of reference. please consult primary references, drug information; a pharmacist and also an institutional guidelines before administering any drug agent. In no case can the author be held responsible for any liability, loss, injury or damageincurredas a consequence, directly or indirectly from the use.

References
1. Micromedex
2. Handbook of injectable drugs 11th Edition Lippincott
3. King's Guide to Parental Admixture
4. Intravenous Medication 2003 19th edition
5. Drug Facts and Comparision
6. Drug package insert
7. "Guidline forinjectable Medications: for intramuscular &/or Intravenous use-1998"
8. Vohra S, Patel R., & Do P. Journal of Pharmacy Practice, August 1998;9:4
9. "The stability of injectable Medication after reconstitution and/or Further dilution" Kirschenbaum BE,& Latiolis CJ, Parenteral special issue 1986; 4(5a): 1.
10. CDC vaccine Internet.

Chapter 48

Managed Care in Pharmacy and the Pharmaceutical Industry

F. Randy Vogenberg, R.Ph., Ph.D. and Rita Marcoux, R.Ph., MBA

48.1 Managed Care

Managed healthcare and federal reimbursement policy shifts have affected pharmacy policy and practice to different degrees over the past fifteen years. This chapter will focus on how specific changes at the federal level have reverberated through pharmacies in all settings including hospitals, long-term care facilities, and retail.

In 2008, the average number of hospital days per 1,000 members of HMOs not owned by multihospital systems grew by 6.6 percent. This was the fifth consecutive year of increases.[1] That is in addition to the virtually unchanged length of hospital stays resulting from the federal reimbursement for Medicare beneficiaries under Diagnosis Related Groupings (DRGs). A corollary to the inpatient reduction has been the rising rate of outpatient or day surgeries being performed in the U.S. Institutional revenue streams today are realized from successful, short hospital stays and single-day surgical procedures. Drugs used in both scenarios must be efficacious, possessing few side effects or other interactions that could interfere with these goals. Pharmacists must be more attuned to patient outcomes being achieved quickly and safely, including avoidance of troublesome returns to the hospital after discharge.

The Institute of Medicine (IOM) is widely cited for its report on the morbidity and mortality of, and cost associated with, medication errors in this country. In response to the IOM's report and numerous articles highlighting the impact on quality of life and economic waste, The Joint Commission has committed to assisting organizations in medication error prevention. The National Patient Safety Goal (NPSG) 8, focusing on medication reconciliation, has been part of its accreditation criteria for hospitals since 2005. Many hospitals have placed pharmacists in the emergency room to manage medication order verification and ordering in their attempt to meet NPSG 8 requirements. However, organizations continue to struggle with the implementation and maintenance of effective processes in support of NPSG 8. Consequently, The Joint Commission decided that NPSG 8 will be a part of the accreditation survey but will not be a factor in the accreditation decision-making process effective January 1, 2009. The Joint Commission will evaluate and refine expectations for organizations so that NPSG 8 will be ready for implementation in 2010.[2]

At the same time that hospital costs and quality are being monitored, patient satisfaction continues to grow in importance for determining who gets the inpatient-care business from payers. This is known as integrating reasonable costs with highest possible quality, which some analysts try to calculate through a cost/quality ratio. Patient surveys to determine the degree of satisfaction with services provided often include questions about drugs and/or pharmacist services, if applicable.

How these many managed-care changes are affecting the three pharmacy settings can be described as follows. Systems of care for a geographic region have emerged through strategic alliances and organizational mergers. Each has reduced redundant services, including general pharmacies, and increased alternatives to hospital and physician care, including specialized pharmacies. This strategy optimizes drug-use outcomes, while maintaining economic efficiency.

In July 1998, a new reimbursement program was implemented for Medicare's Part A services in long-term care, sub-acute care, and home care. This program is known as the Prospective Payment System (PPS) and operates similarly to the way that diagnosis-related groups (DRGs) functioned in hospitals. Rather than being reimbursed on a fee-for-service basis, nursing homes and others must now categorize patients and their needs according to specific assessments required by the Centers for Medicare and Medicaid Services (CMS). The PPS system's daily rates are adjusted for geographic differences in labor costs and case mix. Case mix adjustments are done using a system known as Resource Utilization Groups (RUGs). The RUGs classification assigns patients to groups based on the patient characteristics and services expected to be required. The number of groups within the RUGs has increased from 44 to 66 in RUGs IV. The result of these changes continues to require these organizations to re-evaluate the way in which they do business, including contracting for pharmaceuticals and pharmacy consultative services. Pharmacists who provide drugs or monthly patient-chart reviews will be challenged to maintain high quality in a lowered cost-reimbursement environment. As seen in hospitals, larger organizations that can spread the financial risk over a greater number of patients or services will likely do better than independent operators.

All types of ambulatory and community-based care are growing in this environment. Outpatient visits for day surgery, disease monitoring, and preventive care have continuously grown over the past five years, to the point where most hospitals' occupancy rates can fall below 50 percent. In turn, however, intensive-care units' (ICU) occupancy remains strong and is growing, since people are sicker by the time they reach the hospital. As a result, changes have become necessary, as far as the number of staff and the personnel matrix required to run a more acute-care (compared to maintenance-level) hospital service. Long-term care facilities now offer a wider range of services—including intravenous drug administration—that generate different staffing and pharmacy needs. Similarly, community-based (retail) pharmacists are supplying drugs and information to patients

who otherwise would have been hospitalized ten to fifteen years ago. Furthermore, pharmacists are changing their roles to become more like drug-information consultants and care advisors (both for patients and prescribers).

From another perspective, in multihospital systems of care (compared to independent organizations):

- Outpatient surgeries per day increased
- Outpatient visits per day increased
- Emergency department visits per day increased 2.9 percent in 2007 over 2006
- Average length of stay (ALOS) fell for all facilities
- In 2007, cost per occupied bed increased for the fourth straight year
- Acute-care hospitals staffed an average of 0.18 full-time equivalent (FTE) physician assistants (PAs) per occupied bed in 2007, up 20 percent from 0.15 in 2006

These figures speak to the efficiencies that may be gained from the new order of healthcare delivery, as well as the changes required by hospitals, long-term care facilities, and retail pharmacies.[3–5]

48.2 Specialty Pharmacy and Payor Changes

Outcries over reduced access to prescription drugs have resulted in new formulary regulations. Mandated opening of drug benefits and access to prescription drugs (in general or niche categories) remains a problem for managed care organizations (MCOs)—especially in light of rising costs of brands and biotechnology products. Traditionally, closed formularies and narrow drug-benefit policies had been used to create a consistent level of quality in drug utilization and to contain costs. Today, drug benefit designs use tiered formularies to contain costs. More drug choices in the pharmacies have contributed to double-digit increases in MCOs' pharmacy-segment costs. To compensate for the increased cost of prescription medications, many employers have shifted the cost burden to their employees by increasing the co-pays for drugs at the various tiers. Significant cost differentials can be seen between each of the tiers within the benefit design. Employers have also continued to increase the employees' deductibles to balance the increased cost of healthcare. In 2008, 58 percent of covered employees were in a Preferred Provider Organization Plan. Of these employees, half are enrolled in plans with a family deductible of $1,000 or more.[6] The increasing cost of health care despite insurance is causing many individuals to miss doses of their medication or to stop taking the medication altogether.

The dynamic changes taking place today have forced everyone in the healthcare industry to adopt new approaches in the marketplace. Nowhere are these changes more pronounced than in the pharmacy. The advent of third-party prescription-drug benefit programs by the insurance industry in the early 1980s foretold the evolution of more formal management systems into the traditional physician or pharmacy distribution channel. Pharmacy benefit managers (PBMs) have entered into specialty pharmacy distribution roles previously enjoyed by physicians and community pharmacies. The words "specialty" and "biotechnology or biotech" are often used interchangeably when discussing this group of prescription medications. *Specialty/biotech* refers to a diverse group of expensive drugs, defined by CMS as more than $500/month. On average, these medications cost $600/month.[7] Specialty pharmacy and biologically-derived injectable medications are prescribed for the management of (1) uncommon chronic illnesses such as multiple sclerosis, hepatitis C, hemophilia, and (2) some common diseases such as cancer, arthritis, and osteoporosis. Cancer medications as a group represent the single largest product mix managed by specialty pharmacies. Traditionally, these medications have been administered only in physician offices versus other medications that patients can obtain in a community pharmacy. However, an increasing number of specialty pharmacy medications are in a form that patients can administer themselves.

These products require special handling and specialized patient education and monitoring. The products are self-administered injections and infusions. The patient outlet for obtaining prescription drugs is typically either the traditional retail pharmacy or a mail-order pharmacy. However, many products may not be readily available at the typical local retail pharmacy. These products would have to be ordered by the pharmacy or a product may have a restricted distribution only with select specialty pharmacies. Retail pharmacies often do not keep these drugs in stock because of their high cost, low utilization, and special storage and handling requirements. Also, retail pharmacies are not able to receive favorable pricing because of their low utilization. Within mail order, a specific delivery system evolved into what is known as *specialty pharmacy*. Key services delivered by specialty pharmacies versus traditional retail pharmacies include the ability to negotiate favorable pricing, administrative support, billing and claims, availability of limited distribution product lines, one-stop shopping, and patient monitoring. One overarching key characteristic for the specialty pharmacy is a focus on patient outcomes versus medication dispensing alone.

These medications can have serious side effects that can result in patients not adhering to the prescribed therapy, espe-

cially for the long duration of therapy typically required such as with hepatitis treatment. Examples of issues with the use of these medications include common problems such as rash at the injection site, nausea, or diarrhea. A unique individual response to a single therapy, rather than a predictable outcome, can occur, resulting in no clinical effect or too much of an effect, and death from rare complications due to the underlying biologic intervention that these medications achieve has been reported. Owing to their significant positive and sometimes negative impact on patient care, appropriate use and support of biotechnology medications versus traditional medications must be considered in plan design strategy.

Although the number of patients requiring these medications is small, the cost of treatments for these diseases can range from $6,000 to $400,000 annually, as previous stated. Unlike individual physician offices, specialty pharmacies can purchase larger quantities to save product cost, in addition to offering the large variety of patient support services which accompany these medications.[7] In an effort to appropriately manage patient care and cost, CMS and many employers have removed these products from the medical benefit and are processing the products as part of the prescription benefit. This change has shifted a significant portion of the cost to the patient, as managed care organizations have moved these products to the highest co-pay or specialty tier of their pharmacy benefit.

Today, nearly every traditional PBM, health plan, or insurer offers specialty pharmacy as an option. But what is offered, the number of drugs available, and how they are administered may vary. For example, some PBMs have included a wide variety of drugs in their specialty pharmacy program. This may not be in the patient's best interest, because some of these drugs may not require the same special handling and additional oversight as the biotech drugs, and may be readily available through a retail pharmacy at the network discount, which may be deeper than that from the specialty pharmacy. Other PBMs require a complete "lockout" of the retail pharmacy for these drugs, meaning that they can be obtained only through the specialty pharmacy. Due to exclusive manufacturer distribution contracts, some products are only available from one or a select few specialty pharmacies. Still other PBMs offer different discounts depending on which outlet is used in their network—retail or specialty.

Examples of specialty pharmacy organizations that a health plan or self-insured employer can contract with by longevity and experience in the marketplace include CVS/Caremark, Walgreens, ExpressScripts/Curascript, Magellan/iCore, Medco/Accredo, Americsource Bergen Specialty Group, and BioScrip.

Improved and more stable medication formulation or delivery systems have further expanded the ability to distribute specialty medications directly to patients. This includes oral, topical, and inhaled medications as well as less temperature-dependent formulations of injectables. Just as several hospital-based surgical procedures or technologies have moved to out-of-hospital day surgical or imaging centers, specialty pharmacy medication supply chains have shifted to new sources of delivery, handling, and storage, allowing for easier as well as expanded use of this category of medication by patients.

Key professional practice and benefit management challenges include inconsistent application of coverage, utilization management, health and safety monitoring, member cost sharing, medical plan versus specialty pharmacy plan management, and fragmentation of clinical and patient support programs.

48.3 Certification

Managed-care plans have begun exercising greater selectivity in contracting with medical professionals, in response to employer and government requirements for greater quality assurance. In fact, quality and accountability are major themes heard in today's healthcare marketplace—including managed-care organizations, employers, and payers. Increasingly, both government and private-sector purchasers of healthcare services are searching for ways to differentiate the many healthcare providers in this highly competitive market. While much of the attention is presently focused on the role of physicians, all healthcare professionals are being subjected to ever-increasing scrutiny of their qualifications and performance.

Quality management in managed care covers a broad range of activities, which managed-care plans must undertake to meet their industry's accreditation standards. Among these activities, credentialing of participating health professionals plays a critical role. Credentialing, as a management process, has evolved over the years and has been adapted to meet the unique needs of the managed-care environment. It is, in effect, an objective assessment process intended to both validate each provider's training and experience and serve as the vehicle to evaluate performance. In managed-care credentialing, the emphasis is on individual performance.

The need for managed-care plans to credential network providers is now well-documented. Recent judicial decisions imposing liability for physician malpractice on the plan no longer permit plans to rely on a hospital's credentialing process.[8] Moreover, several empirical studies substantiate the need for greater accuracy in the credentialing process

through the independent verification of credentials information from the primary (original) source of information.[9]

The inclusion of primary-source verification in the credentialing process is an important development for present credentialing practices. Traditionally, hospitals and plans relied upon copies of documentation and other information supplied by the physician. However, the marketplace's demands for quality assurance and pressure from government regulators for greater accountability have focused the industry's attention on increasing the performance standards in this area. This stringent requirement is reflected in the most recent standards adopted by industry-accreditation bodies, including the National Committee for Quality Assurance (NCQA), American Accreditation Program, Inc. (AAPI), Utilization Review Accreditation Commission (URAC), and The Joint Commission. Many of these regulatory boards require re-certification or licensure approximately every three years. These boards are recognized by the federal government and are typically non-profit organizations to avoid potential claims of economic biases related to speed and standards or accreditation. Some of these organizations, particularly the NCQA, release publicly available report cards on the facilities that it certifies yearly, giving its accreditation slightly more weight than organizations that review facilities every few years.

48.4 Credentialing and Accreditation for Pharmacies or Pharmacists

Analogous to existing Joint Commission accreditation requirements, specific documentation around the process of certifying members of the medical staff is a required activity of the hospital. In managed care, NCQA requires a process of certifying members of the medical staff and other primary-care providers who come in contact with patients. Articles in insurance and professional journals underscore the changes of practice for pharmacists and other allied health-provider credentialing. In response to these changes, post-licensing education for pharmacists has expanded to afford pharmacists the opportunity to specialize in specific areas.

As early as 1976, the Board of Pharmaceutical Specialties began offering certification in five specialties. In 1999, the Council on Credentialing in Pharmacy (CCP) was founded. It is a coalition of 13 national organizations with a vested interest in the profession of pharmacy. These organizations focus on the credentialing of programs that impact or are relevant to pharmacy. Over the last 20 years, the organizations that form this coalition have developed standards for credentialing programs. Currently, over 17 certification programs are available for pharmacists through one of these organizations.[10]

As clinical expectations for pharmacists have expanded over the last decade, so has the passage of regulations that oversee the practice. Currently, pharmacists are allowed to immunize patients in 49 states. Pharmacists are recognized as providers in over 45 states and territories. The expanded regulations have broadened the scope of practice to include such activities as collaborative practices with physicians, administration of vaccines, as well as the management of clinics for chronic diseases.[10] Additionally, state boards of pharmacy have modified continuing education requirements for pharmacists that have expanded scopes of practice. In many states, pharmacists are required to attend programs, in a varying number of required hours, in their areas of expertise to satisfy expanded licensure.

CMS has increased the emphasis and pressure for quality of care and cost-effective use of resources that support the expanded practice for pharmacists. A major component of the Medicare Part D program has been Medication Management Therapy (MTM) programs offered by plan sponsors. MTMs are medication assessment and disease management programs designed to monitor patients for medication appropriateness, compliance, and complications. CMS has approved pharmacists as providers for services reimbursed under the MTM provision, and made significant changes in plan sponsor requirements for MTM programs in fiscal year 2010. They also expanded the number of beneficiaries who qualify for this intervention with expanded criteria and have eliminated the opt-in method of patient enrollment. At a minimum, the plan sponsor must offer an annual comprehensive medication review that includes OTC and herbal products to qualifying enrollees targeted at least quarterly for enrollment.[11] MTMs afford pharmacists a new opportunity to market their clinical expertise as recognized providers under CMS. Pharmacists are working independently as well as through their employers to consult with patients and bill plan sponsors for the assessment and interventions.

CMS and managed care continue to place enormous pressure on healthcare professionals to position themselves as quality providers of services (e.g., physicians and pharmacists). Plan sponsors are responsible for measuring and reporting to CMS on the outcomes of their MTM programs. Purchasers are increasingly limiting their contracts to quality health plans and service providers. URAC has developed a number of accreditation programs focused on pharmacy services such as mail order pharmacy, specialty pharmacy, PBM services, and drug therapy management. These accreditation programs are becoming a standard for entry into segments of the market. Board certification, continuing medical education, and other expert training and experience are at an all-time premium. While there may not be an im-

mediate and measurable reimbursement for an investment in quality, market positioning, with an emphasis on quality, remains the best business strategy to preserve market share and maintain future profitability.

48.5 Current and Near Future Issues in Pharmacy Practice

Changes are happening now, and the intensity of these changes will increase for a while longer. Movement from stage two to stage three status in managed care takes less time today than it did three years ago. Even within a six-month period, subtle shifts that impact pharmacists or pharmacy services for prescription drugs can be seen in most markets. Multiple pressures on the pharmacy as a result of this dynamic marketplace put cascading pressure on the pharmacist in the dispensing of drugs and drug information to patients and other providers. This can result in the potential for more medication-related errors by all providers—including the pharmacist. This concern around medication errors has been the subject of several journal articles and the IOM, focusing on both the system cost of these various errors and the opportunities for system improvement to eliminate potential errors through changes in practice patterns. These changes toward quality improvement include the use of automation, new generations of computer software to check for drug-related prescribing errors, and requirements for better training of healthcare professionals that are documented to verify improvement in personal professional practice.

Credentialing of healthcare professionals is increasingly playing an integral role in quality management. Largely in response to consumer pressure for accountability, managed-care plans have been left with little choice but to exercise greater oversight and limit the number of health professionals to those who offer measurable quality services. Accreditation, credentialing, and increased regulation on the various aspects and processes of the dispensing function and practice of pharmacy continue to evolve. These environmental changes have enormous implications for pharmacists who, at the same time, are threatened by less expensive means of dispensing drugs. The market continues to transition to practitioners with advanced degrees in clinical pharmacy. The number of certification programs and specialty areas of practice are expanding as are the regulations that oversee the practice. Pharmacists are now found in collaborative practices, managing hospital clinics, administering vaccines, and as sole practitioners in community settings managing patient medications through MTM programs. With the increase in responsibilities have come some challenges to the profession. The U.S. Food and Drug Administration (FDA) approved Plan B, an emergency contraceptive medication, in 2006 as a new class of medications available without a prescription but under the supervision of the pharmacy for individuals 18 years or older. Pharmacists immediately were charged with managing this product's access as well as appropriate patient instructions and care. In April 2009, the FDA agreed to lower the age to 17 for non-prescription users. This has been an expansion of practice for pharmacists. In addition, some pharmacists are opposed to emergency contraceptive and refused to sell or fill the prescriptions for this product. This issue touched off a number of conscience issues such as the sale of contraceptive agents and dispensing medication that would be used for the right to die. Boards of Pharmacy and states are enacting laws to address the right of pharmacists to refuse to fill a valid prescription based on ethical consideration. The rights of pharmacists vary greatly between states, with some states mandating the filling of prescriptions unless there is a relevant clinical judgment for refusal.

Pharmacists have always been gatekeepers who manage access to legally approved controlled substances. However, they recently have been asked to play a role in the Drug Enforcement Agency's (DEA) war on illicit drugs. A very common cold preparation, pseudoephedrine, remains available to consumers but is managed by store personnel. This product is used to manufacture methamphetamine. Many retail stores have moved this product to the pharmacies to be managed by pharmacy personnel to ensure appropriate and controlled use. Some stores require a photo ID before the product is sold to a consumer.

The pharmacist's role has traditionally been one of distribution, not administration. However, many rural areas lack the necessary health personnel to manage the immunization process. Pharmacists have been identified as a potential key to improved access to immunization in all areas, but especially rural areas because of their easy accessibility. With the exception of Maine, legislation has been passed in 49 states to allow pharmacists to immunize patients. Each state's legislation dictates the breadth of immunizations with some states having passed broad legislation while others have limited scope. This increased responsibility was exceedingly timely as the flu season of 2009 was impacted by the H1N1 virus. States and the federal government are stressing the importance of pneumonia and flu vaccines for vulnerable populations. The additional support of pharmacists in the immunization process should allow demand to be met.

Another area of change has been with the dispensing of medication as written by the physicians. Traditionally, pharmacists filled prescriptions as written by the physician. However, many states enacted generic substitution laws that required pharmacists to dispense generic equivalents unless specified by the physician that a brand medication was nec-

essary. This mandate to fill generically has saved managed care and federal and state governments billions of dollars while having minimal effect on patient care as the two products are chemically equivalent. This practice is generally acceptable to physicians and patients. However, payors have started discussing the possibility of therapeutic substitution of medications in which a product from the same therapeutic class is selected over the prescribed choice of the physician. The selection would be based on formulary criteria and patient history. Physicians and advocacy groups strongly oppose this practice. Pharmacists working in collaboration with physicians may have individual practitioners' approval to intervene, and hospital pharmacists often make therapeutic substitutions within the hospital's formulary. However, pharmacists in these practices have the information necessary to make informed decisions. Until the information exchange between practitioners is developed, pharmacists in the community would find it difficult to gather the information necessary to make informed decisions.

48.6 Landscape of Pharmacy Practice: The Changing Marketplace

Third-party payment for pharmaceutical products is now the predominant form of payment in all types of pharmacy settings. The pharmacy benefit from healthcare insurers is widely prevalent across all types of managed care. The passage of the Medicare Modernization Act of 2003 expanded prescription coverage for those on Medicare with the addition of Part D. Part D coverage went into effect in 2006 and offered prescription benefits to 45 million elderly and disabled beneficiaries.[12] This coverage is available through private plans that are either stand-alone prescription drug plans (PDPs) or Medicare Advantage prescription drug plans (MA-PD). A Medicare Advantage plan includes all Medicare benefits. As of February 2009, CMS reported that 26.7 million beneficiaries had enrolled in a Medicare Part D program.[12]

Consolidation continues to occur within every segment of the healthcare industry. The pace of change continues to be rapid; however, both federal and state regulators have taken mostly conservative positions that have slowed mergers (along with the moribund U.S. economy). Affected market segments employing pharmacists included pharmacy-benefit management (PBM) firms, healthcare insurers, physician-practice management (PPM) companies, hospitals, pharmacy chains, and pharmacy wholesalers.

Consumer advocacy and patient protection was a top priority in the late 1990s, resulting in several pieces of legislation that impacted healthcare-delivery decisions. Managed care organizations and other healthcare providers are working continuously to improve the security of their data systems and managed access to protected health data. The federal courts are increasingly imposing sanctions against organizations for violation of Health Information Portability and Accountability Act provisions. An example of these sanctions include a national pharmacy chain agreeing to a $2.25 million settlement for an HIPAA violation in which their pharmacies were inappropriately disposing of labeled medication vials.[13] The American Recovery and Reinvestment Act (ARRA) of 2009 has significantly increased the monetary penalties for HIPAA violations, further increasing the stress for secure systems and processes. In addition, ARRA extends the application of the main provisions of HIPAA to business associates of the covered entities and requires periodic compliance auditing of covered entities and their business associates. Lastly, individuals must be notified of a breach in their confidential information if the information was in an unsecured format.

Federal reimbursement changes continue to be phased in as a result of the Balanced Budget Act (BBA) of 1997 and CMS, which continues to encourage Medicare and Medicaid beneficiaries to move into managed care where available. The continuing economic burden of health care on state budgets has required significant changes to most Medicaid programs. In 2002, Michigan and Vermont received approval from CMS to implement a preferred drug list for beneficiaries in fee-for-service Medicaid programs. Preferred drug lists (PDL) allowed states to contract with manufacturers for additional supplemental rebates for position on the preferred drug list. Currently, over 40 states have PDLs in place. In addition, states have implemented additional cost containment strategies such as co-pays for certain segments of their programs, limiting the number of monthly prescriptions and implementing quantity limits to manage increasingly tight budgets.

All of these changes to the healthcare marketplace have significantly affected the role of a pharmacist in delivering patient-care services. Pharmacists today, in all settings, face continued pressure to maintain low-cost, high-quality pharmacy services with fewer personnel. Much of the cost pressure will continue to increase, due to the demographics of our aging society along with the physician's reliance on medications as a primary form of treatment for most diseases. Given the number of new drugs, including novel or therapeutically important agents, pharmacists today face an economic and drug-knowledge challenge unlike that of previous generations.

48.7 Colleges of Pharmacy, Lifelong Learning, and Certification

According to the American Association of Colleges of Pharmacy (AACP), there were 111 schools or colleges of phar-

macy with accreditation status and five schools with precandidate status across the United States in July 2009, up from 81 in 2001. Congruent with the increase in the number of schools, applications and enrollment have continued to rise over the last 8 years. Institutions reported to AACP an application to enrollment ratio of 8:1.[14] Additionally, many colleges are expanding the size of their potential graduating class to offer more opportunities for qualified students to earn their degree. The AACP reports that approximately two-thirds of the schools and colleges of pharmacy in the United States require prospective students applying to their program to take the Pharmacy College Admission Test (PCAT).[15] Accreditation Council for Pharmacy Education (ACPE) released new standards for the accreditation of colleges in 2007. The new standards have incorporated feedback from stakeholders and place significant emphasis on developing curriculum that offer students opportunities to develop the competencies and confidence needed to be part of a healthcare team, emphasizing practice and communication skills. The objectives of the curriculum are targeted to developing professionals and lifelong learners. The standards have increased the number of experiential hours required for completion of the program.[16]

The Pharm.D. (Doctor of Pharmacy) is the sole undergraduate professional degree for pharmacists offered in the US as of June 2012. The Pharm.D. curriculum contains an increased number of credit hours in advanced biopharmaceutical sciences, pharmacotherapy, and clinical rotations emphasizing the treatment of disease in various patient-care settings. The Pharm.D. degree is known as a clinical degree, as opposed to a business or research degree track, where the terminal degree would be a Ph.D. For B.Sc. pharmacists who are interesting in acquiring a Pharm.D. degree, many schools offer a two year post-B.Sc. program. Increasingly, non-traditional learning programs have emerged in pharmacy, enabling expanded numbers of students to learn via remote, collaborative, or online courses. These programs lead to the Pharm.D. degree—both for the new terminal entry-level degree, as well as the advanced degree for B.Sc. pharmacists seeking a clinical focus.

48.8 Pharmacy-Support Personnel, and Certification or Registration

The use of support personnel in pharmacy continues to expand, due to several factors, including the shortage of pharmacists, an increasing number of prescriptions filled annually, and a greater demand for medication therapy management provided by pharmacists. As the scope of services performed by the technician has increased, so has the number of states developing regulations governing the education, training, and responsibilities of the pharmacy technician. Currently, 39 states regulate technicians through some type of licensure, registration, or certification process. Of these 39 states, 29 have regulations specific to the mandatory training of technicians. In 14 states, the Board of Pharmacy requires technicians to pass an examination. The CPhT is currently the only nationally-recognized certification by the Pharmacy Technician Certification Board.[10]

Regulation in certain states involves criminal background screenings as well as fingerprinting to check criminal records prior to licensure and certification through state boards of pharmacy. In many states, potential technicians must have a high school diploma or equivalent, maintain a criminal record devoid of felony convictions or pending charges for a duration of five years, and may not have any previous felony conviction involving controlled substances found or used within the pharmacy. Pharmacy technicians may have continuing education requirements to maintain licensure. The Council on Credentialing in Pharmacy estimates that there are over 280,000 technicians regulated by state boards of pharmacy.[17]

Pharmacy technicians hold positions in a wide variety of healthcare settings including community practice, military, long-term care, hospital, and managed care organizations to name a few. The role of the technician has evolved to handle many of the technical aspects of dispensing prescriptions. A pharmacy technician works under the supervision of a pharmacist, who is responsible for the care of the patients. They may handle routine prescription refilling, assist with new-prescription processing, and work under the direct supervision of a pharmacist. Generally, they must obtain annual continuing education to maintain this certification. In many states, this requirement is annual, although some states have a review every two years. State boards of pharmacy usually require between five to ten continuing education credits per year.

Nearly all states put ratios in place to limit the number of supportive personnel that a pharmacist may supervise at any one time. These ratios would include registered or certified technicians, in addition to a pharmacist intern (or extern, in some states). For example, a state may allow no more than three supportive personnel (a one-to-three ratio), provided that at least one of the three supportive personnel is a certified pharmacy technician or an intern.

48.9 Continuing Professional Education: Pharmacists and Support Personnel

Just as with physicians and other licensed professionals, pharmacists have been forced to redefine their roles in the delivery system in the face of dominant market penetration

by managed-care pharmacy programs. Threatened by new distribution channels for prescription drugs, pharmacists are increasingly searching for new direction. The focus on quality management in managed care affords an opportunity for pharmacists to control the redefining of their role in the system and to exploit their major advantage—the patient. The direct patient contact provided by pharmacists has placed them in a unique position to play a vital role in medication therapy management. In effect, pharmacists are positioned to become the driving force in providing "hands-on" service to patients in dispensing drugs, monitoring their treatment, education, specific disease management, and other related cognitive services critical to patient treatment and positive medical outcomes.

As a result, pharmacists in all 50 states are required to achieve a minimum number of continuing-education (CE) hours as a condition for re-licensure by their respective state boards of pharmacy. Pharmacists usually must complete 15 contact hours of continuing education for each calendar or fiscal year. A number of states require a certain number of hours to be live (versus passive or written) CE programs. Other states may require a limited number of hours to be dedicated to selected topics—such as law or AIDS. Individuals who wish to maintain active registration as an immunizing pharmacist, board certified, or specialist may be bound by additional continuing education criteria pursuant to each state's local board of pharmacy. Furthermore in certain states, pharmacists who fail to maintain continuing education accreditation are subject to immediate license revocation upon a state board of pharmacy audit.

48.10 Professional Practice Settings

Consider the typical acute hospital patient today—over age 65 with multisystem diseases—now admitted for one or more acute exacerbations of their underlying diseases. Consider again, how many of these patients are coming from an older adult community, continuing care or long-term care facility? Changes in our healthcare-delivery system, including healthcare reform efforts, have forced providers and consumers to become more astute in their understanding and use of all healthcare services as well as their choice of direct-care clinical provider. Consumers (patients) are now in the challenging position of either developing a better understanding of their healthcare choices or aligning themselves with their family caregiver, primary care physician, or an independent patient advocate who may guide them through and/or refer them to a preferred plan. This may be particularly difficult for those older adults who may be at the highest medical risk and who have the greatest need for accessing healthcare services without advocacy assistance.

In community hospitals, the importance of initial drug assessment, aggressive polypharmacy intervention, and coordination in pharmaceutical care has and is being highlighted for older-adult patients by healthcare professionals, as well as by payors such as CMS. More importantly, a role for the pharmacist on a geriatric assessment team (GAT) has been shown to provide value to the older-adult patient, hospital, and non-pharmacist team members. There are some newer examples such as Programs for the All-inclusive Care of the Elderly (PACE), programs designed to assist the elderly in remaining in the community despite qualifying for nursing home care. Drug therapy is a key component to these programs, and pharmacists can be found as members of the patient's healthcare team. Similar pharmacist roles are being shown in general ambulatory-, pediatric-, oncology-, and cardiology-related care, most recently with the newly granted legal right to administer vaccinations in nearly all states. Many pharmacists have found another potential avenue for practice either in large-scale clinics or in small-scale scenarios in community settings (see Figure 48.1).

Home-care services today are more than just nursing homes, as pharmacists and patients have seen. Home-care services are a spectrum of healthcare services delivered in a variety of settings (see Table 48.1). This is not unlike the change happening in hospitals transforming themselves into integrated or continuing care delivery systems (IDS, CCDS). Home-care services may be a part of that IDS, or, more frequently, part of an affiliated, independent arm of the acute-care hospital (see Table 48.1).

Finally, the availability of on-site medical services in pharmacies or at employer clinics has created new potential integrated mid-level care systems that feature pharmacist-provided care, including MTM. Examples of this include CVS/Caremark and Walgreens, where acquisitions by these corporations have created a combination of retail, PBM/mail order, and mid-level practitioner limited-care sites in hundreds of locations across the U.S.

48.11 The Pharmacist Professional versus Pharmacy Business

The traditional view of pharmacists as "the pharmacy" is no longer accurate. The majority of pharmacists today are employees of an organization. The organization may be a hospital, health system, or chain pharmacy, as well as various forms of a legal business entity (S and C corporations or Limited Liability Corporation). In all cases, there are separate and distinct roles expected from the pharmacist, versus what the pharmacy provides in the delivery of patient care. The pharmacy can (and usually does) include a number of non-pharmacist personnel. Similar to how physician offices today are dominated in number by non-physicians, pharmacies are, likewise, a group of personnel with relatively specialized functions—all working together to deliver pharmaceuticals in an optimum fashion. Even the customers vary widely—from hospital nurses and operating room or clinic physicians (who administer drugs to patients), to hospital and ambulatory patients.

The financial business of the pharmacy has changed, with reimbursement shifts that have driven profits out of drug distribution. Managed care and public sector payers have extracted discounts from retail selling prices to the point where reimbursement formulas are now indexed on

---

Highest-care intensity
  acute care
  subacute/transitional care
  rehabilitation
  nursing home/long-term care
  hospice
  assisted living
  home
Lower-care intensity

Figure 48.1 *Continuum of acute-to-chronic patient-care settings. Intensity of care related to need for hands-on nursing care and/or twenty-four-hour professional-services support. Note: complexity of drug treatment can remain constant across the continuum. Original compilation by F.R. Vogenberg, September 19, 1998. Reviewed December 2002.*

Table 48.1
Spectrum of Home-Care Settings in Which Pharmacy Services May Be Provided

- Adult day care*
- Assisted living*
- Community/public health programs*
- Congregate living
- Continuing-care community (life care)
- Home health care
- Hospice**
- Rehabilitation facilities**
- Respite care*

*Services provided in home or at a facility
**Both in patient and ambulatory/home-based services

near-acquisition prices to retail (plus a fixed fee for dispensing). The shortage of pharmacists is driving their salaries and bonuses as corporations compete to staff their stores to meet the increased prescription volumes. The personnel issue continues to exert pressure on the industry as it strives to meet increasing managed care, consumer, and regulatory demands. In response to these pressures, retailers have increased the rate of implementation of technological advances in automation and computer software. Rural areas and small community hospitals are using telepharmacy to service their patients. A pharmacy technician fills the prescription using scanning technology that enables the pharmacist to see the prescription and medication dispensed. A computer system enabled with audio-visual capability allows the pharmacist in an off-site location, sometimes hundreds of miles away, to verify and approve prescriptions filled by technicians and counsel patients who would otherwise lack access to prescription services. Hospitals have implemented telepharmacy to cover their 11 P.M. to 7 A.M. shift, which traditionally has been difficult and costly to staff. Using this technology, one hospital pharmacist may verify prescriptions at a number of off-site hospitals and approve the dispensing of medications through automated dispensing machines. These automated systems allow nurses to access medications from patient profile-based automated dispensing machines. In addition, the availability of computer physician order entry that directly routes orders to robotic dispensing systems allows pharmacists the opportunity to spend more time on patient floors and in consultation with physicians. Hospital pharmacists are now located on patient floors and in specific clinics, such as anticoagulant, asthma, and diabetes, monitoring patients.

These robotic dispensing systems also assist in processing the ever-increasing volumes at the retail stores. The systems are integrated with interactive voice response systems to decrease the volume of calls handled by store personnel and to facilitate customer service. Many larger chain retailers are developing central prescription processing sites to handle refills and non-emergency prescriptions for a large geographic area of retail stores. These central fill locations are mail order-type facilities able to handle large volumes of prescriptions using the latest prescription processing technology and automated systems. In addition, many of these retail chains have launched call centers consolidating functions and optimizing the workload of store personnel. The call center's staff will assist in third-party processing issues, physician calls, and patient inquiries. The call center allows store personnel to assist in-store customers and be available to offer patient MTM type services. Another advanced technique for managing excess volume in stores has been the

triaging of calls between high-volume and lower-volume stores. Pharmacies with excess pharmacists' capacity are reviewing and managing the prescription processing steps up through the actual dispensing of medication in their stores via the chain computer system. State boards of pharmacy have worked collaboratively with community chains to modify or rewrite regulations so that the practice of pharmacy maximizes the clinical role of pharmacists in the healthcare delivery team while utilizing available resources for the dispensing function of pharmacy.

Lower margins resulting from this reimbursement have caused retail pharmacies to move faster into automated dispensing techniques and to seek to use non-pharmacist personnel to increase the productivity of pharmacists. Other pharmacies have gone into compounding and other specialties in pharmacy that do not have the strict reimbursement provisions seen in the mainstream pharmacy business. By contrast, the pharmacist who is not involved in the distribution of drugs is focused either on direct patient-care monitoring and education or is working as a member of the healthcare team (whose job includes advising others about the appropriate use of medications for individual patients). The role of the individual pharmacist in our emerging healthcare delivery system will continue to be debated and redefined. New national and local programs targeted to pharmacists have begun to capitalize on their strengths and to position pharmacists as quality managers who can contribute to better medical outcomes for patients. Pharmacist academicians and many associations have adopted this patient-care focus as the future value of pharmacists in the community or institutional-delivery settings.

48.12 Issues for Pharmacy in the Near Future

Barriers to expanding the pharmacists' capabilities in this new integrated, patient-oriented environment include database information, consensus on the pharmacist's role, and training opportunities reflective of the changing role of the pharmacist. To assist in achieving a standardized approach and maintaining appropriate levels of quality, long-term care (LTC) and home care has followed other levels of care in moving toward patient-care guidelines and focusing on consistent, cost-effective care. This has led rehabilitation facilities and nursing homes to put best practices into their daily routines, including improved communication of patient data.[18,19]

The need for information and assessment is being pushed in efforts to decrease medication errors in order to improve quality of care and reduce excess cost in the present system. Organizations continue to assist in monitoring healthcare delivery. The FDA has used the MedWatch form as a mechanism to track adverse drug events. The industry continues to see organizations with missions to address medications' safety. For example, The Institute for Safe Medication Practice, formed in 1975, assists healthcare providers with medication error prevention and safe medication use. The organization tracks medication errors and develops strategies and educational programs to help address these potentially life-threatening events.

Information management is an essential component of the integration within healthcare-delivery systems. Some of the obstacles to merging the various databases in healthcare, particularly for pharmacists, have been reported in the medical and information-management literature over many years. Important barriers for the hospital-LTC interface include patients who are members of a health plan, but who do not universally have pharmacy benefits. They also include patients with plan limits (which would mean that some prescription services would not be captured in the claims system). Also, current data captured may not be what is necessary for meaningful outcomes analysis, and the reporting of utilized services are usually incomplete when those services are reimbursed by prospective payment schemes, such as capitation, or the information submitted is not precise enough for clinical evaluation. The challenges encountered using payment data for utilization analysis and quality review may be addressed with CMS's latest initiative on ICD-9-DM. In January 2009, CMS released a final rule that requires the use of ICD-10-CM diagnostic codes beginning in October 2013. A few of the enhancements with ICD-10-DM include greater specificity in diagnosis codes, expanded injury codes, and diagnosis/symptom code combination that will decrease codes submitted. The replacement of ICD-9-CM with the greatly expanded ICD-10-CM code set will help support quality reporting, pay-for-performance, biosurveillance and other activities critical to the management of patient claims.[20]

The information barriers are important to the hospital pharmacist, who is being asked to become more involved (through integrated delivery systems)—both in preventing LTC readmissions and in speeding discharges, as it relates to individual patient drug-therapy issues. Without adequate information from inside the hospital or the outside older-adult sources, it can be difficult to make those decisions on recommendations for patient drug-therapy interventions. This continuous striving to better manage patient care increased in momentum with two CMS initiatives. Two initiatives that link quality of care to reimbursement are Hospital Acquired Conditions (HAC) and Hospital Quality Measure Reporting. Increased morbidity and cost of patient care due to hos-

pital-acquired conditions (HAC) has been documented in a number of studies and cited in the IOM reports. The IOM's report "To Err is Human: Building a Safer Health Systems" estimates that the total national costs of these errors, due to lost productivity, disability, and health care costs, could be between $17 to $29 billion.[21] Under HAC, CMS will no longer pay hospitals at higher rates for the increased cost of care for patients harmed by one of several conditions that they did not have upon hospitalization or for conditions that could have been reasonably prevented. The hospital will be reimbursed as if these conditions did not exist starting on October 1, 2008. The HAC conditions are commonly referred to as never-events and will continually be updated by CMS. Two new conditions are deep venous thrombosis (DVT) and pulmonary embolism (PE) occurring after knee and hip surgery. Medication therapy will be a consideration in managing many of these conditions and patients, further emphasizing the need for pharmacists as part of the team working to prevent HAC events. Furthermore, CMS has issued a Medicaid Directors guidance letter on the coordination of Medicaid payment policies in consideration of the newly enacted Medicare HAC policies. Many states and insurers have followed CMS's lead and developed a list of events that will not be reimbursed.[22]

The second initiative is the Hospital Quality Measure Reporting that is used to develop payment algorithms for hospitals. The program requires most hospitals to submit data for specific quality measures for health conditions common among people with Medicare, and that would typically result in hospitalization. The information gathered is intended for use by consumers in making healthcare decisions, while also encouraging hospitals and providers to continually improve the quality of inpatient care provided to all patients. The information is available to the public at www.hospitalcompare.hhs.gov.

In the near future, patients stand to gain the most from these and other changes in the increasingly better-managed healthcare marketplace. Managed care has injected price competition into all sectors of healthcare delivery. It has also changed provider behaviors, created novel opportunities within the business of healthcare, and moved healthcare toward a defined and measurable standard of quality.[23]

Pharmacists need to be aware of the differing perspectives and common goals in this marketplace as integrated systems evolve. The hospital integrated-care systems will demand that pharmacists perform certain tasks as part of various performance-improvement initiatives. Pharmacists, whether in a retail, hospital, or LTC setting, must be knowledgeable of the healthcare system environment and understand what the desired goal is for the patient, hospital, and payer. Ultimately, all pharmacist providers must communicate and work together, in order for these novel older adult-care systems to truly provide effective patient care (including pharmaceutical care).

Increasingly, capitated or prepayment-reimbursement methods are creating incentives for both providers and payors to promote wellness. This can lead to incomplete data, unusual referral patterns for care, and unreported services (due to billing methods used in prepayment). In contrast to those information problems, some of the outcome goals include increased patient satisfaction, cost-per-case-day reduction, and decreased admission-readmission rates—all of which are more difficult to determine in many current prepayment schemes.[24] For LTC facilities and hospitals, an interface that uses fewer, or avoids, inpatient days stands out as an important element to the success of a continuum of care (or IDS). In some LTC settings, additional value may be created when service and equipment redundancy can be eliminated, which can have the additional benefit of avoiding an emergency room visit or hospital admission.

There are providers, including pharmacists, who are now being asked to deliver patient-oriented care for older-adult patients—regardless of the tradition or existing bureaucracy barrier that has flourished to date. This includes non-complimentary attitudes among the hospital pharmacist, retail pharmacist, or home-care services consultant pharmacist. Today's marketplace has become team-based wellness management, performance assessment, and integration of services along the healthcare continuum.

48.13 Pharmaceutical Wholesaler

Changes in the healthcare system have led drug wholesalers to broaden the services they offer to pharmacies, enabling pharmacists to extend the services they offer to patients. Traditionally, wholesalers served as the middleman—a distribution hub between the pharmaceutical manufacturer and the pharmacy. This industry has undergone merger-and-acquisition activity, leaving a few national leaders and a handful of local or regional firms. Leaders in this industry are the publicly traded corporations McKesson, Cardinal Health, and AmerisourceBergen (ASB), who collectively control 80 percent of all drug wholesaling. The trade association for this segment of the pharmacy industry is the National Wholesale Druggists Association (NWDA).

Wholesalers are developing new services that manage assets and support the needs of manufacturers and pharmacies. The offerings by wholesalers include: decision support software for clinicians, barcode scanning technology, and healthcare information technology software and hardware. As a result, pharmacists are able to offer more patient care-

oriented services in their practice settings. In 1999, chain pharmacies remained the dominant wholesaler customer base (30.5 percent) and independent pharmacies were second (18.3 percent).[25]

Other customers include medical-supply firms, hospital and home-care pharmacies, and physician groups. In a survey done by Wilson Health Information in 2008, it was evident that pharmacy customers most frequently use chain drug stores to fill prescriptions (see Figure 48.2), although independent pharmacies were found to be the most highly satisfying for pharmacy customers, as seen in Figure 48.3. The top-ten medical conditions treated among pharmacy customer households can be seen in Figure 48.4.

Lastly, wholesalers are key players in the new pedigree regulations that are being drafted at the national and state level. The wholesalers will be responsible for verifying the pedigree of products sold to customers and ensuring the pedigree of products purchased on secondary markets. If the federal government's implementation precedes the States', a national standard may ease the burden being placed on wholesalers as the gatekeepers against counterfeit products. However, state-specific requirements varying from a national standard may prevent the distribution of products on a timely basis and impact the availability of products to consumers.

48.14 The Pharmaceutical Industry: Marketplace Description and Changes

The emergence of managed care over the last ten years has had a significant impact on the financing and delivery of healthcare services. The dynamic changes taking place today have forced everyone in the healthcare industry to adopt new approaches in the marketplace. Nowhere are these changes more pronounced than in the pharmacy industry. The advent of third-party prescription drug programs by the insurance industry in the early 1980s foretold the intrusion of purchasers into the traditional healthcare-distribution channels. Group purchasers and their managed-care advisors have now usurped the exclusive "directing" role previously enjoyed by physicians in the healthcare delivery decision-making process.

Pharmacy-benefit management, plan design, and cost issues have been increasing in importance to pharmaceutical companies over the past five years. The 2008 *Takeda Prescription Drug Benefit Cost and Plan Design Survey Report*, produced by the Pharmacy Benefit Management Institute, provides a comprehensive overview of the current state of prescription drug coverage costs and plan designs. Some of the key findings from the report are included below:[26]

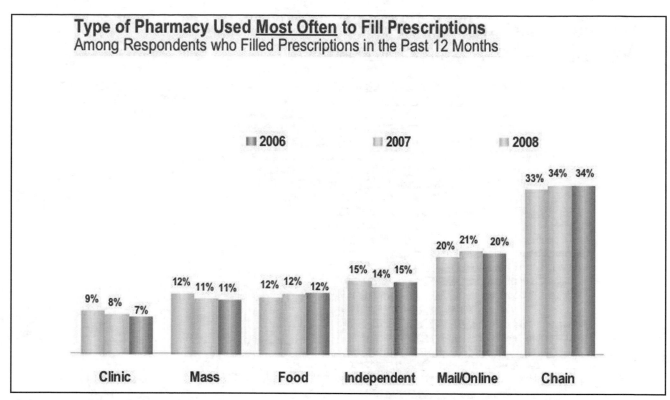

Figure 48.2 *Type of pharmacy used most often to fill prescriptions. ©2008 Wilson Health Information LLC, New Hope, PA. All rights reserved. Permission granted for reproduction.*

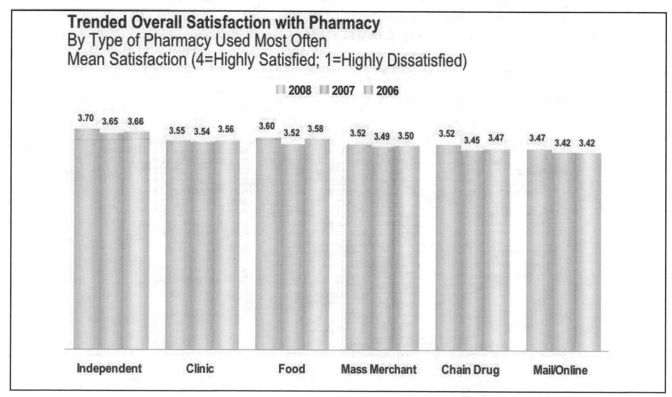

Figure 48.3 *Overall satisfaction with pharmacy used most often. ©2008 Wilson Health Information LLC, New Hope, PA. All rights reserved. Permission granted for reproduction.*

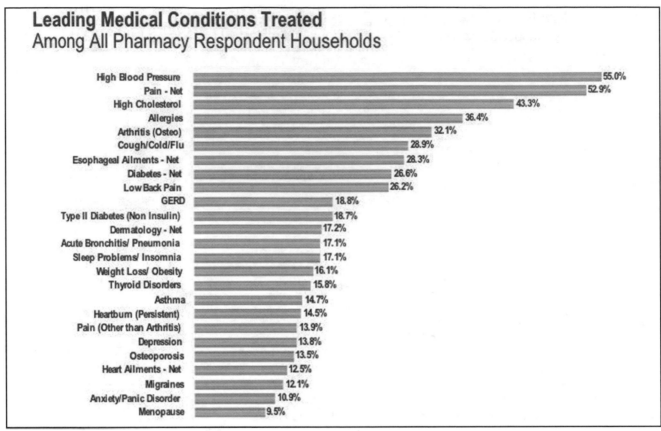

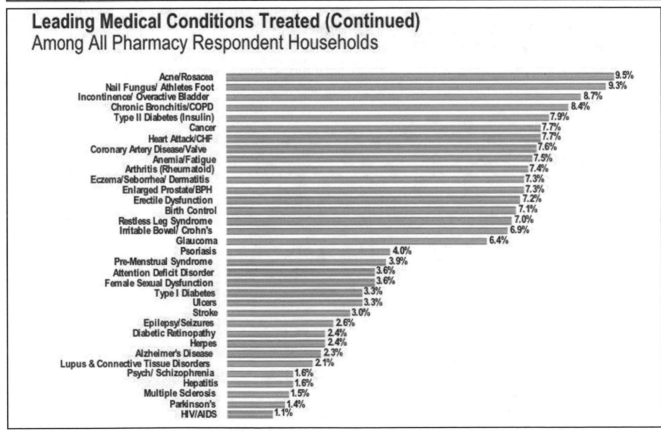

Figure 48.4 *Leading medical conditions as reported by pharmacy customers. ©2008 Wilson Health Information LLC, New Hope, PA. All rights reserved. Permission granted for reproduction.*

- Employers established drug plan designs to share some portion of drug costs with members. On average, members paid 26.6 percent of a retail prescription and 19 percent of a mail prescription.

- Three or more tier plan designs are used by 86.5 percent of employers. The most commonly used cost sharing approach is a three-tier copayment design (generics, preferred brand, and non-preferred brand).

- Employers are using a broad range of utilization programs in benefit design. The most popular tools are: refilling too soon (84.2 percent), quantity limits (81.4 percent), and prior authorization (79.4 percent).

- Drug-specific annual deductibles, maximum annual benefits, or out-of-pocket limits are not included in the majority of employers' plan designs.

- Generic drug use continues to rise. Employers are using incentives for generic dispensing in retail and mail service.

- A total of 93.7 percent of employers offer a mail-service option for maintenance medications for their employees. The mail service is mandatory for maintenance medications for only 12.4 percent of these employers. Less than 31.4 percent of employers use retail settings to dispense maintenance medications while 60 percent of employers using retail pharmacies to dispense maintenance medications are not restricting dispensing to select pharmacies.

Given the changes in practice settings where pharmaceutical care and drugs are delivered to patients, the industry supplying these medications has had to change. One change is the consolidation occurring among manufacturers, as they seek to gain research benefits to fuel future offerings in marketed drugs and increase their clout in the marketing of drugs in a fiercely competitive marketplace. Additionally, the world marketplace has further intensified the competition for long-term survival.

The pharmaceutical drug manufacturers aggressively contract with pharmacy purchasers in the U.S., who themselves are under increasing fiscal pressure to reduce costs. Group purchasing in all pharmacy settings continues to be the norm today. These groups are two to five times larger than they were just five years ago. The need to drive better contracts has forced purchasers to buy bigger volumes of product and drive real, versus promised, purchasing from manufacturers. Manufacturers have become strict about their contracting terms, and require performance in order for the organization to gain discounts or purchase rebates. Competition among manufacturers and the plethora of drug options has caused manufacturers to use multiple strategies to maintain market share and to be able to research new drugs for the future.

An increasingly important market force on manufacturers has been legislation at the state and federal level to introduce pedigree requirements for pharmaceutical products. Pedigree is a record, either paper or electronic, that documents the transaction of the product throughout the course of its manufacturer and sale. The Prescription Drug Marketing Act (PDMA) of 1987 had language to address many of the issues of counterfeit, misbranded, and adulterated drugs. The subsequent amendments to the PDMA added and clarified language on pedigree and extended implementation until January 2010. With the continued extension of the PDMA implementation, individual states began to address the pedigree issue. California's requirement was an electronic pedigree and was scheduled to be implemented on January 1, 2009, but has been delayed until 2011. This delay will allow the FDA to set the national standards with its pedigree implementation in January 2010. The impetus for this legislation is to combat counterfeit drugs that have entered the market and to be able to trace products for recall. With the outsourcing of manufacturing to other countries and many manufacturers based in other countries, the opportunity for counterfeit products of FDA-approved products continues to increase. The recent manufacturing issues with heparin from China and the proliferation of counterfeit sales of high visibility products such as Viagra® have the FDA and manufacturers aligned to implement a system that meets the goal of a safe distribution system. The most promising technology to date for pedigree has been Radio Frequency Identification (RFID), but other electronic and paper systems could be possible as interim steps in the process of a standard national system. Two major hurdles have been the cost of these systems as well as the time to implement a tracing system from the initial ingredient to sale to consumers.

With the continued emphasis on disease outcomes, manufacturers are also aligning themselves with disease prevention-and-treatment programs, where their drug would or could be part of the program. Known as "disease management," these programs are developed and implemented by healthcare organizations in order to achieve better patient outcomes, which bolsters their presence in the marketplace. The synergy for manufacturers and healthcare providers is to use drug products appropriately and achieve a cost-effective, positive outcome for the patient.

Manufacturers have several different types of representatives calling on customers today. They also have staff members who coordinate their resources on behalf of the customer, to achieve sales and product movement. They include the following examples:

- National account managers are responsible for purchasing groups (such as Premier), large health systems (such as Daughters of Charity Health System), or national companies (such as Walgreens).
- Key account managers are responsible for key accounts or influential systems at the local and regional levels.
- Managed-care managers are responsible for working with managed-care organizations at the local, regional, or national levels.
- Sales representatives are responsible for calling on local physicians, their office personnel, and local pharmacists in pharmacies.
- Hospital representatives are responsible for calling on the local hospitals, including teaching institutions. They also work on establishing product inroads with thought leaders in the medical community.
- Specialty representatives are responsible for product niche areas and the respective physicians or pharmacists who would use or purchase such a product. An example would be drugs for transplant patients or a drug for a rare medical condition.

48.15 Manufacturers: Research-Intensive, Biotechnology, and Generic Segments

In 2008, the FDA approved 31 new molecular entities including 21 new drugs, three therapeutic biologics, and seven other biologics. There are nearly 3,000 potential drugs currently in the pipeline. According to the PhRMA, over 600 of these drugs are biotechnology products.[27]

Branded manufacturers saw therapeutic classes converted mostly to generic products as managed-care organizations used their tools to shift market share quickly to newly released generic alternatives (see Table 48.2). As these new drug entities became available, multiple generic manufacturers competed for the market, helping to quickly reduce the cost of these agents. The top generic companies include Apothecon, Mylan, Teva, Abbott Hospital, Watson, Schein, Geneva, Ivax, and Roxane. Interestingly, many of these firms are wholly-owned subsidiaries of research-intensive manufacturers.

For biotechnology and molecular medicine (biopharmaceutical) manufacturers, efforts are underway in Congress to allow follow-on biologics or biosimilar medications

to be approved by the FDA. A biosimilar is a product that attempts to replicate a biologic product, which is a complex product manufactured through living organisms. These biologic products are difficult to replicate, and therefore biosimilar products would not be identical to the original as is the case with current generic products. The legislation in Congress would empower the FDA to create an approval pathway for biosimilars as has been done in other countries such as the European market, where several biosimilars have been available for a 20 to 30 percent savings from the original product.

The focus of the debate on biosimilar products has been the length of market exclusivity and patent time that should be afforded the originator products. Patent protection provides a certainty to market exclusivity and protection from competitors while terms of exclusivity are grayer. Given the large investments made in developing and manufacturing biologic products, this is an important issue to investors as well as the manufacturer regarding its return on investment.

A continuing challenge for manufacturers has been reimportation practices in the United States. Individuals struggling to pay for the cost of their medications have looked to Canada and Mexico for brand name medications at reduced prices. This practice has been supported by legislation in a few states. The passage of the MMA 2003 and the patent expiration on a number of blockbuster medications has diminished the strong push for importation of foreign products. The Medicare Part D programs offer prescription coverage to the largest group of Americans who had no prescription coverage, reducing the need to seek alternative sources of medications. In addition, a FDA study in 2003 found that a majority of U.S. citizens would spend less buying generic versions in the U.S. than branded products in Canada.[28]

Under the 1997 act, companies were permitted to distribute off-label-usage information and health-economic data to professionals. The FDA also relaxed its restrictions regarding direct-to-consumer (DTC) advertising of prescription medications.[3] In October 2002, President Bush signed the Prescription Drug User Fee Act (PDUFA III) that continues funding to the FDA to review activities that might help speed up new drug product approvals. Additionally, President Bush signed an Executive Order in October 2002 to speed the entry of generic drugs into the marketplace and limit branded-product litigation against generic drug-market entry to a single 30-month period. The Prescription Drug User Fee Amendment of 2007 (PDUFA IV) will enable the FDA to significantly expand its post-marketing surveillance of approved drugs and enhance its IT infrastructure to monitor and track adverse drug events.

Table 48.2
First-Time Generic Approvals

Generic Approval	Brand Name and Dosage Form	Generic Name	Use	Market Sales ($M)*
2006	Plavix® tablet	clopidogrel	Inhibit platelet aggregation	2,659
	Flonase® nasal spray	fluticasone	Rhinitis	1,098
	Pravachol® tablet	pravastatin	High cholesterol	1,395
	Zocor® tablet	simvastatin	High cholesterol	3,393
	Zoloft® tablet, oral concentrate	sertaline	Depression	2,664
	Zithromax® oral suspension	azithromycin	Bacterial infections	368
	Wellbutrin XL® tablet (50-mg, 100-mg, 200-mg)	bupropion	Depression	1,431
	Zofran® tablet, orally disintegrating tablet (Zofran ODT®), oral solution	ondansetron	Nausea, vomiting	818
2007	Norvasc®	amlodipine besylate	High blood pressure	2,331
	Ambien® tablet	zolpidem	Insomnia	2,180
	Toprol-XL® extended release tablets	metoprolol succinate	High blood pressure, angina, congestive heart failure	1,200
	Lotrel® tablet	amlodipine besylate/ benazepril	High blood pressure	1,400
	Protonix® tablet	pantoprazole	Gastroesophageal reflux disease, ulcers	2,262
	Coreg® tablet	carvedilol	High blood pressure, congestive heart failure	
	Trileptal® tablet	oxcarbazepine	Seizures	601
2008	Fosamax® tablet	alendronate	Osteoporosis	1,415 weekly
	Wellbutrin XL® tablet (200-mg)	bupropion	Depression	898
	Prilosec® 40-mg capsule	omeprazole	Gastroesophageal reflux disease, ulcers	168
	Risperdal® tablets and oral solution	risperdone	Schizophrenia, bipolar disorder	2,003
	Lamictal®	lamotrigine	Seizures, bipolar disorder	1,938
	Depakote®	divalproex sodium	Seizures, bipolar disorder, migraine	678
	Keppra® tablet	levetiracetam	Seizures	783
	Imitrex®	sumatriptan	Migraines	Tablets: 1,047 Injection: 199

*For Year of First-Time Generic Approval
Data compiled from Medco Drug Reports 2007-2009.

The FDA has been working to review and respond to many of the changes that occurred with the provisions of the PDUFA. The FDA is responsible for overseeing the advertising of drugs and sending regulatory letters to manufacturers to halt the dissemination of volatile letters. The Government Accountability Office's (GAO) 2008 report on *Trends in FDA's Oversight of Direct-to-Consumer Advertising* highlights the difficulty the FDA has had in oversight of this area. The GAO reports that the DTC reviews and advisory letters often arrive after the manufacturer has ceased dissemination of the information.[29] The additional staff hired through the budget expansion in PDUFA IV should help address this area.

Significant challenges continue to plague the FDA. The past decade has seen the agency deal with drug recalls such as Vioxx and the questions on the safety of our food supply with the widespread recall of tainted peanut products. Margaret Hamburg, M.D., has been selected by President Obama as the individual capable of reshaping and redirecting this $2 billion agency. Dr. Hamburg has a history in public health as well as bioterrorism and disease control. To date, her message has been one of safety as well as efficacy, with the underlying message that the FDA is crucial to ensuring the welfare of U.S. citizens through oversight and accountability.

Additionally in June 2009, President Obama signed landmark legislation that gave the FDA increasing authority over the tobacco industry. The new legislation will allow the FDA to ban misleading health claims, restrict marketing campaigns, and increase the health warnings associated with smoking all types of cigarettes as well as monitor the sales of the tobacco products. Critics have voiced concerns that the FDA is currently overburdened with responsibilities and that the added burden of overseeing tobacco will further dilute the FDA's ability to oversee the activities within the pharmaceutical arena.

Consumers continue to switch from brand to generic drugs as they become available. Generic substitution rates of over 70 percent are commonly seen in many health plans. Generic manufacturers capitalized on a significant number of blockbuster branded medications losing patent protection over the last five years. For the generic drug-manufacturing industry, one big event in 1997 was Congress' passage of the Food and Drug Administration Modernization Act (FDAMA). This law included some benefits to generic drug manufacturers, as follows:

- Once the FDA and an applicant company agree on what bioavailability or bioequivalence studies are needed for approval of an Abbreviated New Drug Application (ANDA), the FDA cannot change the rules (without a compelling reason).

- The unavailability of data from the FDA field office can't be used to delay generic drug approvals.

FDAMA also gives certain innovator drugs that treat severe or life-threatening illnesses an extra six months of marketing exclusivity in exchange for manufacturers' conducting pediatric clinical studies of the drug. Congress continues to tinker with FDA legislation and regulation that balances the marketing rights among traditional research-oriented and generic drug firms. Other regulation and legislation that is still debated but not fully resolved includes (1) FDA-proposed guidelines to hold drug manufacturers or any other PBM owner responsible for false or misleading prescription marketing or promotion; (2) a CMS proposal to require hospitals to demonstrate a medication-error rate lower than or equal to 2 percent, in order to receive Medicare funding; and (3) a congressional equal-access bill to prohibit health plans from favoring one type of pharmacy provider (e.g., mail-order over local retail pharmacy) by inclusive contract or by financial incentives, such as co-pay differentials.

A number of class action lawsuits have resulted in billions of dollars in settlements. At the core of many of these suits has been the role of the manufacturer in convincing physicians to prescribe these medications for patients with conditions outside FDA indications. Physicians have always had the authority to prescribe drugs for off-labeled use, but manufacturers are limited to discussing labeled indications. One manufacturer settled a lawsuit alleging that their antipsychotic product was promoted for off-labeled uses and that the manufacturer minimized the risk of diabetes. The manufacturer put aside $1.42 billion for a potential settlement. In another case, the government has assessed a manufacturer $2.3 billion in criminal and civil penalties for violating drug marketing rules.

Another issue facing drug manufacturers is the number of products that have had black box warnings added to their drug labeling. A black box warning is the strongest safety warning the FDA requires and usually gives details as to the risk. Manufacturers are required to change their package insert to include the black box warning, and notification is sent out to prescribers. The anti-smoking drug Chantix® and the newer, second-generation antidepressants as well as some older medications such as propoxyphene and metoclopramide recently received black box warnings for significant adverse drug events.

A patent expiration of some blockbuster drugs valued around $20 billion has occurred over the last decade. Legal maneuvering usually delays the actual marketing of generic products, and research-intensive manufacturers also will license early marketing for as long as possible to a subsidiary or marketing partner, to better manage the profitability of their products. Some of the recent or upcoming drugs losing patent protection are listed in Table 48.3. As the manufacturers of traditional medications strive to develop new products to replace these blockbuster drugs, patent protection has allowed the products of biotechnology companies in the U.S. to remain unchallenged.

48.16 Pharmaceutical Manufacturer Sales and Marketing
A. Organization and Operations
Pharmaceutical companies in the U.S. have traditionally been organized into three operational areas to fulfill their mission: (1) research and development (R&D), (2) sales and marketing, and (3) manufacturing and distribution.

R&D operations are primarily focused on the discovery of new compounds that will be safe and effective in treating targeted disease states. In the past, R&D was accomplished within the organization. Pharmacists are employed in various aspects of R&D, including drug formulation, clinical research, and medical communications about drug information. Companies must spend over $200 million to successfully obtain FDA approval to market a drug in the U.S., including discovery, drug development, and clinical testing. Today, most companies also license new drugs or technology created by startup firms who are more willing to assume risk (in order to capture investor funding). Various biotechnology and pharmaceutical-formulation firms have marketing agreements with traditional manufacturers who offer sales and marketing expertise, as well as recognition in the medical marketplace.

Table 48.3
Anticipated Patent Expirations for 2009-2011

Possible Patent Expiration	Brand name (generic name), manufacturer	Use	2008 US retail sales ($M)
2009	*Ambien CR®* (zolpidem controlled-release), Sanofi-Aventis	Insomnia	986
	Topamax® (topiramate), Ortho-McNeil	Seizure disorders, migraine headache	2,356
	Prevacid® (lansoprazole), Novartis	Ulcers, gastroesophageal reflux disease	2,948
	Adderall XR® (amphetamine salts), Shire	Attention deficit hyperactivity disorder	1,585
	Pulmicort Respules® (budesonide), AstraZeneca	Asthma	876
	Valtrex® (valacyclovir), GlaxoSmithKline	Viral infections	2,020
2010	*Flomax XR®* (tamsulosin), Boehringer Ingelheim	Benign prostatic hypertrophy	1,318
	Effexor XR® (venlafaxine extended-release), Wyeth	Depression, anxiety, panic disorder	2,791
2011	*Xalatan®* (latanoprost opthalmic solution), Pfizer	Glaucoma, ocular hypertension	494
	Aricept® (donepezil), Eisai	Alzheimer's disease	1,224
	Levaquin® (levofloxacin), Ortho-McNeil	Bacterial infections	1,719
	Actos® (pioglitazone), Takeda	Type II diabetes	2,569
	Zyprexa® (olanzapine), Lilly	Schizophrenia, bipolar disorder	1,853
	Lipitor® (atorvastatin), Pfizer	High cholesterol	6,392
	Tazorac® (tazarotene topical), Allergan	Acne	109

Availability dates for first-time generics are subject to significant change as a result of multiple patent protections, patent litigation, pediatric or other exclusivities, at-risk launches, and delays between patent expiration and launch of first-time generics.
Source: Medco Drug Trend Report 2009

Sales and marketing is the other main engine driving pharmaceutical companies. Some players believe that if a company discovers a drug for which there is no other marketplace competition, doctors will prescribe it and patients will purchase it. More commonly, however, marketing and sales expertise is necessary to achieve success in the face of obstacles such as a non-breakthrough drug, pricing problems, or fierce competition. Typical sales personnel are recruited from college with a degree in a health-related area, such as pharmacy, nursing, or medicine. All manufacturers require continuing education in salesmanship and conduct rigorous sales training.

At some point in their career, nearly all marketing personnel have spent time in the field. Marketing, although uniquely different from sales in many other industries, has remained intertwined with sales in the pharmaceutical industry. This is probably due, in part, to the regulation, the nature of the product being sold, and the way in which the product is ordered through the prescriber. Pharmacists do hold sales and marketing positions in most pharmaceutical companies.

Manufacturing and distribution of pharmaceutical products occurs among all types of pharmaceutical manufacturers. Employment of pharmacists in this capacity is common (and currently, there is a high demand for pharmacists to fill this role). Personnel in this area prepare the oral, liquid, and topical drug products that ultimately are sold by the manufacturer to a pharmacy. Actual distribution of the product may go through the drug wholesaler, or direct from the manufacturer to a pharmacy or other licensed customer. Strict regulations surrounding the compounding, manufacture, and distribution of prescription pharmaceutical products demand a wide area of knowledge (of which the pharmacist has a solid, basic understanding).

B. Other Targeted Customer Segments

Other customer segments, sectors or trade categories include federal or state government programs, military, and the Veterans Administration. Manufacturers and wholesalers typically have separate account management and support for conducting business with these categories of pharmaceutical trade.

Unlike the private sector, public and military trade categories operate under different procurement rules and requirements, as well as compliance with legislative or regulatory pricing guidelines. For example, the Federal Supply Schedule (FSS) is a key determinant for authorized purchases of all categories of products, including pharmaceuticals. This includes the VA and the military as well as some federally funded and qualified health centers (FQHCs) or federally qualified programs through legislative mandates.

From a medical and pharmacy practice perspective, professionals follow common standards of patient care as appropriate for their settings of care. In fact, cross-innovation between private and public sector professionals has led to increased roles for pharmacists as an active member of the patient care team. For example, pharmacists who can practice under a physician collaborative agreement evolved largely from VA hospital and clinic practices as well as select academic hospitals around the country.

48.17 Contracting and Change in the Pharmaceutical Industry

Just as pharmacists in pharmacies have changed in response to marketplace pressures, the manufacturers have adjusted personnel and resources to better compete in the future. One strategy is to focus on new drug entities that have no competitors and that offer a clear advancement in the diagnosis or treatment of a disease. Another strategy is to focus on select categories, as opposed to a broad-based range of conditions that may dilute the marketing capabilities of the organization across too many prescriber types. Some manufacturers are renting sales-force personnel through co-promotional alliances, where they do not have to compete in order to achieve faster market-share accumulation.

Other manufacturers are more aggressively forming strategic-marketing alliances and research partnerships to augment their own capabilities, in order to help them speed towards market approval and generate sales dollars. For manufacturers that do not focus on new-drug marketing, competition has remained strong. Most recently, profits had lagged under the weight of purchaser consolidation, driving deeper discounts on multi-source (generic) drug products. This trend is leveling off, while many new drugs are coming off of patent protection and into generic firms, leading to a renewed profit opportunity for these marketers.[30] Manufacturers, pharmacies, and MCOs frequently market the drug-price savings associated with generic drug products to consumers. Now, even single-source, brand-name products may be marketed to consumers in an effort to capture market share by influencing the prescribers of prescription drug products.

Finally, all manufacturers continue to face scrutiny in their marketing practices, due to various federal and state laws or regulation of pharmaceutical products. These include, but are not limited to, the distribution of drug samples, drug advertising (21 C.F.R. 202.1, 201.2), reminder advertising (21 C.F.R. 200.200), direct-to-consumer advertising (21 C.F.R. part 202), and the use of approved drugs for unapproved conditions.

Reimbursement regulations—such as those emanating from the Omnibus Budget Reconciliation Act of 1990

(OBRA), which mandated drug-use rebates to Medicaid—can also affect manufacturers' pricing and marketing position. Managed Care Organizations, as well as federal and state programs, have traditional reimbursement to pharmacies and clients as a percentage off of the average wholesale price (AWP). The MMA 2003 and the Deficit Reduction Act have language requiring reimbursement be based off alternatives to AWP. The Deficit Reduction Act requires pricing using Average Manufacturer Price (AMP), which has traditionally been a confidential price used to calculate federal rebates for the Medicaid Programs. National Pharmacy Organizations have been challenging the use of AMP as a reduction in reimbursement to pharmacy providers. The MMA requires that Medicare reimbursement be based on Average Sale Price, a number submitted by manufacturers quarterly to CMS. In addition, First Data Bank, a national publisher of AWP, has agreed to cease publishing AWP as a part of its settlement in a lawsuit that accused First Data Bank of artificially inflating prices with the wholesaler McKesson. The lawsuit alleges that the actions of FDB and McKesson cost Medicaid agencies, health plans, and private payers in excess of $7 billion. Given the marketplace changes, even regulations may have to be amended or repealed—or new regulations may have to be promulgated—to keep pace with the changing pricing algorithms used to determine fair and reasonable reimbursement.

Fraud and abuse within the healthcare system is another area that has gained local and national attention. HIPAA allowed for the creation of the National Health Care Fraud and Abuse Control Program (HCFAC), which was responsible for recovering $1.8 billion in judgment and settlements in 2007 according to OIG report of recoveries. In the OIG's *Semiannual Report to Congress,* the agency announced it expected to recover over $2.2 billion in recoveries from audits and investigation-related inquiries. CMS expects the new ICD-10-CM codes to improve the fraud and abuse initiatives that have been in place since the enactment of HIPAA in 1996. Responsibility for the security rules and administrative simplification standards of HIPAA has been a CMS responsibility. However, Health and Human Services (HHS) Secretary Kathleen Sebelius has granted authority for administration and enforcement of HIPAA's privacy and security rules to the Office of Civil Rights. CMS retained its authority over the administrative simplification standards of HIPAA.[31]

48.18 Health Care Industry Changes in the Near Future

How will health care or insurance reform and managed care affect hospitals and other care settings? It is useful to review some of the principles in the evolving marketplace influ-

enced by managed care. There are several stages of managed-care presence used by experts to determine the degree of saturation by managed-care organizations (MCOs). One simple model to follow has four stages:

- Stage one represents an unstructured market with virtually no elements of managed healthcare. This is, essentially, the traditional fee-for-service market (which is now starting to enter into the sphere of MCOs).
- Stage two begins to see some elements of managed healthcare—such as system evolution and contracting. Examples of cities that were fully into stage two included Boston, Dallas, Philadelphia, and St. Louis.
- Stage three shows provider and institutional consolidation. Healthcare systems evolve from those changes. Examples of cities that were among the many at this stage included Houston, Salt Lake City, and Phoenix.
- Stage four is distinguished by clear coalitions of caregiver organizations and integrated systems of patient care across the continuum-of-care settings. Of the few cities where this has occurred, Minneapolis, Los Angeles, and Worcester are prime examples.

When examining a region's managed-care evolution, a determining factor is the degree of vertical integration throughout the care system. Key aspects to evaluate include the number of components of care, components in the delivery of care, and the number of system-wide contracts. This is illustrated in Table 48.4.

Future shifts in providing care include moving from a system focused on short-term care to a system focused on a chronic or long-term continuum of care. Aging in the U.S. population continues to place an enormous strain on the resources of the U.S. health care delivery system, including access to drugs and pharmacists. Reimbursement changes, such as prospective-payment systems, are aligning incentives among care providers to utilize the lowest level of care necessary for adequate patient-care outcomes. An increasingly important part of that outcome is related to drug therapy—a paradox for pharmacists and payors, since drug treatment can further increase the ambulatory cost of care. However, if a drug is not available due to access barriers such as cost sharing or if patients do not use it regularly, they will have adverse outcomes and will have to utilize more expensive levels of care, such as the emergency room or hospital.

Table 48.4
Degree of Integration Matched
to Stage of Managed Care

Number of components

(Stage 2)
Including lab and diagnostic imaging only

Number of delivery components

(Stage 3)
Only hospital and physician care contracts

Number of system-wide contracts

(Stage 4)
All components of diagnostic and care delivery
across the continuum of patient-care settings

Integrated information systems are required to aid in refining the treatment process and obtaining patient-outcome information. While pharmacies have long been fully computerized, they remain not fully linked to other segments of the care-delivery system. This lack of connection, even in stage-four cities, remains a major barrier to fully achieving the promises of appropriate drug utilization and receiving any positive impact from pharmacists' patient care. Most MCOs have been spending increasing amounts of money on information systems, especially in those stage-four markets, to remain competitive and achieve the benefits that shared information can bring to geographically separated members of the healthcare system. The focus of various electronic platform initiatives does include pharmacy, but are focused primarily around medical care providers or facilities where most healthcare spending occurs in the U.S.

Group purchasing of drugs by healthcare delivery systems as a single class of trade has emerged since 1998 as a major shift in purchasing policy. Aside from a licensed retail pharmacy, all other care settings can purchase jointly and maximize their purchasing power, while still achieving a measure of cost containment. Employer coalitions and other payors have similarly leveraged group purchasing as part of strategies to optimize drug product and pharmacist services efficiency.

Legislation affecting formularies has remained a problem with MCOs, as part of the historical consumer backlash over reduced access to care, which has once again surfaced in the healthcare reform debate. Mandated opening of drug benefits and access to prescription drugs (in general or in niche categories) has become a new problem for managed care to handle – especially in light of the continually rising costs of health care. Traditionally, closed formularies and narrow drug-benefit policies had been used to create a consistent level of quality in drug utilization and to try to contain costs. Today, open formularies and easier prior approval processes are more the norm. More drug choices along with new biotechnology and molecular medicine therapies in the pharmacies have contributed to almost double-digit increases in MCOs' pharmacy-segment costs. As a result, many plans have changed their budgeting to global costs-of-care assessments and increasingly shared financial risk with physicians for drug-utilization expenditures.

48.19 Summary

Few can accurately predict the future impact on the pharmacist, pharmacy, and pharmaceutical industry with healthcare reform efforts underway in the U.S. Even with health reform passed in some form, it would take more time to begin to deal with the precision necessary for implementation in all state jurisdictions. Given the turmoil and rapid changes in the care delivery system in recent years, it is clear that all pharmacy-related stakeholders will feel some effect of planned system changes on their individual role within the healthcare system. However, some trends have emerged, and experts are attempting to focus change in healthcare, including changes in pharmacy, manufacturer of product, and the pharmacist's role.

Recent and emerging changes in providing pharmacy services include integrated healthcare (merged, alliance) systems; a renewed emphasis on drug-use control to achieve documented, optimal patient outcomes; the privatization of public-sector and not-for-profit institutions or organizations; the expanded use of group-purchasing organizations (GPO) and coalitions for value-based purchasing; the changing role of the pharmacy wholesaler in the distribution system going beyond being just a purveyor of products to becoming a partner in drug distribution with the manufacturer and pharmacy; and general management and legal or regulatory issues particular to pharmacy services as part of a regulated profession.

The use of non-dispensing pharmacist services has been shown to have a significant impact on the quality and cost of patient care by optimizing drug therapy, which, in turn, results in positive patient-care outcomes. To enable the pharmacist to engage in these non-dispensing activities, pharmacy services will necessarily continue the process of automating the preparation and dispensing of drugs. The roles and responsibilities of pharmacy technicians and other non-pharmacist personnel will grow commensurate with changes in pharmacists' direct patient-care responsibilities. In the hospital, clinic, and home-care settings, pharmacists moving to decentralized patient-care areas will require increased use of supportive personnel in non-judgmental tasks of pharmacy operations. These changes will require or have already resulted in regulatory and personnel-development changes in the field of pharmacy. Similarly, increased use of automation in non-hospital settings will require or have already resulted in regulatory approval and retraining of personnel in pharmacy.

As dispensers of medication, pharmacies and pharmacists will be playing a greater role in drug identification and safety, and monitoring for optimal use of medication therapy. As a result, future pharmacy operations will become more patient-centered, regardless of the healthcare-delivery setting. Performance will be measured by the actual data of patient outcomes, collected by the healthcare organization having primary responsibility for providing total health care, and reimbursement will be linked to those measures of outcome performance. Total cost of care and various pre-payment-reimbursement methods will continue, but will allow for compensation of pharmacists separate from product dispensing, in order to achieve successful financial and patient-care outcomes for total health care value that can appeal to both sides (dispensing and clinical) within the current pharmacy profession. In addition, pharmacists are now permitted to administer vaccinations in most states, such as flu vaccine, and play an emerging public health role in pandemic or emergency management planning.

This chapter provided an overview of pharmacy, pharmacists, and manufacturers as they relate to various healthcare-delivery settings reimbursed through managed care. These health professional settings included the retail or community pharmacy and acute-care hospital, as well as the subacute, outpatient, long-term, home, and physician-office care settings. Healthcare professionals in all settings, including pharmacists, need to be aware of the differing perspectives and common goals for providing pharmacy services in the U.S. marketplace, as integrated systems evolve. The integrated-care system, which they are a part of (through a hospital or health plan), will expect pharmacists to perform tasks as part of various performance-improvement initiatives leading towards improved patient care outcomes.

Pharmacists, regardless of the healthcare settings they practice in, must be knowledgeable of the U.S. healthcare-system environment and understand the goals of the patient, hospital, and managed care payer. Ultimately, all pharmacists, as healthcare service providers, must communicate and work together with the entire healthcare organization, in order for the new coordinated care systems to truly provide clinically safe and cost-effective treatment.

Glossary

AACP. American Association of Colleges of Pharmacy.

AAPI. American Accreditation Program, Inc.

ALOS. Average length of stay.

AMP. Average Manufacturer Price.

ANDA. Abbreviated New Drug Application.

ARRA. American Recovery and Reinvestment Act.

BBA. Balanced Budget Act.

capitated payment. A hybrid of traditional MCO payment (where a provider is reimbursed through a fixed payment per member per month) or other performance-based criteria method. A primary-care physician may act as a gatekeeper for referral and institutional medical services, while the member retains some coverage for services not authorized by the gatekeeper or services provided by nonparticipating clinicians or providers.

CCDS. Continuing Care Delivery System.

CCP. Council on Credentialing in Pharmacy.

CCRC. Continuing-care retirement community (or center).

CMS. Center for Medicine and Medical Services, formerly the Health Care Financing Administration (HCFA).

co-pay or **co-payment**. A fixed dollar amount for each dispensed prescription paid for by the patient. The specific amount may vary for brand, as opposed to generic, drugs dispensed.

DME. Durable medical equipment.

DOS. Date of service.

DRG. Diagnosis-related groupings.

FDAMA. Food and Drug Administration Modernization Act.

FFS or fee for service. Payment of a set or negotiated fee for a service from a healthcare provider.

FTE. Full-time Equivalent.

GAT. Geriatric Assessment Team.

GPO. Group Purchasing Organizations.

HAC. Hospital Acquired Conditions.

HCFAC. National Healthcare Fraud and Abuse Control Program.

HDMA. Healthcare Distribution Management Association.

HMO (health maintenance organization). An organized health system that is responsible for both the financing and delivery of comprehensive health services to an enrolled group of patients.

ICD-9-CM. *International Classification of Diseases*, 9th edition, clinical modification.

ICU. Intensive Care Unit.

IDS. Integrated Delivery System.

IOM. Institute of Medicine.

IPA. Independent Practice Association. A legal entity composed of physicians, organized for the purpose of negotiating contracts to provide physician services.

Joint Commission, The. A non-profit accreditation program that focuses on hospitals, long-term, and home care.

LTC. Long-term Care.

MA-PD. Medicare Advantage Prescription Drugs.

MCO (managed-care organization). An organization whose philosophy states that managing the provider delivery system can result in outcomes that manage medical care for the patient.

MTM. Medication Therapy Management.

NCPDP. National Council of Prescription Drug Programs. An organization responsible for the standards of prescription claims submission.

NCQA. National Committee for Quality Assurance. A national organization of employer and managed-care organization providers whose mission is to promote high quality of care in managed-care provider organizations.

NPSG. National Patient Safety Goal.

OOPS. Out-of-pocket costs and expenses.

PA. Physician Assistant.

PACE. Program of all-inclusive care for the elderly.

PBM. Pharmaceutical-benefit manager.

PCAT. Pharmacy College Admission Test.

PDL. Preferred Drug List.

PDMA. Prescription Drug Marketing Act.

PDP. Prescription Drug Plans.

PDUFA. Prescription Drug User Fee Act. A fee legislated by Congress that allows the FDA to charge for review of new drug applications, to fund staffing and computerization initiatives that speed the drug-approval process for new or generic drug products.

PMPM (per member per month). A calculation of total monthly prescription-cost expenditures, divided by the total number of eligible plan members.

POS. Point of service. The claim is adjudicated and payment information is received within seconds of processing.

PPM. Physician-Practice Management.

PPO (preferred provider organization). Entities through which various health plans or carriers contract to purchase healthcare services for patients from a selected group of providers (typically at a better per-patient cost).

PPS (prospective payment system). Capitation is one example.

PSAO. Pharmacy Services Administrative Organization.

RFID. Radio Frequency Identification.

SNF. Skilled-nursing facility.

TEFRA. Tax Equity and Fiscal Responsibility Act of 1982.

TPA. Third-party administrator.

UCR. Usual, customary, and reasonable charges for prescriptions in the community.

Endnotes

1. *Managed Care Digest Series: Hospitals/Systems Digest.* Vol 3. Bridgewater, NJ: Sanofi Aventis; 2008.

2. The Joint Commission. National Patient Safety Goals. 2009. www.jointcommission.org/PatientSafety/NationalPatientSafetyGoals/npsg8_review.htm. Accessed July 27, 2009.

3. *Novartis Pharmacy Benefit Report.* 1998 ed. Totowa, NJ: Emron; 1998.

4. *Managed Care Digest Series: Institutional Digest.* 1998 ed. Kansas City, MO: Hoechst Marion Roussel; 2001.

5. *Managed Care Digest: Integrated Health Systems Digest.* Kansas City, MO: Hoechst Marion Roussel; 2001.

6. Rowland D, Hoffman C, McGinn-Shapiro M. *Health Care and the Middle Class: More Costs and Less Coverage.* The Henry J. Kaiser Foundation; 2009.

7. Jack Hoadley EH, Julietter Cubankski, Tricia Neuman. *Specialty Tiers.* The Henry J. Kaiser Foundation; 2009.

8. *Wickline v. State of California,* 239 Cal. Rptr. 810 (Ct. App. 1986).

9. Porcaro ET. *Final Report of Phase I SBIR Grant #97-P-08080/3-01*1994.

10. The Council on Credentialing in Pharmacy. Scope of Contemporary Pharmacy Practice: Roles, Responsibilities, and Functions of Pharamcists and Pharmacy Technicians. Washington, DC: Council on Credentialing in Pharmacy; 2009.

11. Blum J. Combined Call Letter for 2010. In *Health and Human Services.* Baltimore: Centers for Medicare and Medicaid Services; 2009: 68-73.

12. Medicare: The Medicare Prescription Drug Benefit. In *The Henry J. Kaiser Family Foundation.* Menlo Park, CA: The Henry J. Kaiser Family Foundation; 2009: 1-2.

13. Federal Trade Commission. CVS Caremark Settles FTC Charges: Failed to Protect Medical and Financial Privacy of Customers and Employees; CVS Pharmacy Also Pays $2.25 Million to Settles Allegations of HIPAA Violations. In *Federal Trade Commission.* Washington, DC; 2009.

14. American Association of Colleges of Pharmacy. Academic Pharmacy's Vital Statistics. 2009. www.aacp.org/about/Pages/Vitalstats.aspx, accessed 2009.

15. American Association of Colleges of Pharmacy. Pharmacy College Admission Test. 2009. www.aacp.org/resources/student/pharmacyforyou/admissions/Pages/PCAT.aspx, accessed 2009.

16. Mapping of ACPE Standards: Standards 2000 vs. Standards 2007. www.acpe-accredit.org/pdf/CS_Mapping_of_Standards_2000_vs_Standards_2007.pdf.

17. Exam for the Certification of Pharmacy Technicians. State-By-State Tech Requirements. 2009; www.nhanow.com/pharmacy-technician/requirements.aspx. Accessed June 15, 2012.

18. Cassidy J. Targeting Treatment in Rehabilitation. *Subacute Care.* 1995; 10(4): 31-32.

19. Guidelines leading the way to best practices in long-term care. *Provider.* 1995; 21(12): 43-48.

20. Department of Health and Human Services. HIPAA Administration Simplification: Modifications to Medical Data Code Set Standards to Adopt ICD-10-CM and ICD-10-PCS. In *Department of Health and Human Services.* Washington, DC: Department of Health and Human Services; 2009: 3328-3329.

21. Institute of Medicine. *To Err is Human: Building a Safer Health System.* 1999.

22. Centers for Medicare and Medicaid Services. CMS Proposes to Expand Quality Program for Hospital Inpatient Services. 2008.

23. Navarro RP. Measuring the effect of change. *Medical Interface.* 1995; 8(9): 13.

24. Vogenberg FR, Venable RS, eds. *A Managed Care Primer: Capitation and Constructive Partnerships.* Alexandria, VA: American Society of Consultant Pharmacists; 1995.

25. Coster JM. *Pharmaceutical Marketplace Dynamics.* Alexandria, VA: National Association of Chain Drug Stores; 2002.

26. *The Takeda Prescription Drug Benefit Cost and Plan Design Survey Report.* Lincolnshire, IL: The Pharmacy Benefit Management Institute, Inc.; 2008.

27. Biotechnology Research Continues to Bolster Arsenal Against Disease with 633 Medicines in Development. PhRMA, 2008.

28. Bernstein IBG, Shuren J. The Food and Drug Administration's Counterfeit Drug Initiative. *Journal of Pharmacy Practice*. 2006; 19(4): 250-254.

29. Government Accountability Office. Trends in FDA's Oversight of Direct-to-Consumer Advertising. Washington, DC: Government Accountability Office; 2008: 1-4.

30. Generics: Making a comeback. *Drug Topics supplement*. 1998; 142(15).

31. Office of Inspector General. Semiannual Report to Congress: October 1, 2007 - March 31, 2008. In *Department of Health and Human Services*. Washington, DC; 2008.

Index

Food and Drug Administration Modernization Act of 1997, 16, 52, 616

Food Drug & Cosmetic Act, 8, 14-16, 19-20, 23, 26, 75, 127, 163, 178, 184-185, 191, 209, 317, 542, 574, 582, 617, 619, 625

Foreseeability, 80, 103, 159, 267, 273, 343, 558, 591, 598

Formication, 757, 770

Formularies, 828, 848

Fragmentation pattern, 701

Fragmentation pieces, 701

Fraud, 28-29, 32, 96, 239, 311, 317-318, 544, 555-556, 558-559, 562-563, 569-572, 584, 683-684, 688, 847

Freedom of Information (FOI), 87, 201, 268, 319

Fructosamine, 372, 602

FTC, see Federal Trade Commission

Fulminant hepatic failure, 364, 371, 395-396, 398-399, 402-403

G

Garlic, 17, 541

Gas chromatography, 698, 706, 711-713, 722, 780

Gas phase, 700

Gastric lavage, 172, 649

Gastrointestinal therapy, 35, 406, 488

Gatekeeper, 56

GCP, see Good clinical practice

Generic drugs, 10, 15, 53, 113-114, 140, 147, 210-211, 555, 560, 578, 582-585, 590, 665, 841-842, 844, 846

Genetic polymorphism, 144

Genetics, 29, 38, 136, 143-144, 166, 173, 240, 242, 247, 267, 392, 394, 423, 440, 509-510, 516, 598

Gentamicin, 138, 279, 381-382, 385, 434, 486, 591, 637, 685

Glandulars, 17

Glaucoma, 428, 436, 731, 845

Glucocorticoids, 157, 216, 355, 360, 377

Glucose, 134, 139, 145, 199, 296, 369-378, 404, 422, 510-511, 590, 598, 602, 609-610, 780

Glutathione, 142, 393, 396, 400-401

Glyburide, 376, 486, 644

Glynase, 404

Good Clinical Practice (GCP), 43, 48, 64, 71-72, 74, 100, 104, 171, 274, 349, 370, 420, 441, 446, 545, 593, 616, 640, 646, 657-658, 669, 671-672, 689-690, 692-693, 781, 836

Good Compounding Practices, 601, 616-617, 620-624, 626

Good Manufacturing Practice (GMP), 18-19, 24-25, 534, 541, 551, 601

GPO, see Group purchasing organizations

Group Purchasing Organizations (GPO), 109, 848

Growth hormone, 36, 535, 537-539

Guanethidine, 240, 377

Guidelines for Good Clinical Practice, 71, 74, 333, 349, 443, 593-594, 624

H

H. pylori, 402-403, 603

Halcion, 523

Haldol, 292, 588

Hallucinations, 217-218, 338, 424, 436, 442, 475, 509, 686, 689-693, 750-751, 757, 759, 761-762

Hallucinogens, 686, 750, 761-762

Haloperidol, 348, 420-421, 427-429, 439, 781

Halothane, 391-392, 394-395

Hashish, see Recreational drugs

Hazards, 18, 24, 31, 54, 56, 77, 82, 96, 105, 161, 166-167, 169-171, 208, 215, 238, 240, 256, 261, 263, 289, 305, 334, 341-342, 384, 427, 539, 611, 621-622, 646, 718, 727, 744

Headache pain, 255, 772, 774, 776

Health insurance, 202, 211, 311, 481, 552, 567-568, 571, 601, 609, 638, 828, 847

Health Insurance Portability and Accountability Act of 1996, 311, 552, 571-572, 601, 609, 611, 638, 833, 847

Health profile, 348

Heart attacks, 24, 63-64, 213-214, 218, 220-221, 301, 340-341, 485, 487, 538, 540, 762, 770-771, 773, 775-777

Heart valve disease, 48, 70, 214, 218, 258, 371, 382, 410, 416, 428, 473, 475, 520, 522-523, 536, 574, 605, 644

Heart valvulopathies, 220, 442

Helicobacter pylori, 219, 402, 652

Hemoglobin, 298, 372, 469

Hemolytic anemia, 244

Hemophilia, 491-494, 496-498, 500, 504, 568, 829

Hemorrhage, 7, 217-218, 259, 292, 402, 410, 416, 465, 491, 523, 588, 649
    Intracerebral hemorrhage, 218

Heparin, 44, 136, 138, 140, 157, 217-218, 281, 284, 290, 296-298, 374, 409-416, 484, 487, 501, 590, 592-594, 632-633, 650, 841
    Heparin-Induced Thrombocytopenia (HIT), 409, 411-414, 593
    Low Molecular Weight Heparin (LMWH), 412, 415, 487-488

Hepatic failure, acute, 398

Hepatic injury, 346, 391-392, 395, 397, 405-406

Hepatitis, 24, 30, 98, 108, 143, 186-187, 189, 217-219, 371, 391-393, 395-398, 404-405, 478, 491, 493-497, 500-503, 541, 599, 829
    Acute, 392-393, 398, 404, 493
    Isoniazid, 397

Hepatomegaly, 316, 397-398

Hepatorenal syndrome, 398

Hepatotoxic drugs, 391-393, 396, 403

Hepatotoxicity, 213-214, 217-218, 222, 346, 377, 391-394, 396-401, 403, 405-406, 509-511

Hepatotoxic risk, 393, 403

Herbs, 17-18, 20-22, 24-27, 29-31, 34, 114, 117, 345-346, 353, 355, 359, 363, 435, 533-534, 539-541, 544-545, 598, 600-602, 604, 606, 609-610, 652, 831

Chinese ephedra, 24
Chinese herbs, 34, 355, 541
Fish oils, 17, 541
Ginseng, 17, 20, 28, 345, 429
Hypericum, 345
St. John's Wort, 32, 344-346, 429
Heroin, see Recreational drugs
Hespan, 290
High-risk patients, 301, 339, 605, 607
Histamine activity, 432
Home Care Interface, 645
Home medical equipment (HME), 603
Homeopathy, 541-543
Hospital pharmacy, 224, 247-248, 273, 288, 315-316, 319-320, 324-325, 327-330, 332, 334-335, 341, 343, 373-375, 386, 409, 549-550, 590-595, 607, 626, 629, 631-636, 638, 646, 651, 660, 663-664, 680, 683, 751, 828, 832, 835-838, 842, 849
Human growth hormone, 36, 535, 537-539
Huntington's disease, 440
Hydrocodone, 249, 401-402, 436, 471, 473, 481, 576, 696, 776
Hydrocortisone, 279, 300, 362
Hydromorphone, 213-214, 281, 290, 463, 477, 689, 696, 776
Hypalgesia, 770-771
Hyperlipidemia, 259, 362, 511
Hyperreflexia, 344, 359, 429, 437
Hypertension, 35, 61, 66, 205, 208, 219, 255-256, 259, 347, 360-361, 382-383, 386-388, 466, 573-575, 605, 633, 644, 648, 686, 845
Hyperthermia, 240, 422, 429
Hypoglycemia, 169, 296-297, 369-377, 404, 486-487, 686
Hypoglycemic agent, 236, 370, 377, 403, 486
Hypogonadism, 424
Hypothyroidism, 289, 466
Hypoventilation, 470, 472, 476
Hypoxemia, 355

I

Iatrogenic injuries and disease, 297, 570
Ibuprofen, 180, 201, 241, 249, 251, 271, 401, 583, 752-753, 776-777
ICU, see Intensive care unit
Idiopathic, 217-218, 246, 249, 371, 420, 431, 433, 436, 478
Idiopathic thrombocytopenic purpura, 217-218
Idiosyncratic, 208, 236, 240, 242, 260, 264, 381-382, 393-394, 397-398, 403-404, 428, 439, 479
Idiosyncratic liver damage, 217-218, 222, 342, 393-394, 396-398, 400, 404-406, 494-495, 583
Illinois Motor Vehicle Code, 747-748
Imipramine, 220, 337-338, 346, 437, 687
Imminent hazard, 18, 24, 539
Immune, 22, 69, 219, 240-242, 244-247, 255, 259, 308, 371, 396, 411-413, 415, 484, 494, 496-498, 507, 518, 524, 537, 542, 696, 722

Immunity, 499, 562, 572, 579
Immunization, 216, 309, 370, 600, 606-609, 652, 832
Immunoassay, 414-415, 695-696, 721-722, 727, 734, 753
Immunoassay tests, 695-696, 721-722, 734, 753
Impaired drivers, 741
Impairment of motor activity, 476, 762
Impurities, 761
Incident report, 278-279, 684-685
Inclusion/exclusion criteria, 66-68, 101, 164, 619, 644
IND, see Investigational new drug
Indomethacin, 377, 776
Induction, 123, 141-142, 173, 377, 396, 400-401, 420, 422, 780
Infants, 29, 143, 169-170, 217-219, 294, 299, 313-316, 318-320, 325-326, 329-332, 335, 363, 374-375, 401, 409, 498, 520-525, 590, 615, 730
Inflammation, 99, 140, 217-218, 227, 241, 243, 245, 249, 279, 355, 358-361, 364-365, 396-397, 407, 413, 494
Influenza, 53, 55, 63-64, 122, 216, 219, 225, 398, 401, 535, 606-607, 651, 832, 849
Influenza vaccine, 216, 219, 535, 651, 832, 849
Informed consent, 66, 68, 71, 76-83, 88, 96-98, 100-103, 105-106, 108, 159-160, 305-310, 441-446, 544, 574
  written, 66, 68, 71, 76-83, 88, 96-98, 100-103, 105-106, 108, 159-160, 305-311, 441-446, 544, 574, 609
Ingredient and nutrition labeling, 17-18, 21, 534
Injection, 134-137, 158, 240-241, 247, 287-288, 293, 296, 313-315, 343, 356-357, 361-362, 370, 375, 425, 441, 464, 470, 478, 543, 607, 690, 700, 702, 731, 754-755, 829, 843
Injunctive relief, 557, 559
Injuries
  Accidental, 343, 742, 749
  Alcohol-related, 687, 741-742, 744, 746-747, 756
  Drug, 236, 263, 273, 305-306, 311, 328, 375, 594, 643-648, 652-654, 757, 763
  Legal, 358
  Medical, 3, 160, 278, 305, 363, 634, 698, 775
Innervation, 770
Inordinate amounts, 617-619
Inpatient drug orders, 11, 55, 147-149, 151, 179, 185, 187, 189, 218, 228, 238, 251, 279, 285, 289-291, 310, 322, 325, 334, 396, 466, 486, 587, 623, 633, 635, 639, 653, 667, 716, 780
INR, 289, 392, 409-410, 416, 488, 602-604, 606
Insomnia, 256, 357, 423, 429, 431, 434, 436, 509, 523, 689, 691-693, 843, 845
Institute for Safe Medication Practices (ISMP), 279, 297, 299, 484, 587, 594, 631-632, 638, 665, 837
Institutional Review Board (IRB), 60, 67-69, 72-73, 76-83, 86-90, 95, 99-108, 159-161, 206-207, 544
Insulin, 22, 136, 153, 157, 209, 215, 240-241, 243, 245, 247, 281, 296-297, 369-378, 404, 484, 486-487, 510-511, 590, 652, 686

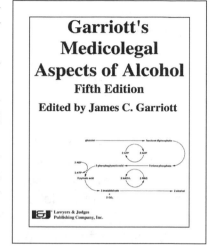

Medical-Legal Aspects of Drugs, Second Edition
Edited by Marcelline Burns, Ph.D.

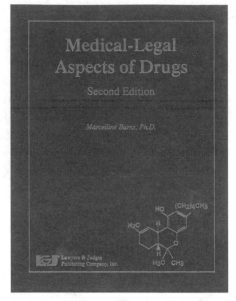

Drug use is at least as long standing as recorded history. Many centuries ago humans, as well as some animal species, discovered medicinal and intoxicant properties of a variety of plants. As predicted in the first edition of *Medical-Legal Aspects of Drugs*, drug use continues to be a problem but there have been significant changes. Drugs of choice and use trends have changed and new issues have surfaced. Drug options have expanded with the discovery and re-discoveries of intoxicating plant materials and the development of new compounds in both legal and illegal laboratories. The use and abuse of drugs will continue.

Medical-Legal Aspects of Drugs addresses the challenge of this dynamic and pervasive problem with accurate, cutting-edge information from acknowledged experts. You'll learn about psychoactive drugs, effects of various kinds of drugs, both legal and illegal, on behavior, and the development of anxiolytics, antidepressants, and antihistamines. These medications, which are effective treatments for depression, insomnia, anxiety, chronic allergic rhinitis, and numerous other disorders, have become popular as raw materials or as intoxicants themselves, producing a host of new issues and problems to be addressed.

Drug use in the workplace, in schools, and in athletics continues to be a widespread problem. You will learn about the effects of drug use on employee performance in the workplace or school. You will also learn about the effects of doping by athletes as they seek improved performance. The drug detection methods and the legal issues surrounding the practice of mandatory testing for drugs are discussed.

Drug use is often linked with criminal activity, including driving under the influence, dealing, manufacture, theft, assault, child or spousal abuse, murder, and other crimes. Drug-related offenses fill our courts, the perpetrators populate our jails, and their crimes devastate families, schools, and communities. This book provides information about prosecution and defense of drug cases, as well as information on drug law enforcement and field sobriety testing and other types of drug testing commonly used by law enforcement agencies. In-depth coverage of drugs and their effect on visual function and on driving behavior is also included, as drug use is often most commonly evident in these areas

Drug use is an international issue. The contributors to *Medical-Legal Aspects of Drugs* offer an international, as well as an American perspective, and much of their knowledge is currently available as written materials only in this text. As a diverse group of uniquely capable experts, their chapters examine the major medical-legal issues surrounding drug use. What they have written will provide legal and criminal justice professionals, employers, school and community personnel, and other interested individuals with essential knowledge about drugs.

Produce Code: 6192 • ISBN: 978-1-933264-08-0 • Pages: 255 • Casebound • 8.5"×11"

Slips, Trips, Missteps and Their Consequences, Second Edition
by Jon R. Abele, Alvin S. Hyde, H. Harvey Cohen, Cindy A. LaRue, and Gary M. Bakken

Falls are the second leading cause of accidental deaths in the United States, but are overlooked in most literature. Of use to primary care physicians, nurses, insurance adjusters, architects, writers of building codes, attorneys, or those who care for the elderly, this book will tell you how, why, and when people will likely fall, what most likely will be injured, and how such injuries come about. It details potential trouble spots, which may cause falls, in buildings, both private and public, and how to prevent or reduce the risk of accidents.

This book answers your questions on how to determine fault and liability between the plaintiff and the defendant in a slip and fall case, applying the traditional premises liability model. The included case studies and examples will help you understand the mechanics and causes of these accidents, and what human factors may be present.

Biomedical factors that increase the likelihood and severity of fall injuries are covered including an extensive chapter on osteoporosis and its relation to falls and fall injury. With the very useful Fall Prevention Manual that is included, you will find potential trouble areas in and around a building before an accident occurs. *Slips, Trips, Missteps and Their Consequences, Second Edition* is peerless in its handling of an important and overlooked subject.

Topics Include

- The incidence of accidental falls
- Classifying falls
- Standing, walking, the environment and gravity
- Human factors in falls
- Environmental factors in falls
- Aging and central nervous system changes
- Osteoporosis and other diseases that cause or contribute to falls
- Medications and iatrogenic causes of falls
- Building design standards and pedestrian traffic
- Fall injuries: spine, head, and extremities
- Preventing falls and injuries
- Premises liability
- Defense techniques and suggestions for slip, trip and/or fall cases<.li>
- Fall Prevention Manual and checklist

Produce Code: 5430 • ISBN: 978-1-933264-01-1 • Pages: 375 • Casebound • 8.5"×11"

Nursing Home Litigation: Pretrial Practice and Trials, Second Edition

Edited by Ruben J. Krisztal, Esq.

A must-have reference for any professional involved in nursing home cases. The litigation of neglect and abuse of the elderly in assisted living and nursing home facilities is unlike any other personal injury litigation. The second edition of *Nursing Home Litigation: Pretrial Practice and Trials* has been significantly expanded and will provide you with a detailed step-by-step look at how nursing home cases should be handled.

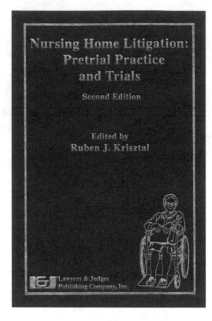

The book's chapters are organized in a way that will help you with your case from pretrial to trial. The first chapter will give you tips and techniques for writing the demand letter. The following chapters provide insight for both the plaintiff's attorney and defense attorney on topics such as interviewing older witnesses, preparing staff for deposition, demonstrative evidence, voir dire, opening and closing arguments.

Also included is a free CD of actual depositions of nurses, administrators, directors of nursing and upper management in nursing homes.

Topics include

- Handling older witnesses: the defense perspecive
- Preparing nursing home staff for deposition
- The preparation and use of demonstrative evidence
- Fighting fraud in long-term care
- Voir dire, opening arguments and closing arguments
- Punitive damages
- The role of nutrition
- The Medicare "super lein"
- CD-ROM of actual depositions of nurses, administrators, directors of nursing and upper management in nursing homes

Produce Code: 5813 • ISBN: 978-1-930056-48-0 • Pages: 627 • Casebound • 6"×9"

Nursing Home Litigation: Investigation and Case Preparation, Second Edition
Edited by Patricia W. Iyer

Each chapter in *Nursing Home Litigation Investigation and Case Preparation, Second Edition* has been revised and updated while new chapters have been added to provide detailed information on even more issues and cases in nursing home litigation. It is an excellent reference for your nursing home or eldercare litigation team including attorneys representing either plaintiffs or defendants, financial consultants, life care planners, and other specialists with perspectives from experienced attorneys, physicians, nursing consultants, pharmacists, and nursing home experts.

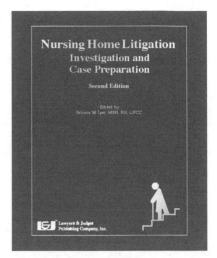

This book is composed of four specialized sections so you can quickly and easily find the information you need. Part One discusses legal strategies you and your team can utilize during the investigation and pretrial phases of nursing home cases including screening cases, special issues unique to assisted living and nursing home cases, and use of Legal Nurse Consultants. Part Two explains the liability issues that arise due to the nature of the nursing home setting including staffing concerns, services provided to residents, administrative liability, direct and indirect medical practitioner responsibility issues. Part Three describes common allegations of injury, illness and other liability issues that occur in nursing home cases including falls, skin trauma, infections, pharmacology issues, pain management, billing fraud, and records tampering. Part Four provides tips for defending nursing home, long-term care and assisted living facilities with information on defense perspectives and strategies on many types of nursing home cases as well as insurance adjusters' perspectives on nursing home cases pertaining to insurance claims.

This comprehensive text is a must-have legal and medical reference for everyone who works with nursing home, assisted living, long-term care, or elder law cases.

Topics include:

- Nursing home liability
- Physician's liability
- Nursing home administration liability
- Defense perspectives
- Claims adjuster's perspectives
- Use of legal nurse consultants
- Screening cases
- Investigation and pretrial considerations
- Nursing practice in long-term care situations
- Overview of the nursing home environment

- Assisted living cases- special considerations
- Falls and restraints
- Skin trauma
- Infections
- Wandering and Elopement
- Pharmacology and the elderly
- Pain management
- Tampering with medical records
- Billing fraud

Produce Code: 5643 • **ISBN: 978-1-933264-00-4** • **Pages: 720** • **Casebound** • **8.5"×11"**